TECHNICAL DRAWING

FREDERICK E. GIESECKE

Late Professor Emeritus of Drawing
Texas A & M University

ALVA MITCHELL

Late Professor Emeritus of Engineering Drawing
Texas A & M University

HENRY CECIL SPENCER

Late Professor Emeritus of Technical Drawing;
Formerly Director of Department
Illinois Institute of Technology

IVAN LEROY HILL

Late Professor Emeritus of Engineering Graphics;
Formerly Chairman of Department
Illinois Institute of Technology

JOHN THOMAS DYGDON

Professor Emeritus of Engineering Graphics;
Formerly Chairman of the Department,
and Director of the Division of Academic Services
and Office of Educational Services
Illinois Institute of Technology

JAMES E. NOVAK

Senior Lecturer and Director,
Engineering Graphics Division
Department of Civil and Architectural Engineering
Illinois Institute of Technology

SHAWNA LOCKHART

PEARSON
Prentice
Hall

Upper Saddle River, New Jersey
Columbus, Ohio

Library of Congress Cataloging in Publication Data

Technical drawing / Frederick E. Giesecke . . . [et al.].—13th ed.
   p. cm.
Includes bibliographical references and index.
ISBN-13: 978-0-13-513527-3
ISBN-10: 0-13-513527-3
1. Mechanical drawing. I. Giesecke, Frederick E. (Frederick Ernest), 1869-1953.
T353.T28 2009
604.2—dc22

2008010987

Editor in Chief: Vernon R. Anthony
Acquisitions Editor: Jill Jones-Renger
Editorial Assistant: Doug Greive
Project Manager: Louise N. Sette
Production Supervision: S4Carlisle Publishing Services
Art Director: Diane Ernsberger
Cover Designer: Bryan Huber
Operations Supervisor: Deidra M. Schwartz
Director, Image Resource Center: Melinda Patelli
Manager, Rights and Permissions: Zina Arabia
Manager, Visual Research: Beth Brenzel
Manager, Cover Visual Research and Permissions: Karen Sanatar
Image Permission Coordinator: Fran Toepfer
Director of Marketing: David Gesell
Senior Marketing Coordinator: Alicia Dysert
Marketing Assistant: Les Roberts

This book was set by S4Carlisle Publishing Services. It was printed and bound by Courier Kendallville, Inc. The cover was printed by Phoenix Color Corp.

Pearson Prentice Hall™ is a trademark of Pearson Education, Inc.
Pearson® is a registered trademark of Pearson plc
Prentice Hall® is a registered trademark of Pearson Education, Inc.

Pearson Education Ltd., London
Pearson Education Singapore Pte. Ltd.
Pearson Education Canada, Inc.
Pearson Education—Japan

Pearson Education Australia Pty. Limited
Pearson Education North Asia Ltd., Hong Kong
Pearson Educación de Mexico, S.A. de C.V.
Pearson Education Malaysia Pte. Ltd.

10 9 8 7 6 5 4 3 2 1
ISBN-10:   0-13-513527-3
ISBN-13: 978-0-13-513527-3

10 9 8 7 6 5 4 3 2 1
School Edition ISBN-10:   0-13-503404-3
ISBN-13: 978-0-13-503404-0

TECHNICAL DRAWING

ABOUT THIS BOOK

The 13th edition of Giesecke's Technical Drawing is a comprehensive introduction and detailed reference for creating 2D documentation drawings.

Expanding on its reputation as a trusted reference for drawing technique, this edition includes even better integration of illustrations with text and consistent navigational features to make it even easier to refer back to important information.

This edition illustrates the application of technical drawing skills to real-world work practice and integrates drawing skills with CAD use in a variety of disciplines.

Updated Content

- Updated to show current ASME standards
- More examples of plastic and sheet metal parts
- CAD coverage focusing on issues that arise in documenting design
- Civil and architectural drawing examples
- Full-color illustrations distinguish explanations from annotations that are part of a technical drawing
- Consistent color use in illustrations helps readers understand drawings. (e.g. cutting planes are always blue, folding lines are always tan, etc.)
- Illustrations are integrated closely with text. (No more page turning to find a figure referred to in the text.)
- Step by Step explanations: Easily understood instructions with illustrations *right next to each step* walk readers through complex constructions.
- Color photos and examples show inspiring real-world applications.
- Full-color solid models help readers visualize and understand orthographic projections.

Teaching/Learning Features

Visually-oriented students and busy professionals will quickly locate content by navigating these consistent chapter features.

- ***Splash Spread*** An attention-getting chapter opener interests readers and provides a context for the chapter content to follow.
- ***References and Web Links*** Applicable references to standards and links to handy Websites are at the start of each chapter.
- ***Foundations Section*** An introductory section set off by a topic heading tab at the top of the page for easy navigation, covers the drawing topic's usage and importance, visualization tips, and theory related to the drawing techniques.
- ***Detail Section*** This is the "brass tacks" part of the book, where detailed explanations of drawing techniques, variations, and examples are organized into quick-read sections, each numbered for quick reference in the detailed Contents.
- ***CAD at Work Section*** This breakout page includes tips related to using the 2D or 3D CAD model to generate drawings.
- ***Portfolio Section*** Examples of finished drawings wrap up the chapter by showing real-world application of topics presented.
- ***Key Words*** Italicized on first reference, keywords are summarized at the end of the chapter.
- ***Chapter Summary***
- ***Review Questions***
- ***Exercises*** The excellent Giesecke problem set features updated exercises including plastic and sheet metal parts, updated assembly drawings from CAD models, and sketching problems.

Supplements

- ***Companion Website*** with new animations and models that match figures in the text.
- ***Problem Workbooks***
- ***Instructors' Materials*** (Online Instructor's Manual, PowerPoint™ slides, and Test Bank.)

USING THIS BOOK

The following features were designed to provide easy navigation and quick reference for students and professionals who look to Giesecke both as helpfully organized teaching text and a lasting reference for technical drawing information.

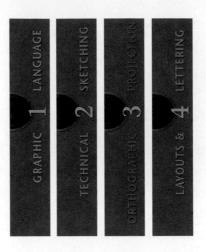

Chapters are keyed in alternating colors to help you locate frequently referenced content by memory.

CHAPTER OPENER SECTIONS

A bold vertical color band and oversized number on the first page of each chapter help you flip to find topics quickly.

Topics that you can expect to learn about in this chapter are listed here.

A large illustration and an interesting overview give you a real-world context for what this chapter is about.

CHAPTER ONE

THE WORLDWIDE GRAPHIC LANGUAGE FOR DESIGN

OBJECTIVES

After studying the material in this chapter, you should be able to:

1. Describe the role of drawings in the design process.
2. Contrast concurrent versus traditional design processes.
3. List five professions that use technical drawings.
4. Describe four creativity techniques.
5. Explain why standards are important.
6. Identify uses of the graphic language.

Refer to the following standards:
- Y14.100—2004 Engineering Drawing Practices
- Y14.2M—1992 Line Conventions and Lettering
- Y14.1—2005 Decimal Inch Drawing Sheet Size and Format
- Y14.1M—2005 Metric Drawing Sheet Size and Format

THE WORLDWIDE GRAPHIC LANGUAGE FOR DESIGN   3

Conceptual Sketch. Conceptual sketches. Exploring many design options through quick sketches is one method that Lunar, recently named one of the top 10 award winning American product design firms by BusinessWeek magazine, uses to create beautiful products and successful brands. *Courtesy of Lunar Design.*

OVERVIEW

Regardless of the language they speak, people all over the world use technical drawings to communicate their ideas. Graphic representation is a basic, natural form of communication that isn't tied to a particular time or place. It is, in a sense, a universal language.

Accomplishing ideas, from the simplest to the most elaborate, requires teamwork. A new product, machine, structure, or system may exist in the mind of the engineer or designer, but before it can become a reality, the idea must be communicated to many different people. The ability to communicate design concepts quickly and accurately through technical drawings is key to meeting project budgets and time constraints. Effective graphic communication is also an advantage in the global marketplace where team members may not always share a spoken or written language.

Like carpenters who learn to use the tools of their trade, engineers, architects, drafters, designers, manufacturers, and technicians learn the tools of technical drawing. They learn specific methods to represent ideas, designs, and specifications in a consistent way that others can understand. By becoming an effective graphic communicator, you can ensure that the product, system, or structure that you envision is produced as you specified.

Check the sites below for engineering graphics supplies and equipment:
- http://www.reprint-graphix.com/
- http://www.eclipse.net/~eesco/draft/draft.htm
- http://www.graphic-design.com/Type/index.html
- Triz40 Design Tools: http://www.triz40.com

Drawing Standards that apply to this chapter are shown here.

Handy Websites that apply to this chapter are shown here.

"FOUNDATIONS" SECTION

This introductory section covers the drawing topic's usage and importance, visualization tips, and theory related to the drawing techniques.

Color at the top of the page makes it easy to flip to the "Foundations" section.

The tab at the top of the page tells the topic of the overview.

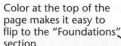

Prisms

A **prism** has two bases, which are parallel equal polygons, and three or more additional faces, which are parallelograms (Figure 3.3). A triangular prism has a triangular base; a rectangular prism has rectangular bases; and so on. (If a prism's bases happen to be parallelograms, the prism is called a parallelepiped, a word rarely heard in everyday conversation.)

A right prism has faces and lateral (side) edges that are perpendicular to the bases; an oblique prism has faces and lateral edges that are angled to the bases. If one end is cut off to form an end that is not parallel to the bases, the prism is said to be *truncated* (a word which simply means "shortened by having a part cut off").

Right square · *Right rectangular* · *Oblique rectangular* · *Right triangular* · *Right pentagonal* · *Oblique hexagonal*

3.3   Right Prisms and Oblique Prisms

Pyramids

A **pyramid** has a polygon for a base and triangular lateral faces which intersect at a common point called the *vertex* (Figure 3.4). The line from the center of the base to the vertex is called the *axis*. If the axis is perpendicular to the base, the pyramid is called a *right* pyramid; otherwise it is an *oblique* pyramid. A triangular pyramid has a triangular base; a square pyramid has a square base; and so on. If a portion near the vertex has been cut off, the pyramid is truncated, or it is referred to as a *frustum*.

Right rectangular · *Right square (truncated)* · *Oblique pentagonal*

3.4   Pyramids

Cylinders

A **cylinder** has a single-curved exterior surface (Figure 3.5). You can think of a cylinder as being formed by taking a straight line and moving it in a circular path to enclose a volume. Each position of this imaginary straight line in its path around the axis is called an *element* of the cylinder.

Right circular · *Oblique circular*

3.5   Cylinder and Oblique Cylinder

Cones

A **cone** has a single-curved exterior surface (Figure 3.6). You can think of it as being formed by moving one end of a straight line around a circle while keeping the other end fixed at a point, the vertex of the cone. An element of the cone is any position of this imaginary straight line.

Right circular · *Right circular (frustum)* · *Oblique circular (truncated)*

3.6   Cones

Spheres

A **sphere** has a double-curved exterior surface (Figure 3.7). You can think of it as being formed by revolving a circle about one of its diameters, somewhat like spinning a coin. The poles of the sphere are the points at the top and bottom of the sphere that would not move while it was spinning. The axis of the sphere is the term for the line between its poles.

Tori

A **torus** is shaped like a doughnut (Figure 3.8). Its boundary surface is double-curved. You can think of it as being formed by revolving a circle (or other curve) around an axis that positioned away from (outside) the curve.

Sphere · *Torus*

3.7   Sphere   3.8   Torus

Ellipsoids

An oblate or prolate **ellipsoid** is shaped like an egg (Figure 3.9). You can think of it as formed by revolving an ellipse about its minor or major axis, respectively.

Oblate Ellipsoid · *Prolate Ellipsoid*

3.9   Ellipsoids

"DETAIL" SECTION

This is the "brass tacks" section of the book, where detailed drawing techniques, variations, and examples are organized into quick-read sections, numbered for quick reference from the Contents.

Content is broken into individual, numbered sections. Pages are white, to differentiate them from other sections.

4.11 NORMAL EDGES

A **normal edge** is a line perpendicular to a plane of projection. It appears as a point on that plane of projection and as a true-length line on adjacent planes of projection (Figure 4.41).

True lenth

4.41 Projections of a Normal Edge. *Courtesy of Giesecke et al., Modern Graphics Communication, 3e, © 2004, pp. 116, 120-122, 124. Reprinted with permission of Pearson Education, Inc.*

4.12 INCLINED EDGES

An **inclined edge** is parallel to one plane of projection but inclined to adjacent planes. It appears as a true-length line on the plane to which it is parallel and as a foreshortened line on adjacent planes. The true-length view of an inclined line always appears as an angled line, but the foreshortened views appear as either vertical or horizontal lines (Figure 4.42).

True length   Foreshortened

4.42 Projections of an Inclined Edge. *Courtesy of Giesecke et al., Modern Graphics Communication, 3e, © 2004, pp. 116, 120-122, 124. Reprinted with permission of Pearson Education, Inc.*

4.13 OBLIQUE EDGES

An **oblique edge** is tipped to all planes of projection. Since it is not perpendicular to any projection plane, it cannot appear as a point in any standard view. Since it is not parallel to any projection plane, it cannot appear true length in any standard view. An oblique edge appears foreshortened and as an angled line in every view (Figure 4.43).

Foreshortened

4.43 Projections of an Oblique Edge. *Courtesy of Giesecke et al., Modern Graphics Communication, 3e, © 2004, pp. 116, 120-122, 124. Reprinted with permission of Pearson Education, Inc.*

4.14 PARALLEL EDGES

When edges are parallel to one another on the object, they will appear as parallel lines in every view, unless they align one behind the other. This information can be useful when you are laying out a drawing, especially if it has a complex inclined or oblique surface that has parallel edges. Figure 4.44 shows an example of parallel lines in drawing views.

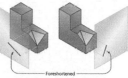

(a) Parallel planes intersected by another plane · (b) Lines 1,2 & 3,4 parallel, and parallel to horizontal plane · (c) Lines 1,2 & 3,4 parallel, & parallel to frontal plane · (d) Lines 1,2 & 3,4 parallel, and oblique to all planes

---

WEB SUPPLEMENT ICONS

This icon of a solid modeled block tells you that a solid model to accompany this figure or topic is available online.

This icon of a film strip tells you that an animation that explains this figure or topic is available online.

SOLID MODEL VISUALIZATION ART

Solid models bring views to life on the page to help you visualize the drawing.

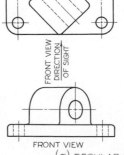

TOP VIEW

R SIDE VIEW DIRECTION OF SIGHT

FRONT VIEW DIRECTION OF SIGHT

FRONT VIEW   R SIDE VIEW

(a) REGULAR VIEWS

"STEP-BY-STEP" ACTIVITIES

Throughout the book, complicated processes are shown as step-by-step activities with each illustration right next to the text that explains it.

Step-By-Step tab identifies these activities.

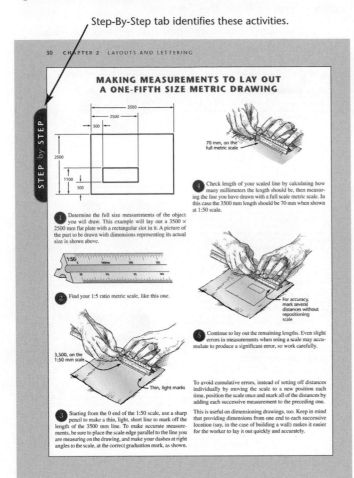

"CAD AT WORK" PAGES

CAD at Work sections break out tips related to using the 2D or 3D CAD model to generate drawings.

A grey header with a "CAD at Work" tab identifies these pages.

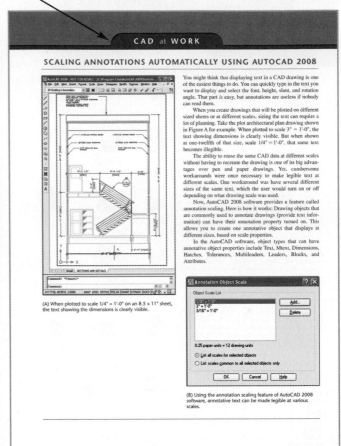

ILLUSTRATIONS

Colored callouts differentiate explanatory text from annotations in technical drawings.
Consistent use of color helps to differentiate the meaning of projection lines, fold lines, and other drawing elements.
A color key is provided for easy reference.

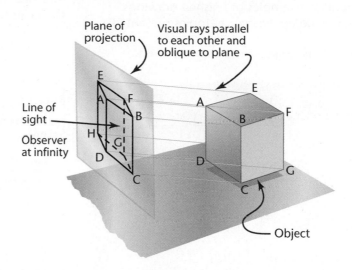

Color Key for Instructional Art

Item	In instructional art	In a technical drawing
Callout arrow	→	*
Dimension line	←——→	←——→ a thin (0.3mm) black line
Projection line	———————	——————— a lightly sketched line
Folding line	— — · — · — · —	—— – – —— used in descriptive geometry
Picture plane on edge	———————	*
Plane of projection	▬▬▬	*
Cutting plane on edge	— — — — —	↑ _ _ _ ↑ (see Chapter 6)
Cutting plane	▬▬▬	*
Reference plane on edge	———————	—— – – —— used in descriptive geometry
Reference plane	▬▬▬	*
Viewing direction arrow	⟹	↑ _ _ _ ↑
Horizon + ground line	———————	———————
Rotation arrow	⤸	30°⤸

* Not a typical feature of technical drawings. (Shown in this book for instructional purposes.)

"PORTFOLIO" PAGES

This section offers examples of finished drawings showing real-world application of topics presented.

Look for the tan pages with a portfolio tab on the outer edge.

A civil drawing showing approval blocks and engineers' stamp. *Courtesy of Perliter and Ingalsbee Consulting Engineers and Calleguas Municipal Water District.*

PORTFOLIO

Window and Door schedules are used in architectural draw... manufacturer and othe information. *Courtesy of Frog Rock D...*

Exercises are easy to find. The color stripe on the outer edge of the page corresponds to the chapter so you can flip to them quickly.

CHAPTER REVIEW PAGE

You will find Key Words, Chapter Summary, and Review Questions sections at the end of each chapter.

KEY WORDS

Visualization
Communication
Documentation
Design Process
Concurrent Engineering
Life Cycle Design
Computer-Aided Design
Computer-Aided Engineering
Computer-Aided Manufacturing
Design for Six Sigma (DFSS)
Define, Measure, Analyze, Improve, Control (DMAIC)
Six Sigma
Quality Function Deployment (QFD)
Product Data Management
Enterprise Data Management
Engineering Change Orders
Ideation
Prototype
Parametric Modeling
Constraint-Based Modeling
Feature-Based Modeling
Rapid Prototyping
Standards
Reverse Engineering
Coordinate Measuring Machine
Functional Decomposition
Patent Drawings
Product Definition

CHAPTER SUMMARY

The members of the engineering design project team must be able to communicate among themselves and with the rest of the project team in order to contribute to the team's success.

The graphic language is the universal language used to design, develop, and construct products and systems throughout the world.

There are two basic types of drawings: artistic and technical.

The design process is the ability to combine ideas, scientific principles, resources, and existing products into a solution for a problem. It consists of five specific stages.

Every technical drawing is based on standards that prescribe what each symbol, line, and arc means.

The basic principles for communicating information using technical drawings are the same whether you are creating drawings by hand or using CAD.

Successful companies hire skilled people who can add value to their team. A thorough understanding of the graphic language is an essential skill that employers value.

REVIEW QUESTIONS

1. When is sketching used as graphic communication?
2. Why are standards so important for members of the engineering design team?
3. What is the design process?
4. What are the five phases of the design process?
5. Describe the difference between concurrent and traditional design process models.
6. What does PDM or EDM stand for? What are some advantages of PDM?
7. When are rapid prototypes useful?
8. List three ways a CAD database can be used.
9. List five techniques you can use to enhance creativity.

EXERCISES

Drawing Exercises

Practice your skills for making measurements, laying out drawing sheets, and forming neat standard lettering with these drawing exercises.

These problems are designed to fit easily on a sheet. (See the inside front cover of this book or the form provided on the Web as a pdf file that you can print to sketch on). Draw all construction lines lightly, using a hard lead (4H to 6H), and all required lines dense black with a softer lead (F to H). Draw your construction lines lightly so that they do not need to be erased.

In exercises 2.1–2.3 you will practice measuring, and in Exercises 2.4–2.6 you will practice drawing layouts.

Exercise 2.1 Measure the lines shown above and list their lengths using millimeters. List the inch measurements for each in square brackets [ ] to the right of the millimeter measurement.

Exercise 2.2 Measure the lines shown above and draw them at Scale 1:2, Scale 2:1, and list their scales below them using the form Scale: X:X.

Exercise 2.3 Measure the overall interior dimensions of your room. Letter the measured length neatly in the first column as shown in the example. In the second column list how long you would draw that line at a scale of 1/4" = 1', third column at 3/8" = 1', fourth column at 1" = 1', fifth column at 1:100 metric scale (10 mm = 1 meter)

EXERCISES

The Giesecke problem set features updated exercises including plastic and sheet metal parts, updated assembly drawings from CAD models, and sketching problems.

ABOUT THIS BOOK

For many decades, *Technical Drawing* has been recognized as an authority on the theories and techniques of graphical communication. Generations of instructors and students have used and retained this book as a professional reference. *Technical Drawing*'s longstanding success can be attributed to its clear and engaging explanation of principles, and to its drawings, which are unsurpassed in detail and accuracy.

While not a departure from its original authoritative nature, this new edition is truly the rebirth of a classic. While its hallmark features continue to shine, the book is thoroughly revised and updated to the latest technologies and practices in the field. More than ever, *Technical Drawing* will prepare students to enter the marketplace of the twenty-first century and serve as a lasting reference.

Shawna Lockhart, author of the 13th edition revision, first used *Technical Drawing* when teaching Engineering Graphics at Montana State University in 1989. Throughout her 15 years as an award-winning professor, she selected this text because, in her words, "It was the most thorough and well-presented text with the best graphic references and exercises on the market."

The quality of the illustrations and drawing examples was established by the original author, Frederick Giesecke, who created the majority of the illustrations in the first edition of *Technical Drawing*, published in 1933.

Giesecke, founder of Texas's first formal architectural education program at what is today Texas A&M University, has been described as "a wunderkind of the first magnitude." He joined the A&M faculty at the age of 17, after graduating in 1886 with a B.S. in Mechanical Engineering and by the age of 19, was appointed head of A&M's Department of Mechanical Drawing.

Studying architectural drawing and design at Cornell University and Massachusetts Institute of Technology, respectively, he also served as head of the Department of Architecture and the official college architect at Texas A&M, designing many campus buildings that are still standing today.

A long-time admirer of Giesecke's legacy, Lockhart was honored to carry on the commitment to clear, engaging, thorough, and well-organized presentation that began with the original author.

Lockhart is known as an early adopter and authority on CAD technologies, as an instructor noted for outstanding dedication to students, and for encouraging a broad spectrum of individuals, particularly women and minorities, to follow careers in engineering related fields. She now works full time to ensure that the Giesecke graphics series continually applies to an evolving variety of technical disciplines.

Frederick E. Giesecke as a cadet in the Texas A&M Corps of Cadets.

Frederick E. Giesecke, founder of Texas's first formal architectural education program.

THE THIRTEENTH EDITION

The Thirteenth Edition of *Technical Drawing* continues its long history as an introduction to technical drawing and an easy-to-use reference for techniques and practices. Twenty-one reviewers advised us on how to make *Technical Drawing* both classic and cutting-edge. New features include:

- A new 4-color design with a user-friendly layout that makes it easy for students to navigate the text. Illustrations are closely integrated with the text.
- Hundreds of new and updated pieces of art
- Updated exercises including plastic and sheet metal parts, updated assembly drawings from CAD models, and sketching problems
- *CAD at Work section* includes tips related to using the 2D or 3D CAD model to generate drawings
- *Portfolio Section* offers examples of finished drawings showing real-world application of topics presented
- More examples of plastic and sheet metal parts, as well as civil and architectural examples

ONLINE RESOURCES

To access supplementary materials online, instructors need to request an instructor access code. Go to www.pearsonhighered .com/irc, where you can register for an instructor access code. Within 48 hours after registering, you will receive a confirming e-mail, including an instructor access code. Once you have received your code, go to the site and log on for full instructions on downloading the materials you wish to use.

SUPPLEMENTS

- *Instructor's Manual and Test Bank:* This manual by Tom Kane of Pueblo Community College includes answers to end-of-chapter problems, chapter worksheets, teaching outlines, and a test bank keyed to each chapter of the book.
- *Instructor's CD-Rom:* This CD contains PowerPoint slides of key text figures and electronic versions of the Instructor's Manual and Test Bank.
- *Website:* www.prenhall.com/giesecke: This website serves as an online study guide for students and features the following:
  - Dozens of animations created from art in the thirteenth edition
  - Self-grading concept questions: true or false, multiple choice, and fill-in-the blank questions for each chapter
  - Chapter summaries and objectives
  - Links to relevant websites for CAD and technical drawing

WORKBOOKS

Three workbooks with additional problems are available. These workbooks are fully class-tested for effectiveness and relevance to the course. They range from having traditional to more modern approaches.

- *Engineering Drawing Problem Series 1 (ISBN: 013658361):* Contains traditional, mechanical workbook problems.
- *Engineering Drawing Problem Series 2 (ISBN: 0136588816):* Contains traditional problems with an emphasis on engineering concepts.
- *NEW 4th Edition Engineering Drawing Problem Series 3 with CD (ISBN: 0135134811):* The new edition of this workbook by Paige Davis and Karen Juneau contains more modern drawing problems as well as a CD with a disk of starter CAD files.

SOFTWARE BUNDLES

This text may be packaged with a student version of CAD software. To request specific bundling information, as well as ISBNs and prices, please contact your local Pearson Professional & Career sales representative. For the name and number of your sales representative, please contact Pearson Faculty Services at 1-800-526-0485.

ACKNOWLEDGMENTS

Sincere thanks to all of the individuals and companies who shared their expertise through drawings and advice with the readers of this book.

Mark Perkins, Joe Evers, Scott Schwartzenberger, Douglas Wintin, David and Caroline Collett, Lee Sutherland, Jeff Zerr, Jeremy Olson, Bryan Strobel, Chad Schipman, Jost Diedrichs, Mary Albini, Kelly Pavlik, Steve Elpel, Erik Renna, Tim Devries, Tom Jungst, Marla Goodman, Cindy Johnson, Robert Rath, Jacob Baron-Taltre, Alex Wilson, Andrea Orr

We gratefully acknowledge the contributions of reviewers for the thirteenth edition of *Technical Drawing:*

Edward Roadarmel, Penn sylvania College of Technology
Ramarathnam Narasimhan, University. of Miami
Douglas C. Hicks, Delaware Technical & Community College
Grant Newman, Olympic College
Gregory Conrey, Southern Polytechnic State University.
Mel Whiteside, Butler Community College
William H. Neely, Montgomery County Community College
Jimmy Vu, Houston Community College
Frank J. Rubino, Middlesex County College
Charles R. Cole, Southern Polytechnic State University.
Adrian Guy Baird, Brigham Young University–Idaho
John Ucker, University of Cincinnati and ITT Technical Institute
Susan Hooper, Portland Community College
Kirk Barnes, Ivy Tech Community College
H. Mike Allen, Tarrant County College
Robert Conn, ITT Technical Institute
David Ball, Waubonsee Community College
Charles W. White, Purdue University
Chuck Bales, Moraine Valley Community College
Keith Andrews, Northeast Alabama Community College
Gregory M. Mocko, Clemson University
Richard Baugher, Southwestern Oklahoma State University

CONTENTS

CHAPTER TEN
TOLERANCING 334

CHAPTER EIGHTEEN
ELECTRONIC DIAGRAMS 620

CHAPTER NINETEEN
STRUCTURAL DRAWING 644

TECHNICAL DRAWING

CHAPTER ONE

THE WORLDWIDE GRAPHIC LANGUAGE FOR DESIGN

OBJECTIVES

After studying the material in this chapter, you should be able to:

1. Describe the role of drawings in the design process.

2. Contrast concurrent versus traditional design processes.

3. List five professions that use technical drawings.

4. Describe four creativity techniques.

5. Explain why standards are important.

6. Identify uses of the graphic language.

Refer to the following standards:
- Y14.100—2004 Engineering Drawing Practices
- Y14.2M—1992 Line Conventions and Lettering
- Y14.1—2005 Decimal Inch Drawing Sheet Size and Format
- Y14.1M—2005 Metric Drawing Sheet Size and Format

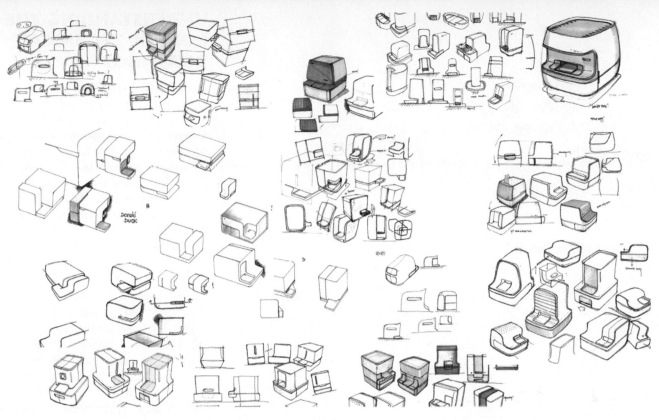

Conceptual Sketch. Conceptual sketches. Exploring many design options through quick sketches is one method that Lunar, recently named one of the top 10 award winning American product design firms by BusinessWeek magazine, uses to create beautiful products and successful brands. *Courtesy of Lunar Design.*

OVERVIEW

Regardless of the language they speak, people all over the world use technical drawings to communicate their ideas. Graphic representation is a basic, natural form of communication that isn't tied to a particular time or place. It is, in a sense, a universal language.

Accomplishing ideas, from the simplest to the most elaborate, requires teamwork. A new product, machine, structure, or system may exist in the mind of the engineer or designer, but before it can become a reality, the idea must be communicated to many different people. The ability to communicate design concepts quickly and accurately through technical drawings is key to meeting project budgets and time constraints. Effective graphic communication is also an advantage in the global marketplace where team members may not always share a spoken or written language.

Like carpenters who learn to use the tools of their trade, engineers, architects, drafters, designers, manufacturers, and technicians learn the tools of technical drawing. They learn specific methods to represent ideas, designs, and specifications in a consistent way that others can understand. By becoming an effective graphic communicator, you can ensure that the product, system, or structure that you envision is produced as you specified.

Check the sites below for engineering graphics supplies and equipment:
- http://www.reprint-draphix.com/
- http://www.eclipse.net/~essco/draft/draft.htm
- http://www.graphic-design.com/Type/index.html
- Triz40 Design Tools: http://www.triz40.com

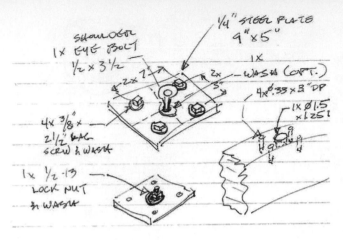

1.1   Computation Sketch Detail.

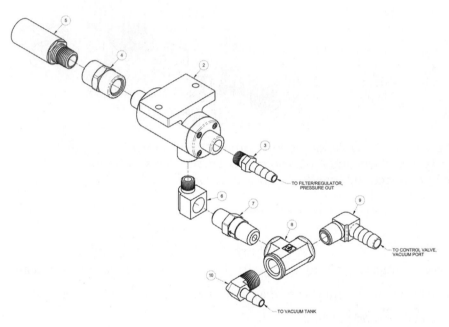

1.2   Excerpt from an Assembly Drawing. *Courtesy of Woods Power-Grip Co., Inc.*

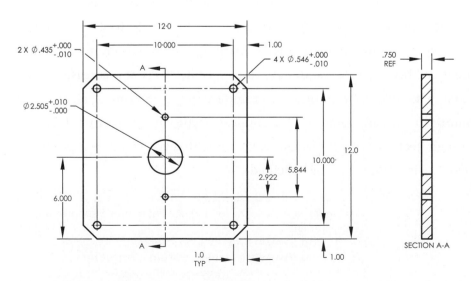

1.3   A Part Drawing. *Courtesy of Dynojet Research, Inc.*

UNDERSTANDING THE ROLE OF TECHNICAL DRAWINGS

Drawings and specifications control the many details of product manufacture, assembly, and maintenance. Both ease in freehand sketching and the ability to use computers to produce technical drawings are valued skills in the global marketplace. Technical drawing requires knowledge of the standards that allow drawings to concisely communicate designs around the world.

Technical drawings can take many forms: idea or concept sketches (such as the Hydropolis drawing on the previous page), computation sketches, design sketches, layout drawings, part drawings, working or construction drawings, electrical drawings, installation drawings, and assembly drawings are all examples. Sketches, 2D CAD drawings and 3D CAD models are all forms of technical drawing. Some of these types of technical drawings are shown in Figures 1.1 through 1.6. Each of these types of drawings and others, have a place in the process of designing and building a product, system, or structure. In general, technical drawings serve one of three purposes:

- Visualization
- Communication
- Documentation

A wide variety of professions use technical drawings to communicate and document designs. Some examples are civil engineering, mechanical engineering, electrical engineering, architecture, bio-resource engineering, landscape design, landscape architecture, industrial design, construction engineering, construction technology, patternmaking, project management, fabrication, and manufacturing. There are many others.

Whether you are designing a bridge, installing underground power lines in a subdivision, or designing a plastic housing for a new toaster, understanding and using technical drawing is a key skill you will need.

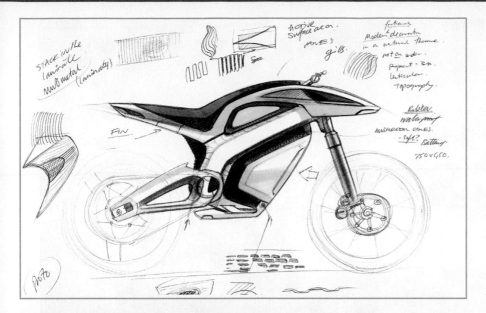

1.4   Design Sketch. *Courtesy of Seymourpowell.*

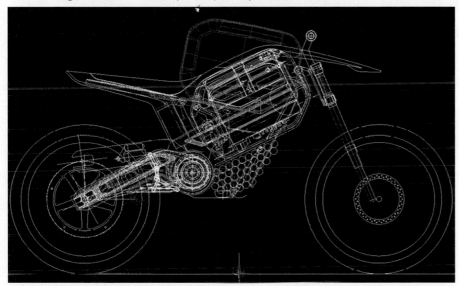

1.5   2D CAD Drawing. *Courtesy of Seymourpowell.*

1.6   Rendered 3D CAD Model. *Courtesy of Seymourpowell.*

Courtesy of Seymourpowell.

Project Velocity

The ENV (Emission Neutral Vehicle) bike began as a top secret project at the Fulham England offices of Seymourpowell. The award winning industrial design firm was selected from a list of four British finalists to showcase groundbreaking technology developed by Intelligent Energy, a leader in fuel cell technology.

The commission began in 2003. First, Seymourpowell facilitated a series of workshops with Intelligent Energy's commercial and technical staff to determine and test a number of potential concepts. They agreed on the idea of a bike to be designed from the fuel cell outward. The bike's form and function would be derived directly from its fuel cell heart.

One early challenge was to accommodate the fuel cell and its hydrogen fuel within a neat and compact unit. Over a period of time, many refinements were made to the bike, both technologically and visually. Early styling iterations with a predatory appearance suggested "Raptor" for the first model, but after the astonishing experience of gliding silently around the park on the bike's first test drive, the name "Eureka" was chosen. Months of hard work, refinement, and exhaustive testing of the technology followed.

ENV the world's first purpose-built hydrogen fuel cell motorbike, was launched in March 2005 at London's Design Museum to extraordinary global acclaim. The sleek, quiet, land pollution-free motorcycle can reach speeds of 50 mph.

Britain's leading motorcycle weekly, MCN, commented: this could be the most important new motorcycle ever. For more information, visit http://www.envbike.com

1.7 Siddartha Meeting Death—Tibet 18th Century *Drawings and paintings are traditionally used to communicate ideas without words, or to clarify what is written. Courtesy of the Art Archive/Musee Guimet Paris/Dagli Orti.*

Artistic and Technical Drawings

Graphic representation has developed along two distinct lines: (1) artistic and (2) technical.

Humans have always used artistic drawings to express aesthetic, philosophic, or other abstract ideas. Before other communications technologies developed, people informed themselves through conversation and by looking at sculptures, paintings, or drawings in public places. Pictures were a principal source of information that everyone could understand. Figure 1.7 is one among countless examples of pictures that tell stories.

Technical drawings are the other distinct form of drawing. From the beginning of recorded history, people have used drawings to represent the design of objects to be built or constructed. Only traces remain of early drawings (such as Figure 1.8) but drawings must have been used, or people could not have designed and built complex structures.

Personal or cultural expression in design is often referred to as aesthetic design, while enhancing product development is considered functional design. Aesthetics and function can work hand in hand to create a product that not only appeals to the senses, but fulfills specific product demands, as shown in Figure 1.9.

Creativity plays a role in both the aesthetic and the functional aspects of design. You will learn about techniques for improving your creativity later in this chapter.

1.8 Chaldean Fortress. This plan view for the design of a fortress drawn by the Chaldean engineer Gudea was engraved on a stone tablet. It is remarkable how similar this plan is to those made by modern architects, although it was "drawn" thousands of years before paper was invented. *From Transactions ASCE, May 1891.*

The Design Process

The organized and orderly approach to solving problems is known as the **design process.** The engineering design process addresses society's needs, desires, and problems by applying scientific principles, experience, and creativity.

A project engineer in a hard hat leans over to examine a blueprint. *Courtesy of Dennis MacDonald/Photo Edit, Inc.*

1.9 The Phillips-Alessi line of kitchen products is an example of design that combines aesthetics and function. *Project developed and created by Philips Design.*

Different types of technical drawings have a specific function in the engineering design process. For example, freehand sketches capture and document the ideation process. Later in the process, CAD models and drawings capture the design and specify the details necessary for manufacture.

The design process for any product requires a clear understanding of the functions and the performance expected of that product. It has been estimated that 70–80 percent of the cost of product development and manufacture is determined during the initial design stages. Although many industrial groups may identify them in their own particular way, one procedure for designing a new or improved product follows these five stages (shown in Figure 1.10):

1. Problem identification: First, a clear statement of the need for and objectives for the design must be written.
2. Ideation: Technical sketches are often used to convey concepts to multidisciplinary teams.
3. Refinement/analysis: Designs may be rethought, based on engineering analysis. CAD models and sketches are useful during the analysis and compromise stage. Accurate 2D or 3D CAD models and drawings are created to refine the design.
4. Implementation/documentation: Production and/or working drawings providing the details of manufacture and assembly are finalized and approved.

Ideally, the design moves through these stages, but as new information becomes available, it may be necessary to return to a previous stage and repeat the process. For example, based on engineering analysis, the familiar phrase "back to the drawing board" might come into play at the compromise solutions stage.

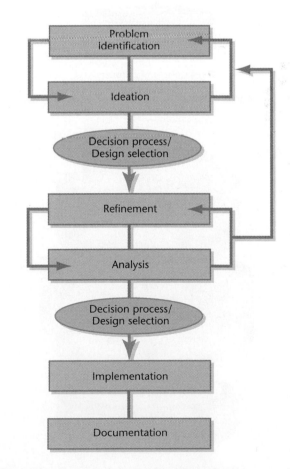

1.10 The Stages of the Design Process

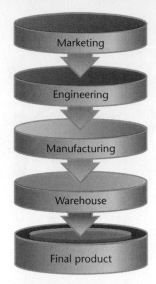

(a) Sequential Process

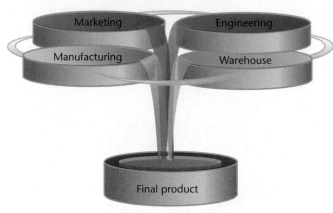

(b) Concurrent Process

1.11 A Model of the Concurrent Design Process

1.12 The Life Cycle of a Product

Concurrent Engineering

Traditionally, design and manufacturing activities have taken place in sequential order rather than concurrently (simultaneously). Designers would spend considerable effort and time analyzing components and preparing detailed part drawings, and then forward them to other departments. For example, the materials department would use the drawing to identify the particular alloys and source vendors to use. The manufacturing department would then identify the processes needed for efficient production. This step by step approach seems logical, but in practice it has been found to be wasteful.

For example, if a manufacturing engineer wanted taper the flange on a part to make it easier to cast in metal, or to choose a different alloy, the design analysis stage would have to be repeated to ensure that the product would still function effectively. These iterations, illustrated in Fig. 1.11a, may be necessary, but they waste resources and more importantly, time. Time is important because early product introduction carries advantages toward a greater market percentage (and hence greater profits) and a longer life before the product becomes obsolete (clearly a concern with consumer electronics).

Concurrent engineering is a systematic approach that integrates the design and manufacture of products with the goal of optimizing all elements involved in the life cycle of the product. Figure 1.11b illustrates the concurrent design process.

Life cycle design means that all aspects of a product (such as design, development, production, distribution, use, and its ultimate disposal and recycling) are considered simultaneously. Figure 1.12 depicts the life cycle of a product from conception to disposal.

The basic goals of concurrent engineering are to minimize product design and engineering changes and to reduce the time and cost involved in taking a product from design concept through production and ultimately to introduction into the marketplace. In concurrent engineering, all disciplines are involved in the early design stages, so the iterations which naturally occur result in less wasted effort and lost time.

Communication between and within disciplines is especially important in a concurrent design process. Effective interaction between engineering, marketing, and service functions, as well as between engineering sub-disciplines, is recognized as crucial to this type of process. Cross-disciplinary communication also helps provide a fertile environment for innovative approaches that can lead to savings in material and production costs.

Computer-Aided Design and Product Development

For both large and small companies, product design often involves preparing analytical and physical models of the product which can be used to study factors such as forces, stresses, deflections, and optimal part shape. The necessity for these types of models depends on how complex the product is. Today, the process of constructing and studying analytical models is simplified by using **computer-aided design** (CAD), **computer-aided engineering** (CAE), and **computer-aided manufacturing** (CAM) techniques. These systems allow rapid design analysis for simple objects as well as complex structures.

Computer-aided design (CAD) allows for a range of activities, from modeling 2D and 3D geometry to creating drawings that document the design for manufacturing and legal considerations.

Computer-aided manufacturing (CAM) provides computerized control for manufacturing processes. Examples might be using a computer interface to control a lathe or generating the path for milling machine tools directly from the CAD model. In more sophisticated systems, CAM can be used in materials handling, assembly, and inspection.

Computer-aided engineering allows users to simulate and analyze structures that will be subject to various temperatures, static loads, or fluctuating loads. Kinematic analysis provides for the study of moving parts. Some of these functions are integrated with CAD software and other packages import data from a CAD system. Using these tools, engineers can simulate, analyze, and test designs efficiently, accurately, and quickly.

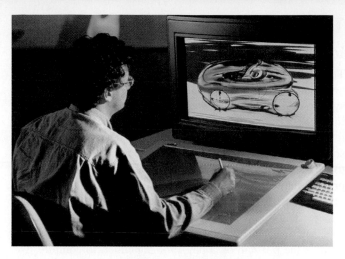

A car designer working with CAD. *Courtesy of Getty Images, Inc.*

Designing Quality Into Products

There are a number of systematic ways that companies try to design "quality" into their products as well as to measure performance and make decisions based on data. Designers may feel that their creative approach to problem solving is stifled when these systems are poorly implemented in the workplace. But when these systems are well implemented, organizations can show quality improvement.

DFSS Design for Six Sigma (DFSS) is an approach that uses engineering and statistical tools to design products in a way that predicts and minimizes customer and manufacturing problems.

DMAIC Define, Measure, Analyze, Improve, and Control (DMAIC) are steps defined in a continuous improvement process that attempts to define and ensure critical quality (CTF) characteristics.

Six Sigma Six Sigma is a process originated at Motorola to improve quality by reducing or eliminating defects.

QFD Quality Function Deployment (QFD) is a tool for decision making that helps companies focus on a customer driven approach and set of product characteristics.

The Digital Database

Computer use continues to change the way products are produced. All of the information to manage, design, analyze, simulate, package, market, and manufacture a product can be shared with a diverse (and perhaps geographically distant) group of users through a single complex digital database.

Product data management (PDM) systems or **enterprise data management** (EDM) systems electronically store the various types of data associated with designing and manufacturing a product. An effective PDM system allows all of the product data to be quickly stored, retrieved, displayed, printed, managed, and transferred to anywhere in the organization. This allows for designs to be optimized or directly modified at any time. Costs, product revisions, and **engineering change orders** (ECOs) can be analyzed, tracked, and implemented

Windchill Extended Enterprise

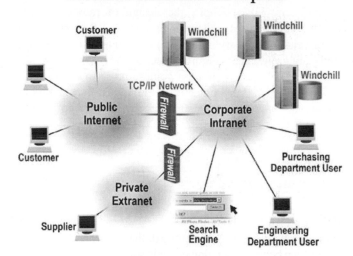

1.13 Product Data Management. PTC's WIndchill is an enterprise-wide product data management system designed to be be extended to service data over the internal network (or intranet). Data from the database would be provided to external users via a secure, password-protected site (to share non-public information with suppliers and other partners in remote locations). *Courtesy of Parametric Technology Corporation.*

quickly. Managing enterprise data requires commitment and planning, but companies who implement PDM effectively can capture product data once and utilize it many ways to achieve a competitive advantage (Figure 1.13).

1.1 ENGINEERING DESIGN STAGE 1

Identify the Customer and the Problem

The basic role of engineering design is to provide solutions for problems and to fulfill needs or wants for products, services, or systems. The engineering design process begins with recognizing or identifying these needs and considering the economic feasibility of fulfilling them. A successful design must not only solve the problem, but meet the needs and wishes of the customer. It follows that any new design and the related design process should ultimately be driven by the needs of the end user. Products must also meet government standards/regulations and adhere to the standards or codes of professional organizations.

Engineering designs range from simple and inexpensive, such as the pull tab on a beverage container, to complex and costly, such as products that meet the needs of air, ground, and space travel. Although a product may be as small as the pull tab on a beverage can, the production tools and dies needed to create it can require considerable engineering and design effort.

Products may be new or may be revised versions of existing products. For example, the design of radios, toasters, watches, automobiles, and washing machines have been similar for years, but the styling and features change to reflect new needs and preferences (Figure 1.14).

Nearly all designs require compromises to meet budget constraints, marketing objectives, and other considerations. The amount of time budgeted to a project is no exception.

1.14 New Design of a Traditional Product: Clear Appliances—*In this unused design by Phillips Co., users could watch their toast brown or water boil through casings made of glass rather than stainless steel. But keeping the insides of the toaster clean was an engineering challenge that meant it never made the production line. Project developed and created by Philips Design.*

1.2 ENGINEERING DESIGN STAGE 2

Generate Concepts

After a problem or need is identified, the design team begins generating possible solutions. During this stage, often called the **ideation** stage, many ideas—reasonable and otherwise—are collected. The ideas may come from individuals or may be developed in team brainstorming sessions. Whether from a group or an individual process, concepts that may not be suitable as solutions can still serve as springboards to generate more ideas.

Technical sketching is frequently used during the ideation stage. The ability to freely create technical sketches lets you present and share ideas and record them so you can refer back to solutions, inspirations, and breakthroughs that come to light during this creative stage of the process. All notes and sketches should be signed, dated, and retained for design documentation and possible patent proof. Figure 1.15 shows an ideation sketch created during the development of the ENV bike.

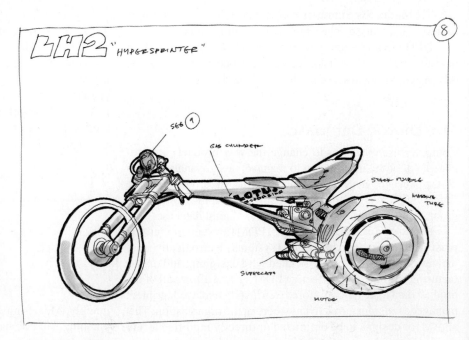

1.15 Ideation Sketch. *Courtesy of Seymourpowell.*

1.3 ENGINEERING DESIGN STAGE 3

Compromise Solutions

After careful consideration of the problem, the design team selects various features of the concepts generated in the ideation stage and combines them into one or more promising compromise solutions. At this point the best solution is evaluated in detail and attempts are made to simplify it so that it performs efficiently and is easy to manufacture, repair, and even dispose of when its lifetime is over.

Refined design sketches are often followed by a study of suitable materials (Figure 1.16) and of motion problems that may be involved. What source of power is to be used: manual, electric motor, or some other means? What type of motion is needed? Is it necessary to translate rotary motion into linear motion, or vice versa? Many of these problems are solved graphically, using schematic drawings in which various parts are shown in skeleton form. For example, pulleys and gears are represented by circles, an arm by a single line, and a path of motion by centerlines (Figure 1.17). Certain basic calculations, such as those related to velocity and acceleration, may also be made at this time.

Preliminary studies are followed by a design layout, usually an accurate CAD drawing that shows actual sizes so that proportions and fits can be clearly visualized, or by a clearly dimensioned layout sketch. An example is shown in Figure 1.18. At this time all parts are carefully designed for strength and

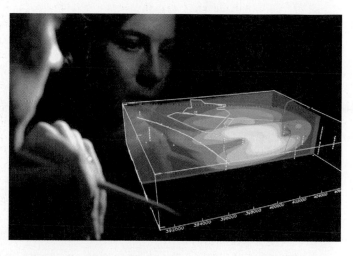

1.16   CAD Model of Iron Aggregate Surface. *Courtesy of Ed Eckstein/Phototake NYC.*

function. Costs are constantly kept in mind, because no matter how well the device performs, it must sell at a profit; otherwise the time and development costs will have been a loss.

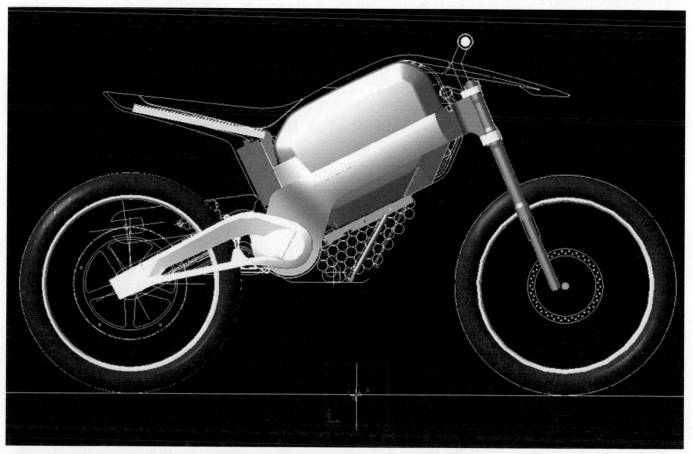

1.17   A CAD Layout Showing Features as Skeletons. *Courtesy of Seymourpowell.*

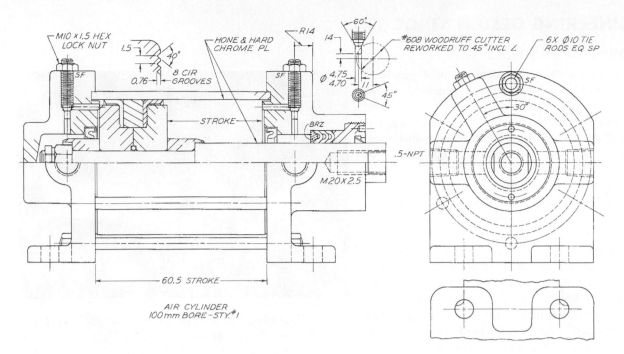

1.18 Design Layout

Figure 1.18 shows the layout of basic proportions of parts and how they fit together in an assembly drawing. Special attention is given to clearances of moving parts, ease of assembly, and serviceability. Standard parts are used wherever possible, because they are less expensive than custom parts. Materials and costs are carefully considered. Although functional considerations must come first, manufacturing problems must be kept constantly in mind.

1.4 ENGINEERING DESIGN STAGE 4

Models and Prototypes

Design teams often construct a model to scale in order to study, analyze, and refine a design. A full-size working model made to final specifications (except, possibly, for materials), is known as a **prototype.** Model-shop craftspeople often work from dimensioned sketches or CAD drawings to create a prototype for use in testing and visualization. The prototype is tested and modified where necessary and the information gained is used to revise the design if necessary. If the prototype is unsatisfactory, it may be necessary to return to a previous stage in the design process and repeat the procedures, bearing in mind what was learned during the testing process. Of course, time and expense considerations always limit the duration of this looping. Eventually the team must reach a decision for the production model.

Figure 1.19 shows a virtual prototype of the safe navigation Mars rover.

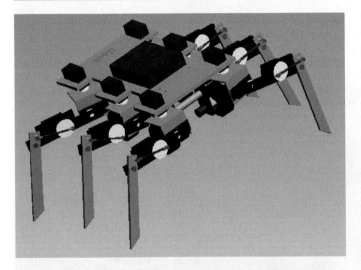

1.19 **3D CAD Model** *This 3D CAD Model of a Design for the Mars Rover is constructed to act as a Virtual Prototype for the Design. Courtesy of Byron Johns.*

1.20 Ayanna Howard and the Safe Navigation Mars Rover Prototype. The Mars rover is a solution to a need in the space program to explore larger areas of the Martian surface. *Courtesy of Michael Grecco/Icon International.*

Accurate 3D CAD models can act as a virtual prototype, sometimes even making it unnecessary to create a physical prototype for testing the design. Using an accurate CAD model, clearances can be checked and mass properties calculated. An added benefit is the ability to create realistic renderings of the model, which can be used for design visualization. The appearance of the part, shaded and rendered using CAD, sometimes looks even better than the final product due to the perfection of the CAD image compared to actual surfaces. Figure 1.20 shows a virtual prototype for a Mars rover design.

Intelligent Models

Parametric, constraint-based or **feature-based modeling** uses variables to constrain the shape of the geometry. Using feature-based modeling, the designer roughly sketches initial shapes and applies drawing dimensions and constraints to create models that have "intelligence." Later, as the design is refined, the model can update as the designer changes the dimensions and constraints so that new models do not have to be created for each design change. In addition, the constraints and dimensions that control this type of 3D CAD model can be calculated based on engineering design data. Sophisticated models can even follow systems of complex physical rules, such as modeling the effect of gravity or other physical laws.

Figure 1.21 shows a rendered 3D CAD model of a braking system used to stop the rotation of a dynomometer drum.

1.21 3D CAD Model of the SAAR Brake. *Courtesy of Dynojet Research, Inc.*

Rapid Prototyping

While refining design ideas, the design team often works concurrently with manufacturing to determine the best ways to make and assemble the necessary parts. After several cycles of refining, analyzing, and synthesizing the best ideas, the final design is ready to go into production. **Rapid prototyping** systems allow designers to generate parts quickly, directly from 3D models, for mockup and testing. For example, you can check useability for humans or explore customer reactions in consumer focus groups by showing them facsimile products created using rapid prototyping. 3D design data can be formatted for use by rapid prototyping equipment. Figure 1.22 shows the prototyped part emerging from the unfused material of the ZPrinter 450 rapid prototyper, which can "print" a color part like the one shown in about four hours. You will learn more about rapid prototyping methods in Chapter 8.

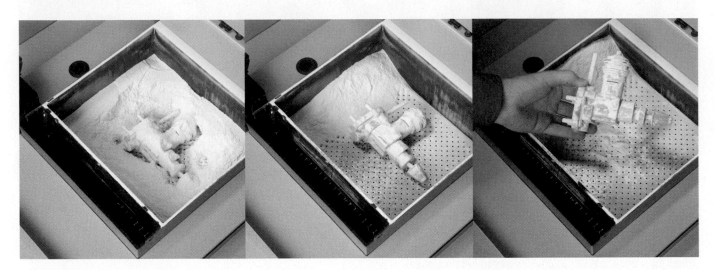

1.22   Rapid Prototyping. *The ZPrinter 450 from Zcorp "printed" the colored part shown in about four hours. Courtesy of Z Corporation.*

1.5 ENGINEERING DESIGN STAGE 5

Production or Working Drawings

To produce or manufacture a product, often a final set of production or working drawings is made, checked, and approved. The drawings, showing the necessary views, include the material, dimensions, required tolerances, notes, and other information needed to describe each part sufficiently for it to be manufactured consistently. These drawings of the individual parts are also known as detail drawings.

Figure 1.23 shows a detail drawing of an air can mounting bracket. An *assembly drawing,* like that shown in Figure 1.24, shows how all the parts go together in the complete product.

Unaltered standard parts that are purchased "off the shelf" do not require detail drawings but are shown conventionally on the assembly drawing and listed with specifications in the parts list.

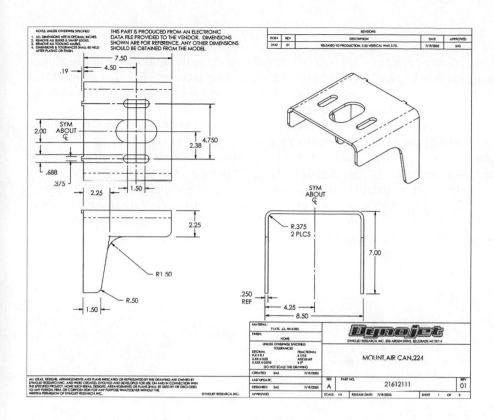

1.23 Detail Drawing for the SAAR Brake Air Can Mounting Bracket. *Courtesy of Dynojet Research, Inc.*

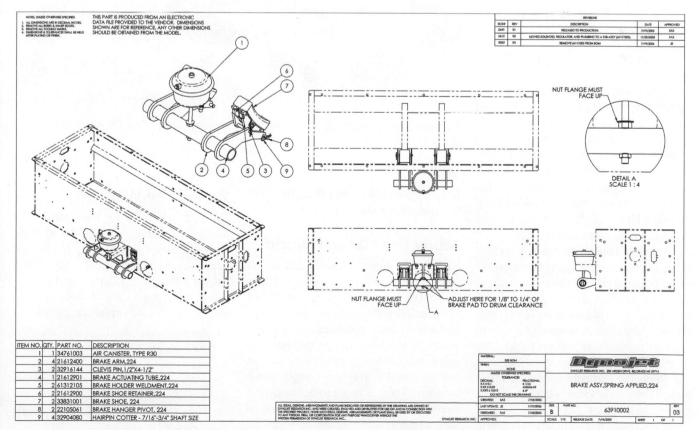

ITEM NO.	QTY.	PART NO.	DESCRIPTION
1	1	34761003	AIR CANISTER, TYPE R30
2	4	21612400	BRAKE ARM,224
3	2	32916144	CLEVIS PIN,1/2"X4-1/2"
4	1	21612901	BRAKE ACTUATING TUBE,224
5	2	61312105	BRAKE HOLDER WELDMENT,224
6	2	21612900	BRAKE SHOE RETAINER,224
7	2	33831001	BRAKE SHOE, 224
8	2	22105061	BRAKE HANGER PIVOT, 224
9	4	32904080	HAIRPIN COTTER - 7/16"-3/4" SHAFT SIZE

1.24 Assembly Drawing for the SAAR Brake. *Courtesy of Dynojet Research, Inc.*

1.6 DRAFTING STANDARDS

There are **standards** that support a uniform, effective graphic language for use in industry, manufacturing, engineering, and science. Technical drawing texts like this book can help you learn them. In the United States, providing these standards has been the work of the American National Standards Institute (ANSI) with the American Society for Engineering Education (ASEE), the Society of Automotive Engineers (SAE), and the American Society of Mechanical Engineers (ASME).

Participants in these organizations help develop the *American National Standard Drafting Manual—Y14*, which is composed of a number of separate sections that are published as approved standards as they are completed (see Appendix 1). These standards are frequently updated in order to communicate information so that it meets the needs of modern industry and engineering practice. They are considered the most authoritative guide to uniform drafting practices in the United States today.

International standards, often defined by the International Standards Organization (ISO) and the ASME or ANSI standards for drawing practices, are similar in many respects. The greatest differences are in the preferred method of projection: first angle versus third angle projection; and in the units of measurement in dimensioning. Third angle projection is the projection method that you will be learning in this text. Where practical, information for both U.S. and international drawings will be presented.

1.7 CREATIVITY TECHNIQUES

Some people are naturally gifted at design and drawing, but everyone can improve their design ability if they learn to use the proper tools and techniques. It is similar to learning to play a musical instrument; it comes more naturally to some people than to others, but everyone can learn to play if they practice.

How do you develop new ideas? Here are some proven techniques you can practice.

Examine Manufactured Products

It is common for design engineers to dismantle manufactured products, evaluate them, and study how their parts are designed to work together. As you use and examine manufactured products, ask yourself how could they be improved. What would you do differently? How could you expand/change the design to guarantee better performance? What could you do to expand the life of the product? How could you make it more efficient, more cost-effective, etc.?

Reverse engineering is a term that refers to designing products based on existing designs, usually through measurement and deconstruction of an existing product. A **coordinate measuring machine** (CMM) aids in speeding the time to reverse engineer some products. A CMM measures the object using a probe or laser and stores the pertinent geometric information into a database where it can be manipulated using CAD.

Functional decomposition is a term for determining the subfunctions involved

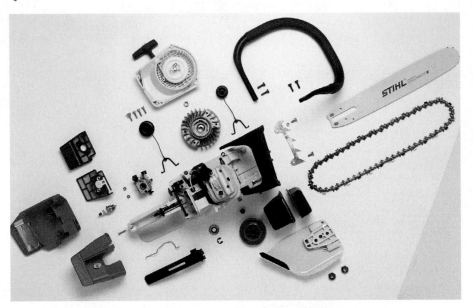

A Chain Saw Disassembled. *Dave King© Dorling Kindersley, Courtesy of Andreas Stihl, Ltd.*

in a design and then using those functions to reconstruct a similar product.

Study the Natural World

Noting how other creatures and organisms function and interact with their surroundings can provide a wealth of information and creativity. Such things as beehives and spiderwebs are masterpieces of structural design that have inspired human designers for centuries. A hummingbird's wings are aerodynamic wonders. There is much to be learned by studying natural forms and expanding on their designs, as Leonardo da Vinci did with his flying machine (Figure 1.25).

Watch the Web

Excellent resources for engineering and design are available on the World Wide Web. Reading technology blogs and news feeds, and visiting engineering sites is a way to stay current and keep in touch with peers. The following Web sites are useful for engineering design:

- http://www.yahoo.com/headlines/ Yahoo's site for the latest technology news and a one-week archive
- http://www.techweb.com/ TechWeb site from CMP media
- http://www.uspto.gov/ U.S. Patent Office on-line search site

1.25 Full-scale wooden replica of the Ornithopter, a flapping-winged flying machine conceived by Leonardo da Vinci. *Courtesy of Peter Chadwick© Dorling Kindersley.*

Research Patent Drawings

Patents can be a great source of ideas. A patent is issued by the U.S. government and grants the holder the "right to exclude others from making, using, or selling" a specific product for a specific time period. The patent process was first developed as a way to promote the disclosure of technical advances. You can research the current state of design for your product idea at the U.S. Patent and Trademark Office's searchable Web site (www.uspto.gov). The U.S. Patent and Trademark Office has strict regulations as to how designs are presented in **patent drawings** so the drawings are easy to reproduce (Figure 1.26).

Design Groups

In order to bring complex products and systems to market, most individuals end up working in a team environment. Teams combine the expertise of individuals familiar with materials, production processes, marketing, finance, and so on, so most projects become a team effort long before a product is produced and marketed. In addition to supplying the varied expertise that it takes to bring an idea from concept to manufacture, interaction between people of varied talents plays an important role in the creative design process. The ability to create and understand technical drawings helps group members contribute to and benefit from team communication.

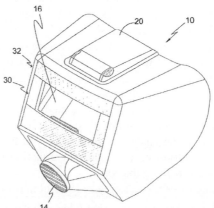

1.26 Patent Drawing for Universal Healthier Helmet

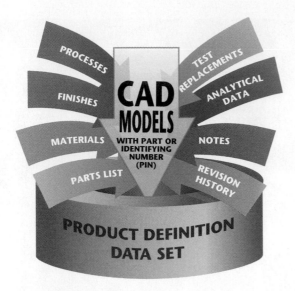

1.27   Possible Contents of a 3D Data Set

1.8 PRODUCT DEFINITION

As stated before, technical graphics play three important roles: visualization, communication, and documentation. Drawings and CAD models are an important part of product definition. **Product definition** refers to the range of digital or hard copy documents that specify the physical and functional requirements for a product. This can range from a 3D CAD model that specifies manufacturing requirements within the CAD file to a dimensioned paper sketch.

Many companies prefer storing information in a digital format because the storage cost is comparatively low and the data can be easily searched, retrieved, and utilized by many individuals. Figure 1.27 represents a range of contents of a product definition data set. From hand sketches to complex 3D models, a thorough understanding of the graphic language is necessary to be a player in the competitive world marketplace.

1.9 SHOWING THE DESIGN PROCESS IN A PORTFOLIO

A portfolio is a representative sample of work that helps communicate your skills and talents, usually to a prospective employer or client. Many companies and individuals post portfolios on the Web to promote their capabilities and accomplishments. Larger companies tend to show more models and completed projects because working drawings may be proprietary information. Individuals, particularly recent students, may focus more on showing correct drawing practices and creative problem solving skills.

Whether you are a consulting engineer, an architect, an industrial designer, or a draftsman, showing samples of your work offers an advantage over just talking about it. Drawings are proof, not only that you have good ideas, but that you have the skill to communicate clearly and accurately throughout the stages of a project, from concept to completion,

If you are seeking an entry level job, don't worry if your portfolio looks like an entry level portfolio. Clean, correct student work is a good indication of your potential. Don't try to cover a lack of well-drawn examples with a more expensive portfolio case, or decorative presentation. Instead, spend that energy completing a project that shows your ability.

A portfolio is an opportunity to tell concise success stories. For example, you may want to show four to six projects, including the design brief (or assigned problem), sketches, development drawings, and final presentation (including working drawings, renderings and physical or 3d models) for each. Your portfolio samples make great talking points in an interview, so take advantage of the chance to show how you tackled challenges such as cutting costs, improving function or solving problems that arose along the way.

Some more tips for creating a successful portfolio are:

1. Less is more. It is assumed that what you show in a portfolio is your best work, so a few good examples are better than a million mediocre examples. Four to six projects are usually plenty.

2. Show correct drawing practices. Especially if you are seeking a drafting position, but even if your strength is creativity, be sure that line weights, dimensioning, notes and other parts of the drawing conform to technical drawing standards.

3. Keep several versions of your current portfolio, including hard copy, digital and Web presence. Use widely accessible formats (such as PDF or PowerPoint) to make your digital portfolio easy to access. Including your Web address in correspondence allows people to view your work or refer back to your samples at their convenience.

4. Never rely entirely on electronic equipment. Even if you have a great digital presentation, bring a portfolio of printed samples. Drawings should be clean and legible. Depending on your discipline, you may want a larger or smaller portfolio case, keeping in mind how convenient it is to transport and view. You may fold large drawings to fit, as long as they are easy to take out and look at.

5. Save good examples as you create them. It is easy to forget what you did last year, or four years ago. Keep copies (both digital and paper) of your best work in a file for portfolio samples and remember to save some development sketches from successful projects, too.

6. Depending on your career goals, let your portfolio reflect the area you want to explore. If you are seeking a creative position and you have related skills (such as artistic drawing or photography) you may want to include appropriate examples. If you are mainly interested in a drafting position, you may want to include more working drawings and models.

Throughout this book, the Portfolio sections give you some exposure to real-world drawings that apply to chapter topics. However, the Portfolio section for this chapter shows how an industrial design student successfully communicated the design process through a well-conceived portfolio page.

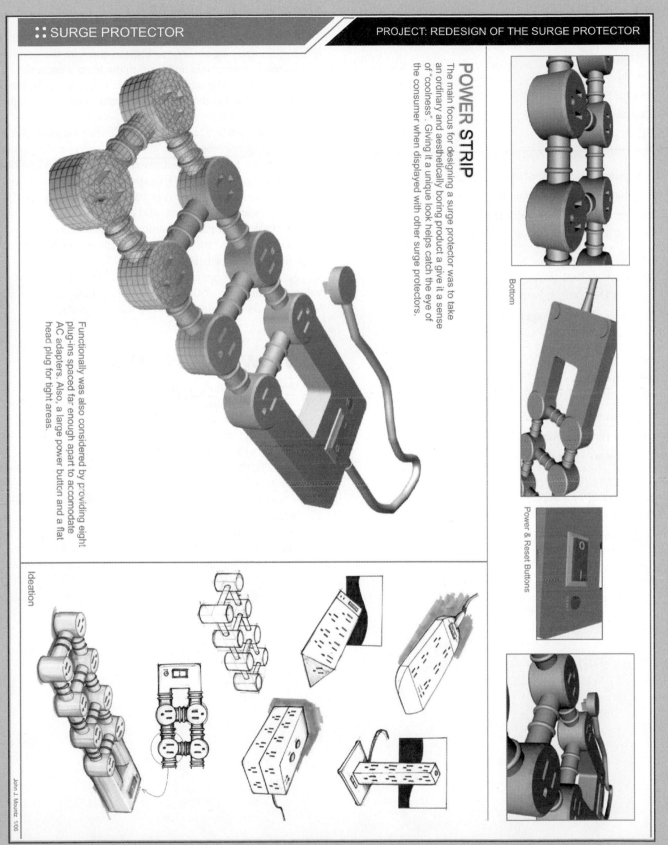

POWER STRIP

The main focus for designing a surge protector was to take an ordinary and aesthetically boring product a give it a sense of "coolness". Giving it a unique look helps catch the eye of the consumer when displayed with other surge protectors.

Functionally was also considered by providing eight plug-ins spaced far enough apart to accomodate AC adapters. Also, a large power button and a flat head plug for tight areas.

Bottom

Power & Reset Buttons

Ideation

John J. Mountz 1/06

PORTFOLIO

This single page from the portfolio of John Mountz begins with the design brief and rationale for the design. It includes initial concepts, more refined sketches, a solid model and details. Mountz showed the final presentation drawing on an additional portfolio page. At the time, he was a student of industrial design Doug Wintin, then Chair of the School of Design at ITT Technical Institute. *Courtesy of John Mountz.*

KEY WORDS

Visualization

Communication

Documentation

Design Process

Concurrent Engineering

Life Cycle Design

Computer-Aided Design

Computer-Aided Engineering

Computer-Aided Manufacturing

Design for Six Sigma (DFSS)

Define, Measure, Analyze, Improve, Control (DMAIC)

Six Sigma

Quality Function Deployment (QFD)

Product Data Management

Enterprise Data Management

Engineering Change Orders

Ideation

Prototype

Parametric Modeling

Constraint-Based Modeling

Feature-Based Modeling

Rapid Prototyping

Standards

Reverse Engineering

Coordinate Measuring Machine

Functional Decomposition

Patent Drawings

Product Definition

CHAPTER SUMMARY

The members of the engineering design project team must be able to communicate among themselves and with the rest of the project team in order to contribute to the team's success.

The graphic language is the universal language used to design, develop, and construct products and systems throughout the world.

There are two basic types of drawings: artistic and technical.

The design process is the ability to combine ideas, scientific principles, resources, and existing products into a solution for a problem. It consists of five specific stages.

Every technical drawing is based on standards that prescribe what each symbol, line, and arc means.

The basic principles for communicating information using technical drawings are the same whether you are creating drawings by hand or using CAD.

Successful companies hire skilled people who can add value to their team. A thorough understanding of the graphic language is an essential skill that employers value.

REVIEW QUESTIONS

1. When is sketching used as graphic communication?
2. Why are standards so important for members of the engineering design team?
3. What is the design process?
4. What are the five phases of the design process?
5. Describe the difference between concurrent and traditional design process models.
6. What does PDM or EDM stand for? What are some advantages of PDM?
7. When are rapid prototypes useful?
8. List three ways a CAD database can be used.
9. List five techniques you can use to enhance creativity.

CHAPTER TWO

LAYOUTS AND LETTERING

OBJECTIVES

After studying the material in this chapter, you should be able to:

1. Identify six types of technical drawings based on the projection system they use.

2. Identify the line patterns used in technical drawings and describe how they are used.

3. Read and measure with the architects' scale, engineers' scale, and metric scale.

4. Identify standard drawing media and sheet sizes.

5. Add lettering to a sketch.

6. Fill in a standard title block with the appropriate information.

7. Lay out a drawing sheet.

Refer to the following standards:

- Y14.100—2004 Engineering Drawing Practices
- Y14.2M—1992 Line Conventions and Lettering
- Y14.1—2005 Decimal Inch Drawing Sheet Size and Format
- Y14.1M—2005 Metric Drawing Sheet Size and Format

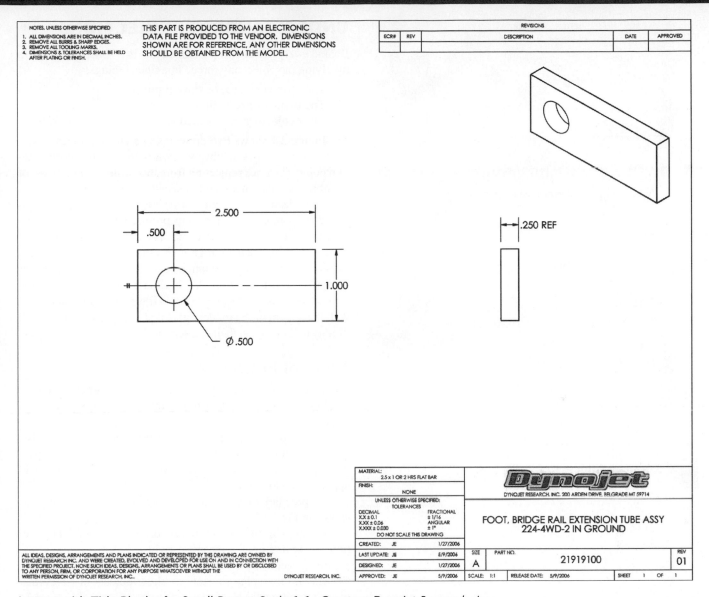

Layout with Title Block of a Small Part at Scale 1:1. *Courtesy Dynojet Research, Inc.*

OVERVIEW

Two dimensional technical drawings, whether they are sketched by hand, drawn using instruments, drawn using a CAD program, or generated from 3D solid models, follow certain rules so that they can be correctly interpreted. Unlike artistic drawings, which communicate self expression and emotional content, technical drawings communicate how to manufacture or construct a product, system, or device. In order to clearly describe this information, technical drawings adhere closely to formal standards.

These formal standards include systems of projection for developing and understanding drawing views.

They also include an "alphabet of lines," where each line of the drawing represents certain information. Lettering is also standardized, to make drawings quick to create and easy to read and reproduce. Standard sheet sizes for drawings include a title block that provides important information such as the drawing name, company information, scale, revision numbers, and approvals for release of the drawing.

Check the sites below for engineering graphics supplies and equipment
- http://www.reprint-draphix.com/
- http://www.eclipse.net/~essco/draft/draft.htm
- http://www.graphic-design.com/Type/index.html

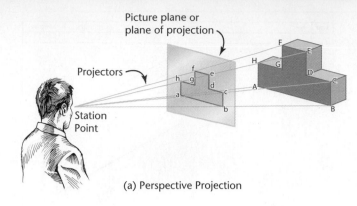

Picture plane or plane of projection

Projectors

Station Point

(a) Perspective Projection

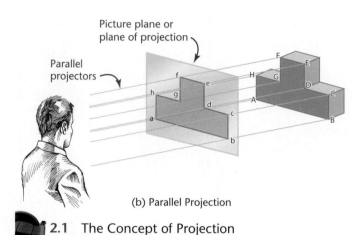

Picture plane or plane of projection

Parallel projectors

(b) Parallel Projection

2.1 The Concept of Projection

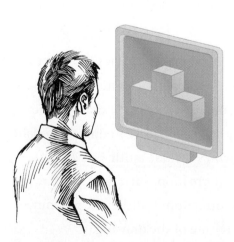

2.2 A View of a 3D Object "Projected" onto a Computer Monitor

UNDERSTANDING PROJECTIONS

Behind every 2D drawing of an object is a space relationship involving the object and three "imagined" things:

1. The observer's eye, or **station point**
2. The **plane of projection**
3. The **projectors** (also called *visual rays* or *lines of sight*).

Figure 2.1 shows two drawings of a shape projected onto a plane as viewed by an observer, whose eye represents the station point. The lines projecting from the corners (or vertices) of the object are the imagined lines, called projectors.

To understand projection, imagine that the drawing is produced by points, called **piercing points,** where the projectors would pierce the projection plane. The drawing may be a two-dimensional representation on a sheet of paper, or it may be a two-dimensional representation shown on your computer screen, as shown in Figure 2.2, but the basic principles are the same. One reason 2D projection skills remain relevant, even with the advent of 3D modeling, is that computer monitors still display a 2D view on their flat screens.

Types of Projections

There are two main types of projection: perspective and parallel. These are broken down into subtypes as shown in Figure 2.3.

In **perspective projections,** the projectors come together at the station point to form a cone, as in Figure 2.1a. Perspective drawings represent objects as we see them or as they would appear in a photograph.

In **parallel projections,** the projectors are parallel, as shown in Figure 2.1b.

Orthographic projections are one type of parallel projection. In orthographic (meaning right-angle) projections, the parallel projectors are perpendicular to the plane of projection. Because orthographic projections show objects in a way that their features can be represented at true size or scaled at a proportion of true size, they are especially useful in specifying the dimensions needed in technical applications.

If the projectors are parallel to each other, but are at an angle *other than 90°* to the plane of projection, the result is called an **oblique projection.**

Technical drawings of 3D objects usually use one of four standard types of projection, shown in Figure 2.3:

- Multiview
- Axonometric (isometric)
- Oblique
- Perspective

Multiview projection shows one or more necessary views. Either of two systems are used to arrange the views in a multiview drawing: Third Angle or First Angle. You will learn about multiview projection in Chapter 4.

Axonometric, oblique, and perspective sketches are methods of showing the object pictorially in a single view. They will be discussed in Chapters 14, 15, and 16.

The main types of projection are listed in Table 2.1.

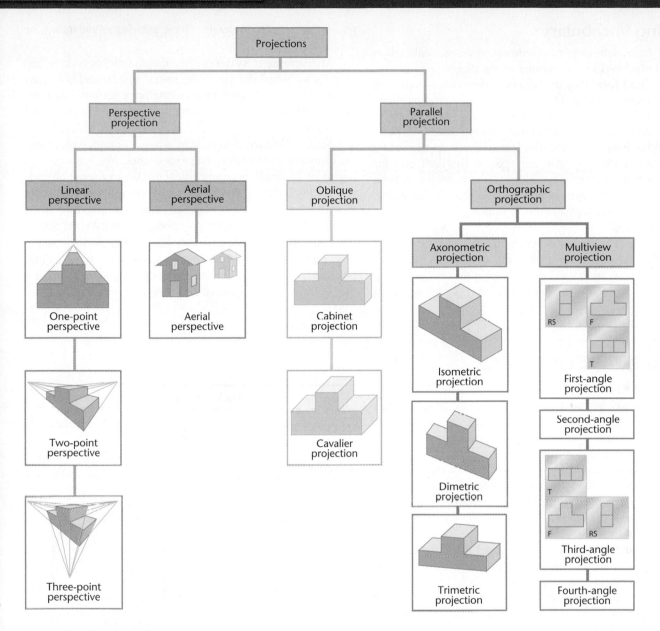

2.3   Classification of Projections

Table 2.1 Classification by Projectors.

Class of Projection	Distance from Observer to Plane of Projection	Direction of Projectors
Perspective	Finite	Radiating from station point
Parallel	Infinite	Parallel to each other
Oblique	Infinite	Parallel to each other and oblique to plane of projection
Orthographic	Infinite	Perpendicular to plane of projection
Axonometric	Infinite	Perpendicular to plane of projection
Multiview	Infinite	Perpendicular to plane of projection

Drawing Vocabulary

Drawing lines, lettering, measurement systems, scale, sheet sizes and title blocks are presented in this chapter.

Drawing Lines Projected drawing views use specific line patterns to represent object features. For example, when showing a three dimensional object, some lines represent the edges of surfaces that are hidden from that viewing direction. These hidden lines have a dashed line pattern to help the reader understand the drawing. Another type of line indicates the location of the center of a symmetric feature, such as a hole. Familiarity with the types of lines used in technical drawings helps you read drawings and create drawings that others can easily understand.

Lettering The shapes of letters that are easy to read and write are described as part of drawing standards. Often freehand sketching is used early in the design process to present ideas and showing notes and information legibly helps present your ideas to others clearly. Good lettering often makes or breaks a sketch.

Measurement Systems Two measurements systems are used for technical drawings: the metric system and U.S. customary units. It is important to be familiar with both measurement systems to create and read drawings that are used worldwide.

Scale Obviously a large item, a house or bridge for example, cannot be shown full size on a paper sheet. To clearly convey important information about particularly large or small objects, you need to select an appropriate sheet size and show drawings to scale (proportionately smaller or larger than the actual size). Standard lettering sizes for drawings depend on the sheet size.

Title Blocks Company information, the drawing scale, sheet size, and other information is included in a standard title block located in the lower right corner of the drawing to make it easy to locate these important details on every drawing layout.

2.1 ALPHABET OF LINES

The meaning of each line on a technical drawing is indicated by its width (thick or thin) and its particular line style. The person who reads the drawing will depend on these line styles to know if a line is visible or hidden, if it represents a center axis, or if it conveys dimension information.

To make your drawings easy to read, make the contrast between thick and thin lines distinct. **Thick lines** (0.6 mm) should be twice the width of **thin lines** (0.3 mm) as shown in Figure 2.4. The line gage in Figure 2.5 shows various widths.

Figure 2.6 shows freehand line technique. You may find it helpful to use 1/8" graph paper at first to get a feel for the length of dashes used in hidden lines and centerlines. Soon you will be able to estimate the lengths by eye.

Figure 2.7 illustrates line styles for technical drawings. All lines (except construction lines) must be sharp and dark. For visible, cutting-plane, and short-break lines use thick lines. Thin drawing lines should be just as sharp and black, but only half the thickness of thick lines. Construction lines and lettering guidelines should be thin and light so that they can barely be seen at arm's length and need not be erased. All lines should be uniform in width and darkness. Ideal lengths of the dashes used to form the line patterns are also shown in Figure 2.7.

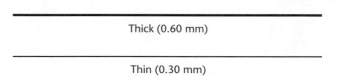

Thick (0.60 mm)

Thin (0.30 mm)

2.4   Thick and Thin Drawing Lines

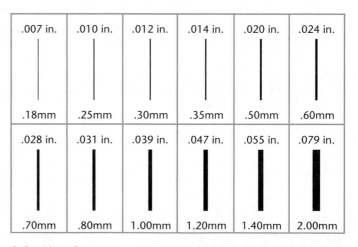

.007 in.	.010 in.	.012 in.	.014 in.	.020 in.	.024 in.
.18mm	.25mm	.30mm	.35mm	.50mm	.60mm
.028 in.	.031 in.	.039 in.	.047 in.	.055 in.	.079 in.
.70mm	.80mm	1.00mm	1.20mm	1.40mm	2.00mm

2.5   Line Gage

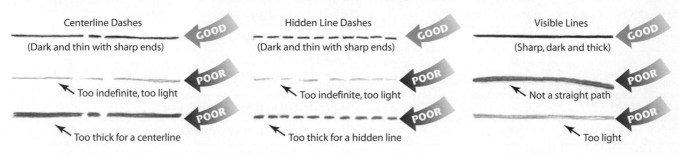

Centerline Dashes	Hidden Line Dashes	Visible Lines
GOOD (Dark and thin with sharp ends)	GOOD (Dark and thin with sharp ends)	GOOD (Sharp, dark and thick)
POOR Too indefinite, too light	POOR Too indefinite, too light	POOR Not a straight path
POOR Too thick for a centerline	POOR Too thick for a hidden line	POOR Too light

2.6   Good and Poor Freehand Line Technique

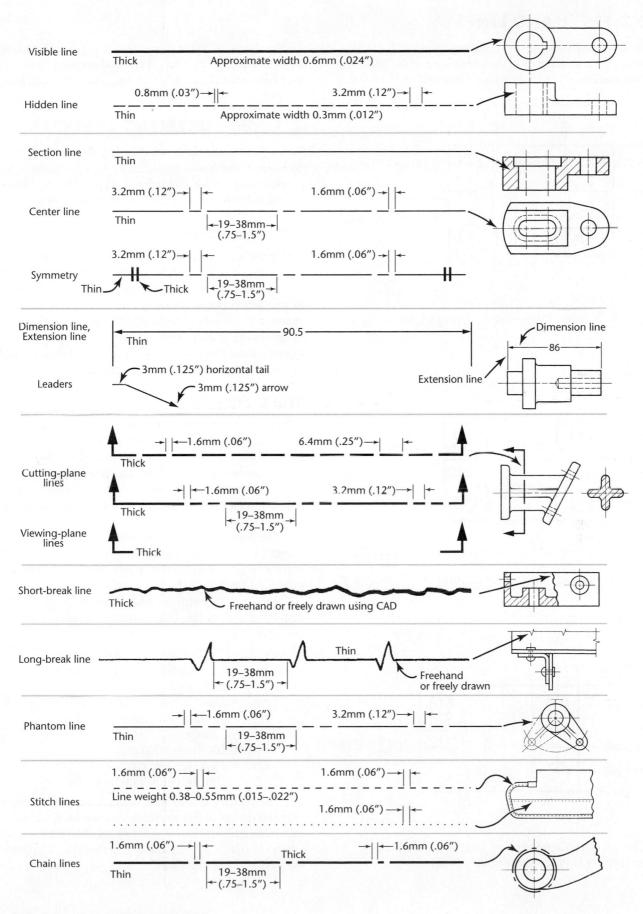

Visible line — Thick — Approximate width 0.6mm (.024")

Hidden line — 0.8mm (.03") — 3.2mm (.12") — Thin — Approximate width 0.3mm (.012")

Section line — Thin

Center line — 3.2mm (.12") — 1.6mm (.06") — Thin — 19–38mm (.75–1.5")

Symmetry — 3.2mm (.12") — 1.6mm (.06") — Thin — Thick — 19–38mm (.75–1.5")

Dimension line, Extension line — Thin — 90.5 — Dimension line — 86 — Extension line

Leaders — 3mm (.125") horizontal tail — 3mm (.125") arrow

Cutting-plane lines — 1.6mm (.06") — 6.4mm (.25") — Thick — 1.6mm (.06") — 3.2mm (.12") — Thick — 19–38mm (.75–1.5")

Viewing-plane lines — Thick

Short-break line — Thick — Freehand or freely drawn using CAD

Long-break line — Thin — 19–38mm (.75–1.5") — Freehand or freely drawn

Phantom line — 1.6mm (.06") — 3.2mm (.12") — Thin — 19–38mm (.75–1.5")

Stitch lines — 1.6mm (.06") — 1.6mm (.06") — Line weight 0.38–0.55mm (.015–.022") — 1.6mm (.06")

Chain lines — 1.6mm (.06") — Thick — 1.6mm (.06") — Thin — 19–38mm (.75–1.5")

2.7   Alphabet of Lines (Full Size)

2.2 FREEHAND LINES

The main difference between an instrument or CAD drawing and a freehand sketch is in the appearance of the lines. A good **freehand line** is not expected to be precisely straight or exactly uniform, as is a CAD or instrument-drawn line. Freehand lines show freedom and variety. Freehand **construction lines** are very light, rough lines. All other lines should be dark and clean.

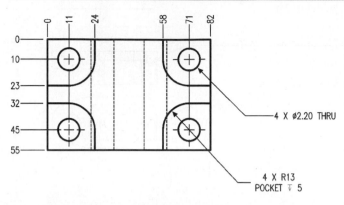

2.8 A Drawing Dimensioned Using Metric Units

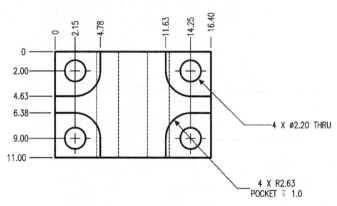

2.9 A Drawing Dimensioned Using U.S. Customary Units

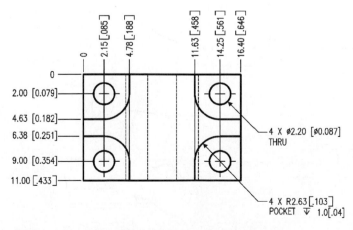

2.10 A Dual Dimensioned Drawing Using U.S. Customary Units as the Primary Units

2.3 MEASUREMENT SYSTEMS

When you create a technical drawing, the item you show will be manufactured or constructed using a particular system of measurement, which you indicate on the drawing. The metric system is the world standard used for measuring lengths.

U.S. Customary Units

U.S. customary units based on inch-foot and yard measurements (where a yard equals exactly 0.9144 meters, there are 3 feet to the yard, and 12 inches to the foot) continue to be used in the United States. Drawings may use either measurement system and still follow ANSI/ASME drawing standards as long as the system of measurement is stated clearly on the drawing. Figure 2.8 and Figure 2.9 show the same part dimensioned with the two different measurement systems.

The Metric System

Today's metric system is the International System of Units, commonly referred to as SI (from the French name, le Système International d'Unités). It was established in 1960 by international agreement and is now the international standard of measurement, with all countries in the world adopting it, although some continue using traditional U.S. units to a greater or lesser degree.

The meter was established by the French in 1791 with a length of one ten-millionth of the distance from the Earth's equator to the pole. A meter equals 39.37 inches or approximately 1.1 yards.

The metric system for linear measurement is a decimal system similar to the U.S. system of counting money. For example,

1 mm	= 1 millimeter (1/1000 of a meter)	
1 cm	= 1 centimeter (1/100 of a meter)	
	= 10 mm	
1 dm	= 1 decimeter (1/10 of a meter)	
	= 10 cm = 100 mm	
1 m	= 1 meter	
	= 100 cm = 1000 mm	
1 km	= 1 kilometer = 1000 m	
	= 100,000 cm = 1,000,000 mm	

The primary unit of measurement for engineering drawings and design in the mechanical industries is the millimeter (mm). Secondary units of measure are the meter (m) and the kilometer (km). The centimeter (cm) and the decimeter (dm) are rarely used on drawings.

Some industries have used a dual dimensioning system of millimeters and inches on drawings. However, this practice can be confusing because the sizes displayed in the two systems may contain rounding errors. If two systems are shown, the primary units are used for all manufacturing measurements and the secondary system units (shown in parentheses) are for general information purposes only. Figure 2.10 shows a drawing using dual dimensioning. Most large manufacturers use all metric dimensions on the drawing for ease and consistency.

Many of the dimensions in the illustrations and the problems in this text are given in metric units. Dimensions that are given in U.S. customary units (inches and feet, either decimal or fractional) can be converted easily to metric values. In standard practice, the ratio 1 in. = 25.4 mm is used. Decimal equivalents tables can be found inside the back cover, and conversion tables are given in Appendix 31. Many handy unit conversion sites are also available on the Web, at sites such as www.onlineconversion.com.

2.4 DRAWING SCALE

Unlike drawing using a computer (where an object is drawn at its actual size so that the information stored in the computer file is accurate) a printed or paper drawing may represent the object at its actual size (full size), or may be larger or smaller than the object, depending on the size of sheet used. **Drawing scale** is the reduction or enlargement of the drawn object relative to the real object (Figure 2.11).

Scale is stated as a ratio of the number of drawing units to the number of actual units. For example, a machine part may be shown on a sheet at half its actual size, a scale of 1:2; a building may be drawn 1/48 of its size, a scale of 1:48 (or in U.S. customary units, 1/4" = 1'); a map may be drawn 1/1200 actual size, a scale of 1" = 100' or 1:1200; or a printed circuit board may be drawn four times its size, a scale of 4:1.

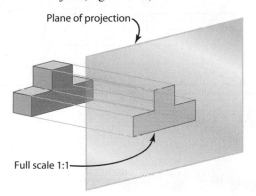
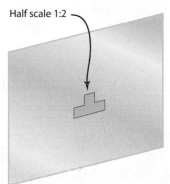
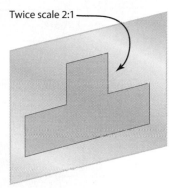

2.11 Reduced and Enlarged Scale. *Many drawings must be shown at reduced scale for the object to fit on the paper.*

2.5 SPECIFYING THE SCALE ON A DRAWING

There are several acceptable methods to note scale on the drawing, but all of them show the relationship of the size of the object as drawn to the size of the actual object. For a part that is shown on the paper at half its actual size, list the scale one of these three ways:

SCALE: 1:2
SCALE: 1/2
SCALE: .5

For machine drawings, the scale indicates the ratio of the size of the drawn object to its actual size, regardless of the unit of measurement used. Expansion or enlargement scales are given as 2:1, 4:1; 5:1, 10:1, and so on. Figure 2.11 illustrates how the actual object relates to a drawing at half size and how that might be noted in the title block of the drawing. Figure 2.12 shows the scale for a 1 to 24 reduction noted in a title block.

Architectural drawings in the U.S. typically list the scale based on the number of fractions of an inch on the drawing that represent one foot on the actual object. For example, SCALE: 1/8" = 1'.

The various scale calibrations available on the metric scale and the engineers' scale provide almost unlimited scale ratios.

Preferred metric scale ratios are 1:1; 1:2; 1:5, 1:10, 1:20, 1:50, 1:100, and 1:200.

Map scales are indicated in terms of proportions such as Scale 1:62500, fractions such as Scale 1/62500, or graphically, such as **400   0   400   800 Ft**

2.12 List Predominant Drawing Scale in the Title Block. *Courtesy of Dynojet Research, Inc.*

2.6 SCALES

Scales are measuring tools used to quickly enlarge or reduce drawing measurements. Figure 2.13 shows a number of scales, including (a) metric, (b) engineers', (c) decimal (d) mechanical engineers', and (e) architects' scales. On a full-divided scale, the basic units are subdivided throughout the length of the scale. On open-divided scales, such as the architects' scale, only the end unit is subdivided.

Scales are usually made of plastic or boxwood. The better wood scales have white plastic edges. Scales can be either triangular or flat. The triangular scales combine several scales on one stick by using each of the triangle's three sides. A scale guard shown in Figure 2.13f can save time and prevent errors by marking the side of the scale currently in use.

Several scales that are based on the inch-foot system of measurement continue in domestic use today, along with the metric system of measurement, which is accepted worldwide for science, technology, and international trade.

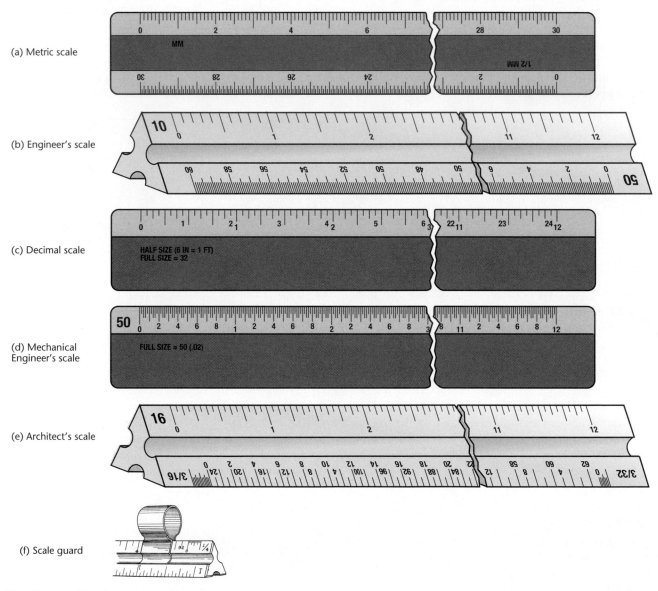

(a) Metric scale

(b) Engineer's scale

(c) Decimal scale

(d) Mechanical Engineer's scale

(e) Architect's scale

(f) Scale guard

2.13 Types of Scales

2.7 METRIC SCALES

Metric scales are available in flat and triangular styles with a variety of scale graduations. The triangular scale illustrated (Figure 2.14) has one full-size scale and five reduced-size scales, all fully divided. Using these scales, a drawing can be made full size, enlarged sized, or reduced sized.

Full Size The 1:1 scale (Figure 2.14a top) is full size, and each division is actually 1 mm in width with the numbering of the calibrations at 10 mm intervals. The same scale is also convenient for ratios of 1:10, 1:100, 1:1000, and so on.

Half Size The 1:2 scale (Figure 2.14a bottom) is one-half size, and each division equals 2 mm with the calibration

numbering at 20-unit intervals. This scale is also convenient for ratios of 1:20, 1:200, 1:2000, and so on.

The remaining four scales on this triangular metric scale include the typical scale ratios of 1:5, 1:25, and 1:75 (Figures 2.14b and c). These ratios may also be enlarged or reduced by multiplying or dividing by a factor of 10. Metric scales are also available with other scale ratios for specific drawing purposes.

Metric scales are also used in map drawing and in drawing force diagrams or other graphical constructions that involve such scales as 1 mm = 1 kg and 1 mm = 500 kg.

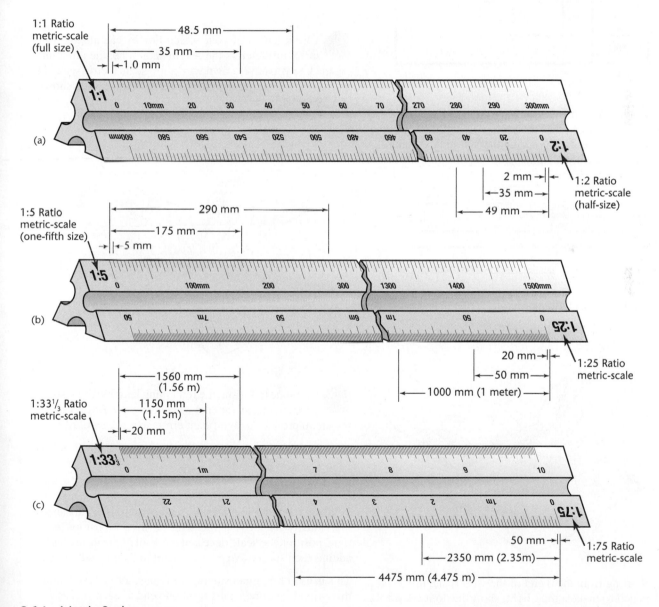

2.14 Metric Scales

STEP by STEP

MAKING MEASUREMENTS TO LAY OUT A ONE-FIFTH SIZE METRIC DRAWING

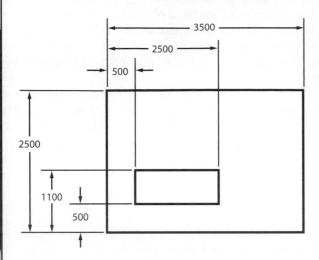

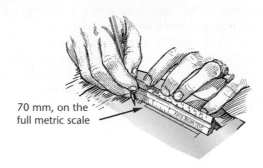

70 mm, on the full metric scale

1 Determine the full size measurements of the object you will draw. This example will lay out a 3500 × 2500 mm flat plate with a rectangular slot in it. A picture of the part to be drawn with dimensions representing its actual size is shown above.

4 Check length of your scaled line by calculating how many millimeters the length should be, then measuring the line you have drawn with a full scale metric scale. In this case the 3500 mm length should be 70 mm when shown at 1:50 scale.

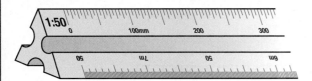

2 Find your 1:5 ratio metric scale, like this one.

For accuracy, mark several distances without repositioning scale

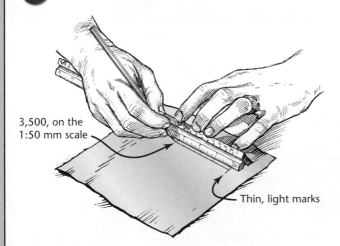

3,500, on the 1:50 mm scale

Thin, light marks

3 Starting from the 0 end of the 1:50 scale, use a sharp pencil to make a thin, light, short line to mark off the length of the 3500 mm line. To make accurate measurements, be sure to place the scale edge parallel to the line you are measuring on the drawing, and make your dashes at right angles to the scale, at the correct graduation mark, as shown.

5 Continue to lay out the remaining lengths. Even slight errors in measurements when using a scale may accumulate to produce a significant error, so work carefully.

To avoid cumulative errors, instead of setting off distances individually by moving the scale to a new position each time, position the scale once and mark all of the distances by adding each successive measurement to the preceding one.

This is useful in dimensioning drawings, too. Keep in mind that providing dimensions from one end to each successive location (say, in the case of building a wall) makes it easier for the worker to lay it out quickly and accurately.

2.8 ENGINEERS' SCALES

An *Engineers' scale* is a decimal scale graduated in units of 1 inch divided into 10, 20, 30, 40, 50, and 60 parts. These scales are also frequently called the civil engineers' scales because they were originally used in civil engineering to draw large scale structures or maps. Sometimes the engineers' scale is referred to as a chain scale, because it derived from a chain of 100 links that surveyors used for land measurements.

Because the engineers' scale divides inches into decimal units, it is convenient in machine drawing to set off inch dimensions expressed in decimals. For example, to set off 1.650" full size, use the 10 scale and simply set off one main division plus 6-1/2 subdivisions (Figure 2.15). To set off the same dimension half size, use the 20 scale, since the 20 scale is exactly half the size of the 10 scale. Similarly, to set off the dimension quarter size, use the 40 scale.

An engineers' scale is also used in drawing stress diagrams or other graphical constructions to such scales as 1" = 20 lb. and 1" = 4000 lb.

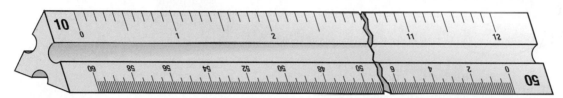

2.15   Engineers' Scale

2.9 DECIMAL INCH SCALES

The widespread use of *decimal inch* dimensions brought about a scale specifically for that use. On its full-size scale, each inch is divided into fiftieths of an inch, or .02". On half- and quarter-size decimal scales, the inches are compressed to half size or quarter size and then are divided into 10 parts, so that each subdivision stands for .1" (Figure 2.16).

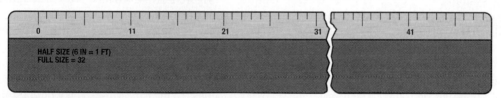

2.16   Decimal Inch Scale

2.10 MECHANICAL ENGINEERS' SCALES

The objects represented in machine drawing vary in size from small parts that measure only fractions of an inch to parts of large dimensions. For this reason, mechanical engineers' scales are divided into units representing inches to full size, half size, quarter size, or eighth size (Figure 2.17). To draw an object to a scale of one-half size, for example, use the mechanical engineers' scale marked half size, which is graduated so that every 1/2" represents 1". In other words, the half-size scale is simply a full-size scale compressed to half size.

These scales are useful in dividing dimensions. For example, to draw a 3.6" diameter circle full size, we need half of 3.6" to use as radius. Instead of using math to find half of 3.6", it is easier to set off 3.6" on the half-size scale.

--- **TIP** ---
Triangular combination scales are available that include full- and half-size mechanical engineers' scales, several architects' scales, and an engineers' scale all on one stick.

2.17 Mechanical Engineers' Scale

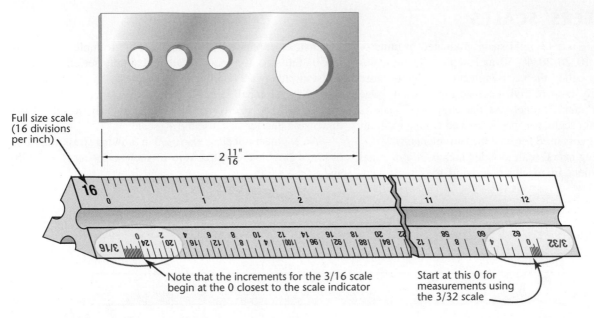

2.18 Architects' Scale

2.11 ARCHITECTS' SCALES

The **architects' scale** is intended primarily for drawings of buildings, piping systems, and other large structures that must be drawn to a reduced scale to fit on a sheet of paper. The full-size scale is also useful in drawing relatively small objects, and for that reason this scale has rather general usage.

Architects' scales have one full-size scale and ten reduced-sized scales. (To fit them all on a three-sided scale, there are two scales on the same edge of the scale, but each starts from the opposite end. Simply find the scale you want, and read the units from the zero closest to that end.

Architects' scales can be used to draw various sizes from full size to 1/128 size. In all of the reduced scales, the major divisions represent feet and their subdivisions represent inches and fractions of inches.

Note that on an architects' scale, the scale marked 3/4 means 3/4 inch = 1 foot, *not 3/4 inch = 1 inch* (that is, it means one-sixteenth size, *not* three-fourths size). Similarly, on an architects' scale, 1/2 means 1/2 inch = 1 foot, *not 1/2 inch = 1 inch*. In other words, on an architects' scale, 1/2 means twenty-fourth-size, *not* half size.

- Full Size: Each division in the full-size scale is 1/16" (Figure 2.18). Each inch is divided into halves, then quarters, eighths, and finally sixteenths. You'll notice that the dividing lines are shorter with each subdivision.

  Measurements smaller than 1/16" must be made by estimating. For example, 1/32" is half of one 1/16", so you would visually estimate halfway between 1/16" division lines. To measure 1/64", you would estimate one fourth of 1/16", and so on.

- Half Size: Use the full-size scale, and divide every dimension by two. (Remember, do not use the 1/2" scale, which is intended for drawing to a scale of 1/2" = 1', not half-size.) To create a half scale drawing using an architects' scale, divide your measurements in half and then lay out the drawing.

- Double Size: Use the full-size scale, and multiply every dimension by 2.

> **TIP**
> AutoCAD software users sometimes become confused using architectural units. When selecting architectural units in which to enter lengths, keep in mind that a value of 1 is one inch, not one foot.

MEASURING WITH AN ARCHITECTS' SCALE

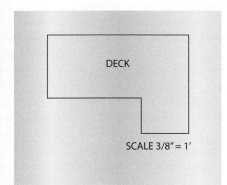

DECK

SCALE 3/8" = 1'

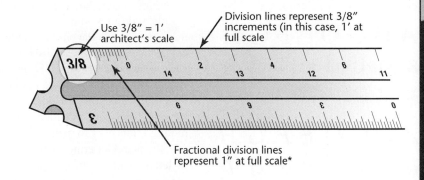

Use 3/8" = 1'
architect's scale

Division lines represent 3/8"
increments (in this case, 1' at
full scale

3/8   0   14   2   13   4   12   6   11

3   6   9   3   0

Fractional division lines
represent 1" at full scale*

1 To make measurements with an architects' scale, first determine which scale to use by reading the scale noted in the title block or noted below the view. In the example above, 3/8 inch = 1 foot.

2 Position the scale so that the 0 value is aligned with the left end of the line being measured and note the division mark nearest to the line's right end (in this case, 2).

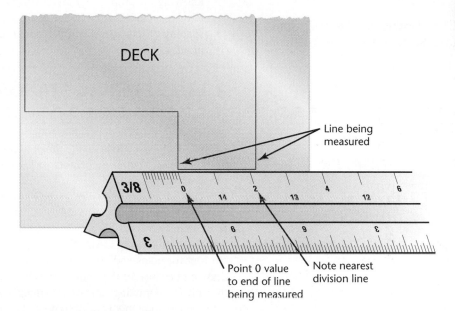

DECK

Line being
measured

3/8   0   14   2   13   4   12   6

3   6   9   3

Point 0 value
to end of line
being measured

Note nearest
division line

3 Slide the scale to the right so that the closest whole division you noted in Step 2 lines up with the right end of the line you are measuring. A fractional portion of the line you are measuring now extends on the left, past the scale's 0 mark.

Counting toward the left, note how many fractional division marks are between zero and the left end of the line. (In this example, there are two.)

Add the fractional value to the whole value that you noted in Step 2. In this example, you noted 2 whole division lines, plus two fractional division lines, so the length of the line is 2'–2" at actual size.

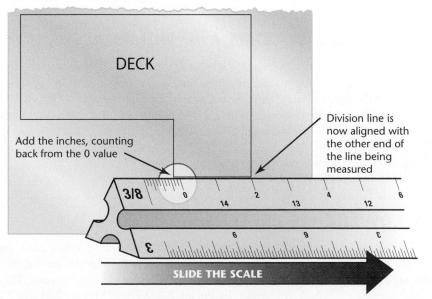

DECK

Add the inches, counting
back from the 0 value

Division line is
now aligned with
the other end of
the line being
measured

3/8   0   14   2   13   4   12   6

3   6   9   3

SLIDE THE SCALE

On architects' scales, there are 12 fractional divisions, because there are 12 inches per foot.

A B C D E F G H
a b c d e f g h

Sans-serif lettering has no serifs,
or spurs, at the ends of the strokes

A B C D E F G H
a b c d e f g h

Roman letters are accented by
thick and thin line weights

A B C D E F G H
a b c d e f g h

Italic letters are slanted,
whether serif or sans serif

2.19 Distinctions Between Roman,
Italic, Serif, and Sans Serif Lettering

2.12 LETTERING

Lettered text is often necessary to completely describe an object or to provide detailed specifications. Lettering should be legible, be easy to create, and use styles acceptable for traditional drawing and CAD drawing.

Engineering drawings use single-stroke sans-serif letters because they are highly legible and quick to draw. (Sans-serif means without serifs, or spurs.) A **font** is the name for a particular shape of letters. The particular font for engineering drawings is called Gothic. Figure 2.19 shows the distinctions between **Roman, italic, serif** and **sans serif** fonts.

Lettering is a standard feature available in computer graphics programs. With CAD software, you can add titles, notes, and dimensioning information to a drawing. Several fonts and a variety of sizes may be selected. When modifications are required, it is easy to make lettering changes on the drawing by editing existing text.

Freehand lettering ability has little relationship to writing ability. You can learn to letter neatly even if you have terrible handwriting. There are three necessary aspects of learning to letter:

- knowing the proportions and forms of the letters (to make good letters, you need to have a clear mental image of their correct shape)
- spacing of letters and words for legibility
- practice

AUTOCAD TXT FONT
ROMAN SIMPLEX
ROMAN DUPLEX
TITLES
TRUE TYPE FONTS

2.20 An Example of Lettering and
Titles Using CAD

2.13 LETTERING STANDARDS

Most hand-drawn notes use lettering about 3 mm (1/8") in height. Light horizontal **guidelines** are useful to produce consistent letter heights. CAD notes are set using the keyboard and sized to be in the range of 3 mm (1/8") tall according to the plotted size of the drawing. Lettering heights vary with the size of the sheet and the intended use of the drawing.

CAD drawings typically use a Gothic lettering style, but often use a Roman style for titles. When adding lettering to a CAD drawing, a good rule of thumb is not to use more than two fonts within the same drawing. See Figure 2.20 for a sample of the fonts available using CAD. You may want to use one font for the titles and a different font for notes and other text. It may be tempting to use many different fonts in a drawing because of the wide variety available, but this tends to look distracting on the drawing. Drawings that use too many lettering styles and sizes have been jokingly referred to as having a "ransom note" lettering style.

2.14 VERTICAL LETTERS AND NUMERALS

There are standard widths for the various letters. The proportions of **vertical** capital letters and numbers are shown in Figure 2.21. In the figure, each letter is shown on a 6-unit-high grid that shows its width in relation to its height. The numbered arrows indicate the traditional order and direction in which the lettering strokes are made.

Aside from the letters I and W, letters are either five or six grid divisions wide, or about as wide as they are tall. This is probably a little wider than your usual writing. It is easier to remember the six-unit letters if you think of them as spelling a name: TOM Q. VAXY. The letter I is a pencil width, and the letter W is eight grid-units wide (1-1/3 times its height).

With the exception of the numeral 1, which uses only a pencil width, all numerals are five units wide.

2.15 LOWERCASE LETTERS

Lowercase letters are rarely used in engineering sketches except for lettering large volumes of notes. Vertical lowercase letters are used on map drawings, but very seldom on machine drawings. Lowercase letters are shown in Figure 2.22. The lower part of the letter (or descender) is usually two-thirds the height of the capital letter.

When large and small capitals are combined, the small capitals should be three-fifths to two-thirds the height of the large capitals. The inclined letters and numbers shown in Figures 2.23 and 2.24 will be discussed in the next section.

Straight-line letters

Letter "i" has short bars

"W" is only letter over 6 units wide. Letters in "TOM Q. VAXY" are 6 units wide—all others are 5, except "I" and "W"

Curved-line letters

The letters O, Q, C, G and D are based on a true circle. The lower portion of of the J and U is elliptical

Curved-line letters and numerals

The 8 is composed of two ellipses. The 3, S, and 2 are based on the 8

Curved-line letters and numerals

Number "1" is a straight line. The 0, 6, and 9 are elliptical

2.21 Vertical Capital Letters and Numerals

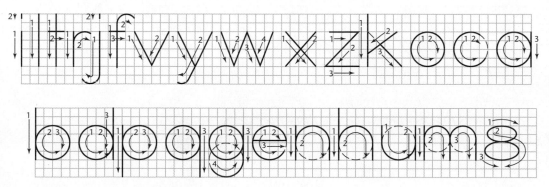

2.22 Vertical Lowercase Letters

Straight-line letters

Letter "i" has short bars

"W" is only letter over 6 grid units wide. Letters in "TOM Q. VAXY" are 6 grid units wide—all others are 5, except "I" and "W"

Curved-line letters

The letters O, Q, C, G and D are based on a true ellipse. The lower portion of of the J and U is elliptical

Curved-line letters and numerals

The 8 is composed of two ellipses. The 3, S, and 2 are based on the 8

Curved-line letters and numerals

Number "1" is a straight line. The 0, 6, and 9 are elliptical

2.23 Inclined Capital Letters and Numerals

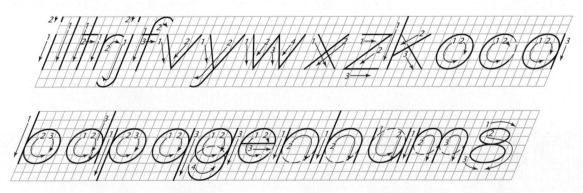

2.24 Inclined Lowercase Letters

2.16 INCLINED LETTERS AND NUMBERS

Inclined (italic) capital letters and numerals, shown in Figure 2.23, are similar to vertical characters, except for the slope. The slope of the letters is about 68° from the horizontal.

While you may practice drawing slanted hand lettering at approximately this angle, it is important in CAD drawings to always set the amount of incline for the letters at the same value within a drawing so that the lettering is consistent. Inclined lowercase letters, shown in Figure 2.24, are similar to vertical lowercase letters.

Keep in mind that only one style of lettering, either vertical or inclined, should be used throughout a drawing.

2.17 FRACTIONS

Fractions are shown twice the height of the corresponding whole numbers. Make the numerator and the denominator each about three-fourths as high as the whole number to allow enough space between them and the fraction bar. For dimensioning, the most commonly used height for whole numbers is 3 mm (1/8"), and for fractions 6 mm (1/4"), as shown in Figure 2.25.

- Never let numerals touch the fraction bar.
- Center the denominator under the numerator.
- Avoid using an inclined fraction bar, except when lettering in a narrow space, as in a parts list.
- Make the fraction bar slightly longer than the widest part of the fraction.

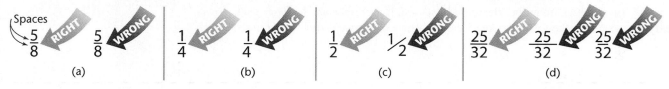

(a)   (b)   (c)   (d)

2.25 Common Errors in Lettering Fractions

2.18 USING GUIDELINES

Use extremely light horizontal **guidelines** to keep letter height uniform, as shown in Figure 2.26. Capital letters are commonly made 3 mm (1/8") high, with the space between rows of lettering being from three-fifths to full height of the letters. Do not use vertical guidelines to space the distance from one letter to the next within a word or sentence. This should be done by eye while lettering. If necessary, use a vertical guideline at the beginning of a column of hand lettered text to help you line up the left edges of the following rows. Beginners can also use randomly spaced vertical guidelines to practice maintaining the correct slant.

Vertical guide lines drawn at random

LETTERING IS EASIER
IF YOU REMEMBER TO
USE GUIDE LINES

Space between lines usually from $\frac{3}{5}$ to total height of letters

2.26 Using Guidelines

TIP

For even freehand letters

- Use 1/8" gridded paper for drawing to make lettering easy.
- Use a scale and set off a series of spaces, making both the letters and the spaces between lines of letters 1/8" high.
- Use a guideline template like the Berol Rapidesign 925 shown in Figure 2.27.
- For whole numbers and fractions, draw five equally spaced guidelines.

REVERSE WITH INKING PEN

$\frac{3}{36}$ $\frac{1}{4}$

$\frac{5}{32}$ $\frac{3}{16}$

$\frac{1}{8}$ $\frac{5}{32}$

$\frac{3}{32}$ $\frac{1}{8}$

Berol.RapiDesign.
R-925
LETTERING AID

2.27 The Berol Rapidesign 925 Template Is Used to Quickly Create Guidelines for Lettering

2.19 SPACING OF LETTERS AND WORDS

Spacing Between Letters

Uniform spacing between letters is done by eye. Contrary to what might seem logical, putting equal distances from letter to letter causes them to appear unequally spaced. The background areas between letters, not the distances between them, should be approximately equal to get results that appear balanced. Figure 2.28 illustrates how using equal spacing from one letter to the next does not actually appear equal. Space your lettering so that background areas appear equal, like the example shown in the bottom half of the figure.

Some combinations, such as LT and VA, may have to be slightly closer than other letters to look correctly spaced. In some cases, the width of a letter may be decreased slightly. For example, the lower stroke of the L may be shortened when followed by A. In typesetting, pairs of letters that need to be spaced more closely to appear correctly are called **kerned pairs.**

Spacing Between Words

Space letters closely within words to make each word a compact unit, but space words well enough apart to be clearly separate from adjacent words. For both uppercase and lowercase lettering, make spaces between words approximately equal to a capital O.

Spacing Between Rows

Be sure to leave space between rows of lettering, usually equal to the letter height. Rows spaced too closely are hard to read. Rows spaced too far apart do not appear to be related.

Using equal spacing from one letter to another does not actually appear equal, as in this example

Space your lettering so that background areas appear equal, like the example shown above

2.28 Visually Balancing Letter Spacing

TIP

Creating letters that appear stable

Certain letters and numerals appear top-heavy when they are drawn with equal upper and lower portions like the example below.

To correct this, reduce the size of the upper portion to give a balanced appearance, as in this example.

If you put the central horizontal strokes of the letters B, E, F, and H at midheight, they will appear to be below center.

To overcome this optical illusion, draw the strokes for B, E, F, and H slightly above the center as you letter, keeping letters uniform, as in the second example below.

The same practice applies to numerals. In the illustrations below, the example at left looks top-heavy. Note how the example at right looks more balanced.

A good example of uniform lettering	RELATIVELY
These examples show what not to do	
Nonuniform style	Relatively
Nonuniform letter height	RELATIVELY RELATIVELY
Nonuniform angle	RELATIVELY RELATIVELY
Nonuniform stroke thickness	RELATIVELY RELATIVELY
Nonuniform letter spacing	RELA TIVELY
Nonuniform word spacing	NOW IS THE TIME FOR EVERY GOOD PERSON TO COME TO THE AID OF HIS OR HER COUNTRY

2.20 LETTERING FOR TITLES

In most cases, the title and related information are lettered in title boxes or title strips as shown in Figure 2.29. The main drawing title is usually centered in a rectangular space, which is easy to do, using CAD.

When lettering by hand, arrange the title symmetrically about an imaginary centerline, as shown in Figure 2.30. In any kind of title, give the most important words prominence by making the lettering larger, heavier, or both. Other data, such as scale and date, can be smaller.

Figure 2.31 shows examples of freehand lettering at actual size.

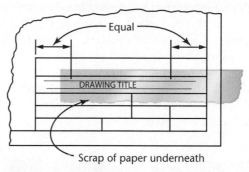

TOOL GRINDING MACHINE
TOOL REST SLIDE
SCALE : FULL SIZE
AMERICAN MACHINE COMPANY
NEW YORK CITY

DRAWN BY ____ CHECKED BY ____

2.29 Balanced Machine-Drawing Title

2.30 Centering Title in Title Box

THE IMPORTANCE OF GOOD LETTERING CANNOT BE OVER-EMPHASIZED. THE LETTERING CAN MAKE OR BREAK AN OTHERWISE GOOD DRAWING.

PENCIL LETTERING SHOULD BE DONE WITH A FAIRLY SOFT SHARP PENCIL AND SHOULD BE CLEAN-CUT AND DARK. ACCENT THE ENDS OF THE STROKES.

2.31 Pencil Lettering (Full Size)

TIP
Lettering with a Pencil

- Since practically all pencil lettering will be reproduced, the letters should be dense black, not gray or blurred. Use a sharp, soft pencil, such as an F, H, or HB to make lettering dark and sharp.
- If you like using wooden pencils, sharpen them to a needle point, then dull the point very slightly.
- Don't worry about making the exact letter strokes unless you find it difficult to make the letters look right, but do use them as a reference if you are having trouble drawing uniform, symmetrical letters.
- Use extremely light, 1/8" (3 mm) horizontal guidelines to regulate the height of letters. A few light, vertical or inclined lines randomly placed help you visually keep the letters uniformly vertical or inclined.

- Draw vertical strokes downward with a finger movement.
- Draw horizontal strokes from left to right with a wrist movement and without turning the paper.
- Draw curved strokes and inclined strokes with a downward motion.

Left-handers: Traditional lettering strokes were designed for right-handed people. Experiment with each letter to find out which strokes are best and develop a system of strokes that works best for you.

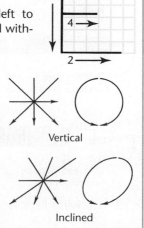

Vertical

Inclined

2.21 DRAWING PENCILS

High-quality drawing pencils help produce good quality technical sketches and drawings. Use light lines for construction lines, lettering guidelines, and precise layout work. Use dark, dense black lines for the final lines, lettering, and arrowheads. Drawings are often reproduced and the lines need to be dark for the copies to turn out well.

Drawing pencils are made of graphite with a polymer binder or clay binder. They are divided into 18 grades from 9H (the hardest) to 7B (the softest) as shown in Figure 2.32. Specially formulated leads of carbon black particles in a polymer binder are also available in several grades for use on polyester film (mylar).

Hard leads are used where accuracy is required, such as on graphical computations and charts and diagrams. For other uses, their lines are apt to be too light.

Medium leads are used for general purpose technical drawing, such as sketching, lettering, arrowheads, and other freehand work on mechanical drawings.

Soft leads are not useful in technical drawing. They make smudged, rough lines that are hard to erase, and the lead dulls quickly. These grades are generally used for artistic drawing.

Which grade of pencil works best for you depends on your hand pressure, the humidity, and the type of paper you are using, among other things. For light lines, use a hard lead in the range of 4H to 6H. For dark lines, use a softer lead in the range of 2H to B.

Mechanical pencils are available with 0.3-, 0.5-, 0.7-, or 0.9-mm-diameter drafting leads in several grades (Figure 2.33). Their thin leads produce uniform-width lines without sharpening. The .5-mm lead is a good general size, or you can use a .7-mm lead for thick lines and .3 mm for thin lines.

9H 8H 7H 6H 5H 4H   3H 2H H F HB B   2B 3B 4B 5B 6B 7B

Hard
The hard leads in this group (left) are used where extreme accuracy is required, as on graphical computations and charts and diagrams. The softer leads in this group (right) are sometimes used for line work on engineering drawings, but their use is limited because the lines are apt to be too light.

Medium
These grades are for general purpose work in technical drawing. The softer grades (right) are used for technical sketching, lettering, arrowheads, and other freehand work on mechanical drawings. The harder leads (left) are used for line work on machine drawings and architectural drawings. The H and 2H leads are widely used on pencil tracings for reproduction.

Soft
These leads are too soft to be useful in mechanical drafting. They tend to produce smudged, rough lines that are hard to erase, and the lead must be sharpened continually. These grades are used for artwork of various kinds, and for full-size details in architectural drawing.

2.32 Lead Grade Chart

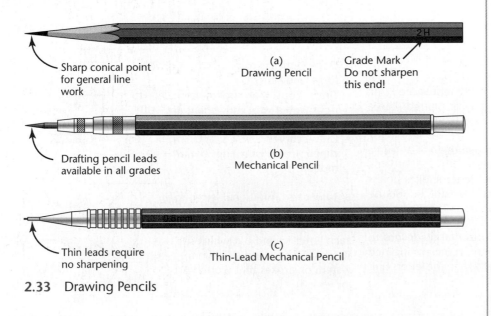

Sharp conical point for general line work

(a)
Drawing Pencil

2H

Grade Mark
Do not sharpen this end!

Drafting pencil leads available in all grades

(b)
Mechanical Pencil

0.5mm

Thin leads require no sharpening

(c)
Thin-Lead Mechanical Pencil

2.33 Drawing Pencils

TIP

You might be surprised how much your drawings benefit from finding a style of pencil that suits your use. Soft pencils, such as HB or F, are mainly used in freehand sketching. Choose a pencil that:

- Is soft enough to produce clear black lines, but hard enough not to smudge too easily
- Is not so soft that the point breaks easily.
- Feels comfortable in your hand.
- Grips the lead without slipping.

Be aware that some lead holders require special sharpeners.

You can sometimes tell the difference in hardness of a mechanical pencil lead just by looking at it. Smaller diameter leads are used for the harder grades and larger diameter leads are used to give more strength to the softer grades.

Plain wooden pencils work great. They are inexpensive, and it is easy to produce thick or thin lines by varying the amount that you sharpen them. An old trick to keep the lead sharp longer is to turn the pencil frequently as you work to wear it down evenly.

Gum erasers and nylon erasers work well to pick up smudges without leaving much eraser dust.

Nylon eraser strips that come in refillable holders like mechanical pencils can be convenient for areas that require some precision. A trick for erasing fine details is to sharpen the end of the eraser strip in a small hand-held pencil sharpener.

2.22 TEMPLATES

Templates are available for a great variety of specialized needs (Figure 2.34). Templates may be found for drawing almost any ordinary drafting symbols or repetitive features.

2.23 THE COMPUTER AS A DRAFTING TOOL

Most people who create technical drawings use CAD. Advantages include accuracy, speed, and the ability to present spatial and visual information in a variety of ways.

However, these advantages don't eliminate the need for drawings to be easily and accurately interpreted. CAD drawings use the same general concepts and follow the same drafting standards as drawings created by hand.

Most CAD drawings are plotted on standard sheet sizes and to similar scales as hand drawings. Both CAD and hand drawings should contrast thick lines for objects with thin lines for hidden, center, and dimensions to make the printed drawing easy to read. CAD drawings

2.34 Drawing Templates. *Courtesy of Chartpak.*

should use correct line patterns. Likewise, lettering on CAD drawings should follow these same general guidelines as for hand drawings.

One benefit of CAD is the ability to draw perfectly straight uniform lines and other geometric elements. Another is the ability to quickly represent the various styles of lines (Figure 2.35). Making changes to a CAD drawing takes about a tenth the time that it takes

to edit a drawing by hand. Using CAD, you can quickly plot drawings to different scales.

Keeping CAD drawing files organized, backing up data regularly, and following conventions for naming files so that you can find them again are important considerations. Even the most skilled CAD users need to also be skilled in freehand sketching, in order to quickly get ideas down on paper.

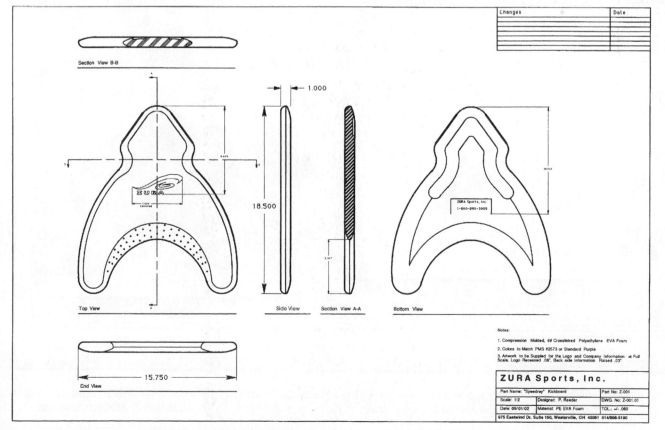

2.35 A Drawing Created Using CAD. *Courtesy of Zura Sports, Inc.*

MODEL SPACE AND PAPER SPACE IN AUTOCAD 2008

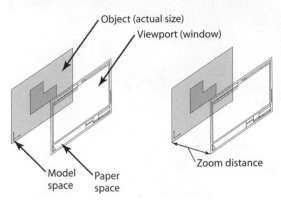

(A) In AutoCAD 2008, paper space allows you to see how various views of the full size model can be shown on a sheet of paper. *Reprinted by permission of Pearson Education, Inc., Upper Saddle River, NJ.*

Using CAD, you can make an accurate model of the device or structure. To do this, you create the object at the actual size that it exists in the real world, using whatever system of measurement that you would use when constructing it.

On paper it is a different matter. You would have to have some really large sheets to print your building full size. AutoCAD 2008 software uses the concept of two "spaces," model space and paper space, to describe how to transform the full size CAD model to proportionate views that fit your sheet of paper.

Understanding scale as it relates to paper drawings or as it relates to creating layouts from a CAD drawing is an important concept for technical drawing because the ultimate goal is for drawings to be interpreted and used in the real world. Therefore, they must be easy to print and read.

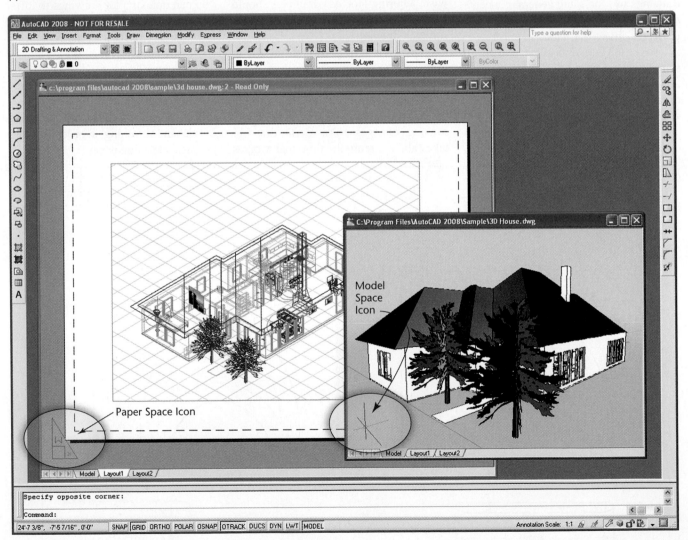

(B) The window at left shows a paper space representation of the full size CAD model in the smaller window at right. Note that AutoCAD uses icons to help users differentiate the two "spaces." *Courtesy of Autodesk, Inc. © 2006-2007. All rights reserved.*

2.24 SKETCHING AND DRAWING MEDIA

Many choices of **media** (paper and other) are available for particular sketching or drawing purposes. Whether you are sketching or are plotting a drawing from a CAD workstation, choose the type of sheet and size that suits your needs.

Small notebooks or sketch pads are useful when working at a site or when it is necessary to quickly record information. Many companies use bound notebooks of graph paper for recording engineering design notes for patent and documentation purposes. Graph paper can be helpful in making neat sketches like the one in Figure 2.36. Paper with 4, 5, 8, or 10 squares per inch is convenient for maintaining proportions.

A sketch pad of plain paper with a master grid sheet showing through underneath works well as a substitute for grid paper. You can create your own master grid sheets using CAD. Specially ruled isometric paper is available for isometric sketching, or you can use CAD to create masters.

The best drawing papers have up to 100% pure rag stock. Their strong fibers hold up well for erasing and folding, and they will not discolor or grow brittle with age. Good drafting paper should have a fine grain (or tooth) to pick up the graphite

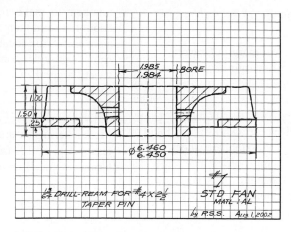

2.36 Sketch on Graph Paper

and produce clean, dense black lines. Paper that is too rough produces ragged, grainy lines, is harder to erase, and wears down pencils quickly. Look for paper that has a hard surface that will not groove too easily under pencil pressure.

2.25 POLYESTER FILMS AND COATED SHEETS

Polyester film is a high quality drafting material available in rolls and standard sized sheets. It is made by bonding a matte surface to one or both sides of a clear polyester sheet. Its transparency and printing qualities are good and it provides an excellent matte drawing surface for pencil or ink, it is easy to erase without leaving ghost marks, and it has high dimensional stability. Its resistance to cracking, bending, and

tearing makes it very durable. Many companies still plot their drawings in ink on polyester film for long-term storage and reproduction.

Even large coated sheets of aluminum (which provides a good dimensional stability) have been used in the aircraft and auto industry for full-scale layouts that were scribed into the coating with a steel point rather than a pencil.

2.26 STANDARD SHEETS

There are ANSI/ASME standards for international and U.S. **sheet sizes.** Table 2.2 describes the height and width of these standard sheets, the letters used to refer to them, and their margins and zones. Note that drawing sheet size is given as height × width. Most standard sheets use what is called a "landscape" orientation.

The use of the basic sheet size, 8.5" × 11.0" or 210 mm × 297 mm, and its multiples permit filing folded prints in standard files with or without correspondence. These sizes can be cut from standard rolls of media.

Table 2.2 Sheet Sizes.

Nearest International Size (mm)	International Number of Zones	International Margin	Standard U.S. Size (in.)	U.S. Number of Zones (width)	U.S. Margin (in.)
A4 210 × 297	6	10	A* 8.5 × 11.0	2 (optional)	.50
A3 297 × 420	6	10	B 11.0 × 17.0	2 (optional)	.50
A2 420 × 594	8	10	C 17.0 × 22.0	4	.50
A1 594 × 841	12	20	D 22.0 × 34.0	4	.50
A0 841 × 1189	16	20	E 34.0 × 44.0	8	.50

May also be used as a vertical sheet size at 11" tall by 8.5" wide.

2.27 STANDARD LAYOUT ELEMENTS

Margins and Borders

Each layout begins with a border drawn inside the sheet margin. Drawings in the U.S. use a .50" margin. Refer to Table 2.2 for international sheet sizes and margins. Some companies use slightly larger sheets to provide for binding drawings into a set. This extra allowance should be added on to the standard sheet size so that the drawing border meets the size standards (see Figure 2.37). Figure 2.38 shows the alternate orientation of an A size drawing.

Zones

You have probably seen **zone numbers** on maps, where the margin is subdivided by letters along one side and by numbers along the other. These are also used along the outer edges of technical drawings so that you can refer to items by the area on the sheet where they are located. This is particularly useful when a client calls with a question. You can use zone numbers to make sure you are talking about the same item. Zone numbers are also useful for locating revisions. You should provide zone numbers on all sheets larger than size B.

Typical Letter Sizes

Most lettering on drawings should be at least 3 mm or .12" (about 1/8") tall. Lettering is typically sized as follows:

Drawing Title, Drawing Size
   6 mm (.24")
CAGE Code
   6 mm (.24")
Drawing Number, Revision Letter
   6 mm (.24")
Section and View Letters
   6 mm (.24")
Zone Letters and Numbers
   6 mm (.24")
Drawing Block Headings
   2.5 mm (.10")
All Others
   3 mm (.12")

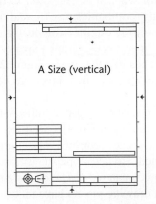

2.38　Vertical Orientation of A Size

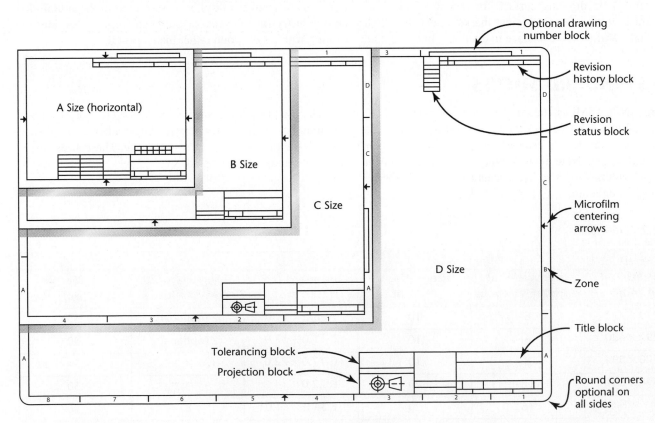

2.37　Typical Sheet Sizes and Borders. *(See the inside front cover for E size and international standard sizes.)*

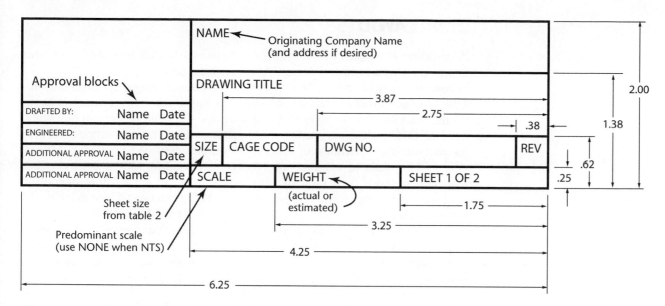

2.39 Title Block for A, B, and C Sized Sheets

Title Block

The title block is located in the lower right corner of the format. Standard areas in the title block provide the following information. Refer to Figure 2.39 for dimensions for a typical title block for A, B, and C sized sheets.*

Name Show the originating company or business (and address if desired). Refer to Figure 2.40.

Drawing Title Briefly describe the item using a singular noun or noun phrase and modifiers if necessary to distinguish it from similar items. Do not use the terms "for" or "or" in the title. For example, "Dust Cap" would be preferred over "Cap or Cover for Dust Protection," which is too wordy.

Drawing Number Give each drawing a unique number, using the company's numbering system.

Sheet Revision Block Track the drawing version using the number of the revision. The original release of the drawing typically shows revision 0.

Approval Block List the name(s) of the person(s) approving the drawing and the date it was approved. Additional areas of this block can be used for various design activities, if separate approval is required. For example, a company may use separate areas for structural design or manufacturing engineering approvals (Figure 2.41).

Scale List the predominant scale for the drawing. Drawings may include details at other scales, which should be noted below the detail. If the drawing is not made to a particular scale, note NONE in the scale area. Refer to Section 2.6.

Drawing Size List the sheet size used for the drawing. This helps track the original size when the drawing is reproduced at a smaller size.

Sheet Number List the number of the sheet in the set, using whole numbers starting at 1. A format that lists this sheet out of the total number helps keep track of the entire set. For example, 1 OF 2.

CAGE Code List the Commercial and Government Entity (CAGE) code if applicable. This is a number assigned to

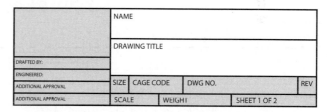

2.40 Company Name and Drawing Title

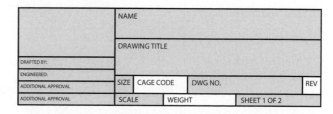

2.41 Approval Block, Scale, Revision, and Drawing Size

2.42 CAGE Code and Weight May Be Listed

entities that manufacture items for the government. The code is assigned based on the original design activity.

Weight List the actual or estimated weight of the part if required (Figure 2.42).

*For more formats, title blocks, revision blocks, and a list of materials blocks, see inside the front cover of this book.

2.28 LAYOUTS

A particular size sheet with a drawing border is called a **layout.** Using a CAD system, you may often be able to select from standard layouts or templates that set the sheet size limits, the border, and even the title block as the starting point for your drawing. Regardless of whether you draw by hand or use CAD or 3D modeling methods, you need to plan your sheet so that the information will fit and show clearly.

When sketching, your layout may be a simple border and title strip along the bottom of the sheet (or you may be using preprinted tablets that have space to record the sketch title, date, and other pertinent data).

When creating a 2D CAD drawing, you may use a drawing template showing the sheet and border and title block, perhaps using different templates or even software interface settings for different types of drawings, such as mechanical/manufacturing, architectural, or civil.

When creating a 2D drawing to plot from a 3D solid model, you may use a layout space that contains different viewports that allow you to show different views of the same 3D model with a border and title block.

2.29 PLANNING YOUR DRAWING OR SKETCH

When laying out a drawing sheet, you will need to consider:

- the size and scale of the object you will show.
- the sheet size.
- the measurement system (units) for the drawing.
- the space necessary for standard notes and title block.

The object you are drawing is the "star" of the sketch. Keep the object near the center of the sheet. It should be boldly drawn, using thick visible lines. Make it large enough to fill most of the sheet and so that details show clearly (Figure 2.43).

Show Details Clearly

Show small objects larger than their actual size to represent the details clearly. If the details are too small, switch to a larger sheet size and use a larger scale. You can also add details at a larger scale if necessary to show features that are smaller than the typical features of the drawing. If you add details at a different scale, label the view, for example, DETAIL A, and note the scale for the detail below it.

Ample space for dimensions and details

Too big for sheet. Leave more space notes and dimensions

DETAIL A

Too small to show details clearly

2.43   Show Details Clearly by Selecting Appropriate Scale and Sheet Size

SHEET LAYOUT

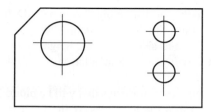

Given drawing

1 To draw the part shown in the given figure, select the sheet size, keeping in mind the size of the objects. Show the part large enough to represent features clearly. Use larger sheets for larger or more detailed objects. (8.5 × 11" will be large enough for the part shown.) Add the border and title block to the sheet using the margin sizes specified in the standards. Refer to Table 2.2.

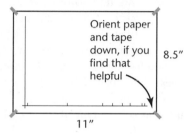

Orient paper and tape down, if you find that helpful

8.5"

11"

2 Determine the units for the drawing. Will it be metric or U.S. Customary (inches, feet and inches)? What system will be used to construct, manufacture, and inspect the actual object? Use that system of measurement for the drawing. This part is in inches.

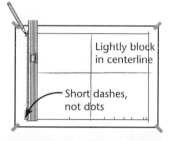

Lightly block in centerline

Short dashes, not dots

Before you begin drawing, determine the scale at which the object will best fit on the sheet.

First, figure the available space within the drawing border. For example the horizontal 8.5 × 11" sheet with a .5" margin leaves 7.5 × 10". If you subtract space for a .375" title strip across the bottom, it leaves 7.125 × 10" for the drawing.

Now, consider the size of the object. Will it fit on the sheet at full-size? Half-size? Do you need to enlarge it to show small features larger than actual size? The 12" gasket shown in the example will fit well at half-size on the 8.5 × 11" sheet selected and still show the details clearly. Use typical scales when possible. Refer to Section 2.5.

Approximately center the object on the sheet. To do this, subtract the size of the scaled drawing from the available sheet space and use half of the difference on each side of the object.

3 One quick technique is to find the center of the available space and lay out the drawing on each side of that centerline. Using CAD, you can easily move the drawing to the center of the sheet visually.

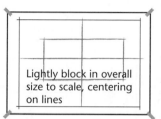

Lightly block in overall size to scale, centering on lines

Sketches do not have to be perfectly centered, but plan ahead so the drawing isn't crammed in one corner of the sheet. Let your drawing be the "star" of the page. Remember to leave enough space around your drawing for notes and dimensions. If you don't, you will run out of room and your layout will look crowded.

4 Lightly add details of the drawing.

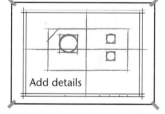

Add details

5 Darken final drawing lines.

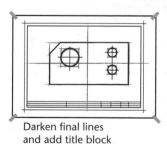

Darken final lines and add title block

TIP
Scale When Using CAD

Keep in mind that when using CAD you will create the object the size that it actually exists in real life. On the plotted sheet, when showing the drawing to scale, it is easy to try a few different scales and see which fits. You can always change the scale later if needed.

STEP by STEP

SCALING ANNOTATIONS AUTOMATICALLY USING AUTOCAD 2008

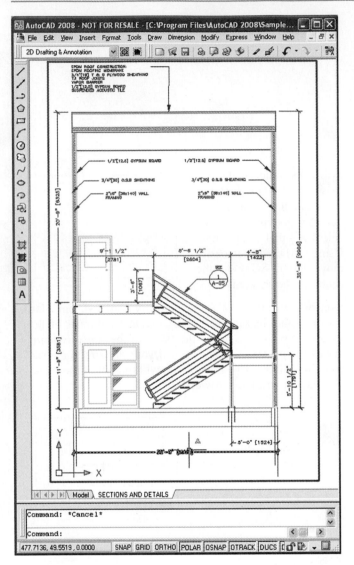

(A) When plotted to scale 1/4" = 1'-0" on an 8.5 x 11" sheet, the text showing the dimensions is clearly visible. *Courtesy of Autodesk, Inc. © 2006-2007. All rights reserved.*

You might think that displaying text in a CAD drawing is one of the easiest things to do. You can quickly type in the text you want to display and select the font, height, slant, and rotation angle. That part *is* easy, but annotations are useless if nobody can read them.

When you create drawings that will be plotted on different sized sheets or at different scales, sizing the text can require a lot of planning. Take the plot architectural plan drawing shown in Figure A for example. When plotted to scale 3" = 1'-0", the text showing dimensions is clearly visible. But when shown at one-twelfth of that size, scale 1/4" = 1'-0", that same text becomes illegible.

The ability to reuse the same CAD data at different scales without having to recreate the drawing is one of its big advantages over pen and paper drawings. Yet, cumbersome workarounds were once necessary to make legible text at different scales. One workaround was have several different sizes of the same text, which the user would turn on or off depending on what drawing scale was used.

Now, AutoCAD 2008 software provides a feature called annotation scaling. Here is how it works: Drawing objects that are commonly used to annotate drawings (provide text information) can have their annotation property turned on. This allows you to create one annotative object that displays at different sizes, based on scale properties.

In the AutoCAD software, object types that can have annotative object properties include Text, Mtext, Dimensions, Hatches, Tolerances, Multileaders, Leaders, Blocks, and Attributes.

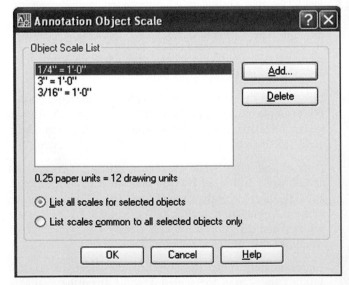

(B) Using the annotation scaling feature of AutoCAD 2008 software, annotative text can be made legible at various scales. *Courtesy of Autodesk, Inc. © 2006-2007. All rights reserved.*

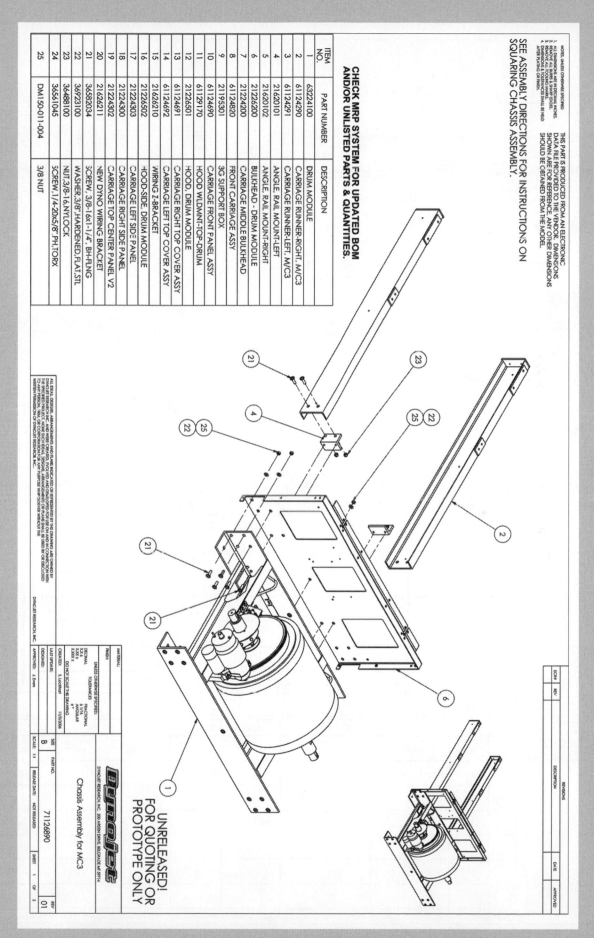

An assembly drawing showing a revision block and a standard title block. *Courtesy of Dynojet Research, Inc.*

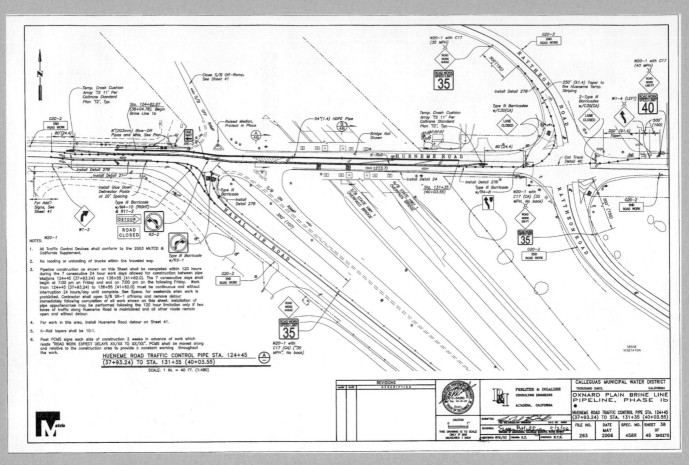

A civil drawing showing approval blocks and engineers' stamp. *Courtesy of Perliter and Ingalsbee Consulting Engineers and Calleguas Municipal Water District.*

WINDOW SCHEDULE

MK	MANUFACTURER/ LINE	TYPE	UNIT SIZE/ MODEL #	R.O.	NOTES
A	PITTSBURG CORNING "LIGHTWISE"	GLASS BLOCK	32X80	33 3/16" X 79 7/8"	8X8 GLASS BLOCK PANEL W/ WHITE VINYL FRAME PATTERN TO BE DETERMINED
B1	SUMMIT VINYL	AWNING	24X24	24" X 24"	PROVIDE AUTOMATIC OPENERS FOR CLERESTORY WINDOWS
B2	SUMMIT VINYL	PICTURE	24X24	24" X 24"	
C	PITTSBURG CORNING "LIGHTWISE"	GLASS BLOCK	24X24	25 3/8" X 25 3/8"	8X8 GLASS BLOCK PANEL W/ WHITE VINYL FRAME PATTERN TO BE DETERMINED
D	KOLBE & KOLBE "TILT N TU	SPECIALTY	48X54	48 1/2" X 54 1/2"	WOOD/ CLAD EXTERIOR
E	SUMMIT VINYL				
F	PITTSBURG "LIGHTWIS				

DOOR SCHEDULE

MK	SIZE	DOOR TYPE	MANUFACTURER/ LINE	STYLE	MATERIAL	SPECIAL HARDWARE	NOTE
1	10070	OVERHEAD DOOR		FLUSH PANEL		AUTOMATIC OPENER	(4) WINDOWS IN UPPER PANEL
2	3068	EXTERIOR DOOR	SOUTHWEST DOOR/ CLASSIC	18 LITE	ALDER		FINISH & TEXTURE TO BE DETERM
3	6080	EXTERIOR DOUBLE FRENCH DOORS	WEATHERSHIELD/ PROSHIELD	SINGLE PANE	VINYL		WHITE FRAME, TEMPERED GLASS
4	5068	EXTERIOR DOUBLE FRENCH DOORS	WEATHERSHIELD/ PROSHIELD	SINGLE PANE	VINYL		WHITE FRAME, TEMPERED GLASS
5	2668	INTERIOR DOOR		SINGLE PANE			TEMPERED GLASS
6	2468	POCKET DOOR		FLUSH HOLLOW CORE	WOOD		FINISH TO BE DETERMINED
7	2468	POCKET DOOR		FLUSH HOLLOW CORE	WOOD		FINISH TO BE DETERMINED

Window and Door schedules are used in architectural drawings to specify the type of window or door, rough opening size, manafacturer and othe information. *Courtesy of Frog Rock Design, LLP.*

KEY WORDS

Station Point
Plane of Projection
Projectors
Piercing Points
Perspective Projections
Parallel Projections
Orthographic Projections
Oblique Projection
Multiview Projection
Drawing Lines
Lettering
Measurement Systems
Scale
Title Blocks
Thick Lines
Thin Lines
Freehand Line
Construction Lines
Drawing Scale
Scales
Engineers' Scale
Decimal Inch
Architects' Scale
Font
Serif
Italic
Roman
Sans Serif
Guidelines
Vertical
Inclined
Kerned Pairs
Media
Sheet Sizes
Zone Numbers
Name
Drawing Title
Drawing Number
Sheet Revision Block
Approval Block
Scale
Drawing Size
Sheet Number
CAGE Code
Weight
Layout

CHAPTER SUMMARY

Now that you have completed this chapter you should be able to:

- Understand the basic principles of projection used in drawings.
- Demonstrate the line weights (thickness) and types (dashed or solid) of lines used in the alphabet of lines that specify meaning in technical drawings.
- List the two main systems of measurement used on drawings.
- Use different types of scales to make measurements.
- Note the scale for a drawing in the title block. Paper drawings are scaled before they are drawn. CAD drawings are scaled when they are to be printed.
- List the advantages of several different drawing media and the qualities that distinguish them.
- Add legible and quick to produce notes and dimensions to sketches using uppercase letters drawn by hand.
- Lay out a sheet and fill in the information in the title block using standard letter shapes.

REVIEW QUESTIONS

1. Draw the alphabet of lines and label each line.
2. Which architects' scale represents a size ratio of 1:24? Which metric scale represents a half size? Which engineers' scale would be used for full size?
3. Which scale type is the only one to use fractions of an inch?
4. What are the main advantages of polyester film as a drawing media?
5. What are the four standard types of projections?
6. Which drawing lines are thick? Which are thin? Which are very light and should not reproduce when copied?
7. What font provides the shape of standard engineering lettering?
8. Describe the characteristics of good freehand lettering.
9. Why should guidelines be used for lettering?
10. List the standard items found in a title block.

EXERCISES

Drawing Exercises

Practice your skills for making measurements, laying out drawing sheets, and forming neat standard lettering with these drawing exercises.

These problems are designed to fit easily on a sheet. (See the inside front cover of this book or the form provided on the Web as a pdf file that you can print to sketch on). Draw all construction lines lightly, using a hard lead (4H to 6H), and all required lines dense black with a softer lead (F to H). Draw your construction lines lightly so that they do not need to be erased.

In exercises 2.1–2.3 you will practice measuring, and in Exercises 2.4–2.6 you will practice drawing layouts.

Exercise 2.1 Measure the lines shown above and list their lengths using millimeters. List the inch measurements for each in square brackets [ ] to the right of the millimeter measurement.

Exercise 2.2 Measure the lines shown above and draw them at Scale 1:2, Scale 2:1, and list their scales below them using the form Scale: X:X.

Exercise 2.3 Measure the overall interior dimensions of your room. Letter the measured length neatly in the first column as shown in the example. In the second column list how long you would draw that line at a scale of 1/4" = 1', third column at 3/8" = 1', fourth column at 1"= 1', fifth column at 1:100 metric scale (10 mm = 1 meter)

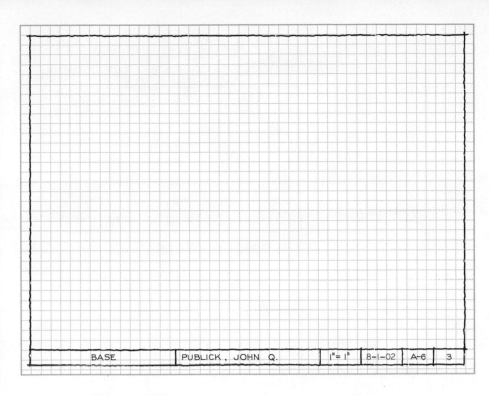

BASE | PUBLICK , JOHN Q. | 1"= 1" | 8-1-02 | A-6 | 3

Exercise 2.4 Create the layout for and 8.5 × 11" sheet as shown at left.

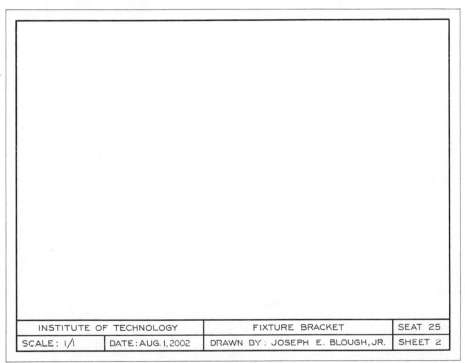

| INSTITUTE OF TECHNOLOGY | FIXTURE BRACKET | SEAT 25 |
| SCALE: 1/1 | DATE: AUG. 1, 2002 | DRAWN BY: JOSEPH E. BLOUGH, JR. | SHEET 2 |

Exercise 2.5 Create the layout for the 210 mm × 297 mm sheet shown at left.

Exercise 2.6 Design a title block and layout for a C-sized sheet. Create a name and logo for your company. Use an attractive but legible font for the titles on your layout. If assigned, design a special north arrow to be used on your drawings.

Lettering Exercises

Layouts for lettering problems are given in Exercises 2.7–2.11. Draw complete horizontal and vertical or inclined guide lines very lightly. Draw the vertical or inclined guide lines through the full height of the lettered area of the sheet. For practice in ink lettering, the last two lines and the title strip on each sheet may be lettered in ink, if assigned by the instructor. Omit all dimensions.

Exercise 2.7 Letter the words to your favorite song, joke, or inspirational quote of 50 words or more. Use 1/8" tall UPPERCASE engineering lettering. Center the words near the middle of the sheet. Make sure to leave a row of space between each row of lettering. Make sure that the subject you choose is professional and appropriate.

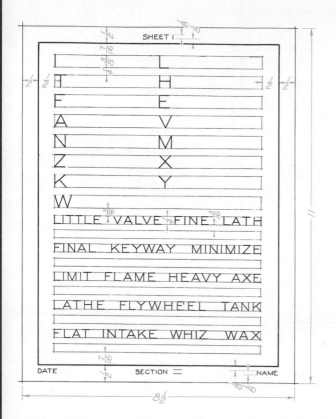

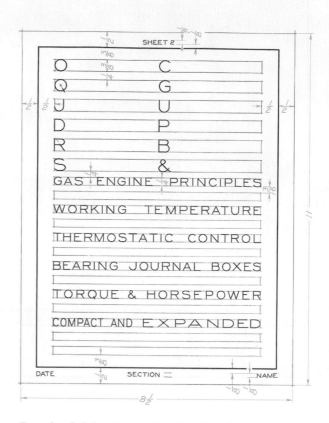

Exercise 2.8 Lay out sheet as shown. Add vertical or inclined guide lines and fill in vertical or inclined capital letters as assigned. For decimal-inch and millimeter equivalents of given dimensions, see inside back cover.

Exercise 2.9 See instructions for Exercise 2.8.

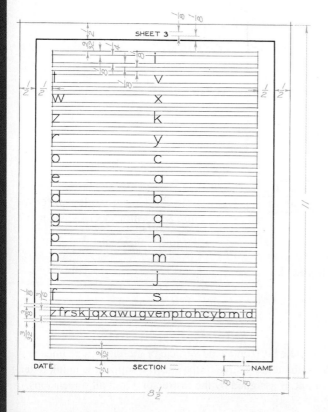

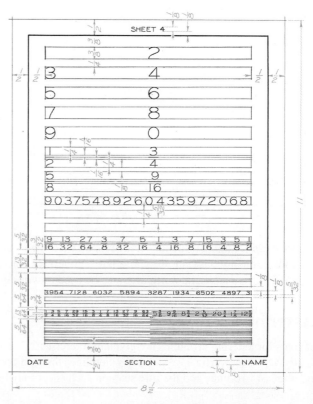

Exercise 2.10 See instructions for Exercise 2.8.

Exercise 2.11 See instructions for Exercise 2.8.

CHAPTER THREE

TECHNICAL SKETCHING

OBJECTIVES

After studying the material in this chapter, you should be able to:

1. Define vertex, edge, plane, surface, and solid.

2. Identify four types of surfaces.

3. Identify five regular solids.

4. Draw points, lines, angled lines, arcs, circles, and ellipses.

5. Apply techniques that aid in creating legible well-proportioned freehand sketches.

6. Apply techniques to draw irregular curves.

7. Create a single view sketch.

8. Create an oblique sketch.

9. Create a one-point perspective sketch.

10. Create an isometric sketch of an object.

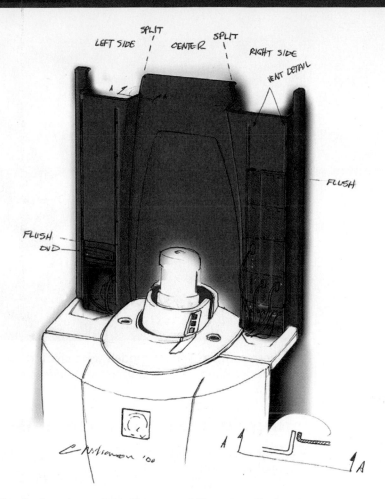

Shaded sketch showing details of wire placement. *Courtesy of Quantum Design.*

OVERVIEW

The ability to envision objects in three dimensions is one of the most important skills for scientists, designers, engineers, and technicians. Learning to visualize objects in space, to use the constructive imagination, is something you can learn by studying technical drawing. People who are extraordinarily creative often possess outstanding ability to visualize, but with practice anyone can improve their ability.

In addition to developing spatial thinking skills, sketching is a valuable tool that allows you to quickly and accurately communicate your ideas. During the development stage of an idea, a picture is often worth a thousand words.

Sketching is also an efficient way to plan your drawing and record notes needed to create a complex object. When you sketch basic ideas ahead of time, you can often complete a final CAD drawing sooner and with fewer errors. Using good technique makes sketching faster, easier, and more legible.

Search the following Web sites for platonic solids (wikipedia, korthalsaltes), convex shapes (ibiblio), and octahedrons (korthalsaltes):
- http://en.wikipedia.org/wiki/Platonic_solid
- http://ibiblio.org/e-notes/3Dapp/Convex.htm
- http://www.korthalsaltes.com/platonic_solids_pictures.html
- http://www.korthalsaltes.com/octahedron.html

These complex surface models were created using 3D CAD. *Courtesy of Professor Richard Palais, University of California, Irvine, and Luc Benard.*

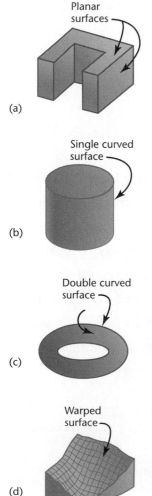

Planar surfaces

(a)

Single curved surface

(b)

Double curved surface

(c)

Warped surface

(d)

3.1 Types of Surfaces

UNDERSTANDING SOLID OBJECTS

Sketches and drawings are used to communicate or record ideas about the shape of three-dimensional objects. Before starting to sketch, it helps to develop a vocabulary for understanding and discussing three-dimensional shapes.

Three-dimensional figures are referred to as **solids.** Solids are bounded by the **surfaces** that contain them. These surfaces can be one of the following four types:

- **Planar**
- **Single-curved**
- **Double-curved**
- **Warped**

Regardless of how complex a solid may be, it is composed of combinations of these basic types of surfaces. Figure 3.1 shows examples of the four basic types of surfaces.

Types of Solids

Polyhedra

Solids that are bounded by plane surfaces are called **polyhedra** (Figures 3.2–3.4). These planar surfaces are also referred to as faces of the object. A *polygon* is a planar area that is enclosed by straight lines.

Regular Polyhedra

If the faces of a solid are equal regular polygons it is called a **regular polyhedron.** There are five regular polyhedra: the tetrahedron, hexahedron, octahedron, dodecahedron, and icosahedron (Figure 3.2).

Tetrahedron (4 triangles)   Hexahedron (cube)   Octahedron (8 triangles)   Dodecahedron (12 pentagons)   Icosahedron (20 triangles)

3.2 Regular Polyhedra

Prisms

A **prism** has two bases, which are parallel equal polygons, and three or more additional faces, which are parallelograms (Figure 3.3). A triangular prism has a triangular base; a rectangular prism has rectangular bases; and so on. (If a prism's bases happen to be parallelograms, the prism is a called a parallelepiped, a word rarely heard in everyday conversation.)

A right prism has faces and lateral (side) edges that are perpendicular to the bases; an oblique prism has faces and lateral edges that are angled to the bases. If one end is cut off to form an end that is not parallel to the bases, the prism is said to be *truncated* (a word which simply means "shortened by having a part cut off").

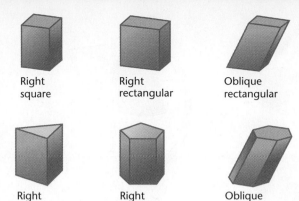

Right
square

Right
rectangular

Oblique
rectangular

Right
triangular

Right
pentagonal

Oblique
hexagonal

3.3 Right Prisms and Oblique Prisms

Pyramids

A **pyramid** has a polygon for a base and triangular lateral faces which intersect at a common point called the *vertex* (Figure 3.4). The line from the center of the base to the vertex is called the *axis*. If the axis is perpendicular to the base, the pyramid is called a *right* pyramid; otherwise it is an *oblique* pyramid. A triangular pyramid has a triangular base; a square pyramid has a square base; and so on. If a portion near the vertex has been cut off, the pyramid is truncated, or it is referred to as a *frustum*.

Right
rectangular

Right square
(truncated)

Oblique
pentagonal

3.4 Pyramids

Cylinders

A **cylinder** has a single-curved exterior surface (Figure 3.5). You can think of a cylinder as being formed by taking a straight line and moving it in a circular path to enclose a volume. Each position of this imaginary straight line in its path around the axis is called an *element* of the cylinder.

Right
circular

Oblique
circular

3.5 Cylinder and Oblique Cylinder

Cones

A **cone** has a single-curved exterior surface (Figure 3.6). You can think of it as being formed by moving one end of a straight line around a circle while keeping the other end fixed at a point, the vertex of the cone. An element of the cone is any position of this imaginary straight line.

Right
circular

Right circular
(frustum)

Oblique circular
(truncated)

3.6 Cones

Spheres

A **sphere** has a double-curved exterior surface (Figure 3.7). You can think of it as being formed by revolving a circle about one of its diameters, somewhat like spinning a coin. The poles of the sphere are the points at the top and bottom of the sphere that would not move while it was spinning. The axis of the sphere is the term for the line between its poles.

Sphere

Torus

3.7 Sphere   **3.8** Torus

Tori

A **torus** is shaped like a doughnut (Figure 3.8). Its boundary surface is double-curved. You can think of it as being formed by revolving a circle (or other curve) around an axis that positioned away from (outside) the curve.

Ellipsoids

An oblate or prolate **ellipsoid** is shaped like an egg (Figure 3.9). You can think of it as formed by revolving an ellipse about its minor or major axis, respectively.

Oblate
Ellipsoid

Prolate
Ellipsoid

3.9 Ellipsoids

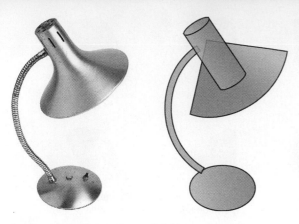

3.10 Identifying Essential Shapes

UNDERSTANDING SKETCHING TECHNIQUES

Analyzing Complex Objects

The ability to break down complex shapes into simpler geometric primitives is an essential skill for sketching and modeling objects.

Before you begin to draw the outline of an object, consider its overall shape and the relationships between its parts. Construction lines can help you preserve the overall dimensions of the object as you sketch.

Bear in mind that you should be thinking in terms of basic shapes whether you are sketching by hand or using a CAD program. Since basic curves and straight lines are the basis of many of the objects that people create, practice in creating the basic elements of a drawing will help you sketch with ease.

Essential Shapes

Look for the essential shapes of objects. If you were to make a clay model of an object, what basic shape would you start with? A ball? A box?

Try squinting your eyes and looking at familiar objects. Do you see their shape as a rectangle? A circle? What other basic shapes do you notice when you look at objects this way?

Think about breaking down more complex objects into their simpler geometric shapes as shown in Figure 3.10. You can block in these shapes using construction lines to show their relationships to one another. Then add details, continuing to pay attention to the spatial relationships between them.

Construction Lines

Artists often begin a sketch by mocking in light guidelines to help them preserve basic shapes and proportions. In technical drawing these are called **construction lines** (Figure 3.11).

It is often helpful to begin a sketch by describing the object's main shapes with construction lines, taking some care to accurately represent the relative size and placement of features.

Use the basic shapes as a guide to place key features. Then use those main features as a "reference map" to place smaller details. For example, the sixth fret line is about halfway up the rectangular guitar neck.

Throughout this chapter you will use light construction lines to draw circles, arcs, and ellipses. Section 3.7 discusses the process of estimating and maintaining the proportions of an object in further detail.

3.11 Using Construction Lines

Contours and Negative Space

The **contours** of an object are the main outlines that separate it from the surrounding space. One way to think about the contours of objects is to look at the contrast between the positive and negative space. Positive space is the space occupied by the object. **Negative space** is the unoccupied space around it.

In Figure 3.12 the space occupied by the contour of a pair of scissors is shown. Note how you can identify specific shapes by looking at the negative space. The individual shapes that make up the negative space are shown in different colors to make them easier for you to see. Some people sketch more accurately when they try to draw the negative space that surrounds the object.

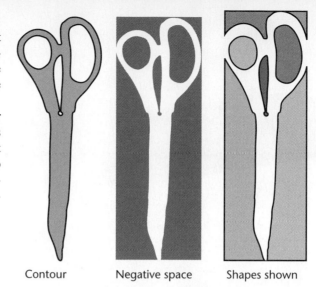

Contour   Negative space   Shapes shown

3.12 Negative Space. *2007 Jupiterimages Corporation.*

TIP

Practice drawing contours

Try sketching the negative spaces that define the shape of a chair. Look at each space as an individual shape. What is the shape of the space between the legs? What is the shape of the space between the rungs and the seat?

Make a sketch of a chair, paying careful attention to sketching the negative spaces of the chair as they really appear. The positive and negative spaces should add up to define the chair.

If you have difficulty, make corrections to your sketch by defining the positive shapes and then check to see if the negative shapes match.

An 8.5-by-11 sheet of Plexiglas (available at most glass stores) is an excellent tool for developing sketching ability. Using a dry erase marker, hold the Plexiglas up in front of an object and trace its contours on the Plexiglas. If you don't move, the outline should match the object's outline exactly. Lower the Plexiglas and look at the orientation of the lines. Are they what you expected?

Try looking at the object and drawing the sketch with the Plexiglas laying on your desktop or knees. Then raise it up and see if your drawing matches the object.

To develop sketching ability, try drawing everyday objects like your toaster, printer, or lamp, as well as exterior and interior views of buildings and equipment.

First try   Examine negative shapes   Note differences   More accurate proportions

3.13   Rubber Stamp

3.14   Hatching. *Reprinted by permission of Pearson Education, Inc., Upper Saddle River, NJ.*

3.15   Stippling. *Reprinted by permission of Pearson Education, Inc., Upper Saddle River, NJ.*

Viewpoint

As you sketch objects, keep in mind that you want to maintain a consistent **viewpoint** like a camera does. This is easier when you are sketching a picture from a book, because you can't move around the object. When you move, you see a different view of the object, depending on where you stand.

Sometimes people have difficulty sketching because they want to show parts of the object that cannot really be seen from a single viewpoint. For example, knowing that the handle of the rubber stamp in Figure 3.13 appears circular from the top, you may be tempted to show it as round, even though it may appear elliptical from your viewpoint.

When you are sketching an object pictorially, temporarily set aside your knowledge of the shapes the object is actually made of and carefully examine the shapes you see from a single, static viewpoint. In this type of sketching, instead of trying to envision the object as it *is*, try only to see it as it *looks*.

Shading

Adding **shading** to your sketch can give it a more realistic appearance because it represents the way the actual object would reflect light. Shading doesn't mean "coloring in." You may only want to shade the most prominently shadowed areas. First identify the darkest and lightest areas on an object. If you want, you can shade various middle tones, placed exactly as they look on the object.

In some ways, shading is like doing a drawing within a drawing, because it is a matter of identifying shapes. When you are shading, instead of identifying the shapes of the object's contours, you are identifying the shape and relative darkness of the shadows.

Hatching lines, shown in Figure 3.14, and stippling, shown in Figure 3.15, are commonly used methods to add shading because they are easier to reproduce with a photocopier than continuous tone pencil shading. In the illustration you can see that shadowed areas are simply darkened by adding more hatching lines or stippling dots.

It is not uncommon for people to draw outlines by hand and add digital shaded fills to a scan of the outline. Marker shading is another popular shading method (Figure 3.16).

Regardless of how you apply shading, darken the outline to define the shape clearly and boldly. Remember that when you are communicating by using a sketch, its subject should be clear. To make the subject—in this case, a rubber stamp—clear, make it stand out with thick bold contour lines.

3.16   Marker Shading in a Concept Sketch. *Courtesy of Douglas Wintin.*

Edges and Vertices

Edges

An **edge** of the solid is formed where two surfaces intersect. Edges are represented in drawings by visible or hidden lines (Figure 3.17).

Vertices

A **vertex** (plural, vertices) of a solid is formed where three or more surfaces intersect. The end of an edge is a vertex. These vertices or "points" are very useful in defining the solid object feature locations that you will sketch (Figure 3.17).

Points and Lines

A **point** is used to represent a location in space, but have no width, height, or depth (Figure 3.12). A point in a drawing is represented by the intersection of two lines (Figure 3.18a), by a short crossbar on a line (Figure 3.18b), or by a small cross (Figure 3.18c). Do not represent points by simple dots on the paper. This makes the drawing look "blobby" and is not as accurate.

A **line** is used in drawings to represent the edge of a solid object. A straight line is the shortest distance between two points and is commonly referred to simply as a "line." If the line is indefinite in extent, in a drawing the length is a matter of convenience, and the endpoints are not marked (Figure 3.19a). If the endpoints of the line are significant, they are marked by small drawn crossbars (Figure 3.19b). Other common terms are illustrated in Figures 3.19c to 3.19i. Either straight lines or curved lines are parallel if the shortest distance between them remains constant. The common symbol for parallel lines is ||, and for perpendicular lines it is ⊥. Two perpendicular lines may be marked with a "box" as shown in Figure 3.19g. Such symbols may be used on sketches, but not on production drawings.

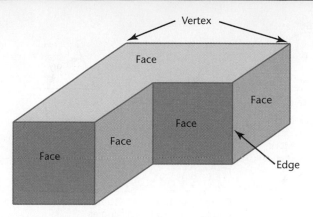

3.17 Edges and Vertices of a Solid

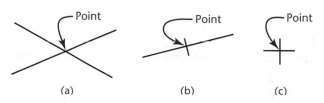

3.18 Showing Points

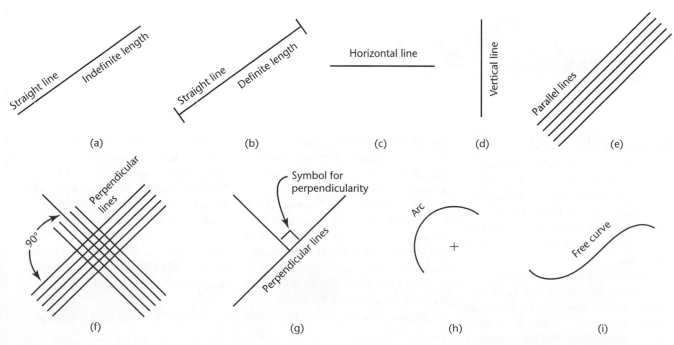

3.19 Showing Lines

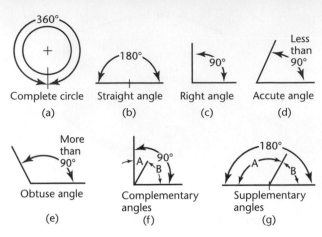

3.20 Showing Angles

Angles

An **angle** is formed by two intersecting lines. A common symbol for angle is ∠.

There are 360 degrees (360°) in a full circle, as shown in Figure 3.20a. A degree is divided into 60 minutes (60'), and a minute is divided into 60 seconds (60"). The angle value 37° 26' 10" is read 37 degrees, 26 minutes, and 10 seconds.

When minutes alone are indicated, the number of minutes should be preceded by 0°, as in 0° 20'.

The different kinds of angles are illustrated in Figure 3.20. Two angles are complementary if they total 90° (Figure 3.20f), and are supplementary if they total 180° (Figure 3.20g).

In sketching, most angles can be estimated. Use a protractor if necessary when drawing odd angles.

Drawings and Sketches

The following are important skills to keep in mind for sketches and drawings:

1. Accuracy. No drawing is useful unless it shows the information correctly.
2. Speed. Time is money in industry. Work smarter and learn to use techniques to speed up your sketching and CAD drawings while still producing neat accurate results.
3. Legibility. A drawing is a means of communication to others, and it must be clear and legible. Give attention to details. Things that may seem picky and small as you are drawing may be significant and save money or even lives when the product is built.
4. Neatness. If a drawing is to be accurate and legible, it must also be clean.

ACCURACY COUNTS

Courtesy of NASA.

Accuracy and legibility in drawings is serious business, as is demonstrated in this article from New Scientist Magazine about the October 2004 Genesis dizzy probe crash.

Dizzy probe crash

You'd think that by now, NASA should be able to tell up from down. Not so in the case of their Genesis space capsule, which crashed into the desert in Utah instead of parachuting gently down so that helicopter stunt pilots could pluck it to safety.

Since its launch in August 2001, the capsule had been collecting precious particles from the solar wind that would have told us something about the composition of the solar system.

But after re-entering Earth's atmosphere on September 8, Genesis plunged into the ground and much of its payload was lost.

On October 15, investigators released their preliminary conclusions, blaming the crash on "a design error that involves the orientation of gravity-switch devices." Huh?

The four small cylindrical switches were designed to sense the re-entry and trigger the parachute. But they were drawn upside down in Lockheed Martin's technical drawings, so they were installed upside down—although NASA's Michael Ryschkewitsch, who led the investigation, is reluctant to use those exact words. The switches never detected the re-entry. Similar devices are installed on another sample-collecting mission called Stardust. Ryschkewitsch believes these are the right way up.

Courtesy of New Scientist magazine.

Freehand Sketching

Freehand sketches are a helpful way to organize your thoughts and record ideas. They provide a quick, low-cost way to explore various solutions to design problems so that the best choices can be made. Investing too much time in creating a detailed layout before exploring your options through sketches can be costly.

The degree of precision needed in a given sketch depends on its use. Quick sketches to supplement verbal descriptions may be rough and incomplete. Sketches can be used to convey important and precise information when they are clearly drawn and annotated.

Freehand sketching requires only pencil, paper, and eraser. Master the techniques in this chapter for showing quick single view, oblique, perspective, and isometric drawings using good freehand line technique and you will possess a valuable tool for communicating your ideas.

The term **freehand sketch** does not mean a sloppy drawing. As shown in Figure 3.21, a freehand sketch shows attention to proportion, clarity, and correct line widths. Figure 3.22 shows an as-built drawing with corrected items sketched on the printed CAD drawing.

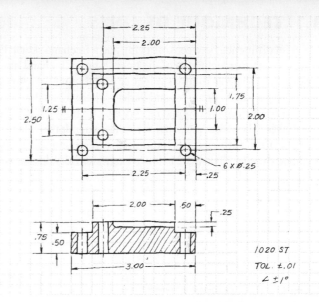

3.21 Sketch on Graph Paper. *Sketches are also used to clarify information about changes in design or provide information on repairing existing equipment.*

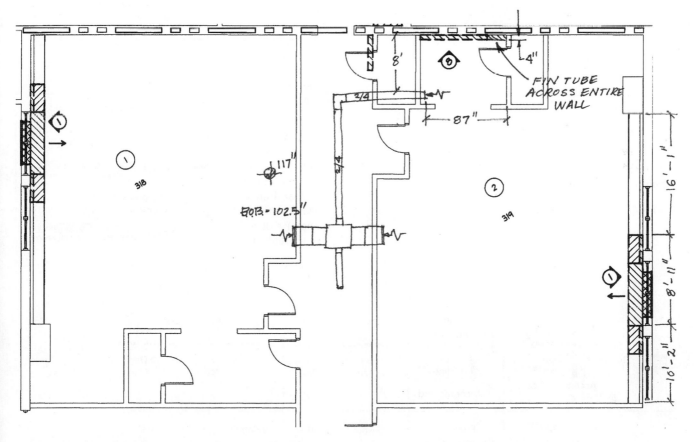

3.22 An As-Built Drawing with Corrected Items Sketched on the Printed CAD Drawing

3.1 TECHNIQUE OF LINES

The chief difference between a drawing and a freehand sketch lies in the character or technique of the lines. A good freehand line is not expected to be as rigidly straight or exactly uniform. A good freehand line shows freedom and variety where a line drawn using CAD or instruments should be very exact. Still, it is important to distinguish between line patterns to make your drawing legible.

The **line patterns** in Figure 3.23 are examples of good freehand quality. Figure 3.24 shows examples of good and poor technique.

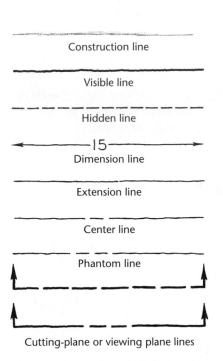

3.23 Freehand Alphabet of Ink Lines (Full Size)

Line Weights

- Make dimension, extension, and centerlines thin, sharp, and black.
- Make hidden lines medium and black.
- Make visible and cutting plane lines thick and black.
- Make construction lines thick and light.

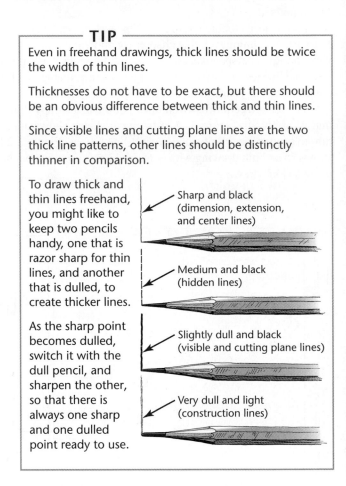

TIP

Even in freehand drawings, thick lines should be twice the width of thin lines.

Thicknesses do not have to be exact, but there should be an obvious difference between thick and thin lines.

Since visible lines and cutting plane lines are the two thick line patterns, other lines should be distinctly thinner in comparison.

To draw thick and thin lines freehand, you might like to keep two pencils handy, one that is razor sharp for thin lines, and another that is dulled, to create thicker lines.

As the sharp point becomes dulled, switch it with the dull pencil, and sharpen the other, so that there is always one sharp and one dulled point ready to use.

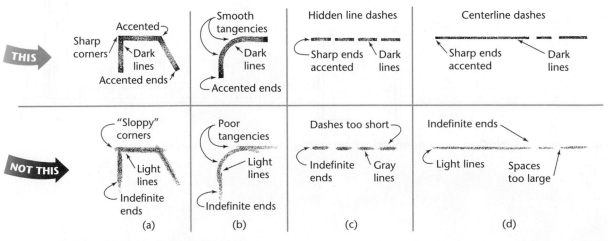

3.24 Technique of Lines (Enlarged)

3.2 SKETCHING STRAIGHT LINES

Most of the lines in an average sketch are straight lines. With practice, your straight lines will naturally improve, but these basics may help you improve quickly.

- Hold your pencil naturally, about 1" back from the point, and approximately at right angles to the line to be drawn.
- Draw horizontal lines from left to right with a free and easy wrist and arm movement.
- Draw vertical lines downward with finger and wrist movements.

Blocking in a Freehand Drawing

Over the years, freehand sketchers have developed all sorts of tricks to improve speed and accuracy. Methods for finding midpoints or quickly blocking in straight vertical and horizontal lines are just a few secrets of the technical sketching craft that can come in handy, even today. When a great idea hits, or you need to sketch quickly at a meeting or on a job site, you might have access to a CAD system, or even a ruler.

TIPS

Drawing Long Freehand Lines

For long freehand lines, make light end marks and lightly sweep your pencil between them, keeping your eye on the mark toward which you are moving. When you are satisfied with the accuracy of your strokes, apply more pressure to make a dark line.

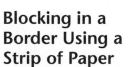

Keep eye on end point →

Keep eye on end point

If your line looks like this you may be gripping your pencil too tightly or trying too hard to imitate mechanical lines

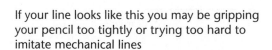

Slight wiggles are OK as long as the line continues on a straight path.

Occasional very slight gaps are fine and make it easier to draw straight.

Blocking in a Border Freehand

Hold your hand and pencil rigidly and glide your fingertips along the edge of the paper to maintain a uniform border.

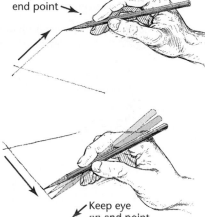

Keep this distance from edge

Finger rigid–slide along edge

Finding a Midpoint Freehand

Use your thumb on your pencil to guess half the distance. Try this distance on the other half. Continue adjusting until you locate the center, then mark it.

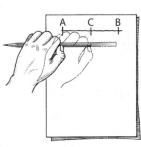

Blocking in a Border Using a Strip of Paper

Mark the distance on the edge of a card or a strip of paper and use it like a ruler to mark at intervals, then draw a final line through the points.

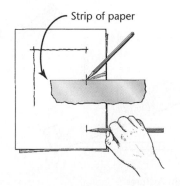

Strip of paper

Folding a Paper to Find a Midpoint

Mark the total distance on the edge of a strip of paper. Then fold the paper to locate its center at the crease. You can fold one half to find quarter points, and so on.

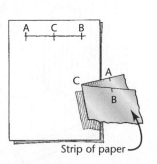

Strip of paper

DIVIDING LINES INTO EQUAL OR PROPORTIONAL PARTS

Proportional Parts

To divide the given line shown into proportions of (for example) 2, 3, and 4 units:

Proportions of 2, 3, and 4 units

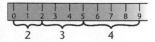

1 Draw a vertical construction line at one end of the line you are dividing.

Sketch vertical line from end

2 Set the zero point of your scale at other end of line.

3 Swing the scale so the desired unit falls on vertical line. In this case it will be the 9th unit, since 2 + 3 + 4 = 9.

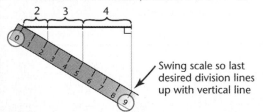

Swing scale so last desired division lines up with vertical line

4 Draw vertical lines upward from the corresponding scale divisions and mark tiny crossbars on the line as shown.

Equal Parts

If you use uniform divisions for the steps above (every third division, for instance) you will get equal parts. Examples of practical applications for dividing lines equally are shown below.

Calculated Proportions

To divide a line into proportions equal to the square of 1, 2, 3, and 4 (1, 4, 9, and 16) find 16 divisions on your scale.

Find desired divisions

(1^2) (2^2) (3^2) (4^2)

1 Set the zero point of your scale at the end of line and draw a light construction line at any convenient angle from one end of the line you are dividing to the appropriate division on the scale. In this case the 4 mark is 16 equal divisions from the 0.

2 Draw construction lines parallel to the end line through each proportionate scale division.

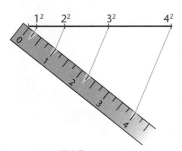

TIP
Exaggerating Closely Spaced Parallel Lines

Sometimes it is helpful to exaggerate the distance between closely spaced parallel lines so there is no fill-in when the drawing is reproduced.

Usually this is done to a maximum of 3 mm or .120". When using CAD it is better to draw the features the actual size and include a detail showing the actual spacing.

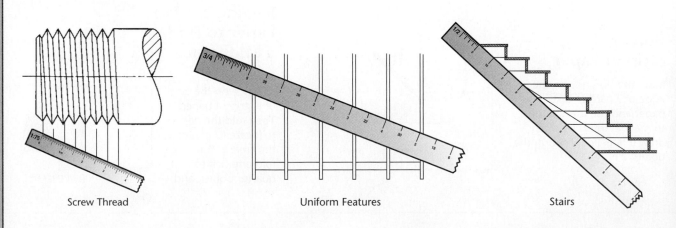

Screw Thread　　　　　Uniform Features　　　　　Stairs

3.25 Many Objects Have Rounded Features that Accurate Circles, Arcs, and Ellipses Are Needed to Represent. *Tim Ridley© Dorling Kindersley.*

3.3 SKETCHING CIRCLES, ARCS, AND ELLIPSES

Circles

Small circles and arcs can be sketched in one or two strokes without any preliminary blocking in.

Circle templates make it easy to sketch accurate circles of various sizes. It may be helpful to experiment with the variety of methods that drafters have devised for sketching accurately sized circles, as the drawing tools available to you may vary under different circumstances. Figure 3.25 shows an object with rounded features to sketch using circles, arcs, and ellipses.

TIP
The Freehand Compass

Using your hand like a compass, you can create circles and arcs with surprising accuracy after a few minutes of practice.

1. Place the tip of your little finger or the knuckle joint of your little finger at the center.
2. "Feed" the pencil out to the radius you want as you would do with a compass.
3. Hold this position rigidly and revolve the paper with your free hand.

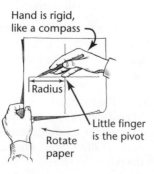

METHODS ARCS FOR SKETCHING CIRCLES

Enclosing Square Method

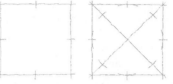

1 Lightly sketch an enclosing square and mark the mid-point of each side.

2 Lightly draw in arcs to connect the midpoints.

3 Darken the final circle.

Centerline Method

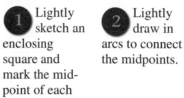

1 Sketch the two centerlines of the circle.

2 Add light 45° radial lines and sketch light arcs across them at an estimated radius distance from the center.

3 Darken the final circle.

Paper Method

Sketch circle through points

1 Mark the estimated radius on the edge of a card or scrap of paper and set off from the center as many points as desired.

2 Sketch the final circle through these points.

STEP by STEP

METHODS FOR SKETCHING ARCS

Radius Method

1 Locate the center of the arc and lightly block in perpendicular lines. Mark off the radius distance along the lines.

2 Draw a 45° line through the center-point and mark off the radius distance along it.

3 Lightly sketch in the arc as shown. Darken the final arc.

Trammel Method

1 Locate the center of the arc and lightly block in perpendicular lines. Mark off the radius distance along the lines.

2 Mark the radius distance on a strip of paper and use it as a trammel.

3 Lightly sketch in the arc, then darken the final arc.

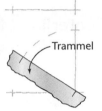

Trammel

Tangent Method

Use these steps to draw arcs sketched to points of tangency.

1 Locate the center of the arc and sketch in the lines to which the arc is tangent.

2 Draw perpendiculars from the center to the tangent lines.

3 Draw in the arc tangent to the lines ending at the perpendicular lines.

4 Darken in the arc and then darken the lines from the points of tangency.

METHODS FOR SKETCHING ELLIPSES

Freehand Method

1 Rest your weight on your upper forearm and move the pencil rapidly above the paper in an elliptical path.

2 Lower the pencil to draw very light ellipses.

3 Darken the final ellipse.

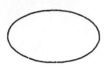

Rectangle Method

1 Lightly sketch an enclosing rectangle.

2 Mark the midpoint of each side and sketch light tangent arcs, as shown.

3 Darken in the final ellipse.

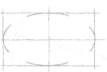
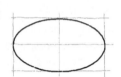

Axes Method

1 Lightly sketch in the major and minor axes of the ellipse.

2 Mark the distance along the axes and lightly block in the ellipse.

3 Darken the final ellipse.

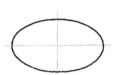

Trammel Method

To sketch accurate ellipses, you can make a trammel.

1 Mark *half* the desired length of the minor axis on the edge of a strip of paper (A-B). Using the same starting point, mark *half* the length of the major axis (A-C). (The measurements will overlap.)

2 Line up the last two trammel points (B and C) on the axes and mark a small dot at the location of the first point (A).

3 Move the trammel to different positions, keeping B and C on the axes, and mark more points at A. Sketch the final ellipse through the points.

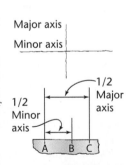

Major axis

Minor axis

1/2 Major axis

1/2 Minor axis

Line up with axes

Mark

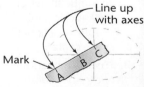
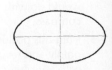

3.26 A Circle Seen as an Ellipse

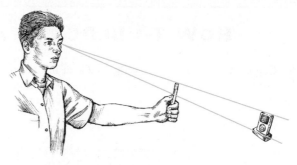

3.27 Estimating Dimensions

Sketching Arcs

Sketching arcs is similar to sketching circles. In general, it is easier to hold your pencil on the inside of the curve. Look closely at the actual geometric constructions and carefully approximate points of tangency so that the arc touches a line or other entity at the right point.

Sketching Ellipses

If a circle is tipped away from your view, it appears as an ellipse. Figure 3.26 shows a coin viewed so that it appears as an ellipse. You can learn to sketch small ellipses with a free arm movement similar to the way you sketch circles, or you can use ellipse templates to help you easily sketch ellipses. These templates are usually grouped according to the amount a circular shape would be rotated to form the ellipse. They provide a number of sizes of ellipses on each template, but usually only include one or two typical rotations.

3.4 MAINTAINING PROPORTIONS

Sketches are not usually made to a specific scale, although it can be handy at times. The size of the sketch depends on its complexity and the size of the paper available. The most important rule in freehand sketching is to keep the sketch in **proportion,** which means to accurately represent the size and position of each part in relation to the whole. No matter how brilliant the technique or how well-drawn the details, if the proportions are off, the sketch will not look right.

To maintain proportions, first determine the relative proportions of height to width and lightly block them in. You can mark a unit on the edge of a strip of paper or use your pencil (as in Figure 3.27) to gage how many units wide and high the object is. Grid paper can help you maintain proportions by providing a ready-made scale (by counting squares). As you block in the medium-sized areas and finally small details, compare each new distance with those already established.

MAINTAINING PROPORTIONS IN A SKETCH

1 If you are working from a given picture, such as this utility cabinet, first establish the relative width compared to the height. One way is to use the pencil as a measuring stick. In this case, the height is about 1-3/4 times the width.

2 Sketch the enclosing rectangle in the correct proportion. This sketch is to be slightly larger than the given picture.

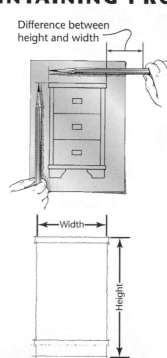

3 Divide the available drawer space into three parts with the pencil by trial. Hold your pencil about where you think one third will be and then try that measurement. If it is too short or long, adjust the measurement and try again. Sketch light diagonals to locate centers of the drawers and block in drawer handles. Sketch all remaining details.

4 Darken all final lines, making them clean, thick, and black.

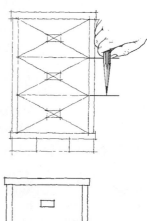

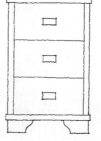

STEP by STEP

HOW TO BLOCK IN AN IRREGULAR OBJECT

1 Capture the main proportions with simple lines.

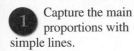

2 Block in the general sizes and direction of flow of curved shapes.

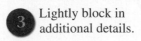
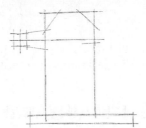

3 Lightly block in additional details.

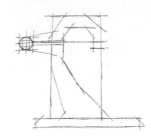

4 Darken the lines of the completed sketch.

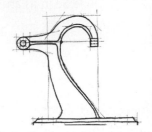

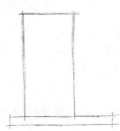

GEOMETRIC METHODS FOR SKETCHING PLANE FIGURES

Sketching a Polygon by the Triangle Method

1 Divide the polygon into triangles as shown. Use the triangles as a visual aid to sketch the shape.

Sketching a Polygon by the Rectangle Method

1 Imagine a rectangle drawn around the polygon as shown below.

2 Sketch the rectangle and then locate the vertices of the polygon (points a, b, c, and so on) along the sides of the rectangle.

3 Join the points to complete the shape.

Visual Aids for Sketching Irregular Figures

1 Visualize shapes made up of rectangular and circular forms by enclosing those features in rectangles.

2 Determine where the centers of arcs and circles are located relative to the rectangles as shown.

3 Sketch the features inside the rectangular shapes you have lightly blocked in and darken the final lines.

Creating Irregular Shapes by Offset Measurements

1 Enclose the shape in a rectangle.

2 Use the sides of the rectangle as a reference to make measurements that locate points along the curve.

Enlarging Shapes Using a Grid of Squares

1 Complex curved shapes can be copied, enlarged, or reduced by hand, if necessary.

2 Draw or overlay a grid of squares on the original drawing.

3 To enlarge, draw the containing rectangle and grid of squares at the desired percentage and transfer the lines of shape through the corresponding points in the new set of squares.

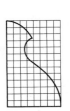
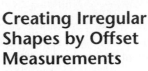

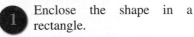

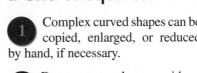
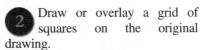

3.5 ONE-VIEW DRAWINGS

Frequently, a single view supplemented by notes and dimensions is enough information to describe the shape of a relatively simple object.

In Figure 3.28, one view of the shim plus a note indicating the thickness as 0.25 mm is sufficient.

Nearly all shafts, bolts, screws, and similar parts should be represented by single views in this way.

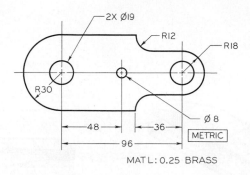

MAT L: 0.25 BRASS

3.28 One-View Drawing of a Shim

SKETCHING A SINGLE VIEW DRAWING

Follow the steps to sketch the single view drawing of the shim shown in Figure 3.28.

1 Lightly sketch the centerlines for the overall width and height of the part. Estimate overall proportions by eye or, if you know the dimensions, use your scale to sketch accurately sized views. Space the enclosing rectangle equally from the margins of the sheet.

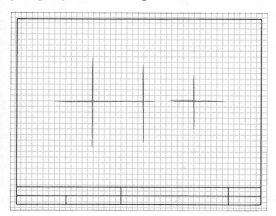

2 Block in all details lightly, keeping the drawing proportions in mind. Use techniques introduced in this chapter to help you.

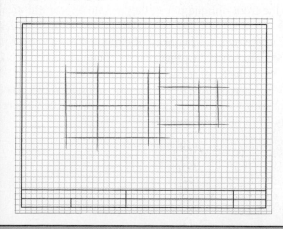

3 Locate the centers of circles and arcs. Block in where they will fit using rectangles. Then sketch all arcs and circles lightly.

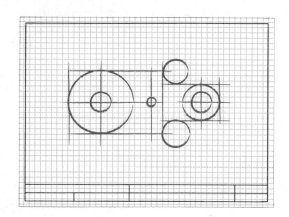

4 Darken your final lines.

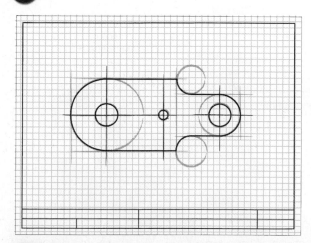

5 Add annotation to the drawing using neat lettering. Fill in the title block or title strip. Note the scale for the sketch if applicable. If not, letter NONE in the Scale area of the title block.

STEP by STEP

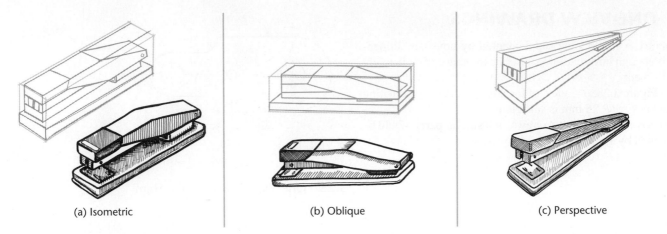

(a) Isometric   (b) Oblique   (c) Perspective

3.29   Three Types of Pictorial Sketches. *Reprinted by permission of Pearson Education, Inc., Upper Saddle River, NJ.*

3.6 PICTORIAL SKETCHING

A **pictorial sketch** represents a 3D object on a sheet of 2D paper by orienting the object so you can see its width, height, and depth in a single view.

Pictorial sketches are used frequently during the ideation phase of engineering design to quickly record ideas and communicate them to others. Their similarity to how the object is viewed in the world around us makes them useful for communicating engineering designs to non-engineers. Later in the design process, pictorial drawings are also often used to show how parts fit together in an assembly and in part catalogs and manuals to make it easy to identify the objects.

This chapter discusses three common methods used to sketch pictorials: isometric sketching, oblique sketching, and perspective sketching. Figure 3.29 shows perspective, isometric, and oblique sketches of a stapler.

Each of the pictorial methods differs in the way points on the object are located on the 2D viewing plane (the piece of paper).

A perspective sketch presents the most realistic looking view. It shows the object much as it would appear in a photograph—portions of the object that are further from the viewer appear smaller, and lines recede into the distance.

An isometric sketch is drawn so that lines do not recede into the distance, but remain parallel. This makes isometric views easy to sketch but takes away somewhat from the realistic appearance.

An oblique sketch shows the front surface of the object looking straight on and is easy to create, but it presents the least realistic representation, as the depth of the object appears to be out of proportion.

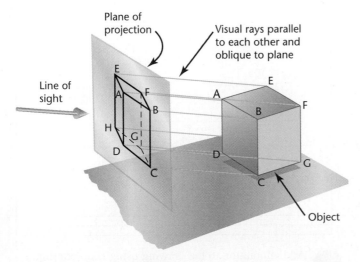

3.30   Oblique Projection Theory

3.7 OBLIQUE SKETCHES

Oblique drawing is an easy method for creating quick pictorials (Figure 3.30). In most oblique sketches, circles and angles parallel to the projection plane are true size and shape and are therefore easy to construct. While circular shapes are easy to sketch in the front oblique plane, they would appear elliptical in the top or sides. Oblique views are primarily a sketching technique used when the majority of circular shapes appear in the front view or when the object can be rotated in order to position circles in the front view.

CAD is not typically used to create oblique views since better-appearing isometric or perspective drawings can be created easily from 3D CAD models.

Appearance of Oblique Drawings

Three things affect the appearance of your oblique sketch are as follows:

1. Which surface of the object you choose to show parallel to the projection plane.
2. The angle and orientation you choose for the receding lines that depict the object's depth.
3. The scale chosen for the receding lines depicting the object's depth (Figure 3.31).

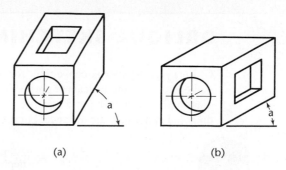

(a) (b)

3.31 Angle of Receding Axis

Choosing the Front Surface

Think about which surface of the object would be the best one to think of as parallel to the plane of projection. For example, a cube has six different surfaces. As you are creating your sketch, any of those six surfaces could be oriented as the "front" of the part. Of course with a cube it wouldn't matter which one you chose. But a cube with a hole through it will make a much better oblique sketch when the round hole is oriented parallel to the projection plane.

Angle of Receding Lines

An angle of 45° is often chosen for the angle of the receding lines because it makes oblique sketches quick and easy. You can use graph paper and draw the angled lines through the diagonals of the grid boxes. An angle of 30° is also a popular choice. It can look more realistic at times. Any angle can be used, but 45° is typical. As shown in Figure 3.32, you can produce different oblique drawings by choosing different directions for the receding lines.

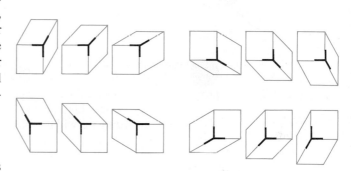

3.32 Variation in Direction of Receding Axis

Depth of Receding Lines

Receding lines with depth in the oblique drawing can be shown at any scale. A drawing that shows the depth at the same scale used for the width and height is called a **cavalier projection,** a term that originated in drawings for medieval fortresses. Oblique drawings are called **cabinet projections** when the depth is represented at half the scale used for the width and height. Figure 3.33 shows a comparison of cavalier projection (Figure 3.33a) and cabinet projection (Figure 3.33d).

Another example of the unnatural appearance of oblique drawing depth is shown in Figure 3.34. This demonstrates that the longer the distance you use for representing the receding axis, the less realistic the appearance of the oblique drawing.

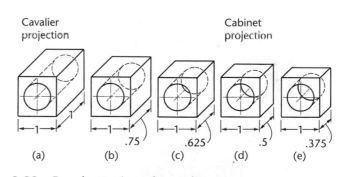

3.33 Foreshortening of Receding Lines

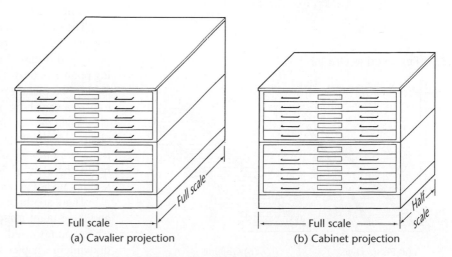

(a) Cavalier projection (b) Cabinet projection

3.34 Comparison of (a) Cavalier and (b) Cabinet Projections

STEP by STEP

OBLIQUE SKETCHING ON GRID PAPER

Ordinary grid paper is convenient for oblique sketching. By counting the grid squares it is easy to make your drawing to scale or proportionate to the object. To draw receding lines at 45° simply sketch diagonally through the grid squares. This will not give a cabinet scale depth projection because the diagonal is not half the distance, but it gives a close and easy approximation.

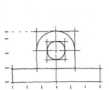

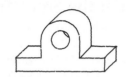

Estimate depth

Any angle

1 Imagine the front shape parallel to the plane of projections, essentially the same as a single view sketch. Lightly sketch a box enclosing the width and height for the "front" view.

2 To establish the depth sketch receding lines diagonally through half as many grid squares as you would use to show the full size dimensions. Sketch all arcs and circles.

3 Darken final lines.

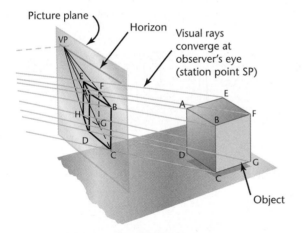

3.35 Perspective Drawing Theory

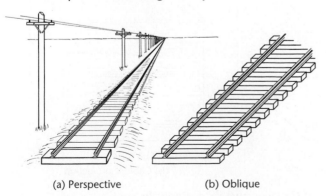

(a) Perspective   (b) Oblique

3.36 Perspective Drawings Appear More Natural Than Oblique Drawings

3.8 SKETCHING ONE POINT PERSPECTIVES

Perspective pictorials most closely approximate the view produced by the human eye. Perspective views are the type of drawing most like a photograph. An example of a perspective drawing can be seen in Figure 3.35. While complex perspective views are time consuming to sketch, they are easy to create from 3D CAD models.

Unlike parallel types of projection, perspective projectors converge. The point at which the projectors converge is called the **vanishing point.** This is clearly seen in Figure 3.36a.

The first rule of perspective is that all parallel lines that are not parallel to the picture plane vanish at a single vanishing point, and if these lines are parallel to the ground, the vanishing point will be on the horizon. Parallel lines that are also parallel to the picture plane remain parallel and do not converge toward a vanishing point.

When the vanishing point is placed above the view of the object in the picture plane, the result is a bird's eye view, looking down onto the object. When the vanishing point is placed below the view of the object, the result is a worm's eye view looking up at the object from below.

There are three types of perspective: one-point, two-point, and three-point perspective, depending on the number of vanishing points used. You will learn more about perspective drawing in Chapter 16.

SKETCHING IN ONE-POINT PERSPECTIVE

To sketch the bearing in one-point perspective (that is, with one vanishing point) follow these steps:

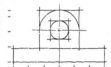

1 Orient the object so that a principal face is parallel to the picture plane. Sketch the true front face of the object, just as in oblique sketching. Select the vanishing point for the receding lines. In many cases it is desirable to place the vanishing point above and to the right of the picture, as shown, although it can be placed anywhere in the sketch. However, if the vanishing point is placed too close to the center, the lines will converge too sharply and the picture will be distorted.

2 Select the vanishing points and sketch receding lines toward the vanishing point.

3 Estimate the depth to look good and sketch in the back portion of the object. Note that the back circle and arc will be slightly smaller than the front circle and arc.

4 Darken all final lines. Note the similarity between the perspective sketch and the oblique sketch earlier in the chapter.

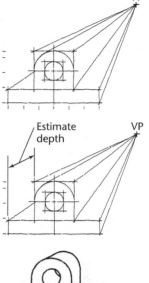

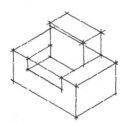

ISOMETRIC SKETCHING FROM AN OBJECT

Positioning the object

To make an isometric sketch from an actual object, first hold the object in your hand and tilt it toward you, as shown in the illustration. In this position the front corner will appear vertical. The two receding bottom edges and those edges parallel to them should appear to be at about 30° with horizontal. The steps for sketching the object follow:

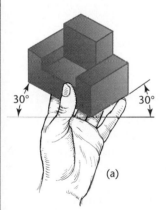

(a)

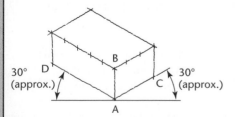

1 Sketch the enclosing box lightly, making AB vertical and AC and AD approximately 30° with horizontal. These three lines are the isometric axes. Make AB, AC, and AD approximately proportional in length to the actual corresponding edges on the object. Sketch the remaining lines parallel to these three lines.

2 Block in the recess and the projecting block.

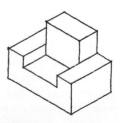

3 Darken all final lines.

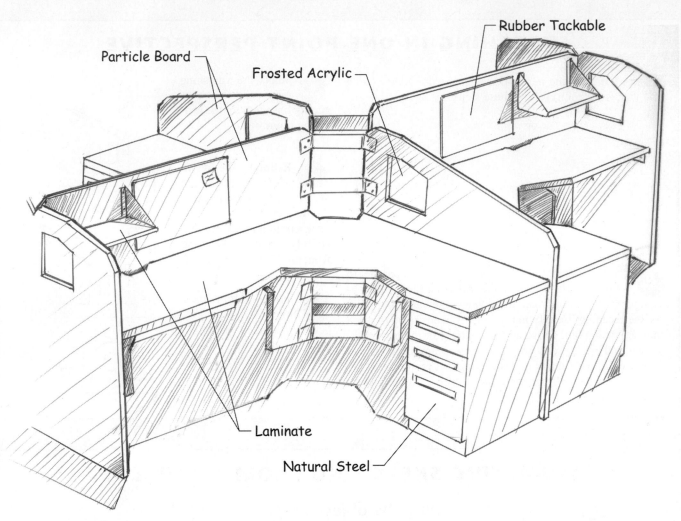

Particle Board

Frosted Acrylic

Rubber Tackable

Laminate

Natural Steel

3.37   Hand sketch to convey custom workstation furniture concept. *Courtesy of Jacob A. Baron-Taltre.*

3.9 DRAWING ON DRAWING

Because CAD helps people produce accurate drawings that are easy to alter, store, and repurpose, computer automation has made the painstaking aspects of hand-rendering technical drawings nearly obsolete. Still, the ability to sketch with clarity is an immediate and universal way to record and communicate ideas.

The ability to think of complex objects in terms of their basic solid components and to identify relationships between various surfaces, edges and vertices is basic to creating both hand-drawn (Figure 3.37) and computer generated technical drawings. By understanding how to represent objects accurately, you can communicate efficiently as part of a team, and increase your constructive visualization ability, or your ability to "think around corners."

"...I want to be able to draw any kind of line I want."

Jacob Baron-Taltre works as a product designer for a mid-sized furniture manufacturer in the Seattle region. He sketches nearly every day at work.

"Sometimes the sketches are very loose . . . just tools for me to work out some detail that I am designing. Other times they are more elaborate and crisp because they will likely be part of a conversation or presentation."

A computer is not the first tool he reaches for when beginning a project.

"Scribbling notes or quick sketches on paper is the fastest way to document the most ideas in the least time. Later, I'll develop some of those ideas more fully by hand and only then begin to use the computer to document the concepts as 2D or 3D CAD work. If a can't draw an idea by hand, I won't likely have more success (if any) using CAD."

Baron-Taltre said he sketches to explore various forms, sizes, and materials.

"CAD is more precise and that precision can be somewhat limiting. When I want to draw a line I want to be able to draw any kind of line I want. In CAD I have to use a specific tool for each line type.

"CAD is a great way to communicate finished thoughts and explore precise relationship. It's also great for quickly building accurate environments and models that can the rotated and examined. You can share these files and edit without having to redraw. Drawing by hand is faster for depicting specific ideas and can be used to communicate with someone in front of you. Plus, you can add detail to key areas of the drawing and leaves out detail in areas needed just for context."

SKETCHING AND PARAMETRIC MODELING

The Design Process

Using CAD parametric modeling in many ways mirrors the design process. To get the rough ideas down, the designer starts by making hand sketches. Then as the ideas are refined, more accurate drawings are created either with instruments or using CAD. Necessary analysis is performed and in response the design may change. The drawings are revised as needed to meet the new requirements. Eventually the drawings are approved so that the parts may be manufactured.

Rough Sketches

Using parametric modeling software, initially the designer roughly sketches the basic shapes on the screen. These sketches do not have to have perfectly straight lines or accurate corners. The software interprets the sketch much as you would interpret a rough sketch given to you by a colleague. If the lines are nearly horizontal or vertical, the software assumes that you meant them thus. If the line appears to be perpendicular it is assumed that it is.

Constraining the Sketch

Using a parametric CAD system, you can start by sketching on the computer screen as though you were sketching freehand. Then the two-dimensional sketch is refined by adding geometric constraints, which tell how to interpret the sketch and by adding parametric dimensions, which control the size of sketch geometry. Once the sketch is refined, it can be created as a 3D feature to which other features can be added. As the design changes, the dimensions and constraints that control the sketch geometry can be changed, and the parametric model will be updated to reflect the new design.

When you are creating sketches by hand or for parametric modeling, think about the implications of the geometry you are drawing. Does the sketch imply that lines are perpendicular? Are the arcs that you have drawn intended to be tangent or intersecting? When you create a parametric model, the software applies rules to constrain the geometry based on your sketch. You can remove, change, or add new constraints, but to use the software effectively you need to accurately depict the geometry you want formed.

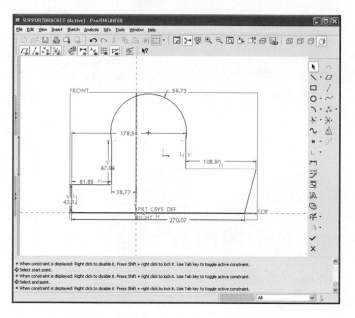

A Rough Sketch in Pro/Engineer Sketcher.

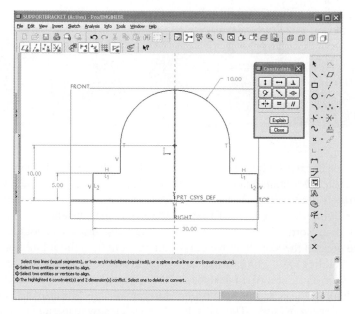

A Constrained Sketch.

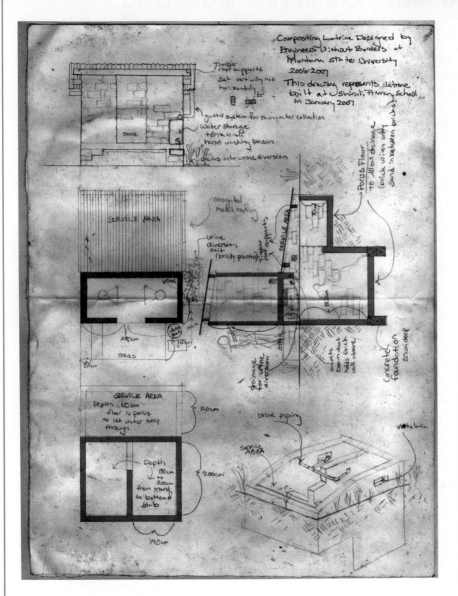

Sketch for a Composting Latrine. *The student chapter of Engineers Without Borders at Montana State University is collaborating with 57 schools in the Khwisero Division of southwestern Kenya to provide sustainable sanitary improvements including wells and composting latrines.* Sketch courtesy of Andrea Orr, Engineers Without Borders, MSU.

Andrea Orr is a student in environment design at Montana State University and a co-fundraiser and co-project designer in the MSU chapter of Engineers without Borders.

She created the sketch above during the building of a composting latrine that she and Chris Allen designed for a school in the Khwisero Division of southwestern Kenya. The sketch showed instructors and local government official how the latrine would work.

Through they had done multiple sketches ahead of time, she and Allen did this complied sketch to clarify their ideas into one concept.

Orr did the sketch outdoors, sitting next to the school building. There was no computer available, because at the remote location, electricity was rarely available. She also did a drawing explaining how to use and maintain the latrine, which was posted inside the finished structure.

Orr said that when she is not working in the field, she still sketches by hand before transferring to CAD.

"There's little bit of vagueness in a hand drawn sketch that keeps it open to creativity," said Orr.

"If you show a sketch to someone they are more likely to offer input and ideas than if it looks like a finished CAD rendering. That's one of the reasons I don't work in CAD until quite a few versions into the project."

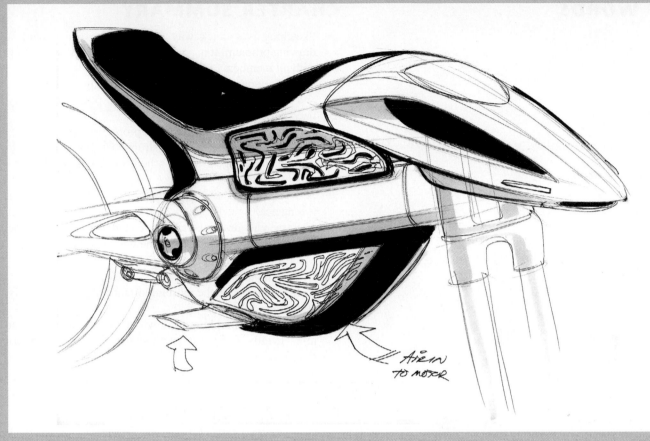

A Sketch for the ENV BIke. *Courtesy of Seymourpowell.*

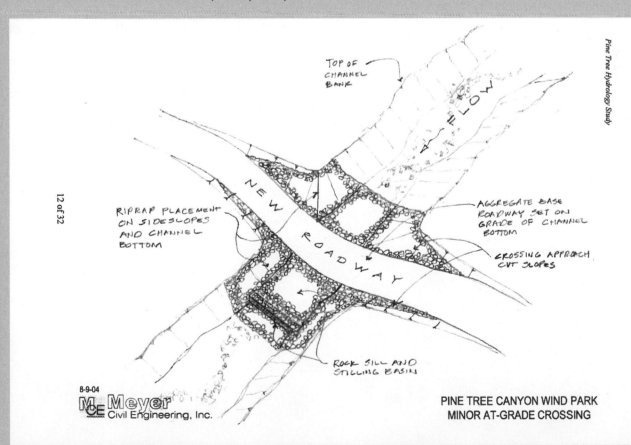

Sketch showing roadway fill details. *Courtesy of Meyer Civil Engineering, Inc.*

KEY WORDS

Solids

Surfaces

Planar

Single-Curved

Double-Curved

Warped

Polyhedra

Regular Polyhedron

Prism

Pyramid

Cylinder

Cone

Sphere

Torus

Ellipsoid

Construction Lines

Contours

Negative Space

Viewpoint

Shading

Hatching

Edge

Vertex

Point

Line

Angle

Freehand Sketch

Line Patterns

Proportion

Pictorial Sketch

Oblique Drawing

Cavalier Projection

Cabinet Projections

Perspective

Vanishing Point

CHAPTER SUMMARY

- Sketching is a quick way of visualizing and solving a drawing problem. It is an effective way of communicating with all members of the design team.
- There are special techniques for sketching lines, circles, and arcs. These techniques should be practiced so they become second nature.
- Using a grid makes sketching in proportion an easy task.
- You can sketch circles by constructing a square and locating the four tangent points where the circle touches the square.
- A sketched line does not need to look like a CAD or mechanical line. The main distinction between CAD and instrumental drawing and freehand sketching is the character or technique of the line work.
- Freehand sketches are made to proportion, but not necessarily to a particular scale.
- Sketching is one of the most important skills for accurately recording ideas.
- Moving your thumb up or down the length of a pencil at arms length is an easy method for estimating proportional size.

REVIEW QUESTIONS

1. What are the advantages of using grid paper for sketching?
2. What is the correct technique for sketching a circle or arc?
3. Sketch the alphabet of lines. Which lines are thick? Which are thin? Which are very light and will not reproduce when copied?
4. What type of 3D drawing can easily be drawn on square grid paper?
5. What is the advantage of sketching an object first before drawing it using CAD?
6. What is the difference between proportion and scale?

SKETCHING EXERCISES

Exercise 3.1 Quick Sketch. © *2007 Jupiterimages Corporation.*

1. Practice the sketching skills and techniques you have learned for construction lines and ellipses. Set a timer for 10 minutes and make quick sketches of these nine different cups.
2. Select one cup and create isometric, oblique, and perspective drawings.
3. Design a new piece of drinkware, using your sketching skills.
4. Select one cup. Draw an enclosing box and shade in the negative space so that the contour of the cup remains white.

(a)   (b)   (c)

(d)   (e)   (f)

(g)   (h)   (i)

Exercise 3.2 Quick Sketch. © *2007 Jupiterimages Corporation.*
See instructions for Exercise 3.1, part 1.

(a)

(b)

(c)

(d)

(e)

(f)

Exercise 3.3 Quick Sketch. © *Jupiterimages Corporation.*
See instructions for Exercise 3.1, part 1.

(a)

(b)

(c)

(d)

(e)

(f)

Exercise 3.4 Sketching. © *Jupiter-images Corporation.*
See instructions for Exercise 3.1, part 1.

(a)

(b)

(c)

(d)

(e)

Exercise 3.5 Divide working space into six equal rectangles and draw visible lines, as shown. Draw construction lines AB through centers C at right angles to required lines; then along each construction line, set off 0.50" spaces and draw required visible lines. Omit dimensions and instructional notes.

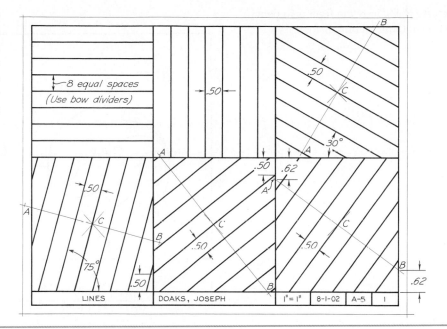

Exercise 3.6 Divide working space into six equal rectangles and draw lines as shown. In the first two spaces, draw conventional lines to match those in Figure 3.23. In remaining spaces, locate centers C by diagonals, and then work constructions out from them. Omit the metric dimensions and instructional notes.

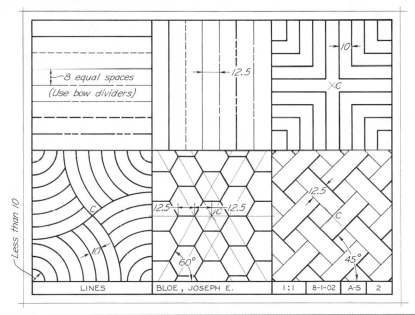

Exercise 3.7 Draw views in pencil, as shown. Omit all dimensions.

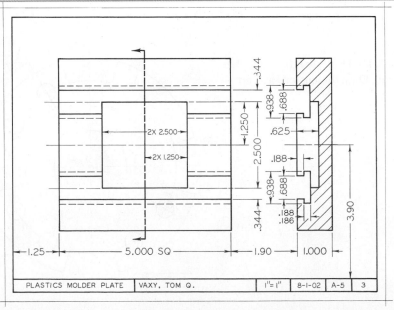

Exercise 3.8 Draw the figures in pencil, as shown. Omit all dimensions.

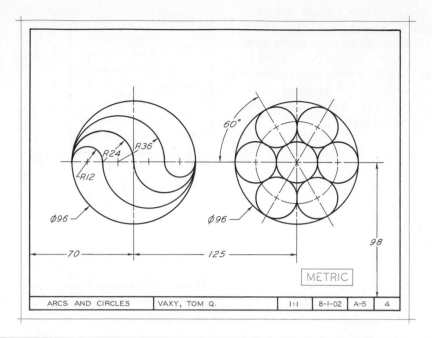

Exercise 3.9 Draw the views in pencil, as shown. Omit all dimensions.

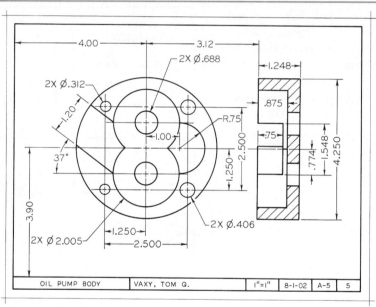

Exercise 3.10 Draw the friction plate using pencil. Omit dimensions and notes.

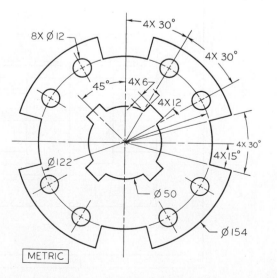

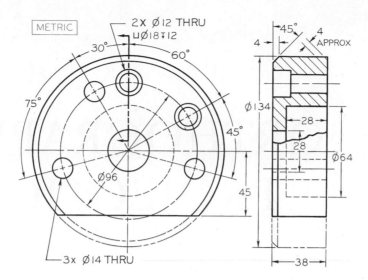

Exercise 3.11 Draw views of the seal cover using pencil. Omit the dimensions and notes.

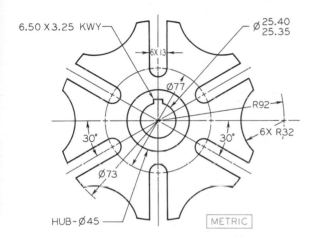

Exercise 3.12 Draw the Geneva cam using pencil. Omit dimensions and notes.

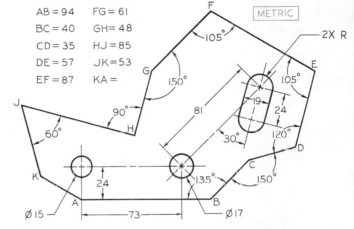

AB = 94	FG = 61
BC = 40	GH = 48
CD = 35	HJ = 85
DE = 57	JK = 53
EF = 87	KA =

Exercise 3.13 Draw accurately in pencil the shear plate. Give the length of KA. Omit the other dimensions and notes.

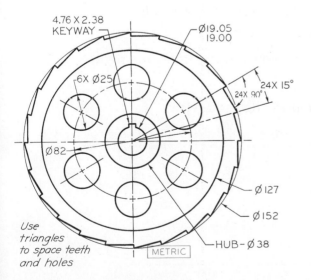

Exercise 3.14 Draw the ratchet wheel using pencil. Omit the dimensions and notes.

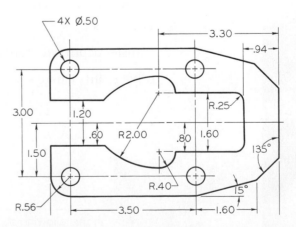

Exercise 3.15 Draw the latch plate using pencil. Omit the dimensions and notes.

CHAPTER FOUR

ORTHOGRAPHIC PROJECTION

---------- **OBJECTIVES** ----------

After studying the material in this chapter, you should be able to:

1. Recognize and sketch the symbol for third-angle projection.

2. List the six principal views of projection.

3. Sketch the top, front, and right-side views of an object with normal, inclined, and oblique surfaces.

4. Understand which views show depth in a drawing that shows top, front, and right-side views.

5. Know the meaning of normal, inclined, and oblique surfaces.

6. Compare and contrast using a CAD program to sketching on a sheet of paper to create 2D drawing geometry.

7. Know which dimensions transfer between top, front, and right-side views.

8. Transfer depth between the top and right-side views.

9. Label points where surfaces intersect.

Refer to the following standard:
*   ANSI/ASME Y14.3—2003 Multiview and Sectional View Drawings

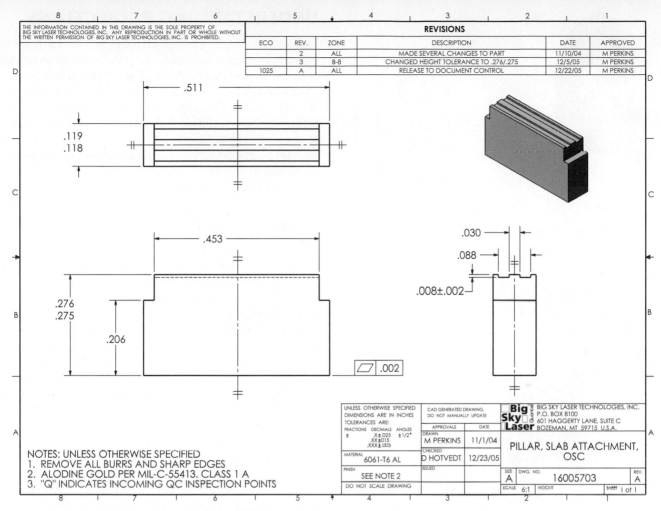

Front, Top, and Right Side Views Generated from a 3D CAD Model. *Courtesy of Big Sky Laser.*

OVERVIEW

A view of an object is called a projection. By projecting multiple views from different directions in a systematic way, you can completely describe the shape of 3D objects.

There are certain standard practices that you must know in order to create sketches and drawings that can be accurately interpreted. For example, you need to know which views to show, how they should be oriented in your drawing, and how to represent key information such as edges, surfaces, vertices, hidden lines, centerlines, and other crucial details.

The standard published in ΛNSI/ASME Y14 3M-1994 is common in the United States where third-angle projection is used. Europe, Asia, and many other places use the first-angle projection system.

Search the following Web sites to learn more about orthographic projections (geomancy) and a biography of Gaspard Mongl (bib math).

- http://wwwgeomancy.org
- http://www.bibmath.net

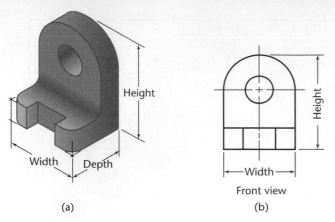

4.1   Front View of an Object

(a)   (b)

Front view

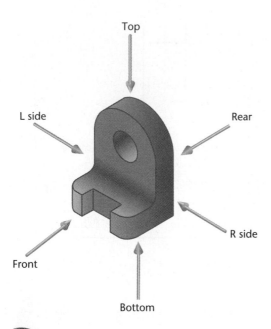

4.2   The Six Principal Views

UNDERSTANDING PROJECTIONS

In order to make and interpret drawings you need to know how to create projections and understand the standard arrangement of views. You also need to be familiar with the geometry of solid objects and be able to visualize a 3D object that is represented in a 2D sketch or drawing. The ability to identify whether surfaces are normal, inclined, or oblique in orientation can help you to visualize objects. Common features such as vertices, edges, contours, fillets, holes, and rounds are shown in a standard way, which makes drawings simpler to create and helps to prevent them from being misinterpreted.

Views of Objects

A photograph shows an object as it appears to the observer, but not necessarily as it is. It cannot describe the object accurately, no matter what distance or which direction it is taken from, because it does not show the exact shapes and sizes of the parts. It would be impossible to create an accurate three-dimensional model of an object using only a photograph for reference because it shows only one view. It is a 2D representation of a 3D object.

Drawings are two dimensional representations as well, but unlike photos, they allow you to record sizes and shapes precisely. In engineering and other fields, a complete and clear description of the shape and size of an object is necessary to be sure that it is manufactured exactly as the designer intended. To provide this information about a 3D object, a number of systematically arranged views are used.

The system of views is called **multiview projection.** Each view provides certain definite information. For example, a front view shows the true shape and size of surfaces that are parallel to the front of the object. An example showing the direction of sight and the resulting front view projection is shown in Figure 4.1. Figure 4.2 shows the same part and the six principal viewing directions, as will be discussed in the next section. Figure 4.3 shows the same six views of a house.

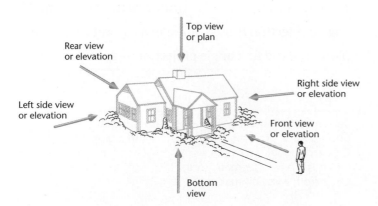

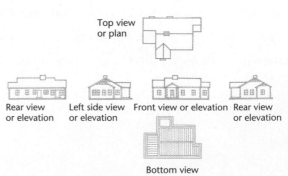

4.3   Six Views of a House

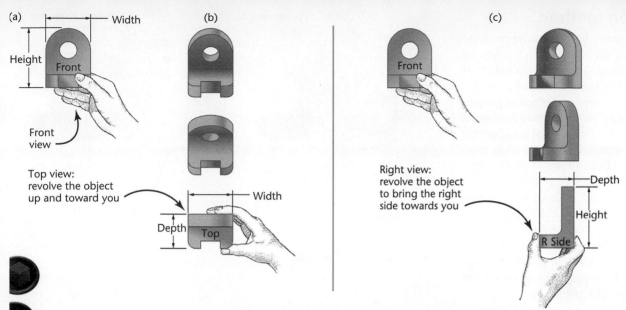

4.4 Revolving the Object to Produce Views. *You can experience different views by revolving an object, as shown. (a) First, hold the object in the front view position. (b) To get the top view, tilt the object toward you to bring the top of the object into your view. (c) To get the right-side view, begin with the object's front view facing you and revolve it to bring the right side toward you. To see views of the rear, bottom, or right side, you would simply turn the object to bring those sides toward you.*

The Six Standard Views

Any object can be viewed from six mutually perpendicular directions, as shown in Figure 4.2. These are called the six **principal views.**

You can think of the six views as what an observer would see by moving around the object. As shown in Figure 4.3, the observer can walk around a house and view its front, sides, and rear. You can imagine the top view as seen by an observer from an airplane and the bottom, or "worm's-eye view," as seen from underneath. The term "plan" may also be used for the top view. The term "elevation" is used for all views showing the height of the building. These terms are regularly used in architectural drawing and occasionally in other fields.

To make drawings easier to read, the views are arranged on the paper in a standard way. The views in Figure 4.3 show the American National Standard arrangement. The top, front, and bottom views align vertically. The rear, left-side, front, and right-side views align horizontally. To draw a view out

of place is a serious error and is generally regarded as one of the worst mistakes in drawing. See Figure 4.4 for a demonstration of how to visualize the different views.

Principal Dimensions

The three principal dimensions of an object are **width, height,** and **depth** (Figure 4.5). In technical drawing, these fixed terms are used for dimensions shown in certain views, regardless of the shape of the object. The terms "length" and "thickness" are not used because they cannot be applied in all cases.

The front view shows only the height and width of the object and not the depth. In fact, any principal view of a 3D object shows only two of the three principal dimensions; the third is found in an adjacent view. Height is shown in the rear, left-side, front, and right-side views. Width is shown in the rear, top, front, and bottom views. Depth is shown in the left-side, top, right-side, and bottom views.

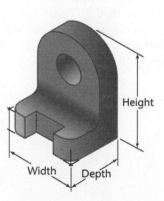

4.5 The Principal Dimensions of an Object

Projection Method

Figure 4.6 shows how to understand the front view of an object drawn using an orthographic projection. Imagine a sheet of glass parallel to the front surfaces of the object. This represents the **plane of projection.** The outline on the plane of projection shows how the object appears to the observer. In orthographic projection, rays (or projectors) from all points on the edges or contours of the object extend parallel to each other and perpendicular to the plane of projection. The word **orthographic** essentially means to draw at right angles.

Examples of top and side views are shown in Figure 4.7. The plane on which the front view is projected is called the **frontal plane.** The plane upon which the top view is projected is the **horizontal plane.** The plane upon which the side view is projected is called the **profile plane.**

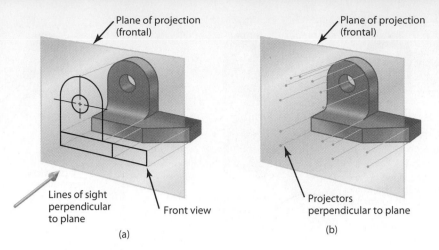

(a)   (b)

4.6 Projection of an Object

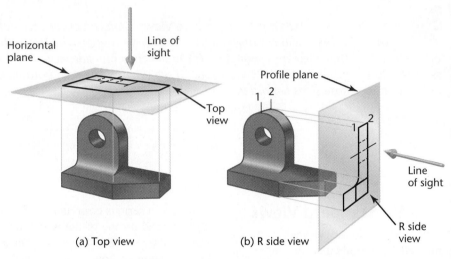

(a) Top view   (b) R side view

4.7 Horizontal and Profile Projection Planes

The Glass Box

One way to understand the standard arrangement of views on the sheet of paper is to envision a **glass box.** If planes of projection were placed parallel to each principal face of the object, they would form a box, as shown in Figure 4.8. The outside observer would see six standard views of the object through the sides of this imaginary glass box.

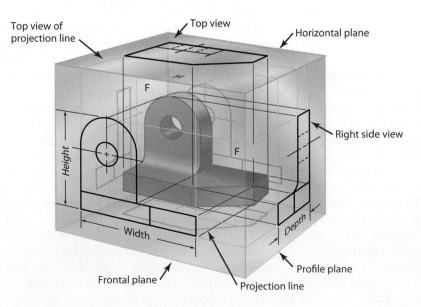

4.8 The Glass Box

To organize the views of a 3D object on a flat sheet of paper, imagine the six planes of the glass box being unfolded to lie flat, as shown in Figure 4.9. Think of all planes except the rear plane as hinged to the frontal plane. The rear plane is usually hinged to the left-side plane. Each plane folds out away from the frontal plane. The representation of the hinge lines of the glass box in a drawing are known as **folding lines.** The positions of these six planes after they have been unfolded are shown in Figure 4.10.

Carefully identify each of these planes and corresponding views with the planes' original position in the glass box.

In Figure 4.10, lines extend around the glass box from one view to another on the planes of projection. These are the projectors from a point in one view to the same point in another view. The size and position of the object in the glass box does not change. This explains why the top view is the same width as the front view and why it is placed directly above the front view. The same relation exists between the front and bottom views. Therefore, the front, top, and bottom views all line up vertically and are the same width. The rear, left-side, front, and right-side views all line up horizontally and are the same height.

Objects do not change position in the box, so the top view must be the same distance from the folding line OZ as the right side view is from the folding line OY. The bottom and left-side views are the same distance from their respective folding lines as are the right-side and the top views. The top, right-side, bottom, and left-side views are all the same distance from the respective folding lines and show the same depth.

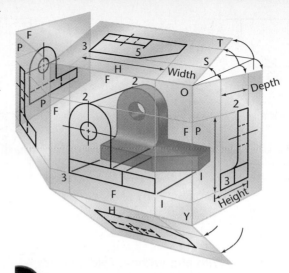

4.9 Unfolding the Glass Box

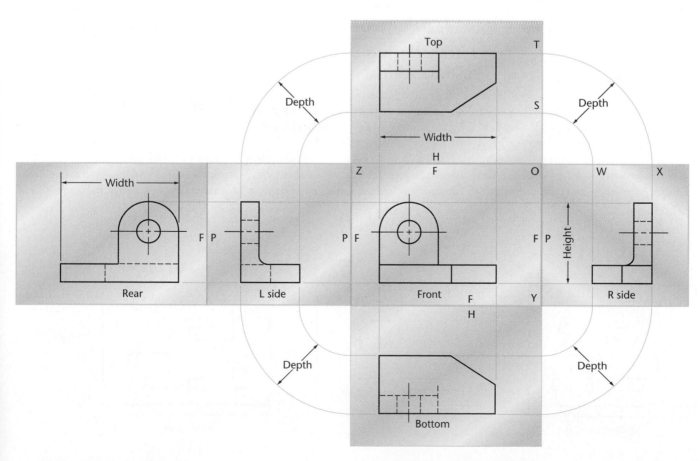

4.10 The Glass Box Unfolded

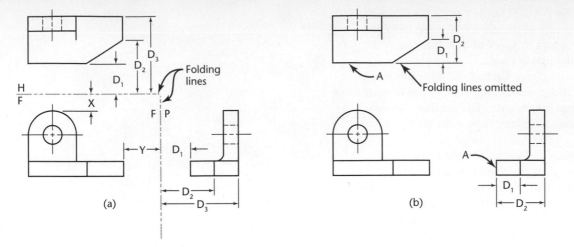

4.11   Views Shown With and Without Folding Lines

The front, top, and right-side views of the object shown in the previous figures are shown in Figure 4.11a, but instead of a glass box, folding lines are shown between the views. These folding lines correspond to the hinge lines of the glass box.

The H/F folding line, between the top and front views, is the intersection of the horizontal and frontal planes. The F/P folding line, between the front and side views, is the intersection of the frontal and profile planes.

While you should understand folding lines, particularly because they are useful in solving problems in descriptive geometry, they are usually left off the drawing, as in Figure 4.11b. Instead of using the folding lines as reference lines for marking depth measurements in the top and side views, you may use the front surface (A) of the object as a reference

line. Note that D1, D2, and all other depth measurements correspond in the two views as if folding lines were used.

Spacing Between Views

Spacing between views is mainly a matter of appearance. Views should be spaced well apart, but close enough to appear related to each other. You may need to leave space between the views to add dimensions.

Transferring Depth Dimensions

The depth dimensions in the top and side views must correspond point-for-point. When using CAD or instruments, transfer these distances accurately.

You can transfer dimensions between the top and side views either with dividers or with a scale, as shown in

Figures 4.12a and 4.12b. Marking the distances on a scrap of paper and using it like a scale to transfer the distance to the other view is another method that works well when sketching.

You may find it convenient to use a 45° miter line to project dimensions between top and side views, as shown in Figure 4.12c. Because the miter line is drawn at 45°, depths shown vertically in the top view Y can be transferred to be shown as horizontal depths in the side view X and vice versa.

Measuring from a Reference Surface

To transfer a dimension from one view to a related view (a view that shares that dimension) you can think of measuring from the edge view of a plane which shows on edge in both views as in Figure 4.13.

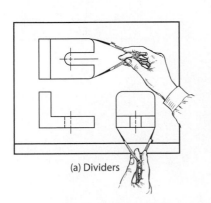

(a) Dividers

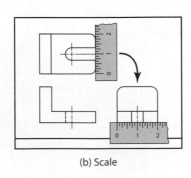

(b) Scale

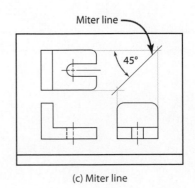

(c) Miter line

4.12   Transferring Depth Dimensions

Necessary Views

Figure 4.14 shows that right- and left-side views are essentially mirror images of each other, only with different lines appearing hidden. Hidden lines use a dashed-line pattern to represent portions of the object that are not directly visible from that direction of sight. Both the right and left views do not need to be shown, so usually the right-side view is drawn. This is also true of the top and bottom views, and of the front and rear views. The top, front, and right-side views, arranged together, are shown in Figure 4.15. These are called the **three regular views** because they are the views most frequently used.

A sketch or drawing should only contain the views needed to clearly and completely describe the object. These minimally required views are referred to as the **necessary views.** Choose the views that have the fewest hidden lines and show essential contours or shapes most clearly. Complicated objects may require more than three views or special views such as partial views.

Many objects need only two views to clearly describe their shape. If an object requires only two views and the left-side and right-side views show the object equally well, use the right-side view. If an object requires only two views and the top and bottom views show the object equally well, choose the top view. If only two views are necessary and the top view and right-side view show the object equally well, choose the combination that fits best on your paper. Some examples are shown in Figure 4.16.

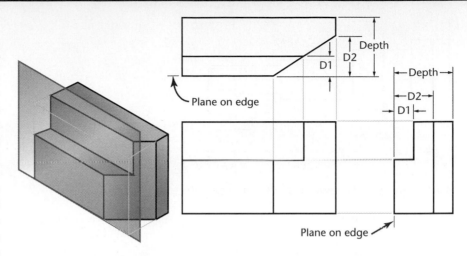

4.13 Transferring Depth Dimensions from a Reference Surface

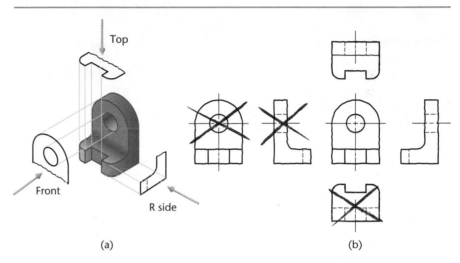

(a)   (b)

4.14 Opposite Views are Nearly Identical

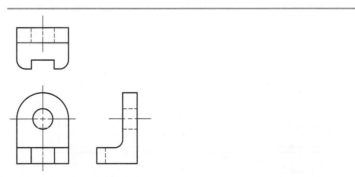

4.15 The Three Regular Views

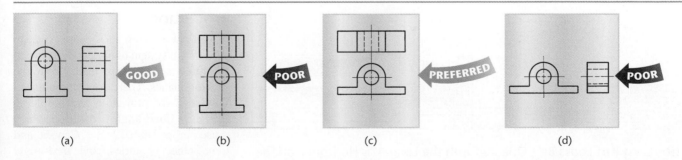

(a)   (b)   (c)   (d)

4.16 Choice of Views to Fit Paper

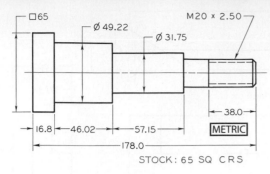

4.17 One-View Drawing of a Connecting Rod

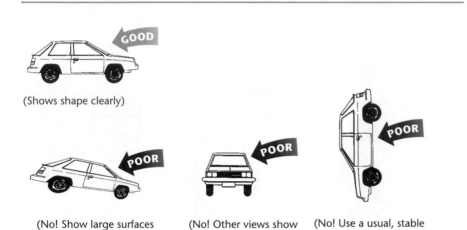

(Shows shape clearly)

(No! Show large surfaces parallel to the view)

(No! Other views show shapes better)

(No! Use a usual, stable or operating position)

4.18 Choice of Front View

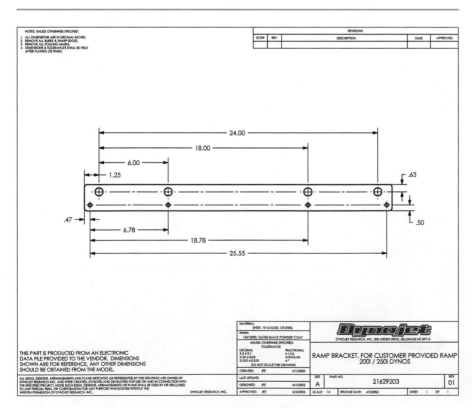

4.19 Long Part Looks Best Oriented with the Long Axis Horizontal on the Sheet. *Courtesy of Dynojet Research, Inc.*

Often, a single view supplemented by a note or by lettered symbols is enough, as shown in Figure 4.17. Objects that can be shown using a single view usually have a uniform thickness. This connecting rod is an exception. It is possible to show it in a single view due to the way it is dimensioned.

Orientation of the Front View

Four views of a compact automobile are shown in Figure 4.18. The view chosen for the front view in this case is the side, not the front, of the automobile.

- The front view should show a large surface of the part parallel to the front viewing plane.
- The front view should show the shape of the object clearly.
- The front view should show the object in a usual, stable, or operating position, particularly for familiar objects.
- When possible, a machine part is drawn in the orientation it occupies in the assembly.
- Usually screws, bolts, shafts, tubes, and other elongated parts are drawn in a horizontal position as shown in Figure 4.19.

CAD software can be used to generate orthographic views directly from a 3D model as shown in Figure 4.20. The pictorial view of this model is shown in Figure 4.21. When using CAD you still need to select a good orientation so that the part shows clearly in the front view. The standard arrangement of views shown in Figure 4.15 should be used. Do not be tempted to rearrange the views of your CAD drawing to fit the sheet better, unless you follow the practices outlined in Chapter 5 for using removed views.

First- and Third-Angle Projection

As you saw earlier in this chapter, you can think of the system of projecting views as unfolding a glass box made from the viewing planes. There are two main systems used for projecting and unfolding the views: **third-angle projection,** which is used in the United States, Canada, and some other countries, and **first-angle projection,** which is primarily used in

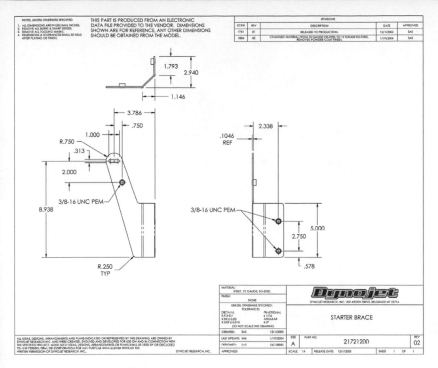

4.20 Computer Generated Multiview Drawing from a CAD Model. *Courtesy of Dynojet Research, Inc.*

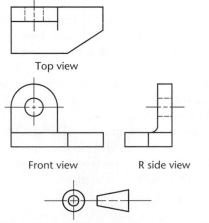

4.21 Pictorial View of the CAD Model Shown in Figure 4.20. *Courtesy of Dynojet Research, Inc.*

Europe and Asia. Difficulty in interpreting the drawing and manufacturing errors can result when a first-angle drawing is confused with a third-angle drawing.

Because of the global nature of technical drawings, you should thoroughly understand both methods. However, since it can be confusing to try to learn both methods intermixed, this text presents third-angle projection throughout. When you are comfortable with creating third-angle projection drawings, revisit this section. You will see that the two drawing methods are very similar and you should be able to extend the same skills to either type of drawing.

Third Angle Projection

Figure 4.22a shows the concept of third-angle orthographic projection. To avoid misunderstanding, international **projection symbols** have been developed to distinguish between first-angle and third-angle projections on drawings. The symbol in Figure 4.22b shows two views of a truncated cone. You can examine the arrangement of the views in the symbol to determine whether first- or third-angle projection was used. On international drawings you should be sure to include this symbol.

To understand the two systems, think of the vertical and horizontal planes of projection, shown in Figure 4.22a, as indefinite in extent and intersecting at 90° with each other; the four angles produced are called the first, second, third, and fourth angles (similar to naming quadrants on a graph.) If the object to be drawn is placed below the horizontal plane and behind the vertical plane, as in the glass box you saw earlier, the object is said to be in the third angle. In third-angle projection, the views are produced as if the observer is outside, looking in.

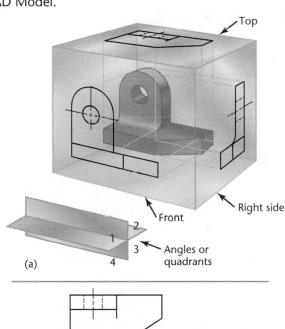

(a)

4.22 Third-Angle Projection

(b) Third angle projection symbol

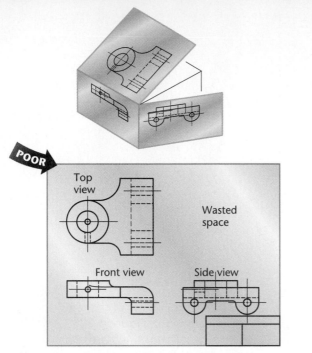

(a) Crowded arrangement of views

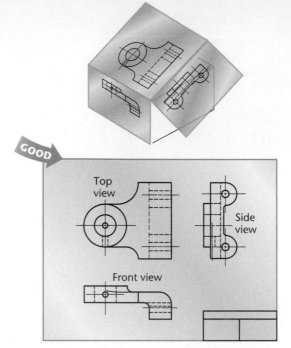

(b) Approved alternate arrangement of views

 4.23   Position of Side View

Alternate Arrangements for Third-Angle Projection

Sometimes drawing three views using the conventional arrangement wastes space. (For example, see the wide flat object in Figure 4.23a.) Using the space on the paper efficiently may prevent the need to use a reduced scale.

For these cases, there is another acceptable arrangement of third angle projection views. Imagine unfolding the glass box as shown in Figure 4.23b. The views are arranged differently, with the right side view aligned with the top view, but these views are still using third angle projection.

In this case, think of the profile (side view) hinged to the horizontal plane (top view) instead of to the frontal plane (front view) so that the side view is beside the top view when unfolded, as shown in Figure 4.23b. Notice the side view is rotated 90° from the orientation shown in the side view in Figure 4.23a when it is in this placement. Note also that you can now directly project the depth dimension from the top view into the side view.

If necessary, you may place the side view horizontally across from the bottom view (so the profile plane is hinged to the bottom plane of the projection).

Similarly, the rear view may be placed directly above the top view or under the bottom view. In this case, the rear plane is considered hinged to the horizontal or bottom plane and rotated to coincide with the frontal plane.

First-Angle Projection

If the object is placed above the horizontal plane and in front of the vertical plane, the object is in the first angle. In first-angle projection the observer looks through the object to the planes of projection. The right-side view is still obtained by looking toward the right side of the object, the front by looking toward the front, and the top by looking down toward the top; but the views are projected from the object onto a plane in each case.

The biggest difference between third-angle projection and first-angle projection is in how the planes of the glass box are unfolded, as shown in Figure 4.24. In first-angle projection, the right-side view is to the left of the front view, and the top view is below the front view, as shown.

You should understand the difference between the two systems and know the symbol that is placed on drawings to indicate which has been used. Keep in mind that you will use third-angle projection throughout this book.

Projection System Drawing Symbol

The symbol shown in Figure 4.25 is used on drawings to indicate which system of projection is used. Whenever drawings will be used internationally you should include this symbol in the title block area.

TIP

You can experiment with these alternative arrangements by trying them out on a paper box.

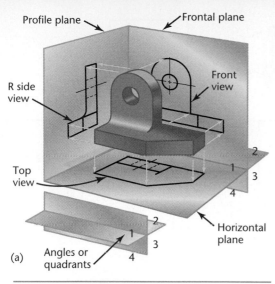

Profile plane — Frontal plane

R side view

Front view

Top view

Horizontal plane

Angles or quadrants

(a)

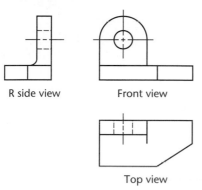

R side view   Front view

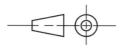

Top view

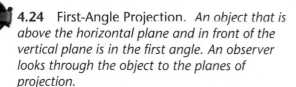

First angle projection symbol

(b)

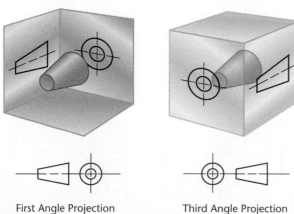

4.24 First-Angle Projection. *An object that is above the horizontal plane and in front of the vertical plane is in the first angle. An observer looks through the object to the planes of projection.*

First Angle Projection   Third Angle Projection

4.25 Drawing Symbols for First- and Third-Angle Projection

Hidden Lines

One advantage of orthographic views over photographs is that each view can show the entire object from that viewing direction. A photograph shows only the visible surface of an object, but an orthographic view shows the object all the way through, as if it were transparent.

Thick, dark lines represent features of the object that are directly visible. Dashed lines represent features that would be hidden behind other surfaces.

Figure 4.26 shows a part that has internal features. When a 3D view of this model is rendered using a transparent material, as shown in Figure 4.27, you can see the internal features. Figure 4.28 shows this part from the front as it would be oriented in an orthographic drawing. The features that are hidden from view are shown in orthographic views using the hidden line pattern as shown in Figure 4.29.

Whenever possible, choose views that show features with visible lines. Use hidden lines where they are needed to make the drawing clear.

Some practices for representing intersections of hidden lines with other lines may be difficult to follow when using CAD. In CAD, adjust the line patterns so that the hidden lines in your drawing have the best appearance possible.

4.26 Shaded Model with Hidden Features

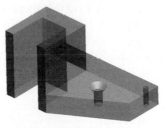

4.27 Transparent Model Showing Hidden Features

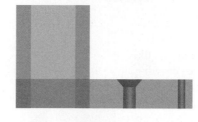

4.28 Front View of Transparent Model

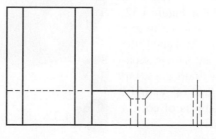

4.29 Front View Projection

CENTERLINES

The centerline pattern is used to:

- show the axis of symmetry for a feature or part
- indicate a path of motion
- show the location for bolt circles and other circular patterns

The centerline pattern is composed of three dashes: one long dash on each end with a short dash in the middle. In the drawing, centerlines are shown as thin and black. Because a centerline is not an actual part of the object, it extends beyond the symmetric feature as shown in Figure 4.30.

The most common shape that needs a centerline is a cylindrical hole. Figure 4.31 shows centerlines in a drawing. In the circular view of a hole, the centerline should form a cross to mark the center location. When a feature is too small for the centerline pattern to be shown with the long-short-long dash pattern, it is acceptable to use a straight line. You will learn more about showing hidden and centerlines in the technique sections.

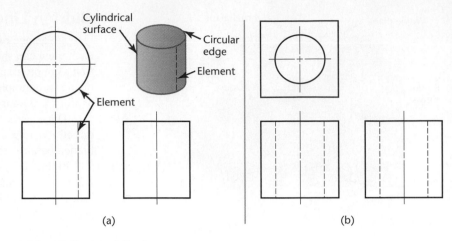

(a)   (b)

4.30   Cylindrical Surfaces

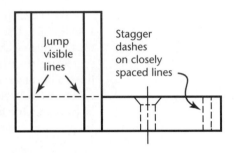

4.31   Hidden Lines

4.1 HIDDEN LINE TECHNIQUE

You can save time and reduce clutter by leaving out hidden lines that aren't necessary as long as you are certain that the remaining lines describe the object clearly and completely. If you omit unnecessary hidden lines, add a note to let the reader know that the lines were left out intentionally and that it is not an error in the drawing.

Sketch hidden lines by eye, using thin dark dashes about 5 mm long and spaced about 1 mm apart. Hidden lines should be as dark as other lines in the drawing, but should be thin.

When hidden lines intersect each other in the drawing, their dashes should meet. In general, hidden lines should intersect neatly with visible lines at the edge of an object. Leave gaps when hidden lines align with a visible lines, so the visible line's length remains clear.

4.2 PRECEDENCE OF LINES

Visible lines, hidden lines, and centerlines (which are used to show the axis of symmetry for contoured shapes, like holes) often coincide on a drawing. There are rules for deciding which line to show. A visible line always takes precedence over and covers up a centerline or a hidden line when they coincide in a view, as shown at A and B in Figure 4.32. A hidden line takes precedence over a centerline, as shown at C. At A and C the ends of the centerline are shown separated from the view by short gaps, but the centerline can be left off entirely. Figure 4.33 shows examples of correct and incorrect hidden lines.

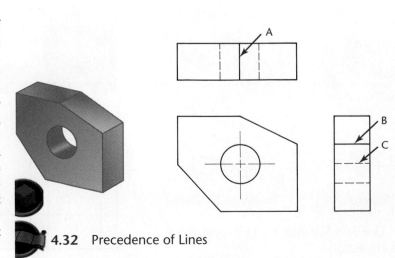

4.32   Precedence of Lines

Correct and incorrect practices for hidden lines

Make a hidden line join a visible line, except when it causes the visible line to extend too far, as shown here.

Leave a gap whenever a hidden line is a continuation of a visible line.

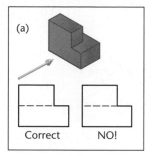

(a)
Correct   NO!

When two or three hidden lines meet at a point, join the dashes, as shown for the bottom of this drilled hole.

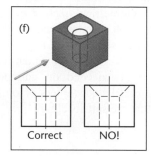

(f)
Correct   NO!

Make hidden lines intersect to for L and T corners.

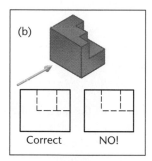

(b)
Correct   NO!

The same rule of joining the dashes when two or three hidden lines meet at a point applics for the top of this counter sunk hole.

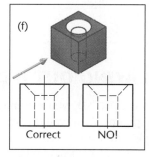

(f)
Correct   NO!

Make a hidden line "jump" a visible line when possible.

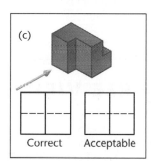

(c)
Correct   Acceptable

Hidden lines should not join visible lines when this makes the visible line extend too far.

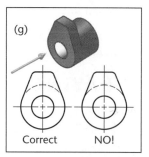

(g)
Correct   NO!

Draw parallel hidden lines so that the dashes are staggered, as in bricklaying.

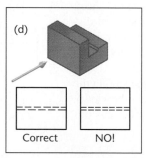

(d)
Correct   NO!

Draw hidden arcs with the arc joining the center line, as in upper example. There should not be a gap between the arc and the center-line, as in the example below with the straightaway joining the centerline.

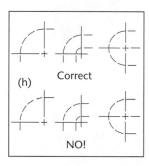

(h)
Correct

NO!

4.33   Correct and Incorrect Practices for Hidden Lines

TIP
Accent the beginning and end of each dash by pressing down on the pencil. Make hidden lines as tidy as you can so they are easy to interpret. Be sure to make hidden line dashes longer than gaps so they clearly represent lines.

4.3 CENTERLINES

Centerlines (symbol: ₵) are used to indicate symmetrical axes of objects or features, bolt circles, and paths of motion as shown in Figure 4.34. Centerlines are useful in dimensioning. They are not needed on unimportant rounded or filleted corners or on other shapes that are self-locating.

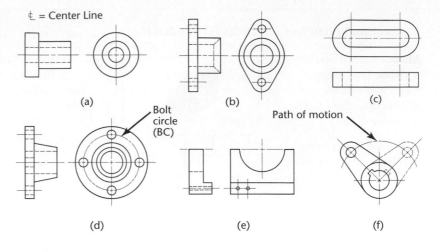

₵ = Center Line

(a)   (b)   (c)

Bolt circle (BC)

Path of motion

(d)   (e)   (f)

4.34   Centerlines

4.4 LAYING OUT A DRAWING

If you use 2D CAD, you can move the views later, keeping them in alignment, so you do not need to give as much attention to placement of the views in the beginning as if you were laying them out by hand. When using 3D CAD to generate views, you should still plan how the sheet will show the information clearly and select the necessary views to best represent the shape of the part. While you can easily change the scale of a CAD drawing after it is created, placing the dimensions and views on the sheet requires some planning. If you consider the purpose of the drawing, the planned scale, and the space that will be required for adding notes and dimensions, you will save the time of having to rearrange their placement later.

STEP by STEP

LAYING OUT A METRIC THREE-VIEW DRAWING

1 Determine space desired between the front and right side views, say 32 mm, C. Add this space to the sum of the length of the views that will be aligned along the long edge of the sheet. (108 + 58 + 32 = 198) To set equal distances to the paper edge, subtract this total from the sheet width, then divide the remaining number by two (266 − 198 = 70, and 70 ÷ 2 = 35). Do the same for the views to be aligned along the short side of the paper, selecting a desired space between the views. Space D need not match C. Remember to leave space for dimensions as you plan your sheet.

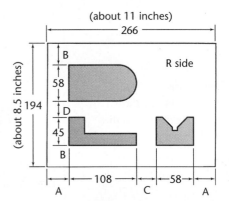

(about 11 inches)
266

(about 8.5 inches)
194

B
58
D
45
B

R side

108   58

A   C   A

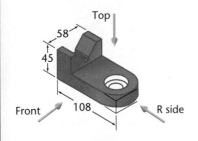

2 Set off vertical and horizontal spacing measurements with light tick marks along the edge of the sheet as shown. Locate centerlines from these spacing marks and construct arcs and circles.

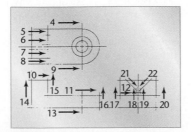

3 Construct the views, drawing horizontal, vertical, and then inclined construction, lines in the order shown above.

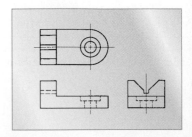

4 Add hidden lines and darken final lines.

4.5 VISUALIZATION

Along with a basic understanding of the system for projecting views, you must be able interpret multiple views to picture the object that they show. In addition to being an indispensable skill to help you capture and communicate your ideas, technical sketching is also a way for others to present their ideas to you.

Even experienced engineers, technicians, and designers can't always look at a multiview sketch and instantly visualize the object represented. You will learn to study the sketch and interpret the lines in a logical way in order to piece together a clear idea of the whole. This process is sometimes called visualization.

Surfaces, Edges, and Corners

To effectively create and interpret multiview projections, you have to consider the elements that make up most solids. **Surfaces** form the boundaries of solid objects. A **plane** (flat) surface may be bounded by straight lines, curves, or a combination of the two. It takes practice to envision flat representations as 3D objects. Take a moment to examine the views shown in Figure 4.35 and try to picture the object. (See solution on page 120).

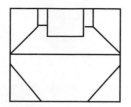

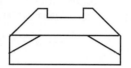

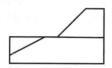

4.35 Three Views of an Object. *Reprinted by permission of Pearson Education, Inc., Upper Saddle River, NJ.*

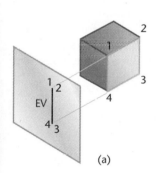 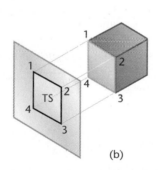 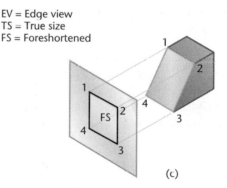

EV = Edge view
TS = True size
FS = Foreshortened

(a) (b) (c)

4.36 Projections of Surfaces

── TIP ──
Using Numbers to Identify vertices

Add lightly drawn numbers to your sketches to keep track of each vertex on the surface you are considering. Each vertex is unique on the part, so each numbered vertex will appear only once in each view. Sometimes two vertices will line up one behind the other as in 4.36a. When this happens you can list them in order with the closest first as in 1, 2 of sometimes it is useful to put numbers for the closest visible vertex outside the shape, and the further hidden vertex inside the shape outline.

4.6 VIEWS OF SURFACES

A plane surface that is perpendicular to a plane of projection appears on edge as a straight line (Figure 4.36a). If it is parallel to the plane of projection, it appears true size (Figure 4.36b). If it is angled to the plane of projection, it appears foreshortened or smaller than its actual size (Figure 4.36c). A plane surface always projects either on edge (appearing as a single line) or as a surface (showing its characteristic shape) in any view.

It can appear foreshortened, but it can never appear larger than its true size in any view.

There are terms used for describing a surface's orientation to the plane of projection. The three orientations that a plane surface can have to the plane of projection are *normal, inclined,* and *oblique*. Understanding these terms will help you picture and describe objects.

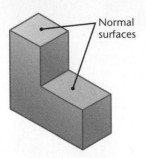

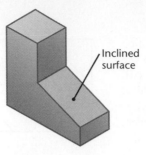

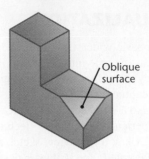

4.37   Normal Surfaces. *Reprinted with permission of Pearson Education.*

4.38   Inclined Surface. *Reprinted with permission of Pearson Education.*

4.39   Oblique Surface. *Reprinted with permission of Pearson Education.*

4.7 NORMAL SURFACES

A **normal surface** is parallel to a plane of projection. It appears true size and true shape on the plane to which it is parallel, and it appears as a true-length vertical or a horizontal line on adjacent planes of projection. Figure 4.37 shows an illustration of normal surfaces.

Practice identifying normal surfaces on CAD drawings. You can download orthographic views of subjects that show many normal surfaces at the following Web sites:
- http://www.constructionsite.come/harlen/8001-81.htm
- http://www.user.mc.net/hawk/cad.htm

4.8 INCLINED SURFACES

An **inclined surface** is perpendicular to one plane of projection, but inclined (or tipped) to adjacent planes. An inclined surface projects an edge on the plane to which it is perpendicular. It appears foreshortened on planes to which it is inclined. An inclined surface is shown in Figure 4.38. The degree of foreshortening is proportional to the inclination. While the surface may not appear true size in any view, it will have the same characteristic shape and the same number of edges in the views in which you see its shape.

4.9 OBLIQUE SURFACES

An **oblique surface** is tipped to all principal planes of projection. Since it is not perpendicular to any projection plane, it cannot appear on edge in any standard view. Since it is not parallel to any projection plane, it cannot appear true size in any standard view. An oblique surface always appears as a foreshortened surface in all three standard views. Figure 4.39 and Figure 4.40 show oblique surfaces.

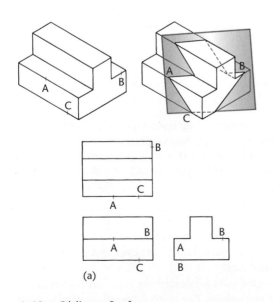

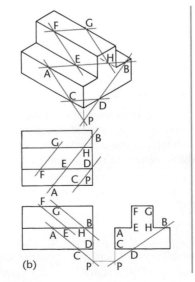

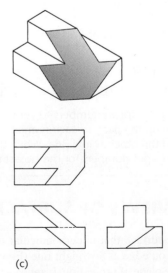

4.40   Oblique Surfaces

4.10 EDGES

The intersection of two plane surfaces of an object produces an **edge,** which shows as a straight line in the drawing. An edge is common to two surfaces, forming a boundary for each. If an edge is perpendicular to a plane of projection, it appears as a point; otherwise it appears as a line. If it is parallel to the plane of projection, it shows true length. If it is not parallel, it appears foreshortened. A straight line always projects as a straight line or as a point. The terms normal, inclined, and oblique describe the relationship of an edge to a plane of projection.

4.11 NORMAL EDGES

A **normal edge** is a line perpendicular to a plane of projection. It appears as a point on that plane of projection and as a true-length line on adjacent planes of projection (Figure 4.41).

4.12 INCLINED EDGES

An **inclined edge** is parallel to one plane of projection but inclined to adjacent planes. It appears as a true-length line on the plane to which it is parallel and as a foreshortened line on adjacent planes. The true-length view of an inclined line always appears as an angled line, but the foreshortened views appear as either vertical or horizontal lines (Figure 4.42).

4.13 OBLIQUE EDGES

An **oblique edge** is tipped to all planes of projection. Since it is not perpendicular to any projection plane, it cannot appear as a point in any standard view. Since it is not parallel to any projection plane, it cannot appear true length in any standard view. An oblique edge appears foreshortened and as an angled line in every view (Figure 4.43).

4.14 PARALLEL EDGES

When edges are parallel to one another on the object, they will appear as parallel lines in every view, unless they align one behind the other. This information can be useful when you are laying out a drawing, especially if it has a complex inclined or oblique surface that has parallel edges. Figure 4.44 shows an example of parallel lines in drawing views.

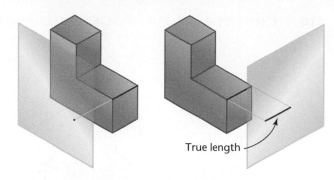

4.41 Projections of a Normal Edge. *Reprinted with permission of Pearson Education, Inc.*

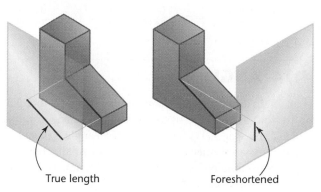

True length   Foreshortened

4.42 Projections of an Inclined Edge. *Reprinted with permission of Pearson Education, Inc.*

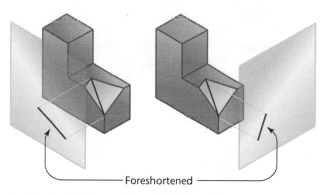

Foreshortened

4.43 Projections of an Oblique Edge. *Reprinted with permission of Pearson Education, Inc.*

(a) Parallel planes intersected by another plane

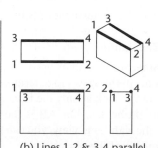

(b) Lines 1,2 & 3,4 parallel, and parallel to horizontal plane

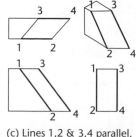

(c) Lines 1,2 & 3,4 parallel, & parallel to frontal plane

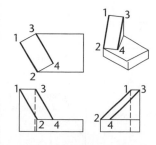

(d) Lines 1,2 & 3,4 parallel, and oblique to all planes

4.44 Parallel Lines

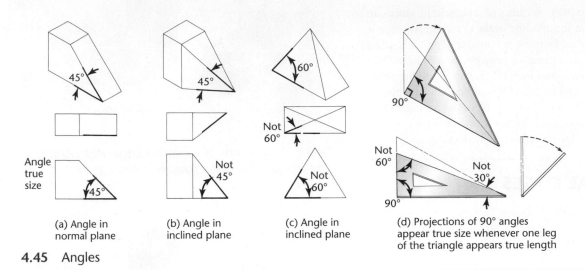

4.45 Angles

4.14 ANGLES

If an angle is in a normal plane (a plane parallel to a plane of projection) it will show as true size on the plane of projection to which it is parallel (Figure 4.45). If an angle is in an inclined plane, it may be projected either larger or smaller than the true angle, depending on its position. The 45° angle is shown oversize in the front view in Figure 4.44b, while the 60° angle is shown undersize in both views in Figure 4.44c.

A 90° angle will project as true size, even if it is in an inclined plane, provided that one leg of it is a normal line.

In Figure 4.44d the 60° angle is projected oversize and the 30° angle is projected undersize. Try this on your own using a 30° or 60° triangle as a model, or even the 90° corner of a sheet of paper. Tilt the triangle or paper to look at an oblique view.

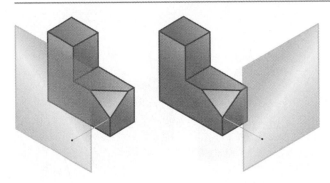

4.46 Views of a Point. *Reprinted with permission of Pearson Education, Inc.*

4.15 VERTICES

A corner, or **point**, is the common intersection of three or more surfaces. A point appears as a point in every view. An example of a point on an object is shown in Figure 4.46.

4.16 INTERPRETING POINTS

A point located in a sketch can represent two things:

*   A vertex
*   The point view of an edge (two vertices lined up one directly behind the other)

4.17 INTERPRETING LINES

A straight visible or hidden line in a drawing or sketch has three possible meanings, as shown in Figure 4.47:

*   An edge (intersection) between two surfaces
*   The edge view of a surface
*   The limiting element of a curved surface

Since no shading is used on orthographic views, you must examine all the views to determine the meaning of the lines. If you were to look at only the front and top views in Figure 4.46, you might believe line AB is the edge view of a flat surface. From the right-side view, you can see that there is a curved surface on top of the object.

If you look at only the front and side views, you might believe the vertical line CD is the edge view of a plane surface. The top view reveals that the line actually represents the intersection of an inclined surface.

4.47 Interpreting Lines

4.18 SIMILAR SHAPES OF SURFACES

If a flat surface is viewed from several different positions, each view will show the same number of sides and a similar shape. This consistency of shapes is useful in analyzing views. For example, the L-shaped surface shown in Figure 4.48 appears L-shaped in every view in which it does not appear as a line. A surface will have the same number of sides and vertices and the same characteristic shape whenever it appears as a surface. Note how the U-shaped, hexagonal, and T-shaped surfaces in Figure 4.49 are recognizable in different views.

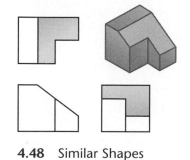

4.48   Similar Shapes

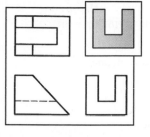 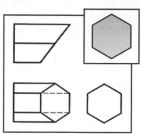 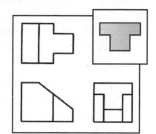

4.49   Similar Shapes

PRACTICE VISUALIZING

Look at the top view (a) and then examine some of the various objects it could represent. As you practice interpreting views, you will get better at visualizing three dimensional objects from projected views.

Notice that the top view alone does not provide all the information, but it does tell you that surfaces a, b and c are not in the same plane. There are many possibilities beyond those shown.

Top view   (a)   (b)   (c)   (d)

4.19 INTERPRETING VIEWS

One method of interpreting sketches is to reverse the mental process used in projecting them. The views of an angle bracket are shown in Figure 4.50a.

The front view (Figure 4.50b) shows the object's L-shape, its height and width, and the thickness of its members. The meanings of the hidden lines and centerlines are not yet clear, and you do not know the object's depth.

The top view (Figure 4.50c) shows the depth and width of the object. It also makes it clear that the horizontal feature is rounded at the right end and has a round hole. A hidden line at the left end indicates some kind of slot.

The right-side view (Figure 4.50d) shows shows the height and depth of the object. It reveals that the left end of the object has rounded corners at the top and

clarifies that the hidden line in the front view represents an open-end slot in a vertical position.

Each view provides certain definite information about the shape of the object, and all are necessary to visualize it completely.

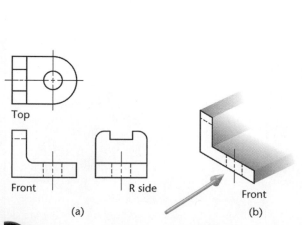 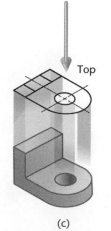 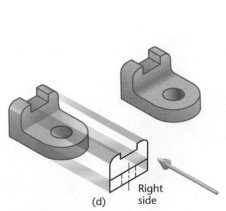

4.50   Visualizing from Given Views

READING A DRAWING

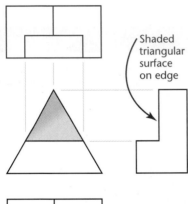

L-shaped shaded surface

1 Visualize the object shown by the three views at left. Since no lines are curved, we know that the object is made up of plane surfaces.

The shaded surface in the top view is a six-sided L-shape. Since you do not see its shape in the front view—and every surface either appears as its shape or as a line—it must be showing on edge as a line in the front view. The indicated line in the front view also projects to line up with the vertices of the L-shaped surface.

Because we see its shape in the top view and because it is an angled line in the front view, it must be an inclined surface on the object. This means it will show its foreshortened shape in the side view as well, appearing L-shaped and six-sided. The L-shaped surface in the right-side view must be the same surface that was shaded in the top view.

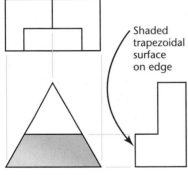

Shaded triangular surface on edge

2 In the front view we see the top portion as a triangular-shaped surface, but no triangular shapes appear in either the top or the side view. The triangular surface must appear as a line in the top view and in the side view.

Sketch projection lines from the vertices of the surface where you see its shape. The same surface in the other views must line up along the projection lines. In the side view, it must be the line indicated. That can help you to identify it as the middle horizontal line in the top view.

Shaded trapezoidal surface on edge

3 The trapezoidal-shaped surface shaded in the front view is easy to identify, but there are no trapezoids in the top and side views. Again the surface must be on edge in the adjacent views.

4 On your own, identify the remaining surfaces using the same reasoning. Which surfaces are inclined, and which are normal? Are there any oblique surfaces?

If you are still having trouble visualizing the object, try picturing the views as describing those portions of a block that will be cut away, as illustrated below.

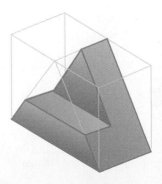

4.20 MODELS

One of the best aids to visualization is an actual model of the object. Models don't necessarily need to be made accurately or to scale. They may be made of any convenient material, such as modeling clay, soap, wood, wire, or Styrofoam, or any material that can easily be shaped, carved, or cut. Some examples of soap models are shown in Figure 4.51.

Rules for Visualizing From a Drawing: Putting it all Together

Reading a multiview drawing is like unraveling a puzzle. When you interpret a drawing, keep these things in mind:

- The closest surface to your view must have at least one edge showing as a visible line.
- A plane surface has a similar shape in any view or appears on edge as a straight line.
- Lines of the drawing represent either an intersection between two surfaces, a surface perpendicular to your view that appears "on edge," or the limiting element of a curved surface.
- No two adjacent areas divided by a visible line in an orthographic view can lie on the same plane in the actual object. Areas not adjacent in a view may lie in the same plane on the object.
- If a line appears hidden, a closer surface is hiding it.
- Your interpretation must account for all of the lines of the drawing. Every line has a meaning.

TIP
Making a Model

Try making a soap or clay model from projected views:

First, look at the three views of the object. Make your block of clay to the same principal dimensions (height, width, and depth) as shown in the views.

Score lines on the frontal surface of your clay block to correspond with those shown on the front view in the drawing. Then do the same for the top and right-side views.

Slice straight along each line scored on the clay block to get a 3D model that represents the projected views.

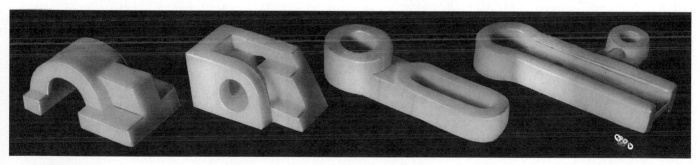

4.51   Soap Models

4.21 PROJECTING A THIRD VIEW

Ordinarily when you are designing a product or system, you have a good mental picture of what the object you are sketching will look like from different directions. However, skill in projecting a third view can be useful for two reasons. First, views must be shown in alignment in the drawing and projected correctly. Secondly, practice in projecting a third view from two given views is an excellent way to develop your visual abilities.

Numbering the vertices on the object makes projecting a third view easy. Points that you number on the drawing represent points on the object where three surfaces come together to form a vertex (and sometimes a point on a contour or the center of a curve).

Once you have located a point in two drawing views, its location in the third view is known. In other words, if a point is located in the front and top view, its location in the side view is a matter of projecting the height of the point in the glass box from the front view and the depth of the point in the glass box from the top view.

In order to number the points or vertices on the object and show those numbers in different views, you need to be able to identify surfaces on the object. Then project (or find) the points in each new view, surface by surface. You can use what you know about edges and surfaces to identify surfaces on the object when you draw views. This will help you to interpret drawings created by others as well as know how to project your own drawings correctly.

PROJECTING A THIRD VIEW

STEP by STEP

Follow the steps to project a third view.

The figure below is a pictorial drawing of an object to be shown in three views. It has numbers identifying each corner (vertex) and letters identifying some of the major surfaces. You are given the top and front view. You will use point numbers to project the side view.

1 To number points effectively, first identify surfaces and interpret the views that are given. Start by labeling visible surfaces whose shapes are easy to identify in one view. Then locate the same surface in the adjacent view. (The surfaces on the pictorial object have been labeled to make it easier.)

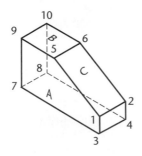

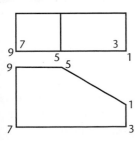

2 Surface A in the front view is a normal surface. It will appear as a horizontal line in the top view. The two rectangular surfaces B and C in the top view are a normal surface and an inclined surface. They will show as a horizontal line and an inclined line in the front view, respectively.

3 After identifying the surfaces, label the vertices of a surface that has an easily recognized shape, in this case, surface A.

Label its vertices with numbers at each corner as shown. If a point is directly visible in the view, place the number outside the corner.

If the point is not directly visible in that view, place the numeral inside the corner. Using the same numbers to identify the same points in different views will help you to project known points in two views to unknown positions in a third view.

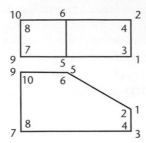

4 Continue on, surface by surface, until you have numbered all of the vertices in the given views as shown. Do not use two different numbers for the same vertex.

5 Try to visualize the right-side view you will create. Then construct the right-side view point by point, using very light lines. Locate point 1 in the side view by drawing a light horizontal projection line from point 1 in the front view. Use the edge view of surface A in the top view as a reference plane to transfer the depth location for point 1 to the side view as shown.

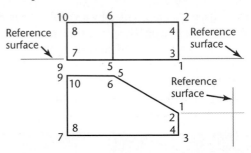

6 Project points 2, 3, and 4 in a similar way to complete the vertical end surface of the object.

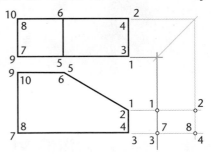

7 Project the remaining points using the same method, proceeding surface by surface.

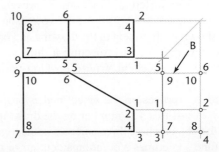

PROJECTING A THIRD VIEW

Continue the steps to project a third view.

 Use the points that you have projected into the side view to draw the surfaces of the object as in this example.

If surface A extended between points 1-3-7-9-5 in the front view where you can see its shape clearly, it will extend between those same points in every other view.

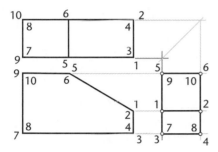

When you connect these points in the side view, they form a vertical line.

This makes sense, because A is a normal surface. As is the rule with normal surfaces, you will see its shape in one standard view (the front in this case) and it will appear as a horizontal or vertical line in the other views.

Continue connecting vertices to define the surfaces on the object, to complete the third view.

 Inspect your drawing to see if all of the surfaces are shown and darken the final lines.

Consider the visibility of surfaces. Surfaces that are hidden behind other surfaces should be shown with hidden lines.

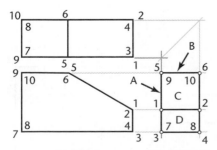

"Ship Arriving Tool Late to Save Drowning Witch" This well-known drawing by artist Roger Price is an example of how a single orthographic view can be difficult to interpret. *Courtesy of "Droodles, The Classic Collection."*

4.22 BECOMING A 3D VISUALIZER

To the untrained person, orthographic projections might not convey the idea of a 3D shape, but with some practice you should now be able to look at projected front, top, and right-side views and envision that they represent the width, depth, and height of an object. Understanding how points, lines, and surfaces can be interpreted and how normal, inclined, or oblique surfaces appear from different views helps you interpret orthographic views to let you form a mental image of the 3D object they represent.

Having an understanding of how orthographic views represent an object gives you the power to start capturing your own 3D concepts on paper in a way that others can accurately interpret. Keep in mind the idea of an unfolded "glass box" to explain the arrangement of views. This clarifies how the views relate to one another and why you can transfer certain dimensions from adjacent views. Using standard practices to represent hidden lines and centerlines helps you further define surfaces, features, and paths of motion.

The better you understand the foundation concepts of projected views, the more fluent you will be in the language of 3D representation and the skill of spatial thinking, regardless of whether you sketch by hand or use CAD.

USING A MITER LINE

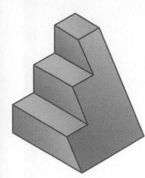

Given two completed views you can use a miter line to transfer the depths and draw the side view of the object shown at left.

1 Locate the miter line a convenient distance away from the object to produce the desired spacing between views.

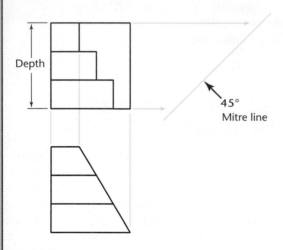

2 Sketch light lines projecting depth locations for points to the miter line and then down into side view as shown.

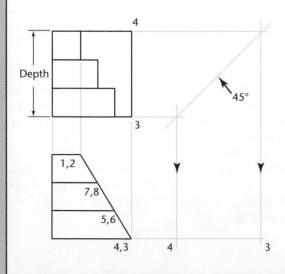

3 Project the remaining points.

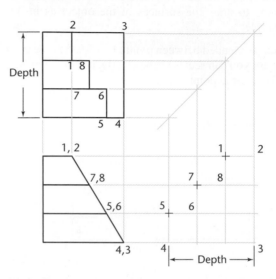

4 Draw view locating each vertex of surface on the projection line and the miter line. To move the right-side view to the right or left, move the top view upward or downward by moving the miter line closer or further from the view. You don't need to draw continuous lines between the top and side views via the miter line. Instead, make short dashes across the miter line and project from these. The 45° miter-line method is also convenient for transferring a large number of points, as when plotting a curve.

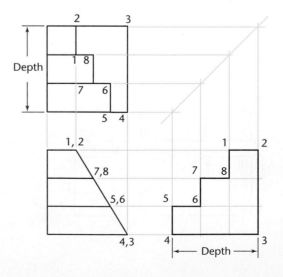

PLACING VIEWS FROM A 3D MODEL

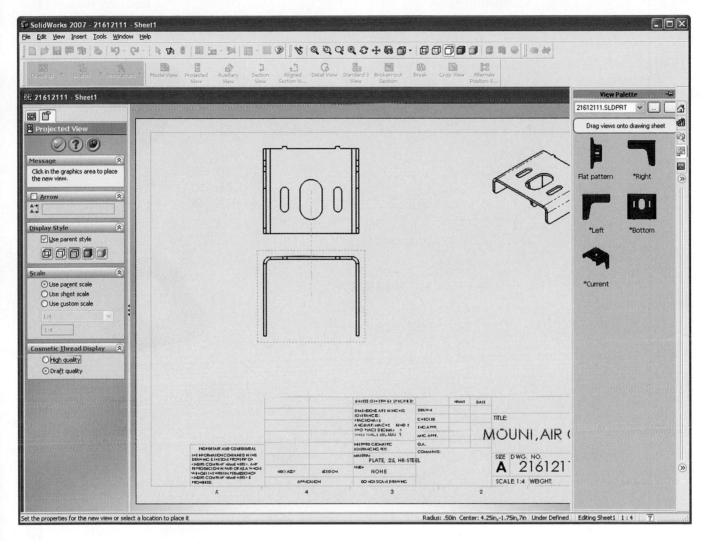

Orthographic Views Generated from a CAD Model. *Courtesy of Solidworks Corporation.*

Once a 3D model is created, most CAD packages allow you to place orthographic views generated from the model. To place a projected view is as easy as selecting the base view and then choosing where to place the projected view. You can also usually turn off hidden lines in each individual view based on whether or not they add useful information. Using CAD to place the 3D views also makes it easy to show views in alignment.

Most 3D CAD software allows you to configure it to show the views in either third-angle or first-angle projection.

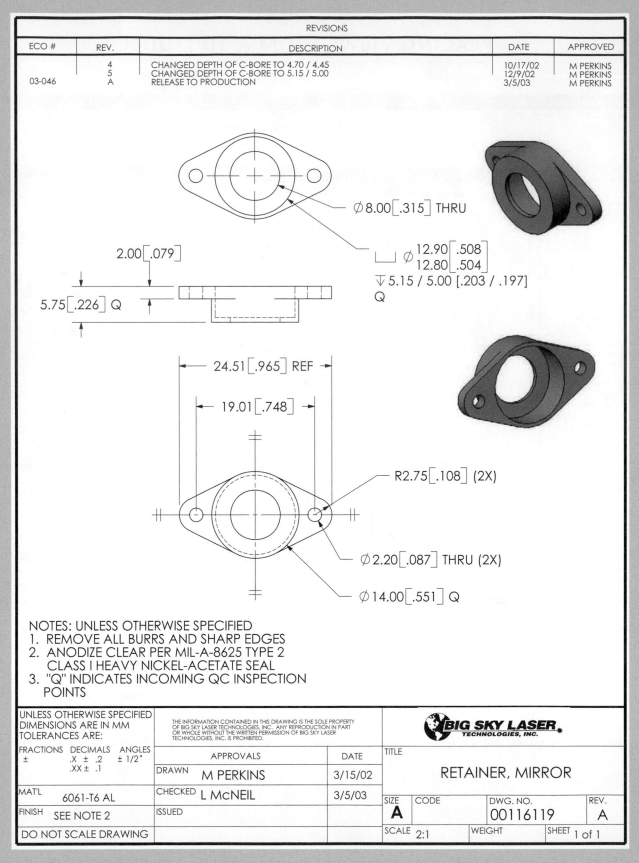

REVISIONS					
ECO #	REV.	DESCRIPTION		DATE	APPROVED
03-046	4	CHANGED DEPTH OF C-BORE TO 4.70 / 4.45		10/17/02	M PERKINS
	5	CHANGED DEPTH OF C-BORE TO 5.15 / 5.00		12/9/02	M PERKINS
	A	RELEASE TO PRODUCTION		3/5/03	M PERKINS

Ø8.00[.315] THRU

Ø 12.90 [.508]
  12.80 [.504]
▽ 5.15 / 5.00 [.203 / .197]
Q

2.00[.079]

5.75[.226] Q

24.51[.965] REF

19.01[.748]

R2.75[.108] (2X)

Ø2.20[.087] THRU (2X)

Ø14.00[.551] Q

NOTES: UNLESS OTHERWISE SPECIFIED
1. REMOVE ALL BURRS AND SHARP EDGES
2. ANODIZE CLEAR PER MIL-A-8625 TYPE 2
   CLASS I HEAVY NICKEL-ACETATE SEAL
3. "Q" INDICATES INCOMING QC INSPECTION
   POINTS

UNLESS OTHERWISE SPECIFIED
DIMENSIONS ARE IN MM
TOLERANCES ARE:

FRACTIONS DECIMALS ANGLES
±   .X ± .2   ± 1/2°
           .XX ± .1

MAT'L   6061-T6 AL

FINISH   SEE NOTE 2

DO NOT SCALE DRAWING

APPROVALS		DATE
DRAWN	M PERKINS	3/15/02
CHECKED	L McNEIL	3/5/03
ISSUED		

BIG SKY LASER
TECHNOLOGIES, INC.

TITLE

RETAINER, MIRROR

SIZE	CODE	DWG. NO.	REV.
A		00116119	A
SCALE 2:1	WEIGHT	SHEET 1 of 1	

Top, Front and Bottom Views of a Mirror Retainer. The bottom view is shown for ease of dimensioning.
Courtesy of Big Sky Laser.

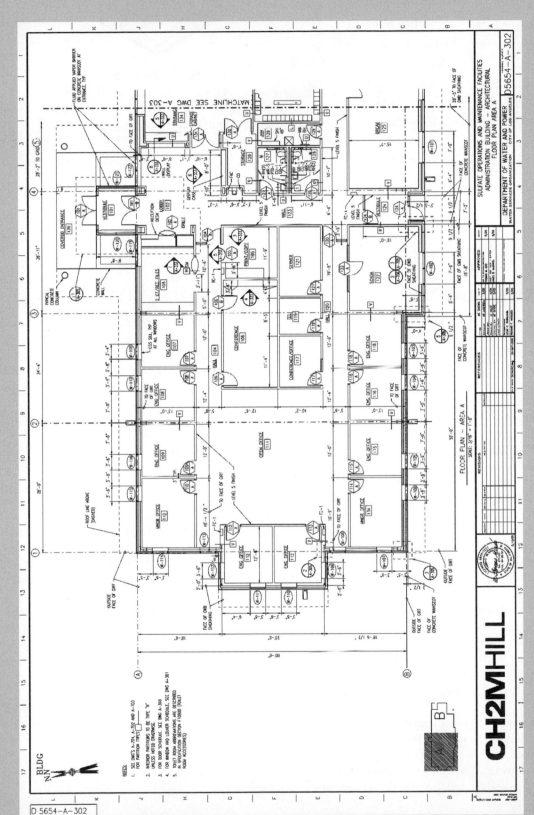

Architectural floor plans show the building as though the roof were cut off and you projected the top orthographic view. *Courtesy of CH2M HILL.*

KEY WORDS

Multiview Projection

Principal Views

Width

Height

Depth

Plane of Projection

Orthographic

Frontal Plane

Horizontal Plane

Profile Plane

Glass Box

Folding Lines

Three Regular Views

Necessary Views

Third-Angle Projection

First-Angle Projection

Projection Symbols

Surfaces

Plane

Normal Surface

Inclined Surface

Oblique Surface

Edge

Normal Edge

Inclined Edge

Oblique Edge

Point

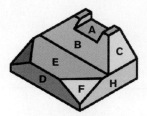

Key to Figure 4.35
Normal Surfaces: A, D, E, H,
Inclined Surfaces: B, C, Oblique
Surfaces: F

CHAPTER SUMMARY

- Orthographic drawings are the result of projecting the image of a 3D object onto one of six standard planes of projection. The six standard views are often thought of as an unfolded glass box. The arrangement of the views in relation to one another is important. Views must project to line up with adjacent views, so that any point in one view projects to line up with that same point in the adjacent view. The standard arrangement of views shows the top, front, and right side of the object.

- Visualization is an important skill for engineers. You can build your visual abilities through practice and through understanding terms describing objects. For example, surfaces can be normal, inclined, or oblique. Normal surfaces appear true size in one principal view and as an edge in the other two principal views. Inclined surfaces appear as an edge view in one of the three principal views. Oblique surfaces do not appear as an edge view in any of the principal views.

- Choice of scale is important for representing objects clearly on the drawing sheet.

- Hidden lines are used to show the intersections of surfaces, surfaces that appear on edge, and the limits of curved surfaces that are hidden from the viewing direction.

- Centerlines are used to show the axis of symmetry for features, paths of motion, and to indicate the arrangement for circular patterns.

- Creating CAD drawings involves applying the same concepts as paper drawing. The main difference is that drawing geometry is stored more accurately using a computer than in any hand drawing. CAD drawing geometry can be reused in many ways and plotted to any scale as necessary.

REVIEW QUESTIONS

1. Sketch the symbol for third-angle projection.
2. List the six principal views of projection.
3. Sketch the top, front, and right-side views of an object of your design having normal, inclined, and oblique surfaces.
4. In a drawing that shows the top, front, and right-side view, which two views show depth? Which view shows depth vertically on the sheet? Which view shows depth horizontally on the drawing sheet?
5. What is the definition of a normal surface? An inclined surface? An oblique surface?
6. What are three similarities between using a CAD program to create 2D drawing geometry and sketching on a sheet of paper? What are three differences?
7. What dimensions are the same between the top and front view: width, height, or depth? Between the front and right-side view? Between the top and right-side view?
8. List two ways of transferring depth between the top and right-side views.
9. If surface A contained corners 1, 2, 3, 4, and surface B contained corners 3, 4, 5, 6, what is the name of the line where surfaces A and B intersect?

MULTIVIEW PROJECTION EXERCISES

The following projects are intended to be sketched freehand on graph paper or plain paper. Sheet layouts such as A-1, found in the back of this book, are suggested, but your instructor may prefer a different sheet size or arrangement. Use metric or decimal inch as assigned. The marks shown on some exercises indicate rough units of either 1/2" and 1/4" (or 10 mm and 5 mm). All holes are through holes. If dimensions are required, study Chapter 9. Use metric or decimal inch dimensions if assigned by the instructor.

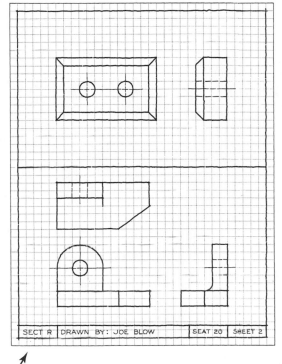

Example of two sketched solutions per 8.5 x 11" sheet

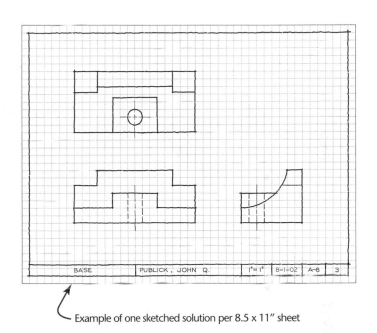

Example of one sketched solution per 8.5 x 11" sheet

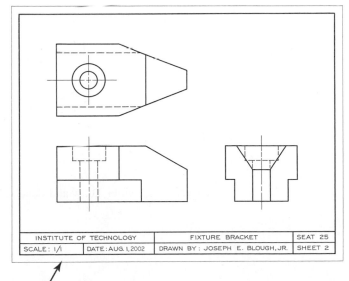

Example of one CAD/instrument solution per 8.5 x 11" sheet

Example Exercise

EXERCISES

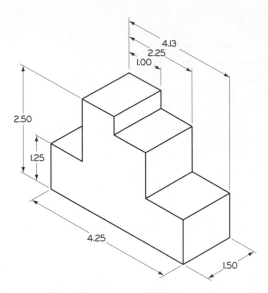

Exercise 4.1 Spacer. Draw and sketch all necessary views.

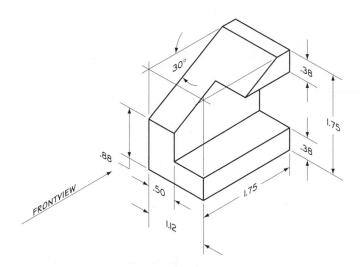

Exercise 4.2 Slide. Draw and sketch all necessary views.

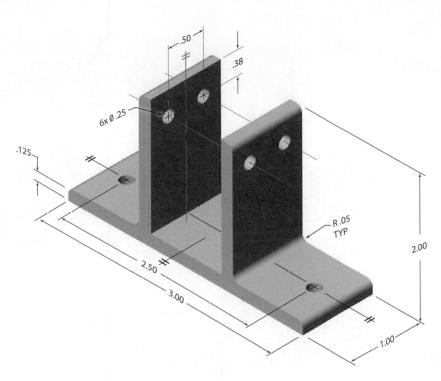

Exercise 4.3 Wall bracket
Create a drawing with the necessary orthographic views for the wall bracket.

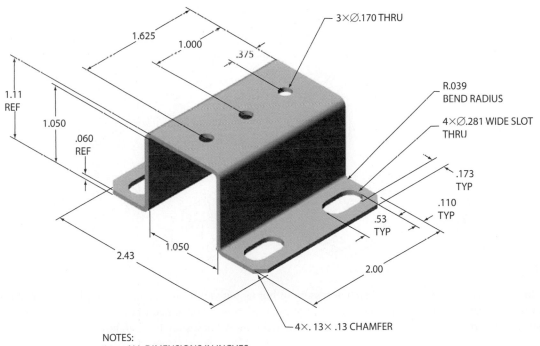

NOTES:
1.   ALL DIMENSIONS IN INCHES
2.   PART IS SYMMETRIC IN 2 AXIS
3.   MAKE FROM .060" THICK SHEET METAL

Exercise 4.4 Sheet metal bracket
Create a drawing the necessary orthographic views for the sheet metal bracket.

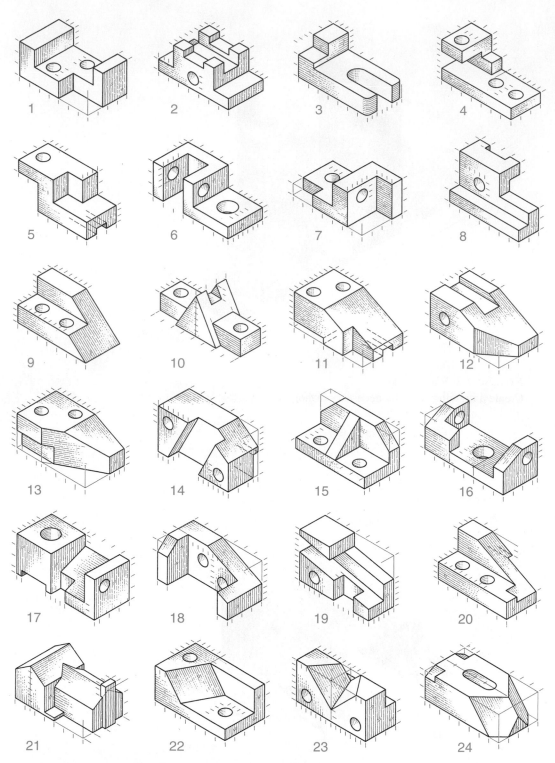

Exercise 4.5 Multiview Sketching Problems. Sketch necessary orthographic views on graph paper or plain paper, showing either one or two problems per sheet as assigned by your instructor. These exercises are designed to fit on 8½ × 11" size A, or metric A4 paper. The units shown may be either .500" and .250" or 10 mm and 5 mm. All holes are through holes.

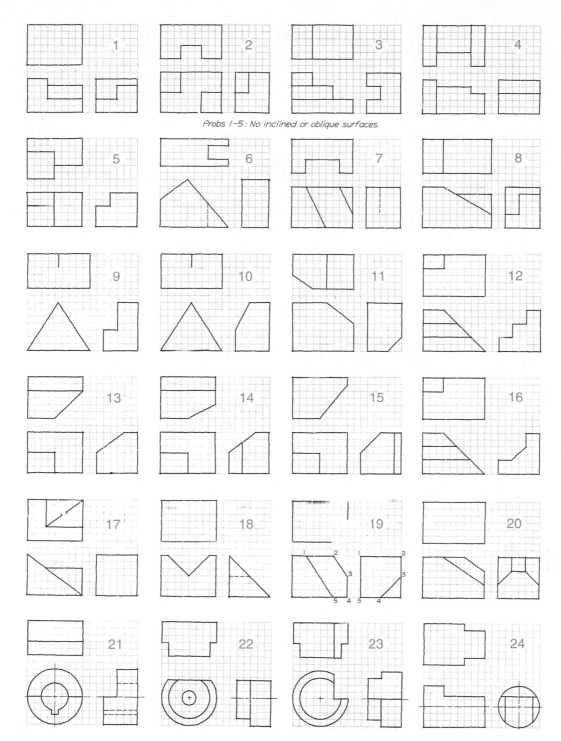

Probs. 1–5: No inclined or oblique surfaces.

Exercise 4.6 Missing-Line Sketching Problems. (1) Sketch given views on graph paper or plain paper showing either one or two problems per sheet as assigned by your instructor. These exercises are designed to fit on 8½ × 11" size A or metric A4 paper. Add missing lines. The squares may be either .250" or 5 mm. See instructions on page 150. (2) Sketch in isometric on isometric paper or in oblique on cross-section paper, if assigned.

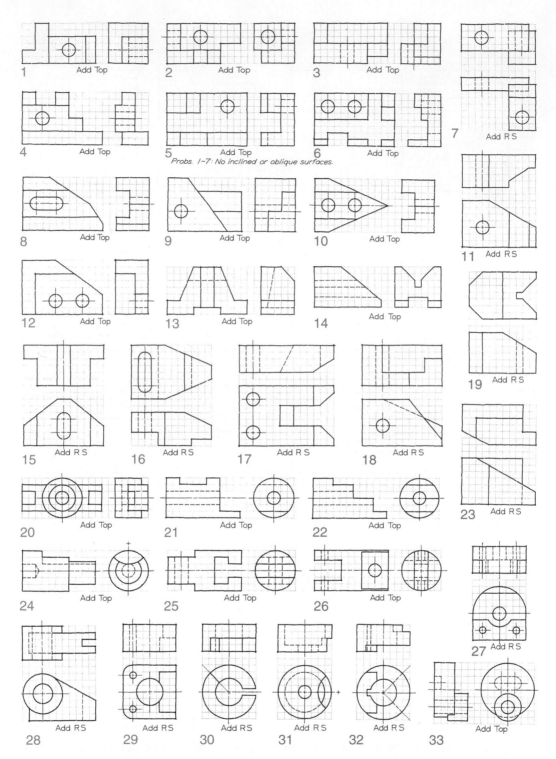

Probs. 1–7: No inclined or oblique surfaces.

Exercise 4.7 Third-View Sketching Problems. Sketch the given views and add the missing views as indicated on graph paper or plain paper. These exercises are designed to fit on 8½ × 11" size A or metric A4 paper. The squares may be either .25" or 5 mm. The given views are either front and right-side views or front and top views. Hidden holes with centerlines are drilled holes.

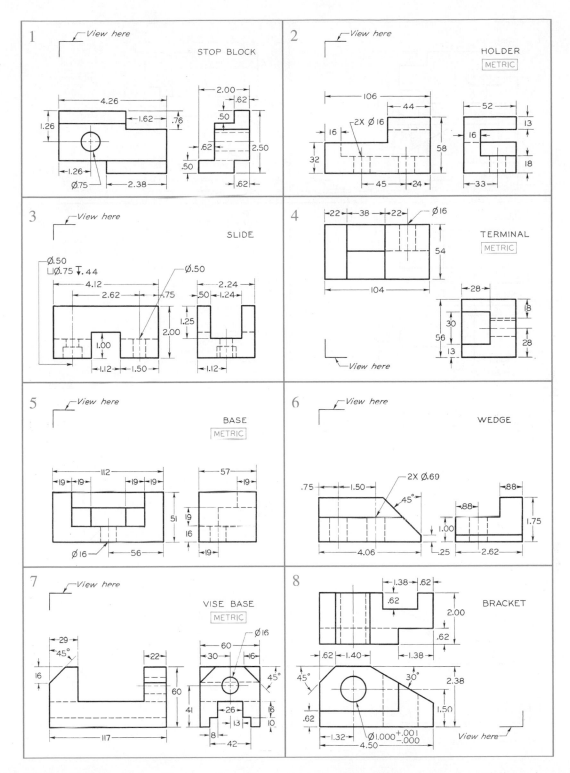

Exercise 4.8 Missing-View Problems. Sketch or draw the given views, and add the missing view. If dimensions are required, study Chapter 9. These exercises are designed to fit on 8½ × 11" size A or metric A4 paper. Use metric or decimal inch dimensions as assigned by the instructor. Move dimensions to better locations where possible. In Exercises 1–5, all surfaces are normal surfaces.

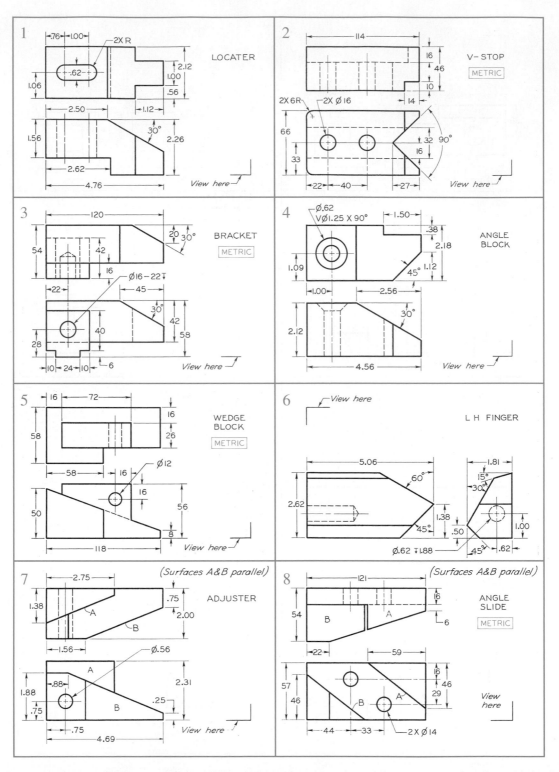

Exercise 4.9 Missing-View Problems. Sketch or draw the given views, and add the missing view. These exercises are designed to fit on 8½ × 11" size A or metric A4 paper. If dimensions are required, study Chapter 9. Use metric or decimal inch dimensions as assigned by the instructor. Move dimensions to better locations where possible.

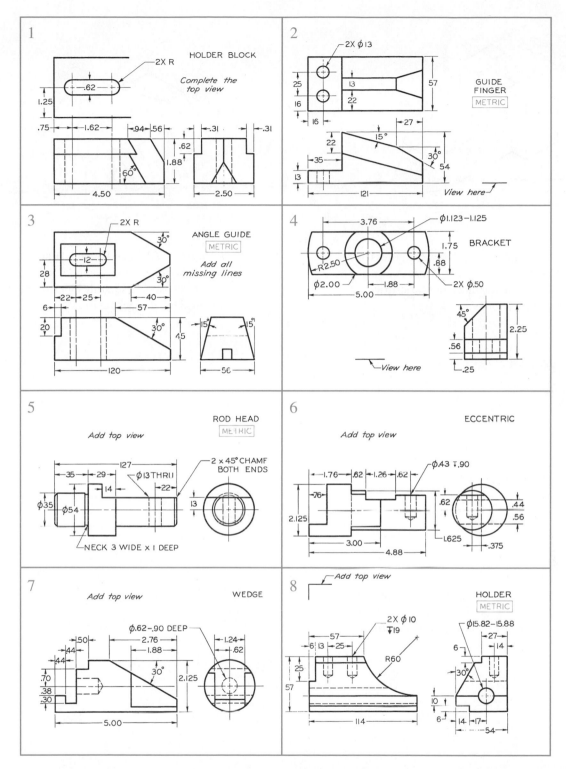

Exercise 4.10 Missing-View Problems. Sketch or draw the given views, and add the missing view. These exercises are designed to fit on 8½ × 11" size A or metric A4 paper. If dimensions are required, study Chapter 9. Use metric or decimal inch dimensions as assigned by the instructor. Move dimensions to better locations where possible.

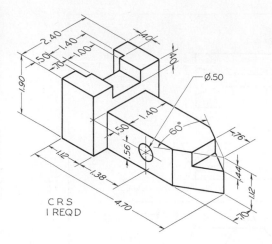

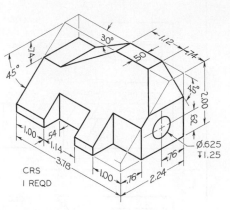

Exercise 4.11 Safety Key. Draw the necessary orthographic views on 8½ × 11" size A or metric A4 paper. Use a title block or title strip as assigned by your instructor.

Exercise 4.12 Tool Holder. Draw the necessary orthographic views on 8½ × 11" size A or metric A4 paper. Use a title block or title strip as assigned by your instructor.

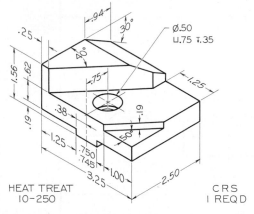

Exercise 4.13 Index Feed. Draw the necessary orthographic views on 8½ × 11" size A or metric A4 paper. Use a title block or title strip as assigned by your instructor.

CHAPTER FIVE

2D DRAWING REPRESENTATION

---------- OBJECTIVES ----------

After studying the material in this chapter, you should be able to:

1. Represent curved surfaces in multiview drawings

2. Show intersections and tangencies of curved and planar surfaces

3. Represent common types of holes

4. Show fillets, rounds, and runout in a 2D drawing

5. Use partial views

6. Apply revolution conventions when necessary for clarity

7. Draw removed views and projected views

8. Show right- and left-hand parts

9. Project curved surfaces by points

10. Show and label an enlarged detail

11. Show conventional breaks

Refer to the following standard:
- ANSI/ASME Y14.3—2003 Multiview and Sectional View Drawings

The CoWorker robot is a 3 ft high Pentium powered robot that can provide a mobile telepresence in remote locations. The CoWorker is made by the iRobot Corporation. *Courtesy of Sam Ogden/Photo Researchers, Inc.*

OVERVIEW

An object that has molded plastic parts like the one shown above has curved surfaces on inside and outside corners in order to make it easier to remove the part from the mold. There are a number of practices for showing curved surfaces in your drawings.

Learning the names of typical features and types of holes that are used in part design and how they are represented in drawing views will make it easier for you to communicate about designs and to understand their documentation requirements.

At times conventional practices are used that are not standard orthographic projections. This is to make it easier to draw or represent objects in your drawings. An example is revolving certain features when it adds to the clarity of the drawing. Another example is

showing "breaks" when a part does not fit well on the sheet because of its long shape, or to avoid unecessary detail.

There is an art to creating drawings that show the information clearly and provide all of the detail necessary to manufacture it. People can read drawings more easily when the least, but still sufficient, information is provided clearly.

The following Web sites show a community for architectural and building systems with cartoons (archmaaik), a drawing archivr of architect and sculptor Amancio d'Alpoim Miranda Guedes (guedes), and free electronic publication for steel construction (search aisc):

- http://archmaaik.net
- http://www.guedes.info/drawings/index.htm
- http://www.aisc.org

PRACTICES FOR 2D DOCUMENTATION DRAWINGS

Now that you are familiar with the basics of orthographic projection and visualizing objects from the information presented in orthographic views, you are ready to make and read more complex 2D drawings. While you might sketch complex designs by hand, it is more likely that you would create these types of drawings using CAD, either as 2D CAD drawings, or generating the 2D CAD drawing from a 3D solid model.

Somtimes practices used to create drawings using 3D CAD differ from those used in creating hand-drawn or 2D CAD drawings. It is necessary to understand the standards and practices in order to create good drawings even when using 3D CAD. The software will not do everything for you.

Common Manufactured Features

Certain features are a part of many engineering designs. Learning their names and shapes, as shown in Figure 5.1 and detailed in Table 5.1, helps you visualize and communicate about them. Some CAD systems may even have prebuilt features that you can place onto a 3D part to create them quickly.

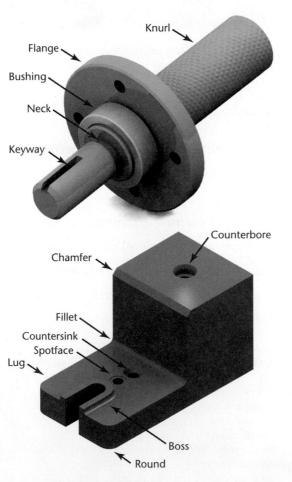

5.1   Commonly Manufactured Features

Table 5.1 Common Manufactured Features.

Feature/Description	Example
Fillet: A rounded interior blend between surfaces. Some uses are to strengthen adjoining surfaces or to allow a part to be removed from a mold.	
Round: A rounded exterior blend between surfaces; used to make edges and corners easier to handle, improve strength of castings, and allow for removal from a mold.	
Counterbore: A cylindrical recess around a hole, usually to receive a bolt head or nut.	
Countersink: A conical-shaped recess around a hole, often used to receive a tapered screw head.	
Spotface: A shallow recess like a counterbore, used to provide a good bearing surface for a fastener.	
Boss: A short raised protrusion above the surface of a part, often used to provide a strong flat bearing surface.	
Lug: A flat or rounded tab protruding from a surface usually to provide a method for attachment.	
Flange: A flattened collar or rim around a cylindrical part to allow for attachment.	
Chamfer: An angled surface, used on cylinders to make them easier to start into a hole, or plates to make them easier to handle.	
Neck: A small groove cut around the diameter of a cylinder, often where it changes diameter.	
Keyway/Keyseat: A shaped depression cut along the axis of a cylinder or hub to receive a key, used to attach hubs, gears, and other parts to a cylinder so they won't turn on it.	
Knurl: A pattern form on a surface to provide for better gripping or more surface area for attachment, often used on knobs and tool handles.	
Bushing: A hollow cylinder that is often used as a protective sleeve or guide, or as a bearing.	

Conventional Representations

Standard orthographic projections don't always show complex shapes as clearly and simply as you may wish, so certain alternative practices, refered to as conventions, are accepted. While "convention" is usually a general term for an accepted method, in the case of conventional representations in technical drawing, it refers particularly to simplified representations that enhance economy and clarity in a drawing. While conventional representations do deviate from true orthographic projection, their methods of simplification are generally recognized and accepted. (See ASME Y14.3-2003.) In other words, conventions are like rules for breaking the rules.

Intersections and Tangencies

To represent complex objects, multiview drawings use standard methods for depicting the way planar and curved surfaces meet. A plane surface can **intersect** or be **tangent** to a contoured surface as shown in Figures 5.2 and 5.3. When a plane surface intersects the contoured surface, a line is drawn to represent the edge formed by that interesection. When the plane surface is tangent to the contoured surface, no line or a thin phantom line pattern is drawn where the surfaces meet, depending on whether the phantom line is needed to aid in visualization.

Removed Views

It is not always possible to show all of the drawing views in alignment on the sheet. This is particularly true of civil and architectural drawings where the size and complexity of the object make it hard to show the level of detail necessary and still fit the views all on one sheet. When this is the case, a removed view can be used. There are two different ways to indicate the viewing direction for removed views. One is to use a view indicator arrow to show the direction of sight as shown in Figure 5.4a. The other is to use a viewing plane line as shown in Figure 5.4b. Clearly label the removed view.

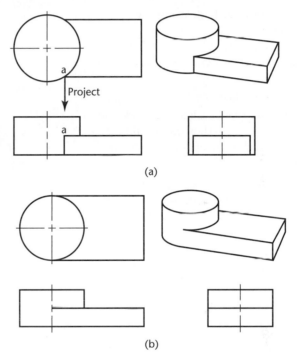

5.2 Intersecting and Tangent Surfaces. *Reprinted by permission of Pearson Education, Inc., Upper Saddle River, NJ.*

5.3 Orthographic Views of Intersecting and Tangent Surfaces. *Reprinted by permission of Pearson Education, Inc., Upper Saddle River, NJ.*

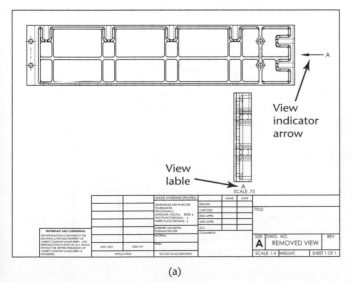

(a)

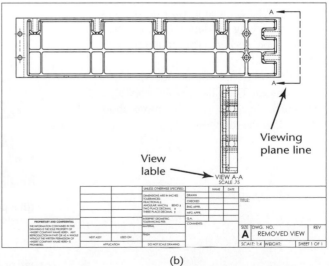

(b)

5.4 Indicating Removed Views

5.1 VISUALIZING AND DRAWING COMPLEX CYLINDRICAL SHAPES

The illustrations in Figure 5.5 show how to visualize cylindrical features being cut from a rectangular block (prism). Compare each illustration showing the material being removed with the drawing.

In Figure 5.5a there is no line where the contoured surface of the rounded top joins the straight planar sides. The top view appears as a rectangle. The centerline for the rounded top is shown in all three views. Consider these questions as you look at Figure 5.5a:

- In this drawing, how many views are necessary?
- Which views are repetitive?
- Is the centerline required to locate the rounded top?

In Figure 5.5b, the material for the center hole is removed. Now hidden lines are added to the top and side view showing the limiting elements of the cylindrical hole. As you look at Figure 5.5b, note:

- In the front view the hole appears round.
- The centerlines in the drawing locate the hole as well as the rounded top, since they are concentric.

In Figure 5.5c, the counterbored holes are created. As you look at Figure 5.5c ask yourself:

- How many lines are used to show the counterbore in the side and top views?
- How many views are necessary?

In Figure 5.5d a portion of the top surface is removed. Notice how those lines appear in the top and side views. How many views are necessary now?

In Figures 5.5a and 5.5b only one view is required.

In Figure 5.5c, the side view or top view or a note specifying the depth of the counterbore would be needed. The counterbore is five lines.

In Figure 5.5d the top or side view or a note is required. The side view is probably a better choice, because it shows more about the shape than the top view.

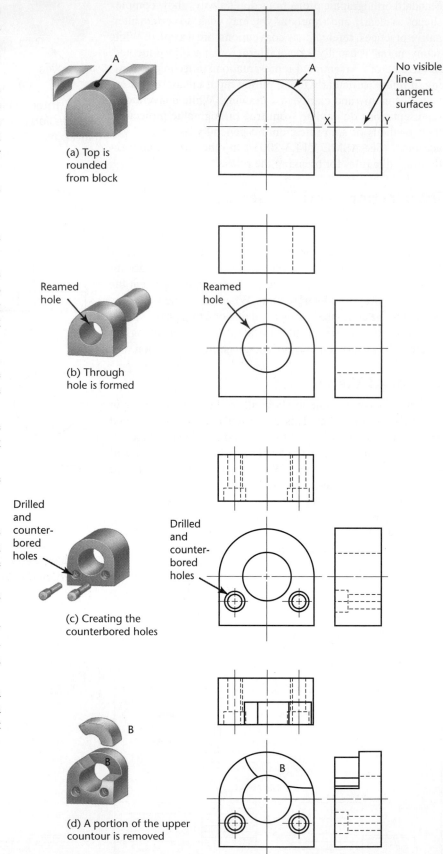

(a) Top is rounded from block

(b) Through hole is formed

(c) Creating the counterbored holes

(d) A portion of the upper countour is removed

5.5 Visualizing and Drawing Cylindrical Shapes

5.2 CYLINDERS WHEN SLICED

Cylinders are often machined to form plane or other types of surfaces. Figure 5.6a shows a single machined cut that created two normal surfaces. Normal surfaces appear true shape in the view where the line of sight is perpendicular to the suface. In the two other views that normal surface appears on edge. The back half remains unchanged.

In Figure 5.6b, two stepped cuts form four normal surfaces. Note that surface 7–8 (top view) is through the center of the cylinder, producing in the side view line 21–24 and in the front view surface 11–14–16–15, which is equal in width to the diameter of the cylinder. Surface 15–16 (front view) is read in the top view as 7–8–ARC 4. Surface 11–14 (front view) is read in the top view as 5–6–ARC 3–8–7–ARC 2.

Figure 5.6c shows a part with two coaxial cylindrical features, which is cut to form a normal surface parallel to the axis of the cylinders.

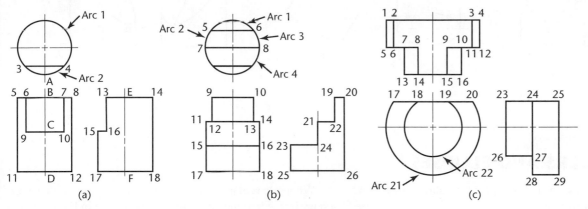

5.6 Showing Views of Cylinders with Planar Surfaces Cut Away

PLOTTING ELLIPSES BY HAND

Given the front and right-side view, project the correct view of the ellipse into the top view. Steps 1–3 apply to both illustrated examples.

Example 1

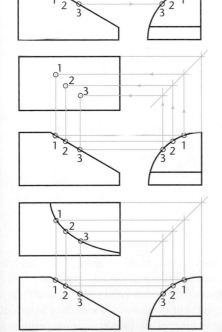

Example 2

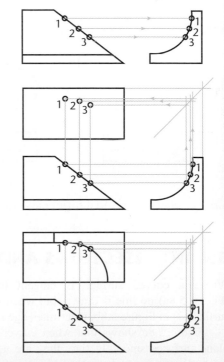

1 Break up the curve into several points and locate them in the adjacent view.

2 Project the points along projection lines into the top view from the front view. Transfer the depth from the side view, using the back surface as a reference plane.

3 Draw the curve through the points.

STEP by STEP

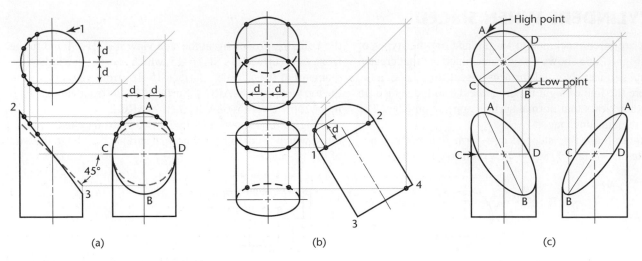

5.7 Elliptical Surfaces on Cylinders

5.3 CYLINDERS AND ELLIPSES

If a cylinder is cut by an inclined plane, as shown in Figure 5.7a, the inclined surface is bounded by an ellipse. This ellipse will appear as a circle in the top view, as a straight line in the front view, and as an ellipse in the side view. Note that circle 1 appears circular in the top view regardless of the angle of the cut. If the cut is at 45° from horizontal, it would also appear as a circle in the side view.

When a circular shape is shown inclined in another view and projected into the adjacent view as shown in Figure 5.7b it will appear as an ellipse, even though the shape is a circle. The inclined ellipse in Figure 5.7c is not shown true size and shape in any of the standard views given. You will learn in Chapter 7 how to create auxiliary views to show the true size and shape of inclined surfaces like these.

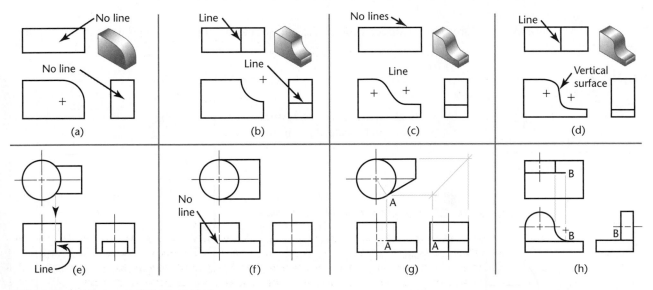

5.8 Intersections and Tangencies

5.4 INTERSECTIONS AND TANGENCIES

Where a curved surface is tangent to a plane surface (Figure 5.8a) no line is drawn, but when it intersects a plane surface, as in Figure 5.8b, a definite edge is formed.

Figure 5.8c shows that when curves join each other or plane surfaces smoothly (i.e., they are tangent), you do not draw a line to show where they come together. If a combination

of curves creates a vertical surface, as in Figure 5.8d, the vertical surface is shown as a line (here in the top view).

When plane surfaces join a contoured surface, don't show a line if they are tangent, but do show a line if they intersect. Figures 5.8e–h show examples of planes joining contoured surfaces.

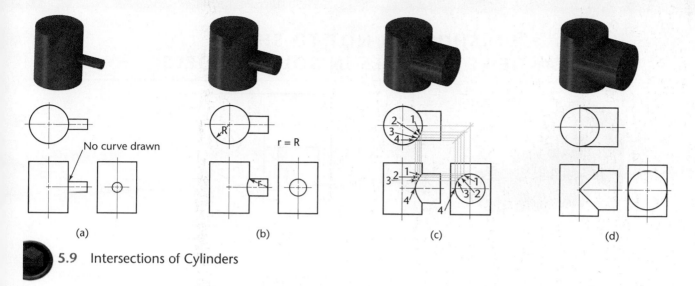

(a)   (b)   (c)   (d)

5.9   Intersections of Cylinders

Intersections of Cylinders

Figure 5.9a shows an example of a small cylinder intersecting a large cylinder. When the intersection is small, its curved shape is not plotted accurately because it adds little to the sketch or drawing for the time it takes. Instead it is shown as a straight line.

When the intersection is larger, it can be approximated by drawing an arc with the radius the same as that of the large cylinder, as shown in Figure 5.9b.

Large intersections can be plotted accurately by selecting points along the curve to project, as shown in Figure 5.9c.

When the cylinders are the same diameter, their intersections appear as straight lines in the adjoining view, as shown in Figure 5.9d. When you are using 3D modeling, the accurate intersection of the surfaces is typically represented. See Figure 5.10.

TIP

Using CAD tools you can locate the center and points on the major and minor axis and use the CAD software's ellipse tool to draw the whole ellipse through the points. Then trim off the extra portion.

A similar technique works when using a template.

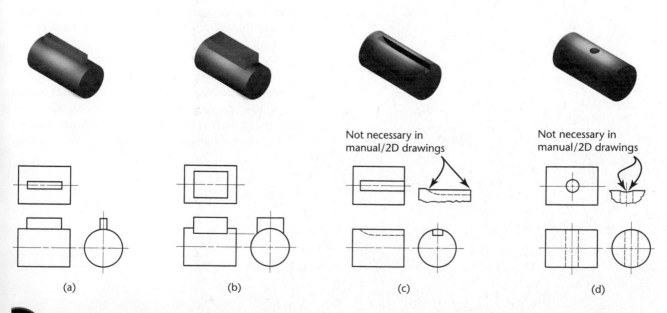

(a)   (b)   (c)   (d)

5.10   Intersections. *(a) and (b) Examples of a narrow prism intersecting a cylinder. (c) and (d) Intersections of a keyseat and cylinder and a small hole and cylinder.*

TO SHOW OR NOT TO SHOW:
TANGENT SURFACES IN SOLID MODELS

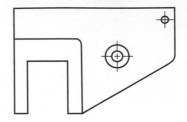

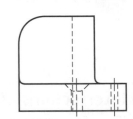

Orthographic drawing views
do not show tangent edges

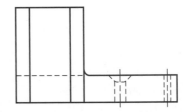

Best: Tangent edges shown as
phantom lines in pictorial view

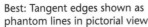

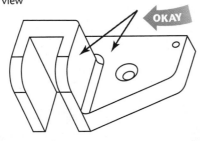

BEST

Okay: Tangent edges shown
as solid lines in pictorial
view

OKAY

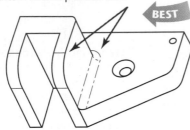

Poor: View is unclear without
tangent edges in pictorial view

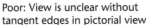

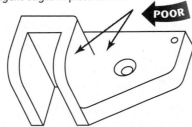

POOR

When you are creating solid models of contoured surfaces, it can be very useful to show the "tangent edges" where the contoured surface intersects the model. These lines that depict where the contoured surface ends and where the planar suface begins are not typically drawn in orthographic drawing views, unless the drawing might be confusing without them. When it is necessary to show the tangent edges, use a phantom line for them.

Using a phantom line to show the tangent edges of the model in the pictorial view is often necessary on parts that have many fillets and rounds, otherwise the view generated by the software may not show the part clearly.

Most CAD software allows you to set the display of tangent edges both for the entire drawing and for individual views.

Even when you are creating drawings using a CAD system you should follow standard drawing conventions. Knowing your CAD software well is important so that you can manage settings like those for tangent edges to show your drawing clearly.

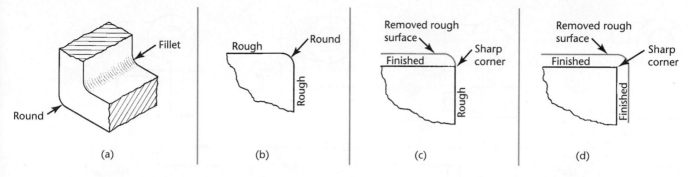

(a)   (b)   (c)   (d)

5.11 Rough and Finished Surfaces

5.5 FILLETS AND ROUNDS

A rounded interior corner is called a fillet. A rounded exterior corner is called a round (Figure 5.11a). Sharp corners are usually avoided in designing parts to be cast or forged because they are difficult to produce and can weaken the part.

Two intersecting rough surfaces produce a rounded corner (Figure 5.11b). If one of these surfaces is machined, as shown in Figure 5.11c, or if both surfaces are machined, as shown in Figure 5.11d, the corner becomes sharp. In drawings, a rounded corner means that both intersecting surfaces are rough. A sharp corner means that one or both surfaces are machined. Do not shade fillets and rounds on multiview drawings. The presence of the curved surfaces is indicated only where they appear as arcs, unless it is done to call attention to them.

3D CAD software varies in its ability to create complex blends for fillets and rounds. Figure 5.12 shows a CAD model with complex fillets. Figure 5.13 shows complex 3D CAD rounds.

5.12 Fillets on a CAD Model. *Courtesy of Ross Traeholt.*

5.13 Rounds on a CAD Model of a Design for a Three Hole Punch. *Courtesy of Douglas Wintin.*

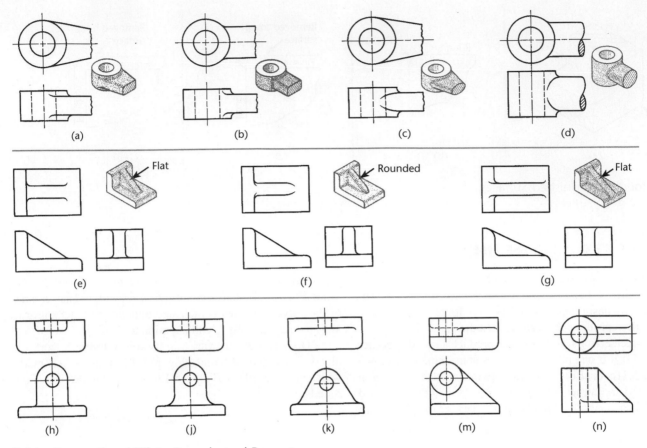

5.14   Conventional Fillets, Rounds, and Runouts

5.6 RUNOUTS

Small curves called **runouts** are used to represent fillets that connect with plane surfaces tangent to cylinders, as shown in Figures 5.14a–5.14d. The runouts, shown in Figure 5.14f, should have a radius equal to that of the fillet and a curvature of about one-eighth of a circle, as shown in Figure 5.15c.

Runouts from different filleted intersections will appear differently due to the shapes of the horizontal intersecting members. Figures 5.14a–5.14g show more examples of conventional representations for fillets, rounds, and runouts. In Figures 5.14e and 5.14f the runouts differ because the top surface of the web is flat in Figure 5.14e, while the top surface of the web in Figure 5.14f is considerably rounded.

When two different sizes of fillets intersect, the direction of the runout is dictated by the larger fillet, as shown in Figures 5.14g and 5.14j.

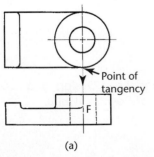
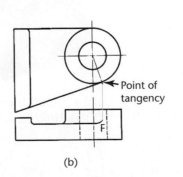
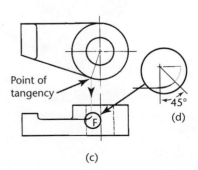

5.15   Runouts

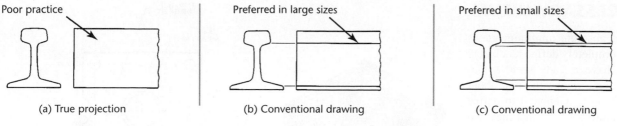

Poor practice

(a) True projection

Preferred in large sizes

(b) Conventional drawing

Preferred in small sizes

(c) Conventional drawing

5.16   Conventional Representation of a Rail

5.7 CONVENTIONAL EDGES

Rounded and filleted intersections eliminate sharp edges and can make it difficult to present the shape clearly. In some cases, as shown in Figure 5.16a, the true projection may be misleading. There is a conventional way of showing rounded and filleted edges for the sake of clarity. Added lines depicting rounded and filleted edges, as shown in Figures 5.16b and 5.16c, give a clearer representation, even though it is not the true projection. Project the added lines from the

intersections of the surfaces as if the fillets and rounds were not present.

Figure 5.17 shows top views for each given front view. The first set of top views have very few lines, even though they are the true projection. The second set of top views, where lines are added to represent the rounded and filleted edges, are quite clear. Note the use of small Y shapes where rounded or filleted edges meet a rough surface. If an edge intersects a finished surface, no Y shape is shown.

George Washington Crossing the Delaware as Seen by a Trout.
Cartoon by Roger Price. Courtesy of "Droodles, The Classic Collection."

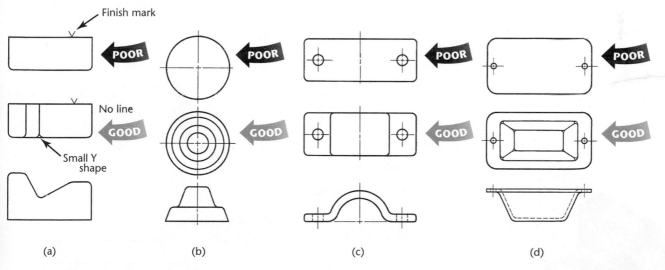

Finish mark

No line

Small Y shape

POOR

GOOD

(a)

POOR

GOOD

(b)

POOR

GOOD

(c)

POOR

GOOD

(d)

5.17   Conventional Edges

5.8 NECESSARY VIEWS

What are the absolute minimum views required to completely define an object?

As you have already seen, sometimes only a single view with a note about the part's thickness is enough to define the shape (Figure 5.18). Sometimes two views are required (Figure 5.19). For complex parts three or more views may be required (Figure 5.20).

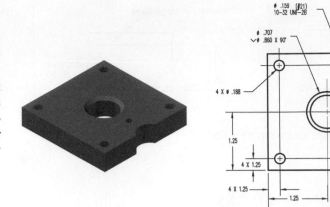

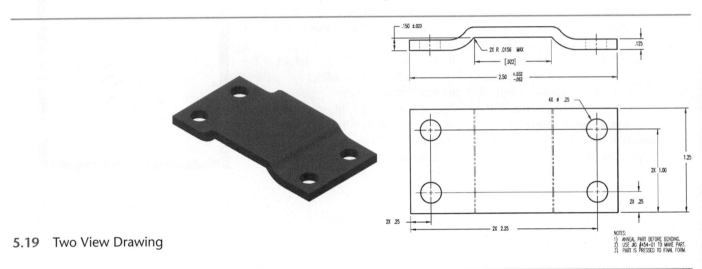

5.18   One View Drawing

5.19   Two View Drawing

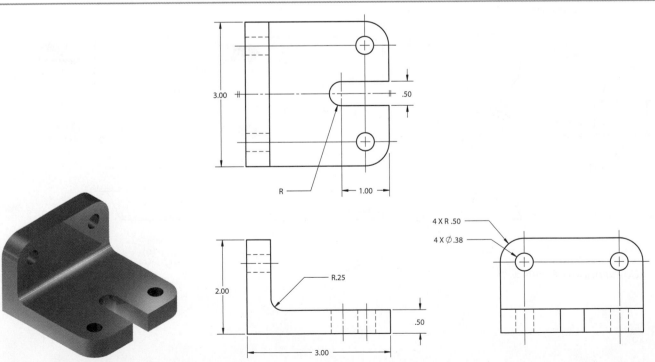

5.20   Three View Drawing

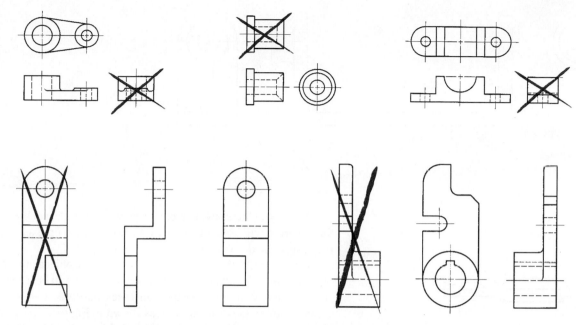

5.21   Three View Drawings Showing Unnecessary Views Eliminated

In each set of views shown in Figure 5.21 three views are shown, but only two of the three are required.

When deciding which views to show, keep in mind the following:

• Show sufficient views to completely describe the shape.

• Show the right-hand view instead of the left-hand view if both show the object equally well.

• Choose the top view rather than the bottom view.

• Show long parts horizontally on the sheet for two reasons: (1) they fit better, (2) they tend to appear even longer when shown vertically.

• Make it your goal to communicate the information clearly. If an additional view helps toward this goal, show it. Keep in mind that drawings are easier to read and update if they are simpler, rather than more complex.

5.9 PARTIAL VIEWS

A view may not need to be complete, but needs to show what is necessary to clearly describe the object. This is called a **partial view** and is used to save sketching time and make the drawing less confusing to read. You can use a break line to limit the partial view, as shown in Figure 5.22a, or limit a view by the contour of the part shown, as shown in Figure 5.22b. If the view is symmetrical, you can draw a half-view on one side of the centerline, as shown in Figure 5.22c, or break out a partial view, as shown in Figure 5.22d. The half-views should be the near side, as shown.

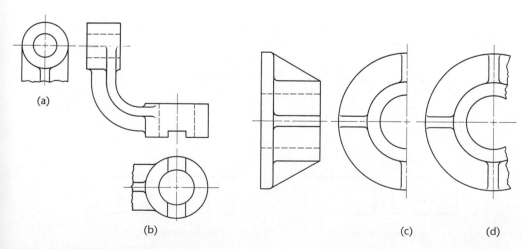

5.22   Partial Views

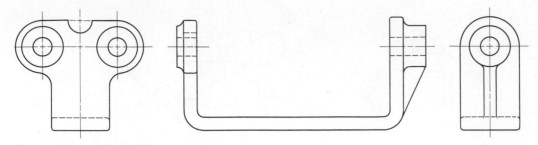

5.23   Partial Side Views

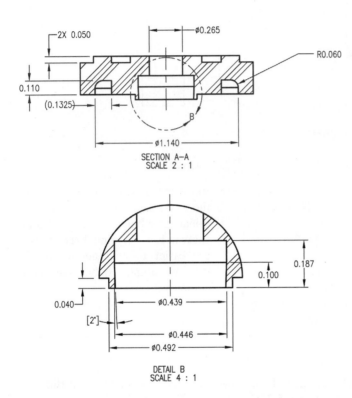

SECTION A–A
SCALE 2 : 1

DETAIL B
SCALE 4 : 1

5.24   Enlarged Detail

When you are drawing a partial view, do not place a break line where it will coincide with a visible or hidden line, as this may cause the drawing to be misinterpreted.

Occasionally the distinctive features of an object are on opposite sides. In either complete side view there will be a considerable overlapping of shapes. In cases like this, two side views are often the best solution, as shown in Figure 5.23. The views are partial views, and certain visible and hidden lines have been omitted for clarity.

Showing Enlarged Details

Figure 5.24 shows drawing details clearly by including detail views drawn at a larger scale. When adding a detail, draw a circle around the features that will be included in the detail as shown in Figure 5.24 (top). Place the detail view on the sheet similarly to a removed view. Label successive details with the word detail followed by letters as in DETAIL A, DETAIL B and so on and note the scale for the detail below its name.

Enlarged details are easy to generate using CAD software.

Conventional Breaks

To shorten the view of a long object, you can use break lines as shown in Figure 5.25. Figure 5.26 shows two views of a garden rake. When the long handle of the rake is shown to scale, the details of the drawing are small and hard to read. By using a break to leave out a portion of the handle, the scale for the ends can be increased to show the details clearly.

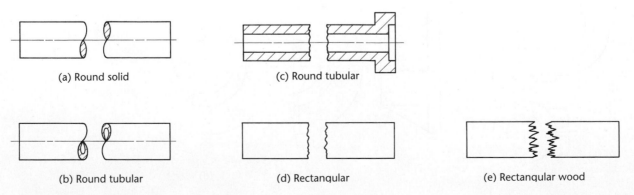

(a) Round solid   (c) Round tubular

(b) Round tubular   (d) Rectangular   (e) Rectangular wood

5.25   Conventional Break

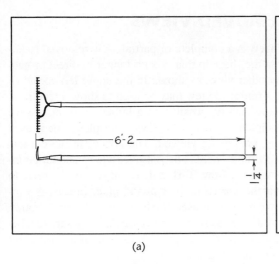

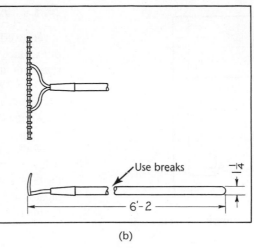

(a)   (b)

5.26 Conventional Breaks Allow for Increased Scale to Show Detail

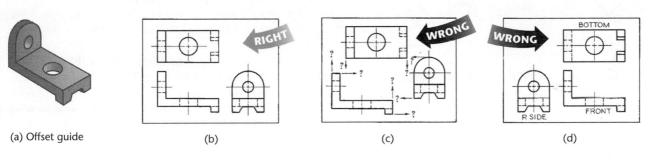

(a) Offset guide   (b)   (c)   (d)

5.27 Alignment of Views

5.10 ALIGNMENT OF VIEWS

Always draw views in the standard arrangement shown in Figure 5.27 to be sure that your drawings are not misinterpreted. Figure 5.27a shows an offset guide that requires three views. Their correct arrangement is shown in Figure 5.27b. The top view should be directly above the front view, and the right-side view directly to the right of the front view—not out of alignment, as in Figure 5.27c.

Never draw the views in reversed positions, with the bottom over the front view or the right side to the left of the front view, as shown in Figure 5.27d. Even though the views do line up with the front view, this arrangement could be misread.

Figure 5.28 shows three views in the correct alignment, but this drawing has a poor choice for the front view. The front view should show the shape of the object clearly. One way to consider this is that the front view shows the most information about the material that would have to be removed from a block.

After design sketches are completed, you will usually follow them with detailed CAD drawings. In finished CAD drawings you should apply the same rules for arranging views, clearly depicting the subject of the drawing, using the proper line patterns and line weights, and following all of the necessary standards as used in drawings created by hand. Many programs allow you to select a standard arrangement of views produced directly from your 3D CAD model.

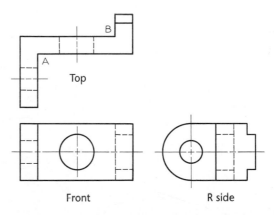

Top

Front   R side

5.28 Three Views in Correct Alignment but Poor Choice of Front View

---

TIP

Because CAD makes it easy to move whole views, it is tempting to place views where they fit on the screen or plotted sheet and not in the standard arrangement. This is not acceptable.

3D CAD software that generates 2D drawing views as projections of the 3D object usually has a setting to select from third angle or first angle projection. Check your software if you are unsure which projection methods are available.

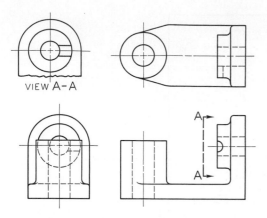

VIEW A–A

5.29 Removed View Using Viewing Plane Line

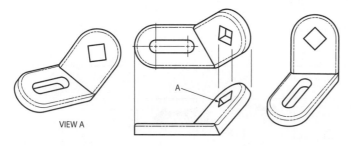

VIEW A

5.30 Removed View Using View Indicator Arrow

5.11 REMOVED VIEWS

A **removed view** is a complete or partial view removed to another place on the sheet so that it is no longer in direct projection with any other view, as shown in the upper left corner of Figure 5.29. A removed view may be used to show a feature of the object more clearly, possibly to a larger scale, or to save drawing a complete regular view. A viewing-plane line is used to indicate the part being viewed. The arrows at the corners show the direction of sight. The removed views should be labeled View A–A or View B–B and so on; the letters refer to those placed at the corners of the viewing-plane line. A view indicator arrow can also be used to show the viewing direction for the removed view, as shown in Figure 5.30. Be sure to label the removed view clearly and provide its scale if it is different from the overall drawing scale.

Architectural drawings often cannot fit even two standard views on the sheet. The sheets are typically labeled to indicate the standard views, as in Figure 5.31. Views are labeled, for example, "Plan" for the top view, "East Elevation" for the side view seen from the east compass direction, and so forth. Additional views use a viewing plane line or arrow to indicate the direction of sight.

In large civil drawings and other complex drawings such as the electrical drawing in Figure 5.32, one entire view may not be able to be shown clearly on a single sheet. For projects that extend sheet to sheet, match lines are often drawn showing how one sheet matches to the previous one.

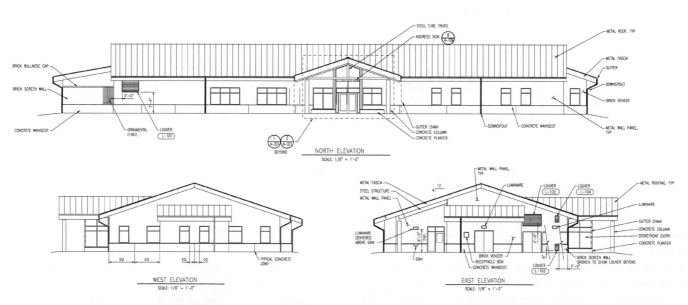

5.31 Architectural Drawing with Views Labeled. *Courtesy of CH2M HILL.*

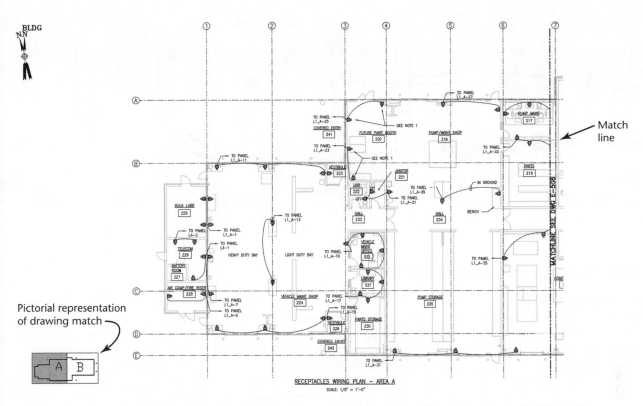

Match line

Pictorial representation of drawing match

5.32 A Portion of a Building Systems Electrical Drawing Using Matchlines. *Courtesy of CH2M HILL.*

5.12 RIGHT-HAND AND LEFT-HAND PARTS

Often parts function in pairs of similar opposite parts. But opposite parts can rarely be exactly alike. For example, the right-front fender of an automobile cannot be the same shape as the left-front fender. A **left-hand part** is not simply a right-hand part turned around; the two parts are mirror images and are not interchangeable.

On sketches and drawings a left-hand part is noted as LH, and a **right-hand part** as RH. In Figure 5.33a, the part in front of the mirror is a right-hand part, and the image shows the left-hand part. No matter how the object is turned, the mirror image will show the left-hand part. Figures 5.33b and 5.33c show left-hand and right-hand drawings of the same object.

Ordinarily you draw only one of two opposite parts and label the one that is drawn with a note, such as LH PART SHOWN, RH OPPOSITE. If the opposite-hand shape is not clear, you should make a separate sketch or drawing to show it clearly and completely.

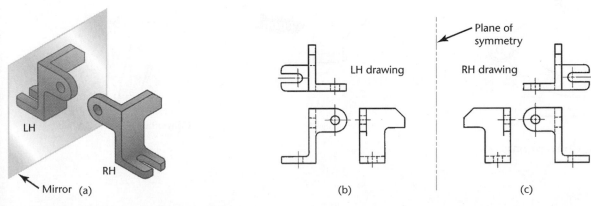

LH

RH

Mirror (a)

LH drawing

Plane of symmetry

RH drawing

(b)   (c)

5.33 Right-Hand and Left-Hand Parts

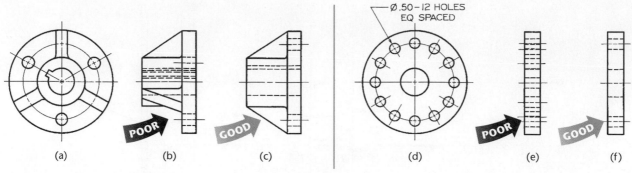

Ø.50–12 HOLES
EQ SPACED

(a)   (b)   POOR   GOOD   (c)   (d)   POOR   GOOD   (e)   (f)

5.34 Revolution Conventions

5.13 REVOLUTION CONVENTIONS

Regular multiview projections are sometimes awkward, confusing, or actually misleading. For example, Figure 5.34a shows an object that has three triangular ribs, three holes equally spaced in the base, and a keyway. The right-side view is a regular projection, but is not recommended—the lower ribs appear in a foreshortened position, the holes do not appear in their true relation to the rim of the base, and the keyway is projected as a confusion of hidden lines.

The method shown in Figure 5.34c is preferred because it is simpler to read

and requires less time to sketch. Each of the features mentioned has been revolved in the front view to lie along the vertical centerline, from which it is projected to the correct side view.

Figures 5.34d and 5.34e show regular views of a flange with several small holes. The hidden holes are confusing and take unnecessary time to show. Figure 5.34f shows the holes revolved for clarity.

Figure 5.35 shows a regular projection with a confusing foreshortening of its inclined arm. In Figure 5.35b, the

lower arm is revolved to line up vertically in the front view so that it projects the true length in the side view and makes the object's symmetry clear.

Revolutions like these are frequently used in connection with sectioning. Revolved sectional views are called aligned sections. You will learn more about them in Chapter 6.

In views generated from 3D CAD models, revolving the features to show their true size is not required, but it is preferred, especially in hand-drawn and 2D CAD drawings.

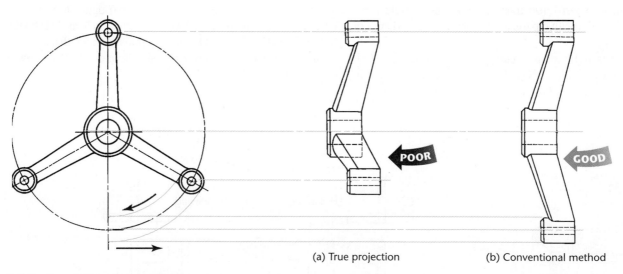

(a) True projection   POOR   GOOD   (b) Conventional method

5.35 Revolution Conventions

Common Hole Features Shown in Orthographic Views

Orthographic views of common hole features are shown in Figure 5.36.
See Table 5.1 on page 134 for descriptions of these common hole features.

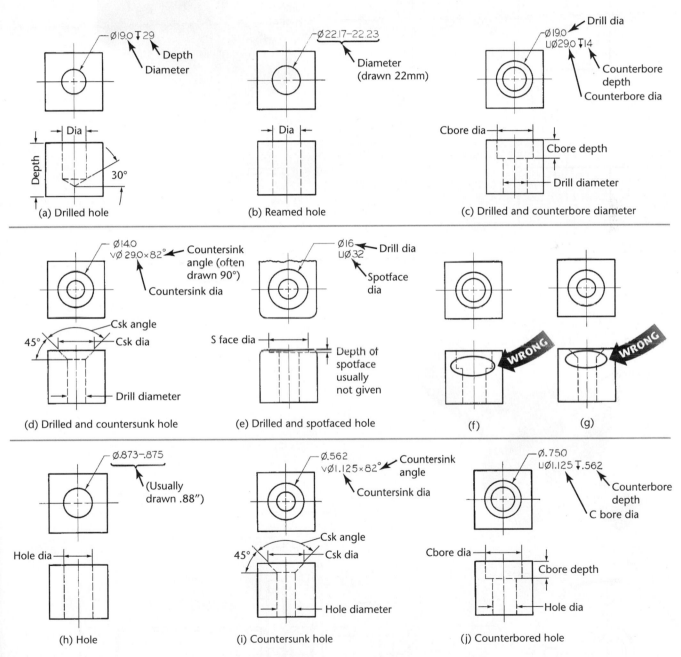

5.36 Representing Holes in Orthographic Views, dimensions for (a)–(e) in metric

Common Features Shown in Orthographic Views

Orthographic views of common features are shown in Figure 5.37. See Table 5.1 for descriptions of common features.

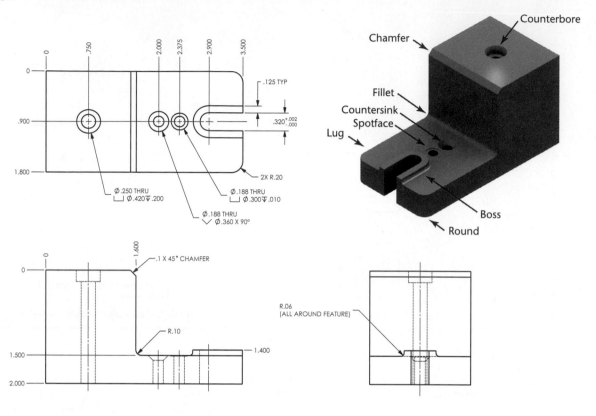

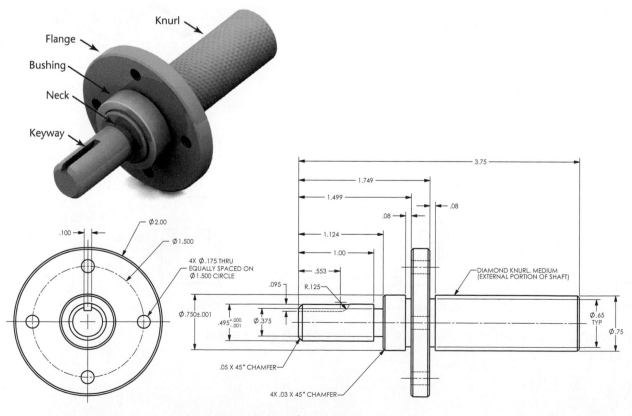

5.37 Representing Common Features in Orthographic Views

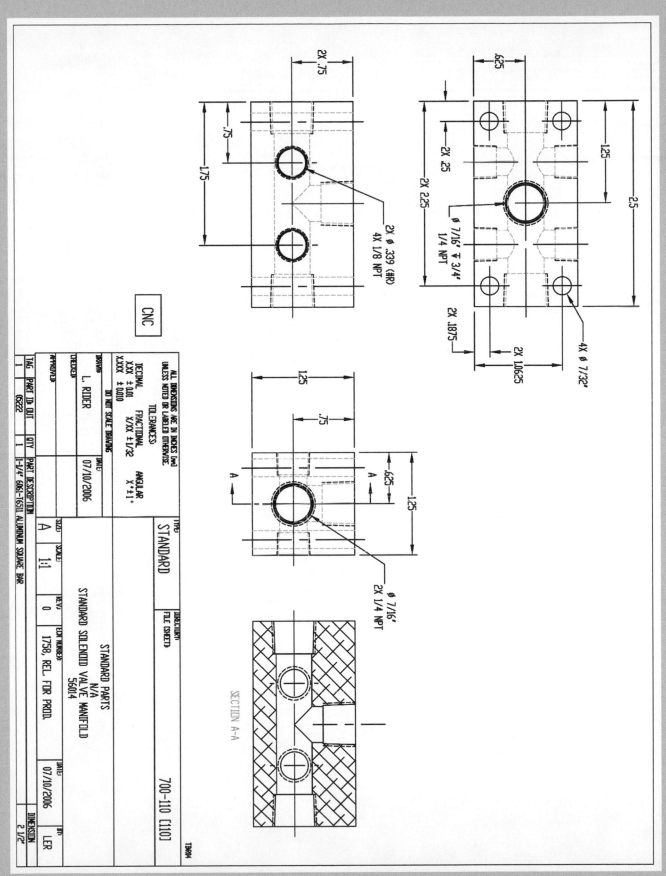

Orthographic Views of a Solenoid Valve Manifold. *This drawing is for a part that has many intersecting holes. Courtesy of Wood's Power-Grip Co., Inc.*

PORTFOLIO

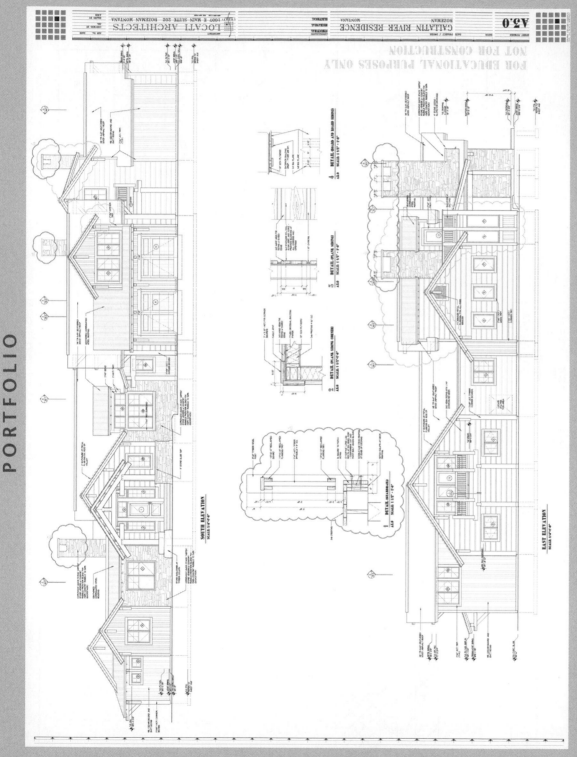

The views in this architectural drawing are too large to fit on a sheet in typical projection so removed views are used. Notice that each view is clearly labeled as to its direction of sight since they are not in projection. *Courtesy of Locati Architects.*

KEY WORDS

Fillet

Round

Counterbore

Countersink

Spotface

Boss

Lug

Flange

Chamfer

Neck

Keyway/Keyseat

Knurl

Bushing

Intersect

Tangent

Runouts

Partial View

Removed View

Left-Hand Part

Right-Hand Part

Revolutions

CHAPTER SUMMARY

1. Irregular curves can be plotted by identifying points on the object. The points can be projected to approximate the boundaries of the curved surface.
2. Drawing conventions define usual practices for the representation of features such as holes, bosses, ribs, webs, lugs, fillets, and rounds.
3. Use the same main practices to arrange drawing views on the sheet for both hand-drawn and CAD drawings. Show and label enlarged details and removed views. Use partial views and leave out hidden lines as long as the object is shown clearly.
4. When curved and planar surfaces intersect, an edge is formed that is represented by a line in the drawing. When curved and planar surfaces are tangent, no edge is formed, so no line is needed. If the drawing is not clear without it, use a phantom line to show tangencies.
5. Common types of holes are through, blind, countersunk, counterbored, and spotfaced.
6. Fillets, rounds, and runout are special types of tangent contours formed on parts with rounded edges.
7. When necessary for clarity, features are sometimes shown in a revolved postion using revolution conventions.
8. Break lines can be used to leave out a section of a part where it is uniform or repetitive. Often this is done to enlarge the scale of the remaining portions of the part so that details can be seen clearly.

REVIEW QUESTIONS

1. If the top view of an object shows a drilled through hole, how many hidden lines would be necessary in the front view to describe the hole? How many if the hole is countersunk? Counterbored?
2. If a plane surface intersects a contoured surface, should you show a line in the drawing to represent that intersection? What about when the planc is tangent?
3. What is a fillet? A round? A lug? A boss? Knurling?
4. How do you show right-hand and left-hand parts?
5. Which is easier, creating an enlarged detail by hand or using a CAD system?

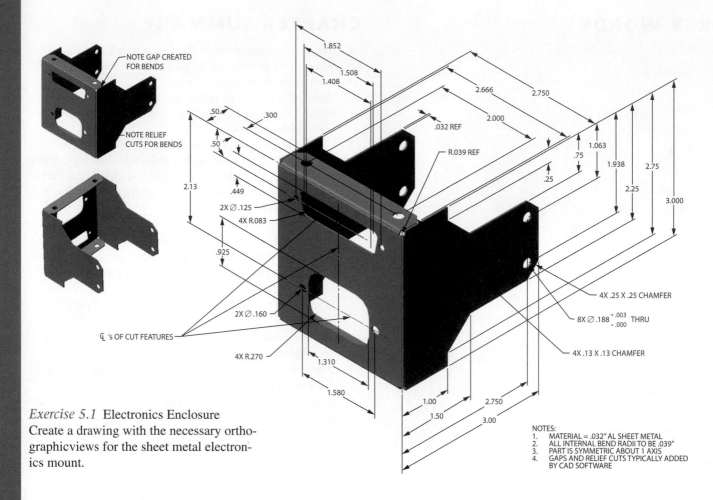

NOTES:
1. MATERIAL = .032" AL SHEET METAL
2. ALL INTERNAL BEND RADII TO BE .039"
3. PART IS SYMMETRIC ABOUT 1 AXIS
4. GAPS AND RELIEF CUTS TYPICALLY ADDED
   BY CAD SOFTWARE

Exercise 5.1 Electronics Enclosure
Create a drawing with the necessary orthographic views for the sheet metal electronics mount.

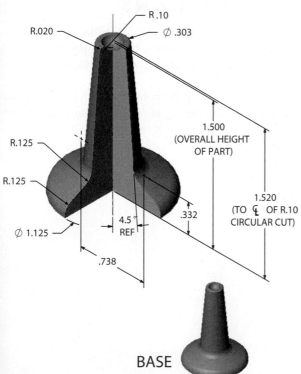

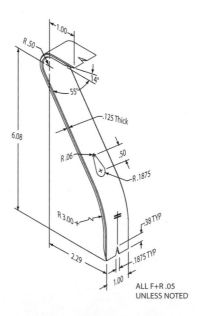

Exercise 5.2 Gyroscope Base
Create a drawing with the necessary orthographic view.

Exercise 5.3 Pry Bar
Create a drawing with the necessary orthographic views for the pry bar.

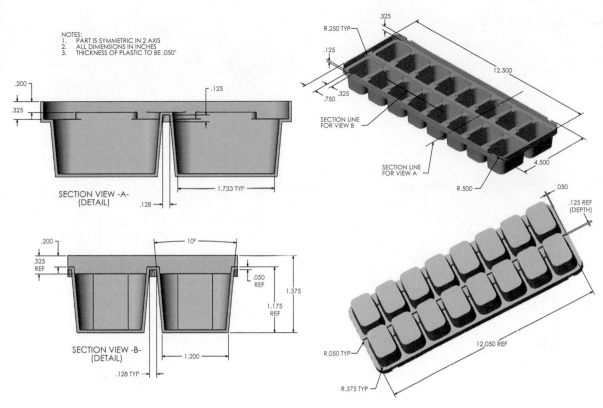

NOTES:
1. PART IS SYMMETRIC IN 2 AXIS
2. ALL DIMENSIONS IN INCHES
3. THICKNESS OF PLASTIC TO BE .050"

SECTION VIEW -A-
(DETAIL)

SECTION VIEW -B-
(DETAIL)

SECTION LINE
FOR VIEW B

SECTION LINE
FOR VIEW A

Exercise 5.4 Ice Cube Tray

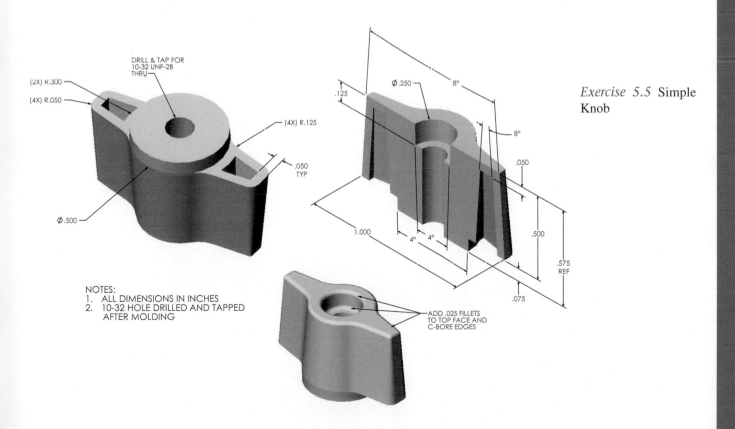

DRILL & TAP FOR
10-32 UNF-2B
THRU

NOTES:
1. ALL DIMENSIONS IN INCHES
2. 10-32 HOLE DRILLED AND TAPPED
   AFTER MOLDING

ADD .025 FILLETS
TO TOP FACE AND
C-BORE EDGES

Exercise 5.5 Simple
Knob

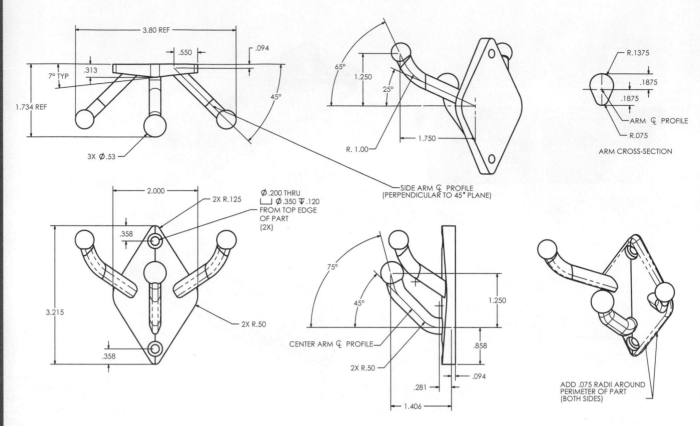

Exercise 5.6 Wall Hanger

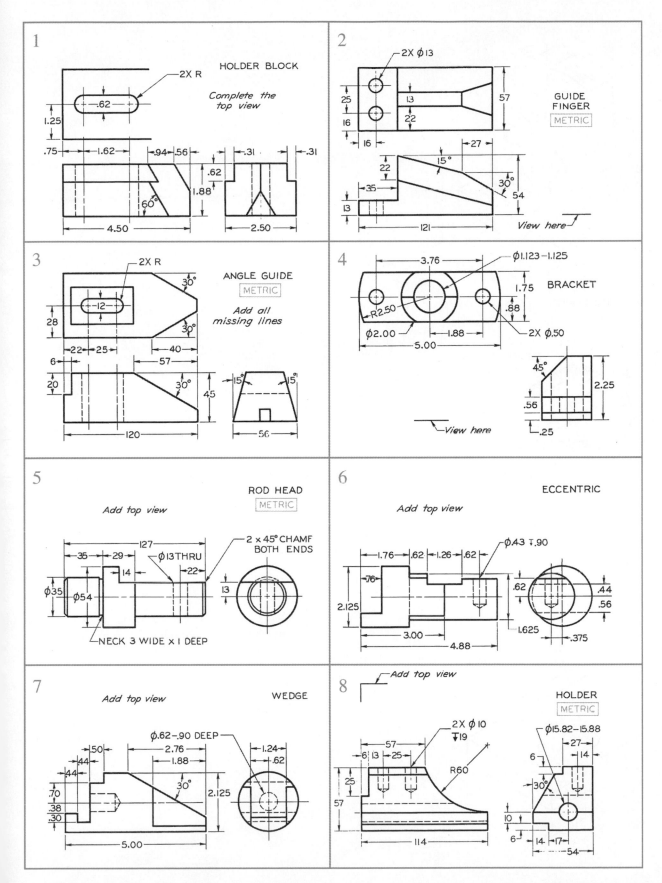

1 HOLDER BLOCK
Complete the top view
2X R
.62
1.25
.75 1.62 .94 .56 .31 .31
.62
60°
1.88
4.50 2.50

2 GUIDE FINGER METRIC
2X ⌀13
25
16
13
22
16
57
27
22 15°
35 30°
13 54
121
View here

3 ANGLE GUIDE METRIC
Add all missing lines
2X R
30°
12
28 30°
22 25 40
6 57
20 30° 45
120 15° 15°
56

4 BRACKET
⌀1.123–1.125
3.76
1.75
.88
R2.50
⌀2.00 1.88 2X ⌀.50
5.00
45°
2.25
.56
View here .25

5 ROD HEAD METRIC
Add top view
127
35 29 ⌀13THRU 22
14
2 x 45° CHAMF BOTH ENDS
13
⌀35 ⌀54
NECK 3 WIDE x I DEEP

6 ECCENTRIC
Add top view
⌀.43 ⊤.90
1.76 .62 1.26 .62
.76
2.125 .62 .44
.56
3.00
4.88 1.625 .375

7 WEDGE
Add top view
⌀.62–.90 DEEP
.50
2.76
.44 1.88 1.24
.44 .62
.70 30°
.38 2.125
.30
5.00

8 HOLDER METRIC
Add top view
2X ⌀ 10
⊤19
⌀15.82–15.88
57 R60 27
6 13 25 14
25 6
30°
57
10
114 6 14 17
54

Exercise 5.7 Missing-View Problems. Sketch or draw the given views, and add the missing view. These exercises are designed to fit on 8½ × 11" A-size or A4 metric size paper. Use a title block or title strip as assigned by your instructor. If dimensions are required, study Chapter 9. Use metric or decimal-inch dimensions as assigned by your instructor. Move dimensions to better locations where possible.

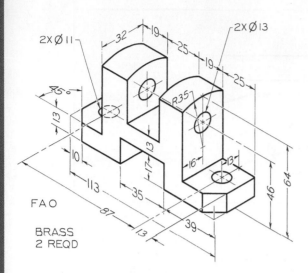

Exercise 5.8 Rod Support*

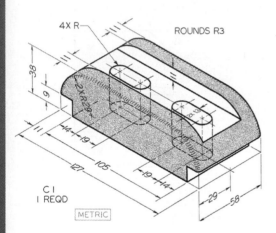

Exercise 5.9 Tailstock*

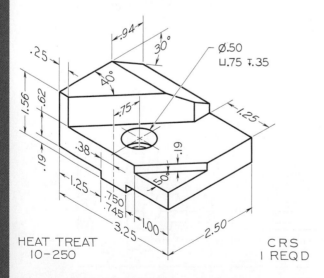

Exercise 5.10 Index Feed*

*Sketch or draw necessary views. These exercises are designed to fit on 8½ × 11" A-size or A4 metric size paper. Use a title block or title strip as assigned by your instructor. If dimensions are required, study Chapter 9. Use metric or decimal-inch dimensions as assigned by your instructor. Move dimensions to better locations where possible.

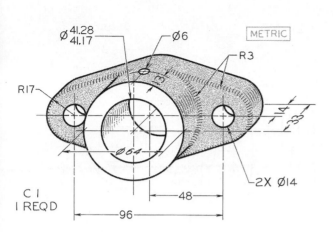

Exercise 5.11 Bearing*

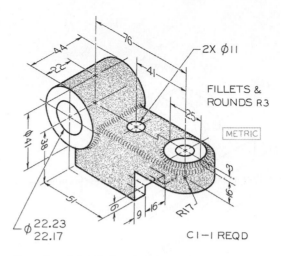

Exercise 5.14 Index Arm*

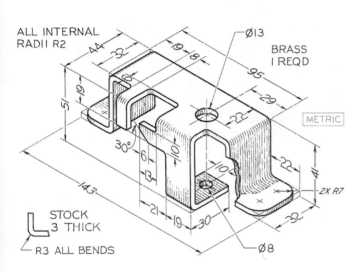

Exercise 5.12 Holder Clip*

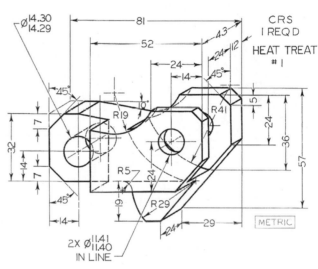

Exercise 5.15 Roller Lever*

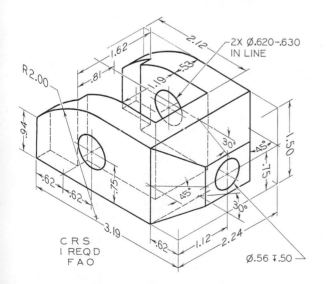

Exercise 5.13 Cam*

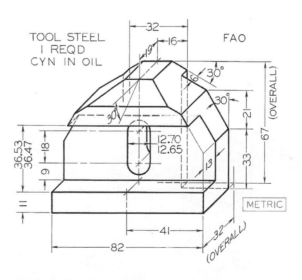

Exercise 5.16 Support*

*Sketch or draw necessary views. These exercises are designed to fit on 8½ × 11" A-size or A4 metric size paper. Use a title block or title strip as assigned by your instructor. If dimensions are required, study Chapter 9. Use metric or decimal-inch dimensions as assigned by your instructor. Move dimensions to better locations where possible.

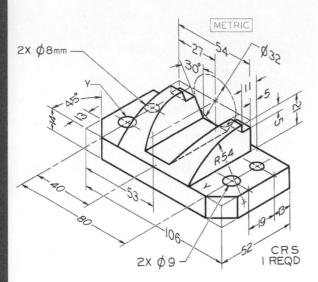

Exercise 5.17 Locating Finger*

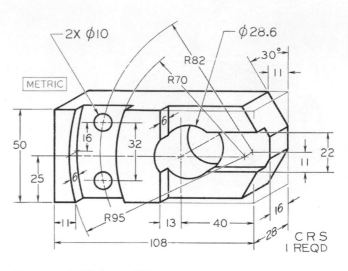

Exercise 5.20 Index Slide*

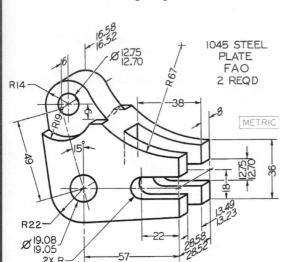

Exercise 5.18 Toggle Lever*

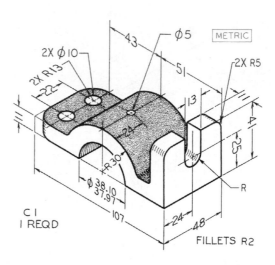

Exercise 5.21 Frame Guide*

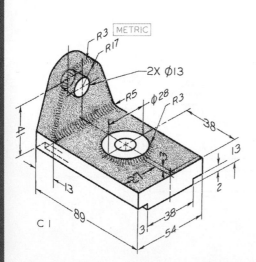

Exercise 5.19 Cut-off Holder*

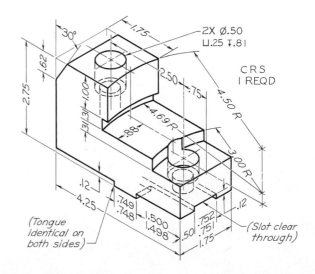

Exercise 5.22 Chuck Jaw*

*Sketch or draw necessary views. These exercises are designed to fit on 8½ × 11" A-size or A4 metric size paper. Use a title block or title strip as assigned by your instructor. If dimensions are required, study Chapter 9. Use metric or decimal-inch dimensions as assigned by your instructor. Move dimensions to better locations where possible.

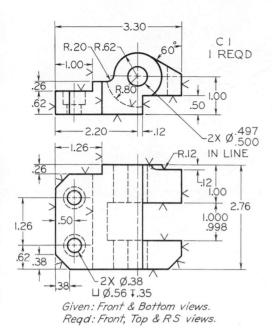

Given: Front & Bottom views.
Reqd: Front, Top & RS views.

Exercise 5.23 **Hinge Bracket***

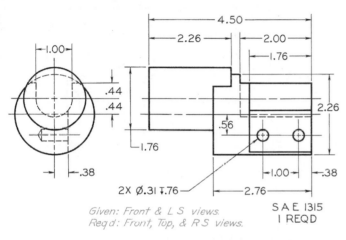

Given: Front & LS views.
Reqd: Front, Top, & RS views.

SAE 1315
1 REQD

Exercise 5.24 **Tool Holder***

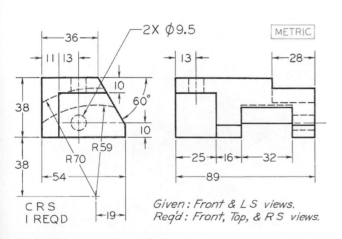

CRS
1 REQD

Given: Front & LS views.
Reqd: Front, Top, & RS views.

Exercise 5.25 **Shifter Block***

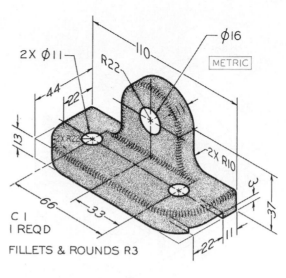

C 1
1 REQD

FILLETS & ROUNDS R3

Exercise 5.26 **Cross-feed Stop***

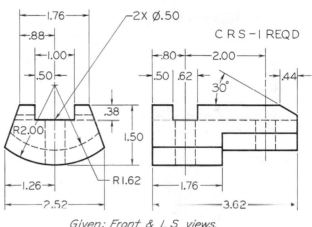

Given: Front & LS views.
Reqd: Front, Top, & RS views.

Exercise 5.27 **Cross Cam***

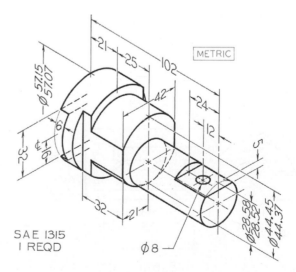

SAE 1315
1 REQD

Exercise 5.28 **Roller Stud***

*Sketch or draw necessary views. These exercises are designed to fit on 8½ × 11" A-size or A4 metric size paper. Use a title block or title strip as assigned by your instructor. If dimensions are required, study Chapter 9. Use metric or decimal-inch dimensions as assigned by your instructor. Move dimensions to better locations where possible.

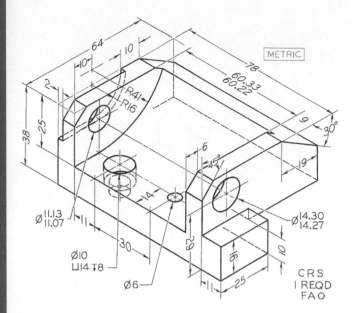

Exercise 5.29 Hinge Block*

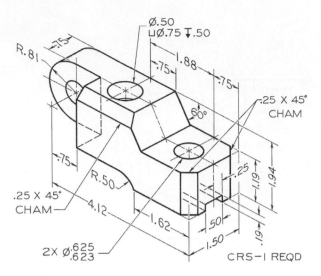

Exercise 5.32 Vibrator Arm*

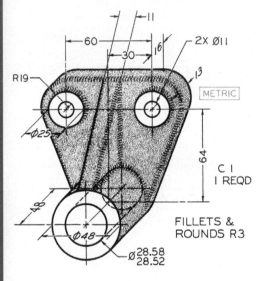

Exercise 5.30 Feed Rod Bearing*

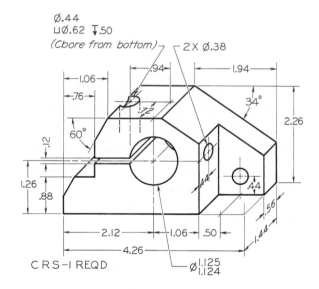

Exercise 5.33 Clutch Lever*

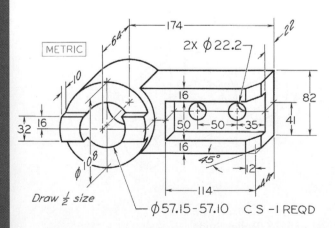

Exercise 5.31 Lever Hub*

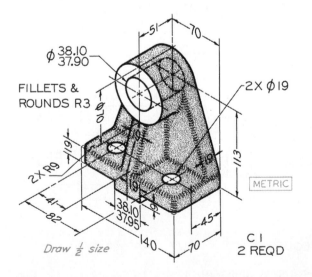

Exercise 5.34 Counter Bearing Bracket*

*Sketch or draw necessary views. These exercises are designed to fit on 8½ × 11" A-size or A4 metric size paper. Use a title block or title strip as assigned by your instructor. If dimensions are required, study Chapter 9. Use metric or decimal-inch dimensions as assigned by your instructor. Move dimensions to better locations where possible.

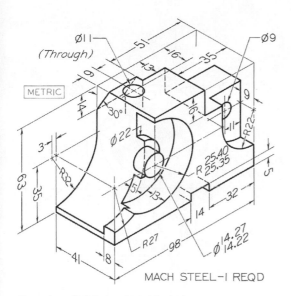

Exercise 5.35 Tool Holder*

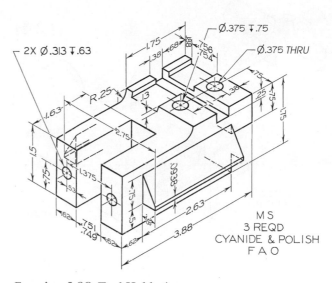

Exercise 5.38 Tool Holder*

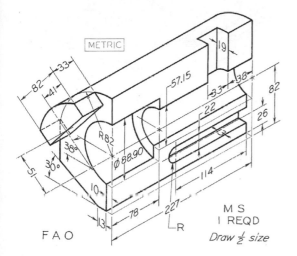

Exercise 5.36 Control Block*

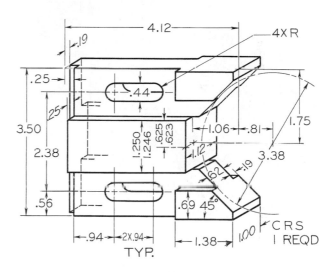

Exercise 5.39 Locating V-Block*

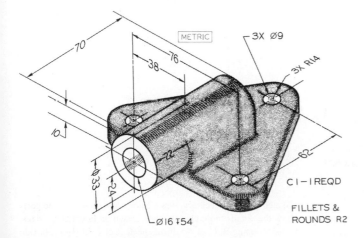

Exercise 5.37 Socket Bearing*

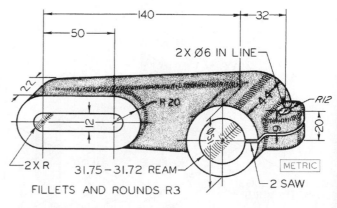

Exercise 5.40 Anchor Bracket*

*Sketch or draw necessary views. These exercises are designed to fit on 8½ × 11" A-size or A4 metric size paper. Use a title block or title strip as assigned by your instructor. If dimensions are required, study Chapter 9. Use metric or decimal-inch dimensions as assigned by your instructor. Move dimensions to better locations where possible.

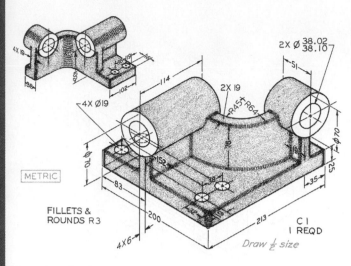

FILLETS & ROUNDS R3

Exercise 5.41 Lead Screw Bracket*

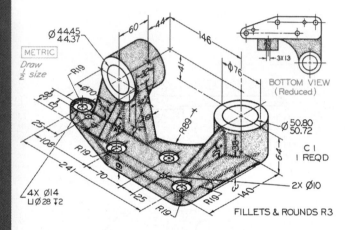

Exercise 5.42 Lever Bracket*

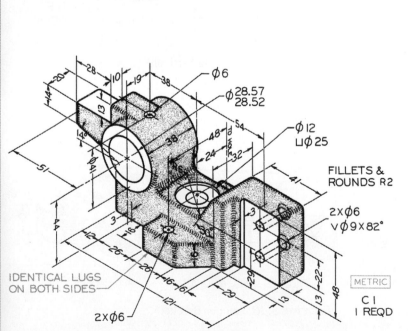

IDENTICAL LUGS ON BOTH SIDES

2×⌀6

Exercise 5.43 Gripper Rode Center*

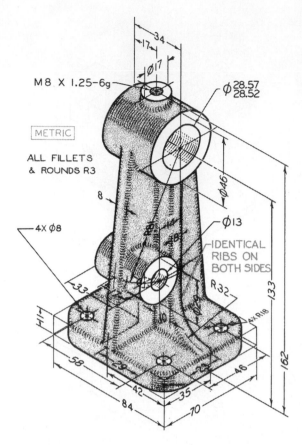

Exercise 5.44 Bearing Bracket*

*Sketch or draw necessary views. Larger and more detailed parts show the details more clearly when drawn on larger sheet sizes. Consider using B, C, or A3 or A2 sheets. Use a title block or title strip as assigned by your instructor. If dimensions are required, study Chapter 9. Use metric or decimal-inch dimensions as assigned by your instructor. Move dimensions to better locations where possible.

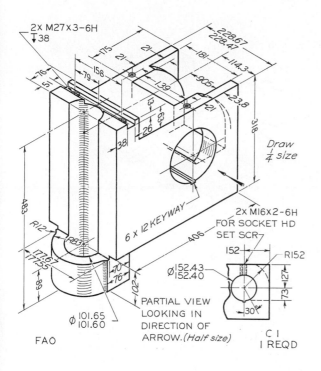

Exercise 5.45 Link Arm Connector*

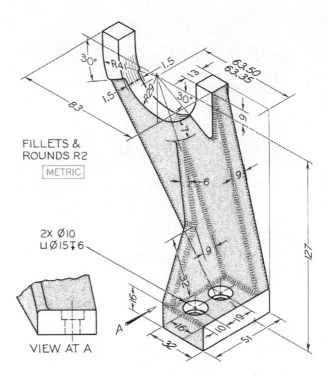

Exercise 5.47 LH Shifter Fork*

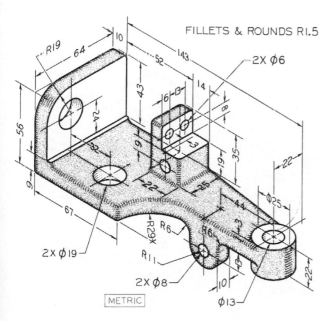

Exercise 5.46 Mounting Bracket*

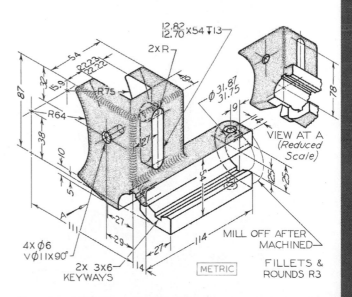

Exercise 5.48 Gear Shift Bracket*

*Sketch or draw necessary views. Larger and more detailed parts show the details more clearly when drawn on larger sheet sizes. Consider using B, C, or A3 or A2 sheets. Use a title block or title strip as assigned by your instructor. If dimensions are required, study Chapter 9. Use metric or decimal-inch dimensions as assigned by your instructor. Move dimensions to better locations where possible.

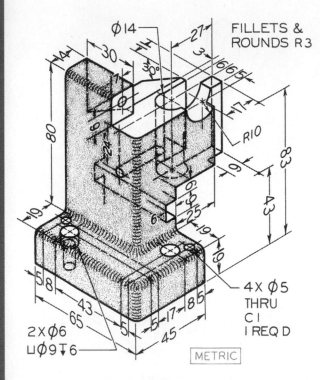

FILLETS &
ROUNDS R3

METRIC

Exercise 5.49 Fixture Base*

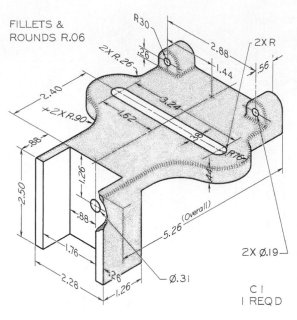

FILLETS &
ROUNDS R.06

C1
1 REQD

Exercise 5.51 Tension Bracket*

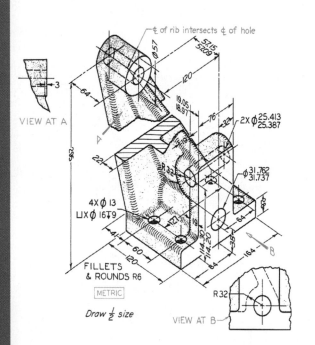

VIEW AT A

FILLETS
& ROUNDS R6

METRIC

Draw ½ size

VIEW AT B

Exercise 5.50 Ejector Base*

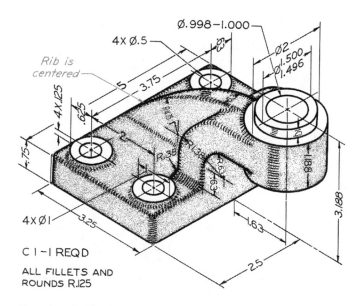

Rib is
centered

C1–1 REQD

ALL FILLETS AND
ROUNDS R.125

Exercise 5.52 Offset Bearing*

*Sketch or draw necessary views. Larger and more detailed parts show the details more clearly when drawn on larger sheet sizes. Consider using B, C, or A3 or A2 sheets. Use a title block or title strip as assigned by your instructor. If dimensions are required, study Chapter 9. Use metric or decimal-inch dimensions as assigned by your instructor. Move dimensions to better locations where possible.

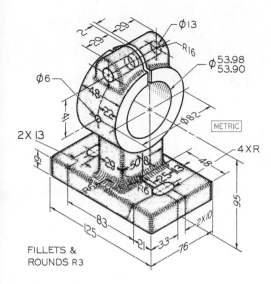

Exercise 5.53 Feed Guide*

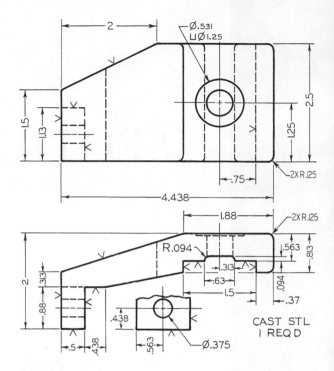

Exercise 5.55 Trip Lever. Given: Front, top, and partial side views. Required: Front, bottom, and left-side views, drawn completely.*

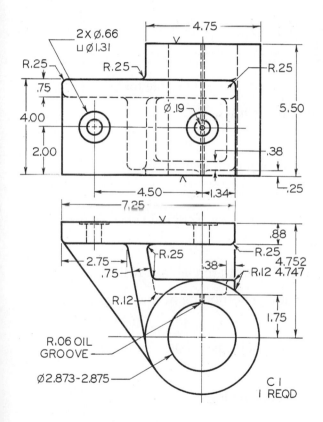

Exercise 5.54 Feed Shaft Bracket. Given: Front and top views. Required: Front, top, and right-side views, half size.*

*Sketch or draw necessary views. Larger and more detailed parts show the details more clearly when drawn on larger sheet sizes. Consider using B, C, or A3 or A2 sheets. Use a title block or title strip as assigned by your instructor. If dimensions are required, study Chapter 9. Use metric or decimal-inch dimensions as assigned by your instructor. Move dimensions to better locations where possible.

CHAPTER SIX

SECTIONAL VIEWS

─────────── **OBJECTIVES** ───────────

After studying the material in this chapter, you should be able to:

1. Understand sections and cutting-plane lines.

2. Apply correct section lining practices.

3. Recognize and draw section lining for ten different materials.

4. Draw a sectional view, given a two-view drawing.

5. Demonstrate correct hidden-line practices for sectional views.

6. Identify seven types of sections.

7. Apply section techniques to create clear interpretable drawings.

8. Demonstrate the proper techniques for sectioning ribs, webs, and spokes.

9. Use hatching when using conventional breaks to show elongated objects.

10. Interpret drawings that include sectional views.

Refer to the following standard:
- ANSI/ASME Y14.3—2003 Multiview and Sectional View Drawings

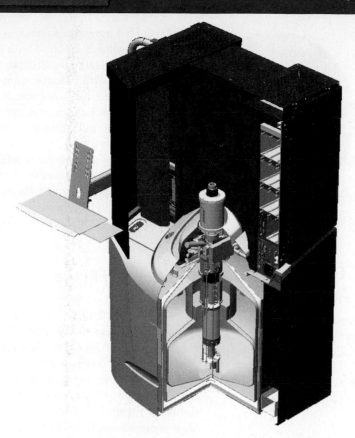

3D Section View of the Superconducting Quantum Interference Device (SQUID). *This isometric section view shows the interior details. Courtesy of Quantum Design.*

OVERVIEW

Technical drawings often represent a single part with a complex interior structure, or many different parts in a mechanical assembly, building, bridge, toy, or other product. When you are creating a drawing, if the interior structure cannot be shown clearly by using hidden lines, you should use a section view to reveal the internal features of the part.

To visualize a section view, think of slicing through the object as if you were cutting through an apple or melon. This familiar cutaway view—looking onto the cut portion of the object—is called a sectional view, or sometimes a cross-section.

Special conventions, some that depart from the practices you have learned for orthographic projection, are used to make section views easier to understand.

3D CAD modeling software often cannot generate section views that meet all of these special conventions, so current practice allows for direct sections of the 3D model. 2D and 3D CAD users need to thoroughly understand sectional views to use them effectively.

Selecting the sectional view that best shows the drawing information is a skill that takes practice.

Search the following Web sites to learn more about standard steel beam cross sections (efunda), standard steel shapes (aisc), and a sample of cross sections from the Visible Human (nlm.nih):
- http://www.efunda.com
- http://www.aisc.org
- http://www.nlm.nih.gov

6.1 Full Section View of a Melon

UNDERSTANDING SECTIONS

Section views are used for three main purposes:

- To document the design and manufacture of single parts that are manufactured as one piece.
- To document how multiple parts are to be assembled or built.
- To aid in visualizing the internal workings of a design.

Sections of Single Parts

If you have ever cut a melon in half, you have created a full section in real life (Figure 6.1). To visualize a section of a single part is no different. Think of the part as being sliced through by the cutting plane, as if the plane were a giant cleaver. Once the object is cut, the closer half is pulled away, showing the inside construction of the part.

Full Sections

When the part is cut fully in half, the resulting view is called a **full section** as shown in Figure 6.2. Figure 6.3 shows a technical drawing of the part from Figure 6.2 that does not use a section view. Notice how confusing all of the hidden lines make it

look. Figure 6.4 shows the same drawing, but this time the typical right-side view is replaced with a right-side section view. Now it is much easier to understand.

In a drawing with a section view, the missing half is imagined to be removed and is not actually shown removed in any view except the section view. A line called the **cutting-plane line** provides the information necessary for understanding where the part was cut.

The cutting-plane line shows where the object was cut and from which direction the section is viewed. The arrows at the ends of the cutting-plane line indicate the direction of sight for the section view. The arrows point *toward the section being viewed* as shown in Figures 6.4 and 6.5, not away from it, as in Figure 6.6.

The Cutting Plane

The cutting-plane is shown in a view adjacent to the sectional view, in this case the front view. In this view, the cutting plane appears edgewise as a thick dashed line called the cutting-plane line. The arrows at the ends of the cutting-plane line indicate the direction of sight for the sectional view as shown in Figure 6.4.

In the section view, the areas that would have been in actual contact with the cutting plane (refer to the visual example shown in Figure 6.2), are shown with **section lining.** Those areas are cross-hatched with thin parallel section lines.

Lines Behind the Cutting Plane

The visible edges of the object behind the cutting plane are generally shown because they are now visible, but they are not cross-hatched with section lining, because they were not cut. Figure 6.7 shows an example of object edges exposed by the cutting plane appearing as visible lines in the section view. In a full section, the location of the cutting plane is obvious from the section itself, so the cutting-plane line is often omitted. Cutting-plane lines should be used wherever necessary for clarity. You will learn about other types of sections that require the cutting plane line in order to be understood, later in this chapter.

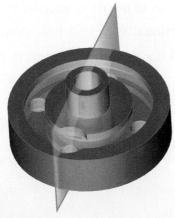

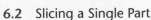
6.2 Slicing a Single Part

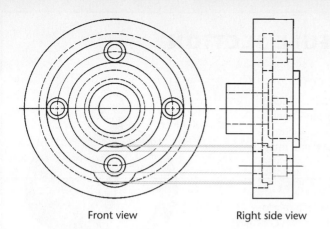

Front view   Right side view

6.3 Front and Right-Side Views. *Parts with a lot of interior detail may have so many hidden lines that their views are confusing.*

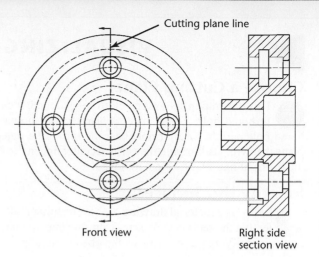

Cutting plane line

Front view   Right side section view

6.4 Front and Right-Side View in Full Section. *Using a section view makes it easier to see interior details.*

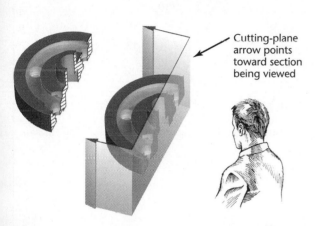

Cutting-plane arrow points toward section being viewed

6.5 Cutting-Plane Line Indicates Direction of Sight

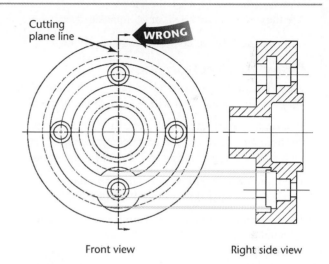

Cutting plane line   WRONG

Front view   Right side view

6.6 Arrows Should Not Point to Removed Portion

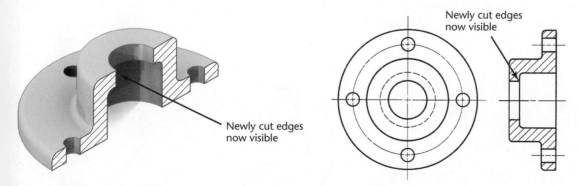

Newly cut edges now visible

Newly cut edges now visible

6.7 Newly Visible Edges Cut by Cutting Plane are Cross-Hatched with Section Lining

VISUALIZING A FULL SECTION

Choose a Cutting Plane

1 This illustration shows a collar to be sectioned. It has a drilled and counterbored hole. To produce a clear section showing both the counterbored hole and the smaller hole near the top of the object, choose a cutting plane that will pass through the vertical center line in the front view and imagine the right half of the object removed.

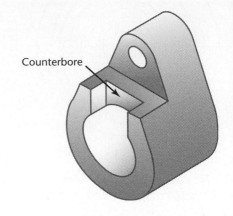

Counterbore

Identify the Surfaces

2 Below is a pictorial drawing of the remaining half. The first step in projecting the section view is making sure that you interpret the object correctly. Identifying the surfaces on the object can help.

Surfaces R, S, T, U, and V have been labeled on the given views and the pictorial view.

Which surface is R in the front view?
Which surface is U in the top view?
Are they normal, inclined, or oblique surfaces?

Can you identify the counterbore in each view?

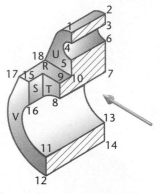

Draw the Section View

3 To draw the section view, omit the portion of the object in front of the cutting plane. You will only be drawing the portion that remains.

Determine which are solid parts of the object the cutting plane will pass through. *Hint: The outside of an object can never be a hole; it must be solid, unless the cutting plane passes through a slot to the exterior.*

The points which will be projected to create the section view have been identified for you in the example shown.

The three surfaces produced by the cutting plane are bounded by points 1-2-3-4 and 5-6-7-8-9-10 and 13-14-12-11. These are shown hatched.

Each sectioned area is completely enclosed by a boundary of visible lines. In addition to the cut surfaces, the sectional view shows all visible parts behind the cutting plane.

No hidden lines are shown. However, the corresponding section shown in this step is incomplete because visible lines are missing.

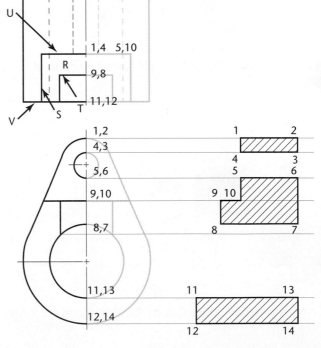

Project the Visible Lines

4 From the direction the section is viewed, the top surface (V) of the object appears in the section as a visible line (12-11-16-15-17).

The bottom surface of the object appears similarly as 14-13-7-6-3-2. The bottom surface of the counterbore appears in the section as line 19-20.

Also, the back half of the counterbore and the drilled hole will appear as rectangles in the section at 19-20-15-16 and 3-4-5-6. These points must also be projected. The finished view is shown at right.

Notice that since all cut surfaces are part of the same object, the hatching must all run in the same direction.

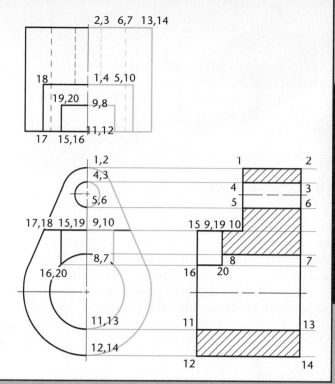

6.1 PLACEMENT OF SECTION VIEWS

Section views can replace the normal top, front, side, or other standard orthographic views in the standard view arrangement. Figure 6.8 shows an example. In this drawing, the front view of the object is shown in section. Only two views are necessary. The front view is shown as a section view and the cutting plane line is shown in the right-side view.

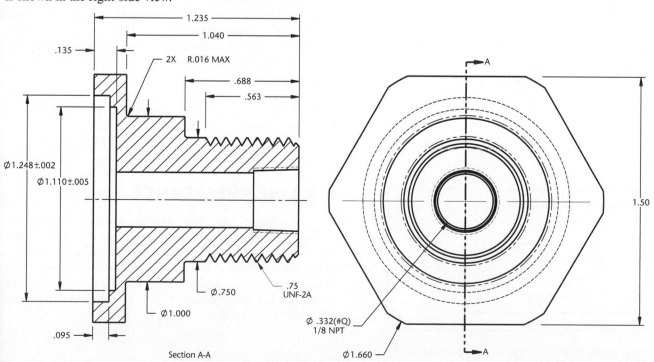

6.8 Section Views Can Replace Standard Orthographic Views. *Courtesy of Wood's Power-Grip. Co. Inc.*

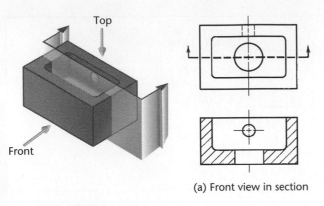

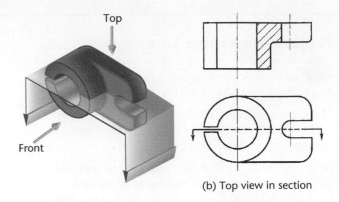

(a) Front view in section

(b) Top view in section

6.9   Front and Top Views in Section

In Figure 6.9a, the object is cut through with a plane parallel to the front view. The front half of the object is imagined removed. The resulting full section may be referred to as the "front view in section" because it occupies the front view position.

In Figure 6.9b, the cutting plane is a horizontal plane (which would appear as a line in the front view). The upper half

of the object is imagined removed. The resulting full section is shown in place of the top view.

When adding a section view to your drawing keep in mind that your purpose is to document and convey information about your design and show the information in the way that best achieves this.

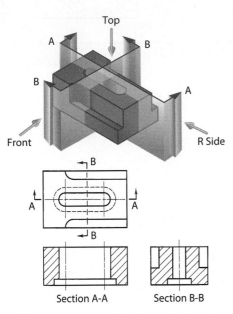

Section A-A   Section B-B

6.10   Front and Side Views in Section

6.2 LABELING CUTTING PLANES

In Figure 6.10, two cutting planes are shown, one a plane parallel to the front view and the other a plane parallel to the side view, both of which appear edgewise in the top view. Each section is completely independent of the other and drawn as if the other were not present.

For section A–A, the front half of the object is imagined removed. The back half is then viewed in the direction of the arrows for a front view, and the resulting section is a front view in section.

For section B–B, the right half of the object is imagined removed. The left half is then viewed in the direction of the arrows for a right-side view, and the resulting section is a right-side view in section. The cutting-plane lines are preferably drawn through an exterior view (in this case the top view, as shown) instead of a sectional view.

The cutting-plane lines in Figure 6.10 are shown for purposes of illustration only. They are generally omitted in cases where the location of the cutting plane is obvious.

6.3 LINE PRECEDENCE

When a cutting-plane line coincides with a centerline, the cutting-plane line takes precedence. When the cutting-plane line would obscure important details in the view, just the ends of the line outside the view and the arrows can be shown as in Figure 6.11. When you do this, be sure to leave a small but visible gap between the lines of the view and the small portion of the cutting-plane line.

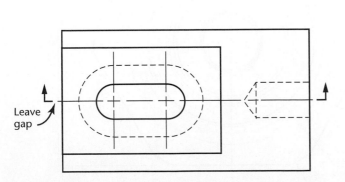

6.11   The Cutting-Plane Line Takes Precedence Over the Centerline

6.4 RULES FOR LINES

When creating section views follow these general rules:

- Show *edges and contours which are now visible behind the cutting plane*; otherwise a section will appear to be made up of disconnected and unrelated parts. (Occasionally, visible lines behind the cutting plane may be omitted, particularly from those generated from 3D models.)
- Omit *hidden lines in section views*. Section views are used to show interior detail without a confusion of hidden lines, so add them only if necessary to understand the part.
- Sometimes hidden lines are necessary for clarity and should be used in such cases, especially if their use will make it possible to omit a view (Figure 6.12d).
- A sectioned area is always completely bounded by a visible outline—never by a hidden line, because in every case the cut surfaces will be the closest surface in the section view and therefore their boundary lines will be visible (Figure 6.12e).
- In a section view of an object, the section lines in all hatched areas for that object must be parallel, not as shown in Figure 6.12f. The use of section lining in opposite directions is an indication of different parts, as when two or more parts are adjacent in an assembly drawing.
- A visible line can never cross a sectioned area in a view of a single part. This would be impossible on the full section of a single part because the section lines are all in the same plane. A line across it would indicate a change of plane (Figure 6.12g). In an assembly section, this would be possible. You will learn about assemblies in a later part of the chapter.

--- **TIP** ---
Learning the rules for section lining saves time. Extra hidden lines and hatching that is denser than necessary take longer to draw and make drawings slower to print. They also make drawings harder to read.

--- **TIP** ---
In CAD, when views can be placed by projection from a 3D model, saving time by omitting a view is not a big concern, but often saving space on the drawing sheet by leaving out a view may be.

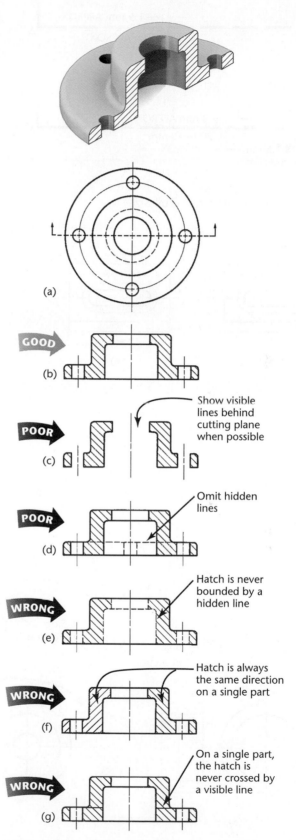

6.12 Right and Wrong Lines in Section Views

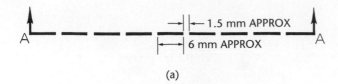

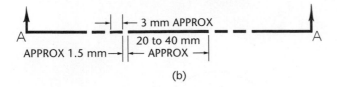

6.13 Cutting-Plane Lines (Full Size)

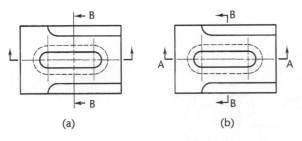

6.14 Alternative Methods for Showing a Cutting Plane

6.5 CUTTING-PLANE LINE STYLE

Figure 6.13a shows the preferred style of line to use for the cutting-plane line. It is made up of equal dashes, each about 6 mm (1/4″) long ending in arrowheads. This form works especially well for drawings. The alternative style, shown in Figure 6.13b, uses alternating long dashes and pairs of short dashes and ends with arrowheads. This style has been in general use for a long time, so you may still see it on drawings. Both lines are drawn the same thickness as visible lines. The arrowheads at the ends of the cutting-plane line indicate the direction in which the cutaway object is viewed (as was shown in Figure 6.5).

Use capital letters at the ends of the cutting-plane line when necessary to help the drawing's reader match each cutting-plane line to its section view. Figure 6.10 showed an example where the cutting plane is labeled and the resulting section view is labeled to match. This most often occurs in the case of multiple sections or removed sections, which are discussed later in the chapter.

An alternative method for showing the cutting plane is to draw the cutting-line pattern and then draw reference arrows pointing to it in the direction of sight (Figure 6.14a).

Especially on architectural drawings, the center of the cutting-plane line is often left out and stylized arrows are used to identify the cutting plane (Figure 6.14b).

Visualizing Cutting-Plane Direction

Correct and incorrect relations between cutting-plane lines and corresponding sectional views are shown in Figure 6.15.

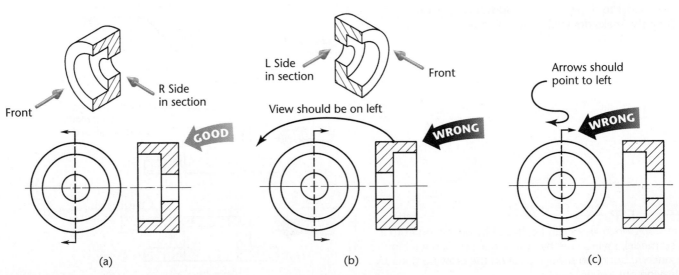

6.15 Correct and Incorrect Cutting-Plane Line Placement

6.6 SECTION LINE TECHNIQUE

The correct method of drawing section lines is shown in Figure 6.16a. When drawing by hand, use a sharp, medium-grade pencil (H or 2H) to draw uniformly thin section lines, or **hatching** (a term meaning closely spaced parallel lines). There should be a marked contrast between the thin section lines and the thick visible outlines of the part.

Draw section lines at 45° from horizontal unless they would be parallel or perpendicular to major edges of the part, in which case use a different angle. Figure 6.16b shows an example of section lines drawn at a different angle to prevent them from being parallel or perpendicular to visible outlines.

Space the lines as evenly as possible by eye (for most drawings, about 2.5 mm (1/32″) apart). The spacing interval depends on the size of the drawing or of the sectioned area, with larger drawings having wider spacing. In a smaller drawing the spacing interval may be as small as 1.5 mm (1/16″) while in a large drawing, it may be 3 mm (1/8″) or more. As a rule, space the lines as generously as possible, yet close enough to clearly distinguish the sectioned areas.

Keep extension lines and dimension values off sectioned areas. If there is no alternative, omit the section lines behind the dimensions (Figure 6.16c).

> ## TIP
> Beginners tend to draw section lines too close together. This is tedious and makes small inaccuracies in spacing obvious. After the first few lines, look back repeatedly at the original spacing to avoid gradually increasing or decreasing the intervals between the lines.

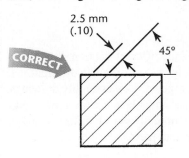

CORRECT

2.5 mm (.10)   45°

- Uniformly spaced by an interval of about 2.5mm
- Not too close together
- Uniformly thin, not varying in thickness
- Distinctly thinner than visible lines
- Do not run beyond or stop short of visible outlines

(a) Correctly drawn section lines

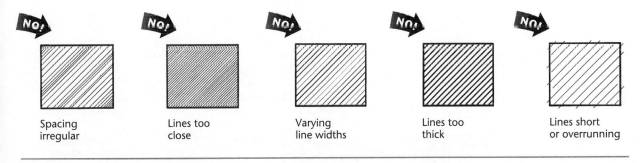

| Spacing irregular | Lines too close | Varying line widths | Lines too thick | Lines short or overrunning |

(b) Direction of Section Lines

If section lines drawn at 45° with horizontal would be parallel or perpendicular (or nearly so) to a prominent visible outline, the angle should be changed to 30°, 60°, or some other angle.

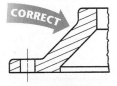 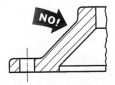 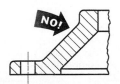

Angle of section lines is adjusted

Lines should not be parallel to outline

Lines should not be perpendicular to outline

(c) Dimensions and Section Lines

Keep extension lines and values for dimensions off crosshatched areas, but when this is unavoidable, the crosshatching should be omitted where the dimension figure is placed.

BEST

Extension lines and dimension values are not on hatched area

O.K.

Section lines are omitted behind dimensioning

Dimensioning should not be on hatched area

6.16 Correct and Incorrect Section Lining Technique

Section Lining Large Areas

When adding section lines to a large area, use outline sectioning, where the center portion of the hatched area is left blank to save time and make the view more legible, as shown in Figure 6.17.

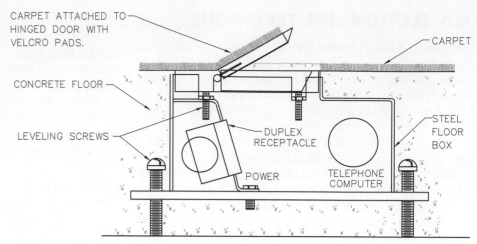

6.17 Outline Sectioning. *Courtesy of Associated Construction Engineering.*

Section Lining Symbols

Section lining symbols (Figure 6.18) may be used to indicate specific materials. These symbols represent general material types only, such as cast iron, brass, and steel. Because there are so many different types of materials (there are hundreds of types of steel, for example), a general name or symbol is not enough. A detailed specification listing the material must be lettered in the form of a note or in the title strip.

The general purpose section lining (which is the same as that for cast iron) may be used to represent any material on the detail drawing for a single part.

Using different section lining patterns helps you distinguish different materials, especially on assembly drawings, but it is acceptable to use the general purpose symbol shown at different angles for different parts.

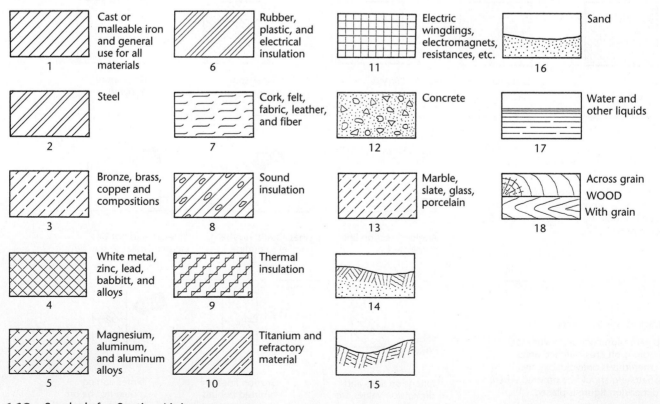

6.18 Symbols for Section Lining

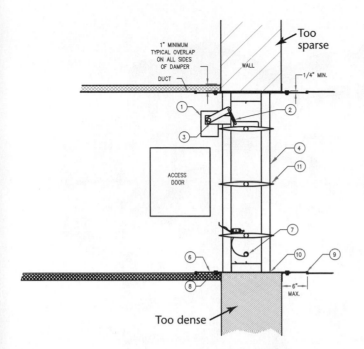

Section Lining in CAD

CAD programs usually include libraries that allow you to select from a variety of section lining patterns, making it easy to use different patterns, angles, and scales for the spacing of the pattern. When using CAD software to hatch an area in the drawing, be careful to specify a scale that relates to the printed drawing scale for that sheet. Otherwise the hatching may turn out so dense that the object appears to be filled in solidly, or so sparse that you do not see any hatching (Figure 6.19).

6.19   Incorrect Hatching in a CAD Drawing

6.7 HALF SECTIONS

Objects that are symmetric can be shown effectively using a special type of section view called a **half section** (Figure 6.20). A half section exposes the interior for one half of the object and the exterior of the other half. This is done by removing one quarter of the object to produce a section view with one half in section and the other half as viewed from the outside. Half sections are not widely used to create detail drawings showing how to make a single part because it can be difficult to show all of the dimensions clearly when some internal features are only partly shown in the sectioned half (Figure 6.20b).

In general,

- Omit hidden lines from both halves of a half section, whenever possible.
- Use a centerline to divide the sectioned half and the unsectioned half, as shown in Figure 6.20b.

Half section drawings are most useful in showing an assembly where it is often necessary to show both internal and external construction in one drawing view and usually without dimensioning. A broken out section may be preferred in some cases.

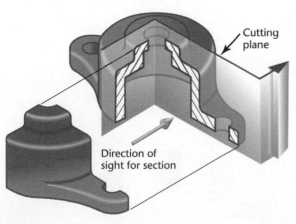

(a) Cutting plane

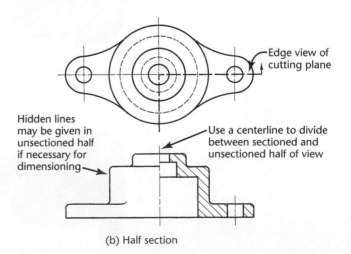

(b) Half section

6.20   Half Section

A 3D broken out section of a diesel engine by Caterpillar reveals its pistons.
Courtesy of Caterpillar, Inc.

6.8 BROKEN OUT SECTIONS

It often happens that only a partial section of a view is needed to expose interior shapes. Such a section, limited by a break line, is called a **broken out section.**

In Figure 6.21, a full or half section is not necessary, and a small broken out section is sufficient to explain the construction.

In Figure 6.22, a half section would have caused the removal of half the keyway. The keyway is preserved by breaking out around it. In this case, the section is limited partly by a break line and partly by a centerline in the drawing.

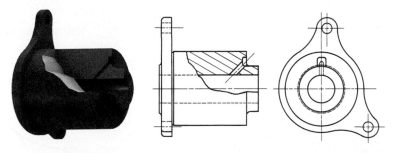

6.21 Broken Out Section

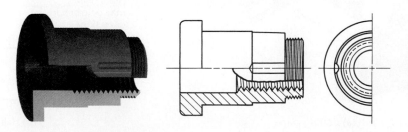

6.22 Break Around Keyway

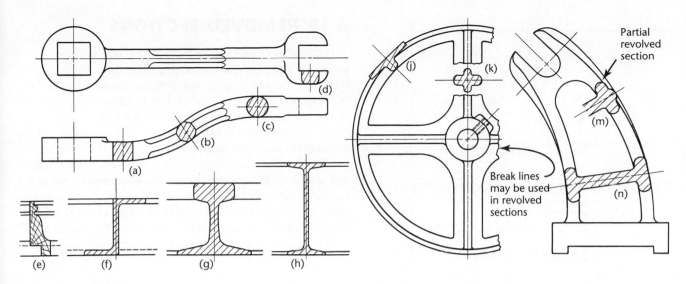

6.23 Revolved Sections

6.9 REVOLVED SECTIONS

You can show the shape of the cross section of a bar, arm, spoke, or other elongated object in the longitudinal view by using a **revolved section.** Figure 6.23 shows examples of how revolved sections look in a drawing.

To create a revolved section, first imagine a cutting plane perpendicular to the centerline or axis of the object, as shown in Figure 6.24a. Next, revolve the plane 90° about a center line at right angles to the axis as shown in Figures 6.24b and 6.24c.

The visible lines adjacent to a revolved section may be broken out if desired, as shown in Figure 6.25.

When you superimpose the revolved section over the top of the view, be sure that any original lines of the view that are covered by the revolved view are removed (Figure 6.26a).

Show the true shape of the revolved section, regardless of the direction of the lines in the view (Figure 6.26b).

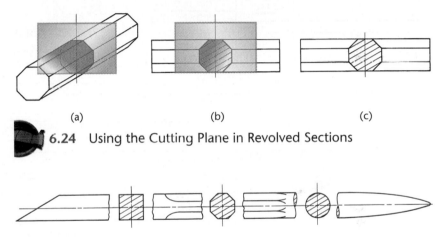

(a)   (b)   (c)

6.24 Using the Cutting Plane in Revolved Sections

6.25 Conventional Breaks Used with Revolved Sections

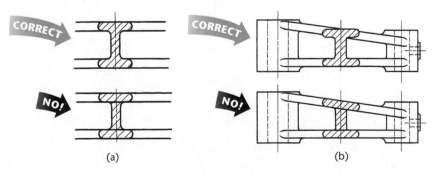

CORRECT   CORRECT

NO!   NO!

(a)   (b)

6.26 Common Errors in Drawing Revolved Sections

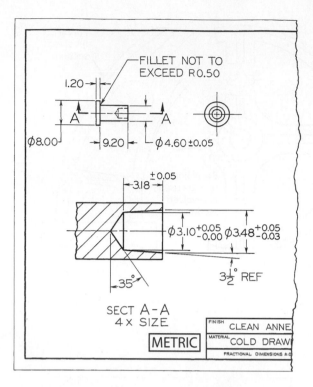

6.27 Removed Section

6.10 REMOVED SECTIONS

A **removed section** (Figure 6.27) is one that is not in direct projection from the view containing the cutting plane—that is, it is not positioned in agreement with the standard arrangement of views. Be sure to keep the section in its normal orientation and do not turn it a different direction on the sheet. If you must rotate the view, use a **rotation arrow** as shown in Figure 6.28 and note the angle the view was rotated.

Removed sections should be labeled, such as section A–A and section B–B, corresponding to the letters at the ends of the cutting-plane line (Figure 6.27). They should be arranged in alphabetical order from left to right on the sheet. Section letters should be used in alphabetical order, but letters I, O, and Q should not be used because they are easily confused with the numeral 1 or the zero. Figure 6.29 shows several removed sections.

6.28 Rotation Arrow Symbol. Use this to label a view that has been rotated. h = letter height in the drawing.

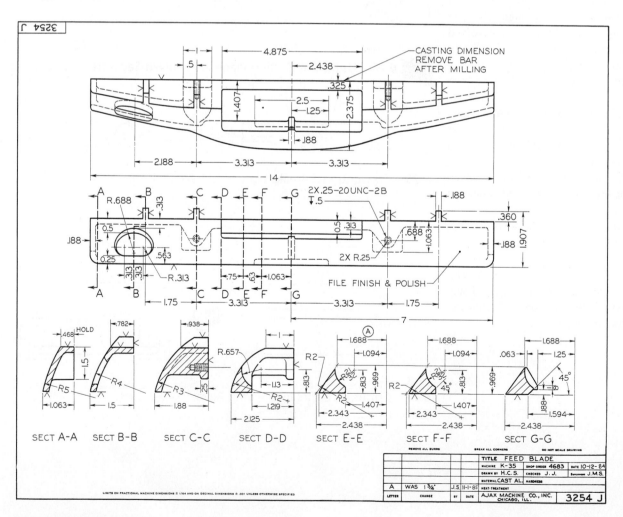

6.29 Removed Sections

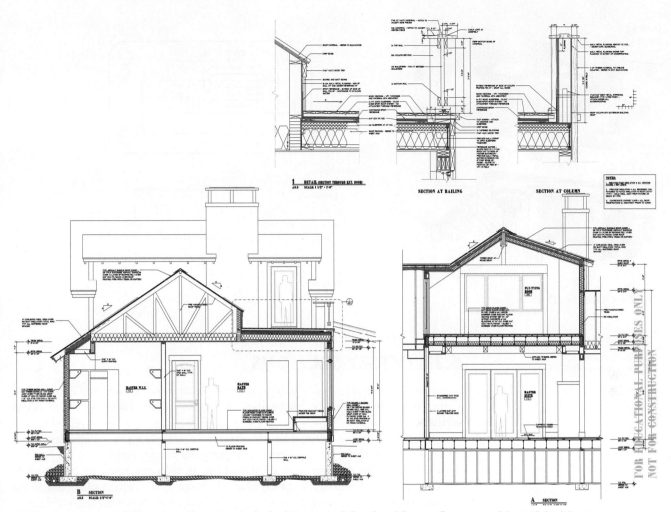

6.30 Architectural Drawing Showing Labeled Removed Section Views. *Courtesy of Locati Architects.*

A removed section is often a **partial section,** where only a portion of the section view is drawn. Removed sections are frequently drawn to an enlarged scale (Figure 6.29) to show detail and provide space for dimensions. When using an enlarged scale be sure to indicate the scale below the section view's title.

A removed section should be placed so that it no longer lines up in projection with any other view. It should be separated clearly from the standard arrangement of views (see Figure 6.30). Whenever possible, removed sections should be on the same sheet as the regular views. If a section must be placed on a different sheet, cross-references should be given on the related sheets. A note should be given below the section title, such as

SECTION B-B ON SHEET 4, ZONE A3

A similar note should be placed on the sheet on which the cutting-plane line is shown, with a leader pointing to the cutting-plane line and referring to the sheet on which the section will be found. Sometimes it is convenient to place removed sections on centerlines extended from the section cuts (Figure 6.31).

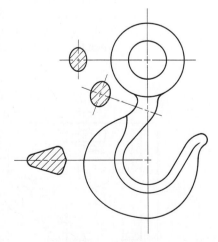

6.31 Removed Sections on Centerlines

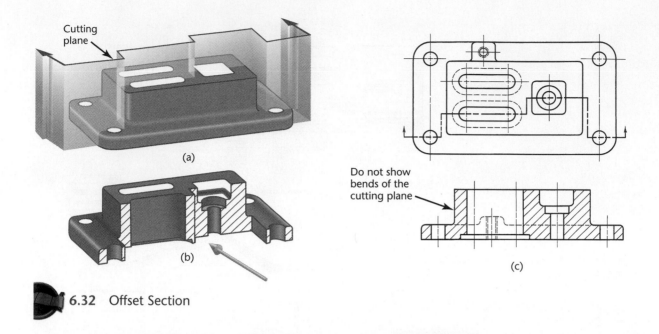

Cutting plane

(a)

(b)

Do not show bends of the cutting plane

(c)

6.32 Offset Section

6.11 OFFSET SECTIONS

In sectioning complex objects, it is often desirable to show features that do not lie in a straight line by "offsetting" or bending the cutting plane. These are called **offset sections.**

In Figure 6.32a the cutting plane is offset in several places to include the hole at the left end, one of the parallel slots, the rectangular recess, and one of the holes at the right end. The front portion of the object is then imagined to be removed (Figure 6.32b). The path of the cutting plane is shown by the cutting-plane line in the top view (Figure 6.32c), and the resulting offset section is shown in the front view.

- The offsets or bends in the cutting plane are all 90°.
- The bends in the cutting plane are never shown in the sectional view.

Figure 6.32 also illustrates how hidden lines in a section eliminate the need for an additional view. In this case, an extra view would be needed to show the small boss on the back if hidden lines were not shown.

Figure 6.33 shows an example of multiple offset sections. Notice that the visible background shapes appear in each sectional view without the use of hidden lines. It is also acceptable to show only the cut portion, but the views are easier to interpret when the lines that are visible behind the cutting plane are shown.

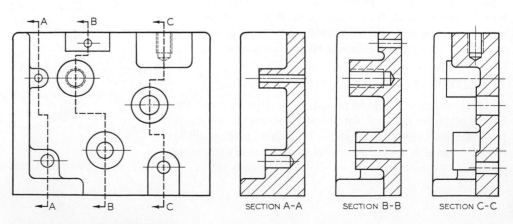

SECTION A-A   SECTION B-B   SECTION C-C

6.33 Three Offset Sections

6.12 RIBS IN SECTION

To avoid a false impression of thickness and solidity, ribs, webs, gear teeth, and other similar flat features are not hatched with section lining even though the cutting plane slices them. For example, in Figure 6.34, the cutting plane A–A slices through the center of the vertical web, or rib, and the web is not sectioned (Figure 6.34a). Do not hatch thin features even though the cutting plane passes lengthwise through them. The incorrect section is shown in Figure 6.34b. Note the false impression of thickness or solidity resulting from section lining the rib.

If the cutting plane passes crosswise through a rib or any thin member, as in section B–B, section line the feature in the usual manner, as in the top view of Figure 6.34c.

If a rib is not sectioned when the cutting plane passes through it flatwise, it is sometimes difficult to tell whether the rib is actually present, as, for example, ribs A in Figures 6.35a and 6.35b. It is difficult to distinguish spaces B as open spaces and spaces A as ribs. In such cases, double-spaced section lining of the ribs should be used (Figure 6.35c). This consists simply of continuing alternate section lines through the ribbed areas, as shown.

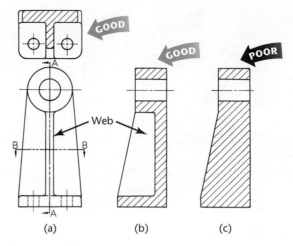

6.34 Web in Section

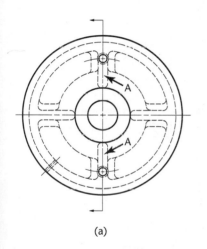

(a)

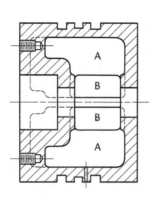

(b) Ribs not section-lined

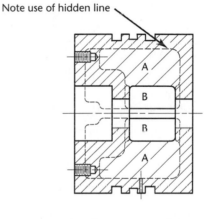

Note use of hidden line

(c) Alternate section lining

6.35 Alternate Sectioning

6.13 ALIGNED SECTIONS

When sectioning parts with angled elements, the cutting plane may be bent to pass through those features. The plane and features are then imagined to be revolved into the original plane. For example, Figure 6.36 shows an **aligned section.** The cutting plane was bent to pass through the angled arm and then revolved to a vertical position (aligned), from where it was projected across to the sectional view.

The angle of revolution should always be less than 90° for an aligned section.

Do not revolve features when the clarity of your drawing is not improved. In the exercises later in the chapter, you will see examples showing when revolution should not be used.

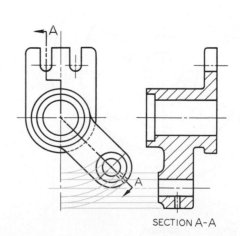

SECTION A-A

6.36 Aligned Section

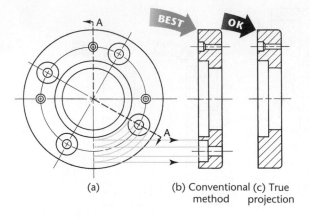

(a)　　　(b) Conventional (c) True
method　　projection

6.37 Aligned Section

In Figure 6.37 the cutting plane is bent to include one of the drilled and counterbored holes in the sectional view. The correct section view in Figure 6.37b gives a clearer and more complete description than does the section in Figure 6.37c, which is shown without any bend in the cutting plane.

In Figure 6.38a, the projecting lugs are not sectioned for the same reason that the ribs are not sectioned. In Figure 6.38b, the projecting lugs are located so that the cutting plane passes through them crosswise; therefore, they are sectioned.

Another example involving rib sectioning and aligned sectioning is shown in Figure 6.39. In the circular view, the cutting plane is offset in circular-arc bends to include the upper hole and upper rib, the keyway and center hole, the lower rib, and one of the lower holes. These features are imagined to be revolved until they line up vertically and are then projected from that position to obtain the section shown in Figure 6.39b. Note that the ribs are not sectioned. If a regular full section of the object were drawn without using the conventions discussed here, the resulting section (Figure 6.39c) would be incomplete and confusing and would take more time to draw.

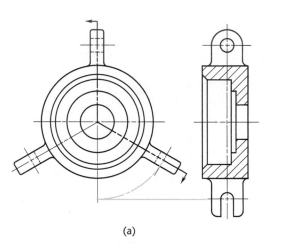

(a)

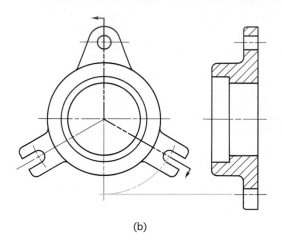

(b)

6.38 Aligned Section

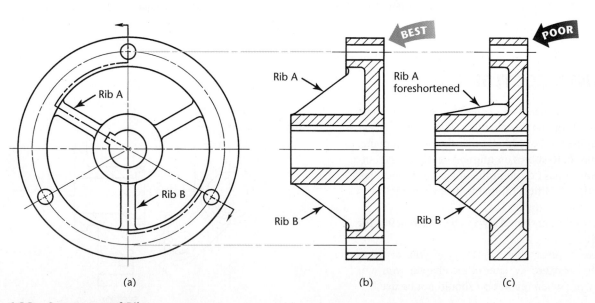

(a)　　　(b)　　　(c)

6.39 Symmetry of Ribs

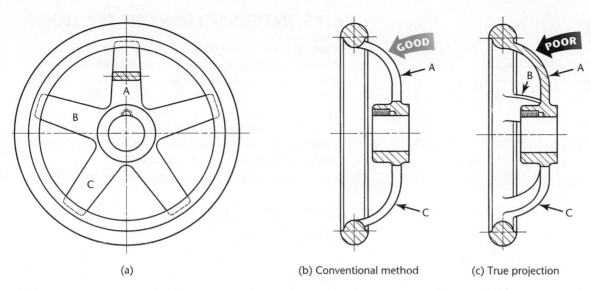

6.40   Spokes in Section

In sectioning a pulley or any spoked wheel (Figure 6.40a), it is standard practice to revolve the spokes if necessary (if there is an odd number) and not to section line the spokes (Figure 6.40b). If the spoke is sectioned, the section gives a false impression of continuous metal (Figure 6.40c). If the lower spoke is not revolved, it will be foreshortened in the sectional view, in which it presents an "amputated" and a misleading appearance.

Figure 6.40 also illustrates correct practice in omitting visible lines in a sectional view. Notice that spoke B is omitted in Figure 6.40b. If it is included, as shown in Figure 6.40c, the spoke is foreshortened, difficult and time-consuming to draw, and confusing to the reader of the drawing.

6.14 PARTIAL VIEWS

If space is limited on the paper or to save time, partial views may be used with sectioning (Figure 6.41). Half views are shown in Figures 6.41a and 6.41b in connection with a full section and a half section, respectively. In each case the back half of the object in the circular view is shown, to remove the front portion of the object and expose the back portion in the section.

Another method of drawing a partial view is to break out much of the circular view, retaining only those features that are needed for minimum representation (Figure 6.41c).

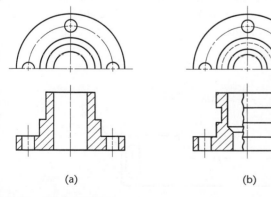

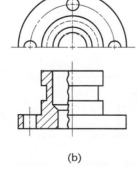

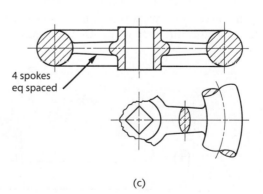

4 spokes eq spaced

(a)   (b)   (c)

6.41   Partial Views

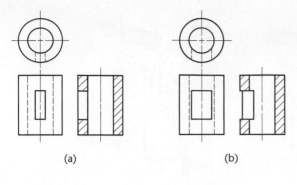

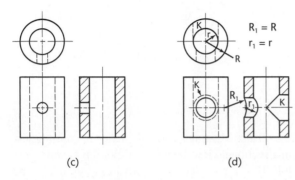

6.42 Intersections

6.15 INTERSECTIONS IN SECTIONS

Where an intersection is small or unimportant in a section, it is standard practice to disregard the true projection of the figure of intersection, as shown in Figures 6.42a and 6.42c. Larger intersections may be projected, as shown in Figure 6.42b, or approximated by circular arcs, as shown for the smaller hole in Figure 6.42d. Note that the larger hole K is the same diameter as the vertical hole. In such cases the curves of intersection (ellipses) appear as straight lines, as shown.

6.16 CONVENTIONAL BREAKS AND SECTIONS

Cross-hatching is often added when showing a conventional break. **Conventional breaks** are used to shorten the view of an object that is too long to show clearly at one scale on the drawing sheet. Figure 6.43 shows examples of hatching on conventional breaks. The parts to be broken must have the same section throughout, or if they are tapered they must have a uniform taper.

The breaks used on cylindrical shafts or tubes are often referred to as "S-breaks" and are usually drawn by eye, although S-break templates are available.

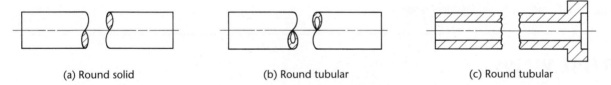

(a) Round solid   (b) Round tubular   (c) Round tubular

6.43 Conventional Breaks Often Show Crosshatching to Show the Cut Material

6.17 ASSEMBLY SECTIONS

Section views are often used to create assembly drawings. Figure 6.44 shows an orthographic drawing for an assembly. Notice that the hatching on different parts is shown using different hatch patterns or hatch at different angles. On the same part the hatching is always at the same angle to help you recognize the parts easily. Solid features that do not have interior structure are not hatched. You will learn more about these types of drawing in Chapter 12.

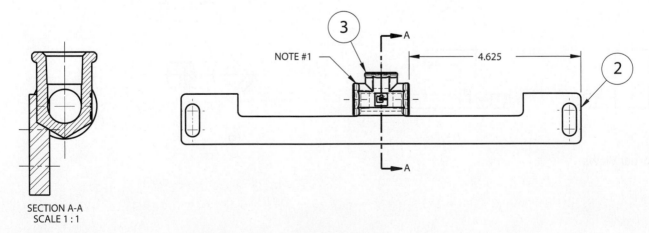

6.44 Assembly Section. *Courtesy of Wood's Power-Grip Co., Inc.*

COMPUTER TECHNIQUES FOR SECTIONS

2D and 3D sectional views are created using CAD. Most CAD systems have a "hatch" command to generate the section lining and hatch patterns to fill an area automatically. A wide variety of hatch patterns are generally available to show materials such as steel, bronze, sand, concrete, and many more.

Creating a full-section view from a 3D model is generally very easy. You often only need to define the cutting plane, viewing direction, scale, and where to place the view on the sheet. Often the hatching for the cut surfaces is generated automatically. Sectioned views other than full sections can be more difficult to create. To create good sectional drawings using CAD, you should have a clear understanding of the standards for showing section views.

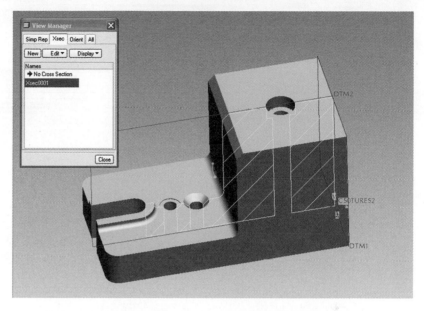

A section created in the 3D model using Pro/Engineer Wildfire Software's View Manager. *Courtesy of PTC.*

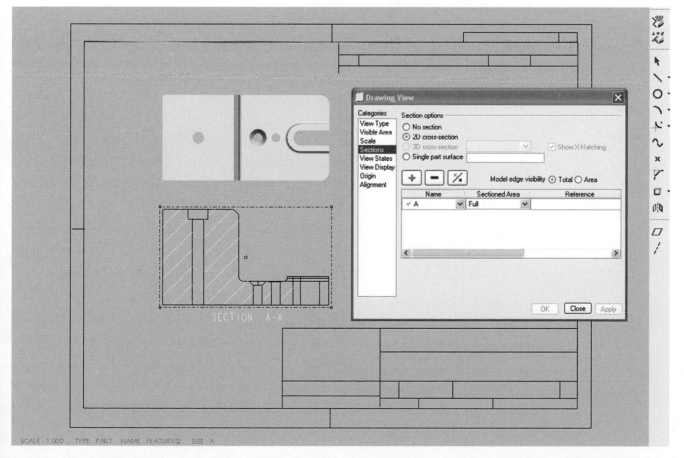

Sections can quickly be shown in orthographic drawings generated from a 3D model using CAD software such as Pro/Engineer. *Courtesy of PTC.*

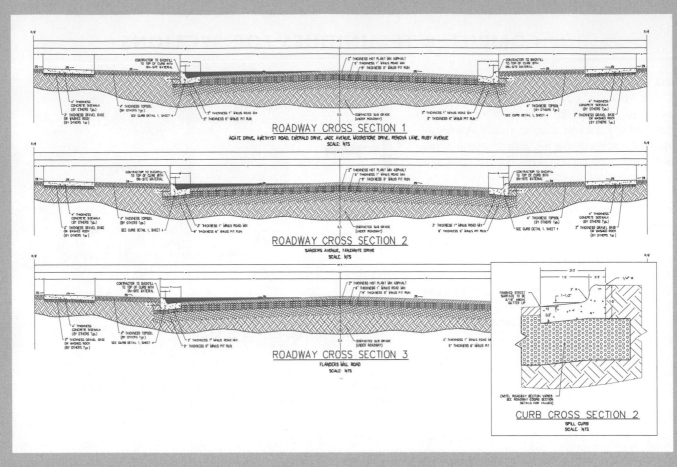

Roadway Sections. (Excerpted from a Larger Drawing). *Courtesy of Locati Architects.*

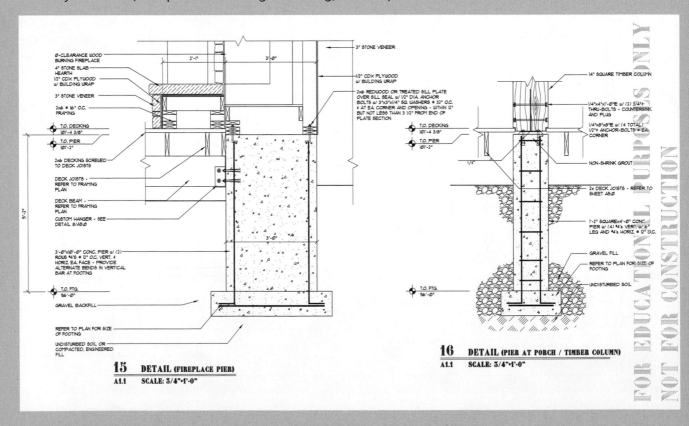

Section Detail. (Excerpted from a Larger Drawing). *Courtesy of Locati Architects.*

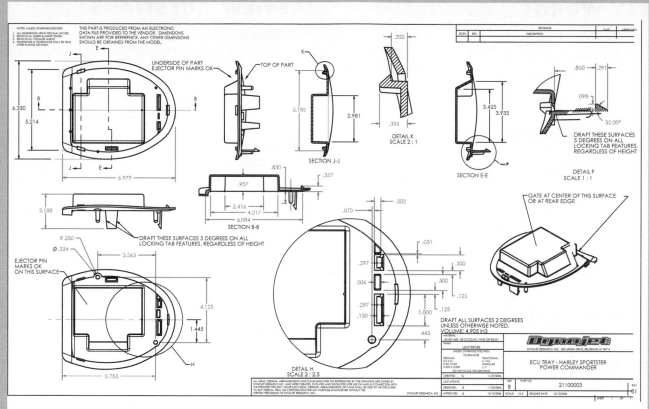

Detail Drawing for an Injection Molded Plastic Part with Removed Section Views. *Courtesy of Dynojet Research, Inc.*

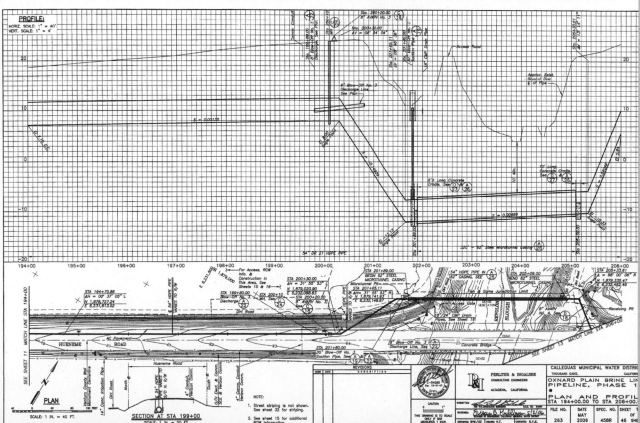

Plan and Profile Drawing with Sections. *Courtesy of Perliter & Ingalsbee Consulting Engineers.*

KEY WORDS

Section Views

Full Section

Cutting-Plane Line

Section Lining

Hatching

Section-Lining Symbols

Half Section

Broken Out Section

Revolved Section

Removed Section

Rotation Arrow

Partial Section

Offset Section

Aligned Section

Conventional Breaks

SUMMARY

Now that you have finished this chapter, you should be able to:

- Show internal details of objects without the need for hidden lines through the use of section views.
- Imagine a variety of objects cut apart along a cutting-plane line.
- Show section lining (hatching) to indicate the solid parts of the object which would be cut by the cutting plane.
- Check that you are not showing hidden lines where they would no longer be needed because the internal surfaces are exposed when the object is imagined cut.
- Use section lining symbols to indicate the material of the object.
- Leave the section lining off ribs, webs, and spokes that are sectioned lengthwise.
- Revolve symmetric features so the sectional view depicts the part's symmetry.
- Use conventional breaks on drawings to show object details when they would appear too small at a scale where the entire object would be shown on the sheet.
- Identify cross section assembly drawings.

REVIEW QUESTIONS

1. What does the cutting-plane line represent?
2. Sketch the section line symbols for ten different materials.
3. List seven different types of sections and sketch an example of each.
4. Which sectional views are used to replace an existing primary view? Which sectional views are used in addition to the primary views?
5. How much of an object is imagined to be cut away in a half section?
6. What type of line is used to show the boundary of a broken out section?
7. Why are hidden lines generally omitted in a sectional view?
8. Why are some symmetrical features, like spokes and webs, revolved in the sectional view?
9. Why is a rib outlined with object lines and not filled with section lining?

SECTIONING EXERCISES

Any of the following exercises may be drawn freehand or with CAD. Study the chapter on dimensioning first if you are going to add dimensions to your drawings. Show cutting-plane lines for practice. Can you tell that in Exercises 6.4 number 2 and number 14 the cutting-planes lines should be shown to make the drawing easy to interpret?

Freehand Sectioning Problems

Exercises 6.1–6.4 are especially suited for sketching on 8.5" × 11" graph paper with appropriate grid squares. Sketch one or two problems per sheet, adding section views as indicated. To make your drawings fit on the paper easily, use each grid square as equal to either 6 mm or 1/4". An example is shown below.
Freehand Sectioning Exercise Example

Exercise 6.1 Freehand Sectioning Problems. Redraw the given views and add the front section view.

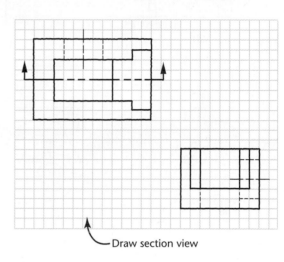

Draw section view

Exercise 6.2 Freehand Sectioning Problems. Redraw the top view, rotate the side view and move it into a position so that you can project the front view in section. Add the front section view. Each grid square equals 6 mm (¼")

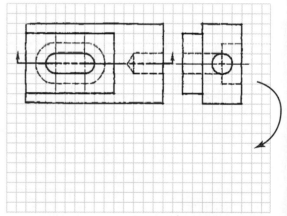

Rotate side view into position

Exercise 6.3 Freehand Sectioning Problems. Use the same directions for exercise 6.2

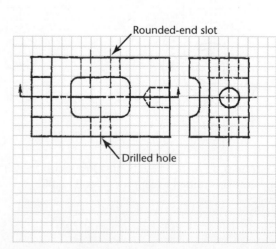

Rounded-end slot

Drilled hole

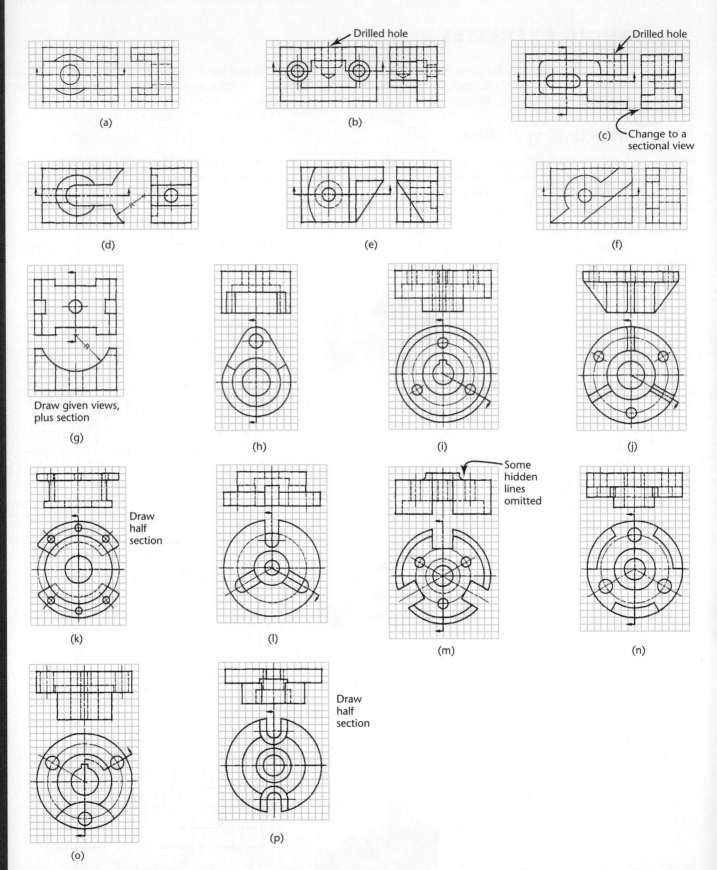

Exercise 6.4 Freehand Sectioning Problems. Sketch views and add sections as indicated by the cutting plane lines. Cutting plane lines can be omitted except for parts B and C.

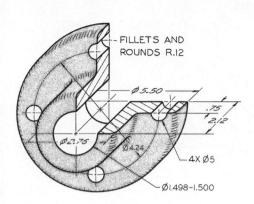

FILLETS AND ROUNDS R.12
Ø5.50
.75
2.12
Ø2.75
Ø4.24
4X Ø5
Ø1.498-1.500

Exercise 6.5 Bearing. Draw necessary views, with full section.*

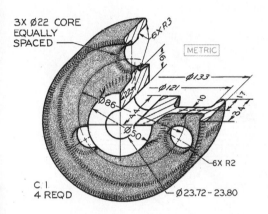

3X Ø22 CORE EQUALLY SPACED
6X R3
METRIC
Ø133
Ø121
Ø86
Ø50
6X R2
C.I. 4 REQD
Ø23.72 - 23.80

Exercise 6.6 Truck Wheel. Draw necessary views, with full section.*

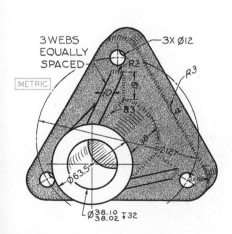

3 WEBS EQUALLY SPACED
3X Ø12
R2
R3
METRIC
R3
Ø12
Ø63.5
Ø38.10 / 38.02 ↧32

Exercise 6.7 Column Support. Draw necessary views, with full section.*

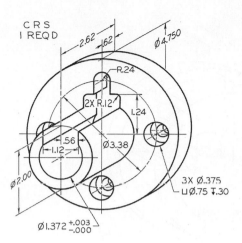

CRS I REQD
2.62
.62
Ø4.750
R.24
2X R.12
1.24
.56
1.12
Ø3.38
Ø2.00
3X Ø.375
⊔Ø.75 ↧.30
Ø1.372 +.003/-.000

Exercise 6.8 Centering Bushing. Draw necessary views, with full section.*

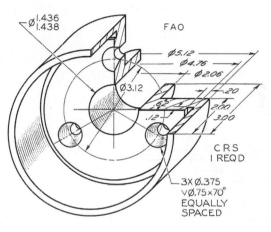

Ø1.436/1.438
FAO
Ø5.12
Ø4.76
Ø2.06
Ø3.12
.62
.20
.12
2.00
3.00
CRS I REQD
3X Ø.375
∨Ø.75×70° EQUALLY SPACED

Exercise 6.9 Special Bearing. Draw necessary views, with full section.*

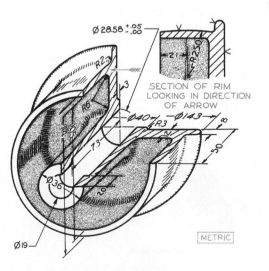

Ø28.58 +.05/-.00
R2.50
.21
SECTION OF RIM LOOKING IN DIRECTION OF ARROW
R2
.3
R6
Ø40
R3
Ø143
.73
Ø36
Ø19
METRIC

Exercise 6.10 Idler Pulley. Draw necessary views, with full section.*

*Leave out dimensions unless assigned by your instructor.

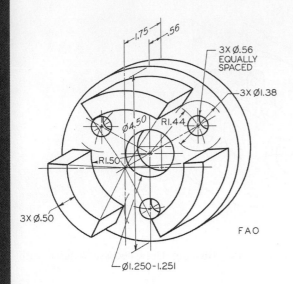

Exercise 6.11 Cup Washer. Draw necessary views, with full section.*

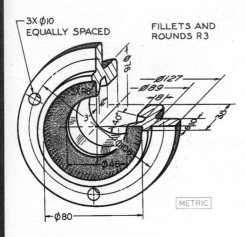

Exercise 6.12 Fixed Bearing Cup. Draw necessary views, with full section.*

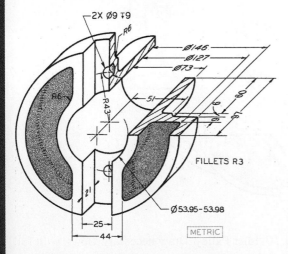

Exercise 6.13 Stock Guide. Draw necessary views, with half section.*

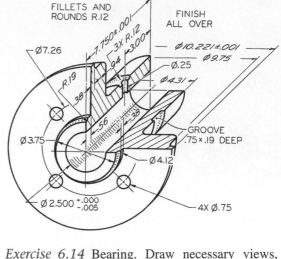

Exercise 6.14 Bearing. Draw necessary views, with half section. Scale: half size.*

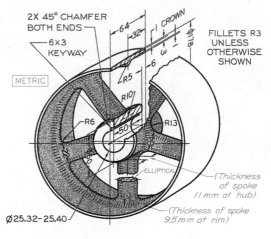

Exercise 6.15 Pulley. Draw necessary views, with full section, and revolved section of spoke.*

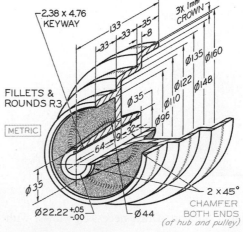

Exercise 6.16 Step-Cone Pulley. Draw necessary views, with full section.*

*Leave out dimensions unless assigned by your instructor.

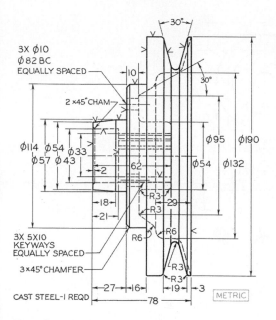

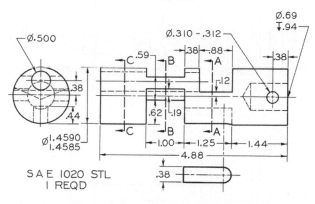

Exercise 6.17 Sheave. Draw two views, including half section.*

Exercise 6.18 Operating Valve. Given: Front, left-side, and partial bottom views. Required: Front, right-side, and full bottom views, plus indicated removed sections.*

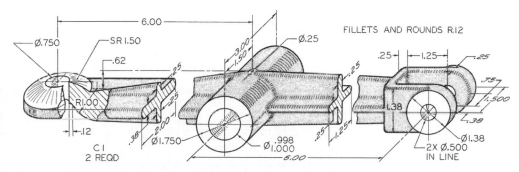

Exercise 6.19 Rocker Arm. Draw necessary views, with revolved sections.*

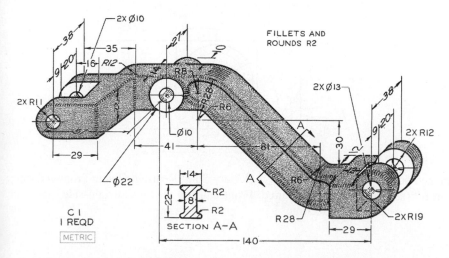

Exercise 6.20 Dash Pot Lifter. Draw necessary views, using revolved section instead of removed section.*

*Leave out dimensions unless assigned by your instructor.

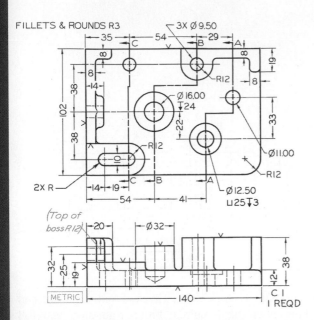

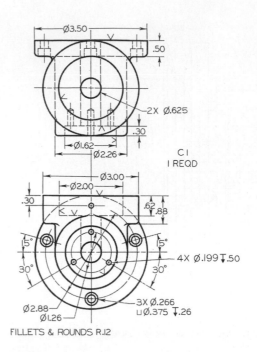

Exercise 6.21 Adjuster Base. Given: Front and top views. Required: Front and top views and sections A–A, B–B, and C–C. Show all visible lines.*

Exercise 6.23 Hydraulic Fitting. Given: Front and top views. Required: Front and top views and right-side view in full section.*

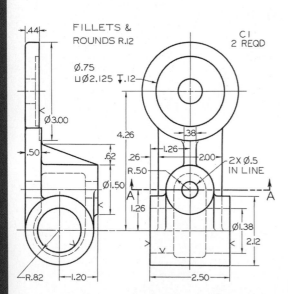

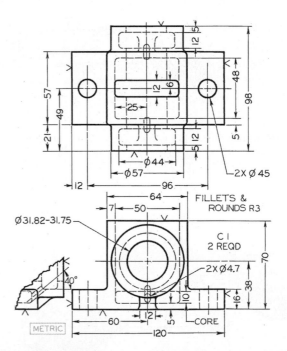

Exercise 6.22 Mobile Housing. Given: Front and left-side views. Required: Front view, right-side view in full section, and removed section A–A.*

Exercise 6.24 Auxiliary Shaft Bearing. Given: Front and top views. Required: Front and top views and right-side view in full section.*

*Leave out dimensions unless assigned by your instructor.

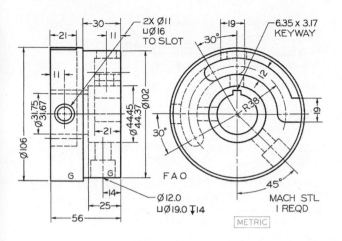

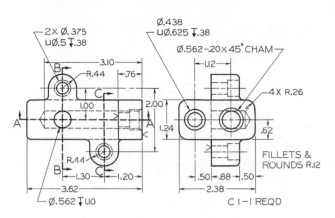

Exercise 6.25 Traverse Spider. Given: Front and left-side views. Required: Front and right-side views and top view in full section.*

Exercise 6.27 Bracket. Given: Front and right-side views. Required: Take front as new top; then add right-side view, front view in full section A–A, and sections B–B and C–C.*

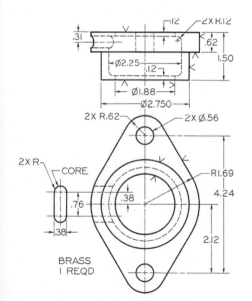

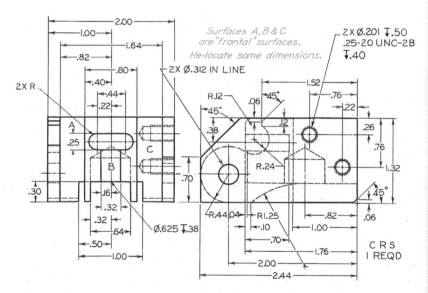

Exercise 6.26 Gland. Given: Front, top, and partial left-side views. Required: Front view and right-side view in full section.*

Exercise 6.28 Cocking Block. Given: Front and right-side views. Required: Take front as new top view; then add new front view, and right-side view in full section. Draw double size.*

*Leave out dimensions unless assigned by your instructor.

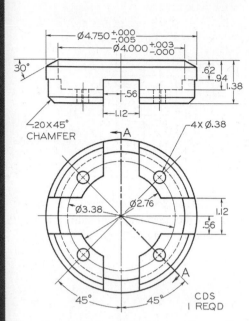

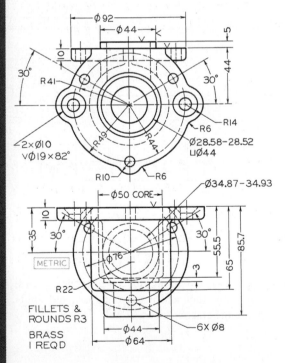

Exercise 6.29 Packing Ring. Given: Front and top views. Required: Front view and section A–A.*

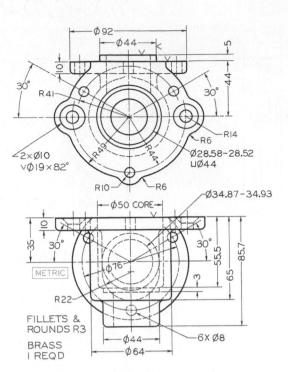

Exercise 6.31 Oil Retainer. Given: Front and top views. Required: Front view and section A–A.*

Exercise 6.30 Strainer Body. Given: Front and bottom views. Required: Front and top views and right-side view in full section.*

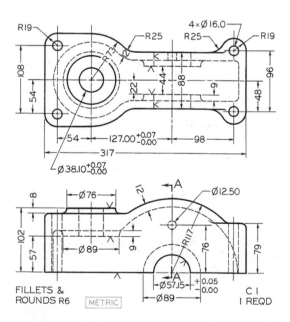

Exercise 6.32 Gear Box. Given: Front and top views. Required: Front in full section, bottom view, and right-side section A–A. Draw half size.*

*Leave out dimensions unless assigned by your instructor.

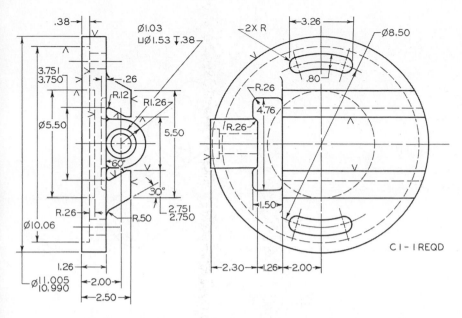

Exercise 6.33 Slotted Disk for Threading Machine. Given: Front and left-side views. Required: Front and right-side views and top full-section view. Draw half size.*

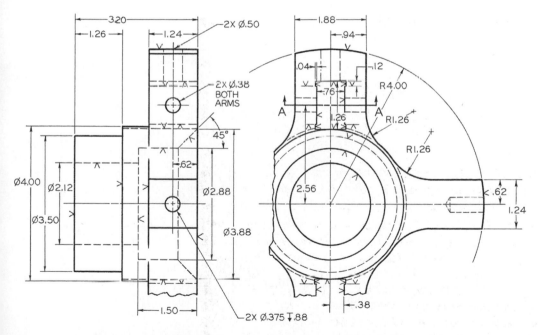

Exercise 6.34 Web for Lathe Clutch. Given: Partial front and left-side views. Required: Full front view, right-side view in full section, and removed section A–A.*

*Leave out dimensions unless assigned by your instructor.

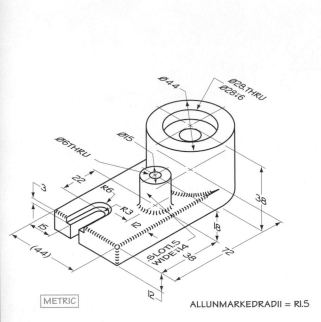

Exercise 6.35 Draw necessary views adding a section view.

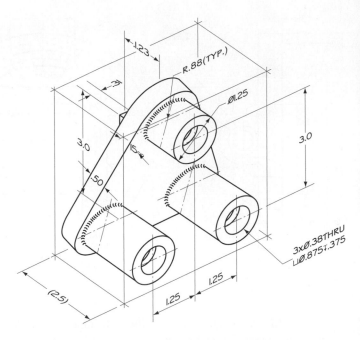

Exercise 6.36 Bushing. Draw necessary views with a broken out section.*

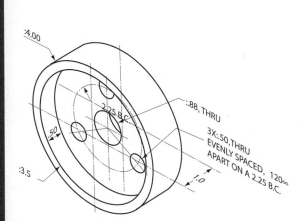

Exercise 6.37 Plastic Spacer. Draw all necessary views using an aligned section.*

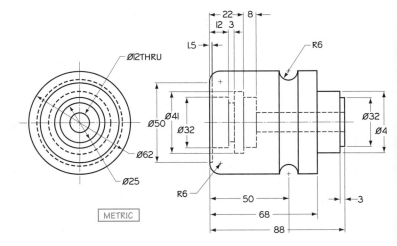

Exercise 6.38 Motor. Draw all required views with one half section.*

*Leave out dimensions unless assigned by your instructor.

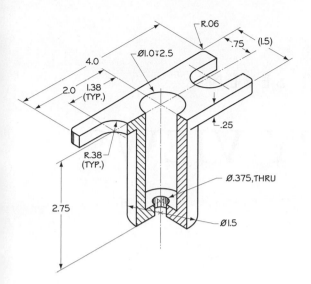

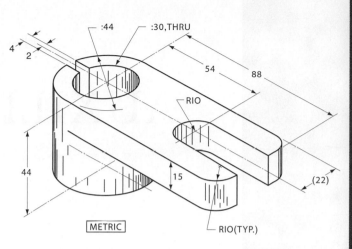

Exercise 6.39 Mounting Pin. Draw the necessary views showing the front view as a half section.*

Exercise 6.40 Clamp. Draw the necessary views showing the front view as a full section.*

---

*Leave out dimensions unless assigned by your instructor.

CHAPTER SEVEN

AUXILIARY VIEWS

───────── **OBJECTIVES** ─────────

After studying the material in this chapter, you should be able to:

1. Create an auxiliary view from orthographic views.

2. Draw folding lines or reference-plane lines between any two adjacent views.

3. Construct depth, height, or width auxiliary views.

4. Plot curves in auxiliary views.

5. Construct partial auxiliary views.

6. Create auxiliary section views.

7. Produce views to show the true length of a line, point view of a line, edge view of a surface, and true size view of a surface.

8. Show the true size of the angle between two planes (dihedral angle).

9. Construct the development of prisms, pyramids, cylinders, and cones.

10. Use triangulation to transfer surface shapes to a development.

11. Create the development of transition pieces.

12. Graphically solve for the intersection of solids.

13. Apply revolution to show true length edges and true size surfaces.

─────────────────────────────

Refer to the following standard:
- ANSI/ASME Y14.3—2003 Multiview and Sectional View Drawings

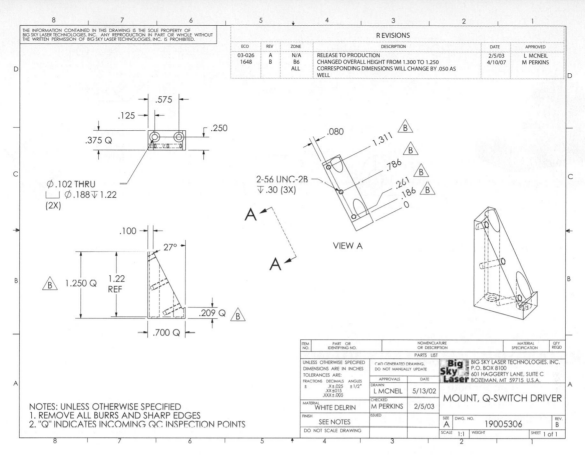

Auxiliary View Drawing. *This switch mount uses an auxiliary view to show the true size of the inclined surface. Courtesy of Big Sky Laser.*

OVERVIEW

Inclined planes and oblique lines do not appear true size or true length in any of the principal planes of projection. To show the true length of an oblique line or the true size of an inclined plane, an auxiliary view must be created. The principles for creating auxiliary views are the same whether you are using traditional drawing, sketching, or CAD: a line of sight and reference plane are defined. With traditional drawing, the view is manually created along line-of-sight projectors. With CAD drawing, the computer generates the view automatically if a 3D model of the object was originally created. Even if you are going to be using a CAD system to generate auxiliary views, it is important to understand the theory of developable surfaces. Some surfaces cannot be developed or "flattened out" to make an exact flat pattern for creating parts from sheet metal, cardboard packaging, or fabric. For example, a sphere can only be approximated. Understanding the development methods can aid you in using your CAD software to the fullest extent.

See the following Web sites:
- http://www.papertoys.com
- http://www.paperedcase.com

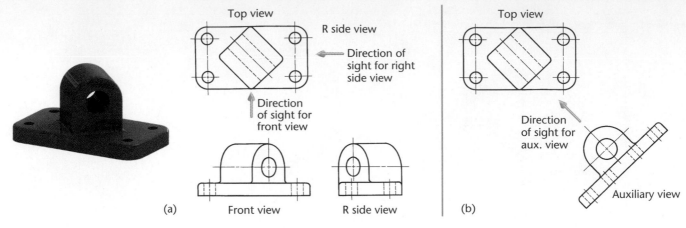

7.1 Regular Views and Auxiliary Views

UNDERSTANDING AUXILIARY VIEWS

Auxiliary views are useful for both design and documentation. Many objects are shaped so that their principal faces are not parallel to the standard planes of projection. For example, in Figure 7.1a the base of the design for the bearing is shown in its **true size** and shape, but the rounded upper portion is at an angle, so it does not appear true size and shape in any of the three regular views. When creating a drawing for documentation, you will often need to show the true size and shape of surfaces and angles. Likewise, you may need to create true size flat patterns for sheet metal, packaging, and other purposes.

To show the true circular shapes, use a direction of sight perpendicular to the plane of the curve, to produce a view as shown in Figure 7.1b. The result is an **auxiliary view:** an orthographic view that is not a standard projection. This view, together with the top view, completely describes the object. The front and right-side views are not necessary.

The Auxiliary Plane

The object shown in Figure 7.2a has an inclined surface (P) that does not appear in its true size and shape in any regular view. To show the inclined surface true size, the direction of sight must be perpendicular to the inclined plane. Or using the glass box model, the auxiliary plane is aligned parallel to the inclined surface P to give a true-size view of it. The **auxiliary plane** in this case is perpendicular to the frontal plane of projection and hinged to it. It is angled to the horizontal (top) and profile (side) viewing planes.

The horizontal and auxiliary planes are unfolded into the plane of the front view, as shown in Figure 7.2. Drawings do not show the planes of the glass box, but you can think of **folding lines** (H/F and F/T) representing the hinges that join the planes. The folding lines themselves are usually omitted in the actual drawing.

Inclined surface P is shown in its true size and shape in the auxiliary view. Note that both the top and auxiliary views show the depth of the object. One dimension of the surface is projected directly from the front view, and the depth is transferred from the top view.

As you learned in Chapter 4, the locations of the folding lines depend on the size of the glass box and the location of the object within it. If the object is further down in the box, distance Y is increased. If the object is moved back in the box, distances X increase but are still equal. If the object is moved to the left inside the glass box, distance Z is increased.

Primary Auxiliary Views

Any view obtained by orthographic projection onto a plane other than the horizontal, frontal, and profile projection planes is an auxiliary view. A **primary auxiliary view** is projected onto a plane that is perpendicular to one of the principal planes of projection and is inclined to the other two. Figure 7.3 shows examples of primary auxiliary views.

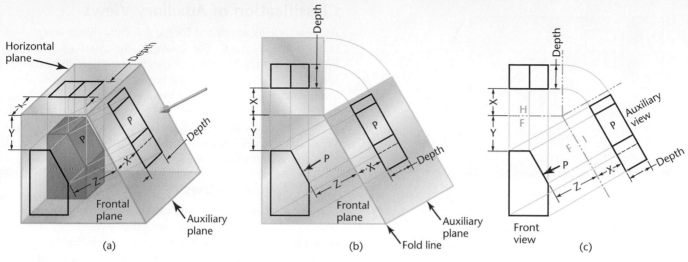

7.2 An Auxiliary View

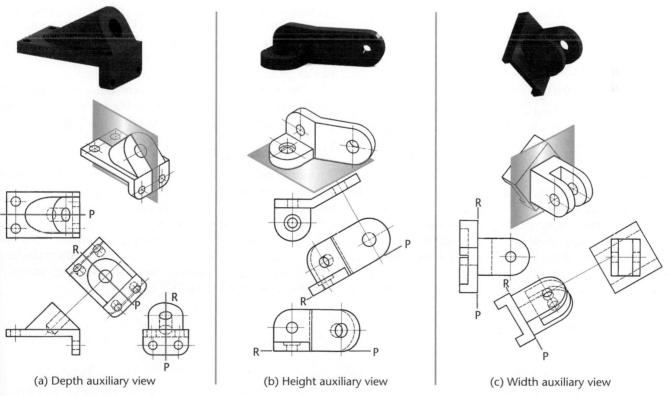

(a) Depth auxiliary view

(b) Height auxiliary view

(c) Width auxiliary view

7.3 Primary Auxiliary Views

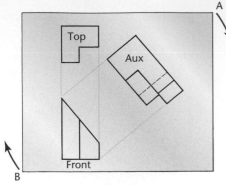

(a) Given drawing

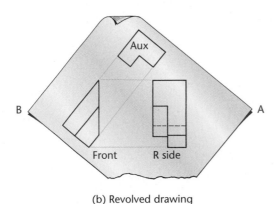

(b) Revolved drawing

7.4 Revolving a Drawing

Visualizing Auxiliary Views as a Revolved Drawing

In Figure 7.4a is a drawing showing top, front, and auxiliary views. Figure 7.4b shows the drawing revolved, as indicated by the arrows, until the auxiliary view and the front view line up horizontally. Although the views remain exactly the same, the names of the views are changed if drawn in this position. The auxiliary view now becomes a right-side view, and the top view becomes an auxiliary view. Sometimes it is easier to visualize and draw an auxiliary view when revolved to the position of a regular view in this manner. In any case, it should be understood that an auxiliary view basically is like any other view.

Classification of Auxiliary Views

Auxiliary views are named for the principal dimension shown in the auxiliary view. For example, the auxiliary views in Figure 7.5 are depth auxiliary views because they show the object's depth. Any auxiliary view projected from the front view, also known as a front adjacent view, is a depth auxiliary view.

Similarly, any auxiliary view projected from the top view, also known as a top adjacent view, is a height auxiliary view; and any auxiliary view projected from a side view, also known as a side adjacent view, is a width auxiliary view.

Depth Auxiliary Views

An infinite number of auxiliary planes can be hinged perpendicular to the frontal plane (F) of projection. Five such planes are shown in Figure 7.5a. The horizontal plane is included to show that it is similar to the others. All these views show the object's depth and therefore are all **depth auxiliary views.**

The unfolded auxiliary planes, shown in Figure 7.5b, show how depth dimensions are projected from the top view to all auxiliary views. The arrows indicate the directions of sight.

The complete drawing, with the outlines of the planes of projection omitted, is shown in Figure 7.5c. Note that the front view shows the height and the width of the object, but not the depth. The principal dimension shown in an auxiliary view is the one not shown in the adjacent view from which the auxiliary view was projected.

Height Auxiliary Views

An infinite number of auxiliary planes can be hinged perpendicular to the horizontal plane (H) of projection. Several are shown in Figure 7.6a. The front view and all these auxiliary views show the height of the object. Therefore, all these auxiliary views are **height auxiliary views.**

The unfolded projection planes are shown in Figure 7.6b, and the complete drawing is shown in Figure 7.6c. Note that in the top view, the only dimension not shown is height.

Width Auxiliary Views

An infinite number of auxiliary planes can also be hinged perpendicular to the profile plane (P) of projection. Some are shown in Figure 7.7a. The front view and all these auxiliary views are **width auxiliary views.**

The unfolded planes are shown in Figure 7.7b, and the complete drawing is shown in Figure 7.7c. In the right-side view, from which the auxiliary views are projected, the only dimension not shown is width.

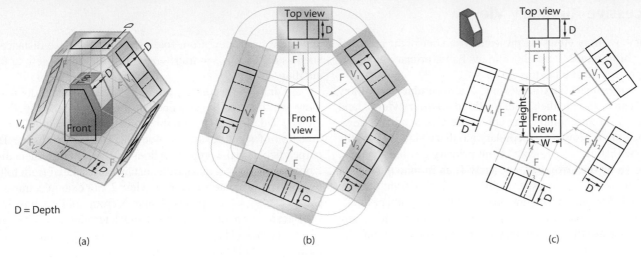

D = Depth

(a)   (b)   (c)

7.5 Depth Auxiliary Views

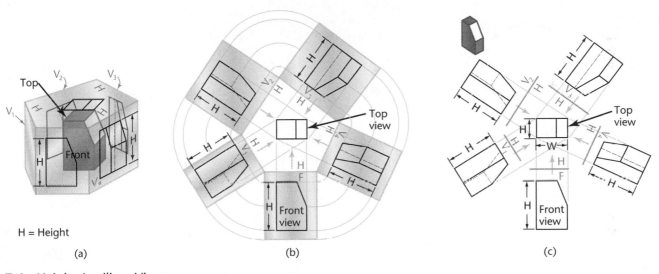

H = Height

(a)   (b)   (c)

7.6 Height Auxiliary Views

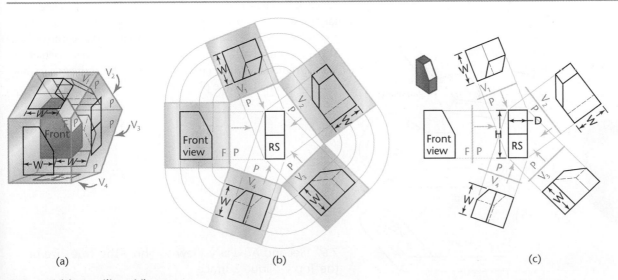

(a)   (b)   (c)

7.7 Width Auxiliary Views

Successive Auxiliary Views

Primary auxiliary views are projected from one of the principal views. In Figure 7.8, auxiliary view 1 is a primary auxiliary view projected from the top view.

From primary auxiliary view 1 a **secondary auxiliary view** 2 can be drawn; then from it a **third auxiliary view** 3, and so on. An infinite number of such successive auxiliary views may be drawn. However, secondary auxiliary view 2 is not the only one that can be projected from primary auxiliary view 1. As shown by the arrows around view 1, an infinite number of secondary auxiliary views, with different lines of sight, may be projected. Any auxiliary view projected from a primary auxiliary view is a secondary auxiliary view. Furthermore, any **succeeding auxiliary view** may be used to project an infinite series of views from it.

In this example, folding lines are more convenient than reference-plane lines. In auxiliary view 1, all numbered points of the object are the same distance from folding line H/1 as they are in the front view from folding line H/F. These distances, such as distance a, are transferred from the front view to the auxiliary view.

To draw the secondary auxiliary view 2, ignore the front view and focus on the sequence of three views: the top view, view 1, and view 2. Draw light projection lines parallel to the direction of sight desired for view 2. Draw folding line 1/2 perpendicular to the projection lines and at any convenient distance from view 1. Transfer the distances measured from folding line H/1 to locate all points in view 2. For example, transfer distance b to locate points 4 and 5 from folding line 1/2. Connect points to draw the object and determine visibility. The closest corner (11) in view 2 will be visible, and the one farthest away (1) will be hidden, as shown.

To draw views 3, 4, and so on, use a similar process. Remember to use the correct sequence of three views.

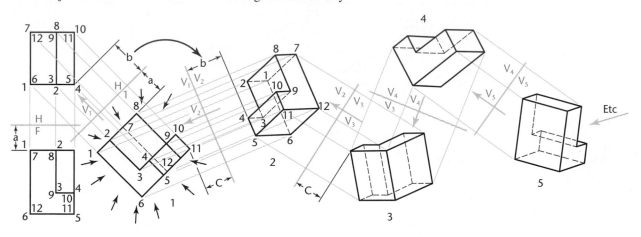

7.8   Successive Auxiliary Views

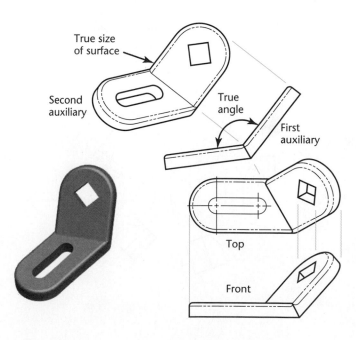

Secondary Auxiliary Views

A secondary auxiliary view is projected from a primary auxiliary view onto a plane that is inclined to all three principal projection planes. As shown in Figure 7.9 a part that has an oblique surface often requires a second auxiliary view to show that surface's true size and shape. In this case, the primary auxiliary view shows the oblique plane on edge.

7.9   Second Auxiliary View to Show the True Size of the Top Oblique Surface

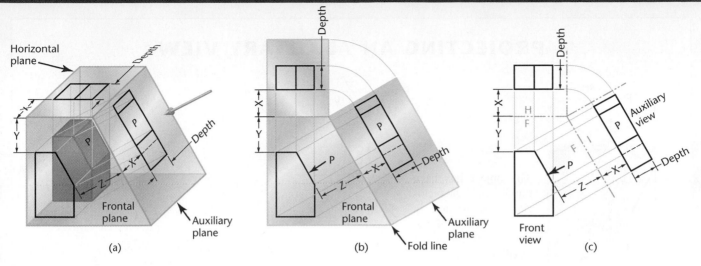

7.10   An Auxiliary View

Reference Planes

In the auxiliary view shown in Figure 7.10c, the folding line represents the edge view of the frontal plane of projection. In this case, the frontal plane is used for transferring distances—that is, depth measurements—from the top view to the auxiliary view.

Instead of using one of the planes of projection, you can use a **reference plane** parallel to the plane of projection and touching or cutting through the object. For example, in Figure 7.11a, a reference plane is aligned with the front surface of the object. This plane appears on edge, or as a line, in the top and auxiliary views. The two reference lines are used in the same manner as folding lines. Dimensions D in the top view and auxiliary views are equal. The advantage of the reference-plane method is that fewer measurements are required because some points of the object lie in the reference plane. Make the reference plane using light lines similar to construction lines.

You can use a reference plane that coincides with the front surface of the object, as shown in Figure 7.11a. When an object is symmetrical, it is useful to select the reference plane to cut through the object, as shown in Figure 7.11b. This way you only have to make half as many measurements to transfer

> **TIP**
>
> If you are using 2D CAD, you can draw half of the view and then mirror the object. You can also use the back surface of the object, as shown in Figure 7.11c, or any intermediate point that would be advantageous.

dimensions because they are the same on each side of the reference plane.

Position the reference plane so it is convenient for transferring distances. Remember the following:

1. Reference lines, like folding lines, are always at right angles to the projection lines between the views.
2. A reference plane appears as a line in two **alternate views,** never in **adjacent views.**
3. Measurements are always made at right angles to the reference lines or parallel to the projection lines.
4. In the auxiliary view, all points are at the same distances from the reference line as the corresponding points are from the reference line in the alternate view, or the second previous view.

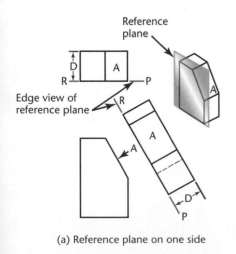

(a) Reference plane on one side

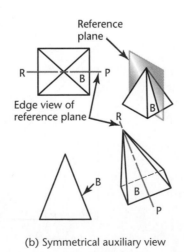

(b) Symmetrical auxiliary view

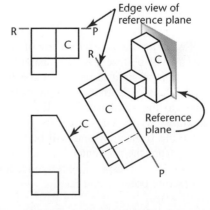

(c) Nonsymmetrical auxiliary view

7.11   Position of the Reference Plane

PROJECTING AN AUXILIARY VIEW

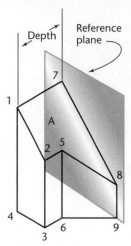

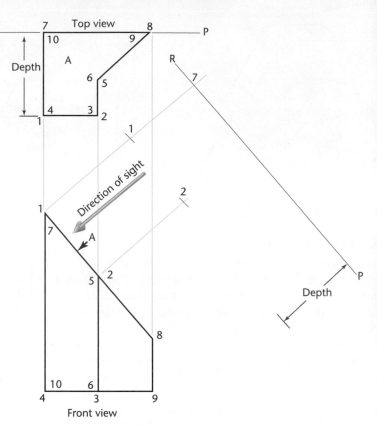

The object has been numbered in the pictorial view to aid in keeping track of the vertices. To create the auxiliary view:

1 Draw two views of the object and determine the direction of sight needed to produce a view which will show the true size of surface A.

Next sketch projection lines parallel to the direction of sight.

Establish a reference plane. In this case the back surface of the object will work well. The reference lines in the top and auxiliary views are at right angles to the projection lines. These are the edge views of the reference plane.

2 Draw the auxiliary view of surface A. It will be true size and shape because the direction of sight is perpendicular to that surface. Transfer depth measurements from the top view to the auxiliary view. Each point in the auxiliary view will be on its projection line from the front view and will be the same distance from the reference line as it is in the top view to the corresponding reference line. Finish projecting points 5 and 8.

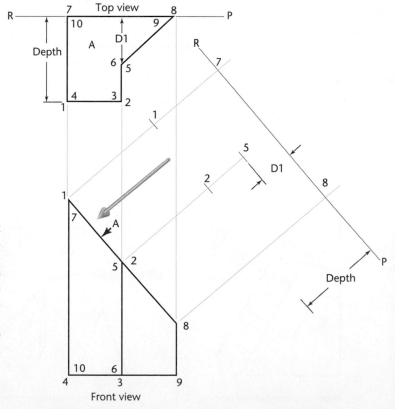

7.1 USING TRIANGLES TO SKETCH AUXILIARY VIEWS

You can use two triangles to quickly draw parallel and perpendicular lines for "accurate" sketches.

- Place two triangles together so that the 90° corners are on the outside, as shown in Figure 7.12.
- Slide them on your drawing until the outer edge of one triangle is along the line to which you want to sketch parallel.
- Hold down the triangle and slide the other along it.
- Draw parallel lines along one edge of the triangle. Draw perpendicular lines along the other edge.

This technique works well as an addition to freehand sketching when you want to show an auxiliary view.

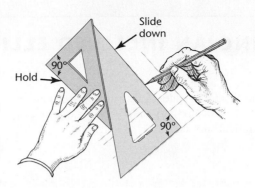

7.12 Triangles Can Be Used to Help Sketch Auxiliary Views

7.2 USING GRID PAPER TO SKETCH AUXILIARY VIEWS

You can use grid paper to help sketch auxiliary views by orienting the lines of the grid paper underneath your vellum or other semitransparent drawing sheet so that the grid is parallel to the inclined edge in the drawing, as shown in Figure 7.13. Use the grid to help sketch lines parallel and perpendicular to the edge in question.

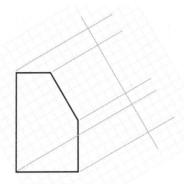

7.13 Sketching Auxiliary Views Using Grid Paper

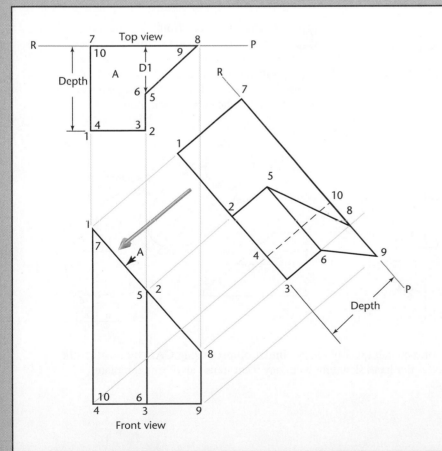

3 Draw surface A true size in the auxiliary view by connecting the vertices in the same order as they are shown connecting in the top view (1-7-8-5-2-1).

Complete the auxiliary view by adding other visible edges and surfaces of the object. Each numbered point in the auxiliary view lies on its projection line from the front view and is the same distance from the reference line as it is in the top view. Note that two surfaces of the object appear as lines in the auxiliary view.

S T E P by S T E P

SHOWING AN INCLINED ELLIPTICAL SURFACE TRUE SIZE

Given the front and side views shown, use these steps to project an auxiliary view showing true size of the elliptical surface.

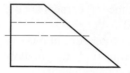

1 Since this is a symmetrical object, use a reference plane through the center of the object, as shown.

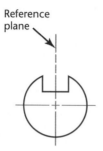

2 Select points on the circle in the side view.

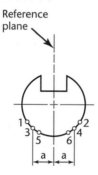

3 Locate the same points on the inclined surface and the left-end surface.

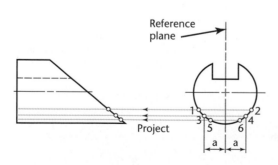

4 Project each point to the auxiliary view along its projection line.

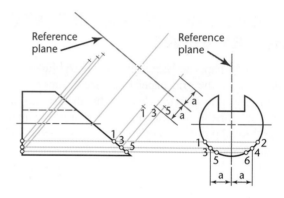

5 Transfer distances from the side view to the auxiliary view. Because the object is symmetrical, two points can be located with each measurement, as shown for points 1–2, 3–4, and 5–6. Project enough points to sketch the curves accurately.

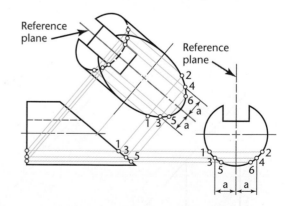

Since the major and minor axes are known, you can quickly create similar ellipses using CAD by locating the major and minor axes or the center and axes. For hand sketching you may want to use an ellipse template.

7.3 USING CAD TO CREATE AUXILIARY VIEWS

Most CAD systems allow you to rotate the grid or to create a new coordinate system (often called the user coordinate system) so that it aligns with the inclined surface. See Figure 7.14. If you are using 3D CAD, you can create auxiliary views by viewing the object perpendicular to the surface you want to show true size.

7.4 CIRCLES AND ELLIPSES IN AUXILIARY VIEWS

Keep in mind that circular shapes appear as elliptical when viewed at an angle other than 90° (straight on to the circular shape). This is frequently the case when constructing auxiliary views (Figure 7.15).

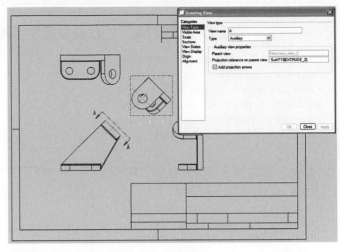

7.14 CAD Software Provides Tools for Generating Auxiliary Views. *Courtesy of Solidworks Corporation.*

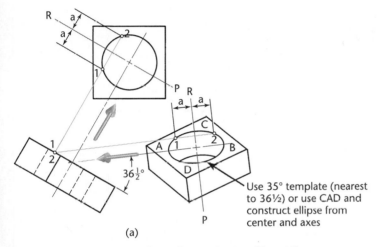

Use 35° template (nearest to 36½) or use CAD and construct ellipse from center and axes

(a)

(b)

7.15 Circles Projected as Ellipses in Auxiliary Views

7.5 HIDDEN LINES IN AUXILIARY VIEWS

Generally, hidden lines should be omitted in auxiliary views, unless they are needed to clearly communicate the drawing's intent. Note the use of hidden lines in Figure 7.16.

> **TIP**
> Your instructor may ask you to show all hidden lines for visualization practice, especially if the auxiliary view of the entire object is shown. Later, when you are familiar with drawing auxiliary views, omit hidden lines when they do not add needed information to the drawing.

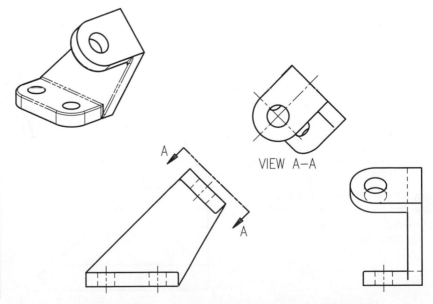

VIEW A–A

7.16 Omit Hidden Lines from Auxiliary Views When Possible

PLOTTING CURVES IN AN AUXILIARY VIEW

Use the following steps to create an auxiliary view that shows the true size and shape of the inclined cut through a piece of molding. The method of plotting points is similar to that explained for the ellipse.

1 Identify some points along the curve shown in the side view. Locate those same points in the front view. The curved shape is the inclined surface.

2 Locate the reference plane and project the points into the auxiliary view.

3 Finish projecting all of the points on the inclined surface and draw its true shape in the auxiliary view.

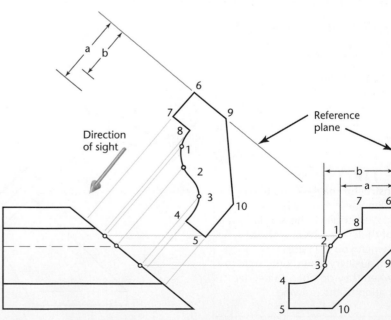

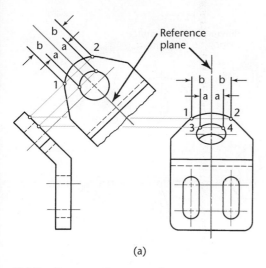

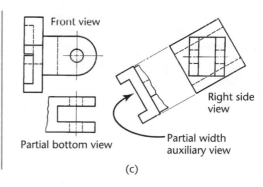

7.17   Reverse Construction

7.6 REVERSE CONSTRUCTION

To complete the regular views, it is often necessary to first construct an auxiliary view where critical dimensions will be shown true size. For example, in Figure 7.17a, the upper part of the right-side view cannot be constructed until the auxiliary view is drawn. First, points are established on the curves and then projected back to the front view.

In Figure 7.17b, the 60° angle and the location of line 1–2 in the front view are given. To locate line 3–4 in the front view and lines 2–4, 3–4, and 4–5 in the side view, you must first construct the 60° angle in the auxiliary view and project it back to the front and side views, as shown.

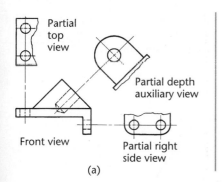

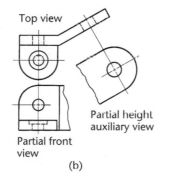

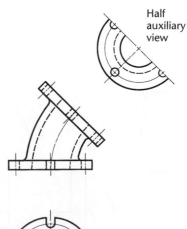

7.18   Partial Views

7.7 PARTIAL AUXILIARY VIEWS

Using an auxiliary view often makes it possible to omit one or more regular views, but auxiliary drawings are time consuming to create and may even be confusing because of the clutter of lines.

Partial views are often sufficient and easier to read. Figure 7.18 shows partial regular views and **partial auxiliary views**. Usually a break line is used to indicate the imaginary break in the views. Do not draw a break line coinciding with a visible line or hidden line.

So that partial auxiliary views (which are often small) do not appear "lost" and unrelated to any view, connect them to the views from which they project, either with a centerline or with one or two thin projection lines as shown in Figure 7.18.

7.8 HALF AUXILIARY VIEWS

If an auxiliary view is symmetrical, and if it is necessary to save space on the drawing or to save time, a **half auxiliary view** may be drawn, as shown in Figure 7.19. In this case, half of a regular view is also shown since the bottom flange is also symmetrical. Note that in each case the near half is shown.

7.19   Half Views

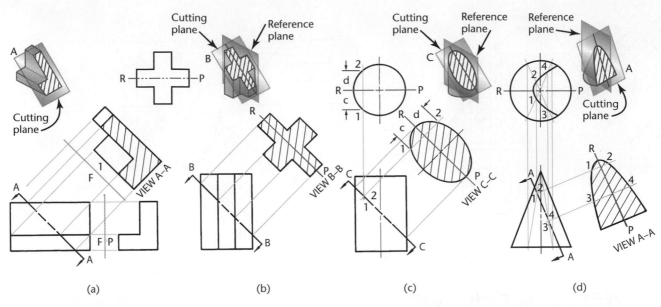

7.20 Auxiliary Sections

7.9 AUXILIARY SECTIONS

An **auxiliary section** is simply an auxiliary view in section. A typical auxiliary section is shown in Figure 7.20. In this example, there is not sufficient space for a revolved section, although a removed section could have been used instead of an auxiliary section. Note the cutting-plane line and the terminating arrows that indicate the direction of sight for the auxiliary section. In an auxiliary section drawing, the entire portion of the object behind the cutting plane may be shown, or the cut surface alone may be shown.

The cutting plane line indicates both the location of the cutting plane and the direction of sight for the auxiliary section. Figures 7.21 and 7.22 show examples of this. Notice that the auxiliary section is shown in alignment. Typically, a centerline is extended to locate the auxiliary sections or a few projection lines are shown in the drawing for this purpose.

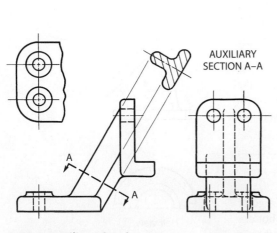

7.21 Auxiliary Section

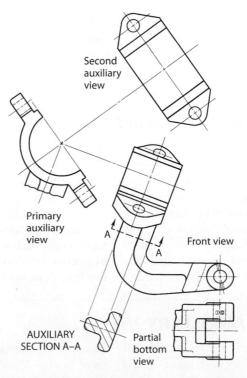

7.22 Secondary Auxiliary View—Partial Views

7.10 VIEWING-PLANE LINES AND ARROWS

When the drawing sheet is too crowded to show the auxiliary view in direction projection you can use a **viewing-plane line** or a **viewing direction arrow** to indicate the direction of sight for the auxiliary view.

A viewing-plane line and a cutting-plane line look essentially the same. The arrows on either end of the line point in the direction of sight for the removed view. The ends of the line are labeled with letters, starting with A, then B, and so on. The auxiliary view, when placed in a removed location, should still be shown in the same orientation it would have if it were aligned in projection. Figure 7.23a shows a removed auxiliary view and viewing-plane line.

A viewing direction arrow for a removed auxiliary view uses the same practices you learned in Chapter 4. Show an arrow pointing in the direction of sight for the removed auxiliary view. Label the removed view and place it in the same orientation it would have when projected, or if it is rotated, show a rotation arrow and specify the amount of rotation.

A centerline can be extended from a hole or other symmetric feature to indicate the alignment of the auxiliary view as shown in Figure 7.23b.

Viewing direction arrows are particularly useful when showing a second auxiliary view in a drawing that is created from a 3D CAD model. Often the primary auxiliary view is not necessary and can be left out if a viewing direction arrow is shown indicating the direction of sight for the second auxiliary view. An example of this use of a viewing direction arrow in a CAD drawing is shown in Figure 7.24.

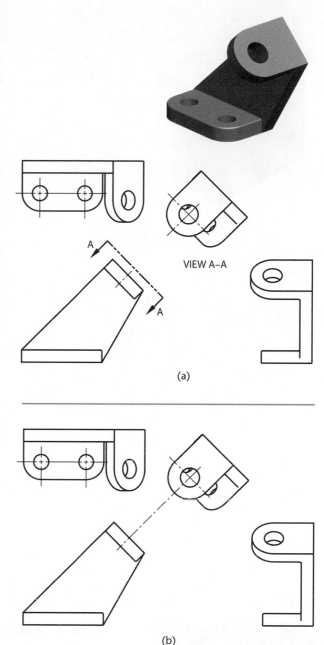

(a)

(b)

7.23 Using a Viewing Plane Line to Show the Direction of Sight for an Auxiliary View—Alternatively a Centerline Can Be Extended to Indicate the Viewing Direction

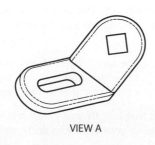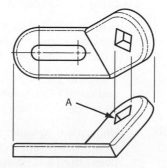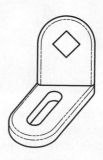

VIEW A

7.24 Arrow to Show the Direction of Sight for the View of an Oblique Surface

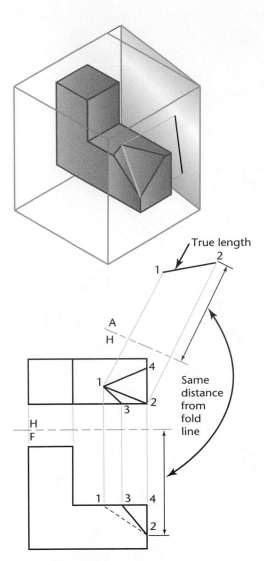

7.25 True Length of a Line

7.11 USES OF AUXILIARY VIEWS

Generally, auxiliary views are used to show the true shape or true angle of features that appear distorted in the regular views. Auxiliary views are often used to produce views which show the following:

1. True length of line
2. Point view of line
3. Edge view of plane
4. True size of plane

You can use the ability to generate views that show the specific things listed above to solve a variety of engineering problems. **Descriptive geometry** is the term for using accurate drawings to solve engineering problems. An accurate CAD drawing database can be used to solve many engineering problems when you understand the four basic views from descriptive geometry. Using 3D CAD, you can often model objects accurately and query the database for lengths and angles. Even so, you will often need the techniques described below to produce views which will help you visualize, create, or display 3D drawing geometry.

7.12 TRUE LENGTH OF A LINE

As shown in Figure 7.25, a line will show true length in a plane of projection that is parallel to the line. In other words, a line will show true length in an auxiliary view where the direction of sight is perpendicular to the line. To show a line true length, make the fold line parallel to the line you want to show true length in the auxiliary view. Whenever a line is parallel to the fold line between two views, it will be true length in the adjacent view.

TIP

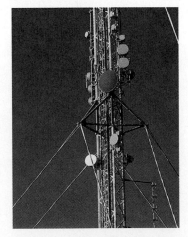

The slope of a guy wire can be determined when you see its true length. Foreshortened views do not show the actual angle

The Need to Show the True Length of a Line in CAD

Whether you are using 2D or 3D CAD or creating a sketch or drawing by hand, it is often necessary to understand how to create a view that shows a certain line true length. For example, a line must appear true length if you want to find its slope.

When you are working in a 3D CAD program, it is generally easy to list the true length of a line or an edge. But knowing the dimension is not the same as being able to show it on a drawing so that others can correctly interpret it.

In order to annotate the dimension on a drawing view where the line in question is shown true length you must understand how to create a view that is parallel to the line.

If you use 2D CAD you will use the same methods explained in this chapter. If you use 3D CAD, reading about how to show a line at true length will help you understand how to create a plane parallel to that line in 3D CAD.

Understanding when a line is true length and when it is foreshortened in a view is also helpful in developing your ability to accurately visualize a 3D object from a 2D drawing.

SHOWING THE TRUE LENGTH OF A HIP RAFTER

The top and front views of the hip rafter (line 1–2) are shown. Use an auxiliary view to show the line true length.

1 Choose the direction of sight to be perpendicular to line 1–2 (front view).

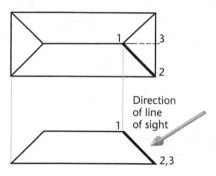

2 Draw the H/F folding line between the top and front view, as shown.

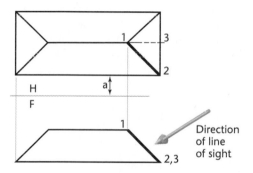

3 Draw the F/1 folding line parallel to line 1–2 and any convenient distance from line 1–2 (front view).

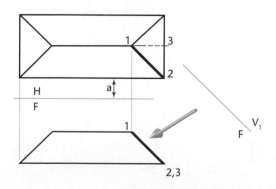

4 Draw projection lines from points 1, 2, and 3 to begin creating the auxiliary view.

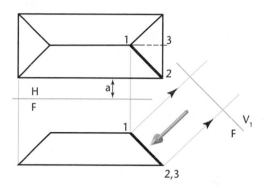

5 Transfer points 1 and 2 to the auxiliary view at the same distance from the folding line as they are in the top view, and along their respective projection lines. The hip rafter (line 1–2) is shown true length in the auxiliary view. Also, triangle 1–2–3 in the auxiliary view shows the true size and shape as that portion of the roof because the direction of sight for the auxiliary view is perpendicular to triangle 1–2–3.

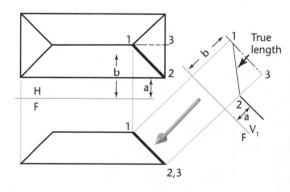

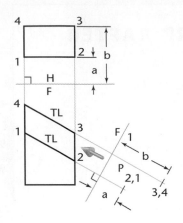

7.26 Point View of a Line

7.13 POINT VIEW OF A LINE

As shown in Figure 7.26, a line will show as a point view when projected to a plane perpendicular it. To show the point view of a line, choose the direction of sight parallel to the line where it is true length.

Showing the Point View of a Line

Refer to Figure 7.27 for the following steps:

1. Choose the direction of sight to be parallel to line 1–2.
2. Draw folding line H/F between the top and front view, as shown.
3. Draw folding line F/1 perpendicular to line 1–2 where it is true length, and any convenient distance from line 1–2 (front view).
4. Draw projection lines from points 1 and 2 to begin creating the auxiliary view.
5. Transfer points 1 and 2 to the auxiliary view at the same distance from the folding line as they are in the top view and along their respective projection lines. They will line up exactly with each other to form a point view of the line.

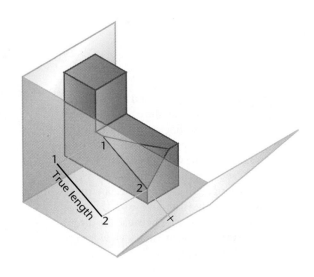

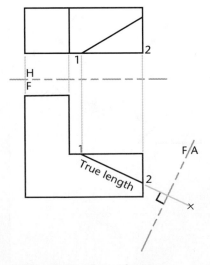

7.27 Point View of a Line

TIP
Viewing a Line as a Point

Draw a line in a plane—for example, a straight line on a sheet of paper. Then tilt the paper to view the line as a point. You will see that when the line appears as a point, the plane containing it appears as a line. (Since your paper will end up being viewed on edge, it may be a little hard to see the line when it is oriented correctly.)

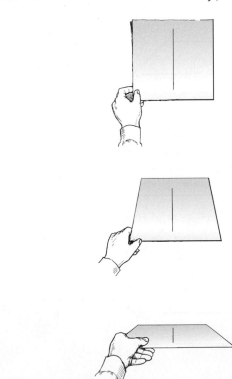

7.14 EDGE VIEW OF A PLANE

As shown in Figure 7.28, a plane will show on edge in a plane of projection that shows a point view of any line that lies entirely within the plane. To get the point view of a line, the direction of sight must be parallel to the line where it is true length. To show the edge view of a plane, choose the direction of sight parallel to a true length line lying in the plane.

Finding the edge view of a plane is a useful tool for the following types of problems:

- Finding the shortest line from a point to a plane. The shortest line will be perpendicular from the point to the plane. This is easiest to show in a view showing the plane on edge.

- Finding the slope of a plane. When you are working in a 3D CAD program, it is easy to create a view from any direction. Understanding how to choose a direction that will produce the most useful view for your purposes is easier yet when you understand these basic principles. Even though you can use CAD inquiry tools to quickly determine the angle between planes, often you may need to document the angle of a plane in a view showing the plane on edge.

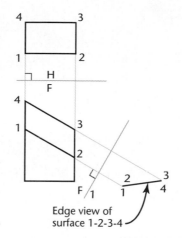

7.28   Edge View of a Surface

Showing the Edge View of a Plane

Refer to Figure 7.29 for the following steps:

1. Choose the direction of sight to be parallel to line 1–2 in the front view where it is already shown true length.
2. Draw folding line H/F between the top and front view, as shown.
3. Draw folding line F/1 perpendicular to true-length line 1–2 and any convenient distance.
4. Draw projection lines from points 1, 2, 3, and 4 to begin creating the auxiliary view.
5. Transfer points 1, 2, 3, and 4 to the auxiliary view at the same distance from the folding line as they are in the top view and along their respective projection lines. Plane 1–2–3–4 will appear on edge in the finished drawing.

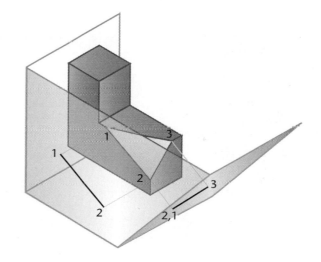

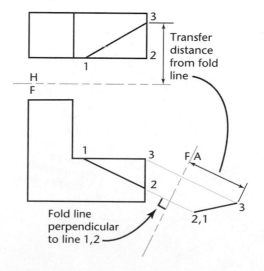

7.29   Edge View of a Plane

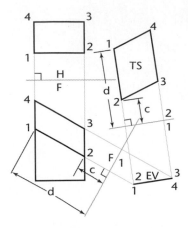

7.30 True Size of an Oblique Surface

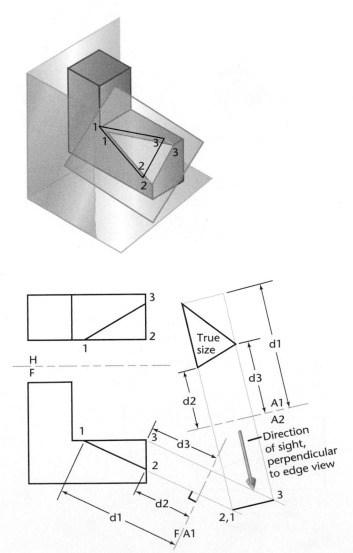

7.31 True Size View of an Oblique Surface

7.15 TRUE SIZE OF AN OBLIQUE SURFACE

As shown in Figure 7.30, a plane will show true size when the plane of projection is parallel to it.

To show the true size view of a plane, choose the direction of sight perpendicular to the edge view of the plane.

Showing the true size of a surface continues from the method presented for showing inclined surfaces true size, where the edge view is already given. But to show an oblique surface true size, you need to first show the oblique surface on edge and then construct a second auxiliary view to show it true size.

Showing the True Size and Shape of an Oblique Surface

To show the true size and shape of an oblique surface, such as surface 1–2–3–4 in Figure 7.31, create a second auxiliary view. In this example folding lines are used, but you can achieve the same results for all of the preceding examples using reference lines.

1. Draw the auxiliary view showing surface 1–2–3–4 on edge, as explained previously.
2. Create a second auxiliary view with the line of sight perpendicular to the edge view of plane 1–2–3–4 in the primary auxiliary view. Project lines parallel to the arrow. Draw folding line 1/2 perpendicular to these projection lines at a convenient distance from the primary auxiliary view.
3. Draw the secondary auxiliary view. Transfer the distance to each point from folding line F/1 to the second auxiliary view—for example, dimensions c and d. The true size TS of the surface 1–2–3–4 is shown in the secondary auxiliary view since the direction of sight is perpendicular to it.

Figure 7.32 shows an example of the steps to find the true size of an oblique surface. The first step, illustrated in Figure 7.32a, shows the oblique surface on edge. Figure 7.32b establishes the direction of sight perpendicular to the edge view. The final true size view of the surface is projected in Figure 7.32c.

Figure 7.33 shows a similar example using the reference plane method.

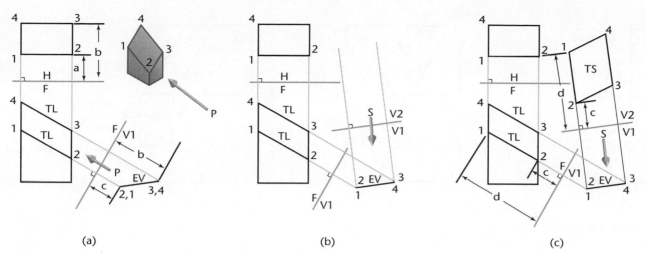

7.32 True Size of Oblique Surface—Folding Line Method

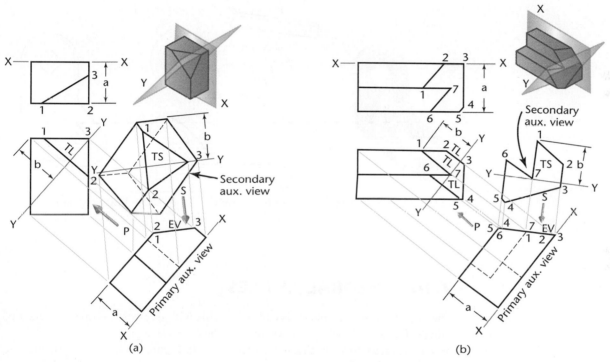

7.33 True Size of an Oblique Surface—Reference Plane Method

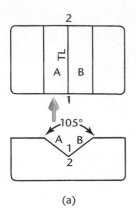

7.34 Dihedral Angles

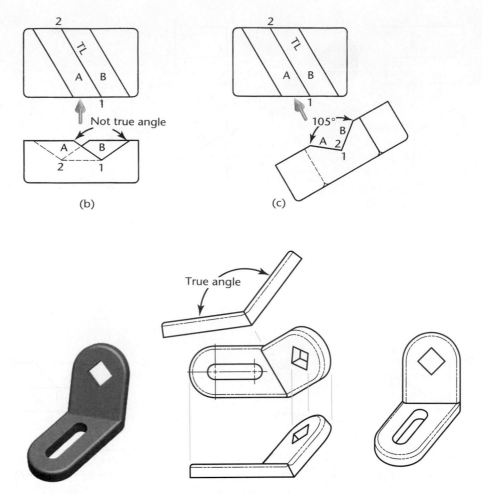

7.35 Using an Auxiliary View to Show the True Angle Between Surfaces (Dihedral Angle)

7.16 DIHEDRAL ANGLES

The angle between two planes is called a **dihedral angle.** Auxiliary views often need to be drawn to show dihedral angles true size, mainly for dimensioning purposes. In Figure 7.34a, a block with a V-groove is shown where the dihedral angle between inclined surfaces A and B is shown true size in the front view.

In Figure 7.34b, the V-groove on the block is at an angle to the front surface so that the true dihedral angle is not shown. Assume that the actual angle is the same as in Figure 7.34a. Does the angle show larger or smaller than in Figure 7.34a? To show the true dihedral angle, the line of intersection (in this case 1–2) must appear as a point. Since the line of intersection for the dihedral angle is in both planes, showing it as a point will produce a view which shows both planes on edge.

This will give you the true-size view of the dihedral angle.

In Figure 7.34a, line 1–2 is the line of intersection of planes A and B. Now, line 1–2 lies in both planes at the same time; therefore, a point view of this line will show both planes as lines, and the angle between them is the dihedral angle between the planes. To get the true angle between two planes, find the point view of the line intersection of the planes.

In Figure 7.34c, the direction of sight is parallel to line 1–2 so that line 1–2 appears as a point, planes A and B appear as lines, and the true dihedral angle is shown in the auxiliary view. Figure 7.35 shows a drawing using an auxiliary view to show the true angle between surfaces.

UNDERSTANDING DEVELOPMENTS AND INTERSECTIONS

A **development** is a flat representation or pattern that when folded together creates a 3D object (Figure 7.36). An **intersection** is the result of two objects that intersect each other (Figure 7.37). Sheet metal construction is the most common application for developments and intersections. The development of surfaces, such as those found in sheet metal fabrication, is a flat pattern that represents the unfolded or unrolled surface of the form. The resulting flat pattern gives the true size of each connected area of the form so that the part or structure can be fabricated. Auxiliary views are a primary tool used in creating developments. Many specialized software packages are available to automate creating developments and intersections. You can also apply what you have learned about auxiliary views to create developments and intersections using your CAD system.

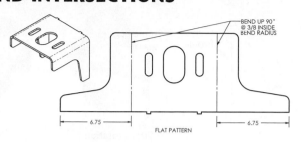

7.36 A Flat Pattern. *Courtesy of Dynojet Research, Inc.*

Surface Terminology

The following terminology describes objects and concepts used in developments and intersections:

A *ruled surface* is one that may be generated by sweeping a straight line, called the **generatrix,** along a path, which may be straight or curved (Figure 7.38). Any position of the generatrix is an **element** of the surface. A ruled surface may be a plane, a single-curved surface, or a warped surface.

A *plane* is a ruled surface that is generated by a line, one point of which moves along a straight path while the generatrix remains parallel to its original position. Many geometric solids are bounded by plane surfaces (Figure 7.39).

A *single curved surface* is a developable ruled surface; that is, it can be unrolled to coincide with a plane. Any two adjacent positions of the generatrix lie in the same plane. Examples are the cylinder (Figure 7.40) and the cone.

A *double curved surface* is generated by a curved line and has no straight-line elements (Figure 7.41). A surface generated by revolving a curved line about a straight line in the plane of the curve is called a **double curved surface of revolution.** Common examples are the **sphere, torus, ellipsoid,** and **hyperboloid.**

A *warped surface* is a ruled surface that is not developable. Some examples are shown in Figure 7.42. No two adjacent positions of the generatrix lie in a flat plane. Warped surfaces cannot be unrolled or unfolded to lie flat. Many exterior surfaces on an airplane or automobile are warped surfaces.

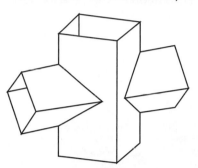

7.37 Intersecting Prisms

7.38 Ruled Surface

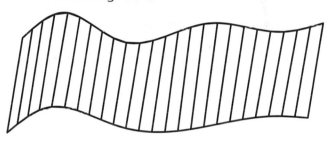

7.39 Plane Surfaces

7.40 Single Curved Surface

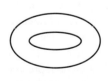

7.41 Double Curved Surface

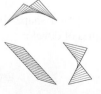

(a) Cylindroid   (b) Conoid   (c) Helicoid   (d) Hyperboloid   (e) Hyperbolic paraboloid

7.42 Warped Surfaces

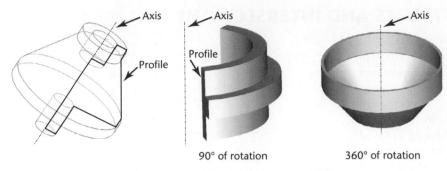

7.43 Solids Formed by Revolution

90° of rotation   360° of rotation

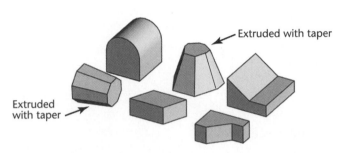

7.44 Solids Formed by Extrusion

Revolved and Extruded Solids

A solid generated by revolving a plane figure about an axis in the plane of the figure is a **revolved solid** (Figure 7.43). Revolved solids that are created from plane figures composed of straight lines are capable of being flattened to create a pattern. Revolving a curved figure creates a double-curved surface, which can have an approximated flat pattern.

An **extruded solid** is one formed by "sweeping" a shape along a linear path as shown in Figure 7.44. Many CAD software platforms also allow you to specify a taper for the surfaces. Extruded solids can have flat patterns formed for them.

Solids bounded by warped surfaces have no group name. The most common example of such solids is the screw thread.

Developable Surfaces

A **developable surface** may be unfolded or unrolled to lie flat. Surfaces composed of single-curved surfaces, of planes, or of combinations of these types are developable.

Warped surfaces and double-curved surfaces are not directly developable. They may be developed by approximating their shape using developable surfaces. If the material used in the actual manufacturing is sufficiently pliable, the flat sheets may be stretched, pressed, stamped, spun, or otherwise forced to assume the desired shape. Nondevelopable surfaces are often produced by a combination of developable surfaces that are then formed slightly to produce the required shape. Figure 7.45 shows examples of developable surfaces.

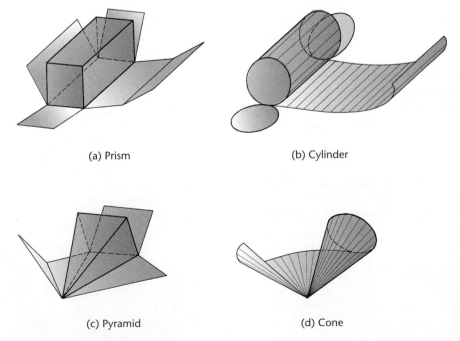

(a) Prism   (b) Cylinder

(c) Pyramid   (d) Cone

7.45 Development of Surfaces

Principles of Intersections

Typical examples of the need for accurate drawings showing the intersections of planes and solids include openings in roof surfaces for flues and stacks; openings in wall surfaces for pipes, chutes, and so on; and the building of sheet metal structures such as tanks and boilers. In such cases, you generally need to determine the true size and shape of the intersection of a plane and one of the more common geometric solids. Figure 7.46 shows an example where you would need to determine the intersection of a solid and a plane to create the correctly shaped opening in the vertical prism—the main flue—where the horizontal prism joins it.

For solids bounded by plane surfaces, you need only find the points of intersection of the edges of the solid with the plane and to join these points, in consecutive order, with straight lines.

For solids bounded by curved surfaces, it is necessary to find the points of intersection of several elements of the solid with the plane and to trace a smooth curve through these points. The intersection of a plane and a circular cone is called a **conic section.** Some typical conic sections are shown in Figure 7.47.

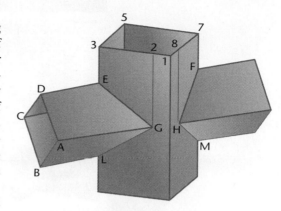

7.46 Intersecting Prisms

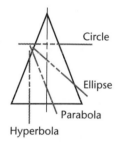    

7.47 Conic Sections

Heating ventilation and air conditioning (HVAC) systems often use ductwork to transfer air through the system. The standard parts shown above are made of 26 gauge galvanized steel and can be purchased "off the self". When ducts must connect at odd angles to fit into existing spaces custom designed developments and intersections are required.

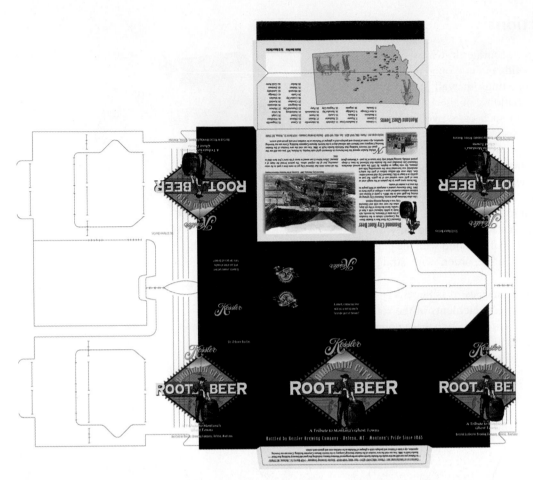

7.48 Flat Pattern for a Root Beer Package. *Courtesy of Kessler Brewing Co.*

7.17 DEVELOPMENTS

The **development of a surface** is that surface laid out on a plane. Practical applications of developments occur in sheet metal work, stone cutting, pattern making, packaging, and package design. See Figure 7.48.

Single curved surfaces and the surfaces of polyhedra can be developed. Developments for warped surfaces and double curved surfaces can only be approximated.

In sheet metal layout, extra material must be provided for laps and seams. If the material is heavy, the thickness may be a factor, and the crowding of metal in bends must be considered. You must also take stock sizes into account and make layouts to economize on material and labor. In preparing developments, it is best to put the seam at the shortest edge and to attach the bases at edges where they match; this will minimize processing such as soldering, welding, and riveting.

It is common to draw development layouts with the inside surfaces up. This way, all fold lines and other markings are related directly to inside measurements, which are the important dimensions in all ducts, pipes, tanks, and vessels. In this position they are also convenient for use in the fabricating shop.

Finding the Intersection of a Plane and a Prism and Developing the Prism

In order to create flat patterns for sheet metal, packaging, and other purposes, you must first determine the true size of the surface. The true size and shape of the intersection of a plane and a prism is shown in the auxiliary view in Figure 7.49. The length AB is the same as AB in the front view, and the width AD is the same as AD in the top view.

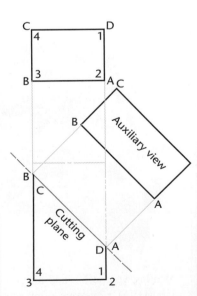

7.49 Auxiliary View Showing True Size and Shape of the Intersection of a Plane and a Prism

DEVELOPING A PRISM

These are the steps to create the development for the prism shown here on this page.

1 Draw the stretchout line, which represents the axis along which the part is unfolded or unrolled. On the stretchout line, transfer the true sizes of the faces 1–2 and 2–3, which are shown true length in the top view. Remember that a line appears true length when the view is perpendicular to the line. In other words, when a line is parallel to the fold line between views, the line is true length in the adjacent view.

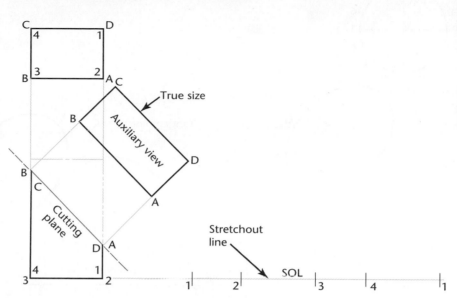

2 Where two surfaces join, draw perpendiculars to the stretchout line and transfer the true height of each respective edge. The front view shows the true heights in this case. Project the heights from the front view, as shown. Complete the development of these surfaces using straight lines to join the points you have plotted. Identify other surfaces that are connected to these and attach their true sizes to the development of the lower base and the upper base. Use an auxiliary view to find the true size of the surface and then draw it in place.

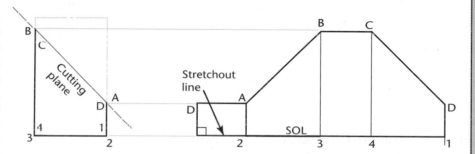

3 When you finish, you will have drawn the development of the entire prism, as shown. If needed, add tabs so that there is material to connect the surfaces when folded up.

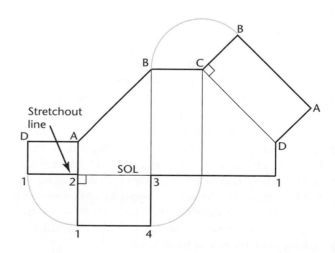

TIP
Cut out and fold up your drawing and check that it forms the flat pattern for the object you are creating. Add gluing tabs to some of the edges if necessary.

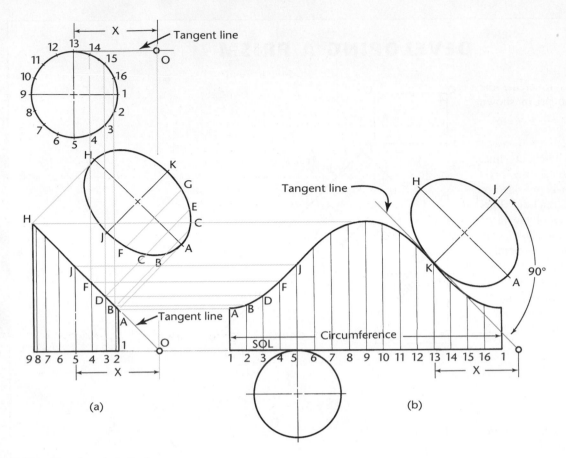

7.50 Plane and Cylinder

Finding the Intersection of a Plane and a Cylinder and Developing the Cylinder

The intersection of a plane and a cylinder is an ellipse whose true size is shown in the auxiliary view of Figure 7.50. The steps for developing a cylinder are as follows:

- Draw elements of the cylinder. It is usually best to divide the base of the cylinder into equal parts, shown in the top view and then projected into the front view.
- In the auxiliary view, the widths BC, DE, and so on are transferred from the top view at 2–16, 3–15, respectively, and the ellipse is drawn through these points, as you practiced earlier in this chapter. The major axis AH shows true length in the front view, and the minor axis JK shows true length in the top view. You can use this information to quickly draw the ellipse using CAD.

- Draw the stretchout line for the cylinder. It will be equal to the circumference of the base, whose length is determined by the formula πd.
- Divide the stretchout line into the same number of equal parts as the circumference of the base and draw an element through each division perpendicular to the line.
- Transfer the true height by projecting it from the front view, as shown in Figure 7.50b.
- Draw a smooth curve through the points A, B, D, and so on.
- Draw the tangent lines and attach the bases as shown in Figure 7.50b.

7.18 HEMS AND JOINTS FOR SHEET METAL AND OTHER MATERIALS

Figure 7.51 shows a wide variety of hems and joints used in fabricating sheet metal parts and other items. Hems are used to eliminate the raw edge as well as to stiffen the material. Joints and seams may be made for sheet metal by bending, welding, riveting, and soldering and for package materials by gluing and stapling.

You must add material for hems and joints to the layout or development. The amount you add depends on the thickness of the material and the production equipment. A good place to find more information is from manufacturers. They can be extremely helpful in identifying specifications related to the exact process you will use in designing a part.

A good way to locate manufacturers and products is through the online Thomas Register: http://www.thomasregister.com/index.html

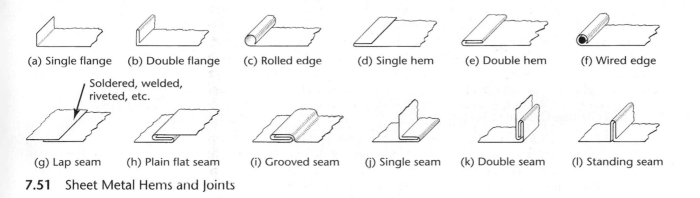

(a) Single flange (b) Double flange (c) Rolled edge (d) Single hem (e) Double hem (f) Wired edge

Soldered, welded, riveted, etc.

(g) Lap seam (h) Plain flat seam (i) Grooved seam (j) Single seam (k) Double seam (l) Standing seam

7.51 Sheet Metal Hems and Joints

7.19 MORE EXAMPLES OF DEVELOPMENTS AND INTERSECTIONS

Developing a Plane and an Oblique Prism

The intersection of a plane and an oblique prism is shown in Figure 7.52a. Where the plane is normal to the prism formed by plane WX (called a right section) it appears as a regular hexagon as shown in the auxiliary view labeled Right section. The oblique section cut by horizontal plane YZ is shown true size in the top view.

The development for this oblique prism is shown in Figure 7.52b. Use the right section to create stretchout line WX. On the stretchout line, set off the true widths of the faces 1–2, 2–3, and so on, which are shown true size in the auxiliary view. Draw perpendiculars through each division. Transfer the true heights of the respective edges, which are shown true size in the front view. Join the points A, B, C, and so on with straight lines. Finally attach the bases, which are shown in their true sizes in the top view, along an edge.

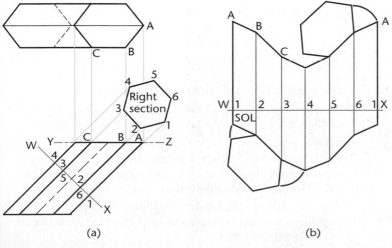

(a)   (b)

7.52 Plane and Oblique Prism

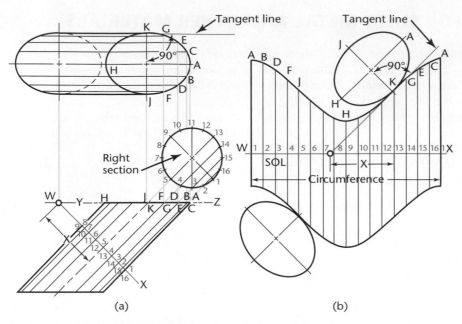

7.53 Plane and Oblique Circular Cylinder

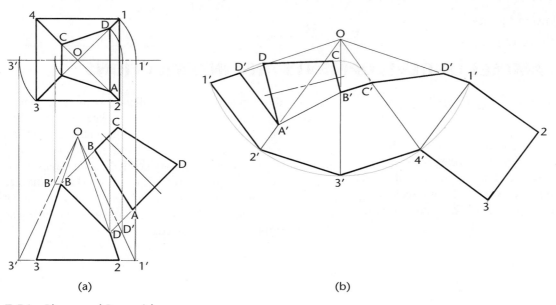

7.54 Plane and Pyramid

Developing a Plane and an Oblique Cylinder

The intersection of a plane and an oblique cylinder are developed similarly to the method for a plane and an oblique prism, as shown in Figure 7.53.

Developing a Plane and a Pyramid

The intersection of a plane and a pyramid is a trapezoid, as shown in Figure 7.54.

Developing a Plane and a Cone

The intersection of a plane and a cone is an ellipse, as shown in Figure 7.55. If a series of horizontal cutting planes is passed perpendicular to the axis, each plane will cut a circle from the cone that will show as true size and shape in the top view. Points in which these circles intersect the original cutting plane are points on the ellipse. Since the cutting plane is shown on edge in the front view (Figure 7.54a), all of these piercing points can be projected from there to the others, as shown in Figure 7.54b.

To develop the lateral surface of a cone, think of the cone as a pyramid having an infinite number of edges. The development is similar to that for a pyramid.

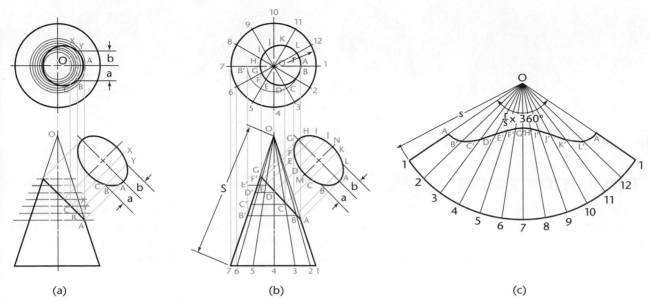

7.55 Plane and Cone

Developing a Hood and Flue

The development of a hood and flue is shown in Figure 7.56. Since the hood is a conical surface, it may be developed as shown in Figure 7.55. The two end sections of the elbow are cylindrical surfaces. The two middle sections of the elbow are cylindrical surfaces, but their bases are not perpendicular to the axes, so they will not develop into straight lines.

Develop them similar to an oblique cylinder. Make auxiliary planes AB and DC perpendicular to the axes so they cut right sections from the cylinders, which will develop into the straight lines AB and CD in the developments. By arranging the developments as shown, the elbow can be constructed from a rectangular sheet of metal without wasting material. The patterns are shown in the right top portion of Figure 7.56 as they will be separated after cutting.

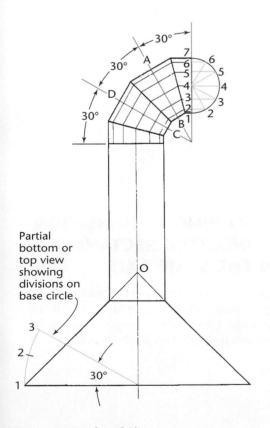

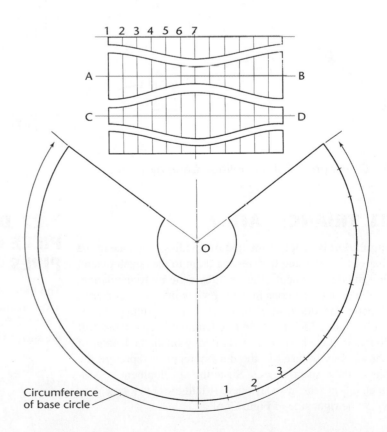

7.56 A Hood and Flue

(a)

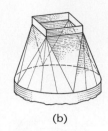
(b)

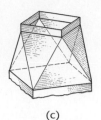
(c)

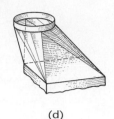
(d)

(e)

7.57 Transition Pieces

7.20 TRANSITION PIECES

A **transition piece** is one that connects two differently shaped, differently sized, or skewed position openings. In most cases, transition pieces are composed of plane surfaces and conical surfaces, as shown in Figure 7.57. You will learn about developing conical surfaces by triangulation next. Triangulation can also be used to develop, approximately, certain warped surfaces. Transition pieces are used extensively in air conditioning, heating, ventilating, and similar construction.

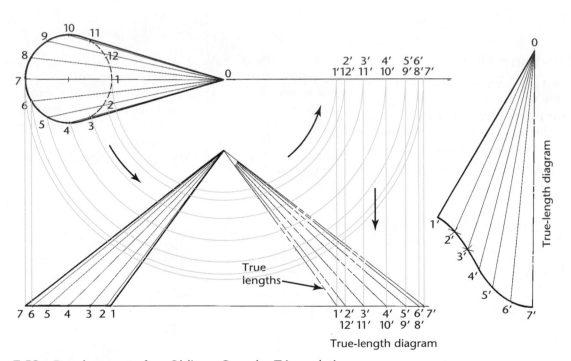

7.58 Development of an Oblique Cone by Triangulation

7.21 TRIANGULATION

Triangulation is simply a method of dividing a surface into a number of triangles and transferring them to the development. To find the development of an oblique cone by triangulation, divide the base of the cone in the top view into any number of equal parts and draw an element at each division point, as shown in Figure 7.58. Find the true length of each element. If the divisions of the base are comparatively small, the lengths of the chords may be used in the development to represent the lengths of the respective arcs. Since the development is symmetrical, it is necessary to lay out only half the development, as shown at the right side of Figure 7.58.

7.22 DEVELOPING A TRANSITION PIECE CONNECTING RECTANGULAR PIPES ON THE SAME AXIS

The transition piece can be a frustum of a pyramid that connects rectangular pipes on the same axis, as shown in Figure 7.59. As a check on the development, lines parallel on the surface must also be parallel on the development.

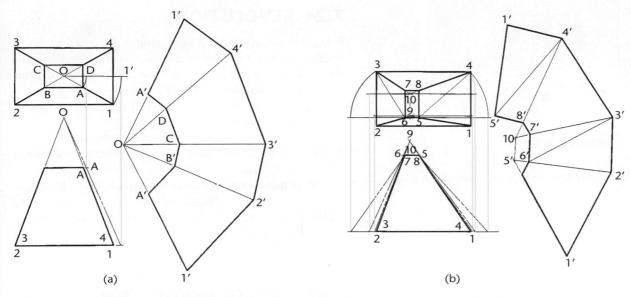

7.59 Development of a Transition Piece—Connecting Rectangular Pipes on the Same Axis

7.23 DEVELOPING A PLANE AND A SPHERE

The intersection of a plane and a sphere is a circle. The diameter of the circle depends on where the plane is located. Any circle cut by a plane through the center of the sphere is called a **great circle.** If a plane passes through the center and is perpendicular to the axis, the resulting great circle is called the **equator.** If a plane contains the axis, it will cut a great circle called a **meridian.**

The surface of a sphere is double curved and is not developable, but it may be developed approximately by dividing it into a series of zones and substituting a portion of a right circular cone for each zone. If the conical surfaces are inscribed within the sphere, the development will be smaller than the spherical surface, but if they are circumscribed about the sphere, the development will be larger. If the conical surfaces are partly

inside and partly outside the sphere, the resulting development is closely approximate to the spherical surface. This method of developing a spherical surface, the **polyconic** method, is shown in Figure 7.60a. It is used on government maps of the United States.

Another method of making an approximate development of the double-curved surface of a sphere is to divide the surface into equal sections with meridian planes and substitute cylindrical surfaces for the spherical sections. The cylindrical surfaces may be inscribed within the sphere, circumscribed about it, or located partly inside and partially outside. This method, the **polycylindric** method (sometimes called the gore method) is shown in Figure 7.60b.

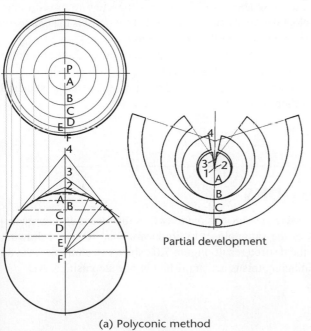

(a) Polyconic method

Partial development

(b) Polycylindric method

Quarter development

7.60 Approximate Development of a Sphere

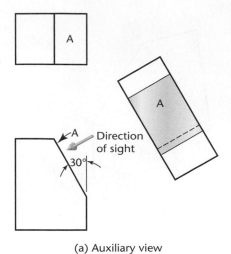

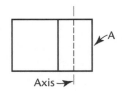

(a) Auxiliary view

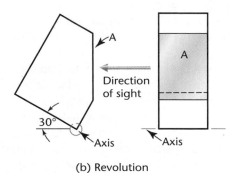

(b) Revolution

7.61 Auxiliary View and Revolution Compared

7.24 REVOLUTION

Revolution, like auxiliary view projection, is a method of determining the true length and true size of inclined and oblique lines and planes. To create the auxiliary view imagine that the object remains stationary and a new viewing plane is added as shown by the arrow in Figure 7.61a. Surface A shows true size and shape in the auxiliary view.

The same view of the object can be obtained by moving the object with respect to the viewing planes, as shown in Figure 7.61b. Here the object is revolved until surface A appears in its true size and shape in the right-side view. Revolution determines true length and true size without creating another view. Instead, revolution positions an object in space to create standard views that show the true size and shape of the inclined or oblique surface.

7.25 AXIS OF REVOLUTION

Imagine the axis of revolution to be perpendicular to the front plane of projection in Figure 7.61b. The **axis of revolution** appears as a point in this view. The object revolves but does not change shape in this view. In the adjacent views in which the axis of revolution if it were drawn would show as a line in true length, the dimensions of the object that are parallel to the axis of revolution do not change. Other dimensions may appear foreshortened.

Creating a Revolved Drawing

To make a drawing using revolution to show the true size of a surface,

1. Select the view that has the inclined surface showing as an edge, or other feature that you want to revolve to produce a true size feature in the adjacent view.
2. Select any point at any convenient position on or outside that view about which to draw the view revolved either clockwise or counterclockwise. That point is the end view, or point view, of the axis of revolution.
3. Draw this first view on the plane of projection. This is the only view that remains unchanged in size and shape.
4. Project the other views from this view using standard orthographic projection techniques.

7.26 PRIMARY AND SUCCESSIVE REVOLUTIONS

The axis of revolution is usually perpendicular to one of the three principal planes of projection. A **primary revolution** is one where the object is revolved about an axis perpendicular to the horizontal, frontal, or profile planes of projection.

Successive revolutions are drawings that use multiple revolutions of the same object to produce a final revolved drawing with the desired result. Figure 7.62 shows an example. As you can imagine, this is accomplished in one step using CAD.

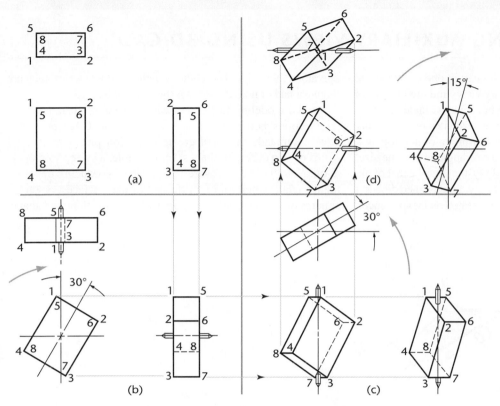

7.62 Successive Revolutions of a Prism

7.27 TRUE LENGTH OF A LINE: REVOLUTION METHOD

A line (edge) appears true length when it is parallel to one of the planes of projection. In Figure 7.63a, line AB (an element of the cone) is oblique to the planes of projection. Line AB appears foreshortened, not true length. If AB is revolved about the axis of the cone until it coincides with either of the contour elements (for example, ABR), it will be shown in its true length in the front view because it will then be parallel to the front plane of projection.

In Figure 7.63b, to show the edge of the pyramid CD true length, revolve it about the axis of the pyramid until it is parallel to the frontal plane of projection and therefore shows true length in the front view. In Figure 7.63c, line EF is shown true length in the front view because it has been revolved about a vertical axis until it is parallel to the front plane of projection.

The true length of a line may also be found by constructing a right triangle or a true length diagram (Figure 7.63d) whose base is equal to the top view of the line and whose altitude is the difference in elevation of the ends. The hypotenuse of the triangle is equal to the true length of the line.

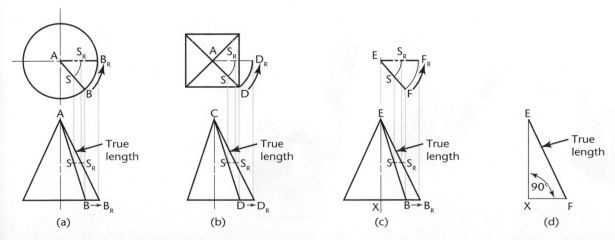

7.63 True Length of a Line—Revolution Method

CREATING AUXILIARY VIEWS USING 3D CAD

Using 3D CAD, any view can be generated in one or two steps, eliminating the need to project auxiliary views and revolve views manually. It is still very important to have a clear understanding of which line of sight will produce a true size view or a view that shows a true dihedral angle. When measuring or dimensioning a view from a CAD screen, if the surface or angle is not true size, the automatic dimension from the CAD system may be that of the apparent, or projected, distance. Incorrectly dimensioned dihedral angles can be an error in CAD drawings created by inexperienced operators. Drawings should show angles true size where they are dimensioned or note it clearly if this is not the case.

Solid modeling techniques can be used to create accurate intersections between various solids. Some CAD programs have commands that will create transition pieces that blend solids of two differing shapes, for example, a sweep/join operation. Not all CAD software is capable of producing developments (flat patterns) of surfaces. Some surfaces, such as spheres or tori, can only be approximated by a flattened shape.

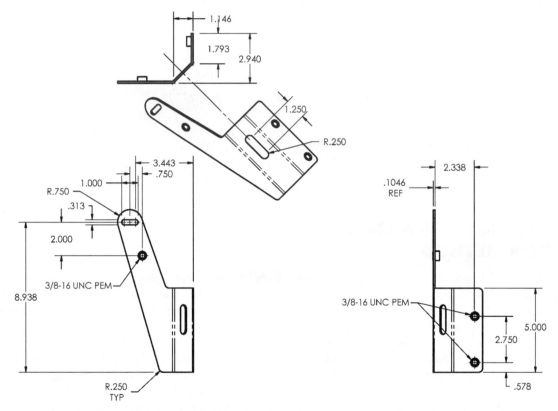

An auxiliary view is used on the drawing for this sheet metal part so that dimensions can be shown where feature to show true size. *Courtesy of Dynojet Research, Inc.*

Views of the solid model from which the detail drawing above were created. *Courtesy of Dynojet Research, Inc.*

KEY WORDS

True Size
Auxiliary View
Auxiliary Plane
Folding Lines
Primary Auxiliary View
Depth Auxiliary Views
Height Auxiliary Views
Width Auxiliary Views
Secondary Auxiliary View
Third Auxiliary View
Succeeding Auxiliary View
Reference Plane
alternate view
adjacent view
Partial Auxiliary Views
Half Auxiliary View
Auxiliary Section
Viewing-Plane Line
Viewing Direction Arrow
Descriptive Geometry
Dihedral Angle
Development
Intersection
Ruled Surface
Generatrix
Element
Plane
Single Curved Surface
Double Curved Surface
Double Curved Surface of Revolution
Sphere
Torus
Ellipsoid
Hyperboloid
Warped Surface
Revolved Solid
Extruded Solid
Developable Surface
Conic Section
Development of a Surface
Transition Piece
Triangulation
Great Circle
Equator
Meridian
Polyconic
Polycylindric
Revolution
Axis of Revolution
Primary Revolution
Successive Revolutions

CHAPTER SUMMARY

- An auxiliary view can be used to create a projection that shows the true length of a line or true size of a plane.
- An auxiliary view can be directly produced using CAD if the original object was drawn as a 3D model.
- Folding lines or reference lines represent the edge views of projection planes.
- Points are projected between views parallel to the line of sight and perpendicular to the reference lines or folding lines.
- A common use of auxiliary views is to show dihedral angles in true size.
- Curves are projected to auxiliary views by plotting them as points.
- A secondary auxiliary view can be constructed from a previously drawn (primary) auxiliary view.
- The technique for creating the development of solids is determined by the basic geometric shape. Prisms, pyramids, cylinders, and cones each have a particular development technique.
- The intersection of two solids is determined by plotting the intersection of each surface and transferring the intersection points to each development.
- Cones and pyramids use radial development. Prisms and cylinders use parallel development.
- Truncated solids, cones, and pyramids are created by developing the whole solid and then plotting the truncated endpoints on each radial element.
- Transition pieces are developed by creating triangular surfaces that approximate the transition from rectangular to circular. The smaller the triangular surfaces, the more accurate the development.
- Revolution moves an object in space, to reveal what would normally be an auxiliary view of the object in a primary view (top, front, right side).
- The main purpose of revolution is to reveal the true length and true size of inclined and oblique lines and planes in a primary view.

REVIEW QUESTIONS

1. What is meant by true length? By true size?
2. Why is a true length line always parallel to an adjacent reference line?
3. If an auxiliary view is drawn from the front view, what other views would show the same depth dimensions?
4. Describe one method for transferring depth between views.
5. What is the difference between a complete auxiliary view and a partial auxiliary view?
6. How many auxiliary views are necessary to draw the true size of an inclined plane? Of an oblique plane?
7. What is the angle between the reference plane line (or folding line) and the direction-of-sight lines?
8. How is the development of a pyramid similar to the development of a cone?
9. When developing a truncated cone or pyramid, why is the complete solid developed first?
10. What descriptive geometry techniques are used to determine the intersection points between two solids?
11. What is a transition piece?
12. What is a stretchout line?
13. Which parts of a development are true size and true shape?
14. What building trades use developments and intersections?
15. What is the purpose of revolution?
16. What is the axis of revolution? What determines where the axis is drawn?
17. What are successive revolutions?

EXERCISES

Auxiliary View Projects

The projects in Exercises 7.2–7.43 are to be drawn with CAD or freehand. If partial auxiliary views are not assigned, the auxiliary views are to be complete views of the entire object, including all necessary hidden lines.

It is often difficult to space the views of an auxiliary view sketch. Make sure to provide enough space for the auxiliary view by lightly blocking in the overall dimensions first and by blocking in the overall dimensions of the auxiliary view. Add more detail after you have established the basic layout of the sketch. If metric or decimal dimensions are to be included, refer to Chapter 9 on dimensioning.

A wide selection of intersection and development projects is provided in Figures 7.44–7.50. These projects are designed to fit A, B size, or A3 sheets. Because developments are used to create patterns, they should be drawn accurately or dimensioned. They can also be solved on most CAD systems, using either 2D or solid modeling.

Design Project

Exercise 7.1 Breakfast cereal has traditionally sold in a rectangular box. The packaging also must keep the product fresh, be reasonably durable, look attractive on the shelf, and be useful for dispensing the product. Create an innovative new packaging for breakfast cereal that meets these requirements. Make your design a sensible candidate for mass production, striving for a low consumer price and the conservation of raw materials. Consider whether to make your packaging disposable, reusable, or refillable. Use the graphic communication skills you have learned so far to represent your design clearly.

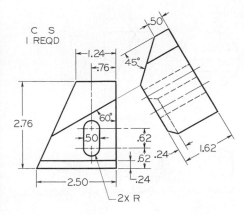

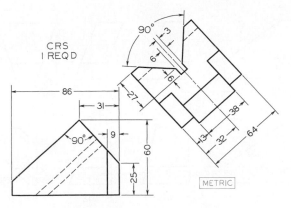

Exercise 7.2 RH Finger. Given: Front and auxiliary views. Required: Complete front, auxiliary, left-side, and top views.

Exercise 7.3 V-Block, Given: Front and auxiliary views. Required: Complete front, top, and auxiliary views.

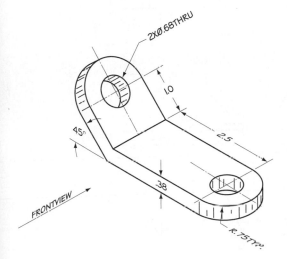

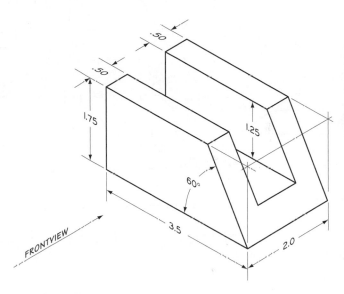

Exercise 7.4 Clamp.

Exercise 7.5 Plastic Slide.

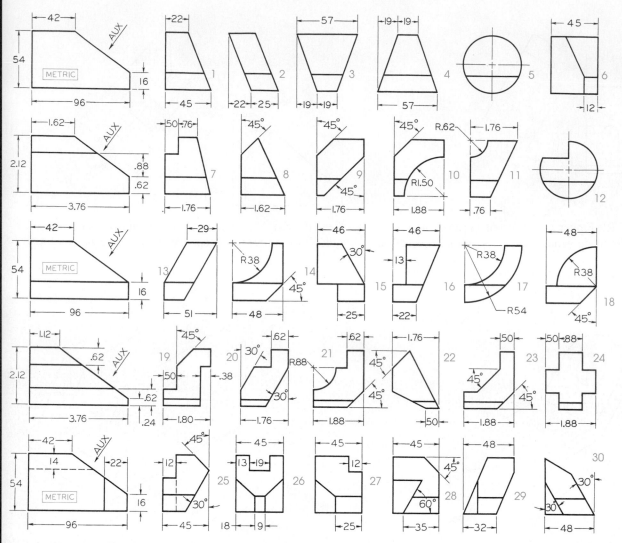

Exercise 7.6 Auxiliary View Problems. Make freehand sketch or instrument drawing of selected problem as assigned. Draw given front and right-side views, and add incomplete auxiliary view, including all hidden lines. If assigned, design your own right-side view consistent with given front view; and then add complete auxiliary view.

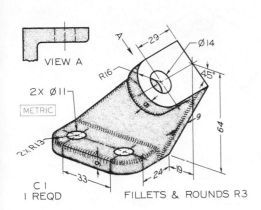

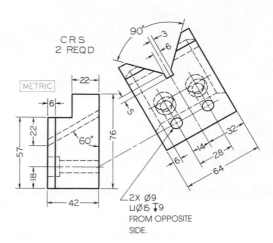

Exercise 7.7 Anchor Bracket. Draw necessary views or partial views.*

Exercise 7.10 Guide Block. Given: Right-side and auxiliary views. Required: Right-side, auxiliary, plus front and top views—complete.*

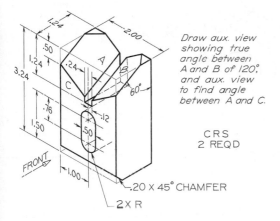

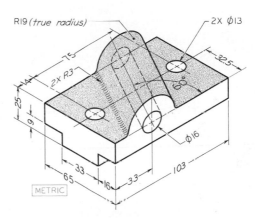

Exercise 7.8 Centering Block. Draw complete front, top, and right-side views, plus indicated auxiliary views.*

Exercise 7.11 Angle Bearing. Draw necessary views, including complete auxiliary view.*

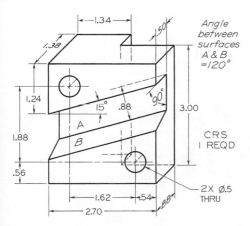

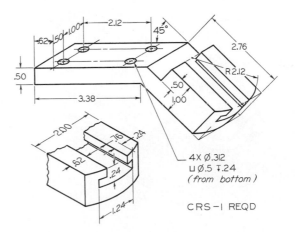

Exercise 7.9 Clamp Slide. Draw necessary views completely.*

Exercise 7.12 Guide Bracket. Draw necessary views or partial views.*

*If dimensions are required, study Chapter 9. Use metric or decimal-inch dimensions as assigned.

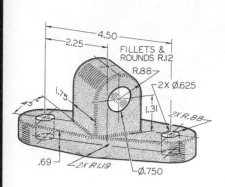

Exercise 7.13 Rod Guide. Draw necessary views, including complete auxiliary view showing true shape of upper rounded portion.*

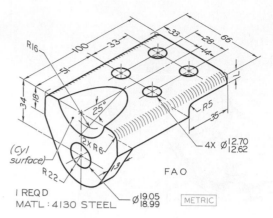

Exercise 7.16 Angle Guide. Draw necessary views, including a partial auxiliary view of cylindrical recess.*

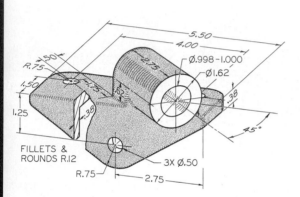

Exercise 7.14 Brace Anchor. Draw necessary views, including partial auxiliary view showing true shape of cylindrical portion (Layout B-4 or A3–4 adjusted.)*

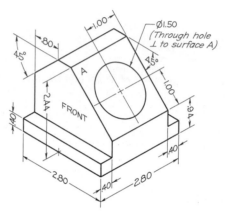

Exercise 7.17 Holder Block. Draw front and right-side views (2.80″ apart) and complete auxiliary view of entire object showing true shape of surface A and all hidden lines.*

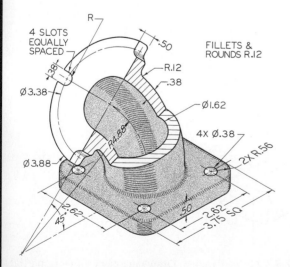

Exercise 7.15 45° Elbow. Draw necessary views, including a broken section and two half views of flanges.*

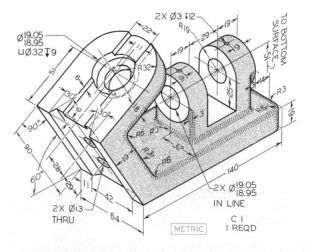

Exercise 7.18 Control Bracket. Draw necessary views, including partial auxiliary views and regular views.*

*If dimensions are required, study Chapter 9. Use metric or decimal-inch dimensions as assigned.

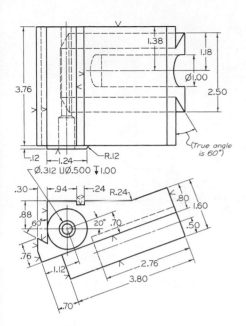

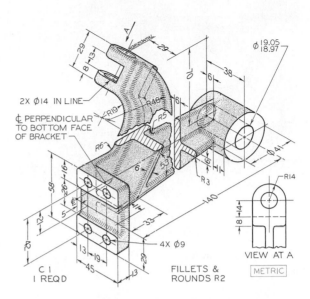

Exercise 7.19 Tool Holder Slide. Draw given views, and add complete auxiliary view showing true curvature of slot on bottom.*

Exercise 7.21 Guide Bearing. Draw necessary views and partial views, including two partial auxiliary views.*

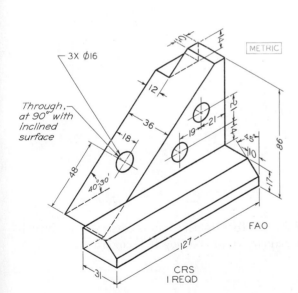

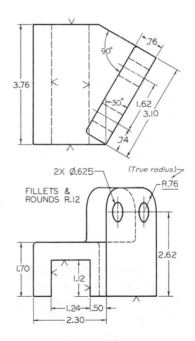

Exercise 7.20 Adjuster Block. Draw necessary views, including complete auxiliary view showing true shape of inclined surface.*

Exercise 7.22 Drill Press Bracket. Draw given views and add complete auxiliary views showing true shape of inclined face.*

*If dimensions are required, study Chapter 9. Use metric or decimal-inch dimensions as assigned.

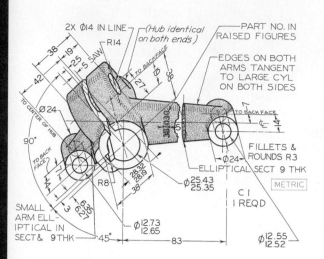

Exercise 7.23 Brake Control Lever. Draw necessary views and partial views.*

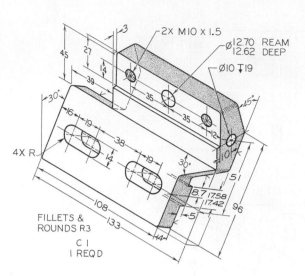

Exercise 7.25 Cam Bracket. Draw necessary views or partial views as needed.*

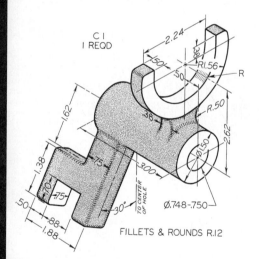

Exercise 7.24 Shifter Fork. Draw necessary views, including partial auxiliary view showing true shape of inclined arm.*

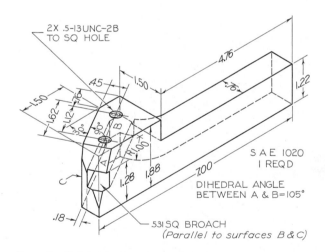

Exercise 7.26 RH Tool Holder. Draw necessary views, including partial auxiliary views showing 105° angle and square hole true size.*

*If dimensions are required, study Chapter 9. Use metric or decimal-inch dimensions as assigned.

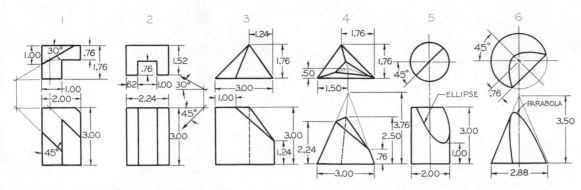

Exercise 7.27 Draw complete secondary auxiliary views, showing the true sizes of the inclined surfaces (except for Problem 2). In Problem 2 draw secondary auxiliary view as seen in the direction of the arrow given in the problem.*

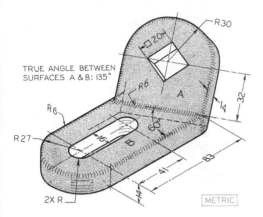

Exercise 7.28 Control Bracket. Draw necessary views including primary and secondary auxiliary views so that the latter shows true shape of oblique surface A.*

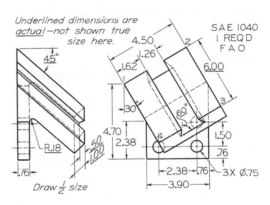

Exercise 7.30 Dovetail Slide. Draw complete given views and auxiliary views, including view showing true size of surface 1–2–3–4.*

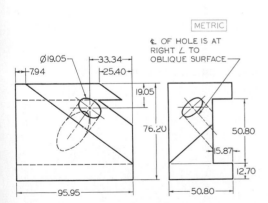

Exercise 7.29 Holder Block. Draw given views and primary and secondary auxiliary views so that the latter shows true shape of oblique surface.*

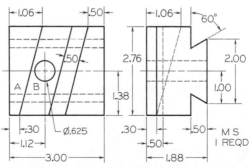

Draw primary aux. view showing angle between planes A and B; then secondary auxiliary view showing true size of surface A.

Exercise 7.31 Dovetail Guide. Draw given views plus complete auxiliary views as indicated.*

*If dimensions are required, study Chapter 9. Use metric or decimal-inch dimensions as assigned.

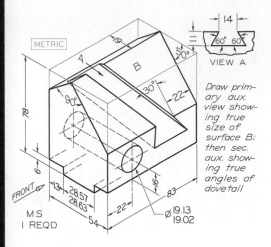

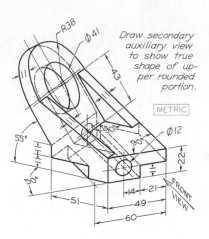

Exercise 7.32 Adjustable Stop. Draw complete front and auxiliary views plus partial right-side view. Show all hidden lines.*

Exercise 7.33 Tool Holder. Draw complete front view, and primary and secondary auxiliary views as indicated.*

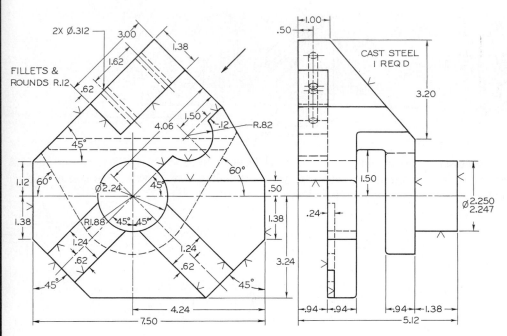

Exercise 7.34 Box Tool Holder for Turret Lathe. Given: Front and right-side views. Required: Front and left-side views, and complete auxiliary view as indicated by arrow.*

---

*If dimensions are required, study Chapter 9. Use metric or decimal-inch dimensions as assigned.

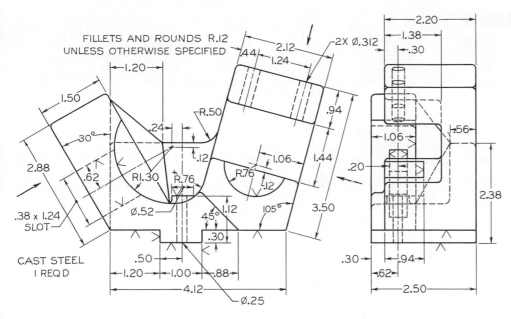

Exercise 7.35 Pointing Tool Holder for Automatic Screw Machine. Given: Front and right-side views. Required: Front view and three partial auxiliary views.*

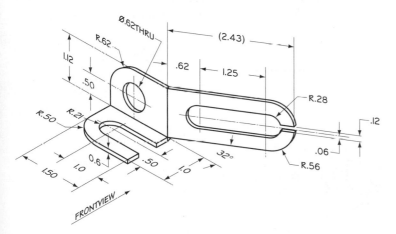

Exercise 7.36 Mounting Clip. Draw all required views. Include at least one auxiliary view.*

*If dimensions are required, study Chapter 9. Use metric or decimal-inch dimensions as assigned.

REVOLUTION PROBLEMS

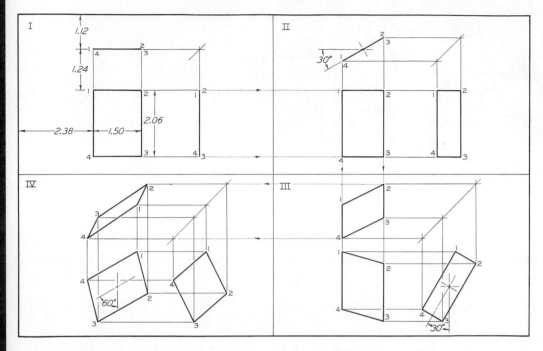

Exercise 7.37 Divide working area into four equal parts, as shown. Draw given views of the rectangle, and then the primary revolution in space II, followed by successive revolutions in spaces III and IV. Number points as shown. Omit dimensions. Use Form 3 title box.

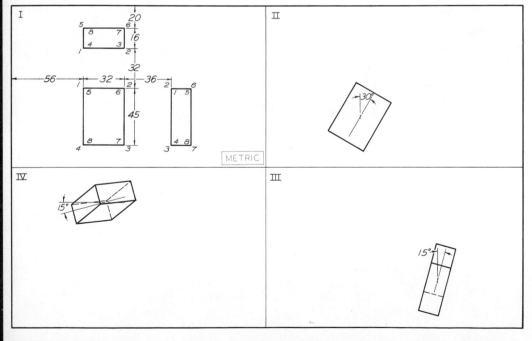

Exercise 7.38 Divide working area into four equal parts, as shown. Draw given views of prism as shown in space I; then draw three views of the revolved prism in each succeeding space, as indicated. Number all corners. Omit dimensions. Use Form 3 title box.

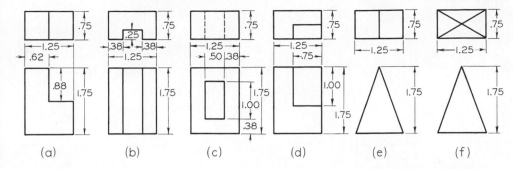

(a) (b) (c) (d) (e) (f)

Exercise 7.39 Divide your sheet into four equal parts as in Exercise 7.37. In the upper left space draw the original drawing as in Figure 7.62a, in the upper right draw a simple revolution as in Figure 7.62b and in the lower two spaces, draw successive revolutions as in Figure 7.62c and 7.62d, but for each problem use a block assigned from Exercise 7.39. Alternative assignment: Divide into two equal spaces. In the left space draw the original views. In the right space draw a simple revolution as in Figure 7.62b, but use an object assigned from Exercise 7.39.

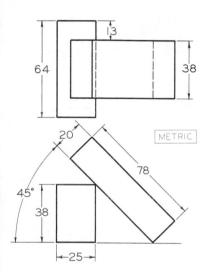

Exercise 7.40 Draw three views of the blocks but revolved 30° clockwise about an axis perpendicular to the top plane of projection. Do not change the relative positions of the blocks.

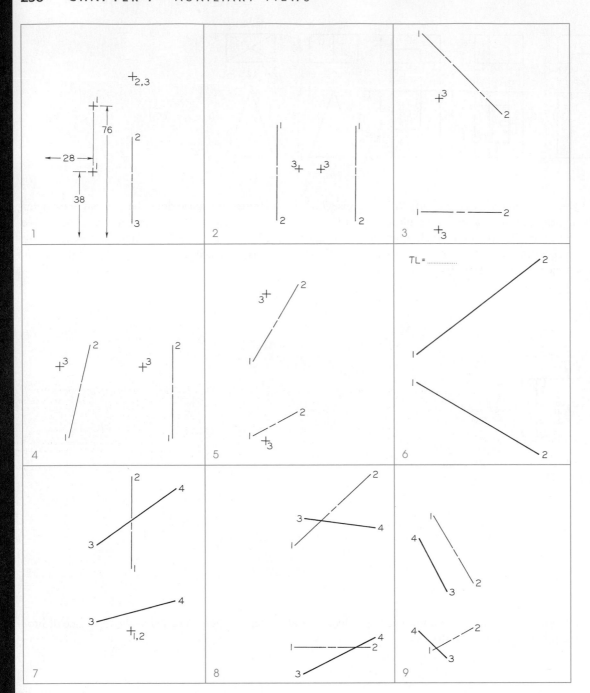

Exercise 7.41 Divide the working area into four equal areas for four problems per sheet to be assigned by the instructor. Data for the layout of each problem are given by a coordinate system in metric dimensions. For example, in Exercise 7.38 no. 1, is located by the scale coordinates (28 mm, 38 mm, 76 mm). The first coordinate locates the front view of the point from the left edge of the problem area. The second one locates the front view of the point from the bottom edge of the problem area. The third one locates either the top view of the point from the bottom edge of the problem area or the side view of the point from the left edge of the problem area. Inspection of the given problem layout will determine which application to use.

1. Revolve clockwise point 1(28, 38, 76) through 210° about the axis 2(51, 58, 94)–3(51, 8, 94).
2. Revolve point 3(41, 38, 53) about the axis 1(28, 64, 74)–2(28, 8, 74) until point 3 is at the farthest distance behind the axis.
3. Revolve point 3(20, 8, 84) about the axis 1(10, 18, 122)–2(56, 18, 76) through 210° and to the rear of line 1–2.
4. Revolve point 3(5, 53, 53) about the axis 1(10, 13, 71)–2(23, 66, 71) to its extreme position to the left in the front view.
5. Revolve point 3(15, 8, 99) about the axis 1(8, 10, 61)–2(33, 25, 104) through 180°.
6. By revolution find the true length of line 1(8, 48, 64)–2(79, 8, 119). Scale: 1:100.
7. Revolve line 3(30, 38, 81)–4(76, 51, 114) about axis 1(51, 33, 69)–2(51, 33, 122) until line 3–4 is shown true length and below the axis 1–2.
8. Revolve line 3(53, 8, 97)–4(94, 28, 91) about the axis 1(48, 23, 81)–2(91, 23, 122) until line 3–4 is in true length and above the axis.
9. Revolve line 3(28, 15, 99)–4(13, 30, 84) about the axis 1(20, 20, 97)–2(43, 33, 58) until line 3–4 is level above the axis.

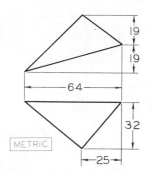

METRIC

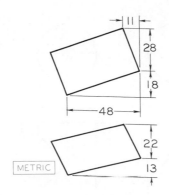

METRIC

Exercise 7.42 Draw three views of a right prism 38 mm high that has as its lower base the triangle shown above. See Figure 7.63.

Exercise 7.43 Draw three views of a right pyramid 51 mm high, having as its lower base the parallelogram shown above. See Figure 7.63.

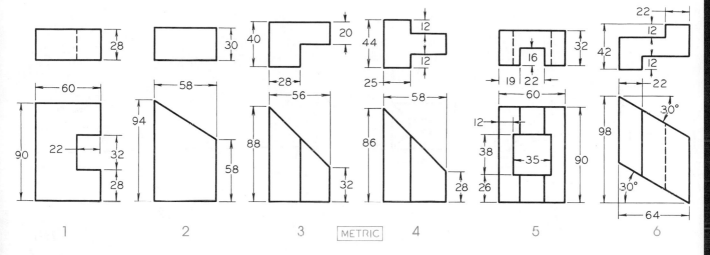

1   2   3   METRIC   4   5   6

Exercise 7.44 Draw given views and develop the lateral surface.

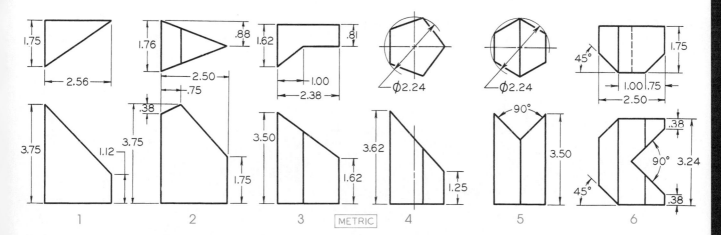

1   2   3   METRIC   4   5   6

Exercise 7.45 Draw given views and develop the lateral surface.

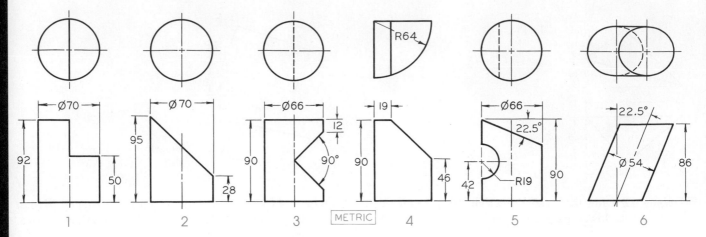

Exercise 7.46 Draw given views and develop the lateral surface.

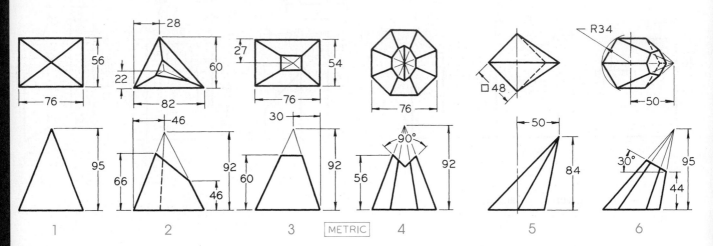

Exercise 7.47 Draw given views and develop lateral surface (Layout A3–3 or B–3).

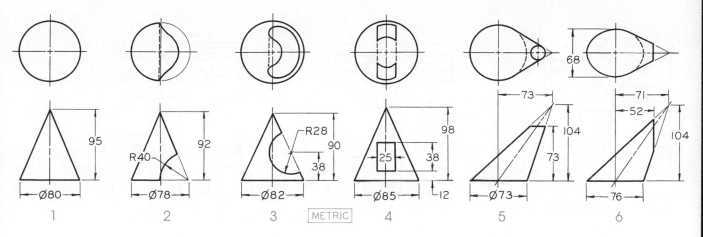

Exercise 7.48 Draw given views and develop lateral surface (Layout A3–3 or B–3).

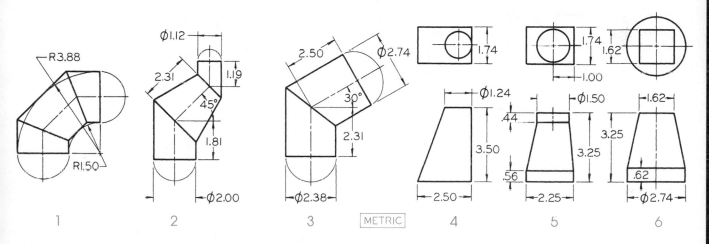

Exercise 7.49 Draw given views of the forms and develop lateral surfaces (Layout A3–3 or B–3).

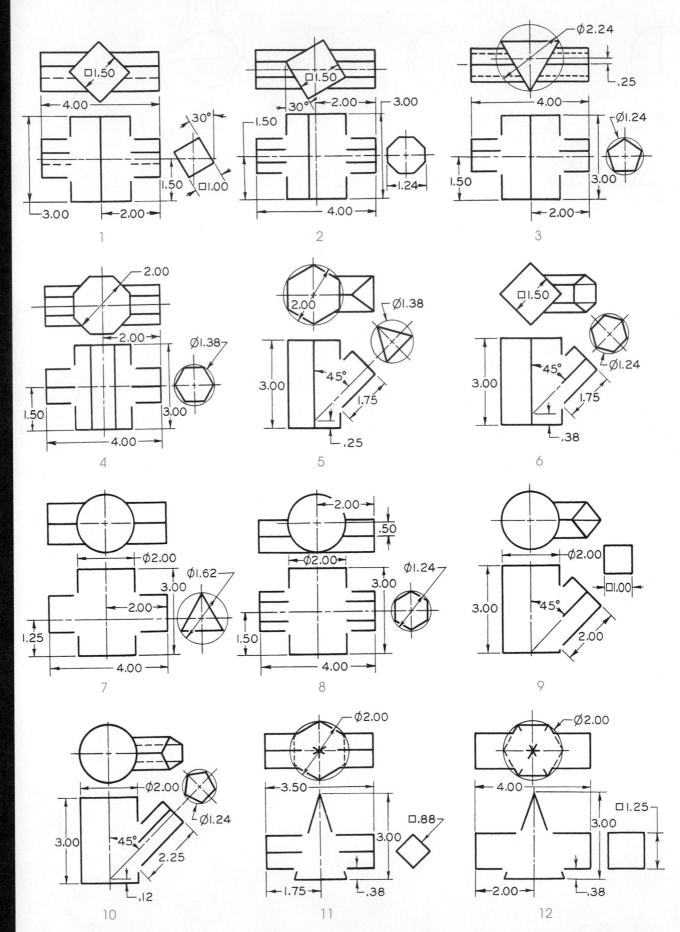

Exercise 7.50 Draw the given views of assigned form and complete the intersection. Then develop the lateral surfaces.

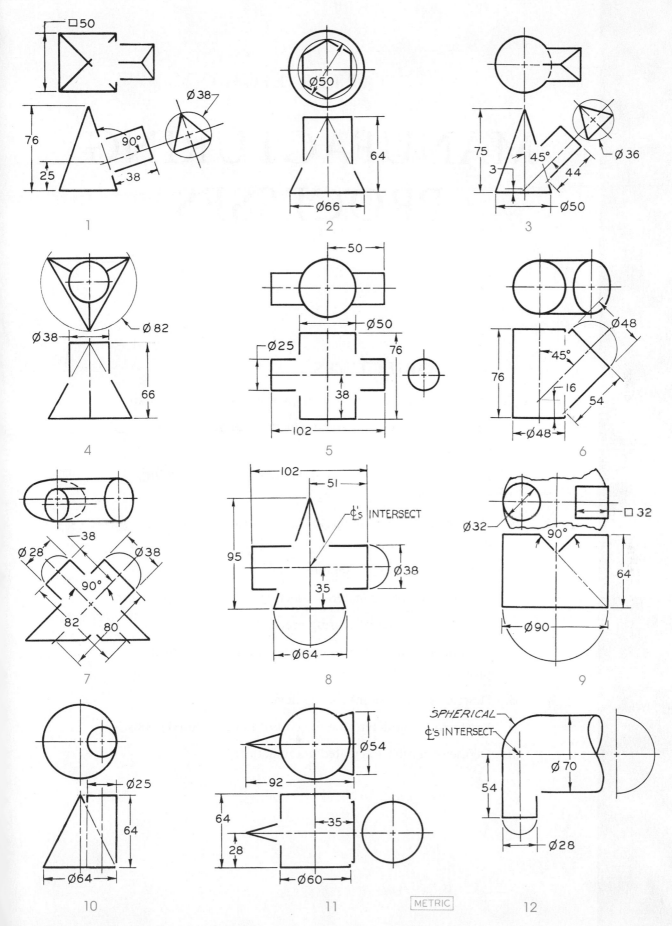

Exercise 7.51 Draw the given views of assigned form and complete the intersection. Then develop the lateral surfaces.

CHAPTER EIGHT

MANUFACTURING PROCESSES

—— OBJECTIVES ——

After studying the material in this chapter, you should be able to:

1. Describe the role of computer aided design in project development.

2. Define rapid prototyping and list four rapid prototyping technologies.

3. Describe the role of design for manufacture, assembly, disassembly and service.

4. Define modeling for assembly.

5. Describe the role of material selection and material properties.

6. List the major manufacturing processes.

7. Look up accuracy and surface finishes for manufacturing processes.

8. Describe the role of measuring devices in production.

9. List factors that determine the cost of manufactured goods.

10. Define computer integrated manufacturing.

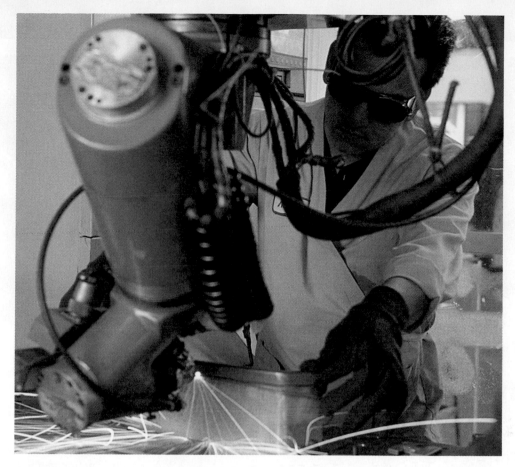

Courtesy of Michael Newman PhotoEdit Inc.

OVERVIEW

Look at the objects around you: your pen, watch, calculator, telephone, chair, and light fixtures. All of these things have been transformed from various raw materials and assembled into the items you see.

Some objects, such as plastic coat hangers, forks, nails, bolts, and metal brackets are made of a single part. However, most objects are assembled from several parts made from different materials. Thousands of assembled products are part of everyday life, from aircraft jet engines (invented in 1939) to ballpoint pens (1938), toasters (1926), washing machines (1910), refrigerators (1931), and photocopiers (1949).

Manufacturing encompasses product design and the selection of raw materials and processes by which goods are manufactured. It is an important part of the world economy, comprising from 20 to 30% of the value of all goods and services produced. The level of manufacturing is directly related to the economic health of a country.

Machines used to manufacture other products are manufactured products themselves. Examples are large presses to shape sheet metal for car bodies, machinery to make bolts and nuts, and sewing machines for making clothing. Servicing and maintaining this machinery during its useful life is an important manufacturing activity.

Engineering drawings, whether created by hand or using CAD, are detailed instructions for manufacturing objects. Drawings define the shape, size, materials, finish, and sometimes the manufacturing process required. This chapter provides information about terms and processes used in manufacturing to aid you in creating documentation drawings that specify the information needed to manufacture a part.

Search the following Web sites to learn more about an online machine shop (emachineshop.com), manufacturing information (americanmachinist.com), and technical standards (ASTM.org).
- http://www.emachineshop.com
- http://www.americanmachinist.com
- http://www.ASTM.org

Conveyor at industrial site

UNDERSTANDING MANUFACTURING

The word "manufacturing" is derived from the Latin *manu factus*, meaning "made by hand." In the modern sense, manufacturing involves making products from raw materials by various processes, machinery, and operations, following a well-organized plan for each activity required. The term manufacturing engineering or production engineering describes this area of industrial activity.

Manufacturing has the important function of adding value. A manufactured item undergoes a number of processes to convert raw material into a useful product, which adds value or marketable price to the product. For example, as the raw material for ceramics, clay has a certain value. When it is used to make a ceramic cutting tool or electrical insulator, value is added to the clay. Similarly, a wire coat hanger or a nail has a value over and above the cost of a piece of wire from which it is made.

Manufacturing may produce **discrete products** (meaning individual parts) or **continuous products.** Nails, gears, balls for bearings, beverage cans, and engine blocks are examples of discrete parts, even though they are mass produced at high production rates. Metal or plastic sheeting, spools of wire, tubes, hose, and pipe are examples of continuous products, which may be cut into individual lengths to become discrete parts.

Manufacturing is generally a complex activity involving a wide variety of resources and activities such as:

- Product design
- Purchasing
- Marketing
- Machinery and tooling
- Manufacturing
- Sales
- Process planning
- Production control
- Shipping
- Materials
- Support services
- Customer service

For manufacturing activities to be responsive to demands and trends:

- A product must fully meet design requirements and product specifications and standards.
- A product must be manufactured by the most environmentally friendly and economical methods.
- Quality must be built into the product at each stage, from design to assembly, rather than relying on quality testing after the product is made. Furthermore, quality should be appropriate to the product's use.

In a highly competitive environment, production methods must be sufficiently flexible so as to respond to changing market demands, types of products, production rates, production quantities, and on-time delivery to the customer.

New developments in materials, production methods, and computer integration of both technological and managerial activities in a manufacturing organization must constantly be evaluated with a view to their appropriate, timely, and economic implementation.

Manufacturing activities must be viewed as a large system, each part of which is interrelated to others. Such systems can now be modeled in order to study the effect of factors such as changes in market demands, product design, and materials. Various other factors and production methods affect product quality and cost.

A manufacturing organization must constantly strive for higher levels of quality and productivity (defined as the optimum use of all its resources: materials, machines, energy, capital, labor, and technology). Output per employee per hour in all phases needs to be maximized. Zero-based part rejection and waste are also an integral aspect of productivity.

The drawings you prepare fit into the overall picture of product realization. They bring an idea to life as a valuable real object. The time you are creating the drawing is the time to consider the many issues involved in manufacturing the part.

The Design Process and Concurrent Engineering

The design process for a product requires a clear understanding of the functions and the performance expected of that product. The product may be new, or it may be a revised version of an existing product. We all have observed, for example, how the design and style of radios, toasters, watches, automobiles, and washing machines have changed. The market for a product and its anticipated uses must be defined clearly, with the assistance of salespeople, market analysts, and others in the organization. Product design is a critical activity because it has been estimated that 70 to 80% of the cost of product development and manufacture is determined at the initial design stages.

As mentioned in Chapter 1, design and manufacturing activities have traditionally taken place sequentially rather than concurrently or simultaneously (Figure 8.1). Designers would spend considerable effort and time in analyzing components and preparing detailed part drawings; these drawings would then be forwarded to other departments in the organization, such as the materials department where, for example, particular alloys and vendor sources would be identified. The specifications would then be sent to a manufacturing department where the detailed drawings would be reviewed and processes selected for efficient production. While this approach seems logical and straightforward, in practice it has been found to be extremely wasteful of resources.

In theory, a product can flow from one department in an organization to another and directly to the marketplace, but in practice there are usually difficulties encountered. For example, a manufacturing engineer may wish to taper the flange on a part to improve its castability, or a different alloy may be desirable, thus necessitating a repeat of the design analysis stage to ensure that the product will still function satisfactorily. These iterations, shown in Figure 8.1a, are certainly wasteful of resources but, more importantly, of time.

There is a great desire, originally driven by the consumer electronics industry, to bring products to market as quickly as possible. The rationale is that products introduced early enjoy a greater percentage of the market and hence profits, and have a longer life before obsolescence (clearly a concern with consumer electronics). For these reasons, concurrent engineering, also called simultaneous engineering, has come to the fore.

A more modern product development approach is shown in Figure 8.1b. While there is a general product flow from market analysis to design to manufacturing, there are recognized iterations that occur in the process. The main difference in the more modern approach is that all disciplines are involved in the early design stages, so that the iterations that naturally occur result in less wasted effort and lost time. A key to the approach is the now well-recognized importance of communication between and within disciplines. That is, while there must be communication between engineering and marketing and service functions, so too must there be avenues of interactions between engineering subdisciplines, for example, design for manufacture, design recyclability, and design for safety.

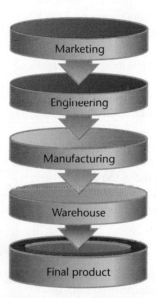

(a) Sequential Process

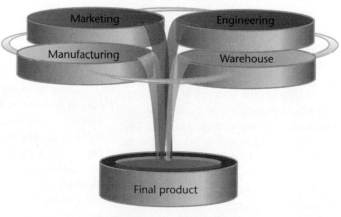

(b) Concurrent Process

8.1   CAD Helps Visualize Complex Designs

The design process begins with the development of an original product concept. An innovative approach to design is highly desirable—and even essential—at this stage for the product to be successful in the marketplace. Innovative approaches can also lead to major savings in material and production costs. The design engineer or product designer must be knowledgeable of the interrelationships among materials, design, and manufacturing, as well as the overall economics of the operation.

Concurrent engineering is a systematic approach integrating the design and manufacture of products with the view of optimizing all elements involved in the life cycle of the product. Life cycle means that all aspects of a product (such as design, development, production, distribution, use, and the product's ultimate disposal and recycling) are considered simultaneously. The basic goals of concurrent engineering are to minimize product design and engineering changes and the time and costs involved in taking the product from design concept to production and introduction of the product into the marketplace.

The philosophy of **life cycle engineering** requires that the entire life of a product be considered in the design stage (i.e., the design, production, distribution, use, and disposal/recycling must be considered simultaneously). Thus a well-designed product is functional (design stage), well manufactured (production), packaged so that it safely arrives to the end user or customer (distribution), functions effectively for its intended life as well as having components that can be easily replaced for maintenance or repair (use), and can be disassembled so that components can be recycled (disposal). Figure 8.2 shows an electromagnet picking up crushed car bodies for recycling.

Although the concept of concurrent engineering appears to be logical and efficient, its implementation can take considerable time and effort when those using it either do not work as a team or fail to appreciate its real benefits. It is apparent that for concurrent engineering to succeed it must:

1. Have the full support of the upper management,

8.2 Car Bodies Crushed for Recycling. *Courtesy of Edward Cross/ Photolibrary.com*

2. Have multifunctional and interactive teamwork, including support groups, and
3. Utilize all available technologies.

There are many examples of the benefits of concurrent engineering. An automotive company, for example, has reduced the number of components in an engine by 30%, and as a result has decreased its weight by 25% and cut manufacturing time by 50%. The concurrent engineering concept can be implemented not only in large organizations but in smaller companies as well. This is particularly noteworthy in view of the fact that 98% of U.S. manufacturing establishments have fewer than 500 employees.

For both large and small companies, product design often involves preparing analytical and physical models of the product, as an aid to studying factors such as forces, stresses, deflections, and optimal part shape. The necessity for such models depends on product complexity. Today, constructing and studying analytical models is simplified through the use of computer-aided design (CAD), computer-aided engineering (CAE), and computer-aided manufacturing (CAM) techniques.

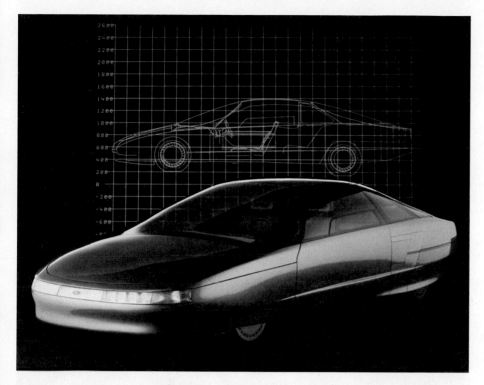

8.3 CAD Helps Visualize Complex Designs. *Ford Motor Company/Dorling Kindersley.*

8.1 COMPUTER-AIDED DESIGN AND PRODUCT DEVELOPMENT

Computer-aided design (CAD) allows the designer to conceptualize objects more easily without having to make costly illustrations, models, or prototypes. These systems are now capable of rapidly and completely analyzing designs, from a simple bracket to complex structures such as the prototype automobile shown in Figure 8.3. The two-engine Boeing 777 passenger airplane was designed completely by computer (paperless design). The airplane was constructed directly from the CAD/CAM models, and no prototypes or mockups were built, unlike previous aircraft. Many companies utilize a simulated 3D model as the "virtual prototype" to improve their design and eliminate costly physical mock-ups.

Computer-Aided Engineering Allows for Future Modification

Using **computer-aided engineering** (CAE), the performance of structures subjected to static or fluctuating loads and various temperatures can now be simulated, analyzed, and tested efficiently, accurately, and more quickly than ever. The information developed can be stored, retrieved, displayed, printed, and transferred anywhere in the organization. Designs can be optimized and modifications can be made directly and easily at any time.

Computer-Aided Engineering Links All Phases of Manufacturing

Computer-aided manufacturing (CAM) involves all phases of manufacturing by utilizing and processing further the large amount of information on materials and processes collected and stored in the organization's database. Computers now assist manufacturing engineers and others in organizing tasks such as programming numerical control of machines; programming robots for materials handling and assembly; designing tools, dies, and fixtures; and maintaining quality control.

On the basis of the models developed using the above-mentioned techniques, the product designer selects and specifies the final shape and dimensions of the product, its dimensional accuracy and surface finish, and the materials to be used. The selection of materials is often made with the advice and cooperation of materials engineers, unless the design engineer is also experienced and qualified in this area. An important design consideration is how a particular component is to be assembled into the final product. To grasp this idea, lift the hood of your car and observe how hundreds of components are put together in a limited space.

8.4 Fiberglass Chassis for a Lotus Car Being Removed from the Mold. *Lotus Cars Ltd./Dorling Kindersley.*

8.5 Car Frames Being Welded on a Robotic Assembly Line. *Courtesy of Adam Lubroth/Stone/ Getty Images Inc.*

The Role of Prototypes and Rapid Prototyping in Product Development

The next step in the production process is to make and test a prototype, that is, an original working model of the product. An important development is rapid prototyping, which relies on CAD/CAM and various manufacturing techniques (using metallic or nonmetallic materials) to quickly produce prototypes in the form of a solid physical model of a part and at low cost. For example, prototyping new automotive components by traditional methods of shaping, forming, machining, and so on, costs hundreds of millions of dollars a year; some components may take a year to produce. See Figure 8.4. **Rapid prototyping** (RP) can cut these costs as well as development times significantly. These techniques are being advanced further so

that they can be used for low-volume economical production of actual parts.

Tests of prototypes must be designed to simulate as closely as possible the conditions under which the product is to be used. These include environmental conditions such as temperature and humidity, as well as the effects of vibration and repeated use and misuse of the product. Computer aided engineering techniques are now capable of comprehensively and rapidly performing such simulations. During this stage, modifications in the original design, materials selected, or production methods may be necessary. After this phase has been completed, appropriate process plans, manufacturing methods, equipment, and tooling are selected

with the cooperation of manufacturing engineers, process planners, and others involved in production. See Figure 8.5.

A **virtual prototype** can serve many of the purposes of a physical model. A 3D solid model can be used to evaluate appearance, customer appeal, fit and clearance for assembled parts, mass properties, kinematics, and other characteristics of the design.

The same information in the CAD database can also be used to direct rapid prototyping processes that generate physical models relatively inexpensively. In the next section, you will learn about these processes and how they operate.

8.2 RAPID PROTOTYPING

Because the volumes contained in a design are fully defined in a solid modeling CAD system, physical models can be created by nontraditional technologies that translate the data into a physical entity. Rapid prototyping systems allow the engineer to develop a prototype directly from a CAD design within minutes or hours instead of the days or weeks it might otherwise take to create a prototype part.

What is it worth to the design process to have an actual part that people can hold in their hands? As a visualization tool and a means for checking the fit with other parts, a physical model is a valuable aid in reducing the time it takes a company to develop an idea from a sketch to a product that is available in the marketplace. Approximately 10% of all manufacturing and design shops spend a minimum of $100,000 per year for prototypes. Confidence in the design and improved ability to communicate with the customer about the design in an understandable way is an important advantage of rapid prototyping. Rapid tooling processes use the same 3D CAD information to produce molds and other tooling that can reduce the time to market even further.

Rapid prototypes are especially useful for prototypes of complex molded parts. Molds for fairly simple plastic parts can cost from $20,000 to $50,000, making them prohibitively expensive to create just to check a design appearance. Using rapid prototyping, single parts can be produced in a matter of hours and used to verify the design. In addition, complex shapes can be created as easily as simpler ones.

Despite its advantages over traditional processes, rapid prototyping is not lightning fast. A part that is 2 by 3 by 1 in. may take three or more hours to create. However, this does not usually depend on the part's complexity, just the size and accuracy built into the prototype file. Parts that would ordinarily have to be molded or cast can be created in the same amount of time required for a rectangular block of about the same dimensions. The complexity of each slice does not have much effect on the time needed to create the part.

Translating the Model

Today's major rapid prototyping systems all work on a similar principle: they slice the CAD model into thin layers, then create the model, layer by layer, from a material that can be fused to the next layer until the entire part is realized.

To send a CAD file to most rapid prototyping systems, often you must export a file in the STL file format. This file type, named for stereolithography, was developed to export CAD data to an early rapid prototyping system. Since then, it has become the de facto standard for exporting CAD data to RP systems.

STL files define the boundaries of the CAD model using triangular facets. This format transforms any model into a standardized definition, but it has the disadvantage of generating a very large file when a realistic shape is required. You generally have the option of setting the size of the facets when you export your model. If the facets are small and the model complex, the resulting STL file will be very large. If a larger size for the triangular facets is used, however, the prototyped part will have noticeable facets on its curved surfaces, as shown in Figure 8.6.

Once the CAD file has been exported, the STL file is read by software that generates thin slices through the model that will be used to create the layers. The accuracy of the model's surface is also limited by the material used in the rapid prototyping process and how small it can make layers and features.

The edge of a prototyped part created by depositing individual layers of material in the horizontal plane and dropping the manufacturing platform down in the vertical direction to create the next layer on top of the first can produce a jagged edge. The size of the jaggies, as these are often called, depends on the thickness of the layer that is deposited. This thickness is limited by the size of the smallest particle that can be fused together. Rapid prototyping systems that have more than three axes of movement can reduce or eliminate the jagged appearance by filling in material on angled edge surfaces.

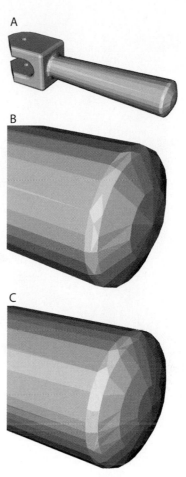

A

B

C

8.6 Faceted Surface on a Prototyped Part. *Reprinted by permission of Pearson Education, Inc., Upper Saddle River, NJ.*

8.7 SLA Rapid Prototyping System. *Courtesy of 3D Systems Corporation.*

8.3 TYPES OF RAPID PROTOTYPING SYSTEMS

Rapid prototyping systems vary in the types of materials used, the size of the model that can be created, and the time it takes to generate a part. If your company owns a rapid prototyping system, the choice of system may be moot. If not, you should consider the design questions that the prototype needs to answer when selecting an appropriate system. The accuracy, size, durability, and time it takes to create a prototype are dependent on the process and material used.

The main categories of rapid prototyping equipment are stereolithography, selective laser sintering, fused deposition modeling, and 3D printing. Most rapid prototyping systems can create parts up to about 10 cu in. in size. Laminate object manufacturing and topographic shell fabrication are two less common methods that allow you to create prototypes of larger parts.

Stereolithography Apparatus (SLA)

SLA uses laser-hardened resins to form the model. Figure 8.7 shows an SLA system from 3D Systems Corporation. The system software controls a focused laser beam in a pool of light-sensitive polymer. The laser hardens each layer in the shape of the cross section or slice of the part. As successive layers are hardened, they are submerged slightly into the resin pool (see Figure 8.7) and the next layer is hardened on top of them. Holes and pockets in the model are formed by uncured resin, which easily pours out of the resulting part. SLA systems create durable parts that can be painted and finished to look very similar to the finished product. The range of accuracy for SLA parts can be up to ±0.002 mm. Because of this accuracy, the prototype parts created using SLA can have relatively smooth surface finishes. SLA is also the most established technology, since it was the first method on the market.

Solid Ground Curing (SGC)

SGC systems are similar to SLA systems except that they use ultraviolet light to cure an entire cross section at once in the polymer pool. A negative of the shape of the cross section is created on a glass plate using electrostatic toner (similar to a copying machine), then used to mask ultraviolet light in the shape of the cross section. These systems are no longer common.

Selective Laser Sintering (SLS)

SLS uses a focused laser to fuse powdered metals, plastics, or ceramics. The fused layer is covered with additional powder and the next layer is fused to it. To form a hole in the prototyped piece, the powdered material is simply not fused in that area. The unfused powder still acts as a base for the next layer, but when the part is completed, the unfused portions are simply poured out. This process has the advantage that models created from powdered metal can sometimes be machined for further refinement. The parts can also be strong enough to be used in certain types of assemblies as one-of-a-kind parts. Figure 8.8 shows an SLS-type rapid prototyping system from 3D Systems. This system can create parts with accuracies of ±50 μm. Other materials, such as a glass-filled nylon, may be used with the sintering process to create parts with varying degrees of flexibility and durability.

Figure 8.9 illustrates an elastomeric material with rubberlike characteristics that makes it suitable for prototyping gaskets and athletic equipment.

Fused Deposition Modeling (FDM)

FDM systems use molten plastic deposited in layers corresponding to cross sections on the part. Because the soft molten plastic cannot be deposited in thin air, to make a hole or an overhang, a second type of plastic is used to create a support structure. Because the two plastics are different materials that do not readily adhere to one another, the support structure can be separated from the actual part. Figure 8.10 shows an FDM system from Stratasys Corporation and some of the parts and support structures that it creates. A part that is about 3 by 2 by 1 in. takes about three hours to create.

8.8 SLS Rapid Prototyping System. *Courtesy of 3D Systems Corporation.*

8.9 Elastomeric Material Used for Prototype Gaskets. *Courtesy of 3D Systems Corporation.*

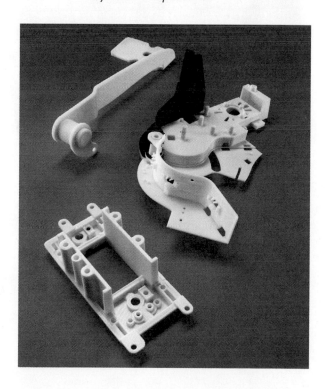

8.10 Fused Deposition Modeling System. *Courtesy of Stratasys, Inc.*

Laminated Object Manufacturing (LOM)

LOM produces solid parts from sheets of material, such as paper or vinyl. LOM systems can be used to create larger prototype parts. Like all rapid prototyping processes, software first generates cross sectional slices through the model. Instead of fusing the layer, however, a computer-controlled laser cuts it from the first sheet of material. Then a heated roller bonds the next sheet to the previous layer, and the next cross section is cut from this sheet. The material that will later be removed is cut into crosshatched shapes to make removal easier. The Helisys LOM-2030H system can create a part with a maximum size of 32 in. length, 22 in. width, and 20 in. height (813 mm length, 559 mm width, and 508 mm height) and a maximum part weight of up to 450 lb (204 kg).

Topographic Shell Fabrication (TSF)

TSF uses layers of high quality silica sand fused together with wax to build shells that can be used to mold rapid prototypes of large scale parts. The sand is deposited in layers and then fused together with molten wax sprayed from a computer-controlled three-axis nozzle. More sand is deposited and then the next layer is fused. The layers range from 0.05-in. to 0.15-in. thick and take about 10 min per square foot of model to print. Once all of the slices have been deposited, the sand/wax shell is smoothed and then lined with plaster or other material. The shell is then used as a temporary mold for creating parts of fiberglass, epoxy, foam, concrete, or other materials. This method is able to handle very large shapes, up to 11 by 6 by 4 ft.

3D Printing

3D printing technology creates 3D physical prototypes by solidifying layers of deposited powder using a liquid binder. These low-cost machines were designed to enable the use of prototypes early and often in the design cycle. At Kodak, for example, a proposed product idea was to be discussed at a 10:30 meeting. At 8:30, the team was asked to bring a model of the idea to the meeting. Z Corporation's 3D printer, similar to that shown in Figure 8.12, was able to build a prototype from the CAD files in time for the meeting.

The relatively low-cost 3D printing systems can be operated safely enough that they can sit next to the regular office printer or copier. See Figure 8.11. Another advantage of Corporation 3D printer systems is that by using a standard inkjet Z print heads, 3D models can be made in full color.

 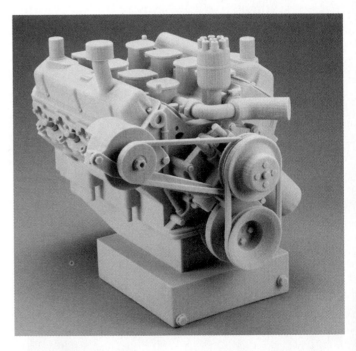

8.11 3D Printing System and a 3D Printer Model. *Courtesy of Z Corporation.*

Rapid Tooling

Rapid prototyping systems were developed to produce parts without having to create a mold or complete intermediate steps needed to manufacture a part. **Rapid tooling** is a similar process, but one that creates the tool (usually a mold for molded plastic or cast metal parts) through a rapid prototyping process, not the part itself. Metal injection molds and molds for cast metal parts are often one of the most expensive and time-consuming parts of the design process. Rapid tooling processes can reduce the amount of time involved in producing these tools. The resulting rapid tool can be used to produce test products and to get products to market early.

Rapid tooling can be accomplished by several different methods. One is direct mold design, in which the tool itself is created using a selective laser sintering-type process. Another method uses rapid prototyping to produce a master part from which a silicone rubber mold is formed. That mold is then used to make other parts. A third method (a more traditional process) uses computer-controlled machining technology to create the cavity in a mold blank to quickly create the mold.

3D Systems' RapidTool process is an example of direct mold design. RapidTool's SLS-type process uses powdered carbon steel pellets coated with a thermal plastic binder. Using a CAD file as input, the SLS process melts (or sinters) the powder to form a green mold shape consisting of metal particles bound by smaller areas of polymer. When the green mold is heated in a furnace, the plastic polymer burns off, leaving only the metal mold as shown in Figure 8.12. The mold is then machined to a tolerance of ± 0.005 in. to eliminate any defects and can be drilled, tapped, welded, and plated like a conventional mold.

Using different materials, cores and molds for sand casting can be created directly using an SLS system, then cured (hardened) in a conventional sand casting oven. Another application is in investment casting. In investment casting, an original shape called a master is used to create the proper shaped opening in a mold. The master is typically made of a wax material so that it will melt out of the mold when molten metal is poured in. Investment casting masters can be produced using SLS processes.

Cores and Cavities

Molded parts are formed by cavities and cores. The **cavity** is the part of the mold that forms the outside shape of the object. The colloquial use of the term mold generally refers to the cavity. Holes that will be formed in molded parts are formed by cores. A **core** is a solid shape that fits inside the mold. It will form a hole in the cooled cast metal or molten plastic. Cores for cast metal parts are often made of packed sand. After the cast metal is cooled, the part is pounded to loosen the particles of sand from one another so they can be poured out through a small hole. This is similar to the way non-hardened resin or unfused powdered metal is poured out of holes in rapid prototypes.

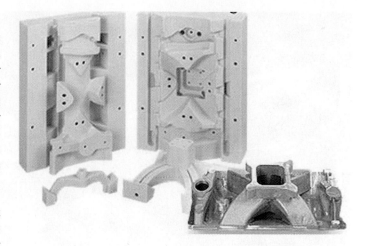

8.12 Rapid Tooling. *Courtesy of Z Corporation.*

Direct Shell Production Casting (DSPC)

DSPC is a system licensed to Soligen Inc. that is used in directly creating molds for metal casting. It is based on 3D printing technologies developed at the Massachusetts Institute of Technology (MIT). First the 3D CAD designed part is used to create a 3D digital model of the mold including the solid cores needed to produce hollow sections. In addition, the CAD file is used to modify the cavity shape by adding fillets and removing features such as small holes that will be machined in the finished casting. If necessary, multiple cavities are defined to produce a mold that forms several parts at once.

To produce the mold, the mold model is sliced into layers. A powder of ceramic material is deposited and liquid binder is "printed" onto the powder in the shape of the cross section of the mold. The process is repeated until the entire mold is printed. Then the mold is fired, producing a rigid ceramic. The unbound powder is removed from the mold to produce the cavities. The mold is then used to produce cast metal parts.

Silicon rubber molds are another way to produce rapid tooling. This process uses an accurately prototyped part that is then coated with silicon rubber to form a mold from which more parts can be molded. The MCP Vacuum Casting System, which uses this process, is capable of producing large plastic parts that weigh as much as 12 lb and span 2 by 3.

Rapid numerical control (NC) machining of mold inserts from a 3D CAD file also promotes rapid tooling. Even though this is more of a traditional process that creates the mold cavity by removing material, the NC machined cavity combined with standard mold blanks can often lead to shorter tooling times for injection molded parts. Metal spraying is another method that can be used in rapid tool production for less complex parts.

Despite the ease with which rapid tooling and rapid prototyping create physical models from CAD data, a strong understanding of traditional and current manufacturing methods will enable you to produce more cost-effective and producible parts.

Courtesy of New York Times.

8.4 DESIGN FOR MANUFACTURE, ASSEMBLY, DISASSEMBLY, AND SERVICE

Design and manufacturing are interrelated, not separate activities. Each part or component of a product must be designed so that it meets design requirements and specifications, and can be manufactured economically and efficiently. This improves productivity and allows a manufacturer to remain competitive.

This area is termed **design for manufacture (DFM)**. DFM is a comprehensive approach to produce goods and integrate the design process with materials, manufacturing methods, process planning, assembly, testing, and quality assurance. Effectively implementing DFM requires a fundamental understanding of the characteristics, capabilities, and limitations of materials, manufacturing processes, and related operations, machinery, and equipment. This includes things like variability in machine performance, dimensional accuracy and surface finish of the workpiece, processing time, and the effect of processing method on part quality.

You must be able to assess the impact of design modifications on manufacturing process selection, assembly, inspection, tools and dies, and product cost. Establishing quantitative relationships is essential in order to optimize the design for ease of manufacturing and assembly at minimum product cost (also called producibility). Computer-aided design, engineering, manufacturing, and process planning techniques, using powerful computer programs, allows such analysis. Expert systems provide capabilities to expedite the traditional iterative process in design optimization.

After individual parts have been manufactured, they have to be assembled into a product. Assembly is an important phase of the overall manufacturing operation and requires consideration of the ease, speed, and cost of putting parts together. Also, many products must be designed so that disassembly is possible, enabling the products to be taken apart for maintenance, servicing, or recycling of their components. Because assembly operations can contribute significantly to product cost, design for assembly (DFA) as well as design for disassembly are now recognized as important aspects of manufacturing. Typically, a product that is easy to assemble is also easy to disassemble. The latest trend now includes design for service, ensuring that individual parts or subassemblies in a product are easy to reach and service.

Methodologies and computer software (CAD) have been developed for DFA utilizing 3D conceptual designs and solid models. In this way, subassembly and assembly times and costs are minimized while maintaining product integrity and performance; the system also improves the product's ease of disassembly. The trend now is to combine design for manufacture and design for assembly into the more comprehensive design for manufacture and assembly (DFMA), which recognizes the inherent interrelationships between design and manufacturing.

There are several methods of assembly, such as using fasteners or adhesive, or by welding, soldering, and brazing, each with its own characteristics and requiring different operations. The use of a bolt and nut, for example, requires preparation of holes that must match in location and size. Hole generation requires operations such as drilling or punching, which take additional time, require separate operations, and produce scrap. On the other hand, products assembled with bolts and nuts can be taken apart and reassembled with relative ease.

Parts can also be assembled with adhesives. This method, which is being used extensively in aircraft and automobile production, does not require holes. However, surfaces to be assembled must match properly and be clean because joint strength is adversely affected by the presence of contaminants such as dirt, dust, oil, and moisture. Unlike mechanical fastening, adhesively joined components, as well as those that are welded, are not usually designed to be taken apart and reassembled, hence are not suitable for the important purposes of recycling individual parts of the product.

Parts may be assembled by hand or by automatic equipment and robots. The choice depends on factors such as the complexity of the product, the number of parts to be assembled, the protection required to prevent damage or scratching of finished surfaces of the parts, and the relative costs of labor and machinery required for automated assembly.

8.5 MATERIAL SELECTION

An ever-increasing variety of materials is now available, each having its own characteristics, applications, advantages, and limitations. The following are the general types of materials used in manufacturing today either individually or in combination.

- **Ferrous metals:** carbon, alloy, stainless, and tool and die steels.
- **Nonferrous metals:** aluminum, magnesium, copper, nickel, titanium, superalloys, refractory metals, beryllium, zirconium, low-melting alloys, and precious metals.
- **Plastics:** thermoplastics, thermosets, and elastomers.
- **Ceramics:** glass ceramics, glasses, graphite, diamond, and diamond-like materials.
- **Composite materials:** reinforced plastics, metal-matrix and ceramic-matrix composites. These are also known as engineered materials.
- **Nanomaterials:** shape-memory alloys, amorphous alloys, superconductors, and various other materials with unique properties.

As new materials are developed, the selection of appropriate materials becomes even more challenging. Aerospace structures, as well as products such as sporting goods, have been at the forefront of new material usage. The trend has been to use more titanium and composites for the airframes of commercial aircraft, with a gradual decline of the use of aluminum and steel. There are constantly shifting trends in the usage of materials in all products, driven principally by economic needs as well as other considerations.

8.6 PROPERTIES OF MATERIALS

When selecting materials for products, we first consider their mechanical properties: strength, toughness, ductility, hardness, elasticity, fatigue, and creep. The strength-to-weight and stiffness-to-weight ratios of material are also important, particularly for aerospace and automotive applications. Aluminum, titanium, and reinforced plastics, for example, have higher values of these ratios than steels and cast irons. The mechanical properties specified for a product and its components should,

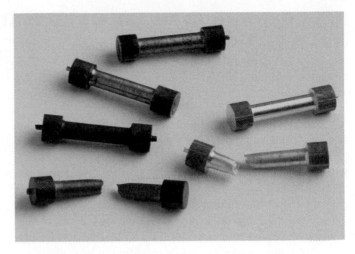

Standard shapes are often used in materials testing to make it easier to compare results. *Courtesy of Clive Streeter © Dorling Kindersley.*

of course, be for the conditions under which the product is expected to function. We then consider the physical properties of density, specific heat, thermal expansion and conductivity, melting point, and electrical and magnetic properties.

Chemical properties also play a significant role in hostile as well as normal environments. Oxidation, corrosion, general degradation of properties, toxicity, and flammability of materials are among the important factors to be considered. In some commercial airline disasters, for example, many deaths have been caused by toxic fumes from burning nonmetallic materials in the aircraft cabin.

Manufacturing properties of materials determine whether they can be cast, formed, machined, welded, and heat treated with relative ease (Table 8.1). Methods used to process materials to the desired shapes can adversely affect the product's final properties, service life, and cost.

Table 8.1 General Manufacturing Characteristics of Various Alloys.

Alloy	Castability	Weldability	Machinability
Aluminum	Excellent	Fair	Good/Excellent
Copper	Fair/Good	Fair	Fair/Good
Gray cast iron	Excellent	Difficult	Good
White cast iron	Good	Very Poor	Very Poor
Nickel	Fair	Fair	Fair
Steels	Fair	Excellent	Fair
Zinc	Excellent	Difficult	Excellent

8.7 COST AND AVAILABILITY OF MATERIALS

Cost and availability of raw and processed materials and manufactured components are major concerns in manufacturing. Competitively, the economic aspects of material selection are as important as the technological considerations of properties and characteristics of materials.

If raw or processed materials or manufactured components are not available in the desired shapes, dimensions and quantities, substitutes and/or additional processing will be required, which can contribute significantly to product cost. For example, if we need a round bar of a certain diameter and it is not available in standard form, then we have to purchase a larger rod and reduce its diameter by some means, such as machining, drawing through a die, or grinding. It should be noted, however, that a product design can be modified to take advantage of standard dimensions of raw materials, thus avoiding additional manufacturing costs.

Reliability of supply, as well as demand, affects cost. Most countries import numerous raw materials that are essential for production. The United States, for example, imports the majority of raw materials such as natural rubber, diamond, cobalt, titanium, chromium, aluminum, and nickel from other countries. The broad political implications of such reliance on other countries are self-evident.

Different costs are involved in processing materials by different methods. Some methods require expensive machinery, others require extensive labor, and still others require personnel with special skills, a high level of education, or specialized training.

8.8 APPEARANCE, SERVICE LIFE, AND RECYCLING

The appearance of materials after they have been manufactured into products influences their appeal to the consumer. Color, feel, and surface texture are characteristics that we all consider when making a decision about purchasing a product.

Time and service-dependent phenomena such as wear, fatigue, creep, and dimensional stability are important. These phenomena can significantly affect a product's performance and, if not controlled, can lead to total failure of the product. Similarly, compatibility of materials used in a product is important. Friction and wear, and corrosion can shorten a product's life or cause it to fail prematurely. Another phenomena that can cause failure is galvanic corrosion between mating parts made of dissimilar metals.

Recycling or proper disposal of materials at the end of their useful service lives has become increasingly important in an age when we are more conscious of preserving resources and maintaining a clean and healthy environment. For example, many new products, such as decking materials, picnic tables, and even stylish interior panels are made from recycled HDPE (high density polyethylene). The proper treatment and disposal of toxic wastes and materials is also a crucial consideration.

RetroPlate flooring. *Courtesy of Retroplate System.*

SUSTAINABILITY APPLAUDED IN NEW MANUFACTURING PRODUCTS

Polishing concrete is a relatively new technique for turning both new and old concrete slabs into attractive, durable, finished floors, thus reducing material use.

In the 1990s, RetroPlate (from Advanced Floor Products, Inc. of Provo, Utah) pioneered a process of grinding, polishing, and chemically hardening concrete which has now been used on more than 100 million square feet of flooring. The highly durable surface is easy to maintain and free of VOC emissions, in addition to reducing impacts from construction and demolitions, according to BuildingGreen, Inc., which highlighted RetroPlate in a list of Top-10 Green Building Products.

The 2006 listing also included PaperStone™ (a composite material made from cellulose fiber and a non-petroleum phenolic resin derived in part from cashew shells) and stylish interior panel products made from recycled materials by 3form, Inc. 3form's 100% post-consumer recycled high-density polyethylene (HDPE) panel product is used in toilet partitions, interior workstations, and interior trim.

BuildingGreen Inc. publishes Environmental Building News™ and the online GreenSpec® Directory, which lists product descriptions for over 2,100 environmentally preferable products selected by BuildingGreen editors.

8.9 MANUFACTURING PROCESSES

Before preparing a drawing for the production of a part, the drafter/designer should consider what manufacturing processes are to be used. These processes will determine the representation the detailed features of the part, the choice of dimensions, and the machining process accuracy.

Many processes are used to produce parts and shapes. There is usually more than one way to manufacture a part from a given material. Table 8.2 lists common methods of production for various features.

Two robots with YAG lasers operating in tandem to machine a complex 3D part. *Courtesy of Maximilian Stock LTD/Phototake NYC.*

Table 8.2 Shapes and Some Common Methods of Production.

Shape of Feature	Production Method
Flat surfaces	Rolling, planing, broaching, milling, shaping, grinding
Parts with cavities	End milling, electrical-discharge machining, electrochemical machining, ultrasonic machining, casting
Parts with sharp features	Permanent mold casting, machining, grinding, fabricating, powder metallurgy
Thin hollow shapes	Slush casting, electroforming, fabricating
Tubular shapes	Extrusion, drawing, roll forming, spinning, centrifugal casting
Tubular parts	Rubber forming, expanding with hydraulic pressure, explosive forming, spinning
Curvature on thin sheets	Stretch forming, peen forming, fabricating, assembly
Opening in thin sheets	Blanking, chemical blanking, photochemical blanking
Cross-sections	Drawing, extruding, shaving, turning, centerless grinding
Square edges	Fine blanking, machining, shaving, belt grinding
Small holes	Laser, electrical discharge machining, electrochemical machining
Surface textures	Knurling, wire brushing, grinding, belt grinding, shot blasting, etching, deposition
Detailed surface feature	Coining, investment casting, permanent-mold casting, machining
Threaded parts	Thread cutting, thread rolling, thread grinding, chasing
Very large parts	Casting, forging, fabricating, assembly
Very small parts	Investment casting, machining, etching, powder metallurgy, nanofabrication, micromachining

(a) Milled Part, (b) Part Turned on a Lathe. *Courtesy of PENCOM.*

Processing Methods

The broad categories of processing methods for materials are:

- **Casting:** expendable molds (sand casting) and permanent molds.
- **Forming and shaping:** rolling, forging, extrusion, drawing, sheet forming, powder metallurgy, and molding.
- **Machining:** turning, boring, drilling, milling, planing, shaping, broaching, grinding, ultrasonic machining; chemical, electrical, and electrochemical machining; and high-energy beam machining.
- **Joining:** welding, brazing, soldering, diffusion bonding, adhesive bonding, and mechanical joining.
- **Finishing:** honing, lapping, polishing, burnishing, deburring, surface treating, coating, and plating.

Selecting a particular manufacturing process, or a series of processes, depends not only on the shape to be produced but also on many other factors pertaining to material properties (Table 8.1). Brittle and hard materials, for example, cannot be shaped easily, whereas they can be cast or machined by several methods. The manufacturing process usually alters the properties of materials. Metals that are formed at room temperature, for example, become stronger, harder, and less ductile than they were before processing.

Two steel mounting brackets are shown in Figure 8.13, one designed for casting, and the other for stamping of sheet metal. Note that there are some differences in the designs, although the parts are basically alike. Each of these two manufacturing

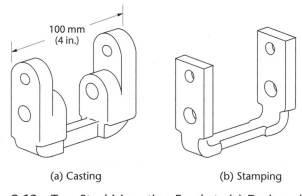

(a) Casting   (b) Stamping

8.13   Two Steel Mounting Brackets (a) Designed for Casting, (b) Designed for Stamping

processes has its own advantages and limitations, as well as production rates and manufacturing costs.

Manufacturing engineers are constantly being challenged to find new solutions to manufacturing problems and cost reduction. For a long time, for example, sheet metal parts were cut and fabricated by traditional tools, punches, and dies. Although they are still widely used, some of these operations are now being replaced by laser cutting techniques. With advances in computer technology, we can automatically control the path of the laser, thus increasing the capability of producing a wide variety of shapes accurately, repeatedly, and economically.

8.10 DO'S AND DON'TS OF PRACTICAL DESIGN

Figures 8.14 and 8.15 show examples in which knowledge of manufacturing processes and limitations is essential for good design.

Casting Design

Figure 8.14 shows drawings of casting designs containing common design flaws alongside preferred alternatives.

Many difficulties in producing good castings result from abrupt changes in section or thickness. In Figure 8.14a, rib thicknesses are uniform so that the metal will flow easily to all parts. Fillet radii are equal to the rib thickness—a good general rule to follow. When it is necessary to join a thin feature to a thicker feature, the thin feature should be thickened as it approaches the intersection, as shown in Figure 8.14b.

In Figures 8.14c, g, and h, coring is used to produce walls with more-uniform sections. In Figure 8.14d, an abrupt change in sections is avoided by making thinner walls and leaving a collar.

Figures 8.14e and f show examples in which the preferred design tends to allow the castings to cool without introducing internal stresses. The less desirable design is more likely to crack as it cools, since there is no give in the design. Curved spokes are preferable to straight spokes, and an odd number of spokes is better than an even number because direct stresses along opposite spokes are avoided.

The design of a part may cause unnecessary trouble and expense for the pattern shop and foundry without any benefit to the design. For example, in the poor designs in Figures 8.14j and k, one-piece patterns would not withdraw from the sand, and two-piece patterns would be necessary. In the preferred examples, the design is just as useful and would be more economical in the pattern shop and foundry.

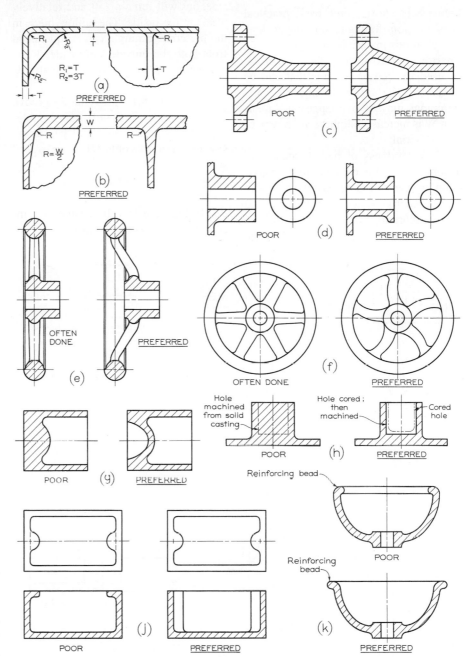

8.14 Casting Design Do's and Don'ts

Practical Considerations

Figure 8.15 shows some basic practical considerations for manufacturing designs using various materials. In Figure 8.15a, a narrower piece of stock sheet metal can be used for certain designs that can be linked or overlapped. In this case, the stampings may be overlapped if dimension W is increased slightly, as shown, to save material.

The hardness of heat treated steel depends on carbon content. To get maximum hardness, it is necessary to rapidly cool (quench) the steel after heating, and it is important that a design can be quenched uniformly. In Figure 8.15b, the solid piece will harden well on the outside, but will remain soft and relatively weak on the inside. The hollow piece in the preferred example can be quenched from both the outside and inside. Thus, a hardened hollow shaft can actually be stronger than a solid one.

In Figure 8.15c, a rounded groove (neck) around a shaft next to a shoulder eliminates a practical difficulty in precision grinding. Not only is it more expensive to grind a sharp internal corner, but sharp corners often lead to cracking and failure.

In Figure 8.15d the design at right eliminates a costly reinforced weld, which would be needed in the design at left. The preferred example has strong virgin metal with a generous radius at the point at where the stress is likely to be most severe. It is possible to make the design on the left as strong as that on the right, but it requires more expense, expertise, and special equipment.

It is difficult to drill into a slanting surface, as shown at left in Figure 8.15e. Drilling is much easier if a boss is provided, as shown at right.

The design at left in Figure 8.15f requires accurate boring or reaming of a blind hole all the way to a flat bottom, which is difficult and expensive. It is better to drill deeper than the hole is to be finished, as shown at the right, to provide room for tool clearance and chips.

In the upper example in Figure 8.15g, the drill and counterbore cannot be used for the hole in the centerpiece because of the raised portion at the right end. In the preferred example, the end is redesigned to provide access for the drill and counterbore.

In the top design in Figure 8.15h, the ends are not the same height, so each flat surface must be machined separately. In the design below, the ends are the same height, the surfaces are in line horizontally, and only two machining operations are necessary. It is always good to simplify and limit the machining as much as possible.

The design at the left in Figure 8.15j requires that the housing be bored for the entire length to receive a pressed bushing. Machining time can be decreased if the cored recess is made as shown, assuming that average loads would be applied in use.

The lower bolt in Figure 8.15k is encircled by a rounded groove no deeper than the root of the thread. This makes a gentle transition from the small diameter at the root of the threads and the large diameter of the body of the bolt, producing less stress concentration and a stronger bolt. In general, sharp internal corners should be avoided because these are points of stress concentration and possible failure.

In Figure 8.15m, a 0.25 in. steel plate is being pulled, as shown by the arrows. Increasing the radius of the inside corners increases the strength of the plate by distributing the load over a greater area.

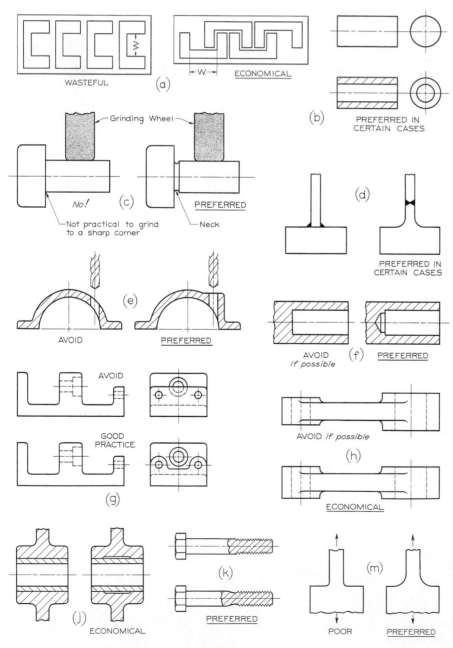

8.15 Practical Design Do's and Don'ts

8.16 Assembly of an Aircraft. *Courtesy AP Wide World Photos.*

8.11 DIMENSIONAL ACCURACY AND SURFACE FINISH

Size, thickness, and shape complexity of the part have a major bearing on the manufacturing process selected to produce it. Flat parts with thin cross sections, for example, cannot be cast properly. Complex parts cannot be formed easily and economically, whereas they may be cast or fabricated from individual pieces.

Tolerances and surface finish obtained in hot-working operations cannot be as good as those obtained in cold-working (room temperature) operations because dimensional changes, warpage, and surface oxidation occur during processing at elevated temperatures. Some casting processes produce a better surface finish than others because of the different types of mold materials used and their surface finish.

The size and shape of manufactured products vary widely. For example, the main landing gear for a twin-engine, 400-passenger Boeing 777 jetliner is 4.3 m (14 ft) high, with three axles and six wheels, made by forging and machining processes (Figure 8.16). At the other extreme is the generation of a 0.05-mm (0.002-in.) diameter hole at one end of a 0.35-mm (0.014-in.) diameter needle, using a process called electrical-discharge machining. The hole is burr-free and has a location accuracy of ±0.003 mm (0.0001 in.).

Another small-scale manufacturing example is given in Figure 8.17, which shows microscopic gears as small as 100 m (0.004 in.) in diameter. These gears have possible applications such as powering microrobots to repair human cells, microknives in surgery, and camera shutters for precise photography. The gears are made by a special electroplating and X-ray etching technique of metal plates coated with a polymer film. The center gear is smaller than a human hair. Such small scale operations are called **nanotechnology** and **nanofabrication** ("nano" meaning one billionth).

8.17 Colored Scanning Electron Micrograph of the Drive Gear (Orange) in a Micromotor. The orange colored gear in this colored scanning electron micrograph is smaller in diameter than a human hair and 100 times thinner than a sheet of paper. The whole micromotor device was etched into the surface of a wafer of silicon by the same techniques used to make silicon chips.

Ultraprecision manufacturing techniques and machinery are now being developed and are coming into more common use. For machining mirrorlike surfaces, for example, the cutting tool is a very sharp diamond tip, and the equipment has very high stiffness and must be operated in a room where the temperature is controlled within 1°C. Highly sophisticated techniques such as molecular-beam epitaxy and scanning-tunneling microscopy are being implemented to obtain accuracies on the order of the atomic lattice ±0.1 nm.

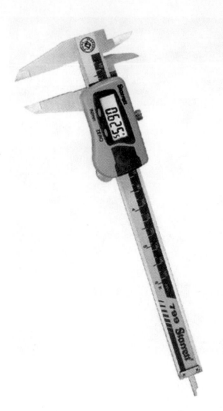

8.18 Digital calipers. *Courtesy of L. S. Starrett Company.*

8.12 MEASURING DEVICES USED IN MANUFACTURING

Although the machinist uses various measuring devices depending on the kind of dimensions (fractional, decimal, or metric) shown on the drawing, it is evident that to dimension correctly, the engineering designer must have at least a working knowledge of the common measuring tools. The **machinists' scale** or steel rule, is a commonly used measuring tool in the shop (Figure 8.18a). The smallest division on one scale of this rule is 1/64″, which is used for common fractional dimensions. Also, many machinists' rules have a decimal scale with the smallest division of .010, which is used for dimensions given on the drawing by the decimal system. For checking the nominal size of outside diameters, the dial or **digital calipers** are used, as shown in Figures 8.18b and 8.18c. It is common practice to check measurements to 0.025 mm (0.0010 in.) with these instruments, and in some instances they are used to measure directly to 0.0025 mm (0.00010 in.). Some digital measuring devices also provide printer/recorders providing a hard copy output of measurements, and even a list of the statistical mean, minimum, and maximum values, and standard deviation.

Most measuring devices in manufacturing are adjustable so they can be used for a range of measurements, but some measuring devices are designed to be used for only one particular dimension. These are called **fixed gages.** A common type of fixed gage is called a "go/no go" gage. An example is shown in Figure 8.19. It has one end finished at a diameter that is sized to fit inside a correctly sized matching hole and the other end sized so that it will not fit in a correctly sized hole. Fixture and gage design is an important specialty area in manufacturing.

8.13 OPERATIONAL AND MANUFACTURING COSTS

The design and cost of tooling, the lead time required to begin production, and the effect of workpiece material on tool and die life are major considerations. Depending on its size, shape, and expected life, the cost of tooling can be substantial. For example, a set of steel dies for stamping sheet metal fenders for automobiles may cost about $2 million.

For parts made from expensive materials, the lower the scrap rate, the more economical the production process will be; thus, every attempt should be made for zero-base waste. Because it generates chips, machining may not be more economical than forming operations, all other factors being the same.

Availability of machines and equipment and operating experience within the manufacturing facility are also important cost factors. If they are not available, some parts may have to be manufactured by outside firms. Automakers, for example, purchase many parts from outside vendors, or have them made by outside firms according to the automaker's specifications.

The number of parts required (quantity) and the required production rate (pieces per hour) are important in determining the processes to be used and the economics of production. Beverage cans or transistors, for example, are consumed in numbers and at rates much higher than telescopes and propellers for ships.

The operation of machinery has significant environmental and safety implications. Depending on the type of operation, some processes adversely affect the environment, such as the use of oil-base lubricants in hot metalworking processes. Unless properly controlled, such processes can cause air, water, and noise pollution. The safe use of machinery is another important consideration, requiring precautions to eliminate hazards in the workplace.

8.19 Go/No Go Gage. *Courtesy of Tom Jungst.*

8.14 CONSEQUENCES OF MATERIAL AND PROCESS SELECTION

Many examples of product failure can be traced to poor selection of material or manufacturing processes or poor control of process variables. A component or a product is generally considered to have failed when:

- It stops functioning (broken shaft, gear, bolt, cable, or turbine blade).
- It does not function properly or perform within required specification limits (worn bearings, gears, tools, and dies).
- It becomes unreliable or unsafe for further use (frayed cable in a winch, crack in a shaft, poor connection in a printed circuit board, or delamination of a reinforced plastic component).

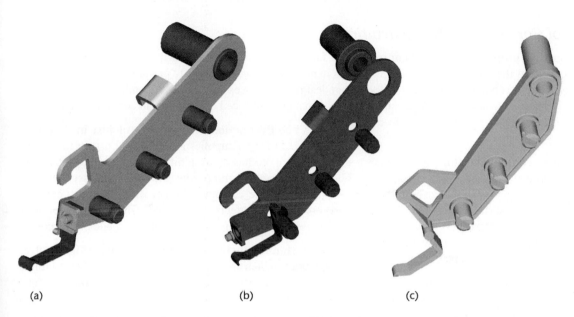

(a)   (b)   (c)

8.20 Net-Shape Manufactured Parts. *Courtesy of Tektronix.*

8.15 NET-SHAPE MANUFACTURING

Since not all manufacturing operations produce finished parts, additional operations may be necessary. For example, a forged part may not have the desired dimensions or surface finish, so additional operations such as machining or grinding may be necessary. Likewise, if it is difficult, impossible, or economically undesirable to produce a part with holes using just one manufacturing process, processes such as drilling may be needed. In another example, the holes produced by a particular manufacturing process may not have the proper roundness, dimensional accuracy, or surface finish, creating a need for additional operations such as honing.

Finishing operations can contribute significantly to the cost of a product. Consequently, the trend has been for net-shape or near **net-shape manufacturing.** In net-shape or near net-shape manufacturing, the part is made as close to the final desired dimensions, tolerances, surface finish, and specifications as possible. Typical examples of these methods are near net-shape forging and casting of parts, stamped sheet metal parts, injection molded plastics, and components made by powder metallurgy techniques.

8.16 COMPUTER-INTEGRATED MANUFACTURING

The major goals of automation in manufacturing facilities are to integrate various operations to improve productivity, increase product quality and uniformity, minimize cycle times, and reduce labor costs. Beginning in the 1940s, automation has accelerated because of rapid advances in control systems for machines and in computer technology.

Few developments in the history of manufacturing have had a more significant impact than computers. Computers are now used in a very broad range of applications, including control and optimization of manufacturing processes, material handling, assembly, automated inspection and testing of products, as well as inventory control and numerous management activities. Beginning with computer graphics and computer aided design and manufacturing, the use of computers has been extended to computer integrated manufacturing (CIM). Computer integrated manufacturing is particularly effective because of its capability for:

- Responsiveness to rapid changes in market demand and product modification.
- Better use of materials, machinery, and personnel, and reduced inventory.
- Better control of production and management of the total manufacturing operation.
- High quality products at low cost.

Major Applications of Computers in Manufacturing

Computer Numerical Control Computer numerical control **(CNC)** is a method of controlling the movements of machine components by direct insertion of coded instructions in the form of numerical data. Numerical control was first implemented in the early 1950s and was a major advance in the automation of machines.

Adaptive Control In **adaptive control (AC)** the parameters in a manufacturing process are adjusted automatically to optimize production rate and product quality, and to minimize cost. Parameters such as forces, temperatures, surface finish, and dimensions of the part are monitored constantly. If they move outside the acceptable range, the system adjusts the process variables until the parameters again fall within the acceptable range.

Industrial Robots **Industrial robots** were introduced in the early 1960s, and they have been replacing humans in operations that are repetitive, boring, and dangerous, thus reducing the possibility of human error, decreasing variability in product quality, and improving productivity. Robots with sensory perception capabilities are being developed (intelligent robots), with movements that simulate those of humans.

Automated Handling of Materials Due to **automated handling of materials,** computers have allowed highly efficient handling of materials and products in various stages of completion (work in progress), such as from storage to machine, from machine to machine, and at the points of inspection, inventory, and shipment.

Automated and Robotic Assembly **Automated and robotic assembly** systems are replacing costly assembly by operators. Products are designed or redesigned so that they can be assembled more easily by machine.

Computer-Aided Process Planning Computer-aided **process planning (CAPP)** is capable of improving productivity in a plant by optimizing process plans, reducing planning costs, and improving the consistency of product quality and reliability. Functions such as cost estimating and work standards (time required to perform a certain operation) can also be incorporated into the system.

Group Technology The concept of **group technology (GT)** is that parts can be grouped and produced by classifying them into families, according to similarities in design and similarities in manufacturing processes to produce the part. In this way, part designs and process plans can be standardized and families of parts can be produced efficiently and economically.

Just in Time Production The principle of **just in time production (JIT)** is that supplies are delivered just in time to be used, parts are produced just in time to be made into subassemblies and assemblies, and products are finished just in time to be delivered to the customer. In this way, inventory carrying costs are low, part defects are detected right away, productivity is increased, and high quality products are made at low cost.

Cellular Manufacturing **Cellular manufacturing** involves workstations, which are manufacturing cells usually containing several machines and with a central robot, each performing a different operation on the part.

Flexible Manufacturing Systems **Flexible manufacturing systems (FMS)** integrate manufacturing cells into a large unit, all interfaced with a central computer. Flexible manufacturing systems have the highest level of efficiency, sophistication, and productivity in manufacturing. Although costly, they are capable of producing parts randomly and changing manufacturing sequences on different parts quickly; thus, they can meet rapid changes in market demand for various types of products.

Expert systems **Expert systems** are basically intelligent computer programs. Expert systems are being developed rapidly with capabilities to perform tasks and solve difficult real-life problems as human experts would.

Artificial Intelligence **Artificial intelligence (AI)** involves the use of machines and computers to replace human intelligence. Computer controlled systems are becoming capable of learning from experience and making decisions that optimize operations and minimize costs. Artificial neural networks, which are designed to simulate the thought processes of the human brain, have the capability of modeling and simulating production facilities, monitoring and controlling manufacturing processes, diagnosing problems in machine performance, conducting financial planning, and managing a company's manufacturing strategy.

8.17 SHARED MANUFACTURING

Although large corporations can afford to implement current technology and take risks, smaller companies generally have difficulty in doing so, due to limited personnel, resources, and capital. More recently, the concept of **shared manufacturing** has been proposed. This consists of a regional or nationwide network of manufacturing facilities with state-of-the-art equipment for training, prototype development, and small-scale production runs to help small companies develop products that compete in the global marketplace.

In view of these advances and their potential, some experts have envisioned the factory of the future in which production could take place with little or no direct human intervention. Although the discussion remains highly controversial, the human role in this system is expected to be confined to supervision, maintenance, and upgrading of machines, computers, and software.

8.18 MANUFACTURING METHODS AND THE DRAWING

In designing a part, consider what materials and manufacturing processes are to be used. These processes will determine the representation of the detailed features of the part, the choice of dimensions, and the machining or processing accuracy. The principal methods of metal forming are:

- **Casting**
- **Machining** from standard stock
- **Welding**
- **Forming** from sheet stock
- **Forging**

A knowledge of these processes, along with a thorough understanding of the intended use of the part, will help determine some basic manufacturing processes.

In sand-casting all cast surfaces remain rough textured, with all corners filleted or rounded. Sharp corners indicate that at least one of the surfaces is finished (i.e., machined further usually to produce a flat surface), and finish marks are shown on the edge view of the finished surface. Plastic parts are similar in many ways to castings because they have filleted and rounded corners and draft to allow the parts to be removed from the mold.

In drawings of parts machined from standard stock, most surfaces are represented as machined. In some cases, as on shafting, the surface existing on the raw stock is often accurate enough without further finishing. Corners are usually sharp, but fillets and rounds are machined when necessary. For example, an interior corner may be machined with a radius to provide greater strength.

On welding drawings, several pieces are cut to size and welded together. Welding symbols (listed in Appendix 32) indicate the welds required. Generally there are no fillets and rounds except those generated during the welding process itself. Certain surfaces may be machined after welding or, in some cases, before welding. Notice that lines are shown where the separate pieces are joined.

On sheet metal drawings, the thickness of the material is uniform and is usually given in the material specification note rather than by a dimension on the drawing. Bend radii and bend reliefs at corners are specified according to standard practice. For dimensions, either the decimal-inch or metric dimensioning systems may be used. Allowances of extra material for joints may be required when the flat blank size is being determined.

For forged parts, separate drawings may be made for the die maker and for the machinist. The forging drawing provides only the information to produce the forging, and the dimensions given are those needed by the die maker. All corners are rounded and filleted and are shown as such on the drawing. The draft is drawn to scale and is usually specified by degrees in a note. A separate drawing for the machinist shows the locations and sizes of drilled holes and information for surface finishes.

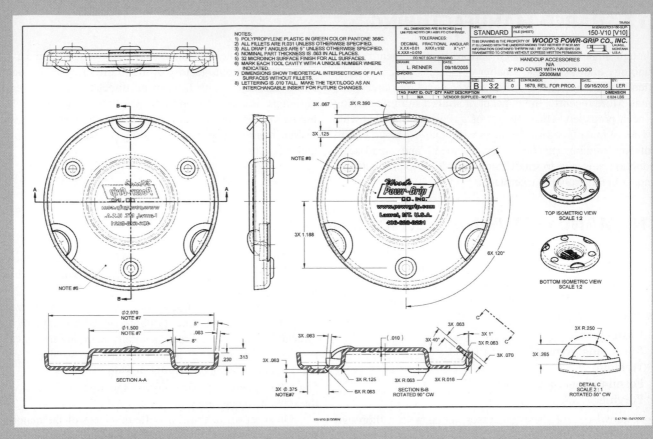

Drawing for a Molded Plastic Part. *Courtesy of Wood's Power-Grip Co., Inc.*

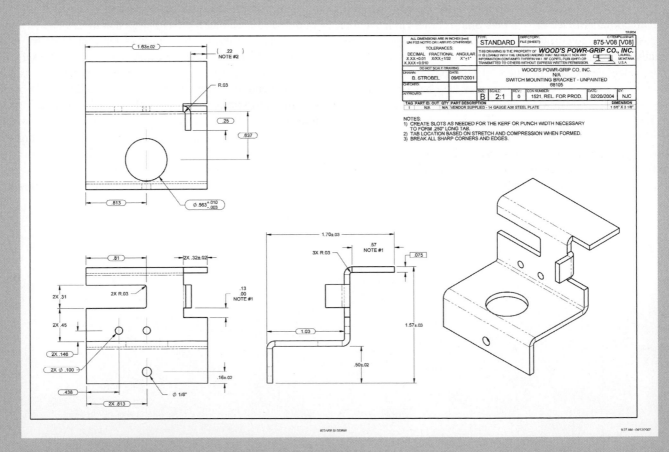

Drawing for a Sheet Metal Part. *Courtesy of Wood's Power-Grip Co., Inc.*

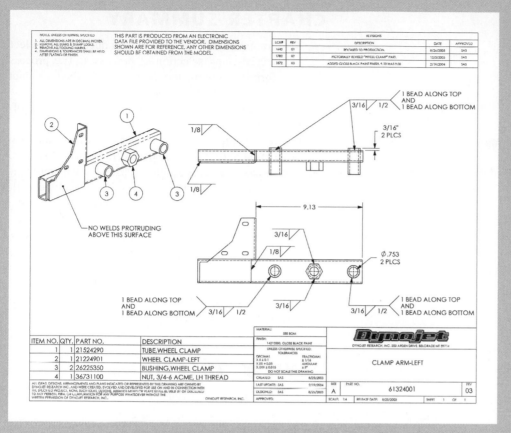

Drawing for a Welded Assembly. *Courtesy of Dynojet Research, Inc.*

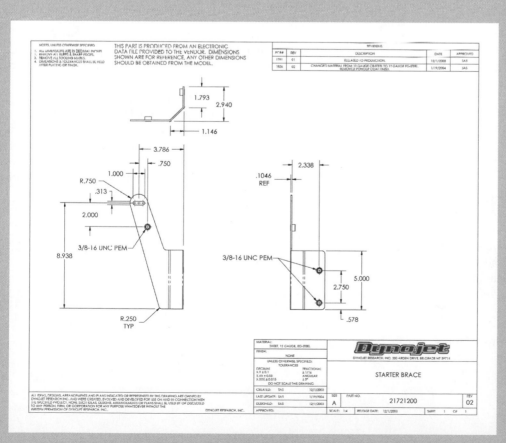

Drawing for a Sheet Metal Part. *Courtesy of Dynojet Research, Inc.*

KEY WORDS

Discrete Products
Continuous Products
Concurrent Engineering
Life Cycle Engineering
Computer-Aided Design
Computer-Aided Engineering
Computer-Aided Manufacturing
Rapid Prototyping
Virtual Prototype
Stereolithography Apparatus (SLA)
Solid Ground Curing (SGC)
Selective Laser Sintering (SLS)
Fused Deposition Modeling (FDM)
Laminated Object Manufacturing (LOM)
Topographic Shell Fabrication (TSF)
3D Printing
Rapid Tooling
Cavity
Core
Direct Shell Production Casting (DSPC)
Design for Manufacture (DFM)
Ferrous Metals
Nonferrous Metals
Plastics
Ceramics
Composite Materials
Nanomaterials
Casting
Forming and Shaping
Machining
Joining
Finishing
Nanotechnology
Nanofabrication
Machinists' Scale
Digital Calipers
Fixed Gages
Net-Shape Manufacturing
Computer Numerical Control (CNC)
Adaptive Control (AC)
Industrial Robots
Automated Handling of Materials
Automated and Robotic Assembly
Computer-Aided Process Planning (CAPP)
Group Technology (GT)
Just in Time Production (JIT)
Cellular Manufacturing
Flexible Manufacturing Systems (FMS)
Expert Systems
Artificial Intelligence (AT)
Shared Manufacturing
Casting
Machining
Welding
Forming
Forging

CHAPTER SUMMARY

- Modern manufacturing involves product design, selection of materials, and selection of processes. The process of transforming raw materials into a finished product is called the manufacturing process.
- The design process requires a clear understanding of the functions and performance expected of that product.
- Concurrent engineering integrates the design process with production to optimize the life cycle of the product.
- Computer-aided design, engineering, and manufacturing are used to construct and study models (prototypes) allowing the designer to conceptualize objects more easily and more cost-efficiently.
- The selection of appropriate materials is key to successful product development.
- Manufacturing processing methods have changed dramatically over the last few decades. More cost and time efficient processes can be implemented using computer-integrated manufacturing.

REVIEW QUESTIONS

1. List the three important phases in the manufacturing process.
2. Define concurrent engineering and explain how it can be used to enhance the design and manufacturing process.
3. Define integrated product development and explain its benefits.
4. Define computer supported cooperative work and discuss its relationship with concurrent engineering.
5. Define modeling for assembly and list at least two benefits for the modern manufacturer.
6. Explain the benefits of rapid prototyping.
7. List four types of materials used in manufacturing today.
8. List the five broad categories of manufacturing processing.
9. Give at least two examples of nanotechnology.
10. List four types of measuring devices.
11. Give three consequences of improper selection of materials and processes.
12. List four application of computer-integrated manufacturing.

CHAPTER NINE

DIMENSIONING

OBJECTIVES

After studying the material in this chapter, you should be able to:

1. Use conventional dimensioning techniques to describe size and shape accurately on an engineering drawing.

2. Create and read a drawing at a specified scale.

3. Correctly place dimension lines, extension lines, angles, and notes.

4. Dimension circles, arcs, and inclined surfaces.

5. Apply finish symbols and notes to a drawing.

6. Dimension contours.

7. Use standard practices for dimensioning prisms, cylinders, holes and curves.

8. List practices for dimensioning a solid model as documentation.

9. Identify guidelines for the do's and don'ts of dimensioning.

Refer to the following standards:
- ANSI/ASME Y14.5M-1994 Dimensioning and Tolerancing
- ASME Y14.41-2003 Digital Product Definition Data Practices

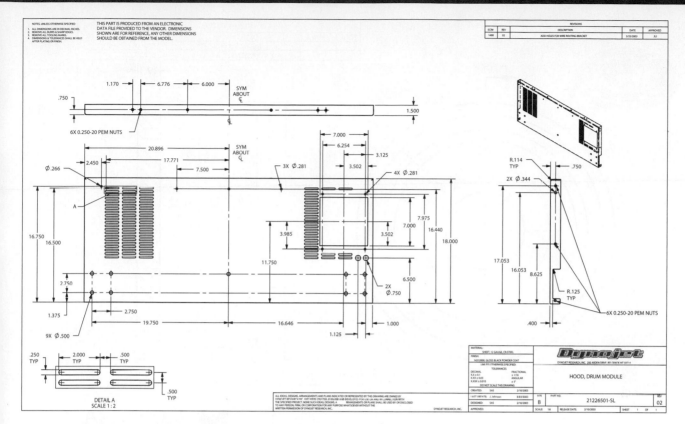

Dimensioned Drawing from Solid Model. This dimensioned drawing for the sheet metal drum module hood was created from a 3D model using Solidworks. Courtesy of Dynojet Research, Inc.

OVERVIEW

It is essential to describe not only the shape of the features you design, but also their sizes and locations. Dimensions and notes define the size, finish, and other requirements to fully define what you want manufactured.

Standards organizations prescribe how dimensions should appear and the general rules for their selection and placement in the drawing and in digital models, but it takes skill and practice to dimension drawings so that their interpretation is clear and unambiguous.

Whether you are creating 2D drawings or 3D models, CAD systems are great for producing dimensions that follow standards for the appearance of the dimensions themselves. However, the job of selecting which dimension to show or where to place it in a drawing takes a level of intelligence that is not part of most CAD systems. Those important decisions are still up to the CAD user—or in other words, *you.*

Learning good practices for dimensioning and tolerancing to define part geometry can also help you to create better 3D solid models. If you have a good understanding of how the sizes and locations of model features will be defined, you can plan ahead to show this information clearly in the model.

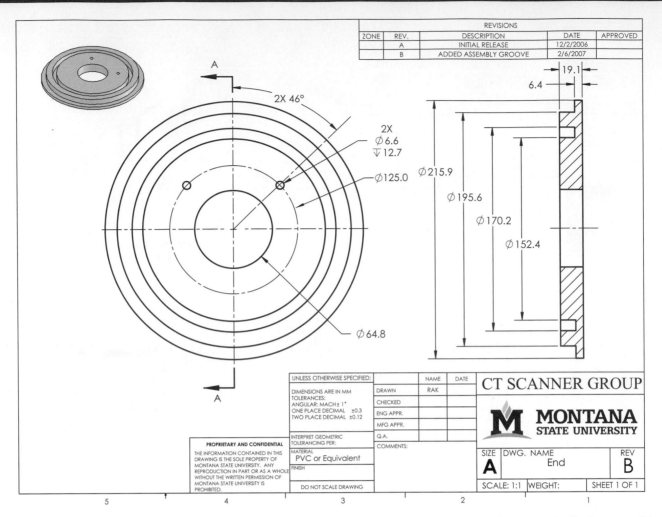

9.1 Automatically Generated Dimensions. *Views and dimensions can be generated automatically from a solid model. Courtesy of Robert Kincaid.*

UNDERSTANDING DIMENSIONING

You have been learning to completely describe an object's shape using different types of drawing views. By providing dimensions, you describe the sizes and locations of design features.

The need for interchangeability of parts is the basis for modern part dimensioning. Drawings for products must be dimensioned so that production personnel all over the world can make mating parts that will fit properly when assembled or when used to replace parts.

The increasing need for precision manufacturing and interchangeability has shifted responsibility for size control to the design engineer or detail drafter. The production worker must properly interpret the instructions given

on the drawings to produce the required part or construct the building or system. You should be familiar with materials and methods of construction and with production requirements in order to create drawings that define exactly what you want to have manufactured.

Practices for dimensioning architectural and structural drawings are similar in many ways to those for dimensioning manufactured parts, but some practices differ. Chapter 19 presents more information about structural drawings and their dimensioning. The portfolio section throughout this book shows a variety of drawings that you can use to familiarize yourself with practices from other disciplines.

Figure 9.1 shows a dimensioned CAD drawing created from a solid model. While CAD can be a great help for proper dimensioning technique, you must provide the intelligence to choose and place the dimensions in order to create a drawing that conveys the design clearly. Even if you are going to transmit 3D CAD files as the product definition, you still need to consider how accurately the parts that you will eventually receive back must match the model definition. Directly specifying tolerances in the model is one way to do this. You will learn more about tolerancing in Chapter 10.

Three Aspects of Good Dimensioning

Dimensions are given in the form of distances, angles, and notes regardless of the dimensioning units being used. For both CAD and hand drawing, the ability to create good dimensioned drawings requires:

Technique of dimensioning The standard for appearance of lines, the spacing of dimensions, the size of arrowheads, and so on, allows others to read your drawing. A typical dimensioned drawing is shown in Figure 9.2. Note the strong contrast between the visible lines of the object and the thin lines used for the dimensions. The dimensions are easily legible because they follow the standards for dimensioning technique.

Placement of dimensions Use logical placement for dimensions according to standard practices so that they are legible, easy to find, and easy for the reader to interpret. Notice that when dimensions are placed in between two views, it is easier to see how the dimension relates to the feature as shown in each view.

Choice of dimensions The dimensions you show affect how your design is manufactured. Dimension first for function and then review the dimensioning to see if you can make improvements for ease of manufacturing without adversely affecting the final result. 3D CAD models can be transmitted as all or part of a digital product definition but this still requires a thorough understanding of the sizes and relationships between the part features.

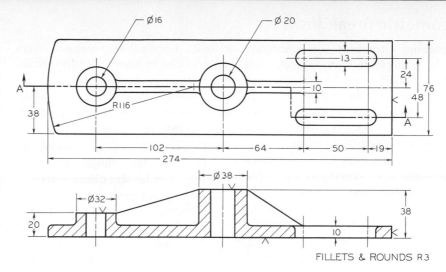

9.2   A Drawing Dimensioned in Millimeters

A drawing released for production should show the object in its completed state, and should contain all necessary information specifying the final part. As you select which dimensions to show, provide functional dimensions that can be interpreted to manufacture the part as you want it built. Keep in mind:

- The finished piece.
- The function of the part in the total assembly.
- How you will inspect the final part to determine its acceptability.
- Production processes.

Also, remember the following points:

- Give dimensions that are necessary and convenient for producing the part.
- Give sufficient dimensions so that none must be assumed.
- Avoid dimensioning to points or surfaces inaccessible to the worker.
- Do not provide unnecessary or duplicate dimensions.

Tolerance

When a finished part is measured, it will vary slightly from the exact dimension specified. **Tolerance** is the total amount that the feature on the actual part is allowed to vary from what is specified by the drawing or model dimension. You will learn a number of ways to specify tolerances in Chapter 10.

A good understanding of tolerance is important to understanding dimensioning, especially when choosing which dimensions to show. For now, keep in mind that tolerance can be specified generally by giving a note on the drawing such as:

ALL TOLERANCES ±.02 INCH
UNLESS OTHERWISE NOTED.

Another method of specifying tolerance is illustrated in the title block shown in Figure 9.3.

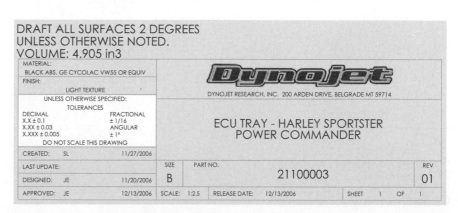

9.3   A Title Block Specifying Tolerances. *Courtesy of Dynojet Research, Inc.*

Geometric Breakdown

Engineering structures are composed largely of simple geometric shapes, such as the prism, cylinder, pyramid, cone, and sphere. They may be exterior (positive) or interior (negative) forms. For example, a steel shaft is a positive cylinder, and a round hole is a negative cylinder.

These shapes result directly from design necessity—keeping forms as simple as possible—and from the requirements of the fundamental manufacturing operations. Forms having plane surfaces are produced by planing, shaping, milling, and so forth, while forms having cylindrical, conical, or spherical surfaces are produced by turning, drilling, reaming, boring, countersinking, and other rotary operations. One way to consider dimensioning of engineering structures involves two basic steps:

1. Give the dimensions showing the sizes of the simple geometric shapes, called **size dimensions**.
2. Give the dimensions locating these elements with respect to each other, called **location dimensions**. Note that a location dimension locates a 3D geometric element and not just a surface; otherwise, all dimensions would have to be classified as location dimensions.

This process of geometric analysis helps you determine the features of the object and the features' relationships to one another, but it is not enough just to dimension geometry. You must also consider the function of the part in the assembly and the manufacturing requirements. This process is similar to that used when modeling designs in 3D CAD.

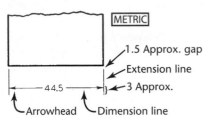

9.4   Dimension Line

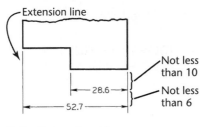

9.5   Extension Lines

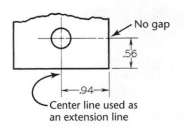

9.6   Centerlines

9.1 LINES USED IN DIMENSIONING

A **dimension line** is a thin, dark, solid line terminated by an arrowhead, indicating the direction and extent of a dimension (Figure 9.4). In a machine drawing, the dimension line is usually broken near the middle to place the dimension value in the line. In structural and architectural drawing, the dimension figure is placed above an unbroken dimension line.

As shown in Figure 9.5, the dimension line nearest the object outline should be spaced at least 10 mm (3/8 in.) away. All other parallel dimension lines should be at least 6 mm (1/4 in.) apart, and more if space is available. The spacing of dimension lines should be uniform throughout the drawing.

An **extension line** is a thin, dark, solid line that extends from a point on the drawing to which a dimension refers (Figure 9.5). The dimension line meets the extension lines at right angles, except in special cases. A gap of about 1.5 mm (1/16 in.) should be left where the extension line would join the object outline. The extension line should extend about 3 mm (1/8 in.) beyond the outermost arrowhead.

A **centerline** is a thin, dark line alternating long and short dashes. Centerlines are commonly used as extension lines in locating holes and other symmetrical features (Figure 9.6). When extended for dimensioning, centerlines cross over other lines of the drawing without gaps. Always end centerlines using a long dash. Refer to Figures 9.4–9.6 for examples of lines used in dimensioning.

DIMENSIONING BY GEOMETRIC BREAKDOWN

To dimension the object shown in isometric at right, use the geometric breakdown as follows:

1 Consider the geometric features of the part.

In this case the features to be dimensioned include:

- two positive prisms
- one positive cylinder
- one negative cone
- six negative cylinders

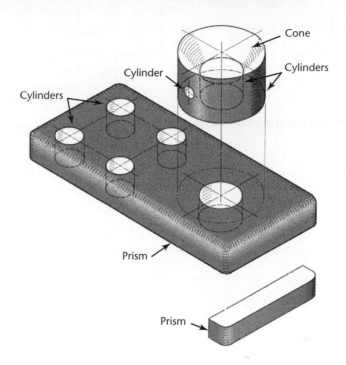

2 Specify the size dimensions for each feature by lettering the dimension values as indicated. (In this illustration, the word "size" indicates the various dimension values.) Note that the four cylinders of the same size can be specified with one dimension. (You will learn more about how to combine information and use symbols to indicate the countersink later in this chapter.)

3 Finally, locate the geometric features with respect to each other. (Actual values would replace the words "size" and "location" in this illustration.) Always check to see that the object is fully dimensioned.

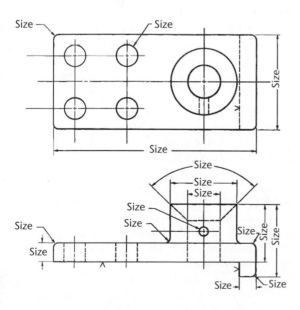

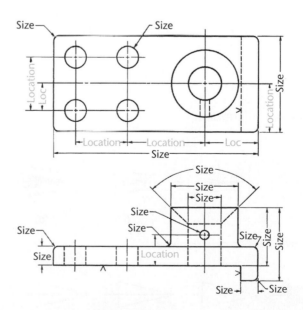

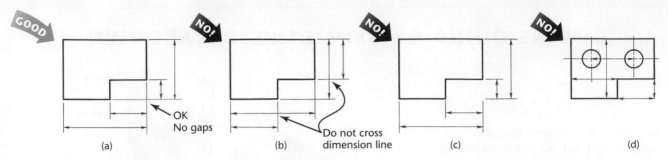

OK
No gaps

Do not cross
dimension line

(a)   (b)   (c)   (d)

9.7 Dimension and Extension Lines

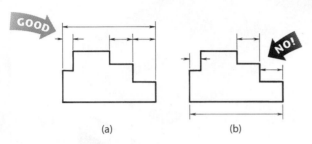

(a)   (b)

9.8 Grouped Dimensions

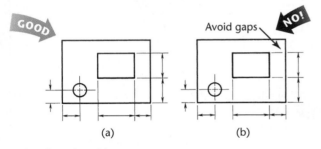

Avoid gaps

(a)   (b)

9.9 Crossing Lines

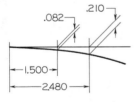

.082   .210

1.500
2.480

9.10 Oblique Extension

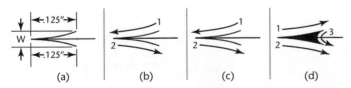

←.125″→
W
←.125″→

(a)   (b)   (c)   (d)

9.11 Arrowheads

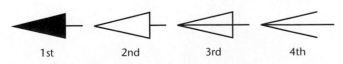

1st   2nd   3rd   4th

9.12 Order of Preference for Arrow Styles on
Mechanical Drawings

9.2 USING DIMENSION AND EXTENSION LINES

Dimension lines and extension lines should follow the guidelines shown in Figure 9.7a. The shorter dimensions are nearest to the object outline. Dimension lines should not cross extension lines, as in Figure 9.7b, which results from placing the shorter dimensions outside. Note that it is perfectly satisfactory to cross extension lines (Figure 9.7a), but they should not be shortened (Figure 9.7c). A dimension line should never coincide with or extend from any line of the drawing (Figure 9.7d). Avoid crossing dimension lines wherever possible.

Dimensions should be lined up and grouped together as much as possible, as in Figure 9.8a, and not as in Figure 9.8b.

In many cases, extension lines and centerlines must cross visible lines of the object (Figure 9.9a). When this occurs, gaps should not be left in the lines (Figure 9.9b).

Dimension lines are normally drawn at right angles to extension lines, but an exception may be made in the interest of clarity, as in Figure 9.10.

9.3 ARROWHEADS

Arrowheads, shown in Figure 9.11, indicate the extent of dimensions. They should be uniform in size and style throughout the drawing, not varied according to the size of the drawing or the length of dimensions. Sketch arrowheads freehand so that the length and width have a ratio of 3:1. The arrowhead's length should be equal to the height of the dimension values (about 3 mm or 1/8 in. long). For best appearance, fill in the arrowhead, as in Figure 9.11d. Figure 9.12 shows the preferred arrowhead styles for mechanical drawings. Most CAD systems allow you to select from a variety of styles.

> **TIP**
> When you are drawing by hand and using the arrowhead method in which both strokes are directed toward the point, it is easier to make the strokes toward yourself.

9.4 LEADERS

A **leader** is a thin, solid line directing attention to a note or dimension and starting with an arrowhead or dot.

A leader should be an inclined straight line drawn at a large angle, except for the short horizontal shoulder (about 3-6 mm or 1/8–1/4 in.) extending from the center of the first or last line of lettering for the note. A leader to a circle should be a radial line, which is a line that would pass through the center of the circle if extended. Figures 9.13a through 9.13d show examples of leader lines. More examples of radial lines are shown in Section 9.22.

Use an arrowhead to start the leader when you can point to a particular line in the drawing, such as the edge of a hole. Use a dot to start the leader when locating something within the outline of the object, such as an entire surface (see Figures 9.13e and 9.13f).

For the Best Appearance, Make Leaders

- near each other and parallel
- across as few lines as possible

Don't Make Leaders

- parallel to nearby lines of the drawing
- through a corner of the view
- across each other
- longer than needed
- horizontal or vertical

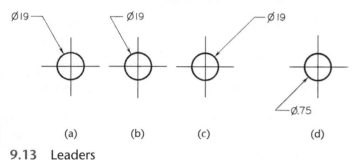

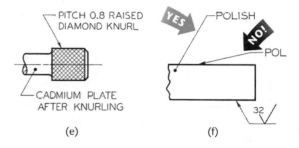

9.13 Leaders

9.5 DRAWING SCALE AND DIMENSIONING

Drawing scale is indicated in the title block as described in Chapter 2. The scale is intended to help you visualize the object by giving an approximate idea of its size, but is not intended to communicate dimensions. Never scale measurements from drawings to find an unknown dimension. Many standard title blocks include a note such as DO NOT SCALE DRAWING FOR DIMENSIONS, as shown in Figure 9.14.

Draw a heavy straight line under any single dimension value that is not to scale (Figure 9.15). Before CAD was widely used, if a change made in a drawing was not important enough to justify correcting the drawing, the practice was simply to change the dimension value. If a dimension does not match the appearance in the drawing, the part is made as dimensioned, not as pictured. If there seems to be an error, many manufacturers check to confirm that the drawing is correct; however, it is your responsibility to specify exactly what you want built. If the entire drawing is not prepared to a standard scale, note NONE in the scale area of the title block. You may see the abbreviation NTS on older drawings, meaning not to scale.

When you create a drawing using CAD, make sure to define dimensions according to the proper standards. Since it is easy to edit CAD drawings, you should generally fix the drawing geometry when making changes, and not merely change dimension values. If you are using a digital model as the sole definition for the part, the model dimensions must be represented accurately.

9.14 Drawing Scale Is Noted in the Title Block. *The drawing should not be scaled for dimensions. Courtesy of Dynojet Research, Inc.*

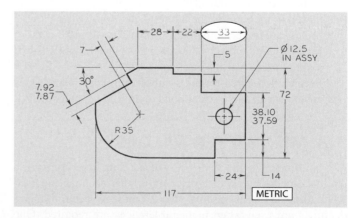

9.15 Draw a Heavy Line Under Any Dimension Value that Is Not to Scale

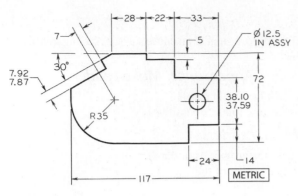

9.16 Unidirectional Dimension Figures

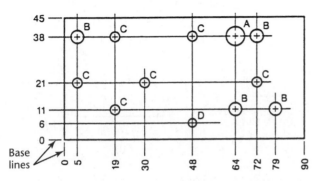

9.17 Rectangular Coordinate Dimensioning May Show Values Reading from the Right. *Reprined from Y14.5M-1994, by permission of The American Society of Mechanical Engineers. All rights reserved.*

9.7 DIMENSION UNITS

Dimension values are shown using the metric system or decimal inch values. Millimeters and decimal inches can be added, subtracted, multiplied, and divided easily compared to fractions. For inch-millimeter equivalents of decimal and common fractions, see the inside back cover of this book.

A note, stating ALL MEASUREMENTS IN MILLIMETER or ALL MEASUREMENTS IN INCHES UNLESS OTHERWISE NOTED is used in the title block to indicate the measurement units, as was shown in Figure 9.14. No units are needed with the dimension values in this case. When indicating dimensions:

- Millimeters are indicated by the lowercase letters mm placed to the right of the numeral, as in 12.5 mm.
- Meters are indicated by the lowercase m, as in 50.6 m.
- Inches are indicated by the symbol ″ placed slightly above and to the right of the numeral.
- Feet are indicated by the symbol ′ similarly placed. It is customary in such expressions to omit the inch mark.

Keeping Dimensions and Lettering Legible at Smaller Scales

The sizes for lettering height, dimension line spacing, and so on, are to be shown that size on the plotted sheet, otherwise the lettering and dimensioning are often illegible. If you are going to use reduced size working prints, increase the lettering, dimension arrows, and other sizes by approximately 50% (depending upon the amount of reduction) to maintain legibility on the smaller print.

9.6 DIRECTION OF DIMENSION VALUES AND NOTES

All dimension values and notes are lettered horizontally and should read from the bottom of the sheet, as oriented by the title block. Figure 9.16 shows the direction for reading dimension values.

The exception is when dimensioning from a baseline as in coordinate dimensioning. Then dimension figures may be aligned with the dimension lines so that they may be read from the bottom or right side of the sheet as shown in Figure 9.17. In both systems, general notes on the sheet and dimensions and notes shown with leaders are always aligned horizontally to read from the bottom of the drawing.

It is standard practice to omit millimeter designations and inch marks on drawings and note the units in the title block except when there is a possibility of misunderstanding. For example, 1 VALVE should be 1″ VALVE.

Either meters or feet and inches and fractional inches are used in architectural and structural work where precision in the thousandths of an inch is not necessary and the steel tape or framing square is used to make measurements. Commodities such as pipe and lumber are identified by standard nominal sizes that are close to the actual dimensions.

In some industries, all dimensions, regardless of size, are given in inches; in others, dimensions up to and including 72 inches are given in inches, and dimensions greater than 72 inches are given in feet and inches. In U.S. structural and architectural drafting, all dimensions of 1 foot or more are usually expressed in feet and inches.

9.8 MILLIMETER VALUES

The millimeter is the commonly used unit for most metric engineering drawings. One-place millimeter decimals are used when tolerance limits permit. Two (or more)–place millimeter decimals are used when higher tolerances are required. One drawing can combine dimensions shown with more and fewer decimal places depending on the necessary tolerance. Keep in mind that 0.1 mm is approximately equal to .004 in. If you are used to working in U.S. customary units, don't provide an unrealistic precision when specifying millimeter values.

Figure 9.18 shows an example drawing dimensioned in millimeters. Figure 9.19 shows various ways that millimeter values can be shown for dimensioning.

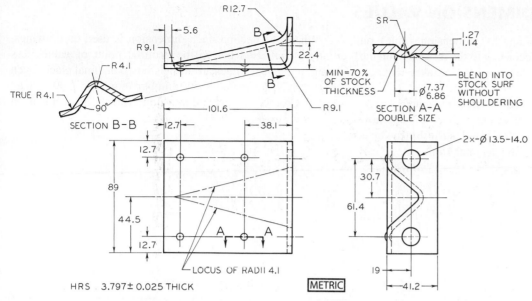

9.18 Complete Millimeter Dimensioning

9.19 Millimeter Dimension Values

9.9 DECIMAL INCH VALUES

Two-place inch decimals are typical when tolerance limits permit. Three or more decimal places are used for tolerance limits in the thousandths of an inch. In two-place decimals, the second place preferably should be an even digit (for example, .02, .04, and .06 are preferred to .01, .03, or .05) so that when the dimension is divided by 2 (for example, when determining the radius from a diameter), the result will still be a two-place decimal. However, odd two-place decimals are used when required for design purposes, such as in dimensioning points on a smooth curve or when strength or clearance is a factor. A typical example of the use of the complete decimal inch system is shown in Figure 9.20.

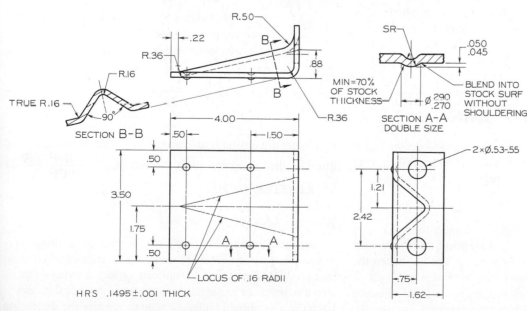

9.20 Complete Decimal Dimensioning

9.10 RULES FOR DIMENSION VALUES

Good hand-lettering is important for dimension values on sketches. The shop produces according to the directions on the drawing, and to save time and prevent costly mistakes, make all lettering perfectly legible.

Make all decimal points bold, allowing ample space. Where the metric dimension is a whole number, do not show either a decimal point or a zero. Where the metric dimension is less than 1 mm, a zero precedes the decimal point.

Where the decimal-inch dimension is used on drawings, a zero is not used before the decimal point of values less than 1 in. Typical values are shown to two decimal places even when they represent a whole number (e.g., use 2.00 instead of 2). Correct decimal dimension values are shown in Figures 9.21a–e.

9.21 Decimal Inch Dimension Values

9.11 RULES FOR ROUNDING DECIMAL DIMENSION VALUES

It is difficult to maintain tolerances smaller than a few thousandths of an inch in manufacturing. In order to provide reasonable tolerances that can be achieved in manufacturing, calculated dimension values for drawings sometimes need to be rounded. Unlike rounding rules used for statistical values, it is preferred to round drawing values to an even number.

When rounding a decimal value to fewer places, regardless of whether the dimension is expressed in inches or metric units, follow these rules:

- If the number following the rounding position is less than 5, make no change.
- If the number following the rounding position is more than 5, round up.
- If the number following the rounding position is a 5, round to an even number. (To do this, note whether the number in the rounding position is even or odd. If the 5 follows an odd number in the rounding position, round up to an even number. If the 5 follows an even number in the rounding position, make no change.)

Examples of Rounded Decimal Values

- 3.4632 becomes 3.463 when rounded to three places. (Make no change, because the 2 following the rounding position is less than 5.)
- 3.4637 becomes 3.464 when rounded to three places. (Round up, because the 7 following the rounding position is more than 5.)
- 8.37652 becomes 8.376 when rounded to three places. (Make no change, because the 6 in the rounding position is even and the number following the rounding position is a 5.)
- 4.375 becomes 4.38 when rounded to two places. (Round up to an even number, because the 7 in the rounding position is odd and the number following the rounding position is a 5.)

9.12 DUAL DIMENSIONING

Dual dimensioning is used to show metric and decimal-inch dimensions on the same drawing. Two methods of displaying the dual dimensions are described below.

Position Method

In the **position method** of dual dimensioning, the millimeter dimension is placed above the inch dimension, and the two are separated by a dimension line, or by an added line when the **unidirectional** system of dimensioning is used. An alternative arrangement is the millimeter dimension to the left of the inch dimension, with the two separated by a slash line, or virgule. Placement of the inch dimension above or to the left of the millimeter dimension is also acceptable. Each drawing should illustrate the dimension identification as $\frac{\text{MILLIMETER}}{\text{INCH}}$ or MILLIMETER/INCH.

Bracket Method

In the **bracket method** of dual dimensioning, the millimeter dimension is enclosed in parentheses. The location of this dimension is optional but should be uniform on any drawing—that is, above or below or to the left or the right of the inch dimension. Each drawing should include a note to identify the dimension values, such as DIMENSIONS IN () ARE MILLIMETERS.

9.13 COMBINATION UNITS

At times when more than one measurement system is used on the same drawing, the main units are indicated through a note in or near the title block. The alternative units are indicated with an abbreviation after the dimension value. Use mm after the dimension value if millimeters, or IN if inches, only when combining two measurement systems on one drawing. In the U.S. to facilitate the changeover to metric dimensions, some drawings are dual-dimensioned in millimeters and decimal inches as shown in Figure 9.22. The second set of units shown in parentheses are for reference only.

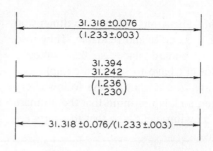

9.22 Dual Dimensioned Drawing in Millimeters. On drawing (*Inch values are given for reference only.*)

9.14 DIMENSION SYMBOLS

A variety of dimensioning symbols shown in Figure 9.23 are used to replace traditional terms or abbreviations. The symbols are preferred because (1) they take less space in the drawing and (2) they are internationally recognized and therefore do not have translation issues if the part is manufactured in a country where a different language is spoken. Traditional terms and abbreviations found in the Appendix can be used if necessary.

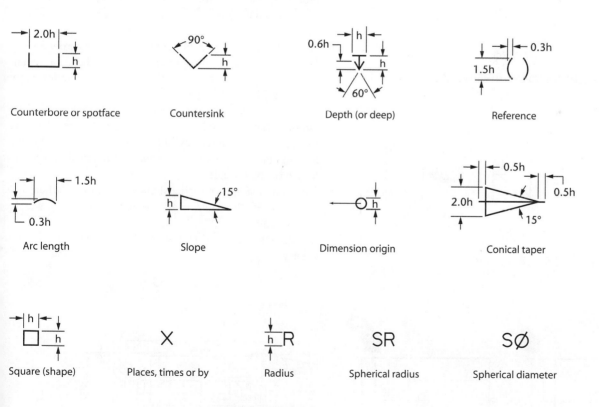

Counterbore or spotface   Countersink   Depth (or deep)   Reference

Arc length   Slope   Dimension origin   Conical taper

Square (shape)   Places, times or by   Radius   Spherical radius   Spherical diameter

h = Letter height

9.23 Form and Proportion of Dimensioning Symbols. *Reprined from Y14.5M-1994, by permission of The American Society of Mechanical Engineers. All rights reserved.*

9.15 PLACING AND SHOWING DIMENSIONS LEGIBLY

Rules for the placement of dimensions help you to dimension your drawings so that they are clear and readable. They also help locate dimensions in standard places so that someone manufacturing the part doesn't have to search a complicated drawing to find a dimension. You cannot always follow every placement rule to the letter, so keep in mind that the ultimate goal is to dimension the drawing clearly so that the parts are built to your specifications.

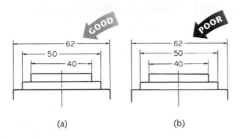

9.24 Staggered Numerals, Metric

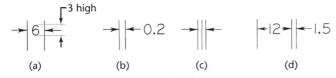

9.25 Fitting Dimension Values in Limited Spaces (Metric Dimensions)

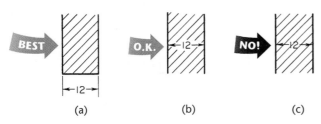

9.26 Dimensions and Section Lines

Rules for Placing Dimensions Properly

- Never letter a dimension value over any line on the drawing; if necessary, break the line.
- In a group of parallel dimension lines, the dimension values should be staggered, as in Figure 9.24a, and not stacked up one above the other, as in Figure 9.24b.
- Do not crowd dimension figures into limited spaces, making them illegible. There are techniques for showing dimension values outside extension lines or in combination with leaders (Figure 9.25). If necessary, add a removed partial view or detail to an enlarged scale to provide the space needed for clear dimensioning.
- Place dimensions between views when possible, but only attached to a single view. This way it is clear that the dimension relates to the feature, which can be seen in more than one view.
- When a dimension must be placed in a hatched area or on the view, leave an opening in the hatching or a break in the lines for the dimension values, as shown in Figure 9.26b and 9.26c.
- Dimensions should not be placed on a view unless it promotes the clarity of the drawing, as shown in Figure 9.27. In complicated drawings such as Figure 9.27c, it is often necessary to place dimensions on a view.
- Avoid dimensioning to hidden lines. (See Figure 9.28.)
- Do not attach dimensions to visible lines where the meaning is not clear, such as the dimension 20 in the top view shown in Figure 9.29b.
- Notes for holes are usually placed where you see the circular shape of the hole, as in Figure 9.29a, but give the diameter of an external cylindrical shape where it appears rectangular. This way it is near the dimension for the length of the cylinder.
- Give dimensions where the shapes are shown—where the contours of the object are defined—as is shown in Figure 9.29.
- Locate holes in the view that shows the shape of the hole clearly.

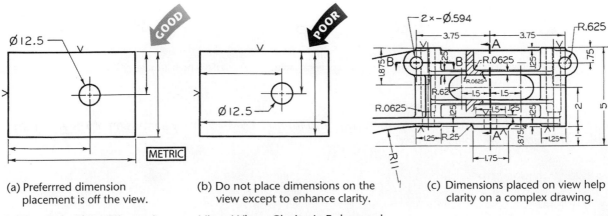

(a) Preferrred dimension placement is off the view.

(b) Do not place dimensions on the view except to enhance clarity.

(c) Dimensions placed on view help clarity on a complex drawing.

9.27 Only Place Dimensions on View When Clarity Is Enhanced

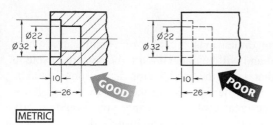

METRIC

9.28 Placement of Dimensions

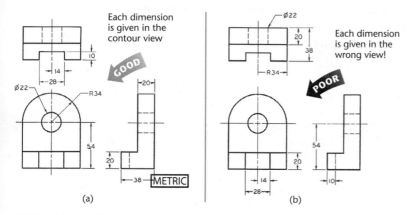

(a)   (b)

9.29 Place Dimensions Where the Contours of the Object Are Defined

---

TIP

Thinking of Dimensioning in Terms of Material Removal

There are many ways to dimension a drawing. If you are having trouble getting started, it may help to consider the overall block of material and what features are to be removed from it, similar to the way you visualize for a sketch. This is especially true when the part is to be manufactured using a process that removes material, such as milling.

Look for the largest portions to be removed and give dimensions for their sizes and locations first. Next add dimensions for the smaller features.

Since the overall dimensions will be the largest, they will be placed furthest from the view. If you are using CAD, it is easy to move dimensions later if you need more space. When you are sketching, block the overall dimension in lightly and leave substantial space between it and the drawing view for placement of shorter dimensions.

Use the rules that you have learned to place dimensions on the view that best shows the shape, and close to where the feature is shown. This makes the drawing easier to read.

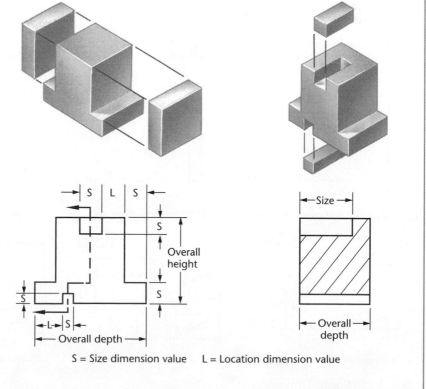

S = Size dimension value   L = Location dimension value

9.16 SUPERFLUOUS DIMENSIONS

All necessary dimensions must be shown, but do not give unnecessary or **superfluous** dimensions. Figure 9.30a–l shows examples of how to omit unnecessary dimensions. Do not repeat dimensions on the same view or on different views, or give the same information in two different ways.

As Figure 9.29b shows, it can be impossible to determine how the designer intended to apply the tolerance when a dimension is given two different ways. When chaining dimensions, one dimension of the chain should be left out if the overall dimension is given, so that the machinist works from one surface only. This is particularly important where an accumulation of tolerances can cause problems with how parts fit or function.

Do not omit dimensions, thinking, for example, that a hole is symmetrical and will be understood to be centered. Note in Figure 9.30b that one of the two location dimensions should be given for the hole at the right side of the part, even though it is centered. As the creator of the drawing, you should specify exactly how the part is to be built and inspected.

As shown in Figure 9.30e, when one dimension clearly applies to several identical features, or a uniform thickness, it need not be repeated, but the number of places should be indicated. Dimensions for fillets and rounds and other noncritical features need not be repeated, nor need the number of places be specified. For example, the radii of the rounded ends in Figure 9.30e need not be repeated.

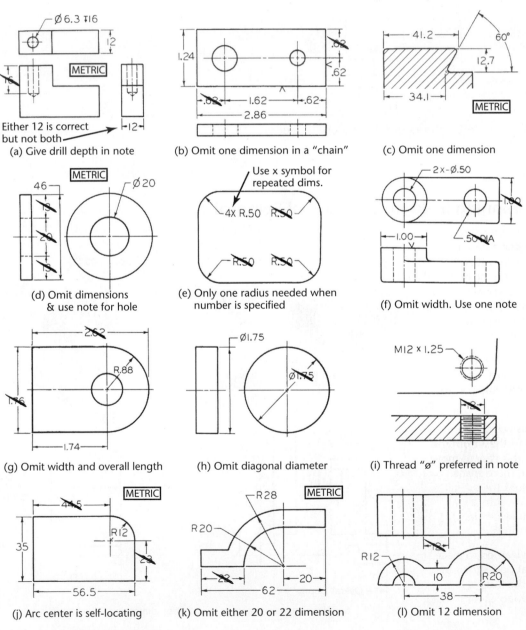

(a) Give drill depth in note

(b) Omit one dimension in a "chain"

(c) Omit one dimension

(d) Omit dimensions & use note for hole

(e) Only one radius needed when number is specified

(f) Omit width. Use one note

(g) Omit width and overall length

(h) Omit diagonal diameter

(i) Thread "ø" preferred in note

(j) Arc center is self-locating

(k) Omit either 20 or 22 dimension

(l) Omit 12 dimension

9.30 Superfluous Dimensions

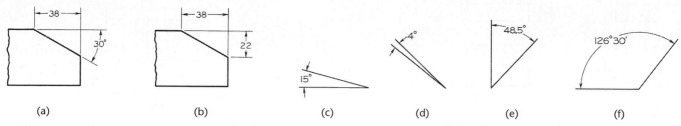

9.31 Dimensioning Angles

9.17 DIMENSIONING ANGLES

Dimension angles by specifying the angle in degrees and a linear dimension as shown in Figure 9.31a. You can also give coordinate dimensions for two legs of a right triangle, as shown in Figure 9.31b. The coordinate method is better when a high degree of accuracy is required. Variations in degrees of angle are hard to control because the amount of variation increases with the distance from the vertex of the angle. Methods of indicating angles are shown in Figure 9.31. The tolerancing of angles is discussed in Chapter 10.

In civil engineering drawings, **slope** represents the angle with the horizontal, whereas **batter** is the angle referred to the vertical. Both are expressed by making one member of the ratio equal to 1, as shown in Figure 9.32. **Grade,** as of a

highway, is similar to slope but is expressed in percentage of rise per 100 feet of run. Thus a 20-foot rise in a 100-foot run is a grade of 20%. In structural drawings, angular measurements are made by giving the ratio of run to rise, with the larger size being 12 in. These right triangles are referred to as bevels.

9.32 Angles in Civil Engineering Projects

9.18 DIMENSIONING ARCS

A circular arc is dimensioned in the view where you see its true shape by giving the value for its radius preceded by the abbreviation R (Figure 9.33). Mark the centers with small crosses to clarify the drawing, but not for small or unimportant radii or undimensioned arcs. When there is room enough, both the radius value and the arrowhead are placed inside the arc. If not, the arrowhead is left inside but the value is moved outside, or

both the arrowhead and value are moved outside. When section lines or other lines are in the way, you can use a leader and place the value and leader outside of the sectioned or crowded area. For a long radius, when the center falls outside the available space, the dimension line is drawn toward the actual center; but a false center may be indicated and the dimension line "jogged" to it (Figue 9.33f).

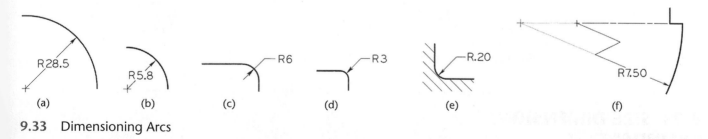

9.33 Dimensioning Arcs

9.19 FILLETS AND ROUNDS

Individual fillets and rounds are dimensioned like other arcs. If there are only a few and they are obviously the same size, giving one typical radius is preferred. However, fillets and rounds are often numerous on a drawing, and they usually are some standard size, such as metric R3 and R6, or R.125 and R.250 when using decimal-inch. In this case, give a general note in the lower portion of the drawing, such as:

FILLETS R6 AND ROUNDS R3 UNLESS OTHERWISE SPECIFIED

or

ALL CASTING RADII R6 UNLESS NOTED

or simply

ALL FILLETS AND ROUNDS R6.

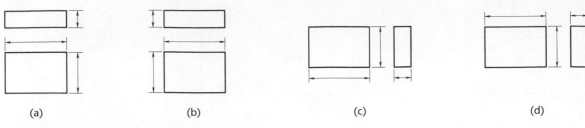

(a)   (b)   (c)   (d)

9.34 Dimensioning Rectangular Prisms

9.20 SIZE DIMENSIONS: PRISMS

The right rectangular prism is probably the most common geometric shape. Front and top views are dimensioned as shown in Figure 9.34a and 9.34b. The height and width are usually given in the front view, and the depth in the top view. The vertical dimensions can be placed on the left or right, usually in-line. Place the horizontal dimension between views as shown and not above the top or below the front view. Front and side views should be dimensioned as in Figures 9.34c and 9.34d. An example of size dimensions for a machine part made entirely of rectangular prisms is shown in Figure 9.35.

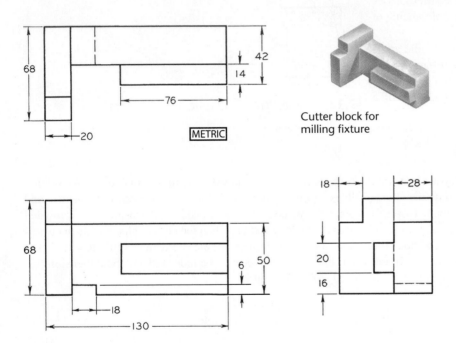

Cutter block for milling fixture

9.35 Dimensioning a Machine Part Composed of Prismatic Shapes

9.21 SIZE DIMENSIONS: CYLINDERS

The right circular cylinder is the next most common geometric shape and is commonly seen as a shaft or a hole. Cylinders are usually dimensioned by giving the diameter and length where the cylinder appears as a rectangle. If the cylinder is drawn vertically, give the length at the right or left, as in Figure 9.36. If the cylinder is drawn horizontally, give the length above or below the rectangular view, as in Figure 9.36.

Do not use a diagonal diameter inside the circular view, except when clarity is improved. Using several diagonal diameters on the same center becomes very confusing.

The radius of a cylinder should never be given because measuring tools, such as the micrometer caliper, are designed to check diameters. Holes are usually dimensioned by means of notes specifying the diameter and the depth, as shown in Figure 9.37, with or without manufacturing operations.

Give the diameter symbol Ø before all diameter dimensions, as in Figure 9.38a (ANSI/ASME Y14.5M-1994). In some cases, the symbol Ø may be used to eliminate the circular view, as shown in Figure 9.38b. The abbreviation DIA following the numerical value was used on older decimal inch drawings.

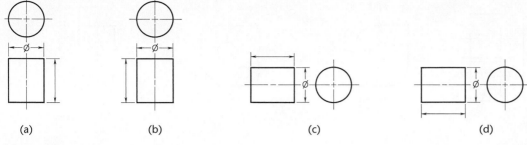

9.36 Dimensioning Cylinders

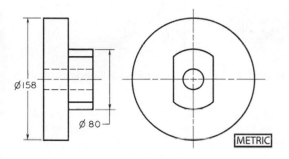

Use "Ø" to indicate circular shape

(a)

Use "Ø" to indicate circular view

(b)

9.37 Use of Ø in Dimensioning Cylinders

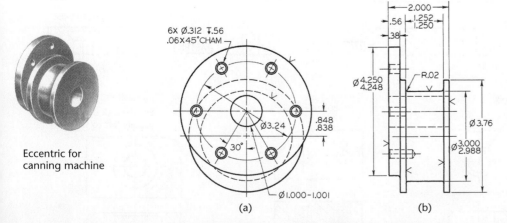

Eccentric for canning machine

(a)

(b)

9.38 Dimensioning a Machine Part that Is Composed of Cylindrical Shapes

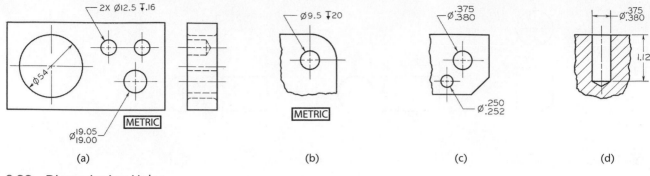

9.39 Dimensioning Holes

9.22 SIZE DIMENSIONING HOLES

Figure 9.39 shows standard symbols used in dimensioning holes. Figure 9.40 shows radial leader lines. Countersunk, counterbored, and tapped holes are usually specified by standard symbols or abbreviations, as shown in Figure 9.41. The order of items in a note corresponds to the order of procedure in the shop in producing the hole. The leader of a note should point to the circular view of the hole, if possible.

When the circular view of the hole has two or more concentric circles, as for counterbored, countersunk, or tapped holes, the arrowhead should touch the outer circle. Draw a **radial leader line,** that is, one that would pass through the center of the circle if it were extended. Figure 9.40 shows good and bad examples of leader lines.

Two or more holes can be dimensioned by a single note and by specifying the number of holes, as shown at the top of Figure 9.41. It is widely acceptable to use decimal fractions for both metric or inch drill sizes, as shown in Figure 9.41b. For numbered or letter-size drills (listed in Appendix 18), specify

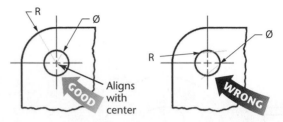

9.40 Good and Bad Examples of Radial Leader Lines

the decimal size or give the number or letter designation followed by the decimal size in parentheses—for example #28 (.1405) or "P" (.3230). Metric drills are all in decimal sizes and are not designated by number or letter.

Specify only the dimensions of the holes, without a note listing whether the holes are to be drilled, reamed, or punched, as shown in Figures 9.41c and 9.41d. The manufacturing technician or engineer is usually better suited to determine the least expensive process to use that will achieve the tolerance required.

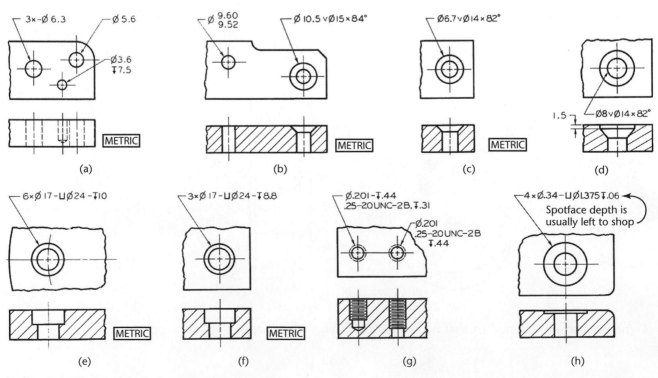

9.41 Standard Symbols for Hole Dimensions

9.23 APPLYING STANDARD DIMENSIONING SYMBOLS

Use standard dimensioning symbols when possible to save space and communicate dimensions clearly. (Refer back to Figure 9.23 for details on how to draw the symbols.) Most CAD software contains a palette of standard symbols. Figure 9.42 shows the application of a variety of standard symbols. Note that Figure 9.42a shows the *basic dimension* symbol used in geometric dimensioning and tolerancing (GD&T). In this case, "basic" does not mean "ordinary." You will learn more about the use of this special symbol in Chapter 10.

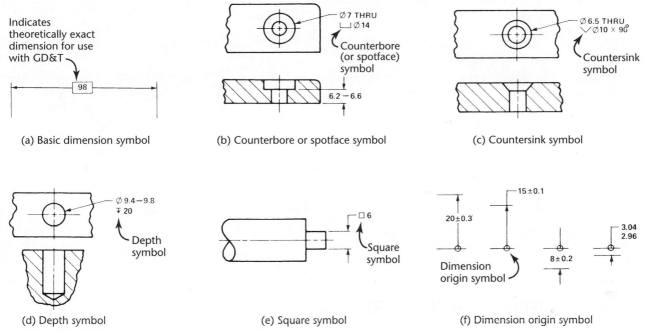

(a) Basic dimension symbol

(b) Counterbore or spotface symbol

(c) Countersink symbol

(d) Depth symbol

(e) Square symbol

(f) Dimension origin symbol

9.42 Use of Dimensioning Symbols. *Reprinted from Y14.5M-1994, by permission of The American Society of Mechanical Engineers. All rights reserved.*

9.24 DIMENSIONING TRIANGULAR PRISMS, PYRAMIDS, AND CONES

To dimension a triangular prism, give the height, width, and displacement of the top edge in the front view, and the depth in the top view, as is shown in Figure 9.43a.

For a rectangular pyramid, give the heights in the front view and the dimensions of the base and the centering of the vertex in the top view, as in Figure 9.43b. If the base is square, you need only give dimensions for one side of the base, preceded by the square symbol, as in Figure 9.43c (or on older drawings you may see it labeled SQ).

For cones, give the altitude and the diameter of the base in the triangular view (Figure 9.43d). For a frustum of a cone, give the vertical angle and the diameter of one of the bases (Figure 9.43e). Another method is to give the length and the diameters of both ends in the front view. Still another is to give the diameter at one end and the amount of taper per foot in a note.

Figure 9.43f shows a two-view drawing of a plastic knob. Overall, it is spherical and is dimensioned by giving its diameter preceded by the abbreviation and symbol for spherical diameter, SØ (in older notations it may be followed by the abbreviation SPHER). The torus-shaped bead around the knob is dimensioned by giving the thickness of the ring and the outside diameter.

Figure 9.43g shows a spherical end dimensioned by a radius preceded by the abbreviation SR. Internal shapes corresponding to the external shapes in Figure 9.43 would be dimensioned similarly.

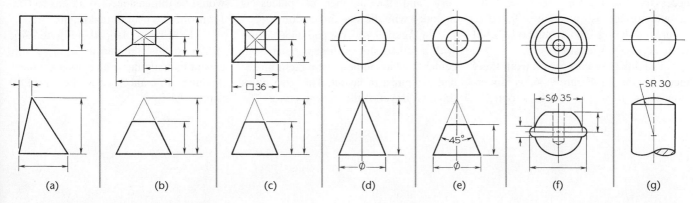

(a) (b) (c) (d) (e) (f) (g)

9.43 Dimensioning Various Shapes

9.25 DIMENSIONING CURVES

One way to dimension curves is to give a group of radii, as shown in Figure 9.44a. Note that in dimensioning the R126 arc, whose center is inaccessible, the center may be moved inward along a centerline and a jog made in the dimension line. Another method is to dimension the outline envelope of a curved shape so that the various radii are self-locating from "floating centers," as shown in Figure 9.44b.

Both circular and noncircular curves may be dimensioned by using coordinate dimensions, or datums, as in Figure 9.44c.

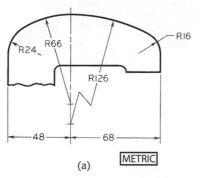

(a) METRIC

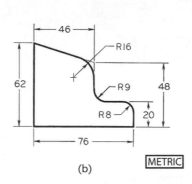

(b) METRIC

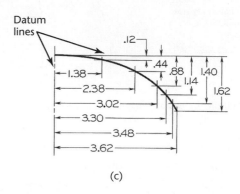

(c)

9.44 Dimensioning Curves

9.26 DIMENSIONING CURVED SURFACES

When angular measurements are unsatisfactory, you may give **chordal dimensions,** as shown in Figure 9.45a, or linear dimensions on the curved surfaces, as shown in Figure 9.45b.

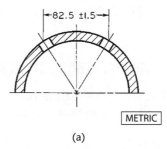

(a) METRIC

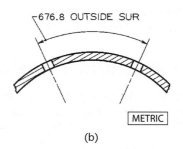

(b) METRIC

9.45 Dimensioning Along Curved Surfaces

9.27 DIMENSIONING ROUNDED-END SHAPES

The method for dimensioning rounded-end shapes depends on the degree of accuracy required. If precision is not necessary, use methods convenient for manufacturing, as in Figures 9.46a–c. Figures 9.46d–g show methods used when accuracy is required.

The link to be cast (or cut from sheet metal or plate) in Figure 9.46a is dimensioned as it would be laid out for manufacture, giving the center-to-center distance and the radii of the ends. Note that only one radius dimension is necessary, and the number of places is included with the size dimension.

In Figure 9.46b, the pad on a casting with a milled slot is dimensioned from center to center to help the pattern maker and machinist in layout. This also gives the total travel of the milling cutter. The

width dimension indicates the diameter of the milling cutter, so give the diameter of a machined slot. A cored slot, however, would be dimensioned by radius to conform with the pattern making procedure.

The semicircular pad in Figure 9.46c is laid out like the pad in Figure 9.46b, except that angular dimensions are used. Angular tolerances can be used if necessary.

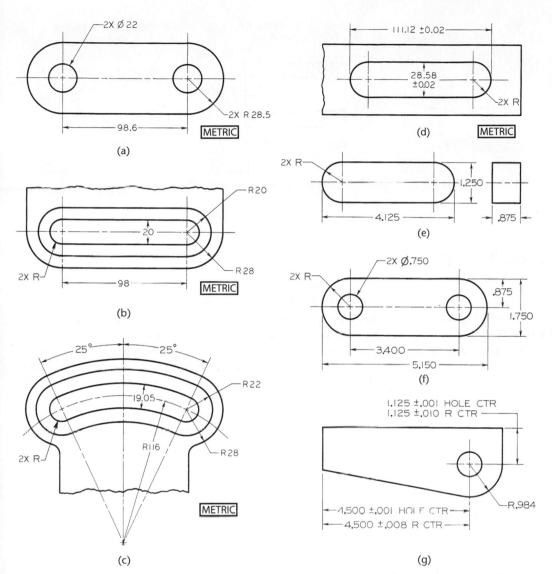

9.46 Dimensioning Rounded-End Shapes. *For accuracy, in Figure 9.46d–g, overall lengths of rounded-end shapes are given, and radii are indicated, but without specific values. The center-to-center distance may be required for accurate location of some holes. In Figure 9.46g, the hole location is more critical than the location of the radius, so the two are located.*

9.28 DIMENSIONING THREADS

Local notes are used to specify dimensions of threads. For tapped holes, the notes should, if possible, be attached to the circular views of the holes, as shown in Figure 9.47. For external threads, the notes are usually placed in the longitudinal views, where the threads are more easily recognized, as in Figures 9.47b and 9.47c. For a detailed discussion of thread notes, see Chapter 11.

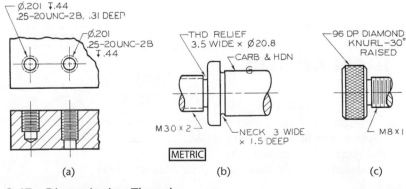

9.47 Dimensioning Threads

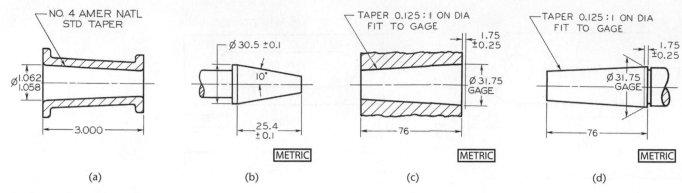

(a) (b) (c) (d)

9.48 Dimensioning Tapers

9.29 DIMENSIONING TAPERS

A taper is a conical surface on a shaft or in a hole. The usual method of dimensioning a taper is to give the amount of taper in a note, such as TAPER 0.167 ON DIA (with TO GAGE often added), and then give the diameter at one end with the length or give the diameter at both ends and omit the length. Taper on diameter means the difference in diameter per unit of length.

Standard machine tapers are used on machine spindles, shanks of tools, or pins, and are described in "Machine Tapers" in ANSI/ASME B5.10-1994. Such standard tapers are dimensioned on a drawing by giving the diameter (usually at the large end), the length, and a note, such as NO. 4 AMERICAN NATIONAL STANDARD TAPER as shown in Figure 9.48a.

For not-too-critical requirements, a taper may be dimensioned by giving the diameter at the large end, the length, and the included angle, all with proper tolerances, as shown in Figure 9.48b. Alternately, the diameters of both ends, plus the length, may be given with necessary tolerances.

For close-fitting tapers, the amount of taper per unit on diameter is indicated as shown in Figure 9.48c and 9.48d. A gage line is selected and located by a comparatively generous tolerance, while other dimensions are given appropriate tolerances as required.

9.30 DIMENSIONING CHAMFERS

A chamfer is a beveled or sloping edge. It is dimensioned by giving the length of the offset and the angle, as in Figure 9.49a. A 45° chamfer also may be dimensioned in a manner similar to that shown in Figure 9.49a, but usually it is dimensioned by note, as in Figure 9.49b.

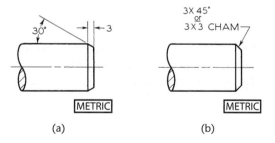

(a) (b)

9.49 Dimensioning Chamfers

9.31 SHAFT CENTERS

Shaft centers are required on shafts, spindles, and other conical or cylindrical parts for turning, grinding, and other operations. Such a center may be dimensioned, as shown in Figure 9.50. Normally the centers are produced by a combined drill and countersink.

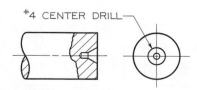

9.50 Shaft Center

9.32 DIMENSIONING KEYWAYS

The methods of dimensioning keyways for Woodruff keys and stock keys are shown in Figure 9.51. Note, in both cases, the use of a dimension to center the keyway in the shaft or collar. The preferred method of dimensioning the depth of a keyway is to give the dimension from the bottom of the keyway to the opposite side of the shaft or hole, as shown. The method of computing such a dimension is shown in Figure 9.51d. Values for A may be found in machinists' handbooks.

For general information about keys and keyways see Appendix 21.

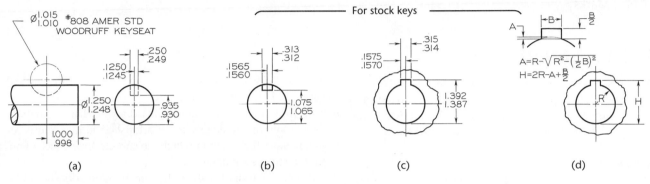

9.51   Dimensioning Keyways

9.33 DIMENSIONING KNURLS

A knurl is a roughened surface to provide a better handgrip or to be used for a press fit between two parts. For handgrip purposes, it is necessary only to give the pitch of the knurl, the type of knurling, and the length of the knurled area, as shown in Figure 9.52a and 9.52b. To dimension a knurl for a press fit, the toleranced diameter before knurling should be given, as shown in Figure 9.52c. A note should be added that gives the pitch and type of knurl and the minimum diameter after knurling (see ANSI/ASME B94.6-1984 (R1995)).

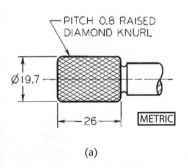

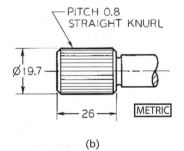

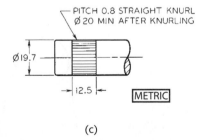

9.52   Dimensioning Knurls

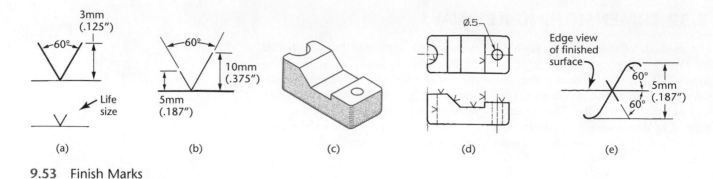

9.53 Finish Marks

9.34 FINISH MARKS

A **finish mark** is used to indicate that a surface is to be machined, or finished, as on a rough casting or forging. To the patternmaker or diemaker, a finish mark means that allowance of extra metal in the rough workpiece must be provided for the machining.

On drawings of parts to be machined from rolled stock, finish marks are generally unnecessary, because it is obvious that the surfaces are finished. Similarly, it is not necessary to show finish marks when the dimension implies a finished surface, such as Ø6.22–6.35 (metric) or Ø2.45–2.50 (decimal-inch).

As shown in Figure 9.53, three styles of finish marks, the general symbol ∨, the new basic symbol √, and the old symbol ✗, are used to indicate an ordinary smooth machined surface. The symbol is like a capital V, made about 3 mm high in conformity with the height of dimensioning lettering. The extended symbol, preferred by ANSI, is like a larger capital with the right leg extended. The short leg is made about 5 mm high and the height of the long leg is about 10 mm. The basic symbol may be altered for more elaborate surface texture specifications.

Figure 9.53c shows a simple casting having several finished surfaces. In Figure 9.53d, two views of the same casting show how the finish marks are indicated on a drawing. The finish mark is shown only on the edge view of a finished surface and is repeated in any other view in which the surface appears as a line, even if the line is a hidden line.

If a part is to be finished all over, finish marks should be omitted, and a general note, such as FINISH ALL OVER or FAO, should be lettered on the lower portion of the sheet.

The several kinds of finishes are detailed in machine shop practice manuals. The following terms are among the most commonly used: finish all over, rough finish, file finish, sand blast, pickle, scrape, lap, hone, grind, polish, burnish, buff, chip, spotface, countersink, counterbore, core, drill, ream, bore, tap, broach, and knurl. When it is necessary to control the surface texture of finished surfaces beyond that of an ordinary machine finish, the symbol √ is used as a base for the more elaborate surface quality symbols.

Finished surfaces can be measured more accurately, so provide dimensions from these when possible, as in Figure 9.54.

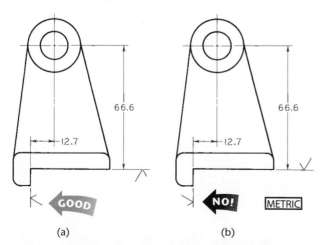

9.54 Correct and Incorrect Marks Showing Dimensions to Finished Surfaces. *The point of the symbol should be directed inward toward the body of metal similar to a tool bit, not upside down, as is shown in Figure 9.54b.*

9.35 SURFACE ROUGHNESS

The demands of automobiles, airplanes, and other machines that can stand heavy loads and high speeds with less friction and wear have increased the need for accurate control of surface quality by the designer, regardless of the size of the feature. Simple finish marks are not adequate to specify surface finish on such parts.

Surface finish is intimately related to the functioning of a surface, and proper specification of finish of surfaces such as bearings and seals is necessary. Surface quality specifications should be used only where needed, since the cost of producing a finished surface becomes greater as the quality of the surface called for is increased. Generally, the ideal surface finish is the roughest that will do the job satisfactorily.

The system of surface texture symbols recommended by ANSI/ASME (Y14.36M-1996) for use on drawings, regardless of the system of measurement used, is now broadly accepted by American industry. These symbols are used to define surface

	Symbol	Symbol
(a)	$\bigvee$	Basic texture surface symbol. Surface may be produced by any method except when the bar or circle, (b) or (d), is specified.
(b)	$\overline{\bigvee}$	Material removal by machining is required. The horizontal bar indicates that material removal by machining is required to reproduce the surface and that material must be provided for that purpose.
(c)	3.5 $\overline{\bigvee}$	Material removal allowance. The number indicates the amount of stock to be removed by machining in millimeters (or inches). Tolerances may be added to the basic value shown or in a general note.
(d)	$\overset{O}{\bigvee}$	Material removal prohibited. The circle in the vee indicates that the surface must be produced by processes such as casting, forging, hot finishing, cold finishing, die casting, powder metalurgy, or injection molding without subsequent removal.
(e)	$\bigvee$	Surface texture symbol. To be used when any surface characteristics are specified above the horizontal line or to the right of the symbol. Surface may be produced by any method except when the bar or circle, (b) or (d), is specified.

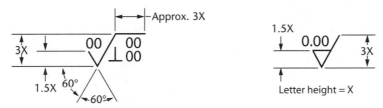

9.55 Surface Texture Symbols and Construction. *Reprinted from Y14.36M-1996, by permission of The American Society of Mechanical Engineers. All rights reserved.*

texture, roughness, and lay. See Figure 9.55 for the meaning and construction of these symbols. The basic surface texture symbol in Figure 9.55a indicates a finished or machined surface by any method, just as does the general V symbol. Modifications to the basic surface texture symbol, shown in Figures 9.55b–d, define restrictions on material removal for the finished surface. Where surface texture values other than roughness average are specified, the symbol must be drawn with the horizontal extension, as shown in Figure 9.55e. Construction details for the symbols are given in Figure 9.55f.

Applications of Surface Roughness Symbols

Applications of the **surface texture symbols** are given in Figure 9.56a. Note that the symbols read from the bottom and/or the right side of the drawing and that they are not drawn at any angle or upside down. Measurements for roughness and waviness, unless otherwise specified, apply in the direction that gives the maximum reading, usually across the lay, as shown in Figure 9.56b.

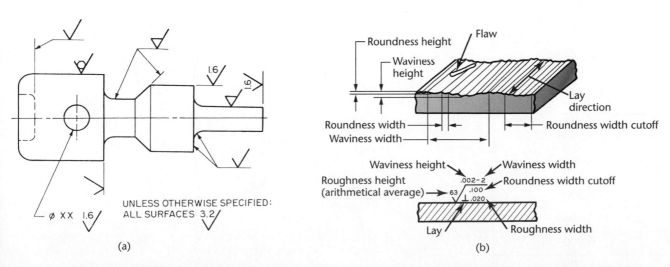

9.56 Application of Surface Texture Symbols and Surface Characteristics. *Reprinted from Y14.36M-1996, by permission of The American Society of Mechanical Engineers. All rights reserved.*

Recommended Roughness and Waviness Values

Recommended roughness height values are given in Table 9.1. When it is necessary to indicate the roughness-width cutoff values, the standard values used are listed in Table 9.2. If no value is specified, the 0.80 value is assumed.

When maximum waviness height values are required, the recommended values to be used are as given in Table 9.3.

Table 9.1 Preferred Series Roughness Average Values.* *Reprinted from Y14.36M-1996, by permission of The American Society of Mechanical Engineers. All rights reserved.*

Micrometers	Micro-inches
0.012	0.5
0.025	1
0.050	2
0.075	3
0.10	4
0.125	5
0.15	6
0.20	8
0.25	10
0.32	13
0.40	16
0.50	20
0.63	25
0.80	32
1.00	40
1.25	50
1.60	63
2.0	80
2.5	100
3.2	125
4.0	180
5.0	200
6.3	250
8.0	320
10.0	400
12.5	500
15	600
20	800
25	1000

Table 9.2 Standard Roughness Sampling Length (Cutoff) Values. *Reprinted from Y14.36M-1996, by permission of The American Society of Mechanical Engineers. All rights reserved.*

Millimeters (mm)	Inches (in.)
0.08	.003
0.25	.010
0.80	.030
2.5	.1
8.0	.3
25.0	1.0
8.0	320
10.0	400
12.5	500
15	600
20	800
25	1000

Table 9.3 Preferred Series Maximum Waviness Height Values. *Reprinted from Y14.36M-1996, by permission of The American Society of Mechanical Engineers. All rights reserved.*

Millimeters (mm)	Inches (in.)
0.0005	.00002
0.0008	.00003
0.0012	.00005
0.0020	.00008
0.0025	.0001
0.005	.0002
0.008	.0003
0.012	.0005
0.020	.0008

* Micrometers are the same as thousandths of a millimeter.

Lay Symbols and Surface Texture Symbols

When you need to indicate lay, the lay symbols in Figure 9.57 are added to the surface texture symbols as shown in the given examples. Selected applications of the surface texture values to the symbols are given and explained in Figure 9.58.

A typical range of surface roughness values that may be obtained from various production methods is included in Chapter 10.

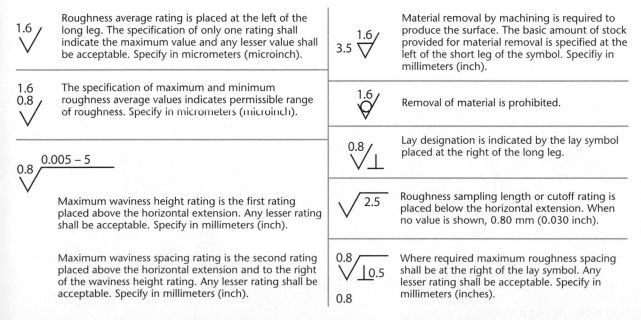

Symbol	Designation	Example	Symbol	Designation	Example
=	Lay parallel to the line representing the surface to which the symbol is applied	Direction of tool marks	X	Lay angular in both directions to the line representing the surface to which the symbol is applied	Direction of tool marks
⊥	Lay perpendicular to the line representing the surface to which the symbol is applied	Direction of tool marks	M	Lay multidirectional	
C	Lay approximately circular to the line representing the surface to which the symbol is applied		R	Lay approximately radial to the line representing the surface to which the symbol is applied	

9.57 Lay Symbols. *Reprinted from Y14.36M-1996, by permission of The American Society of Mechanical Engineers. All rights reserved.*

9.58 Application of Surface Texture Values to Symbol. *Reprinted from Y14.36M-1996, by permission of The American Society of Mechanical Engineers. All rights reserved.*

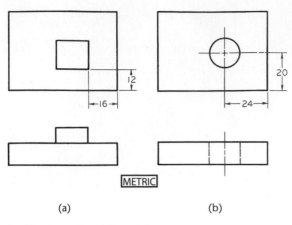

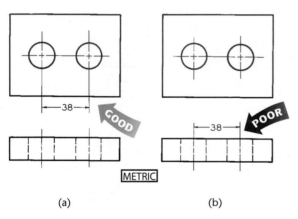

9.59 Location Dimensions

9.60 Locating Holes

9.36 LOCATION DIMENSIONS

After you have specified the sizes of the geometric shapes composing the structure, give **location dimensions** to show the relative positions of these geometric shapes. Figure 9.59a shows rectangular shapes located by their faces. In Figure 9.59b, cylindrical or conical holes or bosses, or other symmetrical shapes, are located by their centerlines. Location dimensions for holes are preferably given where the holes appear circular, as shown in Figure 9.60 and Figure 9.61.

In general, location dimensions should be built from a finished surface or from an important center or centerline. Location dimensions should lead to finished surfaces wherever possible because rough castings and forgings vary in size, and unfinished surfaces cannot be relied on for accurate measurements. The starting dimension, used in locating the first machined surface on a rough casting or forging, must necessarily lead from a rough surface or from a center or a centerline of the rough piece.

When several cylindrical surfaces have the same centerline (as in Figure 9.62b) you do not need location dimensions to show they are concentric; the centerline is enough. Holes equally spaced about a common center may be dimensioned by giving the diameter of the circle of centers, or bolt circle. Use a note such as 3X to indicate repetitive features or dimensions, where the X means *times* and the 3 indicates the number of repeated features. Put a space between the letter X and the dimension as shown in Figure 9.61. Unequally spaced holes are located by means of the bolt circle diameter plus angular measurements with reference to only one of the centerlines. Examples are shown in Figure 9.61.

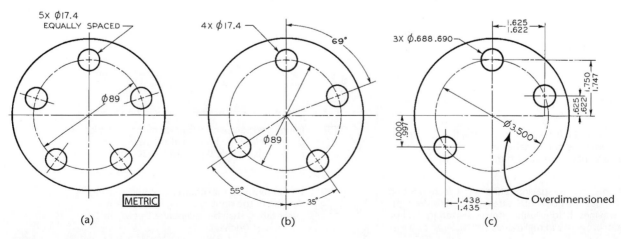

9.61 Locating Holes About a Center

Where greater accuracy is required, **coordinate dimensions** should be given, as shown in Figure 9.61c. In this case, the diameter of the bolt circle is enclosed in parentheses to indicate that it is to be used only as a reference dimension. Reference dimensions are given for information only. They are not intended to be measured and do not govern the manufacturing operations. They represent calculated dimensions and are often useful in showing the intended design sizes.

When several nonprecision holes are located on a common arc, they are dimensioned by giving the radius and the angular measurements from a **baseline,** as shown in Figure 9.62a. In this case, the baseline is the horizontal centerline.

In Figure 9.62b, the three holes are on a common centerline. One dimension locates one small hole from the center; the other gives the distances between the small holes. Note the dimension at X is left off. This method is used when the distance between the small holes is the important consideration. If the relation between the center hole and each of the small holes is more important, then include the distance at X and make the overall dimension a reference dimension.

Figure 9.62c shows another example of coordinate dimensioning. The three small holes are on a bolt circle whose diameter is given for reference purposes only. From the main center,

the small holes are located in two mutually perpendicular directions.

Another example of locating holes by means of linear measurements is shown in Figure 9.62d. In this case, one measurement is made at an angle to the coordinate dimensions because of the direct functional relationship of the two holes.

In Figure 9.62e, the holes are located from two baselines, or datums. When all holes are located from a common datum, the sequence of measuring and machining operations is controlled, overall tolerance accumulations are avoided, and proper functioning of the finished part is assured. The datum surfaces selected must be more accurate than any measurement made from them, must be accessible during manufacture, and must be arranged to facilitate tool and fixture design. It may be necessary to specify accuracy of the datum surfaces in terms of straightness, roundness, flatness, and so on, which you will learn about in the next chapter.

Figure 9.62f shows a method of giving, in a single line, all the dimensions from a common datum. Each dimension except the first has a single arrowhead and is accumulative in value. The overall dimension is separate.

These methods of locating holes are applicable to locating pins or other symmetrical features.

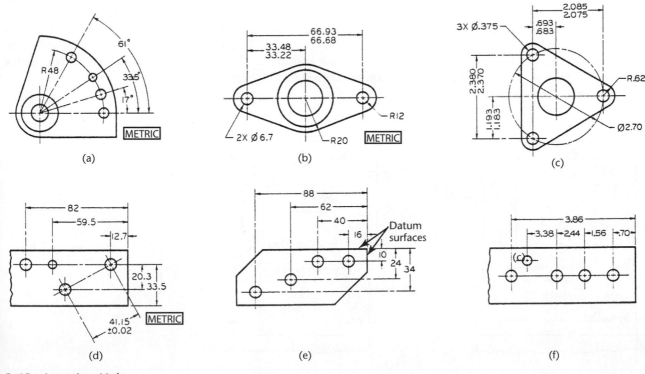

9.62   Locating Holes

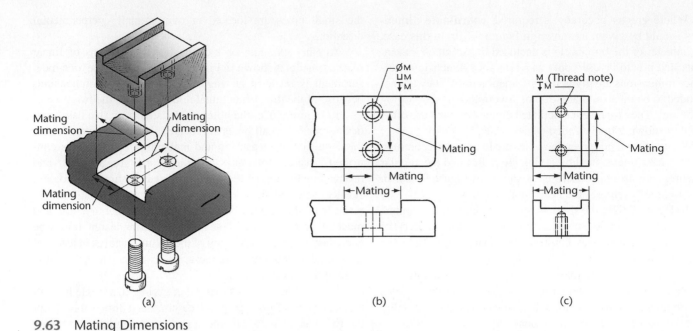

9.63 Mating Dimensions

9.37 MATING DIMENSIONS

In dimensioning a single part, its relation to mating parts must be taken into consideration. For example, in Figure 9.63a a guide block fits into a slot in a base. Those dimensions common to both parts are mating dimensions, as indicated.

These **mating dimensions** should be given on the multiview drawings in the corresponding locations, as shown in Figure 9.63b and 9.63c. Other dimensions are not mating dimensions since they do not control the accurate fitting together of two parts. The actual values of two corresponding mating dimensions may not be exactly the same. For example, the width of the slot in Figure 9.63b may be dimensioned 1/32 in. (0.8 mm) or several thousandths of an inch larger than the width of the block in Figure 9.63c, but these are mating

dimensions figured from a single basic width. Mating dimensions need to be specified in the corresponding locations on the two parts and toleranced to ensure proper fitting of the parts.

In Figure 9.64a, the dimension A is a necessary mating dimension and should appear on both the drawings of the bracket and of the frame. In Figure 9.64b, which shows a redesign of the bracket into two parts, dimension A is not used on either part because it is not necessary to closely control the distance between the cap screws. But dimensions F are now essential mating dimensions and should appear on the drawings of both parts. The remaining dimensions, E, D, B, and C, are not considered to be mating dimensions since they do not directly affect the mating of the parts.

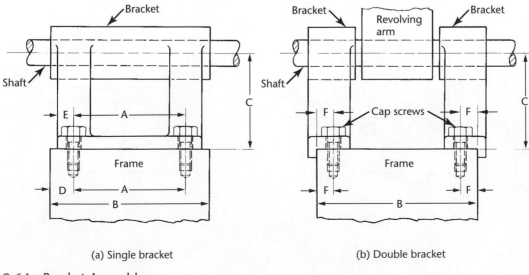

(a) Single bracket (b) Double bracket

9.64 Bracket Assembly

9.38 TABULAR DIMENSIONS

A series of objects having like features but varying in dimensions may be represented by one drawing, as shown in Figure 9.65. Letters are substituted for dimension figures on the drawing, and the varying dimensions are given in tabular form. The dimensions of many standard parts are given in this manner in catalogs and handbooks. Another way to dimension is shown in Figure 9.66.

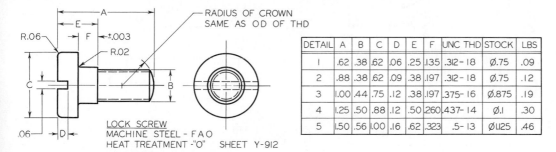

DETAIL	A	B	C	D	E	F	UNC THD	STOCK	LBS
1	.62	.38	.62	.06	.25	.135	.312-18	Ø.75	.09
2	.88	.38	.62	.09	.38	.197	.312-18	Ø.75	.12
3	1.00	.44	.75	.12	.38	.197	.375-16	Ø.875	.19
4	1.25	.50	.88	.12	.50	.260	.437-14	Ø.1	.30
5	1.50	.56	1.00	.16	.62	.323	.5-13	Ø1.125	.46

9.65 Tabular Dimensioning

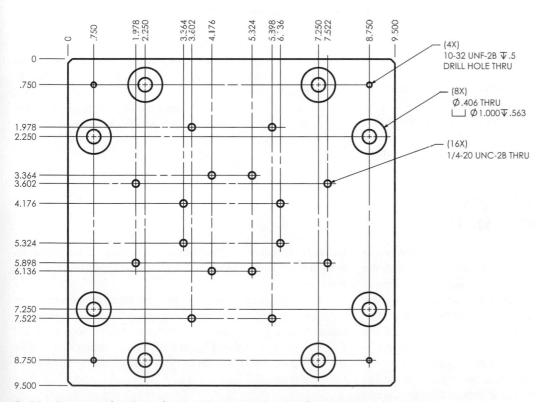

9.66 Rectangular Coordinate Dimensioning Without Dimension Lines

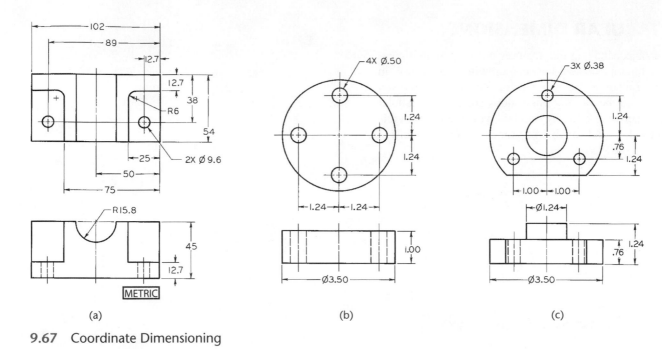

(a)   (b)   (c)

9.67 Coordinate Dimensioning

9.39 COORDINATE DIMENSIONING

Basic coordinate dimensioning practices are generally compatible with the data requirements for tape or computer-controlled automatic production machines.

However, to design for automated production, you should consult the manufacturing machine manuals before making production drawings. What follows are the basic guidelines for coordinate dimensioning.

A set of three mutually perpendicular datum or reference planes is usually required for coordinate dimensioning. These planes either must be obvious or must be clearly identified, as shown in Figure 9.67.

The designer selects as origins for dimensions those surfaces or features most important to the functioning of the part. Enough of these features are selected to position the part in

relation to the set of mutually perpendicular planes. All related dimensions are then made from these planes. Rectangular coordinate dimensioning without dimension lines is shown in Figure 9.68.

- All dimensions should be in decimals.
- Angles should be given, where possible, in degrees and decimal parts of degrees.
- Tools such as drills, reamers, and taps should be left up to the manufacturer unless a certain process is specifically required.
- All tolerances should be determined by the design requirements of the part, not by the capability of the manufacturing machine.

9.40 MACHINE, PATTERN, AND FORGING DIMENSIONS

The pattern maker is interested in the dimensions required to make the pattern, and the machinist is concerned only with the dimensions needed to machine the part. Frequently, a dimension that is convenient for the machinist is not convenient for the pattern maker, or vice versa. Since the pattern maker uses the drawing only once, while making the pattern, and the machinist refers to it continuously, the dimensions should be given primarily for the convenience of the machinist.

If the part is large and complicated, two separate drawings are sometimes made—one showing the pattern dimensions and

the other the machine dimensions. The usual practice, however, is to prepare one drawing for both the pattern maker and the machinist.

For forgings, it is common practice to make separate forging drawings and machining drawings. A forging drawing of a connecting rod, showing only the dimensions needed in the forge shop, is shown in Figure 9.69. A machining drawing of the same part would contain only the dimensions needed in the machine shop.

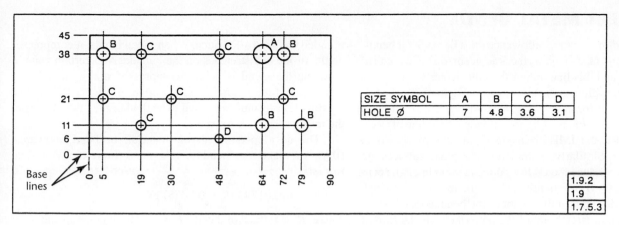

SIZE SYMBOL	A	B	C	D
HOLE Ø	7	4.8	3.6	3.1

1.9.2
1.9
1.7.5.3

9.68 A Hole Table Is Often Used to Dimension Complicated Patterns of Holes. *Reprinted from Y14.5M-1994, by permission of The American Society of Mechanical Engineers. All rights reserved.*

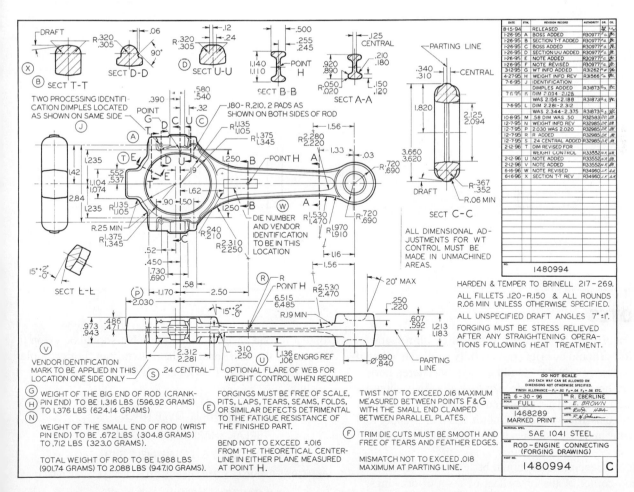

9.69 Forging Drawing of Connecting Rod. *Courtesy of General Motors Corporation.*

9.41 SHEET METAL BENDS

In sheet metal dimensioning, allowance must be made for bends. The intersection of the plane surfaces adjacent to a bend is called the mold line, and this line, rather than the center of the arc, is used to determine dimensions, as shown in Figure 9.70. The following procedure for calculating bends is typical. If the two inner plane surfaces of an angle are extended, their line of intersection is called the IML or inside mold line, as shown in Figure 9.71a–c. Similarly, if the two outer plane surfaces are extended, they produce the OML or outside mold line. The centerline of bend (⊄ B) refers primarily to the machine on which the bend is made and is at the center of the bend radius.

The length, or stretchout, of the pattern equals the sum of the flat sides of the angle plus the distance around the bend measured along the neutral axis. The distance around the bend is called the bend allowance. When metal bends, it compresses on the inside and stretches on the outside. At a certain zone in between, the metal is neither compressed nor stretched, and this is called the neutral axis, as shown in Figure 9.71d. The neutral axis is usually assumed to be 0.44 of the thickness from the inside surface of the metal.

The developed length of material, or bend allowance (BA), to make the bend is computed from the empirical formula

$$BA = (0.017453R + 0.0078T)N$$

where R = radius of bend, T = metal thickness, and N = number of degrees of bend as in Figure 9.71c.

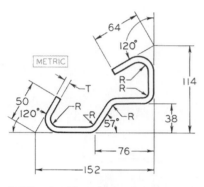

9.70 Profile Dimensioning

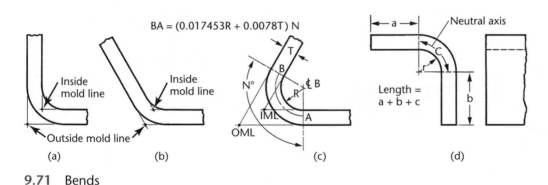

9.71 Bends

9.42 NOTES

It is usually necessary to supplement the direct dimensions with notes. Notes should be brief and carefully worded to allow only one interpretation. Notes should always be lettered horizontally on the sheet and arranged systematically. They should not be crowded and should not be placed between views, if possible. Notes are classified as general notes when they apply to an entire drawing and as local notes when they apply to specific items.

> *General Notes* General notes should be lettered in the lower right-hand corner of the first sheet of a set of drawings, above or to the left of the title block or in a central position below the view to which they apply. If notes are continued

onto a second sheet, that sheet number should be given in a note on the first sheet of the drawing set. For example: NOTES CONTINUED ON PAGE 4.

Examples

FINISH ALL OVER (FAO)

BREAK SHARP EDGES TO R0.8

G33106 ALLOY STEEL-BRINELL 340–380

ALL DRAFT ANGLES 3° UNLESS OTHERWISE SPECIFIED

DIMENSIONS APPLY AFTER PLATING

In machine drawings, the title strip or title block will carry many general notes, including those for materials, general tolerances, heat treatments, and patterns.

Local Notes **Local notes** apply to specific operations only and are connected by a leader to the point at which such operations are performed, as shown in Figure 9.72. The leader should be attached at the front of the first word of a note, or just after the last word, and not at any intermediate place.

Use common abbreviations in notes (such as THD, DIA, MAX) only when they cannot be misunderstood. Avoid less common abbreviations. "When in doubt, spell it out" is a rule of thumb to avoid problems with misunderstood notes.

If a common symbol is available, it is preferred to the abbreviation because symbols are internationally recognized and not language dependent. All abbreviations should conform to ANSI Y14.39-1999. See Appendix 4 for ANSI abbreviations.

In general, leaders and notes should not be placed on the drawing until the dimensioning is substantially completed. Notes and lettering should not touch lines of the drawing or title block. If notes are lettered first, they may be in the way of necessary dimensions and will have to be moved.

When using CAD to add text for drawing notes, keep in mind the final scale to which the drawing will be plotted. You may need to enlarge the text in order for it to be legible when plotted to a smaller scale.

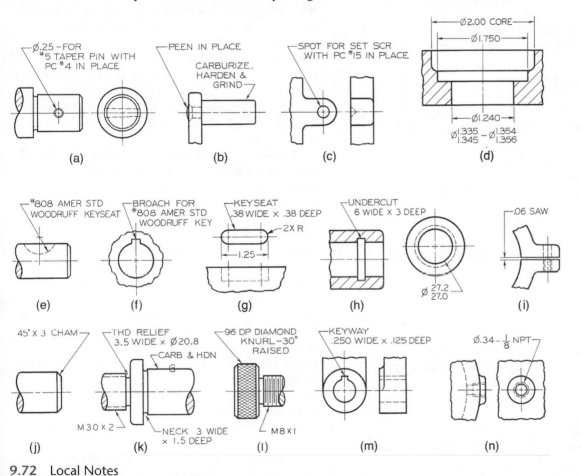

9.72 Local Notes

9.43 STANDARDS

Dimensions should be given, wherever possible, to make use of readily available materials, tools, parts, and gages. The dimensions for many commonly used machine elements—such as bolts, screws, nails, keys, tapers, wire, pipes, sheet metal, chains, belts, ropes, pins, and rolled metal shapes—have been standardized, and the drafter must obtain these sizes from company standards manuals, from published handbooks, from ANSI standards, or from manufacturers' catalogs. Tables of some of the more common items are given in the Appendix.

Such standard parts are not delineated on detail drawings unless they are to be altered for use; they are conventionally drawn on assembly drawings and are listed in parts lists. Common fractions are often used to indicate the nominal sizes of standard parts or tools. If the complete decimal inch system is used, all such sizes are ordinarily expressed by decimals—for example, .250 DRILL instead of 1/4 DRILL. If the all-metric system of dimensioning is used, then the preferred metric drill of the approximate same size (.2480″) will be indicated as 6.30 DRILL.

9.44 DO'S AND DON'TS OF DIMENSIONING

The following checklist summarizes briefly most of the situations in which a beginning designer is likely to make a mistake in dimensioning. Students should check the drawing by this list before submitting it to the instructor.

1. Each dimension should be given clearly so that it can be interpreted in only one way.
2. Dimensions should not be duplicated, nor should the same information be given in two different ways—except for dual dimensioning—and no dimensions should be given except those needed to produce or inspect the part.
3. Dimensions should be given between points or surfaces that have a functional relation to each other or that control the location of mating parts.
4. Dimensions should be given to finished surfaces or important centerlines, in preference to rough surfaces, wherever possible.
5. Dimensions should be given so that it will not be necessary for the machinist to calculate, scale, or assume any dimension.
6. Dimension features should be attached to the view where the feature's shape is best shown.
7. Dimensions should be placed in the views where the features dimensioned are shown true shape.
8. Dimensioning to hidden lines should be avoided wherever possible.
9. Dimensions should not be placed on a view unless clarity is promoted and long extension lines are avoided.
10. Dimensions applying to two adjacent views should be placed between views, unless clarity is promoted by placing some of them outside.
11. The longer dimensions should be placed outside all intermediate dimensions so that dimension lines will not cross extension lines.
12. In machine drawing, all unit marks should be omitted, except when necessary for clarity; for example, 1″ VALVE or 1 mm DRILL.
13. Don't expect production personnel to assume that a feature is centered (as a hole on a plate), but give a location dimension from one side. However, if a hole is to be centered on a symmetrical rough casting, mark the centerline and omit the locating dimension from the centerline.
14. A dimension should be attached to only one view, not to extension lines connecting two views.
15. Detail dimensions should line up in chain fashion.
16. A complete chain of detail dimensions should be avoided; it is better to omit one. Otherwise add a reference to the overall dimension by enclosing it within parentheses.
17. A dimension line should never be drawn through a dimension figure. A figure should never be lettered over any line of the drawing. The line can be broken if necessary.

18. Dimension lines should be spaced uniformly throughout the drawing. They should be at least 10 mm (.38 in.) from the object outline and 6 mm (.25 in.) apart.
19. No line of the drawing should be used as a dimension line or coincide with a dimension line.
20. A dimension line should never be joined end to end with any line of the drawing.
21. Dimension lines should not cross, if avoidable.
22. Dimension lines and extension lines should not cross, if avoidable. (Extension lines may cross each other.)
23. When extension lines cross extension lines or visible lines, no break in either line should be made.
24. A centerline may be extended and used as an extension line, in which case it is still drawn like a centerline.
25. Centerlines should not extend from view to view.
26. Leaders for notes should be straight, not curved, and point to the center of circular views of holes wherever possible.
27. Leaders should slope at 45°, 30°, or 60° with horizontal, but may be made at any convenient angle except vertical or horizontal.
28. Leaders should extend from the beginning or the end of a note, with the horizontal "shoulder" extending from mid-height of the lettering.
29. Dimension figures should be approximately centered between the arrowheads, except in a stack of dimensions, where they should be staggered.
30. Dimension figures should be about 3 mm (.13 in.) high for whole numbers and 6 mm (.25 in.) high for fractions.
31. Dimension figures should never be crowded or in any way made difficult to read.
32. Dimension figures should not be lettered over lines or sectioned areas unless necessary, in which case a clear space should be reserved for the dimension figures.
33. Dimension figures for angles should generally be lettered horizontally.
34. Fraction bars should never be inclined except in confined areas, such as in tables.
35. The numerator and denominator of a fraction should never touch the fraction bar.
36. Notes should always be lettered horizontally on the sheet.
37. Notes should be brief and clear, and the wording should be standard in form.
38. Finish marks should be placed on the edge views of all finished surfaces, including hidden edges and the contour and circular views of cylindrical surfaces.
39. Finish marks should be omitted on holes or other features where a note specifies a machining operation.
40. Finish marks should be omitted on parts made from rolled stock.

41. If a part is finished all over, all finish marks should be omitted and the general note FINISH ALL OVER or FAO should be used.
42. A cylinder is dimensioned by giving both its diameter and length in the rectangular view, except when notes are used for holes. A diagonal diameter in the circular view may be used in cases where it increases clarity.
43. Manufacturing processes are generally determined by the tolerances specified, rather than specifically noted in the drawing. When the manufacturing process must be noted for some reason—such as for dimension holes to be bored, drilled, and reamed—use leaders that preferably point toward the center of the circular views of the holes. Give the manufacturing processes in the order they would be performed.
44. Drill sizes should be expressed in decimals, giving the diameter. For drills designated by number or letter, the decimal size must also be given.
45. In general, a circle is dimensioned by its diameter, an arc by its radius.
46. Diagonal diameters should be avoided, except for very large holes and for circles of centers. They may be used on positive cylinders for clarity.
47. A diameter dimension value should always be preceded by the symbol $\emptyset$.
48. A radius dimension should always be preceded by the letter R. The radial dimension line should have only one arrowhead, and it should pass through or point through the arc center and touch the arc.
49. Cylinders should be located by their centerlines.
50. Cylinders should be located in the circular views, if possible.
51. Cylinders should be located by coordinate dimensions in preference to angular dimensions where accuracy is important.
52. When there are several rough, noncritical features obviously the same size (fillets, rounds, ribs, etc.), it is necessary to give only typical (abbreviation TYP) dimensions or to use a note.
53. When a dimension is not to scale, it should be underscored with a heavy straight line or marked NTS or NOT TO SCALE.
54. Mating dimensions should be given correspondingly on both drawings of mating parts.
55. Pattern dimensions should be given in two-place decimals or in common whole numbers and fractions to the nearest 1/16 in.
56. Decimal dimensions should be used for all machining dimensions.
57. Cumulative tolerances should be avoided where they affect the fit of mating parts.

THE CAD DATABASE AS DESIGN DOCUMENTATION

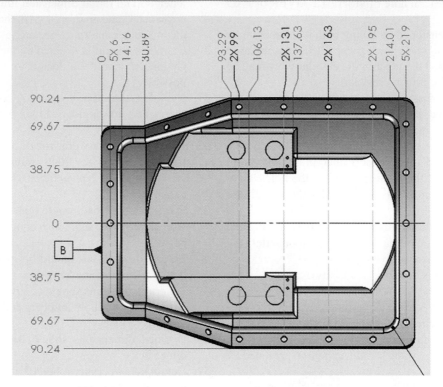

Edrawing software allows you to view 3D and 2D drawings. Many companies transmit and store edrawings as their design record. *Courtesy of Zolo Technologies Inc.*

It is an important advantage of producing an accurate CAD database that you can use the model as a basis for manufacturing. Today's CAD packages offer tools for incorporating tolerances and manufacturing notes into the 3D CAD database itself that improve its ability to document the design. A good understanding of the type of information available in your CAD database combined with the knowledge of how to show critical dimensions and tolerances clearly are important in achieving the most benefit from 3D CAD software.

To use the CAD database as design documentation, companies must consider the legal requirements for maintaining a permanent record of the design. For some industries, a permanent record (or snapshot) of the design used for production must be maintained. A changeable record on the computer may not be considered a legally acceptable practice, or it may be acceptable only if a standard of model/drawing control is met.

ASME Y14.41-2003, Digital Product Definition Data Practices, describes the standard for using a digital product definition to document designs. Some companies use the 3D model with electronic annotations stored in the file or a related database as the final documentation for the product. Other companies produce 2D original drawings from the 3D model to communicate the design for manufacturing and to provide

design documentation for the project. For those companies the 3D model may be stored, but the design record is the fully dimensioned 2D drawings.

Other companies use a combination of the computer files and 2D drawings to document the design. The 2D drawings are used to communicate information about critical tolerances and other information that may not be easily visible in the 3D file. The CAD file serves as the interface to automated manufacturing processes, but the drawing allows the company to call attention to those elements of the design that are critical to its function. Because the manufacturer may not have the same software that was used to create the CAD model, the documentation needs to use a format that can be interpreted by the manufacturer, mold maker, or others who will create or inspect the parts. This is frequently a combination of electronic files in a common 3D format (such as IGES) for the model, and 2D CAD documentation drawings (either printed or in a common 2D file format such as DXF) showing critical dimensions.

Whether the 2D drawings are printed on paper or stored electronically, correctly shown orthographic views still provide much of the basis for communicating and documenting the design. Correctly shown drawing views are also used to communicate information for user manuals and repair manuals, as well as for manufacture and inspection.

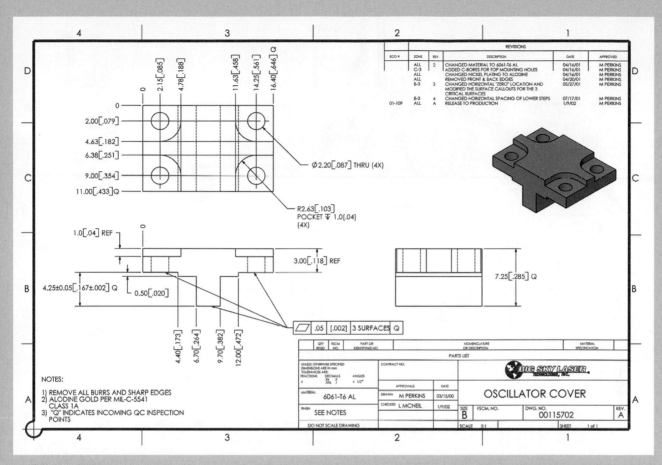

This drawing for a small part shows dimensions in millimeters with the inch values given [in brackets] for reference. *Courtesy of Big Sky Laser.*

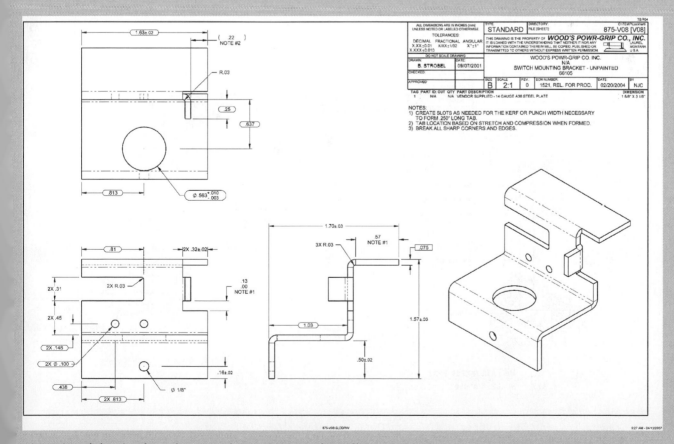

Dimensioned drawing for a sheet metal part. *Courtesy of Wood's Power-Grip Co., Inc.*

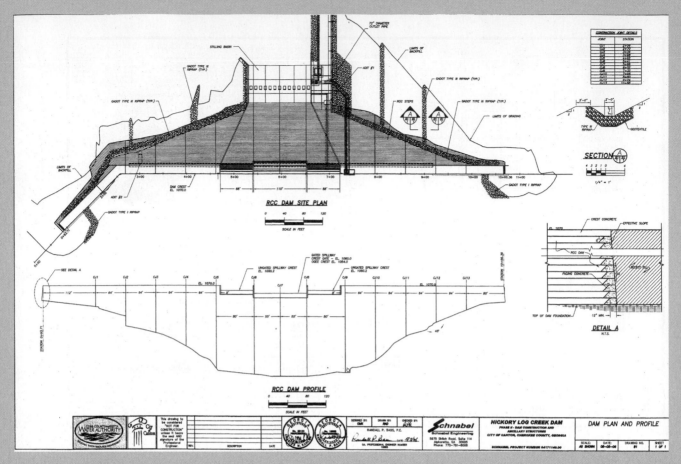

Plan and Profile for Dam Site. *Courtesy of Schnabel Engineering.*

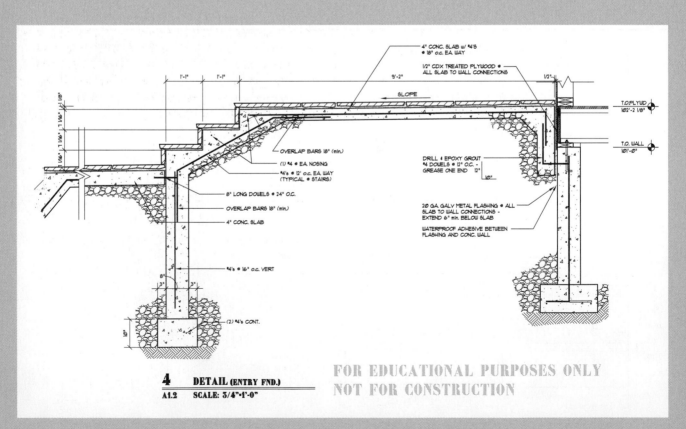

Portion of a Drawing Showing Dimensioned Architectural Details. *Courtesy of Locati Architects.*

KEY WORDS

Dimensions

Tolerance

Size Dimensions

Location Dimensions

Dimension Line

Extension Line

Centerline

Arrowheads

Leader

Dual Dimensioning

Position Method

Unidirectional

Bracket Method

Superfluous

Slope

Batter

Grade

Radial Leader Line

Chordal Dimensions

Finish Mark

Surface Texture Symbols

Location Dimensions

Coordinate Dimensions

Baseline

Mating Dimensions

Local Notes

CHAPTER SUMMARY

- To increase clarity, dimensions and notes are added to a drawing to precisely describe size, location, and manufacturing process.
- Drawings are scaled to fit on a standard sheet of paper. Drawings created by hand are drawn to scale. CAD drawings are drawn full size and scaled when they are printed.
- Dimensions and notes are placed on drawings according to prescribed standards.
- Use good placement practices to make your drawings easy to read.
- Special dimensioning techniques are used for surfaces that have been machined by one of the manufacturing processes.

REVIEW QUESTIONS

1. What are the different units used when a drawing is created using a metric scale? Using an architects' scale?
2. Explain the concept of contour dimensioning.
3. Which type of line is never crossed by any other line when dimensioning an object?
4. How is geometric analysis used in dimensioning?
5. What is the difference between a size dimension and a location dimension?
6. Which dimension system allows dimensions to be read from the bottom and from the right? When can a dimension be read from the left?
7. Draw an example of dimensioning an angle.
8. When are finish marks used? Draw two types.
9. How are negative and positive cylinders dimensioned? Draw examples.
10. How are holes and arcs dimensioned? Draw examples.
11. What are notes and leaders used for?
12. Why is it important to avoid superfluous dimensions?

DIMENSIONING EXERCISES

Most of your practice in dimensioning will be in connection with working drawings assigned from other chapters. However, some dimensioning problems are available here. The problems are designed for 8.5″ × 11″ size sheets and are to be drawn and dimensioned to a full-size scale. Size 297 mm × 420 mm sheets may be used with appropriate adjustments in the title strip layout.

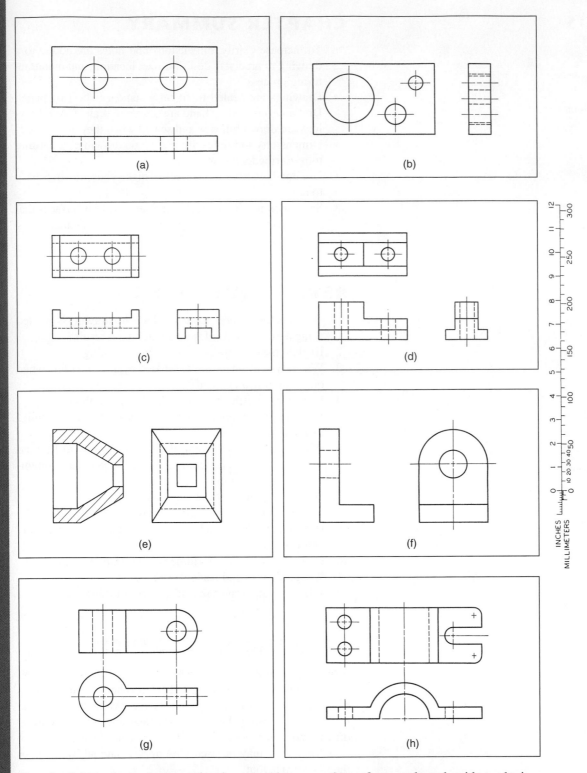

Exercise 9.1 To obtain sizes, use the views on this page and transfer to scale at the side to obtain values completely. Dimension drawing completely in one-place millimeters or two-place inches as assigned, full size. See inside back cover of book for decimal inch and millimeter equivalents.

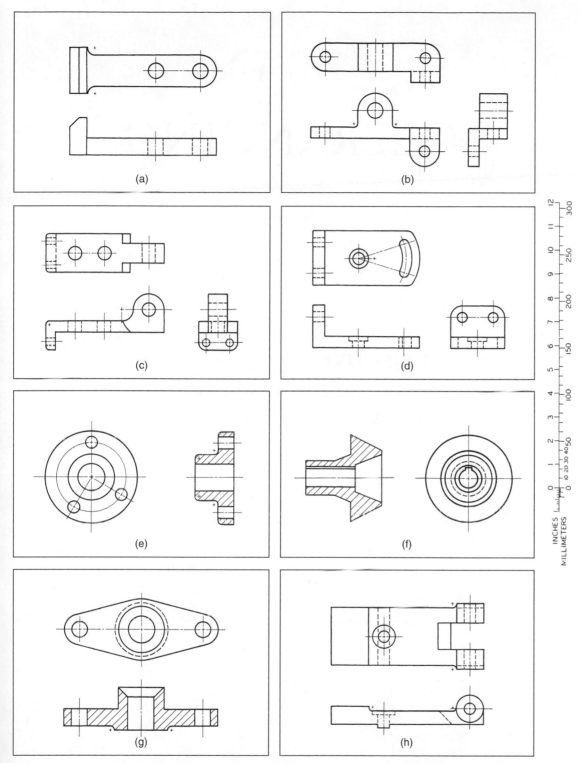

Exercise 9.2 To obtain sizes, use the views on this page and transfer to scale at the side to obtain values completely. Dimension drawing completely in one-place millimeters or two-place inches as assigned, full size. See inside back cover of book for decimal inch and millimeter equivalents.

CHAPTER TEN

TOLERANCING

OBJECTIVES

After studying the material in this chapter, you should be able to:

1. Describe the nominal size, tolerance, limits, and allowance of two mating parts.

2. Identify a clearance fit, interference fit, and transition fit.

3. Describe the basic hole and basic shaft systems.

4. Dimension mating parts using limit dimensions, unilateral tolerances, and bilateral tolerances.

5. Describe the classes of fit and give examples of each.

6. Draw geometric tolerancing symbols.

7. Specify geometric tolerances.

Refer to the following standards:
- ANSI/ASME Y14.5-1994 Dimensioning and Tolerancing
- ANSI B4.1-1967 (R. 1994) Preferred Limits and Fits for Cylindrical Parts
- ANSI B4.2-1978 (R. 1994) Preferred Metric Limits and Fits
- ISO 5459
- ISO 286-1:1988, ISO 286-2:1988
- ISO 1101:1983 (E)

Specifying Tolerance Is Essential to Ensure that Interchangeable Parts Fit Together in Assemblies. *A worker makes notes on a new John Deere engine at a factory in Pune, Maharashtra, India. Courtesy of JOERG BOETHLING/Peter Arnold, Inc.*

OVERVIEW

Interchangeable manufacturing requires effective size control by the engineer or detailer because, in mass production, all parts must fit together properly, regardless of where they are made.

For example, an automobile manufacturer might subcontract parts manufacturing to other companies—both parts for new automobiles and replacement parts for repairs. All parts must be enough alike that each can fit properly in any assembly.

The maximum acceptable amount that an actual part feature can vary from a specified dimension is called tolerance. On technical drawings, tolerances specify the degree of accuracy required for the provided dimensions.

Parts can be made to very precise dimensions, even to a few millionths of an inch or thousandths of a millimeter—as in gage blocks—but highly accurate parts are extremely expensive to produce and there is still some variation between the exact dimension and the actual size of the part. Fortunately, perfectly exact sizes are not needed. The accuracy needed in a part depends on its function.

One aspect of quality is determined by manufacturing tolerances. Products with small variations in shape may fit together more precisely and command higher prices. However, it wouldn't be practical for all products to be manufactured to high precision. For example, a manufacturer of children's tricycles might go out of business if the parts were made with jet engine accuracy—no one would be willing to pay the price.

Waste results when the manufacturing process cannot maintain shape and size within prescribed limits. By monitoring the manufacturing processes and reducing waste, a company can improve profits. This direct relationship to profit is one of the main reasons that tolerancing is critical to manufacturing success.

The Inner Workings of a Watch Are an Example of Parts that Must Fit Precisely in Order to Work. *Courtesy of SuperStock, Inc.*

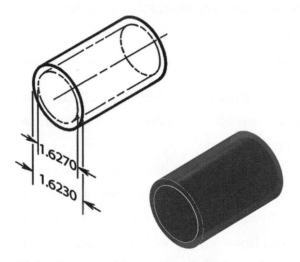

10.1   Upper and Lower Limits of Dimension

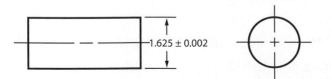

10.2   Direct Limits Used to Specify a Bilateral Tolerance

UNDERSTANDING TOLERANCE

Tolerancing is an extension of dimensioning. It allows you to specify a range of accuracy for the shape, size, and position of every feature of a product, so that the manufactured parts will fit together and function properly when assembled. CAD software often provide features for dimensioning, tolerancing, and checking fits and interferences that aid in the tolerancing process. In order to effectively provide tolerances in your drawings and CAD models, you must:

- Understand the fit required between mating parts.
- Have a clear picture of how inspection measurements are performed.
- Be able to apply tolerance symbols to a drawing or model.

Tolerance

Tolerance is the total amount a specific dimension is permitted to vary (ANSI/ASME Y14.5M-1994). Tolerances are specified so that any two mating parts will fit together. Specify as generous a tolerance as possible that still permits satisfactory function of the part since increased precision makes the part more expensive to manufacture. In this chapter, you will learn several ways of stating the tolerance.

One method of providing a tolerance is to specify the dimension and give a plus or minus range after it. This direct limit applies solely to that feature being controlled by that dimension. Figure 10.1 shows an example of a direct limit. A dimension given as 1.625 ± 0.002 means that the manufactured part may be 1.627 or 1.623 or anywhere between these maximum and minimum limit dimensions. The tolerance (the total amount the actual part feature is allowed to vary from what is specified) is 0.0040.

Quality Control

When you purchase parts or have them manufactured by another company, you must have a way to ensure that the parts are manufactured precisely enough to fit together with their mating parts and perform the intended function.

Before paying for parts, most companies have a process to **quality certify** (QC) the parts against the drawing or model. Larger batches of parts may use statistical methods to control quality where a relevant sample of the parts are inspected instead of all the parts. Some companies require certification from the part vendor rather than inspecting parts themselves.

A tolerance must be specified for each dimension so that it can be determined how accurately the part must be manufactured to be acceptable. The tolerances that you specify are based on the part's function and fit. Figure 10.2 shows the tolerance specified on a drawing.

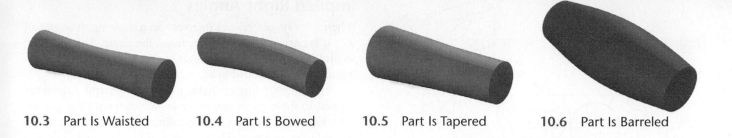

10.3 Part Is Waisted   **10.4** Part Is Bowed   **10.5** Part Is Tapered   **10.6** Part Is Barreled

Variations in Form

Look at the cylinder dimensioned in Figure 10.2. The dimensions specify a **bilateral tolerance** that allow the part to be +.002 or −.002 from the 1.625 dimension specified. The drawing or model of the cylinder specifies the shape and the dimensions and tolerance specify its size and the allowable variation that the size may have.

But what about imperfections of the form? Figures 10.3–10.6 show imperfections of form that may occur in manufacturing cylinders. Of course they are greatly exaggerated in the illustration for clarity. Visually, a difference of a few thousandths of an inch would not be discernable. Since nothing can be made to exact perfection, some of these types of variations will occur in manufacturing. The objective of providing a tolerance is to limit it to an acceptable amount of variation so that the parts will still fit and function.

You can think of tolerance as defining a **perfect form envelope** that the real produced part must fit inside in order to be acceptable. Figure 10.7a illustrates the idea of a part fitting inside the perfect form boundary. The part (in this case a shaft) is represented in green and the upper and lower boundaries are shown as blue areas. The part can be any size that is no larger than the upper boundary and is no smaller than the lower boundary.

Figure 10.7c illustrates the idea of a **bowed** part that extends outside the perfect form boundary. An acceptable part also must not extend beyond the boundary formed by the lower limit. Figure 10.7d illustrates a **waisted** part that extends below the lower limit.

TIP

You can sometimes notice variations in form by placing a machinists' scale along the edge of the part and checking to see if you can slip a feeler gage between the scale and the edge of the part.

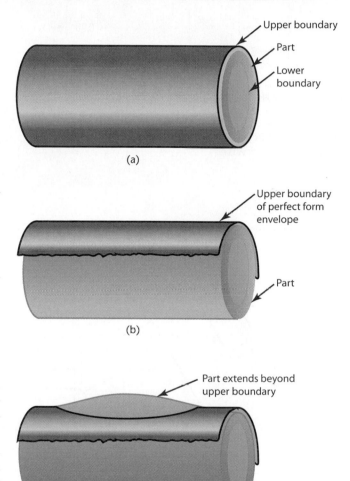

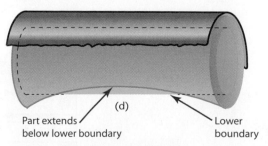

10.7 (a) Fitting (b) Section Showing Fit (c) Part Extends Beyond Perfect Form Boundary (d) Part Extends Beyond Lower Limit (Variations Are Exaggerated for the Purpose of Illustration)

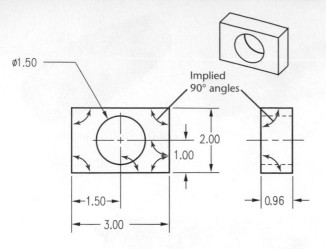

ALL TOLERANCES ±0.002 UNLESS OTHERWISE NOTED.
ANGULAR TOLERANCES ±1°.

10.8   Noted Tolerances Apply to Implied 90° Angles the Same as They Do to Dimensioned Angles that Are Not Noted Otherwise

Implied Right Angles

When lines or centerlines intersect on a drawing at angles of 90°, it is customary not to dimension the angle. This is called an implied 90° angle. If the angle is something other than 90°, it must be dimensioned to be understood clearly.

Implied 90° angles have the same general tolerances applied to them as do any other angles covered by a general note. Figure 10.8 shows a simple dimensioned drawing with a general tolerance note. The tolerance of plus or minus 1 degree applies to the implied 90° angles as well as to the dimensioned angles in the drawing. Figure 10.9 shows a drawing where implied 90° angles are controlled by the tolerance noted in the title block. Later in this chapter you will learn to use geometric dimensioning and tolerancing to control angles with greater precision.

When centerlines and part surfaces are drawn at right angles on a drawing, specific geometric controls or basic dimensions are been shown, as you will learn to do starting in Section 10.11.

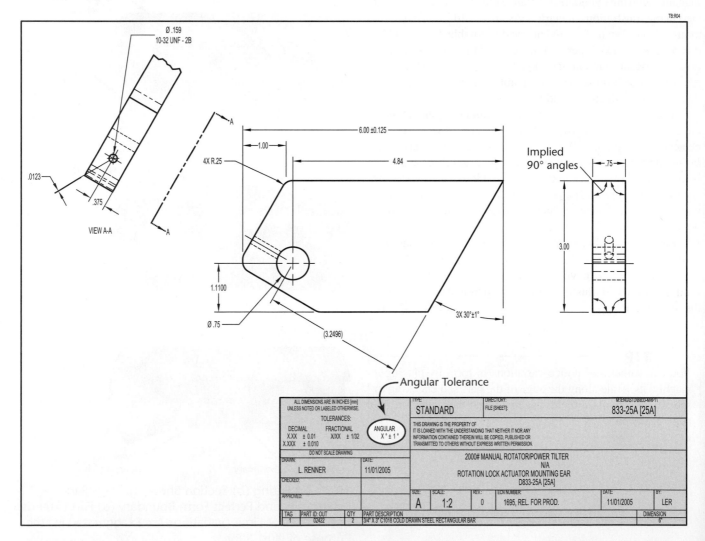

10.9   Tolerance Block Note Is Applied to Implied 90° Angles in the Drawing. *Courtesy of Wood's Power-Grip Co., Inc.*

Fits Between Mating Parts

Fit is the range of tightness or looseness resulting from the allowances and tolerances in mating parts. The loosest fit, or maximum clearance, occurs when the smallest internal part (shaft) is in the largest external part (hole), as shown in Figure 10.10a. The tightest fit, or minimum clearance, occurs when the largest shaft is in the smallest hole, as shown in Figure 10.10b. The difference between the largest allowable shaft size and the smallest allowable hole size (0.002" in this case) is called the **allowance**. There are three general types of fits between parts:

Clearance Fit **Clearance fit** occurs when an internal part fits into an external part with space (or clearance) between the parts. In Figure 10.11 the largest shaft is 1.248" and the smallest hole is 1.250", giving a minimum air space (allowance) of .002" between the

parts. In a clearance fit the allowance is always positive.

Interference Fit An **interference fit** occurs when the internal part is larger than the external part, so the parts must be forced together. In Figure 10.12 the smallest shaft is 1.2513" and the largest hole is 1.2506", so the interference of metal between parts is at least .00070". For the largest shaft and smallest hole, the interference is 0.0019″. In an interference fit the allowance is always negative.

Transition Fit A **transition fit** refers to either a tight clearance or interference. In Figure 10.13 the smallest shaft, 1.2503" will fit into the largest hole, 1.2506". But the largest shaft, 1.2509″, will have to be forced into the smallest hole, 1.2500".

Line fit is sometimes used to indicate limits that are specified so that a clearance or surface contact results when mating parts are assembled.

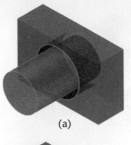
(a)

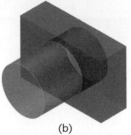
(b)

10.10   Loosest and Tightest Fit

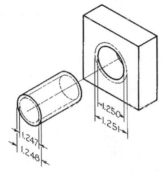
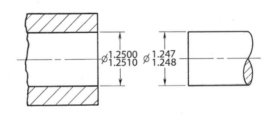

10.11   Clearance Fit

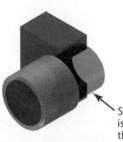
Smallest shaft is still larger than hole size

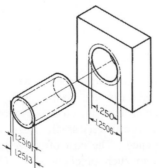
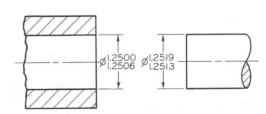

10.12   Interference Fit

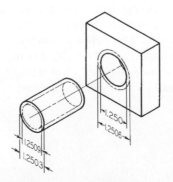
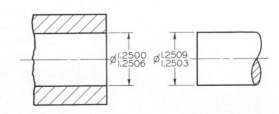

10.13   Transition Fit

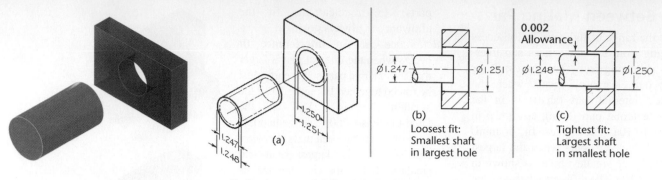

Shaft tolerance = 1.248 – 1.247 = 0.001   Allowance = 1.250 – 1.248 = 0.002
Hole tolerance = 1.251 – 1.250 = 0.001   Max clearance = 1.251 – 1.247 = 0.004

10.14 Specifying Fit Through Limit Dimensions

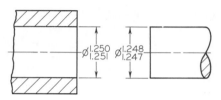

(a) Limit dimensions

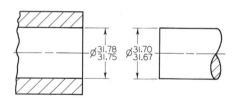

(b) Limit dimensions, metric

10.15   Fits Between Mating Parts

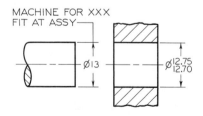

10.16   Noninterchangeable Fit

Specifying Fit Using Limit Dimensions

Limit Dimensions are a method of directly specifying tolerance by providing dimensions for the upper and lower limits of the feature's size.

In the example shown in Figure 10.14, the actual hole may not be less than 1.250" and not more than 1.251". These are the limits for the dimension, and the difference between them (.001") is the tolerance as is indicated in Figure 10.15a.

Likewise, the shaft must be between limits 1.248" and 1.247". The difference between these limits is .001" so the tolerance for the shaft is .001". The minimum clearance is .002", so any shaft will fit inside any hole interchangeably.

In metric dimensions, the limits for the hole are 31.75 mm and 31.78 mm. Their difference, 0.03 mm, is the tolerance (Figure 10.15b). Similarly, the limits for the shaft are 31.70 mm and 31.67 mm, and the difference between them, the tolerance, is 0.03 mm.

When parts are required to fit properly in assembly but are not required to be interchangeable, they are not always toleranced but it is indicated on the drawing that they are to be made to fit at assembly. Figure 10.16 shows an example of this type of note.

Selective Assembly

If allowances and tolerances are specified properly, mating parts are completely interchangeable, but for close fits, it is necessary to specify very small allowances and tolerances. The cost of manufacturing parts to such precision may be very high.

To avoid this expense, either manual or computer-controlled selective assembly is often used. In **selective assembly,** all parts are inspected and classified into several grades according to actual sizes, so that "small" shafts can be matched with "small" holes, "medium" shafts with "medium" holes, and so on. Figure 10.17 shows varation among the sizes of mating parts at an exaggerated size to illustrate the general idea.

Using selective assembly, acceptable fits may be obtained at less expense than by machining all mating parts to highly accurate dimensions. This method is often effective when using transition fits, since either clearance or interference is allowed.

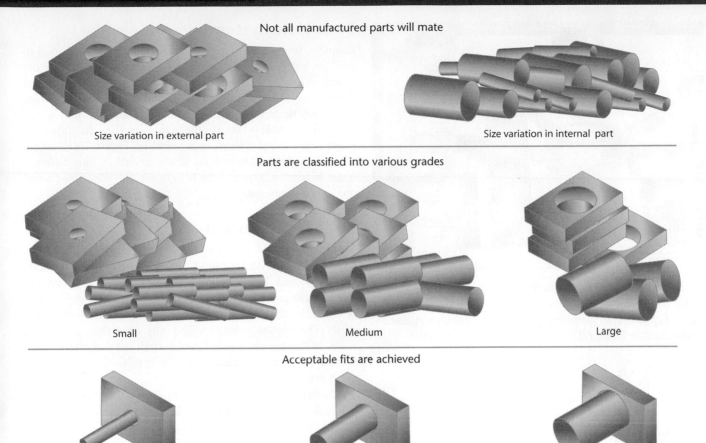

Not all manufactured parts will mate

Size variation in external part

Size variation in internal part

Parts are classified into various grades

Small

Medium

Large

Acceptable fits are achieved

10.17   Selective Assembly. *Difference between the sizes of mating parts is exaggerated for visibility.*

Definitions for Size Designation

You should become familiar with the definitions of size designation terms that apply in tolerancing (ANSI/ASME Y14.5M-1994).

Nominal size   **Nominal size** is used for general identification and is usually expressed in decimals or less often common fractions. In Figure 10.11 the nominal size of both hole and shaft, which is 1-1/4", would be 1.25 inch or 31.75 mm.

Basic size   **Basic size** is the size from which limits of size are determined by applying allowances and tolerances. It is the size from which limits are determined for the size of a feature.

Actual size   **Actual size** is the measured size of the finished part.

Allowance   **Allowance** is the minimum clearance space (or maximum interference) that is specified to achieve a fit between two mating parts. In Figure 10.18, the allowance is the difference between the size of the smallest hole, 1.250", and the size of the largest shaft, 1.248"—or .002". Allowance represents the tightest permissible fit. For clearance fits this difference will be positive, but for interference fits it will be negative.

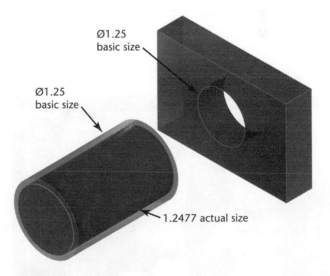

Ø1.25 basic size

Ø1.25 basic size

1.2477 actual size

10.18   Nominal Size, Basic Dimension, Actual Size, Allowance

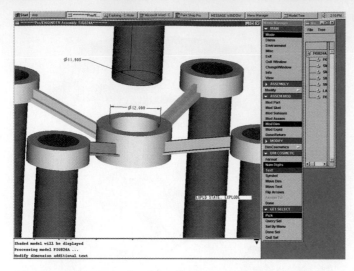

10.19 Tolerances Are Usually Based on the Hole Size Since Holes Are Usually Formed Using Standard Tool Sizes. *Reprinted by permission of Pearson Education, Inc., Upper Saddle River, NJ.*

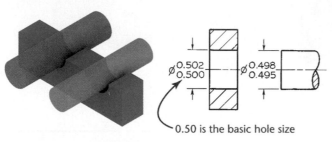

10.20 Basic Hole System

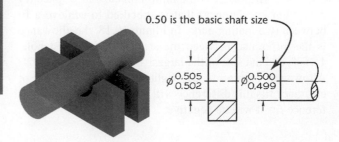

Basic Hole System

Reamers, broaches, and other standard tools are often used to produce holes, and standard plug gages are used to check the actual sizes. On the other hand, shafts are easily machined down to any size desired. Therefore, toleranced dimensions are commonly determined using the **basic hole system,** in which the minimum hole is taken as the basic size. Then the allowance is determined, and tolerances are applied. Figure 10.19 shows a CAD model where several shafts assemble into different holes. Figure 10.20 shows the fit between two parts sized based on the hole diameter.

Basic Shaft System

In some industries, such as textile machinery manufacturing, which use a great deal of cold-finished shafting, the **basic shaft system** is used. It is advantageous when several parts having different fits are required on a single shaft like in Figure 10.21, or when the shaft for some reason can't be machined to size easily. This system should be used only when there is a reason for it. In this system, the maximum shaft is taken as the basic size, an allowance for each mating part is assigned, and tolerances are applied.

In Figure 10.22, the maximum size of the shaft, .500", is the basic size. For a clearance fit, an allowance of .002" is decided upon, giving the minimum hole size of .502". Tolerances of .003" and .001", respectively, are applied to the hole and the shaft to obtain the maximum hole, .505", and the minimum shaft, .499". The minimum clearance is the difference between the smallest hole and the largest shaft and the maximum clearance is the difference between the largest hole and the smallest shaft.

In the case of an interference fit, the minimum hole size would be found by subtracting the desired allowance from the basic shaft size.

10.21 When Several Parts Fit to a Single Shaft Tolerances May Be Based on the Shaft Size. *Reprinted by permission of Pearson Education, Inc., Upper Saddle River, NJ.*

10.22 Basic Shaft System

USING THE BASIC HOLE SYSTEM

1 Determine where mating parts fit. Since the hole will be machined with a standard-size tool, its size will be used to determine the fit. In the figure shown, the minimum size of the hole, .500", is used as the basic size.

2 Determine the type of fit and apply the allowance to the basic size. For a clearance fit, an allowance of .002" is subtracted from the basic hole size, making the maximum shaft size .498" since it is easier to machine the shaft down to a smaller size than to apply the allowance to the hole.

3 Apply the tolerance. Tolerances of .002" and .003", respectively, are applied to the hole and the shaft to obtain the maximum hole of .502" and the minimum shaft of .495". Thus, the minimum clearance is the difference between the smallest hole and the largest shaft and the maximum clearance is the difference between the largest hole and the smallest shaft.

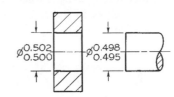

Basic hole fit

STEP by STEP

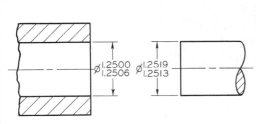

Interference Fit

In the case of an interference fit, the maximum shaft size would be found by adding the desired allowance (the maximum interference) to the basic hole size.

In the figure at left, the basic size is 1.2500". The maximum interference decided upon was .0019″, which when added to the basic size gives 1.2519″, the largest shaft size.

MANUFACTURING TO ONE MILLIONTH OF AN INCH

Gage blocks, used for inspection and calibration, must be manufactured to extremely precise tolerances.

Gage blocks, also known as "Jo blocks" are made from steel, chrome, or ceramic and lapped and honed to accuracies of even just a few millionths of an inch (0.0000254 mm). These precise blocks are used in calibration and inspection. They are often used with a sine bar to precisely measure angles. Using the equation sine Angle = Height/Distance and knowing the fixed distance of the sine bar and the precise height by raising one end of the sine bar on a gage block or stack of gage blocks, you can find precise angles. The angle is typically known and the height of the gage blocks is calculated from the equation. Often tables are used to quickly look up the needed height to produce the required angle for setting up a machine.

Gage blocks are finished so precisely (flatness of around 1 microinch) that they "ring" when slowly slid together and aligned. These blocks are not magnetic. There is some debate as to the exact combination of air pressure, surface tension from the light film of oil or water vapor on the gage blocks, and the interchange of electrons between the atoms of the surfaces of the two blocks being so close together creating an attractive molecular force that hold the blocks together.

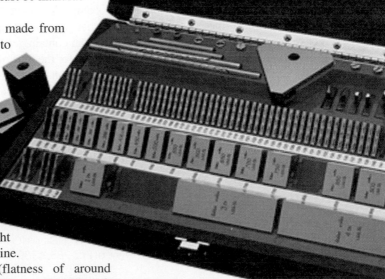

Set of Starrett-Weber gage blocks.
Courtesy of L.S. Starrett Company.

10.1 SPECIFYING TOLERANCES

Every dimension on a drawing should have a tolerance, either direct or by a tolerance note. The primary ways to indicate tolerances in a drawing are

- a general tolerance note;
- a note providing a tolerance for a specific dimension;
- a reference on the drawing to another document that specifies the required tolerances;
- adding limit tolerances to dimensions;
- adding direct plus/minus tolerances to dimensions;
- geometric tolerances.

Many of these tolerancing methods can be used in combination with one another in the same drawing.

10.23 General Tolerance Notes

10.2 GENERAL TOLERANCE NOTES

General notes are usually located in the lower right corner of the drawing sheet near the title block. Often **general tolerance notes** are included in the title block itself. For example, a general tolerance note might state,

"ALL TOLERANCES ±1 MM UNLESS OTHERWISE NOTED. ANGLES ±1 DEGREE."

This indicates that for a dimension value written as 25, for example, any measurement between 24 and 26 on the actual part would be acceptable.

Many companies have standard title blocks that they insert into CAD drawing files that contain general tolerancing standards for the type of production that is common to their industry. Figure 10.23 shows an example of a general tolerance note.

Another way general tolerances are stated is with a table on or near the title block indicating the tolerance by the number of digits used in the dimension as shown in Figure 10.24. For example:

DIGITS	TOLERANCE
.X	±.2 INCH
.XX	±.02 INCH
.XXX	±.001 INCH
X°	±.1°

This type of table indicates that single place decimal dimensions have a tolerance of ±.2. For example, a dimension value written as 3.5 could range anywhere from 3.3 to 3.7 on the actual part and still be acceptable. A dimension written as 3.55 could range from 3.53 to 3.57 on the actual part. And a value written as 3.558 could range from 3.557 to 3.559 and be acceptable. It is uncommon to see more than three decimal places listed for inch drawings because precisions of ±.0001 are very high precision manufacturing and would be unlikely to be indicated merely by a general tolerance note.

10.24 General Tolerance in Title Block. *Courtesy of Dynojet Research, Inc.*

10.3 LIMIT TOLERANCES

Limit tolerances state the upper and lower limits for the dimension range in place of the dimension values as shown in Figure 10.25. Figure 10.26 shows examples of limit tolerances in a drawing. The upper value is always placed above the lower value or, if the two values are written horizontally, to the left of the lower value separated by a dash, as in 32–29.

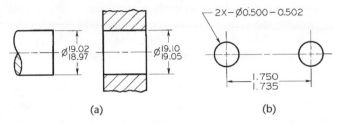

(a)   (b)

10.25 Method of Giving Limits

Single-Limit Dimensioning

It is not always necessary to specify both limits using a single-limit tolerance. The note MIN or MAX is placed after a number to indicate minimum or maximum dimensions desired where other elements of design determine the other unspecified limit. For example, a thread length may be dimensioned as MIN-FULLTHD or a radius dimensioned as R .05 MAX. Other applications include depths of holes and chamfers.

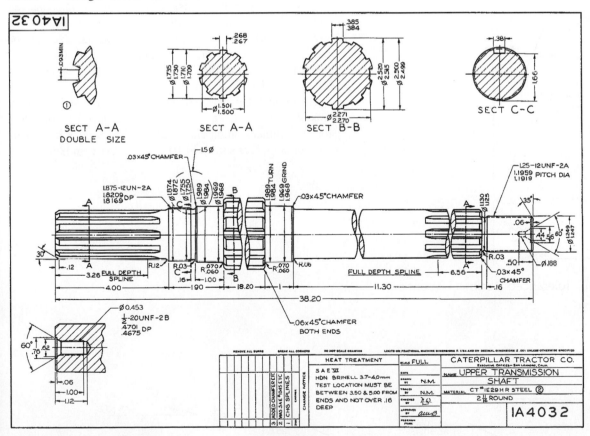

10.26 Limit Dimensions

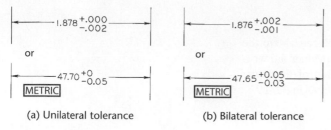

(a) Unilateral tolerance

(b) Bilateral tolerance

10.27   Tolerance Expression

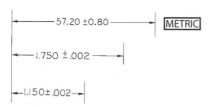

10.28   Bilateral Tolerances

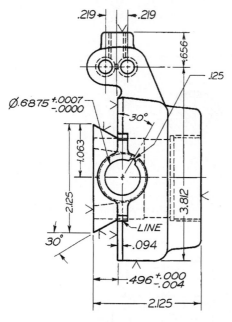

10.29   Plus/Minus Toleranced Decimal Dimensions

10.4 PLUS-OR-MINUS TOLERANCES

In this method the basic size is followed by a plus-or-minus expression for the tolerance (Figure 10.27). The result can be:

- Unilateral where the tolerance only applies in one direction so that one value is zero; or,
- Bilateral where either the same or different values are added and subtracted.

If two unequal tolerance numbers are given—one plus and one minus—the plus is placed above the minus. One of the numbers may be zero. If the plus value and minus value are the same, a single value is given, preceded by the plus-or-minus symbol (±) as shown in Figure 10.28.

The **unilateral system** of tolerances allows variations in only one direction from the basic size. This method is advantageous when a critical size is approached as material is removed during manufacture, as in the case of close-fitting holes and shafts. In Figure 10.27a the basic size is 1.878" (47.70 mm). The tolerance of .002" (0.05 mm) is all in one direction—toward the smaller size. If the dimension is for a shaft diameter, the basic size of 1.878" (47.70 mm) is nearer the critical size, so the tolerance is taken away from the critical size. A unilateral tolerance is always all plus or all minus, but the zeros for the other tolerance value should be shown as in Figure 10.27a.

The **bilateral system** of tolerances allows variations in both directions from the basic size. Bilateral tolerances are usually given for location dimensions or any dimensions that can be allowed to vary in either direction. In Figure 10.27b, the basic size is 1.876" (47.65 mm), and the actual size may be larger by .002" (0.05 mm) or smaller by .001" (0.03 mm). If equal variation in both directions is allowed, the plus-or-minus symbol is used, as shown in Figure 10.28.

Angular tolerances are usually bilateral and given in terms of degrees, minutes, and seconds (Figure 10.29), unless geometric dimensioning and tolerancing is used. Limit tolerances for angles, as shown in 10.30b, are less commonly used.

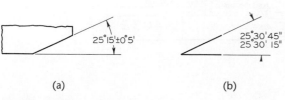

(a)

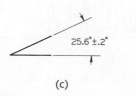

(b)

(c)

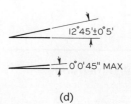

(d)

10.30   Tolerances of Angles

10.5 TOLERANCE STACKING

It is very important to consider the effect of one tolerance on another. When the location of a surface is affected by more than one tolerance value, the tolerances are cumulative. In some cases, for functional reasons, it may be desirable to define dimensions such as X, Y, and Z shown in Figure 10.31a chain fashion, without regard to the overall width of the part. This allows the tolerance to accumulate or "stack up." If the overall width dimension is shown in Figure 10.31a, the part is controlled in too many different ways—it is over-dimensioned. In such cases, if it is shown, the overall dimension should be a **reference dimension** placed inside parentheses to indicate that it is for reference only.

In other cases it may be desired to hold two dimensions (such as X and Y in Figure 10.31a), and the overall width of the part closely by giving the overall width dimension. In that case, a dimension such as Z shown in Figure 10.31a should be omitted or given as a reference dimension only. As a rule, it is best to dimension each surface so that it is affected by only one dimension. This can be done by referring all dimensions to a single datum surface, such as B, as shown in Figure 10.31b.

Chained or Continuous Dimensioning

When dimensions are specified as a chain, the tolerances for the part may add up. A **chained dimension** uses the end of one dimension as the beginning of the next. **Tolerance stacking** refers to the way the tolerance for one dimension is added to the next dimension in the chain and so on from one feature to the next, resulting in a large variation in the location of the last feature in the chain. Figure 10.31a illustrates this effect on a part where the surface labeled A is dimensioned chain fashion. Consider the location of the right end surface relative to the left-hand surface of the part. When features X Y and Z are at their maximum size the surface at the right end of the part can vary within a .015 wide zone. Tolerance stacking is not necessarily bad, if that is the intent for the relative locations of the features. You should be aware of the effect that tolerance has on chained dimensions and specify the tolerances this way when you want the tolerance to accumulate.

Baseline Dimensioning

Baseline dimensioning locates a series of features from a common base feature. Tolerances do not stack up because dimensions are not based on other, toleranced dimensions. Figure 10.31b illustrates how the same part in Figure 10.31a could be dimensioned using baseline dimensioning. Baseline dimensioning can make it easy to inspect the part because features are measured from a common base feature. Dimensioning from a zero point as the base feature can also be a useful technique for dimensioning parts for NC machining.

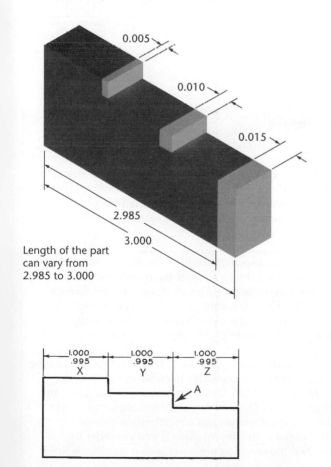

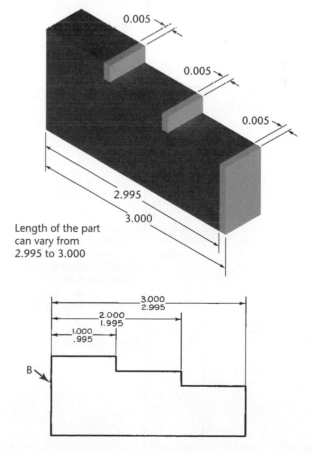

10.31 Cumulative Versus Baseline Tolerances

10.6 USING AMERICAN NATIONAL STANDARD LIMITS AND FIT TABLES

The American National Standards Institute has issued ANSI B4.1-1967 (R1994), "Preferred Limits and Fits for Cylindrical Parts," defining terms and recommending preferred standard sizes, allowances, tolerances, and fits in terms of the decimal inch. This standard gives a series of standard classes of fits on a unilateral-hole basis so that the fit produced by mating parts of a class of fit will produce approximately similar performance throughout the range of sizes. These tables give standard allowances for any given size or type of fit; they also prescribe the standard limits for the mating parts that will produce the fit.

The tables are designed for the basic hole system (see Appendixes 5–9). For coverage of the metric system of tolerances and fits, see Appendixes 13–16.

Table 10.1 gives the three general types of fits, the five subtypes, their letter symbols, and descriptions.

In the fit tables for each class of fit, the range of nominal sizes of shafts or holes is given in inches. To simplify the tables and reduce the space required to present them, the other values are given in thousandths of an inch as in the example shown in Figure 10.32. Minimum and maximum limits of clearance are given; the top number is the least clearance, or the allowance, and the lower number the maximum clearance, or loosest fit. Then, under the heading "Standard Limits," are the limits for the hole and for the shaft that are to be applied to the basic size to obtain the limits of size for the parts, using the basic hole system.

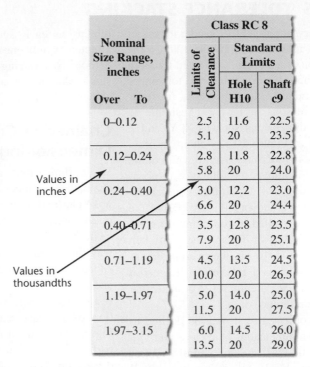

Nominal Size Range, inches Over To	Limits of Clearance	Standard Limits	
		Hole H10	Shaft c9
0–0.12	2.5 5.1	11.6 20	22.5 23.5
0.12–0.24	2.8 5.8	11.8 20	22.8 24.0
0.24–0.40	3.0 6.6	12.2 20	23.0 24.4
0.40–0.71	3.5 7.9	12.8 20	23.5 25.1
0.71–1.19	4.5 10.0	13.5 20	24.5 26.5
1.19–1.97	5.0 11.5	14.0 20	25.0 27.5
1.97–3.15	6.0 13.5	14.5 20	26.0 29.0

Values in inches

Values in thousandths

Column header spans: Class RC 8

10.32 Portion of RC8 Fit Table. *The International Standards Organization (ISO) publishes a similar series of fit tables for metric values.*

Table 10.1 General Fit Types and Subtypes.

Fit Type	Symbol	Subtype	Description
Clearance	RC	Running or sliding fits	Running and sliding fits, (Appendix 7), are intended to provide a similar running performance, with suitable lubrication allowance, throughout the range of sizes. The clearances for the first two classes, used chiefly as slide fits, increase more slowly with diameter than the other classes, so that accurate location is maintained even at the expense of free relative motion.
Locational	LC	Clearance fits	Locational fits (Appendixes 6–8) are fits intended to determine only the location of the mating parts; they may provide rigid or accurate location, as with interference fits, or provide some freedom of location, as with clearance fits. Accordingly, they are divided into three groups: clearance fits, transition fits, and interference fits.
	LT	Transition clearance or interference fits	
	LN	Locational interference fits	
Interference	FN	Force or shrink fits	Force or shrink fits (Appendix 11) constitute a special type of interference fit, normally characterized by the maintenance of constant bore pressures throughout the range of sizes. The interference therefore varies almost directly with diameter and the difference between its minimum and maximum value is small in order to maintain the resulting pressures within reasonable limits.

Milling Machines Can Produce Parts Within Tolerances of .5 mm or a Few Thousands of an Inch. Courtesy of Ron Sherman/Creative Eye/MIRA.com

10.7 TOLERANCES AND MACHINING PROCESSES

Tolerances should be as generous as possible and still permit satisfactory use of the part. The tighter the tolerance, the more expensive it is to manufacture the part. Great savings can be gained from the use of less expensive tools, from lower labor and inspection costs, and from reduced scrapping of material.

Table 10.2 is a chart to be used as a general guide, with the tolerances achievable by the indicated machining processes. You can convert these to metric values by multiplying by 25.4 and rounding to one less decimal place.

Table 10.2 Tolerances Related to Machining Processes.

Range of Sizes From	To and Including	Tolerances								
.000	.599	.00015	.0002	.0003	.0005	.0008	.0012	.002	.003	.005
.600	.999	.00015	.00025	.0004	.0006	.001	.0015	.0025	.004	.006
1.000	1.499	.0002	.0003	.0005	.0008	.0012	.002	.003	.005	.008
1.500	2.799	.00025	.0004	.0006	.001	.0015	.0025	.004	.006	.010
2.800	4.499	.0003	.0005	.0008	.0012	.002	.003	.005	.008	.012
4.500	7.799	.0004	.0006	.001	.0015	.0025	.004	.006	.010	.015
7.800	13.599	.0005	.0008	.0012	.002	.003	.005	.008	.012	.020
13.600	20.999	.0006	.001	.0015	.0025	.004	.006	.010	.015	.025

Process	1	2	3	4	5	6	7	8	9
Lapping and Honing	■	■	■						
Grinding, Diamond Turning, and Boring	■	■	■	■					
Broaching		■	■	■					
Reaming			■	■	■	■			
Turning, Boring, Slotting, Planing, and Shaping					■	■	■		
Milling						■	■	■	
Drilling							■	■	■

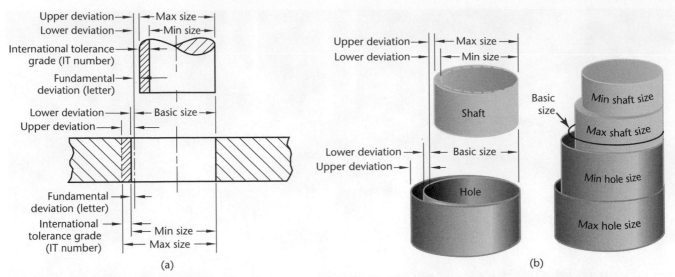

10.33 Terms Related to Metric Limits and Fits. *Reprinted from B4.2-1978, by permission of The American Society of Mechanical Engineers. All rights reseved.*

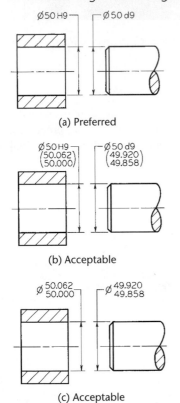

(a) Preferred

(b) Acceptable

(c) Acceptable

10.34 Specifying Tolerances with Symbols for Mating Parts

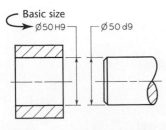

10.35 Specifying Tolerances with Symbols for Mating Parts

10.8 METRIC SYSTEM OF TOLERANCES AND FITS

The preceding material on limits and fits between mating parts applies for both systems of measurement. A system of preferred metric limits and fits by the International Organization for Standardization (ISO) is in the ANSI B4.2 standard. The system is specified for holes, cylinders, and shafts, but it is also adaptable to fits between parallel surfaces of such features as keys and slots. The following terms for metric fits, shown in Figure 10.33a, are somewhat similar to those for decimal inch fits:

Basic size **Basic size** is the size from which limits or deviations are assigned. Basic sizes, usually diameters, should be selected from a table of preferred sizes, as shown in Table 10.3. Figure 10.34 shows examples of preferred and accceptable methods of specifying tolerances on a drawing.

Deviation The **deviation** is the difference between the basic size and the hole or shaft size. This is equivalent to the tolerance in the decimal inch system.

Upper deviation The **upper deviation** is the difference between the basic size and the permitted maximum size of the part. This is comparable to the maximum tolerance in the decimal inch system.

Lower deviation The **lower deviation** is the difference between the basic size and the minimum permitted size of the part. This is comparable to the minimum tolerance in the decimal inch system.

Fundamental deviation The **fundamental deviation** is the deviation closest to the basic size. This is comparable to the minimum allowance in the decimal inch system.

Tolerance The **tolerance** is the difference between the permitted minimum and maximum sizes of a part.

International tolerance grade The **international tolerance grade (IT)** is a set of tolerances that varies according to the basic size and provides a uniform level of accuracy within the grade. For example, in the dimension 50H9 for a close-running fit in Figure 10.35, the IT grade is indicated by the numeral 9. (The letter H indicates that the tolerance is on the hole for the 50 mm dimension.) In all, there are 18 IT grades—IT01, IT0, and IT1 through IT16 (see Figures 10.36 and 10.37)—for IT grades related to machining processes and for the practical use of the IT grades (see also Appendix 10).

Tolerance zone The **tolerance zone** refers to the relationship of the tolerance to basic size. It is established by a combination of the fundamental deviation indicated by a letter and the IT grade number. In the dimension 50H8, for the close-running fit, the H8 specifies the tolerance zone, as shown in Figure 10.38.

Basic hole system The **basic hole system** of preferred fits uses the basic diameter is the minimum size. For the generally preferred hole-basis system, shown in Figure 10.38a, the

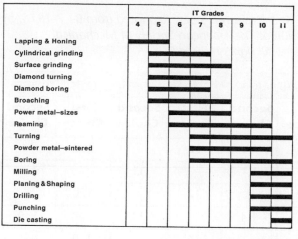

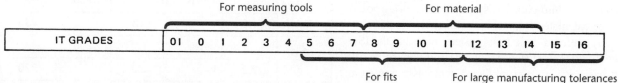

10.36 International Tolerance Grades Related to Machining Processes. *Reprinted from B4.2-1978, by permission of The American Society of Mechanical Engineers. All rights reserved.*

10.37 Practical Use of the International Tolerance Grades

fundamental deviation is specified by the uppercase letter H.

Basic shaft system The basic shaft system of preferred fits is a system in which the basic diameter is the maximum size of the shaft. The fundamental deviation is given by the lowercase letter f, as shown in Figure 10.38b.

Interference fit An interference fit results in an interference between two mating parts under all tolerance conditions.

Transition fit A transition fit results in either a clearance or an interference condition between two assembled parts.

Tolerance symbols **Tolerance symbols** are used to specify the tolerances and fits for mating parts, as shown in Figure 10.38c. For the hole-basis system, the 50 indicates the diameter in millimeters, the capital letter H indicates the fundamental deviation for the hole, and the lowercase letter f indicates the deviation for the shaft. The numbers following the letters indicate the IT grade. Note that the symbols for the hole and shaft are separated by a slash. Tolerance symbols for a 50-mm-diameter hole may be given in several acceptable forms, as shown in Figure 10.39. The values in parentheses are for reference only and may be omitted. For upper and lower limit values, see Appendix 11.

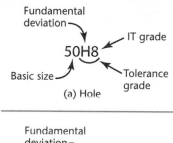

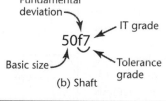

10.38 Applications of Definitions and Symbols to Holes and Shafts. *Reprinted from B4.2-1978, by permission of The American Society of Mechanical Engineers. All rights reserved.*

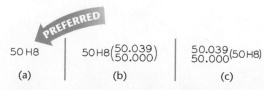

10.39 Acceptable Methods of Giving Tolerance Symbols. *Reprinted from Y14.5M-1994, by permission of The American Society of Mechanical Engineers. All rights reserved.*

10.9 PREFERRED SIZES

The preferred basic sizes for computing tolerances are given in Table 10.3. Basic diameters should be selected from the first choice column since these are readily available stock sizes for round, square, and hexagonal products.

10.10 PREFERRED FITS

The symbols for either the hole-basis or shaft-basis preferred fits (clearance, transition, and interference) are given in Table 10.4. Fits should be selected from this table for mating parts where possible.

For values corresponding to the fits, see Appendixes 11–14. Although second- and third-choice basic size diameters are possible, they must be calculated from tables not included in this text. For the generally preferred hole-basis system, note that the ISO symbols range from H11/c11 (loose running) to H7/u6 (force fit). For the shaft-basis system, the preferred symbols range from C11/h11 (loose fit) to U7/h6 (force fit).

Suppose that you want to use the symbols to specify the dimensions for a free running (hole-basis) fit for a proposed diameter of 48 mm. Since 48 mm is not listed as a preferred size in Table 10.3, the design is altered to use the acceptable 50-mm diameter. From the preferred fit descriptions in Table 10.4, the free-running (hole-basis) fit is H9/d9. To determine the upper and lower deviation limits of the hole as given in the preferred hole-basis table (Appendix 11) follow across from the basic size of 50 to H9 under "Free Running." The limits for the hole are 50.000 and 50.062 mm. Then the upper and lower limits of deviation for the shaft are found in the d9 column under "Free Running." They are 49.920 and 49.858 mm, respectively. Limits for other fits are established in a similar way.

Limits for the shaft-basis dimensioning are determined similarly from the preferred shaft-basis table in Appendix 13. Refer back to Figures 10.34 and 10.39 for acceptable methods of specifying tolerances by symbols on drawings. A single note for the mating parts (free running fit, hole basis) would be H9/d9, as was shown in Figure 10.34.

Table 10.3 Preferred Sizes. *Reprinted from B4.2-1978, by permission of The American Society of Mechanical Engineers. All rights reserved.*

| Basic Size, mm | | Basic Size, mm | | Basic Size, mm | |
First Choice	Second Choice	First Choice	Second Choice	First Choice	Second Choice
1		10		100	
	1.1		11		110
1.2		12		120	
	1.4		14		140
1.6		16		160	
	1.8		18		180
2		20		200	
	2.2		22		220
2.5		25		250	
	2.8		28		280
3		30		300	
	3.5		35		350
4		40		400	
	4.5		45		450
5		50		500	
	5.5		55		550
6		60		600	
	7		70		700
8		80		800	
	9		90		900
				1000	

10.11 GEOMETRIC DIMENSIONING AND TOLERANCING

Geometric tolerances state the maximum allowable variations of a form or its position from the perfect geometry implied on the drawing. The term "geometric" refers to various forms, such as a plane, a cylinder, a cone, a square, or a hexagon. Theoretically, these are perfect forms, but because it is impossible to produce perfect forms, it may be necessary to specify the amount of variation permitted. Geometric tolerances specify either the diameter or the width of a tolerance zone within which a surface or the axis of a cylinder or a hole must be if the part is to meet the required accuracy for proper function and fit. When tolerances of form are not given on a drawing, it is customary to assume that, regardless of form variations, the part will fit and function satisfactorily.

Tolerances of form and position (or location) control such characteristics as straightness, flatness, parallelism, perpendicularity (squareness), concentricity, roundness, angular displacement, and so on.

Methods of indicating geometric tolerances by means of geometric characteristic symbols, rather than by traditional notes, are recommended. See the latest Dimensioning and Tolerancing Standard, ANSI/ASME Y14.5M-1994, for more complete coverage.

Table 10.4 Preferred Fits. *Reprinted from B4.2-1978, by permission of The American Society of Mechanical Engineers. All rights reserved.*

ISO Symbol				
	Hole Basis	**Shaft Basis***	**Description**	
Clearance Fits	H11/c11	C11/h11	**Loose-running** fit for wide commercial tolerances or allowances on external members.	More Clearance →
	H9/d9	D9/h9	**Free-running** fit not for use where accuracy is essential, but good for large temperature variations, high running speeds, or heavy journal pressures.	
	H8/f7	F8/h7	**Close-running** fit for running on accurate machines and for accurate location at moderate speeds and journal pressures.	
Transition Fits	H7/g6	G7/h6	**Sliding** fit not intended to run freely, but to move and turn freely and locate accurately.	
	H7/h6	H7/h6	**Locational clearance** fit provides snug fit for locating stationary parts; but can be freely assembled and disassembled.	
	H7/k6	K7/h6	**Locational transition** fit for accurate location, a compromise between clearance and interference.	
	H7/n6	N7/h6	**Locational transition** fit for more accurate location where greater interference is permissible.	
Interference Fits	H7/p6	P7/h6	**Locational interference** fit for parts requiring rigidity and alignment with prime accuracy of location but without special bore pressure requirements.	← More interference
	1I7/s6	S7/h6	**Medium drive** fit for ordinary steel parts or shrink fits on light sections, the tightest fit usable with cast iron.	
	H7/u6	U7/h6	**Force** fit suitable for parts that can be highly stressed or for shrink fits where the heavy pressing forces required are impractical.	

*The transition and interference shaft-basis fits shown do not convert to exactly the same hole-basis fit conditions for basic sizes in the range from Q through 3 mm. Interference fit P7/h6 converts to a transition fit H7/p6 in the above size range.

10.12 SYMBOLS FOR TOLERANCES OF POSITION AND FORM

Since traditional notes for specifying tolerances of position (location) and form (shape) may be confusing or unclear, may require too much space, and may not be understood internationally, most multinational companies have adopted symbols for such specifications (ANSI/ASME Y14.5M-1994). These ANSI symbols, shown in Table 10.5, provide an accurate and concise means of specifying **geometric characteristics** and tolerances in a minimum of space. A **feature control frame** specifies the tolerance for the geometric characteristic to be controlled and any modifying conditions that are required. The symbols may be supplemented by notes if the precise geometric requirements cannot be conveyed by the symbols. For construction details of the geometric tolerancing symbols, see Appendix 39.

Table 10.5 Geometric Characteristic and Modifying Symbols. *Reprinted from Y14.5M-1994, by permission of The American Society of Mechanical Engineers. All rights reserved.*

Geometric Characteristic Symbols				Modifying Symbols	
	Type of Tolerance	Characteristic	Symbol	Term	Symbol
For individual features	Form	Straightness	—	At maximum material condition	Ⓜ
		Flatness	▱	At least material condition	Ⓛ
		Circularity (roundness)	◯	Projected tolerance zone	Ⓟ
		Cylindricity	⌭	Free state	Ⓕ
For individual or related features	Profile	Profile of a line	⌒	Tangent plane	Ⓣ
		Profile of a surface	⌓	Diameter	⌀
For related features	Orientation	Angularity	∠	Spherical diameter	S⌀
		Perpendicularity	⊥	Radius	R
		Parallelism	//	Spherical radius	SR
	Location	Position	⊕	Controlled radius	CR
		Concentricity	◎	Reference	( )
	Runout	Symmetry	⩵	Arc length	⌒
		Circular runout *	↗	Statistical tolerance	⟨ST⟩
		Total runout *	↗↗	Between *	↔

Arrowheads may be filled or not filled.

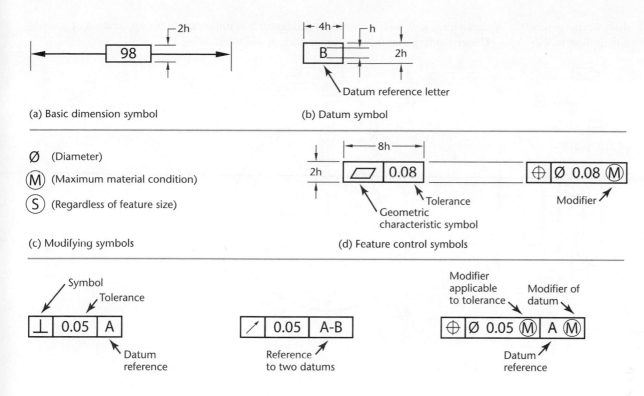

(a) Basic dimension symbol

(b) Datum symbol

Ø (Diameter)

Ⓜ (Maximum material condition)

Ⓢ (Regardless of feature size)

(c) Modifying symbols

(d) Feature control symbols

(e) Feature control symbols with datum references

10.40 Use of Symbols for Tolerance of Position and Form. *Reprinted from Y14.5M-1994, by permission of The American Society of Mechanical Engineers. All rights reserved.*

Figure 10.40 shows combinations of the various symbols and their meanings. The geometric characteristic symbols and the supplementary symbols are explained below with material adapted from ANSI/ASME Y14.5M-1994:

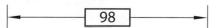

Basic dimension symbol The **basic dimension symbol** is identified by the enclosing frame symbol, as shown in Figure 10.40a. The basic dimension, or size, is the value used to describe the theoretically exact size, shape, or location of a feature. It is the basis from which permissible variations are established either by specifying tolerances on other dimensions, by tolerances given in notes, or by using feature control frames.

▷———Ⓑ *Datum identifying symbol* The **datum identifying symbol** consists of a capital letter in a square frame and a leader line extending from the frame to the concerned feature and terminating with a triangle. The triangle may be filled or not filled. Letters of the alphabet (except I, O, and Q) are used as datum identifying letters.

Ⓜ Ⓟ Ⓛ Ø *Supplementary symbols* **Supplementary symbols** include the symbols for MMC (**maximum material condition**—or minimum hole diameter, maximum shaft diameter) and LMC (least material condition—or maximum hole diameter, minimum shaft diameter), as shown in Figure 10.40c. The abbreviations MMC and LMC are also used in notes (see also Table 10.5).

When needed, the symbol for diameter precedes the specified tolerance in a feature control symbol, as shown in Figure 10.40d. This symbol for diameter should precede the dimension. For narrative notes, you can use the abbreviation DIA for diameter.

Combined symbols **Combined symbols** are found when individual symbols, datum reference letters, and needed tolerances are combined in a single frame, as shown in Figure 10.40e.

Form tolerance The **form tolerance** is given by a feature control symbol made up of a frame around the appropriate geometric characteristic symbol plus the allowable tolerance. A vertical line separates the symbol and the tolerance, as shown in Figure 10.40d. Where needed, the tolerance should be preceded by the symbol for the diameter and followed by the symbol for MMC or LMC.

Reference to a datum The **reference to a datum** is indicated in the feature control symbol by placing the datum reference letter after either the geometric characteristic symbol or the tolerance. Vertical lines separate the entries, and where applicable, the datum reference letter entry includes the symbol for MMC or LMC, as shown in Figure 10.40.

Figure 10.41 shows how geometric dimensioning and tolerance symbols are applied to a drawing. Understanding datum surfaces and features is important to the application of geometric dimensioning and tolerancing.

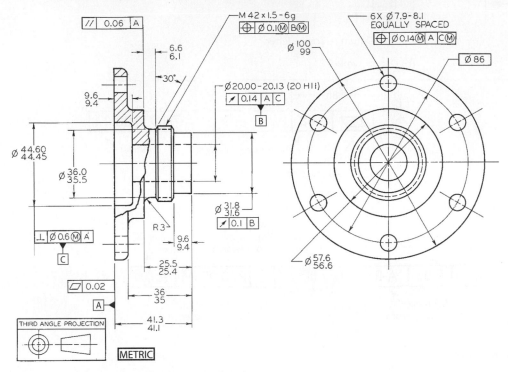

10.41 Application of Symbols to Position and Form Tolerance Dimensions. *Reprinted from Y14.5M-1994, by permission of The American Society of Mechanical Engineers. All rights reserved.*

10.13 DATUM SURFACES AND FEATURES

Datum surfaces and **datum features** are used as references to control other features on the part. For example, when defining the location of a hole, you can specify its distance from a datum surface on the part. Datums should be geometric features on the actual part, such as a point or a plane (or in special cases, an axis) as shown in Figure 10.42. Centerlines on drawings are not used as datums.

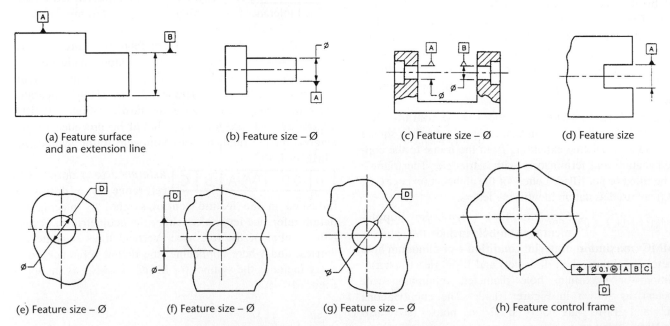

(a) Feature surface and an extension line

(b) Feature size – Ø

(c) Feature size – Ø

(d) Feature size

(e) Feature size – Ø

(f) Feature size – Ø

(g) Feature size – Ø

(h) Feature control frame

10.42 Placement of Datum Feature Symbol. *Reprinted from Y14.5M-1994, by permission of The American Society of Mechanical Engineers. All rights reserved.*

Three mutually perpendicular planes, referred to as the **datum reference frame,** are used to immobilize the part to be inspected and provide a way to make accurate measurements. Datum feature symbols on the drawing identify **primary datum surfaces, secondary datum surfaces,** and **tertiary datum surfaces** (meaning first, second, and third datum surfaces) to create a datum reference frame (Figure 10.43). Figure 10.44 shows the datum reference frame pictorially. Figure 10.45 shows the part oriented on the datum reference frame.

Datums are assumed to be exact, but of course this is not possible in the real world. To simulate the datum reference plane in real life, the person inspecting the part uses a fixture where the primary datum surface on the part makes contact with three points on the fixture. Once the primary datum plane is established, only two additional contact points are needed to establish the secondary datum plane. Once the primary and secondary planes are established, a single additional point will establish the tertiary datum plane. **Datum targets,** as shown in Figure 10.46a, can be added to drawings to specify where these points of contact should occur on the part.

You can find detailed information on datum targets and inspection methods in standard geometric dimensioning and tolerancing texts.

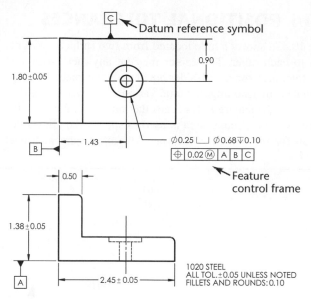

10.43 Datum Reference Symbols Identify Datum Surfaces on a Drawing

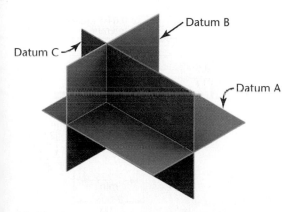

10.44 Datum Reference Frame

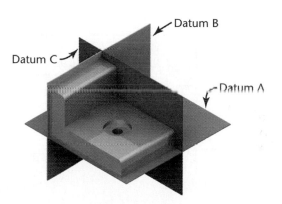

10.45 A Part Oriented on a Datum Reference Frame

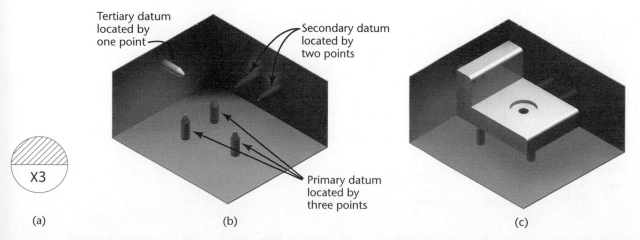

(a)   (b)   (c)

10.46 (a) Datum Target Symbol, (b) Establishing the Datum Reference Frame, (c) Part Immobilized on Datum Reference Frame

10.14 POSITIONAL TOLERANCES

Figure 10.47a shows a hole located from two surfaces at right angles to each other. The center may lie anywhere within a square tolerance zone, with sides equal to the tolerances. Using coordinate dimensioning, the total variation allowed along the diagonals of the square is 1.4 times the indicated tolerance. In contrast, when a circular area is used to specify the allowable variation for the center's location, 57% more parts measure acceptable.

If four holes are dimensioned with rectangular coordinates, as in Figure 10.48a, the tolerance describes a square zone in which the center of the hole must be located (Figure 10.48b and c). This square-shaped zone allows the center of the hole to vary more in the diagonal direction than the stated tolerance value.

In Figure 10.48a, hole A is located from the corner of the part, and the other three are located from A. The tolerances applied to the locations for hole A results in a square tolerance zone. The other three holes are located from the previous hole. Their tolerances produce square zones whose locations vary according to the actual location of hole A. Two of the many possible zone patterns are shown in Figure 10.48b and c.

With the dimensions shown in Figure 10.48a, the resulting parts may not fit with mating parts, even though they meet the drawing tolerances.

Tolerancing features based on their geometry can prevent these problems. Geometric tolerancing controls the shape of the tolerance zone using geometric characteristics in the feature control frame. This is also called **true-position dimensioning**. Using it, the tolerance zone for holes can be a circle, with the size of the circle depending on the variation permitted from true position as specified using a feature control frame.

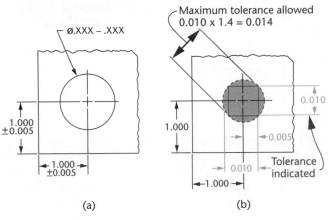

(a)   (b)

10.47 Tolerance Zones

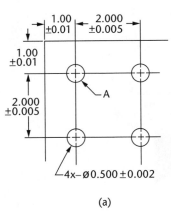

(a)

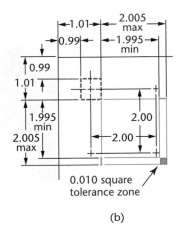

(b)

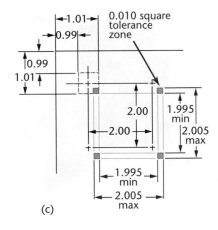

(c)

10.48 Tolerance Zones

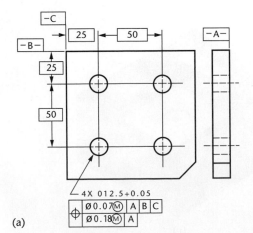

(a)

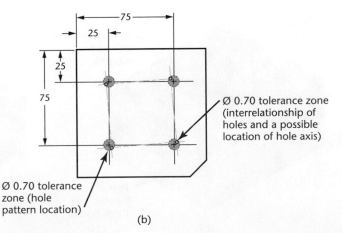

(b)

10.49 True-Position Dimensioning. *Reprinted from Y14.5M-1994, by permission of The American Society of Mechanical Engineers. All rights reserved.*

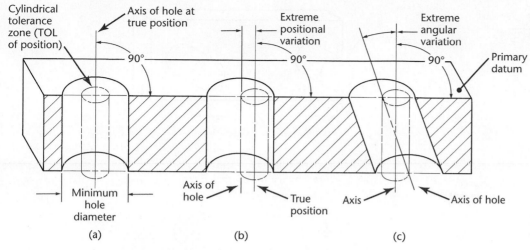

Methods for relating feature control symbols to the feature were shown in Figure 10.41. The following are preferred:

1. Add the symbol to a feature's note or dimension.
2. Run a leader from the symbol to the feature.
3. Attach the side, end, or corner of the symbol frame to an extension line from the feature.
4. Attach a side or end of the symbol frame to the dimension line pertaining to the feature.

A true-position dimension specifies the theoretically exact position of a feature. The location of each feature, such as a hole, slot, or stud, is given by untoleranced basic dimensions identified by an enclosing box. True position is usually established with respect to a datum.

A feature control frame for a positional tolerance describes a cylindrical tolerance zone with a diameter equal to the positional tolerance and a length equal to the length of the feature unless otherwise specified (Figure 10.49). The axis of the hole center must be within the cylindrical zone as shown in Figure 10.50.

The centerline of the hole may coincide with the centerline of the cylindrical tolerance zone (Figure 10.50a). It may be parallel to it but displaced so that it remains within the tolerance cylinder, (Figure 10.50b). Or it may be inclined and remain within the tolerance cylinder (Figure 10.50c).

A positional tolerance specifies that all elements on the hole surface must be on or outside a cylinder whose diameter is equal to the minimum diameter or the maximum diameter of the hole minus the positional tolerance diameter, when the centerline of the cylinder is located at true position.

Special untoleranced basic dimensions locate features at true position, avoiding tolerance accumulation as shown in Figure 10.51.

Features such as slots may vary on either side of a true-position plane, as shown in Figure 10.52.

The exact locations of the true positions are given by untoleranced basic dimensions, ensuring that general tolerances are not applied to them. Add a note to the drawing, such as

GENERAL TOLERANCES DO NOT
APPLY TO BASIC DIMENSIONS.

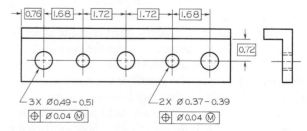

10.51 No Tolerance Accumulation

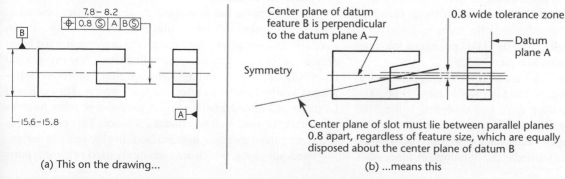

(a) This on the drawing...   (b) ...means this

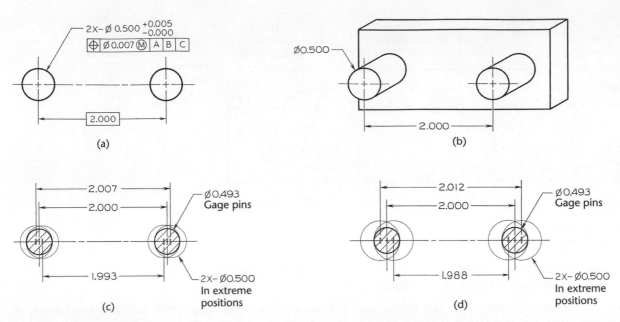

10.53 Maximum and Minimum Material Conditions—Two-Hole Pattern. *Reprinted from Y14.5M-1994, by permission of The American Society of Mechanical Engineers. All rights reserved.*

10.15 MAXIMUM MATERIAL CONDITION

Maximum material condition, or MMC, means that a feature of a finished product contains the maximum amount of material permitted by the toleranced dimensions shown for that feature. Holes, slots, or other internal features are at MMC when at minimum size. Shafts, pads, bosses, and other external features are at MMC when at their maximum size. A feature is at MMC for both mating parts when the largest shaft is in the smallest hole and there is the least clearance between the parts.

In assigning positional tolerance to a hole, consider the size limits of the hole. If the hole is at MMC, or its smallest size, the positional tolerance is not affected, but if the hole is larger, the available positional tolerance is greater. In Figure 10.53a, two half-inch holes are shown. If they are exactly .500" in diameter (MMC, or smallest size) and are exactly 2.000" apart, a gage made of two round pins .500" in diameter fixed in a plate 2.000" apart, as shown in Figure 10.53b, should fit into them. However, the center-to-center distance between the holes may vary from 1.993" to 2.007" as specified by the Ø.007 positional tolerance in the feature control frame in Figure 10.53a.

If the .500" diameter holes are at their extreme positions, as in Figure 10.53c, the pins in the gage would have to be .007" smaller, or .493" in diameter, to fit into the holes. If the .500" diameter holes are located at the maximum distance apart, the .493" diameter gage pins would contact the inner sides of the holes; and if the holes are located at the minimum distance apart,

the .493" diameter pins would contact the outer surfaces of the holes, as shown. If gage-maker's tolerances are not disregarded, the gage pins would have to be .493" in diameter and exactly 2.000" apart if the holes are .500" in diameter, or MMC.

If the holes are .505" in diameter—that is, at maximum size—the same .493" diameter gage pins at 2.000" apart will fit with the inner sides of the holes contacting the inner sides of the gage pins and the outer sides of the holes contacting the outer sides of the gage pins, as shown in Figure 10.53d. When the holes are larger, they may be further apart and still fit the pins. In this case they may be 2.012" apart, which is beyond the tolerance permitted for the center-to-center distance between the holes. Similarly, the holes may be as close together as 1.988" from center to center, which again is outside the specified positional tolerance.

So when holes are at maximum size, a greater positional tolerance becomes available. Since all features may vary in size, it is necessary to make clear on the drawing at what basic dimension the true position applies. In all but a few exceptional cases, when the holes are larger, the additional positional tolerance is available without affecting the function. They can still be freely assembled whether or not the holes or other features are within the specified positional tolerance. This practice has been recognized and used in manufacturing for years in designing fixed-pin gages, which are commonly used to inspect parts and control the least favorable condition of assembly. It has become common practice for both manufacturing and inspection to assume that positional tolerance applies to MMC and that greater positional tolerance becomes permissible when the part is not at MMC.

To avoid misinterpretation as to whether the maximum material condition (MMC) applies, it should be clearly stated on the drawing by adding MMC symbols to each applicable tolerance or by a document referenced on the drawing. When MMC is not specified on the drawing with respect to an individual tolerance, datum reference, or both, the following rules apply:

1. True-position tolerances and related datum references apply at maximum material condition (MMC). For a tolerance of position, regardless of feature size (RFS) may be specified on the drawing with respect to the individual tolerance, datum reference, or both, as applicable.

2. All applicable geometric tolerances—such as angularity, parallelism, perpendicularity, concentricity, and symmetry tolerances, including related datum references, apply regardless of feature size when no modifying symbol is specified. Circular runout, total runout, concentricity, and symmetry are applicable regardless of feature size and cannot be modified to maximum material condition or least material condition (LMC).

3. No element of the actual feature will extend beyond the envelope of the perfect form at maximum material condition. Maximum material condition or least material condition must be specified on the drawing where it is required.

10.16 TOLERANCES OF ANGLES

Bilateral tolerances have traditionally been given on angles, as shown in Figure 10.54. Using bilateral tolerances, the wedge-shaped tolerance zone increases as the distance from the vertex of the angle increases. The use of angular tolerances may be avoided by using gages. Taper turning is often handled by machining to fit a gage or by fitting to the mating part.

If an angular surface is located by a linear and an angular dimension, as shown in Figure 10.55a, the surface must lie within a tolerance zone, as shown in Figure 10.55b. The angular zone will be wider as the distance from the vertex increases. To avoid the accumulation of tolerance further out from the angle's vertex, the **basic angle tolerancing method,** shown in Figure 10.55c, is recommended, (ASME Y14.5M-1994). The angle is indicated as a basic dimension, and no angular tolerance is specified. The tolerance zone is now defined by two parallel planes, resulting in improved angular control, as shown in Figure 10.55d.

Use specific controls such as angular geometric controls or a basic dimension to prevent general tolerances from applying to implied right angles.

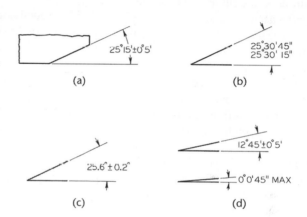

10.54 Tolerances of Angles

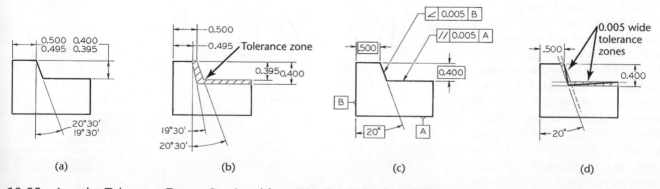

10.55 Angular Tolerance Zones. *Reprinted from Y14.5M-1994, by permission of The American Society of Mechanical Engineers. All rights reserved.*

10.17 FORM TOLERANCES FOR SINGLE FEATURES

Straightness, flatness, roundness, cylindricity, and in some instances, profile, are form tolerances that apply to single features regardless of feature size.

Straightness tolerance The **straightness tolerance** specifies a tolerance zone within which an axis or all points of the considered element must lie (Figure 10.56). Straightness is a condition in which an element of a surface or an axis is a straight line.

Flatness tolerance The **flatness tolerance** specifies a tolerance zone defined by two parallel planes within which the surface must lie (Figure 10.57). Flatness is the condition of a surface having all elements in one plane.

Roundness (circularity) tolerance The **roundness (circularity) tolerance** specifies a tolerance zone bounded by two concentric circles within which each circular element of the surface must lie (Figure 10.58). Roundness is a condition of a surface of revolution in which, for a cone or cylinder, all points of the surface intersected by any plane perpendicular to a common axis are equidistant from that axis. For a sphere, all points of the surface intersected by any plane passing through a common center are equidistant from that center.

Cylindricity tolerance The **cylindricity tolerance** specifies a tolerance zone bounded by two concentric cylinders within which the surface must lie (Figure 10.59). This tolerance applies to both circular and longitudinal elements of the entire surface. Cylindricity is a condition of a surface of revolution in which all points of the surface are equidistant from a common axis. When no tolerance of form is given, many possible shapes may exist within a tolerance zone (Figure 10.60).

Profile tolerance The **profile tolerance** specifies a uniform boundary or zone along the true profile within which all elements of the surface must lie (Figures 10.61 and 10.62). A profile is the outline of an object in a given plane, or 2D, figure. Profiles are formed by projecting a 3D figure onto a plane or by taking cross sections through the figure, with the resulting profile composed of elements such as straight lines, arcs, or other curves.

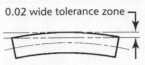

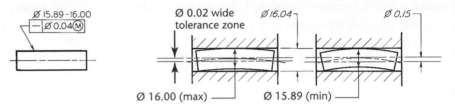

This on the drawing...   Means this

0.02 wide tolerance zone

Each longitudinal element of the surface must be within the specified tolerance size of the perfect form at MMC and lie between two parallel lines (0.02 apart) where the two lines and the nominal axis share a common plane.

Ø 0.02 wide tolerance zone

Ø 16.00 (max)   Ø 15.89 (min)

This on the drawing...   Means this

Each circular element of the figure must be within the specified tolerance size. The centerline of the feature must lie within a cylindrical tolerance zone of 0.04 at MMC. The allowed straightness tolerance increases equal to the amount the feature departs from MMC.

10.56 Specifying Straightness. *Reprinted from Y14.5M-1994, by permission of The American Society of Mechanical Engineers. All rights reserved.*

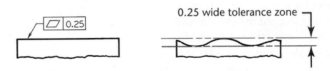

0.25 wide tolerance zone

This on the drawing...   Means this

The surface must be within the specified tolerance of size and must lie between two parallel planes 0.25 apart

10.57 Specifying Flatness. *Reprinted from Y14.5M-1994, by permission of The American Society of Mechanical Engineers. All rights reserved.*

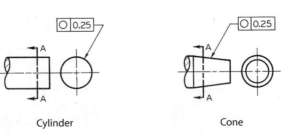

Cylinder   Cone

This on the drawing...

0.25 wide tolerance zone

SECTION A-A

Means this

Each circular element of the surface in any plane perpendicular to a common axis must be within the specified tolerance of size and must lie between two concentric circles — one having a radius 0.25 larger than the other

10.58 Specifying Roundness for a Cylinder or Cone. *Reprinted from Y14.5M-1994, by permission of The American Society of Mechanical Engineers. All rights reserved.*

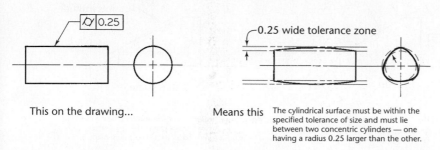

This on the drawing...   Means this   The cylindrical surface must be within the specified tolerance of size and must lie between two concentric cylinders — one having a radius 0.25 larger than the other.

10.59 Specifying Cylindricity. *Reprinted from Y14.5M-1994, by permission of The American Society of Mechanical Engineers. All rights reserved.*

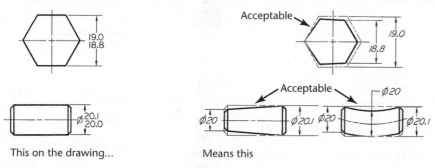

This on the drawing...   Means this

10.60 Acceptable Variations of Form—No Specified Tolerance of Form

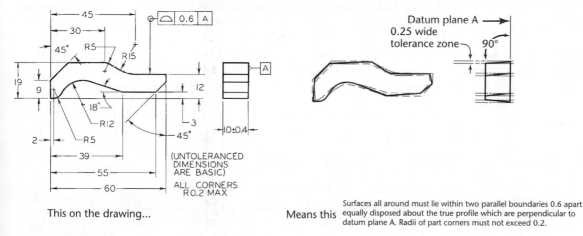

This on the drawing...   Means this   Surfaces all around must lie within two parallel boundaries 0.6 apart equally disposed about the true profile which are perpendicular to datum plane A. Radii of part corners must not exceed 0.2.

10.61 Specifying Profile of a Surface All Around. *Reprinted from Y14.5M-1994, by permission of The American Society of Mechanical Engineers. All rights reserved.*

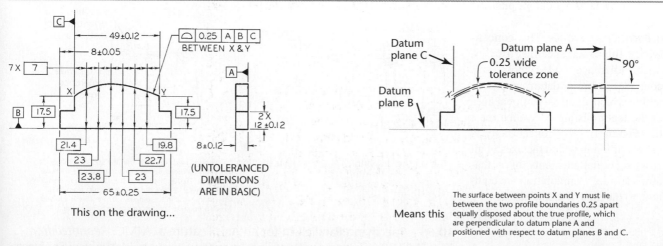

This on the drawing...   Means this   The surface between points X and Y must lie between the two profile boundaries 0.25 equally disposed about the true profile, which are perpendicular to datum plane A and positioned with respect to datum planes B and C.

10.62 Specifying Profile of a Surface Between Points. *Reprinted from Y14.5M-1994, by permission of The American Society of Mechanical Engineers. All rights reserved.*

10.18 FORM TOLERANCES FOR RELATED FEATURES

Angularity, parallelism, perpendicularity, and in some instances, profile, are form tolerances that apply to related features. These tolerances control the attitude of features to one another (ASME Y14.5M-1994).

Angularity tolerance The **angularity tolerance** specifies a tolerance zone defined by two parallel planes at the specified basic angle (other than 90°, in which case use perpendicularity) from a datum plane or axis within which the surface or the axis of the feature must lie (Figure 10.63).

Parallelism tolerance The **parallelism tolerance** specifies a tolerance zone defined by two parallel planes or lines parallel to a datum plane or axis, respectively, within which the surface or axis of the feature must lie (Figures 10.64–10.66). Also, parallelism tolerance may specify a cylindrical tolerance zone parallel to a datum axis within which the axis of the feature must lie.

Perpendicularity tolerance The **perpendicularity tolerance** specifies one of the following:

1. A tolerance zone is defined by two parallel planes perpendicular to a datum plane, datum axis, or axis within which the surface of the feature must lie (Figure 10.67).
2. A cylindrical tolerance zone perpendicular to a datum plane within which the axis of the feature must lie (Figure 10.68).

(Perpendicularity is the condition of a surface, median plane, or axis which is at 90° to a datum plane or axis.)

Concentricity tolerance The **concentricity tolerance** specifies a cylindrical tolerance zone whose axis coincides with a datum axis and within which all cross-sectional axes of the feature being controlled must lie (Figure 10.69). Concentricity is the condition in which the axes of all cross-sectional elements of a feature's surface of revolution are common to the axis of a datum feature.

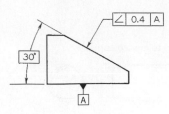

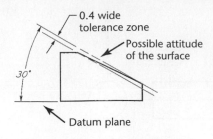

This on the drawing...   Means this   The surface must be within the specified tolerance of size and must lie between two parallel planes 0.4 apart which are inclined at 30° to the datum plane A.

10.63 Specifying Angularity for a Plane Surface. *Reprinted from Y14.5M-1994, by permission of The American Society of Mechanical Engineers. All rights reserved.*

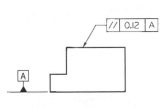

This on the drawing...   Means this   The surface must be within the specified tolerance of size and must lie between two planes 0.12 apart which are parallel to the datum plane A.

10.64 Specifying Parallelism for a Plane Surface. *Reprinted from Y14.5M-1994, by permission of The American Society of Mechanical Engineers. All rights reserved.*

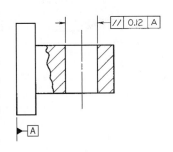
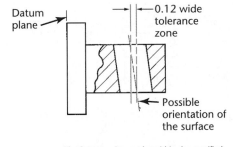

This on the drawing...   Means this   The feature axis must be within the specified tolerance of location and must lie between two planes 0.12 apart which are parallel to the datum plane, regardless of feature size.

10.65 Specifying Parallelism for an Axis Feature RFS. *Reprinted from Y14.5M-1994, by permission of The American Society of Mechanical Engineers. All rights reserved.*

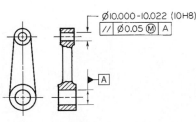

This on the drawing...   Means this   The feature axis must be within the specified tolerance of location. Where the feature is at maximum material condition (10.00), the maximum parallelism tolerance is 0.05 diameter. Where the feature departs from its MMC size, an increase in the parallelism tolerance is allowed which is equal to the amount of such departure.

10.66 Specifying Parallelism for an Axis Feature at MMC. *Reprinted from Y14.5M-1994, by permission of The American Society of Mechanical Engineers. All rights reserved.*

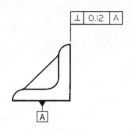

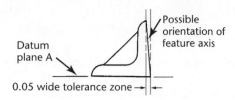

Perpendicularity for a plane surface

The surface must be within the specified tolerance of size and must lie between two parallel planes 0.12 apart which are perpendicular to the datum plane A

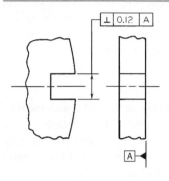

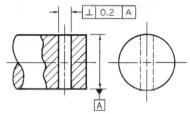

Perpendicularity for a median plane

The feature center plane must be within the specified tolerance of location and must lie between two parallel planes 0.12 apart, regardless of feature size, which are perpendicular to the datum plane A

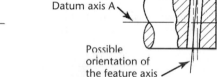

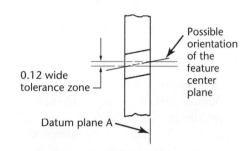

Perpendicularity for an axis

The feature axis must be within the specified tolerance of location and must lie between two planes 0.2 apart, regardless of feature size, which are perpendicular to the datum axis A

10.67 Specifying Perpendicularity. *Reprinted from Y14.5M-1994, by permission of The American Society of Mechanical Engineers. All rights reserved.*

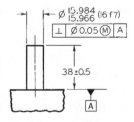

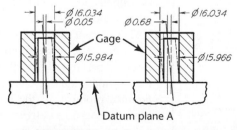

This on the drawing...   Means this

The feature axis must be within the specified tolerance of location. Where the feature is at MMC (15.984) the maximum perpendicularity tolerance is 0.05 diameter. Where the feature departs from its MMC size, an increase in the perpendicularity tolerance is allowed that is equal to the amount of such departure.

10.68 Specifying Perpendicularity for an Axis. Pin, or Boss. *Reprinted from Y14.5M-1994, by permission of The American Society of Mechanical Engineers. All rights reserved.*

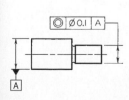

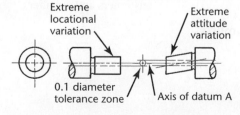

This on the drawing...   Means this

The feature axis must be within a cylindrical zone of 0.1 diameter, regardless of feature size, and whose axis coincides with the datum axis.

10.69 Specifying Concentricity. *Reprinted from Y14.5M-1994, by permission of The American Society of Mechanical Engineers. All rights reserved.*

10.19 USING GEOMETRIC DIMENSIONING AND TOLERANCING

Geometric dimensioning and tolerancing (GDT) has evolved over the last forty years to become an indispensable tool for defining parts and features more accurately. GDT not only considers an individual part and its dimensions and tolerances, but views that part in relation to its related parts. This allows the designer more latitude in defining the part's features more accurately by not only considering the part's dimensions, but its tolerances at the initial design stage. GDT also simplifies the inspection process. This is accomplished through the use of ASME standards (ASME-Y14.5M), as we have discussed previously.

Individually manufactured parts and components must eventually be assembled into products. We take for granted that each part of a lawnmower, for example, will mate properly with its other components when assembled. The wheels will slip into their axles, the pistons will fit properly into their cylinders, and so on. Nothing should be too tight or too loose.

Geometric dimensioning and tolerancing, therefore, is important to both the design and manufacturing processes.

Applying GDT principles to the design process requires five steps.

Step 1 Define the part's functions. It is best to break the part down to its simplest functions. Be as specific as possible. For example, a lawnmower wheel's functions are to: (a) Give the product mobility: (b) Lift the mowing deck off the ground: (c) Add rigidity to the body, etc.

Step 2 List the functions by priority. Only one function should have top priority. This step can be difficult since many parts are designed to incorporate multiple functions. In our lawnmower wheels example, the function with top priority would be to give the product mobility.

Step 3 Define the datum reference frame. This step should be based on your list of priorities. This may mean creating several reference frames, each based on a priority on your list. The frame should be set up in either one, two, or three planes.

Step 4 Control selection. In most cases, several controls will be needed (e.g., runout, position, concentricity, roughness, etc.). Begin with the simplest control. By "simplest" we mean least restrictive. Work from the least restrictive to the most restrictive set of controls.

Step 5 Calculate tolerances. Most tolerances are mathematically based. This step should be the easiest. Apply MMC, RFS, or LMC where indicated. Avoid completing this step first; it should always be your final step.

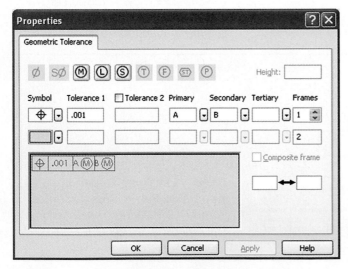

10.70 SolidWorks Dialog Box Aids in Creating Geometric Dimensioning and Tolerancing Symbols. *Courtesy of Solidworks Corporation.*

10.20 COMPUTER GRAPHICS

CAD programs generally allow the user to add tolerances to dimension values in the drawings. See Figure 10.70. Geometric dimensioning and tolerancing symbols, finish marks, and other standard symbols are typically available as a part of the CAD program or as a symbol library.

Geometric dimensioning and tolerancing has become an essential part of today's manufacturing industry. To compete in today's marketplace, companies are required to develop and produce products of the highest quality, at lowest cost, and guarantee on-time delivery. Although considered by most to be a design specification language, GDT is a manufacturing and inspection language as well, providing a means for uniform interpretation and understanding by these various groups. It provides both a national and international contract base for customers and suppliers.

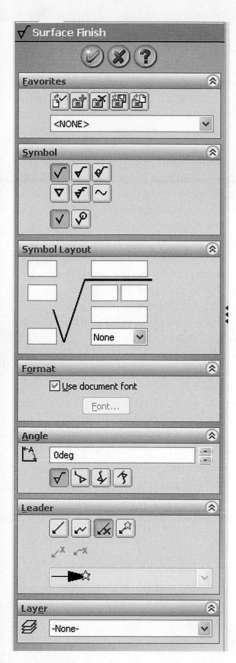

10.71 SolidWorks Software Makes it Easy to Select Surface Finish Symbols. *Courtesy of Solidworks Corporation.*

10.21 TOLERANCES AND DIGITAL PRODUCT DEFINITION

Dimensioning and tolerancing can take place directly in the 3D digital database. The electronic file can be transmitted as the digital product definition specifying the shape, size, and finish to the company that will manufacture and/or assemble the parts.

When you create a 3D model, it represents the ideal geometric shape of the part. The part can be manufactured very precisely, but as precision is increased, so is the price of the part. Adding tolerances to the model informs the manufacturer of the accuracy that is required on the finished part for it to function in your design as you intend. Essentially, you need to tell the manufacturer when to stop trying to achieve the level of perfection that is represented in your model.

When you include annotations in the solid model, the annotation should:

- Be in a plane that is clearly associated with the corresponding surface or view.
- Be clearly associated with the corresponding model geometry.
- Be capable of being printed and meet applicable drawing standards.
- Be possible to display on the screen or turn off.

In general, tolerances and annotations provided directly in the model need to be interpreted to achieve the result that you intend. A combination of drawings and the model, only drawings, or a fully annotated model are all available methods for documenting a design. Each method has its advantages and disadvantages. You should investigate which method is suitable for your use and understand the applicable standards. See Figures 10.71 and 10.72 for examples of tolerancing in CAD.

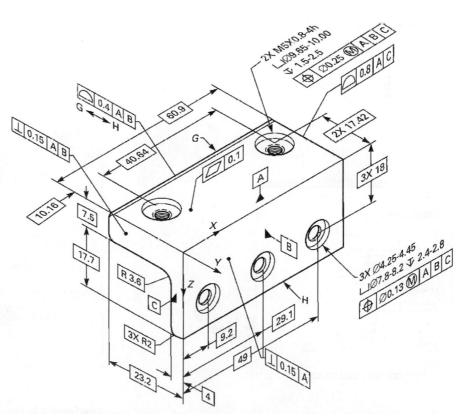

10.72 Tolerances Can be Added Directly to a 3D Model So that It Can be Used as the Digital Product Definition. *Reprinted from Y14.41-2003, by permission of The American Society of Mechanical Engineers. All rights reserved.*

USING PRO/ENGINEER WILDFIRE 3.0 TO PERFORM A FIT STUDY

Tolerances are important to consider, not just for each individual part, but also for the entire assembly of parts. A tolerance accumulation may happen from feature to feature of a part and tolerances may also stack up from part to part in an assembly. One way to analyze the tolerances in the design of your assembly is to do a fit study. Pro/Engineer software has some useful tools for performing a fit study.

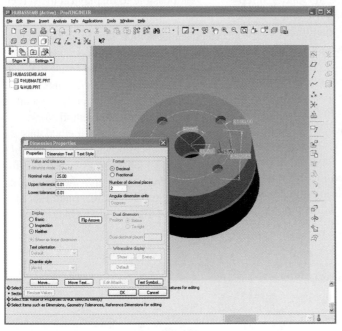

(A)

Dimensions and properties for a 0.25" diameter hole, as seen in Pro/Engineer Wildfire.

Figure A shows the dimensions properties for the size of the 0.25" diameter hole. The upper and lower tolerance for the hole size are set to 0.01". The bottom part has four pins that must fit through the four 0.25" diameter holes. If the locations for the holes are off, the pins may not fit through.

The Wildfire 3 software has a feature called the dimension bounds table that allows you to set a single, group, or all of the dimensions for parts in the assembly to its upper, lower, or nominal size. Figure B shows the dimension bounds table with the value for the R1.00 location dimension for the four holes set to its upper limit. The model automatically regenerates so that the features are sized according to the tolerance applied and the limit set in the bounds table. Saving bounds tables with groups of dimensions set to upper or lower limits helps you analyze the fit for a complex assembly much more quickly than having to change each dimension value in the model and then regenerating the assembly.

Once the bounds table has been used to set the model sizes to the desired dimension limits, you can quickly analyze the interferences in the assembly using the commands available in the software. Figure C shows the interference in this assembly caused by setting the location dimension to its upper limit, when the tolerances for the entire assembly have not been worked out in a way that allows the parts to always fit together. As you can well imagine, the more complex the assembly, the more valuable this CAD tool will be to you.

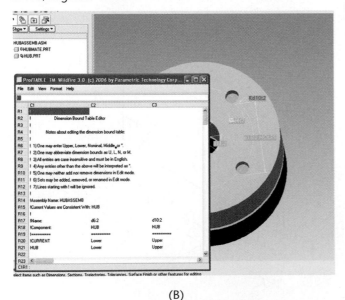

(B)

The Dimension Bounds Table with the value for the R100 location dimension for the four holes set to its upper limit.

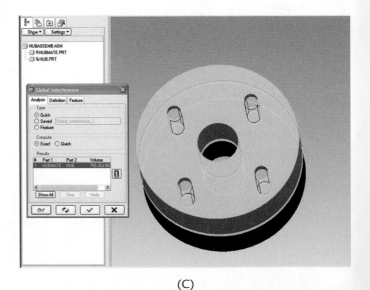

(C)

Interference in the assembly is shown, based on the location dimension limits that you have selected.

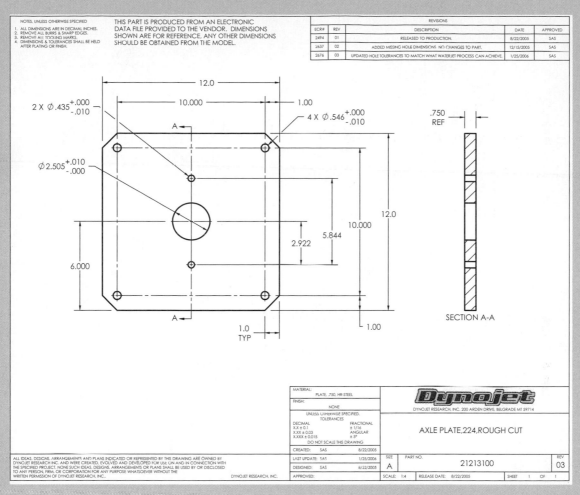

Unilateral Tolerances Are Specified for Hole Sizes. *Courtesy of Dynojet Research, Inc.*

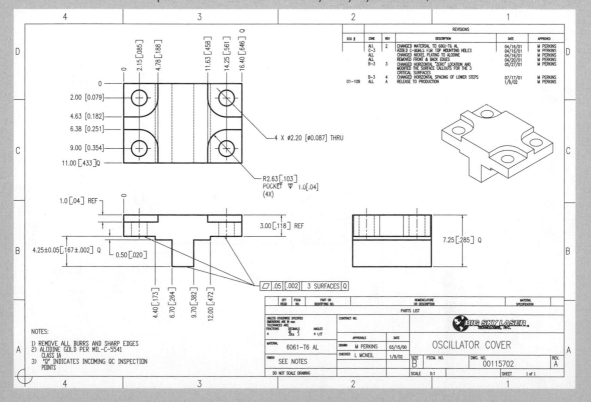

Form Tolerances Are Specified on this Dual Dimensioned Drawing—Big Sky Laser Adds a Q to Indicate Inspection. *Courtesy of Big Sky Laser.*

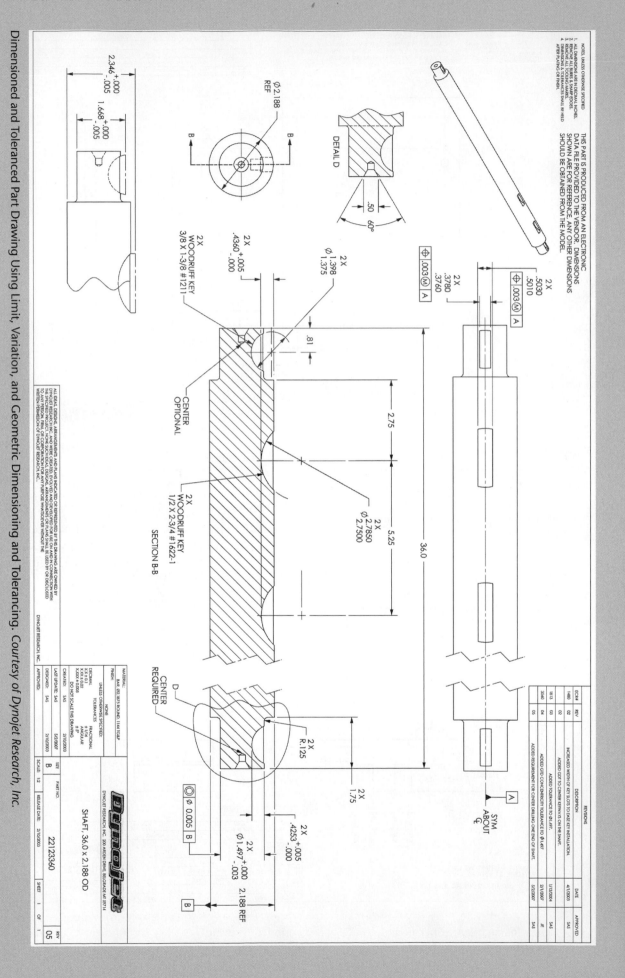

Dimensioned and Toleranced Part Drawing Using Limit, Variation, and Geometric Dimensioning and Tolerancing. *Courtesy of Dynojet Research, Inc.*

KEY WORDS

Tolerance
Quality Certify
Bilateral Tolerance
Perfect Form Envelope
Bowed
Waisted
Fit
Allowance
Clearance Fit
Interference Fit
Transition Fit
Line Fit
Limit Dimensions
Selective Assembly
Nominal Size
Basic Size
Actual Size
Basic Hole System
Basic Shaft System
General Tolerance Notes
Limit Tolerances
Unilateral System
Bilateral System
Angular Tolerances
Reference Dimension
Chained Dimension
Tolerance Stacking
Baseline Dimensioning
Deviation
Upper Deviation
Lower Deviation
Fundamental Deviation
International Tolerance Grade (IT)
Tolerance Zone
Tolerance Symbols
Geometric Tolerances
Geometric Characteristics
Feature Control Frame
Basic Dimension Symbol
Datum Identifying Symbol
Supplementary Symbols
Maximum Material Condition
Combined Symbols
Datum Surfaces
Datum Features
Datum Reference Frame
Primary Datum Surfaces
Secondary Datum Sufaces
Tertiary Datum Surfaces
Datum Targets
True-Position Dimensioning
Basic Angle Tolerancing Method

Straightness Tolerance
Flatness Tolerance
Roundness (Circularity) Tolerance
Cylindricity Tolerance
Profile Tolerance
Angularity Tolerance
Parallelism Tolerance
Perpendicularity Tolerance
Concentricity Tolerance
Geometric Dimensioning and Tolerancing (GDT)

CHAPTER SUMMARY

- Tolerance dimensioning describes the minimum and maximum limits for a size or location of a feature.
- There are several ways of dimensioning tolerances, including limit dimensions, unilateral tolerances, bilateral tolerances, and geometric tolerancing.
- Basic hole tolerance systems are the most commonly used tolerance systems because they assume the hole is nominal size and adjust the shaft to accommodate the tolerance.
- The amount of space between two mating parts at maximum material condition is called the allowance.
- Mating parts with large allowances are classified as having a clearance fit or a running and sliding fit.
- Mating parts with negative allowances are classified as having an interference fit or force fit.
- Mating parts are designed around a nominal size and class of fit. Other tolerances are calculated from these two values.
- High quality parts are often dimensioned with geometric tolerancing to ensure that the size, shape, and relative geometric characteristics are properly defined.
- GDT has become an essential part of today's manufacturing industry. GDT is not only a design language, but an inspection language as well.

REVIEW QUESTIONS

1. What do the two numbers of a limit dimension mean?
2. Draw three different geometric tolerances that reference a datum. Label the information in each box.
3. Why is the basic hole system more common than the basic shaft system?
4. Give five examples of nominal sizes in everyday life. What is the purpose of a nominal size?
5. Give an example of two parts that would require a running and sliding fit. A force fit.
6. List five classes of fit.
7. Can one part have an allowance? Why?
8. Can two parts have a tolerance? Why?
9. Give an example of how GDT could be used as both a design and inspection tool.
10. List the five steps required to apply GDT to the design process.

Design Project

Exercise 10.1 Design a system which will attach under the top of a standard wooden table or desk to contain a computer keyboard. The system should allow the user to store the keyboard underneath the table surface when not in use. Provide a means to prevent the keyboard cable from becoming caught or tangled. Include detailed dimensioning and tolerancing.

Tolerancing Projects

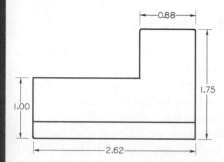

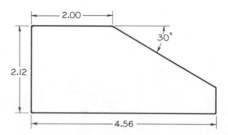

Exercise 10.2 Sketch the figure shown above. Use either limit dimensions, bilateral tolerances, or geometric tolerancing to add a hole to the left end of the part, located .50" from the bottom surface and 2" from the right end of the part. The location should be accurate to ±.005 and its size accurate to within ±.002.

Exercise 10.3 Add geometric dimensioning and tolerancing symbols to the drawing to do the following: a) Control the flatness of the bottom surface to a total tolerance of .001. b) Control perpendicularity of the left surface and bottom surface to .003. c) Control the tolerance for the 30° angle to .01.

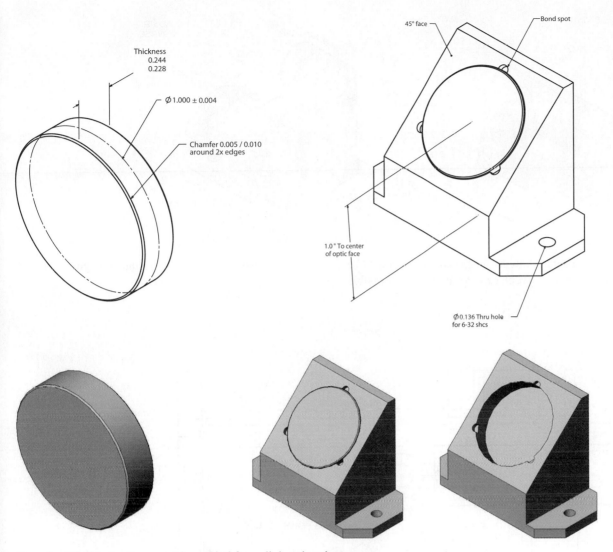

Thickness
0.244
0.228

Ø1.000 ± 0.004

Chamfer 0.005 / 0.010
around 2x edges

45° face

Bond spot

1.0˝ To center
of optic face

Ø0.136 Thru hole
for 6-32 shcs

Exercise 10.4 An optic mount is needed for a dielectric mirror as shown above. The specifications for the design are listed below.

You have been tasked with mounting a dielectric mirror at a 45° angle. This will be done by creating a mount out of 6061-T6 aluminum machined with a 45° face. The face will have a machined c-bore to mount the optic in and three bond spots to attach the optic.

- Reference the provided drawing for stock 1" dielectric mirror.
- The diameter for the c-bore must be .005" to .010" larger than the maximum diameter of the optic.
- The optic must sit at a minimum of .010" and maximum of .020" above the mounting surface.
- The optic will be bonded to the mount using ultraviolet curing adhesive. The adhesive bond spots will be .100" diameter by .050" deep, equally spaced around the perimeter of the optic c-bore.
- The center point of the outer surface of the optic will be located 1 ± .05" from the bottom of the mount.
- The mount will be attached to a laser structure using two 6-32 socket heat cap screws.

Answer these questions:

1. What diameter of c-bore is used to ensure the c-bore is .005" to .010" larger than the maximum diameter of the optic?
2. What depth of c-bore is used to ensure a .010"/.020" protrusion height of the optic?
3. Create a full mechanical drawing with appropriate tolerances for the designed mount.

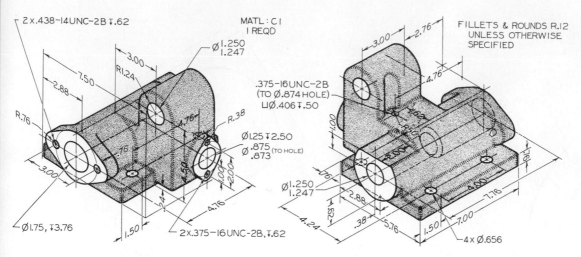

Exercise 10.5 Create a detail drawing for the automatic stop box shown in the two isometric views. Use standardized dimensioning and tolerancing symbols to replace notes as much as possible.

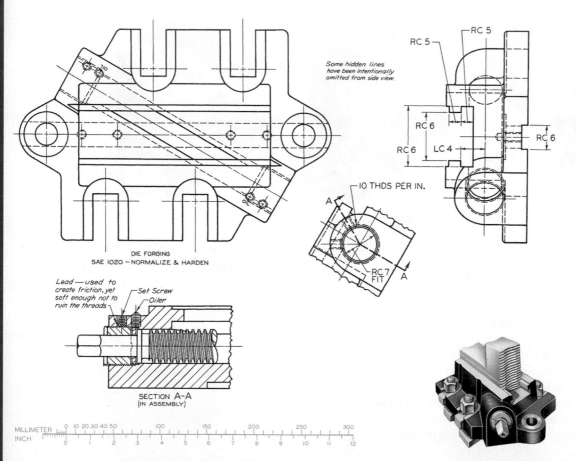

Exercise 10.6 Complete the following for this jaw base for chuck jaw, with top, right-side, and partial auxiliary views shown. (a) Create top, left-side (beside top), front, and partial auxiliary views complete with dimensions, if assigned. Use metric or decimal inch dimensions. Use American National Standard tables for indicated fits or convert for metric values. See Appendixes 5–14 (b) Create solid models for parts and assembly. Make detail drawings for parts and provide tolerances for critical fits. Use a general tolerance note for all other sizes.

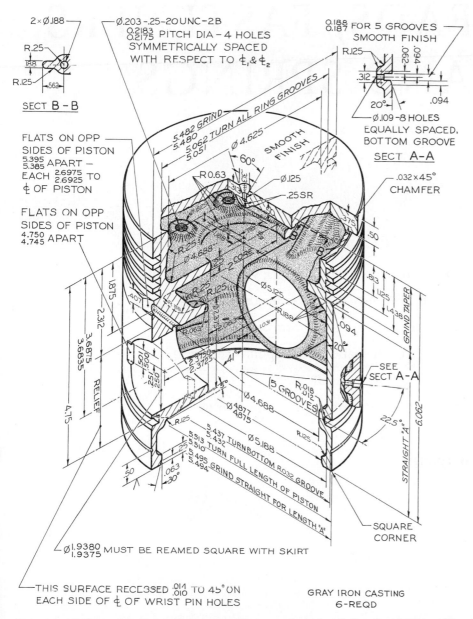

SECT B-B

SECT A-A

Exercise 10.7 For this Caterpillar tractor piston, make a detail drawing full size. If assigned, use the unidirectional decimal inch system, converting all fractions to two-place decimal dimensions, or convert all dimensions to metric. Use standard symbols for dimensioning and tolerancing to replace notes.

CHAPTER ELEVEN

THREADS, FASTENERS, AND SPRINGS

OBJECTIVES

After studying the material in this chapter, you should be able to:

1. Define and label the parts of a screw thread.

2. Identify various screw thread forms.

3. Draw detailed, schematic, and simplified threads.

4. Define typical thread specifications.

5. Identify various fasteners and describe their use.

6. Draw various screw head types.

7. Draw springs.

Refer to the following standards:
- ANSI/ASME B1.1
- ANSI/ASME B1.7M
- ANSI/ASME B1.13M
- ANSI/ASME Y14.6
- ANSI/ASME Y14.6aM

Fasteners. *Courtesy of TwinNut Corp., Germany.*

OVERVIEW

Threaded fasteners are the principal devices used for assembling components. To speed production time and reduce costs, many new types of fasteners are created every year. Existing fasteners are also modified to improve their insertion in mass production. Many companies provide CAD drawings of their fasteners on the Web. When you are using standard fasteners in your designs, save time by downloading drawings or models. Thread is usually dimensioned by giving a thread note in the drawing. This allows you to combine more information in a compact space.

The information in this chapter will prepare you to specify various types of thread and fasteners and use the standard methods of representing them in your drawings.

Web sites related to this chapter
- http://www.mcmaster.com/ A great site for standard parts including fasteners
- http://www.pemnet.com/fastening_products PEM fasteners
- https://sdp-si.com/eStore/ More standard parts with downloadable CAD files

11.1 Thread Used for Attachment. *Courtesy of Arthur S. Aubry/Getty Images, Inc.-Photodisc.*

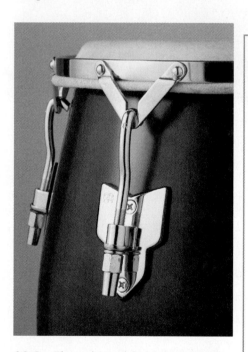

11.2 Thread Used for Adjustment

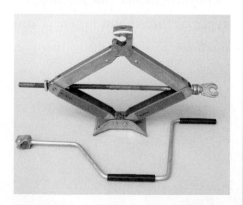

11.3 Thread Used to Transmit Power

UNDERSTANDING THREADS AND FASTENERS

Screw threads are vital to industry. They are designed for hundreds of different purposes. The three basic applications are as follows:

1. To hold parts together (Figure 11.1).
2. To provide for adjustment between parts (Figure 11.2).
3. To transmit power (Figure 11.3).

The shape of the helical (spiral shaped) thread is called the **thread form.** The metric thread form is the international standard, although the unified thread form is common in the United States. Other thread forms are used in specific applications.

CAD drawing programs are often used to automatically depict threads. The thread specification is a special leader note that defines the type of thread or fastener. This is an instruction for the shop technician so the correct type of thread is created during the manufacturing process.

THE STANDARDIZATION OF SCREW THREADS

At one time, there was no such thing as standardization. Nuts made by one manufacturer would not fit the bolts of another. In 1841 Sir Joseph Whitworth started crusading for a standard screw thread, and soon the Whitworth thread was accepted throughout England.

In 1864 the United States adopted a thread proposed by William Sellers of Philadelphia, but the Sellers nuts would not screw onto a Whitworth bolt or vice versa. In 1935 the American standard thread, with the same 60° V form of the old Sellers thread, was adopted in the United States.

Still there was no standardization among countries. In peacetime it was a nuisance; in World War I it was a serious inconvenience; and in World War II the obstacle was so great that the Allies decided to do something about it. Talks began among the Americans, British, and Canadians, and in 1948 an agreement was reached on the unification of American and British screw threads. The new thread was called the Unified screw thread, and it represented a compromise between the American standard and Whitworth systems, allowing complete interchangeability of threads in three countries.

Sir Joseph Whitworth. *Courtesy of National Park Service.*

In 1946 a committee called the International Organization for Standardization (ISO) was formed to establish a single international system of metric screw threads. Consequently, through the cooperative efforts of the Industrial Fasteners Institute (IFI), several committees of the American National Standards Institute, and the ISO representatives, a metric fastener standard was prepared.*

For a listing of ANSI standards for threads, fasteners, and springs, see Appendix 1.

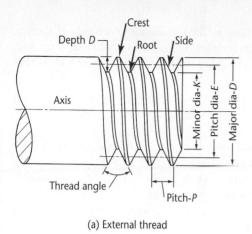
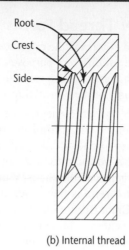

(a) External thread

(b) Internal thread

11.4   Screw Thread Nomenclature

Screw Thread Terms

The following definitions apply to screw threads in general and are shown on the illustration Figure 11.4. For additional information regarding specific Unified and metric screw thread terms and definitions, refer to the appropriate standards.

Screw Thread: A ridge of uniform cross section in the form of a helix on the external or internal surface of a cylinder.

External Thread: A thread on the outside of a member, as on a shaft.

Internal Thread: A thread on the inside of a member, as in a hole.

Major Diameter: The largest diameter of a screw thread (for both internal and external threads).

Minor Diameter: The smallest diameter of a screw thread (for both internal and external threads).

Pitch: The distance from a point on a screw thread to a corresponding point on the next thread measured parallel to the axis. In the U.S., the pitch is equal to 1 divided by the number of threads per inch.

Pitch Diameter: The diameter of an imaginary cylinder passing through the threads where the widths of the threads and the widths of the spaces would be equal.

Lead: The distance a screw thread advances axially in one turn.

Angle of Thread: The angle between the sides of the thread measured in a plane through the axis of the screw.

Crest: The top surface joining the two sides of a thread.

Root: The bottom surface joining the sides of two adjacent threads.

Side: The surface of the thread that connects the crest with the root.

Axis of Screw: The longitudinal centerline through the screw.

Depth of Thread: The distance between the crest and the root of the thread measured normal to the axis.

Form of Thread: The cross section of thread cut by a plane containing the axis.

Series of Thread: The standard number of threads per inch for various diameters.

Electron Microscope View of a Thread Surface. *Courtesy of David Gnizak/Phototake NYC.*

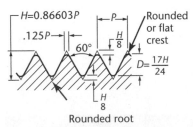

(a) Sharp V

(b) American national

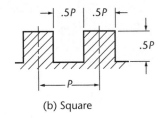

(c) Unified (external)

11.5 Sharp, American National and Unified Screw Thread Forms

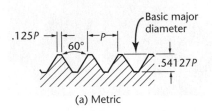

(a) Metric

(b) Square

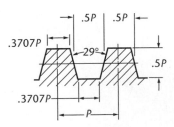

(c) Acme (general purpose)

11.6 Metric, Square, and Acme Screw Thread Forms

Screw Thread Forms

The thread form is the cross sectional shape of the thread. Various forms of threads are used for different purposes. The main uses for threads are to hold parts together, to adjust parts with reference to each other, and to transmit power. Figures 11.5–11.7 show some of the typical thread forms.

Sharp-V thread (60 degrees) useful for certain adjustments because of the increased friction resulting from the full thread face. It is also used on brass pipe work (Figure 11.5a).

American national thread, with flattened roots and crests, is a stronger thread. This form replaced the sharp- V thread for general use. (Figure 11.5b)

Unified thread is the standard thread agreed upon by the United States, Canada, and Great Britain in 1948. It has replaced the American national form. The crest of the external thread may be flat or rounded, and the root is rounded; otherwise, the thread form is essentially the same as the American national. Some earlier American national threads are still included in the new standard, which lists 11 different numbers of threads per inch for the various standard diameters, together with selected combinations of special diameters and pitches. The 11 series includes: the coarse thread series (UNC or NC), recommended for general use; the fine thread series (UNF or NF), for general use in automotive and aircraft work and in applications where a finer thread is required; the extra fine series (UNF or NF), which is the same as the SAE extra fine series, used particularly in aircraft and aeronautical equipment and generally for threads in thin walls; and the eight series of 4, 6, 8, 12, 16, 20, 28, and 32 threads with constant pitch. The 8UN or 8N, 12UN or 12N, and 16UN or 16N series are recommended for the uses corresponding to the old 8-, 12-, and 16-pitch American national threads. In addition, there are three special thread series—UNS, NS, and UN—that involve special combinations of diameter, pitch, and legth of engagement (Figure 11.5c).

Unified extra fine thread series (UNEF) has many more threads per inch for given diameters than any series of the American national or unified. The form of thread is the same as the American national. These small threads are used in thin metal where the length of thread engagement is small, in cases where close adjustment is required, and where vibration is great.

Metric thread is the standard screw thread agreed upon for international screw thread fasteners. The crest and root are flat, but the external thread is often rounded if formed by a rolling process. The form is similar to the American national and unified threads but with less depth of thread. The preferred metric thread for commercial purposes conforms to the ISO basic profile M for metric threads. This M profile design is comparable to the unified inch profile, but the two are not interchangeable. For commercial purposes, two series of metric threads are preferred—coarse (general purpose) and fine—much fewer than previously used (Figure 11.6a).

Square thread is theoretically the ideal thread for power transmission, since its face is nearly at right angles to the axis, but due to the difficulty of cutting it with dies and because of other inherent disadvantages (such as the fact that split nuts will not readily disengage), square thread has been displaced to a large extent by the acme thread. Square thread is not standardized (Figure 11.6b).

Acme thread is a modification of the square thread and has largely replaced it. It is stronger than the square thread, is easier to cut, and has the advantage of easy disengagement from a split nut, as on the lead screw of a lathe (Figure 11.6c).

Standard worm thread (not shown) is similar to the acme thread but is deeper. It is used on shafts to carry power to worm wheels.

Whitworth thread was the British standard and has been replaced by the unified thread. The uses of Whitworth thread correspond to those of the American national thread (Figure 11.7a).

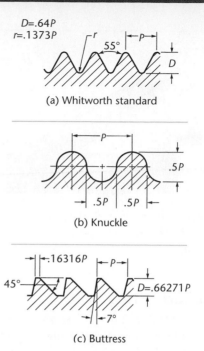

Knuckle Thread is Often Used on Electric Bulbs. *Stephen Oliver © DORLING KINDERSLEY.*

Knuckle thread is usually rolled from sheet metal but is sometimes cast. In modified forms knuckle thread is used in electric bulbs and sockets, bottle tops, etc. (Figure 11.7b).

Buttress thread is designed to transmit power in one direction only. It is commonly used in large guns, in jacks, and in other mechanisms that have high strength requirements (Figure 11.7c).

A number of different thread forms are defined in various ASME standards which specify requirements for the design and selection of screw threads. For example, the old N thread series has been superseded by the UN series.

(a) Whitworth standard

(b) Knuckle

(c) Buttress

11.7 Whitworth Standard, Knuckle, and Buttress Screw Thread Forms

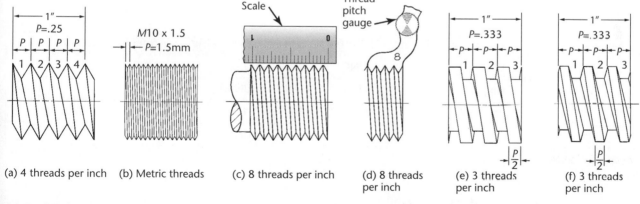

(a) 4 threads per inch (b) Metric threads (c) 8 threads per inch (d) 8 threads per inch (e) 3 threads per inch (f) 3 threads per inch

11.8 Pitch

Thread Pitch

The pitch of any thread form is the distance parallel to the axis between corresponding points on adjacent threads, as shown in Figure 11.8.

For metric threads, this distance is specified in millimeters. The pitch for a metric thread that is included with the major diameter in the thread designation determines the size of the thread—for example, as shown in Figure 11.8b.

For threads dimensioned in inches, the pitch is equal to 1 divided by the number of threads per inch. See Appendix 15 for thread tables giving more information on standard numbers of threads per inch for various thread series and diameters. For example, a unified coarse thread of 1" diameter has eight threads per inch, and the pitch P equals 1/8" (.125").

If a thread has only four threads per inch, the pitch and the threads themselves are quite large, as shown in Figure 11.8a. If there are 16 threads per inch, the pitch is only 1/16" (.063"), and the threads are relatively small, similar to those in Figure 11.8b.

The pitch or the number of threads per inch can be measured with a scale or with a **thread pitch gage.**

An Archimedean Screw.
© 2007 Jupiterimages
Corporation.

The concept of the screw thread seems to have occurred first to Archimedes, the third-century-B.C. mathematician who wrote briefly on spirals and designed several simple devices applying the screw principle. By the first century B.C., the screw was a familiar element but was crudely cut from wood or filed by hand on a metal shaft. Not much was heard of the screw thread until the 15th century.

Leonardo da Vinci understood the screw principle, and created sketches showing how to cut screw threads by machine. In the 16th century, screws appeared in German watches and were used to fasten suits of armor. In 1669, the Frenchman, Besson, invented the screw-cutting lathe, but this method of production did not take hold for another century and a half; nuts and bolts continued to be made largely by hand. Screw manufacturing began in 18th century England, during the Industrial Revolution.

Thread Series

ASME/ANSI Y14.6-2001, Screw Thread Representation, is a standard for drawing, specifying, and dimensioning threads on drawings.

The thread series is the detail of the shape and number of threads per inch composing different groups of fasteners. Table 11.1 shows the thread series for UN thread.

Five series of threads were used in the old ANSI standards:

Coarse thread—A general-purpose thread used for holding. It is designated NC (national coarse).

Fine thread—A greater number of threads per inch it is used extensively in automotive and aircraft construction. It is designated NF (national fine).

8-pitch thread—All diameters have eight threads per inch. It is used on bolts for high-pressure pipe flanges, cylinder-head studs, and similar fasteners. It is designated 8N (national form, 8 threads per inch).

12-pitch thread—All diameters have 12 threads per inch. It is used in boiler work and for thin nuts on shafts and sleeves in machine construction. It is designated 12N (national form, 12 threads per inch).

16-pitch thread—All diameters have 16 threads per inch. It is used where necessary to have a fine thread regardless of diameter, as on adjusting collars and bearing retaining nuts. It is designated 16N (national form, 16 threads per inch).

Table 11.1 Thread Series of UN Thread.

Basic Thread Series	Constant Pitch	Coarse	Fine	Extra Fine	Special Diameter
UN	UN	UNC	UNF	UNEF	UNS
UNJ	UNJ	UNJC	UNJF	UNJEF	UNJS
N	N	NC	NF	NEF	NS
UNR	UNR	UNRC	UNRF	UNREF	UNRS

This series is superseded by the UN series.

Right-Hand and Left-Hand Threads

A right-hand thread is one that advances into a nut when turned clockwise, and a left-hand thread is one that advances into a nut when turned counterclockwise, as shown in Figure 11.9. A thread is always considered to be right-handed (RH) unless otherwise specified. A left-hand thread is always labeled LH on a drawing.

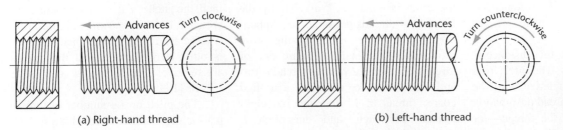

(a) Right-hand thread

(b) Left-hand thread

11.9 Right-Hand and Left-Hand Threads

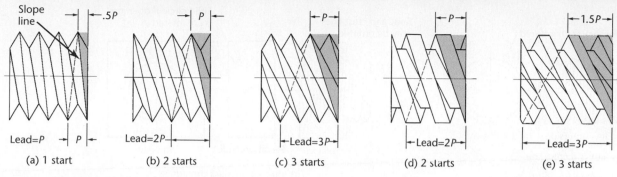

11.10 Multiple Threads

Single and Multiple Threads

A **single thread,** as the name implies, is composed of one ridge, and the lead is therefore equal to the pitch. Multiple threads are composed of two or more ridges running side by side. As shown in Figures 11.10a–c, the slope line is the hypotenuse of a right triangle whose short side equals .5P for single threads, P for double threads, 1.5P for triple threads, and so on. This applies to all forms of threads. In double threads, the lead is twice the pitch; in triple threads, the lead is three times the pitch, and so on. On a drawing of a single or triple thread, a root is opposite a crest; in the case of a double or quadruple thread, a root is drawn opposite a root. Therefore,

in one turn, a double thread advances twice as far as a single thread, and a triple thread advances three times as far. RH double square and RH triple acme threads are shown in Figures 11.10d and 11.10e, respectively.

Multiple threads are used wherever quick motion, but not great power, is desired, as on ballpoint pens, toothpaste caps, valve stems, and so on. The threads on a valve stem are frequently multiple threads to impart quick action in opening and closing the valve. Multiple threads on a shaft can be recognized and counted by observing the number of thread starts on the end of the screw.

American National Thread Fits

For general use, three classes of screw thread fits between mating threads (as between bolt and nut) have been established by ANSI.

These fits are produced by the application of tolerances listed in the standard and are as follows:

Class 1 fit—Recommended only for screw thread work where clearance between mating parts is essential for rapid assembly and where shake or play is not objectionable.

Class 2 fit—Represents a high quality of commercial thread product and is recommended for the great bulk of interchangeable screw thread work.

Class 3 fit—Represents an exceptionally high quality of commercially threaded product and is recommended only in

cases where the high cost of precision tools and continual checking are warranted.

The standard for unified screw threads specifies tolerances and allowances defining the several classes of fit (degree of looseness or tightness) between mating threads. In the symbols for fit, the letter A refers to the external threads and B to internal threads. There are three classes of fit each for external threads (1A, 2A, 3A) and internal threads (1B, 2B, 3B). Classes 1A and 1B have generous tolerances, facilitating rapid assembly and disassembly. Classes 2A and 2B are used in the normal production of screws, bolts, and nuts, as well as in a variety of general applications. Classes 3A and 3B provide for applications needing highly accurate and close-fitting threads.

Metric and Unified Thread Fits

Some specialized metric thread applications are specified by tolerance grade, tolerance position, class, and length of engagement. There are two general classes of metric thread fits. The first is for general-purpose applications and has a tolerance class of 6H for internal threads and a class of 6g for external threads. The second is used where closer fits are necessary and has a tolerance class of 6H for internal threads and a class of 5g6g for external threads. Metric thread tolerance classes of 6H/6g are generally assumed if not otherwise designated

and are used in applications comparable to the 2A/2B inch classes of fits.

The single-tolerance designation of 6H refers to both the tolerance grade and position for the pitch diameter and the minor diameter for an internal thread. The single-tolerance designation of 6g refers to both the tolerance grade and position for the pitch diameter and the major diameter of the external thread. A double designation of 5g6g indicates separate tolerance grades for the pitch diameter and for the major diameter of the external thread.

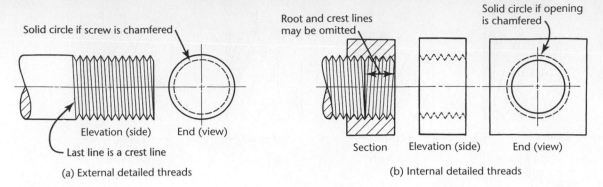

(a) External detailed threads

(b) Internal detailed threads

11.11   Detailed Metric, American National, and Unified Threads

Three Methods for Drawing Thread

There are three methods of representing screw threads on drawings—the schematic, simplified, and detailed methods. Schematic, simplified, and detailed thread symbols may be combined on a single drawing.

Schematic and the more common simplified representations are used to show threads. The symbols are the same for all forms of threads, such as metric, unified, square, and acme, but the thread specification identifies which is to be used.

Detailed representation is a closer approximation of the exact appearance of a screw thread, where the true profiles of the thread's form are drawn; but the helical curves are replaced by straight lines. The true projection of the helical curves of a screw thread takes too much time to draw, so it is rarely used in practice.

Do not use detailed representation unless the diameter of the thread on the drawing is more than 1" or 25 mm and then only to call attention to the thread when necessary. Schematic representation is much simpler to draw and still presents the appearance of thread. Detailed representation is shown in Figure 11.11. Whether the crests or roots are flat or rounded, they are represented by single lines and not double lines. American national and unified threads are drawn the same way. Figure 11.12 shows schematic thread symbols, and Figure 11.13 shows simplified thread symbols.

Figure 11.14 shows detailed directions for drawing schematic and simplified thread.

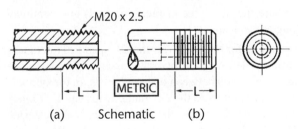

11.12   Schematic Thread Symbols

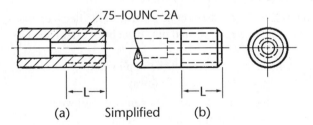

11.13   Simplified Thread Symbols

SHOWING DETAILED THREAD

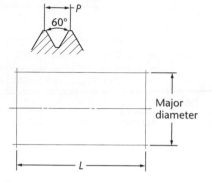

1 Make centerline and lay out length and major diameter as shown at right.

2 Find the number of threads per inch in Appendix 17 for American National and Unified threads. This number depends on the major diameter of the thread and whether the thread is internal or external.

Find P (pitch) by dividing 1 by the number of threads per inch. The pitch for metric threads is given directly in the thread designation. For example, the thread has a pitch of 2 mm.

Establish the slope of the thread by offsetting the slope line $.5P$ for single threads, P for double threads, $1.5P$ for triple threads, and so on. For right-hand external threads, the slope line slopes upward to the left; for left-hand external threads, the slope line slopes upward to the right.

By eye, mark off even spacing for the pitch. If using CAD, make a single thread and array the lines using the pitch as the spacing.

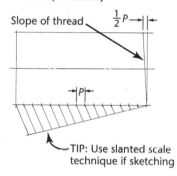

P=Pitch (see tables)

Slope of thread $\frac{1}{2}P$

TIP: Use slanted scale technique if sketching

3 From the pitch points, make crest lines parallel to the slope line. These should be dark, thin lines. Make two V's to establish the depth of thread, and sketch light guidelines for the root of thread, as shown.

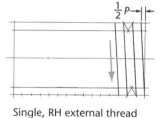

$\frac{1}{2}P$

Single, RH external thread

4 Finish the final 60° V's. The V's should be vertical; they should not lean with the thread.

Make root lines. Root lines will not be parallel to crest lines, but should appear parallel to each other.

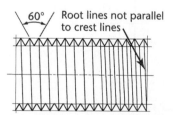

60°   Root lines not parallel to crest lines

5 When the end is chamfered (usually 45° with end of shaft, sometimes 30°), the chamfer extends to the thread depth. The chamfer creates a new crest line, which you make between the two new crest points. It is not parallel to the other crest lines. When finished, all thread root and crest lines should be shown thin, but dark.

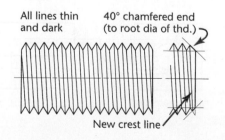

All lines thin and dark   40° chamfered end (to root dia of thd.)

New crest line

MAJOR DIAMETER	#5 (.125) TO #12 (.216)	.25	.3125	.375	.4375	.5	.5625	.625	.6875	.75	.8125	.875	.9375	1.
DEPTH, D	.03125	.03125	.03125	.0468	.0468	.0625	.0625	.0625	.0625	.0781	.0937	.0937	.0937	.0937
PITCH, P	.0468	.0625	.0625	.0625	.0625	.0937	.0937	.0937	.0937	.125	.125	.125	.125	.125

Approximate thread depth table   *(For metric values: 1" = 25.4mm or see inside front cover)*

──────────────── Steps for drawing simplified external threads ────────────────

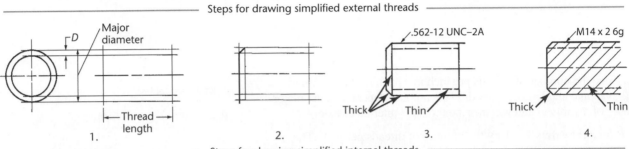

──────────────── Steps for drawing simplified internal threads ────────────────

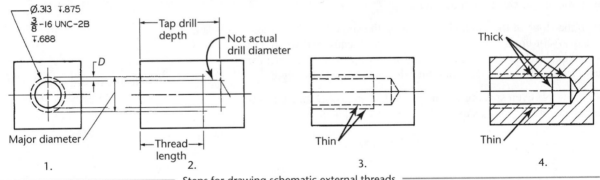

──────────────── Steps for drawing schematic external threads ────────────────

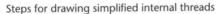

──────────────── Steps for drawing schematic internal threads ────────────────

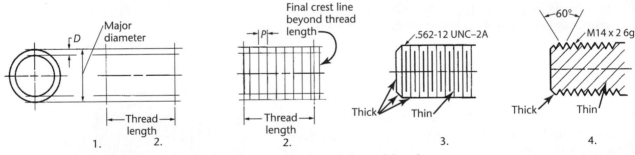

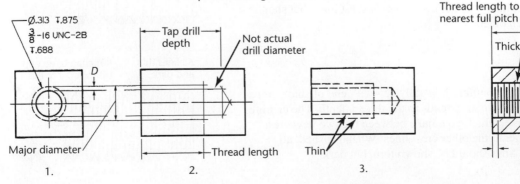

11.14 Steps to Draw Thread Symbols—Simplified and Schematic

11.1 THREAD NOTES

ASME/ANSI Y14.6-2001, Screw Thread Representation, is a standard for representing, specifying, and dimensioning screw threads on drawings. Thread notes for metric, unified, and American national screw threads are shown in Figure 11.15 and 11.16. These same notes or symbols are used in correspondence, on shop and storeroom records, and in specifications for parts, taps, dies, tools, and gages.

Metric screw threads are designated basically by the letter M for metric thread symbol followed by the thread form and nominal size (basic major diameter) in millimeters and separated by the symbol × followed by the pitch, also in millimeters. For example, the basic thread note M10 × 1.5 is adequate for most commercial purposes, as shown in Figure 11.15. If needed, the class of fit and LH for left-hand designation is added to the note. (The absence of LH indicates a RH thread.)

If necessary, the length of the thread engagement is added to the thread note. The letter S stands for short, N means normal, and L means long. For example, the single note M10 × 1.5-6H/6g-N-LH combines the specifications for internal and external mating of left-hand metric threads of 10 mm diameter and 1.5 mm pitch with general-purpose tolerances and normal length of engagement.

If the thread is a multiple thread, the word STARTS, with the number of thread starts all contained in parentheses, should precede the thread form; otherwise, the thread is understood to be single. For example:

(2 STARTS) UNC

would indicate that this is double thread.

A thread note for a blind tapped hole is shown in Figure 11.15b. A tap drill is sized to form a hole that will leave enough material for thread to be cut using a tap in order to form a threaded hole. In practice the tap drill size and depth are omitted and left up to the shop. At times it is desirable to state a tolerance range for the size of the hole prior to threading. This can be stated as follows:

Ø.656–.658 BEFORE THD .75–20–NEF–2B

For tap drill sizes, see Appendix 15.

Thread notes for holes are preferably attached to the circular views of the holes. Thread notes for external threads are preferably given where the threaded shaft appears rectangular, as shown in Figures 11.15c–g. A sample special thread designation is 1.50-7N-LH.

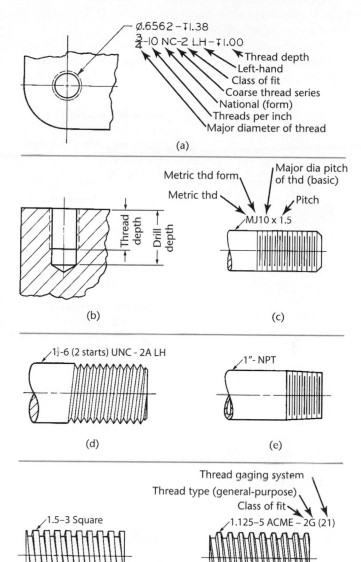

11.15 Thread Notes

General-purpose acme threads are indicated by the letter G, and centralizing acme threads by the letter C. Typical thread notes are 1-4 ACME-2G or 1-6 ACME-4C.

Thread notes for unified threads are shown in Figures 11.15d and e. The letters A and B designate external or internal, respectively, after the numeral designating the class of fit. If the letters LH are omitted, the thread is understood to be right hand. Some typical thread notes are:

-20 (3 STARTS) UNC-2A

-18 UNF-2B

1-16 UN-2A

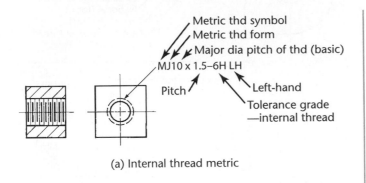

(a) Internal thread metric

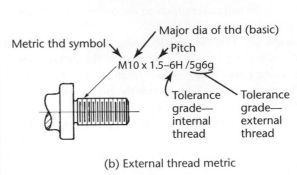

(b) External thread metric

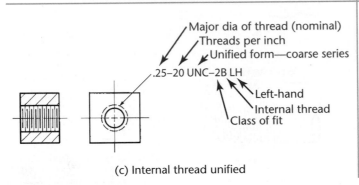

(c) Internal thread unified

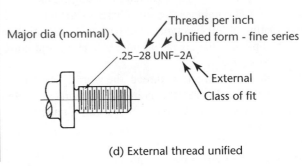

(d) External thread unified

11.16 Thread Notes

11.2 EXTERNAL THREAD SYMBOLS

Simplified representation for external threads are shown in Figures 11.17a and b. The threaded portions are indicated by hidden lines parallel to the axis at the approximate depth of the thread, whether the cylinder appears rectangular or circular. The depth shown is not always the actual thread depth, just a representation of it. Use the table in Figure 11.14 for the general appearance of these lines.

When the schematic form is shown in section, as in Figure 11.18a, show the V's of the thread to make the thread obvious. It is not necessary to show the V's to scale or to the actual slope of the crest lines. To draw the V's, use the schematic thread depth, as shown in Figure 11.15, and determine the pitch by drawing 60° V's.

Schematic threads are indicated by alternate long and short lines, as shown in Figure 11.18b. The short lines representing the root lines are thicker than the long crest lines. Theoretically, the crest lines should be spaced according to actual pitch, but this would make them crowded and tedious to draw, defeating the purpose, which is to save time in sketching them. Space the crest lines carefully by eye, then add the heavy root lines halfway between the crest lines. Generally, lines closer together than about 1/16" are hard to distinguish. The spacing should be proportionate for all diameters. You do not need to use these actual measurements in sketching schematic threads, just use them to get a feel for how far apart to make the lines.

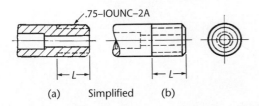

(a) Simplified (b)

11.17 External Thread Symbols for Simplified Thread

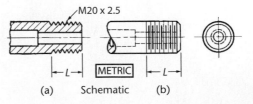

(a) Schematic (b)

11.18 External Thread Symbols for Schematic Thread

11.3 INTERNAL THREAD SYMBOLS

Internal thread symbols are shown in Figure 11.19. Note that the only differences between the schematic and simplified internal thread symbols occur in the sectional views. The representation of the schematic thread in section in Figures 11.19k, 11.19m, and 11.19n is exactly the same as the external representation shown in Figure 11.18b. Hidden threads, by either method, are represented by pairs of hidden lines. The hidden dashes should be staggered, as shown.

In the case of blind tapped holes, the drill depth normally is drawn at least three schematic pitches beyond the thread

length, as shown in Figures 11.19d, 11.19e, 11.19l, and 11.19m. The symbols in Figures 11.19f and 11.19n represent the use of a bottoming tap, when the length of thread is the same as the depth of drill. The thread length you sketch may be slightly longer than the actual given thread length. If the tap drill depth is known or given, draw the drill to that depth. If the thread note omits this information, as is often done in practice, sketch the hole three schematic thread pitches beyond the thread length. The tap drill diameter is represented approximately, not to actual size.

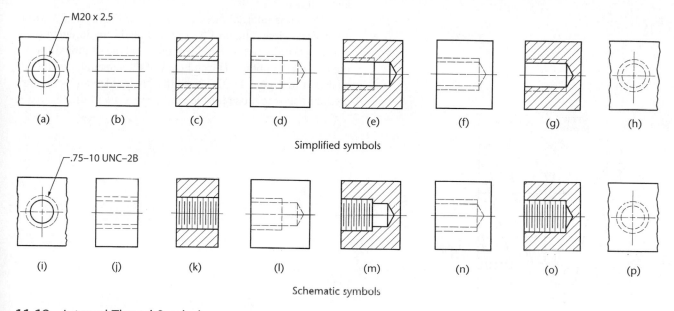

Simplified symbols

Schematic symbols

11.19 Internal Thread Symbols

11.4 DETAILED REPRESENTATION: METRIC, UNIFIED, AND AMERICAN NATIONAL THREADS

The detailed representation for metric, unified, and American national threads is the same, since the flats are disregarded.

Internal detailed threads in section are drawn as shown in Figure 11.20. Notice that for left hand threads the lines slope

upward to the left (Figure 11.20a to 11.20c), while for right hand threads the lines slope upward to the right (Figures 11.20d to 11.20f).

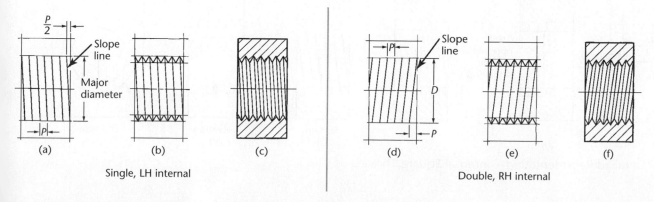

Single, LH internal

Double, RH internal

11.20 Detailed Representation—Internal Metric, Unified, and American

Detailed External Square Thread

Figure 11.21 is an assembly drawing showing an external square thread partly screwed into a nut. When the external and internal threads are assembled, the thread in the nut overlaps and covers up half of the V, as shown at B.

Sometimes in assemblies the root and crest lines may be omitted from the *nut only* portion of the drawing so that it is easier to identify the inserted screw.

Detailed Internal Square Thread

The internal thread construction is the same as in Figure 11.22. Note that the thread lines representing the back half of the internal threads (since the thread is in section) slope in the opposite direction from those on the front side of the screw.

Steps in drawing a single internal square thread in section are shown in Figure 11.22. Note in Figure 11.22b that a crest is drawn opposite a root. This is the case for both single and triple threads. For double or quadruple threads, a crest is opposite a crest. Thus, the construction in Figures 11.22a and b is the same for any multiple of thread. The differences appear in Figure 11.22c, where the threads and spaces are distinguished and outlined.

The same internal thread is shown in Figure 11.22e from an external view. The profiles of the threads are drawn in their normal position, but with hidden lines, and the sloping lines are omitted for simplicity. The end view of the same internal thread is shown in Figure 11.22f. Note that the hidden and solid circles are opposite those for the end view of the shaft.

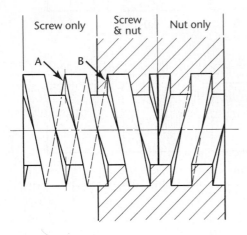

11.21 Square Threads in Assembly

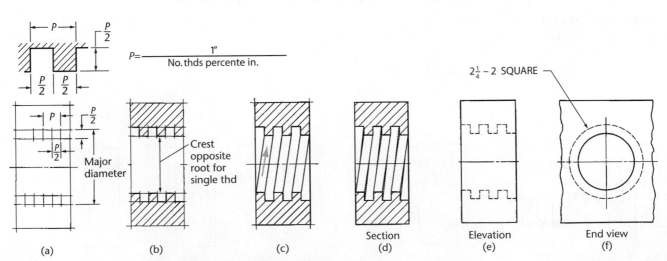

11.22 Detailed Representation—Internal Square Threads

DETAILED REPRESENTATION OF SQUARE THREADS

Detailed representation of external square threads is only used when the major diameter is over about 1" or 25 mm, and it is important to show the detail of the thread on the finished sketch or plotted drawing. The steps to create detailed square thread are as follows.

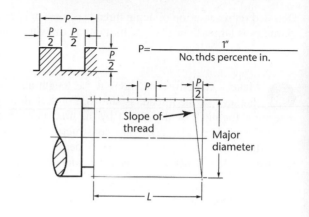

$$P = \frac{1''}{\text{No. thds percent in.}}$$

1 Make a centerline and lay out the length and major diameter of the thread. For U.S. drawings, determine the pitch (P) by dividing 1 by the number of threads per inch (see Appendix 22). For a single right-hand thread, the lines slope upward to the left, and the slope line is offset as for all single threads of any form. On the upper line, use spacing equal to $P/2$, as shown.

2 From the points on the upper line, draw guidelines for root of thread, making the depth as shown.

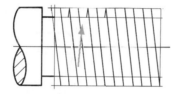

Single, R H external thread

3 Make parallel visible back edges of threads.

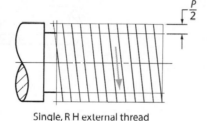

4 Make parallel visible root lines.

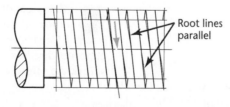

Root lines parallel

5 All lines should be thin and dark.

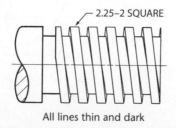

2.25–2 SQUARE

All lines thin and dark

TIP

End view of a shaft

The end view of the shaft illustrated in this Step by Step feature is shown below. Note that the root circle is hidden. When sketching, no attempt is made to show the true projection of any but the major diameter.

If the end of a shaft is chamfered, a solid circle would be drawn instead of the hidden circle.

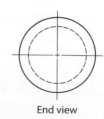

End view

STEP by STEP

DETAILED REPRESENTATION OF ACME THREAD

Detailed representation of acme threads is used only to call attention when details of the thread are important and the major diameter is larger than 1" or 25 mm on the drawing. The steps are as follows.

1 Make a centerline and lay out the length and major diameter of the thread, as shown. For U.S. drawings, determine the pitch by dividing 1 by the number of threads per inch (see Appendix 22). Make construction lines for the root diameter, making the thread depth $P/2$. Make construction lines halfway between crest and root guidelines.

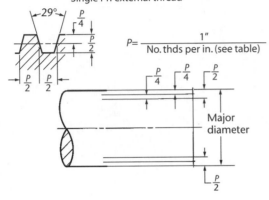

Single r h external thread

$$P = \frac{1''}{\text{No. thds per in. (see table)}}$$

2 Mark off spaces on the intermediate construction lines.

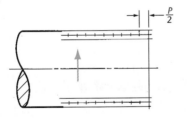

3 Through alternate points, make construction lines for the sides of the threads at 15° (instead of 14 1/2°).

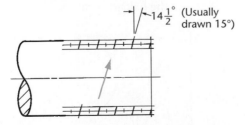

4 Make construction lines for the other sides of the threads, as shown. For single and triple threads, a crest is opposite a root, while for double and quadruple threads, a crest is opposite a crest. Finish tops and bottoms of threads.

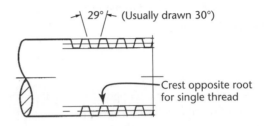

5 Make parallel crest lines.

6 Make parallel root lines, and finish the thread profiles. All lines should be thin and dark. The internal threads in the back of the nut will slope in the opposite direction to the external threads on the front side of the screw.

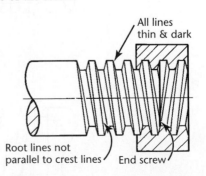

End views of acme threaded shafts and holes are drawn exactly like those for the square thread.

11.5 USE OF PHANTOM LINES

Use phantom lines to save time when representing identical features, as shown in Figure 11.23. Threaded shafts and springs may be shortened without using conventional breaks, but must be correctly dimensioned.

11.23   Use of Phantom Lines

11.6 THREADS IN ASSEMBLY

Threads in an assembly drawing are shown in Figure 11.24. It is customary not to section a stud or a nut or any solid part unless necessary to show some internal shapes. Show these items "in the round," as they would look if they were set in the hole after the assembly was cut to form the section. When external and internal threads are sectioned in assembly, the V's are required to show the threaded connection.

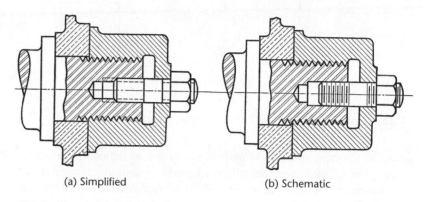

(a) Simplified   (b) Schematic

11.24   Threads in Assembly

11.7 AMERICAN NATIONAL STANDARD PIPE THREADS

The American National Standard for pipe threads, originally known as the Briggs standard, was formulated by Robert Briggs in 1882. Two general types of pipe threads have been approved as American National Standard: taper pipe threads and straight pipe threads.

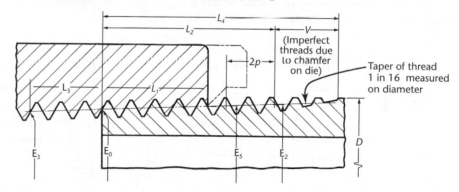

11.25   American National Standard Taper Pipe Thread, ANSI/ASME B1.20.1-1983 (R1992). *Courtesy of The American Society of Mechanical Engineers. All rights reserved.*

The profile of the tapered pipe thread is illustrated in Figure 11.25. The taper of the standard tapered pipe thread is 1 in 16, or .75" per foot measured on the diameter and along the axis. The angle between the sides of the thread is 60°. The depth of the sharp V is .8660p, and the basic maximum depth of the thread is .800p, where f = pitch. The basic pitch diameters, E_0 and E_1, and the basic length of the effective external taper thread, L_2 are determined by the formulas

$$E_0 = D - (.050D + 1.1)\frac{1}{n}$$
$$E_1 = E + .0625L_1$$
$$L_2 = (.80D + 6.8)\frac{1}{n}$$

where D = outer diameter of pipe, E_0 = pitch diameter of thread at end of pipe, E_1 = pitch diameters of thread at large end of internal thread, L_1 = normal engagement by hand, and n = number of threads per inch.

ANSI also recommends two modified tapered pipe threads for (1) dry seal pressure-tight joints (.880 per foot taper) and (2) rail fitting joints. The former is used for metal-to-metal joints, eliminating the need for a sealer, and is used in refrigeration, marine, automotive, aircraft, and ordnance work. The latter is used to provide a rigid mechanical thread joint as is required in rail fitting joints.

While tapered pipe threads are recommended for general use, there are certain types of joints in which straight pipe threads are used to advantage. The number of threads per inch, the angle, and the depth of thread are the same as on the tapered pipe thread, but the threads are cut parallel to the axis. Straight pipe threads are used for pressure-tight joints for pipe couplings, fuel and oil line fittings, drain plugs, free-fitting mechanical joints for fixtures, loose-fitting mechanical joints for locknuts, and loose-fitting mechanical joints for hose couplings.

Pipe threads are represented by detailed or symbolic methods in a manner

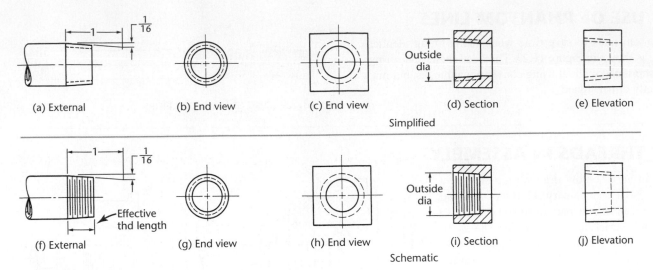

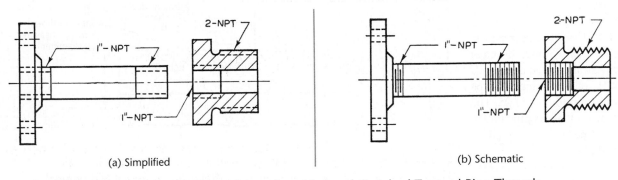

11.26 Conventional Pipe Thread Representation

similar to the representation of unified and American national threads. The symbolic representation (schematic or simplified) is recommended for general use regardless of the diameter, as shown in Figure 11.26. The detailed method is recommended only when the threads are large and when it is desired to show the profile of the thread, as for example, in a sectional view of an assembly.

As shown in Figure 11.26, it is not necessary to draw the taper on the threads unless there is some reason to emphasize it, since the thread note indicates whether the thread is straight or tapered. If it is desired to show the taper, it should be exaggerated, as shown in Figure 11.27, where the taper is drawn 1/16" per 1" on radius (or 6.75" per 1" on diameter) instead of the actual taper of 1/16" on diameter. American National Standard tapered pipe threads are indicated by a note giving the nominal diameter followed by the letters NPT (national pipe taper), as shown in Figure 11.27. When straight pipe threads are specified, the letters NPS (national pipe straight) are used. In practice, the tap drill size is normally not given in the thread note.

11.27 Conventional Representation of American National Standard Tapered Pipe Threads

11.8 BOLTS, STUDS, AND SCREWS

The term bolt is generally used to denote a "through bolt" that has a head on one end, is passed through clearance holes in two or more aligned parts, and is threaded on the other end to receive a nut to tighten and hold the parts together, as shown in Figure 11.28a. A hexagon head cap screw, shown in Figure 11.28b, is similar to a bolt except it often has greater threaded length. It is often used when one of the parts being held together is threaded to act as a nut. The cap screw is screwed on with a wrench. Cap screws are not screwed into thin materials if strength is desired.

A stud, shown in Figure 11.28c, is a steel rod threaded on one or both ends. If threaded on both ends, it is screwed into place with a pipe wrench or with a stud driver. If threaded on

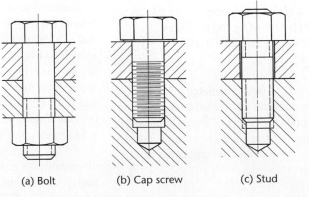

11.28 Bolt, Cap Screw, and Stud

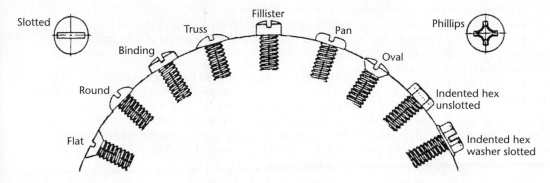

11.29 Types of Screw Heads

one end, it is force fitted into place. As a rule, a stud is passed through a clearance hole in one member, is screwed into another member, and uses a nut on the free end, as shown in Figure 11.28c.

A machine screw is similar to a slotted head cap screw but usually smaller. It may be used with or without a nut. Figure 11.29 shows different screw head types.

A set screw is a screw, with or without a head, that is screwed through one member and whose special point is forced against another member to prevent motion between the two parts.

Do not section bolts, nuts, screws, and similar parts when drawn in assembly because they do not have interior detail that needs to be shown.

11.9 TAPPED HOLES

The bottom of a drilled hole, formed by the point of a twist drill, is cone-shaped, as shown in Figures 11.30a and 11.30b. When an ordinary drill is used to make holes that will be tapped, it is referred to as a tap drill. When drawing the drill point, use an angle of 30° to approximate the actual 31° slope of the drill bit.

The thread length is the length of full or perfect threads. The tap drill depth does not include the cone point of the drill. In Figure 11.30c and 11.30d, the drill depth shown beyond the threads (labeled A) includes several imperfect threads produced by the chamfered end of the tap. This distance varies according to drill size and whether a plug tap or a bottoming tap is used to finish the hole.

A drawing of a tapped hole finished with a bottoming tap is shown in Figure 11.30e. Blind bottom-tapped holes are hard to form and should be avoided when possible. Instead, a relief with its diameter slightly greater than the major diameter of the thread is used, as shown in Figure 11.30f. Tap drill sizes for unified, American national, and metric threads are given in Appendix 15. Tap drill sizes and lengths may be given in the thread note, but are generally left to the manufacturer to determine. Since the tapped thread length contains only full threads, it is necessary to make this length only one or two pitches beyond the end of the engaging screw. In simplified or schematic representation, don't show threads in the bottoms of tapped holes. This way the ends of the screw show clearly.

The thread length in a tapped hole depends on the major diameter and the material being tapped. The minimum engagement length (X), when both parts are steel, is equal to the diameter (D) of the thread. Table 11.2 shows different engagement lengths for different materials.

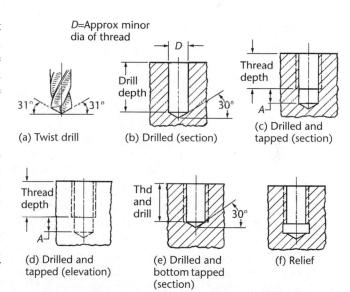

11.30 Drilled and Tapped Holes

Table 11.2 Thread Engagement Lengths for Different Materials.

Screw Material	Material of Parts	Thread Engagement*
Steel	Steel	D
Steel	Cast iron	$1\ 1/2D$
Steel	Aluminum	$2D$

*Requirements for thread engagement vary based on the specific materials. Use these rules of thumb only as guidelines.

TIP

Prevent tap breakage: A chief cause of tap breakage is insufficient tap drill depth. When the depth is too short, the tap is forced against a bed of chips in the bottom of the hole. Don't specify a blind hole when a through hole of not much greater length can be used. When a blind hole is necessary, the tap drill depth should be generous.

Clearance holes: When a bolt or a screw passes through a **clearance hole**, the hole is often drilled 0.8 mm larger than the screw for screws of 3/8" (10 mm) diameter and 1.5 mm larger for larger diameters. For more precise work, the

clearance hole may be only 1/64" (0.4 mm) larger than the screw for diameters up to 10 mm and 0.8 mm larger for larger diameters.

Closer fits may be specified for special conditions. The clearance spaces on each side of a screw or bolt need not be shown on a drawing unless it is necessary to show clearly that there is no thread engagement. When it is necessary to show that there is no thread engagement, the clearance spaces should be drawn about 3/64" (1.2 mm) wide.

11.10 STANDARD BOLTS AND NUTS

American National Standard hexagon bolts and nuts are made in both metric and inch sizes. Square bolts and nuts, shown in Figure 11.31, are only produced in inch sizes. Metric bolts, cap screws, and nuts also come in hexagon form. Square heads and nuts are chamfered at 30°, and hexagon heads and nuts are chamfered at 15–30°. Both are drawn at 30° for simplicity.

Bolt Types Bolts are grouped into **bolt types** according to use: regular bolts for general use and heavy bolts for heavier use or easier wrenching. Square bolts come only in the regular type; hexagon bolts, screws, nuts, and square nuts are available in both regular and heavy.

Metric hexagon bolts are grouped according to use: regular and heavy bolts and nuts for general service and high-strength bolts and nuts for structural bolting.

Finish Square bolts and nuts, hexagon bolts, and hexagon flat nuts are unfinished. Unfinished bolts and nuts are not machined on any surface except for the threads. Hexagon cap screws, heavy hexagon screws, and all hexagon nuts, except hexagon flat nuts, are considered finished to some degree and have a "washer face" machined or otherwise formed on the bearing surface. The washer face is 1/64" thick (drawn 1/32" so that it will be visible on the plotted drawing), and its diameter is 1.5 times the body diameter for the inch series.

For nuts, the bearing surface may also be a circular surface produced by chamfering. Hexagon screws and hexagon nuts have closer tolerances and a more finished appearance but are not completely machined. There is no difference in the drawing for the degree of finish on finished screws and nuts.

Proportions Proportions for both inch and metric are based on the diameter (*D*) of the bolt body. These are shown in Figure 11.32.

For regular hexagon and square bolts and nuts, proportions are:

$$W = 1\tfrac{1}{2}D \qquad H = \tfrac{2}{3}D \qquad T = \tfrac{7}{8}D$$

where *W* = width across flats, *H* = head height, and *T* = nut height.

For heavy hexagon bolts and nuts and square nuts, the proportions are:

$$W = 1\tfrac{1}{2}D + \tfrac{1}{8}\text{" (or + 3 mm)}$$
$$H = \tfrac{2}{3}D \qquad T = D$$

© Dorling Kindersley.

The washer face is always included in the head or nut height for finished hexagon screw heads and nuts.

Threads Square and hex bolts, hex cap screws, and finished nuts in the inch series are usually Class 2 and may have coarse, fine, or 8-pitch threads. Unfinished nuts have coarse threads and are Class 2B. For diameter and pitch specifications for metric threads, see Appendix 20.

Thread lengths For bolts or screws up to 6" (150 mm) long.

$$\text{Thread length} = 2D + \tfrac{1}{4}\text{" (or + 6 mm)}$$

For bolts or screws over in length,

$$\text{Thread length} = 2D + \tfrac{1}{2}\text{" (or + 12 mm)}$$

Fasteners too short for these formulas are threaded as close to the head as practical. For drawing purposes, use approximately three pitches. The threaded end may be rounded or chamfered, but it is usually drawn with a 45° chamfer from the thread depth, as shown in Figure 11.32.

Bolt Lengths Have not been standardized because of the endless variety required by industry. Short bolts are typically available in standard length increments of 1/4" (6 mm), while long bolts come in increments of 1/2" to 1 inch (12 to 25 mm). For dimensions of standard bolts and nuts, see Appendix 20.

11.31   Standard Bolt and Nut.

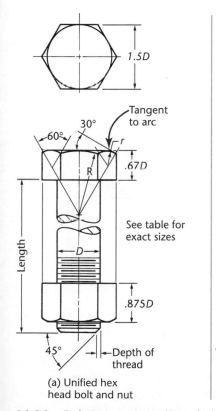

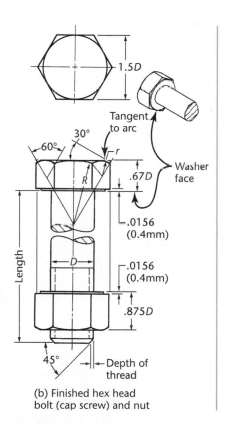

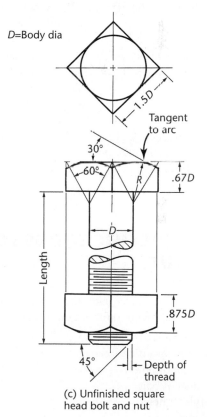

11.32   Bolt Proportions (Regular)

11.11 DRAWING STANDARD BOLTS

Detail drawings show all of the necessary information defining the shape, size, material, and finish of a part. Standard bolts and nuts do not usually require detail drawings unless they are to be altered (for example, by having a slot added through the end of a bolt), because they are usually stock parts that can easily be purchased. But you often need to show them on assembly drawings, which you will learn more about in Chapter 12.

Templates are available to help you add bolts quickly to sketches, or you can use the dimensions from Appendix 18 if accuracy is important, as in figuring clearances. In most cases, a quick representation, where proportions are based on the body diameter, is sufficient. Three typical bolts illustrating the use of these proportions are shown in Figure 11.32.

Many CAD systems have fastener libraries that you can use to add a wide variety of nuts and bolts to your drawings. Often these symbols are based on a diameter of 1 unit so that you can quickly figure a scale at which to insert them. Other systems prompt for the diameter and lengths and create a symbol to your specifications. In 3D models, when nuts and bolts are represented, the thread is rarely shown because it adds to the complexity and size of the drawing and is difficult to model. The thread specification is annotated in the drawing.

Generally, bolt heads and nuts should be drawn "across corners" in all views, regardless of projection. This conventional violation of projection is used to prevent confusion between the square and hexagon heads and nuts and to show actual clearances. Only when there is a special reason should bolt heads and nuts be drawn across flats, as shown in Figure 11.33.

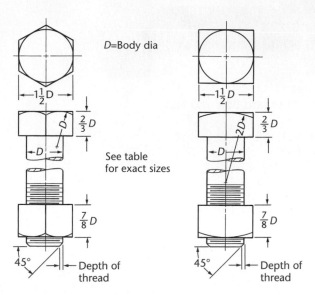

11.33 Bolts "Across Flats"

11.12 SPECIFICATIONS FOR BOLTS AND NUTS

In specifying bolts in parts lists, in correspondence, or elsewhere, the following information must be covered in order:

1. Nominal size of bolt body
2. Thread specification or thread note
3. Length of bolt
4. Finish of bolt
5. Style of head
6. Name

Example (complete decimal inch)
.75-10 UNC- HEXAGON CAP SCREW

Example (abbreviated decimal inch)
HEXCAP SCR

Example (metric)
HEXCAP SCR

Nuts may be specified as follows:

Example (complete)
$\frac{5}{8}$–11 UNC–2B SQUARE NUT

Example (abbreviated)
$\frac{5}{8}$ SQ NUT

Example (metric)
HEX NUT

For either bolts or nuts, REGULAR or GENERAL PURPOSE are assumed if omitted from the specification. If the heavy series is intended, the word HEAVY should appear as the first word in the name of the fastener. Likewise, HIGH STRENGTH STRUCTURAL should be indicated for such metric fasteners. However, the number of the specific ISO standard is often included in the metric specifications—for example, HEXAGON NUT ISO. Finish need not be mentioned if the fastener or nut is correctly named.

SKETCHING HEXAGONAL BOLTS, CAP SCREWS, AND NUTS

1 Determine the diameter of the bolt, the length (from the underside of the bearing surface to the tip), the style of head (square or hexagon), the type (regular or heavy), and the finish before starting to draw.

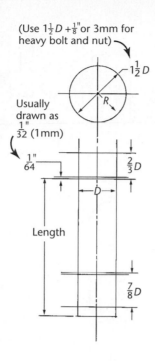

(Use $1\frac{1}{2}D + \frac{1}{8}$" or 3mm for heavy bolt and nut)

$1\frac{1}{2}D$

R

Usually drawn as $\frac{1}{32}$" (1mm)

$\frac{1}{64}$"

$\frac{2}{3}D$

D

Length

$\frac{7}{8}D$

2 Lightly sketch the top view as shown, where D is the diameter of the bolt. Project the corners of the hexagon or square to the front view. Sketch the head and nut heights. Add the 1/64" (0.4 mm) washer face if needed. Its diameter is equal to the distance across flats of the bolt head or nut. Only the metric and finished hexagon screws or nuts have a washer face. The washer face is 1/64" thick, but is shown at about 1/32" (1 mm) for clarity. The head or nut height includes the washer face.

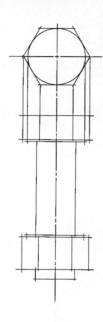

STEP by STEP

3 Represent the curves produced by the chamfer on the bolt heads and nuts as circular arcs, although they are actually hyperbolas. On drawings of small bolts or nuts under approximately 1/2" (12 mm) in diameter, where the chamfer is hardly noticeable, omit the chamfer in the rectangular view.

4 Chamfer the threaded end of the screw at 45° from the schematic thread depth.

5 Show threads in simplified or schematic form for diameters of 1" (25 mm) or less on the drawing. Detailed representation is rarely used because it clutters the drawing and takes too much time.

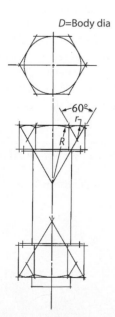

D=Body dia

60°

r

R

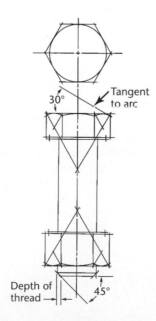

30°

Tangent to arc

Depth of thread

45°

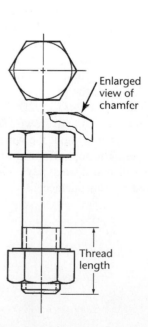

Enlarged view of chamfer

Thread length

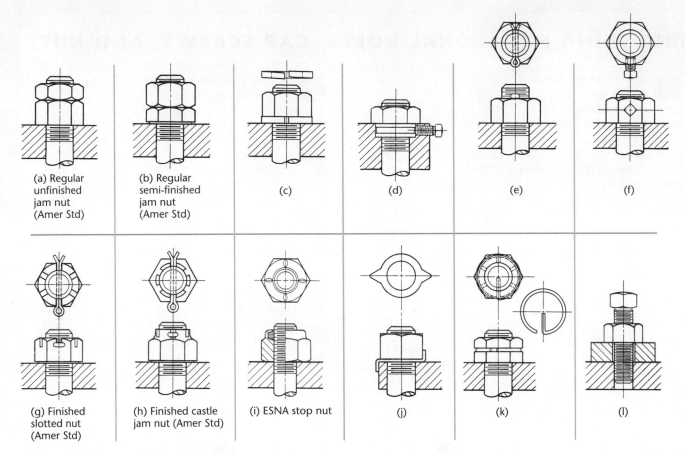

(a) Regular unfinished jam nut (Amer Std)

(b) Regular semi-finished jam nut (Amer Std)

(c)

(d)

(e)

(f)

(g) Finished slotted nut (Amer Std)

(h) Finished castle jam nut (Amer Std)

(i) ESNA stop nut

(j)

(k)

(l)

11.34 Locknuts and Locking Devices

11.13 LOCKNUTS AND LOCKING DEVICES

Many types of special nuts and devices to prevent nuts from unscrewing are available, and some of the most common are shown in Figure 11.34. The American National Standard jam nuts, as shown in Figures 11.34a and 11.34b, are the same as the hexagon or hexagon flat nuts, except that they are thinner. The application shown in Figure 11.34b, where the larger nut is on top and is screwed on more tightly, is recommended. They are the same distance across flats as the corresponding hexagon nuts (1 1/2D or 1"). They are slightly over 1/2D in thickness but are drawn 1/2D for simplicity. They are available with or without the washer face in the regular and heavy types. The tops of all are flat and chamfered at 30°, and the finished forms have either a washer face or a chamfered bearing surface.

The lock washer, shown in Figure 11.34c, and the cotter pin, shown in Figure 11.34e, are very common (see Appendixes 27 and 30). The set screw, shown in Figure 11.34f, is often made to press against a plug of softer material, such as brass, which in turn presses against the threads without deforming them. For use with cotter pins (see Appendix 30), it is recommended to use a hex slotted nut (Figure 11.34g), a hex castle nut (Figure 11.34h), or a hex thick slotted nut or a heavy hex thick slotted nut.

Similar metric locknuts and locking devices are available. See fastener catalogs for details.

Reid Tool is one company that has a free download of its catalog available as CAD files at
* http://www.reidtool.com/download.htm.

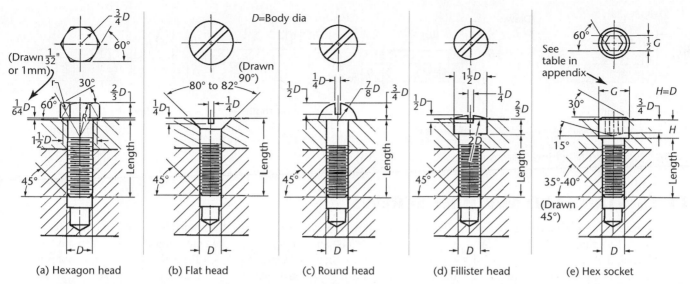

(a) Hexagon head   (b) Flat head   (c) Round head   (d) Fillister head   (e) Hex socket

Hexagon Head Screws Coarse, fine, or 8-thread series, 2A. Thread length = $2D + \frac{1}{4}$" up to 6" long and $2D + \frac{1}{2}$" if over 6" long. For screws too short for formula, threads extend to within $2\frac{1}{2}$ threads of the head for diameters up to 1". Screw lengths not standardized. For suggested lengths for metric hexagon head screws, see Appendix 15.

Slotted Head Screws Coarse, fine, or 8-thread series, 2A. Thread length = $2D + \frac{1}{4}$". Screw lengths not standardized. For screws too short for formula, threads extend to within $2\frac{1}{2}$ threads of the head.

Hexagon Socket Screws coarse or fine threads, 3A. Coarse thread length = $2D + \frac{1}{2}$" where this would be over $\frac{1}{2}L$; otherwise thread length = $\frac{1}{2}L$. Fine thread length = $1\frac{1}{2}D + \frac{1}{2}$" where this would be over $\frac{3}{8}L$; otherwise thread length = $\frac{3}{8}L$. Increments in screw lengths = $\frac{1}{8}$" for screws $\frac{1}{4}$" to 1" long, $\frac{1}{4}$" for screws 1" to 3" long, and $\frac{1}{2}$" for screws $3\frac{1}{2}$" to 6" long.

11.35 Standard Cap Screws—See Appendices 20 and 21

11.14 STANDARD CAP SCREWS

Five types of American National Standard cap screws are shown in Figure 11.35. The first four of these have standard heads, while the socket head cap screws, as shown in Figure 11.35e, have several different shapes of round heads and sockets. Cap screws are normally finished and are used on machine tools and other machines when accuracy and appearance are important. The ranges of sizes and exact dimensions are given in Appendixes 18 and 19. The hexagon head cap screw and hex socket head cap screw are also available in metric.

Cap screws ordinarily pass through a clearance hole in one member and screw into another. The clearance hole need not be shown on the drawing when the presence of the unthreaded clearance hole is obvious.

Cap screws are inferior to studs when frequent removal is necessary. They are used on machines requiring few adjustments. The slotted or socket-type heads are used for crowded conditions.

Actual dimensions may be used in drawing cap screws when exact sizes are necessary. Figure 11.35 shows the proportions in terms of body diameter (*D*) that are usually used. Hexagonal head cap screws are drawn similar to hex head bolts. The points are chamfered at 45° from the schematic thread depth.

Note that screwdriver slots are drawn at 45° in the circular views of the heads, without regard to true projection, and that threads in the bottom of the tapped holes are omitted so that the ends of the screws may be clearly seen. A typical cap screw note is:

Example (complete)

   .375-16 UNC-2A × 2.5 HEXAGON HEAD CAP SCREW

Example (abbreviated)

      .375 × 2.5 HEXHD CAP SCR

Example (metric)

      M20 × 2.5 × 80 HEXHD CAP SCR

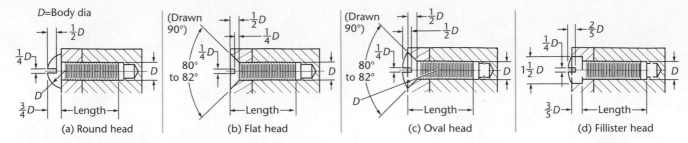

(a) Round head   (b) Flat head   (c) Oval head   (d) Fillister head

11.36 Standard Machine Screws—See Appendix {{20}}

11.15 STANDARD MACHINE SCREWS

Machine screws are similar to cap screws but are usually smaller (.060" to .750" diameter) and the threads generally go all the way to the head. There are eight ANSI-approved forms of heads, which are shown in Appendix 20. The hexagonal head may be slotted if desired. All others are available in either slotted or recessed-head forms. Standard machine screws are produced with a naturally bright finish, not heat treated, and have plain-sheared ends, not chamfered. For similar metric machine screw forms and specifications, see Appendix 20.

Machine screws are used for screwing into thin materials, and the smaller-numbered screws are threaded nearly to the head. They are used extensively in firearms, jigs, fixtures, and dies. Machine screw nuts are used mainly on the round head, pan head, and flat head types and are usually hexagonal.

Exact dimensions of machine screws are given in Appendix 20, but they are seldom needed for drawing purposes. The four most common types of machine screws are shown in Figure 11.36, with proportions based on the diameter (D).

Clearance holes and counterbores should be made slightly larger than the screws.

Typical machine screw notes are:
Example (complete)
NO. 10 (.1900) -32 NF-3 $\times \frac{5}{8}$
FILLISTER HEAD MACHINE SCREW
Example (abbreviated)
NO. 10 (.1900) $\times \frac{5}{8}$ FILH MSCR
Example (metric)
M8 $\times$ 1.25 $\times$ 30 SLOTTED PAN HEAD MACHINE SCREW

11.16 STANDARD SET SCREWS

Set screws, shown in Figure 11.37, are used to prevent motion, usually rotary, between two parts, such as the movement of the hub of a pulley on a shaft. A set screw is screwed into one part so that its point bears firmly against another part. If the point of the set screw is cupped, or if a flat is milled on the shaft, the screw will hold much more firmly. Obviously, set screws are not efficient when the load is heavy or when it is suddenly applied. Usually they are manufactured of steel and case hardened.

Headless set screws have come into greater use because the projecting head of headed set screws has caused many industrial casualties; this has resulted in legislation prohibiting their use in many states.

Metric hexagon socket headless set screws with the full range of points are available. Nominal diameters of metric hex socket set screws are 1.6, 2, 2.5, 3, 4, 5, 6, 8, 10, 12, 16, 20, and 24 mm.

Square head set screws have coarse, fine, or 8-pitch threads and are Class 2A, but are usually furnished with coarse threads since the square head set screw is generally used on the rougher grades of work. Slotted headless and socket set screws have coarse or fine threads and are Class 3A.

Nominal diameters of set screws range from number 0 up through 2"

set-screw lengths are standardized in increments of 1/32" to 1" depending on the overall length of the set screw.

Metric set screw length increments range from 0.5 to 4 mm, again depending on overall screw length.

Set screws are specified as follows:
Example (complete)
.375- 16UNC-2A $\times$ .75 SQUARE HEAD FLAT POINT SET SCREW
Example (abbreviated)
.375- $\times$ 1.25 SQH FP SSCR
.438 $\times$ .750 HEXSOC CUP PT SSCR
$\frac{1}{4}$ -20 UNC 2A $\times \frac{1}{2}$ SLTD HDLS CONE PT SSCR
Example (metric)
M10 $\times$ 1.5 12 HEX SOCKET HEAD SET SCREW

11.37 Set Screws. *Courtesy of Penninsula Components Inc.*

11.17 AMERICAN NATIONAL STANDARD WOOD SCREWS

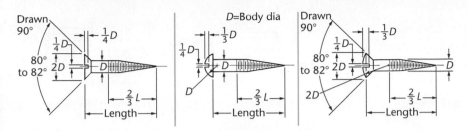

11.38 American National Standard Wood Screws

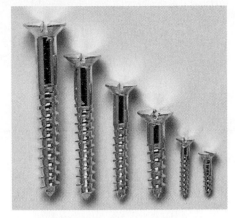

Courtesy of Michael Newman/ PhotoEdit Inc.

Wood screws with three types of heads—flat, round, and oval—have been standardized. The approximate dimensions sufficient for drawing purposes are shown in Figure 11.38.

The Phillips style recessed head is also available on several types of fasteners, as well as on wood screws. Three styles of cross recesses have been standardized by ANSI. A special screwdriver is used, as shown in Figure 11.39q, and this results in rapid assembly without damage to the head.

11.18 MISCELLANEOUS FASTENERS

Many other types of fasteners have been devised for specialized uses. Some of the more common types are shown in Figure 11.39. A number of these are American National Standard round head bolts, including carriage, button head, step, and countersunk bolts.

Helical-coil-threaded inserts, as shown in Figure 11.39p, are shaped like a spring except that the cross section of the wire conforms to threads on the screw and in the hole. These are made of phosphor bronze or stainless steel, and they provide a hard, smooth protective lining for tapped threads in soft metals and plastics.

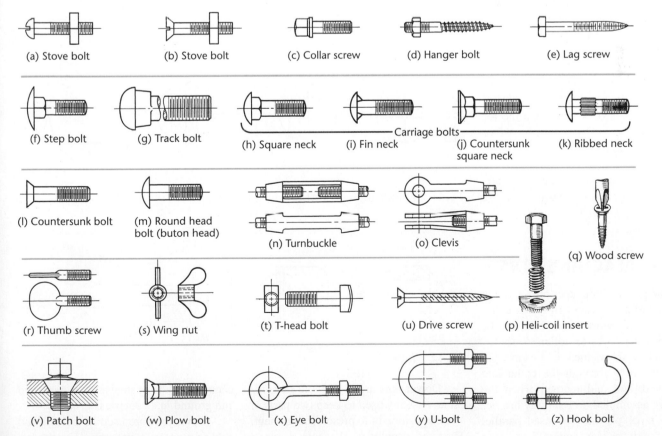

11.39 Miscellaneous Bolts and Screws

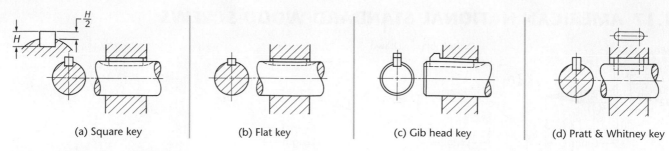

(a) Square key (b) Flat key (c) Gib head key (d) Pratt & Whitney key

11.40 Square and Flat Keys

11.19 KEYS

Keys are used to prevent movement between shafts and wheels, couplings, cranks, and similar machine parts attached to or supported by shafts, as shown in Figure 11.40. A keyseat is in a shaft; a keyway is in the hub or surrounding part.

For heavy-duty functions, rectangular keys (flat or square) are used, and sometimes two rectangular keys are necessary for one connection. For even stronger connections, interlocking splines may be machined on the shaft and in the hole.

A *square key* is shown in Figure 11.40a.

A *flat key* is shown in Figure 11.40b. The widths of keys are generally about one fourth the shaft diameter. In either case, one half the key is sunk into the shaft. The depth of the keyway or the keyseat is measured on the side—not the center—as shown in Figure 11.40a. Square and flat keys may have the top surface tapered 1/8" per foot, in which case they become square taper or flat taper keys.

A *feather key* is rectangular to prevent rotary motion, but permits relative longitudinal motion. Usually feather keys have gib heads, or are fastened so they cannot slip out of the keyway.

A *gib head key* (Figure 11.40c) is the same as a square taper or flat taper key except that a gib head allows its easy removal. Square and flat keys are made from cold-finished stock and are not machined. For dimensions, see Appendix 21.

A *Pratt & Whitney key* (P&W key) is shown in Figure 11.40d. It is rectangular, with semicylindrical ends. Two-thirds of its height is sunk into the shaft keyseat (see Appendix 25).

Woodruff keys are semicircular, as shown in Figure 11.41. This key fits into a semicircular key slot cut with a Woodruff cutter, as shown, and the top of the key fits into a plain rectangular keyway. Sizes of keys for given shaft diameters are not standardized. For average conditions, select a key whose diameter is approximately equal to the shaft diameter. For dimensions, see Appendix 23. See manufacturers' catalogs for specifications for metric counterparts.

Typical specifications for keys are:
.25 × 1.50 SQ KEY
No. 204 WOODRUFF KEY
1/4 × 1/6 × 1-FLAT KEY
No. 10 P&W KEY

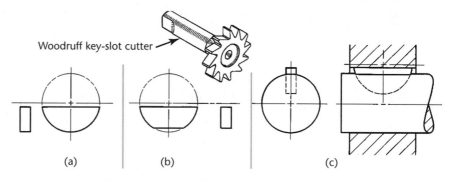

Woodruff key-slot cutter

(a) (b) (c)

11.41 Woodruff Keys and Key-Slot Cutter

11.20 MACHINE PINS

Machine pins include taper pins, straight pins, dowel pins, clevis pins, and cotter pins. For light work, taper pins can be used to fasten hubs or collars to shafts. Figure 11.42 shows the use of a taper pin where the hole through the collar and shaft is drilled and reamed when the parts are assembled. For slightly heavier duty, a taper pin may be used parallel to the shaft as for square keys (see Appendix 29).

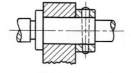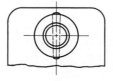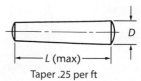

L (max)
Taper .25 per ft

11.42 Taper Pin

Dowel pins are cylindrical or conical and usually used to keep two parts in a fixed position or to preserve alignment. They are usually used where accurate alignment is essential. Dowel pins are generally made of steel and are hardened and ground in a centerless grinder.

Clevis pins are used in a clevis and held in place by cotter pins. For the latter, see Appendix 30.

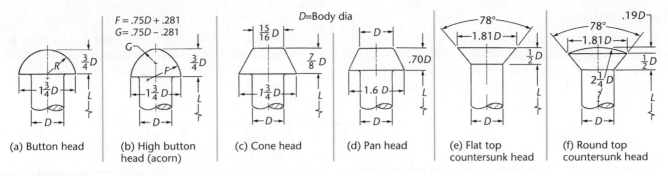

| (a) Button head | (b) High button head (acorn) | (c) Cone head | (d) Pan head | (e) Flat top countersunk head | (f) Round top countersunk head |

11.43 Standard Large Rivets

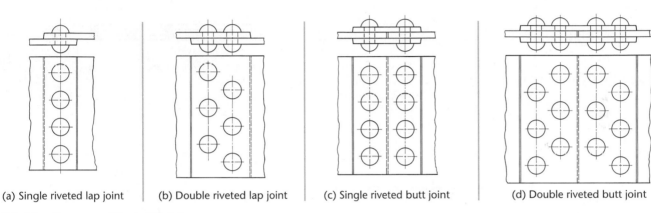

| (a) Single riveted lap joint | (b) Double riveted lap joint | (c) Single riveted butt joint | (d) Double riveted butt joint |

11.44 Common Riveted Joints

11.21 RIVETS

Rivets are regarded as permanent fastenings, unlike removable fastenings, such as bolts and screws. Rivets are generally used to hold sheet metal or rolled steel together and are made of wrought iron, carbon steel, copper, or occasionally other metals.

To fasten two pieces of metal together, holes are punched, drilled, or punched and then reamed, all slightly larger in diameter than the shank of the rivet. Rivet diameters are made from $d = 1.2 \sqrt{t}$ to $d = 1.4\sqrt{t}$, where d is the rivet diameter and t is the metal thickness. The larger rivet diameter size is used for steel and single-riveted joints, and the smaller

may be used for multiple-riveted joints. In structural work it is common to make the hole 1.6 mm (1/16") larger than the rivet.

When the red-hot rivet is inserted, a "dolly bar" with a depression the shape of the driven head is held against the head. A riveting machine is used to drive the rivet and forms the head on the plain end. This causes the rivet to swell and fill the hole tightly.

Large rivets or heavy hex structural bolts are often used in structural work of bridges and buildings and in ship and boiler construction. They are shown in their exact formula proportions in Figure 11.43.

Button heads (Figure 11.43a), and countersunk heads (Figure 11.43e), are the rivets most commonly used in structural work. The button head and cone head are commonly used in tank and boiler construction.

Riveted Joints

Typical riveted joints are shown in Figure 11.44. Note that the rectangular view of each rivet shows the shank of the rivet with both heads made with circular arcs, and the circular view of each rivet is represented by only the outside circle of the head.

Rivet Symbols

Since many engineering structures are too large to be built in the shop, they are built in the largest units possible and then are transported to the desired location. Trusses are common examples of this.

The rivets driven in the shop are called shop rivets, and those driven on the job are called field rivets. However, heavy steel bolts are commonly used on the job for structural work. Solid black circles

are used to represent field rivets, and other standard symbols are used to show other features, as shown in Figure 11.45.

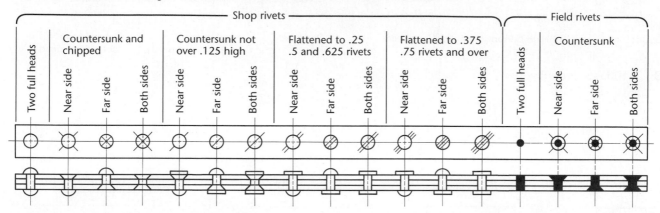

11.45 Conventional Rivet Symbols

Small Rivets

Small rivets are used for light work. American National Standard small solid rivets are illustrated with dimensions that show their standard proportions in Figure 11.46, ANSI/ASME B18.1.1–1972 (R1995). Included in the same standard are tinners', coppers', and belt rivets. Metric rivets are also available. Dimensions for large rivets are in ANSI/ASME B18.1.2-1972 (R1995). See manufacturers' catalogs for additional details.

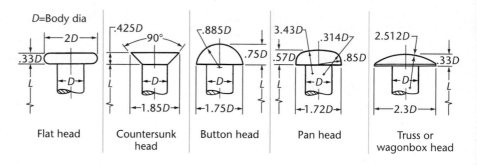

11.46 American National Standard Small Solid Rivet Proportions

Blind Rivets

Blind rivets, commonly known as pop rivets (Figure 11.47), are often used for fastening together thin sheet-metal assemblies. Blind rivets are hollow and are installed with manual or power-operated rivet guns which grip a center pin or mandrel, pulling the head into the body and expanding the rivet against the sheet metal. They are available in aluminum, steel, stainless steel, and plastic. As with any fastener, the designer should be careful to choose an appropriate material to avoid corrosive action between dissimilar metals.

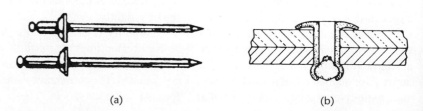

11.47 Blind Rivets (a) Before Installation, and (b) Installed

11.22 SPRINGS

A spring is a mechanical device designed to store energy when deflected and to return the equivalent amount of energy when released, ANSI Y14.13M-1981 (R1992). Springs are commonly made of spring steel, which may be music wire, hard-drawn wire, or oil-tempered wire. Other materials used for compression springs include stainless steel, beryllium copper, and phosphor bronze. Urethane plastic is used in applications where conventional springs would be affected by corrosion, vibration, or acoustic or magnetic forces.

Springs are classified as *helical springs* (Figure 11.48), or *flat springs.*

Springs. *Reprinted by permission of Pearson Education, Inc., Upper Saddle River, NJ.*

Helical Springs

Helical springs are usually cylindrical but may also be conical. There are three types of helical springs.

- **Compression springs** offer resistance to a compressive force.
- **Extension springs** offer resistance to a pulling force.
- **Torsion springs** offer resistance to a torque or twisting force.

On working drawings, true projections of helical springs are not drawn because of the labor involved. Like screw threads, they are drawn in detailed and schematic methods, using straight lines to replace helical curves, as shown in Figure 11.48.

A square wire spring is similar to the square thread with the core of the shaft removed, as in Figure 11.48b. Use standard cross-hatching if the areas in section are large, as in Figure 11.48a and b. Small sectioned areas may be made solid black, as in Figure 11.48c.

In cases where a complete picture of the spring is not necessary, use phantom lines to save time in drawing the coils, as in Figure 11.48d. If the drawing of the spring is too small to be represented by the outlines of the wire, use schematic representation, shown in Figure 11.48e and f.

Compression springs have plain ends, as in Figure 11.49a, or squared (closed) ends, as in Figure 11.49b. The ends may be ground, as shown in Figure 11.49c, or both squared and ground, as in Figure 11.49d. Required dimensions are indicated in the figure. When required, RH or LH is specified for right-hand or left-hand coil direction.

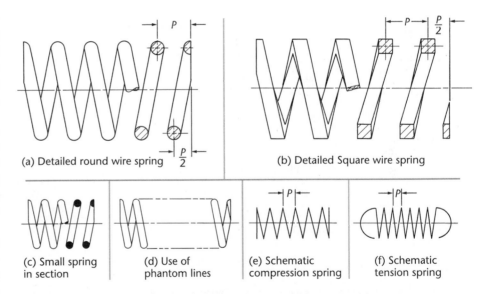

(a) Detailed round wire spring

(b) Detailed Square wire spring

(c) Small spring in section

(d) Use of phantom lines

(e) Schematic compression spring

(f) Schematic tension spring

11.48   Helical Springs

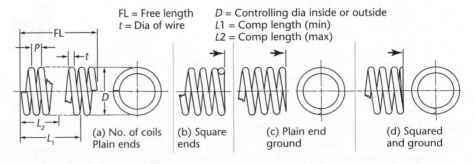

FL = Free length   D = Controlling dia inside or outside
t = Dia of wire   L1 = Comp length (min)
                       L2 = Comp length (max)

(a) No. of coils Plain ends

(b) Square ends

(c) Plain end ground

(d) Squared and ground

11.49   Compression Springs

Extension springs may have many types of ends, so it is necessary to draw the spring or at least the ends and a few adjacent coils, as shown in Figure 11.50.

A typical torsion spring drawing is shown in Figure 11.51. A typical flat spring drawing is shown in Figure 11.52. Other types of flat springs are power springs (or flat coil springs), Belleville springs (like spring washers), and leaf springs (commonly used in automobiles).

Many companies use a printed specification form to provide the necessary spring information, including data such as load at a specified deflected length, load rate, finish, and type of service.

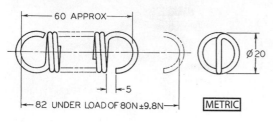

MATERIAL: 2.00 OIL TEMPERED SPRING STEEL WIRE
14.5 COILS RIGHT HAND
MACHINE LOOP AND HOOK IN LINE
SPRING MUST EXTEND TO 110 WITHOUT SET
FINISH: BLACK JAPAN

11.50 Extension Spring Drawing

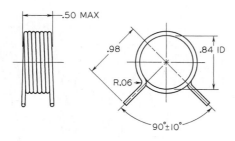

MATERIAL : .059 MUSIC WIRE
6.75 COILS RIGHT HAND NO INITIAL TENSION
TORQUE : 2.50 INCH LB AT 155° DEFLECTION SPRING MUST
DEFLECT 180° WITHOUT PERMANENT SET AND
MUST OPERATE FREELY ON .75 DIAMETER SHAFT
FINISH : CADMIUM OR ZINC PLATE

11.51 Torsion Spring Drawing

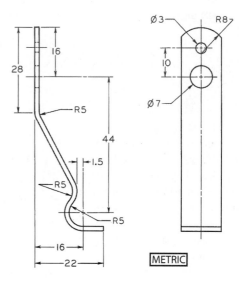

MATERIAL : 1.20 X 14.0 SPRING STEEL
HEAT TREAT : 44-48 C ROCKWELL
FINISH : BLACK OXIDE AND OIL

11.52 Flat Spring

11.23 DRAWING HELICAL SPRINGS

The construction for a schematic elevation view of a compression spring with six total coils is shown in Figure 11.53a. Since the ends are closed, or squared, two of the six coils are "dead" coils, leaving only four full pitches to be set off along the top of the spring.

If there are six total coils, as shown in Figure 11.53, the spacings will be on opposite sides of the spring. The construction of an extension spring with six active coils and loop ends is shown in Figure 11.53c.

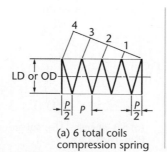

(a) 6 total coils compression spring

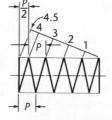

(b) 6.5 total coils compression spring

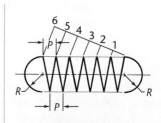

(c) 6.5 total coils extension spring

11.53 Schematic Spring Representation.

Figure 11.54 shows the steps in drawing a detailed section and elevation view of a compression spring. The spring is shown pictorially in Figure 11.54a. Figure 11.54b shows the cutting plane through the centerline of the spring.

Figure 11.54c shows the section with the cutting plane removed. Steps to construct the sectional view are shown in Figures 11.54d–f. Figure 11.54g shows the corresponding elevation view.

If there is a fractional number of coils, such as the five coils in Figure 11.54h, the half-rounds of sectional wire are placed on opposite sides of the spring.

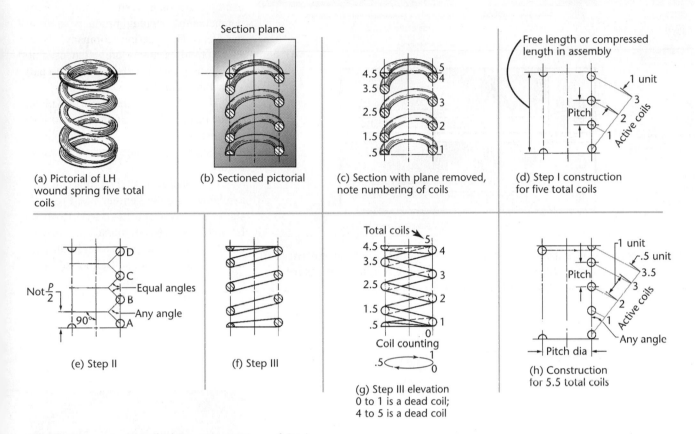

(a) Pictorial of LH wound spring five total coils

(b) Sectioned pictorial

(c) Section with plane removed, note numbering of coils

(d) Step I construction for five total coils

(e) Step II

(f) Step III

(g) Step III elevation
0 to 1 is a dead coil;
4 to 5 is a dead coil

(h) Construction for 5.5 total coils

11.54   Steps in Detailed Representation of Spring

11.24 COMPUTER GRAPHICS

Standard representations of threaded fasteners and springs, in both detailed and schematic forms, are available in CAD symbol libraries. Use of computer graphics frees the drafter from the need to draw time-consuming repetitive features by hand and also makes it easy to modify drawings if required.

In 3D modeling, thread is not usually represented because it can be difficult to create and computer intensive to view and edit. Instead, the nominal diameter of a threaded shaft or hole is usually created along with notation calling out the thread. Sometimes the depth of the thread is shown in the 3D drawing to call attention to the thread and to help in determining fits and clearances.

DOWNLOADING STANDARD FASTENERS

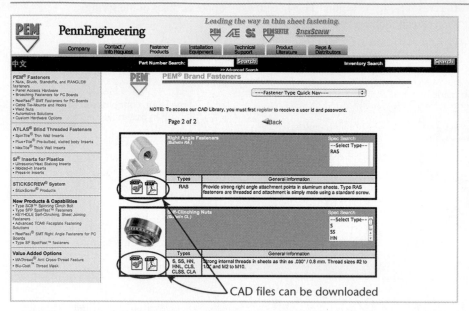

CAD files can be downloaded

(a) PEM brand fasteners, available from Penn Engineering are an example of the many stock fasteners that you can download in CAD file formats for easy insertion into drawings. *Courtesy of PennEngineering.*

Many stock fasteners in standard CAD formats are available to download, ready to use in CAD drawings and models. One example of such a site is http://www.pemnet.com/fastening_products, from the Penn Engineering company. Their PEM brand fasteners are often used to fasten sheet metal parts, such as the part shown in Figure B.

The CAD files that you download can be inserted into your drawings to save drawing time. The stock fastener type is specified in a drawing note as shown in Figure B.

Data sheets in PDF format are also available from the Pemnet site. Figure C shows the cover of a 12-page PDF booklet that lists material, thread size, performance data, and other key data for unified and metric self-clinching nuts that the company carries.

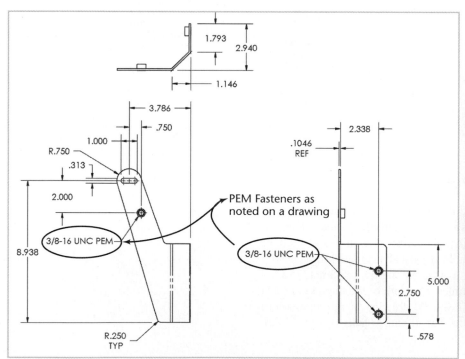

(b) PEM stock fasteners shown on a drawing. *Courtesy of Dynojet Research, Inc.*

(c) Data sheets are often available in PDF format, as in this example from PEM. *Courtesy of PennEngineering.*

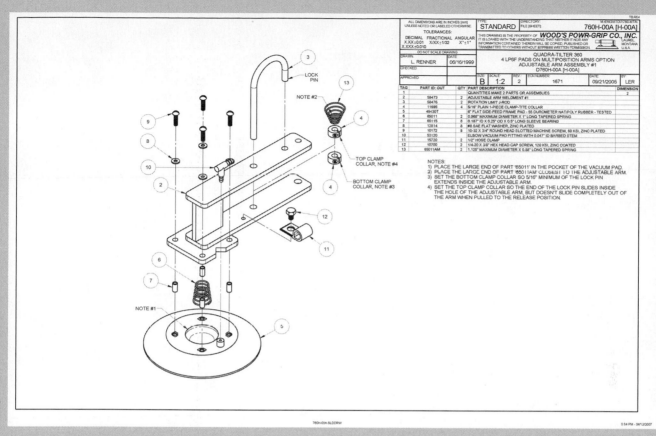

Assembly Drawing Showing Fasteners and Springs. *Courtesy of Wood's Power-Grip Co. Inc.*

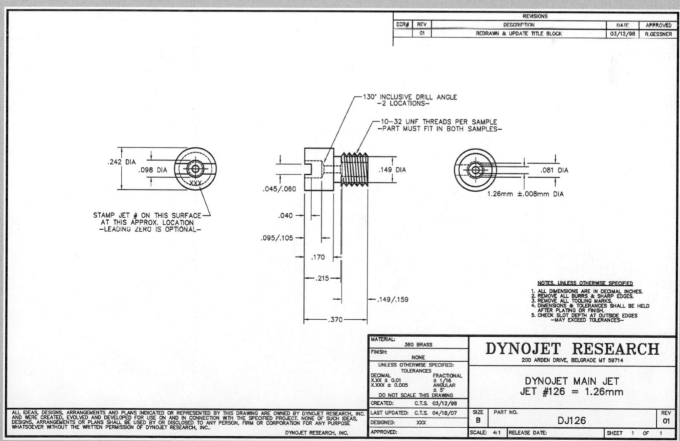

Part Drawing for a Special Purpose Threaded Part (Scale 4:1). *Courtesy of Dynojet Research, Inc.*

PORTFOLIO

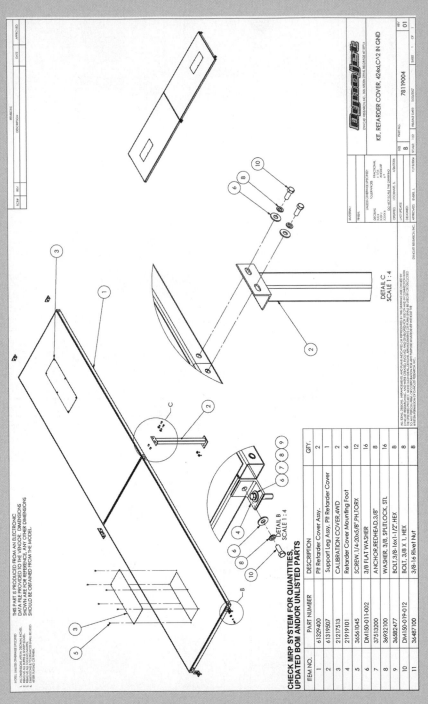

Enlarged Details Show the Fasteners in this Assembly Drawing. *Courtesy of Dynojet Research, Inc.*

KEY WORDS

Thread Form
Screw Thread
External Thread
Internal Thread
Major Diameter
Minor Diameter
Pitch
Pitch Diameter
Lead
Angle of Thread
Crest
Root
Side
Axis of Screw
Depth of Thread
Form of Thread
Series of Thread
Sharp-V thread
American National Thread
Unified Thread
Unified Extra Fine Thread Series
Metric Thread
Square Thread
Acme Thread
Standard Worm Thread
Whitworth Thread
Knuckle Thread
Buttress Thread
Thread Pitch Gage
Coarse Thread
Fine Thread
Single Thread
Multiple Threads
Clearance Holes
Bolt Types
Finish
Thread Lengths
Bolt Lengths
Square Key
Flat Key
Feather Key
Gib Head Key
Pratt & Whitney Key
Woodruff Keys
Compression Springs
Extension Springs
Torsion Springs

CHAPTER SUMMARY

- There are many types of thread forms; however, metric and unified are the most common.
- The method of showing threads on a drawing is called the thread representation. The three types of thread representation are detailed, schematic, and simplified.
- The major diameter, pitch, and form are the most important parts of a thread specification.
- Thread specifications are dimensioned using a leader, usually pointing to the rectangular view of the threaded shaft or to the circular view of a threaded hole. The thread specification tells the manufacturing technician what kind of thread needs to be created.
- The nut and bolt is still the most common type of fastener. Many new types of fasteners are being created to streamline the production process.
- Keys and pins are special fasteners for attachment, for example, a pulley to a shaft.
- The screw head determines what kind of tool will be necessary to install the fastener.

REVIEW QUESTIONS

1. Draw a typical screw thread using detailed representation, and label the parts of the thread.
2. Why are phantom lines used to represent the middle part of a long spring?
3. Draw several types of screw heads.
4. List five types of screws.
5. Why is the simplified thread representation the most commonly used drawing style?
6. List five fasteners that do not have any threads.
7. Write out a metric thread specification and a unified thread specification and label each part of the specification.
8. Which type of thread form is used on a lightbulb?
9. How are multiple threads designated in a thread note?
10. Using the abbreviations in the appendixes, give a specification for a slotted headless flat point set screw.

EXERCISES

Thread and Fastener Projects

Use the information in this chapter and in various manufacturers' catalogs in connection with the working drawings at the end of the next chapter, where many different kinds of threads and fasteners are required. Several projects are included here (Exercises 11.1 to 11.5).

Design Project

Design a system that uses thread to transmit power, for use in helping transfer a handicapped person from a bed to a wheelchair. Use either schematic or detailed representation to show the thread in your design sketches.

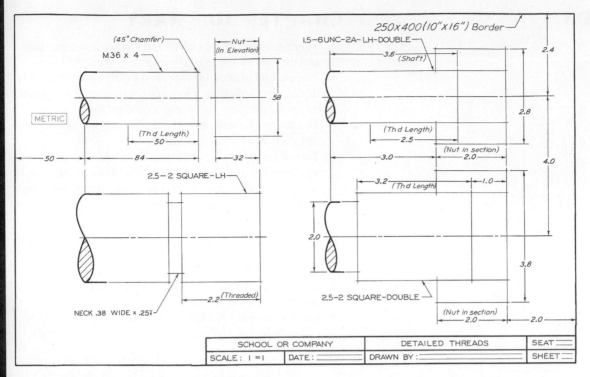

Exercise 11.1 Draw specified detailed threads arranged as shown. Omit all dimensions and notes given in inclined letters. Letter only the thread notes and the title strip. (Some dimensions are given to help you match the sheet layout.)

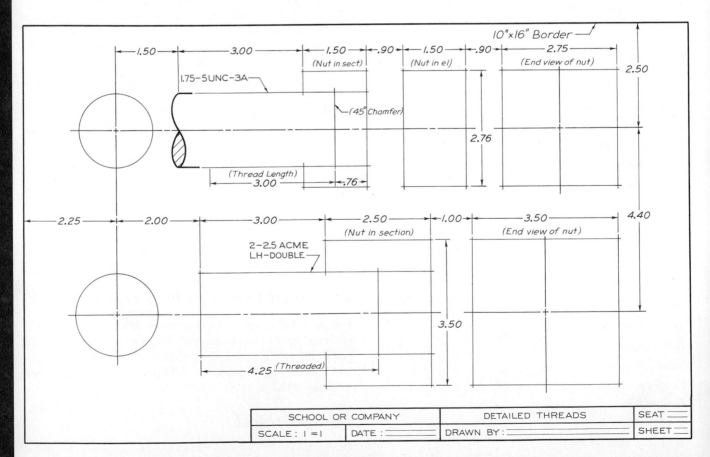

Exercise 11.2 Draw specified detailed notes given in inclined letters. Letter only the thread notes and the title strip. (Some dimensions are given to help you match the sheet layout.)

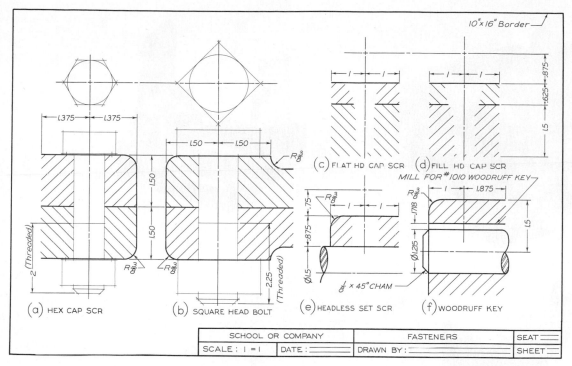

Exercise 11.3 Draw fasteners, arranged as shown. At (a) draw 7/8-9 UNC-2A × 4 Hex Cap Screw. At (b) draw 7 UNC-2A × 41/4 Sq Hd Bolt. At (c) draw 3/8-16 UNC-2A × 11/2 Flat Hd Cap Screw. At (d) draw 7/16-14 UNC-2A × 1 Fill Hd Cap Screw. At (e) draw 1/2 × 1 Headless Slotted Set Screw. At (f) draw front view of No. 1010 Woodruff Key. Draw simplified or schematic thread symbols as assigned. Letter titles under each figure as shown. (Some dimensions are given to help you match the sheet layout.)

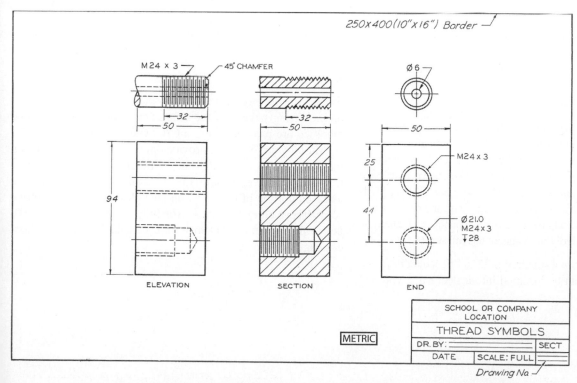

Exercise 11.4 Draw specified thread symbols, arranged as shown. Draw simplified or schematic symbols, as assigned by instructor, using Layout B-5 or A3-5. Omit all dimensions and notes given in inclined letters. Letter only the drill and thread notes, the titles of the views, and the title strip. (Some dimensions are given to help you match the sheet layout.)

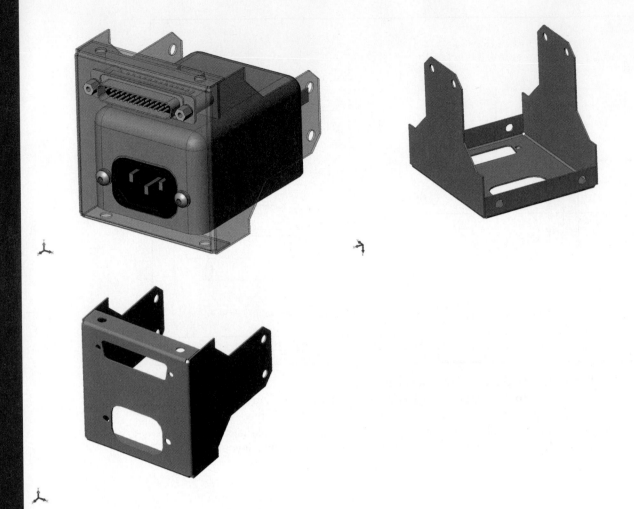

Exercise 11.5 Specify fasteners for attaching the sheet metal and standard electrical components shown. Use the web to research power and electrical connectors.

Exercise 11.6 Captive hardware.

Captive hardware is a term for fasteners that, once installed, cannot be easily or accidentally removed. This is typically achieved by removing a portion of the threading on a screw shaft and then threading the captive hardware into a special sleeve that, once installed, prevents the hardware from backing out. Captive hardware is useful in situations where many fasteners are necessary—for example in sheet metal covers and large panels and when the fastener must be repeatedly unfastened and refastened.

For this exercise, modify a standard 6-32 × .75" socket head cap screw (SHCS) so it can be installed into a sleeve that you will

design. The dimensions for the lock and flat washer are provided on the facing page, and the dimensions from the screw to be modified are provided from a CAD file downloaded from the McMaster-Carr Web site. Provide dimensions for turning down the thread on the 6-32 SHCS and the missing callouts on the captive screw sleeve. Ensure the dimensions provided for the threaded portion of the screw and the clearance for the captive screw sleeve allow the screw to be fully inserted, and allow it to be completely removed from the threaded blank material without causing interference.

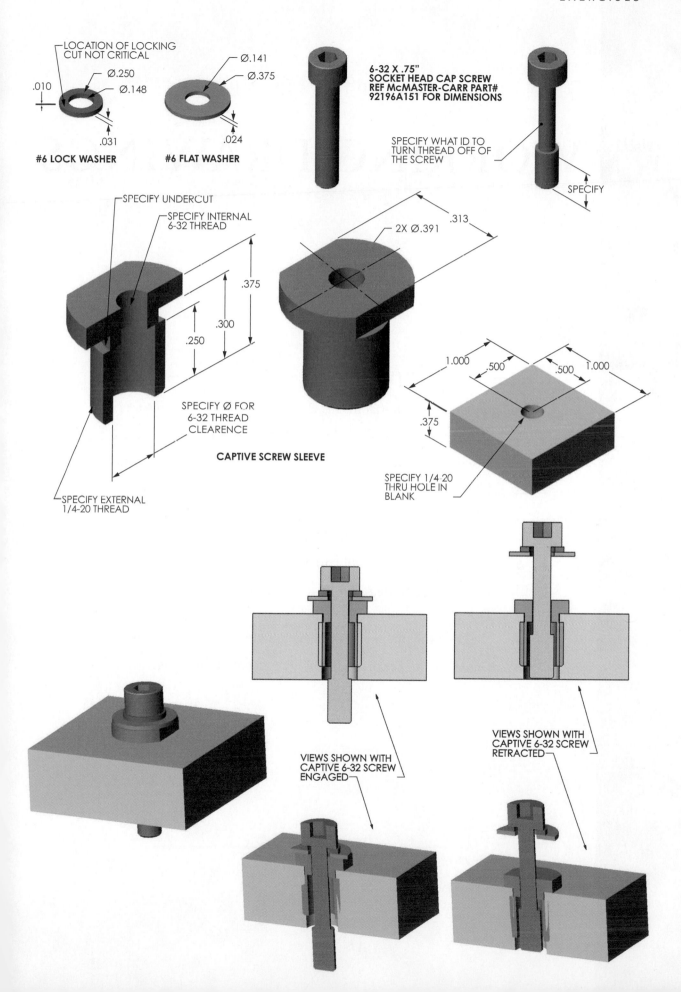

LOCATION OF LOCKING CUT NOT CRITICAL
Ø.250
Ø.148
.010
.031

#6 LOCK WASHER

Ø.141
Ø.375
.024

#6 FLAT WASHER

6-32 X .75" SOCKET HEAD CAP SCREW REF McMASTER-CARR PART# 92196A151 FOR DIMENSIONS

SPECIFY WHAT ID TO TURN THREAD OFF OF THE SCREW

SPECIFY

SPECIFY UNDERCUT
SPECIFY INTERNAL 6-32 THREAD

.375
.300
.250

2X Ø.391
.313

SPECIFY Ø FOR 6-32 THREAD CLEARENCE

CAPTIVE SCREW SLEEVE

SPECIFY EXTERNAL 1/4-20 THREAD

1.000   .500   .500   1.000
.375

SPECIFY 1/4-20 THRU HOLE IN BLANK

VIEWS SHOWN WITH CAPTIVE 6-32 SCREW ENGAGED

VIEWS SHOWN WITH CAPTIVE 6-32 SCREW RETRACTED

CHAPTER TWELVE

WORKING DRAWINGS

WORKING 12 DRAWINGS

OBJECTIVES

After studying the material in this chapter, you should be able to:

1. Define top down, bottom up, and middle out design.

2. Discuss methods of constraining assemblies made using solid modeling and parametric modeling.

3. Identify the elements of a detail drawing.

4. List the parts of an assembly drawing.

5. List six types of assembly drawings.

6. List the role of the record strip and title block in the approval process.

7. Describe the process for revising drawings.

8. Describe the special requirements of a patent drawing.

Refer to the following standards:
- ASME Y14.24-1999 Types and Applications of Engineering Drawings
- ASME Y14.34M-1996 Associated Lists

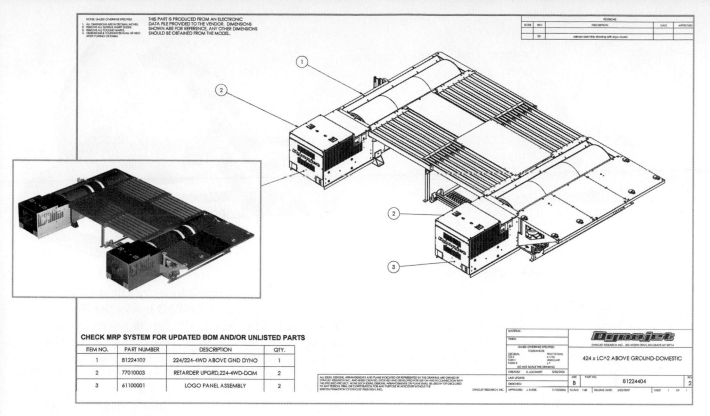

Upper level assembly drawing for a four wheel drive dynamometer (Inset shows 3D model).
Courtesy of Dynojet Research, Inc.

OVERVIEW

Design professionals such as engineers and architects are creators or builders. They use graphics as a means to create, record, analyze, and communicate their design concepts or ideas so that they can be realized or made into real products or structures. The ability to communicate verbally, symbolically, and graphically is essential to building the teams necessary to create large scale projects.

As you learned in Chapter 1, designs progress through five stages. Different types of drawings are required at each stage of the process. Early in the process, ideation sketches communicate and refine concepts for the project. Later, detailed layouts, analysis, and part drawings are created using 2D CAD or solid modeling techniques. Assembly drawings created in 3D CAD or using 2D methods show how multiple parts fit together. They describe the

end result—how the individual pieces that must fit together to work.

Releasing and revising drawings is an important part of the design process. Revisions must be tracked, identified, logged, and saved for future reference. Understanding and using effective methods to manage paper and electronic documents is crucial to retain important information and prevent costly and even dangerous mistakes. You will learn more about managing drawings in Chapter 13.

Check these Web sites for stock component CAD models to add to assemblies:
- http://www.carrlane.com
- http://parts.web2cad.de
- http://www.uspto.gov/web/offices/com/iip/pdf/brochure_05.pdf
- http://www.mycadmash.com/mash.asp lists lots of handy CAD sites

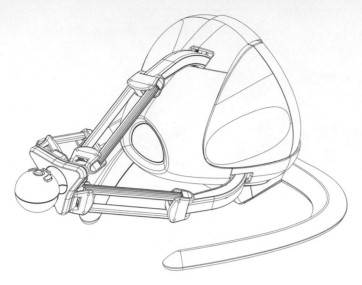

12.1 3D CAD Assembly Model for Lunar Design's Award Winning Design for a 3D Interactive Touch Device for the Home PC. *The Novint Falcon lets users feel weight, shape, texture, dimension, and force effects when playing touch-enabled PC games. It accommodates a variety of controller grips, called end effectors, which allow users to more accurately engage with the experience of the game they are playing, such as feeling their stroke when they hit the golf ball on screen, or gaging how much edge they get on their snowboards as they fly down the slopes. To bring this sophisticated level of 3D touch technology device to market, Lunar Design worked closely with Novint and the commercial haptic developer Force Dimension. Courtesy of Lunar.*

UNDERSTANDING DESIGN, DOCUMENTATION, AND WORKING DRAWINGS

Top Down vs. Bottom Up Design

Methods of accomplishing the design process are sometimes described in terms of three general categories: top down, bottom up, and middle out.

Top down refers to starting the process of designing a product or system by considering the function of the entire system, then breaking that down into subassemblies or component groups based on their major functions. Finally, each part that must be manufactured and assembled to create the design is defined. Layout drawings are often used to facilitate top down design by accurately showing the relationships between major functional items and how those may fit with existing equipment.

Bottom up refers to a design process starting at the part level. Individual components are sized and designed, then the final assembly is built around the design of the parts. This approach is helpful when the components are standardized parts.

Middle out refers to a combination of top down and bottom up design methods, where some parts are standardized and others are designed within the context of fitting into the design of the assembly.

You may prepare detail drawings first or assembly drawings first, depending on your process. Using solid modeling you may create a 2D or 3D layout first and then develop the models for the individual parts. Or you may create part models first and then assemble them together. Some companies use a fully digital documentation process and some create 2D detail drawings and assembly drawings that show how the parts fit together.

Constraining 3D Assembly Models

With **constraint based modeling** software, you use assembly constraints to create relationships between modeled parts. The first part added to the assembly becomes the **parent part.** Other parts are mated to this parent part to build up the assembly. **Mating parts** have features that should fit together. Assembly constraints available in the 3D modeling software let you align mating parts. For example, in the 3D CAD assembly model shown in Figure 12.1, the parts are aligned with one another using assembly constraints, similar to the way you would build the actual device.

If you want two holes to line up, you can use an assembly constraint to align them. If a part changes, it will still be oriented in the assembly so that the holes align. Each software package will offer a similar set of constraint options, so you should become familiar with those available to you. Table 12.1 lists some common assembly constraints and their definitions. Assembly relationships can make your assembly model work for you. As you add parts, use constraints to orient the new part using relationships that will persist in the assembly.

A subordinate assembly, usually called a **subassembly,** is a group of components of a larger machine. Breaking products into subassemblies often makes it easier to coordinate when different designers are working on portions of the same device. Even if you are not using 3D modeling, structuring your drawings into subassemblies provides benefits such as making it easy to reuse subassemblies and track parts. The top down design process focuses on defining all of the subassembly requirements and how those interact in the assembly.

You can create a subassembly in much the same way you create an assembly: by making an assembly of the subassembly components. This subassembly can be added to the main assembly in the same way you add a part.

Organizing the model so that it comes together as it will on the assembly line can be useful in visualizing assembly difficulties. If a group of components are likely to be changed or replaced, linking all the subparts to a main component can make it easy to substitute an alternative design for that group of parts. Planning ahead is essential to creating assemblies efficiently and getting the most out of them.

Table 12.1 Assembly Constraints for 3D Models.

Name	Definition	Illustration
Mate	Mates two planar surfaces together.	
Mate offset	Mates two surfaces together so they have an offset between them.	
Align	Aligns two surfaces, datum points, vertices, or curve ends to be coplanar; also aligns revolved surfaces or axes to be coaxial.	
Align offset	Aligns two planar surfaces with an offset between them.	
Insert	Inserts a "male" revolved surface into a "female" revolved surface, aligning the axes.	
Orient	Orients two planar surfaces to be parallel and facing in the same direction.	
Coordinate system	Places a component into an assembly by aligning its coordinate system with an assembly coordinate system.	

3D Layouts and Skeleton Assemblies

Another method of creating an assembly using 3D CAD software is to start with an assembly framework in the form of an **assembly layout** or **skeleton** that can be used to define the locations of individual parts in the assembly. Using this method, parts are designed so they link to a skeleton framework in the assembly.

A skeleton is a 3D drawing that defines major relationships in the assembly using lines, arcs, curves, and points, as shown in Figure 12.2. By creating the framework for each part up front, all parts do not have to be finished before they can be assembled. Parts can be assembled onto the skeleton at any stage of completion. By allowing the assembly to evolve as the parts are designed and refined, each designer can see the parts the others are creating—or at least the critical relationships between parts—by looking at the assembly.

Working Drawings or Construction Drawings

The term **working drawings** describes a set of **assembly drawings** and detail drawings. A set of civil drawings with site, grading plans, and the many structural details for building a dam or bridge is an example of a set of working drawings.

Architectural drawings are another type of working (or construction) drawings (Figure 12.3). They are given to the contractor to show how to construct the building envisioned by the architect. Working drawings for machines include assembly drawings showing how parts fit together and detail drawings showing how to manufacture the parts. Weldments are a type of assembly drawing showing the welds that must be used to form an assembly from separate pieces of metal.

Drawings, models, and supporting documentation are the specifications for design manufacture. They are given to contractors to perform the work or manufacture individual parts, so they must represent the design accurately. The drawing is a legal document describing what work is to be performed or what parts are to be produced.

A careful process of checking and approving drawings and models helps prevent errors. Take preparing or approving drawings as a serious responsibility. Overlooking what may seem to be small or insignificant details may result in large amounts of wasted money or, worse yet, a person's injury or death.

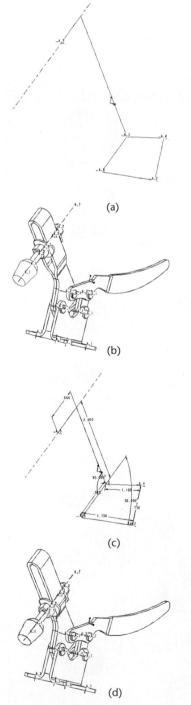

(a)

(b)

(c)

(d)

12.2 Skeleton Model for a Clamp

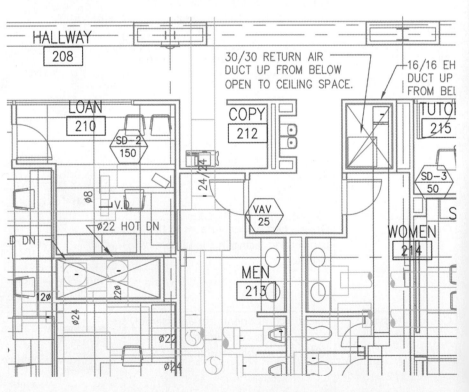

12.3 Portion of a Mechanical System for a Building. *Courtesy of Associated Construction Engineering, Inc.*

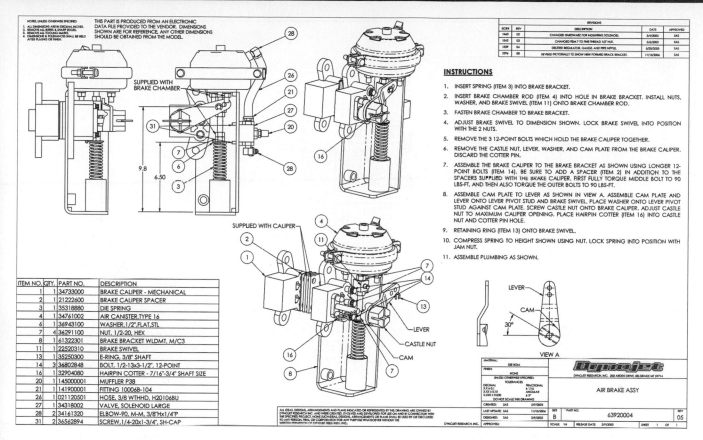

12.4 General Assembly Drawing for an Air Brake Created from a 3D CAD Model. *Courtesy of Dynojet Research, Inc.*

Assembly Drawings

An assembly drawing shows the assembled machine or structure, with all detail parts in their functional positions or as an **exploded view** where you can relate the parts to their functional positions.

There are different types of assembly drawings:

1. Design assemblies, or layouts.
2. General assemblies.
3. Detail assemblies.
4. Working drawing assemblies.
5. Outline or installation assemblies.
6. Inseparable assemblies (as in weldments, and others).

Assembly drawings are often generated from 3D CAD models. For example, the assembly drawing for the air brake in Figure 12.4 was generated from the 3D CAD model of the air brake shown in shaded view in Figure 12.5.

Views

Keep the purpose in mind when you select the views for an assembly drawing. The assembly drawing shows how the parts fit together and suggests the function of the entire unit. A complete set of orthographic views is not required. Often a single orthographic view will show all of the information needed when assembling the parts. The assembly drawing does not need to show how to make the parts, just how to put them together. The assembly worker receives the actual finished parts. The information for each individual part is shown on its detail drawing.

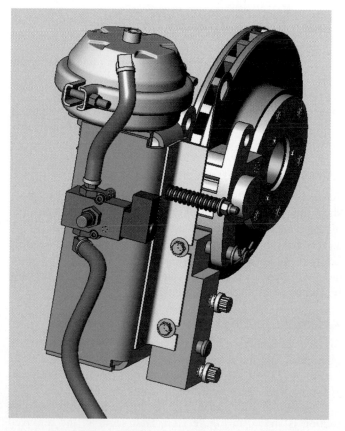

12.5 3D CAD Model for an Air Brake. *Courtesy of Dynojet Research, Inc.*

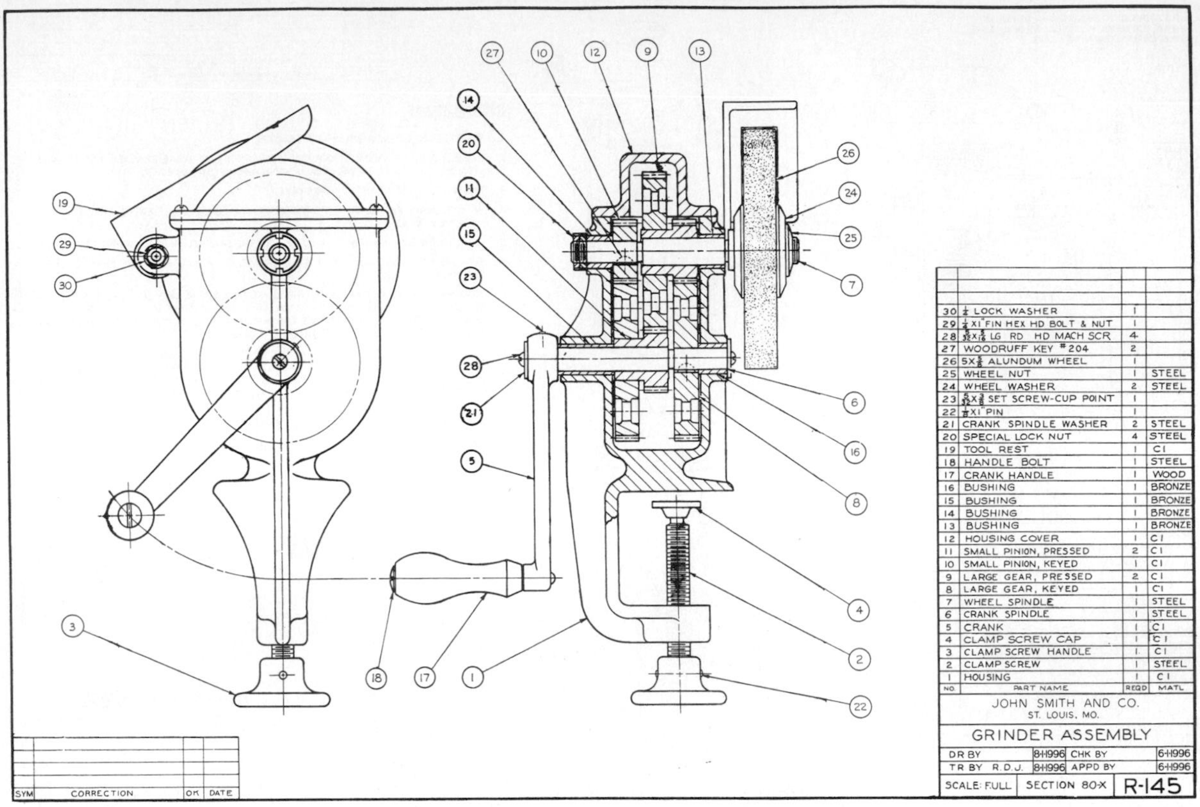

30 1/4 LOCK WASHER 1
29 1/4 X 1" FIN HEX HD BOLT & NUT 1
28 5/32 X 5/16 LG RD HD MACH SCR 4
27 WOODRUFF KEY #204 2
26 5 X 5/8 ALUNDUM WHEEL 1
25 WHEEL NUT 1 STEEL
24 WHEEL WASHER 2 STEEL
23 5/32 X 3/8 SET SCREW-CUP POINT 1
22 1/8 X 1" PIN 1
21 CRANK SPINDLE WASHER 2 STEEL
20 SPECIAL LOCK NUT 4 STEEL
19 TOOL REST 1 CI
18 HANDLE BOLT 1 STEEL
17 CRANK HANDLE 1 WOOD
16 BUSHING 1 BRONZE
15 BUSHING 1 BRONZE
14 BUSHING 1 BRONZE
13 BUSHING 1 BRONZE
12 HOUSING COVER 1 CI
11 SMALL PINION, PRESSED 2 CI
10 SMALL PINION, KEYED 1 CI
9 LARGE GEAR, PRESSED 2 CI
8 LARGE GEAR, KEYED 1 CI
7 WHEEL SPINDLE 1 STEEL
6 CRANK SPINDLE 1 STEEL
5 CRANK 1 CI
4 CLAMP SCREW CAP 1 CI
3 CLAMP SCREW HANDLE 1 CI
2 CLAMP SCREW 1 STEEL
1 HOUSING 1 CI
NO. PART NAME REQD MATL
JOHN SMITH AND CO.
ST. LOUIS, MO.
GRINDER ASSEMBLY
DR BY 8-1-1996 CHK BY 6-1-1996
TR BY R.D.J. 8-1-1996 APPD BY 6-1-1996
SCALE: FULL SECTION 80-X R-145
SYM CORRECTION OK DATE

12.6 Assembly Drawing of a Grinder

Hidden Lines in Assembly Drawings

Typically, hidden lines are not needed on assembly drawings. Keep in mind that the assembly drawing is often used by the worker who is putting the parts together. It needs to be easy to read and show the relationships between parts clearly. Hidden lines can make the drawing difficult to read, so use section or exploded views to show the interior parts in the assembly drawing.

Dimensions in Assembly Drawings

Assembly drawings are not usually dimensioned except to show the relative positions of one feature to the next when that distance must be maintained at the time of the assembly, such as the maximum height of a jack, or the maximum opening between the jaws of a vise. When machining is required in the assembly operation, the necessary dimensions and notes may be given on the assembly drawing.

Assembly Sections

Since assemblies often have parts fitting into or overlapping other parts, 2D and 3D sections are useful views. For example, in Figure 12.6, try to imagine the right-side view drawn in elevation with interior parts represented by hidden lines.

Any kind of section may be used as needed. A broken-out section is shown in Figure 12.6. Half sections and removed sections are also frequently used. Pictorial sections are helpful in creating easy to read assembly drawings.

Detail Drawings or Piece Part Drawings

Drawings of the individual parts are called **piece part drawings, part drawings,** or **detail drawings.** Detail drawings contain all of the necessary information to manufacture any specific part being created for a product or design. Figures 12.7 and 12.8 show detail drawings. The information provided on detail drawings includes:

- All necessary drawing views or accurate 3D model information to fully define the shape.
- Dimensions that can be specified in a drawing or can be measured accurately from a 3D model.
- Tolerances either specified in a drawing or annotated in a 3D model so that how the tolerance applies can be clearly understood.
- The material for the manufactured part.
- Any general or specific notes including heat treatment, painting, coatings, hardness, pattern number, estimated weight, and surface finishes, such as maximum surface roughness.
- Approval or release and revision tracking, whether part of a 2D drawing title and revision block or part of a digital signature system.

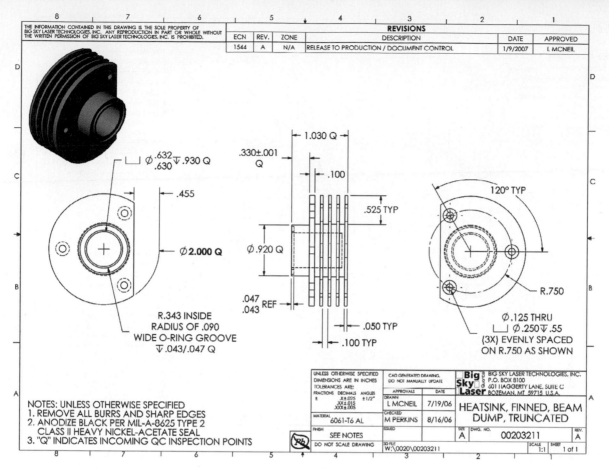

12.7   Part Drawing for a Heat Sink. *Courtesy of Big Sky Laser.*

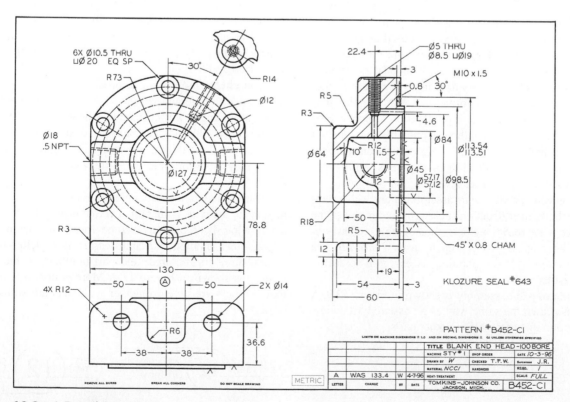

12.8   A Detail Drawing

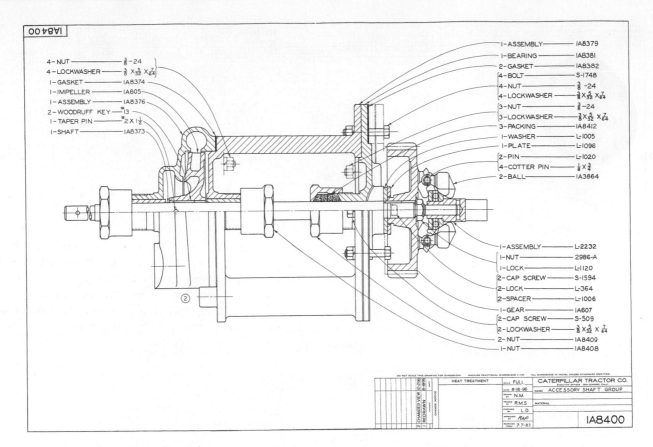

12.9 Subassembly of Accessory Shaft Group

12.1 SUBASSEMBLIES

A set of working drawings includes detail drawings of individual parts and the assembly drawing showing the assembled unit. Often an entire subassembly may be reused in a different design. It is easier to reuse the group of parts in a new design if they are grouped together logically and contained in separate drawings. Your top level assembly drawing will appear cleaner if you keep subassemblies well organized, as the entire subassembly can be identified as a single item on a higher level assembly drawing. Fasteners for the subassembly that attach it to its mating parts in the next higher level assembly drawing are usually shown or listed on the bill of materials (sometimes referred to as BOM) at the higher level.

Structuring your product into assemblies and subassemblies requires thoughtful decision making in order to get the most advantage when retrieving part, subassembly, and assembly drawings later on. If your company uses a product data management system (PDM), planning is essential to seeing downstream results.

An example of a subassembly is shown in Figure 12.9. A subassembly is drawn the same way as an assembly drawing, just for a subgroup that assembles to other parts.

12.2 IDENTIFICATION

Use circled numbers called **balloon numbers** or **ball tags** to identify the parts in the assembly (Figure 12.10). Circles containing the part numbers are placed adjacent to the parts, with leaders terminated by arrowheads touching the parts as shown in Figure 12.11.

The circles are placed in orderly horizontal or vertical rows and not scattered over the sheet. Leader lines should be drawn at an angle, not horizontally or vertically. Do not let leaders cross. Make adjacent leaders parallel or nearly so. For multiple small parts that are easily distinguished, a single leader may have multiple circle item numbers as shown in Figure 12.11.

The circled item number identifies each part. Show information for the part in the parts list that is usually included on the drawing sheet, but may also be a separate document.

Another method of identification is to letter the part names, numbers required, and part numbers, at the end of leaders as shown in Figure 12.9. More commonly, only the part numbers are given, together with standard straight-line leaders.

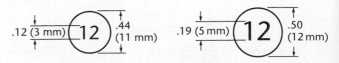

12.10 Identification Numbers

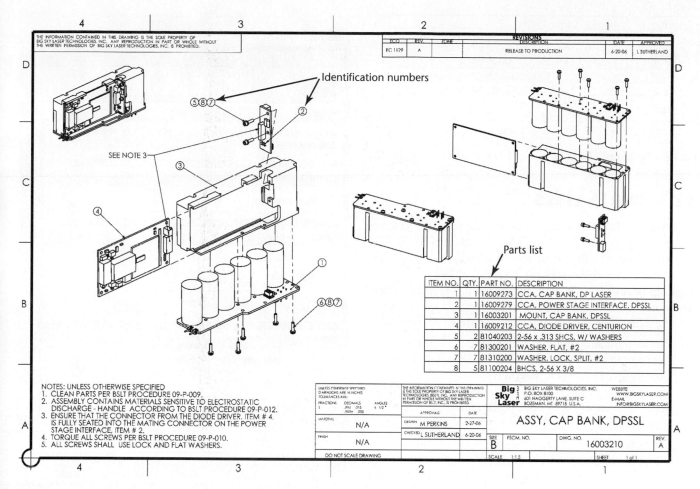

Identification numbers

Parts list

ITEM NO.	QTY.	PART NO.	DESCRIPTION
1	1	16009273	CCA, CAP BANK, DP LASER
2	1	16009279	CCA, POWER STAGE INTERFACE, DPSSL
3	1	16003201	MOUNT, CAP BANK, DPSSL
4	1	16009212	CCA, DIODE DRIVER, CENTURION
5	2	81040203	2-56 x .313 SHCS, W/ WASHERS
6	7	81300201	WASHER, FLAT, #2
7	7	81310200	WASHER, LOCK, SPLIT, #2
8	5	81100204	BHCS, 2-56 X 3/8

NOTES: UNLESS OTHERWISE SPECIFIED
1. CLEAN PARTS PER BSLT PROCEDURE 09-P-009.
2. ASSEMBLY CONTAINS MATERIALS SENSITIVE TO ELECTROSTATIC DISCHARGE - HANDLE ACCORDING TO BSLT PROCEDURE 09-P-012.
3. ENSURE THAT THE CONNECTOR FROM THE DIODE DRIVER, ITEM # 4, IS FULLY SEATED INTO THE MATING CONNECTOR ON THE POWER STAGE INTERFACE, ITEM # 2.
4. TORQUE ALL SCREWS PER BSLT PROCEDURE 09-P-010.
5. ALL SCREWS SHALL USE LOCK AND FLAT WASHERS.

ASSY, CAP BANK, DPSSL

DWG. NO. 16003210

12.11 Identification of Assembly Drawing Items with a Parts List. *Courtesy of Big Sky Laser.*

Multidetail Drawings

When multiple detail drawings are shown on one sheet, identify each part are similar to those used in detail drawings where several details are shown on one sheet, as in Figure 12.12. Place circles containing the part numbers adjacent to the parts, with leaders terminated by arrowheads touching the parts as in Figure 12.11. A portion of a multidetail drawing is shown in Figure 12.12.

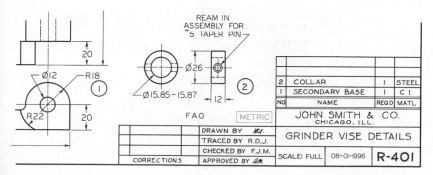

12.12 Portion of a Drawing Showing Identification of Details with a Parts List

ITEM NO.	QTY.	PART NO.	DESCRIPTION
1	1	16009273	CCA, CAP BANK, DP LASER
2	1	16009279	CCA, POWER STAGE INTERFACE, DPSSL
3	1	16003201	MOUNT, CAP BANK, DPSSL
4	1	16009212	CCA, DIODE DRIVER, CENTURION
5	2	81040203	2-56 x .313 SHCS, W/ WASHERS
6	7	81300201	WASHER, FLAT, #2
7	7	81310200	WASHER, LOCK, SPLIT, #2
8	5	81100204	BHCS, 2-56 X 3/8

12.13 Parts List. *Courtesy of Big Sky Laser.*

12.3 PARTS LISTS

A **parts list** or **bill of materials** itemizes the parts of a structure shown on an assembly drawing (ANSI Y14.34M–1996). The title strip alone is sufficient on detail drawings of only one part, but a parts list is necessary on assembly drawings or detail drawings of several parts. Parts can be listed in general order of size or importance or grouped by types.

Parts lists for machine drawings, Figure 12.13 contain:

- Part identification number (PIN).
- Description of each part.
- Quantity required in the assembly.
- The following abbreviations can be used to indicate quantities that are not exactly known: AR indicating *as required*; EST followed by a number for an *estimated quantity.*

For parts lists that contain application data, information for the next assembly level must be included.

Frequently other information is supplied in the parts list, such as material, CAGE code, pattern numbers, stock sizes of materials, and weights of parts.

Automatic BOM Generation

CAD software often allows you to generate the parts list automatically or somewhat automatically. Figure 12.14 shows a dialog box used to automate generation of a parts list.

If you created a 3D assembly model by inserting CAD models for the parts, the software can query the assembly model for quantities and the file names that were inserted to generate the parts list. This is another good reason to use good file management practices and name your parts logically. Most software allows you to type in information, but overriding the information this way makes it harder to automatically update files, losing some of the advantage of using 3D CAD.

Locating the Parts List

If the parts list rests on top of the title box or strip, the order of the items should be from the bottom upward so that new items can be added later, if necessary. If the parts list is placed in the upper-right corner, the items should read downward.

Listing Standard Parts

Standard parts, whether purchased or company produced, are not drawn but are included in the parts list. Bolts, screws, bearings, pins, keys, and so on are identified by the part number from the assembly drawing and are specified by name and size or number.

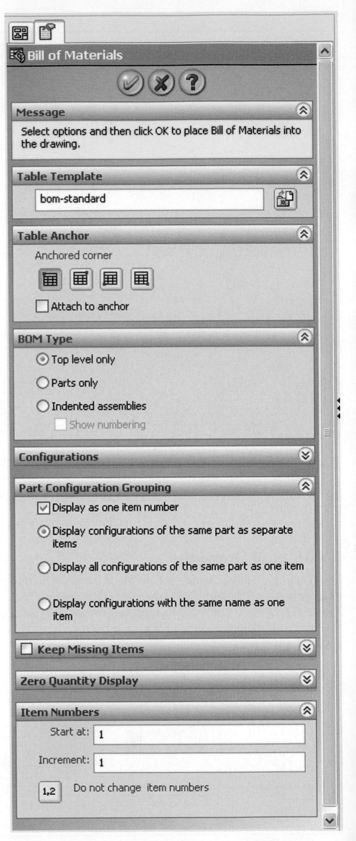

12.14 Solidworks Dialog Box Showing Options For Automatically Inserting a Bill of Materials Table. *Courtesy of Solidworks Corporation.*

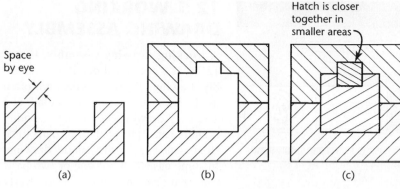

12.15 Section Lining in Assemblies (Full Size)

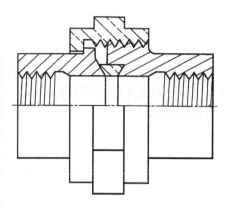

12.16 Symbolic Section Lining

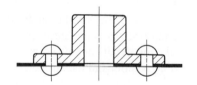

12.17 Solidly Hatching Small Parts

12.4 ASSEMBLY SECTIONS

In assembly sections it is necessary not only to show the cut surfaces but also to distinguish between adjacent parts. Do this by drawing the section lines in opposing directions, as shown in Figure 12.15. The first large area is sectioned at 45° (Figure 12.15a). The next large area, (b), is sectioned at 45° in the opposite direction. Additional areas are then sectioned at other angles, such as 30° or 60° as shown at (c) or at other angles.

In small areas it is necessary to space the section lines closer together. In larger areas space section lining more widely or use outline section lining.

Use the general-purpose section lining for assemblies. You can also give a general indication of the materials used, through using symbolic section lining as shown in Figure 12.16. Refer to Chapter 6 to review section drawing practices.

In sectioning relatively thin parts in an assembly, such as gaskets and sheet metal parts, section lining is ineffective and should be left out or shown in solid black as in Figure 12.17.

In architectural drawings, filling sectioned areas solidly is called **poche,** as shown in Figure 12.18. It is often used to show walls that have been cut through, as on floor plans.

Often solid objects, or parts that do not show required information, are sliced by the cutting plane. Leave these parts unsectioned, or "in the round." This includes bolts, nuts, shafts, keys, screws, pins, ball or roller bearings, gear teeth, spokes, and ribs, among others. See Figure 12.19.

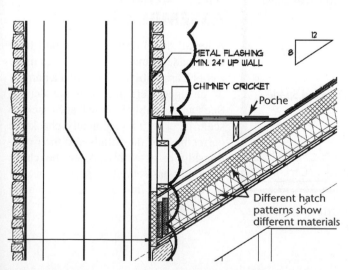

12.18 Use Hatch Patterns to Indicate Material and Poche Small Features *Detail of Drawing. Courtesy of Locati Architects.*

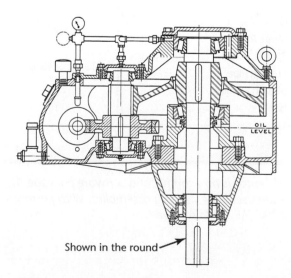

12.19 Assembly Section

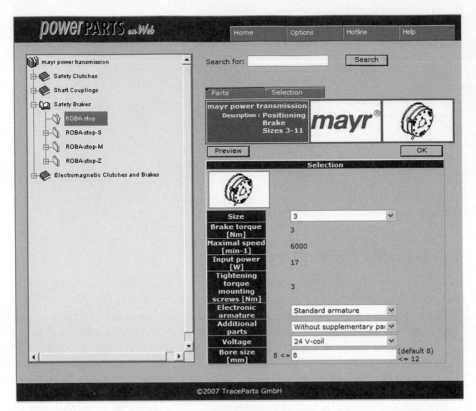

You can save time in creating assemblies by downloading stock parts. Many vendors have models for Web download.

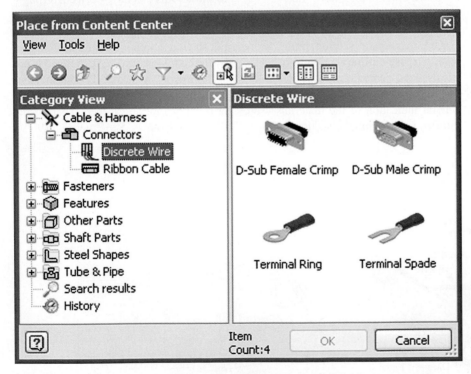

Autodesk Inventor is an example of a software package that features stock parts that are useful for creating assemblies. With permission of Autodesk, Inc. © 2006-2007. All rights reserved.

12.5 WORKING DRAWING ASSEMBLY

A **working drawing assembly,** Figure 12.20, is a combined detail and assembly drawing. These drawings are often used in place of separate detail and assembly drawings when the assembly is simple enough for all of its parts to be shown clearly in the single drawing. In some cases, all but one or two parts can be drawn and dimensioned clearly in the assembly drawing, in which event these parts are detailed separately on the same sheet. This type of drawing is common in valve drawings, locomotive subassemblies, aircraft subassemblies, and drawings of jigs and fixtures.

12.6 INSTALLATION ASSEMBLIES

An assembly made specifically to show how to install or erect a machine or structure is an **installation assembly.** This type of drawing is also often called an outline assembly, because it shows only the outlines and the relationships of exterior surfaces. A typical installation assembly is shown in Figure 12.21. In aircraft drafting, an installation drawing (assembly) gives complete information for placing details or subassemblies in their final positions in the airplane.

12.7 CHECK ASSEMBLIES

After all detail drawings of a unit have been made, it may be necessary to make a **check assembly,** especially if a number of changes were made in the details. Such an assembly is shown accurately to scale in order to graphically check the correctness of the details and their relationship in assembly. After the check assembly has served its purpose, it may be converted into a general assembly drawing.

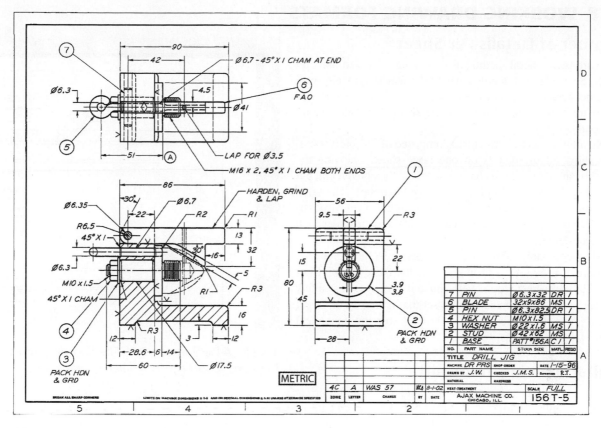

12.20   Working Drawing Assembly of Drill Jig.

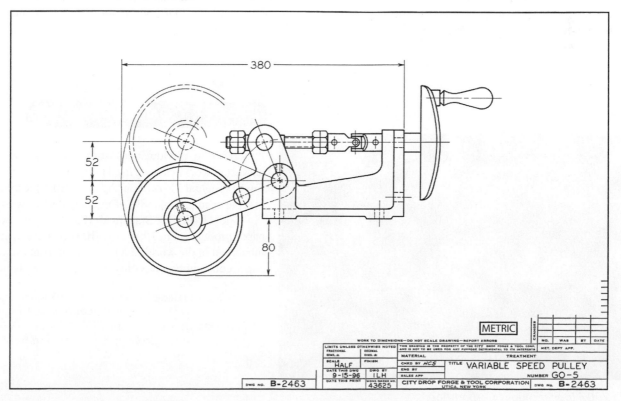

12.21   Installation Assembly

12.8 WORKING DRAWING FORMATS

Number of Details Per Sheet

There are two general methods for grouping detailed parts on sheets. Showing one detailed part per sheet is typically preferred because it is easier to repurpose drawings for other uses and to track revision data when the sheet does not contain extra parts.

Small machines or structures composed of few parts sometimes show all the details on one large sheet. Showing the assembly and all its details on one sheet can be convenient, but it is generally more difficult to revise and maintain. The same scale should be used for all details on a single sheet, if possible. When this is not possible, clearly note the scale under each dissimilar detail.

Most companies show one detail per sheet, however simple or small it may be. For many parts the basic 8.5 × 11" or 210 × 297 mm sheet works well. Since it is easy to lose a few drawings on smaller sheets from a set that is mostly on larger sheets, some companies use all 11 × 17" (or the equivalent metric size) for all parts.

Digital Drawing Transmittal

Electronic file formats such as Portable Document Format (PDF), originally developed by Adobe Systems in 1993, allow the originator to send a document that can be commented on without allowing the original document to be changed.

Several search engines allow you to search for text embedded in the PDF file. This means that PDF can provide advantages not just for storing, but retrieving the information later. Adobe Systems provides a useful document (in PDF format) on using PDF as an archiving standard. You can read it at http://www.adobe.com/products/acrobat/pdfs/pdfarchiving.pdf.

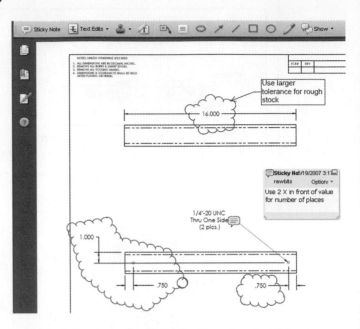

12.22 A Portion of a PDF File Showing Red-Lined Markups. *Courtesy of Dynojet Research, Inc.*

Using electronic files saves trees, makes it quicker to distribute and store documents, and allows others to review documents from various applications. Figure 12.22 shows a drawing stored in PDF format with comments and redlined markups.

PAPER CONSERVATION

According to Worldwatch Institute, 40% of the trees harvested worldwide are used to make paper. The U.S. Environmental Protection Agency (EPA) estimates that paper makes up 38% of municipal solid waste.

The UNESCO Statistical Handbook estimated paper production in 1999 at 1,510 sheets of paper per inhabitant of the world. Even with digital data storage, paper consumption has only increased since then.

Web sites related to paper conservation include:
- http://www2.sims.berkeley.edu/research/projects/how-much-info-2003/print.html
- http://www.lesk.com/mlesk/ksg97/ksg.html

REPORT ALL ERRORS TO FOREMAN								
	NO. REQUIRED	MATERIAL	HEAT TREATMENT	PART NAME	DRAWN BY	UNIT 3134		
	1	SAE 3115	SEE NOTE	FEED WORM SHAFT	H.F.			
				DRAWN FOR	TRACED BY	ALSO USED ON ABOVE MACHINES		
	REPLACED BY	REPLACES	OLD PART NO.	SIMPLEX & DUPLEX (1200)	E.E.Z.			
			563-310	ENGINEERING DEPARTMENT	CHECKED BY	FIRST USED ON LOT	LAST USED ON LOT	
			SCALE	KEARNEY & TRECKER	C.STB.			
			FULL SIZE	CORPORATION	APPROVED BY	**17840 B**		
ALTERATIONS	DATE OF CHG			MILWAUKEE, WISCONSIN, U. S. A.	DATE 8-10-1996			

12.23   TItle Strip

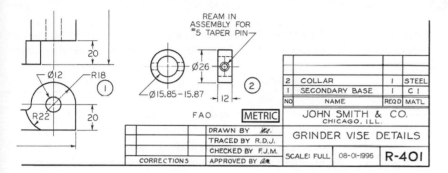

DO NOT SCALE THIS DRAWING FOR DIMENSIONS.		MACHINE FRACTIONAL DIMENSIONS ± 1/64	ALL DIMENSIONS IN INCHES UNLESS OTHERWISE SPECIFIED.		
	HEAT TREATMENT	SCALE FULL	CATERPILLAR TRACTOR CO.		
			EXECUTIVE OFFICES — SAN LEANDRO, CALIF.		
	S A E VIII	DATE 8-10-1996	NAME FIRST, FOURTH & THIRD		
	HDN ROCKWELL C-50-56	DRAWN BY S.G.	SLIDING PINION		
	NOTE 3 TEST LOCATIONS	TRACED BY L.R.	MATERIAL C.T. #1E36 STEEL ② ①		
		CHECKED BY n.w.	UPSET FORGING 3.875 ROUND MAX		
		APPROVED BY amB.	**1A4045**		
		REDRAWN FROM			

12.24   TItle Strip. *Courtesy of Dynojet Research, Inc.*

2	COLLAR	1	STEEL	
1	SECONDARY BASE	1	C I	
NO	NAME	REQD	MATL	
JOHN SMITH & CO.				
CHICAGO, ILL.				
DRAWN BY HL.	GRINDER VISE DETAILS			
TRACED BY R.D.J.				
CHECKED BY F.J.M.				
CORRECTIONS	APPROVED BY am	SCALE: FULL	08-01-1996	**R-401**

12.25   Identifying Details with a Parts List. *Courtesy of Big Sky Laser, Inc.*

Title and Record Strips

Drawings constitute important and valuable information regarding products, so carefully designed, well-kept, systematic files are important.

The function of the title and record strip is to show, in an organized way, all necessary information not given directly on the drawing with its dimensions and notes. The type of title used depends on the filing system in use, the manufacturing processes, and the requirements of the product. The following should generally be given in the title form:

1. Name of the object shown.
2. Name and address of manufacturer.
3. Name and address of the purchasing company, if any.
4. Signature of the person who made the drawing and date of completion.
5. Signature of the checker and date of completion.
6. Signature of the chief drafter, chief engineer, or other official, and the date of approval.
7. Scale of the drawing.
8. Number of the drawing.

Other information may be included, such as material, quantity, heat treatment, finish, hardness, pattern number, estimated weight, superseding and superseded drawing numbers, symbol of machine, and so on, depending on the plant organization and unique aspects of the product. Some typical title blocks are shown in Figures 12.23, 12.24 and 12.25. See the inside back cover for traditional title forms and ANSI-approved sheet sizes.

The title form is usually placed along the bottom of the sheet or in the lower right-hand corner of the sheet, because drawings are often filed in flat, horizontal drawers, and the title must be easily found. However, as many filing systems are in use, the location of the title form depends on your company's organizational preference. Many companies adopt their own title forms or those preferred by ANSI.

To letter items in a title form:

- Use single-stroke vertical or inclined Gothic capitals.
- Letter items according to their relative importance. Use heavier, larger or more widely spaced lettering (or a combination of these) to indicate important items.
- Give the drawing number the most emphasis, followed by the name of the object and name of the company. (Date, scale, and originator's and checker's names are important, but do not need to be prominent.)
- Refer to Chapter 2 for detailed information on title blocks and standard letter heights.

12.9 DRAWING NUMBERS

Every drawing should be numbered. Some companies use serial numbers, such as 60412, or a number with a prefix or suffix letter to indicate the sheet size, as A60412 or 60412-A. The size A sheet is a standard 8.5 × 11". In different numbering schemes, various parts of the drawing number indicate different things, such as model number of the machine and the nature or use of the part. In general, it is best to use a simple numbering system and not to load the number with too many indications.

The drawing number should be lettered 7 mm (.2500") high in the lower-right and upper-left corners of the sheet.

In order to benefit from a CAD system, you must be able to store and retrieve your drawings efficiently. Drawing tracking software allows users to search by part number or text items to retrieve drawing files and CAD models.

12.10 ZONING

To help people locate a particular item on a large or complex drawing, regular ruled intervals are labeled along the margins, often in the right and lower margins only. The intervals on the horizontal margin are labeled from right to left with numerals, and the intervals on the vertical margin are labeled from bottom to top with letters, similar to road maps. Note the zone letters and numbers around the border of Figure 12.26.

12.11 CHECKING DRAWINGS

The importance of accuracy in technical drawing cannot be overstated. Errors sometimes cause tremendous unnecessary expenditures. The signature on the drawing identifies who is responsible for its accuracy.

In small offices, checking is usually done by the designer or by one of the drafters. In large offices, experienced engineers may be employed to devote a major part of their time to checking drawings.

A drawing is carefully checked and signed by the person who made it. It is then checked by the lead designer for function, economy, practicability, fit, tolerances and so on. Corrections, if any, are then made by the original drafter.

The final checker should systematically review the drawing for any remaining errors. They should study the drawing with particular attention to:

1. Soundness of design, with reference to function, strength, materials, economy, manufacturability, serviceability, ease of assembly and repair, lubrication, and so on.
2. Choice of views, partial views, auxiliary views, sections, lettering, and so on.
3. Dimensions, with special reference to repetition, ambiguity, legibility, omissions, errors, and finish marks. Special attention should be given to tolerances.
4. Standard parts. In the interest of economy, as many parts as possible should be standard.
5. Notes, with special reference to clear wording and legibility.
6. Clearances. Moving parts should be checked in all possible positions to ensure freedom of movement.
7. Title form information.

12.12 DRAWING REVISIONS

Changes on drawings may be necessitated by changes in design, changes in tools, desires of customers, or errors in design or in production. An accurate record of all changes made to released drawings is tracked via a revision block. This is important so that the sources of all changes may be understood, verified, and approved.

The record of revisions should show the change, by whom, when, and why the change was made. An engineering change order (ECO) or engineering change request (ECR) is processed to approve and track changes to drawings once they have been released for production. Some companies use a paper record for this and others manage it digitally.

Any changes or additions made to a drawing are tracked by a **revision number.** A symbol can be added to the drawing showing the item affected by the revision.

It is not recommended to remove information by crossing it out.

In rare cases when a dimension is not noticeably affected by a change, it may be underlined with a heavy line to indicate that it is not to scale.

It is important to keep prints or microfilms of each issue on file to show how the drawing appeared before the revision. Issue new prints to supersede old ones each time a change is made.

Digital systems absolutely must use careful backup procedures and, due to data loss concerns, are still not approved in some industries.

If considerable change on a drawing is necessary, it may be necessary to make a new drawing and stamp the old one OBSOLETE and store it in an "obsolete" file. In the title block of the old drawing, enter the words "SUPERSEDED BY" or "REPLACED BY" followed by the number of the new drawing. On the new drawing, under "SUPERSEDES" or "REPLACES," enter the number of the old drawing.

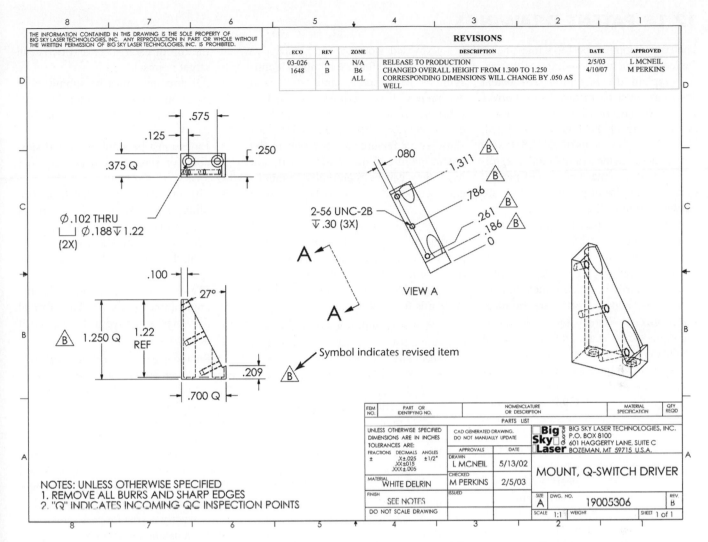

12.26 Symbols Matching the Item in the Revision Block Indicate Revised Features on a Drawing.
Courtesy of Big Sky Laser, Inc.

People use various methods to reference the area on a drawing where the change is made, with the entry in the revision block. The most common is to place numbers or letters in a small circle or triangle near each place where the changes were made and to use the same numbers or letters in the revision block, as shown in Figure 12.26. On zoned drawings the zone of the correction is shown in the revision block. The change should also be described briefly, along with the date and initials of the person making the change.

12.13 SIMPLIFYING DRAWINGS

Drawing time is a considerable part of the total cost of a product. It makes sense to reduce drawing costs by using practices to simplify your drawings without losing clarity. For example, use partial views, half views, thread symbols, piping symbols, and single-line spring drawings when appropriate. Omit lines or lettering on a drawing that are not needed for clarity. In addition to saving production time, this makes drawings easier to read. To simplify drawings:

1. Use word descriptions when practical.
2. Do not show unnecessary views.
3. Use standard symbols such as Ø and standard abbreviations (see Appendix 4 when appropriate).
4. Avoid elaborate, pictorial, or repetitive details. Use phantom lines to avoid drawing repeated features.
5. List rather than draw standard parts such as bolts, nuts, keys, and pins.
6. Omit unnecessary hidden lines.
7. Use outline section lining in large areas to save time and improve legibility.
8. Omit unnecessary duplication of notes and lettering.
9. Use symbolic representation for piping and thread.
10. Use CAD libraries and standard parts when feasible for design and drawings.

Some industries have simplified their drafting practices even more. Learn the practices appropriate to the industry for which you are creating drawings.

12.14 PATENT DRAWINGS

The patent application for a machine or device must include drawings to illustrate and explain the invention. All patent drawings must be mechanically correct and constitute complete illustrations of every feature of the invention claimed. The strict requirements of the U.S. Patent Office facilitate the examination of applications and the interpretation of patents issued. Examples of patent drawings are shown in Figure 12.27.

Drawings for patent applications are pictorial and explanatory in nature; therefore they are not as detailed as working drawings for production purposes. Centerlines, hidden lines, dimension notes, and so forth, are omitted, since specific dimensions, tolerances, and notes are often not required to patent the general design or innovation.

The drawings must contain as many figures as necessary to show the invention clearly. There is no limit on the number of sheets that may be submitted. The drawings can be produced by hand or from the same CAD database used to create the design documentation.

While most engineering drawings are produced with views in alignment on one sheet, patent drawings must show each separate view as one figure on a separate sheet. Figures should be numbered consecutively (i.e., Figure 1, Figure 2, Figure 3A, Figure 3B, etc.). Views, features, and parts are identified by numbers that refer to the descriptions and explanations given in the specification section of the patent application. The reference number for a part or feature should remain the same in every diagram.

Exploded isometric or perspective drawings with reference numbers identifying the parts (i.e., assembly drawings) are preferred. Centerlines are used to illustrate how parts are aligned in exploded views. While the drawing must show every feature that is listed in the patent claims, if standardized parts are used, they can be represented symbolically and do not have to be drawn in detail.

The figures may be plan, elevation, section, pictorial, and detail views of portions or elements, and they may be drawn to an enlarged scale if necessary.

The U.S. Patent Office has basic standards for drawings:

- All sheets within a single application must be the same size, and two sheet sizes are accepted:
  - U.S. size: 8.5 by 11" (216 mm × 279 mm).
  - International size: 210 mm × 297 mm.
- Paper must be single sided.
- Paper must be oriented vertically, so that the short side of the sheet is at the top (called portrait style in printing options).
- No border lines are permitted on the sheets.
- The following minimum margins must be maintained.
  - Top margin: 1" (25 mm).
  - Left margin: 1" (25 mm).
  - Right margin: .675" (15 mm).
  - Bottom margin: .375" (10 mm).
- No labels or drawing lines may extend into the margin except for the specific identification required at the top of each sheet and two scan target points.
- All drawings must be submitted in black and white—no color drawings or photos except in very limited cases.
- Lines must be solid black and suitable for reproduction at a smaller size.
- Shading (either cross hatch or stippling) is used whenever it improves readability. In rare cases when it is necessary to show a feature hidden behind a surface, a lighter solid line is used.
- Sketches are acceptable for the application process, but formal drawings will have to be created if accepted.

Photocopies are accepted since three copies of each drawing must be submitted. The drawings will not be returned so it is *not* a good idea to send an original with the initial patent application.

While the above gives you a basic idea of the standards for patent drawings, the strict requirements of the U.S. Patent Office are carefully documented on their Web site. Be sure to follow their requirements exactly if you are preparing drawings for a patent application.

For more information, log on to the U.S. Patent and Trademark Office's Web site at http://www.uspto.gov.

You can also consult the Guide for Patent Draftsmen, which can be obtained from the Superintendent of Documents, U.S. Government Printing Office, Washington, D.C. 20402.

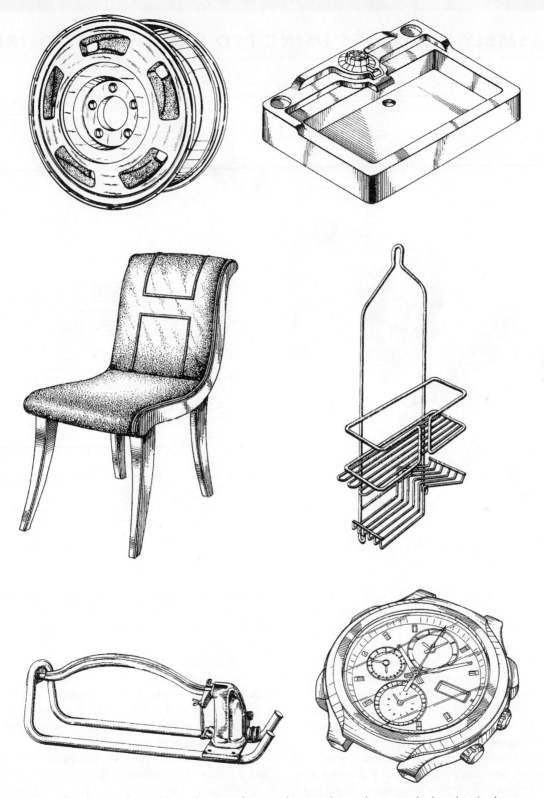

12.27 Patent Drawing Examples *Although several examples are shown here, each drawing is shown on a separate sheet in the patent application. Courtesy of US. Patent and Trademark Office.*

ASSEMBLY DRAWINGS USING PRO ENGINEER WILDFIRE

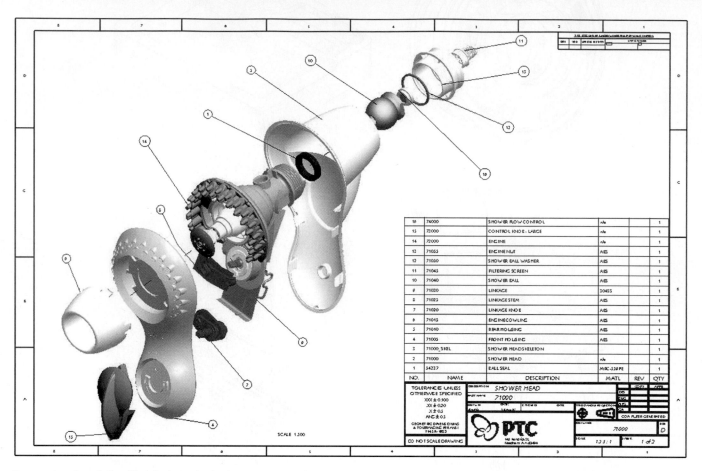

NO.		NAME	DESCRIPTION	MATL	REV	QTY
16	74000		SHOWER FLOW CONTROL	n/a		1
15	73000		CONTROL KNOB - LARGE	n/a		1
14	72000		ENGINE	n/a		1
13	71055		ENGINE NUT	ABS		1
12	71050		SHOWER BALL WASHER	ABS		1
11	71045		FILTERING SCREEN	ABS		1
10	71040		SHOWER BALL	ABS		1
9	71030		LINKAGE	304SS		1
8	71025		LINKAGE STEM	ABS		1
7	71020		LINKAGE KNOB	ABS		1
6	71015		ENGINE COWLING	ABS		1
5	71010		REAR HOLSING	ABS		1
4	71005		FRONT HOLSING	ABS		1
3	71000_SKEL		SHOWER HEAD SKELETON			1
2	71000		SHOWER HEAD	n/a		1
1	54237		BALL SEAL	MRC-330 PE		1

SCALE 1.500

SHOWER HEAD
PART NAME 71000

71000

Example of a Color Shaded Exploded View Assembly from Pro Engineer Wildfire. Courtesy of Parametric Technologies Corporation.

Great looking assembly drawings are only one of the benefits of using 3D CAD for your designs. You can also check to see how parts fit together, perform tolerance studies, and even see how mechanisms you are designing will behave. Additionally, you can analyze the mass properties of your design, determine the volume and surface area of complicated shapes, and produce documentation drawings directly from the part models.

Software like Pro/Engineer Wildfire 3 allows you to use color shaded views of models in the exploded view assembly drawing, as shown in the figure above.

As you decide whether to use a color shaded drawing or a black and white line drawing for an assembly drawing, consider whether and how the drawing will be reproduced. Shaded color views make it easy to identify and visualize the parts, but require color printing and copying to look their best on paper. This doesn't present a problem if you are distributing files electronically.

Even though color shaded drawings look great, there are times when black and white drawings are preferable, or required. For example, patent drawings must be black and white, showing visible lines and not hidden lines. Black and white drawings are also helpful in user manuals, which may be copied or printed in black and white.

With 3D CAD software, it is not difficult to switch between color shaded views, outlines, and views that show hidden lines, to suit the particular need that the drawing will meet.

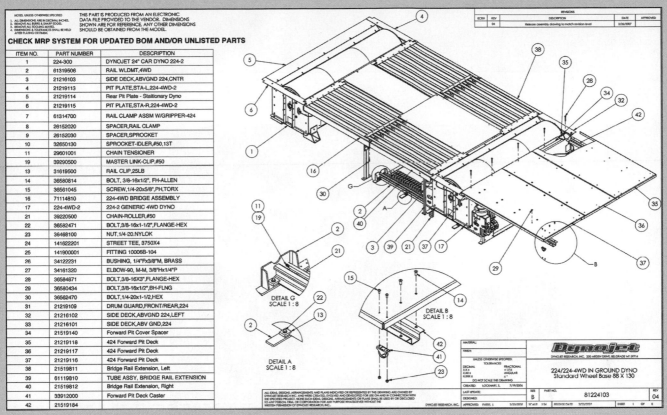

CHECK MRP SYSTEM FOR UPDATED BOM AND/OR UNLISTED PARTS

ITEM NO.	PART NUMBER	DESCRIPTION
1	224-300	DYNOJET 24" CAR DYNO 224-2
2	61319506	RAIL WLDMT,4WD
3	21216103	SIDE DECK,ABVGND 224,CNTR
4	21219113	PIT PLATE,STA-L,224-4WD-2
5	21219114	Rear Pit Plate - Stationary Dyno
6	21219115	PIT PLATE,STA-R,224-4WD-2
7	61314700	RAIL CLAMP ASSM W/GRIPPER-424
8	26152020	SPACER,RAIL CLAMP
9	26152030	SPACER,SPROCKET
10	32850130	SPROCKET-IDLER,#50,13T
11	29601001	CHAIN TENSIONER
19	39290500	MASTER LINK-CLIP,#50
13	31619500	RAIL CLIP,25LB
14	36580814	BOLT, 3/8-16x1/2", FH-ALLEN
15	36561045	SCREW,1/4-20x5/8",PH,TORX
16	71114810	224-4WD BRIDGE ASSEMBLY
17	224-4WD-2	224-2 GENERIC 4WD DYNO
21	39220500	CHAIN-ROLLER,#50
22	36582471	BOLT,3/8-16x1-1/2",FLANGE-HEX
23	36468100	NUT,1/4-20,NYLOK
24	141622201	STREET TEE, 3750X4
25	141900001	FITTING 10006B-104
26	34122231	BUSHING, 1/4"Fx3/8"M, BRASS
27	34161320	ELBOW-90, M-M, 3/8"Hx1/4"P
28	36584671	BOLT,3/8-16X3",FLANGE-HEX
29	36580434	BOLT,3/8-16x1/2",BH-FLNG
30	36562470	BOLT,1/4-20x1-1/2,HEX
31	21219109	DRUM GUARD,FRONT/REAR,224
32	21216102	SIDE DECK,ABVGND 224,LEFT
33	21216101	SIDE DECK,ABV GND,224
34	21519140	Forward Pit Cover Spacer
35	21219118	424 Forward Pit Deck
36	21219117	424 Forward Pit Deck
37	21219116	424 Forward Pit Deck
38	21519811	Bridge Rail Extension, Left
39	61119810	TUBE ASSY, BRIDGE RAIL EXTENSION
40	21519812	Bridge Rail Extension, Right
41	33912000	Forward Pit Deck Caster
42	21519184	

Assembly Drawing for Four Wheel Drive Pit Dyno. *Courtesy of Dynojet Research, Inc.*

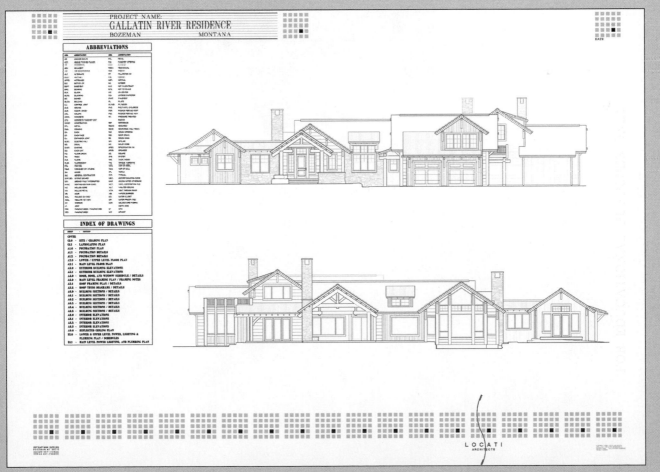

This Cover for a Set of Architectural Plans Lists the Drawings in the Set and Abbreviations Used. *Courtesy of Locati Architects.*

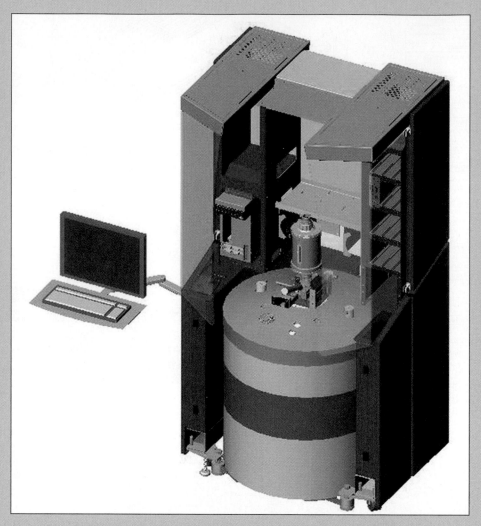

Fully Assembled 3D CAD Model Showing How Parts Fit in Assembly.
Courtesy of Quantum Design.

KEY WORDS

Top Down

Bottom Up

Middle Out

Constraint Based Modeling

Parent Part

Mating Parts

Subassembly

Assembly Layout

Skeleton

Working Drawings

Assembly Drawings

Exploded View

Piece Part Drawings

Part Drawings

Detail Drawings

Balloon Numbers

Ball Tags

Parts List

Bill of Materials

Poche

Working Drawing Assembly

Installation Assembly

Check Assembly

Revision Number

CHAPTER SUMMARY

- The design team moves through five stages during the design process. Each stage helps the team refine the design until it meets all product requirements.
- The final drawings created during the design process include assembly drawings, working drawings, design drawings, and patent drawings.
- There are many revisions to drawings during the design process. The drafter must keep track of each version and what changes were made.
- Models are an important way of testing the way parts are assembled. Both scale models created in a model shop and computer-generated virtual reality models are used by the design team to test their design.
- During the design process, all members of the team must understand their specific roles and how they relate and interact with the rest of the team. Effective teamwork is an essential part of the design process.

REVIEW QUESTIONS

1. What are the special requirements of a patent drawing?
2. What kinds of information are included in an assembly drawing?
3. How is a detail drawing different from an assembly drawing?
4. Why are drawings numbered? Why is this numbering so important?
5. Describe the drawing revision process. Why is it so important to keep track of revisions?
6. How are revised paper drawings stored? How are revised CAD drawings stored?
7. What are the advantages of computer modeling? What are the disadvantages?

DESIGN AND WORKING DRAWING EXERCISES

Design Exercises

The following suggestions for project assignments are of a general and very broad nature, and it is expected that they will help generate many ideas for specific design projects. Much design work is undertaken to improve an existing product or system by utilization of new materials, new techniques, or new systems or procedures. In addition to the design of the product itself, another large amount of design work is essential for the tooling, production, and handling of the product. You are encouraged to discuss with your instructor any ideas you may have for a project.

Each solution to a design problem, whether prepared by an individual student or formulated by a group, should be in the form of a report, which should be typed or carefully lettered, assembled, and bound. It is suggested that the report contain the following (or variations of the following, as specified by your instructor).

1. A title sheet. The title of the design project should be placed in approximately the center of the sheet, and your name or the names of those in the group in the lower right-hand corner. The symbol PL should follow the name of the project leader.
2. Table of contents with page numbers.
3. Statement of the purpose of the project with appropriate comments.
4. Preliminary design sketches, with comments on advantages and disadvantages of each, leading to the final selection of the best solution. All work should be signed and dated.
5. An accurately made pictorial and/or assembly drawing(s), using traditional drawing methods or CAD as assigned, if more than one part is involved in the design.

6. Detail working drawings, freehand, mechanical, or CAD-produced as assigned. The 8.5 ×11" sheet size is preferred for convenient insertion in the report. Larger sizes may be bound in the report with appropriate folding.
7. A bibliography or credit for important sources of information, if applicable.

Exercise 12.1 Design new or improved playground, recreational, or sporting equipment. For example, a new child's toy could be both recreational and educational. Create an assembly drawing.

Exercise 12.2 Design new or improved health equipment. For example, physically handicapped people need special equipment.

Exercise 12.3 Design a cup holder attachment to retrofit cars. It must accommodate a range of cup sizes from 8 oz to 64 oz size.

Exercise 12.4 Design a guitar stand to support either an acoustic or electric guitar. It should be convenient and stable, suitable for use on stage. Allow for quick change of guitars by the musician.

Exercise 12.5 Break up into design teams. See how many different ideas each team can come up with for a new layout of your classroom. Time limit is 20 minutes.

Exercise 12.6 Design a new or improved bike safety lock and chain. Integrate the locking devices into the bike's frame, if possible. Create an assembly drawing showing the features of your design.

Working Drawing Exercises

The problems in Exercises 12.7–12.62 are presented to give you practice in making the type of regular working drawings used in industry. Many exercises, especially assemblies, offer an opportunity to exercise your ability to redesign or improve on the existing design. Due to the variations in sizes and in scales that may be used, you are required to select the sheet sizes and scales, when these are not specified, subject to the approval of the instructor. Standard sheet layouts are shown inside the front cover of this book. (Any of the title blocks shown inside the back cover of this book may be used, with modification if desired, or you may design the title block if assigned by the instructor.)

The statements for each problem are intentionally brief and your instructor may vary the requirements. Use the preferred metric system or the acceptable complete decimal inch system, as assigned.

In problems presented in pictorial form, the dimensions and finish marks are to provide you the information necessary to make the orthographic drawing or solid model. The dimensions given are in most cases those needed to make the parts, but due to the limitations of pictorial drawings they are not in all cases the dimensions that should be shown on the working drawing. In the pictorial problems, the rough and finished surfaces are shown, but finish marks are usually omitted. You should add all necessary finish marks and place all dimensions in the preferred places in the final drawings.

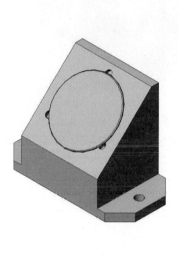

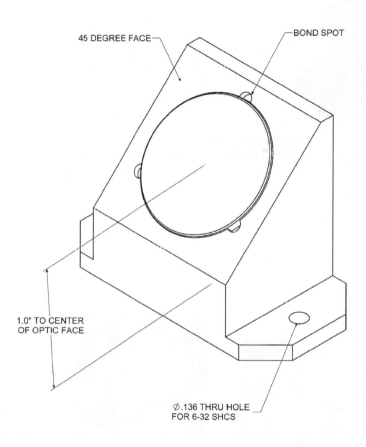

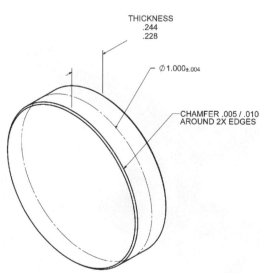

Exercise 12.7 Create part drawings and an assembly for the lens and mount. Maintain the critical distances and precise 45° angle for the lens.

Exercise 12.8 Create an exploded assembly drawing for the gyroscope. Create detail drawings for the parts as assigned by your instructor. Dimensioned parts are shown on the facing page.

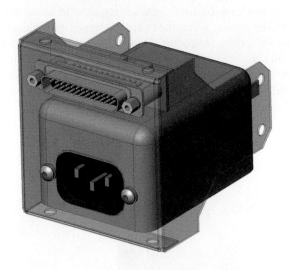

Exercise 12.9 Design the sheet metal housing for the power and D-sub connectors shown. Download stock models for standard parts. Create the flat patterns for the sheet metal if assigned by your instructor.

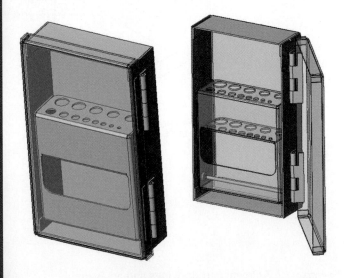

Exercise 12.10 Design a sheet metal drill bit case. Create detailed part and assembly drawings. Develop the flat patterns if assigned. Use "relations" in your model so that you can change the sizes for the holes and overall height, width and depth for the case and automatically update your design to different configurations.

Exercise 12.11 Create an exploded assembly drawing for the clamp. Dimensioned parts are shown on page 442.

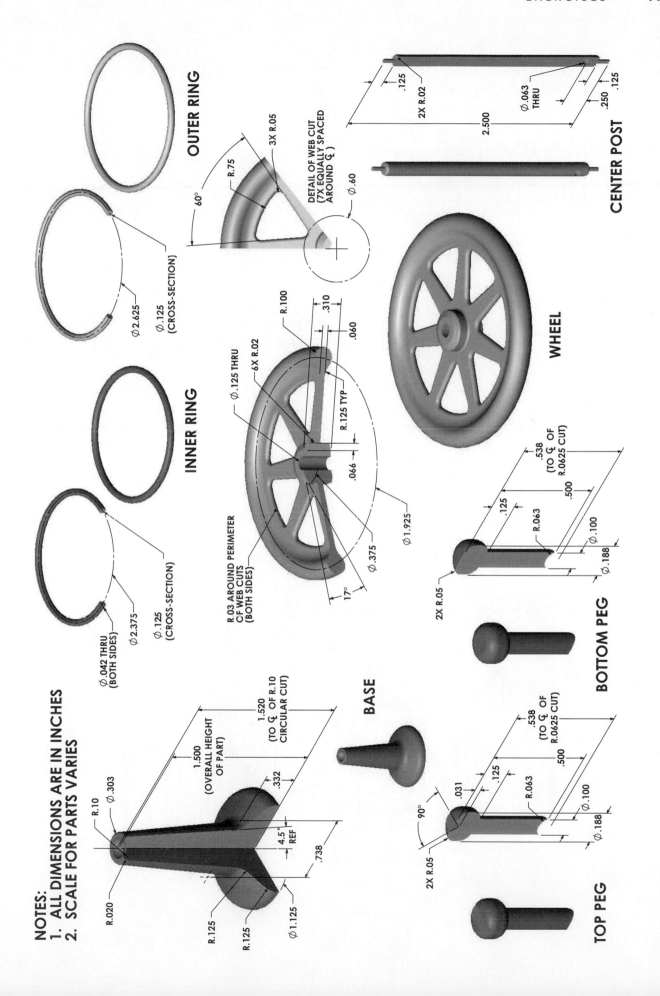

NOTES:
1. ALL DIMENSIONS ARE IN INCHES
2. SCALE FOR PARTS VARIES

OUTER RING

∅ 2.625

∅ .125
(CROSS-SECTION)

60°

R.75

3X R.05

DETAIL OF WEB CUT
(7X EQUALLY SPACED
AROUND ₵)

∅ .60

CENTER POST

.125

2X R.02

∅ .063
THRU

.125

.250

2.500

INNER RING

∅ 2.375

∅ .125
(CROSS-SECTION)

∅ .042 THRU
(BOTH SIDES)

WHEEL

R.100

.310

.060

6X R.02

∅ .125 THRU

R.125 TYP

.066

R.03 AROUND PERIMETER
OF WEB CUTS
(BOTH SIDES)

∅ .375

∅ 1.925

17°

BOTTOM PEG

.538
(TO ₵ OF
R.0625 CUT)

.500

.125

R.063

∅ .100

∅ .188

2X R.05

BASE

1.520
(TO ₵ OF R.10
CIRCULAR CUT)

1.500
(OVERALL HEIGHT
OF PART)

∅ .303

R.10

.332

4.5°
REF

.738

R.020

R.125

R.125

∅ 1.125

TOP PEG

.538
(TO ₵ OF
R.0625 CUT)

.500

.125

.031

90°

R.063

∅ .100

∅ .188

2X R.05

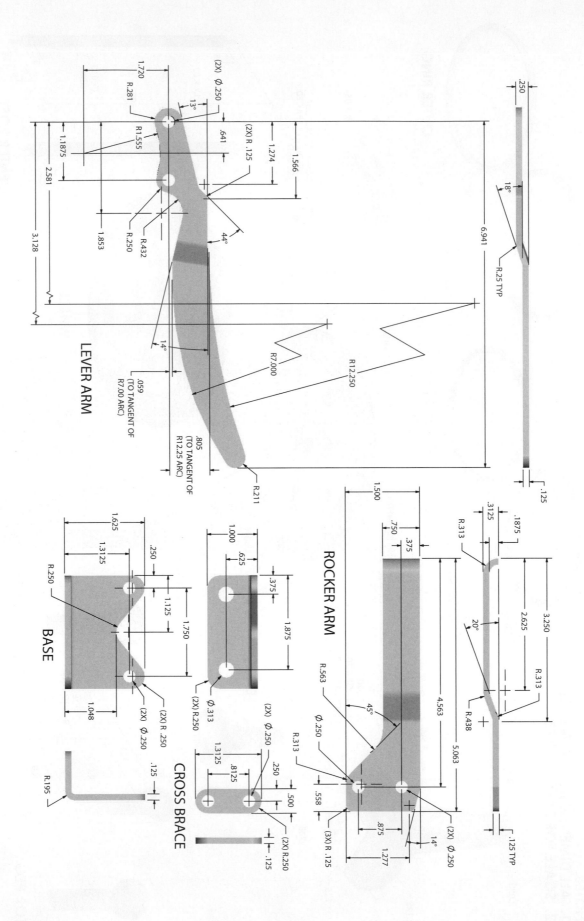

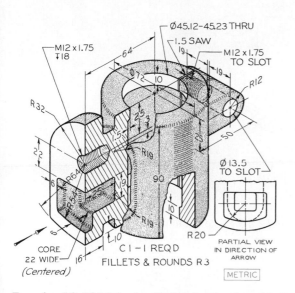

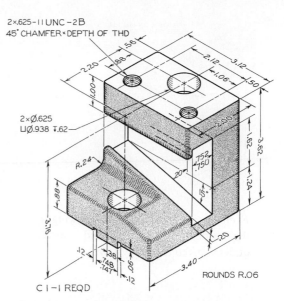

Exercise 12.12 Make detail drawing for the table bracket.

Exercise 12.13 Make detail drawing for the RH tool post. If assigned, convert dimensions to metric system.

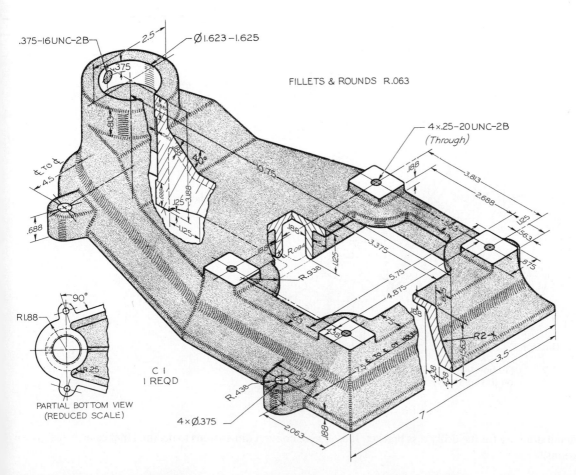

Exercise 12.14 Make detail drawing for the drill press base. Use unidirectional metric or decimal-inch dimensions.

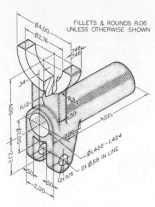

FILLETS & ROUNDS R.06
UNLESS OTHERWISE SHOWN

Exercise 12.15 Make detail drawing for the shifter fork. If assigned, convert dimensions to metric system.

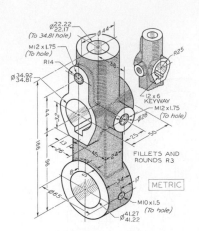

METRIC

FILLETS AND ROUNDS R3

Exercise 12.16 Make detail drawing for the idler arm.

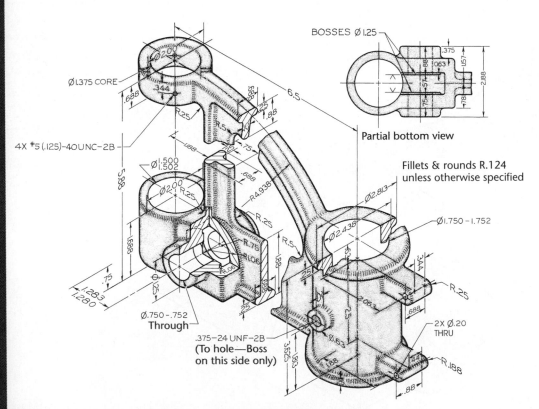

BOSSES Ø 1.25

Partial bottom view

Fillets & rounds R.124 unless otherwise specified

Exercise 12.17 Make detail drawing for the drill press bracket. If assigned, convert dimensions to decimal inches or redesign the part with metric dimensions.

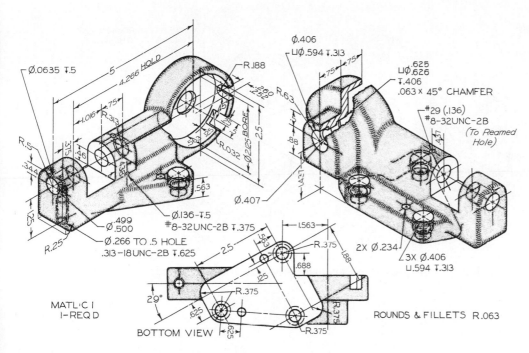

Exercise 12.18 Make detail drawing for the dial holder. If assigned, convert dimensions to decimal inches or redesign the part with metric dimensions.

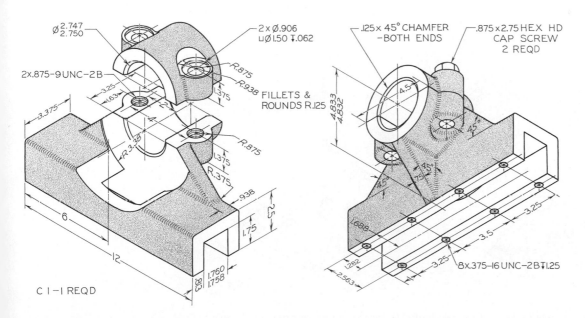

Exercise 12.19 Make detail drawings half size for the rack slide. If assigned, convert dimensions to decimal inches or redesign the part with metric dimensions.

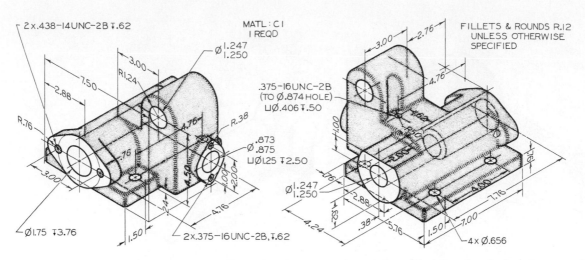

Exercise 12.20 Make detail drawing half size for the automatic stop box. If assigned, redesign the part with metric dimensions.

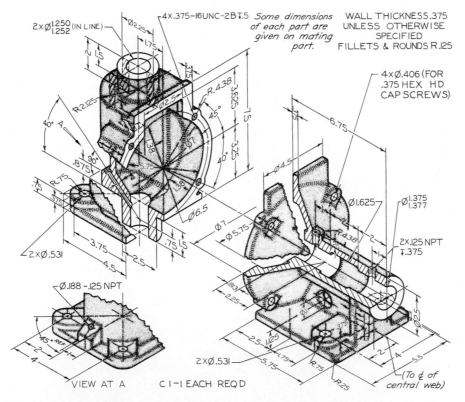

Exercise 12.21 Make detail drawings half size for the conveyer housing. If assigned, convert dimensions to decimal inches or redesign the parts with metric dimensions.

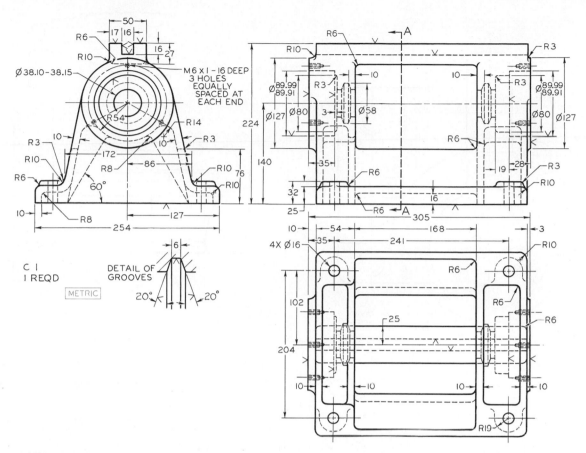

Exercise 12.22 For the spindle housing, draw as follows. Given: Front, left-side, and bottom views, and partial removed section. Required: Front view in full section, top view, and right-side view in half section on A-A. Draw half size. If assigned, dimension fully.

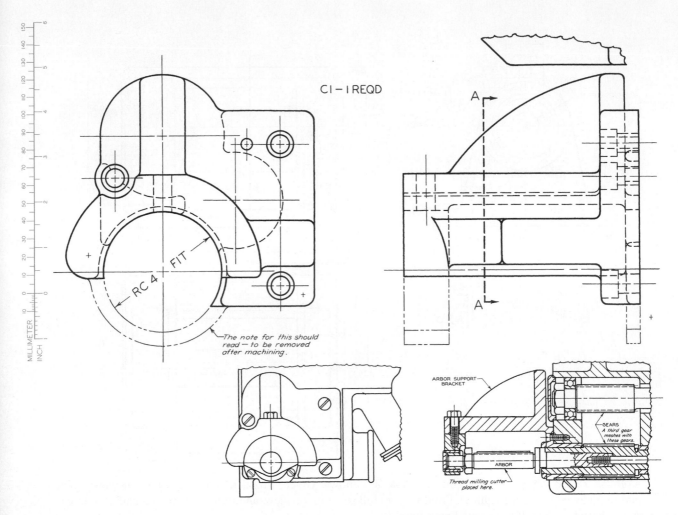

C1 – 1 REQD

A

A

ARBOR SUPPORT
BRACKET

GEARS
A third gear
meshes with
these gears.

ARBOR

Thread milling cutter
placed here.

The note for this should
read – to be removed
after machining.

RC 4 FIT

MILLIMETER
INCH

Exercise 12.23 For the arbor support bracket, draw the following. Given: Front and right-side views. Required: Front, left-side, and bottom views, and a detail section A-A. Use American National Standard tables for indicated fits and if required convert to metric values (see Appendixes 7–16). If assigned, dimension in the metric or decimal inch system.

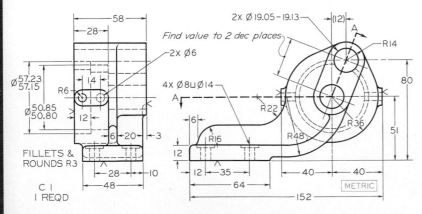

58
28
2X Ø 19.05 – 19.13
(12)
A
Find value to 2 dec places
R14
2X Ø6
Ø 57.23/57.15
14
R6
4X Ø8⊔Ø14
A
80
Ø 50.85/50.80
12
R22
6
R36
R16
6 20 3
R48
51
FILLETS &
ROUNDS R3
12
R16
C 1
1 REQD
28 10
12 35
40 40
48
64
METRIC
152

Exercise 12.24 For the pump bracket for a thread milling machine, draw the following. Given: Front and left-side views. Required: Front and right-side views, and top view in section on A-A. Draw full size. If assigned, dimension fully.

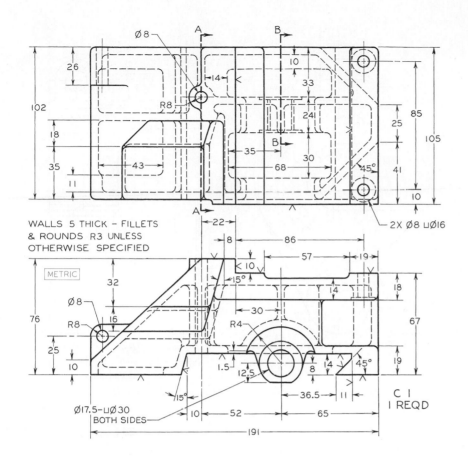

WALLS 5 THICK – FILLETS
& ROUNDS R3 UNLESS
OTHERWISE SPECIFIED

METRIC

C I
I REQD

Exercise 12.25 For the support base for planer, draw the following. Given: Front and top views. Required: Front and top views, left-side view in full section A-A, and removed section B-B. Draw full size. If assigned, dimension fully.

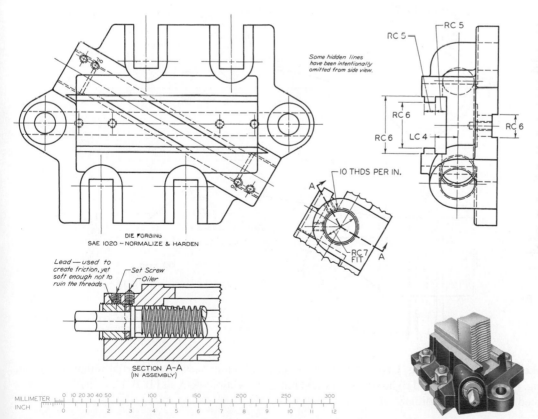

Some hidden lines have been intentionally omitted from side view.

DIE FORGING
SAE 1020 – NORMALIZE & HARDEN

Lead — used to create friction, yet soft enough not to ruin the threads

Set Screw
Oiler

SECTION A-A
(IN ASSEMBLY)

10 THDS PER IN.

RC 7 FIT

RC 5

RC 5

RC 6

RC 6

LC 4

RC 6

Exercise 12.26 For the jaw base for chuck jaw, draw the following. Given: Top, right-side, and partial auxiliary views. Required: Top, left-side (beside top), front, and partial auxiliary views complete with dimensions, if assigned. Use metric or decimal inch dimensions. Use American National Standard tables for indicated fits or convert for metric values. See Appendixes 5–14.

MILLIMETER   0 10 20 30 40 50   100   150   200   250   300
INCH   0   1   2   3   4   5   6   7   8   9   10   11   12

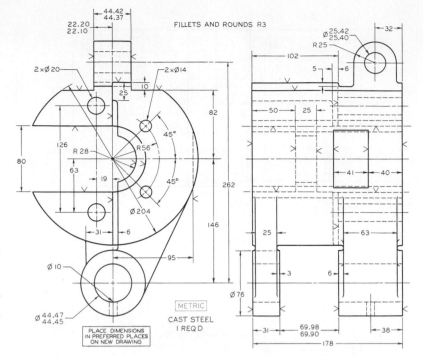

Exercise 12.27 For the fixture base for 60-ton vertical press, draw the following. Given: Front and right-side views. Required: Revolve front view 90° clockwise; then add top and left-side views. Draw half size. If assigned, complete with dimensions.

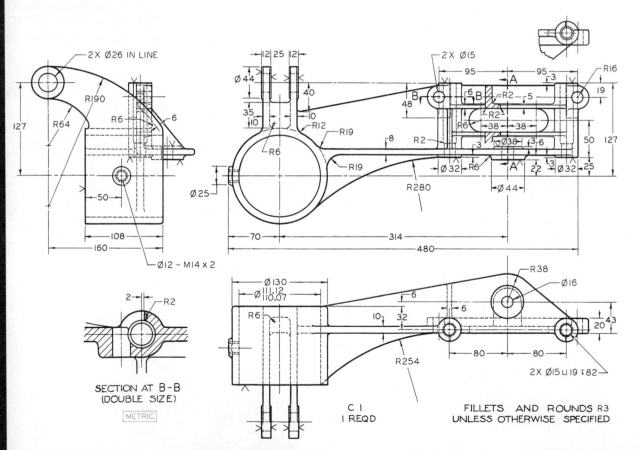

Exercise 12.28 For the bracket, draw the following. Given: Front, left-side, and bottom views, and partial removed section. Required: Make detail drawing. Draw front, top, and right-side views, and removed sections A-A and B-B. Draw half size. Draw section B-B full size. If assigned, complete with dimensions.

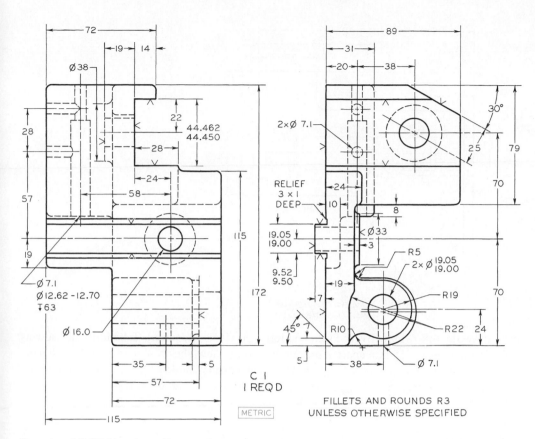

Exercise 12.29 For the roller rest bracket for automatic screw machine, draw the following. Given: Front and left-side views. Required: Revolve front view 90° clockwise; then add top and left-side views. Draw half size. If assigned, complete with dimensions.

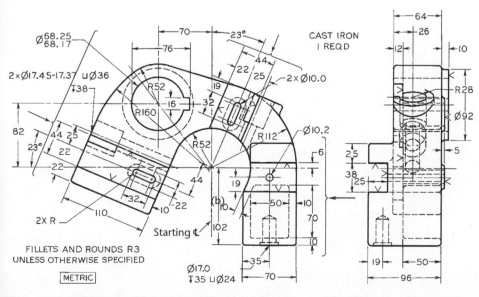

Exercise 12.30 For the guide bracket for gear shaper, draw the following. Given: Front and right-side views. Required: Front view, a partial right-side view, and two partial auxiliary views taken in direction of arrows. Draw half size. If assigned, complete with unidirectional dimensions.

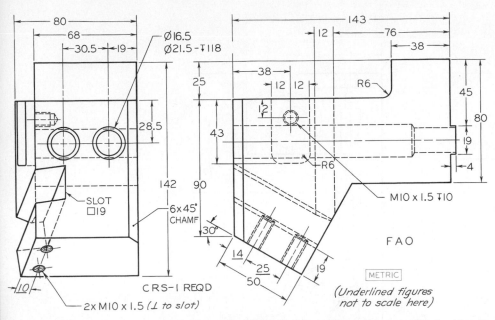

Exercise 12.31 For the rear tool post, draw the following. Given: Front and left-side views. Required: Take left-side view as new top view; add front and left-side views, approx. 215 mm apart, a primary auxiliary view, then a secondary view taken so as to show true end view of 19 mm slot. Complete all views, except show only necessary hidden lines in auxiliary views. Draw full size. If assigned, complete with dimensions.

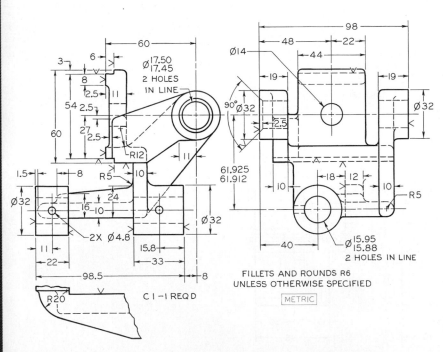

Exercise 12.32 For the bearing for a worm gear, draw the following. Given: Front and right-side views. Required: Front, top, and left-side views. Draw full size. If assigned, complete with dimensions.

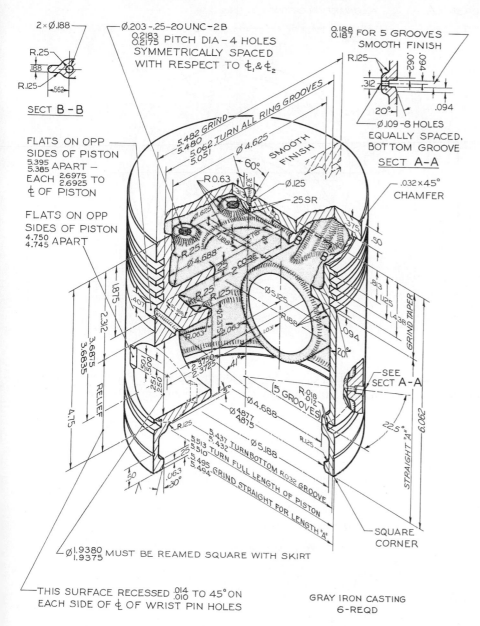

SECT B-B

Ø.203-.25-20UNC-2B
0.2183 PITCH DIA - 4 HOLES
0.2175 SYMMETRICALLY SPACED
WITH RESPECT TO ₵₁ & ₵₂

2 × Ø.188

R.25
.188
R.125 .562

0.188 FOR 5 GROOVES
0.187 SMOOTH FINISH

R.125
.312
.260
.060
20°
.094

Ø.109 -8 HOLES
EQUALLY SPACED,
BOTTOM GROOVE
SECT A-A

FLATS ON OPP
SIDES OF PISTON
5.395 APART—
5.385
EACH 2.6975 TO
2.6925
₵ OF PISTON

FLATS ON OPP
SIDES OF PISTON
4.750 APART
4.745

5.482 GRIND
5.480 5.062 TURN ALL RING GROOVES
5.051

Ø4.625

SMOOTH FINISH

60°

R0.63

Ø.125

.25SR

.032×45°
CHAMFER

.50

.813
1.125
1.438 GRIND TAPER

Ø.625
R.25
Ø4.688
.25
2 CORE
R.25
R.125
Ø5.125
R.188
R.063
2.063
.031
.094
20°

.375

1.875
2.312
3.6875
3.6835
RELIEF
4.75
.501
.500
.251
.250

2.3750
2.3725

4°
5°

SEE
SECT A-A

R.018
R.012
5 GROOVES

Ø4.688

Ø4.877
Ø4.875

Ø5.188

R.125

R.125

R.032 GROOVE
5.437 TURNBOTTOM
5.432
5.513 TURN FULL LENGTH OF PISTON
5.510
.25
5.495 GRIND STRAIGHT FOR LENGTH "A"
5.494

.50
.063
30°

STRAIGHT "A"
22.5°
6.062

SQUARE
CORNER

Ø1.9380 MUST BE REAMED SQUARE WITH SKIRT
1.9375

THIS SURFACE RECESSED .014 TO 45° ON
.010
EACH SIDE OF ₵ OF WRIST PIN HOLES

GRAY IRON CASTING
6-REQD

Exercise 12.33 For the caterpillar tractor piston, draw the following. Make detail drawing full size. If assigned, use unidirectional decimal inch system, converting all fractions to two place decimal dimensions, or convert all dimensions to metric.

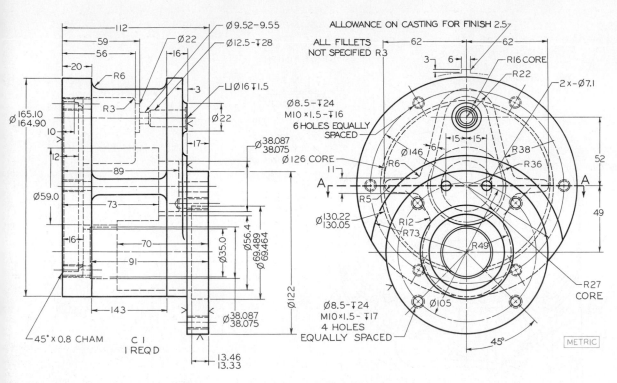

Exercise 12.34 For the generator drive housing, draw the following. Given: Front and left-side views. Required: Front view, right-side view in full section, and top view in full section on A-A. Draw full size. If assigned, complete with dimensions.

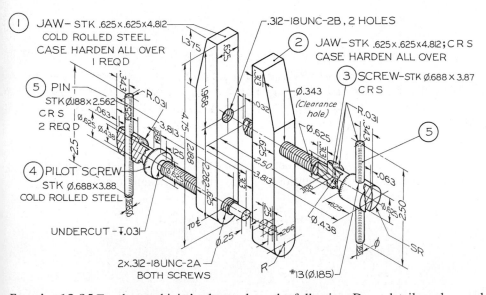

Exercise 12.35 For the machinist's clamp, draw the following. Draw details and assembly. If assigned, use unidirectional two place decimal inch dimensions or redesign for metric dimensions.

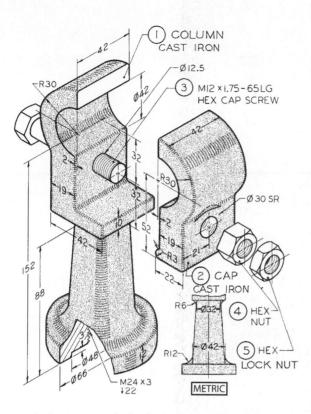

Exercise 12.36 For the hand rail column, draw the following. (1) Draw details. If assigned, complete with dimensions. (2) Draw assembly.

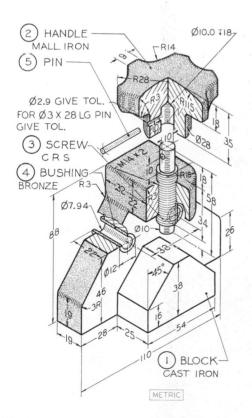

Exercise 12.37 For the drill jig, draw the following. (1) Draw details. If assigned, complete with dimensions. (2) Draw assembly.

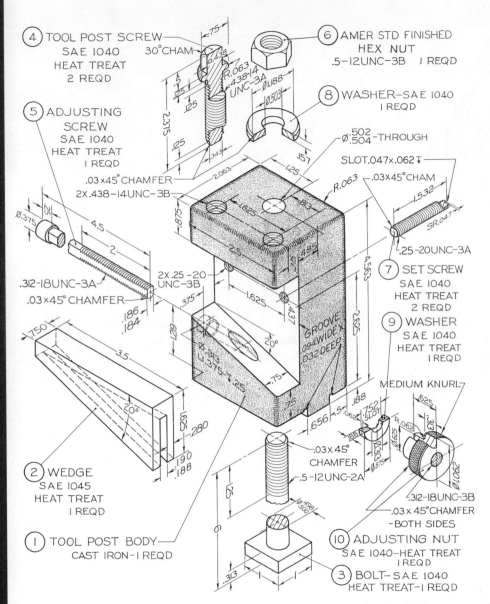

Exercise 12.38 For the tool post, draw the following. (1) Draw details. (2) Draw assembly. If assigned, use unidirectional two place decimals for all fractional dimensions or redesign for all metric dimensions.

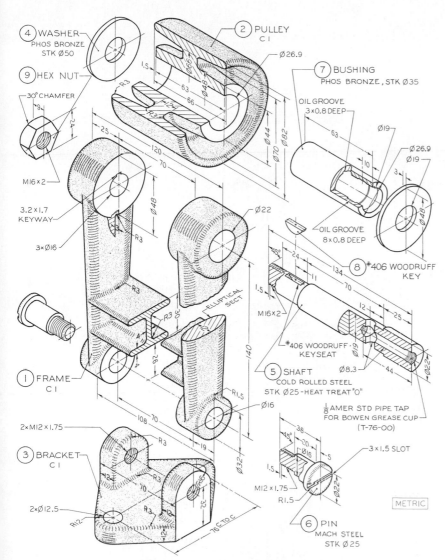

Exercise 12.39 For the belt tightener, draw the following. (1) Draw details. (2) Draw assembly. It is assumed that the parts are to be made in quantity and they are to be dimensioned for interchangeability on the detail drawings. Use tables in Appendixes 11–14 for limit values. Design as follows. (a) Bushing fit in pulley: locational interference fit. (b) Shaft fit in bushing: free running fit. (c) Shaft fits in frame: sliding fit. (d) Pin fit in frame: free running fit. (e) Pulley hub length plus washers fit in frame: allowance 0.13 and tolerances 0.10. (f) Make bushing 0.25 mm shorter than pulley hub. (g) Bracket fit in frame: Same as (e).

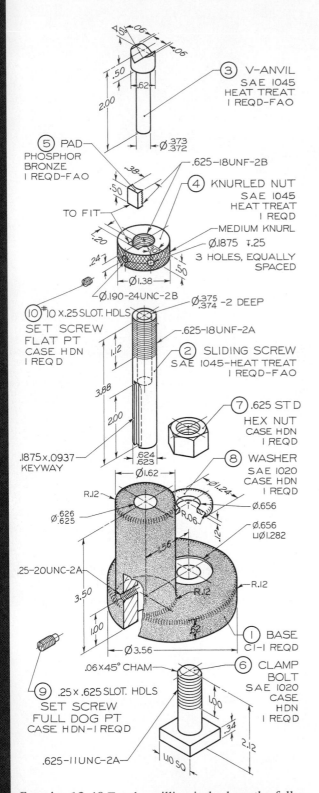

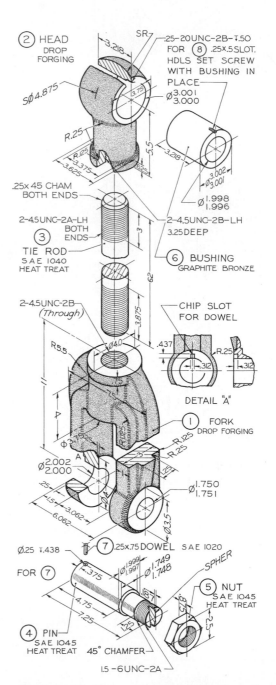

Exercise 12.40 For the milling jack, draw the following. (1) Draw details. (2) Draw assembly. If assigned, convert dimensions to metric or decimal inch system.

Exercise 12.41 For the connecting bar, draw the following. (1) Draw details. (2) Draw assembly. If assigned, convert dimensions to metric or decimal inch system.

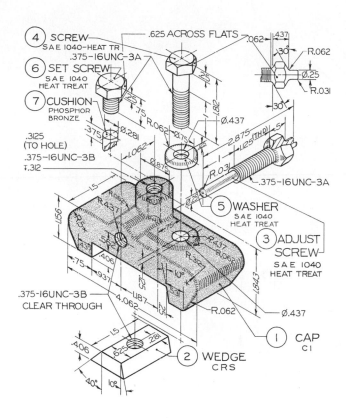

④ SCREW
SAE 1040-HEAT TR
.375-16UNC-3A

⑥ SET SCREW
SAE 1040
HEAT TREAT

⑦ CUSHION
PHOSPHOR
BRONZE

.625 ACROSS FLATS

.062 .437
30 R.062
.25
∅.25
R.031
.182
∅.437
30

.3125
(TO HOLE)
.375-16UNC-3B
⊤.312

.375
∅.281
R.062 ∅.75
.75
.25
.25
1.062
∅.875

2.875 (THD)
1.125 (THD) .5
R.031
∅.25
.375-16UNC-3A

.375-16UNC-3B
CLEAR THROUGH

1.5
R.406
L.156
R.5
R.437
R.437
R.062
R.312
10°
.75 .937 .406
1.187
.125
1.843

4.062

R.062
∅.437

⑤ WASHER
SAE 1040
HEAT TREAT

③ ADJUST
SCREW
SAE 1040
HEAT TREAT

① CAP
C1

1.5
.406
.625 .28
② WEDGE
CRS
40° 10°

Exercise 12.42 For the clamp stop, draw the following. (1) Draw details. (2) Draw assembly. If assigned, convert dimensions to decimal inch system or redesign for metric dimensions.

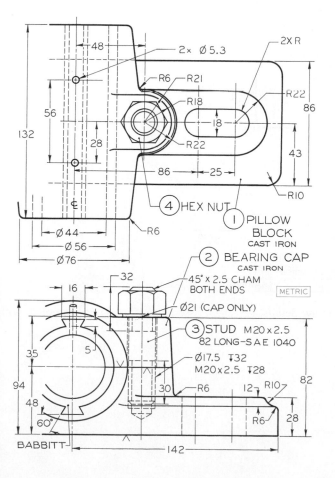

48
2× ∅ 5.3
2X R
R6 R21
R18
R22
56
R22
86
132
28
18
R22
86 25
43
∅ 44
R6
∅ 56
∅ 76
R10

④ HEX NUT
① PILLOW
BLOCK
CAST IRON

② BEARING CAP
CAST IRON

45° × 2.5 CHAM
BOTH ENDS METRIC
∅21 (CAP ONLY)

32
16
35
5
94
48
60°

③ STUD M20 × 2.5
82 LONG-SAE 1040

∅17.5 ⊤32
M20×2.5 ⊤28

30 R6 12 R10
82
R6 28

BABBITT 142

Exercise 12.43 For the pillow block bearing, draw the following. (1) Draw details. (2) Draw assembly. If assigned, complete with dimensions.

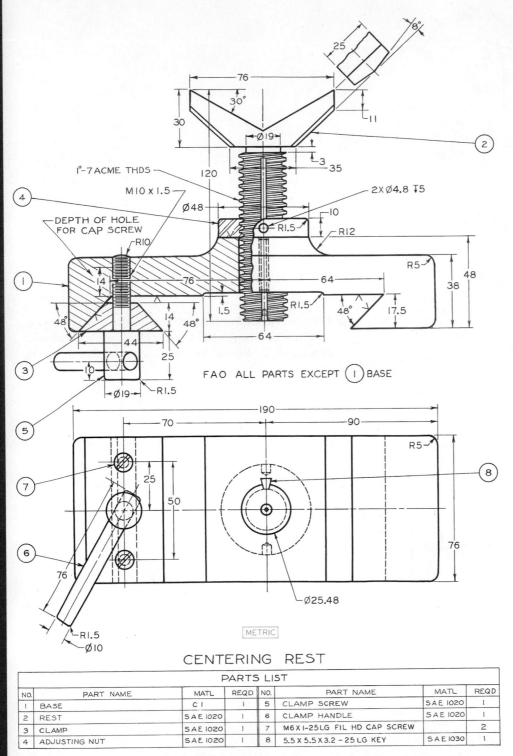

FAO ALL PARTS EXCEPT ①BASE

METRIC

CENTERING REST

NO.	PART NAME	MATL	REQD	NO.	PART NAME	MATL	REQD
			PARTS LIST				
1	BASE	C I	1	5	CLAMP SCREW	S.A.E. 1020	1
2	REST	S.A.E. 1020	1	6	CLAMP HANDLE	S.A.E. 1020	1
3	CLAMP	S.A.E. 1020	1	7	M6 X 1-25 LG FIL HD CAP SCREW		2
4	ADJUSTING NUT	S.A.E. 1020	1	8	5.5 X 5.5 X 3.2 - 25 LG KEY	S.A.E. 1030	1

Exercise 12.44 For the centering rest, draw the following. (1) Draw details. (2) Draw assembly. If assigned, complete with dimensions.

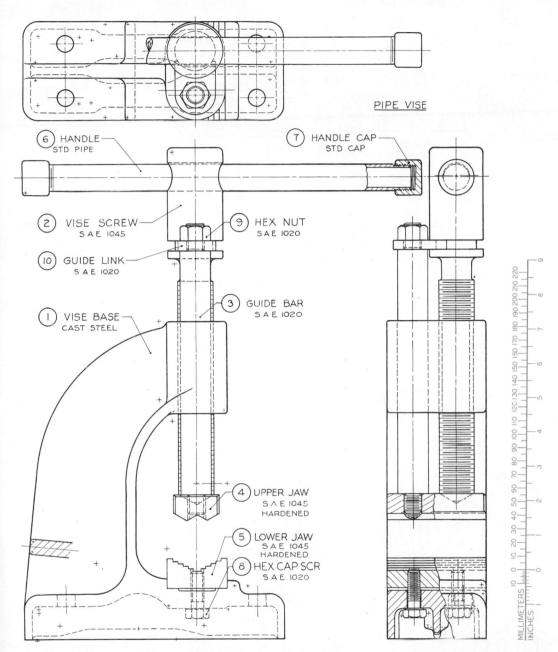

PIPE VISE

(6) HANDLE
   STD PIPE

(7) HANDLE CAP
   STD CAP

(2) VISE SCREW
   S A E 1045

(9) HEX NUT
   S A E 1020

(10) GUIDE LINK
   S A E 1020

(1) VISE BASE
   CAST STEEL

(3) GUIDE BAR
   S A E 1020

(4) UPPER JAW
   S A E 1045
   HARDENED

(5) LOWER JAW
   S A E 1045
   HARDENED

(8) HEX CAP SCR
   S A E 1020

Exercise 12.45 For the pipe vise, draw the following. (1) Draw details. (2) Draw assembly. To obtain dimensions, take distances directly from figure with dividers; then set dividers on printed scale and read measurements in millimeters or decimal inches as assigned. All threads are general purpose metric threads (see Appendix 15) or unified coarse threads except the American National Standard pipe threads on handle and handle caps.

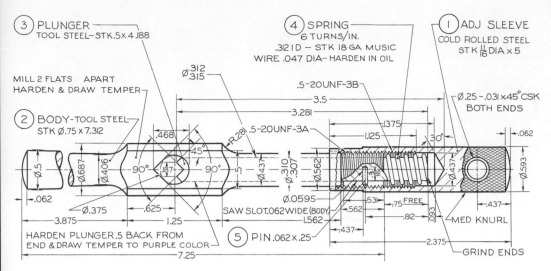

Exercise 12.46 For the tap wrench, draw the following. (1) Draw details. (2) Draw assembly. If assigned, use unidirectional two place decimals for all fractional dimensions or redesign for metric dimensions.

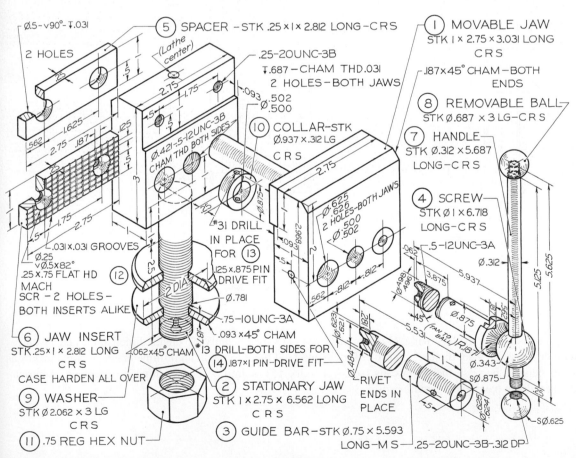

Exercise 12.47 For the machinist's vise, draw the following. (1) Draw details. (2) Draw assembly. If assigned, use unidirectional two place decimals for all fractional dimensions or redesign for metric dimensions.

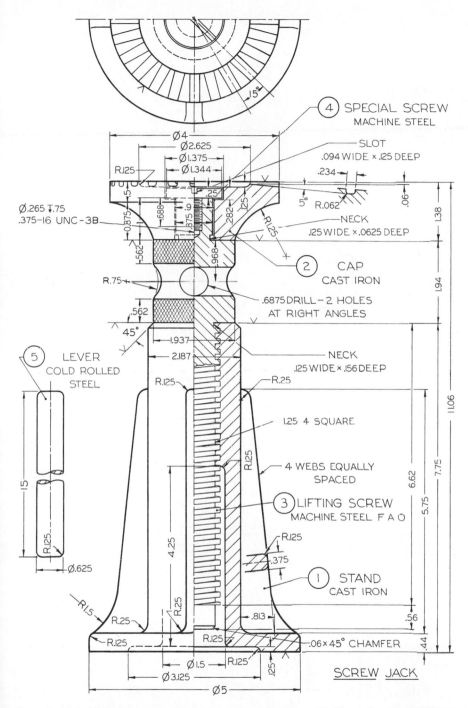

④ SPECIAL SCREW
MACHINE STEEL

Ø4
Ø2.625
Ø1.375
Ø1.344
R.125

SLOT
.094 WIDE × .25 DEEP

.234

Ø.265 ⊤.75
.375−16 UNC−3B

5° R.062

NECK
.125 WIDE × .0625 DEEP

② CAP
CAST IRON

R.75

.6875 DRILL−2 HOLES
AT RIGHT ANGLES

R.25

⑤ LEVER
COLD ROLLED
STEEL

NECK
.125 WIDE × .156 DEEP

R.125

1.937
2.187

R.25

1.25 4 SQUARE

4 WEBS EQUALLY
SPACED

.562

45°

15

③ LIFTING SCREW
MACHINE STEEL F A O

R.125

R.125

Ø.625

.375

① STAND
CAST IRON

R.1.5

R.25

R.125

.813

R.125

.06 × 45° CHAMFER

.56

.44

Ø1.5   R.125

Ø3.125

Ø5

SCREW JACK

Exercise 12.48 For the screw jack, draw the following. (1) Draw details. (2) Draw assembly. If assigned, convert dimensions to decimal inches or redesign for metric dimensions.

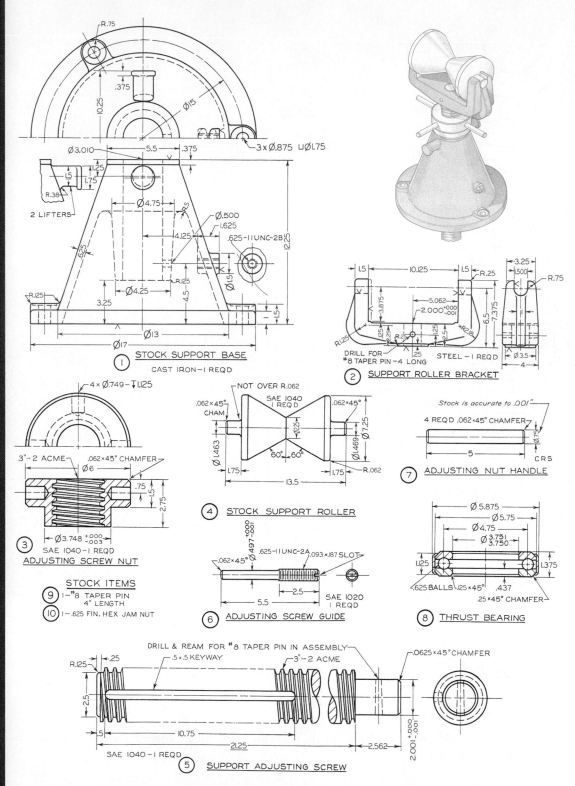

R.75

.375

10.25

Ø15

Ø3.010 — 5.5 — .375 — 3 × Ø.875 ⊔Ø1.75

1.25
1.5
1.75
R.38
2 LIFTERS

Ø4.75
R.5
Ø.500
1.625
.625—11UNC—2B
4.125
12.25
.625
R.125
Ø15
R.125
Ø4.25
4.5
3.25
1.5
R.125
Ø13
Ø17

STOCK SUPPORT BASE
① CAST IRON—1 REQD

1.5 — 10.125 — 1.5 — R.25   3.25
1.500   R.75
3.875
5.062
2.000 +.000 −.001
6.5 7.375
R.125 .25 .25
R.25 2.5 R2.8
DRILL FOR
#8 TAPER PIN—4 LONG   STEEL—1 REQD   Ø3.5
4
② **SUPPORT ROLLER BRACKET**

4 × Ø.749—⊤1.125

NOT OVER R.062
SAE 1040
1 REQD
.062×45° Ø1.25 .062×45°
CHAM
Ø1.463   Ø7.25
60° 60° Ø1.469
1.75 R.062 1.75
13.5
④ **STOCK SUPPORT ROLLER**

Stock is accurate to .001″
4 REQD .062×45° CHAMFER
.75
5
CRS
⑦ **ADJUSTING NUT HANDLE**

3″−2 ACME .062×45° CHAMFER
Ø6
.75
1.5
2.75
③ Ø3.748 +.000 −.003
SAE 1040—1 REQD
ADJUSTING SCREW NUT

Ø.497 +.000 −.001
.062×45° .625—11UNC—2A .093×.187 SLOT
2.5
SAE 1020
5.5   1 REQD
⑥ **ADJUSTING SCREW GUIDE**

Ø5.875
Ø5.75
Ø4.75
Ø3.751 3.750
1.125   1.375
.625 BALLS .25×45° .437
.25×45° CHAMFER
⑧ **THRUST BEARING**

STOCK ITEMS
⑨ 1—#8 TAPER PIN
4″ LENGTH
⑩ 1—.625 FIN. HEX JAM NUT

DRILL & REAM FOR #8 TAPER PIN IN ASSEMBLY
.5 × .5 KEYWAY   3″−2 ACME   .0625×45° CHAMFER
R.125 .25
2.5
.5
10.75
21.25   2.562
2.001 +.000 −.001
SAE 1040—1 REQD
⑤ **SUPPORT ADJUSTING SCREW**

Exercise 12.49 For the stock bracket for cold saw machine, draw the following. (1) Draw details. (2) Draw assembly. If assigned, use unidirectional decimal dimensions or redesign for metric dimensions.

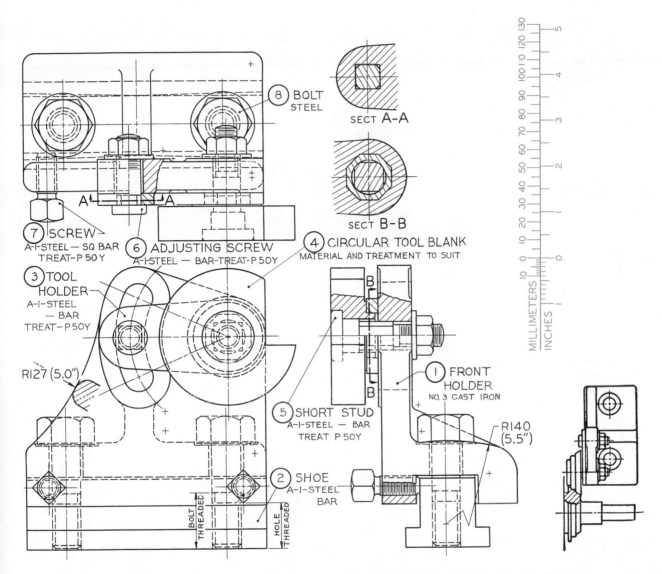

8 BOLT
STEEL

SECT A-A

SECT B-B

7 SCREW
A-I-STEEL — SQ BAR
TREAT-P 50 Y

6 ADJUSTING SCREW
A-I-STEEL — BAR-TREAT-P 50Y

4 CIRCULAR TOOL BLANK
MATERIAL AND TREATMENT TO SUIT

3 TOOL
HOLDER
A-I-STEEL
— BAR
TREAT- P 50 Y

R127 (5.0")

5 SHORT STUD
A-I-STEEL — BAR
TREAT P 50Y

1 FRONT
HOLDER
NO. 3 CAST IRON

R140
(5.5")

2 SHOE
A-I-STEEL
BAR

BOLT THREADED

HOLE THREADED

MILLIMETERS
INCHES

Exercise 12.50 For the front circular forming cutter holder, draw the following. (1) Draw details. (2) Draw assembly. To obtain dimensions, take distances directly from figure with dividers and set dividers on printed scale. Use metric or decimal inch dimensions as assigned.

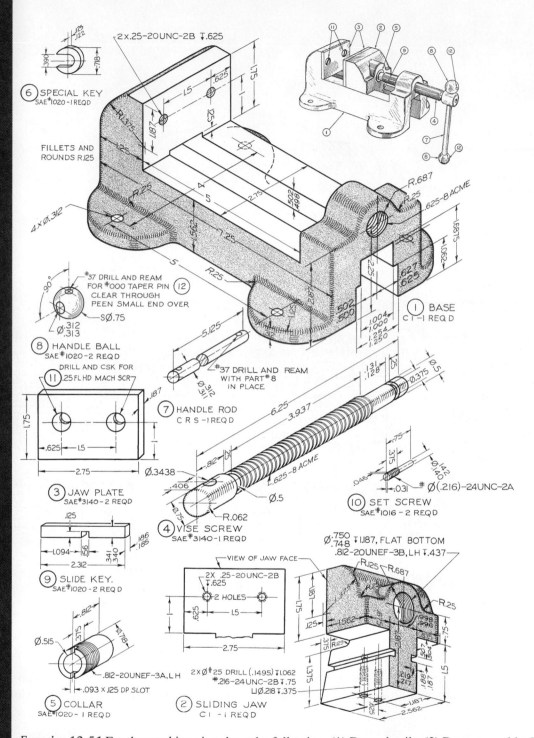

6 SPECIAL KEY
SAE#1020-1 REQD

FILLETS AND ROUNDS R.125

2x.25-20UNC-2B ⊤.625

12 #37 DRILL AND REAM FOR #000 TAPER PIN CLEAR THROUGH PEEN SMALL END OVER
S∅.75

8 HANDLE BALL
SAE#1020-2 REQD

11 DRILL AND CSK FOR .25 FL HD MACH SCR

7 HANDLE ROD
C R S – 1 REQD

#37 DRILL AND REAM WITH PART #8 IN PLACE

3 JAW PLATE
SAE#3140-2 REQD

4 VISE SCREW
SAE#3140-1 REQD

9 SLIDE KEY.
SAE#1020-2 REQD

5 COLLAR
SAE#1020-1 REQD
.812-20UNEF-3A,LH
.093 X.125 DP SLOT

1 BASE
C1-1 REQD

10 SET SCREW
SAE#1016-2 REQD
#∅(.216)-24UNC-2A

VIEW OF JAW FACE
2X .25-20UNC-2B ⊤.625
2 HOLES

∅.750/.748 ⊤1.187, FLAT BOTTOM
.812-20UNEF-3B,LH ⊤.437

2X∅#25 DRILL (.1495)⊤1.062
#.216-24UNC-2B⊤.75
⎿∅.218⊤.375

2 SLIDING JAW
C1 – 1 REQD

.625-8 ACME

Exercise 12.51 For the machine vise, draw the following. (1) Draw details. (2) Draw assembly. If assigned, convert dimensions to the decimal inch system or redesign with metric dimensions.

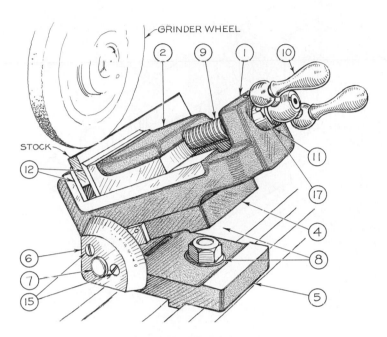

Exercise 12.52 Part (a) For the grinder vise, draw the following. (1) Draw details. (2) Draw assembly. If assigned, convert dimensions to decimal inches or redesign with metric dimensions. See parts (b) and (c) on the following pages.

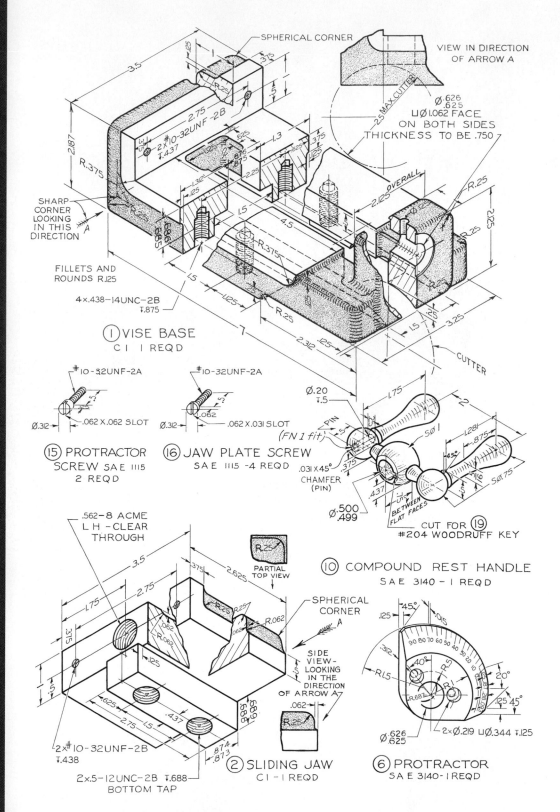

① VISE BASE
C I I REQD

⑮ PROTRACTOR
SCREW SAE 1115
2 REQD

⑯ JAW PLATE SCREW
SAE 1115 -4 REQD

⑩ COMPOUND REST HANDLE
SAE 3140 - I REQD

② SLIDING JAW
C I - I REQD

⑥ PROTRACTOR
SAE 3140 - I REQD

Exercise 12.52 Part (b) For the grinder vise, see Exercise 12.58 part (a) for instructions.

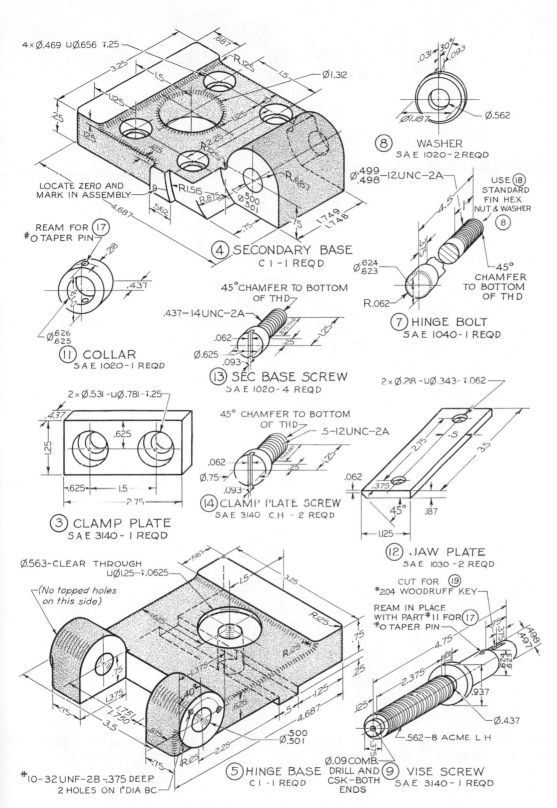

4×∅.469 ⊔∅.656 ⊤.25

.687

R.125   1.5   ∅1.312

3.25

1.5

1.125

.25   .25   R.2.25

.25

R.1.515   R.687

LOCATE ZERO AND
MARK IN ASSEMBLY

9   R.875   ∅.500
.501

.562   .75   .75

4.687   1.749
1.748

④ SECONDARY BASE
C I - I REQD

∅.499 -12UNC-2A
.498

.031   30°
.093

∅1.187   ∅.562

⑧ WASHER
S A E 1020 - 2 REQD

USE ⑱
STANDARD
FIN HEX
NUT & WASHER
⑧

4.5

∅.624
.623

45°
CHAMFER
TO BOTTOM
OF THD

R.062

⑦ HINGE BOLT
S A E 1040 - I REQD

REAM FOR ⑰
#O TAPER PIN

.28

.437

∅.626
.625

⑪ COLLAR
S A E 1020 - I REQD

45°CHAMFER TO BOTTOM
OF THD

.437-14UNC-2A

.062

.25

∅.625   .093   1.25

⑬ SEC BASE SCREW
S A E 1020 - 4 REQD

2 × ∅.531 -⊔∅.781 -⊤.25

.437

.625

1.25   .625   1.5

2.75

③ CLAMP PLATE
S A E 3140 - I REQD

45° CHAMFER TO BOTTOM
OF THD
.5-12UNC-2A

.062

.25   1.25

∅.75   .093

⑭ CLAMP PLATE SCREW
S A E 3140 CH - 2 REQD

2× ∅.218 -⊔∅.343- ⊤.062

2.75   .5   3.5

.062   .375   45°   .187

1.125

⑫ JAW PLATE
S A E 1030 -2 REQD

∅.563-CLEAR THROUGH
⊔∅1.25-⊤.0625

(No tapped holes
on this side)

.687

1.5   3.25

R.125

.75

.375   R.125   .25

1.375   1.25

1.751   .5   4.687
1.750

.75   .500
3.5   2.25   .501

R.125   .75

#10-32UNF-2B -.375 DEEP
2 HOLES ON I"DIA BC

⑤ HINGE BASE
C I - I REQD

CUT FOR ⑲
#204 WOODRUFF KEY

REAM IN PLACE
WITH PART #11 FOR ⑰
#O TAPER PIN

4.75   .75   .498
.375   .497

2.375   .624
.623

.937

∅.437

.125   .562-8 ACME L H

.375

∅.09 COMB.
DRILL AND ⑨ VISE SCREW
CSK-BOTH   S A E 3140 - I REQD
ENDS

Exercise 12.52 Part (c) For the grinder vise, see Exercise 12.58 part (a) for instructions.

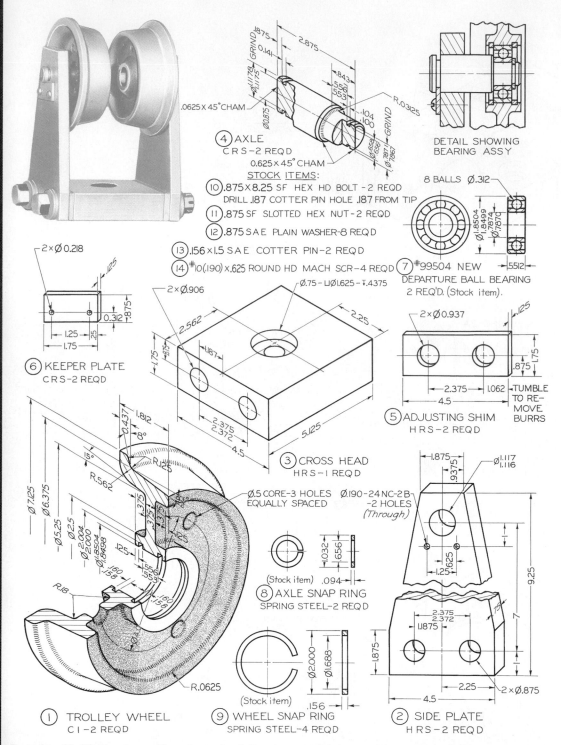

.0625 × 45° CHAM

.875 2.875 GRIND 0.141

Ø1.1179
Ø1.1175

R.0312

.843
.556
.553

.104
.100 GRIND

Ø.875

④ AXLE
C R S – 2 REQD

0.625 × 45° CHAM

DETAIL SHOWING
BEARING ASSY

STOCK ITEMS:
⑩ .875 × 8.25 SF HEX HD BOLT – 2 REQD
DRILL .187 COTTER PIN HOLE .187 FROM TIP
⑪ .875 SF SLOTTED HEX NUT – 2 REQD
⑫ .875 SAE PLAIN WASHER – 8 REQD
⑬ .156 × 1.5 SAE COTTER PIN – 2 REQD
⑭ #10(.190) × .625 ROUND HD MACH SCR – 4 REQD

8 BALLS Ø.312

Ø1.8504
1.8499
.7874
.7870

.5512

⑦ #99504 NEW
DEPARTURE BALL BEARING
2 REQ'D. (Stock item).

2 × Ø 0.218

.125
.875
0.312

1.25 .25
1.75

⑥ KEEPER PLATE
C R S – 2 REQD

2 × Ø.906

Ø.75 – ⊔Ø1.625 – ⊼.4375

2.562 2.25

1.75 1.187

2.375
2.372
4.5

5.125

③ CROSS HEAD
H R S – 1 REQD

2 × Ø0.937

.125
1.75
.875

2.375 1.062
4.5

TUMBLE
TO RE-
MOVE
BURRS

⑤ ADJUSTING SHIM
H R S – 2 REQD

Ø.5 CORE – 3 HOLES
EQUALLY SPACED

.437
1.812
8°
15°
R.125
R.562

Ø7.125
Ø6.375
Ø5.25
Ø2.5
Ø2.004
Ø2.000
Ø1.8504
Ø1.8498

.375
.375
.125

.160
.158
.556
.553
.160
.158

R.18

R.0625

① TROLLEY WHEEL
C I – 2 REQD

.1032
.656

(Stock item) .094

⑧ AXLE SNAP RING
SPRING STEEL – 2 REQD

Ø2.000
Ø1.688

(Stock item) .156

⑨ WHEEL SNAP RING
SPRING STEEL – 4 REQD

Ø.190 – 24 NC – 2 B
– 2 HOLES
(Through)

1.875
.9375 Ø1.117
1.116

.625
1.25

9.25

7

2.375
2.372
1.1875

1.875

2.25 2 × Ø.875
4.5

② SIDE PLATE
H R S – 2 REQD

Exercise 12.53 For the trolley, draw the following. (1) Draw details, omitting parts 7–14. (2) Draw assembly. If assigned, convert dimensions to decimal inches or redesign for metric dimensions.

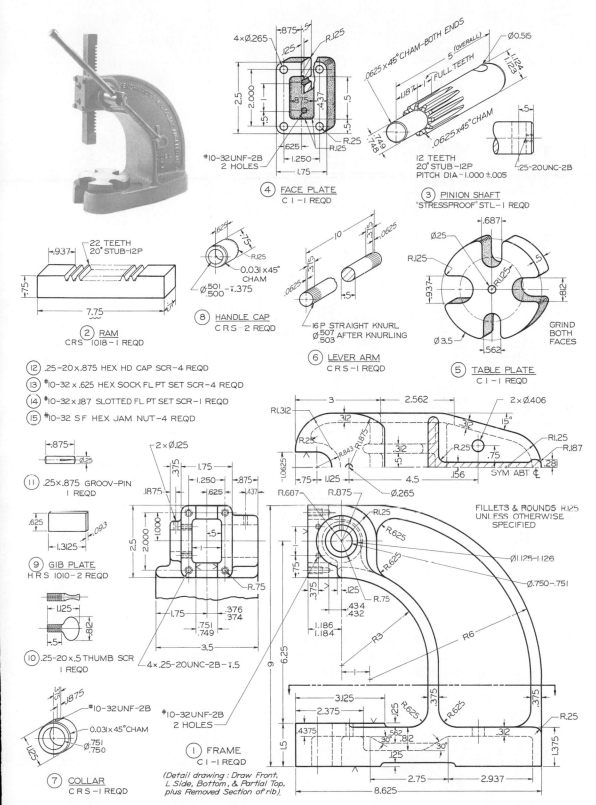

4 FACE PLATE
C I – I REQD

3 PINION SHAFT
"STRESSPROOF" STL – I REQD

12 TEETH
20° STUB – 12P
PITCH DIA – 1.000 ±.005

2 RAM
CRS 1018 – I REQD

22 TEETH
20° STUB – 12P

8 HANDLE CAP
C R S – 2 REQD

6 LEVER ARM
C R S – I REQD

16 P STRAIGHT KNURL
AFTER KNURLING

5 TABLE PLATE
C I – I REQD

GRIND BOTH FACES

12 .25–20×.875 HEX HD CAP SCR–4 REQD

13 #10–32 × .625 HEX SOCK FL PT SET SCR–4 REQD

14 #10–32 × .187 SLOTTED FL PT SET SCR–I REQD

15 #10–32 S F HEX JAM NUT–4 REQD

11 .25×.875 GROOV–PIN
I REQD

9 GIB PLATE
H R S 1010 – 2 REQD

10 .25–20×.5 THUMB SCR
I REQD

7 COLLAR
C R S – I REQD

4× .25–20UNC–2B–↧.5

#10–32UNF–2B
2 HOLES

1 FRAME
C I – I REQD

(Detail drawing : Draw Front,
L Side, Bottom, & Partial Top,
plus Removed Section of rib).

FILLETS & ROUNDS R.125
UNLESS OTHERWISE
SPECIFIED

Exercise 12.54 For the arbor press, draw the following. (1) Draw details. (2) Draw assembly. If assigned, convert dimensions to decimal inches or redesign for metric dimensions.

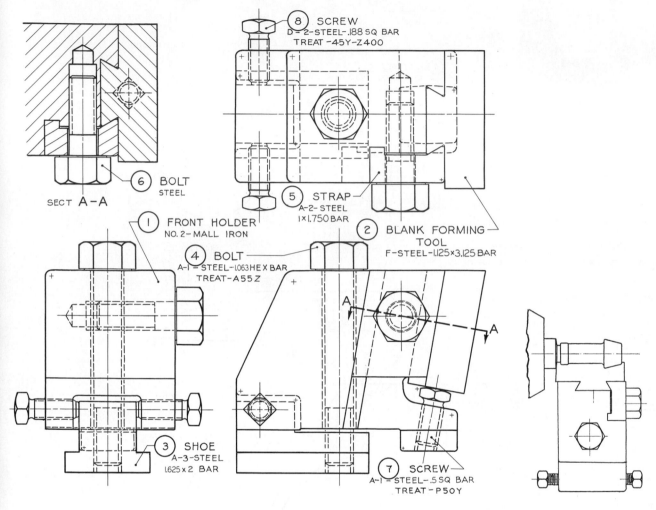

Exercise 12.55 For the forming cutter holder, draw the following. (1) Draw details using decimal or metric dimensions. (2) Draw assembly. Above layout is half size. To obtain dimensions, take distances directly from figure with dividers and double them. At left is shown the top view of the forming cutter holder in use on the lathe.

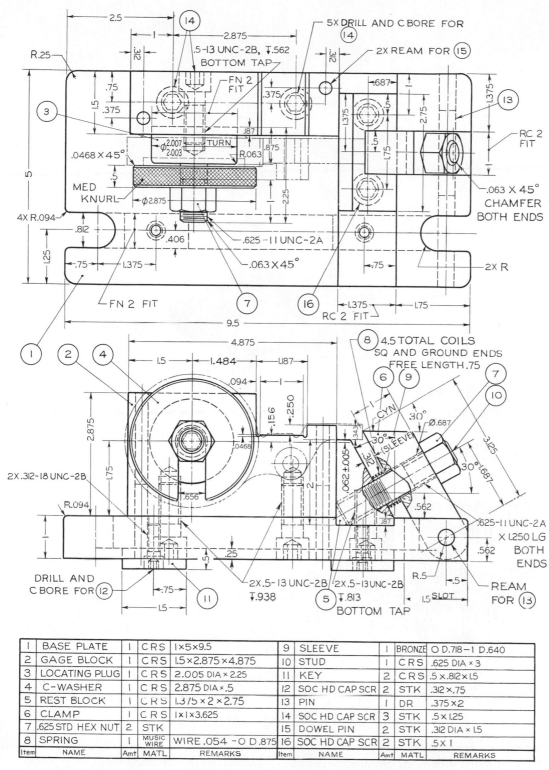

Item	NAME	Amt	MATL	REMARKS	Item	NAME	Amt	MATL	REMARKS
1	BASE PLATE	1	CRS	1×5×9.5	9	SLEEVE	1	BRONZE	O D.718–1 D.640
2	GAGE BLOCK	1	CRS	1.5×2.875×4.875	10	STUD	1	CRS	.625 DIA × 3
3	LOCATING PLUG	1	CRS	2.005 DIA × 2.25	11	KEY	2	CRS	.5 × .812 × 1.5
4	C–WASHER	1	CRS	2.875 DIA × .5	12	SOC HD CAP SCR	2	STK	.312 × .75
5	REST BLOCK	1	CRS	1.375 × 2 × 2.75	13	PIN	1	DR	.375 × 2
6	CLAMP	1	CRS	1×1×3.625	14	SOC HD CAP SCR	3	STK	.5 × 1.25
7	.625 STD HEX NUT	2	STK		15	DOWEL PIN	2	STK	.312 DIA × 1.5
8	SPRING	1	MUSIC WIRE	WIRE .054 – O D .875	16	SOC HD CAP SCR	2	STK	.5 × 1

Exercise 12.56 For the milling fixture for clutch arm, draw the following. (1) Draw details using the decimal inch system or redesign for metric dimensions, if assigned. (2) Draw assembly.

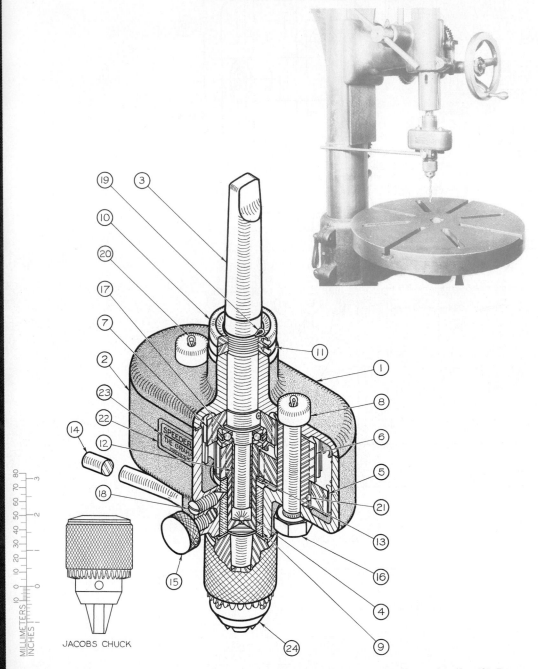

JACOBS CHUCK

Exercise 12.57 Part (a) For the drill speeder, draw the following. (1) Draw details. (2) Draw assembly. If assigned, convert dimensions to decimal inches or redesign with metric dimensions. See parts (b) and (c) on the following pages.

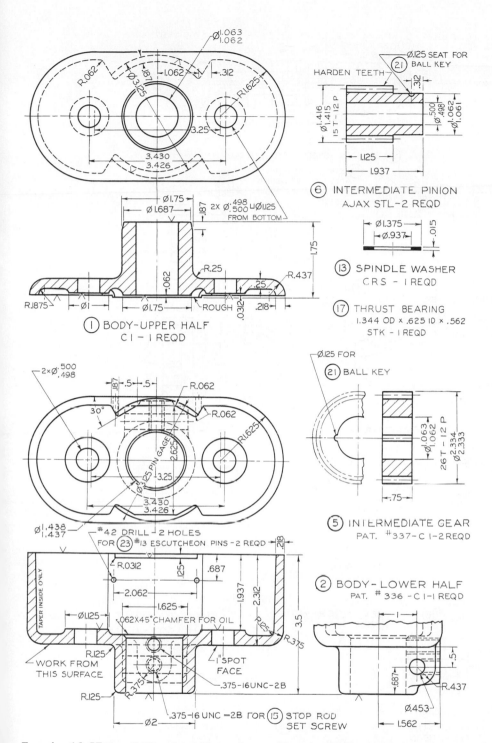

Ø1.063
1.062

HARDEN TEETH
Ø.125 SEAT FOR BALL KEY
21
.312
Ø1.416/1.415
15 T - 12 P
Ø.500/.498
Ø1.062/1.061
1.125
1.937

6 INTERMEDIATE PINION
AJAX STL-2 REQD

R.062
Ø3.125
.187
1.062
.312
R1.625

3.25
3.430
3.426

Ø1.75
Ø1.687
.187
2X Ø.498/.500 ⌴Ø1.125 FROM BOTTOM

1.75
R.25
.062
R.437
R.1875
Ø1
Ø1.75
ROUGH
.0312
.218
.25

1 BODY-UPPER HALF
C1 - 1 REQD

Ø1.375
Ø.937
.015

13 SPINDLE WASHER
C R S - 1 REQD

17 THRUST BEARING
1.344 OD x .625 ID x .562
STK - 1 REQD

Ø.125 FOR
21 BALL KEY

2 X Ø.500/.498
.187
.5
.5
R.062
R.062
R1.625
30°
Ø3.125 PIN GAGE
2.625
3.25
3.430
3.426

Ø1.063/1.062
26 T - 12 P
Ø2.334/2.333
.75

5 INTERMEDIATE GEAR
PAT. #337-C 1-2 REQD

Ø1.438/1.437
#42 DRILL - 2 HOLES
FOR 23 #13 ESCUTCHEON PINS - 2 REQD
.28
R.0312
.125
.687
TAPER INSIDE ONLY
2.062
1.937
2.312
1.625
Ø1.125
.062 X 45° CHAMFER FOR OIL
R.125
R.375
3.5
R.125
WORK FROM THIS SURFACE
R.375
1" SPOT FACE
.375-16UNC-2B
R.125
.375-16 UNC -2B FOR 15 STOP ROD SET SCREW
Ø2

2 BODY-LOWER HALF
PAT. #336-C1-1 REQD

1
.5
.687
R.437
Ø.453
1.562

Exercise 12.57 Part (b) For the drill speeder, see Exercise 12.63 part (a) for instructions.

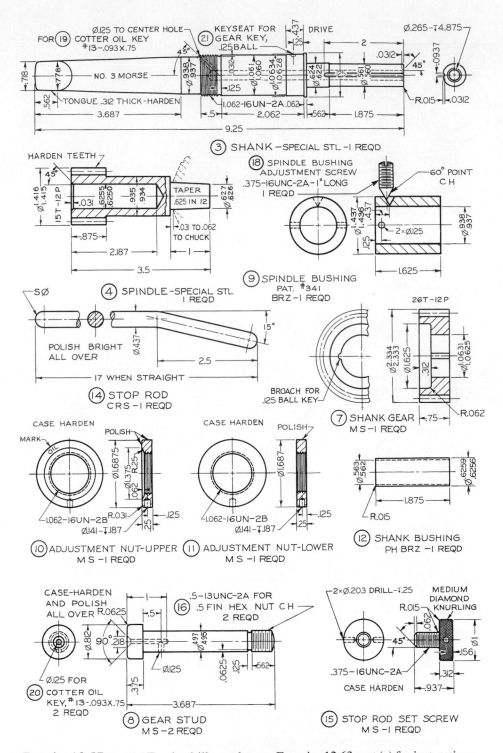

Exercise 12.57 Part (c) For the drill speeder, see Exercise 12.63 part (a) for instructions.

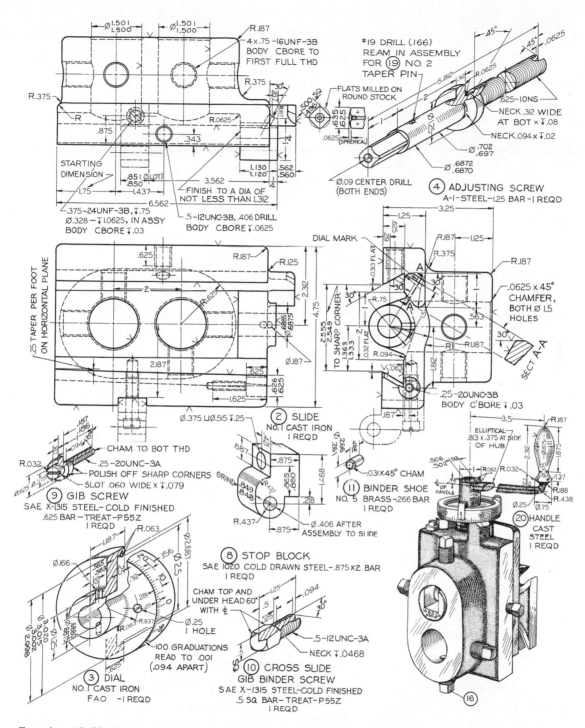

Exercise 12.58 Part (a) For the vertical slide tool, draw the following. (1) Draw details. If assigned, convert dimensions to decimal inches or redesign for metric system. (2) Draw assembly. Take given top view as front view in the new drawing; then add top and right-side views. If assigned, use unidirectional dimensions. See part (b) on the following page.

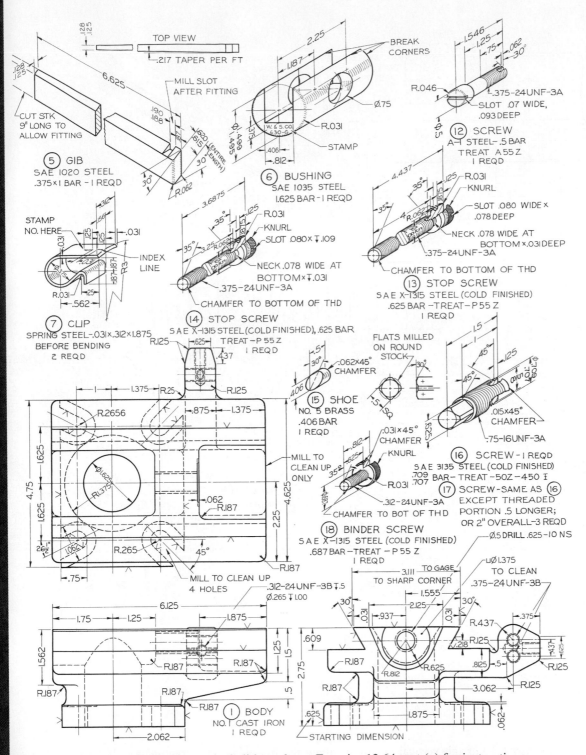

Exercise 12.58 Part (b) For the vertical slide tool, see Exercise 12.64 part (a) for instructions.

Exercise 12.59 Part (a) For the slide tool, draw the following. Consult parts (b), (c), (d), and (e) on the following pages to: (1) Draw details using decimal inch dimensions or redesign with metric dimensions, if assigned. (2) Make an assembly drawing of this slide tool.

PARTS LIST		NO. OF SHEETS ___2___		SHEET NO. ___1___		MACHINE NO. *M-219*					
NAME ___NO. 4 SLIDE TOOL (SPECIFY SIZE OF SHANK REQ'D.)___						LOT NUMBER					
						NO. OF PIECES					

TOTAL ON MACH.	NO. PCS.	NAME OF PART	PART NO.	CAST FROM PART NO.	TRACING NO.	MATERIAL	ROUGH WEIGHT PER PC.	DIA.	LENGTH	MILL	PART USED ON	NO. REQ. FINISH
	1	Body	219-12		D-17417	A-3-S D F						
	1	Slide	219-6		D-19255	A-3-S D F					219-12	
	1	Nut	219-9		E-19256	#10 BZ					219-6	
	1	Gib	219-1001		C-11129	S A E 1020					219-6	
	1	Slide Screw	219-1002		C-11129	A-3-S					219-12	
	1	Dial Bush.	219-1003		C-11129	A-1-S					219-1002	
	1	Dial Nut	219-1004		C-11129	A-1-S					219-1002	
	1	Handle	219-1011		E-18270	(Buy from Cincinnati Ball Crank Co.)					219-1002	
	1	Stop Screw (Short)	219-1012		E-51950	A-1-S					219-6	
	1	Stop Screw (Long)	219-1013		E-51951	A-1-S					219-6	
	1	Binder Shoe	219-1015		E-51952	#5 Brass					219-6	
	1	Handle Screw	219-1016		E-62322	X-1315 C.F.					219-1011	
	1	Binder Screw	219-1017		E-63927	A-1-S					219-6	
	1	Dial	219-1018		E-39461	A-1-S					219-1002	
	2	Gib Screw	219-1019		E-52777	A-1-S		$\frac{1}{4}$-20	1		219-6	
	1	Binder Screw	280-1010		E-24962	A-1-S					219-1018	
	2	Tool Clamp Screws	683-F-1002		E-19110	D-2-S					219-6	
	1	Fill Hd Cap Scr	1-A			A-1-S		$\frac{3}{8}$	$1\frac{3}{8}$		219-6 219-9	
	1	Key	No.404 Woodruff								219-1002	

Exercise 12.59 Part (b) Slide tool parts list.

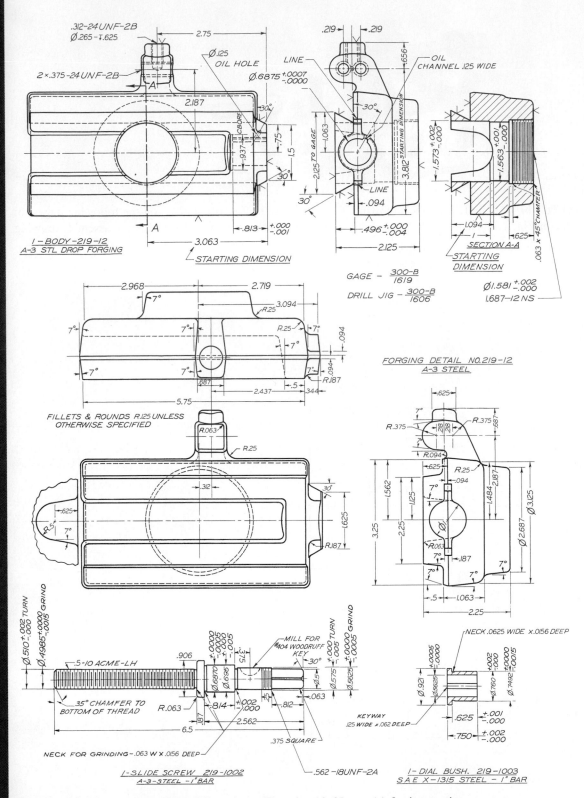

Exercise 12.59 Part (c) For the slide tool, see Exercise 12.65 part (a) for instructions.

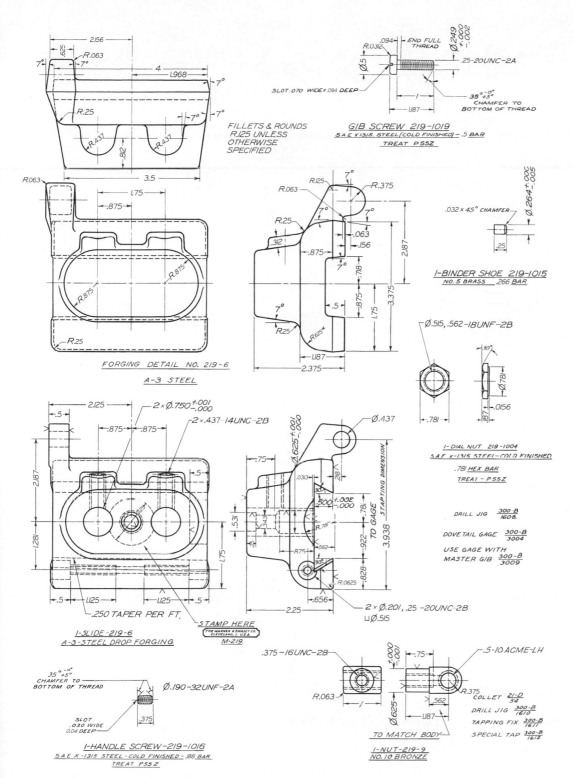

GIB SCREW 219-1019
S.A.E. X-1315 STEEL (COLD FINISHED) - .5 BAR
TREAT P55Z

FILLETS & ROUNDS
R.125 UNLESS
OTHERWISE
SPECIFIED

FORGING DETAIL NO. 219-6

A-3 STEEL

I-BINDER SHOE 219-1015
NO.5 BRASS .266 BAR

I-DIAL NUT 219-1004
S.A.E. X-1315 STEEL-COLD FINISHED
.781 HEX BAR
TREAT - P55Z

DRILL JIG $\frac{300-B}{1608}$

DOVETAIL GAGE $\frac{300-B}{3004}$

USE GAGE WITH
MASTER GIB $\frac{300-B}{3009}$

I-SLIDE -219-6
A-3-STEEL DROP FORGING

STAMP HERE
THE WARNER & SWASEY CO.
CLEVELAND, O. U.S.A.
M-219.

I-HANDLE SCREW-219-1016
S.A.E. X-1315 STEEL - COLD FINISHED - .188 BAR
TREAT P55Z

I-NUT-219-9
NO. 10 BRONZE

COLLET $\frac{21-D}{54}$

DRILL JIG $\frac{300-B}{1610}$

TAPPING FIX. $\frac{300-B}{1611}$

SPECIAL TAP $\frac{300-B}{1612}$

Exercise 12.59 Part (d) For the slide tool, see Exercise 12.65 part (a) for instructions.

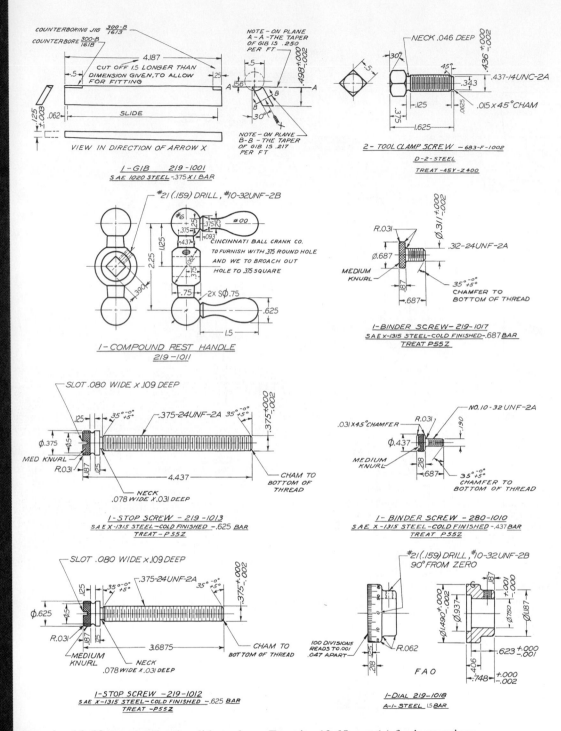

COUNTERBORING JIG $\frac{300-B}{1673}$
COUNTERBORE $\frac{300-B}{1618}$

4.187

CUT OFF 1.5 LONGER THAN
DIMENSION GIVEN, TO ALLOW
FOR FITTING

.5   .25

SLIDE

.062

.125 ±.003

VIEW IN DIRECTION OF ARROW X

NOTE — ON PLANE
A — A — THE TAPER
OF GIB IS .250
PER FT

.5

.498 +.000 −.002

A   .156   A

B   30°

NOTE — ON PLANE
B-B — THE TAPER
OF GIB IS .217
PER FT

1 — GIB   219 - 1001
S A E 1020 STEEL .375 X 1 BAR

NECK .046 DEEP

.436 +.000 −.002

30°   45°

.437 - 14 UNC - 2A

.343

.125   .0625

.375   .015 x 45° CHAM

1.625

2 — TOOL CLAMP SCREW — 683-F-1002
D-2-STEEL
TREAT - 45 Y - Z 400

#21 (.159) DRILL , #10-32 UNF-2B

#6   .125   .375   #00
.375   .250

.093   CINCINNATI BALL CRANK CO.
TO FURNISH WITH .375 ROUND HOLE
AND WE TO BROACH OUT
HOLE TO .375 SQUARE

.437

2.25   1.125

.375

.390   .75   2x S∅.75

.625

1.5

1 — COMPOUND REST HANDLE
219 — 1011

R.031   ∅.311 +.000 −.002

.687   .312 - 24 UNF - 2A

MEDIUM
KNURL   .187

.687   35° +5° −0°
CHAMFER TO
BOTTOM OF THREAD

1 — BINDER SCREW — 219 - 1017
S A E X-1315 STEEL-COLD FINISHED-.687 BAR
TREAT P55 Z

SLOT .080 WIDE x .109 DEEP

.125   35° −0° +5°   .375 - 24 UNF - 2A   35° −0° +5°   .375 +.000 −.002

∅.375   .5

MED KNURL
R.031   .187   .125

NECK
.078 WIDE X .031 DEEP

4.437   CHAM TO
BOTTOM OF
THREAD

1 — STOP SCREW — 219 - 1013
S A E X-1315 STEEL — COLD FINISHED — .625 BAR
TREAT — P 55 Z

.031 x 45° CHAMFER   R.031   NO. 10 - 32 UNF - 2A

∅.437   .190

MEDIUM
KNURL   .28

.687   35° −0° +5°
CHAMFER TO
BOTTOM OF THREAD

1 — BINDER SCREW — 280 - 1010
S A E X-1315 STEEL — COLD FINISHED — .437 BAR
TREAT — P55 Z

SLOT .080 WIDE x .109 DEEP

.125   35° −0° +5°   .375 - 24 UNF - 2A   35° −0° +5°   .375 +.000 −.002

∅.625   .5

R.031   .187   .125

MEDIUM
KNURL   NECK
.078 WIDE X .031 DEEP

3.6875   CHAM TO
BOTTOM OF THREAD

1 — STOP SCREW — 219 - 1012
S A E X-1315 STEEL — COLD FINISHED — .625 BAR
TREAT — P55 Z

#21 (.159) DRILL , #10-32 UNF-2B
90° FROM ZERO

.187   +.001 −.000

∅1.490 +.000 −.002   ∅.937   ∅.750   ∅1.187

100 DIVISIONS
READS TO .001
.047 APART

.28   .125   R.062

.406

FAO

.623 +.000 −.001

.748 +.000 −.002

1 — DIAL 219 - 1018
A-1- STEEL 1.5 BAR

Exercise 12.59 Part (e) For the slide tool, see Exercise 12.65 part (a) for instructions.

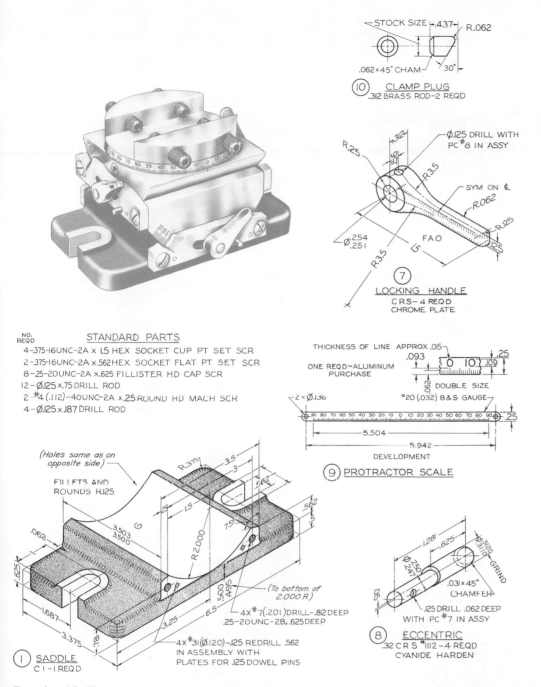

STOCK SIZE .437 R.062
.062×45° CHAM 30°

(10) CLAMP PLUG
.312 BRASS ROD-2 REQD

Ø.125 DRILL WITH
PC #8 IN ASSY
R.25 .312
.150
R.5
SYM ON ℄
R.062
R.25
Ø.254
.251   FAO
R.3.5   .5   .125

(7) LOCKING HANDLE
C R S- 4 REQD
CHROME PLATE

NO. REQD   STANDARD PARTS
4 -.375-16UNC-2A x 1.5 HEX SOCKET CUP PT SET SCR
2 -.375-16UNC-2A x.562 HEX SOCKET FLAT PT SET SCR
8 -.25-20UNC-2A x.625 FILLISTER HD CAP SCR
12 - Ø.125 x.75 DRILL ROD
2 - #4 (.112)-40UNC-2A x.25 ROUND HD MACH SCR
4 - Ø.125 x.187 DRILL ROD

THICKNESS OF LINE APPROX .015   .25
.093   .109
ONE REQD–ALUMINUM   .062
PURCHASE   DOUBLE SIZE
2 × Ø.136   #20 (.032) B & S GAUGE
90 80 70 60 50 40 30 20 10 0 10 20 30 40 50 60 70 80 90 .25
5.504
5.942
DEVELOPMENT

(9) PROTRACTOR SCALE

(Holes same as on
opposite side)
FILLETS AND
ROUNDS R.125
R.375   3.5
3
.062   .562
.625   1.5   75°   .562
3.503   .5
3.500   R 2.000   .5
.062   8   .562
.500   .500
1.687   .495   (To bottom of
2.000 R)
6.5   4x #7(.201)DRILL-.812 DEEP
3.25   .25-20UNC-2B,.625 DEEP
3.375   1.81
4x #31(Ø.120)-.125 REDRILL .562
IN ASSEMBLY WITH
PLATES FOR .125 DOWEL PINS

(1) SADDLE
C I -1 REQD

1.281   .625
Ø.250   Ø.3120
.247   GRIND
SRS   .031×45°
CHAMFER
.125 DRILL .062 DEEP
WITH PC #7 IN ASSY

(8) ECCENTRIC
.312 C R S #1112 -4 REQD
CYANIDE HARDEN

Exercise 12.60 Part (a) For the "any angle" tool vise, draw the following. (1) Draw details using decimal inch dimensions or redesign with metric dimensions, if assigned. (2) Draw assembly. See part (b) on the following page.

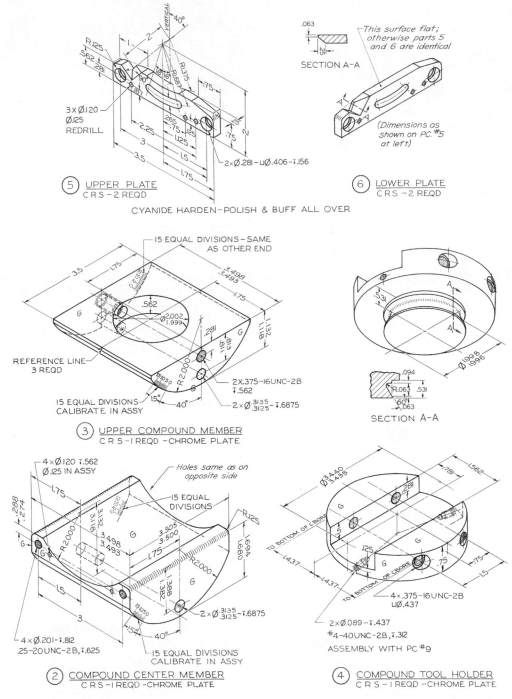

SECTION A-A

⑤ UPPER PLATE
C R S – 2 REQD

⑥ LOWER PLATE
C R S – 2 REQD

CYANIDE HARDEN–POLISH & BUFF ALL OVER

─This surface flat;
otherwise parts 5
and 6 are identical

(Dimensions as
shown on PC. #5
at left)

③ UPPER COMPOUND MEMBER
C R S –1 REQD –CHROME PLATE

SECTION A-A

② COMPOUND CENTER MEMBER
C R S –1 REQD –CHROME PLATE

④ COMPOUND TOOL HOLDER
C R S –1 REQD –CHROME PLATE

Exercise 12.60 Part (b) For the "any angle" tool vise, see Exercise 12.66 part (a) for instructions.

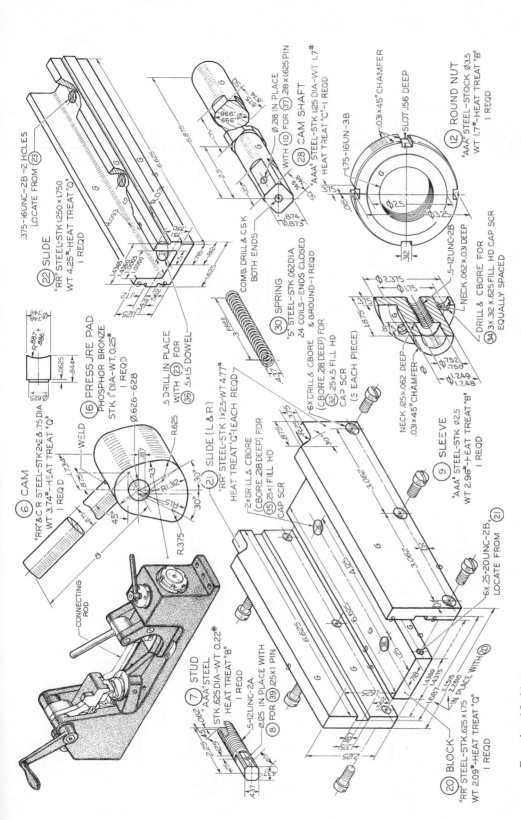

Exercise 12.61 Part (a) For the fixture for centering connecting rod, draw the following. Consult Parts (b) and (c) on the following pages to: (1) Draw details using decimal inch dimensions or redesign with metric dimensions, if assigned. (2) Draw assembly. See parts (b) and (c) on the following pages.

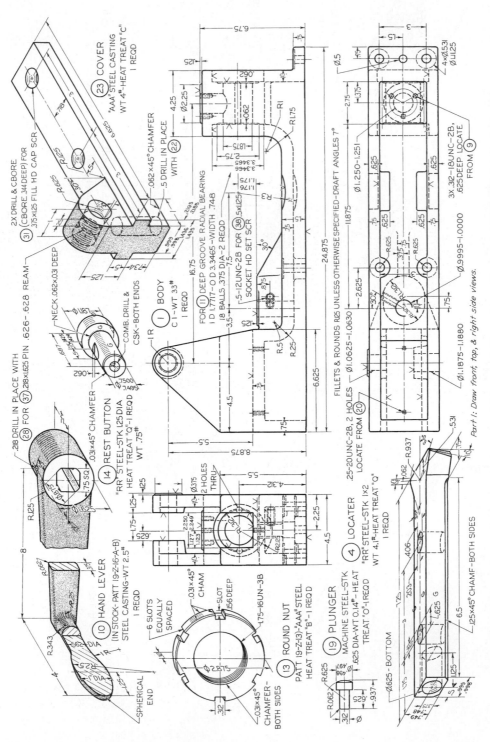

Exercise 12.61 Part (b) For the fixture for centering connecting rod, see Exercise 12.67 part (a) for instructions.

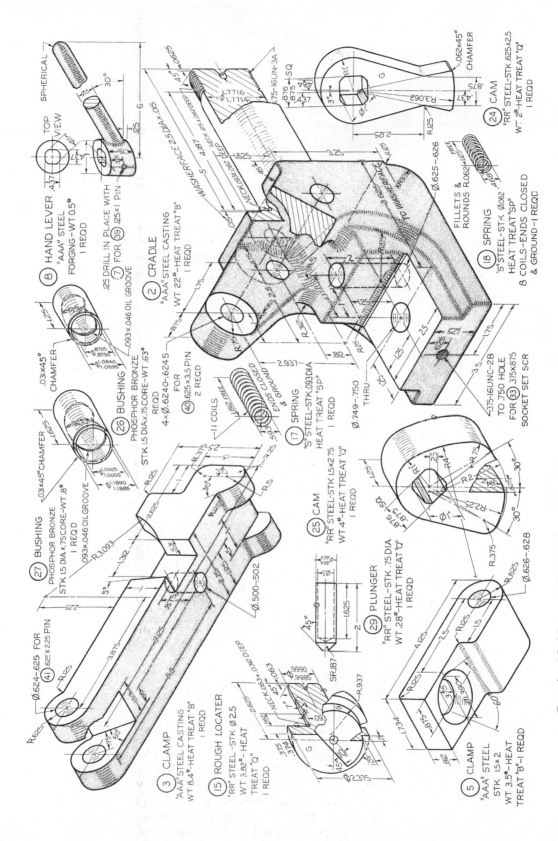

Exercise 12.61 Part (c) For the fixture for centering connecting rod, see Exercise 12.67 part (a) for instructions.

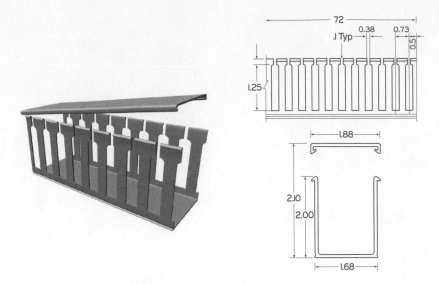

Exercise 12.62 For the plastic open slot wiring duct, front and side views, draw the following. Redraw with metric dimensions reducing the size by 3.

CHAPTER THIRTEEN

DRAWING MANAGEMENT

——— OBJECTIVES ———

After studying the material in this chapter, you should be able to:

1. Understand the importance of document management and control.

2. Understand how an electronic file can be used as both a communication and a storage device.

3. Understand the differences between CD-ROM, optical disk, and other storage options.

4. Describe printing and reproduction methods for technical drawings.

5. Be familiar with the Internet and the World Wide Web and understand how to use them in the product development process.

Refer to the following standards:
- ASME Y14.42-2002 Digital Approval Systems
- ASME Y14.100-2004 Engineering Drawing Practices

The 400 Gigabyte hard drive in the upper right stores more than 100,000 drawings; about 1,000 times as much as the flat file shown at the left Western Digital. The flat file costs 10 times as much. *Courtesy of Mayline Group.*

OVERVIEW

Creating a drawing is part of the process of bringing the concept of a product or system to reality. Approval, management, retention, and storage of the drawing are other very important parts of the process that should not be overlooked. Once a drawing has been created, you must be able to retrieve it to use it effectively.

Managing drawings and other design documentation is both a legal responsibility and an economic one. These records are construed as a contract between a company and the vendors or contractors that manufacture parts or build a structure or system.

For companies to compete in a fast paced marketplace they must be able to respond to changes and innovations that improve efficiency while keeping working documents and archives secure, organized, and conveniently accessible.

A well organized system for storing and retrieving past design efforts can be important for a company's continuing success.

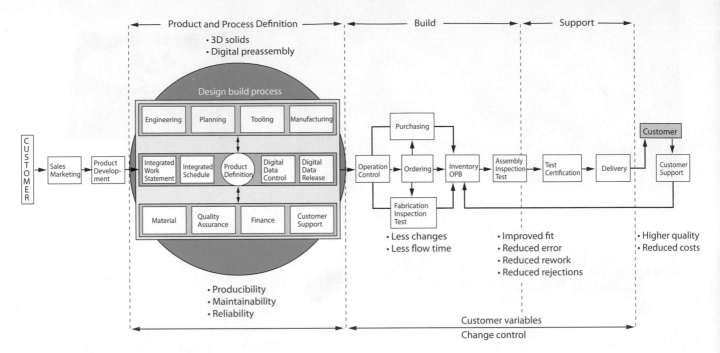

13.1   Boeing's preferred business process illustrates the concurrent nature of the design/build model at the heart of its design process. *Copyright © Boeing. Courtesy of Dynojet Research, Inc.*

MANAGING THE DESIGN PROCESS

Designing a product, structure, or system is an open ended process. As you learned in Chapter 1, a clear needs statement is the starting point. Recognizing the end point or achieving it can be challenging if you do not have a plan for the design process. Two critical items are time and cost.

In order to have a product to market by a particular date, you must allow time in the schedule for all of the stages in the design process, as well as coordinating for the product manufacture or construction. This may involve researching materials and suppliers, coordinating lead times for ordering materials, time for vendors to manufacture parts, incorporate changes, assemble, and market the product, produce user documentation, and a myriad of other details. Figure 13.1 shows a graphical representation of the Boeing Corporation's Preferred Business Process. Notice all of the stages before

the product gets to the customer. If this is to happen on time, careful planning is needed.

Often a **Program Evaluation Review Technique** (PERT) chart or Gantt chart is used to track the time and activity for the project. By working backwards from the ending date, and allotting time to activities, you can develop a plan to meet the critical deadlines and predict the influence on one important activity if a deadline slips somewhere else.

The work of designing the product occurs near the beginning of the process, but it commits a large percentage of the total cost of the product. Figure 13.2 shows a graph of time versus the percentage of the project budget that is committed. Note that even though the conceptual design is not particularly costly, especially when compared with hand tooling for manufacturing, it is at this point that

most of the cost of the project is committed. The difference between the product's success and failure may be determined early on.

Companies use design milestones and design reviews to help ensure that the design process accomplishes its goal in a timely fashion and to minimize the risk in proceeding with the design at that point. Typical milestones may include the following:

Product proposal The **product proposal** is usually driven by marketing and sales in response to consumer needs.

Design proposal The **design proposal** is a plan to meet that need and typically to show the profitability to the company in doing so.

Development plan The **development plan** includes all of the groups involved with the product, such as

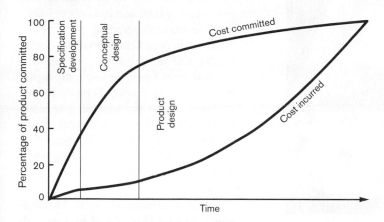

13.2 Early in the design process a large percentage of the life cycle cost of the product is committed. Late in the process, when costs are actually incurred, it may be impossible to reduce costs without major changes to the design. In order to produce products that are viable on the world market, you will want to consider as many alternative designs as possible early in the design process. *Reprinted with permission of the McGraw-Hill Companies from The Mechanical Design Process, Second Edition by David G. Ullman, 1997.*

management, marketing, engineering, manufacturing, service, and sales.

Engineering release **Engineering release** ascertains that satisfactory design reviews have been completed for all of the components, modules, and systems, required in the device or system, and all questions have been answered to the point where it is ready for release. This usually includes several stages of design review both at a product and part level. After this initial engineering release of drawings or a digital database occurs, revisions are tracked and marked on the drawings.

Often companies use a letter to track design revisions before release. For example, at an initial prototype stage the drawing may be marked as revision A. Then as the design is refined a revision B may be indicated. At the initial engineering release, the drawings will then be updated to show release 1 (some companies use 0 as the initial release).

Product release **Product release** requires that each part can be produced and function in the design and the product is now ready for the customer.

Design Review

Entry level employees may be most involved in part reviews to determine if the part that they are working on will function correctly in the entire assembly and can be manufactured cost effectively. You may need to provide the documentation for design decisions; for example, the fastener selections, meeting company standards, analysis, tolerances, and other information.

Documentation drawings can be construed as a contract with the manufacturers and clients, so management of both electronic and printed drawings is a key business practice in all industries that involve technical drawings. *Courtesy of Getty Images-Stock byte.*

UNDERSTANDING DRAWING MANAGEMENT

To control how drawings are released for manufacture, companies and industries have developed procedures to eliminate misunderstandings and costly mistakes. For example, if designs require changes, engineering change orders document these changes so they become a part of the permanent record of the design.

Regulatory bodies, standards organizations, and case law have all contributed to the rules for retaining and producing documentation for your engineering designs. Anyone who works with technical drawings should be familiar with the requirements for record retention in their industry.

Drawing management is obviously important, simply for the sake of convenience and to free designers to use their creative energy toward more lofty pursuits than shuffling through disorganized paperwork. More importantly, though, it plays a key role in providing legal documentation and contributing to a company's overall efficiency and profitability.

Preserving Documentation

Drawings serve as an important part of an agreement between a designer and a producer. You can think of released drawings and 3D CAD models as a contract between you and the company building the structure or system, or the manufacturer producing the part or device. As such, it is crucial to be able to document what was actually provided in this drawing.

Companies may need to produce the **documentation** for various purposes, such as defending themselves against product safety liability and patent infringement lawsuits. In the event of legal issues, you must be able to produce the document as it was provided and in a method that is admissible in a court of law. Because electronically stored files can be altered, they may not be considered an acceptable method for documenting engineering designs.

Whether they are on paper, on mylar, or in electronic format, drawings are important company records and must be managed so that they can be retrieved, reproduced, revised, and retained effectively.

Most legal requests are for copies of all versions of the design, and all copies stored and used within the company. It can be costly and embarrassing if they are not well organized and correct, or if there are multiple versions in use that vary.

Legal Standards for Drawings

Legal standards for how long engineering drawings need to be retained vary from state to state and industry to industry. For example, nuclear power plant drawings may be kept permanently or for hundreds of years, but the drawings for a medical device may be kept only a year or two after the product is obsolete (and no longer being manufactured or sold). In most cases, industry standards groups weigh the risk of record destruction in the context of product and public safety and make recommendations for its members.

The **American Records Management Association** (ARMA) standards for records retention are another source of information about engineering drawing retention. A company—or an individual consultant—needs to understand these standards to determine how long to retain engineering drawing records. Even if the legal standard is less stringent, a court may rule that a firm should meet the industry's common practice to avoid a finding of negligence.

Industries that are regulated by the Food and Drug Administration (FDA) should also be aware of its Guidelines for Electronic Records and Signatures, a ruling that was finalized in early 1998. Regulatory agencies such as the FDA consider engineering drawings "specifications" or "documents" and have clarified their record keeping guidelines to include electronic forms such as graphics files. Companies that are undertaking records management guidelines should be aware of the most current rulings and efforts by industry standards and regulatory groups to encompass electronic media in their recommendations.

Improving Efficiency

Efficient document management is also a key to the effective use of computer-aided design tools and concurrent engineering practices.

Effective storage and retrieval of engineering design documentation can make a difference in a company's ability to succeed in today's world marketplace. The effective use of a 3D design database can provide many benefits outside of just reduced drafting time or a shortened product development cycle.

Understanding the process that paper drawings go through for approval, release, and storage can also help you understand good practices for the approval, release, and storage of your electronic CAD data.

Concurrent engineering, a process that can improve efficiency and profitability by increasing the interplay between steps in the design process, depends on the team's ability to work together on interrelated tasks, often by using a design database. Access to current and accurate information is crucial to the team's ability to work simultaneously on different aspects of the same project.

On team efforts, the individuals involved can use a design database to streamline the design process by bringing the team together. The information kept in a 3D design database can be used either to produce paper drawings or to send as files for NC machining, mold design, or other manufacturing processes. It is also an important part of the engineering design record.

New software tools and processes to manage the flow of design information to and among members of the team are continually being improved.

DRAWING MANAGEMENT IN ENGINEERING ETHICS

The Hyatt Regency Walkways Collapse provides a vivid example of the importance of accuracy and detail in engineering design and shop drawings (particularly regarding revisions), and the costly consequences of errors.

On July 17, 1981, the Hyatt Regency Hotel in Kansas City, Missouri, held a videotaped tea-dance party in their atrium lobby. With many party-goers standing and dancing on the suspended walkways, connections supporting the ceiling rods that held up the second and fourth-floor walkways across the atrium failed, and both walkways collapsed onto the crowded first-floor atrium below. The fourth-floor walkway collapsed onto the second-floor walkway, while the offset third-floor walkway remained intact. The collapse left 114 dead and in excess of 200 injured. Millions of dollars in costs resulted from the collapse, and thousands of lives were adversely affected.

The hotel had only been in operation for approximately one year at the time of the walkways' collapse, and the ensuing investigation of the accident revealed some unsettling facts.

During January and February, 1979, the design of the hanger rod connections was changed in a series of events and disputed communications between the fabricator (Havens Steel Company) and the engineering design team (G.C.E. International, Inc., a professional engineering firm). The fabricator changed the design from a one-rod to a two-rod system to simplify the assembly task, doubling the load on the connector, which ultimately resulted in the walkways' collapse.

The fabricator, in sworn testimony before the administrative judicial hearings after the accident, claimed that his company (Havens) telephoned the engineering firm (G.C.E.) for change approval. G.C.E. denied ever receiving such a call from Havens.

On October 14, 1979 (more than one year before the walkways collapsed), while the hotel was still under construction, more than 2700 square feet of the atrium roof collapsed because one of the roof connections at the north end of the atrium failed.

In testimony, G.C.E. stated that on three separate occasions they requested on-site project representation during

The fabricator of the failed walkway testified that his company had telephoned the engineering design team for change approval, but the engineering firm denied ever receiving such a call. *Courtesy of Texas A & M University.*

the construction phase; however, these requests were not acted on by the owner (Crown Center Redevelopment Corporation), due to additional costs of providing on-site inspection.

Even as originally designed, the walkways were barely capable of holding up the expected load, and would have failed to meet the requirements of the Kansas City Building Code.

Due to evidence supplied at the hearings, a number of principals involved lost their engineering licenses, a number of firms went bankrupt, and many expensive legal suits were settled out of court. The case serves as an excellent example of the importance of meeting professional responsibilities, and what the consequences are for professionals who fail to meet those responsibilities.

Excerpted from "Negligence and The Professional Debate Over Responsibility For Design" A Case History of The Kansas City Hyatt Regency Walkways Collapse. Department of Philosophy and Department of Mechanical Engineering, Texas A&M University http://ethics.tamu. edu/ethicscasestudies.htm

13.1 DRAWING APPROVAL AND RELEASE

Once a drawing is determined to be complete, the title block on the drawing is used to document the change from a draft to a finished drawing. The drawing's creator signs and dates the "drawn by" block, perhaps a checker signs off and dates the "checked by" block, and the engineer approves the drawing for release by signing and dating the "approved by" block. A supervising engineer might also sign off to approve the drawing. On a set of paper drawings the signatures are written manually. When the drawings are approved digitally, approval is indicated by a "symbol of personal identification" according to the ASME Y1.14.42-2002 standard. The **approval indicator** can be any symbols, letters, numbers or a digital signature including bar codes, for example the initials in the title block shown in Figure 13.3.

Once approved, the drawing or set of drawings and contract are released to manufacturing or to the contractor to be produced. Copies of the approved drawings are circulated to various departments within the company as required, and one set of the printed drawings and contract is stored for the permanent record. Figure 13.4 shows a title block used to gather approval signatures on a paper drawing.

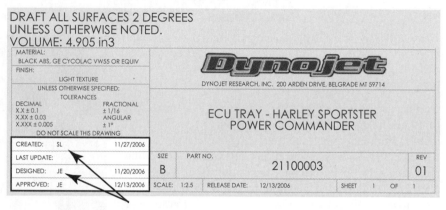

13.3   Electronic Signatures are Used on This Drawing. *Courtesy of Dynojet Research, Inc.*

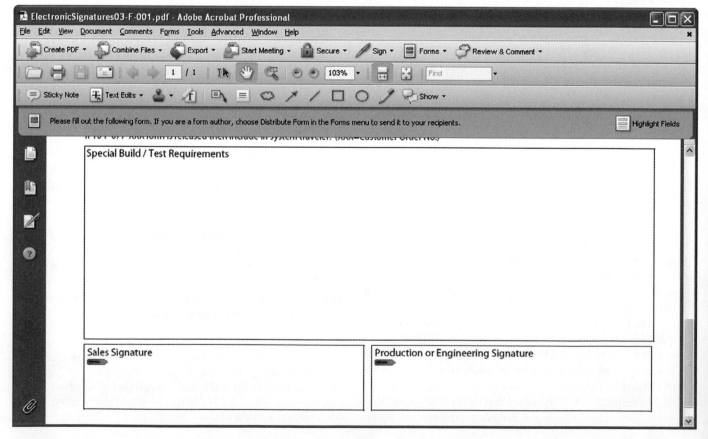

13.4   Electronic Signature Files are Used to Approve This Engineering Order Form. *Courtesy of Big Sky Laser.*

13.2 CHANGE ORDERS

In the imperfect real world, released drawings often require some type of correction during the process of constructing or manufacturing the product or system. After a drawing has been released, an **engineering change order** (ECO), shown in Figure 13.5, is used to document and approve drawing changes. An ECO, also called an engineering change notification (ECN) and sometimes an engineering change request (ECR), details the nature of the change in a separate document. After the ECO is approved, the drawing is revised and the revision noted on the drawing.

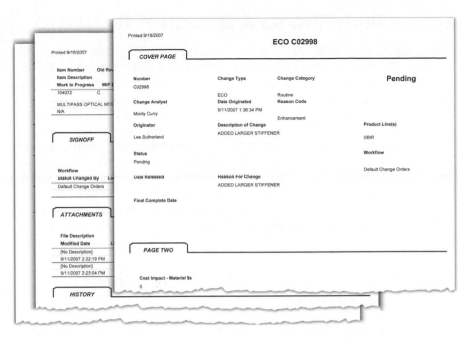

13.5   Engineering Change Order. *Courtesy of Zolo Technologies.*

13.3 REVISION BLOCK

When revised, drawings are not replaced with a new drawing, instead a dated revision block, shown in Figure 13.6, is added to the drawing. A **revision block** describes the change and may also indicate the number of the engineering change order (which contains more information about the change). The revision block requires approval once again. A small number (contained in a triangle or circle) is added to call attention to the revision on the drawing. Some companies also included an easily visible revision number near the drawing number in the title block. Annotating the drawing number helps ensure that two people discussing the print from two different locations can verify that each is looking at the same revision of the drawing.

Once a drawing is revised and approved, a copy is stored for the permanent record. Companies that use printed drawings then must circulate new prints to all who received the previous print so they can update their files. Some companies require that old prints be collected to eliminate the possibility that some departments might continue to use them.

One advantage of a digital database is that when the system is well implemented and properly organized, it is much easier to track which revision is current. Obviously, a poorly implemented digital system is just as prone to confusion as a manual system. Figure 13.7 shows software written at Dynojet Research Inc. to track and approve engineering change requests.

REVISIONS					
ECR#	REV	DESCRIPTION		DATE	APPROVED
1480	02	INCREASED WIDTH OF KEY SLOTS TO EASE KEY INSTALLATION.		4/1/2003	SAS
	02	ADDED GDT TO CENTER KEYWAYS ON THE SHAFT.			
1813	03	ADDED TOLERANCE TO Ø1.497.		1/13/2004	SAS
3560	04	ADDED GTD CONCENTRICITY TOLERANCE TO Ø1.497		2/1/2007	JE
	05	ADDED REQUIREMENT FOR CENTER DRILLING ONE END OF SHAFT.		5/2/2007	SAS

13.6   Revision Block. *Courtesy of Dynojet Research, Inc.*

	Waiting for action	My ECRs	Canceled	All	Search Results		
Date	Status	ECR	Owner	Description of change		Last Comment	
3/23/2007	Complete	5068	slindt	RELEASE TO PRODUCTION These were ...			
4/13/2007	Complete	5100	jrichard	RELEASE 21700004 - This is the 2'' piece...		The install guide is being updated. The ECR for it will ...	
4/16/2007	Complete	5109	jrichard	RELEASE LABOR PART # 19200070 AND ...		all 18 are powder coated	
5/4/2007	Implemented	5211	slindt	RELEASE TO PRODUCTION		Thanks	
5/7/2007	Complete	5199	rick	Add powder coating labor number 19200021...		OK. NEWER DRAWINGS ATTACHED NOW	
5/8/2007	Implemented	5216	jmatter	Remove stock code 54210020, Fuse,1/4A,...		I've got some "1/2 Amp" stickers for LV Tech Support ...	
5/11/2007	New	5238	slindt	RELEASE TO PRODUCTION Will post dat...		Data file is attached.	
5/14/2007	New	5253	slindt	RELEASE TO PRODUCTION Will post dat...		A prototype can be built, and once that prototype is ap...	

13.7   Engineering Change Request Tracking Software. *Courtesy of Dynojet Research, Inc.*

13.4 A DRAWING AS A SNAPSHOT IN TIME

Each of the drawings archived and referenced in the process described above served to document a design at a particular point in time. Some companies continue to print and store a paper copy of the CAD file as their permanent record to provide this documentation. If the electronic CAD file is updated and no longer matches the drawing, the paper copy acts to preserve the design information. In this kind of system, the same approval and archival practices just described are applied to the paper

drawings generated from the CAD database. This is a perfectly acceptable practice if you can retrieve these paper drawings later as needed.

Practices used today allow the same level of control for electronic files that store the design data. Quality standards in some industries allow for electronic documents to serve as the permanent record if they are properly controlled. The process of approval applies to CAD drawings that are "frozen" at each ap-

proval. Instead of storing a paper print, the company stores the electronic file and has backup procedures in place to ensure the future retrieval of the file.

The process just described covers only a portion of the design process and product information that a company needs to control. Sharing, controlling, and storing the electronic files used to document engineering design is important for getting the most value from a companies design effort.

13.5 GOOD PRACTICES FOR ELECTRONIC DRAWING STORAGE

Organized practices for storage, approval, retrieval, file naming, and tracking revision history for electronic CAD data are even more important than they are for paper-based systems. There are many benefits that motivate companies to invest in a 3D CAD database, such as improved communication between functional areas, computer integrated manu-

facturing, shorter design cycle time, cost savings, better access to information, and improved visualization capabilities. If the CAD files and documentation are not well organized, however, many of these benefits may not be realized. Chances are, you will work in a company that has developed and articulated its standards of data management, and

you will be expected to adhere to them. The company may even have invested in data management software. In either case, much of the responsibility for managing data will be yours. Understanding the issues in personal file management will help you devise your own system, if you must, and help you appreciate the pros and cons of various approaches.

13.6 STORING ELECTRONIC FILES

The advent of personal computers on each designer's desktop contributes to the difficulty of managing electronic data. Each designer may organize the files he or she is working on differently, or keep multiple copies of a file in different directories. When others need to view or edit the file, it may be hard to be sure which is the current version. Without a thorough approval process for release of drawings,

the engineer may neglect to track and store the revision history. Even when previous revisions of the drawing are stored electronically, they may not be useful because they don't satisfy the requirements for a static snapshot of the design at the time of release.

Many companies run into difficulties with their CAD data because they start out small and don't implement an

organized system for managing the files. By the time they realize that they require better organization, they have thousands of poorly organized files and many CAD users with poor file storage habits. It is a very important part of your job to manage the product design records that you produce.

13.7 ORGANIZED DIRECTORY STRUCTURES

Using an organized directory structure enables you to retrieve your CAD files and other electronically stored engineering data. Think of a directory on the disk as a kind of file folder. You would not put all of your paperwork loose in your file cabinet; neither should you scatter files over your hard disk.

Most people create a directory structure in a way that makes sense for the types of projects they do. A project-based

directory structure, such as the one shown in Figure 13.8, allows you to store all files related to a particular project in the same directory.

Within each project, you may want to have subdirectories for different parts or different kinds of data associated with the project. A good rule of thumb is to think about situations when you (or others) will want to retrieve the data. Will you think of it in terms of the project?

(Remember that a key to working with assemblies is the availability of the individual part files associated with it.) Or will you think of it in terms of another characteristic? Your CAD file directories may be project based, while other files may be organized differently. Making the directories work as you do will help you find what you need easily.

It is not a good idea to have a single "work" directory where you store all of your files, even if you intend to move them to another project-based directory later. This chore may not get done, or you may not remember which version of the file is current. Nor is it a good practice to store your work files in the directory that contains the application software. (When you install software upgrades, you may accidentally overwrite or delete your work files.) Developing good habits that help you organize your files as you create them will eliminate confusion and save time later.

If you are using a networked computer system, you can store company documents on the network in a directory that others in the company can access. Because CAD files require large amounts of storage space, you need to manage the space on the hard disks and drives available to you. Keeping copies of all files on your personal system should be weighed against the frequency with which you need those files, the time involved in retrieving the files as needed, and the likelihood that the copy of the file on your system will still be current the next time you need it.

If you work for a company that has implemented a system to control their electronic data, you may be required to keep all of your CAD files in a workspace allotted to you on the network server. This makes it possible for the company to control (and regularly back up) this data, and it removes the burden of doing so from each individual employee.

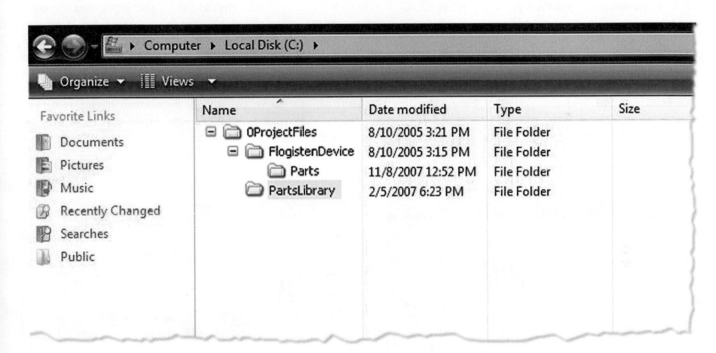

13.8 An Organized Directory Structure

13.8 FILE NAMING CONVENTIONS

File names assigned to your CAD files may be either random or semi random file names, or the name may provide information similar to that in a title block coded within its name. Whichever method you use, it is important to establish a procedure and name the files systematically. If a companywide policy for naming files does not exist, you should develop one for your own files to make them easy to find.

For names that use a code, even without opening the document or studying the model inside, you should be able to identify key information. Multipart file names may be used to indicate, for example, the part, the project it is part of, who created it, and a version number.

If you use numbers for your file names and assign them in a systematic way, users familiar with the system can search for kinds of documents, or for files by name. For example, you may have a sort of Dewey decimal system for types of drawings or documents your

company typically produces, so that numbers starting with 100 are electrical schematics, 200s are assemblies, and so forth. The next set of numbers can further identify the type of file by another set of characteristics, such as project group numbers. A systematic alphanumeric code may work in a similar fashion. When the drawing name/number is not be the same as the CAD file name, it can become confusing. Another disadvantages is that for large numbers of drawings you can run out of values that fit your established code. It can be difficult to imagine a code that suits every type of project or part that may be undertaken.

When drawing names are assigned in a fairly random way, a company may maintain an organized database where users can look to find the particular drawing or file name. Sometimes drawing names are standardized only at the point that a part is approved and released to company archive. If so, the numerical

system used for the CAD file name may also be used for the paper drawing name. Figure 13.9 shows a naming system you might use for CAD files. Figure 13.10 shows part number and drawing tracking software developed at Dynojet Research Inc. for its internal use in tracking drawings and CAD models.

Additional data may be added to the file name over time. The revision number can be added when revision drawings are approved. Once a company has file retention guidelines in place, file names can also incorporate a tag that indicates when it may be removed from long-term storage. This kind of tag is generally added by the group that manages the company's archives, but it demonstrates the role of the file name in encapsulating information and aiding in file management.

Whatever system a company uses is definitely better than having each employee name drawings as he or she pleases.

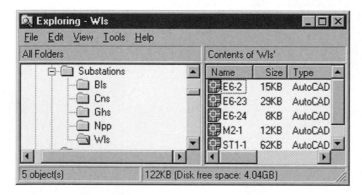

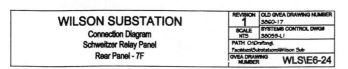

13.9 CAD files can use portions of the file name to code information telling you what the drawing is about. (a) The directory structure is organized around projects. Each filename includes information identifying the project. (b) The drawing title block includes the filename for reference. *Reprinted by permission of Pearson Education, Inc., Upper Saddle River, NJ.*

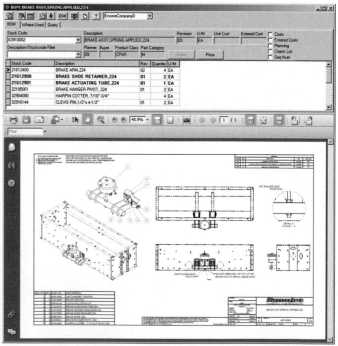

13.10 Part Number and Drawing Tracking Software Allows the User to Search the Description to Find a Drawing or Model. *Courtesy of Dynojet Research, Inc.*

13.9 DRAWING STANDARDS

Like file naming standards, **drawing standards** can help you work more productively and can contribute to the usefulness of the drawings as company records. Engineering drawings are the property of the company, not the individual engineer. As such, their usefulness should not depend on a single individual being able to locate or interpret them.

Company standards may be in place to introduce consistency in the way drawings are constructed. Standardizing the layers in a drawing, for example, can make them more navigable. Architectural engineering firms use layers to organize the many systems, such as plumbing and electrical, that are part of building design. Each of these systems will be assigned a set of layers and layer names so that each drawing can be manipulated in the same way. Notes and drawing text are commonly stored on a separate layer across drawings so this information can be turned on and off as needed when working with the model. Because CAD software carries layer information along with parts, standardizing layer names can prevent unnecessary confusion when files are combined.

The CAD software itself may allow the user to select a CAD standard or check the drawing to see that it matches a CAD standard. Figure 13.11 shows the AutoCAD software's CAD standard dialog box.

The colors used for layers and different drawing elements can also be standardized, as shown in Table 13.1. Center lines may be red, for example. Because color is used to change pen widths on a pen plotter, this kind of standardization can facilitate printing the drawing with the appropriate line weights.

Many other aspects of creating a drawing can be standardized. The borders required for each different sheet size, the information contained in the title block (and how it is to appear), and the fonts and letter sizes to be used for different items are frequently spelled out in a company's drawing standards. The text of certain notes—such as manufacturing standards or safety control notices—are often standardized so that legally appropriate and consistent information is provided in all cases. In addition, libraries of symbols and stock parts may be provided to help you work more efficiently and produce engineering drawings that can easily be understood and reused by others.

The guidelines for drawing standards can be codified and stored with drawing archives as a navigational aid in the future. In some cases, the drafting group will help ensure that drawings meet company standards; in others, it is the responsibility of the designer to check the company's published standards. The standards may be enforced by the records management group responsible for archiving design documents, which will refuse to accept drawings that are not prepared according to standards. While it may be easy to rename a file after it is created to make it consistent with company standards, you should address drawing standards by starting new drawings from a prototype file or seed part that provides the company's common framework.

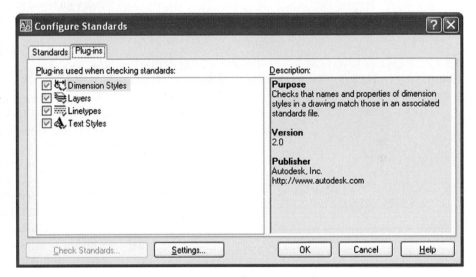

13.11 AutoCAD 2008 Software's Configure Standards Dialog Box. *Certain images and materials contained in this publication were reproduced with the permission of Autodesk, Inc. © 2007. All rights reserved.*

Table 13.1 Standard Base Layers.* *Courtesy of National Oilwell Varco, L.P.*

Line Type	Pen Number	Pen Thickness (AutoCAD)
Center	1	.003
Section	2	.005
Dim, Format	3	.005
Object	4	.009
Hatch	5	.003
Bubbles	6	.004
Material, Symbols, Text	7	.005
Phantom	8	.003
Hidden	9	.003

Note: The layers used for certain drawing elements have been standardized company wide. Each element in the first column is placed on a separate layer in the drawing. Line type, color and line thickness for the various elements are set by layer in the prototype files used to start all drawings.

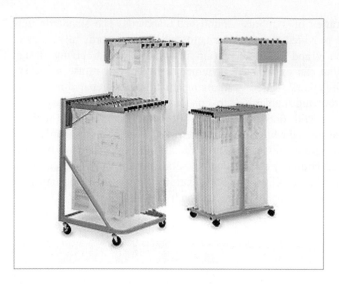

13.12 Paper or Mylar Drawings are Sometimes Stored Clamped into Hanging Racks. *Courtesy of Mayline Group.*

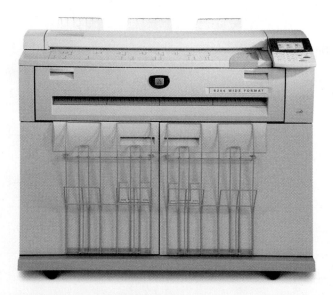

13.13 Xerox Engineering Printer/Copier Model 6024. *Courtesy of Xerox Corporation.*

13.10 STORAGE OF PAPER OR MYLAR DRAWINGS

Paper or mylar drawings may be stored flat in large flat-drawer files or hung vertically in cabinets especially designed for the purpose (Figure 13.12). Exceptionally large drawings are often rolled and stored in tubes in racks or cabinets. Prints are often folded and stored in standard office file cases. Proper control procedures will enable the user of the drawing to find it in the file, to return it to its proper place, and to know where the drawing is when not in the file. Careful revision control processes must be used to ensure the most recent drawing version is being used and the old versions are stored to properly document the design history.

13.11 REPRODUCTION OF DRAWINGS

After the drawings of a machine or structure have been completed, it is usually necessary to supply copies to many different persons and firms. Exact, rapid, and economical reproduction methods must be used to transmit the information on the drawings to the group of drawing users, whether it is storing a PDF file version of the drawing on the Web or computer network or printing the drawing and distributing it. Even when a drawing is plotted from a CAD system, it is frequently faster to use a reproduction process to distribute the drawing. Plots can be created on mylar, or on specialty papers that allow prints to be made directly from the plot. Large format copy machines are also popular for creating distribution drawings of a print. Networks, groupware, Internet and Intranet, and modems are allowing many workplaces to go to a paperless office, where drawings are distributed electronically. However, when there is a need to take drawings into the field, printing is still frequently required.

13.12 PRINTING AND COPYING ENGINEERING DRAWINGS

Of the several processes in use for reproduction, the blueprint is the oldest process used for making prints of large drawings. It is essentially a photographic process in which the original drawing is the negative. The blueprint process, which was the common method used for the reproduction of drawings for many years, has now been replaced to a large extent by other more convenient and efficient processes.

Engineering Printers

High-speed digital engineering printers, such as the one shown in Figure 13.13, are most widely used in the engineering and manufacturing industry. Such printers can produce output from either CAD files, hard copy, or a mixture of both. These printers can also produce multimedia products and digital sorting for automated set production.

Diazo-Moist Prints

Diazo moist prints may be created on special blackprint paper, cloth, or film producing a black-and-white print to a blueprint. Moist diazo prints are fed through a special developer that dampens the coated side of the paper.

The Diazo-Dry Process

The diazo-dry process is a contact method of reproduction which depends on light being transmitted through the original to produce a positive print. Pen or pencil lines, typewritten or any opaque printed matter or image can be reproduced this way. The diazo whiteprint method of reproduction consists of two steps—exposure and dry development by means of ammonia vapors.

Xerography

Xerox prints are positive prints with black lines on a white background (Figure 13.14). A selenium-coated and electrostatically charged plate is used. A special camera is used to project the original onto the plate; hence, reduced or enlarged reproductions are possible. A negatively charged plastic powder is spread across the plate and adheres to the positively charged areas of the image. The powder is then transferred to paper by means of a positive electric charge and is baked onto the surface to produce the final print. Full-sized prints or reductions can be made inexpensively and quickly in the fully automated Xerox or other similar copy machines. Xerography allows for volume print making from original drawings or microfilms.

Fax Technology

Fax machines (sometimes called telecopiers or facsimile machines) can receive or send documents (usually) over standard telephone lines in the office or in the field. A computer can send and receive documents directly, generally as a raster or bitmap type image, avoiding the need for a paper copy of the drawing. Many companies produce all in one copier, printer, and fax machine.

Digital Image Processing

Modern digital techniques have made possible the direct production of drawings on a laser printer from a variety of input sources, including computers and electronic video equipment.

In addition to drawings produced with the assistance of a CAD program, hand-produced drawings may be stored digitally using digital scanning or by manually digitizing the drawing.

Color Laser Printing/Copying

Color laser copiers can reproduce drawings in four colors, with black lettering (Figure 13.15), and some are available with optional built-in computer processing unit and monitor, video player, and film projector to permit convenient viewing and editing of drawings.

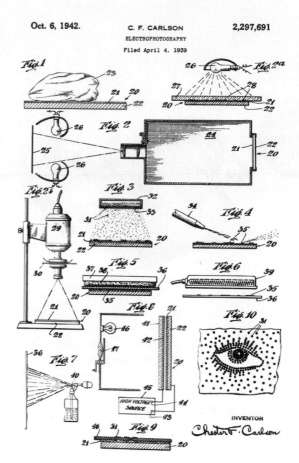

13.14 Patent Drawing for Chester Carlson's Electrophotography Device. *Courtesy of Xerox Corporation.*

13.15   The single pass laser printer uses four separate photoconducting drums and four laser beams one for each color: cyan, magenta, yellow, and black. The four colors of powdery plastic toner are attracted to the positive charges that make up the image. *Courtesy of Xerox Corporation.*

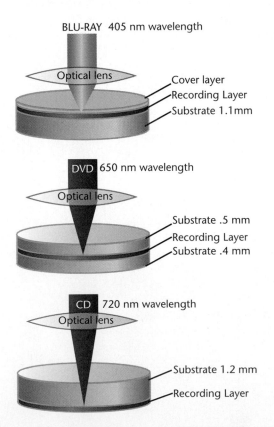

13.16   Blu-Ray disc system compared to DVD and CD Rom

13.13 DIGITAL STORAGE SYSTEMS

CD-ROM

Recordable CD-ROM systems let you store digital information such as CAD drawings, digital audio and video, data, multimedia projects, and other digitally stored records. Write-once-read-many (WORM) CD-ROM storage devices provide excellent storage for CAD documentation. Once the CD has been written it cannot be erased or rewritten. The shelf life for most storage of the media if properly cared for claims to be at least 100 years, so it qualifies as an archival media for permanent storage. CDs are compact and easy to store, and CD-ROM players are standard equipment on many CAD systems. Another advantage of CD-ROM systems is that they are random access storage systems, so that you can go directly to the document you wish to retrieve, unlike tape systems, which must wind through all of the previous tape. Systems that can automatically retrieve from a selection of multiple CDs, called juke box systems, are available for quickly retrieving documents in a network storage situation.

Optical Disk

Optical disk storage systems use optical magnetic media to store capacities up to 4.6 GB (gigabytes) on a single removable disk. They are rewritable media. This means that they are not suitable for archival storage of permanent records. (For more information on other data storage options, refer to Chapter 2.)

DVD

Recordable DVD systems are similar to CD-ROM storage systems. Both use lasers to "read" microscopic bumps created in a spiral pattern on a layered polycarbonate substrate. A DVD holds more data than a CD because it can have more than one spiral in a separate layer. In addition, both sides of the disk can store data. This produces a range of 4.8 to 15.9 GB of storage on a disk.

Blu-Ray

Blu-ray disks (BD) have a data layer that is nearer the surface and therefore closer to the "lens" of the laser. It uses a blue-violet laser to read bumps that are one-fifth the size of those read by the red lasers used by DVD systems. This allows for 50 GB of storage on a single disk (Figure 13.16).

Network Drives

A terabyte (TB) is 1000 GB. Network drives that have fast seek times and allow multiple users to connect at one time are an effective method for storing data. Proper backup procedures are important to ensure that if the hard disk fails you do not lose your data.

13.14 DOCUMENT MANAGEMENT SOFTWARE

Specialized software is available to help manage document revision history, approval, storage, file naming, and other issues of managing digital documentation, such as that produced by CAD systems. Cyco's AutoManager TeamWork ™® is document management software geared to work groups of 5 to 15 people.

Windchill™® is a full scale PDM/PLM solution from PTC corporation and there are many others in every range. In order to have an effective document management system, a lot of planning and setup needs to be done to ensure success. A software package alone will not provide instant success in managing the large

number of files and meeting legal requirements for document storage. It requires setup time, training, and ongoing effort to make it effective. If you are unsure how long different documents must be retained, ARMA is a good place to go for information.

13.15 ELECTRONIC FILES AND THE INTERNET

Most engineering firms use some kind of CAD program, such as AutoCAD, Pro/Engineer Wildfire, SolidEdge, Catia, SolidWorks, or others, to produce the majority of their drawings. These drawings are created and then saved as an electronic file. Unlike hard copy diagrams, these electronic files can be manipulated, revised, and resaved on various storage devices and systems.

Saved electronic files are then categorized and downloaded into an electronic archive. Archived files can then be controlled and managed through a database. In this way, these files can be maintained, retrieved, reviewed, and revised whenever the need arises using this type of control management system.

One of the main advantages of using electronic files is that they can be shared easily with clients, designers, manufacturing staff, marketing management, purchasing agents, and suppliers through e-mail or via the Internet. E-mail

(electronic mail) has become the most widely used electronic tool of the 21st century. It connects the user to the Internet and the World Wide Web. E-mail can be sent around the world or around the corner in a matter of seconds, thereby eliminating the need for phone conversations, mailings, or overnight courier deliveries. E-mails also provide the user with written documentation of all correspondence, which can be read, saved, or forwarded to other users. Electronic files may be attached to e-mails and sent to numerous people at once. This allows the user to communicate and share files with amazing speed. E-mail attachments are limited to a specific file size, based on the restrictions of the Internet provider (IP).

Web sites offer users instant access to the enormous amount of information available on the Web. Through an IP, such as America Online, MSN, Earthlink, ATT, and so on, just to name a few, the user gains access to all of the information

placed on the Web. The user can also create his or her own Web site, placing any information or files he or she would want to share with the Internet community or colleagues. Many engineering firms create their own Web sites and post electronic files and images they wish to be viewed by clients, colleagues, and vendors. Such sites are usually password-protected (i.e., the user must provide a login name and password before gaining access to the site). Many Web sites are interactive (i.e., they respond to the user's commands).

Product designs can be communicated, shared, and interpreted quickly and easily through the Internet. This tremendous communication and design review tool helps shorten the design review process and helps eliminate productivity barriers such as incomplete data, slow fax machines, and overnight packages.

13.16 MICROFILM, MICROFICHE, AND COMPUTER-OUTPUT MICROFILM

Although electronic files have replaced the use of microfilm and microfiche, for the most part, some are still in use as data storage tools.

A microfilm is a photographic image of information, records, or drawings that is stored on film at a greatly reduced scale.

A microfiche is a cardlike film containing many rows of images or records or drawings. Card sizes used for storage are 3 × 5", 4 × 6", and 5 × 8". A typical 4 × 6" microfiche will contain the equivalent of 270 pages of information. The individual cards may be viewed on a reader and, if desired, a full-size copy may be made by using a reader-printer.

Computer-output microfilm (COM) refers to a process used to produce drawings and records on microfilm, with the aid of a computer. A COM unit will produce a microfilm from database information converted to an image on a high-resolution screen that is then photographed. The main advantages of COM are storage capability and speed.

COMMUNICATING YOUR DRAWINGS ELECTRONICALLY

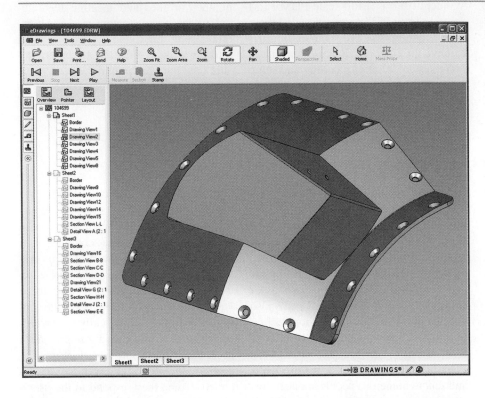

This 212 KB eDrawing can be easily e-mailed to a vendor, who can then view or even rotate the 3D part without any additional software. *Courtesy Zolo Technologies.*

Today, more and more offices are moving towards a totally electronic workplace. This means communicating with coworkers, clients, and vendors through the use of computers and electronic files. Previously, drawings would have been rendered by hand, copied, rolled up into shipping tubes, and then hand delivered or shipped to coworkers, clients, or vendors.

Modern offices no longer want to deal with hard copy diagrams, as they are bulky, costly to ship, take time to reach their destination, and can be damaged easily. Using electronic data to communicate designs saves time, money, and space. Most designers and clients are computer savvy and would prefer to look at designs on screen as opposed to looking at hard copy. Most computer users also want to be able to view designs as more than just static objects.

Communicating electronically to multiple users can pose challenges, though. Compatibility of files, hardware and software requirements, and varying Internet providers can cause communication problems.

SolidWorks offers eDrawings to answer many of these needs. eDrawings allows the user to share and interpret 2D and 3D product design data. With this new technology, the user can create review-enabled documents and send them to an unlimited number of recipients to mark up and measure via e-mail. The recipients do not need to purchase eDrawing Professional themselves. The user can embed eDrawings Viewer into the eDrawing files, allowing recipients the ability to view, mark up, and measure the drawings automatically. Recipients can create, edit, and save reviews by redlining 2D or 3D data and adding written comments; measure geometry in part, assembly, and drawing files when dimensions are omitted from the drawing; explode assemblies by dragging and dropping assembly components with the cursor; and move a cross-sectioning plane through a part or assembly to see design details hidden from view.

eDrawings also permits SolidWorks and AutoCAD integration by allowing the user to generate eDrawings instantly from within the SolidWorks or Auto-CAD software programs.

Getting design information to vendors, suppliers, manufacturers, and coworkers is a large part of the challenge of collaboration. Communication problems often can delay a project. eDrawings offers better communication, smaller file size, and fewer interpretation mistakes by eliminating common communication barriers, by not requiring everyone in the review process to purchase additional software tools. eDrawings makes the files size as small as possible. The ability to rotate 3D models in an eDrawing aids in interpretation, reducing the chance of costly mistakes. eDrawings provide the file in a format that anyone can easily receive and immediately view. This new technology gives the user the capabilities needed to overcome many of the common barriers to effective design communications.

KEY WORDS

Program Evaluation Review Technique

Product Proposal

Design Proposal

Development Plan

Engineering Release

Product Release

Documentation

American Records Management Association

Approval Indicator

Engineering Change Order

Revision Block

Drawing Standards

Drawing Approval

Drawing Release

CHAPTER SUMMARY

- Technical drawings are detailed and often very expensive to create. It is important to understand how to reproduce and manage them safely.
- Past management systems involved physically filing drawings. Most new systems now archive and distribute electronically.
- The blueprint, Diazo-Moist, and Diazo-Dry processes of reproduction are older but still used in many companies.
- Xerography, fax technology, and digital image processing are processes now commonly used that allow great flexibility in control of the drawing.
- Microfilm and microfiche methods store information on a greatly reduced scale and allow for large numbers of drawings to be stored in a small space.
- Digital printers have become the most widely used output devices in the engineering industry.
- CAD files can be used as both storage and communication tools.
- A database can be used to maintain an electronic archive of CAD files.
- The Internet and World Wide Web are tools that can help expedite the product development process.

REVIEW QUESTIONS

1. How do the Diazo-Dry and the Diazo-Moist processes differ?
2. What are some of the benefits and the dangers of using an electronic system to transfer and archive drawings?
3. Explain how CD-ROMs are used in the field of technical drawing.
4. Explain how the Xerography process works.
5. Describe how your class archives and manages its drawings.
6. What are some advantages to using digital printers versus other output devices?
7. How can CAD files be cataloged for future use?
8. List at least three ways in which you can use the Internet to communicate to other people involved in the product development or design process.
9. What is a Web site and how can an engineer or designer use this technology to his or her advantage?

CHAPTER FOURTEEN

AXONOMETRIC PROJECTION

OBJECTIVES

After studying the material in this chapter, you should be able to:

1. Describe the differences between multiview projection, axonometric projection, oblique projection, and perspective.

2. Sketch examples of an isometric cube, a dimetric cube, and a trimetric cube.

3. List the advantages of multiview projection, axonometric projection, oblique projection, and perspective.

4. Create an isometric drawing given a multiview drawing.

5. Use the isometric axes to locate drawing points.

6. Draw inclined and oblique surfaces in isometric.

7. Draw angles, ellipses, and irregular curves in isometric.

Refer to the following standard:
• ASME Y14.4M-1989 Pictorial Drawing

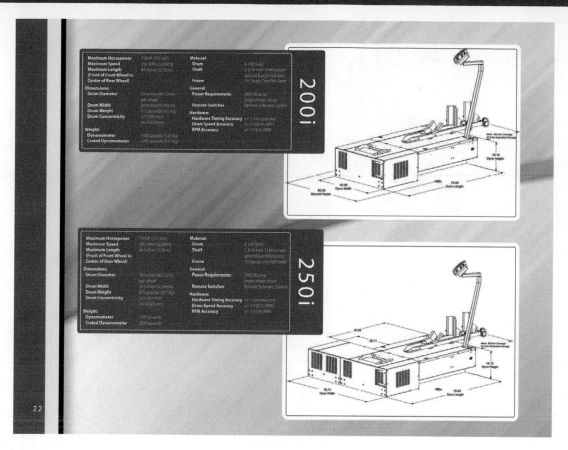

A Portion of a Sales Brochure Showing General Dimensions in Pictorial Drawings. *Courtesy of Dynojet Research, Inc.*

OVERVIEW

Multiview drawing makes it possible to accurately represent the complex forms of a design by showing a series of views and sections, but reading and interpreting this type of representation requires a thorough understanding of the principles of multiview projection. Although multiview drawings are commonly used to communicate information to a technical audience, they do not show length, width, and height in a single view and are hard for a layperson to visualize.

It is often necessary to communicate designs to people who do not have the technical training to interpret multiview projections. Axonometric projections show all three principal dimensions using a single drawing view, approximately as they appear to an observer. These projections are often called pictorial drawings because they look more like a picture than multiview drawings do. Since a pictorial drawing shows only the appearance of an object, it is not usually suitable for completely describing and dimensioning complex or detailed forms.

Pictorial drawings are also useful in developing design concepts. They can help you picture the relationships between design elements and quickly generate several solutions to a design problem.

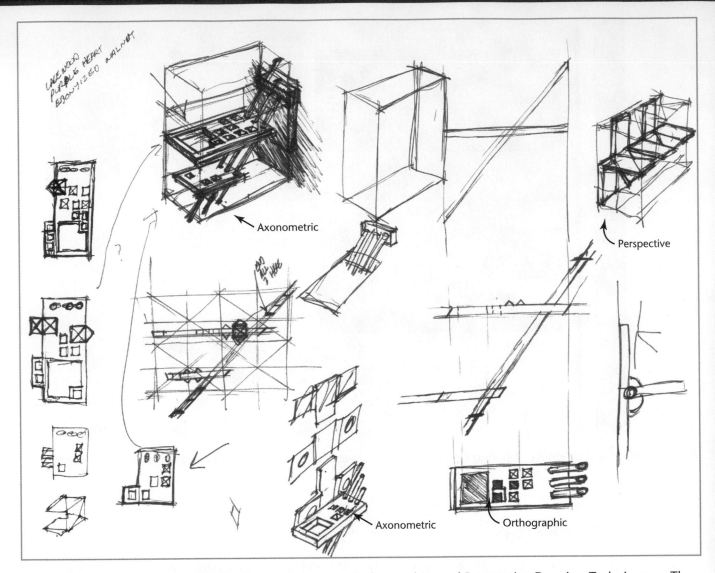

14.1 Sketches for a Wooden Shelf using Axonometric, Orthographic, and Perspective Drawing Techniques—The Axonometric Projections in this Sketch are Drawn in Isometric. *Courtesy of Douglas Wintin.*

UNDERSTANDING AXONOMETRIC DRAWINGS

Various types of pictorial drawings are used extensively in catalogs, sales literature, and technical work. They are often used in patent drawings; piping diagrams; machine, structural, architectural design, and furniture design; and for ideation sketching. The sketches for a wooden shelf in Figure 14.1 are examples of axonometric, orthographic, and perspective sketches.

The most common axonometric projection is **isometric,** which means "equal measure." When a cube is drawn in isometric, the axes are equally spaced (120° apart). Though not as realistic as perspective drawings, isometric drawings are much easier to draw. CAD software often displays the results of 3D models on the screen as isometric projections. Some CAD software allows you to choose between isometric, dimetric, trimetric, or perspective representation of your 3D models on the 2D computer screen. In sketching, dimetric and trimetric sometimes produce a better view than isometric but take longer to draw and are therefore used less frequently.

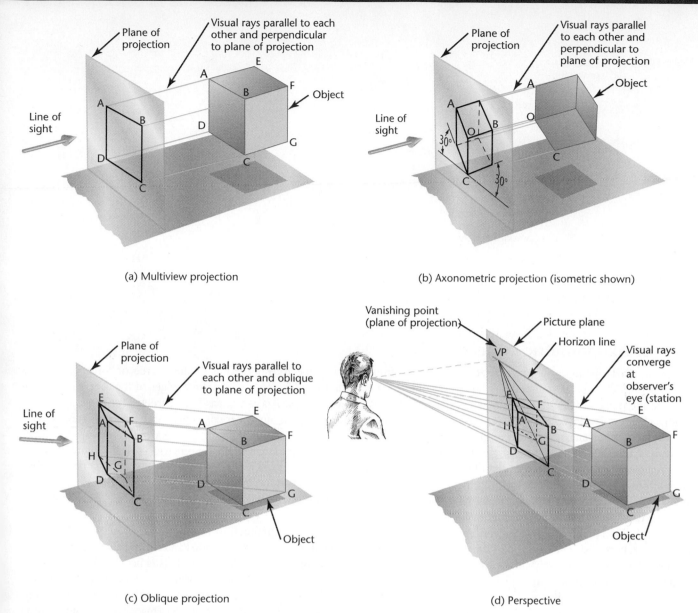

(a) Multiview projection

(b) Axonometric projection (isometric shown)

(c) Oblique projection

(d) Perspective

14.2   Four Types of Projection

Projection Methods Reviewed

The four principal types of projection are illustrated in Figure 14.2. All except the regular multiview projection (Figure 14.2a) are **pictorial** types since they show several sides of the object in a single view. In both **multiview projection** and **axonometric projection** the visual rays are parallel to each other and perpendicular to the plane of projection. Both are types of **orthographic projections** (Figure 14.2b).

In **oblique projection** (Figure 14.2c), the visual rays are parallel to each other but at an angle other than 90° to the plane of projection (see Chapter 15).

In **perspective** (Figure 14.2d), the visual rays extend from the observer's eye, or station point (SP), to all points of the object to form a "cone of rays" (see Chapter 16) so that the portions of the object that are further away from the observer appear smaller than the closer portions of the object.

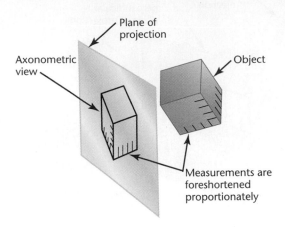

14.3 Measurements are Foreshortened Proportionately based on Amount of Incline

Types of Axonometric Projection

The feature that distinguishes axonometric projection from multiview projection is the inclined position of the object with respect to the planes of projection. When a surface or edge of the object is not parallel to the plane of projection, it appears foreshortened. When an angle is not parallel to the plane of projection, it appears either smaller or larger than the true angle.

To create an axonometric view, the object is tipped to the planes of projection so that all of the principal faces show in a single view. This produces a pictorial drawing that is easy to visualize. But, since the principal edges and surfaces of the object are inclined to the plane of projection, the lengths of the lines are foreshortened. The angles between surfaces and edges appear either larger or smaller than the true angle. There are an infinite variety of ways that the object may be oriented with respect to the plane of projection.

The degree of **foreshortening** of any line depends on its angle to the plane of projection. The greater the angle, the greater the foreshortening. If the degree of foreshortening is determined for each of the three edges of the cube that meet at one corner, scales can be easily constructed for measuring along these edges or any other edges parallel to them (Figure 14.3).

Use the three edges of the cube that meet at the corner nearest your view as the axonometric axes. In Figure 14.4, the axonometric axes, or simply the axes, are OA, OB, and OC. Figure 14.4 shows three axonometric projections.

Isometric projection (Figure 14.4a) has equal foreshortening along each of the three axis directions.

Dimetric projection (Figure 14.4b) has equal foreshortening along two axis directions and a different amount of foreshortening along the third axis. This is because it is not tipped an equal amount to all of the principal planes of projection.

Trimetric projection (Figure 14.4c) has different foreshortening along all three axis directions. This view is produced by an object that is not equally tipped to any of the planes of projection.

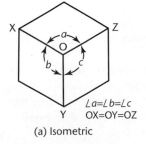

$La = Lb = Lc$
OX = OY = OZ

(a) Isometric

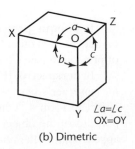

$La = Lc$
OX = OY

(b) Dimetric

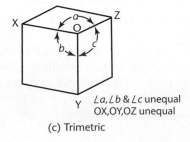

La, Lb & Lc unequal
OX, OY, OZ unequal

(c) Trimetric

14.4 Axonometric Projections

Axonometric Projections and 3D Models

When you create a 3D CAD model, the object is stored so that vertices, surfaces, and solids are all defined relative to a 3D coordinate system. You can rotate your view of the object to produce a view from any direction. However, your computer screen is a flat surface, like a sheet of paper. The CAD software uses similar projection to produce the view transformations, creating the 2D view of the object on your computer screen. Most 3D CAD software provides a variety of preset isometric viewing directions to make it easy for you to manipulate the view. Some CAD software also allows for easy perspective viewing on screen.

After rotating the object you may want to return to a preset typical axonometric view like one of the examples shown in Figure 14.5. Figure 14.6 shows a 3D CAD model.

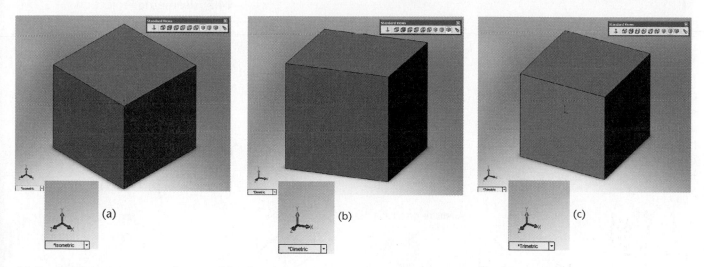

14.5 (a) Isometric View of a 1 inch Cube Shown in SolidWorks, (b) Dimetric View, (c) Trimetric View. *Courtesy of Solidworks Corporation.*

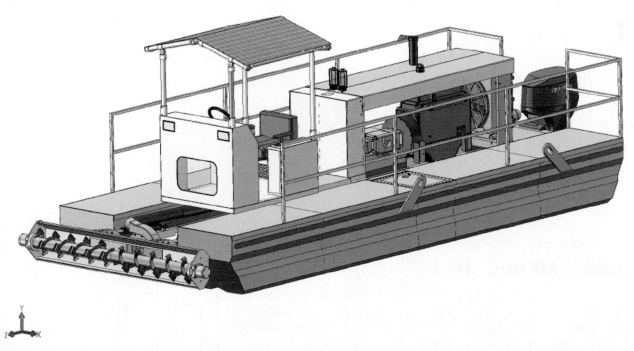

14.6 Complicated 3D CAD Models such as this Dredge from SRS Crisafulli Inc., are Often Viewed on Screen Using Isometric Display—Notice the Coordinate System Display in the Lower Left. *Courtesy of SRS Crisafulli, Inc.*

14.1 ISOMETRIC PROJECTION

In an isometric projection, all angles between the axonometric axes are equal. To produce an isometric projection (isometric means "equal measure"), you orient the object so that its principal edges (or axes) make equal angles with the plane of projection and are therefore foreshortened equally. Oriented this way, the edges of a cube would be projected so that they all measure the same and make equal angles with each other (of 120°) as shown in Figure 14.7.

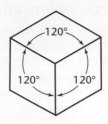

14.7 Isometric Projection

Creating Isometric Projections

Figure 14.8a shows a multiview drawing of a cube. Figure 14.8b shows the cube revolved 45° about an imaginary vertical axis. Now an auxiliary view in the direction of the arrow shows the diagonal of the cube as a point. This creates a true isometric projection. You can continue revolving the cube until the three edges *OX*, *OY*, and *OZ* make equal angles with the front plane of projection and show foreshortened equally. Again, a diagonal through the cube, in this case *OT*, appears as a point in the isometric view and the view produced is a true isometric projection. In this projection the 12 edges of the cube make angles of about 35°16" with the front plane of projection. The lengths of their projected edges are equal to the actual edge length multiplied by $\sqrt{\frac{2}{3}}$ or about 0.816. Thus the projected lengths are about 80 percent of the true lengths or about three-fourths of the true lengths.

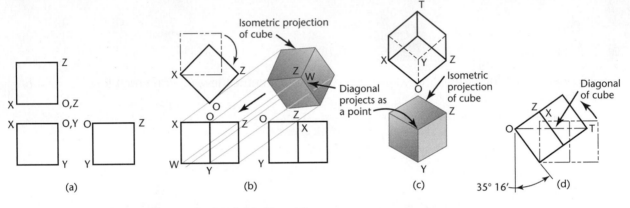

14.8 Isometric Projection as a Second Auxiliary View

14.2 ISOMETRIC AXES

The projections of the edges of a cube make angles of 120° with each other. You can use these as the **isometric axes** from which to make measurements. Any line parallel to one of these is called an isometric line. The angles in the isometric projection of the cube are either 120° or 60°, and all are projections of 90° angles. In an isometric projection of a cube, the faces of the cube, and any planes parallel to them, are called isometric planes. See Figure 14.9.

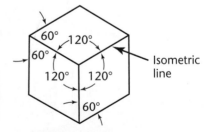

14.9 Isometric Axes

14.3 NONISOMETRIC LINES

Lines of an isometric drawing that are not parallel to the isometric axes are called **nonisometric lines** (Figure 14.10). Only lines of an object that are drawn parallel to the isometric axes are equally foreshortened. Nonisometric lines are drawn at other angles and are not equally foreshortened. Therefore the lengths of features along nonisometric lines cannot be measured directly with the scale.

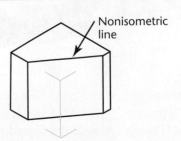

14.10 Nonisometric Edges

14.4 ISOMETRIC SCALES

An **isometric scale** can be used to draw correct isometric projections. All distances in this scale are $\sqrt{\frac{2}{3}} \times$ true size, or approximately 80 percent of true size. Figure 14.11a shows an isometric scale. More commonly, an isometric sketch or drawing is created using a standard scale, as in Figure 14.11b, disregarding the foreshortening that the tipped surfaces would produce in a true projection.

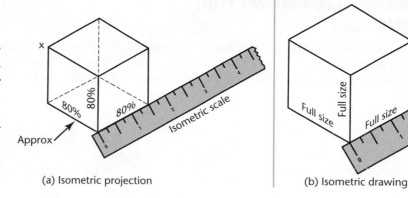

(a) Isometric projection

(b) Isometric drawing

14.11   Isometric and Ordinary Scales

TIP

Making an Isometric Scale

You can make an isometric scale from a strip of paper or cardboard as shown here by placing an ordinary scale at 45° to a horizontal line and the paper scale at 30° to the horizontal line. To mark the increments on the isometric scale, draw straight lines (perpendicular to the horizontal line) from the division lines on the ordinary scale.

Alternatively, you can approximate an isometric scale. Scaled measurements of 9" = 1'-0, or three-quarter-size scale (or metric equivalent) can be used as an approximation.

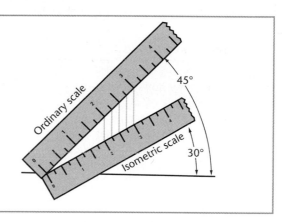

14.5 ISOMETRIC DRAWINGS

When you make a drawing using foreshortened measurements, or when the object is actually projected on a plane of projection, it is called an **isometric projection** (Figure 14.11a). When you make a drawing using the full length measurements of the actual object, it is an **isometric sketch** or **isometric drawing** (Figure 14.11b) to indicate that it lacks foreshortening.

The isometric drawing is about 25 percent larger than the isometric projection, but the pictorial value is obviously the same in both. Since isometric sketches are quicker, as you can use the actual measurements, they are much more commonly drawn.

Positions of the Isometric Axes

The first step in making an isometric drawing is to decide along which axis direction to show the height, width, and depth, respectively. Figure 14.12 shows

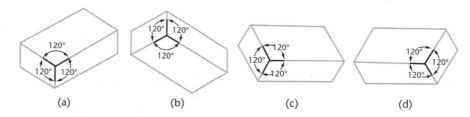

(a)   (b)   (c)   (d)

14.12   Positions of Isometric Axes

four different orientations that you might start with to create an isometric drawing of the block shown. Each is an isometric drawing of the same block, but with a different corner facing your view. These are only a few of many possible orientations.

You may orient the axes in any desired position, but the angle between them must remain 120°. In selecting an orientation for the axes, choose the position from which the object is usually viewed, or determine the position that best describes the shape of the object or better yet, both.

If the object is a long part, it will look best with the long axis oriented horizontally.

TIP

Some CAD software will notify you about the lack of foreshortening in isometric drawings when you print or save them or allow you to select for it.

14.6 MAKING AN ISOMETRIC DRAWING

Rectangular objects are easy to draw using **box construction**, which consists of imagining the object enclosed in a rectangular box whose sides coincide with the main faces of the object.

For example, imagine the object shown in the two views in Figure 14.13 enclosed in a construction box, then locate the irregular features along the edges of the box as shown.

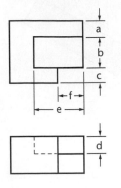
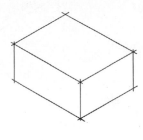
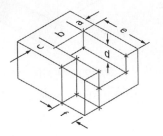
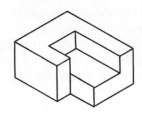

1. Lightly draw the overall dimensions of the box

2. Draw the irregular features relative to the sides of the box

3. Darken the final lines

14.13 Box Construction

Figure 14.14 shows how to construct an isometric drawing of an object composed of all normal surfaces. Notice that all measurements are made parallel to the main edges of the enclosing box—that is, parallel to the isometric axes. No

measurement along a nonisometric line can be measured directly with the scale as these lines are not foreshortened equally to the normal lines. Start at any one of the corners of the bounding box and draw along the isometric axis directions.

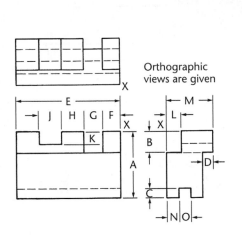
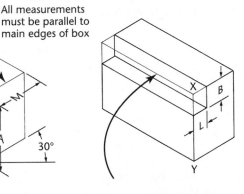

1. Select axes along which to block in height, weight and depth dimensions

2. Locate main areas to be removed from the overall block lightly sketch along isometric axes to define portion to be removed

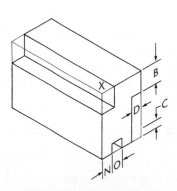
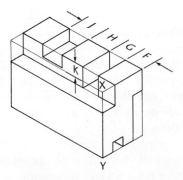
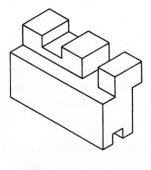

3. Lightly block in any remaining major portions to be removed through the whole block

4. Lightly block in features to be removed from the remaining shape along isometric axes

5. Darken final lines

14.14 Steps in Making an Isometric Drawing of Normal Surfaces

14.7 OFFSET LOCATION MEASUREMENTS

Use the method shown in Figure 14.15a and b to locate points with respect to each another. First draw the main enclosing block, then draw the offset lines (CA and BA) in the full size in the isometric drawing to located corner A of the small block or rectangular recess. These measurements are called **offset measurements**. Since they are parallel to edges of the main block in the multiview drawings, they will be parallel to the same edges in the isometric drawings (using the rule of parallelism).

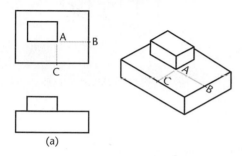

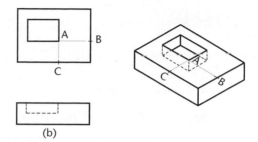

| (a) | (b) |

14.15   Offset Location Measurements

14.8 DRAWING NONISOMETRIC LINES

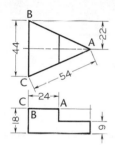

HOW TO DRAW NONISOMETRIC LINES

The inclined lines BA and CA are shown true length in the top view (54 mm), but they are not true length in the isometric view. To draw these lines in the isometric drawing use a construction box and offset measurements.

1 Directly measure dimensions that are along isometric lines (in this case, 44 mm, 18 mm, and 22 mm).

2 Since the 54 mm dimension is not along an isometric axis, it cannot be used to locate point A.

Use trigonometry or draw a line parallel to the isometric axis to determine the distance to point A.

Since this dimension is parallel to an isometric axis, it can be transferred to the isometric.

3 The dimensions 24 mm and 9 mm are parallel to isometric lines and can be measured directly.

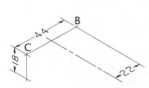

Transfer distance

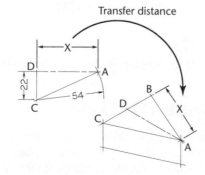

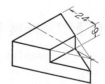

STEP by STEP

TIP

To convince yourself that nonisometric lines will not be true length in the isometric drawing, use a scrap of paper and mark the distance BA (II) and then compare it with BA on the given top view in Figure 14.16a. Do the same for line CA. You will see that BA is shorter and CA is longer in the isometric than the corresponding lines in the given views.

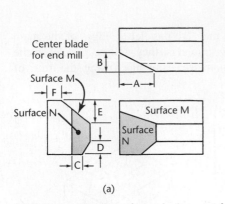

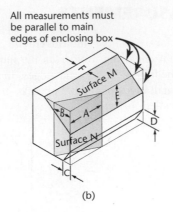

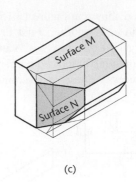

(a) (b) (c)

14.16 Inclined Surfaces in Isometric

Isometric Drawings of Inclined Surfaces

Figure 14.16 shows how to construct an isometric drawing of an object that has some inclined surfaces and oblique edges. Notice that inclined surfaces are located by offset or coordinate measurements along the isometric lines. For example, dimensions *E* and *F* are measured to locate the inclined surface *M*, and dimensions *A* and *B* are used to locate surface *N*.

14.9 OBLIQUE SURFACES IN ISOMETRIC

HOW TO DRAW OBLIQUE SURFACES IN ISOMETRIC

1 Find the intersections of the oblique surfaces with the isometric planes. Note that for this example, the oblique plane contains points A, B, and C.

2 To draw the plane, extend line AB to X and Y, in the same isometric plane as C. Use lines XC and YC to locate points E and F.

3 Finally, draw AD and ED using the rule that parallel lines appear parallel in every orthographic or isometric view.

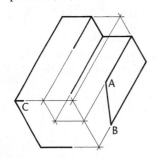

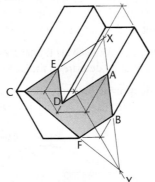

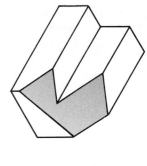

14.10 HIDDEN LINES AND CENTERLINES

Hidden lines are omitted unless they are needed to make the drawing clear. Figure 14.17 shows a case in which hidden lines are needed because a projecting part cannot be clearly shown without them. Sometimes it is better to include an isometric view from another direction than to try to show hidden features with hidden lines.

Draw centerlines if they are needed to indicate symmetry or if they are needed for dimensioning, but in general, use centerlines sparingly in isometric drawings. If in doubt, leave them out, as too many centerlines will look confusing.

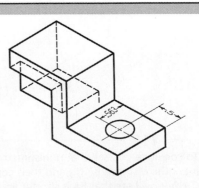

14.17 Using Hidden Lines

14.11 ANGLES IN ISOMETRIC

Angles project true size only when the plane containing the angle is parallel to the plane of projection. An angle may project to appear larger or smaller than the true angle depending on its position.

Since the various surfaces of the object are usually inclined to the front plane of projection, they generally will not be projected true size in an isometric drawing.

HOW TO DRAW ANGLES IN ISOMETRIC

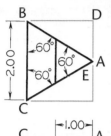
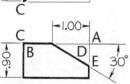

The multiview drawing at left shows three 60° angles. None of the three angles will be 60° in the isometric drawing.

TIP

Checking Isometric Angles

To convince yourself that none of the angles will be 60°, measure each angle in the isometric in Figure 14.17 with a protractor or scrap of paper and note the angle compared to the true 60°. None of the angles shown are the same in the isometric drawing. Two are smaller and one is larger than 60°.

Estimating 30° angles

If you are sketching on graph paper and estimating angles, an angle of 30° is roughly a rise of 1 to a run of 2.

---

1 Lightly draw an enclosing box using the given dimensions, except for dimension *X*, which is not given.

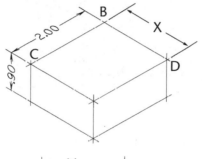

2 To find dimension *X*, draw triangle BDA from the top view full size, as shown.

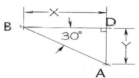

3 Transfer dimension *X* to the isometric to complete the enclosing box. Find dimension *Y* by a similar method and then transfer it to the isometric.

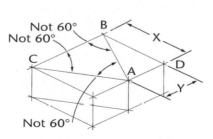

4 Complete the isometric by locating point E by using dimension K, as shown. A regular protractor cannot be used to measure angles in isometric drawings. Convert angular measurements to linear measurements along isometric axis lines.

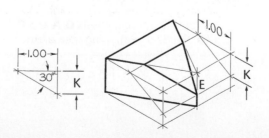

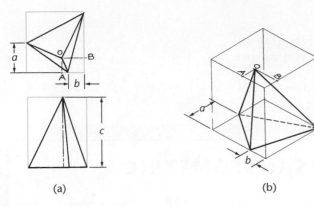

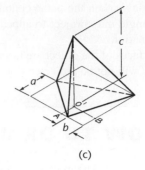

(a)   (b)   (c)

14.18   Irregular Object in Isometric

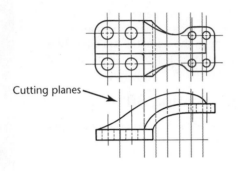

Cutting planes

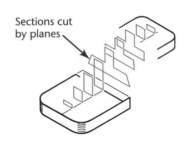

Sections cut
by planes

1. Construct sections in isometric.

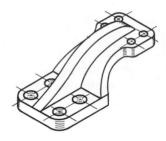

2. Complete the object by drawing lines
through the corners of the sections.

14.19   Using Sections in Isometric

14.12 IRREGULAR OBJECTS

You can use the construction box method to draw objects that are not rectangular (Figure 14.18). Locate the points of the triangular base by offsetting **a** and **b** along the edges of the bottom of the construction box. Locate the vertex by offsetting lines **OA** and **OB** using the top of the construction box.

You can also draw irregular objects using a series of sections. The edge views of imaginary cutting planes are shown in the top and front views of the multiview drawing in Figure 14.19. In the example, all height dimensions are taken from the front view and all depth dimensions from the top view.

--- **TIP** ---
It is not always necessary to draw the complete construction box as shown in Figure 14.18b. If only the bottom of the box is drawn, the triangular base can be constructed as before. The orthographic projection of the vertex **O'** on the base can be drawn using offsets **O'A** and **O'B**, as shown, and then the vertical line **O'O** can be drawn, using measurement **C**.

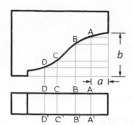

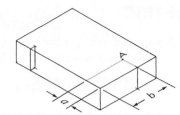

1. Use offset measurements *a* and *b* in the isometric to locate point A on the curve

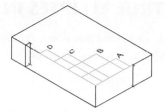

2. Locate points B, C, and D, and so on

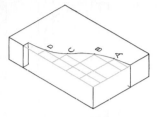

3. Sketch a smooth light freehand curve through the points

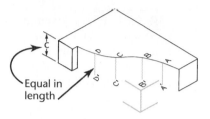

4. Draw a line vertically from point A to locate point A', and so on, making all equal to the height of block (c) then draw a light curve through the points

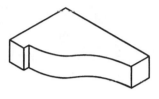

5. Darken the final lines

14.20   Curves in Isometric

14.13 CURVES IN ISOMETRIC

You can draw curves in isometric using a series of offset measurements similar to those discussed in Section 14.7. Select any desired number of points at random along the curve in the given top view, such as points *A*, *B*, and *C* in Figure 14.20. Choose enough points to accurately locate the path of the curve (the more points, the greater the accuracy). Draw offset grid lines from each point parallel to the isometric axes and use them to locate each point in the isometric drawing as in the example shown in Figure 14.20.

Tennis Ball (Factory Reject). *Cartoon by Roger Price.*
Courtesy of Droodles, "The Classic Collection."

14.14 TRUE ELLIPSES IN ISOMETRIC

If a circle lies in a plane that is not parallel to the plane of projection, the circle projects as an ellipse. The ellipse can be constructed using offset measurements.

STEP by STEP

DRAWING AN ISOMETRIC ELLIPSE BY OFFSET MEASUREMENTS

Random Line Method

1 Draw parallel lines spaced at random across the circle.

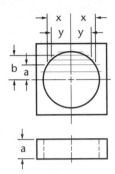

2 Transfer these lines to the isometric drawing. Where the hole exits the bottom of the block, locate points by measuring down a distance equal to the height *d* of the block from each of the upper points. Draw the ellipse, part of which will be hidden, through these points. Darken the final drawing lines.

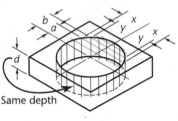

Eight Point Method

1 Enclose the given circle in a square, and draw diagonals. Draw another square through the points of intersection of the diagonals and the circle as shown.

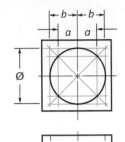

2 Draw this same construction in the isometric, transferring distances a and b. (If more points are desired, add random parallel lines, as above.) The centerlines in the isometric are the conjugate diameters of the ellipse. The 45° diagonals coincide with the major and minor axes of the ellipse. The minor axis is equal in length to the sides of the inscribed square.

When more accuracy is required, divide the circle into 12 equal parts, as shown.

12 point method

Refer to Appendix 39 for detailed methods of constructing the ellipse.

Nonisometric Lines

If a curve lies in a nonisometric plane, not all offset measurements can be applied directly. The elliptical face shown in the auxiliary view lies in an inclined nonisometric plane.

1 Draw lines in the orthographic view to locate points.

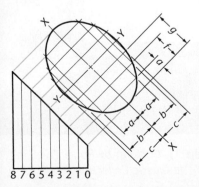

2 Enclose the cylinder in a construction box and draw the box in the isometric drawing. Draw the base using offset measurements and construct the inclined ellipse by locating points and drawing the final curve through them.

Measure distances parallel to an isometric axis (*a*, *b*, etc.) in the isometric drawing on each side of the centerline X–X. Project those not parallel to any isometric axis (*e*, *f*, etc.) to the front view and down to the base, then measure along the lower edge of the construction box, as shown.

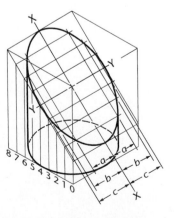

3 Darken final lines.

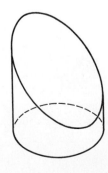

14.15 ORIENTING ELLIPSES IN ISOMETRIC DRAWINGS

Figure 14.21 shows a four center ellipses constructed on the three visible faces of a cube. Note that all of the diagonals are horizontal or at 60° with horizontal. Realizing this makes it easier to draw the shapes.

An approximate ellipse such as this, constructed from four arcs, is accurate enough for most isometric drawings. The four center method can be used only for ellipses in isometric planes. Earlier versions of CAD software, such as AutoCAD Release 10, used this method to create the approximate elliptical shapes available in the software. Current releases use an accurate ellipse.

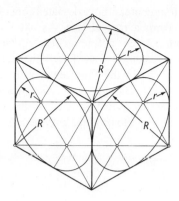

14.21 Four Center Ellipses

DRAWING A FOUR CENTER ELLIPSE

1 Draw or imagine a square enclosing the circle in the multiview drawing. Draw the isometric view of the square (an equilateral parallelogram with sides equal to the diameter of the circle).

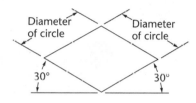

2 Create perpendicular bisectors to each side. They will intersect at four points, which will be centers for the four circular arcs.

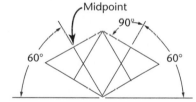

— **TIP** —

Here is a useful rule. The major axis of the ellipse is always at right angles to the centerline of the cylinder, and the minor axis is at right angles to the major axis and coincides with the centerline.

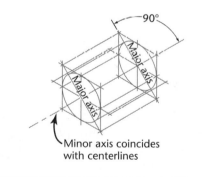

3 Draw the two large arcs, with radius *R*, from the intersections of the perpendiculars in the two closest corners of the parallelogram.

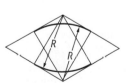

4 Draw the two small arcs, with radius *r*, from the intersections of the perpendiculars within the parallelogram, to complete the ellipse.

— **TIP** —

As a check on the accurate location of these centers, you can draw a long diagonal of the parallelogram as shown in Step 4. The midpoints of the sides of the parallelogram are points of tangency for the four arcs.

More Accurate Ellipses

The four center ellipse deviates considerably from a true ellipse. As shown in Figure 14.22a, a four center ellipse is somewhat shorter and "fatter" than a true ellipse. When the four center ellipse is not accurate enough, you can use a closer approximation called the Orth four center ellipse to produce a more accurate drawing.

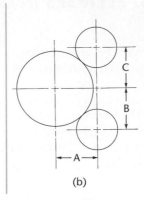
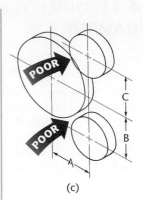

(a) (b) (c)

14.22 Inaccuracy of the Four Center Ellipse

DRAWING AN ORTH FOUR CENTER ELLIPSE

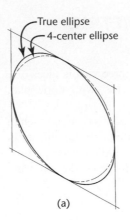

To create a more accurate approximate ellipse using the Orth method, follow the steps for these methods. The centerline method is convenient when starting from a hole or cylinder.

Centerline Method

1 Draw the isometric centerlines. From the center, draw a construction circle equal to the actual diameter of the hole or cylinder. The circle will intersect the centerlines at four points *A*, *B*, *C*, and *D*.

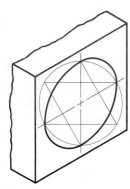

Constuction circle equal to diameter of hole

Isometric center lines

2 From the two intersection points on one centerline, draw perpendiculars to the other centerline. Then draw perpendiculars from the two intersection points on the other centerline to the first centerline.

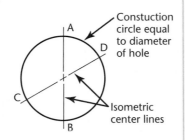

Horizontal

Perpendicular

3 With the intersections of the perpendiculars as centers, draw two small arcs and two large arcs.

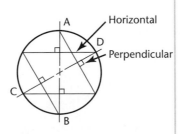

Enclosing Rectangle Method

1 Locate center and block in enclosing isometric rectangle.

2 Use the midpoint of the isometric rectangle (the distance from *A* to *B*) to locate the foci on the major axis.

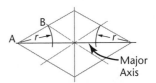

Major Axis

3 Draw lines at 60° from horizontal through the foci (points *C* and *D*) to locate the center of the large arc *R*.

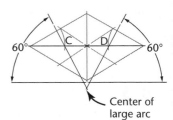

Center of large arc

4 Draw the two large arcs *R* tangent to the isometric rectangle. Draw two small arcs *r*, using foci points *C* and *D* as centers, to complete the approximate ellipse.

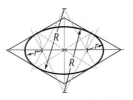

Note that these steps are exactly the same as for the regular four center ellipse, except for the use of the isometric centerlines instead of the enclosing parallelogram. (When sketching, it works fine to just draw the enclosing rectangle and sketch the arcs tangent to its sides.)

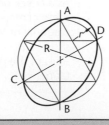

STEP by STEP

Isometric Templates

Special templates like this isometric template with angled lines and ellipses oriented in various isometric planes make it easy to draw isometric sketches.

The ellipses are provided with markings to coincide with the isometric centerlines of the holes—a convenient feature in isometric drawing.

You can also draw ellipses using an appropriate ellipse template selected to fit the major and minor axes.

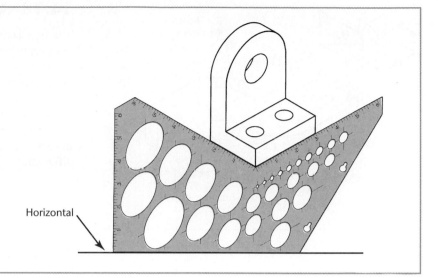

Horizontal

14.16 DRAWING ISOMETRIC CYLINDERS

A typical drawing with cylindrical shapes is shown in Figure 14.23. Note that the centers of the larger ellipse cannot be used for the smaller ellipse, though the ellipses represent concentric circles. Each ellipse has its own parallelogram and its own centers. Notice that the centers of the lower ellipse are drawn by projecting the centers of the upper large ellipse down a distance equal to the height of the cylinder.

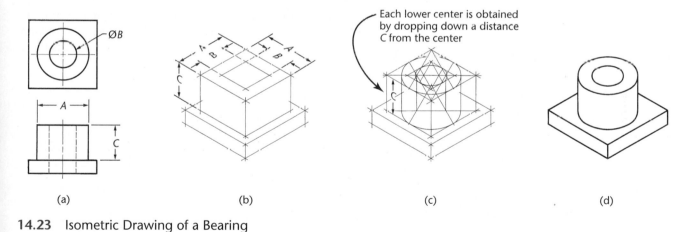

Each lower center is obtained by dropping down a distance C from the center

(a)   (b)   (c)   (d)

14.23   Isometric Drawing of a Bearing

14.17 SCREW THREADS IN ISOMETRIC

Parallel partial ellipses equally spaced at the symbolic thread pitch are used to represent only the crests of a screw thread in isometric (Figure 14.24). The ellipses may be sketched, drawn by the four center method, or created using an ellipse template.

14.24   Screw Threads in Isometric

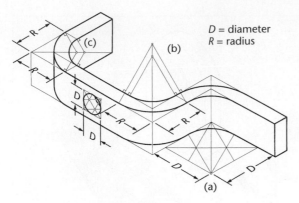

D = diameter
R = radius

14.25 Arcs in Isometric

14.18 ARCS IN ISOMETRICS

The four center ellipse construction can be used to sketch or draw circular arcs in isometric. Figure 14.25a shows the complete construction. It is not necessary to draw the complete constructions for arcs, as shown in Figure 14.25b and c. Measure the radius *R* from the construction corner; then at each point, draw perpendiculars to the lines. Their intersection is the center of the arc. Note that the *R* distances are equal in Figure 14.25b and c, but that the actual radii used are quite different.

14.19 INTERSECTIONS

To draw the elliptical intersection of a cylindrical hole in an oblique plane in isometric (Figure 14.26a), draw the ellipse in the isometric plane on top of the construction box (Figure 14.26b); then project points down to the oblique plane as shown. Each point forms a trapezoid, which is produced by a slicing plane parallel to a lateral surface of the block.

To draw the curve of intersection between two cylinders (Figure 14.27), use a series of imaginary cutting planes through the cylinders parallel to their axes. Each plane will cut elements on both cylinders that intersect at points on the curve of intersection (Figure 14.26b). As many points should be plotted as necessary to assure a smooth curve. For accuracy, draw the ends of the cylinders using the Orth four center construction, with ellipse guides, or by one of the true ellipse constructions.

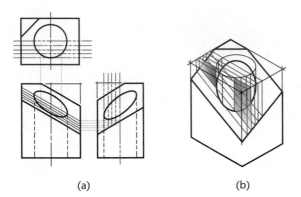

(a)   (b)

14.26 Oblique Plane and Cylinder

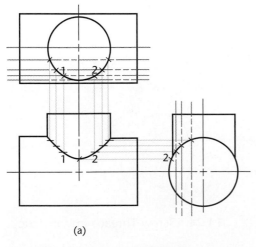

(a)

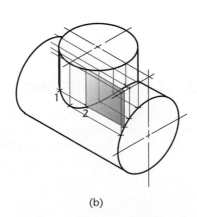

(b)

14.27 Intersection of Cylinders

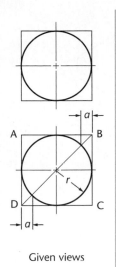

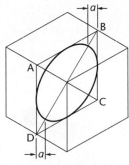

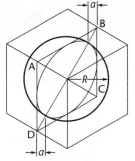

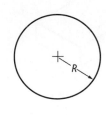

Given views

Determining the radius

Isometric drawing

Isometric projection

1. Draw the the isometric of a great circle parallel to one face of the cube; then determine the radius of the sphere by locating points on the diagonal using measurement *a* to establish the ends of the major axis

2. The diameter of the circle in the isometric drawing is $\sqrt{\frac{2}{3}} \times$ the diameter of the sphere

3. The diameter of the circle in the isometric projection is equal to the true diameter of the sphere

14.28 Isometric of a Sphere

14.20 SPHERES IN ISOMETRIC

The isometric drawing of any curved surface is the envelope of all lines that can be drawn on that surface. For spheres, select the great circles (circles cut by any plane through the center) as the lines on the surface. Since all great circles, except those that are perpendicular or parallel to the plane of projection, are shown as ellipses having equal major axes, their envelope is a circle whose diameter is the major axis of the ellipse.

Figure 14.28 shows two views of a sphere enclosed in a construction cube. Next, an isometric of a great circle is drawn in a plane parallel to one face of the cube. There is no need to draw the ellipse, since only the points on the diagonal located by measurements *a* are needed to establish the ends of the major axis and thus to determine the radius of the sphere.

In the resulting isometric drawing the diameter of the circle is $\sqrt{\frac{2}{3}}$ times the actual diameter of the sphere. The isometric projection is simply a circle whose diameter is equal to the true diameter of the sphere.

14.21 ISOMETRIC SECTIONING

Isometric sectioning is useful in drawing open or irregularly shaped objects. Figure 14.29 shows an isometric full section. It is usually best to draw the cut surface first, then draw the portion of the object that lies behind the cutting plane.

To create an isometric half section, it is usually easiest to make an isometric drawing of the entire object, then add the cut surfaces as shown in Figure 14.30. Since only a quarter of the object is removed in a half section, the resulting pictorial drawing is more useful than a full section.

Isometric broken-out sections are also sometimes used. Section lining in isometric drawing is similar to that in multiview drawing. Section lining at an angle of 60° with horizontal as shown in Figures 14.29 and 14.30 is recommended, but change the direction if 60° would cause the lines to be parallel to a prominent visible line bounding the cut surface, or to other adjacent lines of the drawing.

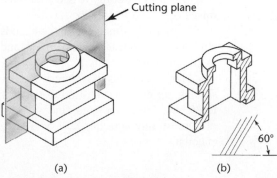

(a)   (b)

14.29 Isometric Full Section

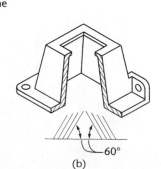

(a)   (b)

14.30 Isometric Half Section

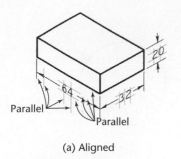

(a) Aligned

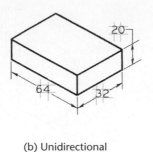

(b) Unidirectional

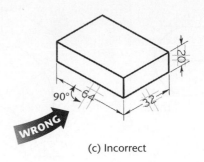

(c) Incorrect

14.31 Numerals and Arrowheads in Isometric (Metric Dimensions)

14.22 ISOMETRIC DIMENSIONING

Isometric dimensions are similar to ordinary dimensions used on multiview drawings but should match the pictorial style. Two methods of dimensioning are approved by ANSI—namely, the pictorial plane (aligned) system and the unidirectional system (Figure 14.31).

Note that vertical lettering is used for either system of dimensioning. Inclined lettering is not recommended for pictorial dimensioning. Figure 14.31a and b show how to draw numerals and arrowheads for the two systems.

In the aligned system, the extension lines, dimension lines, and lettering for the 64 mm dimension are all drawn in the isometric plane of one face of the object (Figure 14.31a). The "horizontal" guidelines for the lettering are drawn parallel to the dimension line, and the "vertical" guidelines are drawn parallel to the extension lines. The barbs of the arrowheads should line up parallel to the extension lines.

In the unidirectional system the extension lines and dimension lines for the 64 mm dimension are drawn in the isometric plane of one face of the object (Figure 14.31b). The lettering for the dimensions is vertical and reads from the bottom of the drawing. This simpler system of dimensioning is often used on pictorials for production purposes. Still, the barbs of the arrowheads should line up parallel to the extension lines, as in Figure 14.31a.

As shown in Figure 14.31c, the vertical guidelines for the letters should not be perpendicular to the dimension lines. The example in Figure 14.31c is incorrect because the 64 mm and 32 mm dimensions are not lettered in the plane of corresponding dimension and extension lines, nor are they in a vertical position to read from the bottom of the drawing. Note how the 20 mm dimension is awkward to read because of its position.

Correct and Incorrect Isometric Dimensioning

Correct practice in isometric dimensioning using the aligned system of dimensioning is shown in Figure 14.32a.

Figure 14.32b shows several incorrect practices. The 3.125 dimension runs to a wrong extension line at the right, so the dimension does not lie in an isometric plane. Near the left side, a number of lines cross each other unnecessarily and terminate on the wrong lines. The upper .5 drill hole is located from the edge of the cylinder when it should be dimensioned from its centerline. Study these two drawings carefully to see additional mistakes in Figure 14.32b.

Isometric dimensioning methods apply equally to fractional, decimal, and metric dimensions.

Many examples of isometric dimensioning are given in the End of Chapter Exercises. Study these to find samples of almost any special case you may encounter.

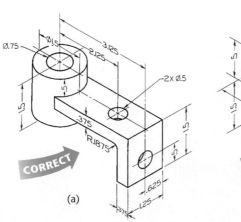

(a)

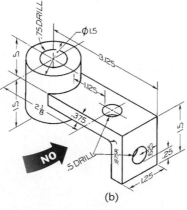

(b)

14.32 Correct and Incorrect Isometric Dimensioning (Aligned System)

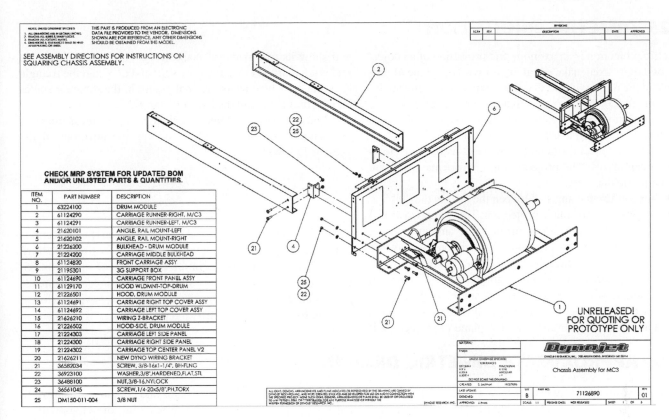

14.33 Exploded Isometric Assembly Drawing. *Courtesy of Dynojet Research, Inc.*

14.23 EXPLODED ASSEMBLIES

Exploded assemblies are often used in design presentations, catalogs, sales literature, and in the shop to show all the parts of an assembly and how they fit together. They may be drawn by any of the pictorial methods, including isometric (Figure 14.33).

14.24 PIPING DIAGRAMS

Isometric and oblique drawings are well suited for representation of piping layouts, as well as for all other structural work to be represented pictorially. An example is shown in Figure 14.34.

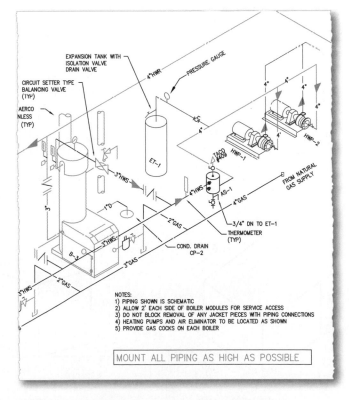

14.34 Portion of an Isometric Piping Diagram. *Courtesy of Associated Construction Engineering.*

14.25 DIMETRIC PROJECTION

A dimetric projection is an axonometric projection of an object where two of its axes make equal angles with the plane of projection and the third axis makes either a smaller or a greater angle (Figure 14.35). The two axes making equal angles with the plane of projection are foreshortened equally, while the third axis is foreshortened in a different proportion.

Usually the object is oriented so one axis is vertical. However, you can revolve the projection to any orientation if you want that particular view.

Do not confuse the angles between the axes in the drawing with the angles from the plane projection. These are two different, but related things. You can arrange the amount that the principal faces are tilted to the plane of projection any way that two angles between the axes are equal and over 90°.

The scales can be determined graphically, as shown in Figure 14.36a, in which *OP*, *OL*, and *OS* are the projections of the axes or converging edges of a cube. If the triangle *POS* is revolved about the axis line *PS* into the plane of projection, it

will show its true size and shape as *PO'S*. If regular full-size scales are marked along the lines *O'P* and *O'S*, and the triangle is counterrevolved to its original position, the dimetric scales may be divided along the axes *OP* and *OS*, as shown.

You can use an architect's scale to make the measurements by assuming the scales and calculating the positions of the axes, as follows:

$$\cos a = \frac{-\sqrt{2h^2v^2 - v^4}}{2hv}$$

where *a* is one of the two equal angles between the projections of the axes, *h* is one of the two equal scales, and *v* is the third scale. Examples are shown in the upper row of Figure 14.35, where length measurements could be made using an architect's scale. One of these three positions of the axes will be found suitable for almost any practical drawing.

14.26 APPROXIMATE DIMETRIC DRAWING

Approximate dimetric drawings, which closely resemble true dimetrics, can be constructed by substituting for the true angles shown in the upper half of Figure 14.35 angles that can be obtained with the ordinary triangles and compass, as shown in the lower half of the figure. The resulting drawings will be accurate enough for all practical purposes.

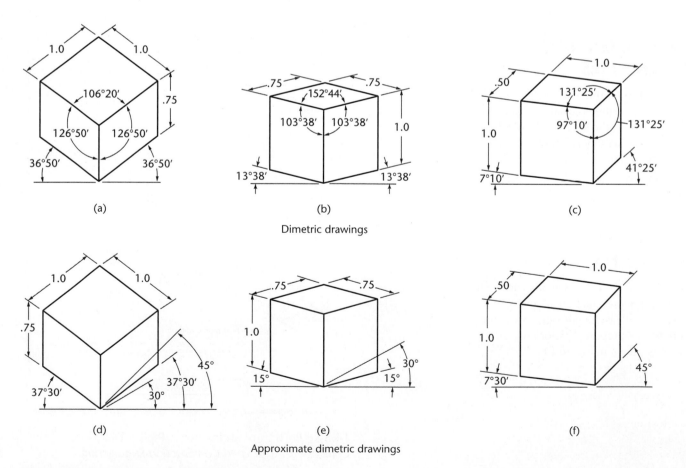

Dimetric drawings

Approximate dimetric drawings

14.35 Undertstanding Angles in Dimetric Projection

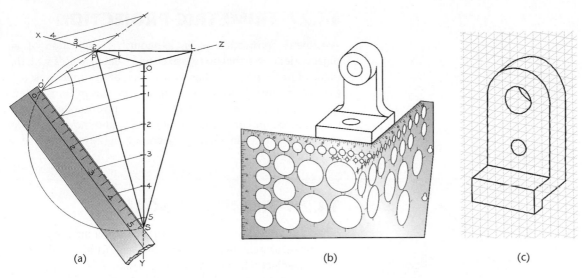

(a)   (b)   (c)

14.36 Dimetric Drawings

HOW TO MAKE DIMETRIC DRAWINGS

STEP by STEP

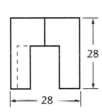

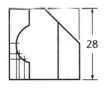

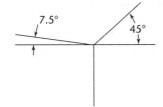

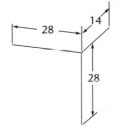

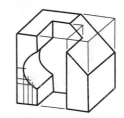

① To make a dimetric drawing for the views given, draw two intersecting axis lines at angles of 7.5° and 45° from horizontal. Draw the third axis direction vertically through them.

② The dimensions for the principal face are measured full size. The dimension for the receding axis direction will be at half scale.

③ Block in the features relative to the surfaces of the enclosing box. The offset method of drawing a curve is shown in the figure.

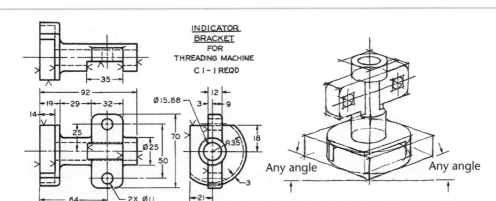

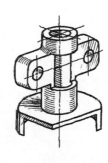

An Approximate Dimetric Drawing

Follow these steps to make a dimetric sketch with the position similar to that in Figure 14.35e where the two angles are equal.

① Using whichever angle produces a good drawing of your part, block in the dimetric axes. An angle of 20° from horizontal tends to show many parts well.

② Block in the major features, foreshorten the dimensions along the two receding axes by approximately 75 percent.

③ Darken the final lines.

14.27 TRIMETRIC PROJECTION

A trimetric projection is an axonometric projection of an object oriented so that no two axes make equal angles with the plane of projection. In other words, each of the three axes, and the lines parallel to them, have different ratios of foreshortening. If the three axes are selected in any position on paper so that none of the angles is less than 90°, and they are not an isometric nor a dimetric projection, the result will be a trimetric projection.

14.28 TRIMETRIC SCALES

Since the three axes are foreshortened differently, each axis will use measurement proportions different from the other two. You can select which scale to use as shown in Figure 14.37. Any two of the three triangular faces can be revolved into the plane of projection to show the true lengths of the three axes. In the revolved position, the regular scale is used to set off inches or fractions thereof. When the axes have been counter-revolved to their original positions, the scales will be correctly foreshortened, as shown.

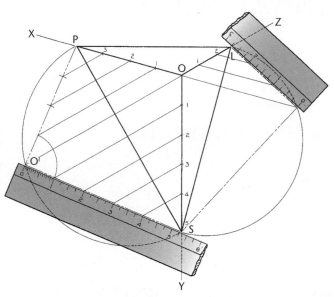

14.37   Trimetric Scales

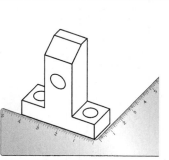

> **TIP**
>
> You can make scales from thin card stock and transfer these dimensions to each card for easy reference. You might even want to make a trimetric angle from Bristol Board or plastic, as shown here, or six or seven of them, using angles for a variety of positions of the axes.

14.29 TRIMETRIC ELLIPSES

The trimetric centerlines of a hole, or the end of a cylinder, become the conjugate diameters of an ellipse when drawn in trimetric. The ellipse may be drawn on the conjugate diameters or you can determine the major and minor axes from the conjugate diameters and construct the ellipse on them with an ellipse template or by any of the methods shown in Appendix 4.48–4.50.

One advantage of trimetric projection is the infinite number of positions of the object available. The angles and scales can be handled without too much difficulty, as shown in Sections 14.30 and 14.31. However, in drawing any axonometric ellipse, keep the following in mind:

1. On the drawing, the major axis is always perpendicular to the centerline, or axis, of the cylinder.
2. The minor axis is always perpendicular to the major axis; on the paper it coincides with the axis of the cylinder.

3. The length of the major axis is equal to the actual diameter of the cylinder.

The directions of both the major and minor axes, and the length of the major axis, will always be known, but not the length of the minor axis. Once it is determined, you can construct the ellipse using a template or any of a number of ellipse constructions. For sketching you can generally sketch an ellipse that looks correct by eye.

In Figure 14.38a, locate center O as desired, and draw the horizontal and vertical construction lines that will contain the major and minor axes through O. Note that the major axis will be on the horizontal line perpendicular to the axis of the hole, and the minor axis will be perpendicular to it, or vertical.

Use the actual radius of the hole and draw the semicircle, as shown, to establish the ends A and B of the major axis. Draw AF and BF parallel to the axonometric edges WX and YX, respectively, to locate *F*, which lies on the ellipse. Draw a vertical line through *F* to intersect the semicircle at *F'* and join *F'* to *B'*, as shown. From *D'*, where the minor axis, extended, intersects the semicircle, draw *D'E* and *ED* parallel to *F'B* and *BF*, respectively. Point *D* is one end of the minor axis. From center *O*, strike arc *DC* to locate *C*, the other end of the minor axis. On these axes, a true ellipse can be constructed, or drawn with an ellipse template.

See Appendix xx for additional methods for constructing ellipses.

In constructions where the enclosing parallelogram for an ellipse is available or easily constructed, the major and minor axes can be determined as shown in Figure 14.38b. The directions of both axes and the length of the major axis are known. Extend the axes to intersect the sides of the parallelogram at *L* and *M*, and join the points with a straight line. From one end *N* of the major axis, draw a line *NP* parallel to *LM*. The point *P* is one end of the minor axis. To find one end *T* of the minor axis of the smaller ellipse, it is only necessary to draw *RT* parallel to *LM* or *NP*.

The method of constructing an ellipse on an oblique plane in trimetric is similar to that shown in the Step by Step in Section 14.17 for drawing an isometric ellipse by offset measurements.

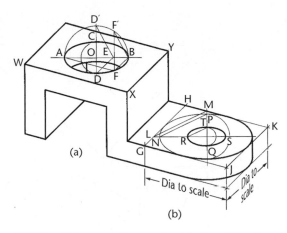

14.38 Ellipses in Trimetric. *Method (b). Courtesy of Professor H. E. Grant.*

TIP

When you are creating a trimetric sketch of an ellipse, it works great to block in the trimetric rectangle that would enclose the ellipse and sketch the ellipse tangent to the midpoints of the rectangle.

PRESENTATION DRAWING

The MARGE (Mars Autonomous Rover for Geoscience Exploration) aeroshell, shown at right, is part of a NASA Scout mission proposal developed by Malin Space Science Systems and the Raytheon Company in 2005 and 2006. The blunt, conical MARGE aeroshell is an integrated system providing safe delivery of its payload, two small, autonomous rovers, to the surface of Mars. The aeroshell is about 2.4 meters in diameter.

Shown here is the part of the system which provides aerobraking for the spacecraft's initial descent from orbit, the terminal rocket descent phase just before landing, and the final soft touchdown with the surface. With the protective backshell (where the parachute is located) and rovers removed, you can clearly see the components of the propulsion and control systems integrated into the rover egress deck, and color coded for clarity. In addition to aerobraking and rocket-powered descent, the MARGE aeroshell design incorporates crushable foam layers of increasing density to cushion the final touchdown with the planet surface. After the descent and landing phase is complete, clamps are disengaged and the rovers drive off the lip of the aeroshell under their own power.

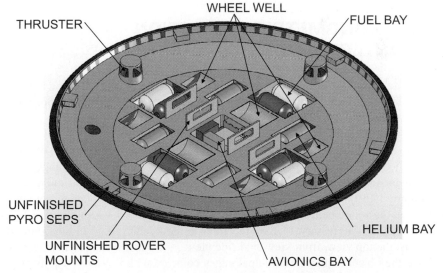

Shaded isometric views of 3D models are often used as presentation drawings. This isometric view of a proposed design for the MARGE Aeroshell was used as a presentation drawing to communicate the features of a concept developed by Malin Aerospace. *Courtesy of Malin Space Science Systems, Inc.*

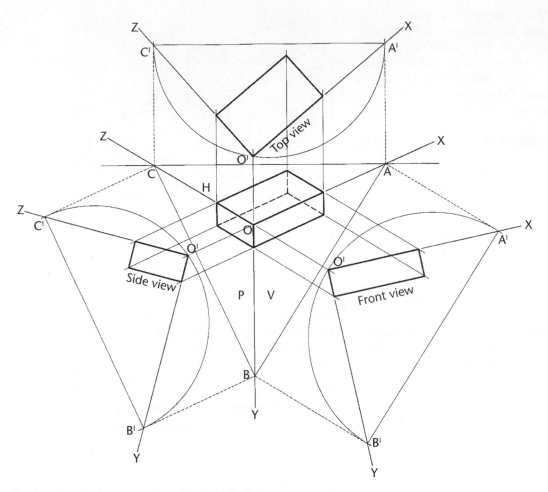

14.39   Views from an Axonometric Projection

14.30 AXONOMETRIC PROJECTION USING INTERSECTIONS

Before the advent of CAD engineering scholars devised methods to create an axonometric projection using projections from two orthographic views of the object. This method, called the method of intersections, was developed by Professors L. Eckhart and T. Schmid of the Vienna College of Engineering and was published in 1937.

To understand their method of axonometric projection, study Figure 14.39 as you read through the following steps. Assume that the axonometric projection of a rectangular object is given, and it is necessary to find the three orthographic projections: the top view, front view, and side view.

Place the object so that its principal edges coincide with the coordinate axes, and the plane of projection (the plane on which the axonometric projection is drawn) intersects the three coordinate planes in the triangle *ABC*.

From descriptive geometry, we know that lines *BC*, *CA*, and *AB* will be perpendicular, respectively, to axes *OX*, *OY*, and *OZ*. Any one of the three points *A*, *B*, or *C* may be assumed anywhere on one of the axes in order to draw triangle *ABC*.

To find the true size and shape of the top view, revolve the triangular portion of the horizontal plane *AOC*, which is in front of the plane of projection, about its base *CA*, into the plane of projection. In this case, the triangle is revolved inward to the plane of projection through the smallest angle made with it. The triangle would then be shown in its true size and shape, and you could draw the top view of the object in the triangle by projecting from the axonometric projection, as shown (since all width dimensions remain the same).

In the figure, the base *CA* of the triangle has been moved upward to *C'A'* so that the revolved position of the triangle will not overlap its projection.

The true sizes and shapes of the front view and side view can be found similarly, as shown in the figure.

Note that if the three orthographic projections, or in most cases any two of them, are given in their relative positions, as shown in Figure 14.39, the directions of the projections could be reversed so that the intersections of the projecting lines would determine the axonometric projection needed.

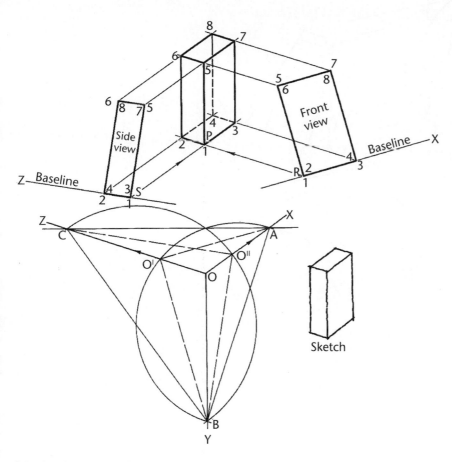

14.40   Axonometric Projection

Use of an Enclosing Box to Create an Isometric Sketch using Intersections

To draw an axonometric projection using intersections, it helps to make a sketch of the desired general appearance of the projection as shown in Figure 14.40. Even for complex objects the sketch need not be complete, just an enclosing box. Draw the projections of the coordinate axes *OX*, *OY*, and *OZ* parallel to the principal edges of the object, as shown in the sketch, and the three coordinate planes with the plane of projection.

Revolve the triangle *ABO* about its base *AB* as the axis into the plane of projection. Line *OA* will revolve to *O'A*, and this line, or one parallel to it, must be used as the baseline of the front view of the object. Draw the projecting lines from the front view to the axonometric parallel to the projection of the unrevolved *Z*-axis, as indicated in the figure.

Similarly, revolve the triangle *COB* about its base *CB* as the axis into the plane of projection. Line *CO* will revolve to *CO''*. Use this line, or one parallel to it, as the baseline of the side view. Make the direction of the projecting lines parallel to the projection of the unrevolved *X* axis, as shown.

Draw the front view baseline at a convenient location parallel to *O' X*. Use the parallel line you drew (*P3*) as the base and draw the front view of the object. Draw the side view baseline at a convenient location parallel to *O'' C*. Use it as the base (*P2*) for the side view of the object, as shown. From the corners of the front view, draw projecting lines parallel to *OZ*. From the corners of the side view, draw projecting lines parallel to *OX*. The intersections of these two sets of projecting lines determine the axonometric projection. It will be an isometric, a dimetric, or a trimetric projection, depending on the form of the sketch used as the basis for the projections.

If the angles formed by the three coordinate axes are equal, the projection is isometric; if two of them are equal, the projection is dimetric; and if none of the three angles are equal, the result is a trimetric projection.

To place the desired projection on a specific location on the drawing (Figure 14.40), select the desired projection *P* of point 1, for example, and draw two projecting lines *PR* ands *PS* to intersect the two baselines and thereby to determine the locations of the two views on their baselines.

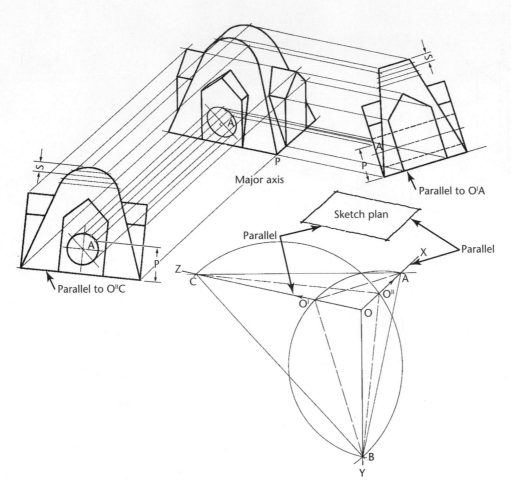

14.41 Axonometric Projection

Another example of this method of axonometric projection is shown in Figure 14.41. In this case, it was only necessary to draw a sketch of the plan or base of the object in the desired position.

To understand how the axonometric projection in Figure 14.41was created, examine the figure while reading through these steps.

Draw the axes with *OX* and *OZ* parallel to the sides of the sketch plan, and the remaining axis *OY* in a vertical position.

Revolve triangles *COB* and *AOB*, and draw the two baselines parallel to *O"C* and *O'A*.

Choose point *P*, the lower front corner of the axonometric drawing, at a convenient place, and draw projecting lines toward the baselines parallel to axes *OX* and *OZ* to locate their positions. You can draw the views on the baselines or even cut them apart from another drawing and fasten them in place with drafting tape.

To draw the elliptical projection of the circle, use any points, such as *A*, on the circle in both front and side views. Note that point *A* is the same altitude, *P*, above the baseline in both views. Draw the axonometric projection of point *A* by projecting lines from the two views. You can project the major and minor axes this way, or by the methods shown in Figure 14.38.

True ellipses may be drawn by any of the methods shown in the Appendix or with an ellipse template. An approximate ellipse is fine for most drawings.

14.31 COMPUTER GRAPHICS

Pictorial drawings of all sorts can be created using 3D CAD (Figures 14.42, 14.43). To create pictorials using 2D CAD, use projection techniques similar to those presented in this chapter. The advantage of 3D CAD is that once you make a 3D model of a part or assembly, you can change the viewing direction at any time for orthographic, isometric, or perspective views. You can also apply different materials to the drawing objects and shade them to produce a high degree of realism in the pictorial view.

14.42 Shaded Dimetric Pictorial View from a 3D Model. *Courtesy of Robert Kincaid.*

ITEM NO.	PART NAME	QTY.
1	Outer Tube	1
2	End	1
3	Top	1
4	Inner Tube	1
5	Heat exchanger	1
6	Assem Sampler	1
7	Fan	1
8	Sample Bottom	1
9	HX Mounting Plate	1
10	Cooling Hose	1
11	Door	1

DIMENSIONS ARE IN MM
TOLERANCES:
FRACTIONAL±
ANGULAR: MACH± BEND ±
TWO PLACE DECIMAL ±
THREE PLACE DECIMAL ±

	NAME	DATE
DRAWN		
CHECKED		
ENG APPR.		
MFG APPR.		
Q.A.		
COMMENTS:		

MATERIAL N/A

FINISH N/A

DO NOT SCALE DRAWING

MONTANA STATE UNIVERSITY

SIZE **A** DWG. NAME. Assem Round Encloser REV.

SCALE:1:1 WEIGHT: SHEET 1 OF 1

14.43 Isometric Assembly Drawing. *Courtesy of PTC.*

ISOMETRIC SKETCHES USING AUTOCAD SOFTWARE

Need a quick isometric sketch? AutoCAD software has special drafting settings for creating an isometric style grid.

Figure A shows the Drafting Settings dialog box in AutoCAD. When you check the button for Isometric Snap, the software calculates the spacing needed for an isometric grid. You can use it to make quick pictorial sketches like the example shown in Figure B. Piping diagrams are often done this way, although they can also be created using 3D tools.

Even though the drawing in Figure B looks 3D, it is really drawn in a flat 2D plane. You can observe this if you change the viewpoint so you are no longer looking straight onto the view.

The Ellipse command in AutoCAD has a special Isocircle option that makes drawing isometric ellipses easy. The isocircles are oriented in different directions depending on the angle of the snap cursor. Figure C shows isocircles and snap cursors for the three different orientations. In the software, you press CTRL and E simultaneously to toggle the cursor appearance.

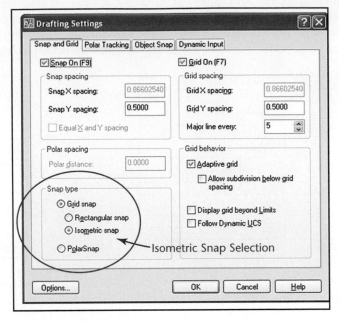

(A) Selecting isometric snap in the AutoCAD drafting settings dialog box.

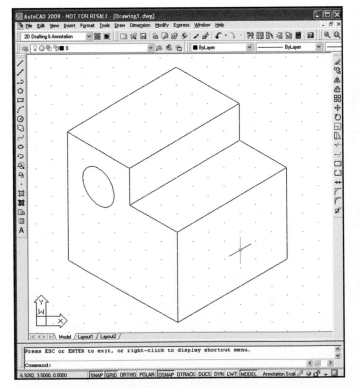

(B) A pictorial sketch created from a flat drawing using isometric snap.

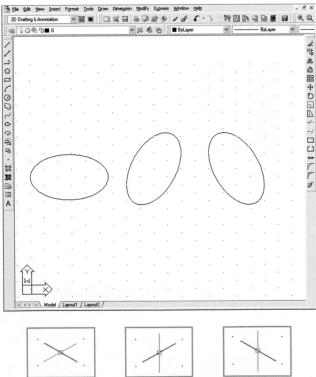

Center cursor   Right cursor   Left cursor

(C) Variously oriented isometric circles and the corresponding snap cursors used to create them.

KEY WORDS

Isometric

Pictorial

Multiview Projection

Axonometric Projection

Orthographic Projections

Oblique Projection

Perspective

Foreshortening

Isometric Projection

Dimetric Projection

Trimetric Projection

Isometric Axes

Nonisometric Lines

Isometric Scale

Isometric Projection

Isometric Sketch

Isometric Drawing

Box Construction

Offset Measurements

Isometric Sectioning

Isometric Dimensions

Exploded Assemblies

CHAPTER SUMMARY

- Axonometric projection is a method of creating a pictorial representation of an object. It shows all three dimensions of length, width, and height in one view.
- Isometric is the easiest of the axonometric projections to draw and is therefore the most common pictorial drawing. Isometric drawings created with CAD are often called 3D models.
- The spaces between the axes of an isometric drawing each are 120°. Isometric axes are drawn at 30° to the horizontal and vertical.
- The only lines on an isometric drawing that are to scale are parallel to the three isometric axes.
- An axonometric drawing is created by rotating an object about imaginary vertical and horizontal axes until three adjacent views, usually the top, front, and right side view, can all be seen at the same time.
- Inclined surfaces and oblique surfaces must be determined by plotting the endpoints of each edge of the surface.
- Angles, irregular curves, and ellipses require special construction techniques for accurate representation.
- A common method of drawing an object in isometric is by creating an isometric box and drawing the features of the object within the box.
- Unlike perspective drawing, in which parallel lines converge on a vanishing point, parallel lines are drawn parallel in axonometric drawings.

REVIEW QUESTIONS

1. Why is isometric drawing more common than perspective drawing in engineering work?
2. What are the differences between axonometric projection and perspective?
3. What type of projection is used when creating a 3D model with CAD?
4. At what angles are the isometric axes drawn?
5. What are the three views that are typically shown in an isometric drawing?
6. Which type of projection places the observer at a finite distance from the object? Which types place the observer at an infinite distance?
7. Why is isometric easier to draw than dimetric or trimetric?
8. Is the four circle ellipse a true ellipse or an approximation?
9. Is an ellipse in CAD a four circle ellipse or a true conic section?

EXERCISES

Axonometric Problems

Exercises 14.1–14.9 are to be drawn axonometrically. The earlier isometric sketches may be drawn on isometric paper, and later sketches should be made on plain drawing paper.

Since many of the exercises in this chapter are of a general nature, they can also be solved using CAD. Your instructor may assign you to use CAD for specific problems.

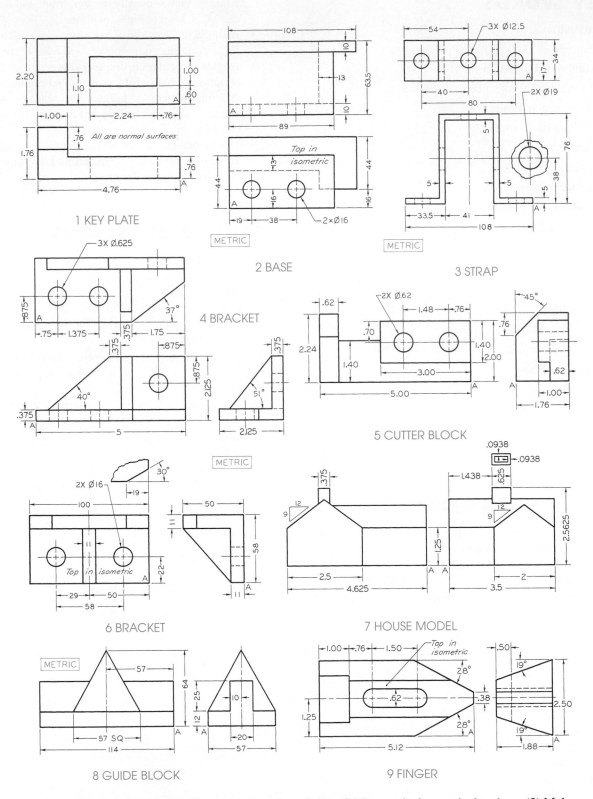

1 KEY PLATE

All are normal surfaces

METRIC

2 BASE

3 STRAP

4 BRACKET

5 CUTTER BLOCK

METRIC

6 BRACKET

7 HOUSE MODEL

METRIC

8 GUIDE BLOCK

9 FINGER

Exercise 14.1 (1) Make freehand isometric sketches. (2) Use CAD to make isometric drawings. (3) Make dimetric drawings. (4) Make trimetric drawings with axes chosen to show the objects to best advantage. Dimension your drawing only if assigned by your instructor.

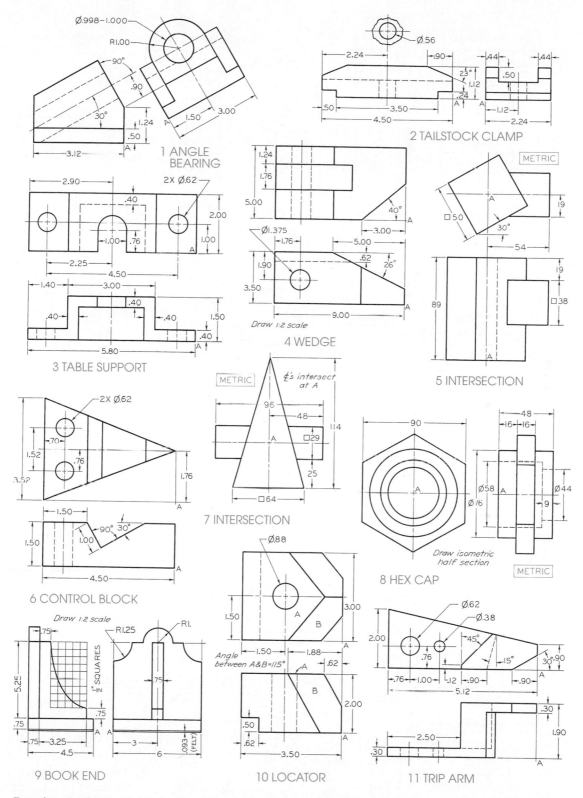

Ø.998–1.000
R1.00
90°
.90
30°
1.24
.50
3.12

1 ANGLE BEARING

Ø.56
2.24
.90
.44
.44
23°
.50
1.12
.24
A
A
.50
3.50
1.12
4.50
2.24

2 TAILSTOCK CLAMP

2.90
2X Ø.62
.40
2.00
1.00
1.00
.76
A
2.25
4.50
1.40
3.00
.40
.40
.40
.40
1.50
.40
A
5.80

3 TABLE SUPPORT

1.24
1.76
5.00
40°
A
3.00
Ø1.375
1.76
5.00
.62
26°
1.90
A
3.50
9.00

Draw 1:2 scale

4 WEDGE

METRIC
A
□50
30°
19
54
89
19
□38
A

5 INTERSECTION

2X Ø.62
.70
1.52
.76
3.52
1.76
A
1.50
90° 30°
1.50
1.00
A
4.50

6 CONTROL BLOCK

METRIC
₵'s intersect at A
96
48
114
A
□29
25
□64

7 INTERSECTION

90
A
48
16 16
Ø58 A
Ø16
Ø44
9

Draw isometric half section

8 HEX CAP
METRIC

Draw 1:2 scale
.75
R1.25
R1.
5.25
.75
½" SQUARES
.75
.75
A A
.75 3.25
3
.093 (FELT)
4.5
6

9 BOOK END

Ø.88
1.50
A
B
Angle between A&B=115°
A
1.50
1.88
.62
B
2.00
.50
.62
3.50
3.00
A
2.00
A

10 LOCATOR

Ø.62
Ø.38
2.00
45°
.76
15°
30°
.90
.76 1.00 .12 .90 .90
5.12
A
.30
2.50
1.90
.30
A

11 TRIP ARM

Exercise 14.2 (1) Make freehand isometric sketches. (2) Use CAD to make isometric drawings. (3) Make dimetric drawings. (4) Make trimetric drawings with axes chosen to show the objects to best advantage. Dimension your drawing only if assigned by your instructor.

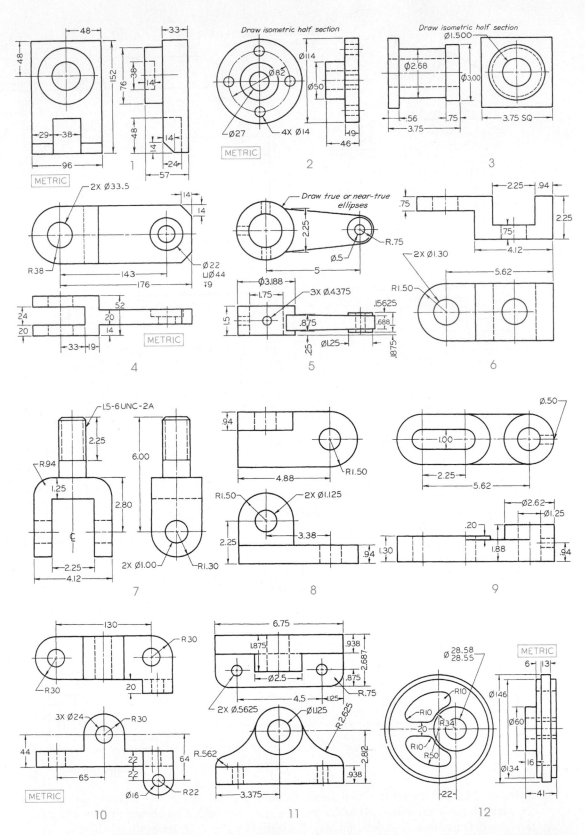

Exercise 14.3 (1) Make freehand isometric sketches. (2) Use CAD to make isometric drawings. (3) Make dimetric drawings. (4) Make trimetric drawings with axes chosen to show the objects to best advantage. Dimension your drawing only if assigned by your instructor.

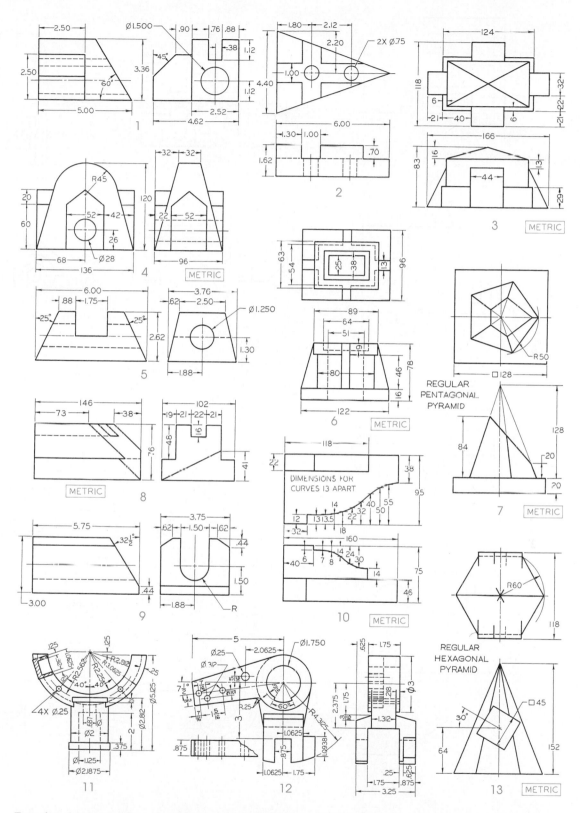

Exercise 14.4 (1) Make freehand isometric sketches. (2) Use CAD to make isometric drawings. (3) Make dimetric drawings. (4) Make trimetric drawings with axes chosen to show the objects to best advantage. Dimension your drawing only if assigned by your instructor.

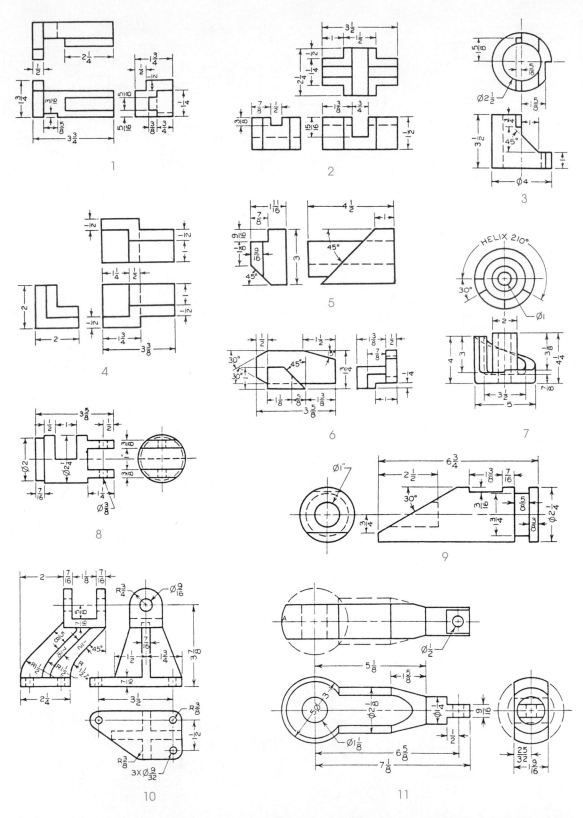

Exercise 14.5 (1) Make freehand isometric sketches. (2) Use CAD to make isometric drawings. (3) Make dimetric drawings. (4) Make trimetric drawings with axes chosen to show the objects to best advantage. Dimension your drawing only if assigned by your instructor.

Exercise 14.6 Draw the nylon collar nut as follows. (1) Make an isometric freehand sketch. (2) Make an isometric drawing using CAD.

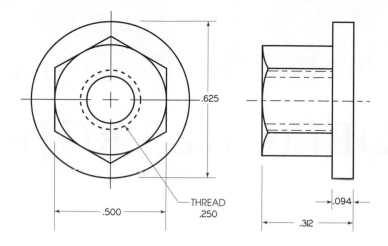

Exercise 14.7 Draw the plastic T-handle plated steel stud as follows. (1) Make a diametric drawing using CAD. (2) Make a trimetric drawing using CAD.

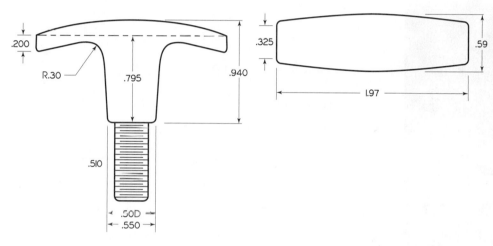

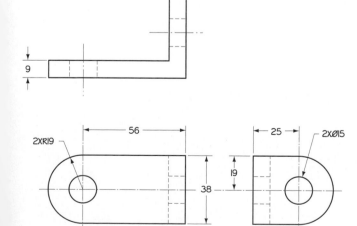

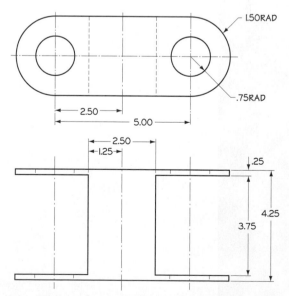

Exercise 14.8 Draw the mounting plate as follows. (1) Make an isometric freehand sketch. (2) Make isometric drawings using CAD.

Exercise 14.9 Draw the hanger as follows. (1) Make an isometric freehand sketch. (2) Make isometric drawings using CAD.

CHAPTER FIFTEEN

OBLIQUE PROJECTION

OBJECTIVES

After studying the material in this chapter, you should be able to:

1. Create an oblique projection.

2. List the advantages and disadvantages of oblique projection.

3. Draw cavalier and cabinet oblique drawings.

4. Select the best view for circular shapes in an oblique drawing.

5. Describe why CAD software does not automatically create oblique drawings.

Refer to the following standard:
- ASME Y14.4M-1989 Pictorial Drawing

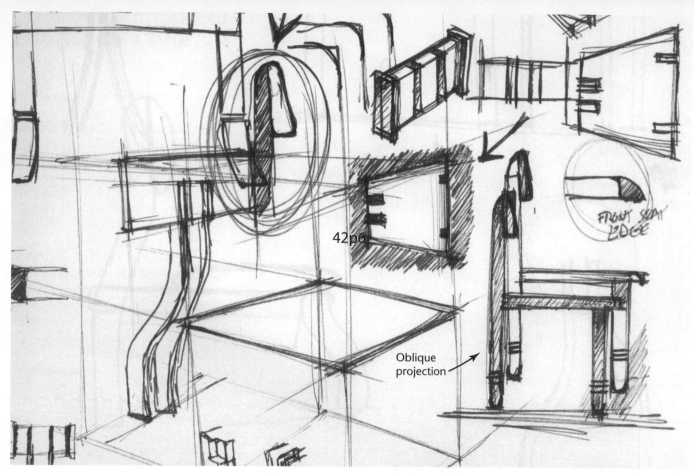

42p6

Oblique
projection

Oblique Projection in a Sketch. *Courtesy of Douglas Wintin.*

OVERVIEW

An oblique projection is a drawing where the projectors are parallel to each other but are at an angle other than 90° (oblique) to the plane of projection.

Oblique drawings are primarily used as a sketching technique. The front view in an oblique projection is the same as the front view in a multiview drawing, so circles and angles parallel to the front plane show as true size and shape and are therefore easy to draw. The downside is that while drawing circles in the front surface is easier, they are more difficult to draw in the top or side surfaces.

Oblique projection does not look as realistic as axonometric projection because the depth appears distorted. Using a proportion of the depth measurement makes the object's depth look more realistic. Oblique drawings are rarely created using CAD since it is more accurate to create a 3D model representing the actual shape and then show views of it using either isometric or perspective projection.

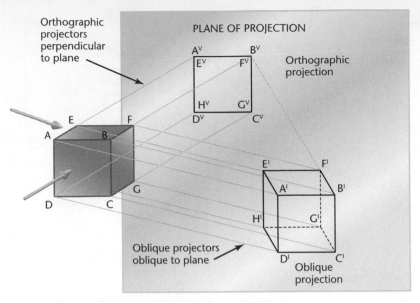

15.1   Comparison of Oblique and Orthographic Projections

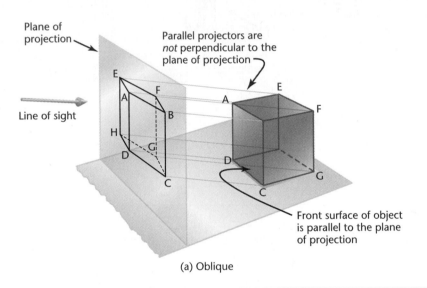

(a) Oblique

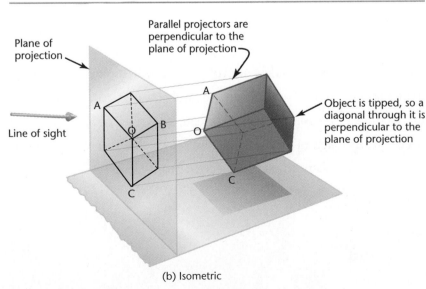

(b) Isometric

15.2   Comparison of Oblique and Isometric Projections

UNDERSTANDING OBLIQUE PROJECTIONS

In **oblique projections**, the projectors are parallel to each other but are not perpendicular to the **plane of projection.** To create an oblique projection, orient the object so that one of its principal faces is parallel to the plane of projection as illustrated in Figure 15.1. Bear in mind that the goal is to produce an informative drawing. Orient the surface showing the most information about the shape of the object so it is parallel to the plane of projection.

Figures 15.2, 15.3, and 15.4 show comparisons between oblique projection, orthographic projection, and isometric projection for a cube and a cylinder. In oblique projection, the front face is identical in the front orthographic view.

If an object is placed with one of its faces parallel to the plane of projection, the projected view will show the face true size and shape. This makes oblique drawings easier than isometric or other axonometric projection such as diametric or trimetric for many shapes. Surfaces that are not parallel to the plane of projection will not project in true size and shape.

In axonometric drawings, circular shapes nearly always project as ellipses because the principal faces are inclined to the viewing plane. If you position the object so that those surfaces are parallel to the viewing plane and draw an oblique projection, the circles will project as true shape and are easy to draw.

Oblique projections show the object from an angle where the projectors are not parallel to the viewing plane. An axis (like AB of the cylinder in Figure 15.3) projects as a point (A^VB^V) in the orthographic view where the line of sight is parallel to AB. But in the oblique projection, the axis projects as a line $A'B'$. The more nearly the direction of sight approaches being perpendicular to the plane of projection, the closer the oblique projection moves toward the orthographic projection, and the shorter $A'B'$ becomes.

Directions of Projectors

In Figure 15.5, the projectors make an angle of 45° with the plane of projection; so line *CD'*, which is perpendicular to the plane, projects true length at *C'D'*. If the projectors make a greater angle with the plane of projection, the oblique projection is shorter, and if the projectors make a smaller angle with the plane of projection, the oblique projection is longer. Theoretically, *CD'* could project in any length from zero to infinity.

Line *AB* is parallel to the plane and will project in true length regardless of the angle the projectors makes with the plane of projection.

In Figure 15.1, the lines *AE*, *BF*, *CG*, and *DH* are perpendicular to the plane of projection and project as parallel inclined lines *A'E*, *B'F*, *C'G*, and *D'H'* in the oblique projection. These lines on the drawing are called the receding lines. They may be any length, depending on the direction of sight.

What angle will these lines be in the drawing measured from horizontal? In Figure 15.6, line *AO* is perpendicular to the plane of projection, and all the projectors make angles of 45° with it; therefore, all the oblique projections like *BO*, *CO*, and *DO* are equal in length to line *AO*. You can select the projectors at any angle and still produce any desired angle with the plane of projection. The directions of the projections *BO*, *CO*, *DO*, and so on, are independent of the angles the projectors make with the plane of projection. Traditionally, the angle used is 45° (*CO* in the figure), 30°, or 60° with horizontal.

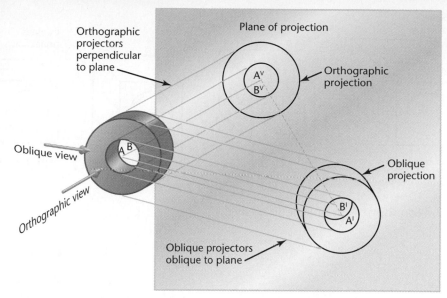

15.3 Circles Parallel to Plane of Projection

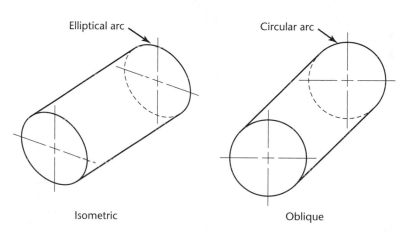

15.4 Comparison of Oblique and Isometric Projections for a Cylinder

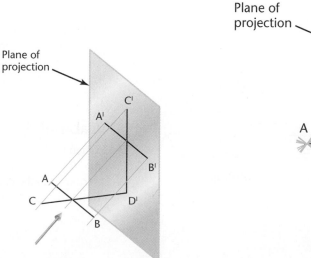

15.5 Lengths of Projections

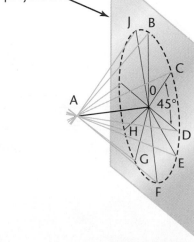

15.6 Directions and Projections

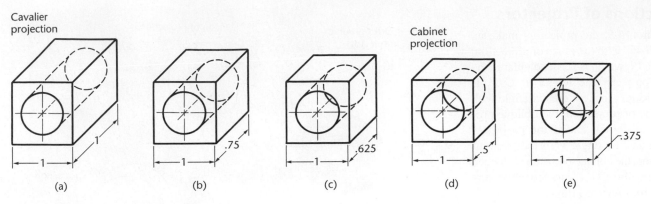

Cavalier projection

Cabinet projection

(a)   (b)   (c)   (d)   (e)

15.7 Foreshortening of Receding Lines

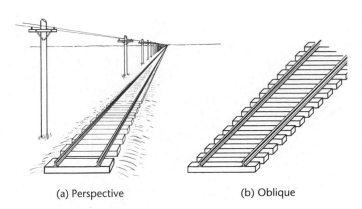

(a) Perspective   (b) Oblique

15.8 Unnatural Appearance of Oblique Drawing

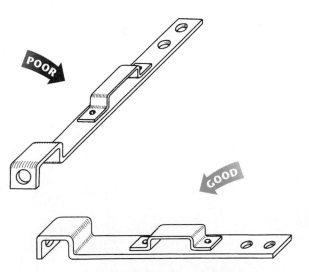

POOR

GOOD

15.9 Long Axis Parallel to Plane of Projection

15.1 LENGTH OF RECEDING LINES

Theoretically, **oblique projectors** can be at any angle to the plane of projection other than perpendicular or parallel. The difference in the angle you choose causes **receding lines** of oblique drawings to vary in angle and in length from near zero to near infinity. However, many of those choices would not produce very useful drawings. Figure 15.7 shows a variety of oblique drawings with different lengths for the receding lines.

Since we see objects in perspective (where receding parallel lines appear to converge) oblique projections look unnatural to us. The longer the object in the receding direction, the more unnatural the object appears. For example, the object shown in Figure 15.7a is an isometric drawing of a cube where the receding lines are shown full length. They appear to be too long and they appear to widen toward the rear of the block. Figure 15.8b shows how unnatural the familiar pictorial image of railroad tracks leading off into the distance would look if drawn in an oblique projection. To give a more natural appearance, show long objects with the long axis parallel to the view, as shown in Figure 15.9.

Cavalier Projection

When the receding lines are true length—(the projectors make an angle of 45° with the plane of projection)—the oblique drawing is called a **cavalier projection** (Figure 15.7a). Cavalier projections originated in the drawing of medieval fortifications and were made on horizontal planes of projection. On these fortifications the central portion was higher than the rest, and it was called cavalier because of its dominating and commanding position.

Cabinet Projection

When the receding lines are drawn to half size (Figure 15.7d), the drawing is known as a **cabinet projection**. This term is attributed to the early use of this type of oblique drawing in the furniture industries.

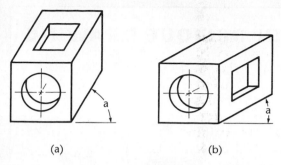

(a)   (b)

15.10   Angle of Receding Axis

15.2 ANGLES OF RECEDING LINES

Typically 45° is a good angle to choose for receding lines, since this makes it is easy to sketch through the diagonal of squares on grid paper or using the snap feature in CAD. Other common angles for the receding lines are 30° or 60°, but any convenient angle may be used.

Choose an angle based on the shape of the object and the location of its significant features. For example, the larger angle used in Figure 15.10a shows a better view of the rectangular recess on the top of the object, while the smaller angle in Figure 15.10b shows a feature on the side of the object.

15.3 CHOICE OF POSITION

Orient the view so that important shapes are parallel to the viewing plane as shown in Figure 15.11. In Figure 15.11a and c, the circles and circular arcs are shown in their true shapes and are easy to draw. In Figure 15.11b and d they are not shown in true shape and must be plotted as free curves or ellipses.

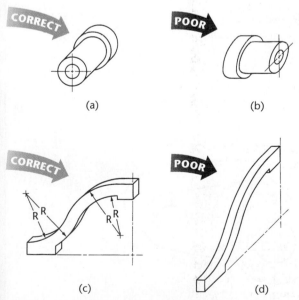

(a)   (b)

(c)   (d)

15.11   Essential Contours Parallel to Plane of Projection

STEP by STEP

USING BOX CONSTRUCTION TO CREATE AN OBLIQUE DRAWING

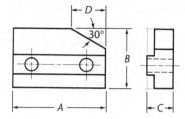

Follow these steps to draw a cavalier drawing of the rectangular object shown in the two orthographic views.

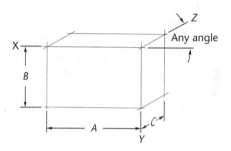

1 Lightly block in the overall width (*A*) and height (*B*) to form the enclosing rectangle for the front surface. Select an angle for the receding axis (*OZ*) and draw the depth (*C*) along it.

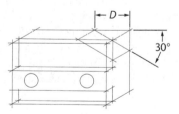

2 Lightly block in the details of the front surface shape including the two holes which will appear round. Add the details of the right side surface shape. Extend lines along the receding axis connecting the edges to form the remaining surface edges.

3 Darken the final lines.

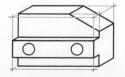

USING SKELETON CONSTRUCTION IN OBLIQUE DRAWING

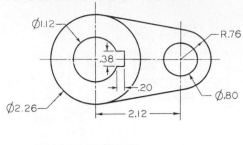

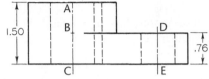

Oblique drawings are especially useful for showing objects that have cylindrical shapes built on axes or centerlines. Construct an oblique drawing of the part shown using projected centerlines using these steps.

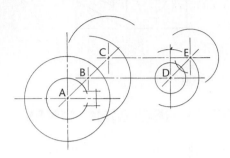

3 Build the drawing from the location of these centerlines.

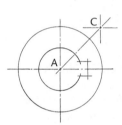

1 Position the object in the drawing so that the circles shown in the given top view are parallel to the plane of projection. This will show true shape in the oblique view. Draw the circular shape in the front plane of the oblique view and extend the center axis along the receding axis of the oblique drawing.

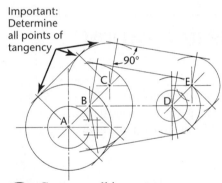

Important: Determine all points of tangency

4 Construct all important points of tangency.

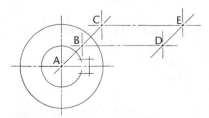

2 Add the centerline skeleton as shown.

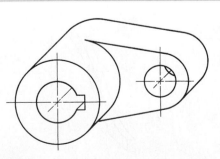

5 Darken the final cavalier drawing.

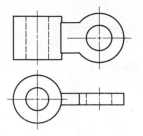

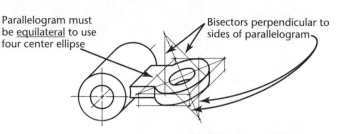

(a) Object with circles in different planes

(b) Use of four center ellipse

15.12 Circles and Arcs Not Parallel to Plane of Projection

15.4 ELLIPSES FOR OBLIQUE DRAWINGS

It is not always possible to orient the view of an object so that all of its rounded shapes are parallel to the plane of projection. For example, the object shown in Figure 15.12a has two sets of circular contours in different planes. Both cannot be simultaneously placed parallel to the plane of projection, so in the oblique projection, one of them must be viewed as an ellipse.

If you are sketching, you can just block in the enclosing rectangle and sketch the ellipse tangent to its sides. Using CAD, you can draw the ellipse by specifying its center and major and minor axes. In circumstances where a CAD system is not available, if you need an accurate ellipse, you can draw them by hand using one of the following methods.

Alternate Four Center Ellipses

Normal four center ellipses can be made only in equilateral parallelograms so they cannot be used in an oblique drawing where the **receding axis** is foreshortened. Instead, use this alternate four center ellipse to approximate ellipses in oblique drawings.

Draw the ellipse on two centerlines, as shown in Figure 15.13. This is the same method as is sometimes used in isometric drawings, but in oblique drawings it appears slightly different according to the different angles of the receding lines.

First, draw the two centerlines. Then, from the center, draw a construction circle equal to the diameter of the actual

hole or cylinder. The circle will intersect each centerline at two points. From the two points on one centerline, draw perpendiculars to the other centerline. Then, from the two points on the other centerline, draw perpendiculars to the first centerline. From the intersections of the perpendiculars, draw four circular arcs, as shown.

Four Center Ellipse for Cavalier Drawings

For cavalier drawings, you can use the normal four center ellipse method to draw ellipses (Figure 15.12b). This method can be used only in cavalier drawing because the receding axis is drawn to full scale forming an equilateral parallelogram.

To approximate the ellipse in the angled plane, draw the enclosing parallelogram. Then draw the perpendicular bisectors to the four sides of the parallelogram. The intersections of the perpendicular bisectors will be centers for the four circular arcs that form the approximate ellipse. If the angle of the receding lines is anything other than 30° from horizontal, as in this case, the centers of the two large arcs will not fall in the corners of the parallelogram.

When using a CAD system, you can quickly construct accurate ellipses and do not need these methods, but knowing them may be helpful for drawing in the field, or under other circumstances where CAD may not be readily available.

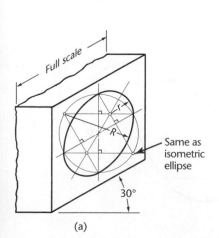

(a)

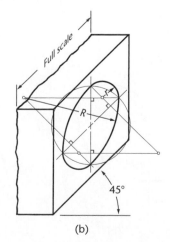

(b)

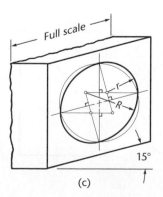

(c)

15.13 Alternate Four Center Ellipse

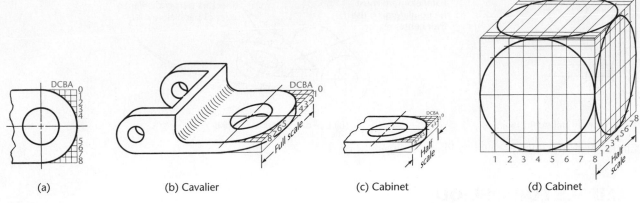

(a)   (b) Cavalier   (c) Cabinet   (d) Cabinet

15.14   Use of Offset Measurements

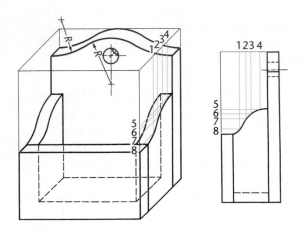

15.15   Use of Offset Measurements

15.5 OFFSET MEASUREMENTS

Circles, circular arcs, and other curved or irregular lines can be drawn using **offset measurements,** as shown in Figure 15.14. Draw the offsets on the multiview drawing of the curve (Figure 15.14a), and transfer them to the oblique drawing (Figure 15.14b). In this case, the receding axis is full scale; therefore all offset measurements are drawn full scale. The four center ellipse could be used, but this method is more accurate.

In a cabinet drawing (Figure 15.14c) or any oblique drawing where the receding axis is at a reduced scale, the offset measurements along the receding axis must be drawn to the same reduced scale. The four center ellipse cannot be used when the receding axis is not full scale. A method of drawing ellipses in a cabinet drawing of a cube is shown in Figure 15.14d.

Figure 15.15 shows a free curve drawn by means of offset measurements in an oblique drawing. This also illustrates hidden lines used to make the drawing clearer.

Offset measurements can be used to draw an ellipse in an inclined plane as shown in Figure 15.16. In Figure 15.16a, parallel lines represent imaginary cutting planes. Each plane cuts a rectangular surface between the front of the cylinder and the inclined surface. These rectangles are shown in the oblique drawing in Figure 15.16b. The curve is drawn through the corner points. The final cavalier drawing is shown in Figure 15.16c.

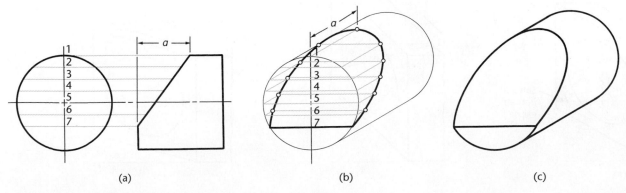

(a)   (b)   (c)

15.16   Use of Offset Measurements

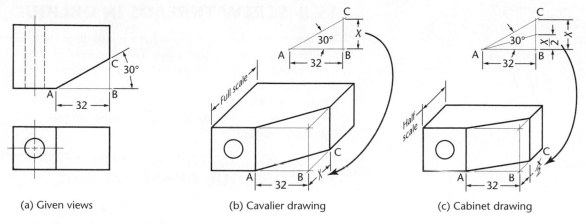

(a) Given views   (b) Cavalier drawing   (c) Cabinet drawing

15.17 Angles in Oblique Projection

15.6 ANGLES IN OBLIQUE PROJECTION

When an angle that is specified in degrees lies in a receding plane, convert the angle into linear measurements to draw the angle in an oblique drawing. Figure 15.17a shows a drawing with an angle of 30° specified.

To draw the angle in the oblique drawing, you will need to know distance X. The distance from point A to point B is given as 32 mm. This can be measured directly in the cavalier drawing (Figure 15.17b). Find distance X by drawing the right triangle ABC (Figure 15.17c) using the dimensions given, which is quick and easy using CAD.

You can also use a mathematical solution to find the length of the side: The length of the opposite side equals the tangent of the angle times the length of the adjacent side. In this case, the length is about 18.5 mm. Draw the angle in the cavalier drawing using the found distance.

Remember that all receding dimensions must be reduced to match the scale of the receding axis. Thus, in the cabinet drawing in Figure 15.17b, the distance BC must be half the side BC of the right triangle in Figure 15.17c.

15.18 Oblique Half Section

15.7 OBLIQUE SECTIONS

Sections are often useful in oblique drawing, especially to show interior shapes. An oblique half section is shown in Figure 15.18. Oblique full sections are seldom used because they do not show enough of the exterior shapes. In general, all the types of sections for isometric drawing may be applied to oblique drawing.

Meat Cereals. *Courtesy of Randall Munroe, xkcd.com.*

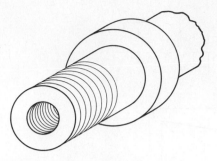

15.19 Screw Threads in Oblique

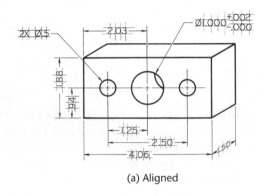

(a) Aligned

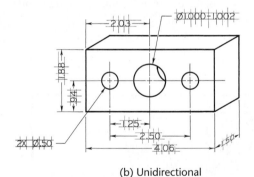

(b) Unidirectional

15.20 Oblique Dimensioning

15.8 SCREW THREADS IN OBLIQUE

To show screw thread in a cavalier oblique projection, use parallel partial circles spaced equally to the symbolic thread pitch for only the crests (Figure 15.19). For a cabinet oblique projection, the space would be one half of the symbolic pitch. If you are not using CAD and the thread is positioned to require ellipses, you can draw them using an ellipse template or the four center method.

15.9 OBLIQUE DIMENSIONING

You can dimension oblique drawings in a way similar to that used for isometric drawings. Follow the general principles of dimensioning that you learned in Chapter 9.

As shown in Figure 15.20, all dimension lines, extension lines, and arrowheads must lie in the planes of the object to which they apply. You should also place the dimension values in the corresponding planes when using the aligned dimensioning system (Figure 15.20a). For the preferred unidirectional system of dimensioning, all dimension figures are horizontal and read from the bottom of the drawing (Figure 15.20b). Use vertical lettering for all pictorial dimensioning.

Place dimensions outside the outlines of the drawing except when clarity is improved by placing the dimensions directly on the view.

15.10 COMPUTER GRAPHICS

Using CAD you can easily create oblique drawings by using a snap increment and drawing similarly to the method used on grid paper. If necessary, adjust for desired amount of foreshortening along the receding axis as well as the preferred direction of the axis. You can use CAD commands to draw curves, ellipses, elliptical arcs, and other similar features easily. However if you have a need for a complicated detailed pictorial, it is often easier and more accurate to create a 3D model rather than an oblique view.

QUICK OBLIQUE DRAWING USING AUTOCAD

You can use the snap tool available in the AutoCAD software to make a quick oblique drawing. An oblique drawing is a 2D drawing that gives the appearance of 3D by showing the object angled so that it shows all of the major surfaces in one pictorial view.

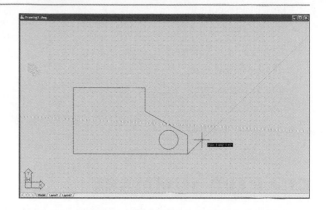

To Create a Quick Oblique Drawing

Use methods similar to that for creating a sketch on paper:

1. Draw the front view of the object.
2. Use the snap increment or the polar tracking to draw one of the receding lines showing the depth of the object.
3. Copy the front surface to the back.
4. Add the receding edges.

3D solid models are rarely ever shown in oblique views. It is as quick and easy to create a 3D solid model and produce a view of that as it is to make an oblique sketch, but depending on your need, you may choose either option.

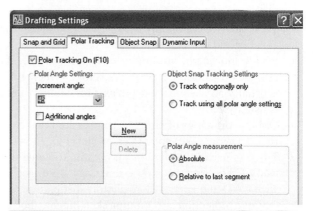

To Create a Solid Model

1. Draw the front view.
2. Use the region command to create 2D areas from the drawing lines.
3. Subtract the areas that are holes from the exterior.
4. View the drawing from an angle so that you can see the results when you produce the 3D part.
5. Extrude the region to create a 3D solid.
6. Orbit the drawing to change your 3D viewpoint.

   Which drawing appears most realistic?
   Which do you think is most useful?

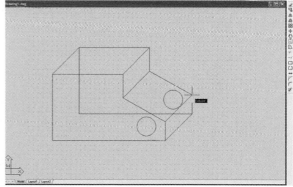

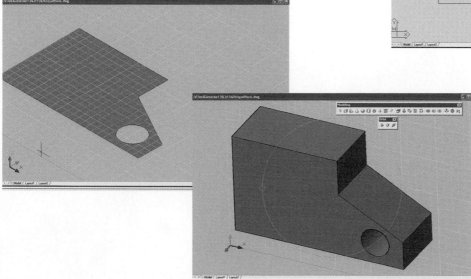

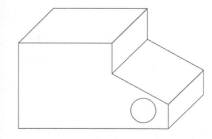

Reproduced with the permission of Autodesk, Inc.

KEY WORDS

Oblique Projections
Plane of Projection
Oblique Projectors
Receding Lines
Cavalier Projection
Cabinet Projection
Receding Axis
Offset Measurements

CHAPTER SUMMARY

- Oblique projection makes drawing circles in the projection plane easier than with other pictorial projection methods.
- There are two commonly used types of oblique projection: cavalier and cabinet.
- Width and height are drawn true size and true shape in oblique projection. The depth axis for cavalier (full depth) is usually 30°, while the depth axis for cabinet (half depth) is usually 45°.
- Oblique drawings of circular features are often created by first drawing a skeleton of centerlines.
- There is usually no reason for creating oblique drawings using CAD, since isometric drawings are easier to make with CAD and appear more photorealistic.
- Oblique projection is a common sketching method because the front view is true size and true shape and easier to draw.

REVIEW QUESTIONS

1. What is the primary advantage of an oblique projection?
2. Which is the most photorealistic: isometric, perspective, or oblique projection? Which is the least photorealistic?
3. If a hockey puck were to be drawn using oblique projection, how should it be positioned to appear as a circle?
4. Can an angle on an oblique drawing be measured in the front view? In the right side view? In the top view?
5. Why are oblique drawings seldom created with CAD software?
6. What is the first thing that should be drawn when creating an oblique drawing?
7. Describe how to plot an irregular curve in an oblique drawing.

EXERCISES

Oblique Projection Problems

Exercises to be drawn in oblique—either cavalier or cabinet—are given in Exercises 15.1–15.6. They may be drawn freehand using graph paper or plain drawing paper as assigned by the instructor, or they may be drawn with instruments. In the latter case, all construction lines should be shown on the completed drawing.

Since many of the problems in this chapter are of a general nature, they can also be solved on most CAD systems. The instructor may ask you to use CAD on specific problems.

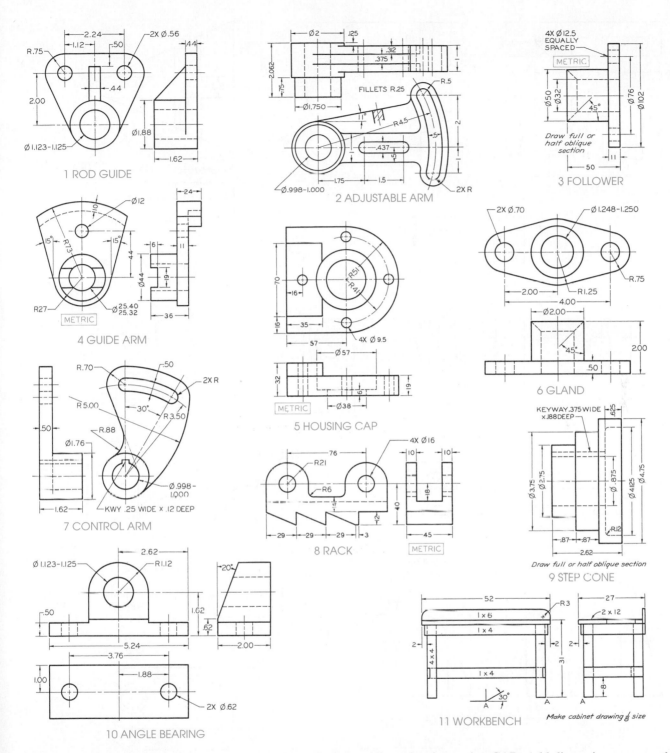

1 ROD GUIDE

2 ADJUSTABLE ARM

3 FOLLOWER

4 GUIDE ARM

5 HOUSING CAP

6 GLAND

7 CONTROL ARM

8 RACK

9 STEP CONE

10 ANGLE BEARING

11 WORKBENCH

Exercise 15.1 (1) Make freehand oblique sketches. (2) Make oblique drawings using CAD. Add dimensions to your drawing only if assigned by your instructor.

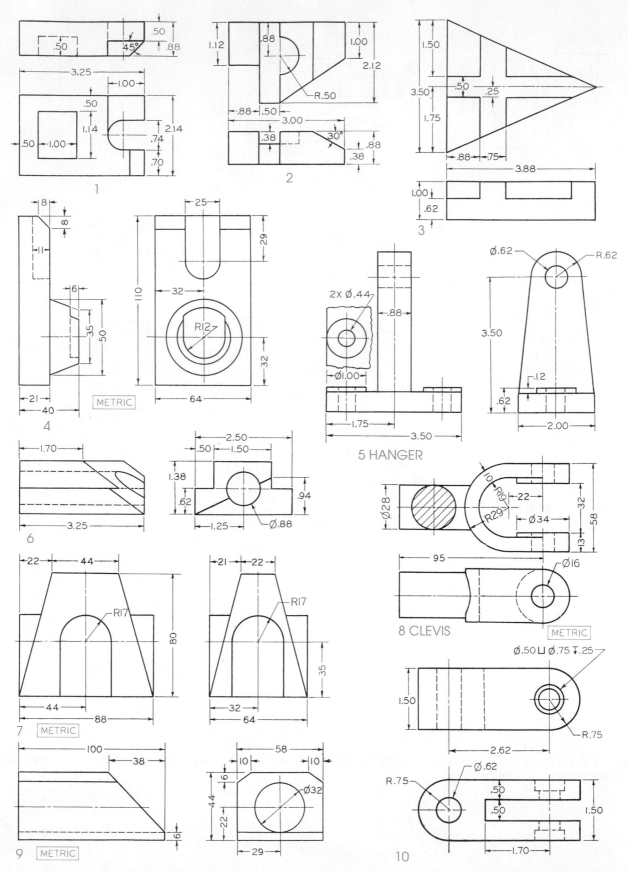

Exercise 15.2 (1) Make freehand oblique sketches. (2) Make oblique drawings using CAD. Add dimensions to your drawing only if assigned by your instructor.

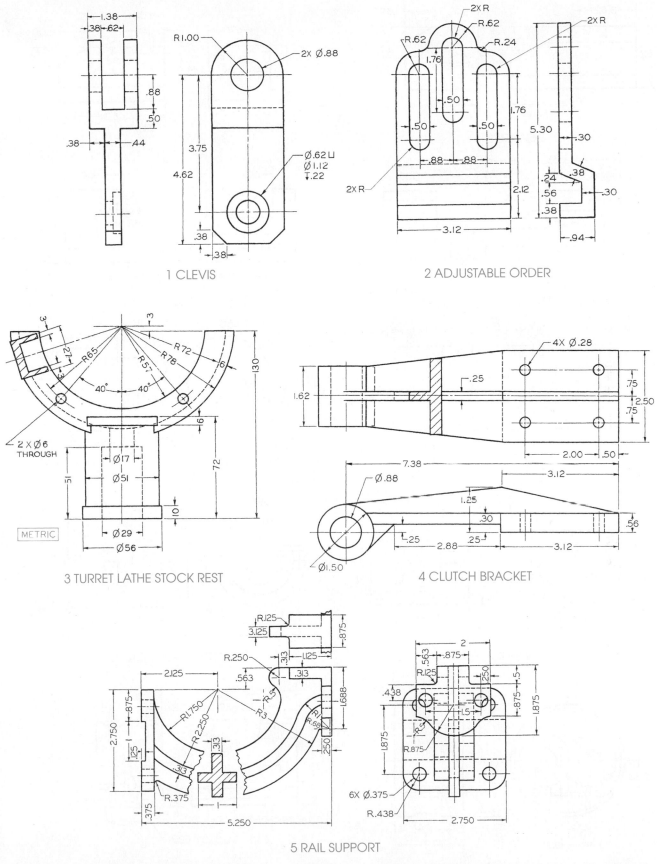

1 CLEVIS

2 ADJUSTABLE ORDER

3 TURRET LATHE STOCK REST

4 CLUTCH BRACKET

5 RAIL SUPPORT

Exercise 15.3 (1) Make freehand oblique sketches. (2) Make oblique drawings using CAD. Add dimensions to your drawing only if assigned by your instructor.

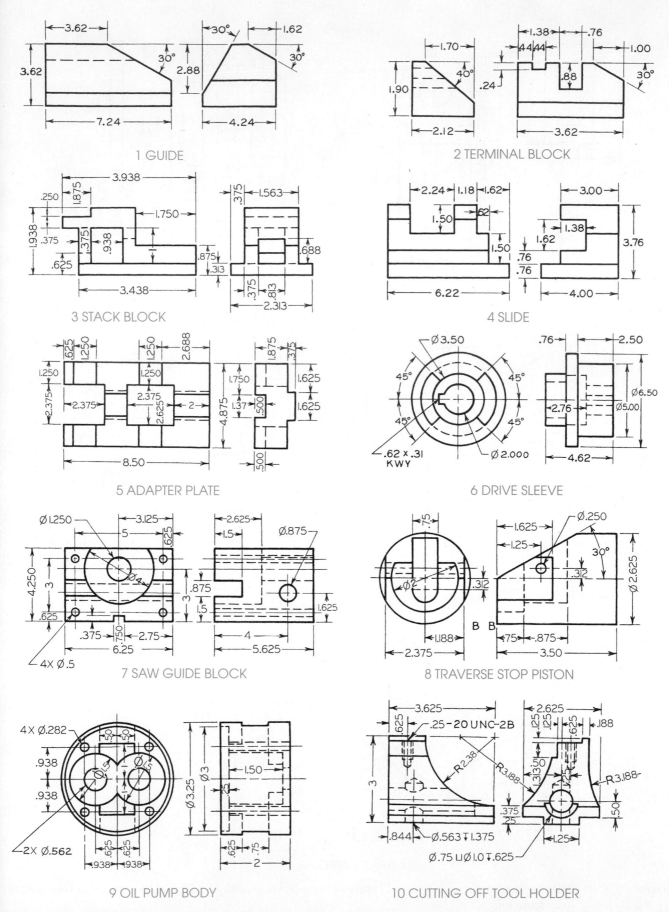

1 GUIDE

2 TERMINAL BLOCK

3 STACK BLOCK

4 SLIDE

5 ADAPTER PLATE

6 DRIVE SLEEVE

7 SAW GUIDE BLOCK

8 TRAVERSE STOP PISTON

9 OIL PUMP BODY

10 CUTTING OFF TOOL HOLDER

Exercise 15.4 (1) Make freehand oblique sketches. (2) Make oblique drawings using CAD. Add dimensions to your drawing only if assigned by your instructor.

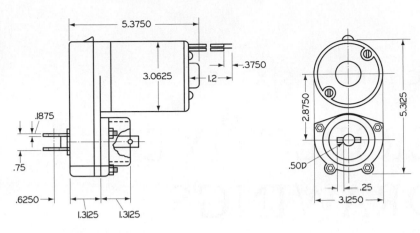

Exercise 15.5 For the linear actuator, make an oblique drawing. If requested by your instructor, add the overall dimensions.

CHAPTER SIXTEEN

PERSPECTIVE DRAWINGS

OBJECTIVES

After studying the material in this chapter, you should be able to:

1. Identify a drawing created using perspective projection.

2. List the differences between perspective projection and axonometric projection.

3. Create a drawing using multiview perspective.

4. Describe three types of perspective.

5. Measure distances in perspective projection.

Refer to the following standard:
*   ANSI/ASME Y14.4M-1989 Pictorial Drawing

The large red pipes of a thermal energy plant in Iceland vanish toward the horizon in this photograph. *Courtesy of Paul Chesley/Getty Images Inc.-Stone Allstock.*

OVERVIEW

Perspective, or central projection, is the most realistic-looking of the pictorial drawing styles because it is closest to the way humans see. An ordinary photograph shows the view in perspective, with objects in the foreground appearing larger, and objects in the background diminishing until they appear to vanish.

Architects, industrial designers, illustrators, and engineers should understand the basic principles of perspective because this method is used in creating sophisticated presentation drawings and in basic design sketching.

Unlike axonometric projection, where projection lines from the object remain parallel to one another, perspective projection shows parallel edges as converging at vanishing points, as we would view them in a photograph. To make complex and accurate perspective drawings you can project every point and edge of an object from a multiview drawing.

The three types of perspective are one point, two point, and three point perspective. CAD software can easily render perspective projections from 3D models, but it is still important to understand the basic principles that produce the view.

For further information about perspective drawing, visit
- http://www.artyfactory.com/perspective_drawing/perspective_1.htm
- http://www.termespheres.com/perspective.html
- http://www.khulsey.com/perspective_basics.html

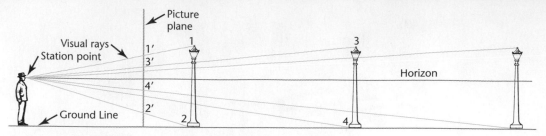

16.1 Looking Through the Picture Plane

UNDERSTANDING PERSPECTIVES

A **perspective drawing** involves four main elements:

- The observer's eye.
- The object being viewed.
- The plane of projection.
- The projectors from the observer's eye to all points on the object.

The plane of projection is placed between the observer and the object, as shown in Figure 16.1. The perspective view is produced where the **perspective projectors** pierce the plane of projection.

Figure 16.1 shows an observer looking along a boulevard and through an imaginary plane of projection. This plane is called the **picture plane** (PP). The position of the observer's eye is called the **station point** (SP). The lines from the station point to the various points in the scene are the projectors, or visual rays.

The visual rays pierce the picture plane giving perspectives of the points. Together, these piercing points form the perspective view of the object or the scene as viewed by the observer. Figure 16.2 shows the perspective view of the objects projected into the picture plane from the point of view of the observer in Figure 16.1. Each lamp post projects smaller than the preceding one as it is further from the observer. A lamp post in the picture plane would be projected in true length.

In Figure 16.1, a line represents the horizon. The horizon represents the eye level of the observer (SP). In Figure 16.1, the ground plane is the edge view of the ground on which the object usually rests. In Figure 16.2, the **ground line** (GL) is the intersection of the ground plane with the picture plane.

Lines that are parallel to each other but not parallel to the picture plane, such as curb lines, sidewalk lines, and lines along the tops and bottoms of the lamp posts, all converge toward a single point on the horizon. This point is called the **vanishing point** (VP) of the lines.

Some rules to learn for perspective are:

- All parallel lines that are not parallel to the picture plane vanish at a point.
- If these lines are parallel to the ground, the vanishing point will be on the horizon.
- Lines that are parallel to the picture plane, such as the vertical axis of each lamp post, remain parallel to one another and do not converge toward a vanishing point.

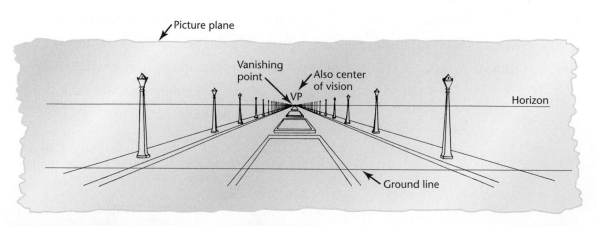

16.2 A Perspective

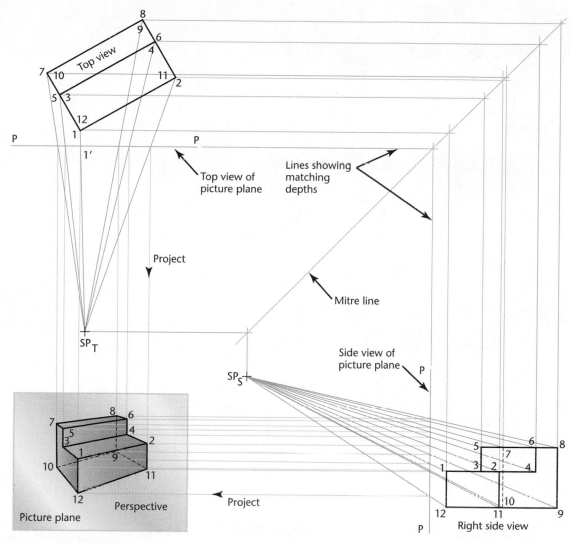

16.3 Multiview Method of Drawing Perspective

16.1 PERSPECTIVE FROM A MULTIVIEW PROJECTION

It is possible to draw a perspective from a multiview projection, as shown in Figure 16.3. The upper portion of the drawing shows the top view of the station point, the picture plane, the object, and the visual rays. The right-side view shows the same station point, picture plane, object, and visual rays.

In the front view, the picture plane coincides with the plane of the paper, and the perspective view is drawn on it. Depth measurements are transferred from the top view to the side view, using the usual multiview projection techniques.

To show point 1 in the perspective view, you would:

1. Draw a visual ray in the top view from SP_T to point 1 on the object in the top view.
2. Draw a projection line downward into the perspective view where your ray crosses the picture plane (1').
3. Locate point 1 in the perspective view where your vertical line meets a similar projection line from the side view.

Find the perspective locations of other points in the same way and then draw the visible and hidden lines between the endpoints you projected into the perspective view.

Examine the perspective drawing shown in Figure 16.4. All parallel lines that are also parallel to the picture plane (the vertical lines) remain parallel and do not converge. The other two sets of parallel lines converge toward vanishing points. If the converging lines from the edges in the perspective view were extended, they would meet at two vanishing points (one for each set of parallel lines).

It is possible to construct the perspective of any object this way, but this method is rather cumbersome because the top and side views usually show the object in an angled position.

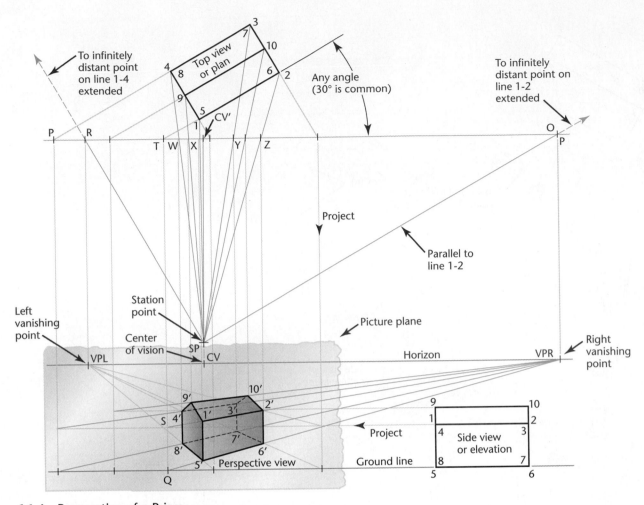

16.4 Perspective of a Prism

16.2 NON-ROTATED SIDE VIEW METHOD FOR PERSPECTIVE

Figure 16.4 shows a simpler construction for a perspective. The upper portion of the drawing shows the top views of the station point, picture plane, and the object. The lines SP-1, SP-2, SP-3, and SP-4 are the top views of the visual rays.

Details of the actual side view for the given top view are not required. Any side view drawn in that location can provide the necessary height measurements.

The perspective view is drawn on the picture plane where the front view would usually be located.

The side view shows the edge view of the ground line on which the object is resting.

The perspective view shows the intersection of the ground plane with the picture plane. In the perspective view, the horizon shows as a horizontal line. Since the horizon plane passes through the observer's eye, or SP, it is drawn at the level of the eye—that is, at the

distance above the ground line representing (to scale) the height of the eye above the ground.

The **center-of-vision** (CV), is the orthographic projection (or front view) of the station point on the picture plane of the perspective view. Since the **horizon** is at eye level, the center-of-vision will always be on the horizon, except in three point perspectives.

As shown in Figure 16.4, you would locate the center-of-vision (CV1) in the top view by projecting a perpendicular line from the station point (SP) to the picture plane (PP). You would locate CV in the front view by projecting downward from CV1 to the horizon.

Note that vertical heights can be measured only in the picture plane. If the front vertical edge 1'-5' of the object were actually situated in the picture plane, the vertical height would be full size. If the vertical edge is behind the

picture plane, you can extend a plane of the object, such as surface 1-2-5-6, forward until it intersects the picture plane (line TQ). The line TQ is called a measuring line. The true height (SQ) of line 1-5 can be measured with a scale or projected from the side view as shown.

If your drawing area is not large enough, one vanishing point, such as VPR, may be off the sheet. By using one vanishing point VPL and projecting down from the piercing points in PP, vanishing point VPR may be eliminated. The second vanishing point allows for checking so it is best to draw it if space permits.

Drawing perspective views of horizontal lines that are not parallel to the picture plan is not difficult, if you understand the process. Steps for finding line 1'-2' in the perspective view are detailed on the next page.

DRAWING PERSPECTIVES OF HORIZONTAL STRAIGHT LINES THAT ARE NOT PARALLEL TO THE PICTURE PLANE

1 Find the piercing point of line 1-2.

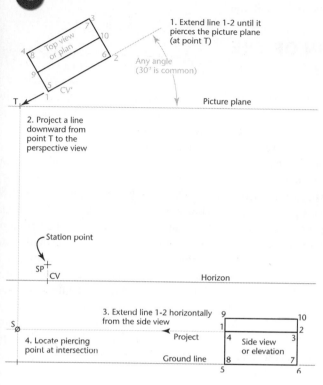

1. Extend line 1-2 until it pierces the picture plane (at point T)

Any angle (30° is common)

Picture plane

2. Project a line downward from point T to the perspective view

Station point

SP   CV

Horizon

3. Extend line 1-2 horizontally from the side view

Project

4. Locate piercing point at intersection

Ground line

Side view or elevation

2 Find the vanishing point for line 1'-2'.

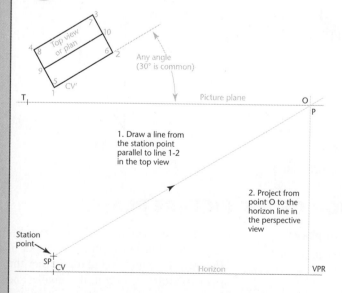

Any angle (30° is common)

Picture plane

1. Draw a line from the station point parallel to line 1-2 in the top view

2. Project from point O to the horizon line in the perspective view

Station point

SP   CV

Horizon   VPR

3 Draw a line from the piercing point of line 1-2 in the perspective view (point S) to its vanishing point.

Station Point

SP   CV   Horizon   VPR

S

Infinite line from piercing point to vanishing point

Side view or elevation

Ground line

4 Locate the endpoints of the line 1-2 in the perspective view.

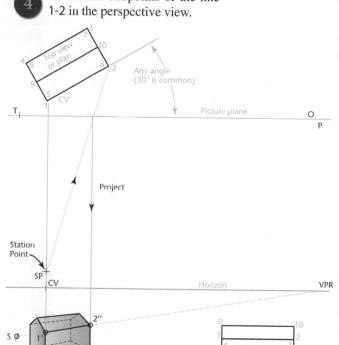

Top view or plan

Any angle (30° is common)

Picture plane

Project

Station Point

SP   CV   Horizon   VPR

S

Side view or elevation

Ground line

5 After you draw all horizontal edges in the perspective, draw the vertical and inclined edges to complete the perspective as shown in Figure 16.5.

Project down from the piercing points of the visual rays in the picture plane (PP) to find the endpoints of line 1-2 as it appears in the perspective view (1′ and 2′). Or draw the perspectives of the remaining horizontal edges of the object to find where they intersect. Better yet, use both methods to check your work.

STEP by STEP

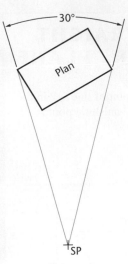

16.5 Distance from Station Point to Object

16.3 DRAWING AN ANGULAR PERSPECTIVE

Since objects are defined principally by edges that are straight lines, drawing a complex perspective is just a series of drawings of the perspective of lines. If you can draw the perspective of a line, you can draw the perspective of any object, no matter how complex.

16.4 POSITION OF THE STATION POINT

The centerline of the cone of visual rays should be directed toward the approximate center, or center of interest, of the object. In two point perspective, (Figure 16.4), locating the station point (SP) in the plan view slightly to the left and not directly in front of the center of the object produces a better view, as if the object is seen at a glance without turning the head. Use a cone of rays with its vertex at the station point and a vertical angle of about 30° entirely enclosing the object, as shown in Figure 16.5 to produce this effect.

The station point (SP) does not appear in the perspective view in Figure 16.4, because the station point is in front of the picture plane. The orthographic projection center-of-view (CV) of station point (SP) in the picture plane shows the height of the station point measured from the ground plane. It also shows the altitude of the station point since the horizon is at eye level.

Draw the horizon in the perspective view at the same level above the ground line that you want to use as the height of the station point. Most small and medium-size objects, such as machine parts or furniture, look best when the station point is slightly above the top of the object. Large objects, such as buildings, are usually viewed from a station point at about the height of the eye above the ground, or about 5'6".

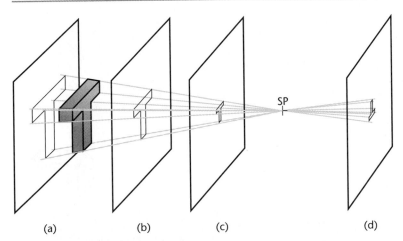

(a)   (b)   (c)   (d)

16.6 Location of Picture Plane

16.5 LOCATION OF THE PICTURE PLANE

The picture plane can be placed:

- In front of the object, as in Figure 16.6b and Figure 16.6c, which is the most common.
- Behind the object, as in Figure 16.7a.
- Behind the station point (SP), as in Figure 16.6d, in which case the perspective is reversed, like a camera lens.

The perspectives in Figure 16.6 differ in size but not in proportion. As in Figures 16.6b and 16.6c, the further the plane is from the object, the smaller the perspective drawing will be. This distance controls the scale of the perspective. Usually the object is placed with the front corner in the picture plane to make vertical measurements easier.

16.6 BIRD'S EYE VIEW OR WORM'S EYE VIEW

The horizon is level with the observer's eye, so controlling the location for the horizon line controls whether the perspective view appears from above or below the object. The horizon line is defined by the **observer's point of view.**

To produce a perspective view that shows the objects as though looking down from above, place the object below the horizon line. To produce a perspective view that shows the object as though looking up from below, place the object above the horizon line. This is not the case in three point perspective (see Section 16.11). The differences in effect produced by placing the object on, above, or below the horizon are shown in Figure 16.7.

16.7 THE THREE TYPES OF PERSPECTIVES

Perspective drawings are classified according to their number of vanishing points. This is determined by the position of the object with respect to the picture plane.

If the object is situated with one face parallel to the plane of projection, only one vanishing point is required, and the result is a one point perspective, or parallel perspective.

If the object is situated at an angle with the picture plane but with vertical edges parallel to the picture plane, two vanishing points are required, and the result is a two point perspective, or an angular perspective. This is the most common type of perspective drawing.

If the object is situated so that principal faces or edges are parallel to the picture plane, three vanishing points are necessary, and the result is a three point perspective.

16.8 ONE POINT PERSPECTIVE

In one point perspective, orient the object so two sets of its principal edges are parallel to the picture plane (essentially a flat surface parallel to the picture plane) and the third set is perpendicular to the picture plane. This third set of parallel lines will converge toward a single vanishing point in perspective.

Figure 16.8 shows the object with one face parallel to the picture plane. If desired, this face could be placed in the picture plane. The piercing points of the eight edges perpendicular to the picture plane (PP) are found by extending them to PP and then projecting downward to the level of the lines as projected across from the elevation view.

To find the vanishing points (VP) of these lines, draw a **visual ray** from the station point (SP) parallel to the lines (like Step 2 on page 569). The vanishing point of all lines perpendicular to the picture plane (PP) is in the center-of-view (CV). Connect the eight piercing points with the vanishing point (which is also the center-of-view) to find the directions for the perspective lines of the eight edges.

To show the actual lengths of the edges of the object along the perspective lines, draw horizontal lines from the endpoints

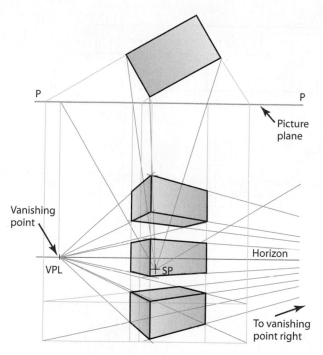

16.7   Object and Horizon

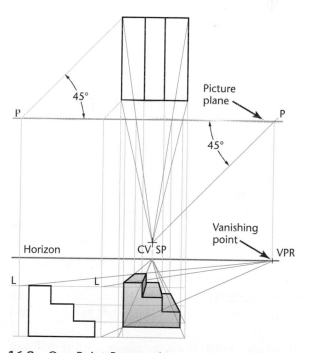

16.8   One Point Perspective

of one of the edges in the top view and at any desired angle with the picture plane (for this example, 45°). Find the piercing points and the vanishing point VPR of these lines and draw the perspectives of the lines. The intersections of these lines with the perspectives of the corresponding edges of the object produce the length of the receding edges. Use them to complete the perspective of the object.

Building interiors are sometimes shown using parallel perspective.

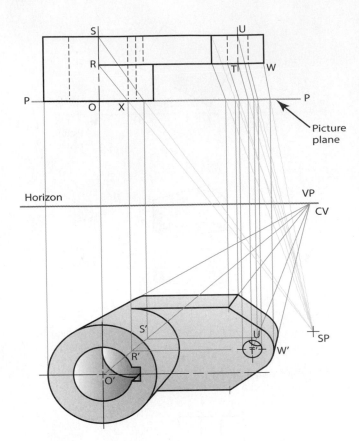

16.9 ONE POINT PERSPECTIVE OF A CYLINDRICAL SHAPE

A one point perspective representing a cylindrical machine part is shown in Figure 16.9. The front surface of the cylinder is placed in the picture plane. All circular shapes are parallel to the picture plane and they project as circles and circular arcs in the perspective. The station point (SP) is located in front and to one side of the object. The horizon is placed above the ground line. The single vanishing point is on the horizon in the center-of-view.

The two circles and the keyway in the front surface of the object are drawn true shape because they lie in parallel to the view as they are in the picture plane. The circles are drawn with the center at point O′. To locate the center of the large arc in perspective (R′), draw a visual ray from SP to R in the top view. Then, from the intersection of the ray with the picture plane (X), project down to the centerline of the large cylinder, to find the center of the arc in the perspective.

To find the radius T′W′ at the right end of the perspective view, draw visual rays SP-T and SP-W, and from their intersections with the picture plane (PP), project down to T′ and W′ on the horizontal centerline of the hole.

16.9   One Point Perspective

16.10 TWO POINT PERSPECTIVE

In two point perspective, the object is oriented so that one set of parallel edges is vertical and has no vanishing point, while the two other sets have vanishing points. Two point perspectives are often used to show buildings in an architectural drawing, or large structures in civil engineering, such as dams or bridges, especially for client presentation drawings.

The perspective drawing of a small building is shown in Figure 16.10. To make it easier to draw two point perspective:

1. Show an edge of the object in the picture plane so that measurements may be made directly from it.
2. Orient the object so that its faces make unequal angles with the picture plane; for example, one angle may be 30° and the other 60°.

The front corner (AB) lies in the picture plane (PP). It will be full scale in the perspective view (A′B′). To draw it, project downward from the top view (plan view) and across from the side view (elevation view). Draw visual rays from the station point to the corners of the building in the top view. Project these corners to the picture plane in the top view (S and R). Now draw the vertical lines (S-C′ and R-E′) from the intersections S and R to locate the corners in the perspective view where they will appear as vertical lines. The perspectives of the tops of the windows and the door are determined by the lines A′-VPR and A′-VPL. Their widths and lateral spacings are determined by projecting downward from the intersections with the picture plane of the respective visual rays. The bottom lines of the windows are determined by the lines V′-VPR and V′-VPL.

Find the perspective view of the roof ridge line by joining N′, the point where the ridge line pierces the picture plane, and VPR. Find the ridge endpoints O′ and Q′ by projecting down from the intersections of the visual rays with the picture plane, or by drawing the perspectives of any two lines intersecting at the vanishing points. Complete the perspective of the roof by joining the points O′ and Q′ to the end of the eaves.

> **TIP**
> When multiview drawings are already available, tape their top (plan) and side (elevation) views in position, and use them to construct the perspective. When you are finished, remove the taped portions.

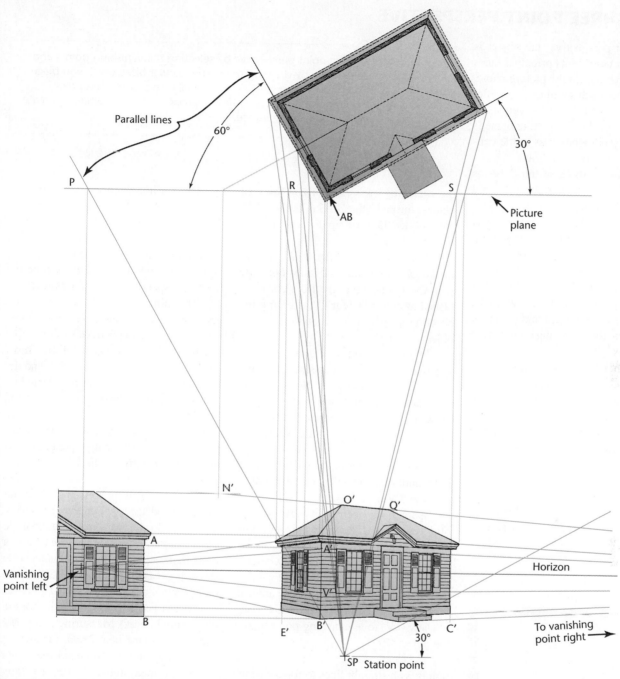

16.10   Two Point Perspective Drawing of a Building

16.11 THREE POINT PERSPECTIVE

In three point perspective, the object is placed so that none of its principal faces or edges are parallel to the picture plane. This means that each set of three parallel edges will have a separate vanishing point (Figure 16.11). The picture plane is approximately perpendicular to the centerline of the cone of visual rays.

In this figure, think of the paper as the picture plane, with the object behind the paper and placed so that all its edges make an angle with the picture plane. The center-of-view (CV) represents the orthographic location of your eye, or the station point, on the picture plane. The vanishing points P, Q, and R are lines drawn from a station point parallel to the principal axes of the object and then projected to locate their piercing points in the picture planes.

Remember that to find the vanishing point of a line in any type of perspective you draw a visual ray, or line, from the station point parallel to that edge of the object. Then find the piercing point of this ray in the picture plane. When the object is rectangular, these lines to the vanishing points are at right angles to each other exactly as the axes are in axonometric projection. The lines PQ, QR, and RP are perpendicular, respectively, to CV-R, CV-P, and CV-Q and are

> ### TIP
> You can sketch a three point perspective by selecting the vanishing points and finding the center of view by drawing the perpendicular bisectors. If you place the object at the center-of-view, the edge lines will recede from that point toward the vanishing points. You can estimate proportionate distances to create a sketch that has a pleasing appearance.

the vanishing traces, or horizon lines, of planes through the station point (SP) parallel to the principal faces of the object.

The imaginary corner O is assumed in the picture plane and may coincide with CV; but as a rule the front corner is placed at one side near CV, showing the observer's position relative to the object's corner.

In this method you draw the perspective directly from measurements and not projected from views. Now that you have the background information, follow these steps to create a general three point perspective of the drawing shown in Figure 16.11.

Near the center of the paper, make a light mark that you will use as the center-of-view (CV).

Above the center-of-view (for a bird's eye view), sketch a horizontal line to use as the horizon line.

Extend a light line from the center-of-view (CV) to the right and left vanishing points on the horizon line (Q and P).

Extend a light line from the center-of-view (CV) to a vanishing point below the object (R).

Connect these three vanishing points with straight lines to form a triangle. Perpendicular lines from each vanishing point to the opposite side will cross at the center-of-view (CV).

Construct the station points by extending these perpendicular bisectors to find SP_1 and SP_2.

Draw lines SP_1-R, SP_1-Q, SP_2-P, and SP_2-Q.

Draw a line from vanishing point Q parallel to SP-R. This will be the front line of the perspective object.

Draw a line from vanishing point P parallel to SP_2-Q. This will be the left line of the perspective object.

Extend a line from the intersection of the two lines you just drew (from point O) to vanishing point R. This will be the height perspective line of the object.

The dimensions of the object are given by the three views, and these will be set off on measuring lines GO, EO, and OF. The measuring lines EO and OF are drawn parallel to the vanishing trace PQ, and the measuring line GO is drawn parallel to RQ. These measuring lines are actually the lines of intersection of principal surfaces of the object, extended, with the picture plane (PP). Since these lines are in the picture plane (PP), true measurements of the object can be made along them.

Three measuring points M1, M2, and M3 are used along with the measuring lines. To locate M1, revolve triangle CV-R-Q about RQ as an axis. Since it is a right triangle, it can be constructed true size using R as the center and R-SP1 as the radius and drawing arc SP1-M1, as shown. M1 is the measuring point for the measuring line GO. Measuring points M2 and M3 are found in a similar manner.

Height dimensions, from the given views, are measured full size or to any desired scale, along measuring line GO, at points 3, 2, and 1. From these points, draw lines to M1. Heights on the perspective drawing are the intersections of these lines with the perspective front corner (O) of the object. Similarly, the true depth of the object is set off on measuring line EO from 0 to 5, and the true width is set off on measuring line OF from 0 to 8. Construct the intermediate points in a similar manner.

8:12 Train as seen by 8:12 1/2 Commuter by Roger Price, reprinted from "Droodles, The Classic Collection."

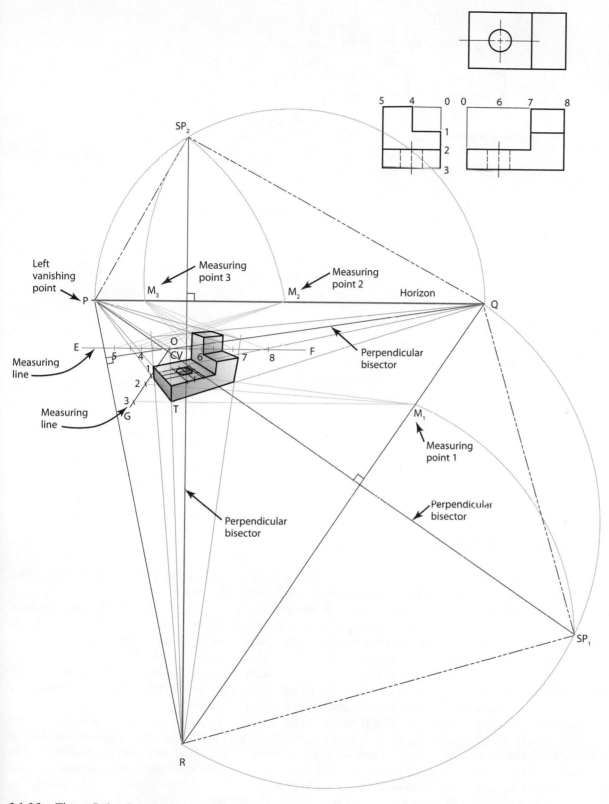

16.11   Three Point Perspective

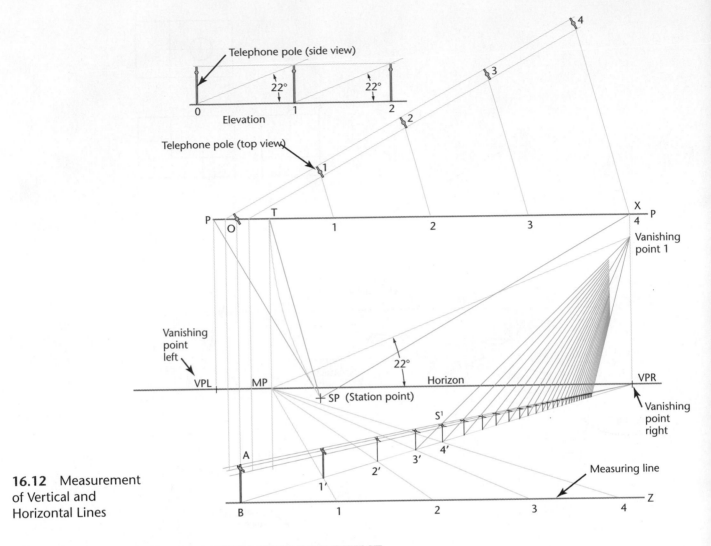

16.12 Measurement of Vertical and Horizontal Lines

16.12 MEASUREMENTS IN PERSPECTIVE

Remember: All lines in the picture plane are shown in their true lengths, and all lines behind the picture plane are foreshortened.

To draw the perspective of a line of telephone poles (Figure 16.12) use the following method.

Use line OB which represents the line of intersection of the picture plane (PP) with the vertical plane containing the poles. In this line, the height (AB) of a pole is measured directly to the desired scale. All the heights in the perspective drawing of all the poles can be constructed by drawing lines from A and B to the vanishing point (VPR).

To locate the bottoms of the poles along the line B-VPR, measure along the picture plane (PP) the distances 0-1, 1-2, 2-3, . . . , equal to the distance from pole to pole.

Draw the lines 1-1, 2-2, 3-3, . . . , that form a series of isosceles triangles

0-1-1, 0-2-2, 0-3-3, ... The lines 1-1, 2-2, 3-3, . . . , are parallel to each other and, therefore, have a common vanishing point (MP). Locate the vanishing point by drawing from the station point (SP) a line to point T (SP–T) parallel to the lines 1-1, 2-2, 3-3, . . . , and finding its piercing point in the picture plane (PP) to use as the measuring point (MP). Since line SP-X is parallel to the line of poles 1-2-3, . . . , the triangle SP-X-T is an isosceles triangle, and T is the top view of MP. Locate point T by measuring the distance X-T equal to SP-X or by drawing the arc SP-T with its center at X and radius SP-X.

From the measuring point MP, find the piercing points in the picture plane (PP) of lines 1-1, 2-2, 3-3, . . . , and draw their perspectives as shown. Since these lines are horizontal lines, their piercing points are in a horizontal ground line BZ

in the picture plane at the bottom of the drawing.

The true distances between the poles can be measured along line BZ. BZ is used as a measuring line. Use the intersections 1′, 2′, 3′, . . . , of the perspectives of the lines 1-1, 2-2, 3-3, . . . , with the line B-VPR to provide the spacing of the poles.

Only a few measurements may be made along the measuring line BZ that are within the limits of the drawing. For additional measurements, you can use the diagonal method of spacing as shown.

Since all diagonals from the bottom of each pole to the top of the succeeding pole are parallel, they have a common vanishing point VPI. This information leads to using the diagonal method to make measurements.

16.13 **DIRECT MEASUREMENTS ALONG INCLINED LINES**

The method of direct measurements may also be applied to lines inclined to the picture plane (PP) and to the ground plane, as illustrated in Figure 16.13. It shows line XE, which pierces the picture plane (PP) at X. If you revolve the end of the house about a vertical axis XO into the picture plane (PP), line XE will be shown true length and tipped as shown at XY. This line XY may be used as the measuring line for XE. Next find the corresponding measuring point MP. The line YE is the horizontal base of an isosceles triangle having its vertex at X, and a line drawn parallel to it through SP will determine MP, as described for Figure 16.13.

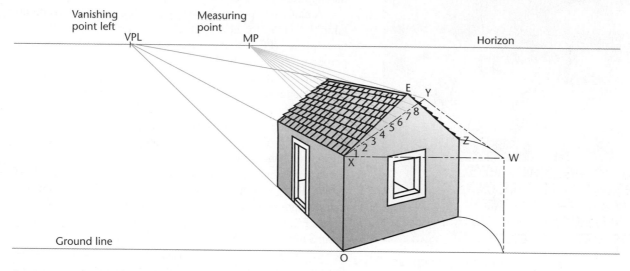

16.13   Measurement of Inclined Lines

PERSPECTIVE SKETCHING

As you create perspective sketches, lightly blocking in the ground line, horizon line, and vanishing point makes it easier to create a realistic pictorial appearance and is quicker than trying to draw angles of the receding lines through repeated trial and error.

Bear in mind that the distance between the ground line and the horizon line alter the appearance of the view. If you select more commonly seen placements for the ground line, horizon line, and vanishing points, your perspectives will appear more as the subject would appear in real life.

To familiarize yourself with perspectives that look realistic, examine existing drawings, paintings, and photographs, and practice identifying the ground line, horizon line, and vanishing point.

You can place a sheet of tracing paper over a photo and, using a ruler, extend projectors from the receding lines to find the vanishing point. Or draw directly on the photos in old newspapers that you are planning to recycle. Eventually, you won't need a ruler to quickly identify the vanishing point for an image. Remember, the vanishing point may not always be on the paper.

Editor's note: Mr. Munroe has been missing for several days. We have received no submissions from him for some time, but we found this single panel on his desk in a folder labeled 'MY BEST IDEA EVER'. It is clearly part of a work in progress, but we have decided to post it in lieu of a complete comic.

Known for Drawing Stick Figures in his "Webcomic of Romance, Sarcasm, Math and Language" xkcd Creator Randall Munroe Uses Perspective Drawing Skill in this Cartoon. *Courtesy of xkcd.com*

16.14 VANISHING POINTS OF INCLINED LINES

To find the vanishing point of an inclined line, determine the piercing point in the picture plane (PP) of a line drawn from the station point (SP) parallel to the given line.

Figure 16.14 shows the perspective of a small building. Use this method to determine the vanishing point of the inclined roof line C'E'.

A plane that passes through the station point and is parallel to the end of the house (plan view) would intersect the picture plane (PP) in the line XY, through VPL, and be perpendicular to the horizon.

Since the line drawn from SP parallel to C'E' (in space) is in the plane SP-X-Y, it will pierce the picture plane (PP) at some point T in XY. To find the point T, revolve plane SP-X-Y about the line XY as an axis into the picture plane (PP). The point SP will fall on the horizon at point O in the top view and MR in the front view.

From point MR, draw the revolved position of the line SP-T (now MR-T) making an angle of 30° with the horizon and determining point T. This point T is the vanishing point of the line C'E' and of all lines parallel to that line. The vanishing point S of the line D'E' is in line XY, because D'E' is in the same vertical plane as the line C'E'. Vanishing point S is as far below the horizon as T is above the horizon, because the line E'D' slopes downward at the same angle at which the line C'E' slopes upward.

16.15 INCLINED LINES IN PERSPECTIVE, JOINING ENDPOINT METHOD

The perspective drawing of inclined lines can be found without finding the vanishing points, by finding the perspectives of the endpoints and joining them. The perspective of any point may be determined by finding the perspectives of any two lines intersecting at the point. Obviously, it would be best to use horizontal lines, parallel to lines whose vanishing points are already in the drawing. For example, in Figure 16.14, to find the perspective of the inclined line EC, the point E' is the intersection of the horizontal lines R'-VPR and B'-VPL. The point C' is already established, since it is in the picture plane (PP); but if it were not, it could be easily found in the same manner. The perspective of the inclined line EC is the line joining the perspectives of the endpoints E' and C'.

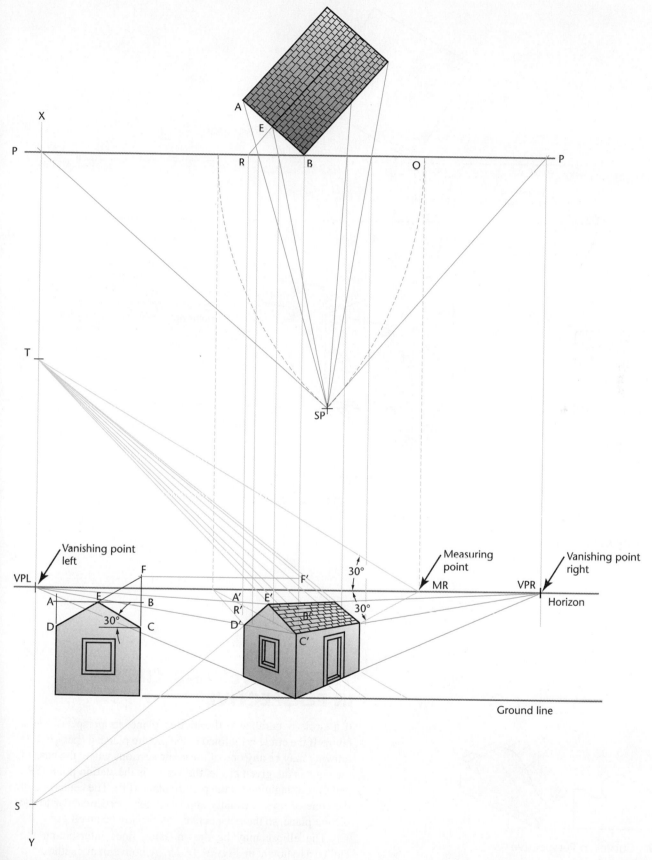

16.14 Vanishing Points of Inclined Lines

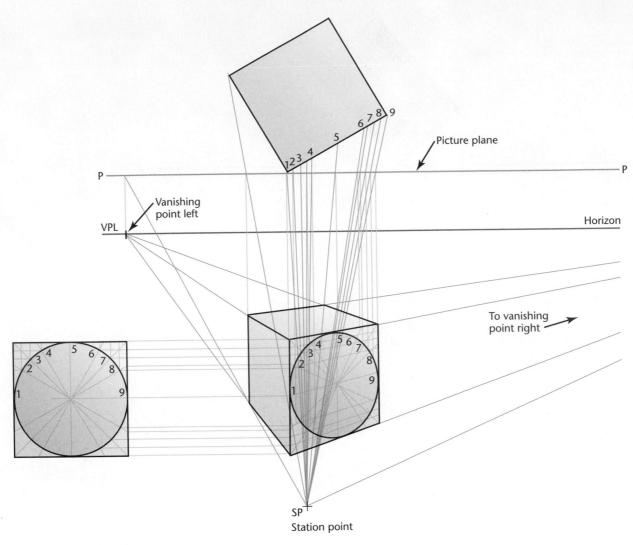

16.15 Circles in Perspective

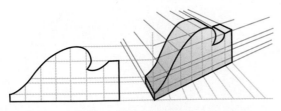

16.16 Curves in Perspective

16.16 CURVES AND CIRCLES IN PERSPECTIVE

If a circle is parallel to the picture plane, its perspective is a circle. If the circle is inclined to the picture plane, its perspective drawing may be any one of the conic sections where the base of the cone is the given circle, the vertex is the station point (SP), and the cutting plane is the picture plane (PP). The centerline of the cone of rays is usually approximately perpendicular to the picture plane, so the perspective will usually be an ellipse.

The ellipse may be drawn using lines intersecting the circle, as shown in Figure 16.15. A convenient method for determining the perspective of any planar curve is shown in Figure 16.16.

16.17 THE PERSPECTIVE PLAN METHOD

You can draw a perspective by first drawing the perspective of the plan of the object (Figure 16.17a), then adding the vertical lines (Figure 16.17b), and finally adding the connecting lines (Figure 16.17c). When the drawing is complicated, the superimposition of the perspective on the perspective plan causes a confusion of lines. Often drawing the perspective of the plan either above or below its normal location can help when you are using it to locate the vertical measurements. One possible position of the perspective plan is shown in Figure 16.17. The use of the perspective plan below the perspective is shown in Figure 16.18.

The chief advantages of the perspective plan method over the ordinary plan method are that the vertical lines of the perspective can be spaced more accurately and that a considerable portion of the construction can be made above or below the perspective drawing, avoiding lots of confusing lines.

When the perspective plan method is used, you can omit the ordinary plan view and measuring points that would be used to determine distances along horizontal edges in the perspective.

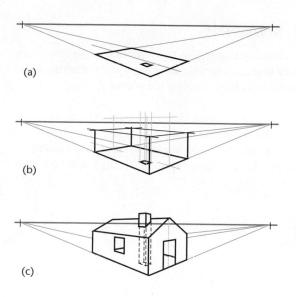

(a)

(b)

(c)

16.17 Building upon the Perspective Plan

16.18 PERSPECTIVE DIAGRAM

You can use drawing methods to figure out the spacing of vanishing points and measuring points. You can also calculate the locations. In Figure 16.19, a simple diagram of the plan layout shows the position of the object, the picture plane, the station point, and the constructions for finding the vanishing points and measuring points for the problem in Figure 16.18. The complete plan need not be drawn. Use a diagram drawn to any small convenient scale. Vanishing points and measuring points should be measured in the perspective to the larger scale desired.

Often structures are oriented in one of a limited number of simple positions with reference to the picture plane, such as $30° \times 60°$, $45° \times 45°$, and $20° \times 70°$. You can create a table of measurements for locating vanishing points and measuring points to avoid tedious construction of each drawing.

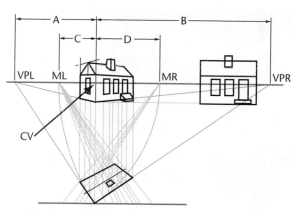

16.18 Perspective Plan Method

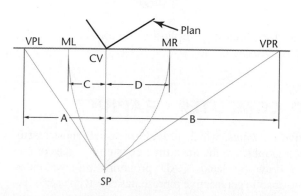

16.19 Perspective Diagram

16.19 SHADING

Shading pictorial drawings can be very effective in describing the shapes of objects in display drawings, patent drawings, and other pictorial drawings. Ordinary working drawings are not shaded.

Since the purpose of an industrial pictorial drawing is to show clearly the shape, the shading should be simple, should reproduce well, and should be limited to producing a clear picture. Some of the common types of shading are shown in

Figure 16.20. Pencil or ink lines are drawn mechanically (Figure 16.20a) or freehand (Figure 16.20b). Two methods of shading fillets and rounds are shown in Figure 16.20c and d. Shading produced with pen dots is shown in Figure 16.20e, and pencil "tone" shading shown in Figure 16.20f gives poor results using xerographic copying.

Examples of line shading on pictorial drawings often used in industrial sales literature are shown in Figures 16.21 to 16.22.

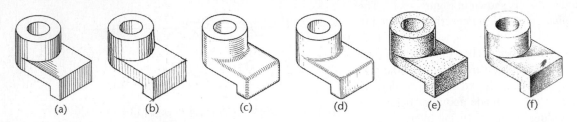

(a)   (b)   (c)   (d)   (e)   (f)

16.20 Methods of Shading

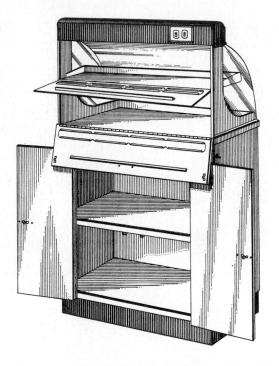

16.21 Surface Shading Applied to Pictorial Drawing of Display Case

16.22 A Line-Shaded Drawing of an Adjustable Support for Grinding.

16.20 COMPUTER GRAPHICS

Perspective drawings, which provide pictorials most resembling photographs, are the most time-consuming types of pictorials to draw by hand. CAD programs produce either wireframe or solid perspective representations, with user selection of viewing distance, focal point, z-axis convergence, and arc resolution scale. Historically, perspectives were used more

in architectural applications than in engineering drawing. Increasingly widespread access to sophisticated CAD programs makes perspective drawing a viable alternative for pictorial representations of a variety of objects.

PERSPECTIVE VIEWS IN AUTOCAD

AutoCAD software uses an interactive command called Dview (dynamic viewing) that you can use to show 3D models and drawings in perspective. The Dview command uses a camera and target to create parallel and perspective views. You can use the camera option to select a new camera position with respect to the target point at which the camera is aimed. The Dview distance option is used to create a perspective view such as the one shown in Figure A by increasing the distance between the camera and the object to calculate a new view. The off option of the command turns perspective viewing off again.

Notice that the grid squares in the figure appear larger closer to the viewing direction and smaller when they are farther away. Specifying a distance that is too close can fill up the entire view with the object.

The zoom option of the Dview command acts like a normal zoom command when perspective viewing is off. When perspective viewing is on, you use the zoom dynamically by moving the slider bar shown in Figure B to adjust the camera lens to change the field of view. The default is to show the view similar to what you would see through a 35 mm camera with a 50 mm lens.

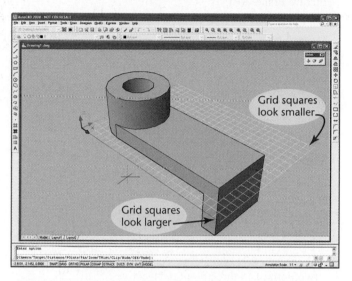

(A) A perspective view created using the DView command in AutoCAD. *With permission of Autodesk, Inc. © 2006-2007. All rights reserved.*

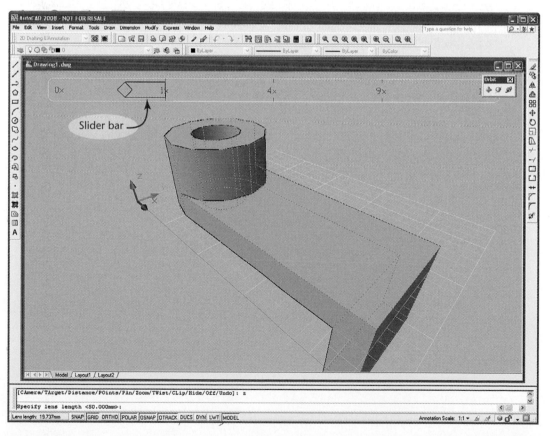

(B) Using the zoom slider to adjust field of view. *With permission of Autodesk, Inc. © 2006-2007. All rights reserved.*

KEY WORDS

Perspective Drawing

Perspective Projectors

Picture Plane (PP)

Station Point (SP)

Ground Line (GL)

Vanishing Point (VP)

Center-of-Vision (CV)

Horizon

Angular Perspective

Observer's Point of View

Visual Ray

CHAPTER SUMMARY

- The most realistic pictorial drawing is perspective.
- There are three types of perspective projection: one point, two point, and three point perspective.
- In perspective projection, parallel edges converge to one or more vanishing points, which appear similar to how the human eye sees an object.
- Perspective projection can be produced by projection from two orthographic views (usually top and right side).
- Location and relationship between the vanishing points, the picture plane, and the object determine the appearance of the perspective view.
- In one point perspective, the object is placed so that two of the three primary axes of the object are parallel to the picture plane.
- In two point perspective, the object is placed so that only one of the three primary axes of the object is parallel to the picture plane.
- In three point perspective, the object is placed so that none of the three primary axes of the object are parallel to the picture plane.

REVIEW QUESTIONS

1. What is the primary advantage of a perspective projection?
2. Why is perspective projection rarely used in engineering?
3. What is the purpose of the picture plane?
4. What is the station point?
5. How does the distance between the station point and the ground line affect the final perspective drawing?
6. What is the relationship between the station point and the horizon?
7. What type of perspective is often used for rendering interior spaces in architectural drawings?
8. What tools are available to assist the drafter in creating perspective drawings on paper?

EXERCISES

Perspective Exercises

Since many of the exercises in this chapter are of a general nature, they can also be solved on most computer graphics systems. If a system is available, the instructor may choose to assign specific problems to be completed by this method.

In addition to Exercises 16.1–16.6, many suitable problems for perspective are found among the axonometric and oblique problems at the ends of Chapters 14 and 15.

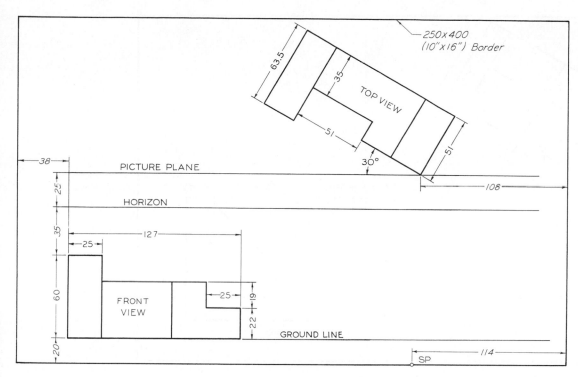

Exercise 16.1 Draw views in perspective on a size B or A3 sheet of paper, vellum, or film, with your name, date, class, and other information lettered below the border as specified by the instructor. Omit dimensions. (The dimensions given from the sheet border are to assist you in placing the views.)

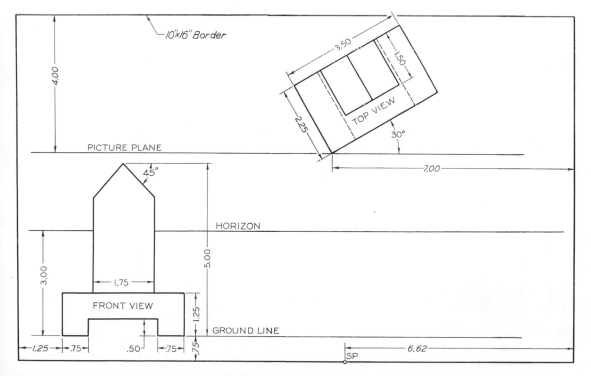

Exercise 16.2 Draw views in perspective on a size B or A3 sheet of paper, vellum, or film, with your name, date, class, and other information lettered below the border as specified by the instructor. Omit dimensions. (The dimensions given from the sheet border are to assist you in placing the views.)

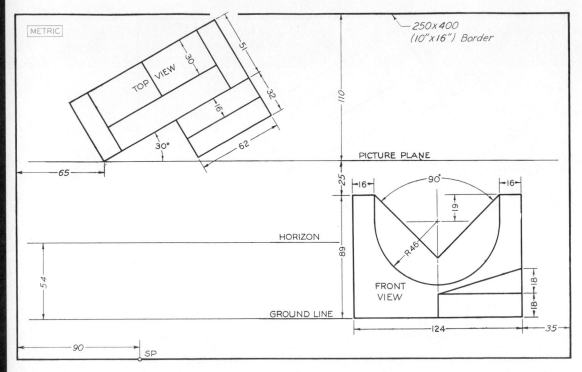

Exercise 16.3 Draw views in perspective on a size B or A3 sheet of paper, vellum, or film, with your name, date, class, and other information lettered below the border as specified by the instructor. Omit dimensions. (The dimensions given from the sheet border are to assist you in placing the views.)

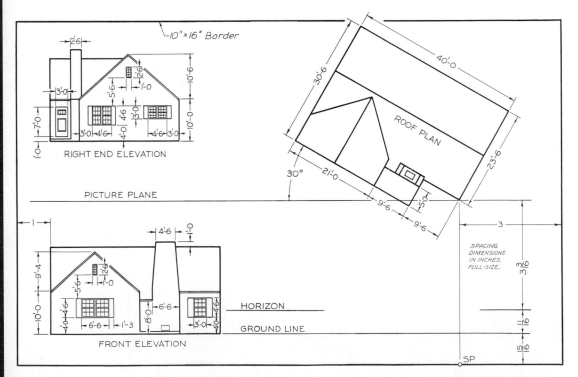

Exercise 16.4 Draw views in perspective on a size B or A3 sheet of paper, vellum, or film, with your name, date, class, and other information lettered below the border as specified by the instructor. Omit dimensions. (The dimensions given from the sheet border are to assist you in placing the views.)

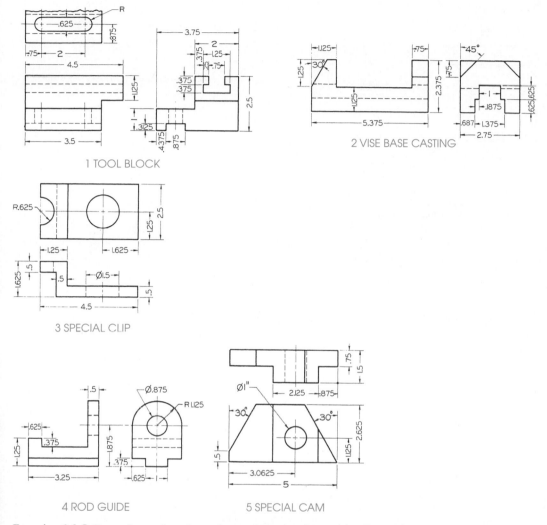

1 TOOL BLOCK

2 VISE BASE CASTING

3 SPECIAL CLIP

4 ROD GUIDE

5 SPECIAL CAM

Exercise 16.5 Draw front elevation, plan and perspective on size B or A3 paper. Determine the arrangement on the sheet to produce the most effective perspective in each case.

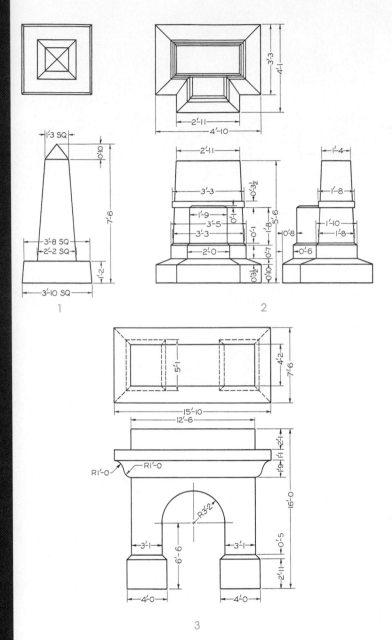

Exercise 16.6 Draw front elevation, plan and perspective. Select both sheet size and scale.

CHAPTER SEVENTEEN

GEARS AND CAMS

—— OBJECTIVES ——

After studying the material in this chapter, you should be able to:

1.   Define the characteristics of a spur gear, worm gear, and bevel gear.

2.   Calculate the gear ratio and rpm of two mating gears, given the pitch diameters.

3.   Define the principal spur gear terms.

4.   Draw a spur gear.

5.   Describe the relationship between a cam profile and a displacement diagram.

6.   Draw a cam profile, given a displacement profile drawing.

7.   List the types of cam followers.

See the following standards:
- ANSI Y14.7.1-1971 Gear Drawing Standards, Part 1: For Spur, Helical, Double Helical and Rack
- ANSI Y14.7.2-1978 Gear and Spline Drawing Standards, Part 2: Bevel and Hypoid Gears
- AGMA 933-B03 Basic Gear Geometry

Four Spur Gears with Meshing Teeth. *Courtesy of Takeshi Takahara/Photo Researchers, Inc.*

OVERVIEW

Gears, pulleys and belts, chains and sprockets, cams, linkages, and other devices are commonly used to transmit power and motion from one machine member to another. Understanding the function of these devices will help you create correct drawings and specifications for them.

Gears are one of the most common drive transfer mechanisms. Gears can change rotation direction, rotation speed, and axis orientation. The complex shape of a gear tooth is the result of mathematical computation. Drawing gears exactly on paper or with CAD requires considerable theoretical knowledge. However, often it is not necessary to represent details of gear teeth. Advanced CAD software programs often can generate gear models based on the parameters for the gear. Having an understanding of gear terminology before you start drawing a gear will help you provide the necessary information whether you draw by hand or use CAD.

Cams change rotational motion into reciprocating motion. Both gears and cams are commonly used in automobile engines and transmissions.

The American Gear Manufacturers Association (AGMA) was founded in 1916. AGMA produces standards for gear design and manufacture for American and global markets. They publish specific standards for gear types such as spur gears used in vehicles, plastic gears, bevel gears, and many others. AGMA 933-B03 is their standard for basic gear geometry. For more information when designing gears, check their Web site at www.AGMA.org for relevant standards.

Search the following Web sites to learn more about designing gears (agma), stock drive products (sdp-si), and an interactive gear template generator (woodgears.ca):

- http://www.agma.org
- http://www.sdp-si.com/
- http://woodgears.ca/gear_cutting/template.html

Spur Gear. *Courtesy of Big Sky Laser.*

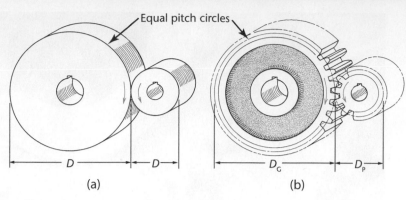

Equal pitch circles

(a)   (b)

17.1 Friction Gears and Toothed Gears

UNDERSTANDING GEARS

Gears are used to transmit power and rotating or reciprocating motion from one machine part to another. They may be classified according to the position of the shafts that they connect. Parallel shafts, for example, may be connected by **spur gears, helical gears,** or **herringbone gears.** Intersecting shafts may be connected by **bevel gears** having either straight, skew, or spiral teeth. Nonparallel, nonintersecting shafts may be connected by **helical gears, hypoid gears,** or a worm and **worm gear.** A spur gear meshed with a rack will convert rotary motion to reciprocating motion.

ANSI/AGMA publishes detailed standards for gear design and drawing. Refer to these standards for current design specification and inspection practices for all of the gear types discussed in this chapter.

Using Gears to Transmit Power

The **friction wheels** shown in Figure 17.1a transmit motion and power from one shaft to another parallel shaft. However, friction wheels are subject to slipping, and a great deal of pressure is required between them to create the necessary frictional force; therefore, they are usually used for low power applications, such as CD ROM drives. Spur gears (Figure 17.2b) have teeth on the cylindrical surfaces that fit together and transmit the same motion and power without slipping and with reduced bearing pressures.

If a friction wheel of diameter D turns at n **rpm** (revolutions per minute), the linear velocity, v, of a point on its periphery will be πDn, since $Dn = c$ (circumference).

Example

Let
$$D = 3 \text{ inches}$$
$$n = 100 \text{ rpm}$$
Then
$$v = \pi Dn = \pi(3)(100) \text{ in./min}$$
$$= 942 \text{ in./min}$$
or
$$\frac{942}{12} = 78.5 \text{ ft/min}$$

But the **pitch circles** of a pair of mating spur gears correspond exactly to the outside diameters of the friction wheels, and since the gears turn in contact without slipping, they must have the same linear velocity at the pitch line.

Therefore
$$\pi D_G n_G = \pi D_P n_P$$

or
$$\frac{D_G}{D_P} = \frac{n_P}{n_G} = m_G$$

where D_G = **pitch diameter** of larger gear (called the wheel)
D_P = pitch diameter of smaller gear (called the **pinion**)
n_G = rpm of gear
n_P = rpm of pinion
m_G = **gear ratio**

The gear ratio is also expressed as n_P/n_G or D_G/D_P.

Example

Let
$$D_G = 27'' \quad \text{and} \quad D_P = 9''$$
Then
$$\text{Gear ratio} = m_G = 27:9$$
$$= 3:1 \text{ (read as 3 to 1)}$$

Example

For the same gear pair, let $n_P = 1725$ rpm. Find n_G.

$$\frac{n_P}{n_G} = \frac{D_G}{D_P} \qquad \frac{n_G}{n_P} = \frac{D_P}{D_G}$$
$$n_G = n_P \frac{D_P}{D_G} = 1725 \cdot \frac{9}{27}$$
$$= \frac{1725}{3}$$
$$= 575 \text{ rpm}$$

The teeth on mating gears must be of equal width and spacing, so the number of teeth on each gear, N, is directly proportional to its pitch diameter, or

$$\frac{N_G}{N_P} = \frac{D_G}{D_P} = \frac{n_P}{n_G} = m_G$$

Spur Gear Definitions and Formulas

Proportions and shapes of gear teeth are well standardized, and the terms illustrated and defined in Figure 17.2 are common to all spur gears. The dimensions relating to tooth height are for full-depth $14\frac{1}{2}°$ or $20°$ involute teeth.

To make gears operate smoothly with a minimum of noise and vibration, the curved surface of the tooth profile uses a

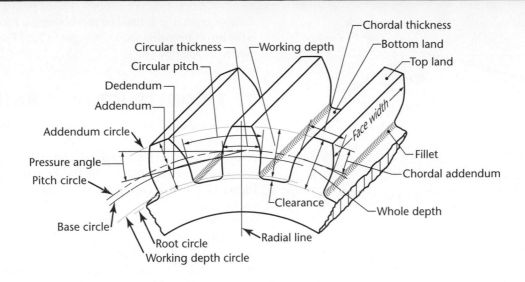

Term	Symbol	Definition	Formula
Addendum	a	Radial distance from pitch circle to top of tooth.	$a = 1/P$
Base circle		Circle from which involute profile is generated.	
Chordal addendum	a_c	Radial distance from the top of a tooth to the chord of the pitch circle.	$a_c = a + \frac{1}{2}D\,[1\text{-cos}\,(90°/N)]$
Chordal thickness	t_c	Thickness of a tooth measured along a chord of the pitch circle.	$t_c = D\sin\,(90°/N)$
Circular pitch	p	Distance measured along pitch circle from a point on one tooth to corresponding point on the adjacent tooth; includes one tooth and one space.	$p = \pi D/N$ $p = \pi/P$
Circular thickness	t	Thickness of a tooth measured along the pitch circle: equal to one-half the circular pitch.	$t = p/2 = \pi/2P$
Clearance	c	Distance between top of a tooth and bottom of mating space: equal to the dedendum minus the addendum.	$c = b - a = 0.157/P$
Dedendum	b	Radial distance from pitch circle to bottom of tooth space.	$b = 1.157/P$
Diametral pitch	P	A ratio equal to the number of teeth on the gear per inch of pitch diameter.	$P = N/D$
Number of teeth	N_G or N_P	Number of teeth on the gear or pinion.	$N = P \times D$
Outside diameter	D_o	Diameter of addendum circle: equal to pitch diameter plus twice the addendum.	$D_o = D + 2a = (N + 2)/P$
Pitch circle		An imaginary circle that corresponds to the circumference of the friction gear from which the spur gear is derived.	
Pitch diameter	D_G or D_P	Diameter of pitch circle of gear or pinion.	$D = N/P$
Pressure angle	ϕ	Angle that determines direction of pressure between contacting teeth and designates shape of involute teeth—e.g. $14\frac{1}{2}°$ involute; also determines the size of base circle.	
Root diameter	D_R	Diameter of the root circle; equal to pitch diameter minus twice the dedendum.	$D_R = D - 2b =$ $(N - 2.314)/P$
Whole depth	h_t	Total height of the tooth; equal to the addendum plus the dedendum.	$h_t = a + b = 2.157/P$
Working depth	h_k	Distance a tooth projects into mating space; equal to twice the addendum.	$h_k = 2a = 2/P$

17.2 Spur Gear Terminology

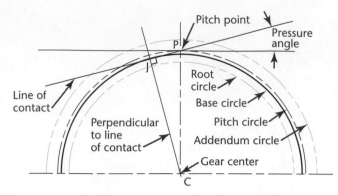

17.3   Construction of a Base Circle

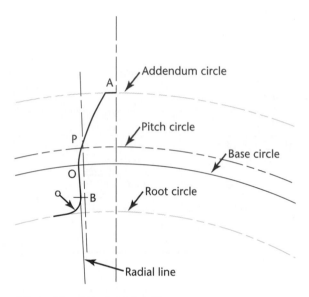

17.4   The Involute Profile

17.5   Shaded Model of Involute Shaped Spur Gear Teeth. *It is not typical to model gear teeth in detail as it creates an unnecessarily large and complex model.*

definite geometric form. The most common form in use today is the **involute** profile shown in Figure 17.2. (The word *involute* means "rolled inward.")

17.1 CONSTRUCTING A BASE CIRCLE

The involute tooth form depends on the pressure angle, which is ordinarily 14½° or 20°. This pressure angle determines the size of the **base circle;** from this the involute curve is generated.

To calculate the base circle for the spur gear as shown in Figure 17.3, follow these steps. At any point on the pitch circle, such as point *P* (the pitch point) draw a line tangent to the pitch circle; draw a second line through *P* at the required pressure angle (frequently approximated at 15° on the drawing). This line is called the line of contact. Next, draw a line perpendicular to the line of contact from the center, *C*. Then draw the base circle with radius *CJ* tangent to the line of contact at *J*.

17.2 THE INVOLUTE TOOTH SHAPE

If the exact shape of the tooth is desired, the portion of the profile from the base circle to the **addendum** circle can be drawn as the involute of the base circle. In Figure 17.4, the tooth profile from *A* to *O* is an involute of the base circle. See Appendix 20 if you need to refer to the method of construction. The part of the profile below the base circle, line *OB*, is drawn as a radial line (a straight line drawn from the gear center) that terminates in the fillet at the **root circle.** The fillet should be equal in radius to one and one-half times the clearance from the tip of the tooth to the bottom of the mating space. See Figure 17.5.

17.3 APPROXIMATE INVOLUTE USING CIRCULAR ARCS

Involute curves can be closely approximated with two circular arcs, as shown in Figure 17.6. This method, originally devised by G. B. Grant, uses a table of arc radii, an involute odontograph, for gears with various numbers of teeth. To use this method, draw the base circle as described above, and set off the spacing of the teeth along the pitch circle. Then draw the face of the tooth from *P* to *A* with the face radius *R*, and draw the portion of the flank from *P* to *O* with the flank radius *r*. Draw both arcs from centers located on the base circle. The table in Figure 17.2 gives the correct face and flank radii for gears of one **diametral pitch.** For other pitches, divide the values in the table by the diametral pitch. For gears with more than 90 teeth, use a single radius (let *R* = *r*) computed from the appropriate formula given in Figure 17.6, then divide by diametral pitch. Below the base circle, complete the flank of the tooth with a radial line *OB* and a fillet.

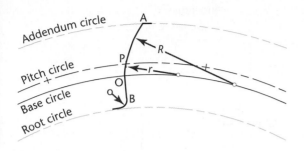

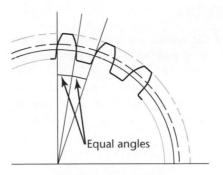

17.7 Spacing Gear Teeth

No. of Teeth (N)	14½°		20°	
	R (in.)	r (in.)	R (in.)	r (in.)
12	2.87	0.79	3.21	1.31
13	3.02	0.88	3.40	1.45
14	3.17	0.97	3.58	1.60
15	3.31	1.06	3.76	1.75
16	3.46	1.16	3.94	1.90
17	3.60	1.26	4.12	2.05
18	3.74	1.36	4.30	2.20
19	3.88	1.46	4.48	2.35
20	4.02	1.56	4.66	2.51
21	4.16	1.66	4.84	2.66
22	4.29	1.77	5.02	2.82
23	4.43	1.87	5.20	2.98
24	4.57	1.98	5.37	3.14
25	4.70	2.08	5.55	3.29
26	4.84	2.19	5.73	3.45
27	4.97	2.30	5.90	3.61
28	5.11	2.41	6.08	3.77
29	5.24	2.52	6.25	3.93
30	5.37	2.63	6.43	4.10
31	5.51	2.74	6.60	4.26
32	5.64	2.85	6.78	4.42
33	5.77	2.96	6.95	4.58
34	5.90	3.07	7.13	4.74
35	6.03	3.18	7.30	4.91
36	6.17	3.29	7.47	5.07
37–39	6.36	3.46	7.82	5.32
40–44	6.82	3.86	8.52	5.90
45–50	7.50	4.46	9.48	6.76
51–60	8.40	5.28	10.84	7.92
61–72	9.76	6.54	12.76	9.68
73–90	11.42	8.14	15.32	11.96
91–120	0.118N		0.156N	
121–180	0.122N		0.165N	
Over 180	0.125N		0.171N	

17.6 Wellman's Involute Odontograph for Drawing Gear Teeth Using Circular Arcs

17.4 SPACING GEAR TEETH

Suppose that number of teeth (N) = 20 and diametral pitch (P) = 4 for a 14½° involute tooth. The values from Table 17.2 are $R = 4.02$ and $r = 1.56$. These must be divided by P; yielding $r = 4.02/4 = 1.005''$ and $r = 1.56/4 = 0.39''$. Note that these values are for a full-size drawing.

Space the teeth around the periphery by laying out equal angles (Figure 17.7). The number of spaces should be $2N$, twice the number of teeth, to make the space between teeth equal to the tooth thickness at the pitch circle. In the example, since $N = 20$, $a = 360°/2N = 360°/40 = 9°$, the angle subtended by each tooth and each space.

When the pressure angle is 20° and the height of the tooth is reduced, the teeth are called **stub teeth.** Stub teeth are drawn in the same manner as other teeth except that $a = 0.8/P$, $b = 1/P$, and the pressure angle is 20°. The main advantage of stub teeth is that they are stronger than the 14½° standard full-depth teeth.

TIP

The Divide command in the AutoCAD software is very handy for dividing a circle or other geometry into any number of equal divisions. You can also use it to insert a block at the same time. A polar array is another useful command for creating gears.

Involute Gear Hob. Spur gears with involute tooth shapes are usually manufactured using a hobbing machine. This machine cuts gear teeth by rotating the gear blank and a cutter like the one shown at a fixed speed ratio. The cross sectional profile of the sides of the teeth on the cutter generate the involute tooth shape for the gear. Very small gears normally must be milled instead. *Courtesy of Hobsource.*

17.5 RACK TEETH

Gear teeth formed on a flat surface are called a **rack.** In the involute system, the sides of rack teeth are straight and are inclined at an angle equal to the pressure angle. To mesh with a gear, the linear pitch of the rack must be the same as the **circular pitch** of the gear, and the rack teeth must have the same height proportions as the gear teeth. See Figure 17.8.

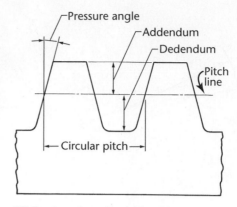

17.8 Involute Rack Teeth

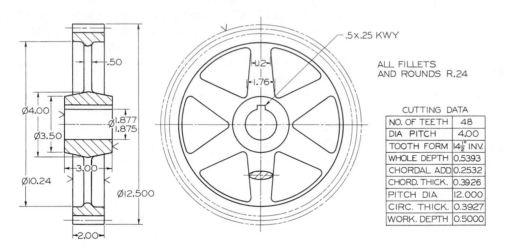

17.9 Working Drawing of a Spur Gear

CUTTING DATA	
NO. OF TEETH	48
DIA PITCH	4.00
TOOTH FORM	14½° INV.
WHOLE DEPTH	0.5393
CHORDAL ADD.	0.2532
CHORD. THICK.	0.3926
PITCH DIA	12.000
CIRC. THICK.	0.3927
WORK. DEPTH	0.5000

17.6 WORKING DRAWINGS OF SPUR GEARS

A typical working drawing of a spur gear is shown in Figure 17.9. Since the teeth are cut to standard shape, it is not necessary to show individual teeth on the drawing. Instead, draw the addendum and root circles as phantom lines and the pitch circle as a centerline.

The drawing actually shows only a **gear blank**—a gear complete except for teeth. Since the machining of the blank and the cutting of the teeth are separate operations, the necessary dimensions are arranged in two groups: the blank dimensions are shown on the views, and the cutting data are given in a note or table.

Before laying out the working drawing, calculate the gear dimensions. For example, if the gear must have 48 teeth

of 4 diametral pitch, with 14½° full-depth involute profile, as in Figure 17.9, calculate the following items in this order: **pitch diameter, addendum, dedendum, outside diameter, root diameter, whole depth, chordal thickness,** and **chordal addendum.**

The dimensions shown in Figure 17.9 are the minimum requirements for the spur gear. The chordal addendum and chordal thickness are given to aid in checking the finished gear. Other special data may be given in the table, according to the degree of precision required and the manufacturing method.

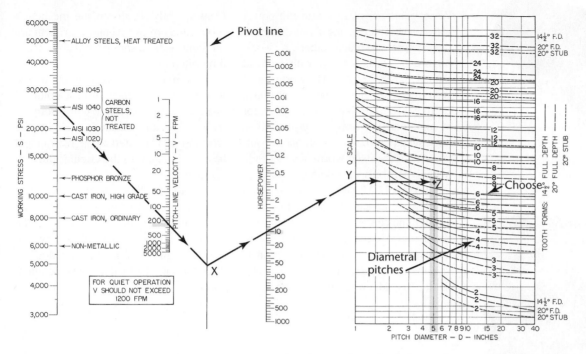

17.10   Chart for Design of Cut Spur Gears. *The chart is based on the Lewis equation, with the Barth velocity modification, and assumes gear face width equal to three times the circular pitch.*

17.7 SPUR GEAR DESIGN

Spur gear design normally begins with selecting pitch diameters to suit the required speed ratio, center distance, and space limitations. The size of the teeth (the diametral pitch) depends on the gear speeds, gear materials, horsepower to be transmitted, and the selected tooth form. The complete analysis and design of precision gears is complex and beyond the scope of this textbook, but the chart in Figure 17.10 gives suitable diametral pitches for ordinary cut spur gears.

Example To determine the diametral pitch and face width for a 5″ pitch diameter (G10400 carbon steel) pinion with 14½° full-depth teeth that must transmit 10 hp (horsepower) at 200 rpm.

Calculate the pitch in line velocity V as follows:

$$V = \pi/12(D_p n_p)$$

$$= 0.262 \times 5 \times 200 = 262 \text{ fpm (ft/min)}$$

On the chart, draw a straight line from 25,000 psi on the working stress scale through 262 fpm on the velocity scale to intersect the pivot line at X. From X, draw a second straight line through 10 on the horsepower scale to intersect the Q scale at Y. From this point, enter the graph of pitches and go to the ordinate for 5″ pitch diameter. The junction point Z falls slightly above the curve for 14½° full-depth teeth of 6 diametral pitch; hence, choose 6 diametral pitch for the gears.

For good proportions the face width of a spur gear should be about three times the circular pitch, and this proportion is incorporated in the chart. For 6 diametral pitch the circular pitch is $\pi/6$ or .5236″, and the face width is $3 \times .5236$ or 1.5708 inch. This width should be rounded to 1⅝ inch (1.625″).

When both the pinion and the gear are of the same material, the smaller gear is the weaker, and the design should be based on the pinion. When the materials are different, the chart should be used to determine the horsepower capacity of each gear.

17.11 Worm

A Waverly Guitar Tuner. *Worms are often designed so they can easily turn the gear, but the gear cannot turn the worm. Guitar machines, often called tuners, use worm gears so that the guitar can be tuned by turning the worm, but the strings are kept taut as the gear cannot turn the worm. Courtesy of Stewart-MacDonald Company.*

17.8 WORM GEARS

Worm gears are used to transmit power between nonintersecting shafts that are at right angles to each other. A worm (Figure 17.11) is a screw with a thread shaped like a rack tooth. The worm wheel is similar to a helical gear that has been cut to conform to the shape of worm for more contact. Worm gearing offers a large speed ratio, since with one revolution, a single-thread worm advances the worm wheel only one tooth and a space.

Figure 17.12 shows a worm and a worm wheel engaged. The section taken through the center of the worm and perpendicular to the axis of the worm wheel shows that the worm section is identical to a rack and that the wheel section is identical to a spur gear.

Consequently, in this plane the height proportions of thread and gear teeth are the same as for a spur gear of corresponding pitch.

Pitch (p) The axial pitch of the worm is the distance from a point on one thread to the corresponding point on the next thread measured parallel to the worm axis. The pitch of the worm must be exactly equal to the circular pitch of the gear.

Lead (L) The lead is the distance that the thread advances axially in one turn. The lead is always a multiple of the pitch. Thus, for a single-thread worm, the lead equals the pitch; for a double-thread worm, the lead is twice the pitch, and so on.

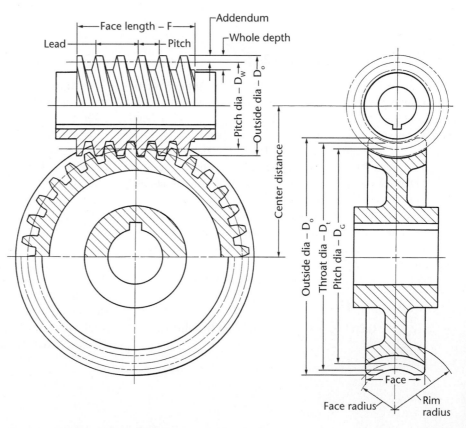

17.12 Double-Thread Worm and Worm Gear

Lead angle (λ) The lead angle is the angle between a tangent to the helix at the pitch diameter and a plane perpendicular to the axis of the worm. The lead angle can be calculated from

$$\tan l = \frac{L}{pD_W}$$

where

D_W = pitch diameter of the worm

The speed ratio of worm gears depends only on the number of threads on the worm and the number of teeth on the gear. Therefore,

$$m_G = \frac{N_G}{N_W}$$

where

N_G = number of teeth on the gear
N_W = number of threads on the worm

For 14½° standard involute teeth and single-thread or double-thread worms, the following proportions are the recommended practice of the AGMA. All formulas are expressed in terms of

circular pitch *p* instead of diametral pitch *P*. It is easier to machine the worm and the hob used to cut the gear if the circular pitch has an even rational value such as 5/8″.

For the worm:

Pitch diameter	$D_w = 2.4p \times 1.1$ (recommended value, but it may vary)
Whole depth	$h_t = 0.686p$
Outside diameter	$D_o = D_w + 0.636p$
Face length	$F = p(4.5 + N_G/50)$

For the gear:

Pitch diameter	$D_G = p(N_G/\pi)$
Throat diameter	$D_t = D_G + 0.636p$
Outside diameter	$D_o = D_t + 0.4775p$
Face radius	$R_f = \frac{1}{2}D_w - 0.318p$
Rim radius	$R_r = \frac{1}{2}D_w + p$
Face width	$F = 2.38p \times 0.25$
Center distance	$C = \frac{1}{2}(D_G + D_w)$

17.9 WORKING DRAWINGS OF WORM GEARS

In an assembly drawing, the engaged worm and gear can be shown as in Figure 17.12, but usually the gear teeth are omitted and the gear blank represented conventionally, as shown in the lower half of the circular view. On detail drawings, the worm and gear are usually drawn separately, as shown in Figures 17.13 and 17.14. Although their dimensioning depends on the production method, it is standard practice to dimension

the blanks on the views and give the cutting data in a table, as shown. Note that dimensions that closely affect the engagement of the gear and worm have been given as three-place decimal or limit dimensions; other dimensions, such as rim radius, face lengths, and gear outside diameter, have been rounded to convenient two-place decimal values.

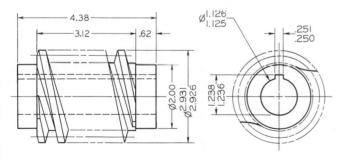

CUTTING DATA	
NO. OF THREADS	2
PITCH DIA	2.533
AXIAL PITCH	0.625
LEAD-R H	1.250
LEAD ANGLE	8°56'
PRESSURE ANGLE	14½°
WHOLE DEPTH	0.429

17.13 Working Drawing of a Worm

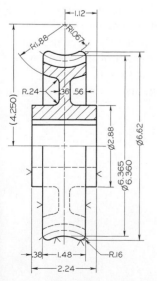

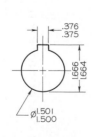

CUTTING DATA	
NO. OF TEETH	30
PITCH DIA	5.967
ADDENDUM	0.199
WHOLE DEPTH	0.429
NO. OF THREADS	2
AXIAL PITCH	0.625
LEAD-R H	1.250
LEAD ANGLE	8°56'
PRESSURE ANGLE	14½°

17.14 Working Drawing of a Worm Gear

17.15 Bevel Gears. *Courtesy of Stock Drive Products/ Sterling Instruments.*

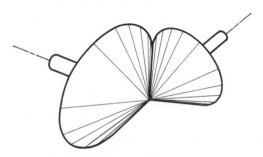

17.16 Friction Cones

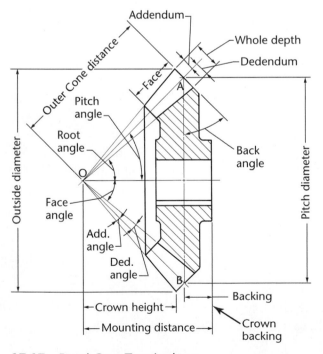

17.17 Bevel Gear Terminology

17.10 BEVEL GEARS

Bevel gears (Figure 17.15) are used to transmit power between shafts whose axes intersect. The analogous friction drive would consist of a pair of cones with a common apex at the point where their axes intersect, as in Figure 17.16. The axes may intersect at any angle, but right angles are most common. Bevel gear teeth have the same involute shape as teeth on spur gears, but they are tapered toward the cone apex; hence, the height and width of a bevel gear tooth vary with the distance from the cone apex. Spur gears are interchangeable (a spur gear of given pitch will run properly with any other spur gear of the same pitch and tooth form) but this is not true of bevel gears, which must be designed in pairs and will run only with each other.

The speed ratio of bevel gears can be calculated from the same formulas given for spur gears.

17.11 BEVEL GEAR DEFINITIONS AND FORMULAS

Since the design of bevel gears is very similar to that of spur gears, many spur gear terms are applied with slight modification to bevel gears. Just as in spur gears, the pitch diameter D of a bevel gear is the diameter of the base of the pitch cone, the circular pitch p to the teeth is measured along this circle and the diametral pitch P is also based on this circle.

The important dimensions and angles of a bevel gear are illustrated in Figure 17.17. The pitch cone is shown as the triangle AOB, and the pitch angle is $\frac{1}{2}$ angle AOB. The root and face angle lines do not actually converge at point O but are often drawn as if they do for simplicity. Figure 17.17 shows that the pitch angle of each gear depends on the relative diameters of the gears. When the shafts are at right angles, the sum of the pitch angles for the two mating gears equals 90°.

Therefore, the pitch angles, Γ (gamma), are determined from the following equations:

$$\tan \Gamma_G = \frac{D_G}{D_P} = \frac{N_G}{N_P}$$

and

$$\tan \Gamma_G = \frac{D_P}{D_G} = \frac{N_P}{N_G}$$

In the simplified formulas given here, tooth proportions are assumed equal on both gears, but in modern practice bevel gears are often designed with unequal addenda and unequal tooth thicknesses to balance the strength of gear and pinion. Refer to AGMA standards for more details.

Terms for bevel gear definitions and formulas are given in Table 17.1.

17.12 WORKING DRAWINGS OF BEVEL GEARS

Like those for spur gears, working drawings of bevel gears give only the dimensions of the gear blank. Data necessary for cutting the teeth are given in a note or table. A single sectional view will usually provide all necessary information (Figure 17.18). If a second view is required, only the gear blank is drawn, and the tooth profiles are omitted. Two gears are shown in their operating relationship. On detail drawings, each gear is usually drawn separately, as in Figure 17.17, and fully dimensioned. Placement of the gear-blank dimensions depends largely on the manufacturing methods used in producing the gear, but the scheme shown is commonly followed.

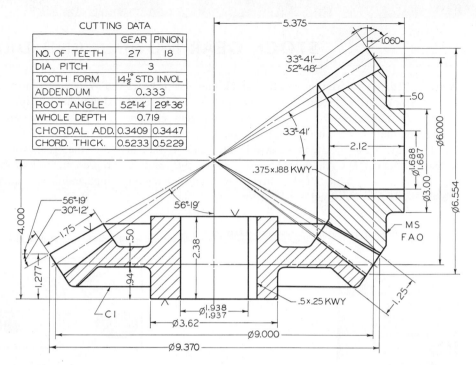

17.18 Working Drawing of Bevel Gears

Table 17.1 Bevel Gear Terms, Definitions, and Formulas.

Term	Symbol	Definition	Formula
Addendum	a	Distance from pitch cone to top of tooth; measured at large end of tooth.	$a = 1/P$
Addendum angle	α	Angle subtended by addendum; same for gear and pinion.	$\tan \alpha = a/A$
Back angle		Usually equal to the pitch angle.	
Backing	Y	Distance from base of pitch cone to rear of hub.	
Chordal addendum Chordal thickness	$\left.\begin{array}{c} a_c \\ \\ t_c \end{array}\right\}$	For bevel gears, the formulas given for spur gears can be used if D is replaced by $D/\cos \Gamma$ and N is replaced by $N \cos \Gamma$.	
Crown backing	Z	More practical than backing for shop use; dimension Z given on drawings instead of Y.	$Z = Y + a \sin \Gamma$
Crown height	X	Distance, parallel to gear axis, from cone apex to crown of the gear.	$X = \frac{1}{2}D_o/\tan \Gamma_o$
Dedendum	b	Distance from pitch cone to bottom of tooth; measured at large end of tooth.	$b = 1.188/P$
Dedendum angle	δ	Angle subtended by dedendum; same for gear and pinion.	$\tan \delta = b/A$
Face angle	Γ_o	Angle between top of teeth and the gear axis.	$\Gamma_o = \Gamma + \alpha$
Face width	F	Should not exceed A or $10/P$, whichever is smaller.	
Mounting distance	M	A dimension used primarily for inspection and assembly purposes.	$M = Y + \frac{1}{2}D/\tan \Gamma$
Outer cone distance	A	Slant height of pitch cone; same for gear and pinion.	$A = D/2 \sin \Gamma$
Outside diameter	D_o	Diameter of outside or crown circle of the gear.	$D_o = D + 2a \cos \Gamma$
Pitch diameter	D_G	Diameter of base of pitch cone of gear or pinion.	$D_G = N_G/P$
	D_P		$D_P = N_P/P$
Root angle	Γ_R	Angle between the root of the teeth and the gear axis.	$\Gamma_R = \Gamma - \delta$

STOCK GEAR MODELS AND DRAWINGS

A great Web site where you can find stock models for gears is the Stock Drive Products/Sterling Instruments site at https://sdp-si.com (Figure A). Once you have registered, you can search their site for useful standard parts that you might purchase for a design. After you have located a part, you can download 2D or 3D CAD data. Figure B shows the compatible file types available for download. Detailed data sheets are available for download in PDF format. You can even use a Web viewer to view and rotate the 3D model before you download it (Figure C).

When gears are ordered to use as standard parts in an assembly, a detailed gear drawing is not necessary. A table showing the gear information is often sufficient. Simplified representations of the shape—for example, the exterior envelope and/or base curves—may be used to represent the gear.

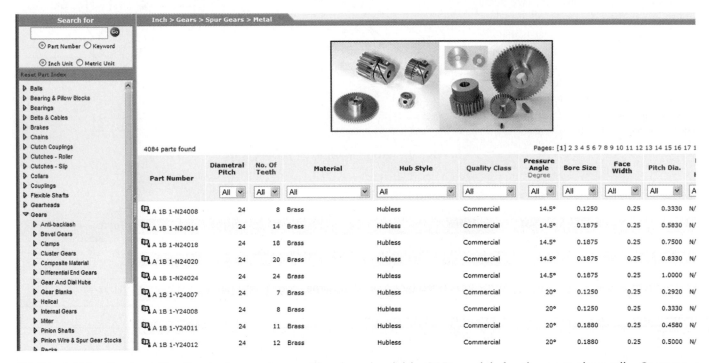

(A) Stock Drive Product/Sterling Instruments provides downloadable CAD models for the parts they sell. *Courtesy of Stock Drive Products/Sterling Instruments.*

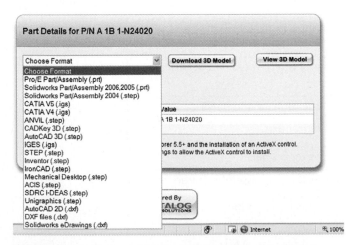

(B) Several CAD formats are available for download. *Courtesy of Stock Drive Products/Sterling Instruments.*

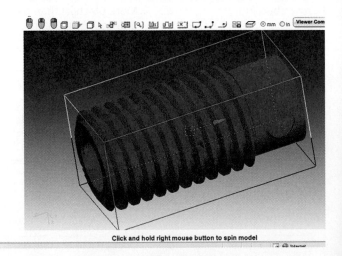

(C) An interactive viewer allows you to view and rotate the 3D model via the Web. *Courtesy of Stock Drive Products/Sterling Instruments.*

Camshafts. *Courtesy of Andrew Wakeford/Getty Images, Inc.-Photodisc.*

Billet Steel Cams for Ford 4.6/5.4L SOHC V-8. *Courtesy of Crane Cams, Inc.*

17.13 CAMS

Cams can produce unusual and irregular motions that would be difficult to produce otherwise. Figure 17.19a shows the basic principle of the cam. A shaft rotating at uniform speed carries an irregularly shaped disk called a cam; a reciprocating member, called the **cam follower,** presses a small roller against the curved surface of the cam. (The roller is held in contact with the cam by gravity or a spring.) Rotating the cam causes the follower to reciprocate with a cyclic motion according to the shape of the **cam profile.**

Figure 17.19b shows an automobile valve cam which operates a flat-faced follower. Figure 17.19c shows a disk cam with the roller follower attached to a linkage to transmit motion to another part of the device.

The following sections discuss how to draw a cam profile that will cause the follower to produce the particular motion that is needed.

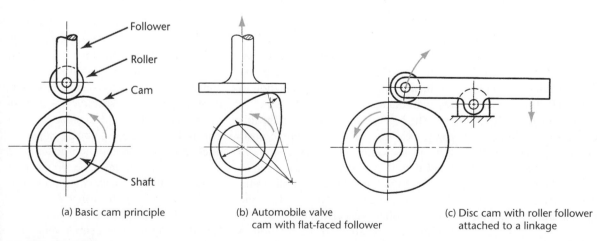

(a) Basic cam principle

(b) Automobile valve cam with flat-faced follower

(c) Disc cam with roller follower attached to a linkage

17.19 Disk Cams

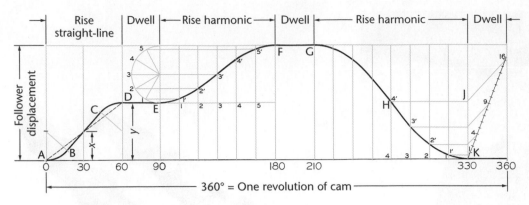

17.20 Displacement Diagram with Typical Curves

17.14 DISPLACEMENT DIAGRAMS

Since the motion of the follower is your first concern, its rate of speed and its various positions should be carefully planned in a displacement diagram before the cam profile is constructed. A **displacement diagram** (Figure 17.20) is a curve showing the displacement of the follower as ordinates on a baseline that represents one revolution of the cam. Draw the follower displacement to scale, but you can use any convenient length to represent the 360° of cam rotation.

The motion of the follower as it rises or falls depends on the shape of the curves in the displacement diagram. In this diagram, four commonly employed types of curves are shown. If a straight line is used, such as the dashed line *AD* in Figure 17.20, the follower will move

with a uniform velocity, but it will be forced to start and stop very abruptly, producing high acceleration and unnecessary force on the follower and other parts. This straight-line motion can be modified as shown in the curve *ABCD*, where arcs have been introduced at the beginning and at the end of the period.

The curve shown at *EF* gives harmonic motion to the follower. To construct this curve, draw a semicircle with a diameter equal to the desired rise. Divide the circumference of the semicircle into equal arcs. (The number of divisions should be the same as the number of horizontal divisions.) Then find points on the curve by projecting horizontally from the divisions on the semicircle to the corresponding ordinates.

The parabolic curve shown at *GHK* gives the follower constantly accelerated and decelerated motion. The half of the curve from *G* to *H* is exactly the reverse of the half from *H* to *K*. To construct the curve *HK*, divide the vertical height from *K* to *J* into distances proportional to 1^2, 2^2, 3^2, or 1, 4, 9, and so on. The number of vertical divisions should be the same as the number of horizontal divisions. Find points on the curve by projecting horizontally from the divisions on the line *JK* to the corresponding ordinates. The parabolic curve and curves of higher polynomial equations produce smoother follower motion than those of the other curves discussed.

17.15 CAM PROFILES

The general method for constructing a cam profile is shown in Figure 17.21. The disk cam rotating counterclockwise on its shaft raises and lowers the roller follower, which is constrained to move along the straight line *AB*. The displacement diagram at the bottom of the figure shows the desired follower motion.

With the follower in its lowest or initial position, the center of the roller is at *A*, and *OA* is the radius of the base circle. The diameter of the base circle is determined from design parameters that are not discussed here.

Since the cam must remain stationary while it is being drawn, you can obtain an equivalent rotative effect by imagining that the cam stands still while the follower rotates about it in the opposite direction.

Therefore, the base circle is divided into 12 equal divisions corresponding to the divisions used in the displacement diagram. These divisions begin at zero and are numbered in an opposite direction to the cam rotation.

The points 1, 2, and so on, on the follower axis *AB* indicate successive positions of the center of the roller and are located by transferring ordinates such as *x* and *y* from the displacement diagram. So, when the cam has rotated 60°, the follower roller must rise a distance *x* to position 2, and after 90° of rotation, a distance *y* to position 3, and so on.

Note that while the center of the roller moved from its initial position *A* to position 2, for example, the cam rotated 60° counterclockwise. Therefore, point 2

must be revolved clockwise about the cam center *O* to the corresponding 60° tangent line to establish point 2′. In this position, the complete follower would appear as shown by the phantom outline. Points represent consecutive positions of the roller center, and a smooth curve drawn through these points is called the pitch curve. To obtain the actual cam profile, the roller must be drawn in a number of positions, and the cam profile drawn tangent to the roller circles, as shown. The best results are obtained by first drawing the pitch curve very carefully and then drawing several closely spaced roller circles with centers on the **pitch curve,** as shown between points *5′* and *6′*.

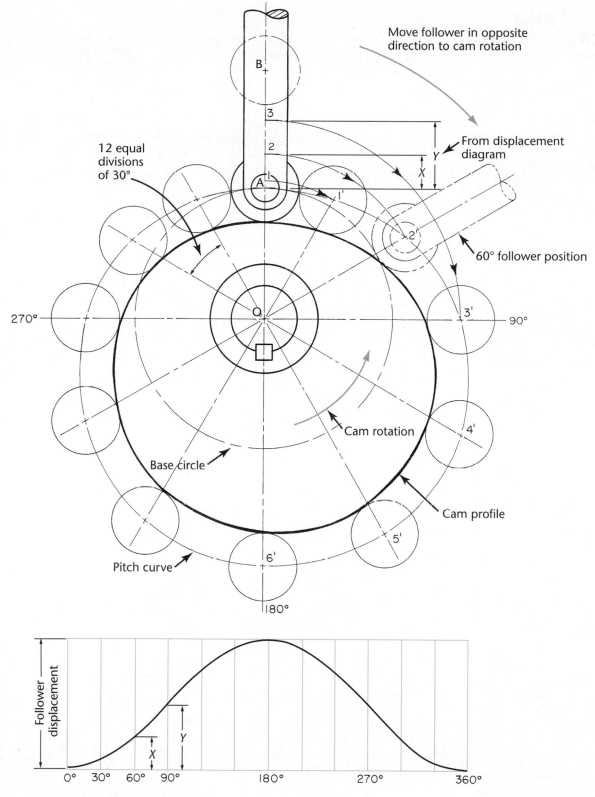

Move follower in opposite direction to cam rotation

From displacement diagram

60° follower position

12 equal divisions of 30°

Cam rotation

270°

90°

180°

Base circle

Cam profile

Pitch curve

Follower displacement

0° 30° 60° 90°   180°   270°   360°

17.21 Disk Cam Profile Construction

17.16 OFFSET AND PIVOTED CAM FOLLOWERS

If the follower is offset as shown in Figure 17.22, an offset circle is drawn with center O and radius equal to the amount of offset. As the cam turns, the extended centerline of the follower will always be tangent to this offset circle. The equiangular spaces are stepped off on the offset circle, and tangent lines are then drawn from each point on the offset circle, as shown.

If the roller is on a pivoted arm, as shown in Figure 17.23a, then the displacement of the roller center is along the circular arc AB. The height of the displacement diagram (not shown) should be made equal to the rectified length of arc AB. Ordinates from the diagram are then transferred to arc AB to locate the roller positions $1, 2, 3, \ldots$. As the follower is revolved about the cam, pivot point C moves in a circular path of radius OC to the consecutive positions C_1, C_2, and so on. Length AC is constant for all follower positions; hence, from each new position of point C, the follower arc of radius R is drawn as shown at the 90° position. The roller centers $1, 2, 3$, are now revolved about the cam center O to intersect the follower arcs at $1', 2', 3'$. After the pitch curve is completed, the cam profile is drawn tangent to the roller circles.

The construction for a flat-faced follower is shown in Figure 17.23b. The initial point of contact is at A, and points $1, 2, 3$, represent consecutive positions of the follower face. Then for the 90° position, point 3 must be revolved 90°, as shown, to position $3'$, and the flat face of the follower is drawn through point $3'$ at right angles to the cam radius. When this procedure has been repeated for each position, the cam profile will be enveloped by a series of straight lines, and the cam profile is drawn inside and tangent to these lines. Note that the point of contact, initially at A, changes as the follower rises. At 90°, for example, contact is at D, a distance X to the right of the follower axis.

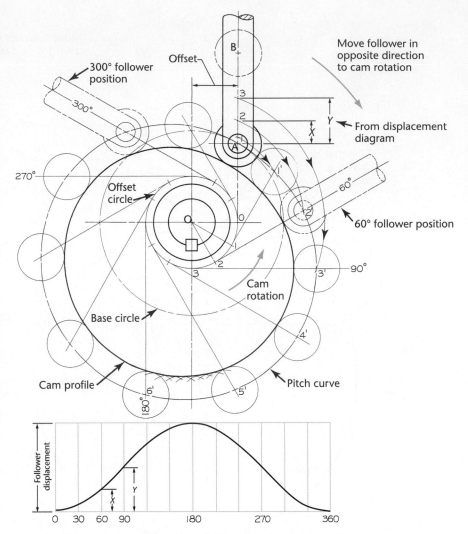

17.22 Disk Cam Profile with Offset Follower Construction

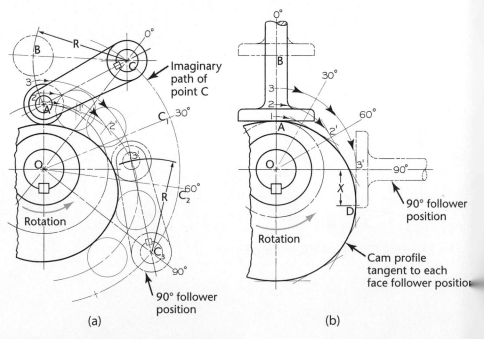

(a)   (b)

17.23 Pivoted and Flat-Faced Followers

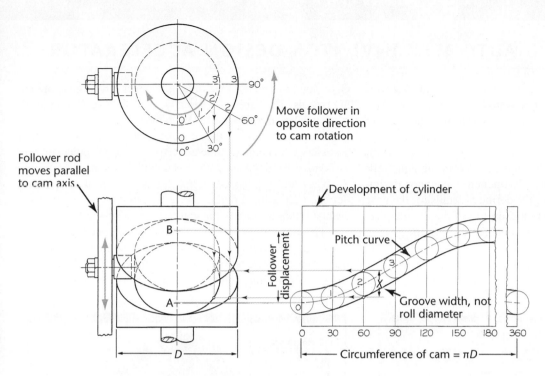

Follower rod moves parallel to cam axis

Move follower in opposite direction to cam rotation

Development of cylinder

Pitch curve

Groove width, not roll diameter

Follower displacement

Circumference of cam = πD

17.24   Cylindrical Cam

17.17 CYLINDRICAL CAMS

When the follower movement is in a plane parallel to the camshaft, some form of cylindrical cam must be employed. In Figure 17.24, for example, the follower rod moves vertically parallel to the cam axis as the attached roller follows the groove in the rotating cam cylinder.

A cylindrical cam of diameter D is required to lift the follower rod a distance AB with harmonic motion in 180° of cam motion and to return the rod in the remaining 180° with the same motion. The displacement diagram is drawn first and conveniently placed directly opposite the front view. The 360° length of the diagram must be made equal to πD so

that the resulting curves will be a true development of the outer surface of the cam cylinder. The pitch curve is drawn to represent the required motion, and a series of roller circles is then drawn to establish the sides of the groove tangent to these circles. This completes the development of the outer cylinder and actually provides all information needed for making the cam; hence, it is not uncommon to omit the curves in the front view.

To complete the front view, points on the curves are projected horizontally from the development. For example, at 60° in the development, the width of the groove measured parallel to the cam axis

is X, a distance slightly greater than the actual roller diameter. This width X is projected to the front view directly below point 2, the corresponding 60° position in the top view, to establish two points on the outer curves. The inner curves for the bottom of the groove can be established in the same manner, except that the groove width X is located below point 2′, which lies on the inner diameter. The inner curves are only approximate because the width at the bottom of the groove is actually slightly greater than X, but the exact bottom width can only be determined by drawing a second development for the inner cylinder.

17.18 OTHER DRIVE DEVICES

When the distance between drive and driven shafts makes the use of gears impractical, devices such as belt and pulley or chain and sprocket drives are often employed. Layout and detailing standards vary somewhat from one company to another, but design procedures and specification methods may be obtained from almost any good textbook or handbook on mechanical design.

GEARS USING AUTODESK INVENTOR DESIGN ACCELERATOR

When you know the design requirements for a gear pair, you can use a CAD package, such as Autodesk Inventor, to automatically generate the 3D models from the information. It can be very time-consuming to create drawings of gears and cams by hand, whereas using CAD frees you to spend more time on other aspects of your designs. Figure A shows the Autodesk Inventor software's Spur Gear Component Generator design tab which you can use to enter the defining details for the gear pair. Clicking the Preview option shows the values and a pictorial representation of the dimensional features for the gear as shown in Figure B.

Once you have entered the data, just select OK to generate the 3D models. They are automatically assembled so that the teeth mesh as shown in Figure C. Each gear is a separate part, for which you can list the data and generate the table of information necessary to manufacture the gear. You can also simulate motion to aid in inspecting how your design will function.

Gear drawings specify the information needed to manufacture the gear using a table. Figure D shows an example of the gear table that can be automatically generated using the software.

The Inventor software's Design Accelerator has similar powerful tools for designing bolted connections, shafts, spur gears, bevel gears, worm gears, bearings, spring, belts, pins, welds, hubs, beams, and columns, among other useful items.

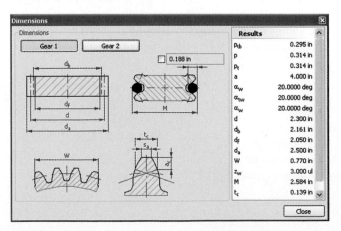

(A) Autodesk Inventor spur gear component generator design tab

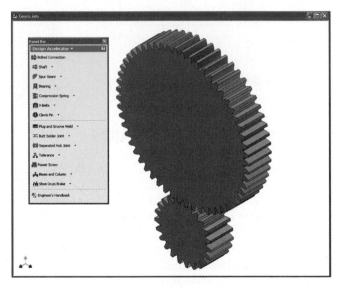

(C) 3D model

(B) Preview shows values and a representation of dimensional features

Gears

		Gear 1	Gear 2
Type of model		Component	Component
Number of Teeth	N	23 ul	57 ul
Unit Correction	x	0.0000 ul	0.0000 ul
Pitch Diameter	d	2.300 in	5.700 in
Outside Diameter	d_a	2.500 in	5.900 in
Root Diameter	d_f	2.050 in	5.450 in
Base Circle Diameter	d_b	2.161 in	5.356 in
Work Pitch Diameter	d_w	2.300 in	5.700 in
Facewidth	b	1.000 in	1.000 in
Facewidth Ratio	b_r	0.4348 ul	0.1754 ul
Addendum	a^*	1.0000 ul	1.0000 ul
Clearance	c^*	0.2500 ul	0.2500 ul
Root Fillet	r_f^*	0.3500 ul	0.3500 ul

(D) Table of information needed to manufacture the gear

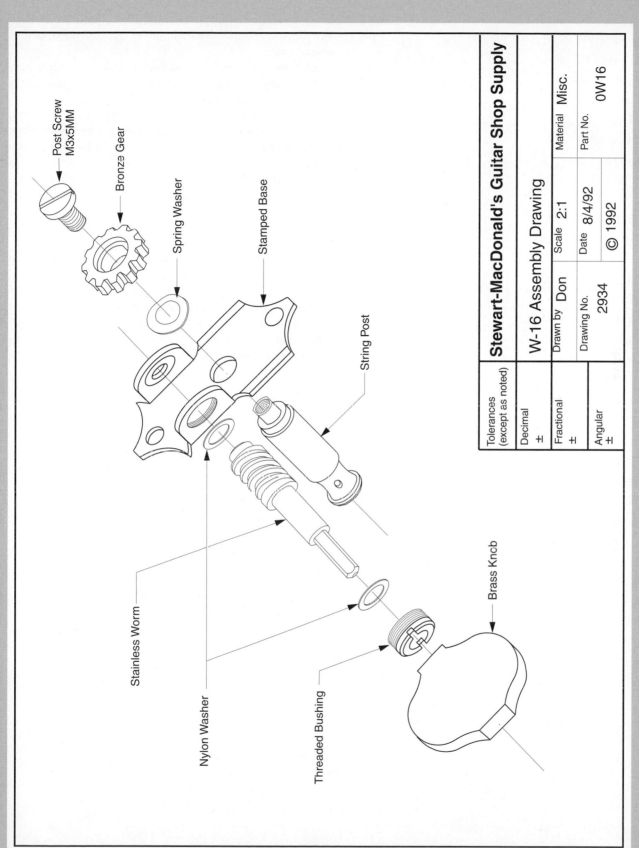

Post Screw
M3x5MM

Bronze Gear

Spring Washer

Stamped Base

String Post

Stainless Worm

Nylon Washer

Threaded Bushing

Brass Knob

Stewart-MacDonald's Guitar Shop Supply

W-16 Assembly Drawing

Drawn by Don	Scale 2:1	Material Misc.
Drawing No.	Date 8/4/92	Part No.
2934	© 1992	0W16

Tolerances (except as noted)
Decimal ±
Fractional ±
Angular ±

PORTFOLIO

Assembly Drawing for Waverly Tuner. *Courtesy of Stewart MacDonald Co.*

KEY WORDS

Gears

Spur Gears

Helical Gears

Herringbone Gears

Bevel Gears

Helical Gears

Hypoid Gears

Worm Gears

Friction Wheels

rpm

Pitch Circles

Pitch Diameter

Pinion

Gear Ratio

Involute

Base Circle

Addendum

Root Circle

Diametral Pitch

Stub Teeth

Rack

Circular Pitch

Gear Blank

Pitch Diameter

Dedendum

Root Diameter

Whole Depth

Chordal Thickness

Chordal Addendum

Cam

Cam Follower

Cam Profile

Displacement Diagram

Pitch Curve

CHAPTER SUMMARY

- Gears transmit power from one rotating shaft to another. The purpose of a gear is to change the rpm, direction, or axis orientation.
- Exact drawings for gears are difficult to draw on paper or with CAD because of complex tooth shape. A table of gear data is typically all that is needed to define the shape.
- Once the mathematical calculations for a gear are complete, the construction of a gear profile is begun by constructing four circles: the addendum circle, pitch circle, base circle, and root circle.
- The involute profile is the most common gear tooth profile.
- Advanced CAD programs can automate the construction of gear teeth.
- The most common gear type is the spur gear. Spur gear axes are parallel to each other.
- The axes of worm gears and bevel gears are positioned 90° to each other.
- Cams change rotating motion into reciprocating motion. The displacement curve defines the linear follower movement as the cam rotates through 360° of rotary motion.
- When gears are ordered as standard parts to use in an assembly, you do not need a detailed drawing. A table showing the gear information is often sufficient.

REVIEW QUESTIONS

1. What is the purpose of a gear?
2. What is the geometric shape most commonly used for a gear tooth profile?
3. What are the four circles used to draw a gear?
4. Which types of gears have shafts that are perpendicular to each other?
5. Describe how to draw a cam profile, given a displacement diagram.
6. What is the purpose of a cam follower?
7. How many total degrees of rotation are shown on a cam displacement diagram?
8. Why is the cam follower position always the same at the starting point and the ending point?

EXERCISES

Gearing and Cam Exercises

The following exercises provide practice in laying out and making working drawings of the common types of gears and cams. Where paper sizes are not given, select both scale and sheet layout. If assigned, convert the design layouts to metric dimensions. The instructor may choose to assign specific problems to be completed using CAD.

Gearing

Exercise 17.1 Draw the following by hand or using CAD, as assigned by your instructor.

   a. A 12-tooth IDP pinion engages a 15-tooth gear. Make a full-size drawing of a segment of each gear showing how the teeth mesh. Construct the 14½° involute teeth exactly, noting any points where the teeth appear to interfere. Label gear ratio m_G on the drawing. Include dimensions, notes, and cutting data as assigned by your instructor.

   b. Follow the instructions for Part a but use 13 or 14 teeth, or any number of teeth as assigned by your instructor.

   c. Follow the instructions for Part a but use 20° stub teeth instead of involute teeth.

   d. Follow the instructions for Part a but use a rack in place of the 12-tooth pinion.

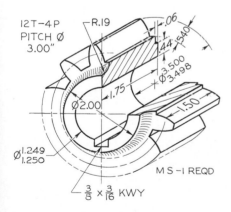

Exercise 17.2 Make a display drawing of the pinion shown above. Show two views, drawing the teeth by the odontograph method shown in Figure 17.6. Draw double size. Omit dimensions.

Exercise 17.3 A spur gear has 60 teeth of 5 diametral pitch. The face width is 1.50″. The shaft is 1.19″ in diameter. Make the hub 2.00″ long and 2.25″ in diameter. Calculate accurately all dimensions, and make a working drawing of the gear. Show six spokes, each 1.12″ wide at the hub, tapering to .75″ wide at the rim and .50″ thick. Use your own judgment for any dimensions not given. Draw half size.

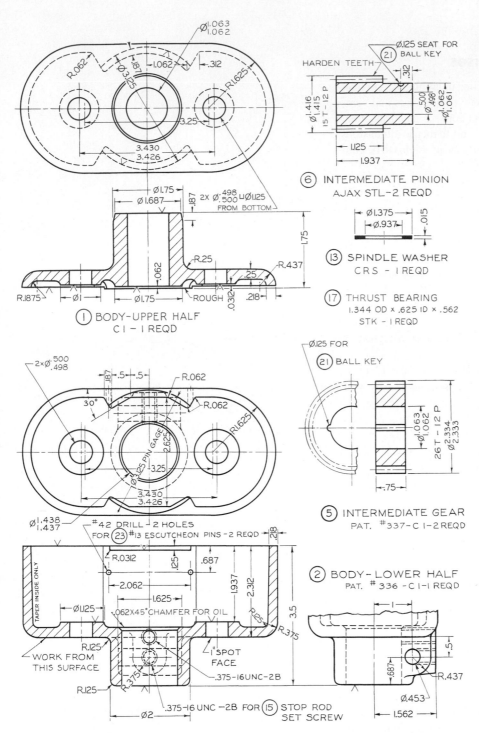

Exercise 17.4 Draw the following.

a. Make a pictorial display of the intermediate pinion shown in Part 6 above. Show the gear as an oblique half section, similar to Exercise 17.2. Draw four-times size, reducing the 30° receding lines by one-half, as in cabinet projection. Draw the teeth by the odontograph method.

b. Make a working drawing of the intermediate pinion shown in Part 6 of the figure. Check the gear dimensions by calculation.

c. Make a working drawing of the intermediate gear shown in Part 5 of the figure. Check the gear dimensions by calculation.

d. Follow instructions for Part a, but use the pinion shown in Exercise 17.2.

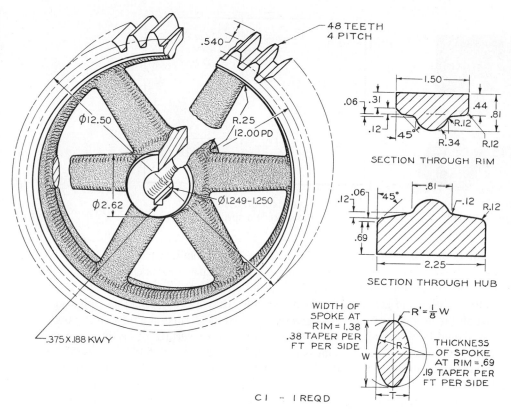

48 TEETH
4 PITCH

.540

Ø12.50

R.25
12.00 PD

Ø2.62

Ø1.249-1.250

.375 X .188 KWY

1.50

.06 .31
.12
45°
.44
.81
R.12
R.34   R.12

SECTION THROUGH RIM

.81

.12 .06 45°
.12 R.12
.69

2.25

SECTION THROUGH HUB

WIDTH OF
SPOKE AT
RIM = 1.38
.38 TAPER PER
FT PER SIDE

R' = ⅛ W

W   R

THICKNESS
OF SPOKE
AT RIM = .69
.19 TAPER PER
FT PER SIDE

T

CI - I REQD

Exercise 17.5 Make a pictorial display of the spur gear shown above. Show the gear as an oblique half section, similar to Exercise 17.2. Draw four-times size, reducing the 30° receding lines by one-half, as in cabinet projection. Draw the teeth by the odontograph method.

Exercise 17.6 Draw the following by hand or using CAD, as assigned by your instructor.

   a. A pair of bevel gears has teeth of 4 diametral pitch. The pinion has 13 teeth, the gear 25 teeth. The face width is 1.12″. The pinion shaft is .94″ in diameter, and the gear shaft is 1.19″ in diameter. Calculate accurately all dimensions, and make a working drawing showing the gears engaged as in Figure 17.18. Make the hub diameters approximately twice the shaft diameters. Select key sizes from Appendix 21. The backing for the pinion must be .62″, and for the gear 1.25″. Use your own judgment for any dimensions not given.

   b. Make a working drawing of the pinion.

   c. Make a working drawing of the gear.

   d. Show two views of the pinion in Part b. Follow the general instructions in that problem.

   e. Follow instructions in Part a but use 5 diametral pitch and 30 and 15 teeth. The face is 1.00″. Shafts: pinion, 1.00″ diameter; gear, 1.50″ diameter. Backing: pinion .50″ gear, 1.00″.

   f. Follow instructions in Part a but use 4 diametral pitch, both gears 20 teeth. Select the correct face width. Shafts: 1.38″ diameter. Backing: 0.75″.

(a) Counter shaft end used on a trough conveyor

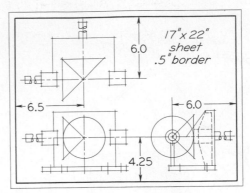

(b) Layout for an assembly drawing of a similar unit.

Exercise 17.7 Make a half-scale assembly drawing of the complete unit (a suggested layout with full size dimension for view placement is shown). The following full-size dimensions are sufficient to establish the position and general outline of the parts; the minor detail dimensions, web and rib shapes, and fillets and rounds should be designed with the help of the photograph in Part a of the figure

The gears are identical in size and are similar in shape to the one in Figure 17.17. There are 24 teeth of 3 diametral pitch in each gear. Face width, 1.50″. Shafts, 2.00″ diameter, extending 7.00″ beyond left bearing, 4.00″ beyond rear (break shafts as shown). Hub diameters, 2.75″. Backing, 1.00″. Hub lengths, 3.25″. The front gear is held by a square gib key and a .38″ set screw. The collar on front shaft next to right bearing is .75″ thick, 2.25″ outside diameter, with a .38″ set screw.

On the main casting, the split bearings are 2.75″ diameter, 3.00″ long, and 10.00″ apart. Each bearing cap is held by two 1/2″ bolts, 3.50″ apart, center to center. Oil holes have a layout for an assembly drawing of a similer unit. pipe tap for plug or grease cup. Shaft centerlines are 6.50″ above bottom surface, 8.00″ from the rear surface of casting. The main casting is 11.50″ high, and its base is 16.00″ long, 8.75″ wide, and .75″ thick. All webs, ribs, and walls are uniformly .50″ thick. In the base are eight holes (not shown in the photograph) for 1/2″ bolts, two outside each end, and two inside each end.

First block in the gears in each view, and then block in the principal main casting dimensions. Fill in details only after principal dimensions are clearly established.

Exercise 17.8

  a.   The worm and worm gear shown in Figure 17.12 have a circular pitch of .62″, and the gear has 32 teeth of 14½° involute form. The worm is double threaded. Make an assembly drawing similar to Figure 17.12. Draw the teeth on the gear by the odontograph method of Figure 17.6. Calculate dimensions accurately, and use AGMA proportions. Shafts: worm, 1.12″ diameter; gear, 1.62″ diameter.
  b.   Make a working drawing of the worm in Part a.
  c.   Make a working drawing of the gear in Part a.
  d.   Make a working drawing of the worm in Part a, but make the worm single threaded.

Exercise 17.9

  a.   A single-thread worm has a lead of .75″. The worm gear has 28 teeth of standard form. Make a working drawing of the worm. The shaft is 1.25″ in diameter.
  b.   Make a working drawing of the gear in Part a. The shaft is 1.50″ in diameter.

Cams

Exercise 17.10 Draw the following for the 90° roller follower at right.

a. For the setup in the figure at right, draw the displacement diagram and determine the cam profile that will give the radial roller follower this motion: up 1.50″ in 120°, dwell 60°, down in 90°, dwell 90°. Motions are to be unmodified straight line and of uniform velocity. The roller is .75″ in diameter, and the base circle is 3.00″ in diameter. Note that the follower has zero offset. The cam rotates clockwise.

b. Instructions are the same as for Part a, except that the straight line motions are to be modified by arcs whose radii are equal to one-half the rise of the follower.

c. Instructions are the same as for Part a, except that the upward motion is to be harmonic and the downward motion parabolic.

d. Instructions are the same as for Part a, except that the follower is offset 1.00″ to the left of the cam centerline. Full size dimensions for suggested view placement are given in the example layout.

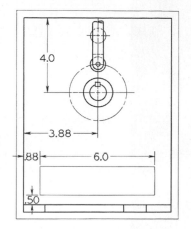

Exercise 17.11 For the 90° flat-faced follower in the figure at right, draw the displacement diagram, and determine the cam profile that will give the flat-faced follower this motion: dwell 30°, up 1.50″ on a parabolic curve in 180°, dwell 30°, down with harmonic motion in 120°. The base circle is 3.00″ in diameter. After completing the cam profile, determine the necessary width of face of the follower by finding the position of the follower where the point of contact with the cam is farthest from the follower axis. The cam rotates counterclockwise.

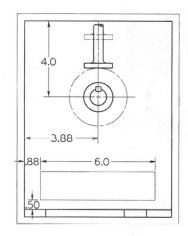

Exercise 17.12 Draw the following for the 45° roller following at right.

a. For the setup in the figure at right, draw the displacement diagram, and determine the cam profile that will swing the pivoted follower through an angle of 30° with the same motion as prescribed in Exercise 17.11. The radius of the follower arm is 2.75″, and in its lowest position the center of the roller is directly over the center of the cam. The base circle is 2.50″ in diameter, and the roller is .75″ in diameter. The cam rotates counterclockwise.

b. Follow instructions for Part a, except that the motion is: up 1.50″ in 120°, dwell 60°, down in 90°, dwell 90°.

c. Follow instructions for Part a, except that the motion is to be: dwell 30°, up 1.50″ on a parabolic curve in 180°, dwell 30°, down with harmonic motion in 120°.

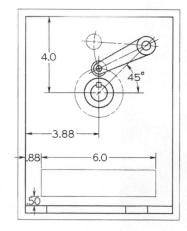

Exercise 17.13 Draw the following by hand or using CAD, as given by your instructor.

a. Using an arrangement like Figure 17.24, construct a half development and complete the front view for the following cylindrical cam. Cam, 2.50″ diameter, 2.50″ high. Roller, .50″ diameter; cam groove, .38″ deep. Camshaft, .62″ diameter; follower rod, .62″ wide, .31″ thick. Motion: up 1.50″ with harmonic motion in 180°, down with the same motion in remaining 180°. Cam rotates counterclockwise. Assume lowest position of the follower at the front center of cam.

b. Follow instructions for Part a, but construct a full development for the following motion: up 1½″ with parabolic motion in 120°, dwell 90°, down with harmonic motion in 150°.

CHAPTER EIGHTEEN

ELECTRONIC DIAGRAMS

OBJECTIVES

After studying the material in this chapter, you should be able to:

1. Identify common component symbols on an electronic schematic diagram.

2. Draw a schematic diagram using standardized symbols.

3. Draw connecting and crossover paths.

4. Identify interrupted and uninterrupted lines.

5. Designate terminals and numerical values of components.

Refer to the following standards:
- ANSI/IEEE 200-1975 (R1989)
- ASME/IEEE 91-1984 / 91A-1991 Graphic Symbols for Logic Functions (Includes IEEE Std 91a-1991 Supplement, and IEEE Std 91-1984)
- ASME/IEEE 315A-1986 Standards Graphic Symbols for Electrical and Electronics Diagrams
- ASME 14.24-1999 Types and Applications of Engineering Drawings

A mobile phone transmitter atop a building in Chicago, Illinois. *Courtesy of Roger Tully/Getty Images Inc.-Stone Allstock.*

OVERVIEW

As all types of designs become more closely integrated with computer controls, it is increasingly uncommon for a device to be purely mechanical. A wide variety of drawings are necessary for the fabrication of electrical machinery, switching devices, chassis for electronic equipment, cabinets, housings, and other "mechanical" elements associated with electrical equipment. Some of these drawings are based on the principles given in Chapter 12, "Working Drawings."

While more and more circuits are contained within integrated circuit chips, many devices still require point-to-point connections. These connections are represented on schematic diagrams, block diagrams, and wiring diagrams.

Every discrete component can be represented with a unique graphic symbol. Components with terminals or numeric values are labeled. Specialized circuit design software allows users to create drawings that also provide for simulations and analysis of electronic circuit. An example is SPICE type software. SPICE is an acronym for Simulations Program with Integrated Circuit Emphasis.

Many standard CAD programs include libraries of electronic symbols that make drawing schematic diagrams easier and less time consuming to draw. For paper drawings, plastic templates are available to reduce drawing time.

Search the following websites to learn more about standards.
- http://shop.ieee.org/ieeestore/ provides a catalog of the IEEE standards.
- http://www.dscc.dla.mil/Programs/MilSpec/ listing and links to military specifications and standards.
- http://www.techstreet.com/cgi-bin/publishers.tmpl listing of a wide array of standards publishers.

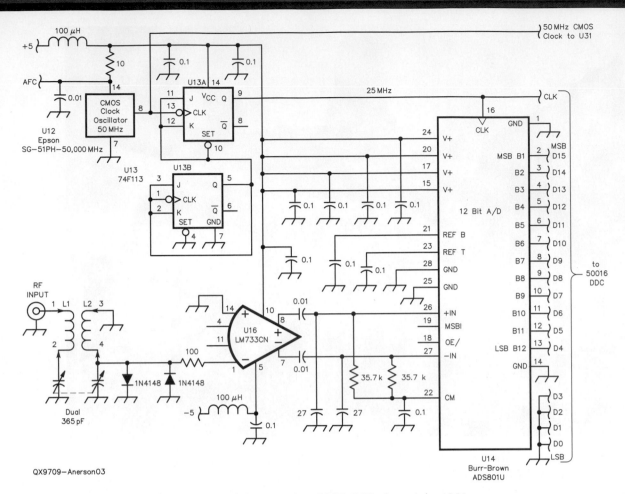

QX9709—Anerson03

18.1 Schematic Diagram. *Courtesy of September 1997 QEX: Copyright ARRL.*

UNDERSTANDING ELECTRONIC DIAGRAMS

Figure 18.1 shows a schematic diagram. Figures 18.2 and 18.3 show a first floor lighting diagram for an architectural project. There are wide a variety of electrical and electronic drawings and diagrams. As is the case in all types of technical drawing communication, you will need to become familiar with specialized industrial practice for the drawings you prepare. A wiring diagram for a second floor house plan looks quite different from a logic diagram. This chapter is intended to introduce you to the types of drawings and general practices and symbols used in electronic diagrams.

Other standards should be referred to as required. The U.S. government has developed a series of standards to be used by military contractors, for example MIL-STD-681 Identification Coding and Application of Hook Up and Lead Wires. In other applications, adherence to standards developed by Underwriters' Laboratory (UL) may be required, particularly where safety considerations may dictate a special printed circuit board layout or component spacing. Standards are updated as they evolve, so research the current applicable standards for the type of drawing you are creating.

Standard Symbols

The symbols approved by the American National Standards Institute (ANSI) are published in "Graphic Symbols for Electrical and Electronic Diagrams," ANSI/IEEE 200-1975 (R1989). In addition, modern printed circuitry techniques, which are used extensively in electronic equipment, require specially prepared diagrams or drawings. Much of the material in this chapter is extracted or adapted from that standard.

CAD Symbol Libraries

You can create or purchase libraries of standard electronic symbols for use in electronic diagrams. CAD symbol libraries should follow approved standards just as manually created drawings would. When you create CAD drawings showing electronic symbols, consider the final size of the plotted drawing. Make sure that symbols you create or add to drawings meet minimum size standards as set out in ANSI 14.2M.

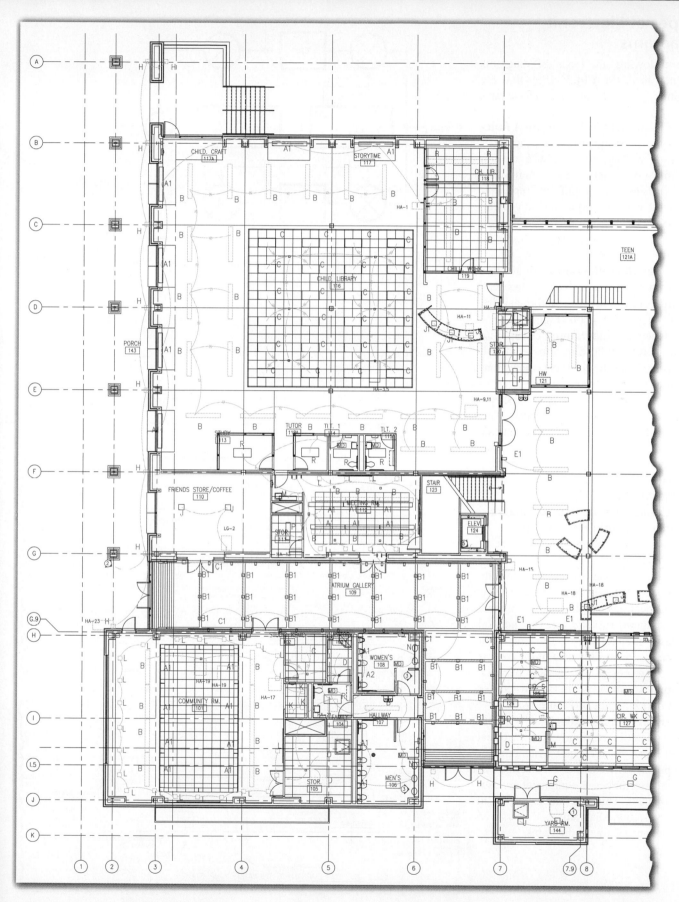

18.2 Portion of a Single Line Diagram Showing the First Floor Lighting Plan for a Public Library. *Courtesy of Associated Construction Engineering.*

Types of Electronic Diagrams

The following are types of diagrams defined in ANSI Y14.24-1999 that are commonly used in the electronics industry.

Functional block diagram A **functional block diagram** shows the functions of major elements in a circuit, assembly or system using a simplified form. It is used to simplify the representation of complex equipment by using blocks or rectangles to depict stages, units, or groups of components in a system (Figure 18.3).

Single line diagram A **single line diagram** shows the path of an electrical/electronic circuit in a general format using single lines and symbols (Figure 18.4).

Schematic diagram or circuit diagram A **schematic diagram or circuit diagram** shows the electrical connections and functions of a specific circuit arrangement. It does not depict the physical shape, size or arrangement of the elements. This type of drawing is used to communicate the design, construction, and maintenance information for electronic equipment. It facilitates tracing the circuit to convey its function (Figure 18.5).

Connection or wiring diagram A **connection or wiring diagram** shows the connections of an installation or its component devices or parts. It may cover internal or external connections, or both, and contains the level of detail to show the connections involved. The connection diagram usually shows general physical arrangement of the component devices or parts. This type of diagram is used to represent the wiring between component devices in electrical or electronic equipment (Figure 18.6).

Interconnection diagram An **interconnection diagram** shows only external connections between unit assemblies or equipment. The internal connections of the unit assemblies or equipment are usually omitted. This diagram is similar to the connection diagram; both serve to supplement schematic diagrams.

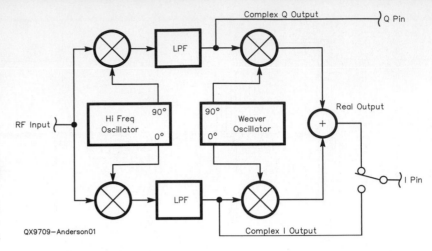

QX9709—Anderson01

18.3 Functional Block Diagram for a Digital Downconverter. *Courtesy of September 1997 QEX: Copyright ARRL.*

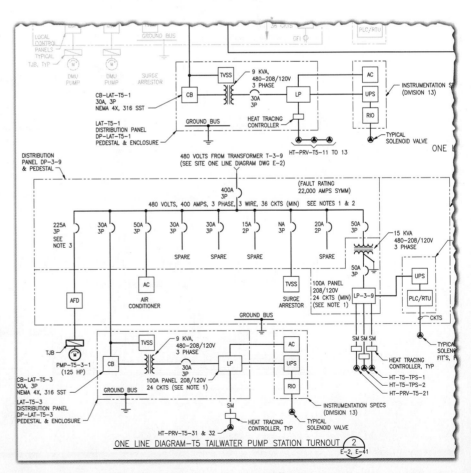

18.4 Single Line Diagram. *Courtesy of CH2MHILL.*

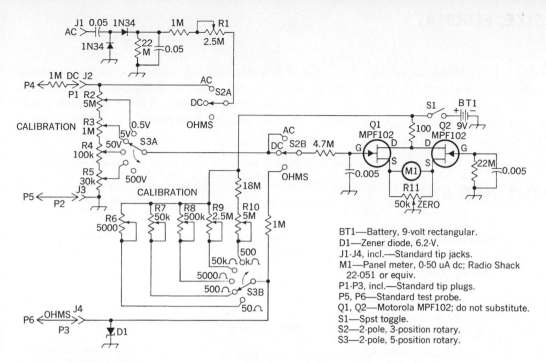

18.5 Schematic Diagram of a FET (field-effect transistor) VOM (volt-ohm-milliammeter). *Courtesy of American Radio Relay League.*

BT1—Battery, 9-volt rectangular.
D1—Zener diode, 6.2-V.
J1-J4, incl.—Standard tip jacks.
M1—Panel meter, 0-50 uA dc; Radio Shack 22-051 or equiv.
P1-P3, incl.—Standard tip plugs.
P5, P6—Standard test probe.
Q1, Q2—Motorola MPF102; do not substitute.
S1—Spst toggle.
S2—2-pole, 3-position rotary.
S3—2-pole, 5-position rotary.

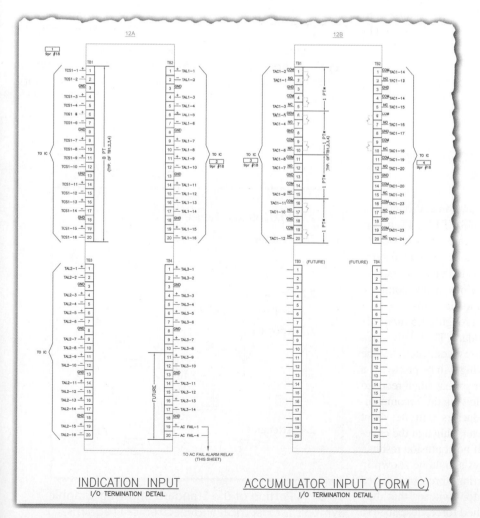

INDICATION INPUT
I/O TERMINATION DETAIL

ACCUMULATOR INPUT (FORM C)
I/O TERMINATION DETAIL

18.6 Portion of a Connection Diagram. *Courtesy of Golden Valley Electric Association.*

18.1 DRAWING SIZE, FORMAT, AND TITLE

The title for the types of the drawing should include the standardized wording in the definition and a description of the application, for example:

SINGLE-LINE DIAGRAM—AM–FM RECEIVER SCHEMATIC DIAGRAM— 250-WATT AMATEUR TRANSCEIVER

It is often useful to include some basic wiring information on schematic diagrams, such as connection details of transformers and switches. For combined forms such as this, don't alter the title, but describe the primary function of the diagram.

18.2 LINE CONVENTIONS AND LETTERING

As in any drawing for reproduction, select line thicknesses and letter sizes according to the amount of reduction or enlargement involved so that all parts of the drawing will be legible.

ANSI recommends a line of medium thickness for general use on electrical diagrams. A thin line may be used for brackets, leader lines, and so on. To emphasize special features such as main **signal paths,** a thicker line may be used to provide the desired contrast. For recommended line thickness and lettering, refer to ANSI/ASME Y14.2M.

Line conventions for electrical diagrams are shown in Figure 18.7. Lettering on electrical diagrams should meet the same standards as for other drawings. Refer to Chapter 2 to review lettering practices. For most sheet sizes, a letter height of 3 mm (.125″) is typical.

For general use	Medium
Mechanical connection, shielding, & future circuits line	Medium
Bracket-connecting dash-line	Medium

Use of these line thicknesses optional

Brackets, leader lines, etc.	Thin (0.3 mm)
Boundary of mechanical grouping	Thin (0.3 mm)
For emphasis	Thick (0.6 mm)

18.7 Line Conventions for Electronic Diagrams. *Reprinted from ASME Y14.15-1966 9R1973, by permission of the American Society of Mechanical Engineers. All rights reserved.*

18.3 STANDARD SYMBOLS FOR ELECTRONIC DIAGRAMS

Symbols Symbols should conform to an internationally or nationally approved standard, such as ANSI/IEEE 315, a portion of which is shown in Figure 18.8. On rare occasions when no standard symbol is available, you can devise a special symbol (or augment a standard symbol), provided that you include an explanatory note. Appendix 36 provides many common schematic symbols for electrical/electronic diagrams.

Size of symbols Symbols should be drawn roughly 1.5 times the size of those shown in the IEEE 315A standard. The relative proportions of the symbols and relative sizes compared to one another should be maintained. If the drawing will be printed at a reduced scale, the symbols must be larger so that when reduced they will still be completely illegible. Following this recommendation, circular envelopes for semiconductors will be about 16 mm or .62″ to 19 mm or .75″ in diameter, although the envelope for semiconductors may be omitted if no confusion results.

Switches and relays Switches and relays should be shown in the "normal" position—with no operating force or applied energy. If exceptions are necessary, as for switches that may operate in several positions with no applied force, describe the conditions in an explanatory note on the drawing.

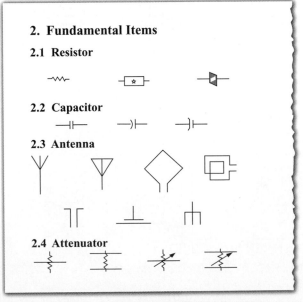

2. Fundamental Items

2.1 Resistor

2.2 Capacitor

2.3 Antenna

2.4 Attenuator

18.8 A Portion of the Standard Showing Graphic Symbols for Electrical and Electronics Diagrams. *Courtesy of IEEE.*

18.4 ABBREVIATIONS

Abbreviations on electrical diagrams should conform to ANSI/ASME Y1.1. (See Appendix 4.)

18.5 GROUPING PARTS

When parts or components are naturally grouped, as in separately obtained subassemblies or assembled components such as relays, tuned circuit transformers, hermetically sealed units, and printed circuit boards, indicate the group using dashed-line to enclose them in a "box," as in Figure 18.9. You can also group components by showing extra space from adjacent circuitry.

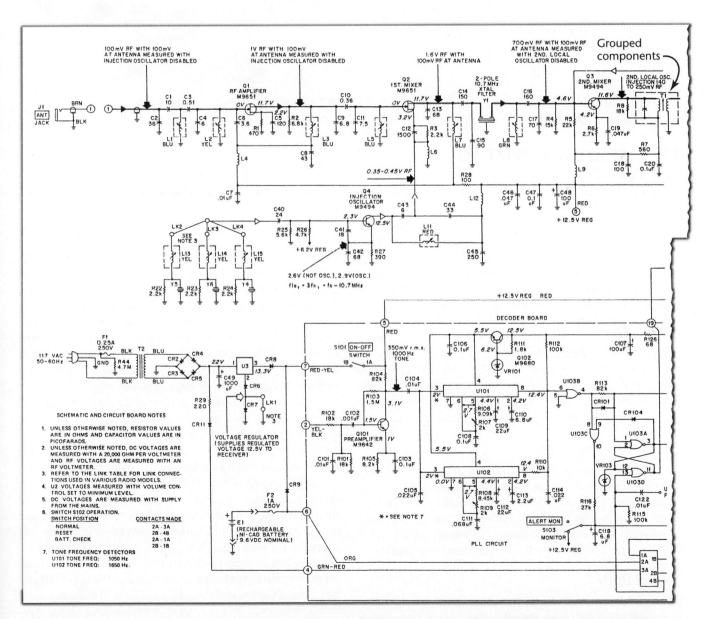

18.9   Portion of a Maintenance-Type Schematic Diagram of FM Weather Monitor Radio. *Copyright Motorola, Inc. 1980. All rights reserved.*

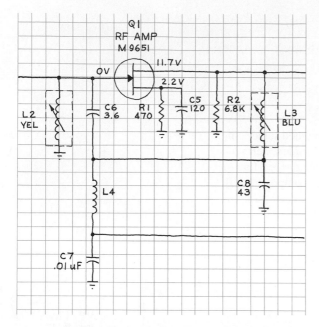

18.10 A Portion of a Preliminary Freehand Sketch of a Schematic Diagram

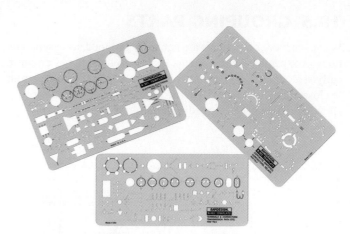

18.11 Electronic Symbol Templates. *Courtesy of Chartpak, Inc.*

18.6 ARRANGEMENT OF ELECTRICAL/ELECTRONIC SYMBOLS

Figure 18.10 shows a freehand sketch of a schematic diagram. It helps to use grid paper when sketching schematics, since it is easier to keep components lined up and makes a neater sketch. Rearrange details to improve the final diagram if it is redrawn. Templates, such as those shown in Figure 18.11, save time when drawing symbols.

CAD can help you to produce complicated schematic drawings efficiently. As a minimum, CAD software provides standard symbol libraries that make it quick to place the symbols into a drawing. On the more complex side, CAD packages may automatically route traces, and simulate the circuit function. Figure 18.12 shows an example drag and drop CAD symbol palette. Figure 18.13 shows circuit simulation software.

Symbol Arrangement

Arrange the various parts and symbols to balance blank areas and lines. Provide sufficient blank spaces adjacent to symbols to allow for reference designations and notes. Exceptionally large spaces give an unbalanced effect but may be necessary to provide for later circuit additions. Of course, using CAD, it is easy to move and stretch the existing drawing to add space.

Signal Path

Arrange schematic and single-line diagrams so that the signal or transmission path from input to output proceeds from left to right and from top to bottom when possible. Supplementary circuits, such as a power supply or an oscillator circuit, are usually drawn below the main circuit.

Stages of an electronic device are groups of components or a semiconductor, which together perform one function of the device. For example, the sketch in Figure 18.10 shows the RF (radio frequency) amplifier stage of the FM Weather Monitor Radio, whose schematic was shown in Figure 18.9. Other stages that can be seen in Figure 18.9 are the first and second mixer stages associated with transistors Q2 and Q3; the limiter/detector stage, containing integrated circuit U1; and finally the audio output stage, U2, and speaker. The power supply, which rectifies alternating current through **diodes** CR2–CR5 to produce direct current voltage, regulated through integrated circuit U3, is shown at the lower left, along with a rechargeable battery backup power supply, E1.

Also shown in the lower portion of the diagram is the circuitry contained on a separate tone decoder printed circuit board (within the dashed lines).

With experience in drawing electronic circuits you are able to visualize fairly accurately the space required by the circuitry involved in each stage. Generally, you should keep the semiconductor symbols arranged in horizontal lines and group the associated circuitry in a reasonably symmetrical arrangement about them. This way each stage is confined to an area of the drawing.

Note that the signal path from input to output follows from left to right and top to bottom. The input is at the upper left and the output at the lower right in Figure 18.10. The signal path is clearly designated by a heavier than normal line. This is typical of maintenance-type schematic diagrams, which are drawn to be easily read and interpreted by service technicians. Heavier lines in the drawing are used for emphasis, but do not have any other significance. Supplementary circuitry (in this case the power supply) is in the lower portion of the diagram.

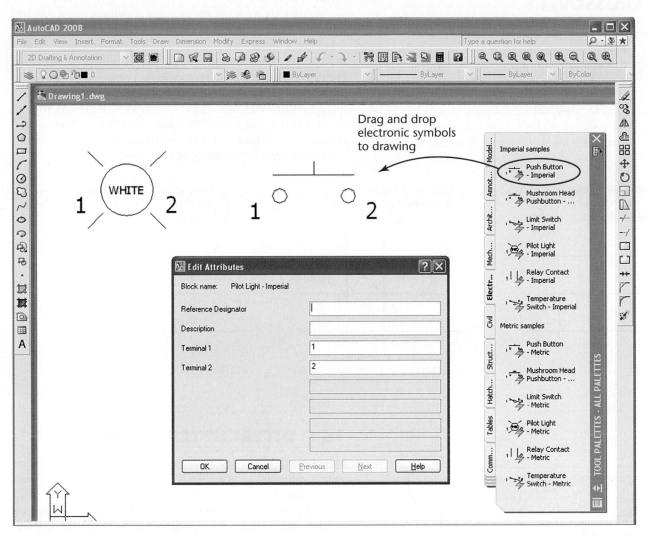

18.12   AutoCAD Software Provides a Convenient Tool Palette to Use for Inserting Symbols. *Reprinted with permission of Autodesk, Inc. © 2006-2007. All rights reserved.*

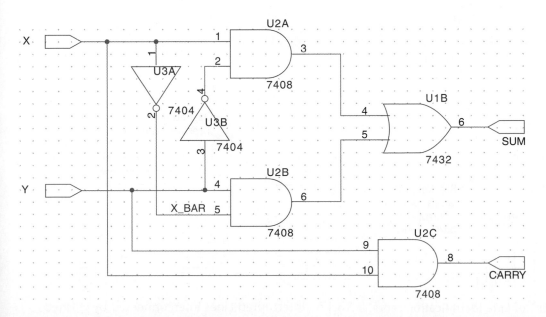

18.13   A simple circuit design created in ORCAD. *Circuits created in ORCAD allow simulation of their function. Courtesy of Cadence.*

18.7 CONNECTIONS AND CROSSOVERS

Connecting lines (for conductors) are typically drawn horizontally or vertically, minimizing bends and **crossovers.** Avoid using long interconnecting lines. You can use interrupted paths to prevent the need for long, awkward interconnecting lines or in cases where a diagram occupies more than one sheet. When parallel connecting lines must be drawn close together, the spacing between lines should not be less than .06″ *after reduction.* Group parallel lines with similar functions and with at least double spacing between groups to make the drawing easier to interpret.

At times it is impossible to avoid drawing a line representing a conductor wire across another conductor wire, where the wires cross but do not connect. These crossovers must clearly depict that the conductors *do not* make a connection. Figure 18.14a shows the recommended practice, in which the termination of a line signifies a connection. If more than three lines come together, as at Z, the dot symbol is necessary. You can avoid this by staggering the connecting lines. The looped crossovers in Figure 18.14c are no longer standard but are still used when there is possibility of confusion.

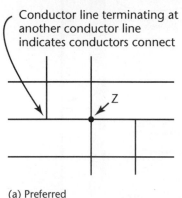

(a) Preferred   (b) Acceptable for showing connections   (c) Used to call attention to the crossover

18.14 Crossovers

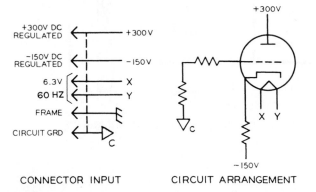

CONNECTOR INPUT   CIRCUIT ARRANGEMENT

18.15 Identification of Interrupted Lines. *Reprinted from ASME Y14.15-1966 9R1973, by permission of the American Society of Mechanical Engineers. All rights reserved.*

18.8 INTERRUPTED PATHS

Interrupted paths may be used for either a single line or groups of lines to simplify a diagram (Figures 18.15 and 18.16). Label these carefully with letters, numbers, abbreviations, or other identification so that their destinations are unmistakable. Grouped lines are also bracketed as well as labeled (Figure 18.16). When convenient, interrupted grouped lines may be connected by dashed lines (Figure 18.17).

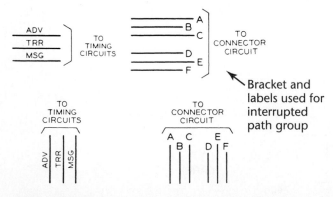

18.16 Typical Arrangement of Line Identifications and Destinations. *Reprinted from ASME Y14.15-1966 9R1973, by permission of the American Society of Mechanical Engineers. All rights reserved.*

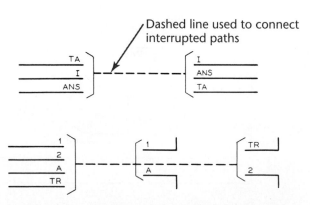

18.17 Interrupted Lines Interconnected by Dashed Lines. *Reprinted from ASME Y14.15-1966 9R1973, by permission of the American Society of Mechanical Engineers. All rights reserved.*

18.9 TERMINALS

Terminal circles need not be shown unless they are needed for clarity and identification.

When actual physical markings appear on or near **terminals** of a component, they may be shown on the electrical diagram. Otherwise assign arbitrary reference numbers or letters to the terminals and add a simple diagram that associates the numbers or letters with the actual arrangement of terminals on the component (Figures 18.18, 18.19, and 18.20b). Figure 18.20a is a pictorial explanation of Figure 18.20b.

Terminal identification for rotary variable resistors follows similar practices, but it is often desirable to indicate the direction of rotation as well, usually as clockwise or counterclockwise, as viewed from the knob or actuator end of the control. Any other arrangement must be explained by a note or diagram. The letters CW placed near the terminal adjacent to the movable contact identify the extreme clockwise position of the movable terminal (Figure 18.21a). When terminals are numbered, number 2 is assigned to the movable contact (Figure 18.21b). Additional fixed taps are assigned sequential numbers, as in Figure 18.21c.

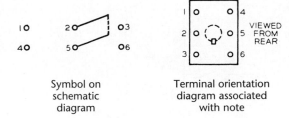

Symbol on schematic diagram   Terminal orientation diagram associated with note

18.18 Terminal Identification—Toggle Switch. *Courtesy of IEEE.*

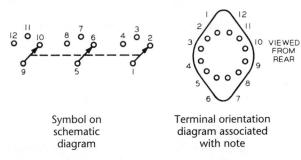

Symbol on schematic diagram   Terminal orientation diagram associated with note

18.19 Terminal Identification—Rotary Switch. *Courtesy of IEEE.*

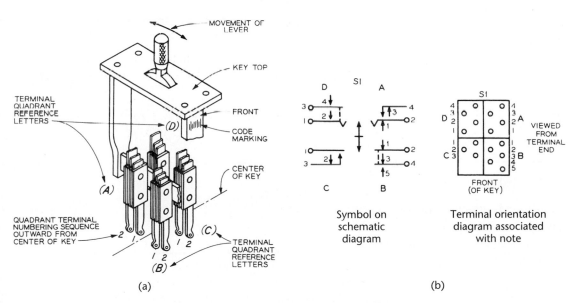

(a)   (b)

18.20 Terminal Identification—Lever-Type Key. *Courtesy of IEEE.*

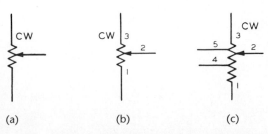

(a)   (b)   (c)

18.21 Terminal Identification for a Variable Resistor. *Courtesy of IEEE.*

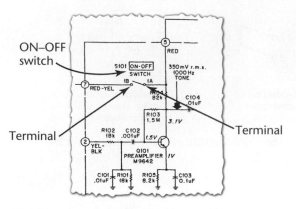

18.22 Terminal Identification and On-Off Switch. *Courtesy of Motorola, Inc.*

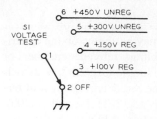

(a) Functions shown at symbol

(b) Functions shown in tabular form

18.23 Position-Function Relationship for Rotary Switches, Optional Methods. *Courtesy of IEEE.*

Switch S101 of Figure 18.22 illustrates the use of terminal symbols and their identification. Switch position, as it affects function, should also be shown on a schematic diagram. Depending on complexity, the designation may range from the simple on-off of switch S101 in Figure 18.22 to the functional labeling of the terminals in Figure 18.23a or to the tabular form of function listing 3 (Figure 18.23b).

The tabular forms use dashes to indicate which terminals are connected for each position. For example, in Figure 18.24, position 2 connects terminal 1 to terminal 3, terminal 5 to terminal 7, and terminal 9 to terminal 11.

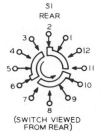

(a) Symbol on schematic diagram

(b) Functions shown in tabular form

18.24 Position-Function Relationships for Rotary Switches Using the Tabular Method. *Courtesy of IEEE.*

18.10 COLOR CODING

Terminals or leads are frequently identified by colors or symbols, which should be indicated on the diagram. Figure 18.25 shows how the colors of the insulated wire leads are noted near each terminal. Colors are shown on the drawing using the following codes:

Black:	BLK
Blue:	BLU
Brown:	BRN
Gray:	GRA
Green:	GRN
Orange:	ORN
Red:	RED
Violet:	VIO
White:	WHT
Yellow:	YEL

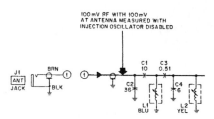

18.25 Color Coding. *Courtesy of Motorola, Inc.*

18.11 DIVISION OF PARTS

For clarity, draw sections of multi-element parts separately in a schematic diagram. Indicate subdivisions with suffix letters. For the rotary switch in Figure 18.26, the first portion S1A of switch S1 is identified as S1A FRONT and S1A REAR, viewed as usual from the actuator end.

An example using suffixes is shown in Figure 18.27. Here the two piezoelectric crystals A and B are enclosed in one unit, Y1. They are then referred to as Y1A and Y1B.

Another way to identify parts of components that are functionally separated on the diagram is with the PART OF prefix (Figure 18.28a). If the portion is indicated as incomplete by a short-break line, as in Figure 18.28b, the words PART OF may be omitted.

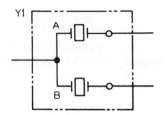

18.27   Identification of Parts by Suffix Letters. *Courtesy of IEEE.*

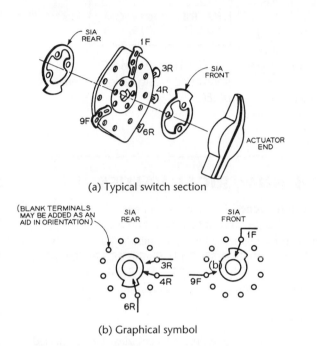

(a) Typical switch section

(b) Graphical symbol

18.26   Development of a Graphical Symbol—Rotary Switch. *Courtesy of IEEE.*

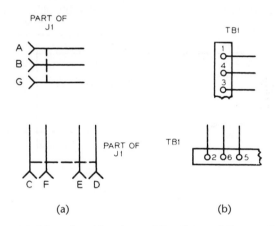

(a)   (b)

18.28   Identification of Portions of Items. *Courtesy of IEEE.*

18.12 ELECTRON TUBE PIN IDENTIFICATION

Electron tubes are generally not used in new designs but are still commonly seen in high-power amplifiers. You may see their symbols in maintenance diagrams used while troubleshooting or modifying existing equipment. Electron tube pins are conventionally numbered clockwise from the tube base key

or other point of reference, with the tube viewed from the bottom. In the recommended method of pin identification on a diagram, the corresponding numbers are shown immediately outside the tube envelope, adjacent to the connecting line (Figures 18.29 and 18.30).

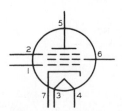

18.29   Terminal Identification for Electron Tube Pins. *Courtesy of IEEE.*

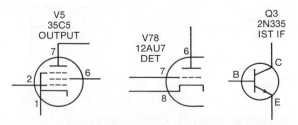

18.30   Reference Designation, Type Number, and Function for Electron Tubes and Semiconductors. *Courtesy of IEEE.*

18.13 REFERENCE DESIGNATIONS

In electrical diagrams it is essential to identify each separately replaceable part with appropriate combinations of letters and numbers. Portions not separately replaceable are frequently identified, as in the previous examples. In electronics and communications, the recognized form is the appropriate letter followed by a number (the same size and on the same line) with no separating hyphen or space. This is followed by any required suffix, again with no hyphen.

Numbers assigned for each category (resistances, capacitances, inductances, etc.) should start in the upper left corner of the diagram proceeding left to right,

then top to bottom, ending at the lower right corner. If parts are deleted in revision, the remaining components should not be renumbered. The numbers not used should be listed in a table (Figure 18.31). If the circuit contains many parts, it may also be helpful to include, as shown, the highest numbers used in each category.

Semiconductors, such as transistors and integrated circuits, are identified by the reference designation and the type number. It is often helpful to include the function below the type number. All this information should be placed near (preferably above) the symbol.

HIGHEST REFERENCE DESIGNATIONS	
R65	C35
REFERENCE DESIGNATIONS NOT USED	
R7, R9 R60, R62	C11, C14 C19, C23

18.31 Highest and Omitted Reference Designations. *Courtesy of IEEE.*

18.14 NUMERICAL VALUES

Along with reference designations, numerical values for resistance, capacitance, and inductance should be shown, preferably in the form using the fewest numerals. To do this, you can combine the multipliers shown in Figure 18.32a and the symbols in Figure 18.32b and 18.32c. Note that commas are not used in four-digit numbers: 4700 is recommended, not 4,700.

Inductance

According to magnitude, inductance may be expressed in henries (H), millihenries (mH or MILLI H), or microhenries (μH or UH). Following the principle of minimizing the number of numerals, $2\,\mu$H is preferable to .002 mH, and 5 mH is better than either .005 H or 5000 UH.

To avoid repeating units of measurement, use a note such as:

UNLESS OTHERWISE SPECIFIED, RESISTANCE VALUES ARE IN OHMS AND CAPACITANCE VALUES ARE IN MICROFARADS.

Part Value Placement

For clarity, locate numerical values immediately adjacent to the symbol. Suggested forms are shown in Figure 18.33.

Multiplier	Prefix	Symbol	
		Method 1	Method 2
10^{12}	tera	T	T
10^9	giga	G	G
10^6 (1,000,000)	mega	M	M
10^3 (1,000)	kilo	k	k
10^{-3} (.001)	milli	m	MILLI
10^{-6} (.000001)	micro	μ	U
10^{-9}	nano	n	N
10^{-12}	pico	p	P
10^{-15}	femto	f	F
10^{-18}	atto	a	A

(a) Multipliers

Range in Ohms	Express as	Example
Less than 1,000	ohms	.031 470
1,000 to 99,999	ohms or kilohms	1800 15,853 10 k 22 K
100,000 to 999,999	kilohms or megohms	380 k .38 M
1,000,000 or more	megohms	3.3 M

(b) Resistance

Range in Picofarads	Express as	Example
Less than 10,000	picofarads	152.4 pF 4700 pF
10,000 or more	microfarads	.015 μF 30 UF

(c) Capacitance

18.32 Numerical Values for Components

18.33 Methods of Reference Designation and Part Value Placement. *Courtesy of IEEE.*

18.15 FUNCTIONAL IDENTIFICATION AND OTHER INFORMATION

It sometimes contributes to the readability of a diagram to include special functional identification of certain parts or stages. In particular, where functional designations (TUNER, OUTPUT, etc.) are to be shown on a panel or **chassis** surface, they should also be shown on the electrical diagram in an appropriate place.

Test points may be identified by the words TEST POINT on the drawing. If several are to be shown, the abbreviated form TP1, TP2, or M1, M2, and so on may be used (Figure 18.9).

Still other information that may be shown on schematic diagrams, if desired, includes the following:

1. DC resistance of **transformer** windings and coils.
2. Critical input or output impedance values.
3. Voltage or current wave shapes at selected points.
4. Wiring requirements for critical **ground** points, shielding pairing, and so on.
5. Power or voltage ratings of parts.
6. Indication of operational controls or circuit functions.

18.16 INTEGRATED CIRCUITS

An **integrated circuit** is a semiconductor wafer or chip that has been processed to produce a microminiature replacement for discrete components, such as transistors, diodes, **resistors,** capacitors, and connecting wiring.

Integrated circuits are widely used in consumer products, such as calculators, personal computers, radios, and televisions, as well as in mainframe computers, microprocessors, and many other industrial applications.

A typical integrated circuit, housed in a "DIP" (dual in-line package) less than an inch in length (Figure 18.34a), contains circuitry replacing all the discrete components shown in Figure 18.34b. To simplify the representation of the circuitry, use a schematic symbol, as shown in Figure 18.34c.

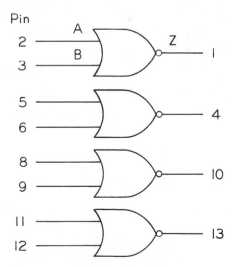

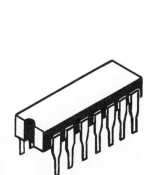

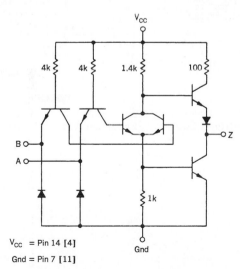

V_{CC} = Pin 14 [4]
Gnd = Pin 7 [11]

(a) Pictorial representation of component

(b) Schematic representation (1/4 of circuit shown)

(c) Symbolic representation

18.34 A Typical Dual In-Line Package Integrated Circuit Representation. *Courtesy of Motorola, Inc.*

18.17 PRINTED CIRCUITS

In the interests of miniaturization and mass production, **printed circuit** boards are widely used in the electronics industry, replacing expensive and tedious hand-wiring manufacturing methods. See Figure 18.35.

A variety of procedures have been developed for fabricating these boards. Their name is derived from an early method of production, depositing (printing) a pattern of conductive ink on a base of insulating material. The method now most commonly used consists of etching a wiring pattern on copper-coated phenolic, glass-polyester, or glass-epoxy material.

Single-sided printed circuit (PC) boards have a component side and a foil side. The component side often has part designations silk-screened on the board; on the foil side, the component leads are soldered onto the copper foil.

If CAD is not being used, once the electronic designer has decided on the physical arrangement of components to be mounted on the printed circuit board, a freehand layout sketch is made.

It is important to maintain close tolerances in the production of printed circuit artwork, so that the various electronic components' leads will fit properly in the spaces provided for them on the finished board. CAD circuit design software should be utilized whenever possible to provide optimum PC board designs with minimal effort.

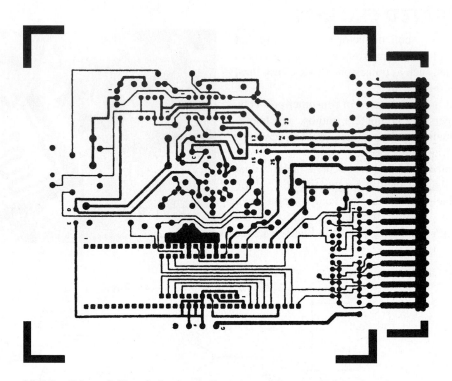

18.35 Printed Circuit Pattern. *Courtesy of Pearson Education, Inc.*

18.18 COMPUTER GRAPHICS

CAD greatly simplifies the process of producing printed circuit artwork. Sophisticated programs let you reduce the physical size of the board and minimize the need for crossover jumper wires.

Double-sided printed circuit boards are common, and many compact designs require multilayer boards, in which the conductive paths are sandwiched between insulating layers. These board layouts (Figure 18.36) require precise registration of the artwork for each layer to ensure proper alignment of corresponding features, such as holes that are to be "plated through" from side to side.

A CAD component layout program allows you to create the best possible parts placement in the shortest possible time Microminiature surface-mount components, which have short solder tab connections instead of wire leads and so do not require drilled mounting holes, are used with increasing frequency. The small size of these parts requires a high degree of accuracy in board layout and design that CAD systems can easily provide.

CAD systems are capable of providing full-size or scaled artwork along with other data required to set up automated soldering and drilling equipment required to produce a finished printed circuit board.

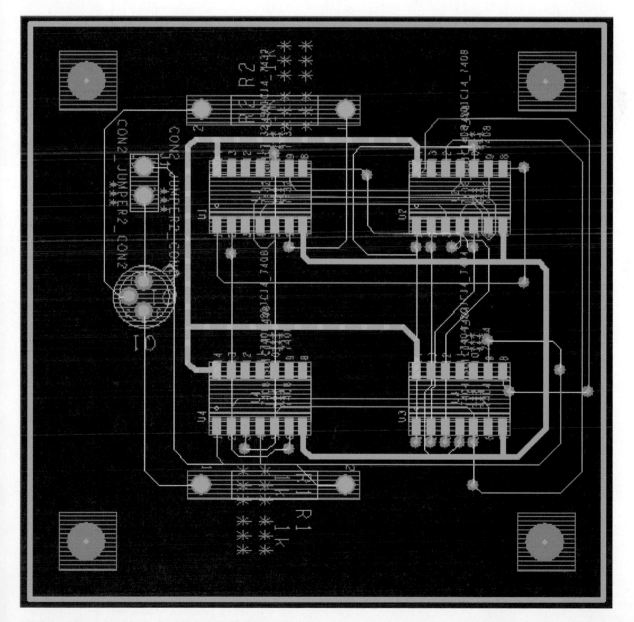

18.36 The ORCAD Software's PCB Editor Supports Autorouting of Board Components. *Courtesy of Cadence.*

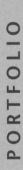

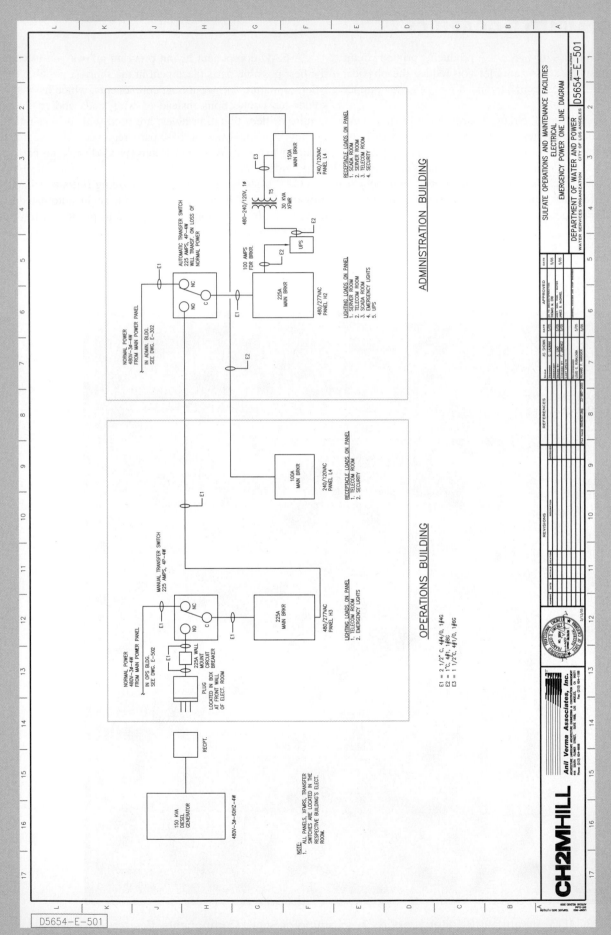

Block Diagram. *Courtesy of CH2M Hill.*

KEY WORDS

Functional Block Diagram

Single Line Diagram

Schematic Diagram or Circuit Diagram

Connection or Wiring Diagram

Interconnection Diagram

Signal Paths

Switches and Relays

Stages

Diodes

Crossovers

Interrupted Paths

Terminals

Semiconductors

Chassis

Transformer

Ground

Integrated Circuit

Resistors

Printed Circuit

CHAPTER SUMMARY

- Schematic diagrams show the signal path between discrete components.
- Wiring diagrams show point-to-point wiring connections.
- Block diagrams show simplified representations of subsystems. Each subsystem is designated by a separate rectangular box.
- Unique graphic symbols are assigned to every electronic component. CAD programs store these symbols in a library. Pencil schematic drawings can be created using plastic template guides.
- Computer graphics programs can automate much of the drawing work when using the computer to generate a printed circuit board layout.
- Letters and numbers are placed next to components to indicate connection points, terminal pin designations, and reference values.

REVIEW QUESTIONS

1. In what direction does the signal path flow in a schematic diagram?
2. What is the difference between a block diagram and a schematic diagram?
3. What does each box represent in a block diagram?
4. In a schematic diagram, what does a large dot mean when two lines cross?
5. How are a component's terminal pins identified in a schematic diagram?
6. Draw the representation of a wire that stops and then continues at a different location.
7. What type of electronic drawing shows parts in three dimensions?
8. What are the names of each side of a printed circuit board? Which side contains the soldered connections?
9. Draw the schematic symbols for 10 electronic components.
10. What is the schematic symbol for chassis ground?

EXERCISES

All of the following problems may also be solved using CAD or freehand. If freehand sketches are assigned, 8.5″ × 11″ grid paper with .25″ grid squares is suggested. Refer to Appendix 36 for standard graphical symbols.

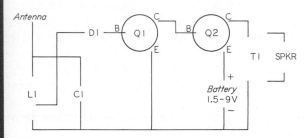

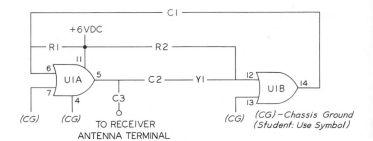

Exercise 18.1 The circuit shown is suitable for classroom or laboratory demonstrations. After a local radio station is tuned with a regular 9-volt battery in place, other devices, such as photoelectric cells and homemade batteries, are substituted.

Make a freehand or CAD schematic diagram of the circuit, approximately twice the size of the figure. Use standard symbols and show component values and reference designations, following recommended practices.

Components List

C1	10-365 PF variable capacitor
D1	Germanium diode
L1	Loopstick antenna coil with center tap
T1	Output transformer: 2500 ohm primary, 3–4 ohm secondary
Q1	NPN type RF transistor (B = base, C = collector, E = emitter)
Q2	PNP type audio transistor

Exercise 18.2 The unit shown is used to calibrate the tuning dials of shortwave communications receivers by providing a check signal every 100 kHz throughout the commonly used bands.

Reproduce the schematic diagram approximately double size, freehand or using CAD, as assigned. Add standard symbols and include reference designations, component values, and other data following recommended practices.

Components List

Capacitors

C1	1000 PF
C2	7–45 PF trimmer
C3	10 PF

Crystal

Y1	100 kHz

Resistors (ohms)

R1	56K
R2	56K

Integrated Circuit

U1	HEP 570 (quad 2-input gate)

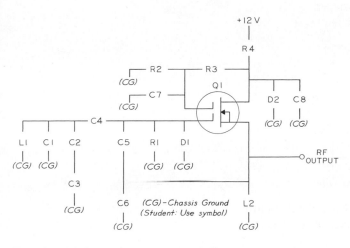

Exercise 18.3 The circuit above is for a variable frequency oscillator (VFO) that may be used with transmitters operating in the 80 m amateur radio ("ham") band.

Make a freehand or CAD schematic diagram, approximately twice the size of the figure. Use standard symbols and include reference designations and component values, following recommended practices.

Components List

Capacitors

C1	100 PF trimmer
C2	50 PF
C3	150 PF variable
C4	470 PF
C5, C6	1000 PF
C7, C8	.1 UF

Resistors (ohms)

R1, R2, R3	22K
R4	270

Coils

L1	6 UH ceramic or air core
L2	1 MH RF choke

Semiconductors

D1	1N914 silicon diode
D2	6 V, 1 W zener diode
Q1	40673 dual-gate MOSFET transistor

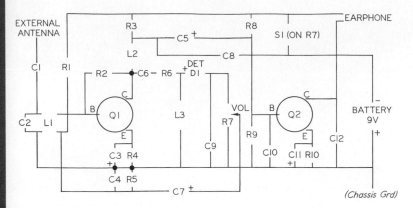

(Chassis Grd)

Exercise 18.4 Make a freehand or CAD schematic diagram of the circuit shown approximately double size. Use standard symbols and show reference designations and component values, following recommended practices.

Note: By rearranging slightly a few connecting lines, you can eliminate the three dot symbols.

Components List

Capacitors		Resistors (ohms)	
C1	10 PF	R1	47K
C2	10–365 PF	R2	82K
	variable	R3	2200
C3	90 UF	R4	1000
C4	.005 UF	R5	10K
C5	5 UF	R6	82
C6	.001 UF	R7	10K variable (potentiometer)
C7	5 UF	R8	82K
C8	.01 UF	R9	5600
C9	.005 UF	R10	3900
C10	.005 UF		
C11	90 UF		
C12	.005 UF		

Coils

L1   Loopstick antenna (same symbol as magnetic core transformer)

L2   Magnetic core, .5 MILLI H

L3   Magnetic core, 1.0 MILLI H

Transistors

(E = emitter, B = base, C = collector)

Q1   PNP type, RF-AF amplifier

Q2   PNP type, audio amplifier

Miscellaneous

S1   On-off switch (mounted on R7)

D1   Diode detector

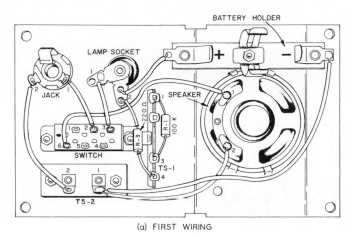

(a) FIRST WIRING

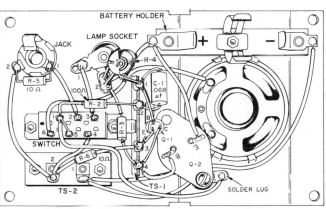

(b) FINAL WIRING

Exercise 18.5 Figures a and b are pictorial wiring diagrams of a transistorized code practice oscillator. The unit provides for practicing International Morse Code either by listening to an audible tone over headphones or speaker or by watching a flashing light.

Study the illustrations and the components list carefully, making preliminary sketches of connections. Then make a complete schematic diagram of the circuit following recommended practices and including component values and reference designations.

Note: Terminal strips TS-1 and TS-2 and the battery holder are for mechanical function and convenience in wiring. They should not be shown in a schematic diagram.

Components List

Capacitors

C1	.068 UF

Resistors (ohms)

R1	100K
R2	100
R3	220
R4	50K variable (potentiometer)
R5	10
R6	10

Transistors

(E = emitter, B = base, C = collector)

Q1	NPN type, oscillator
Q2	PNP type, amplifier

Miscellaneous

Battery	"C" Type, $1\frac{1}{2}$ volt
Battery holder	
Jack	2-conductor (for headphones)
Key	Telegraph key (not shown—connected between terminals 1 and 2 of TS-2)

Lamp, 1.5 V
Lamp socket
Speaker

Switch	3-position slide switch

Connections
Position one (OFF-LIGHT)—terminals 1–5, 3–4
Position two (SPEAKER)—terminals 1–6, 2–4
Position three (PHONES)—terminals 2–5
Terminal strips TS-1 and TS-2

CHAPTER NINETEEN

STRUCTURAL DRAWING

---------- **OBJECTIVES** ----------

After studying the material in this chapter, you should be able to:

1. Create a structural truss or floor plan drawing.

2. Label and specify the size and shape of steel structural members.

3. Identify, draw, and label various structural steel shapes.

4. Identify, draw, and label high strength bolts used in structural joints.

5. Identify welding symbols used in steel fabrication of structural components.

6. Identify and read concrete and brick construction details.

Refer to the following standards:
- http://www.ascelibrary.org/ Search and browse to view tables of contents and abstracts from this comprehensive online library of over 33,000 papers from ASCE journals for all disciplines of civil engineering. Full text is available to subscribers.
- http://www.forestprod.org/awc/index.html Estore for American Wood Council design standards.
- http://www.awc.org/Standards/wsdd.html Estore for wood structural design data.
- http://www.awc.org/standards/nds.html Estore for national design standard for wood construction.
- http://www.strongtie.com/products/Alpha_list.html.
- http://afandpa.org/ American Forest and Paper Association Web site.
- http://www.aisc.org/ American Institute of Steel Construction.

An engineer works with a laptop computer near an unfinished bridge. *Courtesy of Getty Images, Inc.*

OVERVIEW

Structural drawing consists of the preparation of design and construction drawings for buildings, bridges, domes, tanks, towers, and other civil structures. A structural member is essentially one that is bearing a load. Structural drawing is a very large field made up of a wide variety of disciplines. Although the basic drawing principles are the same as for those of machines and machine parts, some methods of representation are different in structural drafting.

Ordinarily, the structural engineer determines the form and shape of a structure, as well as the sizes of the main members to be used. Detail drawings are often made under the engineer's supervision. In many cases, creating detail drawings is a position that provides a stepping-stone to greater responsibility.

Structural drawing can appear in plan or elevation. The location, size, shape, material, and fastening details must be clearly defined. Inaccurate or ambiguous structural drawings can cause building failure and endanger human life. Structural drawings are an essential part of engineering design. Nearly every commercial building uses structural steel in its construction. Residential construction often uses structural wood members.

Many computer graphics programs can enhance the drawing process by providing structural strength calculations for each structural element in a drawing. To ensure safety, meticulous proofing and checking is performed by every member of the team.

STRUCTURAL DRAWINGS

A spider web is one of nature's fine examples of a structure. The web is made of many parts connected to form a unit strong enough to support the spider. Most building or civil project structures also have many interconnecting parts, such as beams, girders, and columns, that form a framework strong enough to support loads (Figures 19.1 and 19.2).

Structural drawings include foundation plans, wall section and framing details, structural steel framing and details, beam and column drawings and details, and others.

Structural drawings are created using either 2D or 3D CAD software. 3D CAD offers better visualization, as well as analytical and simulation capabilities, but due to the complexity of large structures, 3D CAD requires a considerable modeling effort. Wireframe 3D models can sometimes reduce the amount of modeling effort and still provide sufficient information. Structural analysis of piping is an example where 3D wireframe models are used. 2D CAD provides the ability to make accurate orthographic drawings and easily reuse standard details.

The materials most commonly used in construction are wood, glass, structural steel, aluminum, concrete (plain, reinforced, and prestressed), structural clay products, and stone masonry (plain and reinforced). Each of these materials presents its own benefits and challenges as a construction material. Each material also has standard members that are manufactured in stock sizes and shapes. CAD software often provides libraries for these stock parts and features.

19.1   A Silver Argiope Spider on its Doily-like Web. *The doily-like stabilimentum in the middle of the web has a disputed purpose. Some think it is there to hide the spider, or foil predators, or possibly to reflect ultraviolet light and attract insects. Courtesy of Darlyne A. Murawski/National Geographic Image Collection.*

19.2   Glass Ceiling by Architect I.M. Pei Creates Abstract of Spider's Web While an Alexander Calder Mobile Hangs from it. *National Gallery, Washington, D.C. Courtesy of Jacqueline Mia Foster/Photoedit, Inc.*

19.1 WOOD CONSTRUCTION

Many different types of wood are used as structural timber, including ash, birch, cedar, cypress, Douglas fir, elm, oak, pine, poplar, redwood, and spruce. Information concerning the strength properties of the various types and grades can be obtained from 1986 Wood Structural Design Data—with 1992 Revisions. The ANSI/AF&PA NDS-2005 National Design Specification for Wood Construction, published by the American Wood Council (AWC) contains detailed connection information. http://www.awc.org/standards/nds.html (see Figure 19.3).

Nominal Sizes for Wood Products

The surface of a wood product is finished, or "dressed," by milling or planing. Due to wood loss in surfacing, a 1″ thick designation for a thickness is actually ³/4″ for dry lumber and 25/32″ for **green lumber.** Lumber is considered "green" if its moisture content exceeds 19 percent. Table 19.1 shows dressed thickness for various sizes of dry and green wood.

Symbols for Finished Surfaces on Wood Products

Symbols are used to indicate requirements for finished surfaces on wood.

S2S: surface two sides.
S2E: surface two edges.
S4S: all four faces are to have finished surfaces.

The working drawings must show whether standard dressed, standard rough, or special sizes are to be used.

Wood is commonly used for sills, columns, studs, joists, rafters, **purlins, trusses,** and sheathing in homes and other buildings. Methods of fastening timber members include nails, screws, lag screws, drift bolts, bolts, steel plates, and various special timber connectors.

Ordinarily, a structural timber is cut so that the wood fibers, or grain, runs parallel to the length. The strength resistance of wood is not the same in a direction perpendicular to the grain as it is parallel to the grain. Therefore, in designing connections, the direction of the force to be transmitted must be taken into account. Also, proper spacing, edge distance, and end distance must be maintained for screws, bolts, and other connectors.

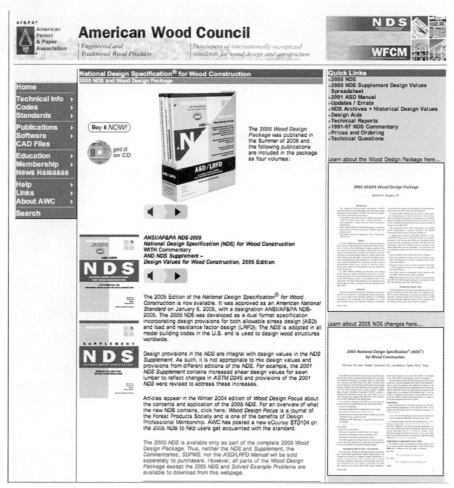

19.3 The American Wood Council publishes the National Design Specification for Wood Construction (NDS). *Courtesy of the American Wood Council.*

Table 19.1 Nominal and Dressed Sizes for Dry and Green Wood.

Nominal Size	Dressed Thickness, Dry	Dressed Thickness, Green
1″	3/4″	25/32″
2″ to 4″	subtract 1/2″	subtract 7/16″
5″, 6″, and 7″	subtract 1/2″	subtract 3/8″
8″	subtract 3/4″	subtract 1/2″

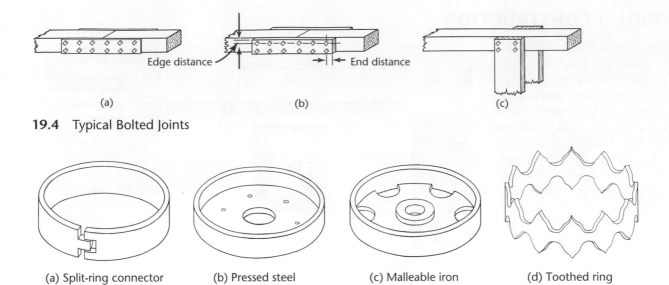

Edge distance ⟶ ⟵ End distance

(a)   (b)   (c)

19.4 Typical Bolted Joints

(a) Split-ring connector

(b) Pressed steel shear plate

(c) Malleable iron shear plate

(d) Toothed ring connector

19.5 Metal Connectors for Timber Structures

Wood Joints

Typical bolted **joints** are shown in Figure 19.4. Either steel or wood splice plates may be used to transmit the forces (Figures 19.4a and 19.4b). A detail without splice plates is shown in Figure 19.4c. Many specialty connectors and shear plates are available.

Connector Designs

Each type of connection requires a different design. Figure 19.5 shows split-ring metal connectors. Figure 19.6 shows how split ring connections install. Figure 19.7 shows a drawing of the left half of a timber roof truss using this type of connector. Only the left half is drawn, since the truss is symmetrical. The views of the top and bottom chords show the relative positions of the connecting members of the structure. In truss drawings, the view of the top chord is an auxiliary view. It is also customary to show the lower chord using a section taken just above the lower chord with the line of sight downward.

Metal Ring Connectors

Metal ring connectors can be installed in wood of proper grade and moisture content to provide increased resistance to shearing loads. The method consists of using either a toothed ring, called an alligator, or a split ring (Figure 19.5a) to connect wood to wood or wood to metal joints.

Toothed Rings

Place the toothed ring (Figure 19.5d) between two members to connect. Draw the two members together by tightening the bolt so that the teeth of the ring are forced into the two members. The ring assists in transmitting stress from one member to the other.

Split Rings

Cut a groove into each of the two members to connect. Place the ring in the grooves. Fasten the two members together using a bolt, as shown in Figure 19.6.

The open joint of the ring should be in a direction at right angles to that of the stress, so that as the stress applied the ring is deformed slightly and transmits the pressure to the wood within the ring as well as to that without. With this connection, the tensile and shearing strengths of wood are developed to a higher degree than by other methods of connection, and it is possible to use timber in tension much more economically.

It is standard practice to show ring connectors by solid lines, as shown in Figure 19.7.

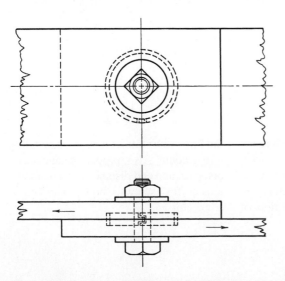

19.6 Method of Installing Split-Ring Connectors

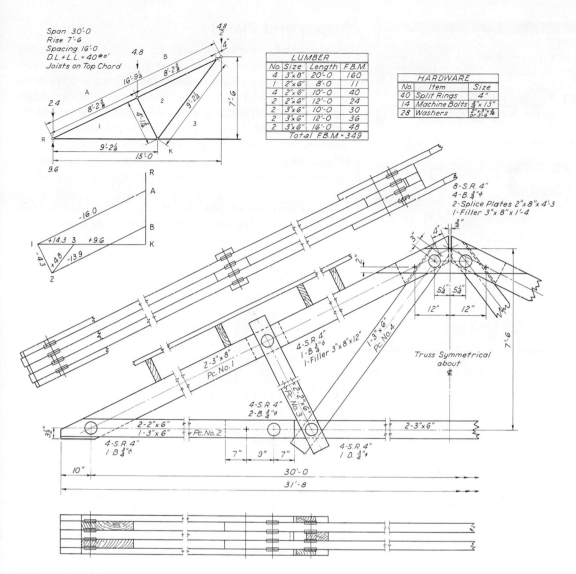

19.7 A Roof Truss.

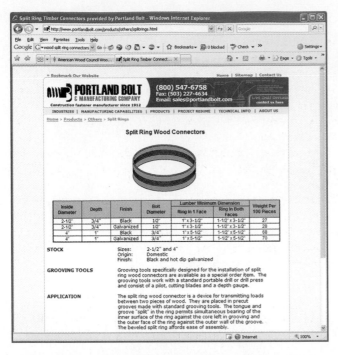

19.8   Design and Sizing Information Is Easy to Find on the World Wide Web. *Courtesy of Portland Bolt and Manufacturing Company (www.portlandbolt.com).*

Straps and Plates

Many specialty straps and plates are available for connecting wood members to wood or other materials (Figure 19.8). Figure 19.9 shows a drawing detail specifying a strap tie hold-down. Figure 19.10 shows a manufacturer's installation detail. Simpson Strong-Tie Co. is one manufacturer that provides a custom menu for AutoCAD that allows you to easily insert orthographic views of their connectors in your drawings (Figure 19.11). Use the resources available from manufacturing companies to save time and effort in drawing repetitive detail.

Another resource you can find on the Web is the Truss Plate Institute, which provides design and verification services as well as a variety of publications for connecting wood structural members. You can find their resources at http://www.tpinst.org.

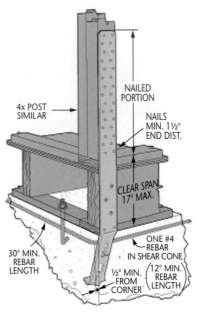

19.10   Pictorial drawing showing installation specifications. *Courtesy of Simpson Strong-Tie Co., Inc.*

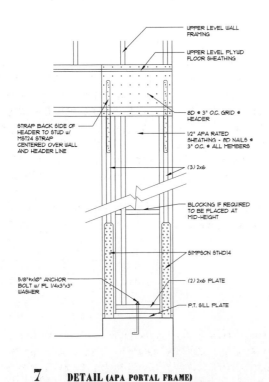

19.9   Drawing detail Calling for Simpson STHD Strap Tie Hold-Down. *Courtesy of Locati Architects.*

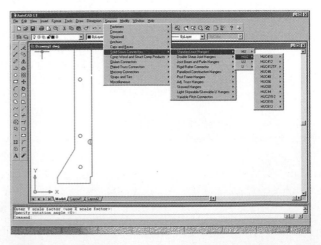

19.11   Simpson Strong-Tie Co., Inc. Provides a Custom AutoCAD Menu. *Courtesy of Simpson Strong-Tie Co., Inc.*

19.2 STRUCTURAL STEEL

Structural steel drawings are ordinarily one of two types: engineering **design drawings** made by the design engineer, and manufacturing (shop) drawings usually made by the steel fabricator. For a more complete treatment of this subject, consult Detailing for Steel Construction (published by the American Institute of Steel Construction, Chicago, IL).

Design drawings show the overall dimensions of the structure, such as the location of columns, beams, angles, and other structural shapes, and list the sizes of these members. Detail in the form of typical cross sections, special connections required, and various notes are also included.

For example, a building floor plan shows the steel columns in cross section and the beam or girder framing using single heavy lines, as shown in Figure 19.12. Members framing from column to column, providing end support for other beams, are called **girders,** while smaller beams framing between girders are called **filler beams.** The designer's plans are sent to the steel fabricator who will furnish the steel for the job. From these plans the fabricator makes the necessary detailed shop drawings and erection plans. Before shop work begins, the fabricator's drawings are sent to the design engineer for final checking and approval. The design engineer is the authority who makes any changes necessary to ensure the required strength and safety of connections. Once the fabricator receives shop drawings approved by the engineer, the shop work can begin.

Shop drawings consist of detail drawings of all parts of the entire structure, showing exactly how the parts are to be made. These drawings show all dimensions necessary for fabrication, usually calculated to the nearest 1/16″. They also show the location of all holes needed for connections, the details of connection parts, and the required sizes of all material. Notes specify fabrication or construction methods on the detail drawings whenever such items are not covered by separate written specifications. Fabrication, shop methods, and field construction methods, must be fully understood by the detailer.

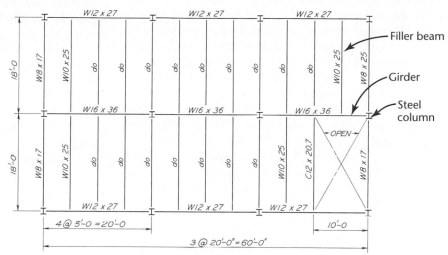

19.12   Typical Steel Floor Design Plan

19.13   Piece Mark

The design of details and connections is an important part of the engineering of the structure. The connections of the various members must be sufficient to transmit the forces in these members. Connection details should be drawn to a scale large enough to show them without crowding. Overall lengths of members are not always drawn to scale in order to show connections clearly. Break lines can be very useful. Show all necessary dimensions. Measurements should never be made from detail drawings by the shop or in the field by the workers making the piece.

Piece Marks

A system is used to mark each piece that is separately handled. This mark is called the **piece mark** and should be shown wherever the member appears on the drawings (Figure 19.13). The piece mark is also painted on the member in the shop and later serves as a shipping mark and erection mark in the field for final assembly of the member in the structure.

Erection Plans

Erection plans made by the steel fabricator are assembly drawings for the steel structure. They show how the steel parts fit together. The piece marks of the individual members are shown on the erection plan to make it easy to identify individual parts. Only show as much detail as needed so that a skilled worker can assemble the parts. The detail drawings fully describe each member and how it connects, so this information is not needed in the erection plan. Line diagrams show the steel members using heavy straight lines. When the assembly is complex, more detail is needed. Draw the assembly views to scale. Like detail shop drawings, workers should never measure from the drawing to obtain dimensions. Use notes on these drawings to indicate how the structure is to be assembled. Cross sections of structural steel shapes are given in Figure 19.14.

An erection plan for the roof steel framing on a building addition is shown in Figure 19.15. This structure is for a paper roofing products pulp mill. New steel is shown by full lines. Existing roof members are shown by dashed lines. Connections to existing steel members are shown in sectional views. The timber framing for the support of large roof ventilators is also shown.

19.3 STRUCTURAL STEEL SHAPES

Structural steel is available in many standard shapes that are formed by the mill by rolling steel billets under high temperatures. (Aluminum and magnesium shapes are also available, but are not covered in this text.) Here are some of the available shapes: square, flat, round bars; plates; equal-leg and unequal-leg angles, American Standard and miscellaneous channels; S, W, M, and HP shapes for beams, columns, and bearing piles; structural tees mill cut from W, S, or M shapes; and standard strong and extra strong pipe and tubing in square, rectangular, or circular cross sections. Figure 19.14 shows some typical cross sections of these shapes and how they are designated or listed in the bill of materials. Use the correct designation on both the design and the detailed drawings every place the structural member appears. For example, designate a wide **flange** section of 14″ nominal depth, weighing 53 lb per ft and having an overall length of 26″-2 $\frac{1}{8}$″ as W14 × 53 × 26″-2 $\frac{1}{8}$″.

Most CAD programs have structural shape symbol libraries available. Templates are also available to save time in drawing structural symbols if you are drawing by hand.

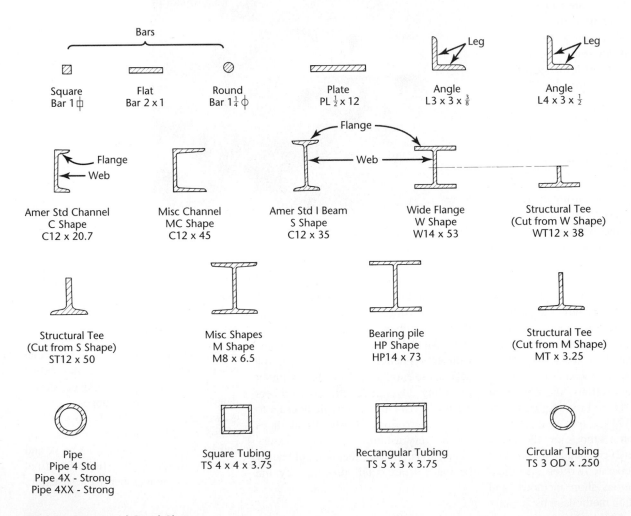

19.14 Structural Steel Shapes

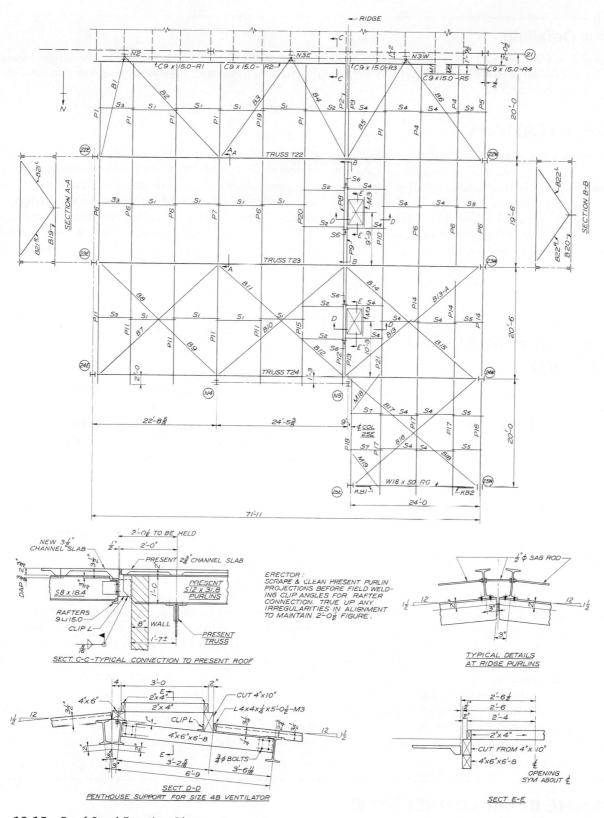

19.15   Roof Steel Erection Plan

> **TIP**
> ## Scales for Detailing
> Often scales of $\frac{3}{4}'' = 1''-0$, or $1'' = 1''-0$ are convenient for showing steel details. The details need to be large enough to show clearly. Due to the length of steel members, break lines may be necessary. In some cases scale in any direction may need to be exaggerated to show details.

19.4 SPECIFICATIONS

Dimensions, weights, and properties of rolled steel structural shapes, rolling mill practice, and miscellaneous data for designing and estimating is listed in the Manual of Steel Construction (American Institute of Steel Construction, AISC). This is the authoritative manual for structural steel drafting.

Fifteen types or grades of **structural steel** are available. These differ in chemical composition and physical properties. An ASTM (American Society for Testing Materials) specification defines each type. There are considerable variations in the strengths and costs of the various grades. Economical selection of steel grade depends on physical properties of steels, such as strengths, ductilities, corrosion resistance, and costs. Specify the type by giving the ASTM designation on the drawing. The most commonly used grade is ASTM A36; the number 36 specifies that the guaranteed minimum yield strength is 36 ksi (36,000 lb/in²). Many lightweight cold-formed C and Z section shapes are also available.

19.5 WELDED AND BOLTED CONNECTIONS

The main members of a steel structure are joined together in the field to build the structure. Most joints are welded connections to the main members. Open holes are provided for field bolts that join the members together. Connections are made of angles or connection plates that attach to the main members by riveting or by bolting with either ordinary or high strength steel bolts in either bearing-type or slip-critical-type connections. High strength bolts must be field tightened by a definite amount of torque applied to the wrench. Formerly, shop riveting and field riveting were used exclusively in structural work.

19.6 RIVETED CONNECTIONS

Although riveting is seldom used now, you may find reference to riveted joints in original plans of structures that require new additions or modifications. Structural rivets are made of soft carbon steel and are available in diameters ranging from $1/2''$ to $1 1/4''$. Rivets driven in the shop are called shop rivets, and those driven in the field (at the construction site) are called field rivets. Rivets are usually of the button-head type and are driven hot, into holes $\frac{1}{16}''$ larger than the rivet diameter. The length of a rivet is the thickness (grip) of the parts being connected, plus the length of the shank necessary to form the driven head and to fill the hole. Excess shank length will produce capped heads, whereas lengths too short will not permit the formation of a full head. Shop rivets are ordinarily driven by large riveting machines that are part of the permanent shop equipment.

Field rivets are heated in a forge at the construction site. The heated rivet is held firmly in the hole with a dolly bar while the pneumatic hammer or rivet gun forms a round, smooth head.

A shop drawing for a riveted roof truss is shown in Figure 19.16. Only the left half is drawn, since the truss is symmetrical about the centerline. Note the use of the gage lines (lines passing through rivets or holes like centerlines) of the members. Locate gage lines close to the centroid of the axes of the members, and at the joints where members intersect. These gage lines should intersect at a single point to avoid unnecessary moment stresses due to off center locations (eccentricities). The open holes indicate where the field splices are to be—usually at the centerline of the truss (℄) for the top chord and at $5'-2\frac{5}{16}$ from the centerline for the bottom chord.

19.7 FRAME BEAM CONNECTIONS

AISC recommends certain standard connections for attaching beams. These connections are ordinarily adequate to transmit the end forces that beams carry. You should know the strength of these connections and use them only when they are sufficient. For complete information, see the AISC Manual of Steel Construction, Allowable Stress Design (ASD) and Load Resistance Factor Design (LRFD). This manual provides details for standard framed beam connections using $\frac{3}{4}''$, $\frac{7}{8}''$, and $1''$ diameter bolted or riveted connections, and allowable loads for both slip-critical-type and bearing-type connections. The fasteners may have a regular or a staggered arrangement. The holes may be either standard round or oversized slotted ones.

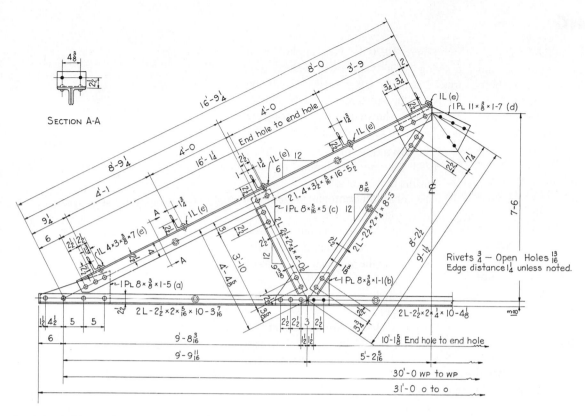

19.16   A Riveted Truss.

Figure 19.17 shows standard two-angle framed beam connections in a typical detail drawing of a floor beam. This drawing illustrates several important features. Shop rivets are shown as open circles on shop drawings. Holes for field rivets or bolts are blacked in solid. Gage lines are always shown. Line up holes or rivets on these lines when possible rather than "breaking the gage."

It is necessary to locate the **gage line** of an angle for each leg, unless it has already been shown for the identical angle elsewhere on the drawing. The edge distance, from end rivet or hole to the end of the angle, must be given at one end; the billed length of the piece is worked out to provide the necessary edge distance at the other end. It is not necessary that the beam extend the full length of the distance back-to-back of end angles. It is shown "set back" at both ends; the length of beam called for is 1" less than the $13'-7\frac{3}{4}''$ distance.

Below the drawing, the mark B25 is the piece or shipping mark that appears on the erection plan and is to be painted on the member in the shop for identification. The end connection angles are fully detailed at the left end of the beam and are given the assembly mark aa. At the right end where these same angles are again used, only the assembly mark 2–aa, to indicate two angles, is needed. The value $10'-1\frac{1}{4}''$ is called an **extension figure.** This is the distance from the back of the left-end angles to the center of the group of four holes. Note that this dimension is on the same horizontal line as the $3'-4\frac{1}{2}''$ figure just to the left. It is customary, in giving feet and inches, to give the foot mark (′) after dimensions in feet, but not to give the (″) inch mark, designating inches.

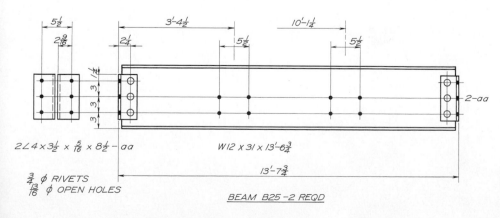

$\frac{3}{4} \phi$ RIVETS
$\frac{13}{16} \phi$ OPEN HOLES

$2L 4 \times 3\frac{1}{2} \times \frac{5}{16} \times 8\frac{1}{2} - aa$

$W12 \times 31 \times 13' - 6\frac{3}{4}$

$13' - 7\frac{3}{4}$

BEAM B25 –2 REQD

19.17   Floor Beam Shop Drawing

19.8 WELDING

Welding is a common method for connecting steel members of buildings and bridges. Most steel fabricators have bolt, welding, and riveting equipment available. Some handle only welded fabrication. The **fillet weld** is most common in structural steel fabrication. Use standard weld symbols to simplify making the shop drawings. For additional information, refer to Chapter 22 and to the relevant specification in the AISC Manual of Steel Construction. When a structure is to be welded, it should be designed throughout for this method of fabrication. It is not economical to merely substitute welding for riveting.

A beam with end connection angles shop welded to the **beam web** is shown in Figure 19.18. The remaining legs of the angles are to be welded to the connecting columns in the field, as shown in the end view. This view pertains only to field erection. Open holes in the far legs facilitate positioning for the bolts.

A shop drawing of a diagonal bracing between two columns is shown in Figure 19.19. Here the diagonal members are shop welded to gusset plates that are to be bolted to the column flanges as a permanent installation in the field.

Figure 19.20 is the complete shop drawing for a symmetrical welded roof truss. Because it is symmetrical, only the left half of the structure needs to be shown. Symmetry is shown on the drawing by the note Sym. abt. ℄. In this drawing:

- The **clip angles** marked aa are to be used for the attachment of roof purlins to the truss.
- The only **plate material** is the small gusset plate marked pb.
- Most of the connections of web **members** to chords are made by fillet welding the angles to the webs of the chords.
- The **chords** are of structural tee (WT) type.
- The top chords are joined at the ridge by butt welding, which is also used at the end of the truss where the chords join.
- **Weld symbols** and **member marks** are used.
- Sizes and quantities are listed in the **bill of material** (BoM).
- The drawing is uncluttered and clear, with lots of important information conveyed under the heading General Notes.

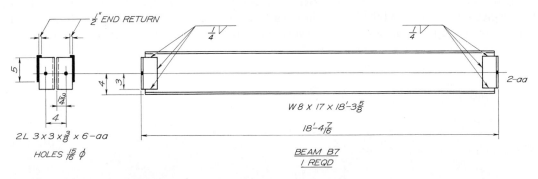

19.18 Detail of Welded Beam

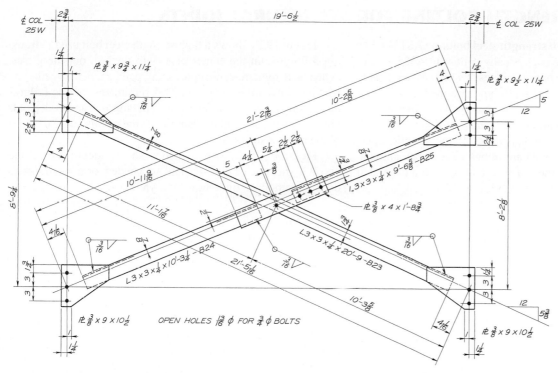

19.19 Details of Column Bracing

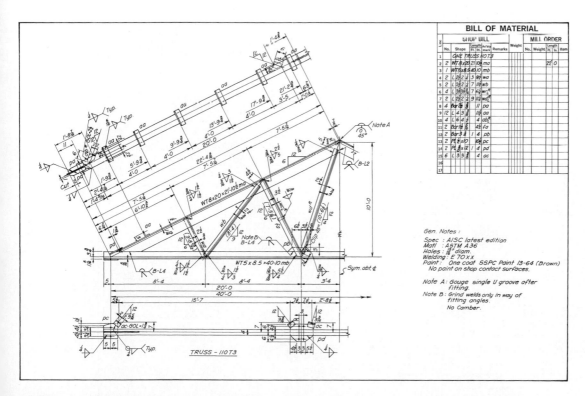

19.20 A Welded Roof Truss. *Courtesy of American Institute of Steel Construction, Inc.*

19.9 HIGH STRENGTH BOLTING FOR STRUCTURAL JOINTS

Two common types of **high strength steel bolts** are ASTM A325 and A490. The A449 type is physically similar to A325, except that A325 requires the use of special nuts. These bolts are treated by quenching and tempering. A325 bolts are made of medium carbon steel, while A490 are made of alloy steel. Metric high strength structural bolts, nuts, and washers are available. Consult a manufacturer's catalog or Appendix 20 for specifications. During installation, these bolts are tightened a certain amount, either using the "turn of the nut method" or with a calibrated torque wrench.

Figure 19.21 shows a high strength steel bolt used to transmit a force from the center plate into the two outside plates. When fully tightened, the connecting parts are held together by friction, preventing joint slip. This minimizes fatigue failures due to impact or stress reversals. The slip resistance depends not only on the amount of clamping force but also on the nature of the contact surfaces.

Figure 19.21 shows hardened washers under both head and nut. Whether one or two washers are needed, or none, depends on the method of tightening, the yield stress of the material

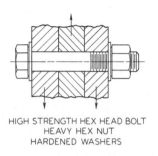

HIGH STRENGTH HEX HEAD BOLT
HEAVY HEX NUT
HARDENED WASHERS

19.21 High Tensile Strength Steel Bolt

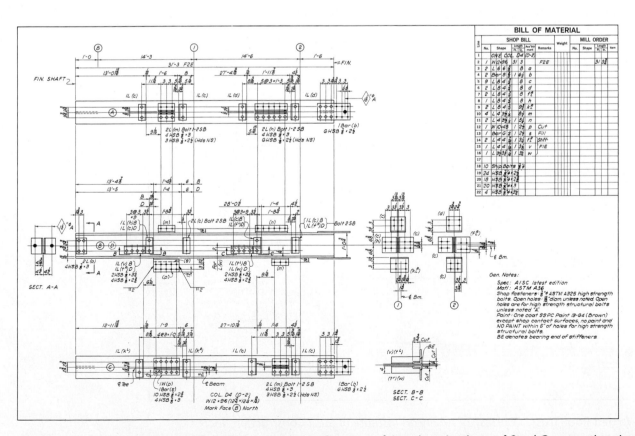

19.22 Steel Column Detail—Bolted Connections. *Courtesy of American Institute of Steel Construction, Inc.*

being joined, and whether the joint is to be the "slip-critical" or "bearing" type.

A bearing-type connection relies on the strength of the bolt shank bearing against the material, and no allowance is made for friction due to clamping action. Specifications for accepted practice, along with installation and inspection procedures, design examples, and reference tables, are covered in High Strength Bolting for Structural Joints (published by Bethlehem Steel Corporation, Bethlehem, PA).

Figure 19.22 shows the complete shop drawing of a steel column of two-floor height. The floors are indicated by reference lines B, 1, and 2 of the drawing. High strength bolts are used to attach connection material to the W12 × 96 column shaft. The top views at levels 1 and 2 show the outstanding legs of the angles in sectional plan views. Open holes are shown by the round dots located by dimensions taken from the column centerlines. The open holes are for the insertion of field bolts in beam connections when the entire assembly is erected.

Faces A, B, C, and D are designated. Viewing a column from above, designate the faces in counterclockwise order, with faces A and C designating the flanges. For web faces B and D, usually only face B needs to be drawn. However, when the connections on face D are exceptionally complicated, it should be drawn as an additional **elevation** view.

Note how the drawing shows shop bolts and their designation "HSB" (high strength bolts).

At the top of this column, splice connection material is provided by Bars (b), for attachment of the shaft above. All material for this column is listed in the bill of material on the drawing.

19.10 ACCURACY OF DIMENSIONS

An important part of the structural drawing is accurate dimensioning. If there are incorrect dimensions on the drawings, they will result in serious errors and misfits when members are assembled in the field. Correction of such errors not only entails considerable expense but often delays the completion of the work. Since in ordinary steel work dimensions are given to the closest 1/16", considerable precision is demanded.

Consider the effect of tolerance stacking on the fit of steel members. Review the dimensioning and tolerancing practices in Chapters 9 and 10. Using baseline dimensioning can aid in defining the shape so that tolerances don't accumulate.

Using CAD, you can accurately list dimensions for the lengths of angled members that would have required trigonometric calculation prior to the advent of CAD.

Don't let the ability of CAD to list accurate dimensions cause you to overlook the fact that real world fabrication will necessarily have some variation from the exact dimension value.

19.11 CONCRETE CONSTRUCTION

Concrete is made by mixing sand (fine aggregate) and gravel (coarse aggregate) or other fine and coarse aggregates with Portland cement and water. Its strength varies with the quality and relative quantities of the materials; the manner of mixing, placing, and curing; and the age of the concrete.

The compressive strength of concrete depends on the mix design, but concrete has been manufactured to develop an ultimate strength at 28 days as high as 7,000 psi. The material's tensile strength is limited to about one tenth its compressive strength. **High strength concrete,** used in high-rise construction, has a compressive strength up to 17,000 psi.

Portland cement is a controlled, manufactured product, in contrast to natural cements. Its name is derived from its color, which resembles the color of a famous stone found on the island of Portland in southern England.

Since the tensile strength of plain concrete is very limited, its use as a building material can be improved by embedding steel reinforcing bars so that the steel resists the tension and the concrete mainly resists the compression. The two materials act together in resisting forces and flexure. Concrete combined with steel in this way is called **reinforced concrete.**

When the steel is pretensioned before the superimposed load is applied, producing an interior force within the member, the material is called **prestressed concrete.** The type of steel used in prestressed concrete is flexible but very strong.

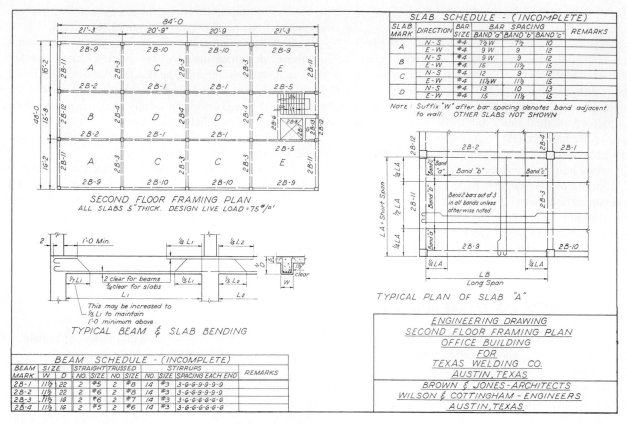

19.23   Engineering Drawing for a Two-Way Slab and Beam Floor

19.12 REINFORCED CONCRETE DRAWINGS

The design of the reinforcing for a reinforced concrete structure and preparation of the corresponding drawings are complicated. To simplify and to secure uniformity throughout engineering offices, the American Concrete Institute (Detroit, MI) publishes a Manual of Standard Practice for Detailing Reinforced Concrete Structures.

The manual recommends the preparation of two sets of drawings: an engineering drawing and a placing drawing. The engineering drawing is prepared by the manufacturer that fabricates the reinforcing steel. It shows the general arrangement of the structure, the sizes and reinforcements of the several members, and such other information as may be necessary for the correct interpretation of the designer's ideas. The drawing is also used for making forms with precise dimensions before placing the reinforcing bars and casting concrete.

The placing drawing shows the sizes and shapes of the several rods, stirrups, hoops, ties, and so on, and arranges them in tabular forms for reference by the building contractor.

An engineering drawing for a two-way slab and beam floor of a multistory building is shown in Figure 19.23. For examples of placing drawings, consult the American Concrete Institute manual referred to earlier.

Figure 19.24 shows the detail design drawing for a reinforced concrete pier, one of the supporting members for a highway bridge. Note that the steel bars, even though embedded, are shown by full lines and that concrete is always stippled in cross section. Unlike shop drawings for structural steel, concrete drawings are ordinarily made to scale in both directions. Usually, a scale of $1/4''$ to the foot is adequate, although when the structure is complicated, scales of $3/8''$ or $1/2''$ to the foot may be used. Avoid a cluttered appearance (usually the result of crowding the drawing with notes) by using tables and schedules for listing bar sizes and other necessary data. Cover important points in a single set of notes, as shown in Figure 19.24.

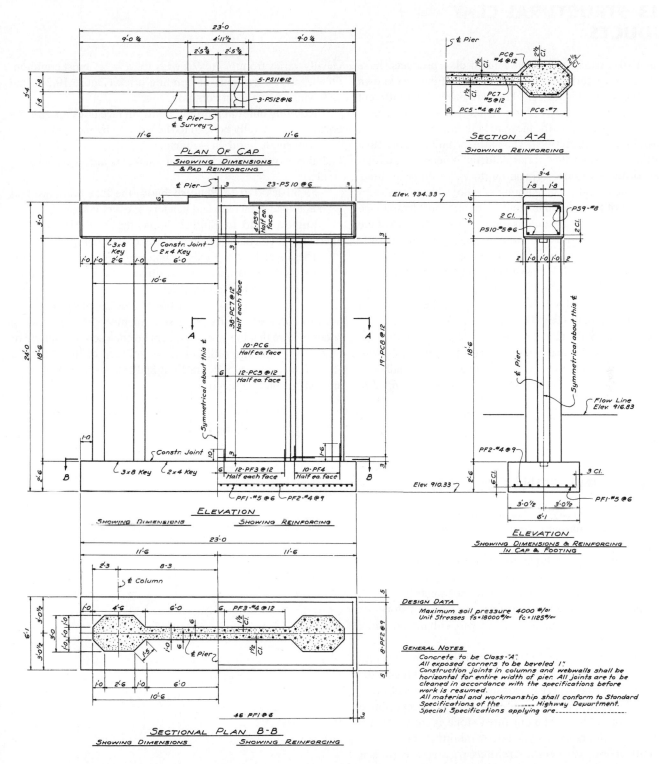

19.24 Reinforced Concrete Pier Deck Girder. *Courtesy of American Concrete Institue, Manual of Standard Practice for Detailing Reinforce Concrete Structure, ACI 315-80.*

19.13 STRUCTURAL CLAY PRODUCTS

Brick and tile, which are manufactured clay products, have been in use for centuries and comprise some of the best known forms of building construction. They are made from different types of clay and in many different shapes, forms, and colors (Figure 19.25). Traditionally, they are built into masonry forms by skilled brick or tile masons, who place the units one at a time in a soft mortar. After the mortar hardens, it becomes an integral part of the structure. Typical mortars contain sand, lime, Portland cement, and water. Although the compressive and tensile strengths of the clay units themselves are considerable, the overall strength of the structure is limited by the strength of the mortar joints. The result is a structure of high compressible strength and relatively low tensile strength.

As with concrete, it is possible to reinforce brick and tile masonry by embedding steel rods, thus adding greatly to tension resistance and strength. This material is called reinforced brick (or tile) masonry (**RBM).**

Information on the manufacture, weight and strength properties, and various uses and applications of structural clay products can be found in the Brick Institute of America handbooks *Principles of Brick Engineering* and *Principles of Tile Engineering*.

Bricks are made in various sizes, with the $2\frac{1}{4} \times 3\frac{3}{4} \times 8''$ building brick being most common. Thickness of mortar joints usually varies from $1/4''$ to $3/4''$ with $3/8''$ and $1/2''$ most common. Of the several methods of bonding brick (Figure 19.26), the following are the most common:

Running bond In **running bond,** all face brick are stretchers and are generally bonded to the backing by metal ties.

American bond In **American bond,** the face brick are laid alternatively, five courses of stretchers and one course of headers.

Flemish bond In **Flemish bond,** the face brick are laid with alternate stretchers and headers in every course.

English bond In **English bond,** the face brick are laid alternately, one course of stretchers and one course of headers.

These standard methods of bonding are frequently modified to produce various artistic effects. Typical brick lintel arches are shown in Figure 19.26.

In addition to its use as a basic building material, tile is used in fireproofing structural steel members. Most building codes require that the steel members be enclosed in concrete or masonry so that fire will not cause collapse of the structure. Hollow tile units, which are light and relatively inexpensive, are well adapted to this use.

19.14 STONE CONSTRUCTION

Natural stone—generally limestone, marble, sandstone, or granite—is used in masonry construction, most commonly for ornamental facing.

Ashlar masonry Ashlar masonry (also spelled *ashler*) is formed of stones cut accurately to rectangular faces and laid in regular courses or at random with thin mortar joints.

Rubble masonry Rubble masonry is formed of stones of irregular shapes laid in courses or at random with mortar joints of varying thickness.

Manufactured stone Manufactured stone is concrete made of fine aggregate for the facing and coarse aggregate for the backing. The fine aggregate consists of screenings of limestone, marble, sandstone, or granite, to present an appearance similar to natural stone. Manufactured stone is made of any desired shape, with or without architectural ornament.

Architectural terra cotta Architectural terra cotta is a hard-burned clay product and is used primarily for architectural decoration and for wall facing and wall coping.

Brick, stone, tile, and terra cotta are combined in many different ways in masonry construction. A few examples are shown in Figure 19.25.

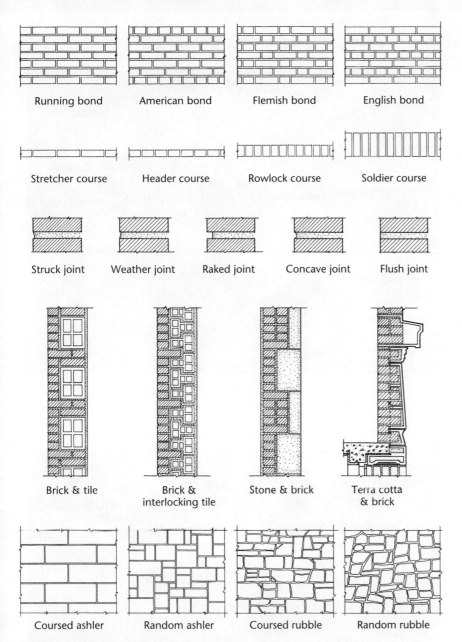

Running bond   American bond   Flemish bond   English bond

Stretcher course   Header course   Rowlock course   Soldier course

Struck joint   Weather joint   Raked joint   Concave joint   Flush joint

Brick & tile   Brick & interlocking tile   Stone & brick   Terra cotta & brick

Coursed ashler   Random ashler   Coursed rubble   Random rubble

19.25 Methods of Laying and Bonding Brick, Tile, and Stone

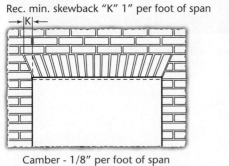

Rec. min. skewback "K" 1" per foot of span

→|K|←

Camber - 1/8" per foot of span

Brick units - tapered sides and ends

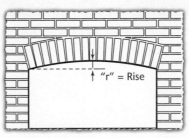

"r" = Rise

Brick units - tapered sides only

19.26 Typical Lintels.

CAD TOOLS FOR STRUCTURAL DRAWINGS

Structural drawings use a variety of standard symbols and methods of representation. A number of CAD symbol libraries are available that allow users to quickly generate drawings of structural steel shapes, connecting members, and steel erection plans. Once plans have been created, other programs are available to automatically calculate areas and perform finite element analysis on the design.

3D constraint-based software platforms often provide very sophisticated steel shapes that can be inserted to create assemblies that are easy to modify.

SDS/2 software from Design Data lets you designate the material edge distance, cope criteria, and other connection parameters to create 3D models of a structure. The software's automatic detailing feature makes it simple to produce 2D detail drawings, so the information can be communicated to the crew erecting the structure.

Construction of the 3rd Avenue Bridge over the Bronx River. *Courtesy of Design Data and GeniFab, Inc.*

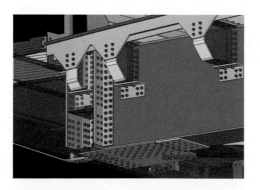

Detail of a bolted connection for the Bridge Structure. *Courtesy of Design Data and GeniFab, Inc.*

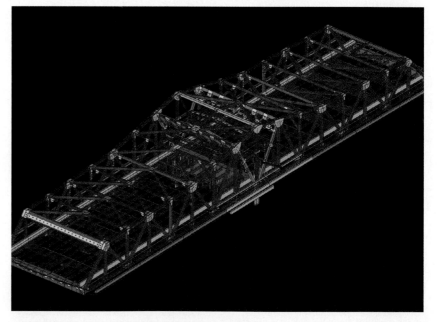

3D Model of the Bridge Structure Created in SDS2 Software. *Courtesy of Design Data and GeniFab, Inc.*

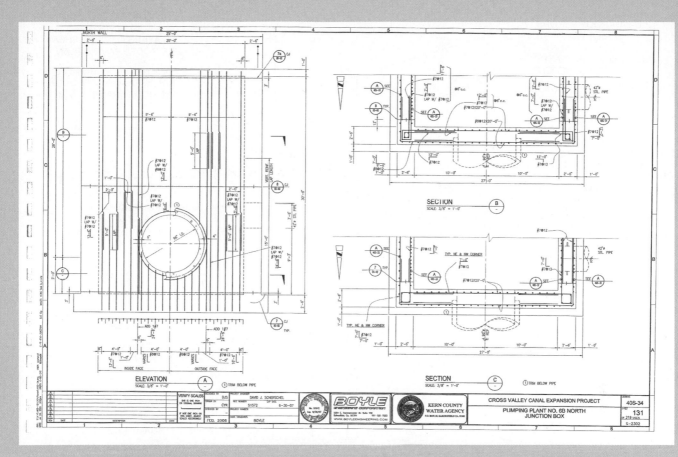

Reinforced concrete structure. *Courtesy of Kun County Water Agency and Boyle Inc.*

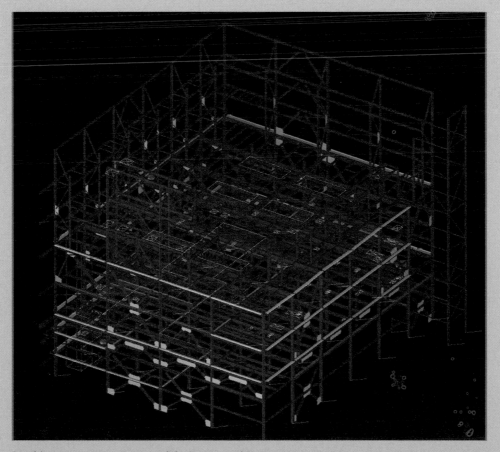

Steel beam construction model. *Courtesy of Sarwer Hasan.*

PORTFOLIO

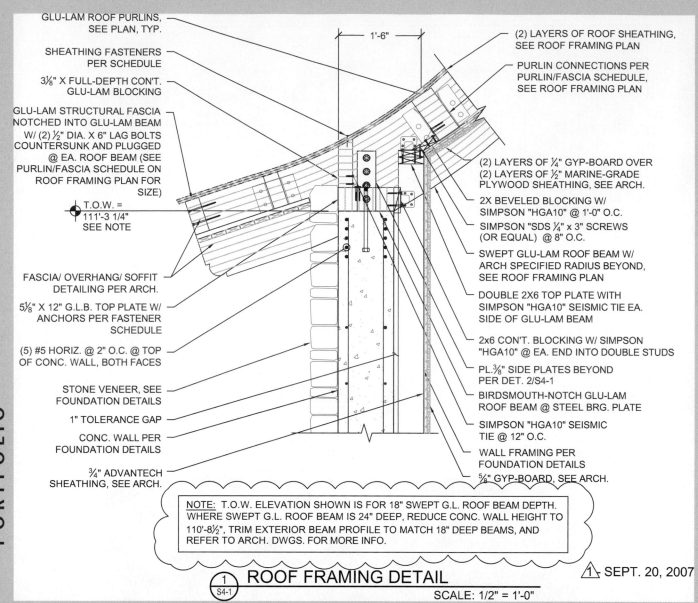

GLU-LAM ROOF PURLINS, SEE PLAN, TYP.

SHEATHING FASTENERS PER SCHEDULE

3⅛" X FULL-DEPTH CON'T. GLU-LAM BLOCKING

GLU-LAM STRUCTURAL FASCIA NOTCHED INTO GLU-LAM BEAM W/ (2) ½" DIA. X 6" LAG BOLTS COUNTERSUNK AND PLUGGED @ EA. ROOF BEAM (SEE PURLIN/FASCIA SCHEDULE ON ROOF FRAMING PLAN FOR SIZE)

T.O.W. = 111'-3 1/4" SEE NOTE

FASCIA/ OVERHANG/ SOFFIT DETAILING PER ARCH.

5⅛" X 12" G.L.B. TOP PLATE W/ ANCHORS PER FASTENER SCHEDULE

(5) #5 HORIZ. @ 2" O.C. @ TOP OF CONC. WALL, BOTH FACES

STONE VENEER, SEE FOUNDATION DETAILS

1" TOLERANCE GAP

CONC. WALL PER FOUNDATION DETAILS

¾" ADVANTECH SHEATHING, SEE ARCH.

1'-6"

(2) LAYERS OF ROOF SHEATHING, SEE ROOF FRAMING PLAN

PURLIN CONNECTIONS PER PURLIN/FASCIA SCHEDULE, SEE ROOF FRAMING PLAN

(2) LAYERS OF ¼" GYP-BOARD OVER (2) LAYERS OF ½" MARINE-GRADE PLYWOOD SHEATHING, SEE ARCH.

2X BEVELED BLOCKING W/ SIMPSON "HGA10" @ 1'-0" O.C.

SIMPSON "SDS ¼" x 3" SCREWS (OR EQUAL) @ 8" O.C.

SWEPT GLU-LAM ROOF BEAM W/ ARCH SPECIFIED RADIUS BEYOND, SEE ROOF FRAMING PLAN

DOUBLE 2X6 TOP PLATE WITH SIMPSON "HGA10" SEISMIC TIE EA. SIDE OF GLU-LAM BEAM

2x6 CON'T. BLOCKING W/ SIMPSON "HGA10" @ EA. END INTO DOUBLE STUDS

PL.⅜" SIDE PLATES BEYOND PER DET. 2/S4-1

BIRDSMOUTH-NOTCH GLU-LAM ROOF BEAM @ STEEL BRG. PLATE

SIMPSON "HGA10" SEISMIC TIE @ 12" O.C.

WALL FRAMING PER FOUNDATION DETAILS

⅝" GYP-BOARD, SEE ARCH.

NOTE: T.O.W. ELEVATION SHOWN IS FOR 18" SWEPT G.L. ROOF BEAM DEPTH. WHERE SWEPT G.L. ROOF BEAM IS 24" DEEP, REDUCE CONC. WALL HEIGHT TO 110'-8½", TRIM EXTERIOR BEAM PROFILE TO MATCH 18" DEEP BEAMS, AND REFER TO ARCH. DWGS. FOR MORE INFO.

1 **ROOF FRAMING DETAIL**
S4-1

SCALE: 1/2" = 1'-0"

△ SEPT. 20, 2007

Construction detail for attaching a glu-lam beam to a concrete wall. *Courtesy of Hicks Engineering PC.*

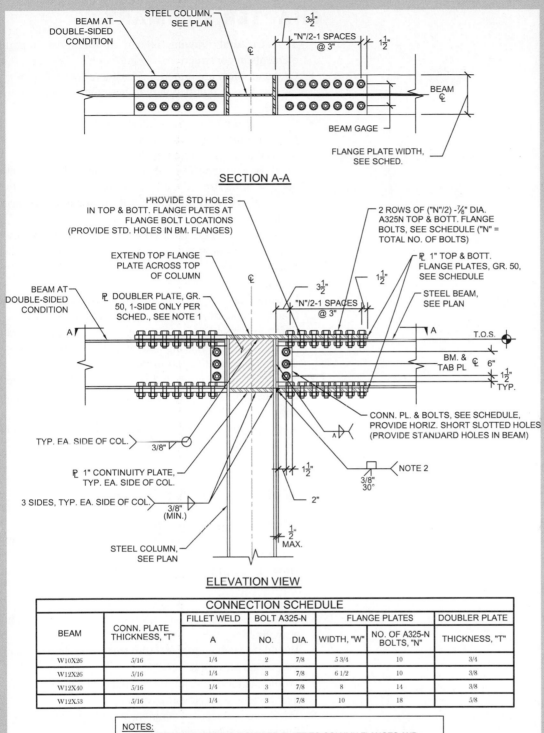

SECTION A-A

ELEVATION VIEW

CONNECTION SCHEDULE							
BEAM	CONN. PLATE THICKNESS, "T"	FILLET WELD	BOLT A325-N		FLANGE PLATES		DOUBLER PLATE
		A	NO.	DIA.	WIDTH, "W"	NO. OF A325-N BOLTS, "N"	THICKNESS, "T"
W10X26	5/16	1/4	2	7/8	5 3/4	10	3/4
W12X26	5/16	1/4	3	7/8	6 1/2	10	3/8
W12X40	5/16	1/4	3	7/8	8	14	3/8
W12X53	5/16	1/4	3	7/8	10	18	5/8

NOTES:
1. PROVIDE C.J.P. WELD @ DOUBLER PLATE TO COLUMN FLANGES AND CONTINUITY PLATES (4-SIDES).

2. REMOVE BACK-UP BAR, GRIND BOTTOM OF WELD SMOOTH, & INSTALL 3/8" REINFORCING WELD. SHOP FULL PEN. WELDS TO BE 100 % INSPECTED IN ACCORDANCE WITH 2003 IBC. SECTIONS 1701.4.5 & 1703.

④ **BOLTED FLANGE PLATE MOMENT CONN. DETAIL**
S6-2   SCALE: 1/2" = 1'-0"

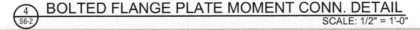

Detail showing welded and bolted connections. *Courtesy of Hicks Engeneering PC.*

KEY WORDS

Structural Drawings

Green Lumber

Purlins

Trusses

Joints

Design Drawings

Girders

Filler Beams

Shop Drawings

Piece Mark

Erection Plans

Flange

Structural Steel

Gage Line

Extension Figure

Fillet Weld

Beam Web

Clip Angles

Plate Material

Members

Chords

Weld Symbols

Member Marks

Bill of Material

High Strength Steel Bolts

Elevation

High Strength Concrete

Reinforced Concrete

Prestressed Concrete

RBM

Running Bond

American Bond

Flemish Bond

English Bond

Ashlar Masonry

Rubble Masonry

Manufactured Stone

Architectural Terra Cotta

CHAPTER SUMMARY

- The structural drawing is one of the most important elements in construction drawings.
- Cost and safety are important considerations when designing a structure that people will use, such as a building or bridge.
- Structural drawings are precise, detailed instructions for general contractors, who must create the structure according to the information in the drawings.
- Steel is commonly used in commercial construction because of its strength and durability. Steel shape and size designations are different from those for other materials, such as wood.
- Structural drawings show both plan and elevation views.
- Details about how structural members are connected and fastened to each other are critical parts of a structural drawing.
- Structural drawings use more notes about size, shape, location, and fastening details than other types of drawings.
- Safety is dependent on correctly following the engineer's design. Careful proofing and checking of every note and detail is an essential part of the engineering process.
- The list of materials, including their size, shape, and detail information, is often included in a material schedule that appears in table form in a corner of the drawing.
- When components are welded together, standard welding symbols and notes must be used.

REVIEW QUESTIONS

1. List five structural materials.
2. Draw four different structural steel shapes and label each shape.
3. How is reinforced concrete different from regular concrete?
4. What is shown in the plan view of a structural drawing?
5. What is shown in the elevation view of a structural drawing?
6. Would the spacing for steel roof trusses be shown in a plan view or an elevation view?
7. Would the individual members of a roof truss be shown in a plan view or an elevation view?
8. What are the most common fastening techniques for joining structural steel?

EXERCISES

The following problems are intended to offer practice in drawing and dimensioning simple structures and in illustrating methods of construction. They may be completed by hand or using CAD.

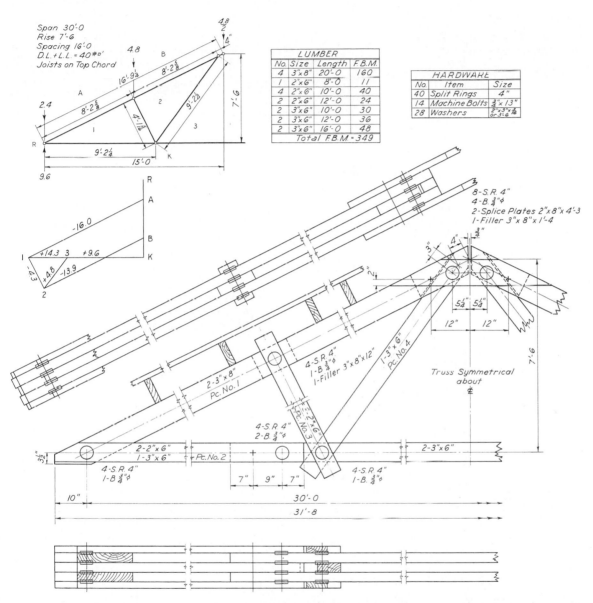

Exercise 19.1 Calculate point-to-point lengths (the distances between centers of joints) of the web members of the roof truss based on a design by Timber Engineering Company. Make a detailed drawing of web member piece No. 4.

Exercise 19.2 Make a complete detail of the top chord member of the truss shown for a 30° angle of inclination.

Exercise 19.3 Assuming riveted construction, with rivets of $\frac{3}{4}''$ or 20 mm diameter, make a complete shop drawing for a typical filler beam of the steel floor design plan to the right. Detail the same beam for welded construction. Consult the AISC Manual of Steel Construction.

Exercise 19.4 Assuming the column size to be W8 × 31, detail the W16 × 36 girder at the center of the drawing to the right.

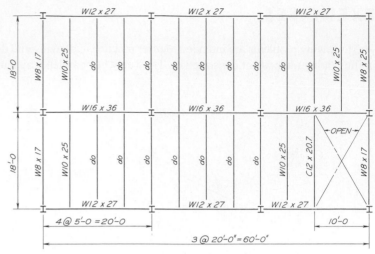

Typical Steel Floor Design Plan

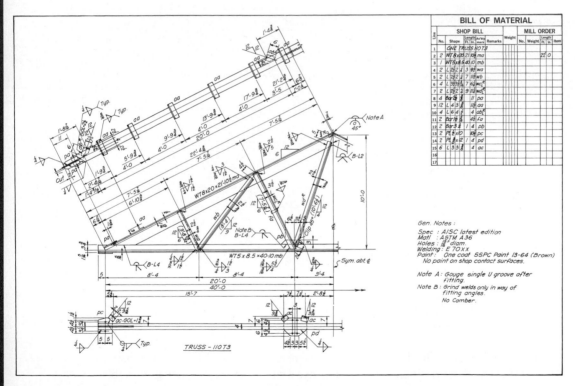

A Welded Roof Truss. *Courtesy of American Institute of Steel Construction.*

Exercise 19.5 Make a complete detail for a truss of the same length, but change the height from 10′–0 to 6′–8. Use angle members of the same cross section sizes as those shown, but of different lengths, as needed.

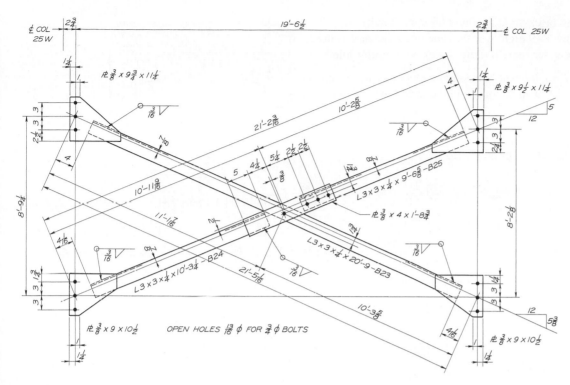

Exercise 19.6 Make a similar bracing detail as for the detail drawing of column bracing above, also changing the distance between column centers from 20′–0 to 18′–6.

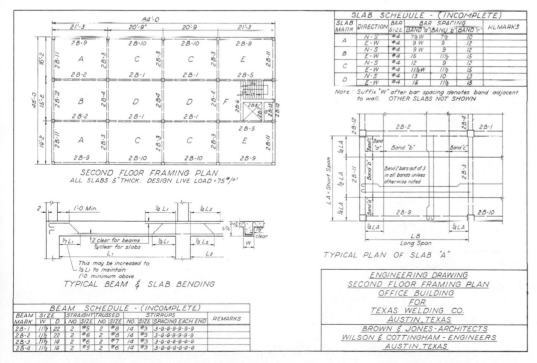

Exercise 19.7 Draw cross sections through panel D in both directions for the engineering drawing for a two-way slab and beam floor shown above. Include the supporting beams in each cross section, and show all dimensions, size and spacing of reinforcing steel, and dimensions to locate the ends of bars and the points of bend for the bent bars. Also show and locate the stirrups in these views.

Exercise 19.8 Detail the brickwork surrounding a window frame for an opening 4'–07/8" wide by 6'–9 high. Use the type of curved arch lintel as shown above. Assume standard-size building brick with mortar joints.

Exercise 19.9 Consult *Principles of Tile Engineering*, and draw a cross-sectional view through a 12" wall of composite brick and tile construction.

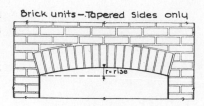

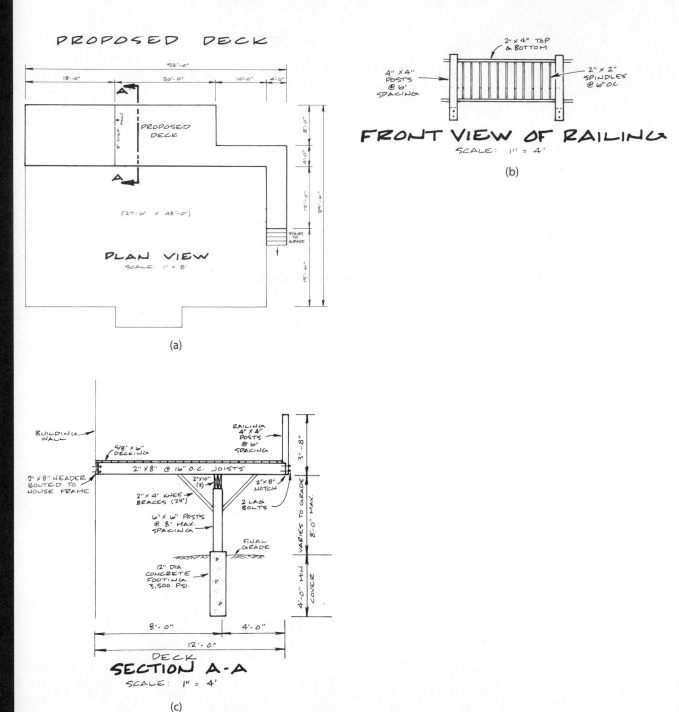

(a)

(b)

(c)

Exercise 19.10 Referring to the figure above, redraw a complete detail of this proposed deck, changing the total width of the deck from 12' to 14' and the length from 52' to 54'.

Exercise 19.11 Referring to Part b of the figure above, adjust the dimensions on the posts from 4 × 4' to 6' × 6'. Redraw a complete detail of the railing view and Section A–A.

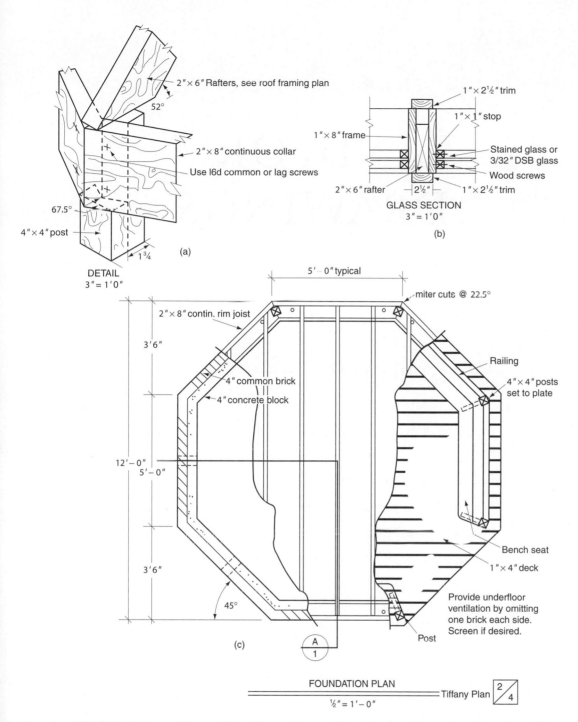

2" × 6" Rafters, see roof framing plan

52°

2" × 8" continuous collar

Use l6d common or lag screws

67.5°

4" × 4" post

1 3/4

(a)

DETAIL
3" = 1'0"

1" × 2½" trim

1" × 1" stop

1" × 8" frame

Stained glass or
3/32" DSB glass

Wood screws

2" × 6" rafter   2½"   1" × 2½" trim

GLASS SECTION
3" = 1'0"

(b)

5' – 0" typical

miter cuts @ 22.5°

2" × 8" contin. rim joist

3'6"

4" common brick

4" concrete block

Railing

4" × 4" posts
set to plate

12'–0"
5'–0"

Bench seat

1" × 4" deck

3'6"

Provide underfloor
ventilation by omitting
one brick each side.
Screen if desired.

45°

Post

(c)

A
1

FOUNDATION PLAN
½" = 1'–0"

Tiffany Plan

2
4

Exercise 19.12 Referring to Part a of the figure above, adjust the post dimensions from 4 × 4″ to 6 × 6″. Redraw a complete detail of Part a.

Exercise 19.13 Referring to Part c of the figure above, insert the adjustments made to the post detail in Exercise 19.12 and redraw the complete foundation plan.

CHAPTER TWENTY

LANDFORM DRAWINGS

OBJECTIVES

After studying the material in this chapter, you should be able to:

1. Read and draw a plat, topographic contour map, street contour map, and highway plan and profile.

2. Read the elevation of a tract of land using contour lines.

3. Identify the scale and compass orientation of a topographic map.

4. Read and notate property boundaries on a land survey map.

5. Create a profile map from contour lines.

3D Geologic Terrain Model. *Courtesy of Howard Architectural Models, Inc.*

OVERVIEW

Drawings and maps show natural and man-made features on the Earth's surface. Topographic drawings use orthographic projection, just as technical drawings do, where the direction of sight is perpendicular to the plane of the map. Survey monuments placed on the ground allow you to locate features with respect to definite point locations.

The U.S. Coast and Geodetic Survey, the U.S. Department of Interior, and the U.S. Geological Survey (USGS) all produce contour maps of land boundaries. More detailed maps are created by local communities when subdividing property for residential and commercial construction. Highways and public works, such as dams and bridges, may require detailed topographic drawings of a given geographic area. Topographic drawings use contour lines to show elevation in the plan view. Profile drawings show the sectional elevation of a specified datum plane. Many topographic drawings become legal documents used in resolving disputes over property boundaries. USGS partners with businesses like TopoZone and Microsoft's TerraServer-USA to provide map content online.

Search the following Web sites for landform mapping information:
- http://www.topozone.com/viewmaps.asp Topozone.
- http://terraserver-usa.com Microsoft's TerraServer-USA.
- http://www.geocommunicator.gov/GeoComm/index.shtm BLM's National Integrated Land System (NILS) site.
- http://www.blm.gov/cadastral/Manual/73man/ Download the BLM 1973 Manual of Surveying Instructions.
- http://erg.usgs.gov/isb/pubs/booklets/symbols/ Explains topographic map symbols.

UNDERSTANDING LANDFORM DRAWINGS

A landform drawing or map's purpose determines the features and details to show and the scale to use. Many types of maps and drawings are used to locate features on the Earth's surface.

Since the shape of the Earth is spherical, any representation on a plane (such as a piece of paper) is distorted because spheres can only be developed into a flat plane by approximation. When drawing large areas, you can define control or reference points using spherical coordinates for latitude and longitude (meridians and parallels) as reference lines to minimize the distortion. In drawing small areas to a relatively large scale, the distortion due to the Earth's curvature is so slight that it may be neglected.

Definitions

Useful map and landform drawing terms include the following.

Plat A plat is a map of a small area, plotted from a land **survey.** It does not ordinarily show elevations. Plats are drawn to calculate areas, and land locate property lines, locate building projects and facilities (Figure 20.1).

Traverse A traverse consists of a series of intersecting straight lines of accurately measured lengths. At the points of intersection, the deflection angles between adjacent lines are measured and recorded. From the starting point you can calculate rectangular coordinates of the other

intersection points using trigonometry. A closed traverse is a closed polygon that allows you to check the accuracy of the surveyed information based on whether or not the last angle and distance meet back at the starting point of the loop. The land survey plat of Figure 20.1 shows a closed traverse.

Elevations are vertical distances above a common **datum,** or reference plane or point. The elevation of a point on the surface of the ground is usually determined by differential leveling from some other point of known elevation. Commonly, elevations are referenced to the mean sea level.

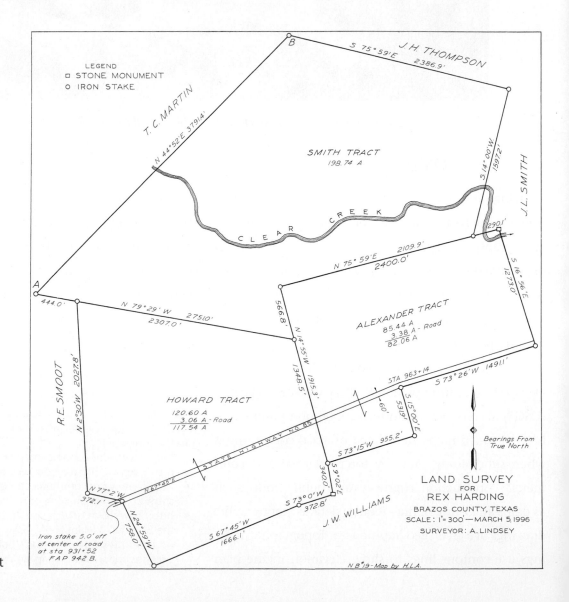

20.1 Land Survey Plat

Profile A profile is a line contained in a vertical plane, and it depicts the relative elevations of various points along the line. For example, if a vertical section were to be cut into the Earth, the top line of this section would represent the ground profile (Figure 20.2).

Contours are lines drawn on a map to locate, in the plan view, points of equal ground elevation. On a single contour line, therefore, all points have the same elevation (Figure 20.2).

Hatchures are short, parallel, or slightly divergent lines drawn in the direction of the slope. They are closely spaced on steep slopes and converge toward the tops of ridges and hills. Hatchures are shade lines used to show relief on older maps.

Monuments are special installations of stone or concrete to mark the locations of points accurately determined by precise surveying. It is intended that monuments be permanent or nearly so, and they are usually tied in by references to nearby natural features, such as trees and large boulders.

Cartography is the science or art of mapmaking.

Topographic maps (Figure 20.3) depict:

1. Water, including seas, lakes, ponds, rivers, streams, canals, and swamps.
2. Relief, or elevations, of mountains, hills, valleys, cliffs, and the like.
3. Culture, or human constructions, such as towns, cities, roads, railroads, airfields, and boundaries.

Hydrographic maps convey information concerning bodies of water, such as shoreline locations; relative elevations of points of lake, stream, or ocean beds; and sounding depths.

Cadastral maps are accurately drawn maps of cities and towns, showing property lines and other features that control property ownership.

Military maps contain information of military importance in the area represented.

Nautical maps and charts show navigational features and aids, such as locations of buoys, shoals, lighthouses and beacons, and sounding depths.

Aeronautical maps and charts show prominent landmarks, towers, beacons, and elevations for the use of air navigators.

Engineering maps are made for special projects as an aid to locations and construction.

Landscape maps are used in planning installations of trees, shrubbery, drives, and other garden features in the artistic design of area improvements.

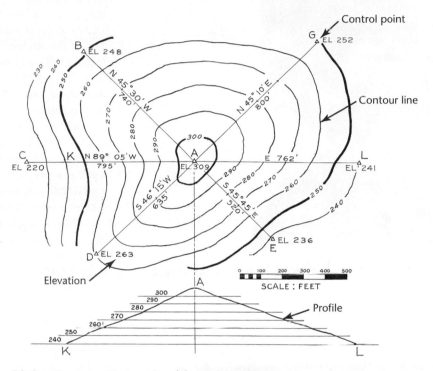

20.2 Contours Determined from Control Points

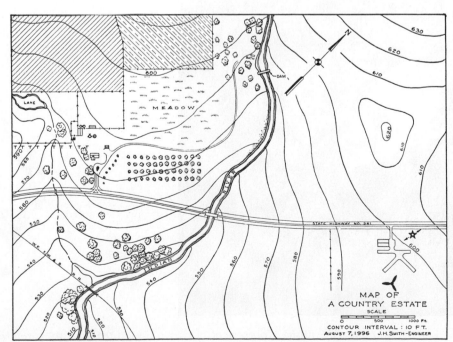

20.3 A Topographic Map

20.4 Trimbal S6 Total Station. *Courtesy of Trimble Navigation Limited.*

GETTING INFORMATION FOR MAPS

A survey is the basis of all maps and topographic drawings. Several surveying methods are used to obtain the information necessary to make a map.

Electronic Survey Instruments Most surveys use electronic survey instruments to measure distances and angles. To measure to a distant point, the surveyor aims the instrument toward the point, where a passive reflector or prism has been set. The instrument generates either a modulated infrared light signal focused into a narrow beam, or a laser beam, aimed directly at the reflector. When the reflector bounces the beam back to the aiming head, the beam's travel time is measured electronically and directly converted into the distance to the point. One advantage of electronic measurement over the distance-taping method is that it is not necessary to stop traffic to take measurements. Electronic instruments measure distances of up to 4 mi with accuracies from .01 to .03 ft which is more than sufficient for topographic surveying. Figure 20.4 shows a Trimbal S6 total station. This type of instrument is often used to gather survey data.

Global positioning system (GPS) receivers calculate the receiver's position by interpreting data received from four different satellites concurrently through a process called trilateration (which is similar to triangulation). Figure 20.5 shows a GPS satellite. Twenty-four satellites orbit the earth in a pattern called a **GPS satellite constellation** (see Figure 20.6). These satellites each broadcast a signal that includes the precise time from the satellite's onboard atomic clock. The distance to the satellite from the position of your GPS receiver can be calculated based on the time delay in receiving the signal. From any position on Earth your receiver should be able to locate four satellites and using trilateration calculate very accurately your position on the surface of the Earth. Most modern maps of large areas are prepared using GPS positioning and satellite imagery.

20.5 GPS Satellite GPS IIR-M. *Courtesy of Lockheed Martin Space Systems.*

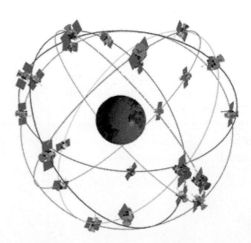

20.6 GPS Satellite Constellation. *Courtesy of Aerospace Corporation (http://www.aero.org).*

GPS SURVEYS

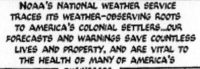

© NAS. KING FEATURES SYNDICATE.

While GPS has revolutionized surveying, the vertical accuracy of GPS measurements (elevations) has not been as good as the horizontal accuracy (latitude and longitude). Knowledge of elevations is critical to surveyors, engineers, coastal managers, developers, and those who make resource or land-use management decisions.

Because forces such as sea level rise, subsidence (i.e., land sinking), and geological events constantly change the surface of the Earth, it is necessary to periodically resurvey areas to correct for changes. State and local governments spend tens of millions of dollars each year adjusting engineering projects that are continually affected by changing land surfaces, so a fast, yet accurate, method for determining elevations is needed. Height Modernization, which uses GPS in conjunction with other new and existing technologies to increase the accuracy of elevation measurements, is one such method.

This article looks at the evolution of the Height Modernization (HtMod) Program within NOAA's National Geodetic Survey (NGS) and how the program is contributing to a state of the art National Spatial Reference System.

NGS HtMod Guidelines

NGS, in cooperation with the GPS community, only recently developed standards, specifications, and techniques to enable GPS to attain the accuracy levels required for most applications using height information. These guidelines, which are available on the NGS Web site, provide detailed instructions for the amount of survey control required as a base from which to start the modernization of elevation data. NGS also provides instructions on how surveys must be carried out to ensure that results meet the requirements. Meeting these specifications is important to ensure that HtMod surveys can be tied to the NSRS.

A requirement of the NGS guidelines is that known horizontal and vertical survey control points must encircle the project area at certain maximum distances. Then, a survey network is planned with many interconnections, to tie old and new points together. High-quality GPS receivers, antennas, and tripods must be used and strict data collection and data processing procedures followed. This methodology replaces the old method of using spirit leveling alone to determine differences in elevation.

Mark Trail image courtesy of artist-writer Jack Elrod and King Features Syndicate. Story courtesy NOAA.gov.

20.7 Disto A8 Laser Distance Meter Allows Measurement of Distances up to 200 m (650 ft) with Precision of ±1.5 mm (.06"). *Courtesy of Leica Geosystems, Switzerland.*

Photogrammetry and Satellite imagery are widely used for map surveying. They use actual photographs of the Earth's surface and manufactured objects on the Earth. Aerial photogrammetry, via aircraft or satellite, is used for purposes such as governmental and commercial surveying, explorations, and property valuation. It has the advantage of being easy to use in difficult terrain with steep slopes, where ground surveying would be difficult or nearly impossible.

The use of aerial photographs is called **aerial photogrammetry;** photographs taken from ground stations with the axis of the camera lens nearly horizontal is called **terrestrial photogrammetry.** By combining the results of both types of observations, it is possible to determine the relative positions of objects in a horizontal plane and their relative elevations.

Photogrammetry can be the basis of contour mapping as well as plan mapping. Generally, aerial photographs are used by forming a mosaic of photographs, which must each overlap slightly. Photogrammetry offers the distinct advantage that a large area can be mapped from a single clear photograph. Photogrammetry can be used in connection with ground surveying by photographing control points already located on the ground by precise surveying.

For large land developments and large construction projects, new technologies for producing topographic maps have evolved. Some state highway departments and most engineering firms that specialize in surveying and mapping now make use of aerial photography with computers, terrain digitizers, stereoplotters, GIS, and various photolaboratory techniques. In high volume work situations, expensive equipment may save enough time to justify its cost.

Laser Distance Meters typically calculate distance based on the difference in phase between the internal reference laser pulse and the external laser pulse reflected from the targeted object or a reflector plate attached to it. An example of this type of device is shown in Figure 20.7.

Optical Mechanical systems are less used today. Before electronic measurement systems became affordable, an optical instrumental method called the **stadia** method was used in mapmaking. A stadia transit is an optical instrument used with a stadia rod. By sighting visually on the rod and using a conversion factor, the instrument reading could be converted to distance. An example of this type of device is shown in Figure 20.8.

Steel Tape Short distances are ordinarily measured by **steel tape,** with driven stakes marking the points between field measurements.

Scaled Measurements are made on rare occasions. In this method, distances are determined by measuring aerial photographs, when the scale is known.

For additional information, refer to publications such as the Manual of Surveying Instructions for the Survey of the Public Lands of the United States, prepared and published by the Bureau of Land Management (U.S. Government Printing Office, Washington, D.C., expected revision in 2007). Many governmental agencies also publicize information about maps and geographic data on the Web.

20.8 Optical Mechanical System. *Courtesy of David White.*

RISE OF THE THREE GORGES DAM

November 7, 2006

April 17, 1987

*Article courtesy of
http://svs.gsfc.nasa.gov/
vis/a000000/a003400/
a003433/
http://earthobservatory.
nasa.gov/Newsroom/Ne
wImages/images.php3?
img_id=17674*

Satellite Imagery of the
Three Gorges Dam.
Courtesy of NASA.

Some call it the eighth wonder of world; others say it's the next Great Wall of China. Upon completion in 2009, the Three Gorges Dam will be the world's largest hydroelectric power generator. One of the few man-made structures so enormous that it's actually visible to the naked eye from space, NASA's Landsat satellite has had a closer look, providing detailed, vivid views of the dam since its inception in 1994.

The dam is built along the Yangtze River, the third largest in the world, stretching more than 3,900 miles across China before reaching its mouth near Shanghai. Historically, the river has been prone to massive flooding, overflowing its banks about once every 10 years. During the Twentieth Century alone, Chinese authorities estimate that some 300,000 people were killed from Yangtze River floods. The dam is designed to greatly improve flood control on the river and protect the 15 million people and 3.7 million acres of farmland in the lower Yangtze flood plains.

Observations from the NASA-built Landsat satellites provide an overview of the dam's construction. The earliest data set, from 1987, shows the region prior to the start of construction. By 2000, construction along each riverbank was underway, but sediment-filled water still flowed through a narrow channel near the river's south bank. The 2004 data shows development of the main wall and the partial filling of the reservoir, including numerous side canyons. By mid-2006, construction of the main wall was completed and a reservoir more than 2 mi (3 km) across had filled just upstream of the dam.

CONTOURS	
Topographic	
Index	—6000—
Approximate or indefinite	
Intermediate	
Approximate or indefinite	
Supplementary	
Depression	
Cut	
Fill	
Continental divide	
Bathymetric	
Index***	
Intermediate***	
Index primary***	
Primary***	
Supplementary***	

20.9 USGS Topographic Map Symbols. *Courtesy of USGS. For a complete set see their Web site http://erg.usgs.gov/isb/pubs/booklets/symbols/*

20.10 Timely Map Symbol Template. *Courtesy of Timely Products Co., Inc.*

20.1 SYMBOLS

Various natural and man-made features are designated by special symbols. A list of the most commonly used map symbols is given in Appendix 33. Figure 20.9 shows an example of some commonly used symbols. You can find a full set on the Web at http://erg.usgs.gov/isb/pubs/booklets/symbols/. Templates like that shown in Figure 20.10 can save time in hand drawing map symbols.

20.2 BEARINGS

The **bearing** of a line is its angle from magnetic north. Bearings are listed by referencing the angle the line makes departing from either the North or the South toward either the East or West. In Figure 20.11, the bearing for traverse line AB is N 44°52′E, meaning that if you were standing at point A facing North, you would turn 44°52′ toward the East to face point B. (If you were at point B, you would use the opposite directions to face point A, facing South and turning 44°52′ toward the West.)

Once the bearings of the lines of a traverse have been determined, the angles between them can be computed by adding or subtracting. Electronic survey instruments are used to calculate the bearings of lines because compass readings are not accurate. Magnetic north and true north are not the same and local magnetism may affect the position of the compass needle.

20.3 ELEVATION

If GPS is not used to provide elevation, an optical instrument called a level, equipped with a telescope for sighting long distances, can be used to determine differences in elevation in the field. The process is called **differential leveling.** When the instrument is leveled, the line of sight of its telescope is horizontal. A level rod, graduated in feet and decimals of feet, may be held on various points. Instrument readings of the rod then serve to determine the differences in elevations of the points.

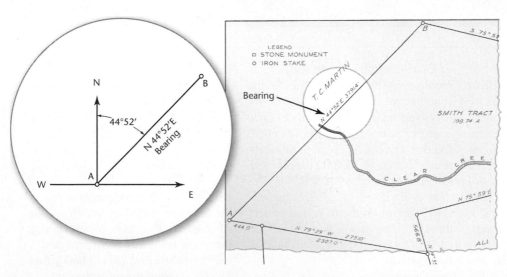

20.11 Bearings Specify an Angle and Direction from North or South toward East or West *The bearing N44°52′ E means that if you were at point A facing north, you would turn 44°52′ toward the east to face point B.*

20.4 CONTOURS

Contours are map lines showing points of equal ground elevation. Figure 20.12 shows a comparison between a contour map and a satellite image which were both available from the TopoZone Web site.

A contour interval is the vertical distance between horizontal planes passing through successive contours. For example, in Figure 20.13 the contour interval is 10′. The contour interval should not change on any one map. It is customary to show every fifth contour by a line heavier than those representing intermediate contours.

For contour lines keep in mind:

- If extended far enough, every contour line will close.
- At streams, contours form Vs pointing upstream.
- Even spacing between successive contours means that the ground slopes uniformly.
- Uneven spacing between contours means that the slope changes frequently.
- Widely spaced contours indicate a gentle slope.
- Closely spaced contours indicate steep slopes.

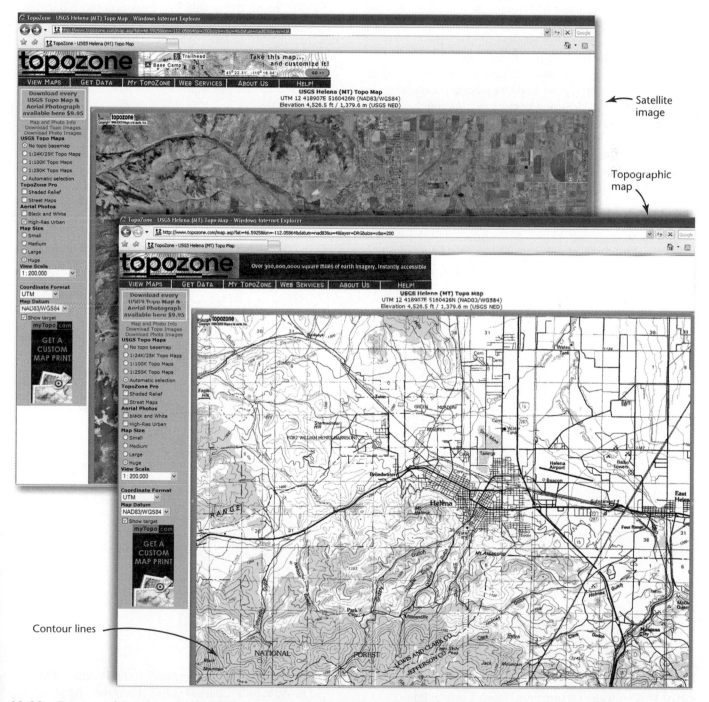

Satellite image

Topographic map

Contour lines

20.12 Topographic Map with Contours and Satellite Imagery. *Courtesy of TopoZone at www.topozone.com*

Interpolating Elevation Data

Locations of points on contour lines are determined by interpolation. In Figure 20.13, the locations and elevations of seven control points have been determined. The goal is to draw the contour lines assuming the slope of the surface of the ground is uniform between station A and the six adjacent stations, using a contour interval of 10′. The locations of the intersection of the contour lines with the straight lines joining the point A and the six adjacent points, was calculated as follows.

The horizontal distance between stations A and B is 740′. The difference in elevation of those stations is 61′. The difference in elevation of station A and contour 300 is 9′; therefore, contour 300 crosses line AB at a distance from station A of 9/61 of 740, or 109.1′. Contour 290 crosses the line AB at a distance from contour 300 of 10/61 of 740, or 121.3′. This 121.3′ distance between contour lines is constant along the line AB and can be measured without more calculations.

You can interpolate points where the contours cross the other lines of the survey the same way. After interpolating the elevations you can draw the contour lines through points of equal elevation as shown.

After contours have been plotted, you can draw a profile of the ground line in any direction. In Figure 20.13, the profile of line KAL is shown in the lower or front view. It is customary, as shown here, to draw the profile using an exaggerated vertical scale to emphasize the varying slopes. Terrain can also be described by online models such as in Figure 20.14.

Contour lines may be plotted from recorded elevations of points on the ground, as in Figure 20.15a. This figure illustrates a checkerboard survey, in which lines are drawn at right angles to each other, dividing the survey into 100 ft squares, and where elevations have been measured at the corners of the squares. The contour interval is taken as 2′, and the slope of the ground between adjacent stations is assumed to be uniform.

The points where the contour lines cross the survey lines can be located approximately by inspection, by graphical methods, or by the numerical method explained for Figure 20.13.

You can also find the points of intersection that contour lines make with survey lines by constructing a profile of each line of the survey, as shown for line 1 in Figure 20.15b. Draw horizontal lines at elevations where you want to show contours. The points where the profile line intersects these horizontal lines are the elevations of points where corresponding contour lines cross the survey line 1. These can be projected upward, as shown, to locate these points.

The profile of any line can be constructed from the contour map by the converse of the process just described.

3D Terrain Models

Electronic survey data containing elevations can often be downloaded directly to 3D terrain modeling software. Most of these software solutions produce a surface model of the terrain formed of many small triangles and are thus called a Triangulated Irregular Network or TIN. Contours, profiles, cut and fill calculations, and other information can be generated semiautomatically from the TIN. An example is shown in Figure 20.14.

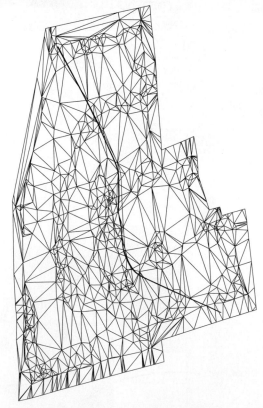

20.14 TIN 3D Terrain Model Produced in Autodesk Civil 3D 2008. *Used with permission of Autodesk, Inc. © 2006-2007. All rights reserved.*

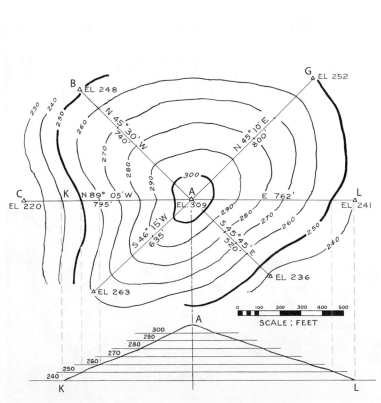

20.13 Contours Determined from Control Points

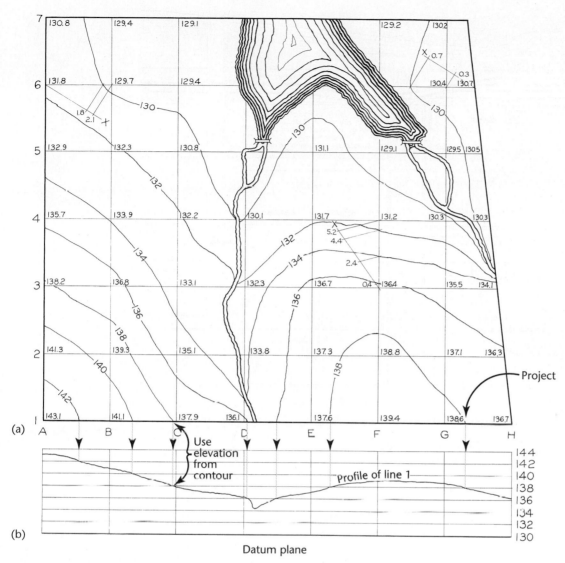

20.15 Contours Determined from Readings at Regular Intervals

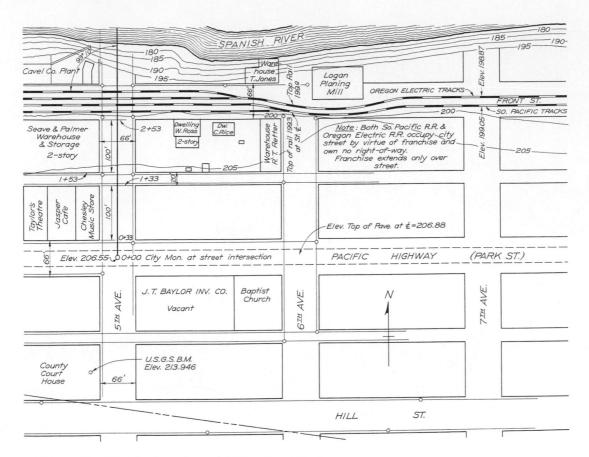

20.16 A City Plan for Location of a New Road Project

20.5 CITY MAPS

The special use of a map determines what features are to be shown. Maps of city areas may be put to many uses. Figure 20.16, a city plan for location of a new road construction, shows only those features of importance to the location and construction of the road. The transit line starts at the centerline intersection of Park St. and 5th Ave., and it is marked as station 0 + 00. From here it extends north over the railroad yard to cross the river. Features near the transit line, such as buildings, are shown and identified by name. Street widths are important and are shown. Contour lines between the railroad yard and the river indicate the steeply sloping terrain.

Subdivisions Plats

Maps perform an important function for those who plan the layout of lots and streets. For example, Figure 20.17a shows an original layout of these features for a new residential area. An examination of the contours will show that this layout is not satisfactory, since the directions of the streets do not fit the natural ground slopes. Streets should be arranged so that the subdivision can be entered from a low point and so that a maximum number of lots will be above street grade. The layout in Figure 20.17b is a decided improvement, for in it the streets curve to fit the topography and the entrance is located at a low point.

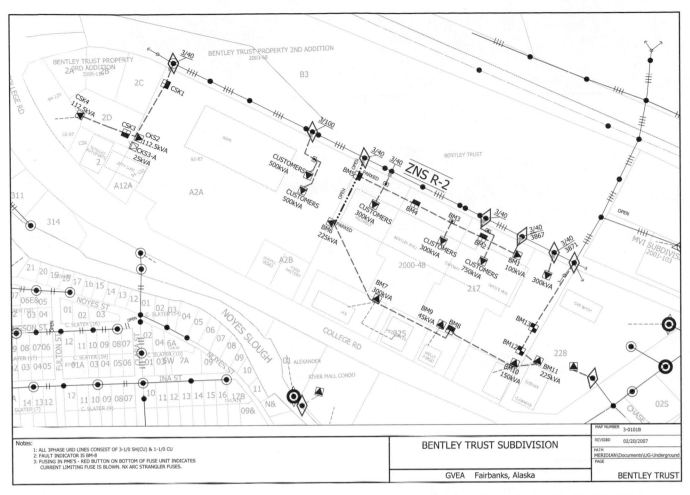

20.18   Above Ground and Underground Power are Located from Subdivision Plats. *Courtesy of Golden Valley Electric Association.*

Uses for Subdivision Plats

Utilities and other information are often referenced to locations from subdivision plats. A subdivision plat showing the locations of above ground and underground power is shown in Figure 20.18. Subdivision plats are recorded legal documents, and they are often available from County clerks and recorders offices. These drawings are used as reference for property boundaries, for landscape development, and other uses.

Landscape Drawings

Maps have a definite use in landscape planning. Figure 20.19 is a landscape drawing showing a proposed layout of deck, water feature, and trees for beautification of an outdoor space.

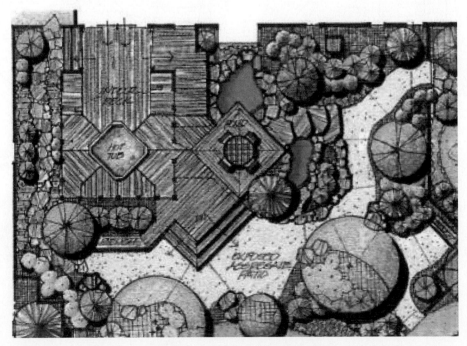

20.19   A Landscape Drawing. *Courtesy of Hispanic Business, Inc.*

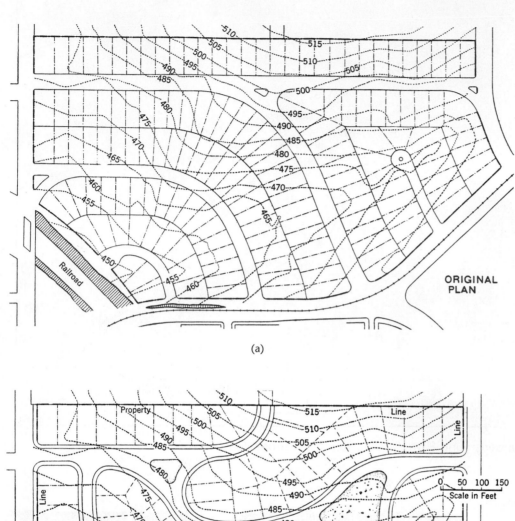

(a)

(b)

20.17 Adjustment of Streets to Topography *From Land Subdivision, ASCE Manual No. 16 of Engineering Practice with permission from ASCE.*

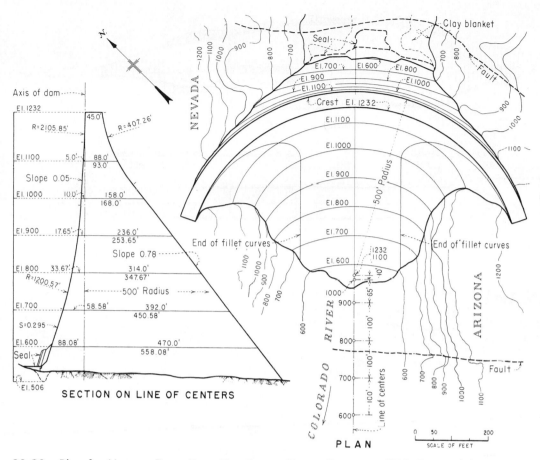

20.20   Plan for Hoover Dam *From Treatise on Dams. Courtesy of U.S. Dept. of the Interior, Bureau of Reclamation.*

20.6 STRUCTURE LOCATION PLANS

Maps arc used to plan construction projects to locate construction features so they fit the topography of the area. A project location plan for a dam is shown in Figure 20.20. This map shows the important natural features, contours, a plan view of the structure, and a cross section through Hoover Dam.

To show the complete construction drawings for a large bridge project may take hundreds of drawings, but one of the most important early drawings is a general arrangement plan and elevation in the form of a line diagram. Figure 20.21 is an example. It shows a plan and elevation of a large bridge structure.

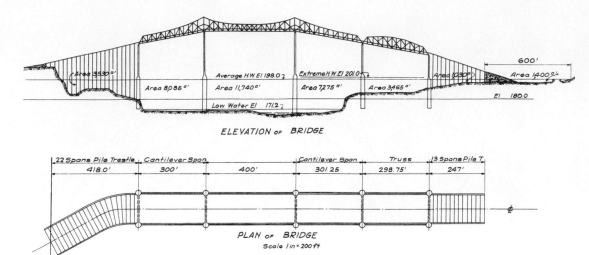

20.21 Plan and Elevation of a Bridge Structure

20.7 HIGHWAY PLANS

Before highway construction starts, it is necessary to plan the horizontal and vertical location and alignments. Commonly both the plan view and profile are drawn on the same sheet as in Figure 20.22.

The topographical plan at the top of the figure shows such features as trees, fences, and farmhouses along the right of way as shown in Figure 20.22. The transit line, locating the centerline of the new road, is drawn with stations located every 100 ft, 50 m, or some other convenient spacing. Data for creating the horizontal curves in the field are calculated and listed on the drawing.

Reading the information on the drawing, notice that the point of curve (P.C.) at station 17 + 00 is the point at which the line begins to curve with a 600′ radius, for a curve length of 400′. The central angle is 38°12′, and the degree of curve (the angle subtended by a 100′ chord) is shown as 9°33′. The reverse curve of 800′ radius begins at station 21 + 00. Note also the North point and the bearing N73°E of the transit line.

The vertical alignment is shown in profile below the plan view. Note the station numbers listed below the profile. The scale of this view is larger in a vertical than in a horizontal direction to exaggerate the elevations so they show easily. The existing ground profile along the centerline of the road is shown, as well as the profile of the proposed vertical alignment. The symbol P.I. denotes the point of intersection of the grade lines, and

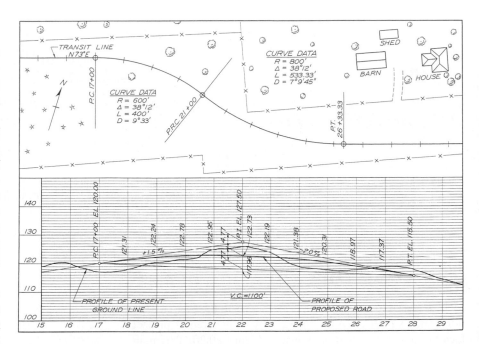

20.22 A Highway Plan and Profile

grade slopes are given in percentages. A 1 percent grade would rise vertically 1′ in each 100′ of horizontal distance. Station 22 + 00, therefore, is the intersection point of an upgrade of 1.5 percent and a downgrade of −2 percent.

To provide a smooth transition between these grades, a vertical curve (V.C.) of 1100′ length was used. This curve is parabolic and tangent to grade at

stations 17 + 00 and 28 + 00. The straight line joining these points has an elevation 117.96′ directly below the P.I. At this point the parabolic curve must pass through the midpoint of the vertical distance, at a height of 4.77′ below the P.I.

The final profile elevations are given in Figure 20.22. Calculations are given in Table 20.1.

TIP

Ordinates to parabolas, measured from tangents, are proportional to the squares of the horizontal distances from the points of tangency. Therefore, it is possible to calculate the elevations of points along the curve by first determining the grade elevations and then subtracting the parabolic curve ordinates.

Table 20.1 Calculation of Vertical Curve Elevations.

Station	Tangent Elevations	Ordinate	Curve Elevations
18	121.50	.19 a	121.31
19	120.00	.76	122.24
20	124.50	1.72	122.78
21	126.00	3.05	122.95
22	127.50	4.77	122.73
23	125.50	3.31	122.19
24	120.50	2.12	121.38
25	121.50	1.19	120.31
26	119.50	.53	118.97
27	117.50	.13	117.37

20.8 UNITED STATES MAPS

Maps of the United States, prepared by the U.S. Coast and Geodetic Survey and the U.S. Geological Survey, are excellent examples of topographic mapping. Such maps cover large areas, for example a large scale of 1 : 62,500, very nearly one mile to the inch. The contour interval in this example is 20′. At this size, it is impossible to show small features like fences clearly. Maps at large scales can show only the main features of the terrain, such as contours, roads, railroads, rivers, lakes, and streams. USGS maps are quite reliable because they are based on precise surveying.

The U.S. Geological Survey has prepared a series of standard topographic maps that cover the United States, Puerto Rico, Guam, American Samoa, and the U.S. Virgin Islands. Each unit of survey (map) is a **quadrangle** bounded by parallels of latitude and meridians of longitude. Quadrangles covering 7½ minutes of latitude and longitude are published at a scale of 1 : 24,000 (1″ = 2000′). Quadrangles covering 15 minutes of latitude and longitude are published at a scale of 1 : 62,500 (1′ = 1 mi, approximately.)

Maps (27 × 41″) showing the status of various phases of mapping and the areas covered by aerial photography in the United States at a scale of 1 : 5,000,000 (1″ = 80 mi, approximately) are available on request from the U.S. Geological Survey, Reston, VA 22092.

Figure 20.23 shows the National Atlas Web site. You can create and download custom maps there, at http://www.nationalatlas.gov/natlas/Natlasstart.asp.

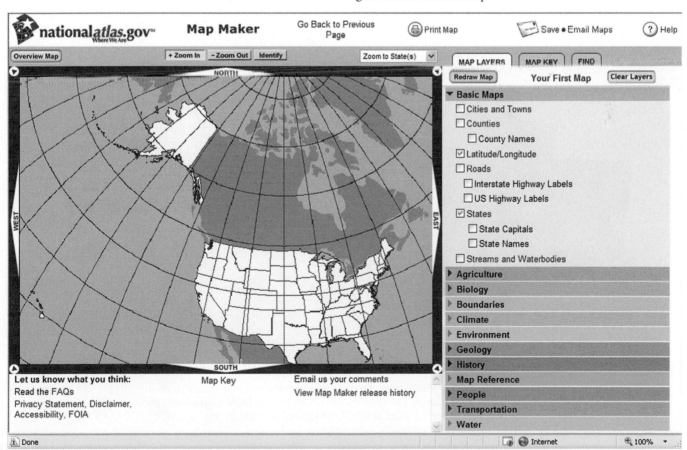

20.23 The National Atlas *Available on the World Wide Web at http://www.nationalatlas.gov/natlas/Natlasstart.asp. Courtesy of National Atlas of the United States.*

CONTOUR MAPS FROM 3D DATA

CAD software like Autodesk's Civil 3D 2008 allows you to create contour maps by entering site data like those shown in Figure A. This can even be downloaded directly into the CAD software from a total station survey instrument.

Using Civil 3D 2008 software, you can show point descriptions, contour lines, grid lines, and features such as bodies of water or structures and produce topographic pictorial drawings.

Planners are able to lay out roads and subdivisions using specialized software features that provide the contractor with earthwork calculations for individual lots or the entire site.

The same survey data that produces contour maps can be used to produce profiles like those shown in Figure B. Profiles generated from a TIN that can be used for earthwork calcunlations. Street intersections and features such as cul de sacs can be automatically generated.

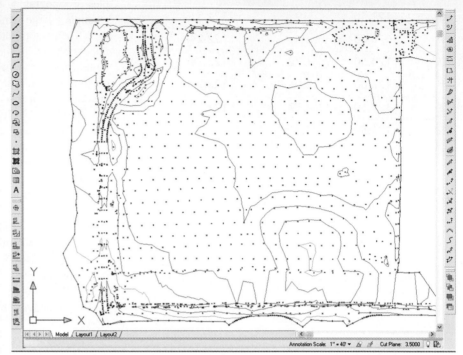

(A) Autodesk Civil 3D 2008 software provides tools to generate contour maps from survey data. *Courtesy of Autodesk, Inc. © 2006-2007. All rights reserved.*

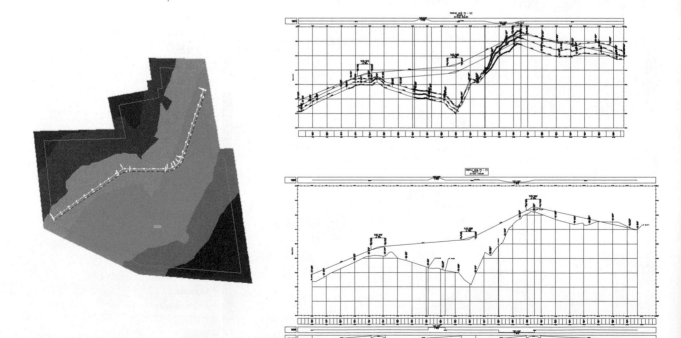

(B) Profiles can be generated across any alignment once the TIN for site has been created. The profiles shown above are from alignments shown in the colored contour map at left. *Courtesy of Autodesk, Inc. © 2006-2007. All rights reserved.*

This portion of a site plan shows contours, lot boundaries, utility easement and the primary view directions. *Courtesy of Locati Architects.*

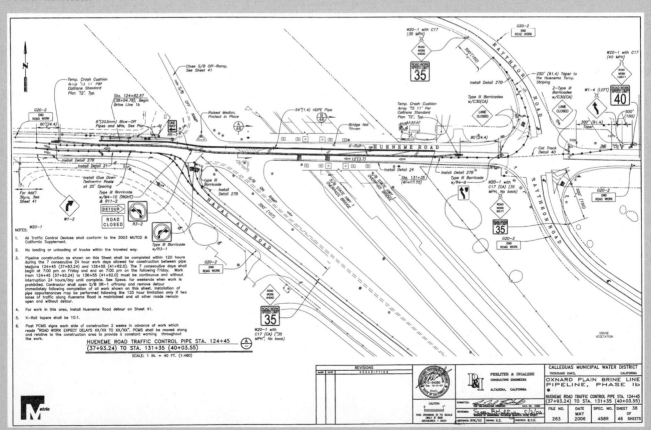

Highway signage and barricades along with trees, shrubs, fences, are located on this pipeline contstruction traffic control drawing. *Coutesy of Perliter and Ingalsbee Consulting Engineers and Calleguas Municipal Water District.*

KEY WORDS

Plat

Survey

Traverse

Elevations

Datum

Profile

Contours

Hatchures

Monuments

Cartography

Topographic Maps

Hydrographic Maps

Cadastral Maps

Military Maps

Nautical Maps

Aeronautical Maps

Engineering Maps

Landscape Maps

Electronic Survey Instruments

Global Positioning System (GPS)

GPS Satellite Constellation

Photogrammetry and Satellite Imagery

Aerial Photogrammetry

Terrestrial Photogrammetry

Laser Distance Meters

Optical Mechanical Systems

Stadia

Steel Tape

Scaled Measurements

Bearing

Differential Leveling

Quadrangle

CHAPTER SUMMARY

- Topographic drawings represent three dimensions on a 2D plan view.
- Land surveys denote the boundaries of tracts of land. Boundaries are defined by bearing and length.
- Contour lines are used to show elevation on a plan drawing. Each contour line represents one elevation level. Closely spaced contour lines indicate a steep slope. Widely spaced contour lines indicate a flatter slope.
- A profile drawing of elevation is created by drawing a cutting-plane datum on the plan view and transferring distances and elevation from the plan to the profile drawing. Profile drawings are often used to determine fill and cut slopes for roadways and railways.
- Land subdivision drawings show roads, property boundaries, and major landscape landmarks like parks, streams, buildings, and large trees.
- Computer graphics workstations can model 3D surfaces from satellite photographs. Computers model surfaces by creating a wire frame structure and then applying solid color contours to the wire frame surface.

REVIEW QUESTIONS

1. What is the purpose of a plat drawing? Is it a plan or an elevation?
2. What is the topographic notation for a plat boundary that runs exactly east and west for 1503.4 ft?
3. What are the lines that indicate elevation on a topographic map?
4. What is the purpose of a profile drawing?
5. If contour lines are very close together, would the slope be steep or gentle?

Topographic Drawing Exercises

The following problems are given to afford practice in topographic drawing. They may be completed by using either traditional drawing methods or a CAD program. The drawings are designed for a Size B or A3 sheet. The position and arrangement of the titles should conform approximately to those of Figure 20.1.

Exercise 20.1 Draw symbols of six of the common natural surface features (streams, lakes, etc.) and six of the common development features (roads, buildings, etc.) shown in Appendix 33.

Exercise 20.2 Draw, to assigned horizontal and vertical scales, profiles of any three of the six lines shown in Figure 20.12.

Exercise 20.3 Assuming the slope of the ground to be uniform and assuming a horizontal scale of $1'' = 200'$ and a contour interval of $5'$, plot, by interpolation, the contours of Figure 20.12.

Exercise 20.4 Using the elevations shown in Figure 20.13a and a contour interval of $1'$, plot the contours to any convenient horizontal and vertical scales, and draw profiles of lines 3 and 5 and of any two lines perpendicular to them. Check, graphically, the points in which the contours cross these lines.

Exercise 20.5 Using a contour interval of $1'$ and a horizontal scale of $1'' = 100'$, plot the contours from the elevations given (above) at $100'$ stations; check, graphically, the points in which the contours cross one of the horizontal lines and one of the vertical lines, using a vertical scale of $1'' = 10'$; sketch, approximately, the drainage channels.

Exercise 20.6 Use CAD to draw a plat of the survey shown in Figure 20.1. If the drawing is accurate, the plat will close. Plot your final drawing on as large a sheet as practical. Determine a standard scale at which to show the drawing. Make sure the text labeling your drawing lines appears legible and at a standard height.

Exercise 20.7 Draw a topographic map of a country estate similar to that shown in Figure 20.3.

Exercise 20.8 Calculate profile elevations for a vertical curve $800'$ long to join grades of $+3.00$ percent and -3.00 percent. Assume grade elevations at points of tangency to be $100.00'$.

144.7	139.2	143.1	144.6	144.3	143.5	142.2
142.5	138.0	139.0	141.3	142.7	139.3	139.1
140.7	137.5	136.1	138.6	138.0	136.1	137.2
138.8	136.5	135.0	136.2	135.7	135.9	136.1
139.1	136.4	134.6	133.5	133.7	134.1	135.8
135.3	134.5	133.0	132.7	132.0	131.9	132.3
135.9	134.0	132.7	131.3	130.8	129.6	131.5

CHAPTER TWENTY-ONE

PIPING DRAWINGS

OBJECTIVES

After studying the material in this chapter, you should be able to:

1. Identify cast iron, brass, copper, and thermoplastic pipe and tubing fittings.

2. Draw and label common pipe joints using ANSI/ASME standard designations.

3. Draw a multiview or pictorial piping drawings using standard schematic symbols.

4. Draw the schematic symbols for valves and identify flow direction.

Refer to the following standards:
- ANSI Y32.2.3-1949 Reaffirmed 1999 Graphic Symbols for Pipe Fittings, Valves and Piping Removed February 11, 2003. Historical reference only.
- AWWA C110/A21.10-03: Ductile-Iron and Grey-Iron Fittings for Water
- ISA-5.1-1984 (R1992) Instrumentation Symbols and Identification

A complex arrangement of pipes and tubes at a gas processing plant. *Ron Sherman/Creative Eye/MIRA.com*

OVERVIEW

Pipe is made of aluminum, brass, clay, concrete (made both with ordinary aggregates and in combination with other materials), copper, glass, iron, lead, plastics, rubber, wood, and other materials or combinations of materials. Cast iron, steel, wrought iron, brass, copper, and plastic pipes are most commonly used for transporting water, steam, oil, or gases. Pipe is also used for structural elements such as columns and handrails.

Building plans for industrial plants, commercial buildings, and residences all use piping diagrams to describe the distribution path of the gases and liquids these buildings require. Special schematic symbols simplify each type of pipe connection. CAD libraries provide piping symbol for quick insertion into drawings. Piping symbol templates are also available to simplify the process of hand sketching.

Search the following Web sites for piping information:
- http://dev.awwa.org/ American Water Works Association
- http://dev.awwa.org/bookstore/product.cfm?id=20375 AWWA Piping Handbook
- http://www.acipco.com/adip/fittings/flanged/ff.cfm#app Some standard fittings

Courtesy of GILLIANNE TEDDER/Photolibrary.com

UNDERSTANDING PIPING DRAWINGS

Standard Symbols

To make drawings of piping systems quick to produce and easy to read, a standard set of symbols shown in Appendix 34 has been developed to represent the various pipe fittings and valves. Figure 21.1 shows a few of the standard symbols. CAD systems have standard symbols available and templates for drawing piping symbols are a convenient time-saver when you are sketching piping.

Types of Drawings

Two types of drawings are common for piping systems: single line and double line.

Single line drawings show the centerline of the pipe as shown in Figure 21.2b.

Double line drawings show two lines representing the pipe diameter as shown in Figure 21.2a.

Either type of drawing can be created using orthographic drawings, orthographic section views, or pictorial drawings. An example of an orthographic drawing of a piping system is shown in Figure 21.3. In complicated systems, where a large amount of piping of various sizes is run in close proximity and where clearances are important, the use of double-line multiview drawings, made accurately to scale, is desirable.

	Flanged	Screwed	Bell & Spigot	Welded	Soldered
Joint	─╫─	─┼─	─⊂─	─✕─	─◯─
Elbow					
Elbow (45°)					

21.1   Standard Piping Symbols *See Appendix 34*

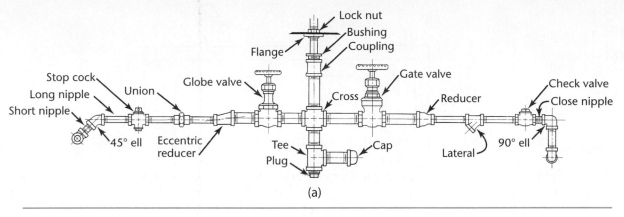

(a)

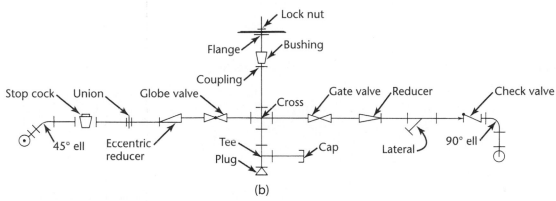

(b)

21.2 Piping Symbols Used in a (a) Double Line Drawing; (b) Single Line Drawing

21.3 Piping System Drawing Created Using CAD. *Courtesy of Softdesk, Inc.*

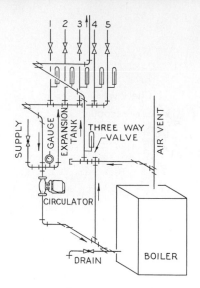

21.4 Schematic Drawing of Piping Connecting Boiler to Heating Coils

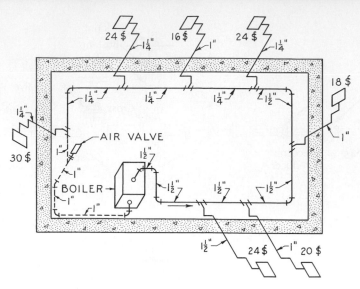

21.5 A One-Pipe Steam Heating System

Axonometric projections are also used for piping drawings. Figure 21.4 shows an oblique projection used for a piping diagram. The drawing shown in Figure 21.5 is a modified form of oblique projection generally used in representing the piping arrangement for heating systems. In these cases, the pipe mains are shown in plan and the risers in oblique projection in various directions to make the representation as clear as possible.

In most installations, some pipes are vertical and some are horizontal. If the vertical pipes are revolved into the horizontal plane or if the horizontal pipes are revolved into the vertical plane by turning some of the fittings, the entire installation can be shown in one plane as shown in Figure 21.6c. This is called a **developed piping drawing.**

Showing the relative positions of component parts in all views reduces the probability of interference when the piping is erected and is almost a necessity where piping components are prefabricated in a shop and sent to the job in finished dimensions. Prefabrication is common for large systems and large pipe sizes. Most piping 2 1/2" and larger is shop fabricated.

3D CAD is useful for creating piping drawings. Showing the centerline of the pipe along with the valve may often be all that is necessary. Extrude the pipe diameter along the centerline to produce a drawing that shows the entire pipe when more detail is needed. Automated interference checking, available in 3D CAD, can help eliminate errors in the design.

Dimensioning Piping Drawings

In dimensioning a piping drawing, give distances from center to center (c to c), center to end (c to e), or end to end (e to e) of fittings or valves and the lengths of all straight runs of pipe as shown in Figure 21.7. Fully dimensioned single line drawings are not always drawn to scale. You may find it useful to use break lines and omit portions of the straight pipe.

Allowances in pipe lengths for makeup in fittings and valves must be made in preparing a bill of materials.

Show the centerlines in double line drawings if they are to be dimensioned.

Show the size of the pipe for each run by a numeral or by a note at the side of the pipe. Use a leader when necessary for clarity.

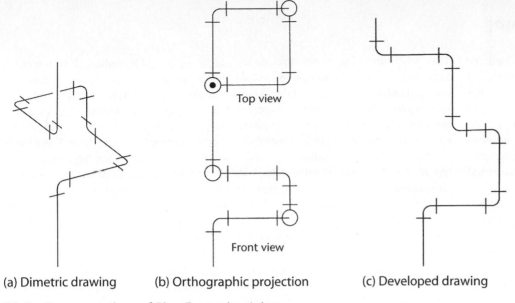

(a) Dimetric drawing   (b) Orthographic projection   (c) Developed drawing

21.6   Representations of Pipe Expansion Joint

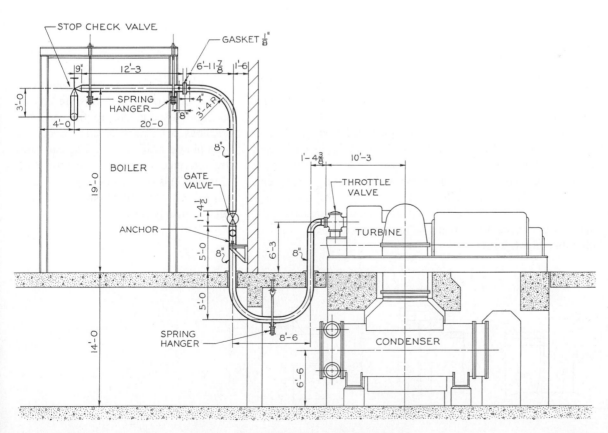

21.7   A Dimensioned Piping Drawing—Side View of Steam Piping

21.1 STEEL AND WROUGHT IRON PIPE

Steel or wrought iron pipe is used for water, steam, oil, and gas. Until the early 1930s, it was available in only three weights, known as "standard," "extra strong," and "double extra strong." At that time increasing pressures and temperatures, particularly for steam service, made the availability of more diversified wall thicknesses desirable.

The American National Standards Institute/American Society of Mechanical Engineers (ANSI/ASME) has developed dimensions for 10 different **schedules** of pipe (see Appendix 38). The table in Appendix 38 shows dimensions for nominal sizes from 1/8″ to 24″. Dimensions have not been established for all schedules. In the different schedules, the outside diameters (O.D.) are maintained for each nominal size to facilitate threading and the uniform use of fittings and valves.

Certain of the schedule dimensions correspond to the dimensions of "standard" and "extra strong" pipe. These are shown in **boldface** type in the appendix.

The schedule dimensions shown for Schedules 30 and 40 correspond to standard pipe and those for Schedule 80 correspond to extra strong pipe. There are no schedule dimensions corresponding to double extra strong pipe. Some of the established schedule dimensions may not always be commercially available, so investigate before specifying pipe on drawings. Generally, schedules 40, 80, and 160 are readily available.

Note that the actual outside diameter of pipe in nominal sizes 1/8″ to 12″ inclusive is larger than the nominal size, whereas the outside diameter of pipe in nominal sizes 14″ and larger corresponds to the nominal size. Pipe in nominal sizes 14″ and larger is commonly referred to as O.D. pipe.

Pipe may be welded or seamless. Welded pipe is available in schedules 40 and 80 in the smaller sizes. Lap welded pipe is made in sizes up to and including 2″. Butt welded pipe is available as furnace-welded material, where a formed length is heated in a furnace and then welded, in

sizes up to and including 3″. Butt welded pipe is also available as continuous welded pipe, where the finished pipe is continuously heated, formed, and welded from a roll of strip steel, in sizes up to and including 4″. Seamless pipe is made in both small and large sizes.

Many applications require the use of alloys to withstand pressure-temperature conditions without having to be excessively thick. Many alloys are available in both ferritic and austenitic material. Refer to the specifications of the American Society for Testing Materials (ASTM) for these alloys and for dimensional tolerances.

Steel pipe is available as **black pipe** or as **galvanized pipe.** Galvanized pipe is used for water distribution, and black pipe for natural gas.

Steel or wrought iron pipe comes in lengths up to about 40′ in the small sizes, with the length decreasing with increasing size and wall thickness.

21.2 CAST IRON PIPE

Cast iron (C.I.) pipe is used for water or gas service and as soil pipe. For water and gas pipe, it is generally available in sizes from 3″ to 60″ inclusive and in standard lengths of 12′. Various wall thicknesses satisfy different internal pressure requirements. The dimensions and the pressure ratings of the various classes are shown in Appendix 39.

Generally, water and gas pipes are connected with **bell and spigot joints**

(Figure 21.8a) or **flanged joints** (Figure 21.8b) although other types of joints (Figure 21.8c) are also used.

As soil pipe, cast iron pipe is available in sizes 2″ to 15″ inclusive, in standard lengths of 5′, and in service and extra heavy weights. Soil pipe is generally connected with bell and spigot joints, but soil pipe with threaded ends is available in sizes up to 12″.

Using cast iron pipe, designers consider both the internal pressure and the external loading, due to fill and other loadings, such as roads and tracks. Cast iron pipe is brittle and settling can cause fracture unless the joints are sufficiently flexible. This is why flange joints are not usually used for buried pipes unless they are adequately supported.

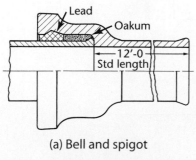

(a) Bell and spigot

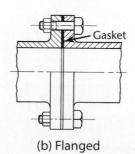

(b) Flanged

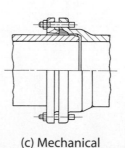

(c) Mechanical

21.8 Cast Iron Pipe Joints

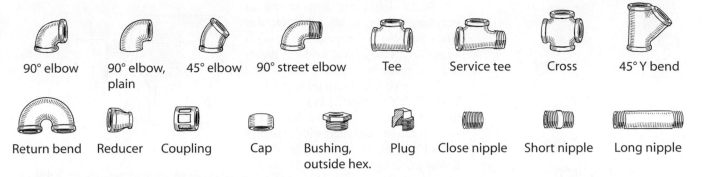

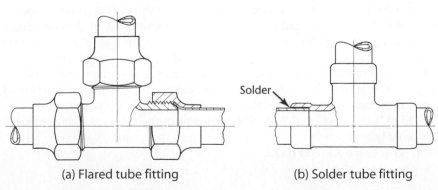

21.9 Screwed Fittings

21.3 SEAMLESS BRASS AND COPPER PIPE

Pipe made of brass and copper is available in approximately the same dimensions as "standard" and "extra strong" steel pipe. It is used in plumbing for supply, soil, waste drain, and vent lines. It is also particularly suitable for process work where formation of scale or oxidation in steel pipe would be troublesome. Brass pipe and copper pipe are available in straight lengths up to 12′.

Brass pipe, generally known as **red brass pipe,** is an alloy of approximately 85 percent copper and 15 percent zinc. Copper pipe is practically pure copper with less than 0.1 percent of alloying elements.

Brass pipe and copper pipe should be joined with fittings of copper-base alloy to avoid galvanic action resulting in corrosion. Where screwed joints are used, fittings similar to cast or malleable iron fittings are available (Figure 21.9).

Flanged fittings of brass and copper are of different dimensions than fittings made of ferrous material. Refer to dimensional standards published by the American National Standards Institute (ANSI/ASME B16.24-1991) for dimensions of brass and copper fittings.

21.4 COPPER TUBING

Copper tubing is often used in applications for nonferrous construction in sizes below 2″. It is suitable for process work, for plumbing, and for heating systems (particularly radiant heating).

Copper tubing is made as **hard temper** and as **soft tubing.** Hard temper tubing is much stiffer than soft tubing and is used when rigidity is desired. Soft tubing is easy to bend and is used where bending during assembly is required. Neither hard nor soft temper tubing has the rigidity of iron or steel pipe and must be supported at frequent intervals. Where multiple runs of parallel tubes are used over distances of 20′ or more, parallel runs of soft tubing are laid in a trough to provide continuous support.

Copper tubing joints are usually made with **flared joints** (Figure 21.10a), or **solder joints** (Figure 21.10b). There are several types of flared joints, but the basic design of making a metal-to-metal joint is common to all. Fittings, such as tees, elbows, and couplings, are available for flared joints.

(a) Flared tube fitting   (b) Solder tube fitting

21.10   Copper Pipe Fittings

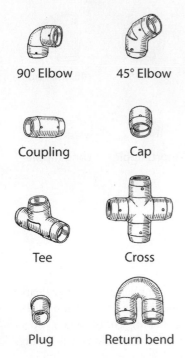

90° Elbow   45° Elbow

Coupling   Cap

Tee   Cross

Plug   Return bend

21.11 Solder Fittings

Solder joints are also known as **capillary joints** because the **annular space** between the tube and the fitting is so small that the molten solder is drawn into the space by capillary action. The solder may be introduced through a hole in the fitting (Figure 21.11) or through the outer end of the annular space. Fittings can be purchased with a factory-assembled ring of solder in the fitting. Solder joints may be made with soft solder (usually 50/50 or 60/40 tin and lead) or with silver solder. Silver solder has a higher melting point than soft solder, makes a stronger joint, and is suitable for higher operating temperatures.

Copper pipe or tubing has an upper operating temperature limit of 406°F. If solder fittings are used, the upper temperature limit depends on the softening point of the solder rather than the temperature limit of the base material.

Copper tubing can be connected to threaded pipe or fittings using **adapters.** Adapters are available with either male or female pipe threads and with

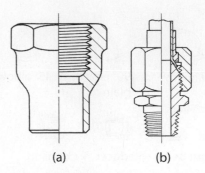

(a)   (b)

21.12 Adapters—Copper Tube to Threaded Pipe

either flared or solder connections for the tubing. Two types are shown in Figure 21.12.

Copper tubing is available in straight lengths up to 20′ or in coils of 60′ for soft temper material. Hard temper material is available in straight lengths only, since it cannot be coiled. Installation costs for coiled material are lower, because fewer joints are needed. Copper tubing is available in both O.D. and nominal sizes.

21.5 PLASTIC AND SPECIALTY PIPES

Pipe and tubing of other material, such as aluminum and stainless steel, are also available. A wide variety of plastic pipe, both rigid and flexible, is used in construction. Plastic pipe is lightweight, corrosion proof, resistant to many chemicals, and has a smooth inner surface which offers low flow resistance.

PVC (polyvinyl chloride) pipe and fittings are available in Schedule 40 and extra heavy Schedule 80. Schedule 80 is used where higher working pressures are present and may be threaded. Schedule 40 should not be threaded, and is normally assembled with slip fittings and solvent. The maximum temperature rating for PVC is 140°F (110°C).

CPVC (chlorinated polyvinyl chloride) pipe is similar to PVC and has a higher maximum temperature rating, 180°F (132°C). Both PVC and CPVC pipe are commonly available in sizes ranging from 1/2″ to 4″ inside diameter (I.D.).

Black polyethylene flexible pipe, approved by the National Sanitation Foundation for use with drinking water, has a rated working pressure of 100 psi when not exposed to direct sunlight. It is available in sizes from 1/2″ to 2″ I.D. (inside diameter). Black polyethylene pipe should not be used on hot water lines or exposed to temperatures greater than 100°F (88°C). It is often used for underground lawn sprinkler systems.

HDPE (high density polyethylene) is available in sizes from 1/2″ to 63″ in a variety of wall thicknesses and shapes.

The applications of these materials vary according to their physical properties and temperature-pressure limitations. Regardless of the material used in a piping system, the procedure followed in the design of the system and the creation of the necessary drawings remains basically the same.

21.6 PIPE FITTINGS

Pipe fittings are used to join lengths of pipe, to provide changes of direction, to provide branch connections at different angles, or to effect a change in size. They are made of cast iron, malleable iron, cast or forged steel, nonferrous alloys, and other materials for special applications. Pipe fittings are available in different weights and should be matched to the pipe they are used with. Ferrous fittings are made for threaded, welded, or flanged joints. Nonferrous fittings are made for threaded, solder, flared, or flanged joints. The common types of fittings for threaded joints were shown in Figure 21.9. Common fittings for solder joints were shown in Figure 21.11. Fittings for welded joints are shown in Figure 21.13, and for flanged joints in Figure 21.14.

Where both or all ends of a fitting are the same nominal size, the fitting is designated by the nominal size and the description—for example, a 2″ **screwed tee.** Where two or more ends of a fitting are not the same nominal size, the fitting is designated as a **reducing fitting,** the dimensions of the run precede those of the branches, and the dimension of the larger opening precedes that of the smaller opening—for example, a 2 × 1½ × 1″ **screwed reducing tee.** See Figure 21.15 for typical designations.

The threads of screwed fittings conform to the pipe thread with which they are to be used, either male or female.

Dimensions of 125 lb cast iron screwed fittings, 250 lb cast iron screwed fittings, 125 lb cast iron flanged fittings, and 250 lb cast iron flanged fittings are shown in Appendixes 40–43 and 45.

 90° elbow 45° elbow

 Tee  Cap

 Return bend Reducing nipple

 Welding nipple

21.13 Butt Welded Fittings

 90° elbow Tee Cross 45° lateral 90° long radius, elbow 45° elbow 90° base elbow Taper reducer Return bend

21.14 Flanged Fittings

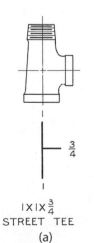 IXIX¾ STREET TEE (a)

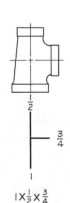 IX½X¾ TEE (b)

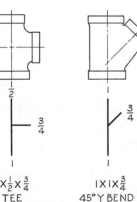 IXIX¾ 45° Y BEND (c)

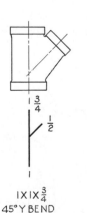 IXIX¾ 45° Y BEND (d)

 IXIX½X½ CROSS (e)

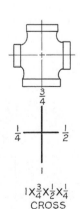 IX¾X½X¼ CROSS (f)

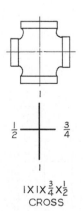 IXIX¾X½ CROSS (g)

21.15 Designating Sizes of Fittings

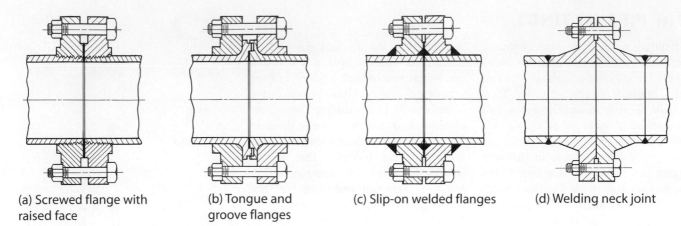

(a) Screwed flange with raised face

(b) Tongue and groove flanges

(c) Slip-on welded flanges

(d) Welding neck joint

21.16 Special Types of Flanged Joints

21.7 PIPE JOINTS

The joints between pipes, fittings, and valves may be **screwed, flanged, welded,** or, for nonferrous metallic materials, **soldered.** Plastic pipes may be screwed together or fastened with slip joints and solvent or with compression fittings.

The American National Standard pipe threads were illustrated in Figures 11.25–11.27, and tabular dimensions are shown in Appendix 38. The threads of the American Petroleum Institute (API) differ somewhat from the American National Standard pipe threads. Refer to the API Standards for these differences.

Threaded joints can be made up tightly by simply screwing the cleaned threads together. However, it is common practice to use **pipe compound,** as it lubricates the threads and enables them to be screwed together more tightly. It also serves to seal irregularities, providing a tighter joint. Pipe compound is applied to the male thread only, to avoid forcing it into the pipe and to prevent contamination or obstruction.

Flanged Joints

Flanged joints are made by bolting two flanges together with a resilient **gasket** between the flange faces. Flanges may be attached using a screwed joint or by welding, lapping the pipe, or being cast integrally with the pipe, fitting, or appliance.

The faces of the flanges between which the gasket is placed have different standard facings, such as flat face, $1/16''$ raised face, $1/4''$ raised face, male and female, tongue and groove, and ring joints. Flat face and $1/16''$ raised face are standard for cast iron flanges in the 125 lb and 250 lb classes, respectively. The other types of facing are standard for steel flanges.

The number and size of the bolts joining these flanges vary with the size and the working pressure of the joint. Bolting for Class 125 cast iron and Class 250 cast iron flanges is shown in Appendixes 43 and 46, respectively.

For dimensions of the various flange facings and for flange and bolting dimensions of the various sizes and pressure standards of steel flanges, refer to the American National Standard for Steel Pipe Flanges and Flanged Fittings (ANSI/ASME B16.5-1988), which is too extensive to be included here. Some special types of flanged joints are shown in Figure 21.16.

Welded Joints

Piping construction using welding joints is in almost universal use today, particularly for higher pressure and temperature conditions. Such joints may either be socket welded or butt welded (Figure 21.13). Socket welded joints are limited to use in small sizes. The contours of the butt welded joints shown in Figure 21.17a and c are those shown in ANSI/ASME B16.25-1992.

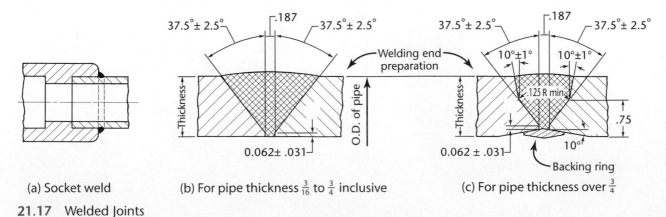

(a) Socket weld

(b) For pipe thickness $\frac{3}{16}$ to $\frac{3}{4}$ inclusive

(c) For pipe thickness over $\frac{3}{4}$

21.17 Welded Joints

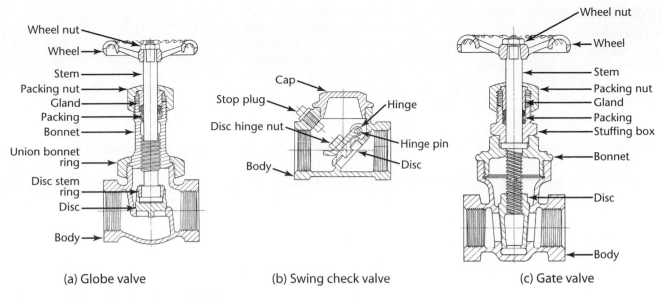

(a) Globe valve   (b) Swing check valve   (c) Gate valve

21.18 Globe, Check Valves, and Gate

21.8 VALVES

Valves are used to stop or regulate the flow of fluids in a pipe line. The more common types are **gate valves, globe valves,** and **check valves.** Other types, such as **pressure-reducing valves** and **safety valves,** are used to maintain a desired lower pressure on the downstream side of the valve or to prevent undesirable overpressure, respectively.

Globe Valves

Globe valves have approximately spherical bodies with the seating surface at either a right or an acute angle to the centerline of the pipe (Figure 21.18a). In a globe valve the flowing fluid makes abrupt turns in the body resulting in higher pressure loss than in a gate valve.

Globe valves are commonly used for close regulation of flow and are less subject to cutting action in throttling service than gate valves.

Inside screw and outside screw and yoke (OS & Y) type valves are also available. Angle valves and needle valves are special designs of the general class of globe valves (Figure 21.18c).

Check Valves

Check valves are used to limit fluid flow to only one direction. **Swing check valves** use a disk that may be hinged to swing partially out of the stream (Figure 21.18b). **Lift check valves** use a disk that is guided so that it rises vertically from its seat.

Gate Valves

Gate valves have full-sized straightway openings that offer small resistance to the flow of fluid. The gate, or disk, may rise on the stem (inside screw type) (Figure 21.18c), or the gate may rise with the stem, which in turn rises out of the body (rising stem, or outside screw and yoke type). Inside screw type valves are used in the smaller sizes and lower pressures.

Seating may be on nonparallel seats, in which case the disk is solid and wedge shaped. There is also a type of gate valve that uses parallel seats. In this type, two disks are hung loosely on the stem and are free of the seats until an adjusting wedge reaches a lug at the closed position of the valve, when further movement of the stem causes the wedge to spread the disks and form a tight joint on the parallel seats. These valves are used only on low-pressure and low-temperature services.

Solenoid Actuated Valves

A thermostatically controlled heating system is an example of process control. When you set your home thermostat to a particular value, the heating system is controlled typically using solenoid actuated valves in order to try to meet the set temperature value. Solenoid valves are electromechanical devices often used to regulate the flow of liquid or gas.

Drawings for process control often combine electronic and piping elements to show how the process is controlled. Figure 21.19a shows a cross sectional view of a two-way, two position, normally closed solenoid valve. Figure 21.19b shows a schematic diagram for a two-way, two position, normally closed solenoid flow control valve.

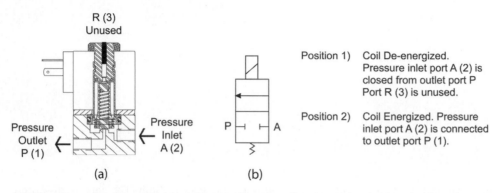

21.19 Two Way Two Position, Normally Closed Solenoid Valve. *Courtesy of Spartan Scientific.*

21.9 AMERICAN NATIONAL STANDARD CODE FOR PRESSURE PIPING

The American National Standards Institute has adopted an American National Standard Code for Pressure Piping (ANSI/ASME B31.1-1995). This compilation of recommended practices and minimum safety standards covers various types of piping, such as power piping, industrial gas and air piping, oil refinery piping, oil transportation piping, refrigerating piping, chemical industry process piping, and gas transmission and distribution piping.

PIPING DRAWING FOR A FIELD INSTRUMENT

MSE Technology Applications, Inc. (MSE) designed a field instrument to expedite the process of sorting drums containing volatile organic compounds (VOCs). The previous sorting process used a gas chromatograph/mass spectrometer (GC/MS) which was time consuming and relatively expensive. Drums were required to pass two independent field measurements before they could be transported. Figure A is a schematic diagram showing the valves, filters, piping and other features for the instrumentation.

From each drum a headspace gas sample was drawn and analyzed first by a field ready Flame Ionization Detector (FID) VOC meter. A second field instrument, a Photo Ionization Detector (PID) VOC meter equipped with a 10.6-eV lamp analyzed the headspace gas a second time. If the sum of the two VOC measurements were less than 500 ppmv, the waste was designated less than 500 ppmv flammable VOCs and therefore allowed to be shipped. Tests of the device showed the portable field instruments provided a confident approach to sampling and analyzing headspace gas in drums, saving time and avoiding the costly GC/MS analysis previously used.

The actual equipment, when assembled, looked very similar to the 3D CAD model shown in Figure B.

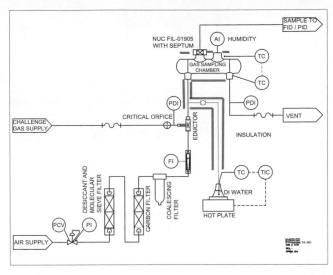

(A) Drum simulation and setup diagram. *Courtesy of MSE Technology Applications, Inc.*

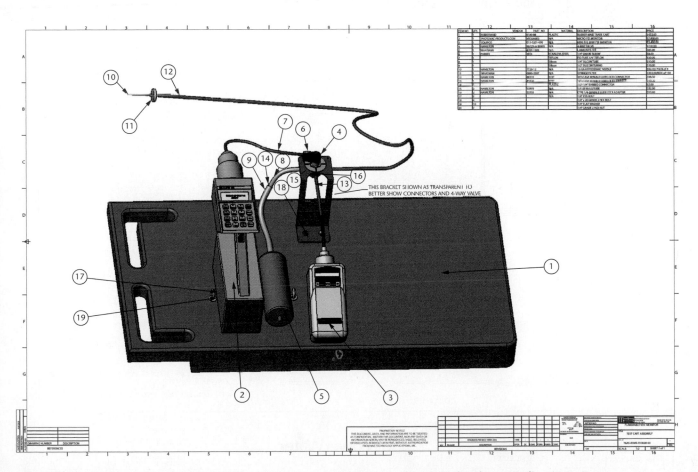

(B) Assembly drawing and parts list from the 3D CAD model. *Courtesy of MSE Technology Applications, Inc.*

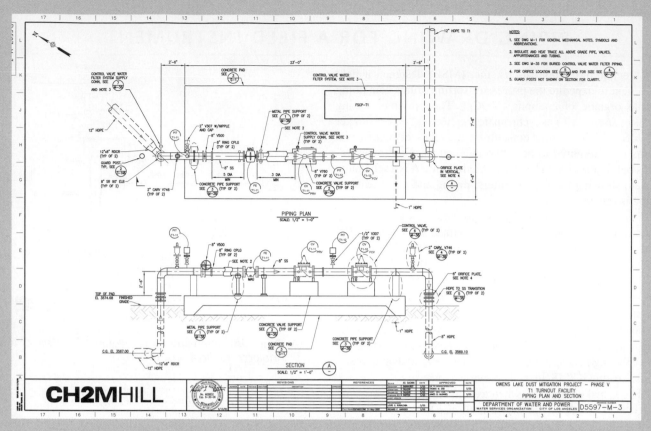

Double line piping plan and elevation drawing. *Courtesy of CH2M Hill.*

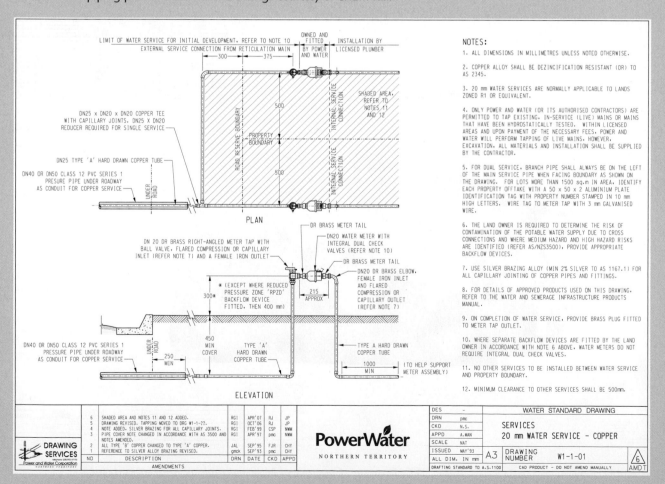

Courtesy of Power and Water Corporation.

KEY WORDS

Single line Drawings

Double line Drawings

Developed Piping Drawing

Schedules

Black Pipe

Galvanized Pipe

Bell and Spigot Joints

Flanged Joints

Red Brass Pipe

Hard Temper

Soft Tubing

Flared Joints

Solder Joints

Capillary Joints

Annular Space

Adapters

PVC

CPVC

HDPE

Screwed Tee

Reducing Fitting

Screwed Reducing tee

Screwed

Flanged

Welded

Soldered

Pipe Compound

Gasket

Gate Valves

Globe Valves

Check Valves

Pressure-Reducing Valves

Safety Valves

Swing Check Valves

Lift Check Values

CHAPTER SUMMARY

- Steel and wrought iron pipes are commonly used for water, steam, oil, and gas. Steel provides the strength necessary for the high pressures commonly associated with these substances.
- Cast iron is primarily used for water, gas, and waste. Cast iron is durable for all but the highest pressures. Cast iron pipe typically uses threaded fittings.
- Copper tubing is typically used for water and compressed air. Copper tubing can be connected with solder joints or with compression fittings.
- Plastic pipe and fittings are lightweight, corrosion resistant, and have a smooth inner surface. They are often used as a substitute for metallic pipe.
- Single line drawings and simplified symbols are commonly used to represent pipes and fittings on a pipe drawing. Piping drawings are usually not drawn to scale.
- Valves control the flow of material through a pipe.
- A library of computer piping symbols can speed the creation and modification of CAD piping drawings.

REVIEW QUESTIONS

1. What pipe material would be used for the highest pressures?
2. What types of fittings are commonly used with cast iron pipe? With copper tubing?
3. What fitting would join two pipes at 90° or 45°?
4. What fitting would join two pipes at 180°?
5. What fitting would join four pipes together at one joint?
6. What fitting would connect two pipes of different diameter?
7. What is the purpose of a valve?
8. How is flow direction indicated on a piping drawing?
9. Why is a library of piping symbols important when drawing with CAD?
10. Draw and label five single-line piping symbols.

EXERCISES

Piping Drawing Problems

Exercise 21.1 Make a double-line drawing, similar to Figure 21.12a, showing the following fittings: a union, a 45° Y bend, an eccentric reducer, a globe valve, a tee, a stopcock, and a 45° ell. Use ½″ and 1″ wrought steel pipe and 125 lb cast iron screwed fittings.

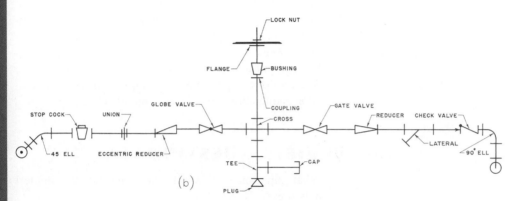

(b)

Exercise 21.2 Make a single-line drawing, similar to the figure above, showing the following fittings: a 45° ell, a union, a 45° Y bend, an eccentric reducer, a tee, a reducer, a gate valve, a plug, a cap, and a cross.

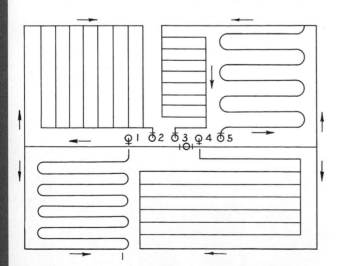

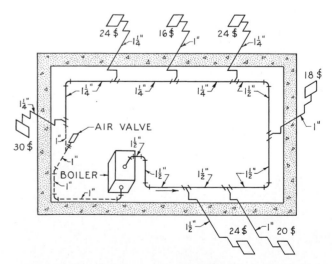

Exercise 21.3 Make a single-line drawing of the system of pipe coils and grids shown. Show, by their respective standard symbols, the elbows and tees that must be used to connect pipes meeting at right angles if welding is not used to make the joints.

Exercise 21.4 Make an oblique projection, similar to that in Figure 21.5, of the one-pipe steam heating system shown. Show the pipes by single lines, the fittings by their standard symbols, and the boiler and radiators as parallelepipeds.

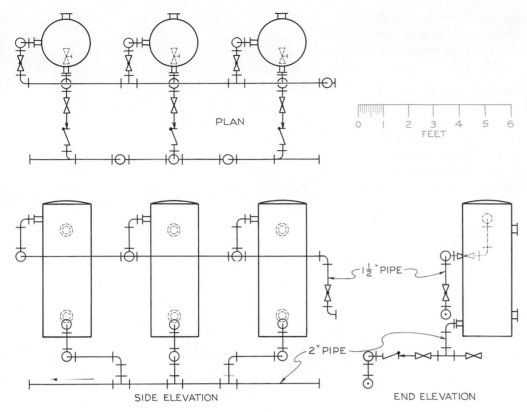

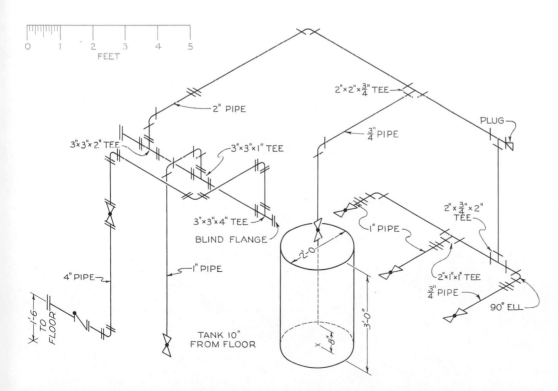

Exercise 21.5 Make a single-line isometric drawing of the piping layout shown. Use a scale of 3/4″ = 1′−0. (Make the drawing similar to the isometric layout shown in Exercise 21.6.)

Exercise 21.6 Make a single-line multiview drawing of the piping layout shown. Use a scale of 1″ = 1′−0. (This drawing should be similar to the piping layout in Exercise 21.5.)

Exercise 21.7 Make a double-line multiview drawing of the piping layout in Exercise 21.5 to a scale of your own selection. (This drawing should be similar to the two-line piping drawing in Figure 21.3a.)

Exercise 21.8 Make a double-line multiview drawing of the piping layout in Exercise 21.6 to a scale of your own selection. Use Schedule 80 wrought steel pipe throughout, with Class 250 cast iron flanged fittings where pipe is larger than 2″ and Class 250 cast iron screwed fittings where pipe is 2″ and smaller. (This drawing should be similar to the two-line piping drawing in Figure 21.3a.)

CHAPTER TWENTY-TWO

WELDING REPRESENTATION

OBJECTIVES

After studying the material in this chapter, you should be able to:

1. Describe the various welding processes.

2. Draw the common welding symbols.

3. Dimension a welding drawing using standard ANSI welding notation.

4. Identify and draw a fillet weld, groove weld, back weld, spot weld, seam weld, projection weld, and flash weld.

5. Describe the use of welding symbols in CAD drawings.

Refer to the following standards:
- AWS A2.4-2007 Standard Symbols for Welding, Brazing, and Nondestructive Examination.
- AWS A1.1-2001, Metric Practice Guide for the Welding Industry.
- AWS A3.0-1994 Standard Welding Terms and Definitions.

An Automobile Frame is Welded on a Robotic Automobile Assembly Line. *Courtesy of Vladimir Pcholkin/Stone/ Getty Images.*

OVERVIEW

For fastening parts together permanently rather than using bolts, screws, rivets, or other fasteners, welding is often the method of choice. Welding is widely used in fabricating machine parts or other structures that formerly would have been formed by casting or forging. Structural steel frames for buildings, ships, and other structures are often welded. Welding is one of few machine processes that adds material to a workpiece, rather than removing it.

Welding symbols on a mechanical drawing provide precise instructions for the welder. The weld type and the location of each weld must be clearly defined using standardized symbols. CAD libraries of welding symbols can simplify the drawing process. Welding templates can speed the process of drawing by hand.

Check the sites below for Web resources:
- Examples for students and links about ASME codes and standards: http://www.asme.org/Codes/About/Links/Links_Codes_Standards.cfm
- Americal Welding Societies homepage: www.AWS.org

UNDERSTANDING WELDMENT DRAWINGS

Welding is used extensively and for a wide variety of attachment purposes. A series of "Standard Welding Symbols" were developed in 1947 to provide an accurate method of showing the exact types, sizes, and locations of welds on construction drawings of machines or structures. Before these standards were developed, notes on the drawing such as "To be welded throughout" or "To be completely welded," gave responsibility for welding control to the welding shop, which was dangerously vague and could be unnecessarily expensive, since shops would often "play it safe" by welding more than necessary.

Welding Processes

The principal methods of welding are:

- **Gas welding**
- **Arc welding**
- **Resistance welding**

Gas Welding The oxyacetylene method is generally known as gas welding. Gas welding originated in 1895, when the French chemist Le Châtelier discovered that the combustion of acetylene gas with oxygen produced a flame hot enough to melt metals. This discovery was soon followed by the development of practical methods to produce and transport oxygen and acetylene and the construction of torches and welding rods.

Arc Welding the electric arc method is generally known as arc welding, In arc welding, the heat of an electric arc is used to fuse the metals that are to be welded or cut. Gas metal arc welding **(GMAW)** is often known by its subtypes metal inert gas welding **(MIG)** and metal active gas welding **(MAG).**

This type of welding uses a wire electrode that is fed along with a shielding gas through the welding gun. Gas tungsten arc welding **(GTAW)** often known as tungsten inert gas welding **(TIG)** and plasma arc welding are processes that conduct the arc through a heated gas called a plasma, to produce strong high-quality welds. Arc and gas welding are important construction processes in industry.

Resistance Welding Electric resistance welding is generally called resistance welding. In resistance welding, two pieces of metal are held together under some pressure, and a large amount of electric current is passed through the parts. The resistance of the metals to the passage of the current causes great heating at the junction of the two pieces, resulting in the welding of the metals.

Standard Symbols

The text and illustrations of this chapter are based primarily on ANSI/AWS A2.4-2007 Standard Symbols for Welding, Brazing, and Nondestructive Examination. You may also want to refer to AWS A1.1-2001, Metric Practice Guide for the Welding Industry, and ANSI/AWS A3.0-1994, Standard Welding Terms and Definitions.

Welding drawings are a special type of assembly drawing as weldments are composed of a number of separate pieces fastened together as a unit. The welds themselves are not drawn but are clearly and completely indicated by the welding symbols. Figure 22.1 shows a drawing using standard welding symbols. Most CAD packages provide standard welding symbols that can quickly be inserted into your drawing.

The joints are all shown in the drawing as they would appear before welding. Dimensions are given to show the sizes of the individual pieces to be cut from stock. Each component piece is identified by encircled numbers and by specifications in the parts list.

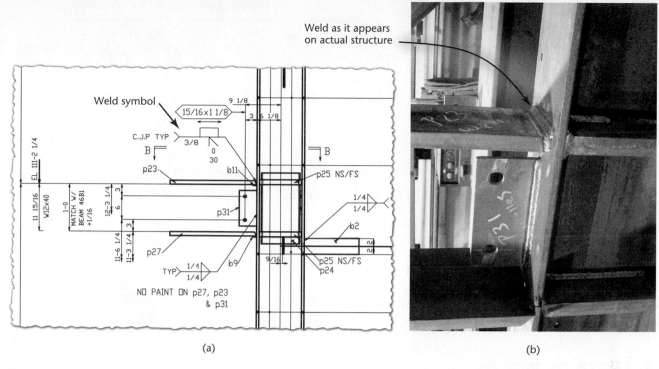

(a)

(b)

22.1   a. Portion of a weldment drawing. *Courtesy of Midwest Steel Industries.*

b. Picture of welded structure (photo has been rotated to the same orientation as the drawing in part a.)

UNDERSTANDING A WELDING SYMBOL

A welding symbol added to the drawing has many different features that specify each detail of the weld. The items that can be specified are:

- Type of weld
- Process
- Depth of bevel, size or strength for some weld types
- Groove weld size
- Finishing designator
- Contour
- Groove angle
- Root opening
- Length of weld
- Number and **pitch** (center to center spacing) of welds
- Whether the weld is to be field welded (done on site)
- All around indicator
- Which side of the material is to be welded

That's a lot of information contained in one symbol. The next sections provide more detail about the information contained in the symbol you will add to your drawings. Figure 21.1 shows an example of a weld symbol used on a drawing and the actual welded part. Figure 22.2 points out features of a weld to which the symbol may refer.

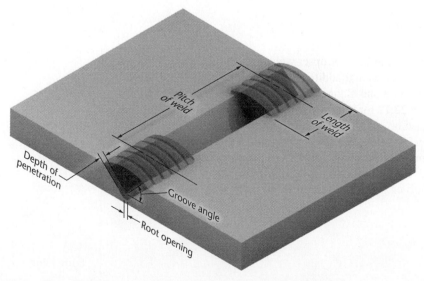

22.2   Features of a weld

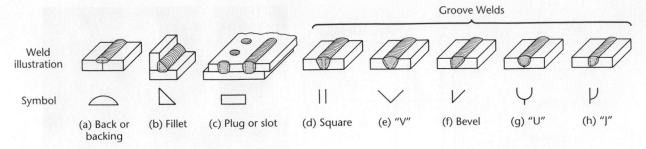

Weld illustration

Symbol

(a) Back or backing   (b) Fillet   (c) Plug or slot   (d) Square   (e) "V"   (f) Bevel   (g) "U"   (h) "J"

22.3 Basic Welds and Symbols

22.1 TYPES OF WELDED JOINTS

There are five basic types of welded joints: **butt joint, corner joint, T-joint, lap joint,** and **edge joint.** They are classified according to the positions of the parts being joined. Table 22.1 shows illustrations of the types of welded joints.

A number of different types of welds are applicable to each type of joint, depending on the thickness of metal, the strength of joint required, and other considerations.

22.2 TYPES OF WELDS

The four types of arc and gas welds are shown in Figure 22.3:

- **Back or backing weld.**
- **Fillet weld.**
- **Plug or slot weld.**
- **Groove weld.**

Groove welds are further classified as square, V, bevel, U, and J, as shown Figure 22.3d through h.

More than one type of weld may be applied to a single joint. For example, a V weld may be on one side and a back weld on the other side. Frequently, the same type of weld is used on opposite sides, forming such welds as a double-V, a double-U, or a double-J.

The four basic resistance welds are:

- **Spot weld.**
- **Projection weld.**
- **Seam weld.**
- **Flash or upset weld.**

Except for the flash or upset weld, the corresponding symbols for these welds and additional basic weld symbols for surfacing, groove, and flange joints are given in Figure 22.4. See Section 22.12 for the use of the square groove weld symbol for the flash or upset resistance weld. Supplementary symbols are shown in Figure 22.5. Depending on your field and the particular project, you may need only to use a simple symbol composed of the minimum elements (the arrow and the weld symbol) or you may need to use the additional components.

Table 22.1 Basic Types of Welded Joints.

Type of Joint	Example
Butt joint	
Corner joint	
T-joint	
Lap joint	
Edge joint	

Spot or projection	Seam	Surfacing	Groove		Edge	Scarf
			Flare	Flare bevel		
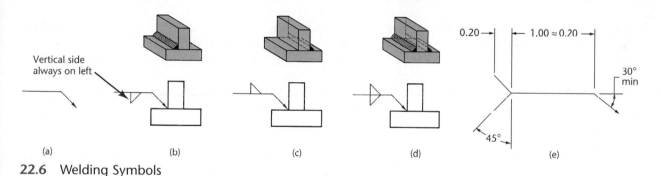						

22.4 Additional Basic Weld Symbols

Weld all around	Field weld	Melt-thru	Consumable insert (square)	Backing or spacer matl	Contour		
					Flush	Convex	Concave

22.5 Supplementary Symbols

22.6 Welding Symbols

22.3 WELDING SYMBOLS

The basic element of the symbol is the "bent" arrow, as shown in Figure 22.6a. The arrow points to the joint where the weld is to be made (Figure 22.6b). Attached to the reference line, or shank, of the arrow is the weld symbol for the desired weld. The symbol would be one of those illustrated in Figures 22.3 and 22.4. In this case, a fillet weld symbol has been used.

The weld symbol is placed below the reference line if the weld is to be on the **arrow side** of the joint, as in Figure 22.6b, or above the reference line if the weld is to be on the **other side** of the joint, as in Figure 22.6c. If the weld is to be on both the arrow side and the other side of the joint, weld symbols are placed on both sides of the reference line (Figure 22.6d). This rule for placement of the weld symbol is followed for all arc or gas weld symbols. Dimensions for creating a weld symbol are shown in Figure 22.6e.

When a joint is represented by a single line on a drawing, as in the top and side views of Figure 22.7b, the arrow side of the joint is regarded as the "near" side to the reader of the drawing, according to the usual conventions of technical drawing.

For the plug, slot, seam, and projection welding symbols, the arrow points to the outer surface of one of the members at

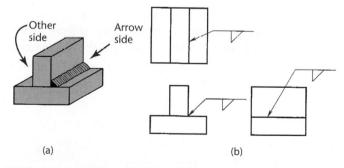

(a) (b)

22.7 Arrow Side and Other Side

the centerline of the weld. In such cases, the arrow side of the joint is the one to which the arrow points, or the "near" side to the reader (see Sections 22.8 and 22.12).

Note that for all fillet or groove symbols, the vertical side of the symbol is always drawn on the left as shown in Figure 22.6b.

For best results, welding symbols should be drawn using CAD or a template, but in certain cases where necessary, they may be drawn freehand.

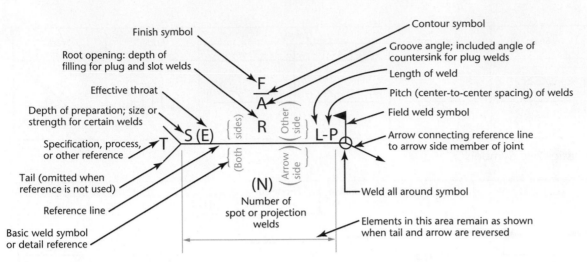

22.8 The Standard Locations of the Elements of the Welding Symbol

The complete welding symbol, enlarged, is shown in Figure 22.8. See Appendix {{32}} for additional welding symbol details.

Reference to a specification, process, or other supplementary information is indicated by any desired symbol in the tail of the arrow (Figure 22.9a). Otherwise, a general note may be placed on the drawing, such as

UNLESS OTHERWISE INDICATED, MAKE ALL WELDS PER SPECIFICATION NO. XXX

If no reference is indicated in the symbol, the tail may be omitted.

To avoid repeating the same information on many welding symbols on a drawing, general notes may be used, such as

FILLET WELDS UNLESS OTHERWISE INDICATED

or

ROOT OPENINGS FOR ALL GROOVE WELDS UNLESS OTHERWISE INDICATED

Welds extending completely around a joint are indicated by an open circle around the elbow of the arrow (Figure 22.9b). When the weld all around symbol is not used, the welding symbol is understood to apply between abrupt changes in direction of the weld, unless otherwise shown. A short vertical staff with a solid triangular flag at the elbow of the arrow indicates a weld to be made "in the field" (on the site) rather than in the fabrication shop (Figure 22.9c).

Spot, seam, flash, or upset symbols usually do not have arrow-side or other-side significance and are simply centered on the reference line of the arrow (Figure 22.10a through c). Spot and seam symbols are shown on the drawing as indicated in Figure 22.10d and e. Note that the required process must be specified in the tail of the symbol (RSW = resistance spot weld, EBW = electron beam weld).

For bevel or J-groove welds, the arrow should point with a definite change of direction, or break, toward the member that is to be beveled or grooved (Figure 22.11a and b). In this case, the upper member is grooved. The break is omitted if the location of the bevel or groove is obvious.

Lettering for the symbols should be placed to read from the bottom or from the right side of the drawing in accordance with the aligned system (Figure 22.11c through e). Dimensions may be indicated on a drawing in the fractional, decimal inch, or metric system.

When a joint has more than one weld, the combined symbols are used (Figure 22.11f through h).

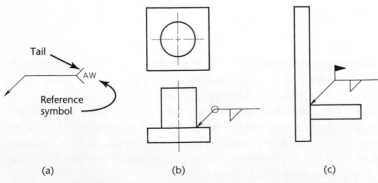

(a)   (b)   (c)

22.9 The Standard Locations of the Elements of the Welding Symbol

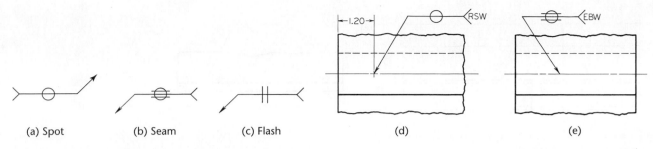

22.10 Spot, Seam, and Flash Welding Symbols

(a) Spot (b) Seam (c) Flash (d) (e)

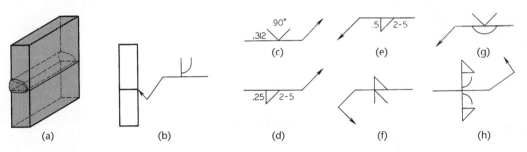

22.11 Welding Symbols

(a) (b) (c) (d) (e) (f) (g) (h)

22.4 FILLET WELDS

The usual fillet weld has equal legs (Figure 22.12a). The size of the weld is the length of one leg, as indicated in Figure 22.12b by a dimension figure (fraction, decimal inch, or metric) at the left of the weld symbol. For fillet welds on both sides of a joint, the dimensions may be indicated on one side or both sides of the reference line (Figure 22.12c). The lengths of the welds and the pitch (center to center spacing of welds) are indicated as shown. When the welds on opposite sides are different in size, the sizes are given as shown in Figure 22.12d. If a fillet weld has unequal legs, the weld orientation is shown on the drawing, if necessary,

and the lengths of the legs are given in parentheses to the left of the weld symbol, as in Figure 22.12e. If a general note is given on the drawing, such as

ALL FILLET WELDS UNLESS OTHERWISE NOTED

the size dimensions are omitted from the symbols.

No length dimension is needed for a weld that extends the full distance between abrupt changes of direction. For each abrupt change in direction, an additional arrow is added to the symbol, except when the weld all around symbol is used.

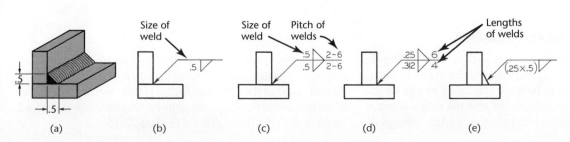

22.12 Dimensioning of Fillet Welds

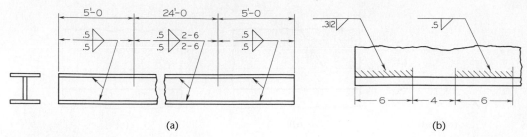

22.13 Lengths of Fillet Welds

Fillet Weld Length

Lengths of fillet welds may be indicated by symbols in conjunction with dimension lines (Figure 22.13a). The extent of fillet welding may be shown graphically with section lining if desired (Figure 22.13b).

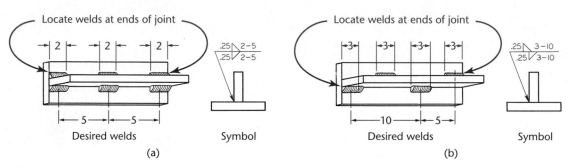

22.14 Intermittent Welds

Intermittent Fillet Welding

Chain intermittent fillet welding is indicated as shown in Figure 22.14a. If the welds are staggered, the weld symbols are staggered (Figure 22.14b).

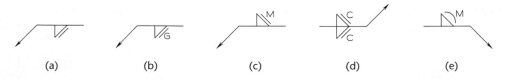

22.15 Surface Contour of Fillet Welds

Surface Contour and Fillet Welds

Unfinished flat-faced fillet welds are indicated by adding the **flush** symbol (see Figure 22.5), to the weld symbol (Figure 22.15a). If fillet welds are to be made flat-faced by mechanical means, add the flush-contour symbol and the user's standard finish symbol to the weld symbol (Figure 22.15b through d).

These finish symbols indicate the method of finishing (C = chipping, G = grinding, M = machining, R = rolling, H = hammering) and not the degree of finish. If fillet welds are to be finished to a **convex** contour, the convex contour symbol is added, together with the finish symbol (Figure 22.15e).

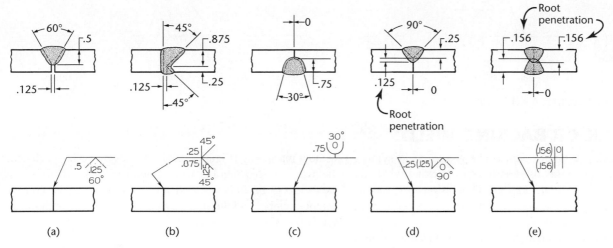

22.16 Groove Welds

22.5 GROOVE WELDS

In Figure 22.16, various groove welds are shown above and the corresponding symbolic representations below. The sizes of the groove welds (depth of the V, bevel, U, or J) are indicated on the left of the weld symbol. For example, in Figure 22.16a, the size of the V-weld is .50″, in Figure 22.16b the sizes are .25″ and .875″, in Figure 22.16c the size is .75″, and in Figure 25.16d the size is .25″. For the symbol in Figure 22.16d the size is followed by .125″, which is the additional "root penetration" of the weld. In Figure 22.16e, the root penetration is .156″ from zero, or from the outside of the members. Note the overlap of the root penetration in this case.

The root opening or space between members, when not covered by a company standard, is shown within the weld symbol. In Figure 22.16a and b, the root openings are .125″. In Figure 22.16c through e, the openings are zero.

The groove angles, when not covered by a company standard, appear just outside the openings of the weld symbols (Figure 22.16a and b).

A general note may be used on the drawing to avoid repeating the symbols, such as

ALL V-GROOVE WELDS TO HAVE 60° GROOVE ANGLE
UNLESS OTHERWISE SHOWN

However, when the dimensions of one or both of two opposite welds differ from the general note, both welds should be completely dimensioned.

When single-groove or symmetrical double-groove welds extend completely through, the size need not be added to the welding symbol. For example, in Figure 22.16a, if the V-groove extended entirely through the joint, the depth or size would be simply the thickness of the stock and would not need to be indicated in the welding symbol.

Surface Contour of Groove Welds

When groove welds are to be approximately flush without finishing, add the flush contour symbol (see Figure 22.5) to the weld symbols (Figs. 22.17a and b). If the welds are to be machined, add the flush contour symbol and the user's standard finish symbol to the weld symbol (Figure 22.17c and d). These finish symbols indicate the method of finishing (*C* = chipping, *G* = grinding, *M* = machining) and not the degree of finish. If a groove weld is to be finished with a convex contour, add the convex contour and finish symbols, as in Figure 22.17e.

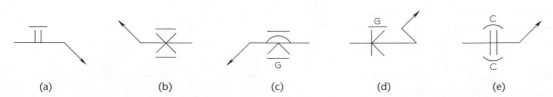

22.17 Surface Contour of Groove Welds

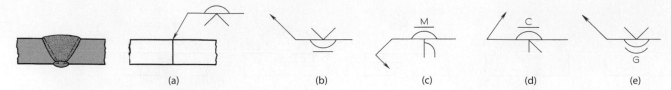

22.18   Back or Backing Weld Symbols

22.6 BACK OR BACKING WELDS

A back or backing symbol opposite the groove weld symbol indicates bead type welds used as back or backing welds on single groove welds (Figure 22.18a). Dimensions for back or backing welds are not shown on the symbol, but may be shown, if necessary, directly on the drawing.

A flush contour symbol included in the weld symbols indicates that the back or backing welds are to be approximately flush without machining (Figure 22.18b). If they are to be machined, the user's finish symbol is added (Figures 22.18c and d). If the welds are to be finished with a convex contour, the convex contour symbol and the finish symbol are included in the weld symbol, as shown in Figure 22.18e.

22.7 SURFACE WELDS

The surface weld symbol indicates a surface to be built up with single- or multiple-pass bead type welds (Figure 22.19). Since this symbol does not indicate a welded joint, there is no arrow-side or other-side significance, so the symbol is always drawn below the reference line. Indicate the minimum height of the weld deposit at the left of the weld symbol, except where no specific height is required. When a specific area of a surface is to be built up, give the dimensions of the area on the drawing.

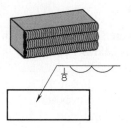

22.19   Surface Weld Symbol

22.8 PLUG AND SLOT WELDS

The same symbol is used for plug welds and slot welds. Figure 22.20a and d show the hole or slot that is made to receive the weld. If it is in the arrow-side member, place the weld symbol below the reference line as shown Figure 22.20b and c. If it is in the other-side member, place the weld symbol above the line as shown in Figure 22.20e and f.

Place the size of a plug weld (which is the smallest diameter of the hole, if countersunk) at the left of the weld symbol. If the included angle for the countersink of a plug welds is in accordance with the user's standard, omit it; otherwise, place it adjacent to the weld symbol as shown in Figure 22.20b and c.

A plug weld is understood to fill the depth of the hole unless its depth is indicated inside the weld symbol as shown in Figure 22.21a. The pitch of plug welds is shown at the right of the weld symbol (Figure 22.21b). If the weld is to be approximately flush without finishing, add the flush contour symbol as in Figure 22.21c. If the weld is to be made flush by mechanical means, a finish symbol is added (Figure 22.21d). Flush contour and finish symbols are used the same way for slot welds and for plug welds.

Indicate the depth of filling for slot welds the same way as for plug welds (Figure 22.21a). The size and location dimensions of slot welds cannot be shown on the welding symbol. Show them directly on the drawing (Figure 22.20f) or in a detail with a reference to it on the welding symbol as shown in Figure 22.21e.

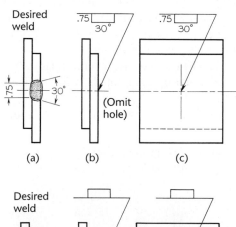

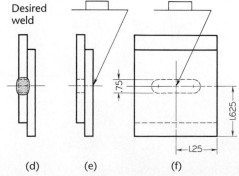

22.20   Plug and Slot Welds

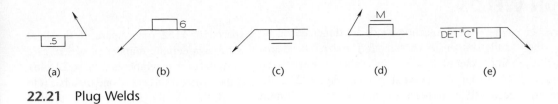

22.21 Plug Welds

22.9 SPOT WELDS

The spot weld symbol, with the required welding process indicated in the tail, may or may not have arrow-side or other-side significance. Show dimensions on the same side of the reference line as the symbol, or on either side when the symbol is centered on the reference line and no arrow-side or other-side significance is intended.

The size of a spot weld is its diameter. Show this value at the left of the weld symbol on either side of the reference line (Figure 22.22a). If you need to indicate the minimum acceptable shear strength in pounds per spot, instead of the size of the

weld, place this value at the left of the weld symbol, and indicate pitch at the right of the weld symbol as shown in Figure 22.22b. In this case the spot welds are 3″ apart.

If a joint requires a certain number of spot welds, give the number in parentheses above or below the symbol, as in Figure 22.22c. If the exposed surface of one member is to be flush, add the flush contour symbol above the symbol if it is the other-side member, and below it if it is the arrow-side member, as in Figure 22.22d. Figure 22.22e shows the welding symbol used in conjunction with ordinary dimensions.

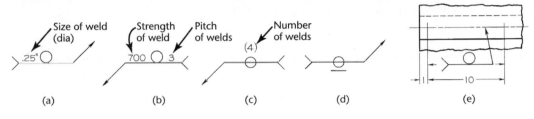

22.22 Spot Welds

22.10 SEAM WELDS

The seam weld symbol, with the welding process indicated in the tail, may or may not have arrow-side or other-side significance. Dimensions are shown on the same side of the reference line as the symbol, or on either side when the symbol is centered on the reference line and no arrow-side or other-side significance is intended.

The size of the seam weld is its width. Show this value at the left of the weld symbol, on either side of the reference line (Figure 22.23a). If you need to indicate the minimum acceptable shear strength in pounds per linear inch, instead of the size of the weld, place this value at the left of the weld symbol, and show the length of a seam weld at the right of the weld symbol

as in Figure 22.23b. In this case, the seam weld is 5″ long. If the weld extends the full distance between abrupt changes of direction, no length dimension in the symbol is given.

The pitch of intermittent seam welding is the distance between centers of lengths of welding. Show the pitch at the right of the length figure (Figure 22.23c). In this case, the welds are 2″ long and spaced 4″ center to center.

When the exposed surface of one member is to be flush, add the flush-contour symbol above the symbol if it is the other-side member and below it if it is the arrow-side member (Figure 22.23d). Figure 22.23e shows the welding symbol used in conjunction with ordinary dimensions.

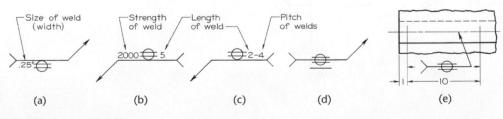

22.23 Seam Welds

22.11 PROJECTION WELDS

In projection welding, one member is embossed in preparation for the weld (Figure 22.24a). When welded, the joint appears in section, as in Figure 22.24b. The weld symbols, in this case, are placed below the reference lines (Figure 22.24c) to indicate that the arrow-side member is the one that is embossed. The weld symbols would be placed above the lines if the other member were embossed.

Projection welds are dimensioned by either size or strength. The size is the diameter of the weld. This value is shown to the left of the weld symbol (Figure 22.24d). If you need to indicate the minimum acceptable shear strength in pounds per weld, place the value at the left of the weld symbol (Figure 22.24e). Indicate the pitch at the right of the weld symbol (Figure 22.24e). In this case, the welds are

spaced 6″ (152 mm) apart. If the joint requires a definite number of welds, give the number in parentheses (Figure 22.24e). If the exposed surface of one member is to be flush, add the flush contour symbol (Figure 22.24f). Figure 22.24g shows the welding symbol used in conjunction with ordinary dimensions. The welding process reference is required in the tail of the symbol.

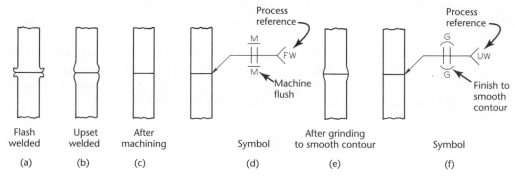

22.24 Projection Welds

22.12 FLASH AND UPSET WELDS

Flash and upset weld symbols have no arrow-side or other-side significance, but the supplementary symbols do. A flash-welded joint is shown in Figure 22.25a, and an upset welded joint in Figure 22.25b. The joint after machining flush is shown in Figure 22.25c. The complete symbol (Figure 22.25d) includes the weld symbol together with the flush contour and machining symbols.

If the joint is ground to smooth contours (Figure 22.25e), the resulting welding drawing and symbol would be constructed as in Figure 22.25f, which includes convex-contour and grind symbols. In either Figure 22.25d or 22.25f, the joint may be finished on only one side, if desired, by indicating the contour and machining symbols on the appropriate side of the reference

line. The dimensions of flash and upset welds are not shown on the welding symbol. Note that the process reference for flash welding (FW) or upset welding (UW) must be placed in the tail of the symbol.

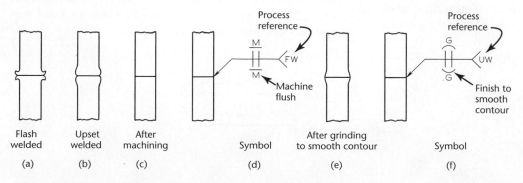

22.25 Flash and Upset Welds

22.13 WELDING APPLICATIONS

A typical example of welding fabrication for machine parts is shown in Figure 22.26. In many cases, especially when only one or a few identical parts are required, it is cheaper to produce by welding than to make patterns and sand castings and do the necessary machining. Thus, welding is particularly adaptable to custom-built constructions.

Welding is also suitable for large structures that are difficult or impossible to fabricate entirely in the shop, and it is coming into greater use for steel structures, such as building frames, bridges, and ships. A welded beam is shown in Figure 19.18, and a welded assembly of diagonal bracing between two columns is shown in Figure 19.19. A welded truss is shown in Figure 22.27. It is easier to place members in such a welded truss so that their center of gravity axes coincide with the working lines of the truss than is the case in a riveted truss. Compare this welded truss with the riveted truss in Figure 19.15.

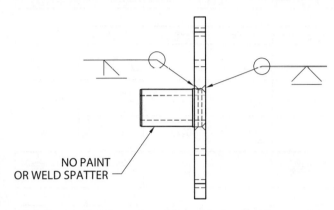

22.26   Application of welding fabrication for machine parts
Courtesy of Dynojet Research, Inc.

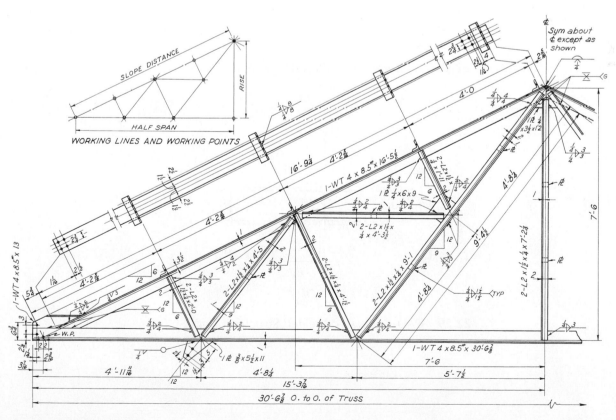

22.27   A Welded Truss

22.14 WELDING TEMPLATES

Welding templates can simplify drawing welding symbols by hand (which may be done in pencil or ink). They have all the forms needed for drawing the arrow, weld symbols, and supplementary symbols, as well as an illustration of the complete composite welding symbol for quick reference.

22.15 COMPUTER GRAPHICS

Welding symbols libraries available in CAD (Figure 22.28) allow for rapid application of accurate, uniform symbols that are in compliance with AWS standards (Figure 22.29). In addition to standard symbols, many CAD programs permit the operator to create custom symbols as required.

BASIC WELDING SYMBOLS AND THEIR LOCATION SIGNIFICANCE						
LOCATION SIGNIFICANCE	FLANGE CORNER	SQUARE	GROOVE V	BEVEL	U	J
ARROW SIDE						
OTHER SIDE						
BOTH SIDES	NOT USED					
NO ARROW SIDE OR OTHER SIDE SIGNIFICANCE	NOT USED		NOT USED	NOT USED	NOT USED	NOT USED

LOCATION SIGNIFICANCE	GROOVE FLARE-V	FLARE-BEVEL	FILLET	PLUG OR SLOT	SPOT OR PROJECTION	SEAM
ARROW SIDE						
OTHER SIDE						
BOTH SIDES				NOT USED	NOT USED	NOT USED
NO ARROW SIDE OR OTHER SIDE SIGNIFICANCE	NOT USED	NOT USED	NOT USED	NOT USED		

LOCATION SIGNIFICANCE	BACK OR BACKING	SURFACING	SCARF FOR BRAZED JOINT	FLANGE EDGE	SUPPLEMENTARY SYMBOLS	
ARROW SIDE	GROOVE WELD SYMBOL				ALL AROUND	ALL AROUND
OTHER SIDE	GROOVE WELD SYMBOL	NOT USED			FIELD	FIELD
BOTH SIDES	NOT USED	NOT USED		NOT USED	TAIL	
NO ARROW SIDE OR OTHER SIDE SIGNIFICANCE	NOT USED	NOT USED	NOT USED	NOT USED	TEXT 2-5 / 2-5	

22.28 Computervision Production Drafting

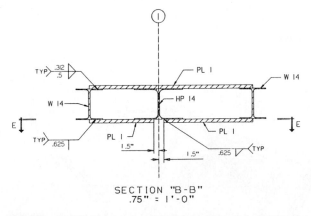

SECTION "B-B"
.75" = 1'-0"

22.29 CAD-Generated Welded Structural Detail

WELD SYMBOLS FROM CAD

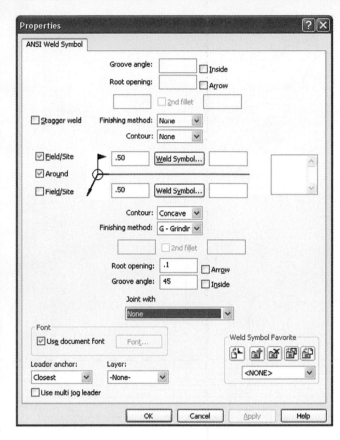

(A) SolidWorks Weld Symbol Dialog Box

Most CAD systems provide a way to quickly generate weld symbols to place in your drawing. The Solidworks dialog box shown in Figure A allows you to select the symbol for type and size of weld, field placement, whether to add the all around symbol, special indications for contour and finish method. Once you have made you selections, the weld symbol as shown in Figure B is automatically generated based on your selections and you have only to click to place it in your drawing.

Specialized software like Design Data's SDS/2 allows you to design and model connections between members based on parameters that you define for each job. You can designate the material, edge distance, cope criteria and other connection specifications, and SDS/2 will automatically generate connections. You can model all of the details using the software's 3D modeler for example the fillet welds shown in figure C. 2D drawings can be taken directly from the model, providing an accurate fit in the field.

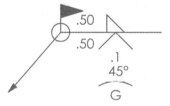

(B) Automatically Generated Weld Symbol

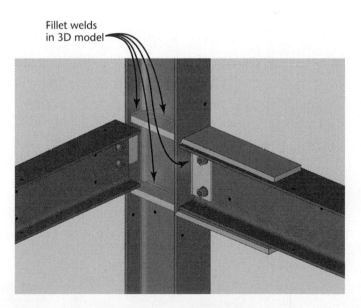

(C) Fillet welds in a 3D model. *Courtesy of Paul Hergett, Midwest Steel Industries.*

PORTFOLIO

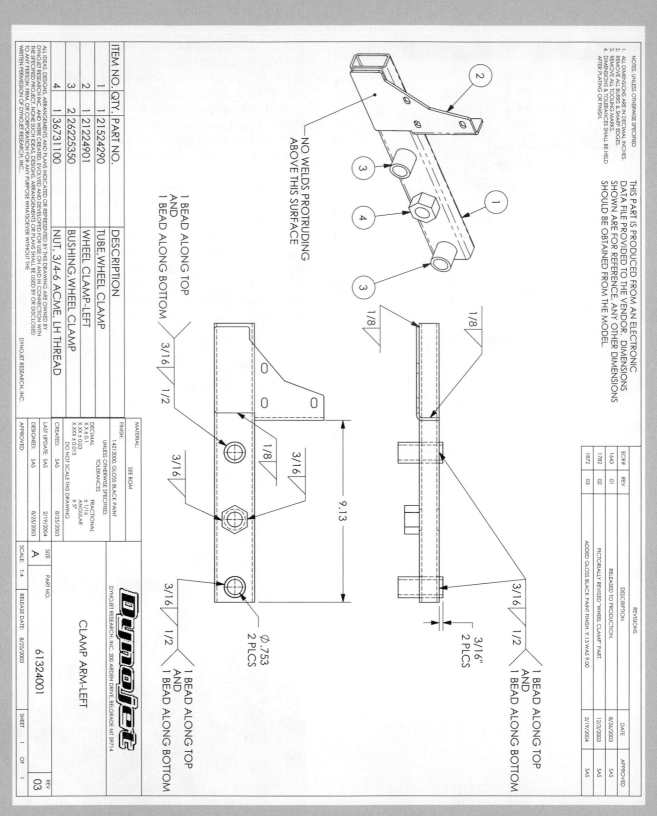

Welding symbols specify the welds for attaching the tubes, bushing, nut, and plate for the clamp arm.
Courtesy of Dynojet Research, Inc.

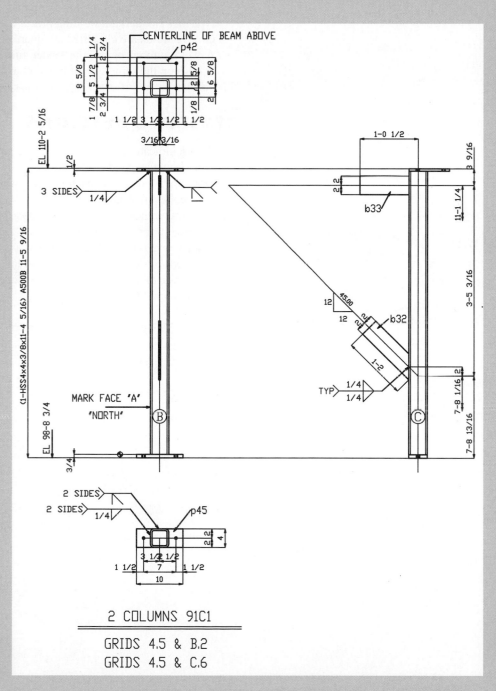

Welding symbols specify how plates attach to structural beam in this drawing created from a 3D model using SOSZ software. *Courtesy of Paul Hergett, Midwest Steel Industries.*

KEY WORDS

Gas Welding

Arc Welding

Resistance Welding

GMAW

MIG

MAG

GTAW

TIG

Welding Drawings

Pitch

Butt Joint

Corner Joint

T-Joint

Lap Joint

Edge Joint

Back or Backing Weld

Fillet Weld

Plug or Slot Weld

Groove Weld

Spot Weld

Projection Weld

Seam Weld

Flash or Upset Weld

Arrow Side

Other Side

Flush

CHAPTER SUMMARY

- The four basic types of arc and gas welds are back, fillet, plug, and groove.
- The four basic types of resistance welds are spot, projection, seam, and flash.
- The welding symbol defines the location of the weld, the type of weld, and the welding process.
- Groove welds are classified as square, V, bevel, U, and J.
- A weld symbol below the leader line indicates that the weld is on the same side of the joint as the leader arrow.

REVIEW QUESTIONS

1. Which indicates the weld is on the opposite side, the weld type shown above the line, or below the line?
2. Draw the shapes for the following weld symbols: fillet, square, bevel, V, U, J.
3. List five names describing the ways the material can be oriented in forming a joint.
4. List the five types of groove welds.
5. Draw a typical welding symbol and label its parts.
6. What type of weld would join two pieces at 90°?
7. What is a field weld?

EXERCISES

Welding Drawing Exercises

The following problems are given to familiarize the student with some applications of welding symbols to machine construction and to steel structures.

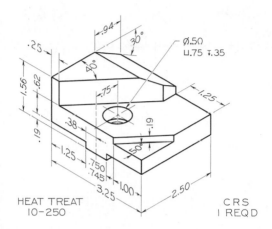

HEAT TREAT
10-250

CRS
I REQD

Exercise 22.1 Change to a welded part. Make working drawing, using appropriate welding symbols.

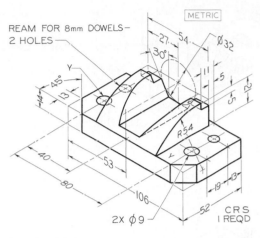

Exercise 22.3 Same instructions as for Exercise 22.1.

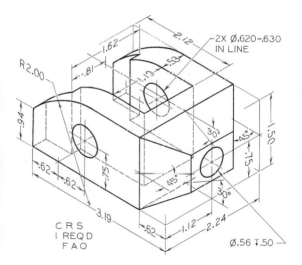

CRS
I REQD
FAO

Exercise 22.2 Same instructions as for Exercise 22.1.

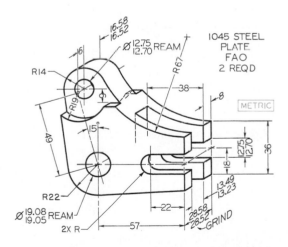

1045 STEEL
PLATE
FAO
2 REQD

Exercise 22.4 Same instructions as for Exercise 22.1.

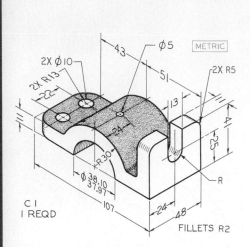

Exercise 22.5 Same instructions as for Exercise 22.1.

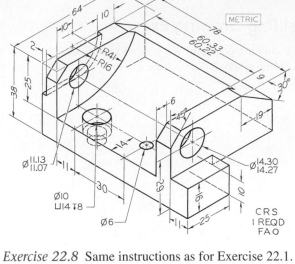

Exercise 22.8 Same instructions as for Exercise 22.1.

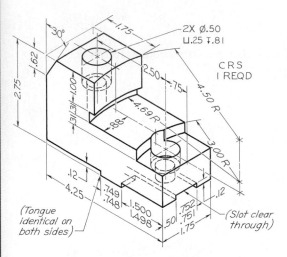

Exercise 22.6 Same instructions as for Exercise 22.1.

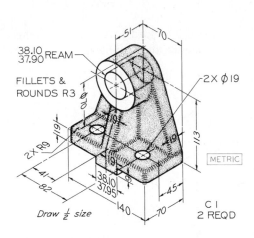

Exercise 22.9 Same instructions as for Exercise 22.1.

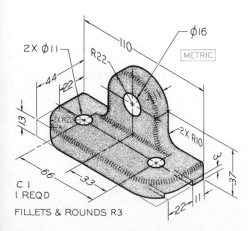

Exercise 22.7 Same instructions as for Exercise 22.1.

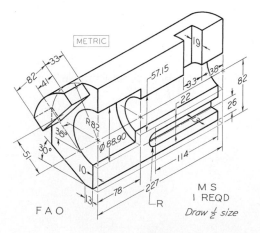

Exercise 22.10 Same instructions as for Exercise 22.1.

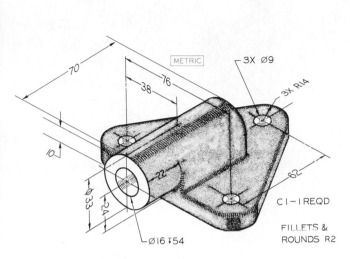

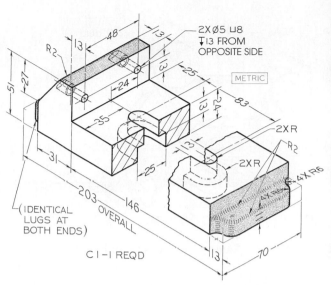

Exercise 22.11 Same instructions as for Exercise 22.1.

Exercise 22.14 Same instructions as for Exercise 22.1.

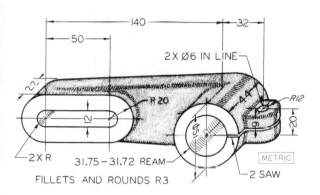

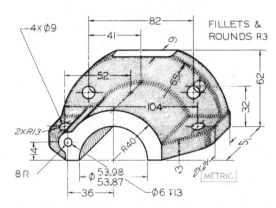

Exercise 22.12 Same instructions as for Exercise 22.1.

Exercise 22.15 Same instructions as for Exercise 22.1.

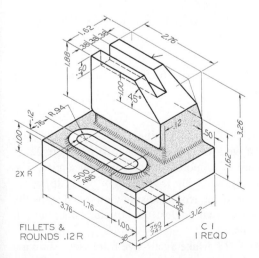

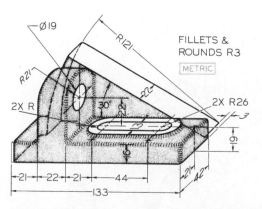

Exercise 22.13 Same instructions as for Exercise 22.1.

Exercise 22.16 Same instructions as for Exercise 22.1.

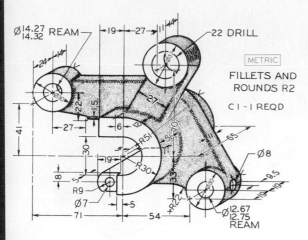

Exercise 22.17 Same instructions as for Exercise 22.1.

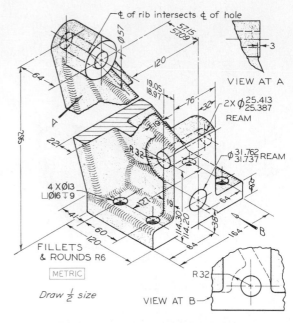

Exercise 22.20 Same instructions as for Exercise 22.1.

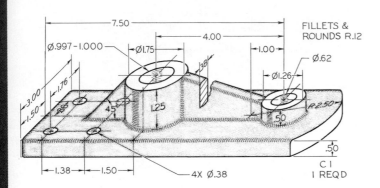

Exercise 22.18 Same instructions as for Exercise 22.1.

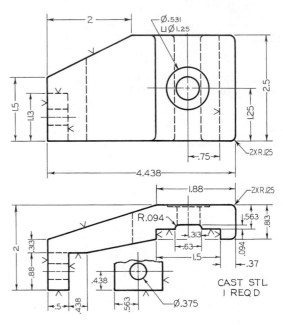

Exercise 22.21 Figure 6.116. Same instructions as for Exercise 22.1.

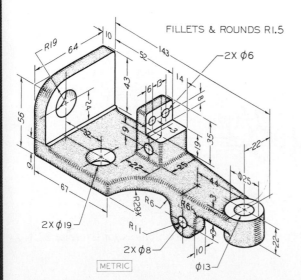

Exercise 22.19 Same instructions as for Exercise 22.1.

Exercise 22.22 Make a half-size drawing of the joint at the center of the lower chord of the truss in Figure 22.27 where the chord is supported by two vertical angles. The chord is a structural tee, cut from an, $8 \times 5\frac{1}{4}$, 17 lb, wide-flange shape. Draw the front and side views, and show the working lines, the two angles, the structural tee, and all welding symbols.

Exercise 22.23 Make a half-size front view, showing the welding symbols, of any joint of the truss in Figure 22.27 in which three or four members meet.

Exercise 22.24 Draw half-size front, top, and left-side views of the end joint of the truss in Figure 22.27 showing the welding symbols.

APPENDICES

CONTENTS

1 LIST OF STANDARDS ORGANIZATIONS

American National Standards Institute, 11 West 42nd St., New York, NY. 10036. For complete listing of standards, see ANSI catalog of American National Standards. http://webstore.ansi.org

Standards from the following developers are availabe at http:webstore.ansi.org/sdo.aspx.

AAMI	Association for the Advancement of Medical Instrumentation
ABYC	American Boat & Yacht Council
ABMA	American Bearing Manufacturers Association
ABNT	Brazilian Technical Standards Association
ACC	American Chemistry Council
ACHC	Accreditation Commission for Health Care
ADA	American Dental Association
AGA	American Gas Association
AGMA	American Gear Manufacturers Association
AIAA	American Institute of Aeronautics and Astronautics
AIAG	Automotive Industry Action Group
AIHA	American Industrial Hygiene Association
AIIM	Association for Information and Image Management
AHAM	Association of Home Appliance Manufacturers
AMT	The Association for Manufacturing Technology
APTA	American Public Transportation Association
ARI	Air-Conditioning and Refrigeration Institute
ARMA	Association for Information Management Professionals
APSP	Association of Pool and Spa Professionals
ASA	Acoustical Society of America
ASABE	American Society of Agricultural and Biological Engineers
ASHRAE	American Society of Heating, Refrigerating and Air-Conditioning Engineers, Inc.
ASME	American Society of Mechanical Engineers
ASQ	American Society of Quality
ASSE	The American Society of Safety Engineers
ASTM	ASTM International
ATIS	Alliance for Telecommunications Industry Solutions
AWS	American Welding Society
BHMA	Builders Hardware Manufacturers Association
CAM-I	Consortium for Advanced Manufacturing - International
CITRA	Center for International Regulatory Assistance
CGA	Compressed Gas Association, Inc

CLSI	Clinical and Laboratory Standards Institute
CSA	Canadian Standards Association
DIN	DIN Deutsches Institutü for Normung
DMIA	Document Management Industries Association
DOD	U.S. Department of Defense
ESTA	Entertainment Services and Technology Association
ETSI	European Telecommunications Standards Institute
GISC	Glazing Industry Secretariat Committee
GEIA	Government Electronics & Information Technology Association
GTEEMC	Georgia Tech Energy and Environmental Management Center
HL7	Health Level Seven
IAPMO	International Association of Plumbing and Mechanical Officials
IESNA	Illuminating Engineering Society of North America
I3A	International Imaging Industry Association
ICBO	International Conference of Building Officials
ICC	International Code Council
IEC	International Electrotechnical Commission
IEEE	Institute of Electrical and Electronics Engineers
IESO	Indoor Environmental Standards Organization
IFI	Industrial Fasteners Institute
IICRC	Institute of Inspection, Cleaning and Restoration Certification
INCITS	International Committee for Information Technology
IPC	Association Connecting Electronics Industries
ISA	Instrument Society of America
ISO	International Organization for Standardization
JIS	Japanese Industrial Standards
KOK	Metric eBooks
LIA	Laser Institute of America
MSS	Manufacturers Standardization Society of the Value & Fittings Industry, Inc.
MTS	Institute for Market Transformation to Sustainability
NACE	National Association of Corrosion Engineers
NAESB	North American Energy Standards Board
NADCA	North American Die Casting Association
NASPO	North American Security Products Organization
NECA	National Electrical Contractors Association

NETA	InterNational Electrical Testing Association
NFPA	National Fire Protection Association
NFPA	National Fluid Power Association
NISO	National Information Standards Organization
NPES	National Printing Equipment and Supply Association, Inc.
NPPC	National Pork Producers Council
NSF	NSF International
OEOSC	Committee for Optics and Electro-Optical Instruments
OLA	Optical Laboratories Association
ON	Austrian Standards Institute
OPEI	Outdoor Power Equipment Institute
PCC	ANSI Partially Controlled Collections
QUEST	Quest Forum: Quality Excellence for Suppliers of Telecommunicatons
SAI	Standards Australia
SCTE	The Society of Cable Telecommunications Engineers
SEMI	Semiconductor Equipment and Materials International
SES	Standards Engineering Society
SIA	Scaffold Industry Association
SIA	Security Industry Association
SIS	Swedish Standards Institute
SPC	Chinese Standards
TAPPI	Technical Association for the Pulp, Paper, and converting Industry
TCA	Tile Council of North America
WMMA	Wood Machinery Manufacturers Association
WPC	Washington Publishing Company
X9	X9, Inc.

2 TECHNICAL TERMS

"The beginning of wisdom is to call things by their right names."

—CHINESE PROVERB

n *means* a noun; v *means* a verb

acme (n) Screw thread form.

addendum (n) Radial distance from pitch circle to top of gear tooth.

allen screw (n) Special set screw or cap screw with hexagon socket in head.

allowance (n) Minimum clearance between mating parts.

alloy (n) Two or more metals in combination, usually a fine metal with a baser metal.

aluminum (n) A lightweight but relatively strong metal. Often alloyed with copper to increase hardness and strength.

anneal (v) To heat and cool gradually, to reduce brittleness and increase ductility.

arc weld (v) To weld by electric arc. The work is usually the positive terminal.

babbitt (n) A soft alloy for bearings, mostly of tin with small amounts of copper and antimony.

bearing (n) A supporting member for a rotating shaft.

bevel (n) An inclined edge, not at a right angle to the joining surface.

bolt circle (n) A circular centerline on a drawing, containing the centers of holes about a common center.

bore (v) To enlarge a hole with a boring mill.

boss (n) A cylindrical projection on a casting or a forging.

brass (n) An alloy of copper and zinc.

braze (v) To join with a hard solder of brass or zinc.

Brinell (n) A method of testing hardness of metal.

broach (n) A long cutting tool with a series of teeth that gradually increase in size which is forced through a hole or over a surface to produce a desired shape.

bronze (n) An alloy of eight or nine parts copper and one part tin.

buff (v) To finish or polish on a buffing wheel composed of fabric with abrasive powders.

burnish (v) To finish or polish by pressure upon a smooth rolling or sliding tool.

burr (n) A jagged edge on metal resulting from punching or cutting.

bushing (n) A replaceable lining or sleeve for a bearing.

calipers (n) Instrument (of several types) for measuring diameters.

cam (n) A rotating member for changing circular motion to reciprocating motion.

carburize (v) To heat a low-carbon steel to approximately 2000°F in contact with material that adds carbon to the surface of the steel, and to cool slowly in preparation for heat treatment.

case harden (v) To harden the outer surface of a carburized steel by heating and then quenching.

castellate (v) To form like a castle, as a castellated shaft or nut.

casting (n) A metal object produced by pouring molten metal into a mold.

BOSS

cast iron (n)   Iron melted and poured into molds.

center drill (n)   A special drill to produce bearing holes in the ends of a workpiece to be mounted between centers. Also called a "combined drill and countersink."

COMBINED DRILL
& C SINK

chamfer (n)   A narrow inclined surface along the intersection of two surfaces.

CHAMFER

chase (v)   To cut threads with an external cutting tool.

chill (v)   To harden the outer surface of cast iron by quick cooling, as in a metal mold.

chip (v)   To cut away metal with a cold chisel.

chuck (n)   A mechanism for holding a rotating tool or workpiece.

coin (v)   To form a part in one stamping operation.

cold rolled steel (CRS) (n)   Open hearth or Bessemer steel containing 0.12–0.20% carbon that has been rolled while cold to produce a smooth, quite accurate stock.

collar (n)   A round flange or ring fitted on a shaft to prevent sliding.

COLLAR

color harden (v)   Same as *case harden,* except that it is done to a shallower depth, usually for appearance only.

cotter pin (n)   A split pin used as a fastener, usually to prevent a nut from unscrewing.

counterbore (v)   To enlarge an end of a hole cylindrically with a *counterbore.*

COUNTERBORE

countersink (v)   To enlarge an end of a hole conically, usually with a *countersink.*

COUNTERSINK

crown (n)   A raised contour, as on the surface of a pulley.

cyanide (v)   To surface-harden steel by heating in contact with a cyanide salt, followed by quenching.

dedendum (n)   Distance from the pitch circle to the bottom of the tooth space.

development (n)   Drawing of the surface of an object unfolded or rolled out on a plane.

diametral pitch (n)   Number of gear teeth per inch of pitch diameter.

die (n)   (1) Hardened metal piece shaped to cut or form a required shape in a sheet of metal by pressing it against a mating die, (2) Also used for cutting small male threads. In a sense, a die is the opposite of a tap.

die casting (n)   Process of forcing molten metal under pressure into metal dies or molds, producing a very accurate and smooth casting.

die stamping (n)   Process of cutting or forming a piece of sheet metal with a die.

dog (n)   A small auxiliary clamp for preventing work from rotating in relation to the face plate of a lathe.

dowel (n)   A cylindrical pin, commonly used to prevent sliding between two contacting flat surfaces.

DOWEL

draft (n)   The tapered shape of the parts of a pattern to permit it to be easily withdrawn from the sand or, on a forging, to permit it to be easily withdrawn from the dies.

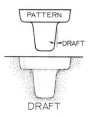

PATTERN

DRAFT

DRAFT

draw (v)   To stretch or otherwise to deform metal. Also to temper steel.

drill (v)   To cut a cylindrical hole with a drill. A *blind hole* does not go through the piece.

drill press (n)   A machine for drilling and other hole forming operations.

drop forge (v)   To form a piece while hot between dies in a drop hammer or with great pressure.

face (v)   To finish a surface at right angles, or nearly so, to the centerline of rotation on a lathe.

(FAO) (v)   An instruction on a drawing to employ the desired surface finish on all surfaces.

feather (key) (n)   A flat key, which is partly sunk in a shaft and partly in a hub, permitting the hub to slide lengthwise of the shaft.

file (v)   To finish or smooth with a file.

fillet (n)   An interior rounded intersection between two surfaces.

fin (n)   A thin extrusion of metal at the intersection of dies or sand molds.

fit (n)   Degree of tightness or looseness between two mating parts, as a *loose fit,* a *snug fit,* or a *tight fit.*

fixture (n)   A special device for holding the work in a machine tool, but not for guiding the cutting tool. Compare to *jig.*

flange (n)   A relatively thin rim around a piece.

flash (n)   Same as *fin*.

flask (n)   A box made of two or more parts for holding the sand in sand molding.

flute (n)   Groove, as on twist drills, reamers, and taps.

forge (v)   To force metal while it is hot to take on a desired shape by hammering or pressing.

galvanize (v)   To cover a surface with a thin layer of molten alloy, composed mainly of zinc, to prevent rusting.

gasket (n)   A thin piece of rubber, metal, or some other material, placed between surfaces to make a tight joint.

gate (n)   The opening in a sand mold at the bottom of the *sprue* through which the molten metal passes to enter the cavity or mold.

graduate (v)   To set off accurate divisions on a scale or dial.

grind (v)   To remove metal by means of an abrasive wheel, often made of carborundum. Use chiefly where accuracy is required.

harden (v)   To heat steel above a critical temperature and then quench in water or oil.

heat-treat (v)   To change the properties of metals by heating and then cooling.

interchangeable (adj.)   Refers to a part made to limit dimensions so that it will fit any mating part similarly manufactured.

jig (n)   A device for guiding a tool in cutting a piece. Usually it holds the work in position. Compare to *fixture*.

journal (n)   Portion of a rotating shaft supported by a bearing.

kerf (n)   Groove or cut made by a saw.

key (n)   A small piece of metal sunk partly into both shaft and hub to prevent rotation.

keyseat (n)   A slot or recess in a shaft to hold a key.

keyway (n)   A slot in a hub or portion surrounding a shaft to receive a key.

knurl (v)   To impress a pattern of dents in a turned surface with a knurling tool to produce a better hand grip.

lap (v)   To produce a very accurate finish by sliding contact with a *lap,* or piece of wood, leather, or soft metal impregnated with abrasive powder.

lathe (n)   A machine used to shape metal or other materials by rotating against a tool.

lug (n)   An irregular projection of metal, but not round as in the case of a *boss,* usually with a hole in it for a bolt or screw.

malleable casting (n)   A casting that has been made less brittle and tougher by annealing.

mill (v)   To remove material by means of a rotating cutter on a milling machine.

mold (n)   The mass of sand or other material that forms the cavity into which molten metal is poured.

MS (n)   Machinery steel, sometimes called *mild steel,* with a small percentage of carbon. Cannot be hardened.

neck (v)   To cut a groove called a *neck* around a cylindrical piece.

normalize (v)   To heat steel above its critical temperature and then to cool it in air.

pack harden (v)   To *carburize,* then to *case harden.*

pad (n)   A slight projection, usually to provide a bearing surface around one or more holes.

pattern (n)   A model, usually of wood, used in forming a mold for a casting. In sheet metal work a pattern is called a *development.*

peen (v)   To hammer into shape with a ballpeen hammer.

pickle (v)   To clean forgings or castings in dilute sulphuric acid.

pinion (n)   The smaller of two mating gears.

pitch circle (n)   An imaginary circle corresponding to the circumference of the friction gear from which the spur gear was derived.

plane (v)   To remove material by means of the *planer.*

planish (v)   To impart a planished surface to sheet metal by hammering with a smooth-surfaced hammer.

plate (v)   To coat a metal piece with another metal, such as chrome or nickel, by electrochemical methods.

polish (v)   To produce a highly finished or polished surface by friction, using a very fine abrasive.

profile (v)   To cut any desired outline by moving a small rotating cutter, usually with a master template as a guide.

punch (v)   To cut an opening of a desired shape with a rigid tool having the same shape, by pressing the tool through the work.

quench (v)   To immerse a heated piece of metal in water or oil to harden it.

rack (n)   A flat bar with gear teeth in a straight line to engage with teeth in a gear.

ream *(v)*   To enlarge a finished hole slightly to give it greater accuracy, with a *reamer.*

relief *(n)*   An offset of surfaces to provide clearance for machining.

rib *(n)*   A relatively thin flat member acting as a brace or support.

rivet *(v)*   To connect with rivets or to clench over the end of a pin by hammering.

round *(n)*   An exterior rounded intersection of two surfaces.

SAE   Society of Automotive Engineers.

sandblast *(v)*   To blow sand at high velocity with compressed air against castings or forgings to clean them.

scleroscope *(n)*   An instrument for measuring hardness of metals.

scrape *(v)*   To remove metal by scraping with a hand scraper, usually to fit a bearing.

shape *(v)*   To remove metal from a piece with a *shaper.*

shear *(v)*   To cut metal by means of shearing with two blades in sliding contact.

sherardize *(v)*   To galvanize a piece with a coating of zinc by heating it in a drum with zinc powder, to a temperature of 575–850°F.

shim *(n)*   A thin piece of metal or other material used as a spacer in adjusting two parts.

solder *(v)*   To join with solder, usually composed of lead and tin.

spin *(v)*   To form a rotating piece of sheet metal into a desired shape by pressing it with a smooth tool against a rotating form.

spline *(n)*   A keyway, usually one of a series cut around a shaft or hole.

SPLINED HOLE

spotface *(v)*   To produce a round spot or bearing surface around a hole, usually with a *spotfacer.* The spotface may be on top of a boss or it may be sunk into the surface.

SPOTFACE

sprue *(n)*   A hole in the sand leading to the *gate* which leads to the mold, through which the metal enters.

steel casting *(n)*   Like cast iron casting except that in the furnace scrap steel has been added to the casting.

swage *(v)*   To hammer metal into shape while it is held over a *swage,* or die, which fits in a hole in the *swage block,* or anvil.

sweat *(v)*   To fasten metal together by the use of solder between the pieces and by the application of heat and pressure.

tap *(v)*   To cut relatively small internal threads with a *tap.*

taper *(n)*   Conical form given to a shaft or a hole. Also refers to the slope of a plane surface.

taper pin *(n)*   A small tapered pin for fastening, usually to prevent a collar or hub from rotating on a shaft.

TAPER PIN

taper reamer *(n)*   A tapered reamer for producing accurate tapered holes, as for a taper pin.

temper *(v)*   To reheat hardened steel to bring it to a desired degree of hardness.

template or templet *(n)*   A guide or pattern used to mark out the work, guide the tool in cutting it, or check the finished product.

tin *(n)*   A silvery metal used in alloys and for coating other metals, such as tin plate.

tolerance *(n)*   Total amount of variation permitted in limit dimension of a part.

trepan *(v)*   To cut a circular groove in the flat surface at one end of a hole.

tumble *(v)*   To clean rough castings or forgings in a revolving drum filled with scrap metal.

turn *(v)*   To produce, on a lathe, a cylindrical surface parallel to the centerline.

twist drill *(n)*   A drill for use in a drill press.

undercut *(n)*   A recessed cut or a cut with inwardly sloping sides.

UNDERCUT

upset *(v)*   To form a head or enlarged end on a bar or rod by pressure or by hammering between dies.

web *(n)*   A thin flat part joining larger parts. Also known as a *rib.*

weld *(v)*   Uniting metal pieces by pressure or fusion welding processes.

Woodruff (key) *(n)*   A semicircular flat key.

WOODRUFF KEYS

wrought iron *(n)*   Iron of low carbon content useful because of its toughness, ductility, and malleability.

3 CAD/CAM GLOSSARY*

access time (or disk access time)   One measure of system response. The time interval between the instant that data is called for from storage and the instant that delivery is completed—i.e., read time. See also *response time.*

alphanumeric (or alphameric)   A term that encompasses letters, digits, and special characters that are machine-processable.

alphanumeric display (or alphameric display)   A workstation device consisting of a CRT on which text can be viewed. An alphanumeric display is capable of showing a fixed set of letters, digits, and special characters. It allows the designer to observe entered commands and to receive messages from the system.

American Standard Code for Information Interchange (ASCII)   An industry standard character code widely used for information interchange among data processing systems, communications systems, and associated equipment.

analog   Applied to an electrical or computer system, this denotes the capability to represent data in continuously varying physical quantities.

annotation   Process of inserting text or a special note or identification (such as a flag) on a drawing, map, or diagram constructed on a CAD/CAM system. The text can be generated and positioned on the drawing using the system.

application program (or software)   A computer program or collection of programs to perform a task or tasks specific to a particular user's need or class of needs.

archival storage   Refers to memory (disks or printouts) used to store data on completed designs or elements outside of main memory.

array (*v*)   To create automatically on a CAD system an arrangement of identical elements or components. The designer defines the element once, then indicates the starting location and spacing for automatic generation of the array. (*n*) An arrangement created in the above manner. A series of elements or sets of elements arranged in a pattern—i.e., matrix.

ASCII   See *American National Standard Code for Information Exchange.*

assembler   A computer program that converts (i.e., translates) programmer-written symbolic instructions, usually in mnemonic form, into machine-executable (computer or binary coded) instructions. This conversion is typically one-to-one (one symbolic instruction converts to one machine executable instruction). A software programming aid.

associative dimensioning   A CAD capability that links dimension entities to geometric entities being dimensioned. This allows the value of a dimension to be automatically updated as the geometry changes.

attribute   A nongraphic characteristic of a part, component, or entity under design on a CAD system. Examples include: dimension entities associated with geometry, text with text

nodes, and nodal lines with connect nodes. Changing one entity in an association can produce automatic changes by the system in the associated entity; e.g., moving one entity can cause moving or stretching of the other entity.

automatic dimensioning   A CAD capability that computes the dimensions in a displayed design, or in a designated section, and automatically places dimensions, dimensional lines, and arrowheads where required. In the case of mapping, this capability labels the linear feature with length and azimuth.

auxiliary storage   Storage that supplements main memory devices such as disk storage.

benchmark   The program(s) used to test, compare, and evaluate in real time the performance of various CAD/CAM systems prior to selection and purchase. A *synthetic* benchmark has preestablished parameters designed to exercise a set of system features and resources. A *live* benchmark is drawn from the prospective user's workload as a model of the entire workload.

bit   The smallest unit of information that can be stored and processed by a digital computer. A bit may assume only one of two values: 0 or 1 (i.e., ON/OFF or YES/NO). Bits are organized into larger units called *words* for access by computer instructions.

Computers are often categorized by word size in bits, i.e., the maximum word size that can be processed as a unit during an instruction cycle (e.g., 16-bit computers or 32-bit computers). The number of bits in a word is an indication of the processing power of the system, especially for calculations or for high precision data.

bit rate   The speed at which bits are transmitted, usually expressed in bits per second.

boot up   Start up (a system).

B-spline   A sequence of parametric polynomial curves (typically quadratic or cubic polynomials) forming a smooth fit between a sequence of points in 3D space. The piecewise defined curve maintains a level of mathematical continuity dependent upon the polynomial degree chosen. It is used extensively in mechanical design applications in the automotive and aerospace industries.

bug   A flaw in the design or implementation of a software program or hardware design that causes erroneous results or malfunctions.

byte   A sequence of adjacent bits, usually eight, representing a character that is operated on as a unit. Usually shorter than a word. A measure of the memory capacity of a system, or of an individual storage unit (as a 300 megabyte disk).

CAD   See *computer-aided design.*

CAD/CAM   See *computer-aided design/computer-aided manufacturing.*

CAE   See *computer-aided engineering.*

CAM   See *computer-aided manufacturing.*

Extracted from the CA/CAM Glossary, 1983 edition, published by the Computercision Corporation, Bedford, MA 01730; reproduced with permission of the publisher.

cathode ray tube (CRT)   A CRT displays graphic representations of geometric entities and designs and can be of various types: storage tube, raster scan, or refresh. These tubes create images by means of a controllable beam of electrons striking a screen. The term *CRT* is often used to denote an entire display device using this technology.

central processing unit (CPU)   The computer brain of a CAD/CAM system that controls the retrieval, decoding, and processing of information, as well as the interpretation and execution of operating instructions—the building blocks of application and other computer programs. A CPU is composed of arithmetic, control, and logic elements.

character   An alphabetical, numerical, or special graphic symbol used as part of the organization, control, or representation of CAD/CAM data.

characters per second (cps)   A measure of the speed with which an alphanumeric terminal can process data.

chip   See *integrated circuit.*

code   A set of specific symbols and rules for representing data (usually instructions) so that the data can be understood and executed by a computer. A code can be in binary (machine) language, assembly language, or a high-level language. Frequently refers to an industry-standard code such as ANSI, ASCII, IPC, or Standard Code for Information Exchange.

color display   A CAD/CAM display device. Color raster-scan displays offer a variety of user-selectable, contrasting colors to make it easier to discriminate among various groups of design elements on different layers of a large, complex design. Color speeds up the recognition of specific areas and subassemblies, helps the designer interpret complex surfaces, and highlights interference problems. Color displays can be of the penetration type, in which various phosphor layers give off different colors (refresh display) or the TV-type with red, blue, and green electron guns (raster-scan display).

command   A control signal or instruction to a CPU or graphics processor, commonly initiated by means of a menu/tablet and electronic pen or by an alphanumeric keyboard.

command language   A language for communicating with a CAD/CAM system in order to perform specific functions or tasks.

communication link   The physical means, such as a telephone line, for connecting one system module or peripheral to another in a different location in order to transmit and receive data. See also *data link.*

compatibility   The ability of a particular file hardware module or software program, code, or language to be used in a computer system without prior modification or special interfaces. *Upward compatible* denotes the ability of a system to interface with new hardware or software modules or enhancements (i.e., the system vendor provides with each new module a reasonable means of transferring data, programs, and operator skills from the user's present system to the new enhancements).

compiler   A computer program that converts or translates a high-level, user-written language (e.g., PASCAL, COBOL, C++, or FORTRAN) or source, into a language that a computer can understand. The conversion is typically one to many (i.e., one user instruction to many machine-executable instructions). A software programming aid, the compiler allows the designer to write programs in an English-like language with relatively few statements, thus saving program development time.

component   A physical entity, or a symbol used in CAD to denote such an entity. Depending on the application, a component might refer to an IC or part of a wiring circuit (e.g., a resistor), or a valve, elbow, or vee in a plant layout, or a substation or cable in a utility map. Also applies to a subassembly or part that goes into higher level assemblies.

computer-aided design (CAD)   A process that uses a computer system to assist in the creation, modification, and display of a design.

computer-aided design/computer-aided manufacturing (CAD/CAM)   Refers to the integration of computers into the entire design-to-fabrication cycle of a product or plant.

computer-aided engineering (CAE)   Analysis of a design for basic error checking, or to optimize manufacturability, performance, and economy (for example, by comparing various possible materials or designs). Information drawn from the CAD/CAM design database is used to analyze the functional characteristics of a part, product, or system under design and to simulate its performance under various conditions. In electronic design, CAE enables users to detect and correct potentially costly design flaws. CAE permits the execution of complex circuit loading analyses and simulation during the circuit definition stage. CAE can be used to determine section properties, moments of inertia, shear and bending moments, weight, volume, surface area, and center of gravity. CAE can precisely determine loads, vibration, noise, and service life early in the design cycle so that components can be optimized to meet those criteria. Perhaps the most powerful CAE technique is finite element modeling. See also *kinematics.*

computer-aided manufacturing (CAM)   The use of computer and digital technology to generate manufacturing-oriented data. Data drawn from a CAD/ CAM database can assist in or control a portion or all of a manufacturing process, including numerically controlled machines, computer-assisted parts programming, computer-assisted process planning, robotics, and programmable logic controllers, CAM can involve production programming, manufacturing engineering, industrial engineering, facilities engineering, and reliability engineering (quality control). CAM techniques can be used to produce process plans for fabricating a complete assembly, to program robots, and to coordinate plant operation.

computer graphics   A general term encompassing any discipline or activity that uses computers to generate, process, and display graphic images. The essential technology of CAD/CAM systems. See also *computer-aided design.*

computer network   An interconnected arrangement or configuration of two or more systems. See also *network.*

computer program   A specific set of software commands in a form acceptable to a computer and used to achieve a desired result. Often called a *software program or package.*

configuration A particular combination of a computer, software and hardware modules, and peripherals at a single installation and interconnected in such a way as to support certain applications.

connector A termination for a cable entering or leaving a PC board.

convention Standardized methodology or accepted procedure for executing a computer program. In CAD, the term denotes a standard rule or mode of execution undertaken to provide consistency. For example, a drafting convention might require all dimensions to be in metric units.

core (core memory) A largely obsolete term for *main storage*.

CPU See *central processing unit*.

CRT See *cathode ray tube*.

cursor A visual tracking symbol, usually an underline or cross hairs, for indicating a location or entity selection on the CRT display. A text cursor indicates the alphanumeric input; a graphics cursor indicates the next geometric input. A cursor is guided by an electronic or light pen, joystick, keyboard, etc., and follows every movement of the input device.

cycle A preset sequence of events (hardware or software) initiated by a single command.

data base A comprehensive collection of interrelated information stored on some kind of mass data storage device, usually a disk. Generally consists of information organized into a number of fixed-format record types with logical links between associated records. Uses include operating systems instructions, standard parts libraries, completed designs and documentation, source code, graphic and application programs, as well as current user tasks in progress.

data communication The transmission of data (usually digital) from one point (such as a CAD/CAM workstation or CPU) to another point via communication channels such as telephone lines.

data link The communication line(s), related controls, and interface(s) for the transmission of data between two or more computer systems. Can include modems, telephone lines, or dedicated transmission media such as cable or optical fiber.

data tablet A CAD/CAM input device that allows the designer to communicate with the system by placing an electronic pen or stylus on the tablet surface. There is a direct correspondence between positions on the tablet and addressable points on the display surface of the display screen. Typically used for indicating positions on the display screen, for digitizing input of drawings, or for menu selection. See also *graphic tablet*.

debug To detect, locate, and correct any bugs in a system's software or hardware.

dedicated Designed or intended for a single function or use. For example, a dedicated workstation might be used exclusively for engineering calculations or plotting.

default The predetermined value of a parameter required in a CAD/CAM task or operation. It is automatically supplied by the system whenever that value (e.g., text, height, or grid size) is not specified.

device A system hardware module external to the CPU and designed to perform a specific function—i.e., a display screen, plotter, printer, etc. See also *peripheral*.

diagnostics Computer programs designed to test the status of a system or its key components and to detect and isolate malfunctions.

dial up To initiate station-to-station communication with a computer via a dial telephone, usually from a workstation to a computer.

digital Applied to an electrical or computer system, this denotes the capability to represent data in the form of digits.

digitize For computer systems these are binary digits in the form of 1's or 0's. To convert a drawing into digital form (i.e., coordinate locations) so that it can be entered into the database for later processing. A digitizer, available with many CAD systems, implements the conversion process. This is one of the primary ways of entering existing drawings, crude graphics, lines, and shapes into the system.

digitizer A CAD input device consisting of a data tablet on which is mounted the drawing or design to be digitized into the system. The designer moves a puck or electronic pen to selected points on the drawing and enters coordinate data for lines and shapes by simply pressing down the digitize button with the puck or pen.

dimensioning, automatic A CAD capability that will automatically compute and insert the dimensions of a design or drawing, or a designated section of it.

direct access (linkage) Retrieval or storage of data in the system by reference to its location on disk, without the need for processing on a CPU.

direct-view storage tube (DVST) Graphics display device using long-lasting, flicker free image with high resolution and no refreshing. It handles an almost unlimited amount of data. However, display dynamics are limited since DVSTs do not permit selective erase. The image is not as bright as with refresh or raster. Also called *storage tube*.

directory A named space on the disk or other mass storage device in which are stored the names of files and some summary information about them.

discrete components Components with a single functional capability per package—for example, transistors and diodes.

disk (storage) A device on which large amounts of information can be stored in the database. Synonymous with *magnetic disk storage* or *magnetic disk memory*.

display A CAD/CAM workstation device for rapidly presenting a graphic image so that the designer can react to it, making changes interactively in real time.

dot matrix plotter A CAD peripheral device for generating graphic plots. Consists of a combination of wire nibs (styli) spaced 100 to 300 or more styli per inch, which place dots of ink where needed to generate a drawing. Because of its high speed, it is typically used in electronic design applications.

drum plotter An electromechanical pen plotter that draws an image on paper or film mounted on a rotatable drum. In this CAD peripheral device a combination of plotting-head movement and drum rotation provides the motion.

dynamic (motion) Simulation of movement using CAD software, so that the designer can see 3D representations of the parts in a piece of machinery as they interact dynamically. Thus, any collision or interference problems are revealed at a glance.

edit   To modify, refine, or update an emerging design or text on a CAD system. This can be done online interactively.

electrostatic plotter   Plotter that uses an electronic charge on the paper to pick up toner particles.

element   The basic design entity in computer-aided design whose logical, positional, electrical, or mechanical function is identifiable.

enhancements   Software or hardware improvements, additions, or updates to a CAD/CAM system.

entity   A geometric primitive—the fundamental building block used in constructing a design or drawing, such as an arc, circle, line, text, point, spline, figure, or nodal line. Or a group of primitives processed as an identifiable unit. Thus, a square may be defined as a discrete entity consisting of four primitives (vectors), although each side of the square could be defined as an entity in its own right. See also *primitive*.

feedback   (1) The ability of a system to respond to an operator command in real time either visually or with a message on the display. This message registers the command, indicates any possible errors, and simultaneously displays the updated design. (2) The signal or data fed back to a commanding unit from a controlled machine or process to denote its response to a command. (3) The signal representing the difference between actual response and desired response and used by the commanding unit to improve performance of the controlled machine or process. See also *prompt*.

figure   A symbol or a part that may contain primitive entities, other figures, nongraphic properties, and associations. A figure can be incorporated into other parts or figures.

file   A collection of related information in the system that may be accessed by a unique name. May be stored on a disk or other mass storage media.

file protection   A technique for preventing access to or accidental erasure of data within a file on the system.

firmware   Computer programs, instructions, or functions implemented in user-modifiable hardware, i.e., a microprocessor with read-only memory. Such programs or instructions, stored permanently in programmable read-only memories, constitute a fundamental part of system hardware. The advantage is that a frequently used program or routine can be invoked by a single command instead of multiple commands as in a software program.

flatbed plotter   A CAD/CAM peripheral device that draws an image on paper, glass, or film mounted on a flat table. The plotting head provides all the motion.

flat-pattern generation   A CAD/CAM capability for automatically unfolding a 3D design of a sheet metal part into its corresponding flat-pattern design. Calculations for material bending and stretching are performed automatically for any specified material. The reverse flat-pattern generation package automatically folds a flat-pattern design into its 3D version. Flat-pattern generation eliminates major bottlenecks for sheet metal fabricators.

flicker   An undesired visual effect on a display screen when the refresh rate is low.

font, line   Repetitive pattern used in CAD to give a displayed line appearance characteristics that make it more easily distinguishable, such as a solid, dashed, or dotted line. A line font can be applied to graphic images in order to provide meaning, either graphic (e.g., hidden lines) or functional (roads, tracks, wires, pipes, etc.). It can help a designer to identify and define specific graphic representations of entities that are view-dependent. For example, a line may be solid when drawn in the top view of an object but, when a line font is used, becomes dotted in the side view where it is not normally visible.

font, text   Sets of typefaces of various styles and sizes. In CAD, fonts are used to create text for drawings, special characters such as Greek letters, and mathematical symbols.

FORTRAN   *FOR*mula *TRAN*slation, a high-level programming language used primarily for scientific or engineering applications.

fracturing   The division of IC graphics by CAD into simple trapezoidal or rectangular areas for pattern-generation purposes.

function key   A specific square on a data tablet, or a key on a function key box, used by the designer to enter a particular command or other input. See also *data tablet*.

function keyboard   An input device located at a CAD/CAM workstation and containing a number of function keys.

gap   The gap between two entities on a computer-aided design is the length of the shortest line segment that can be drawn from the boundary of one entity to the other without intersecting the boundary of the other. CAD/CAM design-rules checking programs can automatically perform gap checks.

graphic tablet   A CAD/CAM input device that enables graphic and location instruments to be entered into the system using an electronic pen on the tablet. See also *data tablet*.

grid   A network of uniformly spaced points or crosshatch used for locating and digitizing a position, inputting components to assist in the creation of a design layout, or constructing precise angles. For example, the coordinate data supplied by digitizers is automatically calculated by the CPU from the closest grid point. The grid determines the minimum accuracy with which design entities are described or connected. In the mapping environment, a grid is used to describe the distribution network of utility resources.

hard copy   A copy on paper of a displayed image—for example, a drawing, printed report, plot, listing, or summary. Most CAD/CAM systems can automatically generate hard copy through an online printer or plotter.

hardware   The physical components, modules, and peripherals comprising a system—computer disk, magnetic tape, CRT terminal(s), plotter(s), etc.

hard-wired link   A technique of physically connecting two systems by fixed circuit interconnections using digital signals.

host computer   The primary or controlling computer in a multicomputer network. Large-scale host computers typically are equipped with mass memory and a variety of peripheral devices, including magnetic tape, line printers, card readers, and possibly hard-copy devices. Host computers may be used to support, with their own memory and processing capabilities, not only graphics programs running on a CAD/CAM system but also related engineering analysis.

IC   See *integrated circuit*.

IGES   See *Initial Graphics Exchange Specification*.

Initial Graphics Exchange Specification (IGES)   A CAD/CAM database specification. IGES attempts to standardize communication of drawing and geometric product information between computer systems.

initialize   To set counters, switches, and addresses on a computer to zero or to other starting values at the beginning of, or at predetermined stages in, a program or routine.

input (data)   (1) The data supplied to a computer program for processing by the system. (2) The process of entering such data into the system.

input devices   A variety of devices (such as data tablets or keyboard devices) that allow the user to communicate with the CAD/CAM system, for example, to pick a function from many presented, to enter text and/or numerical data, to modify a picture, or to construct the desired design.

input/output (I/O)   A term used to describe a CAD/CAM communications device as well as the process by which communications take place in a CAD/CAM system. An I/O device is one that makes possible communications between a device and a workstation operator or between devices on the system (such as workstations or controllers). By extension, input/output also denotes the process by which communications takes place. Input refers to the data transmitted to the processor for manipulation, and output refers to the data transmitted from the processor to the workstation operator or to another device (i.e., the results). Contrast with the other major parts of a CAD/CAM system: the CPU or central processing unit, which performs arithmetic and logical operations, and data storage devices (such as memories, disks, or tapes).

insert   To create and place entities, figures, or information into an emerging design on the display.

instruction set   (1) All the commands to which a CAD/CAM computer will respond. (2) The repertoire of functions the computer can perform.

integrated circuit (IC)   A tiny complex of electronic components and interconnections comprising a circuit that may vary in functional complexity from a simple logic gate to a microprocessor. An IC is usually packaged in a single substrate such as a slice of silicon. The complexity of most IC designs and the many repetitive elements have made computer-aided design an economic necessity. Also called a *chip*.

integrated system   A CAD/CAM system that integrates the entire product development cycle—analysis, design, and fabrication—so that all processes flow smoothly from concept to production.

interactive   Denotes two-way communications between a CAD/CAM system or workstation and its operators. An operator can modify or terminate a program and receive feedback from the system for guidance and verification. See also *feedback*.

interface (n)   (1) A hardware and/or software link that enables two systems, or a system and its peripherals, to operate as a single, integrated system. (2) The input devices and visual feedback capabilities that allow bilateral communication between the designer and the system. The interface to a large computer can be a communications link (hardware) or a combination of software and hardwired connections. An interface might be a portion of storage accessed by two or more programs or a link between two subroutines in a program.

I/O   See *input/output*.

jaggies   A CAD jargon term used to refer to straight or curved lines that appear to be jagged or sawtoothed on the display screen.

joystick   A CAD data-entering device employing a hand-controlled lever to manually enter the coordinates of various points on a design being digitized into the system.

key file   A disk file that provides user-defined definitions for a tablet menu. See *menu*.

kinematics   A computer-aided engineering (CAE) process for plotting or animating the motion of parts in a machine or a structure under design on the system. CAE simulation programs allow the motion of mechanisms to be studied for interference, acceleration, and force determinations while still in the design stage.

layering   A method of logically organizing data in a CAD/CAM database. Functionally different classes of data (e.g., various graphic/geometric entities) are segregated on separate layers, each of which can be displayed individually or in any desired combination. Layering helps the designer distinguish among different kinds of data in creating a complex product such as a multilayered PC board or IC.

layers   User-defined logical subdivisions of data in a CAD/CAM database that may be viewed on the CRT individually or overlaid and viewed in groups.

learning curve   A concept that projects the expected improvement in operator productivity over a period of time. Usually applied in the first 6 months to 1 year of a new CAD/CAM facility as part of a cost-justification study, or when new operators are introduced. An accepted tool of management for predicting manpower requirements and evaluating training programs.

library, graphics (or parts library)   A collection of standard, often-used symbols, components, shapes, or parts stored in the CAD database as templates or building blocks to speed up future design work on the system. Generally an organization of files under a common library name.

light pen   A handheld photosensitive CAD input device used on a display screen for identifying display elements, or for designating a location on the screen where an action is to take place.

line font   See *font, line*.

line smoothing   An automated mapping capability for the interpolation and insertion of additional points along a linear entity yielding a series of shorter linear segments to generate a smooth curved appearance to the original linear component. The additional points or segments are created only for display purposes and are interpolated from a relatively small set of stored representative points. Thus, data storage space is minimized.

machine   A computer, CPU, or other processor.

machine instruction   An instruction that a machine (computer) can recognize and execute.

machine language   The complete set of command instructions understandable to and used directly by a computer when it performs operations.

macro   (1) A sequence of computer instructions executable as a single command. A frequently used, multistep operation can be organized into a macro, given a new name, and remain in the system for easy use, thus shortening program development time. (2) In Computer-vision's IC design system, macro refers to macroexpansion of a cell. This system capability enables the designer to replicate the contents of a cell as primitives without the original cell grouping.

magnetic disk   A flat circular plate with a magnetic surface on which information can be stored by selective magnetization of portions of the flat surface. Commonly used for temporary working storage during computer-aided design. See also *disk*.

magnetic tape   A tape with a magnetic surface on which information can be stored by selective polarization of portions of the surface. Used in CAD/CAM for back up storage of completed design files and other archival material.

mainframe (computer)   A large central computer facility.

main memory/storage   The computer's general-purpose storage from which instructions may be executed and data loaded directly into operating registers.

mass storage   Auxiliary large-capacity memory for storing large amounts of data readily accessible by the computer. Commonly a disk or magnetic tape.

matrix   A 2D or 3D rectangular array (arrangement) of identical geometric or symbolic entities. A matrix can be generated automatically on a CAD system by specifying the building block entity and the desired locations. This process is used extensively in computer-aided electrical/electronic design.

memory   Any form of data storage where information can be read and written. Standard memories include RAM, ROM, and PROM. See also *programmable read-only memory; random access memory; read-only memory; storage*.

menu   Preprogrammed commands or a series of commands, that initiate the particular function or command indicated when selected.

merge   To combine two or more sets of related data into one, usually in a specified sequence. This can be done automatically on a CAD/CAM system to generate lists and reports.

microcomputer   A smaller, lower-cost equivalent of a full-scale minicomputer. Includes a microprocessor (CPU), memory, and necessary interface circuits. Consists of one or more ICs (chips) comprising a chip set.

microprocessor   The central control element of a microcomputer, implemented in a single integrated circuit. It performs instruction sequencing and processing, as well as

all required computations. It requires additional circuits to function as a microcomputer. See *microcomputer*.

minicomputer   A general-purpose, single processor computer of limited flexibility and memory performance.

mirroring   A CAD design aid that automatically creates a mirror image of a graphic entity by flipping the entity or drawing on its *x* or *y* axis.

mnemonic symbol   An easily remembered symbol that assists the designer in communicating with the system.

model, geometric   A complete, geometrically accurate 3D or 2D representation of a shape, a part, a geographic area, a plant or any part of it, designed on a CAD system and stored in the database. A mathematical or analytic model of a physical system used to determine the response of that system to a stimulus or load. See *modeling, geometric*.

modeling, geometric   Constructing a mathematical or analytic model of a physical object or system for the purpose of determining the response of that object or system to a stimulus or load. First, the designer describes the shape under design using a geometric model constructed on the system. The computer stores a mathematical model later used for other CAD functions such as design optimization.

modeling, solid   A type of 3D modeling in which the solid characteristics of an object under design are built into the database so that complex internal structures and external shapes can be realistically represented. This makes computer-aided design and analysis of solid objects easier and clearer.

modem   *MO*dulator-*DEM*odulator, a device that converts digital signals to analog signals, and vice versa, for long-distance transmission over communications circuits such as telephone lines, dedicated wires, optical fiber, or microwave.

module   A separate and distinct unit of hardware or software that is part of a system.

mouse   A handheld data entering device used to position a cursor on a data tablet.

multiprocessor   A computer whose architecture consists of more than one processing unit. See *central processing unit; microcomputer*.

network   An arrangement of two or more interconnected computer systems to facilitate the exchange of information in order to perform a specific function. For example, a CAD/CAM system might be connected to a mainframe computer for file sharing and storage.

numerical control (NC)   A technique of operating machine tools or similar equipment in which motion is developed in response to numerically coded commands. These commands may be generated by a CAD/CAM system. Also, the processes involved in generating the data necessary to guide a machine tool in the manufacture of a part.

off-line   Refers to peripheral devices not currently connected to and under the direct control of the system's computer.

online   Refers to peripheral devices connected to and under the direct control of the system's computer, so that operator-system interaction, feedback, and output are all in real time.

operating system   A structured set of software programs that control the operation of the computer and associated peripheral devices in a CAD/CAM system, as well as the execution of computer programs and data flow to and from peripheral devices. May provide support for activities and programs such as scheduling, debugging, input/output control, accounting, editing, assembly, compilation, storage assignment, data management, and diagnostics. An operating system may assign task priority levels, support a file system, provide drives for I/O devices, support standard system commands or utilities for online programming, process commands, and support both networking and diagnostics.

overlay   A segment of code or data to be brought into the memory of a computer to replace existing code or data.

paint   To fill in a bounded graphic figure on a raster display using a combination of repetitive patterns or line fonts to add meaning or clarity. See *font, line.*

paper-tape punch/reader   An outdated peripheral device that can read as well as punch a perforated paper tape generated by a CAD/CAM system. These tapes were the principal means of supplying data to an NC machine.

parallel processing   Executing more than one element of a single process concurrently on multiple processors in a computer system.

password protection   A security feature of certain CAD/CAM systems that prevents access to the system or to files within the system without first entering a password, i.e., a special sequence of characters.

PC board   See *printed circuit board.*

pen plotter   An electromechanical CAD output device that generates hard copy of displayed graphic data by means of a ballpoint pen or liquid ink.

peripheral (device)   Any device, distinct from the basic system modules, that provides input to and/or output from the CPU. May include printers, keyboards, plotters, graphics display terminals, and analog-to-digital converters.

permanent storage   A method or device for storing the results of a completed program outside the CPU.

photo plotter   A CAD output device that generates high-precision artwork masters photographically for PC board design and IC masks.

pixel   The smallest portion of a display screen that can be individually referenced. An individual dot on a display image. Typically, pixels are evenly spaced, horizontally and vertically, on the display.

plotter   A CAD peripheral device used to output for external use the image stored in the database. Plotter types include pen, drum, electrostatic, and flatbed.

postprocessor   A software program or procedure that formats graphic or other data processed on the system for some other purpose. For example, a postprocessor might format cutter centerline data into a form that a machine controller can interpret.

precision   The degree of accuracy. Generally refers to the number of significant digits of information to the right of the decimal point for data represented within a computer

system. Thus, the term denotes the degree of discrimination with which a design or design element can be described in the database.

preplaced line (or bus)   A run (or line) between a set of points on a PC board layout that has been predefined by the designer and must be avoided by a CAD automatic routing program.

preprocessor   A computer program that takes a specific set of instructions from an external source and translates it into the format required by the system.

primitive   A design element at the lowest stage of complexity. A fundamental graphic entity. It can be a vector, a point, or a text string. The smallest definable object in a display processor's instruction set.

printed circuit (PC) board   A baseboard made of insulating materials and an etched copper-foil circuit pattern on which are mounted ICs and other components required to implement one or more electronic functions. PC boards plug into a rack or subassembly of electronic equipment to provide the brains or logic to control the operation of a computer, or a communications system, instrumentation, or other electronic systems. The name derives from the fact that the circuitry is connected not by wires but by copper-foil lines, paths, or traces actually etched onto the board surface. CAD/CAM is used extensively in PC board design, testing, and manufacture.

process simulation   A program utilizing a mathematical model created on the system to try out numerous process design iterations with real-time visual and numerical feedback. Designers can see what is taking place at every stage in the manufacturing process. They can therefore optimize a process and correct problems that could affect the actual manufacturing process downstream.

processor   In CAD/CAM system hardware, any device that performs a specific function. Most often used to refer to the CPU. In software, it refers to a complex set of instructions to perform a general function. See also *central processing unit.*

productivity ratio   A widely accepted means of measuring CAD/CAM productivity (throughput per hour) by comparing the productivity of a design/engineering group before and after installation of the system or relative to some standard norm or potential maximum. The most common way of recording productivity is Actual Manual Hours/Actual CAD Hours, expressed as 4 : 1, 6 : 1, etc.

program (*n*)   A precise sequential set of instructions that direct a computer to perform a particular task or action or to solve a problem. A complete program includes plans for the transcription of data, coding for the computer, and plans for the absorption of the results into the system. (*v*) To develop a program. See also *computer program.*

Programmable Read-Only Memory (PROM)   A memory that, once programmed with permanent data or instructions, becomes a ROM. See *read-only memory.*

PROM   See *programmable read-only memory.*

prompt   A message or symbol generated automatically by the system to inform the user of (a) a procedural error or incorrect input to the program being executed or (b) the next expected action, option(s), or input.

puck   A handheld, manually controlled input device that allows coordinate data to be digitized into the system from a drawing placed on the data tablet or digitizer surface. A puck has a transparent window containing cross hairs.

RAM   See *random access memory*.

random access memory (RAM)   A main memory read/write storage unit that provides the CAD/CAM operator direct access to the stored information. The time required to access any word stored in the memory is the same as for any other word.

raster display   A CAD workstation display in which the entire display surface is scanned at a constant refresh rate. The bright, flicker-free image can be selectively written and erased. Also called a digital TV display.

raster scan (video)   Similar to conventional television, it involves a line-by-line sweep across the entire CRT surface to generate the image. Raster-scan features include good brightness, accuracy, selective erase, dynamic motion capabilities, and the opportunity for unlimited color. The device can display a large amount of information without flicker.

read-only memory (ROM)   A memory that cannot be modified or reprogrammed. Typically used for control and execute programs. See also *programmable read-only memory*.

real time   Refers to tasks or functions executed so rapidly by a CAD/CAM system that the feedback at various stages in the process can be used to guide the designer in completing the task. Immediate visual feedback makes possible real time, interactive operation of a CAD/CAM system.

rectangular array   Insertion of the same entity at multiple locations using the system's ability to copy design elements and place them at user-specified intervals to create a rectangular arrangement or matrix. A feature of PC and IC design systems.

refresh (or vector refresh)   A CAD display technology that involves frequent redrawing of the displayed image to keep it bright, crisp, and clear. Refresh permits a high degree of movement in the displayed image as well as high resolution. Selective erase or editing is possible at any time without erasing and repainting the entire image. Substantial amounts of high-speed memory are required.

refresh rate   The rate at which the graphic image on a display is redrawn, i.e., the time needed for one refresh of the displayed image.

registration   The degree of accuracy in the positioning of one printed layer or overlay from CAD or artwork, relative to another layer, as reflected by the clarity and sharpness of the resulting image.

repaint   A CAD feature that automatically redraws a displayed design.

resolution   The smallest spacing between two display elements that will allow the elements to be distinguished visually, usually given in dots per inch in printing.

response time   The elapsed time from initiation of an operation at a workstation to the receipt of the results at that workstation. Includes transmission of data to the CPU, processing, file access, and transmission of results back to the initiating workstation.

restart   To resume a computer program interrupted by operator intervention.

restore   To bring back to its original state a design currently being worked on in a CAD/CAM system after editing or modification that the designer now wants to cancel or rescind.

resume   A feature of some application programs that allows the designer to suspend the data-processing operation at some logical break point and restart it later from that point.

reticle   The photographic plate used to create an IC mask. See also *photo plotter*.

robotics   The use of computer-controlled manipulators or arms to automate a variety of manufacturing processes such as welding, material handling, painting, and assembly.

ROM   See *read-only memory*.

rotate   To turn a displayed 2D or 3D construction about an axis through a predefined angle relative to the original position.

routine   A computer program, or a subroutine in the main program. The smallest separately compilable source code unit. See *computer program: source*.

rubber banding   A CAD capability that allows a component to be tracked (dragged) across the screen, to a desired location, while simultaneously stretching all related interconnections to maintain signal continuity. During tracking, the interconnections associated with the component stretch and bend, providing an excellent visual guide for optimizing the location of a component to best fit into the flow of the PC board, or other entity, minimizing total interconnect length and avoiding areas of congestion.

scale (*v*)   To enlarge or diminish the size of a displayed entity without changing its shape, i.e., to bring it into a user-specified ratio to its original dimensions. Scaling can be done automatically by a CAD system. (*n*) Denotes the coordinate system for representing an object.

scissoring   The automatic erasing of all portions of a design that lie outside user-specified boundaries.

scroll   To automatically roll up, as on a spool, a design or text message to permit the sequential viewing of a message or drawing too large to be displayed all at once on the screen. New data appear on the screen at one edge of the screen as other data disappear at the opposite edge. Graphics can be scrolled up, down, left, or right.

selective erase   A CAD feature for deleting portions of a display without affecting the remainder or having to repaint the entire display.

shape fill   The automatic painting-in of an area, defined by user-specified boundaries, on an IC or PC board layout, for example, the area to be filled by copper when the PC board is manufactured. Can be done online by CAD.

smoothing   Fitting together curves and surfaces so that a smooth, continuous geometry results.

software   The collection of executable computer programs including application programs, operating systems, and languages.

source A text file written in a high-level language and containing a computer program. It is easily read and understood by people but must be compiled or assembled to generate machine-recognizable instructions. Also known as *source code*. See also *high-level language*.

source language A symbolic language comprised of statements and formulas used in computer processing. It is translated into object language (object code) by an assembler or compiler for execution by a computer.

spline A subset of a B-spline wherein a sequence of curves is restricted to a plane. An interpolation routine executed on a CAD/CAM system automatically adjusts a curve by design iteration until the curvature is continuous over the length of the curve. See also *B-spline*.

storage The physical repository of all information relating to products designed on a CAD/CAM system. It is typically in the form of a magnetic disk.

storage memory A memory device for storing a large amount of data, e.g., disk. It is not randomly accessible as main memory is.

stretch A CAD design/editing aid that enables the designer to automatically expand a displayed entity beyond its original dimensions.

string A linear sequence of entities, such as characters or physical elements, in a computer-aided design.

stylus A handheld pen used in conjunction with a data table to enter commands and coordinate input into the system. Also called an *electronic pen*.

surface machining Automatic generation of NC tool paths to cut 3D shapes. Both the tool paths and the shapes may be constructed using the mechanical design capabilities of a CAD/CAM system.

symbol Any recognizable sign, mark, shape, or pattern used as a building block for designing meaningful structures. A set of primitive graphic entities (line, point, arc, circle, text, etc.) that form a construction that can be expressed as one unit and assigned a meaning. Symbols may be combined or nested to form larger symbols and/or drawings. They can be as complex as an entire PC board or as simple as a single element, such as a pad. Symbols are commonly used to represent physical things. For example, a particular graphic shape may be used to represent a complete device or a certain kind of electrical component in a schematic. To simplify the preparation of drawings of piping systems and flow diagrams, standard symbols are used to represent various types of fittings and components in common use. In computer-aided mapping, a symbol can be a diagram, design, letter, character, or abbreviation placed on maps and charts, that, by convention or reference to a legend, is understood to stand for or represent a specific characteristic or feature. In a CAD environment, symbol libraries contribute to the quick maintenance, placement, and interpretation of symbols.

syntax (1) A set of rules describing the structure of statements allowed in a computer language. To make grammatical sense, commands and routines must be written in conformity to these rules. (2) The structure of a computer command language, i.e., the English-sentence structure of a CAD/CAM command language, e.g., verb, noun, modifiers.

system An arrangement of CAD/CAM data processing, memory, display, and plotting modules—coupled with appropriate software—to achieve specific objectives. The term CAD/CAM system implies both hardware and software. See also *operating system* (a purely software term).

tablet An input device on which a designer can digitize coordinate data or enter commands into a CAD/CAM system by means of an electronic pen. See also *data tablet*.

task (1) A specific project that can be executed by a CAD/CAM software program. (2) A specific portion of memory assigned to the user for executing that project.

template The pattern of a standard, commonly used component or part that serves as a design aid. Once created, it can be subsequently inserted instead of redrawn whenever needed. A standard part in the database library that can be retrieved and inserted intact into an emerging drawing on the CRT.

temporary storage Memory locations for storing immediate and partial results obtained during the execution of a program on the system.

terminal See *workstation*.

text editor An operating system program used to create and modify text files on the system.

text file A file stored in the system in text format that can be printed and edited online as required.

throughput The number of units of work performed by a CAD/CAM system or a workstation during a given period of time. A quantitative measure of system productivity.

time sharing The use of a common CPU memory and processing capabilities by two or more CAD/CAM terminals to execute different tasks simultaneously.

tool path Centerline of the tip of an NC cutting tool as it moves over a part produced on a CAD/CAM system. Tool paths can be created and displayed interactively or automatically by a CAD/CAM system, and reformatted into NC tapes, by means of postprocessor, to guide or control machining equipment. See also *surface machining*.

trackball A CAD graphics input device consisting of a ball recessed into a surface. The designer can rotate it in any direction to control the position of the cursor used for entering coordinate data into the system.

tracking Moving a predefined (tracking) symbol across the surface of the display screen with a cursor, light pen, or electronic pen.

transform To change an image display screen by, for example by scaling, rotating, translating, or mirroring.

transformation The process of transforming a CAD display image. Also the matrix representation of a geometric space.

translate (1) To convert CAD/CAM output from one language to another, for example, by means of a postprocessor. (2) Also, by an editing command, to move a CAD display entity a specified distance in a specified direction.

trap The area that is searched around each digitized point to find a hit on a graphics entity to be edited. See also *digitize*.

turnaround time The elapsed time between the moment a task or project is input into the CAD/CAM system and the moment the required output is obtained.

turnkey A CAD/CAM system for which the supplier/vendor assumes total responsibility for building, installing, and testing both hardware and software, and the training of user personnel. Also, loosely, a system that comes equipped with all the hardware and software required for a specific application or applications. Usually implies a commitment by the vendor to make the system work and to provide preventive and remedial maintenance of both hardware and software. Sometimes used interchangeably with standalone, although standalone applies more to system architecture than to terms of purchase.

tutorial A characteristic of CAD/CAM systems. If the user is not sure how to execute a task, the system will show the user how to do it. A message is displayed to provide information and guidance.

utilities Another term for system capabilities and/or features that enable the user to perform certain processes.

vector A quantity that has magnitude and direction and that, in CAD, is commonly represented by a directed line segment.

verification (1) A system-generated message to a workstation acknowledging that a valid instruction or input has been received. (2) The process of checking the accuracy, viability, and/or manufacturability of an emerging design on the system.

view port A user-selected, rectangular view of a part, assembly, etc., that presents the contents of a window on the display screen. See also *window*.

window A temporary, usually rectangular, bounded area on the display screen that is user-specified to include particular entities for modification, editing, or deletion.

wireframe graphics A computer-aided design technique for displaying a 3D object as a series of lines outlining its surface.

wiring diagram (1) Graphic representation of all circuits and device elements of an electrical system and its associated apparatus or any clearly defined functional portion of that system. A wiring diagram may contain not only wiring system components and wires but also nongraphic information such as wire number, wire size, color, function, component label, and pin number. (2) Illustration of device elements and their interconnectivity as distinguished from their physical arrangement. (3) Drawing that shows how to hook things up.

word A set of bits (typically 16 to 32) that occupies a single storage location and is treated by the computer as a unit. See also *bit*.

working storage That part of the system's internal storage reserved for intermediate results (i.e., while a computer program is still in progress). Also called *temporary storage*.

workstation The work area and equipment used for CAD/CAM operations. It is where the designer interacts (communicates) with the computer. Frequently consists of a display and an input device as well as, possibly, a digitizer and a hard copy device.

write To transfer information from CPU main memory to a peripheral device, such as a mass storage device.

write-protect A security feature in a CAD/CAM data storage device that prevents new data from being written over existing data.

zero The origin of all coordinate dimensions defined in an absolute system as the intersection of the baselines of the x, y, and z axes.

zero offset On an NC unit, this feature allows the zero point on an axis to be relocated anywhere within a specified range, thus temporarily redefining the coordinate frame of reference.

zoom A CAD capability that proportionately enlarges or reduces a figure displayed on a screen.

4 ABBREVIATIONS FOR USE ON DRAWINGS AND IN TEXT— AMERICAN NATIONAL STANDARD

(Selected from ANSI/ASME Y1.1–2003)

Abbreviations & Word

A

Word	Abbr	Word	Abbr	Word	Abbr
abbreviation	ABBR	advisory	ADVSY	alternating current	AC
about	ABT	aerodynamic	AERODYN	alternation	ALT
above	ABV	aeronautic	AERO	alternative	ALTNV
above baseline	ABL	aeronautical national taper pipe thread	ANPT	alternator	ALTNTR
abrasive	ABRSV	after	AFT	altimeter	ALTM
absolute	ABS	aggregate	AGGR	aluminum	AL
absorption	ABSORB	aileron	AIL	aluminum conductor steel reinforced	ACRS
accelerate	ACCEL	air blast circuit breaker	ABCB	amalgam	AMLG
accelerator	ACLTR	air circuit breaker	ACB	ambient	AMB
accelerometer	ACCLRM	air cleaner	AIRCLNR	amendment	AMEND
acceptor	ACPTR	air condition	AIRCOND	American	AMER
access	ACS	air cooled	ACLD	American Gage Design Standard	AGDS
access opening	AO	air escape	AE	American National Standard Code for Information	ASCII
access panel	AP	air header	AHDR	American Standard Elevator Code	ASEC
accessory	ACCESS	air scoop	AS	American Steel Wire Group	ASWG
account	ACCT	air shutoff	ASHOF	American Wire Gage	AWG
accumulate	ACCUM	air shutter	AIRSHTR	ammeter	AMM
accumulator	ACC	air starting	ASTRG	ammonia	AMNA
acetate	ACTT	air-break switch	ABSW	ammonium nitrate	AMNIT
acetylene	ACET	aircraft	ACFT	amount	AMT
acoustic	ACST	airframe	AFR	amperc	AMP
acoustical tile ceiling	ATC	airport	APRT	ampere hour	AMPHR
across	ACR	airtight	AT	ampere hour meter	AHM
across flats	ACRFLT	alarm	ALM	amplifier	AMPL
acrylic	ACRYL	alarm check valve	ACV	amplitude	AMPTD
actual	ACTL	alclad	ALCD	amplitude modulation	AM
actuate	ACTE	alcohol	ALC	analog	ANLG
actuating	ACTG	alignment	ALIGN	analog to digital	AD
actuator	ACTR	alkaline	ALK	analog to digital converter	ADC
adapter	ADPTR	alkalinity	ALKY	analysis	ANAL
addendum	ADD	all terrain vehicle	ATV	analyze	ANALY
additional	ADDL	allocate	ALLOC	anchor	ANC
additive	ADDT	allowance	ALLOW	anchor bolt	AB
address	ADRS	alloy	ALY	anechoic	ANCH
adhesive	ADH	alloy steel protective plating	ASPP	angle order	ANLOR
adjacent	ADJ	alphabetical	ALPHA	angle stop valve	ASV
adjustable speed	ADJSP	alteration	ALTRN		
administer	ADMIN	altered	ALTRD		
adsorbent	ADSORB	alternate	ALTN		
advance	ADV				

angular	ANLR	arrange	ARR	automatic phase lock	APL
anhydrous	ANHYD	arrester	ARSR	automatic reclosing	AUTORECL
anneal	ANL	arsine	ARS	automatic starter	AUTOSTRT
annode	A	article	ART	automatic stop and check valve	AUTOSCV
announcing	ANCG	articulated	ARTCLD	automatic transformer	AXFMR
annunciator	ANN	artificial	ARTF	automatic volume control	AVC
anodize	ANDZ	artillery	ARTY	automatic zero set	AZS
answer	ANS	as required	AR	automation	AUTOMN
antenna	ANT	as soon as possible	ASAP	automobile	AUTO
antifriction bearing	AFB	asbestos	ASB	automotive	AUTOM
antifriction metal	AFM	asbestos covered metal	ACM	auxiliary	AUX
antilogarithm	ANTILOG	asphalt A	ASPH	auxilliary power unit	APU
apartment	APT	asphalt plank floor	ASPHPF	auxiliary register	AUXR
aperature	APERT	asphalt roof shingles	ASPHRS	auxiliary switch	ASW
apparatus	APPAR	asphalt tile base	ATB	auxiliary switch (breaker) normally closed	ASC
apparent	APRNT	aspirator	ASPRTR		
appearance	APP	assemble	ASSEM		
appendix	APPX	assembly	ASM		
application	APPL	assembly	ASSY	auxilliary switch (breaker) normally open	ASO
applied	APLD	assign	ASGN	availability	AVLBL
applique	APLQ	assignment	ASGMT	available	AVAIL
approach	APRCH	assistance	ASSTN	avenue	AVE
approval	APPVL	assistant	ASST	average	AVG
approve	APPV	associate	ASSOC	average diameter	AVGDIA
approved	APVD	association	ASSN	aviation	AVN
approximate	APPROX	assorted	ASRT	avoirdupois	AVPD
April	APR	astronomical unit	AU	awning	AWN
aqueous	AQ	asymmetric	ASYM	axial flow	AXFL
arbitrary	ARB	asymptote	ASYMP	axial pitch	AXP
arc weld	ARCW	at a later date	ALD	axial pressure angle	APA
arccosecant	ARCCSE	atomic hydrogen weld	ATW	azimuth	AZ
arccosine	ARCCOS	atomic weight	ATWT		
arccotangent	ARCCOT	atomizing	ATMG	*B*	
architectural projected window	APW	attach	ATCH	babbitt	BAB
		attack	ATCK	backview	BV
archive	ARCH	attention	ATTN	backwater valve	BWV
arcing	ARNG	attenuation	ATTEN	baffle	BAF
arcsecant	ARCSEC	attitude	ATTD	baggage	BAG
arcsine	ARCSIN	audible	AUD	balance	BAL
arctangent	ARCTAN	audio frequency	AF	balanced line driver	BLD
arithmetic	ARITH	auditor	AUDTR	balanced voltage	BALV
arithmetic average	AA	augment	AGMT	balancing coil	BALCL
arithmetic logic unit	ALU	August	AUG	balancing rheostat	BALRHEO
arithmetic unit	ARITHU	authorize	AUTH	balancing set	BALS
armament	ARMT	automatic check valve	AUTOCV	ball stop	BSP
armature	ARM	automatic phase control	APC	ballast	BLST

band elimination	BDELIM	biology	BIO	brass	BRS
band filter cutoff	BFCO	biparting doors	BIPD	brass divider strip	BDS
bandstop filter	BSFL	bipost	BPT	braze	BRZ
bandwidth	BW	Birmingham Wire Gage	BWG	brazier	BRAZ
barred	BRRD	bits per inch	BPI	brazing	BRZG
barrel tile roof	BTR	bits per second	BPS	break	BRK
barrier, waterproof	BWP	bituminous	BITUM	break jaw	BJ
base diameter	BDIA	black	BLK	breaker	BRKR
base helix angle	BHA	black enamel slate	BES	breaking	BRKG
base pitch	BP	black iron	BI	brezier head	BRAZH
basement	BSMT	black oil finish state	BOFS	bridge	BRDG
basic	BSC	blacken	BLKN	bright	BRT
basket	BSKT	blackening	BLKNG	brilliance	BRIL
battery	BTRY	blanket	BLKT	Brinell hardness	BH
bearing	BRG	blanking	BLKG	Brinell hardness number	BHN
before	BFR	blanking die	BLKGD	British Standard	BSI
bell crank	BELCRK	bleeder	BLDR	British Standard Wire	
belling	BLNG	blend	BLN	Gage	SWG
bellmouth	BLMTH	blocking oscillator	BO	British thermal unit	BTU
bellows	BLWS	blower	BLO	broach	BRCH
below	BLW	blowtorch	BLWT	broadband	BRDG
bench	BNCH	blue	BLU	brown	BRN
bench mark	BM	blue indicating light	BIL	buckram	BUCK
bend down	BDN	blue tool steel	BTS	buffer amplifier	BA
bend radius	BR	board	BD	buffing	BFG
bend up	BUP	bobbin	BOB	building	BLDG
bending	BNG	body on chassis	BOC	built in	BLTIN
bent	BT	boiler	BLR	bulkhead	BHD
berth	BTH	boiler feed water	BFW	bulldozer	BDZR
Bessemer	BESS	boiler pressure	BOPRESS	bulletin	BULL
between	BETW	boiling	BOG	bulletproof	BPRF
bevel	BEV	bolster	BOLS	bullnose	BN
beveled wood siding	BWS	bolted on base	BOBS	bundle	BDL
beverage	BVGE	bonded	BND	burlap	BRLP
bidirectional	BIDIR	bonding	BNDG	burner	BNR
billet steel	BLSTL	bonnet	BNT	burning	BRNG
bimetallic	BMTLC	booster	BSTR	burnish	BNSH
binary	BIN	bootstrap	BTST	burster	BRSTR
binary digit	BIT	bottle	BTL	bus selector	BSLR
binary divide	BDV	bottom	BOT	bushel	BU
binder	BDR	bottoming	BOTMG	bushing	BSHG
binding	BDG	boundary	BDY	bushing potential device	BPD
binding head	BDGH	bouyant	BYNT	business	BUS
binocular	BNCLR	bracket	BRKT	butane	BUTN
biological	BIOL	braid	BRD	butt weld	BTWLD
biological electronics	BIONICS	brake	BK	butterfly	BTFL

button	BTN	commercial and government entity code	CAGE	cradle	CRDL
button head	BTNHD			crankshaft	CSHAFT
buzzer	BUZ	commission	COMSN	crash position indicator	CPI
Bypass	BYP	communication and data	C&D	crimp	CRP
		communications satellite	COMSAT	crosshead	CRSHD
C		compact disk	CD	crossover	CRSVR
cable	CBL	comparator buffer	CB	cruising	CRUIS
cable television	CATV	compatible single side band	CSSB	cryogenics	CRYOG
cable termination equipment	CTE			cryptography	CRYPTO
		compiler	COMP	crystalline	CRYST
calibration	CAL	compressor	COMPR	cubic feet per minute	CFM
cam timing contact	CTC	computer-aided design	CAD	cubic feet per second	CFS
camera control unit	CCU	computer-aided manufacturing	CAM	curve	CRV
cannister	CSTR			cushing	CSHG
capable	CPBL	concentric	CONC	cyanide	CYN
capacitance	CAP	concession	CON	cycle	CY
carbide steel	CS	concrete splash block	CSB	cylinder	CYL
carrier operated relay	COR	concurrent	CNCR		
carrying	CRYG	condition	COND	*D*	
cartridge	CRTG	conference	CONF	damper	DMPR
casing	CSG	conical	CONL	damping	DPG
castellate	CSTL	connection	CONN	dated	DTD
casting	CSTG	consecutive	CONSEC	datum	DAT
category	CAT	console	CSL	daughterboard	DTRBD
cathode ray oscilloscope	CRO	constant current transformer	CCT	deaerating	DEARTG
cathode ray tube	CRT			dealer	DLR
caution	CAUT	constant output amplifier	COA	decelerate	DCLR
Celsius	C	constant speed drive	CSD	decible	DB
center tap	CT	contact	CONT	decimal	DEC
center to center	C to C	contact potential difference	CPD	decision	DECN
centerline	CL	continental horsepower	CONTHP	declutch	DCLU
central processing equipment	CPE	continued	CONTD	decode	DCD
central processing unit	CPU	control power switch	CSW	decoder	DCDR
ceramic tile base	CTB	control read only memory	CROM	decompression	DECOMPN
change in design	CID	control shift register	CSR	decontamination	DECONTN
chrome vanadium	CRVAN	control transmitter	CX	decrease	DECR
chromium plate	CRPL	controlled rectifier	CR	decrement	DECRT
chronometer	CRNMTR	convection	CONVN	dedendum	DED
circuit switching unit	CSU	convector	CONVR	deep drawn	DD
circulating water pump	CWP	convergence	CONVG	defective	DEF
coarse	CRS	corrosion	CRSN	deflating	DFL
coated	CTD	corrosive	CRSV	deflect	DEFL
coating	CTG	corrugated wire glass	CWG	defrost	DRF
cold drawn copper	CDC	cosecant	CSC	degaussing	DEGUSG
cold water	CW	countersink	CSK	degree	DEG
color code	CC	countersink other side	CSKO	dehydrator	DYHR
combining	COMB	countersunk head	CSKH	delay	DLY

delete	DELE	diesel belt drive	DBD	document	DOC
delineation	DEL	diesel engine	DENG	does not apply	DNA
delivery	DLVY	diesel mechanical	DM	domestic	DOM
deluxe	DLX	diesel oil	DO	door closer	DCL
demagnetize	DMGZ	diethanolamine	DEA	door stop	DST
demodulator	DEMOD	differential thermocouple		door switch	DSW
demodulator band filter	DBF	voltmeter	DTVM	doppler velocity and	
demolition	DML	digital analog converter	DAC	position	DOVAP
denatured	DNTRD	digital block AND OR gate	DBAO	dots per inch	DPI
denote	DEN	digital to analog	DA	double	DBL
density	DENS	digital voltmeter	DVM	double acting	DBLACT
dental	DNTL	dimmer	DMR	double acting door	DAD
department	DEPT	diode resistor		double based solid	
deposit	DEP	transistor logic	DRTL	propellant	DBSP
depot installed	DEPINST	diode transistor logic	DTL	double end	DE
depression	DEPR	dipstick	DPSK	double face	DBLF
depth	D	direct current	DC	double pole back connected	DPBC
depth	DP	direct drive	DDR	double pole double throw	DPDT
derivative	DERIV	direct memory access	DMA	double pole double throw	
derrick	DRK	directly	DRCTY	switch	DPDTSW
describe	DESCR	disable	DSBL	double pole front	
description	DESCP	discontinue	DSCONT	connected	DPFC
desiccant	DSCC	discrete Fourier transform	DFT	double pole single throw	DPST
design	DSGN	discriminator	DSCRM	double pole single throw	
design specification	DSPEC	disengaging	DSENGA	switch	DPSTSW
designation	DES	disk operated system	DOS	double pole switch	DPSW
destination	DESTN	dispenser	DISP	double secondary current	
destructive readout	DRO	dispensing	DSPNSG	transformer	DSCT
destructor	DESTR	display	DSPL	double side band	DSB
detached	DTCH	disposition	DISPN	double sided	DS
detail	DET	distance	DIST	double single sideband	DSSB
detent	DTT	distance measuring		double throw	DT
determination	DETN	equipment	DME	double wall	DBLW
develop	DVL	distill	DSTL	double wall fiberboard	DWLFBD
developed length	DEVLG	distillate	DISTLT	doubler	DBLR
development	DEV	distilled water	DW	dovetail	DVTL
deviation	DEVN	distinguish	DISTING	dowel	DWL
device	DVC	distortion	DISTN	down	DN
dial indicating	DLINDG	distress	DTRS	downdraft	DNDFT
dial lock	DLOCK	distribution amplifier	DAMP	dozen	DOZ
diameter bolt circle	DBC	distribution panel	DPNL	drafting	DFTG
diamond	DMD	distributor	DISTR	drafting machine	DFMACH
dither		DTER	draw bar pull	DBP
diamond pyramid		diver	DVR	drawer	DWR
hardness	DPH	diverter	DIV	drawing	DWG
diazo print	DRP	do not use	DNU	drawing change notice	DCN
diesel	DSL	docking	DCKG	drawn	DWN

dredger	DRGR	electric discharge tube	EDT	emitter	E
dressed (lumber)	DRS	electric dynamometer	EDYNMT	emitter	EMTR
dresser	DRSR	electric motor driven	EMD	emitter coupled logic	ECL
dressing	DRSG	electric water cooler	EWC	empennage	EMP
drill	DR	electrical discharge machining	EDM	employee	EMPL
drill jig	DJ	electrical metallic tubing	EMT	emulator	EMU
drive fit	DF	electrical resistance	ER	emulsion	EMUL
drive unit	DRU	electrical specification	ESPEC	enable	ENBL
driver	DRVR	electrical time, superquick	ETSQ	enamel	ENAM
drop manhole	DMH	electrocardiogram	ECG	encapsulation	ENCAP
drop wood siding	DWS	electrode	ELCTD	enclose	ENCL
dry chemical	DCHEM	electrohydraulic	ELHYD	encode	ENCD
dry pipe valve	DPV	electrolyte	ELCTLT	encoder	ENCDR
drying	DYG	electromagnetic	EM	end cell switch	ECSW
dual speed drive	DSD	electromechanical	ELMCH	end half	EHF
dull black finish slate	DBFS	electromotive force	EMF	end to end	EE
dummy	DUM	electron	ELCTRN	endless tangent screw	ETS
dumping	DMPG	electron coupled oscillator	ECO	endstone	ESTN
duplex	DX	electron type semiconductor material	N	engine drive	ED
damping	DPG			engineering change notice	ECN
duplexer	DPLXR	electronic control	ELECTC	engineering change proposal	ECP
duplicate	DUP	electronic standard	ESTD		
duty cycle	DTYCY	electronic switching	ES	engineering change request	ECR
dwelling	DWEL	electronic voltmeter	EVN	engineering field change	EFC
dynamic	DYN	electronic voltohmmeter	EVOM	engineering release notice	ERN
dynamometer	DYNMT	electronically operated valve	ELV	engineering support activity	ESA
dynamotor	DYNM	electronics	ELEX	engineering work order	EWO
E		electronics switching system	ESS	equivalent focal length	EQFL
each	EA	electronik	ELEK	equivalent series resistance	ESR
each way	EW	electropneumatic	ELPNEU		
ebony asbestos	EBASB	electrostatic discharge	ESD	erased	ERS
eccentric	ECC	electrostatic discharge resistive	ESOS	erecting	ERCG
economize	ECON			erector	ERCR
edge thickness	ET	element	ELEM	escape	ESC
edgewise	EDGW	elestrostatic discharge sensitive	ESDS	especially	ESP
education	EDUC			estimate	EST
effective	EFF	elevate	ELEV	estimated completion date	ECD
effective focal length	EFFL	elevation	EL	et cetera	ETC
ejection	EJN	eliminate	ELIM	evacuate	EVAC
ejector	EJCTR	elliptical	ELP	evaluate	EVAL
elastic	ELAS	elliptical head	ELPH	evaluation	EVLTN
elbow	ELB	elongate	ELNG	evaporate	EVAP
electric	ELEC	emboss	EMB	ever lock	EVRLK
electric contact	ELCTC	emergency power supply	EMPS	examination	EXAM
electric contact ring	ELCTRG	emission	EMSN	excavate	EXC
electric contact brush	ELCTCBR				

excessive	EXCSV	fairing	FAIR	figure	FIG
exchange	EXCH	familiar	FAM	filament center tap	FCT
exciter	EXCTR	fan in	FNI	filament ground	FG
exclusive	EXCL	fan out	FNO	file finish	FF
execute	EXEC	far side	FS	file support equipment	FSE
exercise	EXER	fast operate (relay)	FO	fillet	FIL
exhaust	EXH	fast time constant	FTC	filling	FILL
exhaust gas temperature	EGT	fastener	FSTNR	fillister head	FILH
exhaust vent	EXHV	fault	FLT	film processing	FLMPRS
existing	EXST	fault isolation test	FIT	film sound	FLMSD
exit guide vane	EGV	feasible	FSBL	filter	FL
expand	EXP	February	FEB	filter	FLTR
expanded binary coded		Federal	FED	final assembly	FA
decimal interchange	EBCDIC	Federal Stock Number	FSN	finger	FGR
expansion joint	EXPJT	Federal Supply Catalog		finish	FNSH
expedite	EXPED	Identification List	FSCIL	finish all over	FAO
expendable	EXPEN	Federal Supply Code for		finish one side	F1S
explanation	EXPL	Manufacturers	FSCM	finish two sides	F2S
explode	EXPLD	feedback	FDBK	fire alarm bell	FABL
explosion	EXPLN	feedback potentiometer	FPOT	fire control system	FCS
explotation	EXPLTN	feedback resistance	FBR	fire extinguisher	FEXT
exponent	EXPNT	feeder	FDR	fire hose	FH
exposure	EXPSR	feedwater	FDW	fire hose cabinet	FHC
extender	EXTND	feedwater pump	FWP	fire hose rack	FHR
extension	EXT	feeler	FELR	fire hydrant	FHY
extra	EX	female pipe thread	FPT	fire resistant	FRES
extra fine	EF	female	FEM	fire room	FRM
extra heavy	XHVY	female flared	FFL	firebrick	FBCK
extracting	EXTG	female thread	FTHRD	fireplug	FPL
extreme	EXTM	ferrule contact	FERCON	fireproof	FPRF
extremely low frequency	ELF	fiberboard	FBRBD	firmware	FMW
extrude	EXTR	fiberboard, corrugated	FBDC	first in first out	FIFO
eyelet	EYLT	fiberboard, double wall	FDWL	first reduction	1 RED
eyepiece	EYPC	fiberboard, solid	FBDS	first stage	1 STG
F		fibrous	FBRS	fiscal year	FY
fabricate	FAB	field	FLD	fission	FSSN
face width	FW	field decelerator	FDE	fitted	FTD
faceplate	FP	field discharge	FDI	fitting	FTG
facility	FACIL	field dynamic braking	FDB	fixed	FXD
facing	FCG	field effect transistor	FET	fixed autotransformer	FATR
facisimile	FAX	field force, decreasing	FFD	fixed point	FXP
factor	FAC	field force, increasing	FFI	fixture	FXTR
factory	FCTY	field manual	FM	flagstone	FLGSTN
Fahrenheit	F	field service modification		flame	FLM
failure	FLR	work order	FSMWO	flame resistant	FLMRES
failure rate	FR	field switch	FSW	flame tight	FLMTT
		field weakening	FWK		

flameproof	FLMPRF	follow	FOL	from below	FRBEL
flammable	FLMB	follow up	FLWP	front connection	FC
flange	FLG	foot per second	FPS	front end	FRTN
flapper	FLPR	food service	FDSVC	front of board	FOB
flared	FLRD	foot board	FBM	front upset jaw	FUJ
flared tube fitting	FTF	foot per minute	FPM	fuel air ratio	FARATIO
flared tube fitting gasket seal	FTFGS	foot pound force	FTLB	fuel indicator reading	FIR
		for example	EG	fuel injection pump	FIP
flaring	FLRG	forced draft	FD	fuel oil pump	FOP
flashless	FLHLS	forged	FGD	fuel tank	FTK
flash welding	FLW	forged steel	FST	fuel transfer pump	FTP
flat bar	FB	forging	FORG	fueling	FLNG
flat filister head	FFILH	forked	FKD	fulcrum	FUL
flat nose	FN	forman	FMAN	full dog point	FDP
flat trim template	FTT	formation	FORM	full indicator movement	FIM
flat work	FLWK	former	FRMR	full load	FLLD
flathead	FLH	formula translation	FORTRAN	full load amperes	FLA
flatten	FLN	forward	FWD	full scale	FSC
flexible	FLEX	foundation	FDN	fully heat treated	FHT
flip-flop complementary	FFC	foundry	FDRY	function	FCTN
floating	FLTG	four conductor	4/C	fundamental	FUND
floating point instruction set	FIS	four dimensional	4D	funnel	FUNL
flood light	FLDT	four pole	4P	furnish	FURN
flooding	FLDNG	four pole double throw switch	4PDTSW	fuse	FZ
flotation	FLOT			fuse box	FUBX
flow rate	FLRT	four pole single throw switch	4PSTSW	fuse holder	FUHLR
flow switch	FLSW	four pole switch	4PSW	fuselage	FUSLG
fluid flow	FDFL	four stage	4STG	future	FUT
fluid pressure line	FDPL	four way	4WAY	*G*	
fluked	FLKD	four wire	4W	gage	GA
fluorescent	FLUOR	foyer	FOY	gage board	GABD
flurry	FLRY	fractional	FRAC	gage code number	GCN
flush metal threshold	FMT	fragment	FRAG	gain time control	GTC
flush mount	FLMT	framework	FRWK	gallery	GALL
flush threshold	FT	free cutting brass	FCB	galley	GALY
flush type	FLTP	free height	FRHGT	gallon	GAL
flush valve	FV	free machining steel	FMS	gallons per minute	GPM
fluted	FLTD	freeboard	FREEBD	gallons per second	GPS
fluted socket	FLUOSC	freezer	FRZR	galvanize	GALV
fluted socket head	FLUSOCH	freight	FRT	galvanized steel	GALVS
flutter	FLUT	french fry	FRFY	galvanized steel wire rope	GSWR
flyweight	FLYWT	frequency	FREQ		
flywheel	FLYWHL	fresh water drain collecting tank	FWDCT	galvanometer	GALVNM
focal	FOC			galvennealed	GALVND
foggy	FGY	friction	FRICT	gang punch	GP
folding	FLDG	fringe	FRNG	garage	GAR

garbage	GBG	glider	GLI	ground	GND
garbage in garbage out	GIGO	globe stop valve	GSV	ground fault interrupter	GFI
garboard	GARBD	globe valve	GLV	ground glass	GGL
gas operated	GOPR	glossary	GLOSS	grown junction	GJ
gas turbine	GTRB	glow plug	GLPG	guarantee	GUAR
gas weld	GASW	glycerin	GLYCN	guard rail	GDR
gas, nonpersistent	GNP	gold	GLD	guidance	GDNC
gaseous mixture	GM	governing	GOVG	guide	GDE
gaseous oxygen	GOX	government	GOVT	gunmetal	GMET
gasket	GSKT	Government Industry		gusset	GUS
gasoline	GAS	Data Exchange Program	GIDEP	gutter	GUT
gasoline engine	GENG	governor	GOV	gymnasium	GYM
gasproof	GPF	grab rod	GR	gypsum	GYP
gastight	GT	gradient	GRAD	gypsum plaster ceiling	GPC
gate	G	granite	GRAN	gypsum plaster wall	GPW
gate turnoff	GTO	grommet	GROM	gypsum sheathing board	GSB
gate valve	GTV	granolithic base	GRB	gypsum wallboard	GWB
galvanized iron	GALVI	granolithic finished floor	GFF	gyrocompass	GCMPS
gear rack	GRK	granulated	GNLTD	gyroscope	GYRO
gear shaft	GRSHFT	graphic	GRPH	*H*	
gearbox	GRBX	graphic kilovolt ampere		half dog point	1/2DP
gearcase	GRC	meter	GVA	half hard	1/2H
gearing	GRG	graphic varmeter	GRVA	half round	1/2RD
general	GENL	graphite	GPH	hammer	HMR
general contractor	GENCONT	grater	GRTR	hand control	HNDCONT
general note	GN	grating	GRTG	hand rail	HNDRL
general plan equipment		gravel	GVL	hand reset	HNDRST
requirement	GPER	gravel surface buildup		handbook	HDBK
generation	GEN	roof	GSBR	handhold	HH
generator field	GFLD	gray	GRA	handicap	HDCP
geological	GEOL	gray	GY	handle	HDL
geomagnetism	GEOMAG	gray iron	GI	handling	HDLG
geometry	GMTRY	grease	GRS	handling room	HR
German silver	GS1L	grease nozzle	GNOZ	handshake	HDSHK
gimbal	GMBL	greatest common divisor	GCD	handwheel	HNDWL
glass	GL	green	GRN	hanger	HGR
glass block	GLB	green indicating lamp	GIL	hanging	HNG
glaze	GLZ	Greenwich mean time	GMT	hard chromium	HDCR
glazed all tile base	GWTB	grind	GRD	hard disk	HD
glazed facing unit	GFU	groove	GRV	hard drawn	HDDRN
glazed structural facing unit	GSFU	grooved	GRVD	harden	HDN
glazed structural unit base	GSUB	groover	GRVR	harden and grind	HG
glazed structural units	GSU	grooving	GRVG	hardness	HDNS
glazed wall tile	GWT	gross combined weight		hardness assurance	HA
glazed wallboard	GLWB	rating	GCWR	hardness critical item	HCI
glide slope	GLS	gross vehicle weight	GVW	hardness critical process	HCP
		gross weight	GRWT		

hardware	HDW	high frequency oscillator	HFO	horn gap switch	HGSW
hardware cloth	HDWC	high grade plow steel	HGPS	horsepower	HP
hardwood	HDWD	high humidity	HIHUM	horsepower hour	HPHR
harmonic	HMNC	high intensity	HINT	hose connector	HCONN
harness	HARN	high level language	HLL	hose thread	HSTH
hatch	H	high point	HPT	hospital	HOSP
haversine	HAV	high potential	HIPOT	hot brine pump	HBPUMP
hazardous	HAZ	high potential test	HIPOTT	hot galvanize	HGALV
head crank	HC	high pressure steam	HPS	hot leg	HLG
header	HDR	high speed radar	HSR	hot rolled pickled and oiled	HRPO
heading	HDG	high speed steel	HSS	hot rolled steel	HRS
headless	HDLS	high temperature	HTM	hot side	HSD
headlining	HLNG	high tensile	HTNSL	hot water heater	HWH
headquarters	HQ	high tensile cast iron	HTCI	hot water, circulating	HWC
headset	HDST	high tensile strength	HTS	house	HSE
heat exchange	HE	high tension	HT	household	HSHLD
heat resisting	HTRES	high voltage	HV	housing	HSG
heat shield	HTSHLD	high voltage regulator	HVR	hovering	HVRNG
heat sink	HTSK	high-frequency current	HFCUR	howitzer	HOW
heat treat	HTTR	highpass filter	HPFL	humid	HMD
heated	HTD	highway	HWY	hunting	HNTG
heater	HTR	hinge jaw	HJ	hybrid	HYB
heating	HTG	hinge pillar	HPLR	hydrated	HYDTD
heavy	HVY	hoist	HST	hydraulic	HYDR
height	HGT	holddown	HLDN	hydrocyanic acid	HCN
height by width by length	HXWXL	holder	HLDR	hydroelectric	HYDRELC
helical	HLCL	holding	HLDG	hydro-form dye	HFD
helical compression	HLCPS	hollow	HOL	hydrogen ion	
helical extension	HLEXT	homing	HOM	concentration	pH
helicopter	HLCPTR	hone finish monolithic		hydrometer	HYDM
helipotentiometer	HPOT	floor	HFMF	hydrophone	HYPH
helix angle	HLXA	honeycomb	HNYCMB	hydrostatic	HYDRST
helper	HLP	honorary	HON	hyperbola	HYPERB
herringbone	HGBN	hookup	HKP	hyperbolic sine	SINH
Hertz	Hz	hopper	HPR	hyperbolic tangent	TANH
heterodyne	HET	horizon	HRZN	hyperfine structure	HFS
heavy machine gun	HMG	horizontal	HORIZ	hypergolic clean	HGC
hexagon	HEX	horizontal center		hypotenuse	HYP
hexagonal head	HEXHD	of gravity	HCG		
hexagonal socket	HEXSOC	horizontal centerline	HCL	*I*	
hexagonal socket head	HEXSOCH	horizontal impulse	HZMP	ideal lowpass filter	ILPFL
high altitude platform	HAP	horizontal impulse		idler	IDL
high carbon steel	HCS	reaction	HIR	ignition	IGN
high carbon steel, heat		horizontal reaction	HZRN	current source	IGEN
treated	HCSHT	horizontal reference line	HRL	ignitor	IGNTR
high fidelity	HFI	horizontal volute		illuminate	ILLUM
high frequency	HF	spring suspension	HVSS	illustrate	ILLUS

illustrated parts breakdown	IPB	indicate	IND	inside frosted	IF
illustrated parts catalog	IPC	indicator transmitter	INDTR	inside mold line	IML
imaginary	IMAG	indirectly	IDRTY	inside of metal	IM
imitation	IMIT	individually	INDV	inside radius	IR
immediate	IMMED	inductance	L	inside trim template	ITT
immersion	IMRS	inductance capacitance	LC	insignia	ISGN
impact	IMP	inductance capacitance resistance	LCR	insoluble	INSOL
impedance	IMPD			inspect	INSP
impedor	IMPR	inductance regulator	INDREG	inspection check fixture	ICF
impeller	IMPLR	induction compass	ICMPS	inspection check template	ICT
imperfect	IMPF	inductor	IDCTR	install	INSTL
imperial	IMPRL	inductosyn	ISYN	installer	INSTLR
impingement	IGMT	industrial	INDL	instantaneous automatic gain control	IAGC
implement	IMPL	inert	INRT		
impose	IMPS	inert gas	INRTG	instantaneous automatic volume control	IAVC
impression	IMPRSN	inertial	INRTL		
improved plow steel	IMPPS	inertial guidance	IG	instantaneous overload	IOL
improvement	IMPROV	inertial measurement unit	IMU	instantaneous relay	INSTRLY
impregnate	IMPRG	infinite	INF	instruct	INSTR
impulse	IMPLS	inflatable	IFL	instrumentation	INSTM
impulse conductor	IC	information	INFO	insufficient	INSUF
that is	IE	ingot	IGT	insulate	INSUL
in accordance with	IAW	inhibit	INHB	insulated gate field effect transistor	IGFET
inboard	INBD	initial	INIT		
incandescent	INCAND	initial velocity	IV	intake	INTK
incendiary	INCND	inject	INJ	integral	INT
inch	IN	inlet	INL	integrating	INTEG
inch pound	INLB	inner	INR	intelligence	INTEL
incinerator	INCIN	inner back end	IBE	intensity	INTEN
inclined	INCLN	inner bottom	IB	intercept	INTCP
inclosure	INCLS	inner front end	IFE	interchangeable	INTCHG
include	INCL	inoperative	INOP	interchanger	INTCHGR
incoherent	INCOH	inorganic	INORG	intercommunication	ICM
incoming	INCM	input	INP	intercommunication	INTERCOM
incomplete	INCOMP	input output	IO	interconnection	INTCON
incomplete sequence (relay)	IS	input output buffer	IOB	intercooler	INCLR
incorporated	INC	input output element	IOE	intercylinder	INTCYL
incorrect	INCOR	input output register	IOR	interface	INTFC
increase	INCR	input translator	INXLTR	interface control drawing	ICD
incubator	INCBR	inquiry	INQ	interference	INFRN
indent	INDT	inscription	INSC	interference	INTRF
indentification	IDENT	insecticide	ICTDC	interior	INTR
indentured parts list	IPL	inseparate	INSEP	interlock	INTLK
independent	INDEP	insert	INSR	intermediate	INTMD
indeterminate	INDET	insert screw thread	INST	intermediate power amplifier	IPA
index	IDX	inside	INS	intermittent	INTMT

intermittent duty	IDTY	*J*		kinetic energy	KE
intermodulation distortion	IMD	jacket	JKT	knee brace	KB
internal	INTL	jacket water	JW	knife blade	KNBL
internal combustion engine	ICE	jackscrew	JKSCR	knife edge	KNED
		jamming	JAMG	knife switch	KNSW
internal pipe thread	IPT	janppaned	JAP	Koroseal	KRAL
International Annealed Copper Standard	IACS	January	JAN	*L*	
		jet propelled	JP	label	LBL
International Pipe Standard	IPS	jettison	JTSN	laboratory	LAB
		job order	JO	labyrinth	LBYR
International Standard Thread (metric)	IST	joggle	JOG	labyrinth pack	LBYRPK
		joiner	J	lacquer	LAQ
International Standards Organization	ISO	joint	JT	ladder	LAD
		joint bar	JTB	lagging	LAG
interphase transformer	INTPHTR	joint compound	JC	lampholder	LPHLDR
interpolation	INTRPL	journal	JNL	laminate	LAM
interpole	INTPO	July	JUL	lampblack	LMPBLK
interpret	INTPR	junction	JCT	landing	LDG
interrogate	INTRG	junction box	JB	landmark	LDMK
interrupt	INTRPT	junction field effect transistor	JFET	lantern	LTRN
interrupted continuous wave	ICW	June	JUN	lanyard	LNYD
intersect	INTSCT	junior	JR	lapping	LPG
intership	INTSHP	*K*		large	LGE
interstage	INTSTG	cathode	K	last in first out	LIFO
interval	INTVL	Kalamein	KAL	latch	LCH
intervalometer	INTVLM	Kalamein door	KALD	lateral	LATL
intricate	INTRC	Kalamein door and frame	KDF	latitude	LAT
intrinsic *i*-type semiconductor material	I	keene cement plaster	KCB	lattice	LTC
		keene cement plaster ceiling	KCPC	launch	LANH
introduction	INTRO	keeping	KPG	launcher	LCHR
invariant	INVAR	kerosene	KRSN	laundry	LAU
inventory	INVN	key locker	KL	lavatory	LAV
inverse	INVS	key pulsing	KPLS	layer	LYR
inverse time limit	ITL	keyboard	KYBD	layout	LYT
inverse time relay	ITR	keypunch	KP	lead angle	LA
invert	INVT	keyseat	KST	lead coated metal	LCM
inverter	INV	keyway	KWY	leader	LDR
involute	INVLT	kick plate	KPL	leading edge radius	LER
inward	INWD	kickoff (relay)	KO	leakoff	LOFF
ionosphere	IONO	kiln dried	KD	least material condition	LMC
iron core reactor	ICR	kilovolt ampere hour	KVAH	leather	LTHR
iron pipe	IP	kilovolt ampere hour meter	KVAHM	leaves	LVS
irregular	IRREG	kilovolt ampere meter	KVAM	left bank	LBK
isolate	ISOL	kilowatt hour meter	KWHM	left hand	LH
isolation	ISLN	kinescope	KINE	left hand drive	LHDR
isosceles	ISOS			left hand side	LHS
issue	ISS				

left male	LM	linoleum	LINOL	long side	LSD
left right indicator	LRI	lintel	LNTL	long taper	LTPR
left side	LS	liquid	LIQ	long wheelbase	LWB
length	LG	liquid fuel	LIQFL	longeron	LONGN
length between perpendiculars	LBP	liquid in glass	LQGLS	longitude	LONG
length of curve	LCRV	liquid oxygen	LOX	longitudinal expansion joint	LEJ
length of lead (actual)	LOL	liquid rocket engine	LRE	longleaf yellow pine	LLYP
length overall	LOA	liquor	LQR	loop control (relay)	LPC
length to diameter ratio	LGC	lithograph	LITHO	looper	LPR
lengthening	LNG	litter	LIT	louvered door	LVD
letter	LTR	lizard	LIZ	low alloy steel	LS
level	LVL	load inducing relay	LIRLY	low coolant	LCOLNT
lever	LVR	load limiting resistor	LLRES	low frequency	LF
library	LBRY	load ratio control	LRC	low frequency oscillator	LFO
license	LIC	load resistor (relay)	LR	low level	LL
lifesaving	LSVG	load shifting ratio	LSR	low level logic	LLL
lift up door	LUD	load update subset	LUS	low pass	LP
lifting	LFT	load waterline	LWL	low power output	LPO
lifting eye	LE	local	LCL	low speed	LSP
light	LT	local apparent time	LAPT	low stream	LSTM
light activated semi-conductor controlled rectifier	LASCR	local area network	LAN	low temperature	LTEMPT
		local oscillator	LO	low torque	LTQ
light amplification simulated emission radiation	LASER	local sidereal time	LSDT	low voltage	LV
		local standard time	LST	low voltage protection	LVP
		localizer	LOC	lower	LWR
light emitting diode	LED	locate	LCT	lower deck	LDK
light switch	LTSW	lock pillar	LPLR	lower sideband	LSB
light tank	LTTK	lock washer	LKWASH	lowest	LWST
lighter than air	LTA	locked	LKD	lowest useable frequency	LUF
lighting	LTG	locked closed	LKDC	lowest useable high frequency	LUHF
lightproof louver	LPL	locked in device	LID	lowpass filter	LPFL
lightproof shade	LPS	locked open	LKDO	lubricant	LUBT
lightproof vent	LPTR	locked rotor	LKROT	lubricate	LUB
lightweight concrete	LWC	locker	LKR	lubricating oil	LUBO
lighweight insulating concrete	LWIC	locking	LKG	lubricating oil pump	LOP
lignum vitae	LGNMVTE	locknut	LKNT	lumber	LBR
limit	LIM	lockscrew	LKSCR	lumers per watt	LPW
limit switch	LIMSW	locksmith	LSMITH	luminous	LUM
limited	LTD	lockup	LKUP	lunar orbit rendezvous	LOR
limiting	LMTG	lockwire	LKWR	*M*	
limiter	LMTR	locomotive	LOCO	machine	MACH
line drawing	LD	logarithm	LOG	machine screw	MSCR
line of sight	LOS	logarithm, natural	LN	machine steel	MST
linear	LIN	logarithmic amplifier	LOAMP	machined surface	MASU
linkage	LKGE	logic	LGC	machinery	MCHRY
		logic unit	LU		

machinist	MCHST	manuscript	MS	medium pressure	MP
magnesium thorium	MAGTHOR	manuvering	MANUV	megabyte	MEG
magnetic	MAG	marble base	MRB	melamine	MEL
magnetic amplifier	MAGAMP	marble floor	MRF	member	MBR
magnetic modulator	MAGMOD	marble threshold	MRT	membrane	MEMB
magnetic particle inspection	MPI	March	MAR	memorandum	MEMO
magneto	MGN	margin	MARG	memory	MEM
magnetohydrodynamics	MHD	marginal (relay)	MGL	merchandise	MDSE
magnetometer	MGTMTR	marked	MKD	merchantable	MERCH
magnetomotive force	MMF	marker	MKR	mercurial	MRCL
magnetron	MAGN	markings	MKGS	meridian	MER
magnetude	MAGTD	masking	MASK	meshing	MSHG
magnify	MGF	masonry	MSNRY	message	MSG
mahogany	MAH	master oscillator power amplifier	MOPA	message generator	MSGG
mainframe	MNFRM	master switch	MSW	messenger	MESS
maintenance	MAINT	mastic	MSTC	metal	MET
maintenance and repair	MR	mastic joint	MJ	metal anchor	MA
maintenance parts kit	MPK	matched	MTCHD	metal anchor slots	MAS
maintenance parts list	MPL	material	MATL	metal awning type window	MATW
major	MAJ	material test specification	MTS	metal base	METB
makeup	MKUP	mathematical	MATH	metal casement window	MCW
makeup feed	MUFD	matrix	MAT	metal clad switch gear	MCSWGR
male and female	MF	matrix output amplifier	MOA	metal corner bead	MCB
male flared	MFLRD	maximum	MAX	metal covered door	MCD
male pipe thread	MPT	maximum capacity	MAXCAP	metal curb	METC
male thread	MTHRD	maximum material condition	MMC	metal door	METD
malfunction	MALF			metal flashing	METF
malleable	MAL	maximum permissible exposure	MPE	metal grille	METG
malleable iron	MI	maximum working pressure	MWP	metal interface amplifier	MIA
management	MGT	maximum working voltage	MWV	metal lath and plaster	MLP
manager	MGR	mean aerodynamic chord	MAC	metal mold	METM
managing	MNG	mean effective pressure	MEP	metal mount	MMT
mandrel	MDRL	mean time between failures	MTBF	metal oxide semiconductor	MOS
manhole	MH	mean time to failure	MTTF	metal oxide semiconductor field effects tra	MOSFET
manifold	MANF	mean time to first failure	MTTFF	metal oxide semiconductor transistor	MOST
manual	MNL	mean time to repair	MTTR	metal partition	METP
manual change order	MCO	mean variation	MV	metal rolling door	MRD
manual change request	MCR	mean width ratio	MWR	metal roof	METR
manual gain control	MGC	measure	MEAS	metal strip	METS
manual overload	MANOVLD	mechancial	MECH	metal thick oxide silicon	MTOS
manual volume control	MVC	mechanize	MECZ	metal through wall flashing	MTWF
manually operated	MNLOPR	median	MDN	metallic	MTLC
manufacture	MFR	medical	MED	metallize	MTLZ
manufactured	MFD	medium	MDM	meter	M
manufacturing	MFG	medium high frequency	MHF	meter	MTR

meter killogram second	MKS	momentary	MOM	narrow band	NB
meterological	METRL	monitor	MON	narrow gage	NG
method	MTHD	monograph	MONOG	national	NATL
mezzanine	MEZZ	monophonic	MONO	National coarse thread	NC
microammeter	MCAM	Montana	MT	National Electrical Code	NEC
microcomputer	MCMPTR	month	MO	National Electrical Code Standards	NECS
microcurrent	MCKT	mooring	MRG		
microelectronics	MELEC	mop rack	MOPR	National Electrical Safety Code	NESC
microelement	MELEM	most significant bit	MSB		
microfunctional circuit	MFC	mostly	MSLY	National extra fine thread	NEF
micrometer	MIC	motherboard	MTHBD	National fine thread	NF
microminiature	MMIN	motion	MTN	National gas outlet thread	NGO
microprocessor	IMPRCS	motor	MOT	National pipe thread	NP
microscope	MICR	motor belt drive	MBD	national stock number	NSN
microwave early warning	MEW	motor can	MOCAN	National taper pipe thread	NPT
middle	MDL	motor circuit switch	MCSW		
midget	MDGT	motor direct	MD	National Wire Gage	NWG
miles per gallon	MPG	motor direct connected	MDC	natural	NAT
miles per hour	MPH	motor v-belt	MVB	natural black slate	NBS
military	MIL	motorcycle	MC	nautical	NAUT
military standard	MIL-STD	motorized	MTZ	nautical mile	NMI
milliammeter	MAM	mounted	MTC	naval	NAV
mineral	MNRL	mounting	MTG	naval bronze	NAVBRZ
mineral surface roof	MSR	mounting center	MTGC	Navy Primary Standards	NPS
miniature	MINTR	movable	MVBL	Navy Secondary Standards	NSS
minimum	MIN	movement	MVT	navy standard flange	NFL
minimum discernable signal	MDS	moving	MVG	needle	NDL
mirror	MIR	muffler	MUF	negative	NEG
miscellaneous	MISC	multifrequency pulsing	MFP	negative positive innegative negative	NPIN
missile	MSL	multigage	MG		
miter	MIT	multilith	MULTH	negative positive negative positive	NPNP
miter end	ME	multimeter	MULTR		
mixing	MXG	multiplane	MLTPL	negative positive negative transistor	NPN
mixing flow	MXFL	multiple	MULT		
mixture	MXT	multiple unit	MU	negative temperature coefficient	NTC
mobile	MBL	multiplex	MUX		
mode transducer	MXDCR	multispeed	MLTSP	neon indicating light	NEIL
model	MOD	munitions	MUN	neoprene	NPRN
modification work order	MWO	music wire	MUW	net weight	NTWT
modulator demodulator	MODEM	music wire gage	MWG	network	NTWK
moisture	MSTRE	muzzle	MZL	neutral	NEUT
mold line	ML	*N*		neutron	NTN
molded	MLD	nacelle	NAC	next higher assembly	NHA
molding	MLDG	name plate	NPL	nickel	NKL
molecular weight	MOLWT	namely	VIZ	nickel copper	NICOP
molecule	MOL	narrow	NAR	nickel copper alloy	NCA
				nickel silver	NISIL

nickel steel	NS	normal overload	NOL	oil pressure	OPRS
nipple	NIP	normal pressure angle	NPA	oil pump	OP
nitride steel	NITSTL	normal temperature and		oil ring	OR
no drawing	ND	pressure	NTP	oil seal	OSL
no load	NLD	normally open	NO	oil switch	OS
no voltage release	NVR	not applicable	NA	oiltight	OT
noise generator	NGEN	not in contact	NIC	on center	OC
no lead	NL	not to scale	NTS	one stage	OSTG
nomenclature	NOMEN	notched	NCH	one way	OW
nominal	NOM	notice of revision	NOR	opaque	OPA
noncombustible	NCOMBLE	November	NOV	open close open	OCO
noncorrosive metal	NCM	nozzle	NOZ	open end	OE
noncoupled	NCPLD	nuclear	NUC	open hearth	OH
nondestructive evaluation	NDE	numeral	NUM	open jointed	OJ
nondestructive inspection	NDI	nut plate	NTPL	open type control	
nondestructive readout	NDRO	nylon	NYL	circuit contacts	OTCCC
nondestructive testing	NDT	*O*		opening	OPNG
nonelectric	NELEC	object	OBJ	openside	OPSD
nonenclosure	NENCL	objective	OBJV	operate	OPR
nonflammable	NFLMB	oblique	OBL	operational	OPNL
nonfused	NFSD	obscure	OB	opposite	OPP
nonhygroscopic	NH	observation	OBSV	optical character recognition	OCR
nonlinear	NLNR	obsolete	OBS	optimum	OPT
nonmetallic	NM	obstruction	OBSTN	optimum working frequency	OWF
nonoscillating	NOSC	obverse	OBV	optional	OPTL
nonpetroleum	NPET	occupy	OCC	orange	O
locknut pipe thread	NPSL	octahedral	OCTAHDR	orange	ORN
straight thread pipe		October	OCT	orange indicating light	OIL
couplings	NPSC	odometer	ODOM	order	ORD
tight joints	NPTF	of true position	OTP	organization	ORG
taper pipe thread railing		office	OFC	orientation	ORIENT
fixtures	NPTR	officer	OFCR	orifice	ORF
thread for press-tight		official	OFCL	origin	ORIG
joins	NPSF	offset	OFS	original equipment	
nonreactive relay	NR	ohmmeter	OHM	manufacturer	OEM
nonreinforced concrete		oil circuit breaker	OCB	oscillating	OSCG
pipe	NRCP	oil cleaner	OCLNR	oscillator	OSC
nonreversible	NRVSBL	oil cooled	OCLD	oscillogram	OSCGRM
nonself	NSLF	oil cooler	OCLR	oscilloscope	SCOPE
nonslip thread	NST	oil dipstick	ODPSK	other design activity	ODA
nonstandard	NONSTD	oil filter	OFL	ounce	OZ
nonsynchronous	NONSYN	oil immersed	OI	ounce inch	OZIN
nontight	NT	oil level	OLVL	ouside helix angle	OHA
normal	NORM	oil nozzle	ONOZ	out to out	OO
normal charge	NLCHG	oil pan	OPN	outerback end	OBE
normal circular pitch	NCP	oil plug	OPLG	outlet	OUT
normal diametral pitch	NDP			output transistor	OUTXLTR

outside diameter	OD	parity bit	PBIT	perpendicular	PERP
outside diameter tube	ODT	parkerized	PARK	person	PER
outside face	OF	parking	PRKG	personnel	PERS
outside mold line	OML	parkway	PKWY	perspective	PERSP
outside screw and yoke	OSY	part indentification		petroleum	PETRO
outside trim template	OTT	number	PIN	pewter	PWTR
oval head	OVH	part number	PN	phantom	PHM
oval point	OVP	part of	PO	pharmacy	PHAR
overall	OA	partial	PART	phase	PH
overflow	OVFL	partition	PTN	phase shift	PSH
overfrequency relay	OFR	partly	PTLY	phase shift driver	PSHD
overhanging	OVHG	parts kit	PRTKT	phenoic	PHEN
overhaul	OVHL	party	PTY	Phillips head	PHH
overhead	OVHD	passenger	PASS	phonograph	PHONO
overload	OVLD	passivate	PSV	phosphor bronze	PHBRZ
overload relay	ORLY	passive	PSIV	phosphorescent	PHOS
overpower	OVPWR	paste	PST	photocopy	PHOC
override	OVRD	patent	PAT	photodiode	PDIO
oversize	OVS	patent pending	PATPEND	photoelectric	PELEC
overspeed	OVSP	pattern	PATT	photoelectric cell	PEC
overtravel	OVTR	peak inverse (reverse)		photograph	PHOTO
overvoltage	OVV	voltage	PRV	phototransistor	PXSTR
oxide	OXD	pedestal	PED	physical	PHYS
oxygen	OXY	pencil	PCL	physiological	PHYSIOL
P		pendant	PEND	pickup	PU
		pendular	PNDLR	picture	PIX
package	PKG	penetrate	PEN	piece mark	PCMK
padder capacitor	PAD	pentaerythryte		pierce	PRC
paint	PNT	tetranitrate	PETN	pierced aluminum	
painted	PTD	pentagon	PNTGN	plank	PAP
pallet	PLL	pentode	PENT	pierced steel plank	PSP
pan head	PNH	percent	PCT	pigment	PGMT
panel	PNL	percussion	PERC	pigtail	PGT
panic bolt	PANB	perforate	PERF	piling	PLG
panoramic	PAN	performance	PRFM	pillow block	PLBLK
paper	PPR	performance evaluation		pilot	PLT
parabola	PRB	and review technic	PERT	pilot light	PLTLT
parabolic	PRBLC	Performance Operational		pinion end	PE
paraboloid	PRBD	Maintenance Site	POMSEE	pintle	PTL
parachute	PRCHT	perimeter acquisition		pioneer	PION
paragraph	PARA	radar	PACR	pipe plug	PPG
parallax	PRX	periodic	PERD	pipe rail	PR
parallel	PRL	peripheral	PRPHL	pipe sleeve	PSL
parameter	PRMTR	peripheral command		pipe tap	PT
parametric amplifier	PARAMP	indicator	PCI	pipeline	PPLN
parchment	PCHT	periscope	PERIS	pipette	PPE
parenthesis	PAREN	permanent	PERM		
		permeability	PERMB		

piping	PP	port side light	PSLT	preference	PREF
pistol	PSTL	portable	PORT	preferred	PFD
piston	PSTN	position	POSN	prefocus	PRFCS
pitch diameter	PD	positioner	PSNR	preformed	PREFMD
pivot	PVT	positive	POS	preformed beam	PFB
places	PL	positive displacement	PDISPL	preheat	PHT
plain washer	PW	positive negative intrinsic positive	PNIP	preheater	PHR
planar	PLNR			preinserted	PINSTD
planar epitaxial passivated transistor	PEP	positive negative positive negative	PNPN	preliminary	PRELIM
plane	PLN	positive negative positive transistor	PNP	premium	PREM
planet	PLNT			premolded	PRMLD
planetary	PLNTY	post indicator valve	PIV	premolded expansion joint	PEJ
plank	PLK	potable water	POTW	preparation	PREP
planning	PLNG	potential	POT	prescription	PRESCR
plaque	PLQ	potential switch	PSW	present	PRES
plaster	PLAS	pound	LB	preservation	PSVTN
plastic	PLSTC	pound force foot	LBFT	preservative	PSVTV
plate glass	PLGL	pound force inch	LBIN	press	PRS
plated	PLD	pound force per square foot	PSF	press fit	PRFT
platform	PLATF	pound force per square inch	PSI	pressboard	PBD
plating	PLTG	pound per cubic foot	PCF	pressed	PRSD
pliers	PLR	pound per horsepower	PHP	pressed metal	PRSDMET
plotting	PLOT	powder	PDR	presser	PRSR
plow steel rope	PSR	powder	PWD	pressure	PRESS
plumbing	PLMB	power	PWR	pressure gage	PG
plunger	PLGR	power amplifier	PA	pressure vessel	PV
plus or minus	PORM	power circuit breaker	PCB	pressurize	PRSRZ
pneumatic	PNEU	power control unit	PCU	prevent	PVNT
pnpn transistor magnetic logic	PTML	power driven	PDVN	previous	PREV
		power factor	PF	primary	PRI
pocket	PKT	power supply	PWRSPLY	Primary Coolant System	PCS
point of compound curve	PCC	power supply unit	PSU	prime	PRM
point of intersection	PI	power switchboard	PSWDB	prime mover	PMVR
polarity	PLRT	power takeoff	PTO	primer	PRMR
polish	POL	powerhouse	PWRH	priming	PRM
polyester	POLYEST	practice	PRAC	printed circuit	PC
polyethylene	POLTHN	preamplifier	PREAMP	printed wiring assembly	PWA
polyethylene insulated conductor	PIC	prebent	PRBNT	printed wiring board	PWB
polystyrene	PS	precast	PRCST	printer	PTR
polytetrafluorethylene	PTFE	precedence	PREC	printing	PRNTG
polyvinyl chloride	PVC	precharge	PRCH	printout	PTOUT
pontoon	PON	precipitate	PPT	prism	PSM
popping	POP	precipitation	PRECP	private automatic branch exchange	PABX
porcelain	PORC	precipitin	PRCPTN	probability	PROB
porro	POR	precision	PRCN	procedure	PROC
		prefabricated	PREFAB		

process	PRCS	pulse code modulation	PCM	quarter hard	1/4H
processing	PRCSG	pulse count modulation	PCTM	quarter phase	QTRPH
processing unit	PROCU	pulse duration modulation	PDM	quarter phase	1/4PH
procurement	PRCMT	pulse frequency modulation	PFM	quarter round	QTRRD
production	PROD	pulse interval modulation	PIM	quarter round	1/4RD
program	PRGM	pulse per minute	PPM1N	quartz	QTZ
program register	PRGMRGTR	pulse position modulation	PPM	quaternary	QUAT
programmable logic array	PLA	pulse time modulation	PTM	question	QUEST
programmable logic controller	PLC	pulse time multiplex	PTMUX	quick break	QB
		pulse width modulation	PWM	quick disconnect	QDISC
programmable unijunction transistor	PUJT	pulverizer	PULV	quick firing	QF
		pump discharge	PDISCH	quick opening device	QOD
programming	PRGMG	punch	PCH	quiescent	QUIES
progress	PROG	punching	PCHG	quintuple	QUIN
project	PROJ	purchase	PURCH	quotation	QUOT
projectile	PJCTL	purge	PRG		
projection	PJCTN	purging	PRNG	*R*	
projector	PJTR	purification	PRFCN	rabbet	RAB
proof	PRF	purifier	PUR	rachet	RCHT
proofread	PRFRD	purple indicating light	PIL	radial	RDL
propane	PRPN	push button	PB	radiated emission	RE
propellant	PRPLT	push pull plate	PPP	radiation	RADN
propeller	PROP	push rod	PRD	radiator	RDTR
proportion	PROPN	pyrogen unit	PYGN	radio detection and ranging	RADAR
proposal	PRPSL	pyrometer	PYROM		
proposed	PRPSD	pyrotechnic	PYRO	radio direction finding	RDF
propulsion	PRPLN	*Q*		radio frequency	RF
prosthetic	PRSTC	quadrangle	QUAD	radio frequency choke	RFC
protect	PTCT	quadrant	QDRNT	radio frequency interference	RHI
protection	PROT	quadrature	QDRTR		
protective device	PROTDEV	quadruple	QUADR	radio inertial	RIN
prototype	PROTO	qualified products list	QPL	radio telegraph	RTLG
protractor	PROTR	quality	QUAL	radio telephony	RTEL
provision	PROV	quality assurance	QA	radio teletype	RTT
proximity	PROX	quality conformance inspection	QCI	radioactive	RAACT
p-type hole semi-conductor material	P			radioactive liquid waste	RALW
		quality control	QC	radius	RAD
publication	PUBN	quantitative	QUANT	railcar	RLCR
pull button	PLB	quantity	QTY	railing	RLG
pull button switch	PBSW	quantum amplification stimulated emission	QUASER	railroad	RR
pull rod	PLRD			railway	RY
pulley	PUL	quarry	QRY	raised	RSD
pulsation	PLSN	quarry tile base	QTB	raised face diameter	RFD
pulsator	PLSR	quart	QT	raised face height	RFH
pulse	PLS	quarter	QTF	ramjet	RMJ
pulse amplitude modulation	PAM	quarter hard	QTH	random	RNDM
				random access memory	RAM
				range	RNG

rating	RTG	recording kilovolt ampere meter	RKVAM	reliability	RELBL
rattail	RTTL	recording tachometer	RTM	relief	RLF
raw material	RM	recording varmeter	RVARM	relief valve	RV
rayon	RYN	recoverability	RECY	relieve	RLV
reacting volt ampere meter	RVA	recovery	RCVY	relocated	RELOC
reaction	RCTN	recreation	RCN	remote	RMT
reactivate	REACTVT	rectangle	RECT	remote control system	RCS
reactive	REAC	recurrent	RCUR	remove	RMV
reactive factor meter	RFM	red fuming nitric acid	RFNA	removeable	REM
reactive voltmeter	RVM	red indicating lamp	RIL	renewable	RNWBL
reactor core	RCO	redesignate	REDSG	repair	RPR
read write	RW	reduce	RDC	repeat	RPT
readar	RDR	reducer	RDCR	repeater	RPTR
reading	RDNG	reduction	RDCN	repeating coil	RPTC
readout	RDOUT	reduction of area	RA	repeller	RPLR
ready	RDY	reentry	REY	repetition	RPTN
real time	RT	refacer	RECR	replace	REPL
real time input output transducer	RIOT	reference	REF	replenishing	RPLNG
reamer	RMR	reference designation	REFDES	replenishment	RPNSM
rebabbit	RBBT	reference line	REFL	report	RPRT
recall	RCL	refined	RFND	reproduce	REPRO
receive	RCV	reflected	REFLD	reproducer	RPDR
received	RCVD	reflective insulation	Rl	reproducing unit	RU
receiver	RCVR	reflex	RFLX	republic	REPB
receiving	RCVG	refractory	RFRC	repulsion	RPLSN
receptacle	RCPT	refrigerant	RFGT	request	REQ
reception	RCPTN	refrigerate	REFR	request for price quotation	RPQ
recess	REC	regardless of feature size	RFS	required	REQD
recharger	RECHRG	regenerate	REGEN	requirement	REQT
reciprocate	RECIP	register	RGTR	requisition	REQN
recirculate	RECIRC	register drive	RD	rescind	RESC
reclaiming	RCLMG	regular	RGLR	rescue	RSQ
reclined	RCLD	regulate	RGLT	rescue boat	RSQB
reclose	RECL	regulator	RGLTR	research and development	R&D
recognition	RECOG	reheater	RHR	reserve	RSV
recoiless	RCLS	reid vapor pressure	RVP	reserve feed water	RFW
recommend	RECM	reinforce	REINF	reservoir	RSVR
recompression	RCMPRS	reinforced concrete culvert pipe	RCCP	residual	RESID
recondense	RECOND			residual field	RESFLD
recondition	RCNDT	reinforced concrete pipe	RCP	resiliant	RESIL
reconnaissance	RECON	reject	REL	resistance	R
record	RCD	relate	RLT	resistance capacitance	RC
record and report	RAR	relation	RLTN	resistance capacitance coupled	RCCPLD
recording ammeter	RAMM	relaxation	RLXN	resistance inductance	RL
recording demand meter	RDM	relay	RLY	resistance inductance capacitance	RLC
		relay block	RB		

resistor	RES	ridge	RDG	safe working pressure	SWP
resistor capacitor transistor logic	RCTL	rigging	RGNG	safety	SAF
		right angle	RTANG	safety valve	SV
resistor transistor logic	RTL	right hand drive	RHDR	salinity	SAL
resolution	RESOLN	right hand side	RHS	salvage	SALV
resolver	RSLVR	right side	RS	same size	SS
resonant	RESN	rigid	RGD	sampling	SMPLG
respective	RSPV	ring counter	RCNTR	sandblast	SDBL
respectively	RESP	rivet	RVT	sanitary	SAN
respirator	RSPTR	roasting	RSTG	saponify	SAPON
respond	RSPD	rocker	RKR	satellite	SATL
response	RSPS	rocker arm	RKRA	saturate	SAT
restore	RST	rocket	RKT	sawtooth	ST
restorer	RESTR	Rockwell hardness	RH	saybold second furol	SSF
restrict	RSTR	rod control	RCONT	saybolt second universal	SSU
retain	RET	rod drive	RDDR	scale	SC
retainer	RTNR	Roebling Wire Gage	RWG	scale model	SCMOD
retard	RTD			scanning	SCNG
retardation coil	RTDC	rolled	RLD	scanning electron microscope	SEM
retension	RETNN	roller	RLR		
reticle	RTCL	roofing	RFG	scattered	SCTD
reticulated grating	RG	root mean square	RMS	scavenge	SCAV
retract	RETR	root sum square	RSS	schedule	SCHED
retrieve	RTRV	rotary	RTRY	schematic	SCHEM
retroactive	RETRO	rotate	ROT	science	SCI
retrogressive	RETROG	rotator	ROTR	scintillator	SCINT
return	RTN	rotometer	ROTOMT	scleroscope	SCLER
return head	RHD	rotor	RTR	scooter	SCTR
return to zero	RZ	rough	RGH	scope	SCP
reverberation control of gain	RCG	rough opening	RO	scraper	SRPR
		round	RND	screen door	SCD
reverse	RVS	round head	RDH	screw	SCR
reverse acting	RACT	round trips per hour	RTPH	screw down	SCRDN
reverse current	REVCUR	route	RTE	screwdriver	SCDR
reversible	RVSBL	routine	ROUT	sealed	SLD
revision	REV	rubber	RBR	seamless	SMLS
revolution indicating system	RIS	rubber insulation	RINSUL	seamless steel tubing	SSTU
		rubber tile floor	RTF	second	SEC
revolution per minute	RPM	rudder	RUD	section	SECT
revolution per second	RPS	runway	RWY	sector	SCTR
revolve	RVLV	rust preventative	RPVNTV	sector scan indicator	SSI
rewind	RWND	rustproof	RSTPF	securing	SECRG
rheostat	RHEO	*S*		security	SCTY
rhodium	RHOD	saddle	SDL	sedan	SED
rhombic	RHOMB	safe operating area	SOAR	screw	SSCR
ribbed	RIB	safe practice data sheet	SPDS	segment	SEG
ribbon	RBN				

select	SEL	settling	SETLG	silenging	SILG
self cleaning	SLFCLN	sewage	SEW	silicomanganese steel	SMS
self closing	SELFCL	hyperbolic secant	SECH	silicon precision alloy transistor	SPAT
self contained	SCNTN	sexless (connector)	SXL	silicon unilateral diffused transistor	SUDT
self destroying	SD	sextant	SXTN	silver	SIL
self locking	SLFLKG	sextuple	SXT	silver brazing union	SBU
self propelled	SELFPROP	shaft	SFT	silver solder	SILS
self sealing	SLFSE	shaft extension	SFTEXT	similar	SIM
self tapping	SLFTPG	shaft gear	SHFGR	sine	SIN
selsyn	SELS	shank	SHK	single	SGL
semiconductor	SEMICOND	shape	SHP	single base solid propellant	SBSP
semiconductor controlled switch	SCS	sharpener	SHRP	single beam klystron	SBK
semiconductor unilateral switch	SUS	shearing	SHRNG	single conductor	IC
semiconductory bilateral switch	SBS	sheathing	SHTHG	single conductor cable	SCC
		sheave	SHV	single cylinder	SCYL
semifireproof	SFPRF	sheet	SH	single end	SE
semifixed	SFXD	shell	SHL	single face	SIF
semiflush	SFLS	shield	SHLD	single feeder	SFDR
semiphore	SMPHR	shift	SHF	single groove insulation	SG
semitrailer	STLR	shipment	SHPT	single groove single petticoat insulation	SGSP
sender	SDR	shipping	SHPNG	single pole	SP
sending	SNDG	shipping center	SHCR	single pole double throw	SPDT
sense	SEN	shock absorber	SHABS	single pole double throw switch	SPDTSW
sense amplifier	SA	shop replaceable unit	SRU	single side band	SSB
sensitive	SENS	short circuit	SHORT	single sideboard	SSBD
sensitized	SNTZD	short leaf yellow pine	SLYP	single signal	SSIG
sensitizing	SNTZG	short taper	STPR	single swing blocking oscillator	SSBO
sensor	SNSR	short time constant	SHTC	sinter	SNTR
separate	SEP	short wheelbase	SWB	situation	SIT
sequence	SEQ	shot blast	SHBL	sketch	SK
sequential coding	SECO	shoulder	SHLDR	skirted	SKD
serial	SER	shower and toilet	SHT	skylight	SLT
serial number	SERNO	shown	SHN	slate shingle roof	SSR
serrate	SERR	shrapnel	SHRAP	sleeve	SLV
server	SVR	shredder	SHRDR	sleeving	SLVG
service	SVCE	shroud	SHRD	slice	SLC
service bulletin	SB	shroud fin	SHRDF	sliding	SL
service ceiling	SRVCLG	shunt trip	SHTR	sliding expansion joint	SEJ
service factor amperes	SFA	shut down	SHTDN	slinger	SLGR
serving	SERG	shut off valve	SOV	slip joint	SJ
servomechanism	SERVO	shuttle	SHTL	slope	SLP
screw	SSCR	side light	SILT	slotted	SLTD
servomotor	SVTR	siding	SDG	slow speed	SLSP
setter	SETR	signal	SIG		
setting	SET	signal to noise ratio	SNR		
		signaling	SNLG		

sludge	SLG	stabilized meter oscillator	STAMO	storage address register	SAR
small	SM	stabilized shunt	STSH	storeroom	STRM
smoot face structural clay tile	SFSCT	stable	STB	stormwater	STW
		stainless	STNLS	stowage	STWG
smooth neck	SMNK	stainless steel	SST	straight	STR
smooth surface built up roof	SSBR	stairway	STWY	straight line frequency	SLF
snatch	SNH	stamp	STP	straight line wavelength	SLWL
snubber	SNBR	stanchion	STAN	strand	STRD
socket	SLK	standard	STD	strapped	STRP
socket head	SCH	standard intruction set	SIS	strategic	STRAT
socket welding	SWLDG	standard military drawing	SMD	stratosphere	STRATO
soda fountain	SDFTN	standardization	STDZN	streamline	STRLN
software	SFW	standby	STBY	stringer	STGR
soil stack	SSK	standoff	STDF	stripped	STPD
solder	SLDR	starboard	STBD	stroboscope	STBSCP
solenoid	SOL	start and stop	STSP	strong	STRG
solenoid valve	SOLV	starter	START	strongback	STRBK
solid fiberboard	SFB	starting	STG	structural	STRL
solid height	SOLHGT	statement	STMT	structural carbon steel hard	SCSH
solid neutral	SN	station	STA	structural carbon steel medium	SCSM
soluble	SLBL	stator	STTR	structural carbon steel soft	SCSS
solution	SOLN	statuary bronze	STBRZ	structural clay tile	SCT
solvent	SLVT	status	STAT	structure	STRUCT
sound	SND	steady	STDY	stuffing	STFG
sound navigation and ranging	SONAR	steam generator	STGEN	subassembly	SUBASSY
		steam working pressure	STWP	subcaliber	SUBCAL
sound recorder reproducer	SRR	steaming	STMG	subject	SUBJ
soundproof	SNDPRF	steel	STL	submarine	SUB
source	SCE	steel basement window	SBW	submerged	SUBMG
source control drawing	SOCD	steel cadmium plated	SCDP	submersible	SBM
source control number	SOCN	stellite	STLT	subminiature	SUBMIN
spacer	SPCR	stepdown	STPDN	subsequent	SUBQ
special	SPCL	stepdown and stepup	SDNSU	subsoil drain	SSD
special treatment steel	STS	stepup	STU	substation	SUBSTA
specific gravity	SPGR	stereophonic	STEREO	substitute	SUBST
specification	SPEC	sterilizer	STER	substrate	SBSTR
speedometer	SPDOM	stiffener	STIF	substructure	SUBSTR
speed converter	SPCONV	stimulate	STML	succeeding	SUC
spider	SPDR	stirrup	STIR	suction	SUCT
spooling	SPG	stitch	STC	sufficient	SUF
spot face	SF	stock	STK	suffix	SUFF
spot face other side	SFO	stock number	SNO	summary	SMY
sprayed acoustical ceiling	SAC	stock order	SO	summing	SUM
stabilization	STBLN	stoke	STRK	sump tank	SMTK
stabilize	STAB	stone	STN	sunny	SNY
stabilized local oscillator	STALO	storage	STOR	supercharge	SPCHG

superheater	SUPHTR	Systeme International		terminal	TERM
superhetrodyne	SUPERHET	d'Unites	SI	terminal block	TBLK
superimposed current	SUPCUR	*T*		terminal protective	
superintendent	SUPT	table lookup	TLU	device	TPD
supersede	SUPSD	table solution	TABSOL	terneplate	TRPL
supersensitive	SUPSENS	tables of equipment	TE	terohmmeter	TOHM
superstructure	SUPERSTR	tabulate	TAB	tertiary	TER
supervise	SUPV	tabulator simulator	TABSYM	test equipment	TSTEQ
supplement	SUPPL	tachometer	TACH	test link	TLK
suppression	SUPPR	tachometer voltmeter	TVM	test specification	TSPEC
surface	SURF	tackle	TKL	tester	TSTR
surface four sides	S4S	tactical	TAC	testing	TSTG
surface one side	S1S	tally	TLY	testing and popping	TSPOP
surface one side and one		tandem	TDM	tetrachloride	TET
edge	S1SE	tangent	TAM	tetrofluorethylene	TETFLEYNE
surface two sides	S2S	tanker	TKR	textile	TXTL
surgical	SURG	taper	TPR	theoretical	THEOR
survey	SURV	taper shank	TS	theoretical point of fog	TPF
survival	SRVL	tappet	TPT	therm	THM
suspend	SUSP	tapping	TPG	thermal	THRM
suspended acoustical		technical bulletin	TB	thermal converter	THC
plaster ceiling	SAPC	technical note	TN	thermal demand	
suspended acoustical tile		technical report	TR	transmitter	TDX
ceiling	SATC	technical	TECH	thermistor	THMS
suspended plaster ceiling	SPC	teeth	T	thermoid	TH
suspended sprayed		telecommunications	TELECOM	thermometer	THERM
acoustical ceiling	SSAC	telemeter	TLM	thermostat	THERMO
sustaining	STNG	telemeter transmitter	TMX	thermostatic	THRMSTC
sweat	SWT	telemetry	TLMY	thick	THK
swinging bracket	SWGBKT	telephone	TEL	thick film	THKF
swinging door	SWGD	telephone booth	TELB	thickener	THKNR
switch	SW	telescope	TLSCP	thicker	THKR
switch gear	SWGR	television	TV	thickness	THKNS
switch stand	SWS	television interference	TVI	thimble	TMB
switchboard	SWBD	temper	TEM	thin film	TF
switchgear block	SGB	temperature	TEMP	thin film transistor	TFT
switchover	SWOV	temperature differential	TD	thinner	TNR
swivel	SWVL	temperature indicating		thowout	THWT
symbol	SYM	controlling	TIC	thread	THD
symmetrical	SYMM	temperature meter	TM	thread	TRD
symposium	SYMP	temperature switch	TSW	thread both ends	TBE
syncho switch	SSW	tempered	TMPD	thread cutting	TC
synchro tie	SYNTI	tempering	TMPRG	thread one end	TOE
synchronize	SYNC	template	TEMPL	threaded neck	THDNK
synchronous	SYN	tensile	TNSL	threaded piece	THDPC
synthetic	SYNTH	tension	TNSN	three conductor	3C
system	SYS	tentative	TNTV	three phase	3PH

three pole	3P	torsion	TRSN	treble	TRB
three pole double throw	3PDT	torsional	TORNL	triangle	TRNGL
three pole double throw switch	3PDTSW	total	TOT	tributary	TRIB
		total dynamic head	TDH	trick wheel	TRKWHL
three pole single throw	3PST	total indicator reading	TIR	trigger	TRIG
three way	3WAY	total load	TLLD	trim after forming	TAF
three wire	3W	total time	TT	trimmer	TRMR
throat	THRT	totalize	TOTLZ	trinitrotoluene	TNT
throttle	THROT	totalizing relay	TOR	triode	TRI
through	THRU	tower	TWR	triple	TPL
thrower	THWR	tracer	TRCR	triple throw	3T
thrust	THR	tracking	TRKG	triple wall	TPLW
thrust line	TL	trade name	TRN	triplex	TRX
thyristor	THYR	traffic	TRFC	tripped	TRP
ticket	TKT	trailer	TRLR	trolley	TRLY
tightening	TTNG	trailing	TRG	troposphere	TROPO
tile shingle roof	TSR	trainer	TRNR	throttle reset	TRST
tiller	TLR	trajectory	TRAJ	truck	TRK
tilting	TLG	tranparent	TRANS	true airspeed	TAS
timber	TMBR	transcribe	TRSCB	true position	TP
timed	TMD	transcriber	TRSBR	true position tolerance	TPTOL
time delay closing	TDC	transcribing	TRSBG	truncated Whitworth coarse thread	TWC
time delay opening	TDO	transferred electronic logic	TEDL	truncated Whitworth fine thread	TWF
time meter	TIM				
time of flight	TMFL	transistor driver core memory	TDCM	truncated Whitworth special thread	TWS
time opening	TO				
time since new	TSN	transistor transistor logic	TTL	trunnion	TRUN
time since overhaul	TSO	transistor under test	TUT	truss head	TRH
timer	TMR	transistorized	TSTRZ	tubing	TBG
timing	TMG	transition	TRNSN	tune controlled gain	TCG
tinned	TND	transmit gain control	TGC	tuned plate tuned grid	TPTG
tobin bronze	TOBBRZ	transportation	TRANSP	tuned radio frequency	TRF
toboggan	TOB	transpose	TRNPS	tungsten	TUNG
toggle	TGL	transposition	TPSN	tuning	TUN
tolerance	TOL	transverse	TRANSV	tunnel	TNL
tone and alarm	TNALM	transverse expansion joint	TEJ	tunnel diode	TNLDIO
tongue	TNG				
tongueless	TGLS	trapezoid	TRAP	tunnel diode logic	TDL
top and bottom bolt	TBB	travel limit	TRVLMT	turbine	TURB
top of frame	TFR	traveler	TRVLR	turnbuckle	TRNBKL
topping	TOPG	traveling	TRVLG	turned	TRND
torpedo	TORP	traveling wave tube	TWT	turning	TURN
torpedo battery	TBATT	traversing	TRAV	turning gear	TRNGR
torque	TRQ	treated	TRTD	turning light	TRNLT
torque differential receiver	TDR	treated hard pressed fiberboard	THPFB	turntable	TRNTBL
				turret	TUR
torquemeter	TORM	treatment	TRTMT	twin sideband	TWSB

twist drill gage	TDG	unijunction transistor	UJT	value	VAL
twisted	TW	uninterruptible power		value engineering	VE
twisted pair	TWPR	supply	UPS	valve	V
two conductor	2C	union bonnet	UNB	valve box	VB
two digit	2DIG	unit check	UK	valve seat	VST
two phase	2PH	unit heater	UH	valve stem	VSTM
two stage	2STG	unit under test	UUT	vane axial	VNXL
two way	2WAY	unit weight	UWT	vaporize	VPR
two wire	2W	United States gage	USG	vaporproof	VAPPRF
type mode series	TMS	universal	UNIV	var hour meter	VARHM
type plate	TYPL	universal product code	UPC	varactor	VRCTR
typesetting	TYPSTG	universal time coordinated	UTC	variable	VAR
typesetting lead	TSL	unknown	UNK	variable floating point	VFLPT
typical	TYP	unless otherwise		variable frequency	VF
		specified	UOS	variable	
U		unlimited	UNLIM	frequency clock	VFREQCLK
ultimate	ULT	unloading	UNL	variable frequency	
ultrahigh frequency	UHF	unlocking	UNLKG	oscillator	VFO
ultrasonic frequency	UF	unmarked	UNMKD	variable gain amplifier	VGA
ultraviolet	UV	unmounted	UNMTD	variable resistor	VARISTOR
unbleached	UBL	unregulated	UNRGLTD	variable threshold logic	VTL
unbleached muslin	UMUS	unsensitized	USTZD	variable voltage	
unclamp	UNCLP	unsuppressed	UNSUPPR	transformer	VARITRAN
undefined	UNDEF	until cooler	UC	varistor	VRIS
under	UND	untreated	UTRTD	varmeter	VARM
undercurrent	UNDC	untreated hard pressed		varnish	VARN
underfrequency	UNDF	fiberboard	UHPFB	varying	VRYG
underfrequency relay	UFR	untwist	UNTW	vegetable	VEG
underground	UGND	updraft	UPDFT	vehicle	VEH
underheat	UHT	upper	UPR	velocity	VEL
underload	UNDVD	upper and lower	UL	vendor item control	
undersize	US	upper control limit	UCL	drawing	VICD
undervoltage	UNDV	upright	URT	vent pipe	VP
undervoltage device	UVD	upward	UPWD	ventilate	VENT
underwater	UWTR	USA standard	USAS	verbatim	VERB
underwater battery	UB	use as required	UAR	verification	VERIF
undetermined	UNDETM	used on	UO	verify	VRFY
unfinished	UNFIN	used with	UW	vernier	VERN
unglazed ceramic		utensil	UTN	versatile	VERST
mosaic tile	UCMT	utility	UTIL	versed sine	VERS
unified	UN	*V*		versus	VS
Unified coarse thread	UNC			vertex	VTX
Unified extra fine thread	UNEF	vacuum	VAC	vertical	VERT
Unified fine thread	UNF	vacuum induction melt		vertical center of buoyancy	VCB
Unified sideband	USB	vacuum induction	VIMVAR	vertical center of gravity	VCG
Unified special thread	UNS	vacuum tube	VT	vertical centerline	VCL
uniform	UNIF	vacuum tube voltmeter	VTVM	vertical centrifugal	VCE

vertical impulse	VIMP	voltage control transfer	VCT	watertight	WTRTT
vertical ladder	VL	voltage controlled oscillator	VCO	waterwheel	WWHL
vertical radius	VTR			watt demand meter	WDM
vertical reference line	VRL	voltage detector	VDET	watthour	WH
vertical volute spring suspension	VVSS	voltage drop	VD	watthour demand meter	WHDM
		voltage regulator	VR	watthour meter	WHM
very high frequency	VHF	voltage relay	VRLY	watthour meter with contact device	WHC
very high frequency direction finding	VHFDF	voltage standing wave ratio	VSWR	wattmeter	WM
		voltage tunable magnetron	VTN	wavelength	WL
very high frequency omnidirectional radio	VOR	voltage variable capacitor	VVC	weakened plane joint	WPJ
		voltammeter	VAM	weapon	WPN
very high frequency omnirange localizer	VORLOC	voltmeter	VM	weather	WEA
very large scale integration	VLSI	volume	VOL	weather seal	WSL
		volume unit	VU	weather stripping	WS
very long range	VLR	volumetric	VLMTRC	weatherproof	WTHPRF
very low altitude	VLA	volute	VLT	weathertight	WEAT
very low frequency	VLF	vulcanize	VULC	webbing	WBG
vestibule	VEST			week	WK
vestigial sideband	VSB	*W*		weight	WT
vestigial sideband modulation	VSM	wafer	WFR	welded	WLD
		wagon	WAG	welder	WLDR
vibrate	VIB	waiting	WTG	weldless	WLDS
Vickers hardness	VH	wake light	WKLT	West	W
video	VID	wall receptacle	WR	wheel	WHL
video amplifier	VIDAMP	wallboard	WLB	wheelbase	WB
video display terminal	VDT	walseal	WLSL	whistle	WSTL
video frequency	VIDF	wardrobe	WRB	white	WHT
video integration	VINT	warehouse	WHSE	white indicating lamp	WIL
village	VIL	warning	WRN	white scale	WHS
violet	VIO	warping	WKPU	width	WD
viscometer	VISMR	warranty	WARR	width across flats	WAF
viscosity index	VI	wash fountain	WF	winch	WN
visible	VSBL	Washbun and Moen Gage	WMGA	wind direction	WDIR
visual	VIS	washer	WSHR	winder	WNDR
visual flight rules	VFR	washing	WSHG	winding	WDG
visual glide slope	VGS	water	WTR	windlass	WNDLS
vital load center	VLC	water chiller	WCHR	window	WDO
vitreous	VIT	water closet	WC	window unit	WU
voice	VO	water cooled	WCLD	windshield	WSHLD
voice coil	VC	water cooler	WCR	wire assembly	WA
voice operated transmitter keyer	VOX	water jacket	WJ	wire bound	WBD
		water pump	WP	wire gage	WG
volatile Organic Compound	VOC	water turbine	WTURB	wire glass	WGL
volt ohm milliammeter	VOM	waterproof	WTRPRF	wire wound	WW
volt per mil	VMIL	waterproof shroud	WPS	wiring	WRG
voltage adjusting rheostat	VADJR	waterproofing	WPG		

with blowout	WBL	wrong direction	WRDIR	transmitter	XMTR
without	WO	wrought	WRT	cross point	XPT
without blowout	WOBO	wrought brass	WBRS	explosive	XPL
wood awning type window	WATW	wrought iron	WI	cross section	XSECT
		X		extra strong	XSTR
wood block floor	WBF	experimental testing	X	crystal	XTAL
wood boring	WDBOR	crossarm	XARM	crystal oscillator	XTLO
wood casement window	WCW	cross bracing	XBRA	extraordinary wave	XWAVE
wood cutting	WCTG	crossbar	XBAR	double extra strong	XXSTR
wood furring strips	WFS	crossbar tandem	XBT	*Y*	
wood panel	WDP	cross connection	XCO	yard	YD
wood shingle roof	WSR	cross country	XCY	year	YR
wooden box	WBX	cross connection	XCONN	yellow	Y
woodruff	WDF	transceiver	XCVR	yellow indicating lamp	YIL
working pressure	WPR	transducer	XDCR	yellow light	YLT
working steam pressure	WSP	transfer	XFR	yellow varnished cambric	YVC
working voltage	WV	transformer	XFMR	yield point	YP
workshop	WKS	crosshair	XHAIR	yield strength	YS
worm gear	WMGR	crossing	XING	*Z*	
worm shaft	WMSFT	translator	XLTR	zero adjusted	ZA
worm wheel	WMWHL	extra long wheel base	XLWB	zero temperature coefficient	ZTC
wound	WND	transmission	XMSN		
wrecker	WRK	transmit	XMT		
wringer	WRGR	transmittal	XMTL		
wrist pin	WSTPN	transmitted	XMTD		

5 USEFUL FORMULAS FOR GEOMETRIC ENTITIES

Formulas for Circles

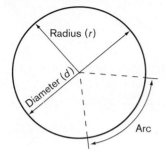

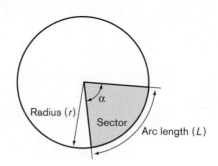

Circle*

Area	$A = \pi r^2$
	$A = 3.141 r^2$
	$A = 0.7854 d^2$
Radius	$r = d/2$
Diameter	$d = 2r$
Circumference	$C = 2\pi r$
	$C = \pi d$
	$C = 3.141 d$

*Note: 22/7 and 3.141 are different approximations for π.

Sector of a Circle

Area	$A = \dfrac{3.141 r^2 \alpha}{360}$
Arc (length)	$L = \dfrac{2\pi r}{360} \alpha$
	$L = 0.01745 r\alpha$
Angle	$\alpha = \dfrac{L}{0.01745 r}$
Radius	$r = \dfrac{L}{0.01745 \alpha}$

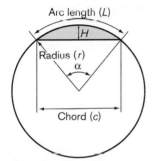

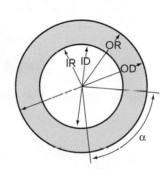

Segment of a Circle

Area	$A = \dfrac{1}{2}(r \bullet L - c(r - h))$
Arc (length)	$L = 0.01745 r\alpha$
Angle	$\alpha = \dfrac{57.296 L}{r}$
Height	$H = r - \dfrac{1}{2}\sqrt{4r^2 - c^2}$
Chord	$c = 2r \sin\alpha$

Circular Ring

Ring area	$A = 0.7854 (OD^2 - ID^2)$
Ring sector area	$a = 0.00873 \, \alpha(OR^2 - IR^2)$
	$a = 0.00218 \, \alpha(OD^2 - ID^2)$

OD = outside diameter
ID = inside diameter
α = ring sector angle
OR = outside radius
IR = inside radius

Formulas for Triangles

Any Triangle

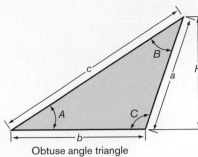

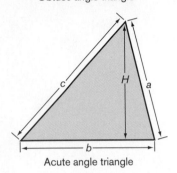

Obtuse angle triangle

Acute angle triangle

Area $\quad A = 1/2bH = \dfrac{Hb}{2}$

$$A = \sqrt{S(S-a)(S-b)(S-c)}$$

$$S = 1/2\,(a + b + c)$$

Perimeter $\quad P = a + b + c$

Height $\quad H = \dfrac{2}{b}\sqrt{S(S-a)(S-b)(S-c)}$

Sum of angles $180° = A + B + C$

Equilateral Triangle

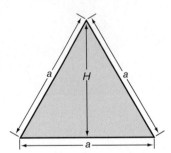

Area $\quad A = a^2\,\dfrac{\sqrt{3}}{4} = 0.433a^2$

$$A = 0.577H^2$$

$$A = \dfrac{a^2}{2} \text{ or } \dfrac{aH}{2}$$

Perimeter $\quad P = 3a$

Height $\quad H = \dfrac{a}{2}\sqrt{3} = 0.866a$

Right Triangle

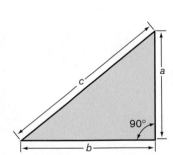

Area $\quad A = \dfrac{ba}{2}$

Perimeter $\quad P = a + b + c$

Height $\quad a = \sqrt{c^2 - b^2}$

Base $\quad b = \sqrt{c^2 - a^2}$

Hypotenuse $\quad c = \sqrt{a^2 - b^2}$

Formulas for Four Sided Polygons

Square

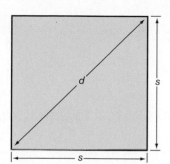

Area $A = s^2$
$A = 0.5d^2$
Side $s = 0.707d$
Diagonal $d = 1.414s$
Perimeter $P = 4s$

Rectangle

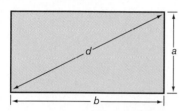

Area $A = ab$

Side a $a = \sqrt{d^2 - b^2}$

Side b $b = \sqrt{d^2 - a^2}$

Diagonal $d = \sqrt{a^2 - b^2}$

Perimeter $P = 2(a + b)$

Parallelogram

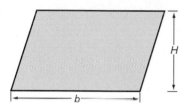

Area $A = Hb$
Height $H = A/b$
Base $b = A/H$

Trapezoid

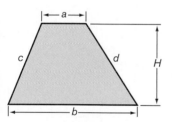

Area $A = 1/2(a + b) \cdot H$
Perimeter $P = a + b + c + d$

Trapezium

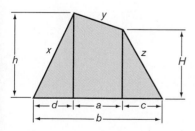

Area $A = \dfrac{a(H + h) + cH + dh}{2}$

Area   Another method is to divide the area into two triangles, find the area of each, and add the areas together.

Perimeter $P = b + x + y + z$

Formulas for Ellipses and Parabolas

Ellipse

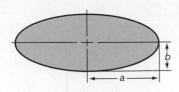

Area $A = \pi ab$
$A = 3.142ab$

Perimeter $P = 6.283 \cdot \dfrac{\sqrt{a^2 + b^2}}{2}$

Parabola

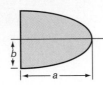

Area $A = 2/3\ ab$

Formulas for Regular Polygons

Multisided

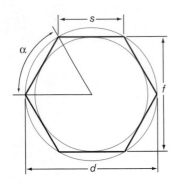

Area $A = n\dfrac{s \cdot \frac{1}{2}f}{2}$

n = number of sides

Side $s = 2\sqrt{\frac{1}{2}d^2 - \frac{1}{2}f^2}$

Flats f = distance across flats; diameter of inscribed circle
Diagonal d = diameter of circumscribed circle
Perimeter P = sum of the sides
Angle $\alpha = 360/n$

Hexagon

Area $A = 0.866f^2$
$A = 0.650d^2$
$A = 2.598s^2$
Side $s = 0.577f$
$s = 0.5d$
Flats $f = 1.732s$
$f = 0.866d$
Diagonal $d = 2s$
$d = 1.155f$
Perimeter $P = 6s$
Angle $\alpha = 60°$

Octagon

Area $A = 0.828f^2$
$A = 0.707d^2$
$A = 4.828s^2$
Side $s = 0.414f$
$s = 0.383d$
Flats $f = 2.414s$
$f = 0.924d$
Diagonal $d = 2.613s$
$d = 1.083f$
Perimeter $P = 8s$
Angle $\alpha = 45°$

Formulas for 3D Shapes

Cube

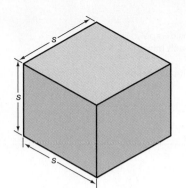

Volume	$V = s^3$
Surface area	$SA = 6s^2$
Side	$s = \sqrt[3]{V}$

Rectangular Prism

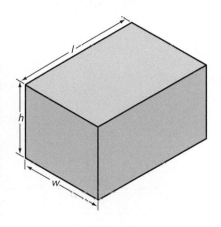

Volume	$V = lwh$
Surface area	$SA = 2(lw + lh + wh)$
Length	$l = V/hw$
Width	$w = V/lh$
Height	$h = V/lw$

Cone (Right Circular)

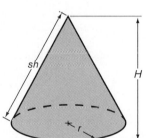

Volume $V = 1/3\ AH$*
A = area of base
$V = 1/3\pi r^2 H$
r = radius of base

Slant height $sh = \sqrt{r^2 + H^2}$

Surface area $SA = (1/2\text{ perimeter of base} \cdot sh) + \pi r^2$
$SA = \pi r(sh) + \pi r^2$
Lateral surface area $LSA = \pi r(sh)$

*Note: True for any cone or pyramid

Pyramid

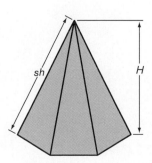

Volume $V = 1/3\ AH$
A = area of base
Surface area $SA = (1/2\text{ perimeter of base} \cdot sh) + A$

Slant height $sh = \sqrt{r^2 + h^2}$

r = radius of circle circumscribed around base

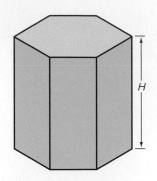

Prism

Volume $V = AH$*
A = area of base
(see multisided polygon)

Surface area SA = (area of each panel) + $2A$

*Note: True for any prism or cylinder with parallel bases.

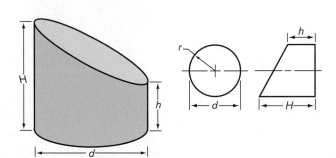

Cylinder (Right Circular)

Volume $V = Ah$
$V = \pi r^2 h$
$V = 0.7854 d^2 h$

Surface area $SA = \pi dh + 2\pi r^2$
$SA = 2\pi rh + 2\pi r^2$
$SA = 6.283 rh + 6.283 r^2$

Lateral surface area $LSA = 2\pi rh$

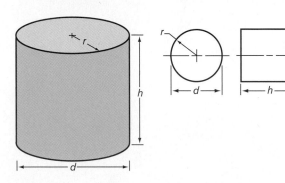

Frustrum of a Cylinder

Volume $V = \pi r^2 \dfrac{H + h}{2}$

$V = 1.5708 r^2 (H + h)$
$V = 0.3927 d^2 (H + h)$

Lateral surface area $LSA = \pi r(H + h)$
$LSA = 1.5708 d(H + h)$

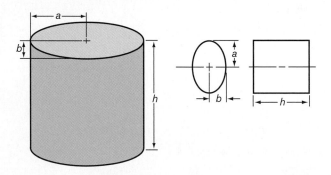

Elliptical Cylinder

Volume $V = \pi abh$

Lateral surface area $LSA = \pi h \sqrt{a^2 + b^2}$

6 GEOMETRIC CONSTRUCTIONS

A6.1 ■ Triangles

A triangle is a plane figure bounded by three straight sides, and the sum of the interior angles is always 180° (Figure A6.1). A right triangle (Figure A6.1d) has one 90° angle, and the square of the hypotenuse is equal to the sum of the squares of the two sides (Figure A6.1c). As shown in Figure A6.1f, any triangle inscribed in a semicircle is a right triangle if the hypotenuse coincides with the diameter.

A6.2 ■ Quadrilaterals

A *quadrilateral* is a plane figure bounded by four straight sides (Figure A6.2). If the opposite sides are parallel, the quadrilateral is also a *parallelogram.*

A6.3 ■ Polygons

A *polygon* is any plane figure bounded by straight lines (Figure A6.3). If the polygon has equal angles and equal sides, it can be inscribed in or circumscribed around a circle and is called a *regular polygon.*

A6.4 ■ Circles and Arcs

A *circle* is a closed curve, all points of which are the same distance from a point called the center (Figure A6.4a).

Circumference refers to the circle or to the distance around the circle. This distance equals the diameter multiplied by π or 3.1416. Other definitions are illustrated in Figure A6.4b–e.

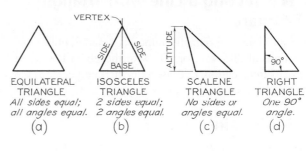

EQUILATERAL TRIANGLE
All sides equal; all angles equal.
(a)

ISOSCELES TRIANGLE
2 sides equal; 2 angles equal.
(b)

SCALENE TRIANGLE
No sides or angles equal.
(c)

RIGHT TRIANGLE
One 90° angle.
(d)

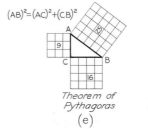

$(AB)^2 = (AC)^2 + (CB)^2$

Theorem of Pythagoras
(e)

RIGHT TRIANGLE IN A SEMICIRCLE
Assume any point C on semicircle. ∠ACB = 90°.
(f)

A6.1 Triangles

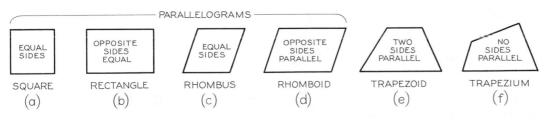

PARALLELOGRAMS

SQUARE — EQUAL SIDES
(a)

RECTANGLE — OPPOSITE SIDES EQUAL
(b)

RHOMBUS — EQUAL SIDES
(c)

RHOMBOID — OPPOSITE SIDES PARALLEL
(d)

TRAPEZOID — TWO SIDES PARALLEL
(e)

TRAPEZIUM — NO SIDES PARALLEL
(f)

A6.2 Quadrilaterals

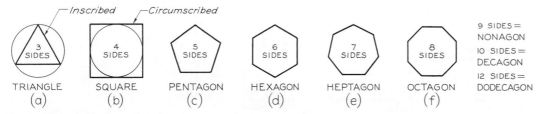

Inscribed   Circumscribed

TRIANGLE — 3 SIDES
(a)

SQUARE — 4 SIDES
(b)

PENTAGON — 5 SIDES
(c)

HEXAGON — 6 SIDES
(d)

HEPTAGON — 7 SIDES
(e)

OCTAGON — 8 SIDES
(f)

9 SIDES = NONAGON
10 SIDES = DECAGON
12 SIDES = DODECAGON

A6.3 Regular Polygons

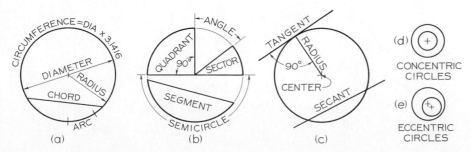

CIRCUMFERENCE = DIA × 3.1416
DIAMETER RADIUS CHORD ARC
(a)

ANGLE QUADRANT 90° SECTOR SEGMENT SEMICIRCLE
(b)

TANGENT RADIUS 90° CENTER SECANT
(c)

(d) CONCENTRIC CIRCLES

(e) ECCENTRIC CIRCLES

A6.4 The Circle

A6.5 ■ Bisecting a Line or Circular Arc

Figure A6.5a shows the given line or arc AB to be bisected.

I. From A and B draw equal arcs with radius greater than half AB.

II. and III. Join intersections D and E with a straight line to locate center C.

A6.6 ■ Bisecting a Line with Triangle and T-Square

As shown in Figure A6.6, from endpoints A and B, draw construction lines at 30°, 45°, or 60° with the given line; then through their intersection, C, draw a line perpendicular to the given line to locate the center D, as shown.

A6.7 ■ Bisecting an Angle

Figure A6.7 shows the given angle BAC to be bisected.

I. Strike large arc R.

II. Strike equal arcs r with radius slightly larger than half BC, to intersect at D.

III. Draw line AD, which bisects the angle.

A6.8 ■ Transferring an Angle

Figure A6.8 shows the given angle BAC to be transferred to the new position at A'B'.

I. Use any convenient radius R, and strike arcs from centers A and A'.

II. Strike equal arcs r, and draw side A'C'.

A6.9 ■ Drawing a Line Through a Point and Parallel to a Line

With given point P as center, and any convenient radius R, strike arc CD to intersect the given line AB at E (Figure A6.9a). With E as center and the same radius, strike arc R' to intersect

the given line at G. With PG as radius and E as center, strike arc r to locate point H. The line PH is the required line.

Preferred Method As shown in Figure A6.9b, move the triangle and T-square as a unit until the triangle lines up with given line AB; then slide the triangle until its edge passes through the given point P. Draw CD, the required parallel line.

A6.10 ■ Drawing a Line Parallel to a Line and at a Given Distance

Let AB be the line and CD the given distance. As shown in Figure A6.10a, draw two arcs with points E and F near A and B,

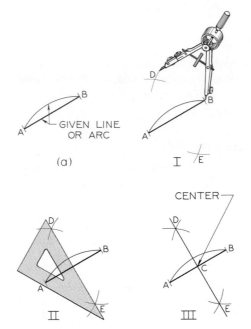

A6.5   Bisecting a Line or a Circular Arc

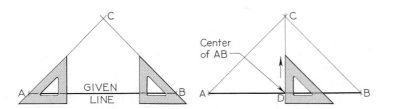

A6.6   Bisecting a Line with Triangle and T-Square

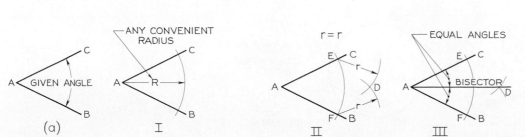

A6.7   Bisecting an Angle

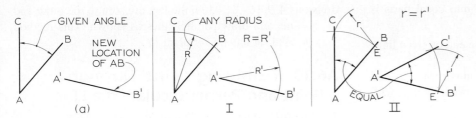

A6.8 Transferring an Angle

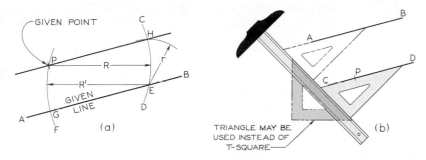

A6.9 Drawing a Line Through a Point Parallel to a Line

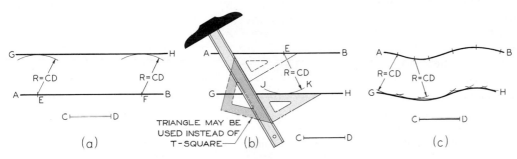

A6.10 Drawing a Line Parallel to a Line at a Given Distance

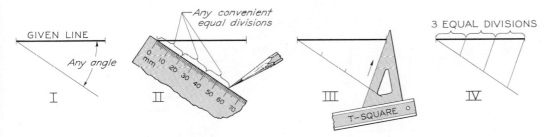

A6.11 Dividing a Line into Equal Parts

respectively, as centers, and CD as radius. The line GH, tangent to the arcs, is the required line.

Preferred Method   With any point E of the line as center and CD as radius, strike an arc JK (Figure A6.10b). Move the triangle and T-square as a unit until the triangle lines up with the given line AB; then slide the triangle until its edge is tangent to the arc JK, and draw the required line GH.

As shown in Figure A6.10c, with centers selected at random on the curved line AB and with CD as radius, draw a series of arcs; then draw the required line tangent to these arcs.

A6.11 ■ Dividing a Line into Equal Parts

There are two methods for dividing a line into equal parts. The first method is shown in Figure A6.11:

I. Draw a light construction line at any convenient angle from one end of line.

II. With dividers or scale, set off from intersection of lines as many equal divisions as needed (in this case, three).

III. Connect last division point to the other end of line, using triangle and T-square, as shown.

IV. Slide triangle along T-square and draw parallel lines through other division points, as shown.

The second method for dividing a line into equal parts is shown in Figure A6.12:

I. Draw vertical construction line at one end of given line.
II. Set zero of scale at other end of line.
III. Swing scale up until third unit falls on vertical line, and make tiny dots at each point, or prick points with dividers.
IV. Draw vertical construction lines through each point.

Some practical applications of this method are shown in Figure A6.13.

A6.12 ■ Dividing a Line into Proportional Parts

Let it be required to divide the line AB into three parts proportional to 2, 3, and 4.

Preferred Method   Draw a vertical line from point B (Figure A6.14a). Select a scale of convenient size for a total of nine units and set the zero of the scale at A. Swing the scale up until the ninth unit falls on the vertical line. Along the scale, set off points for 2, 3, and 4 units, as shown. Draw vertical lines through these points.

Draw a line CD parallel to AB and at any convenient distance (Figure A6.14b). On this line, set off 2, 3, and 4 units, as shown. Draw lines through the ends of the two lines to intersect at the point O. Draw lines through O and the points 2 and 5 to divide AB into the required proportional parts.

Given AB, divide into proportional parts, in this case proportional to the square of x, where $x = 1, 2, 3, \ldots$ (Figure A6.14c). Set zero of scale at end of line and set off

divisions 4, 9, 16, ... Join the last division to the other end of the line, and draw parallel lines as shown. This method may be used for any power of x.

A6.13 ■ Drawing a Line Through a Point and Perpendicular to a Line

The line AB and a point P (Figure A6.15) are given.

When the Point Is Not on the Line   From P, draw any convenient inclined line, as PD (Figure A6.15a). Find center C of line PD, and draw arc with radius CP. The line EP is the required perpendicular.

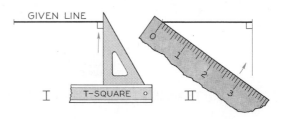

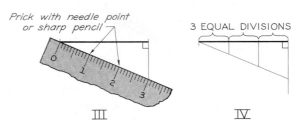

A6.12   Dividing a Line into Equal Parts

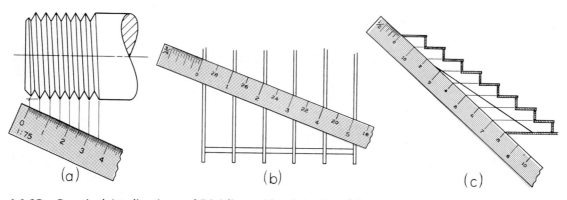

A6.13   Practical Applications of Dividing a Line into Equal Parts

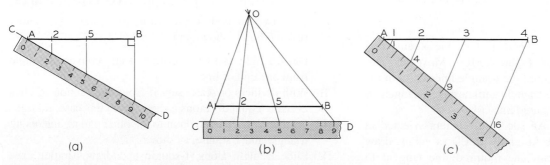

A6.14   Dividing a Line into Proportional Parts

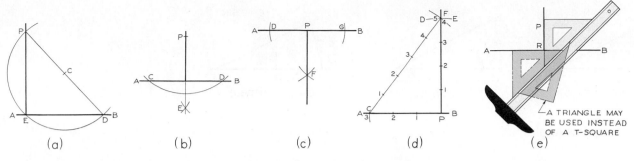

(a)   (b)   (c)   (d)   (e)

A6.15   Drawing a Line Through a Point and Perpendicular to a Line

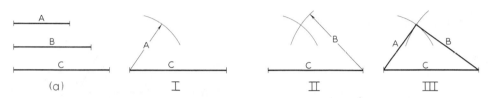

A6.16   Drawing a Triangle with Sides Given

With P as center, strike an arc to intersect AB at C and D (Figure A6.15b). With C and D as centers and radius slightly greater than half CD, strike arcs to intersect at E. The line PE is the required perpendicular.

When the Point Is on the Line   With P as center and any radius, strike arcs to intersect AB at D and G (Figure A6.15c). With D and G as centers and radius slightly greater than half DG, strike equal arcs to intersect at F. The line PF is the required perpendicular.

As shown in Figure A6.15d, select any convenient unit of length (for example, 6 mm or ¼"). With P as center and 3 units as radius, strike an arc to intersect the given line at C. With P as center and 4 units as radius, strike arc DE. With C as center and 5 units as radius, strike an arc to intersect DE at F. The line PF is the required perpendicular.

This method makes use of the 3–4–5 right triangle and is frequently used in laying off rectangular foundations of large machines, buildings, or other structures. For this purpose a steel tape may be used and distances of 30', 40', and 50' measured as the three sides of the right triangle.

Preferred Method   Move the triangle and T-square as a unit until the triangle lines up with AB (Figure A6.15e); then slide the triangle until its edge passes through the point P (whether P is on or off the line), and draw the required perpendicular.

A6.14 ■ Drawing a Triangle with Sides Given

Given the sides A , B, and C, as shown in Figure A6.16a:

I. Draw one side, as C, in desired position, and strike arc with radius equal to side A.
II. Strike arc with radius equal to side B.
III. Draw sides A and B from intersection of arcs, as shown.

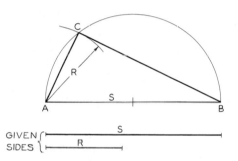

GIVEN SIDES {   S   R

A6.17   Drawing a Right Triangle

A6.15 ■ Drawing a Right Triangle with Hypotenuse and One Side Given

Given sides S and R (Figure A6.17), with AB as a diameter equal to S, draw a semicircle. With A as center and R as radius, draw an arc intersecting the semicircle at C. Draw AC and CB to complete the right triangle.

A6.16 ■ Laying Out an Angle

Many angles can be laid out directly with the triangle, or they may be laid out with the protractor. Other methods, for which considerable accuracy is required, are discussed next (Figure A6.18).

Tangent Method   The tangent of angle θ is y/x and $y = x \tan \theta$. To construct the angle, assume a convenient value for x, preferably 10 units of convenient length (Figure A6.18a). (The larger the unit, the more accurate will be the construction.) Find the tangent of angle θ in a table of natural tangents, multiply by 10, and set off $y = 10 \tan \theta$.

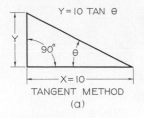
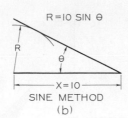
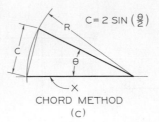

TANGENT METHOD (a)   SINE METHOD (b)   CHORD METHOD (c)

A6.18 Laying Out Angles

EXAMPLE To set off $31\frac{1}{2}°$, find the natural tangent of $31\frac{1}{2}°$, which is 0.6128. Then

$$y = 10 \text{ units} \times 0.6128 = 6.128 \text{ units.}$$

Sine Method Draw line x to any convenient length, preferably 10 units (Figure A6.18b). Find the sine of angle θ in a table of natural sines, multiply by 10, and strike arc R = 10 sin θ. Draw the other side of the angle tangent to the arc, as shown.

EXAMPLE To set off $25\frac{1}{2}°$, find the natural sine of $25\frac{1}{2}°$, which is 0.4304. Then

$$R = 10 \text{ units} \times 0.4305 = 4.305 \text{ units.}$$

Chord Method Draw line x to any convenient length, and draw arc with any convenient radius R—say 10 units (Figure A6.18c). Find the chordal length C in a table of chords (see a machinists' handbook), and multiply the value by 10 since the table is made for a radius of 1 unit.

EXAMPLE To set off 43° 20′, the chordal length C for 1 unit radius, as given in a table of chords equals 0.7384; and if $R = 10$ units, then $C = 7.384$ units.

If a table is not available, the chord C may be calculated by the formula $C = 2 \sin θ/2$.

EXAMPLE Half of 43°20′ = 21°40′. The sine of 21°40′ = 0.3692. $C = 2 \times 0.3692 = 0.7384$ for a 1 unit radius. For a 10 unit radius, $C = 7.384$ units.

A6.17 ■ Drawing an Equilateral Triangle

Side AB is given. With A and B as centers and AB as radius, strike arcs to intersect at C (Figure A6.19a). Draw lines AC and BC to complete the triangle.

Preferred Method Draw lines through points A and B, making angles of 60° with the given line and intersecting C (Figure A6.19b).

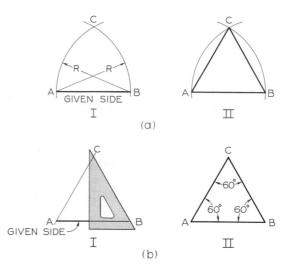

A6.19 Drawing an Equilateral Triangle

A6.18 ■ Drawing a Square

One side AB (Figure A6.20a) is given. Through point A, draw a perpendicular (see Figure A6.15c). With A as center and AB as radius, draw the arc to intersect the perpendicular at C. With B and C as centers and AB as radius, strike arcs to intersect at D. Draw lines CD and BD.

Preferred Method One side AB (Figure A6.20b) is given. Using the T-square or parallel straightedge and 45° triangle, draw lines AC and BD perpendicular to AB and the lines AD and BC at 45° with AB. Draw line CD.

Preferred Method Given the circumscribed circle (distance "across corners"), draw two diameters at right angles to each other (Figure A6.20c). The intersections of these diameters with the circle are vertexes of an inscribed square.

Preferred Method Given the inscribed circle (Figure A6.20d) (distance "across flats," as in drawing bolt heads), use the T-square (or parallel straightedge) and 45° triangle and draw the four sides tangent to the circle.

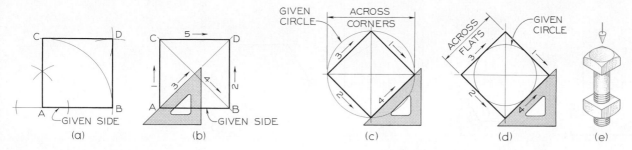

A6.20 Drawing a Square

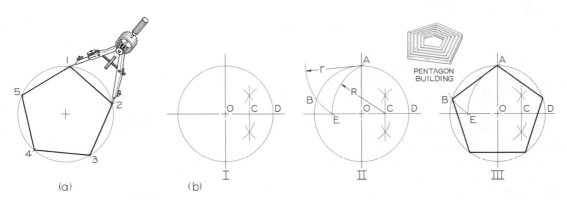

A6.21 Drawing a Pentagon

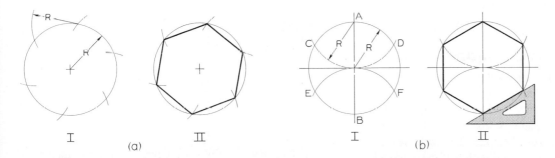

A6.22 Drawing a Hexagon

A6.19 ■ Drawing a Regular Pentagon

Given the circumscribed circle, do the following:

Preferred Method Divide the circumference of the circle into five equal parts with the dividers, and join the points with straight lines (Figure A6.21a).

Geometrical Method As shown in Figure A6.21b:

I. Bisect radius OD at C.
II. With C as center and CA as radius, strike arc AE. With A as center and AE as radius, strike arc EB.
III. Draw line AB; then set off distances AB around the circumference of the circle, and draw the sides through these points.

A6.20 ■ Drawing a Hexagon

The circumscribed circle (Figure A6.22) as given. Each side of a hexagon is equal to the radius of the circumscribed circle (Figure A6.22a). Therefore, using the compass or dividers and the radius of the circle, set off the six sides of the hexagon around the circle, and connect the points with straight lines. As a check on the accuracy of the construction, make sure that opposite sides of the hexagon are parallel.

Preferred Method This construction (Figure A6.22) is a variation of the one shown in Figure A6.22a. Draw vertical and horizontal centerlines. With A and B as centers and radius equal to that of the circle, draw arcs to intersect the circle at C, D, E, and F, and complete the hexagon as shown.

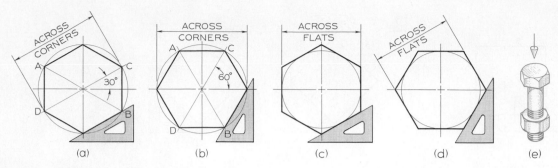

A6.23   Drawing a Hexagon

Given the circumscribed circle (distance "across corners") (Figure A6.23a and b), draw vertical and horizontal centerlines, and then diagonals AB and CD at 30° or 60° with horizontal; finally, with the 30° × 60° triangle and the T-square, draw the six sides as shown.

Given the inscribed circle (distance "across flats") (Figure A6.23c and d), draw vertical and horizontal center lines; then with the 30° × 60° triangle and the T-square or straightedge, draw the six sides tangent to the circle. This method is used in drawing bolt heads and nuts. For maximum accuracy, diagonals may be added, as in Figure A6.23a and b.

As shown in Figure A6.24, use the 30° × 60° triangle and the T-square or straightedge; draw lines in the order shown in Figure A6.24a, where the distance AB ("across corners") is given or, as shown in Figure A6.24b, where a side CD is given.

A6.21 ■ Drawing an Octagon

Given an inscribed circle, or distance "across flats" (Figure A6.25a), use a T-square or straightedge and a 45° triangle to draw the eight sides tangent to the circle, as shown.

Given a circumscribed square, or distance "across flats" (Figure A6.25b), draw diagonals of square; then with the corners of the given square as centers and with half the diagonal as radius, draw arcs cutting the sides as shown in I. Using a T-square and 45° triangle, draw the eight sides, as shown in II.

A6.22 ■ Drawing a Circle Through Three Points

I. Let A, B, and C be the three given points not in a straight line (Figure A6.26). Draw lines AB and BC, which will be chords of the circle. Draw perpendicular bisectors EO and DO intersecting at O (see Figure A6.26).
II. With center at O, draw required circle through the points.

A6.23 ■ Finding the Center of a Circle

Draw any chord AB, preferably horizontal as shown (Figure A6.26b). Draw perpendiculars from A and B, cutting the circle at D and E. Draw diagonals DB and EA whose intersection C will be the center of the circle. This method uses the principle that any right triangle inscribed in a circle cuts off a semicircle.

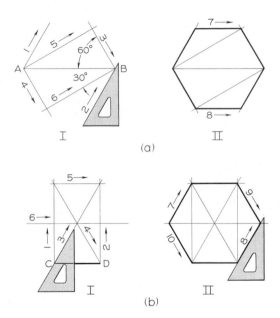

A6.24   Drawing a Hexagon

Another method, slightly longer, is to reverse the procedure of Figure A6.26a. Draw any two nonparallel chords and draw perpendicular bisectors. The intersection of the bisectors will be the center of the circle.

A6.24 ■ Drawing a Circle Tangent to a Line at a Given Point

Given a line AB and a point P on the line (Figure A6.27a):
I. At P, erect a perpendicular to the line.
II. Set off the radius of the required circle on the perpendicular.
III. Draw a circle with radius CP.

A6.25 ■ Drawing a Tangent to a Circle Through a Point

Preferred Method   Given point P on the circle (Figure A6.28a), move the T-square and triangle as a unit until one side of the triangle passes through the point P and the center of the circle; then slide the triangle until the other side passes through point P, and draw the required tangent.

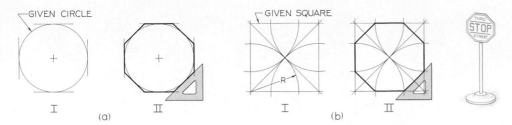

A6.25 Drawing an Octagon

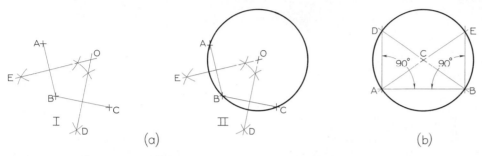

A6.26 Finding Center of Circle

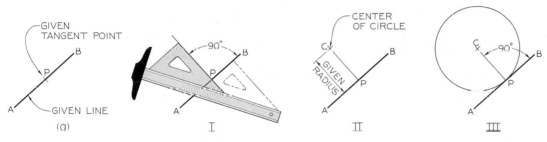

A6.27 Drawing a Circle Tangent to a Line

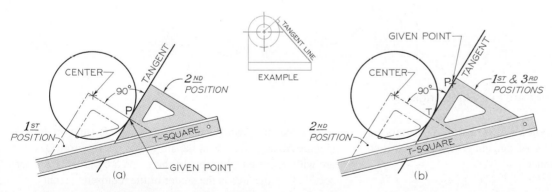

A6.28 Drawing a Tangent to a Circle Through a Point

Given point P outside the circle (Figure A6.28b), move the T-square and triangle as a unit until one side of the triangle passes through point P and, by inspection, is tangent to the circle; then slide the triangle until the other side passes through the center of the circle, and lightly mark the point of tangency T. Finally, move the triangle back to its starting position, and draw the required tangent.

In both constructions either triangle may be used. Also, a second triangle may be used in place of the T-square.

A6.26 ■ Drawing Tangents to Two Circles

Move the triangle and T-square as a unit until one side of the triangle is tangent, by inspection, to the two circles (Figure A6.29a and b); then slide the triangle until the other side passes through the center of one circle, and lightly mark the point of tangency. Then slide the triangle until the slide passes through the center of the other circle, and mark the point of tangency. Finally, slide

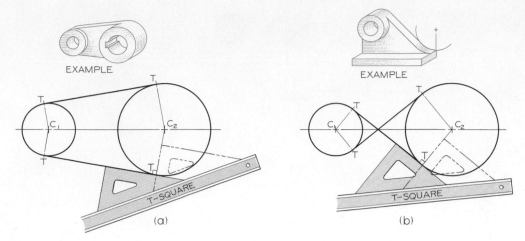

A6.29 Drawing Tangents to Two Circles

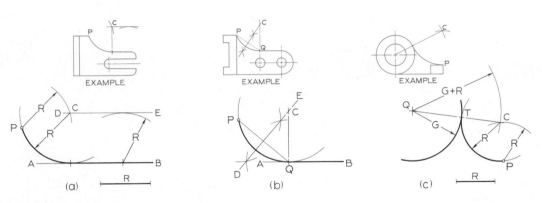

A6.30 Tangents

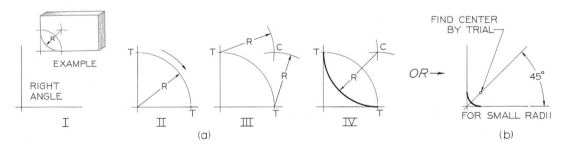

A6.31 Drawing a Tangent Arc in a Right Angle

the triangle back to the tangent position, and draw the tangent lines between the two points of tangency. Draw the second tangent line in a similar manner.

A6.27 ■ Drawing an Arc Tangent to a Line or Arc and Through a Point

Given line AB, point P, and radius R (Figure A6.30a), draw line DE parallel to the given line and distance R from it. From P draw arc with radius R, cutting line DE at C, the center of the required tangent arc.

Given line AB, with tangent point Q on the line and point P (Figure A6.30b), draw PQ, which will be a chord of the required arc. Draw perpendicular bisector DE, and at Q erect a perpendicular to the line to intersect DE at C, the center of the required tangent arc.

Given arc with center Q, point P, and radius R (Figure A6.30c), from P, strike arc with radius R. From Q, strike arc with radius equal to that of the given arc plus R. The intersection C of the arcs is the center of the required tangent arc.

A6.28 ■ Drawing an Arc Tangent to Two Lines at Right Angles

I. Two lines are given at right angles to each other (Figure A6.31a).
II. With given radius R, strike arc intersecting given lines at tangent points T.
III. With given radius R again, and with points T as centers, strike arcs intersecting at C.
IV. With C as center and given radius R, draw the required tangent arc.

For small radii, such as $\frac{1}{8}R$ for fillets and rounds, it is not practicable to draw complete tangency constructions. Instead, draw a 45° bisector of the angle and locate the center of the arc by trial along this line (Figure A6.31b).

Note that the center C can be located by intersecting lines parallel to the given lines, as shown in Figure A6.10b. The circle template can also be used to draw the arcs R for the parallel line method of Figure A6.10b. While the circle template is convenient to use for small radii up to about $\frac{5}{8}''$ or 16 mm, the diameter of the template circle is precisely equal twice the required radius.

A6.29 ■ Drawing an Arc Tangent to Two Lines at Acute or Obtuse Angles

I. Two lines intersecting not making 90° with each other (Figure A6.32a and b) are given.
II. Draw lines parallel to given lines, at distance R from them, to intersect at C, the required center.
III. From C, drop perpendiculars to the given lines, respectively, to locate tangent points T.
IV. With C as center and with given radius R, draw the required tangent arc between the points of tangency.

A6.30 ■ Drawing an Arc Tangent to an Arc and a Straight Line

I. An arc with radius G and a straight line AB (Figure A6.33a and b) are given.
II. Draw a straight line and an arc parallel, respectively, to the given straight line and arc at the required radius distance R from them, to intersect at C, the required center.
III. From C, drop a perpendicular to the given straight line to obtain one point of tangency T. Join the centers C and O with a straight line to locate the other point of tangency T.
IV. With center C and given radius R, draw the required tangent arc between the points of tangency.

A6.31 ■ Drawing an Arc Tangent to Two Arcs

I. Arcs with centers A and B and required radius R (Figure A6.34a and b) are given.
II. With A and B as centers, draw arcs parallel to the given arcs and at a distance R from them; their intersection C is the center of the required tangent arc.

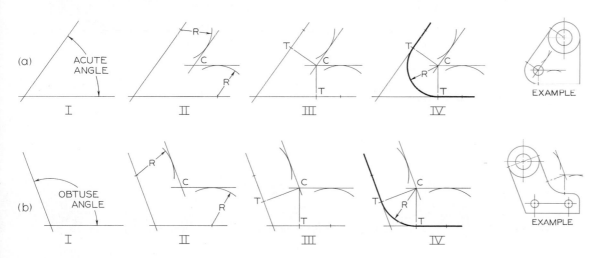

A6.32   Drawing Tangent Arcs

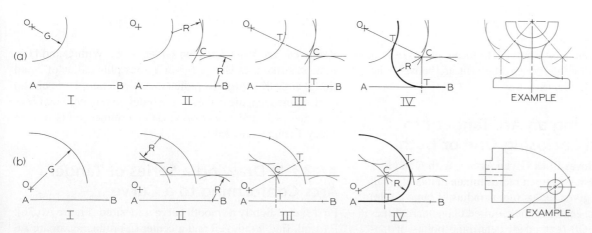

A6.33   Drawing an Arc Tangent to an Arc and a Straight Line

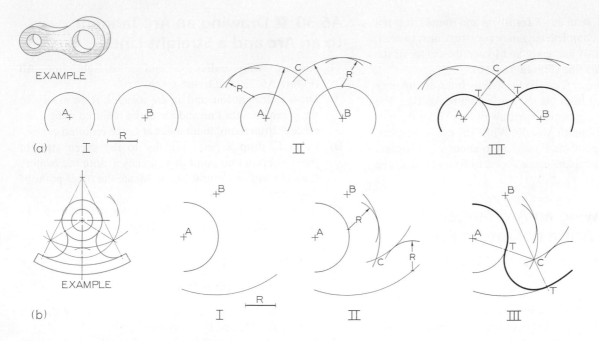

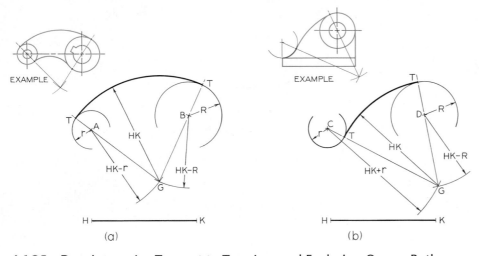

A6.34 Drawing an Arc Tangent to Two Arcs

A6.35 Drawing an Arc Tangent to Two Arcs and Enclosing One or Both

III. Draw lines of centers AC and AC to locate points of tangency T, and draw the required tangent arc between the points of tangency, as shown.

A6.32 ■ Drawing an Arc Tangent to Two Arcs and Enclosing One or Both

Required Arc Encloses Both Given Arcs With A and B as centers, strike arcs HK – r (given radius minus radius of small circle) and HK – R (given radius minus radius of large circle) intersecting at G, the center of the required tangent arc. Lines of centers GA and GB (extended) determine points of tangency T (Figure A6.35a).

Required Arc Encloses One Given Arc With C and D as centers, strike arcs HK + r (given radius plus radius of small circle) and HK – R (given radius minus radius of large circle) intersecting at G, the center of the required tangent arc. Lines of centers GC and GD (extended) determine points of tangency T (Figure A6.35b).

A6.33 ■ Drawing a Series of Tangent Arcs Conforming to a Curve

First sketch lightly a smooth curve as desired (Figure A6.36). By trial, find a radius R and a center C, producing an arc AB that closely follows that portion of the curve. The successive

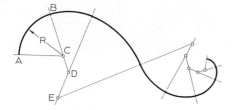

A6.36   Drawing a Series of Tangent Arcs Conforming to a Curve

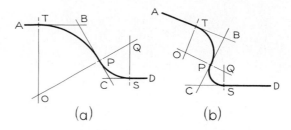

(a)   (b)

A6.38a   Drawing Two Curves Tangent to Three Intersecting Lines

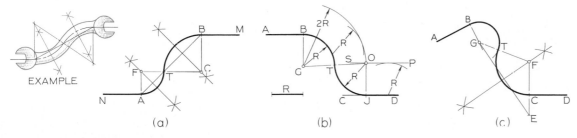

EXAMPLE

(a)   (b)   (c.)

A6.37   Drawing an Ogee Curve

centers D, E, and so on will be on lines joining the centers with the points of tangency, as shown.

A6.34 ◾ Drawing an Ogee Curve

Connecting Two Parallel Lines   Let NA and BM be the two parallel lines. Draw AB, and assume inflection point T (at midpoint if two equal arcs are desired) (Figure A6.37a). At A and B, erect perpendiculars AF and BC. Draw perpendicular bisectors of AT and BT. The intersections F and C of these bisectors and the perpendiculars, respectively, are the centers of the required tangent arcs.

Let AB and CD be the two parallel lines, with point B as one end of the curve and R the given radii (Figure A6.37b). At B, erect perpendicular to AB, make BG = R, and draw the arc as shown. Draw line SP parallel to CD at distance R from CD. With center G, draw the arc of radius 2R, intersecting line SP at O. Draw perpendicular OJ to locate tangent point J, and join centers G and O to locate point of tangency T. Using centers G and O and radius R, draws the two tangent arcs as shown.

Connecting Two Nonparallel Lines   Let AB and CD be the two nonparallel lines (Figure A6.37c). Erect perpendicular to AB at B. Select point G on the perpendicular so that BG equals any desired radius, and draw the arc as shown. Erect perpendicular to CD at C and make CE = BG. Join G to E and bisect it. The intersection F of the bisector and the perpendicular CE, extended, is the center of the second arc. Join centers of the two arcs to locate tangent point T, the inflection point of the curve.

A6.35 ◾ Drawing a Curve Tangent to Three Intersecting Lines

Let AB, BC, and CD be the given lines (Figure A6.38a and b). Select point of tangency P at any point on line BC. Make BT equal to BP, and CS equal to CP, and erect perpendiculars at the

points P, T, and S. Their intersections O and Q are the centers of the required tangent arcs.

A6.36 ◾ Rectifying a Circular Arc

To *rectify* an arc is to lay out its true length along a straight line. The constructions are approximate, but well within the range of accuracy of drawing instruments.

To Rectify a Quadrant of a Circle, AB   Draw AC tangent to the circle BC at 60° to AC, as shown (Figure A6.39a). The line AC is almost equal to the arc AB; the difference in length is about 1 in 240.

To Rectify Arc, AB   Draw tangent at B (Figure A6.39b). Draw chord AB and extend it to C, making BC equal to half AB. With C as center and radius CA, strike the arc AD. The tangent BD is slightly shorter than the given arc AB. For an angle of 45° the difference in length is about 1 in 2,866.

Use the bow dividers and, beginning at A, set off equal distances until the division point nearest B is reached (Figure A6.39c). At this point, reverse the direction and set off an equal number of distances along the tangent to determine point C. The tangent BC is slightly shorter than the given arc AB. If the angle subtended by each division is 10°, the error is approximately 1 in 830.*

A6.37 ◾ Setting Off a Given Length Along a Given Arc

To transfer distances from the tangent line to the arc, reverse the preceding method (Figure A6.39c).

---

*If the angle θ subtending an arc of radius R is known, the length of the arc is $2\pi R\dfrac{\theta}{360°} = 0.01745R\theta$.

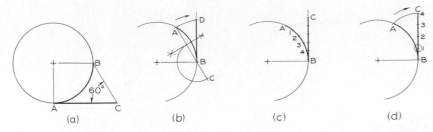

A6.39   Rectifying Circular Arcs

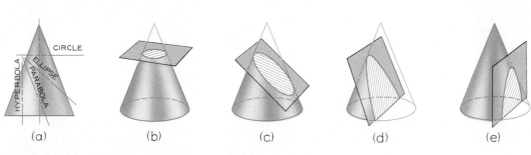

A6.40   Conic Sections

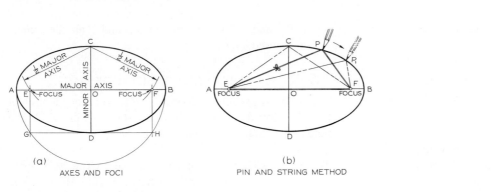

A6.41   Ellipse Constructions

To set off the length BC along the arc BA, draw BC tangent to the arc at B (Figure A6.39d). Divide BC into four equal parts. With center at 1, the first division point, and radius 1–C, draw the arc CA. The arc BA is practically equal to BC for angles less than 30°. For 45° the difference is approximately 1 in 3,232, and for 60° it is about 1 in 835.

A6.38 ■ The Conic Sections

The conic sections are curves produced by planes intersecting a right circular cone (Figure A6.40). Four types of curves are produced: the *circle*, *ellipse*, *parabola*, and *hyperbola*, according to the position of the planes, as shown. These curves were studied in detail by the ancient Greeks and are of great interest in mathematics, as well as in technical drawing. For equations, see any text on analytic geometry.

A6.39 ■ Ellipse Construction

The long axis of an ellipse is the major axis and the short axis is the minor axis (Figure A6.41). The foci E and F are found by striking arcs with radius equal to half the major axis and with center at the end of the minor axis. Another method is to

draw a semicircle with the major axis as diameter, and then to draw GH parallel to the major axis and GE and HF parallel to the minor axis as shown.

An *ellipse* is generated by a point moving so that the sum of its distances from two points (the foci) is constant and equal to the major axis. As shown in Figure A6.41b, an ellipse may be constructed by placing a looped string around the foci E and F and around C, one end of the minor axis, and moving the pencil point P along its maximum orbit while the string is kept taut.

A6.40 ■ Drawing a Foci Ellipse

Let AB be the major axis and CD the minor axis (Figure A6.42). This method is the geometrical counterpart of the pin-and-string method. Keep the construction very light, as follows:

I.   To find foci E and F, strike arcs R with radius equal to half the major axis and with centers at the ends of the minor axis.

II. Between E and O on the major axis, mark at random a number of points (spacing those on the left more closely), equal to the number of points desired in each quadrant of the ellipse. In this figure, five points were deemed sufficient. For large ellipses, more points should be used—enough to

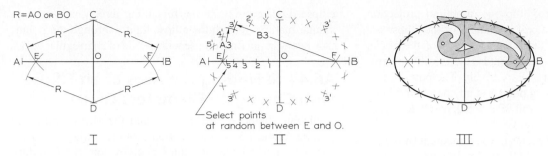

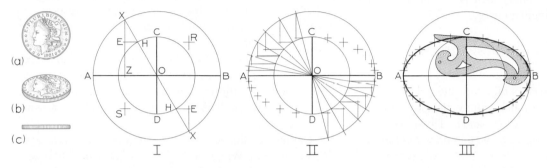

A6.42   Drawing a Foci Ellipse

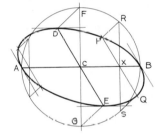

(a)

(b)

(c)

A6.43   Drawing a Concentric Circle Ellipse

ensure a smooth, accurate curve. Begin construction with any one of these points, such as 3. With E and F as centers and radii A–3 and B–3, respectively (from the ends of the major axis to point 3), strike arcs to intersect at four points 3', as shown. Using the remaining points 1, 2, 4, and 5, for each find four additional points on the ellipse in the same manner.

III.   Sketch the ellipse lightly through the points; then heavy in the final ellipse with the aid of an irregular curve.

A6.41 ■ Drawing a Concentric Circle Ellipse

If a circle is viewed so that the line of sight is perpendicular to the plane of the circle, as shown for the silver dollar in Figure A6.43a, the circle will appear as a circle, in true size and shape. If the circle is viewed at an angle, as shown in Figure A6.43b, it will appear as an ellipse. If the circle is viewed edgewise, it appears as a straight line, as shown in Figure A6.43c. The case shown in Figure A6.43b is the basis for the construction of an ellipse by the concentric circle method, which follows. (Keep the construction very light.)

I.   Draw circles on the major and minor axes, using them as diameters; draw any diagonal XX through center O. From the points X, where the diagonal intersects the large circle, draw lines XE parallel to the minor axis, and from the points H, where the diagonal intersects the small circle, draw lines HE parallel to the major axis. The intersections E are points on the ellipse. Two additional points, S and R, can be found by extending lines XE and HE, giving a total of four points from the one diagonal XX.

II.   Draw as many additional diagonals as needed to provide a sufficient number of points for a smooth and symmetrical

ellipse, each diagonal accounting for four points on the ellipse. Notice that where the curve is sharpest (near the ends of the ellipse), the points are constructed closer together to determine the curve better.

III.   Sketch the ellipse lightly through the points, and then heavy in the final ellipse with the aid of an irregular curve.*

---

*In Figure A6.43, part I, the ordinate EZ of the ellipse is to the corresponding ordinate XZ of the circle as b is to a, where b represents the semiminor axis and a the semimajor axis. Thus, the area of the ellipse is equal to the area of the circumscribed circle multiplied by b/a; hence, it is equal to πab.

A6.42 ■ Drawing an Ellipse on Conjugate Diameters: The Oblique Circle Method

Let AB and DE be the given conjugate diameters (Figure A6.44). Two diameters are conjugate when each is parallel to the tangents at the extremities of the other. With center at C and radius CA, draw a circle; draw the diameter GF perpendicular to AB, and draw lines joining points D and F and points G and E.

A6.44   Oblique Circle Ellipse

Assume that the required ellipse is an oblique projection of the circle just drawn; the points D and E of the ellipse are the oblique projections of the points F and G of the circle, respectively; similarly, the points P and Q are the oblique projections of the points R and S, respectively. The points P and Q are determined by assuming point X at any point on AB and drawing the lines RS and PQ, and RP and SQ, parallel, respectively, to GF and DE and FD and GE.

Determine at least five points in each quadrant (more for larger ellipses) by assuming additional points on the major axis and proceeding as explained for point X. Sketch the ellipse lightly through the points; then heavy in the final ellipse with the aid of an irregular curve.

A6.43 ■ Drawing a Parallelogram Ellipse

Given the major and minor axes, or the conjugate diameters AB and CD, draw a rectangle or parallelogram with sides parallel to the axes, respectively (Figure A6.45a and b). Divide AO and AJ into the same number of equal parts, and draw *light* lines through these points from the ends of the minor axis, as shown. The intersection of like-numbered lines will be points on the

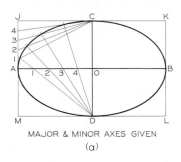

MAJOR & MINOR AXES GIVEN
(a)

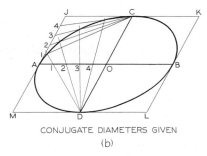

CONJUGATE DIAMETERS GIVEN
(b)

A6.45 Parallelogram Ellipse

ellipse. Locate points in the remaining three quadrants in a similar manner. Sketch the ellipse lightly through the points; then heavy in the final ellipse with the aid of an irregular curve.

A6.44 ■ Finding the Axes of an Ellipse with Conjugate Diameters Given

Conjugate diameters AB and CD and the ellipse are given (Figure A6.46a). With intersection O of the conjugate diameters (center of ellipse) as center, and any convenient radius, draw a circle to intersect the ellipse in four points. Join these points with straight lines, as shown; the resulting quadrilateral will be a rectangle whose sides are parallel, respectively, to the required major and minor axes. Draw the axes EF and GH parallel to the sides of the rectangle.

An ellipse only is given (Figure A6.46c). To find the center of the ellipse, draw a circumscribing rectangle or parallelogram about the ellipse; then draw diagonals to intersect at center O as shown. The axes are then found as shown in Figure A6.46a.

Conjugate diameters AB and CD only are given (Figure A6.46c). With O as center and CD as diameter, draw a circle. Through center O and perpendicular to CD, draw line EF. From points E and F, where this perpendicular intersects the circle, draw lines FA and EA to form angle FAE. Draw the bisector AG of this angle. The major axis JK will be parallel to this bisector, and the minor axis LM will be perpendicular to it. The length AH will be one half the major axis, and HF one half the minor axis. The resulting major and minor axes are JK and LM, respectively.

A6.45 ■ Drawing a Tangent to an Ellipse

Concentric Circle Construction   To draw a tangent at any point on an ellipse, such as E, draw the ordinate at E to intersect the circle at V (Figure A6.47a). Draw a tangent to the circumscribed circle at V, and extend it to intersect the major axis extended at G. The line GE is the required tangent.

To draw a tangent from a point outside the ellipse, such as P, draw the ordinate PY and extend it. Draw DP, intersecting the major axis at X. Draw FX and extend it to intersect the ordinate through P at Q. Then, from similar triangles QY:PY = OF:OD. Draw a tangent to the circle from Q, find the point of tangency R, and draw the ordinate at R to intersect the ellipse at Z. The line ZP

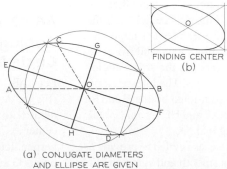

FINDING CENTER
(b)

(a) CONJUGATE DIAMETERS AND ELLIPSE ARE GIVEN

(c) CONJUGATE DIAMETERS GIVEN

A6.46   Finding the Axes of an Ellipse

is the required tangent. As a check on the drawing, the tangents RQ and ZP should intersect at a point on the major axis extended. Two tangents to the ellipse can be drawn from point P.

Foci Construction   To draw a tangent at any point on the ellipse, such as point 3, draw the focal radii E–3 and F–3, extend one, and bisect the exterior angle, as shown in Figure A6.47b. The bisector is the required tangent.

To draw a tangent from any point outside the ellipse, such as point P, with center at P and radius PF, strike an arc as shown. With center at E and radius AB, strike an arc to intersect the first arc at points U. Draw the lines EU to intersect the ellipse at the points Z. The lines PZ are the required tangents.

A6.46 ■ Ellipse Templates

To save time in drawing ellipses and to ensure uniform results, ellipse templates are often used (Figure A6.48a). These are plastic sheets with elliptical openings in a wide variety of sizes, and they usually come in sets of six or more sheets.

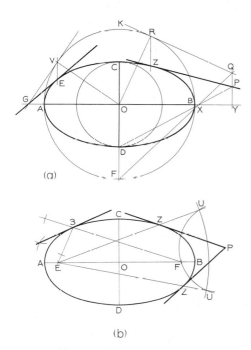

(a)

(b)

A6.47   Tangents to an Ellipse

Ellipse guides are usually designated by the ellipse angle, the angle at which a circle is viewed to appear as an ellipse. In Figure A6.48b, the angle between the line of sight and the edge view of the plane of the circle is found to be about 49°; hence the 50° ellipse template is indicated. Ellipse templates are generally available in ellipse angles at 5° intervals, such as 15°, 20°, and 25°. The 50° template provides a variety of sizes of 50° ellipses, and it is only necessary to select the one that fits. If the ellipse angle is not easily determined, you can always look for the ellipse that is approximately as long and as "fat" as the ellipse to be drawn.

A simple construction for finding the ellipse angle when the views are not available is shown in Figure A6.48c. Using center O, strike arc BF; then draw CE parallel to the major axis. Draw diagonal OE, and measure angle EOB with a protractor. Use the ellipse template nearest to this angle; in this case a 35° template is selected.

Since it is not feasible to have ellipse openings for every exact size that may be required, it is often necessary to use the template somewhat in the manner of an irregular curve. For example, if the opening is too long and too "fat" for the required ellipse, one end may be drawn and then the template may be shifted slightly to draw the other end. Similarly, one long side may be drawn and then the template may be shifted slightly to draw the opposite side. In such cases, leave gaps between the four segments, to be filled in freehand or with the aid of an irregular curve. When the differences between the ellipse openings and the required ellipse are small, it is only necessary to lean the pencil slightly outward or inward from the guiding edge to offset the differences.

For inking the ellipses, a technical drawing pen with a "0" or "00" size designation is recommended (Figure A6.48d).

A6.47 ■ Drawing an Approximate Ellipse

For many purposes, particularly where a small ellipse is required, the approximate circular arc method is perfectly satisfactory (Figure A6.49). Such an ellipse is sure to be symmetrical and may be quickly drawn.

Given axes AB and CD,

I. Draw line AC. With O as center and OA as radius, strike the arc AE. With C as center and CE as radius, strike the arc EF.

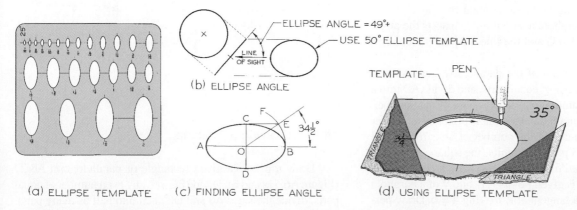

(b) ELLIPSE ANGLE

(a) ELLIPSE TEMPLATE   (c) FINDING ELLIPSE ANGLE

(d) USING ELLIPSE TEMPLATE

A6.48   Using the Ellipse Template

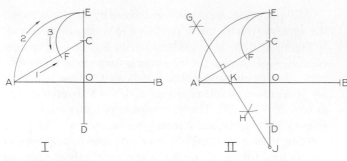

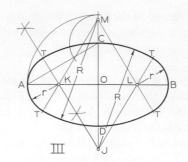

A6.49   Drawing an Approximate Ellipse

II. Draw perpendicular bisector GH of the line AF; the points K and J, where it intersects the axes, are centers of the required arcs.
III. Find centers M and L by setting off OL = OK and OM = OJ. Using centers K, L, M, and J, draw circular arcs as shown. The points of tangency T are at the junctures of the arcs on the lines joining the centers.

A6.48 ■ Drawing a Parabola

The curve of intersection between a right circular cone and a plane parallel to one of its elements is a parabola (see Figure A6.50d). The parabola is used to reflect surfaces for light and sound, for vertical curves in highways, for forms of arches, and approximately for forms of the curves of cables for suspension bridges. It is also used to show the bending moment at any point on a uniformly loaded beam or girder.

A *parabola* is generated by a point moving so that its distances from a fixed point, the focus, and from a fixed line, the directrix, remain equal.

Focus F and directrix AB are given. A parabola may be generated by a pencil guided by a string (Figure A6.50a). Fasten the string at F and C; its length is GC. The point C is selected at random; its distance from G depends on the desired extent of the curve. Keep the string taut and the pencil against the T-square, as shown.

Given focus F and directrix AB, draw a line DE parallel to the directrix and at any distance CZ from it (Figure A6.50b). With center at F and radius CZ, strike arcs to intersect the line DE in the points Q and R, which are points on the parabola. Determine as many additional points as are necessary to draw the parabola accurately, by drawing additional lines parallel to line AB and proceeding in the same manner.

A tangent to the parabola at any point G bisects the angle formed by the focal line FG and the line SG perpendicular to the directrix.

Given the rise and span of the parabola (Figure A6.50), divide AO into any number of equal parts, and divide AD into a number of equal parts amounting to the square of that number. From line AB, each point on the parabola is offset by a number of units equal to the square of the number of units from point O. For example, point 3 projects 9 units (the square of 3). This method is generally used for drawing parabolic arches.

To find the focus, F, given points P, R, and V of a parabola (Figure A6.50), draw a tangent at P, making a = b. Draw perpendicular bisector of AP, which intersects the axis at F, the focus of the parabola.

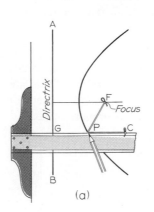

(a)

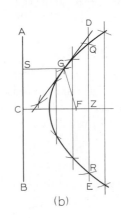

(b)

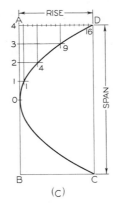

(c)

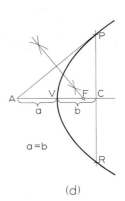

(d)

A6.50   Drawing a Parabola

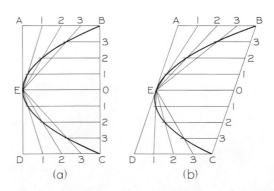

(a)   (b)

A6.51   Drawing a Parabola

Draw a parabola given rectangle or parallelogram ABCD (Figure A6.51a and b). Divide BC into any even number of equal parts, divide the sides AB and DC each into half as many parts, and draw lines as shown. The intersections of like-numbered lines are points on the parabola.

A6.49 ■ Joining Two Points by a Parabolic Curve

Let X and Y be the given points (Figure A6.52). Assume any point O, and draw tangents XO and YO. Divide XO and YO into the same number of equal parts, number the division points as shown, and connect corresponding points. These lines are tangents of the required parabola and form its envelope. Sketch a light smooth curve, and then heavy in the curve with the aid of an irregular curve.

These parabolic curves are more pleasing in appearance than circular arcs and are useful in machine design. If the tangents OX and OY are equal, the axis of the parabola will bisect the angle between them.

A6.50 ■ Drawing a Hyperbola

The curve of intersection between a right circular cone and a plane making an angle with the axis smaller than that made by the elements is a hyperbola (see Figure A6.53e). A *hyperbola* is generated by a point moving so that the difference of its distances from two fixed points, the foci is constant and equal to the transverse axis of the hyperbola.

Let F and F′ be the foci and AB the transverse axis (Figure A6.53a). The curve may be generated by a pencil guided by a string, as shown. Fasten a string at F′ and C; its length is FC minus AB. The point C is chosen at random; its distance from F depends on the desired extent of the curve.

Fasten the straightedge at F. If it is revolved about F, with the pencil point moving against it and with the string taut, the hyperbola may be drawn as shown.

To construct the curve geometrically, select any point X on the transverse axis produced (Figure A6.53b). With centers at F and F′ and BX as radius, strike the arcs DF. With the same centers, F and F′, and AX as radius, strike arcs to intersect the arcs first drawn in the points Q, R, S, and T, which are points of the required hyperbola. Find as many additional points as are necessary to draw the curves accurately by selecting other points similar to point X along the transverse axis and proceeding as described for point X.

To draw the tangent to a hyperbola at a given point P, bisect the angle between the focal radii FP and F′P. The bisector is the required tangent.

To draw the asymptotes HCH of the hyperbola, draw a circle with the diameter FF′ and erect perpendiculars to the transverse axis at the points A and B to intersect the circle in the points H. The lines HCH are the required asymptotes.

A6.51 ■ Drawing an Equilateral Hyperbola

Let the asymptotes OB and OA, at right angles to each other, and the point P on the curve be given (Figure A6.54).

In an equilateral hyperbola, the asymptotes, which are at right angles to each other, may be used as the axes to which

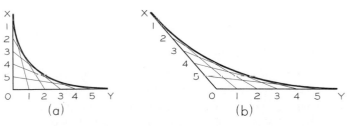

A6.52   Parabolic Curves

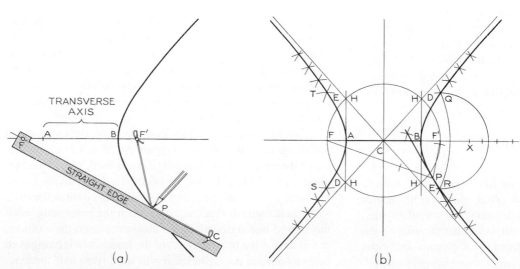

A6.53   Drawing a Hyperbola

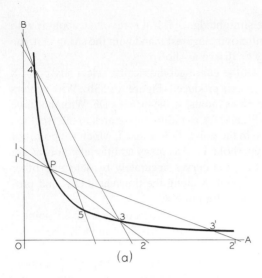

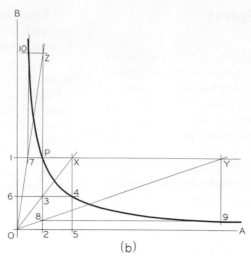

A6.54 Equilateral Hyperbola

the curve is referred. If a chord of the hyperbola is extended to intersect the axes, the intercepts between the curve and the axes are equal (Figure A6.54a). For example, a chord through given point P intersects the axes at points 1 and 2, intercepts P–1 and 2–3 are equal, and point 3 is a point on the hyperbola. Likewise, another chord through P provides equal intercepts P–1' and 3'–2', and point 3' is a point on the curve. Not all chords need be drawn through given point P, but as new points are established on the curve, chords may be drawn through them to obtain more points. After enough points are found to ensure an accurate curve, the hyperbola is drawn with the aid of an irregular curve.

In an equilateral hyperbola, the coordinates are related so their products remain constant. Through given point P, draw lines 1–P–Y and 2–P–Z parallel, respectively, to the axes (Figure A6.54b). From the origin of coordinates O, draw any diagonal intersecting these two lines at points 3 and X. At these points draw lines parallel to the axes, intersecting at point 4, a point on the curve. Likewise, another diagonal from O intersects the two lines through P at points 8 and Y, and lines through these points parallel to the axes intersect at point 9, another point on the curve. A third diagonal similarly produces point 10 on the curve, and so on. Find as many points as necessary for a smooth curve, and draw the parabola with the aid of an irregular curve. It is evident from the similar triangles O–X–5 and O–3–2 that lines P–1 × P–2 = 4–5 × 4–6.

The equilateral hyperbola can be used to represent varying pressure of a gas as the volume varies, since the pressure varies inversely with the volume; that is, pressure × volume is constant.

A6.52 ■ Drawing a Spiral of Archimedes

To find points on the curve, draw lines through the pole C, making equal angles with each other, such as 30° angles (Figure A6.55). Beginning with any one line, set off any distance, such as 2 mm or $\frac{1}{16}$" set off twice that distance on the next line, three times on the third, and so on. Through the points thus determined, draw a smooth curve, using irregular curve.

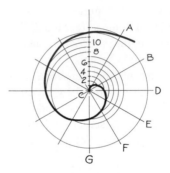

A6.55 Spiral of Archimedes

A6.53 ■ Drawing a Helix

A *helix* is generated by a point moving around and along the surface of a cylinder or cone with a uniform angular velocity about the axis, and with a uniform linear velocity about the axis, and with a uniform velocity in the direction of the axis (Figure A6.56). A cylindrical helix is generally known simply as a helix. The distance measure parallel to the axis traversed by the point in one revolution is called the lead.

If the cylindrical surface on which a helix is generated is rolled out onto a plane, the helix becomes a straight line (Figure A6.56a). The portion below the helix becomes a right triangle, the altitude of which is equal to the lead of the helix; the length of the base is equal to the circumference of the cylinder. Such a helix, therefore, can be defined as the shortest line that can be drawn on the surface of a cylinder connecting two points not on the same element.

To draw the helix, draw two views of the cylinder on which the helix is generated (Figure A6.56b). Divide the circle of the base into any number of equal parts. On the rectangular view of the cylinder, set off the lead and divide it into the same number of equal parts as the base. Number the divisions as shown (in this case 16). When the generating point has moved one sixteenth of the distance around the cylinder, it will have risen one sixteenth of the lead; when it has moved halfway around the cylinder, it will have risen half the lead;

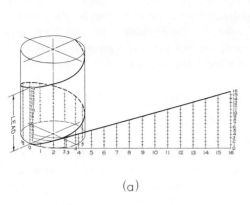
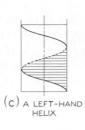
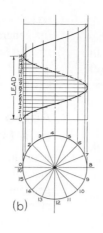
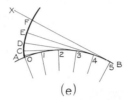
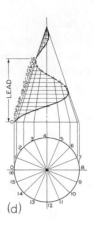

A6.56 Helix

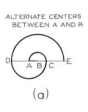
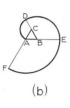
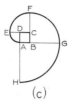

A6.57 Involutes

and so on. Points on the helix are found by projecting up from point 1 in the circular view to line 1 in the rectangular view, from point 2 in the circular view to line 2 in the rectangular view, and so on.

Figure A6.56b is a right-hand helix. In a left-hand helix (Figure A6.56c), the visible portions of the curve are inclined in the opposite direction—that is, downward to the right. The helix shown in Figure A6.56b can be converted into a left-hand helix by interchanging the visible and hidden lines.

The helix finds many applications in industry, as in screw threads, worm gears, conveyors, spiral stairways, and so on. The stripes of a barber pole are helical in form.

The construction for a right-hand conical helix is shown in Figure A6.56d.

A6.54 ■ Drawing an Involute

An *involute* is the path of a point on a string as the string unwinds from a line, polygon, or circle.

To Draw an Involute of a Line Let AB be the given line. With AB as radius and B as center, draw the semicircle AC (Figure A6.57a). With AC as radius and A as center, draw the semicircle CD. With BD as radius and B as center, draw the semicircle DE. Continue similarly, alternating centers between A and B, until a figure of the required size is completed.

To Draw an Involute of a Triangle Let ABC be the given triangle. With CA as radius and C as center, strike the arc AD (Figure A6.57b). With BD as radius and B as center, strike the arc DE. With AE as radius and A as center, strike the arc EF. Continue similarly until a figure of the required size is completed.

To Draw an Involute of a Square Let ABCD be the given square. With DA as radius and D as center, draw the 90° arc AE (Figure A6.57c). Proceed as for the involute of a triangle until a figure of the required size is completed.

To Draw an Involute of a Circle A circle may be regarded as a polygon with an infinite number of sides (Figure A6.57d). The involute is constructed by dividing the circumference into a number of equal parts, drawing a tangent at each division point, setting off along each tangent the length of the corresponding circular arc (Figure A6.39c), and drawing the required curve through the points set off on the several tangents.

An involute can be generated by a point on a straight line that is rolled on a fixed circle (Figure A6.57e). Points on the required curve may be determined by setting off equal distances 0–1, 1–2, 2–3, and so on, along the circumference, drawing a tangent at each division point, and proceeding as explained for Figure A6.57d.

The involute of a circle is used in the construction of involute gear teeth. In this system, the involute forms the face and a part of the flank of the teeth of gear wheels; the outlines of the teeth of racks are straight lines.

A6.55 ■ Drawing a Cycloid

A *cycloid* generated by a point P in the circumference of a circle that rolls along a straight line (Figure A6.58).

Given the generating circle and the straight line AB tangent to it, make the distances CA and CB each equal to the semicircumference of the circle (see Figure A6.58). Divide these distances and the semicircumference into the same number of equal parts (six, for instance) and number them consecutively, as shown. Suppose the circle rolls to the left;

when point 1 of the circle reaches point 1′ of the line, the center of the circle will be at D, point 7 will be the highest point of the circle, and the generating point 6 will be at the same distance from the line AB as point 5 is when the circle is in its central position. Hence, to find the point P′, draw a line through point 5 parallel to AB and intersect it with an arc drawn from the center D with a radius equal to that of the circle. To find point P″, draw a line through point 4 parallel to AB, and intersect it with an arc drawn from the center E, with a radius equal to that of the circle. Points J, K, and L are found in a similar manner.

Another method that may be employed is shown in the right half of Figure A6.57. With center at 11′ and the chord 11–6 as radius, strike an arc. With 10′ as center and the chord 10–6 as radius, strike an arc. Continue similarly with centers 9′, 8′, and 7′. Draw the required cycloid tangent to these arcs.

Either method may be used; however, the second is the shorter one and is preferred. It is evident, from the tangent

arcs drawn in the manner just described, that the line joining the generating point and the point of contact for the generating circle is a normal of the cycloid. The lines 1′–P″ and 2′–P′, for instance, are normals; this property makes the cycloid suitable for the outlines of gear teeth.

A6.56 ■ Drawing an Epicycloid or a Hypocycloid

If the generating point P is on the circumference of a circle that rolls along the convex side of a larger circle, the curve generated is an epicycloid (Figure A6.59a). If the circle rolls along the concave side of a larger circle, the curve generated is a hypocycloid (Figure A6.59b). These curves are drawn in a manner similar to the cycloid (Figure A6.58). Like the cycloid, these curves are used to form the outlines of certain gear teeth and are, therefore, of practical importance in machine design.

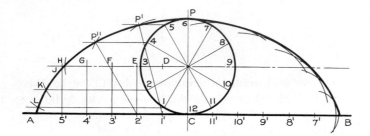

A6.58 Cycloid

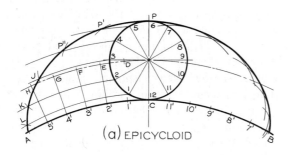

(a) EPICYCLOID

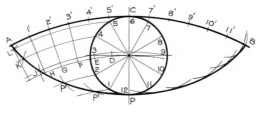

(b) HYPOCYCLOID

A6.59 Epicycloid and Hypocycloid

7 Running and Sliding Fits[a]—American National Standard

RC 1   *Close sliding fits* are intended for the accurate location of parts which must assemble without perceptible play.

RC 2   *Sliding fits* are intended for accurate location, but with greater maximum clearance than class RC 1. Parts made to this fit move and turn easily but are not intended to run freely, and in the larger sizes may seize with small temperature changes.

RC 3   *Precision running fits* are about the closest fits which can be expected to run freely and are intended for precision work at slow speeds and light journal pressures, but they are not suitable where appreciable temperature differences are likely to be encountered.

RC 4   *Close running fits* are intended chiefly for running fits on accurate machinery with moderate surface speeds and journal pressures, where accurate location and minimum play are desired.

Basic hole system. **Limits are in thousandths of an inch.** Limits for hole and shaft are applied algebraically to the basic size to obtain the limits of size for the parts. Data in **boldface** are in accordance with ABC agreements. Symbols H5, g5, etc., are hole and shaft designations used in ABC System.

Nominal Size Range, inches Over To	Class RC 1 Limits of Clearance	Standard Limits Hole H5	Shaft g4	Class RC 2 Limits of Clearance	Standard Limits Hole H6	Shaft g5	Class RC 3 Limits of Clearance	Standard Limits Hole H7	Shaft f6	Class RC 4 Limits of Clearance	Standard Limits Hole H8	Shaft f7
0–0.12	0.1 0.45	+0.2 −0	−0.1 −0.25	0.1 0.55	+0.25 −0	−0.1 −0.3	0.3 0.95	+0.4 −0	−0.3 −0.55	0.3 1.3	+0.6 −0	−0.3 −0.7
0.12–0.24	0.15 0.5	+0.2 −0	−0.15 −0.3	0.15 0.65	+0.3 −0	−0.15 −0.35	0.4 1.12	+0.5 −0	−0.4 −0.7	0.4 1.6	+0.7 −0	−0.4 −0.9
0.24–0.40	0.2 0.6	+0.25 −0	−0.2 −0.35	0.2 0.85	+0.4 −0	−0.2 −0.45	0.5 1.5	+0.6 −0	−0.5 −0.9	0.5 2.0	+0.9 −0	−0.5 −1.1
0.40–0.71	0.25 0.75	+0.3 −0	−0.25 −0.45	0.25 0.95	+0.4 −0	−0.25 −0.55	0.6 1.7	+0.7 −0	−0.6 −1.0	0.6 2.3	+1.0 −0	−0.6 −1.3
0.71–1.19	0.3 0.95	+0.4 −0	−0.3 −0.55	0.3 1.2	+0.5 −0	−0.3 −0.7	0.8 2.1	+0.8 −0	−0.8 −1.3	0.8 2.8	+1.2 −0	−0.8 −1.6
1.19–1.97	0.4 1.1	+0.4 −0	−0.4 −0.7	0.4 1.4	+0.6 −0	−0.4 −0.8	1.0 2.6	+1.0 −0	−1.0 −1.6	1.0 3.6	+1.6 −0	−1.0 −2.0
1.97–3.15	0.4 1.2	+0.5 −0	−0.4 −0.7	0.4 1.6	+0.7 −0	−0.4 −0.9	1.2 3.1	+1.2 −0	−1.2 −1.9	1.2 4.2	+1.8 −0	−1.2 −2.4
3.15–4.73	0.5 1.5	+0.6 −0	−0.5 −0.9	0.5 2.0	+0.9 −0	−0.5 −1.1	1.4 3.7	+1.4 −0	−1.4 −2.3	1.4 5.0	+2.2 −0	−1.4 −2.8
4.73–7.09	0.6 1.8	+0.7 −0	−0.6 −1.1	0.6 2.3	+1.0 −0	−0.6 −1.3	1.6 4.2	+1.6 −0	−1.6 −2.6	1.6 5.7	+2.5 −0	−1.6 −3.2
7.09–9.85	0.6 2.0	+0.8 −0	−0.6 −1.2	0.6 2.6	+1.2 −0	−0.6 −1.4	2.0 5.0	+1.8 −0	−2.0 −3.2	2.0 6.6	+2.8 −0	−2.0 −3.8
9.85–12.41	0.8 2.3	+0.9 −0	−0.8 −1.4	0.8 2.9	+1.2 −0	−0.8 −1.7	2.5 5.7	+2.0 −0	−2.5 −3.7	2.5 7.5	+3.0 −0	−2.5 −4.5
12.41–15.75	1.0 2.7	+1.0 −0	−1.0 −1.7	1.0 3.4	+1.4 −0	−1.0 −2.0	3.0 6.6	+2.2 −0	−3.0 −4.4	3.0 8.7	+3.5 −0	−3.0 −5.2

[a]From ANSI B4.1-1967 (R1994). For larger diameters, see the standard.

7 Running and Sliding Fits[a]—American National Standard (continued)

RC 5 ⎫
RC 6 ⎬ *Medium running fits* are intended for higher running speeds, or heavy journal pressures, or both.

RC 7   *Free running fits* are intended for use where accuracy is not essential, or where large temperature variations are likely to be encountered, or under both these conditions.

RC 8 ⎫ *Loose running fits* are intended for use where wide commercial tolerances may be necessary, together with an allowance,
RC 9 ⎬ on the external member.

Nominal Size Range, inches Over To	Class RC 5 Limits of Clearance	Class RC 5 Standard Limits Hole H8	Class RC 5 Standard Limits Shaft e7	Class RC 6 Limits of Clearance	Class RC 6 Standard Limits Hole H9	Class RC 6 Standard Limits Shaft e8	Class RC 7 Limits of Clearance	Class RC 7 Standard Limits Hole H9	Class RC 7 Standard Limits Shaft d8	Class RC 8 Limits of Clearance	Class RC 8 Standard Limits Hole H10	Class RC 8 Standard Limits Shaft c9	Class RC 9 Limits of Clearance	Class RC 9 Standard Limits Hole H11	Class RC 9 Standard Limits Shaft
0–0.12	0.6 1.6	+0.6 −0	−0.6 −1.0	0.6 2.2	+1.0 −0	−0.6 −1.2	1.0 2.6	+1.0 −0	−1.0 −1.6	2.5 5.1	+1.6 −0	−2.5 −3.5	4.0 8.1	+2.5 −0	−4.0 −5.6
0.12–0.24	0.8 2.0	+0.7 −0	−0.8 −1.3	0.8 2.7	+1.2 −0	−0.8 −1.5	1.2 3.1	+1.2 −0	−1.2 −1.9	2.8 5.8	+1.8 −0	−2.8 −4.0	4.5 9.0	+3.0 −0	−4.5 −6.0
0.24–0.40	1.0 2.5	+0.9 −0	−1.0 −1.6	1.0 3.3	+1.4 −0	−1.0 −1.9	1.6 3.9	+1.4 −0	−1.6 −2.5	3.0 6.6	+2.2 −0	−3.0 −4.4	5.0 10.7	+3.5 −0	−5.0 −7.2
0.40–0.71	1.2 2.9	+1.0 −0	−1.2 −1.9	1.2 3.8	+1.6 −0	−1.2 −2.2	2.0 4.6	+1.6 −0	−2.0 −3.0	3.5 7.9	+2.8 −0	−3.5 −5.1	6.0 12.8	+4.0 −0	−6.0 −8.8
0.71–1.19	1.6 3.6	+1.2 −0	−1.6 −2.4	1.6 4.8	+2.0 −0	−1.6 −2.8	2.5 5.7	+2.0 −0	−2.5 −3.7	4.5 10.0	+3.5 −0	−4.5 −6.5	7.0 15.5	+5.0 −0	−7.0 −10.5
1.19–1.97	2.0 4.6	+1.6 −0	−2.0 −3.0	2.0 6.1	+2.5 −0	−2.0 −3.6	3.0 7.1	+2.5 −0	−3.0 −4.6	5.0 11.5	+4.0 −0	−5.0 −7.5	8.0 18.0	+6.0 −0	−8.0 −12.0
1.97–3.15	2.5 5.5	+1.8 −0	−2.5 −3.7	2.5 7.3	+3.0 −0	−2.5 −4.3	4.0 8.8	+3.0 −0	−4.0 −5.8	6.0 13.5	+4.5 −0	−6.0 −9.0	9.0 20.5	+7.0 −0	−9.0 −13.5
3.15–4.73	3.0 6.6	+2.2 −0	−3.0 −4.4	3.0 8.7	+3.5 −0	−3.0 −5.2	5.0 10.7	+3.5 −0	−5.0 −7.2	7.0 15.5	+5.0 −0	−7.0 −10.5	10.0 24.0	+9.0 −0	−10.0 −15.0
4.73–7.09	3.5 7.6	+2.5 −0	−3.5 −5.1	3.5 10.0	+4.0 −0	−3.5 −6.0	6.0 12.5	+4.0 −0	−6.0 −8.5	8.0 18.0	+6.0 −0	−8.0 −12.0	12.0 28.0	+10.0 −0	−12.0 −18.0
7.09–9.85	4.0 8.6	+2.8 −0	−4.0 −5.8	4.0 11.3	+4.5 −0	−4.0 −6.8	7.0 14.3	+4.5 −0	−7.0 −9.8	10.0 21.5	+7.0 −0	−10.0 −14.5	15.0 34.0	+12.0 −0	−15.0 −22.0
9.85–12.41	5.0 10.0	+3.0 −0	−5.0 −7.0	5.0 13.0	+5.0 −0	−5.0 −8.0	8.0 16.0	+5.0 −0	−8.0 −11.0	12.0 25.0	+8.0 −0	−12.0 −17.0	18.0 38.0	+12.0 −0	−18.0 −26.0
12.41–15.75	6.0 11.7	+3.5 −0	−6.0 −8.2	6.0 15.5	+6.0 −0	−6.0 −9.5	10.0 19.5	+6.0 −0	−10.0 13.5	14.0 29.0	+9.0 −0	−14.0 −20.0	22.0 45.0	+14.0 −0	−22.0 −31.0

[a]From ANSI B4.1-1967 (R1994). For larger diameters, see the standard.

8 Clearance Locational Fits[a]—American National Standard

LC *Locational clearance fits* are intended for parts which are normally stationary but which can be freely assembled or disassembled. They run from snug fits for parts requiring accuracy of location, through the medium clearance fits for parts such as spigots, to the looser fastener fits, where freedom of assembly is of prime importance.

Basic hole system. **Limits are in thousandths of an inch.** Limits for hole and shaft are applied algebraically to the basic size to obtain the limits of size for the parts. Data in **boldface** are in accordance with ABC agreements. Symbols H6, H5, etc., are hole and shaft designations used in ABC System.

Nominal Size Range, inches Over To	Class LC 1 Limits of Clearance	Class LC 1 Standard Limits Hole H6	Class LC 1 Standard Limits Shaft h5	Class LC 2 Limits of Clearance	Class LC 2 Standard Limits Hole H7	Class LC 2 Standard Limits Shaft h6	Class LC 3 Limits of Clearance	Class LC 3 Standard Limits Hole H8	Class LC 3 Standard Limits Shaft h7	Class LC 4 Limits of Clearance	Class LC 4 Standard Limits Hole H10	Class LC 4 Standard Limits Shaft h9	Class LC 5 Limits of Clearance	Class LC 5 Standard Limits Hole H7	Class LC 5 Standard Limits Shaft g6
0–0.12	0 / 0.45	+0.25 / -0	+0 / -0.2	0 / 0.65	+0.4 / -0	+0 / -0.25	0 / 1	+0.6 / -0	+0 / -0.4	0 / 2.6	+1.6 / -0	+0 / -1.0	0.1 / 0.75	+0.4 / -0	-0.1 / -0.35
0.12–0.24	0 / 0.5	+0.3 / -0	+0 / -0.2	0 / 0.8	+0.5 / -0	+0 / -0.3	0 / 1.2	+0.7 / -0	+0 / -0.5	0 / 3.0	+1.8 / -0	+0 / -1.2	0.15 / 0.95	+0.5 / -0	-0.15 / -0.45
0.24–0.40	0 / 0.65	+0.4 / -0	+0 / -0.25	0 / 1.0	+0.6 / -0	+0 / -0.4	0 / 1.5	+0.9 / -0	+0 / -0.6	0 / 3.6	+2.2 / -0	+0 / -1.4	0.2 / 1.2	+0.6 / -0	-0.2 / -0.6
0.40–0.71	0 / 0.7	+0.4 / -0	+0 / -0.3	0 / 1.1	+0.7 / -0	+0 / -0.4	0 / 1.7	+1.0 / -0	+0 / -0.7	0 / 4.4	+2.8 / -0	+0 / -1.6	0.25 / 1.35	+0.7 / -0	-0.25 / -0.65
0.71–1.19	0 / 0.9	+0.5 / -0	+0 / -0.4	0 / 1.3	+0.8 / -0	+0 / -0.5	0 / 2	+1.2 / -0	+0 / -0.8	0 / 5.5	+3.5 / -0	+0 / -2.0	0.3 / 1.6	+0.8 / -0	-0.3 / -0.8
1.19–1.97	0 / 1.0	+0.6 / -0	+0 / -0.4	0 / 1.6	+1.0 / -0	+0 / -0.6	0 / 2.6	+1.6 / -0	+0 / -1	0 / 6.5	+4.0 / -0	+0 / -2.5	0.4 / 2.0	+1.0 / -0	-0.4 / -1.0
1.97–3.15	0 / 1.2	+0.7 / -0	+0 / -0.5	0 / 1.9	+1.2 / -0	+0 / -0.7	0 / 3	+1.8 / -0	+0 / -1.2	0 / 7.5	+4.5 / -0	+0 / -3	0.4 / 2.3	+1.2 / -0	-0.4 / -1.1
3.15–4.73	0 / 1.5	+0.9 / -0	+0 / -0.6	0 / 2.3	+1.4 / -0	0 / -0.9	0 / 3.6	2.2 / -0	+0 / -1.4	0 / 8.5	+5.0 / -0	+0 / -3.5	0.5 / 2.8	+1.4 / -0	-0.5 / -1.4
4.73–7.09	0 / 1.7	+1.0 / -0	+0 / -0.7	0 / 2.6	+1.6 / -0	+0 / -1.0	0 / 4.1	+2.5 / -0	+0 / -1.6	0 / 10	+6.0 / -0	+0 / -4	0.6 / 3.2	+1.6 / -0	-0.6 / -1.6
7.09–9.85	0 / 2.0	+1.2 / -0	+0 / -0.8	0 / 3.0	+1.8 / -0	+0 / -1.2	0 / 4.6	+2.8 / -0	+0 / -1.8	0 / 11.5	+7.0 / -0	+0 / -4.5	0.6 / 3.6	+1.8 / -0	-0.6 / -1.8
9.85–12.41	0 / 2.1	+1.2 / -0	+0 / -0.9	0 / 3.2	+2.0 / -0	+0 / -1.2	0 / 5	+3.0 / -0	+0 / -2.0	0 / 13.0	+8.0 / -0	+0 / -5	0.7 / 3.9	+2.0 / -0	-0.7 / -1.9
12.41–15.75	0 / 2.4	+1.4 / -0	+0 / -1.0	0 / 3.6	+2.2 / -0	+0 / -1.4	0 / 5.7	+3.5 / -0	+0 / -2.2	0 / 15.0	+9.0 / -0	+0 / -6	0.7 / 4.3	+2.2 / -0	-0.7 / -2.1

[a]From ANSI B4.1-1967 (R1994). For larger diameters, see the standard.

8 Clearance Locational Fits[a]—American National Standard (continued)

Nominal Size Range, inches Over To	Class LC 6 Limits of Clearance	Class LC 6 Hole H9	Class LC 6 Shaft f8	Class LC 7 Limits of Clearance	Class LC 7 Hole H10	Class LC 7 Shaft e9	Class LC 8 Limits of Clearance	Class LC 8 Hole H10	Class LC 8 Shaft d9	Class LC 9 Limits of Clearance	Class LC 9 Hole H11	Class LC 9 Shaft c10	Class LC 10 Limits of Clearance	Class LC 10 Hole H12	Class LC 10 Shaft	Class LC 11 Limits of Clearance	Class LC 11 Hole H13	Class LC 11 Shaft
0–0.12	0.3 / 1.9	+1.0 / -0	-0.3 / -0.9	0.6 / 3.2	+1.6 / -0	-0.6 / -1.6	1.0 / 3.6	+1.6 / -0	-1.0 / -2.0	2.5 / 6.6	+2.5 / -0	-2.5 / -4.1	4 / 12	+4 / -0	-4 / -8	5 / 17	+6 / -0	-5 / -11
0.12–0.24	0.4 / 2.3	+1.2 / -0	-0.4 / -1.1	0.8 / 3.8	+1.8 / -0	-0.8 / -2.0	1.2 / 4.2	+1.8 / -0	-1.2 / -2.4	2.8 / 7.6	+3.0 / -0	-2.8 / -4.6	4.5 / 14.5	+5 / -0	-4.5 / -9.5	6 / 20	+7 / -0	-6 / -13
0.24–0.40	0.5 / 2.8	+1.4 / -0	-0.5 / -1.4	1.0 / 4.6	+2.2 / -0	-1.0 / -2.4	1.6 / 5.2	+2.2 / -0	-1.6 / -3.0	3.0 / 8.7	+3.5 / -0	-3.0 / -5.2	5 / 17	+6 / -0	-5 / -11	7 / 25	+9 / -0	-7 / -16
0.40–0.71	0.6 / 3.2	+1.6 / -0	-0.6 / -1.6	1.2 / 5.6	+2.8 / -0	-1.2 / -2.8	2.0 / 6.4	+2.8 / -0	-2.0 / -3.6	3.5 / 10.3	+4.0 / -0	-3.5 / -6.3	6 / 20	+7 / -0	-6 / -13	8 / 28	+10 / -0	-8 / -18
0.71–1.19	0.8 / 4.0	+2.0 / -0	-0.8 / -2.0	1.6 / 7.1	+3.5 / -0	-1.6 / -3.6	2.5 / 8.0	+3.5 / -0	-2.5 / -4.5	4.5 / 13.0	+5.0 / -0	-4.5 / -8.0	7 / 23	+8 / -0	-7 / -15	10 / 34	+12 / -0	-10 / -22
1.19–1.97	1.0 / 5.1	+2.5 / -0	-1.0 / -2.6	2.0 / 8.5	+4.0 / -0	-2.0 / -4.5	3.0 / 9.5	+4.0 / -0	-3.0 / -5.5	5 / 15	+6 / -0	-5 / -9	8 / 28	+10 / -0	-8 / -18	12 / 44	+16 / -0	-12 / -28
1.97–3.15	1.2 / 6.0	+3.0 / -0	-1.2 / -3.0	2.5 / 10.0	+4.5 / -0	-2.5 / -5.5	4.0 / 11.5	+4.5 / -0	-4.0 / -7.0	6 / 17.5	+7 / -0	-6 / -10.5	10 / 34	+12 / -0	-10 / -22	14 / 50	+18 / -0	-14 / -32
3.15–4.73	1.4 / 7.1	+3.5 / -0	-1.4 / -3.6	3.0 / 11.5	+5.0 / -0	-3.0 / -6.5	5.0 / 13.5	+5.0 / -0	-5.0 / -8.5	7 / 21	+9 / -0	-7 / -12	11 / 39	+14 / -0	-11 / -25	16 / 60	+22 / -0	-16 / -38
4.73–7.09	1.6 / 8.1	+4.0 / -0	-1.6 / -4.1	3.5 / 13.5	+6.0 / -0	-3.5 / -7.5	6.0 / 16.0	+6 / -0	-6 / -10	8 / 24	+10 / -0	-8 / -14	12 / 44	+16 / -0	-12 / -28	18 / 68	+25 / -0	-18 / -43
7.09–9.85	2.0 / 9.3	+4.5 / -0	-2.0 / -4.8	4.0 / 15.5	+7.0 / -0	-4.0 / -8.5	7.0 / 18.5	+7 / -0	-7 / -11.5	10 / 29	+12 / -0	-10 / -17	16 / 52	+18 / -0	-16 / -34	22 / 78	+28 / -0	-22 / -50
9.85–12.41	2.2 / 10.2	+5.0 / -0	-2.2 / -5.2	4.5 / 17.5	+8.0 / -0	-4.5 / -9.5	7.0 / 20.0	+8 / -0	-7 / -12	12 / 32	+12 / -0	-12 / -20	20 / 60	+20 / -0	-20 / -40	28 / 88	+30 / -0	-28 / -58
12.41–15.75	2.5 / 12.0	+6.0 / -0	-2.5 / -6.0	5.0 / 20.0	+9.0 / -0	-5 / -11	8.0 / 23.0	+9 / -0	-8 / -14	14 / 37	+14 / -0	-14 / -23	22 / 66	+22 / -0	-22 / -44	30 / 100	+35 / -0	-30 / -65

[a]From ANSI B4.1-1967 (R1994). For larger diameters, see the standard.

9 Transition Locational Fits[a]—American National Standard

LT Transition fits are a compromise between clearance and interference fits, for application where accuracy of location is important, but either a small amount of clearance or interference is permissible.

Basic hole system. **Limits are in thousandths of an inch.** Limits for hole and shaft are applied algebraically to the basic size to obtain the limits of size for the mating parts. Data in **boldface** are in accordance with ABC agreements. "Fit" represents the maximum interference (minus values) and the maximum clearance (plus values). Symbols H7, js6, etc., are hole and shaft designations used in ABC System.

Nominal Size Range, inches Over To	Class LT 1 Fit	Class LT 1 Hole H7	Class LT 1 Shaft js6	Class LT 2 Fit	Class LT 2 Hole H8	Class LT 2 Shaft js7	Class LT 3 Fit	Class LT 3 Hole H7	Class LT 3 Shaft k6	Class LT 4 Fit	Class LT 4 Hole H8	Class LT 4 Shaft k7	Class LT 5 Fit	Class LT 5 Hole H7	Class LT 5 Shaft n6	Class LT 6 Fit	Class LT 6 Hole H7	Class LT 6 Shaft n7
0–0.12	−0.10 / +0.50	+0.4 / −0	+0.10 / −0.10	−0.2 / +0.8	+0.6 / −0	+0.2 / −0.2							−0.5 / +0.15	+0.4 / −0	+0.5 / +0.25	−0.65 / +0.15	+0.4 / −0	+0.65 / +0.25
0.12–0.24	−0.15 / +0.65	+0.5 / −0	+0.15 / −0.15	−0.25 / +0.95	+0.7 / −0	+0.25 / −0.25							−0.6 / +0.2	+0.5 / −0	+0.6 / +0.3	−0.8 / +0.2	+0.5 / −0	+0.8 / +0.3
0.24–0.40	−0.2 / +0.8	+0.6 / −0	+0.2 / −0.2	−0.3 / +1.2	+0.9 / −0	+0.3 / −0.3	−0.5 / +0.5	+0.6 / −0	+0.5 / +0.1	−0.7 / +0.8	+0.9 / −0	+0.7 / +0.1	−0.8 / +0.2	+0.6 / −0	+0.8 / +0.4	−1.0 / +0.2	+0.6 / −0	+1.0 / +0.4
0.40–0.71	−0.2 / +0.9	+0.7 / −0	+0.2 / −0.2	−0.35 / +1.35	+1.0 / −0	+0.35 / −0.35	−0.5 / +0.6	+0.7 / −0	+0.5 / +0.1	−0.8 / +0.9	+1.0 / −0	+0.8 / +0.1	−0.9 / +0.2	+0.7 / −0	+0.9 / +0.5	−1.2 / +0.2	+0.7 / −0	+1.2 / +0.5
0.71–1.19	−0.25 / +1.05	+0.8 / −0	+0.25 / −0.25	−0.4 / +1.6	+1.2 / −0	+0.4 / −0.4	−0.6 / +0.7	+0.8 / −0	+0.6 / +0.1	−0.9 / +1.1	+1.2 / −0	+0.9 / +0.1	−1.1 / +0.2	+0.8 / −0	+1.1 / +0.6	−1.4 / +0.2	+0.8 / −0	+1.4 / +0.6
1.19–1.97	−0.3 / +1.3	+1.0 / −0	+0.3 / −0.3	−0.5 / +2.1	+1.6 / −0	+0.5 / −0.5	−0.7 / +0.9	+1.0 / −0	+0.7 / +0.1	−1.1 / +1.5	+1.6 / −0	+1.1 / +0.1	−1.3 / +0.3	+1.0 / −0	+1.3 / +0.7	−1.7 / +0.3	+1.0 / −0	+1.7 / +0.7
1.97–3.15	−0.3 / +1.5	+1.2 / −0	+0.3 / −0.3	−0.6 / +2.4	+1.8 / −0	+0.6 / −0.6	−0.8 / +1.1	+1.2 / −0	+0.8 / +0.1	−1.3 / +1.7	+1.8 / −0	+1.3 / +0.1	−1.5 / +0.4	+1.2 / −0	+1.5 / +0.8	−2.0 / +0.4	+1.2 / −0	+2.0 / +0.8
3.15–4.73	−0.4 / +1.8	+1.4 / −0	+0.4 / −0.4	−0.7 / +2.9	+2.2 / −0	+0.7 / −0.7	−1.0 / +1.3	+1.4 / −0	+1.0 / +0.1	−1.5 / +2.1	+2.2 / −0	+1.5 / +0.1	−1.9 / +0.4	+1.4 / −0	+1.9 / +1.0	−2.4 / +0.4	+1.4 / −0	+2.4 / +1.0
4.73–7.09	−0.5 / +2.1	+1.6 / −0	+0.5 / −0.5	−0.8 / +3.3	+2.5 / −0	+0.8 / −0.8	−1.1 / +1.5	+1.6 / −0	+1.1 / +0.1	−1.7 / +2.4	+2.5 / −0	+1.7 / +0.1	−2.2 / +0.4	+1.6 / −0	+2.2 / +1.2	−2.8 / +0.4	+1.6 / −0	+2.8 / +1.2
7.09–9.85	−0.6 / +2.4	+1.8 / −0	+0.6 / −0.6	−0.9 / +3.7	+2.8 / −0	+0.9 / −0.9	−1.4 / +1.6	+1.8 / −0	+1.4 / +0.2	−2.0 / +2.6	+2.8 / −0	+2.0 / +0.2	−2.6 / +0.4	+1.8 / −0	+2.6 / +1.4	−3.2 / +0.4	+1.8 / −0	+3.2 / +1.4
9.85–12.41	−0.6 / +2.6	+2.0 / −0	+0.6 / −0.6	−1.0 / +4.0	+3.0 / −0	+1.0 / −1.0	−1.4 / +1.8	+2.0 / −0	+1.4 / +0.2	−2.2 / +2.8	+3.0 / −0	+2.2 / +0.2	−2.6 / +0.6	+2.0 / −0	+2.6 / +1.4	−3.4 / +0.6	+2.0 / −0	+3.4 / +1.4
12.41–15.75	−0.7 / +2.9	+2.2 / −0	+0.7 / −0.7	−1.0 / +4.5	+3.5 / −0	+1.0 / −1.0	−1.6 / +2.0	+2.2 / −0	+1.6 / +0.2	−2.4 / +3.3	+3.5 / −0	+2.4 / +0.2	−3.0 / +0.6	+2.2 / −0	+3.0 / +1.6	−3.8 / +0.6	+2.2 / −0	+3.8 / +1.6

[a] From ANSI B4.1-1967 (R1994). For larger diameters, see the standard.

10 Interference Locational Fits[a]—American National Standard

LN   *Locational interference fits* are used where accuracy of location is of prime importance and for parts requiring rigidity and alignment with no special requirements for bore pressure. Such fits are not intended for parts designed to transmit frictional loads from one part to another by virtue of the tightness of fit, as these conditions are covered by force fits.

Basic hole system. **Limits are in thousandths of an inch.** Limits for hole and shaft are applied algebraically to the basic size to obtain the limits of size for the parts. Data in **boldface** are in accordance with ABC agreements. Symbols H7, p6, etc., are hole and shaft designations used in ABC System.

Nominal Size Range, inches Over To	Class LN 1			Class LN 2			Class LN 3		
	Limits of Interference	Standard Limits		Limits of Interference	Standard Limits		Limits of Interference	Standard Limits	
		Hole H6	Shaft n5		Hole H7	Shaft p6		Hole H7	Shaft r6
0–0.12	0	+0.25	+0.45	0	+0.4	+0.65	0.1	+0.4	+0.75
	0.45	−0	+0.25	0.65	−0	+0.4	0.75	−0	+0.5
0.12–0.24	0	+0.3	+0.5	0	+0.5	+0.8	0.1	+0.5	+0.9
	0.5	−0	+0.3	0.8	−0	+0.5	0.9	0	+0.6
0.24–0.40	0	+0.4	+0.65	0	+0.6	+1.0	0.2	+0.6	+1.2
	0.65	−0	+0.4	1.0	−0	+0.6	1.2	−0	+0.8
0.40–0.71	0	+0.4	+0.8	0	+0.7	+1.1	0.3	+0.7	+1.4
	0.8	−0	+0.4	1.1	−0	+0.7	1.4	−0	+1.0
0.71–1.19	0	+0.5	+1.0	0	+0.8	+1.3	0.4	+0.8	+1.7
	1.0	−0	+0.5	1.3	−0	+0.8	1.7	−0	+1.2
1.19–1.97	0	+0.6	+1.1	0	+1.0	+1.6	0.4	+1.0	+2.0
	1.1	−0	+0.6	1.6	−0	+1.0	2.0	−0	+1.4
1.97–3.15	0.1	+0.7	+1.3	0.2	+1.2	+2.1	0.4	+1.2	+2.3
	1.3	−0	+0.7	2.1	−0	+1.4	2.3	−0	+1.6
3.15–4.73	0.1	+0.9	+1.6	0.2	+1.4	+2.5	0.6	+1.4	+2.9
	1.6	−0	+1.0	2.5	−0	+1.6	2.9	−0	+2.0
4.73–7.09	0.2	+1.0	+1.9	0.2	+1.6	+2.8	0.9	+1.6	+3.5
	1.9	−0	+1.2	2.8	−0	+1.8	3.5	−0	+2.5
7.09–9.85	0.2	+1.2	+2.2	0.2	+1.8	+3.2	1.2	+1.8	+4.2
	2.2	−0	+1.4	3.2	−0	+2.0	4.2	−0	+3.0
9.85–12.41	0.2	+1.2	+2.3	0.2	+2.0	+3.4	1.5	+2.0	+4.7
	2.3	−0	+1.4	3.4	−0	+2.2	4.7	−0	+3.5

[a]From ANSI B4.1-1967 (R1994). For larger diameters, see the standard.

11 Force and Shrink Fits[a]—American National Standard

APPENDICES 817

FN 1   *Light drive fits* are those requiring light assembly pressures, and produce more or less permanent assemblies. They are suitable for thin sections or long fits, or in cast-iron external members.

FN 2   *Medium drive fits* are suitable for ordinary steel parts, or for shrink fits on light sections. They are about the tightest fits that can be used with high-grade cast-iron external members.

FN 3   *Heavy drive fits* are suitable for heavier steel parts or for shrink fits in medium sections.

FN 4 ⎫
FN 5 ⎭   *Force fits* are suitable for parts which can be highly stressed, or for shrink fits where the heavy pressing forces required are impractical.

Basic hole system. **Limits are in thousandths of an inch.** Limits for hole and shaft are applied algebraically to the basic size to obtain the limits of size for the parts. Data in **boldface** are in accordance with ABC agreements. Symbols H7, s6, etc., are hole and shaft designations used in ABC System.

Nominal Size Range, inches Over To	Class FN 1 Limits of Interference	Class FN 1 Hole H6	Class FN 1 Shaft	Class FN 2 Limits of Interference	Class FN 2 Hole H7	Class FN 2 Shaft s6	Class FN 3 Limits of Interference	Class FN 3 Hole H7	Class FN 3 Shaft t6	Class FN 4 Limits of Interference	Class FN 4 Hole H7	Class FN 4 Shaft u6	Class FN 5 Limits of Interference	Class FN 5 Hole H8	Class FN 5 Shaft x7
0–0.12	0.05 / 0.5	+0.25 / −0	+0.5 / +0.3	0.2 / 0.85	+0.4 / −0	+0.85 / +0.6				0.3 / 0.95	+0.4 / −0	+0.95 / +0.7	0.3 / 1.3	+0.6 / −0	+1.3 / +0.9
0.12–0.24	0.1 / 0.6	+0.3 / −0	+0.6 / +0.4	0.2 / 1.0	+0.5 / −0	+1.0 / +0.7				0.4 / 1.2	+0.5 / −0	+1.2 / +0.9	0.5 / 1.7	+0.7 / −0	+1.7 / +1.2
0.24–0.40	0.1 / 0.75	+0.4 / −0	+0.75 / +0.5	0.4 / 1.4	+0.6 / −0	+1.4 / +1.0				0.6 / 1.6	+0.6 / −0	+1.6 / +1.2	0.5 / 2.0	+0.9 / −0	+2.0 / +1.4
0.40–0.56	0.1 / 0.8	+0.4 / −0	+0.8 / +0.5	0.5 / 1.6	+0.7 / −0	+1.6 / +1.2				0.7 / 1.8	+0.7 / −0	+1.8 / +1.4	0.6 / 2.3	+1.0 / −0	+2.3 / +1.6
0.56–0.71	0.2 / 0.9	+0.4 / −0	+0.9 / +0.6	0.5 / 1.6	+0.7 / −0	+1.6 / +1.2				0.7 / 1.8	+0.7 / −0	+1.8 / +1.4	0.8 / 2.5	+1.0 / −0	+2.5 / +1.8
0.71–0.95	0.2 / 1.1	+0.5 / −0	+1.1 / +0.7	0.6 / 1.9	+0.8 / −0	+1.9 / +1.4				0.8 / 2.1	+0.8 / −0	+2.1 / +1.6	1.0 / 3.0	+1.2 / −0	+3.0 / +2.2
0.95–1.19	0.3 / 1.2	+0.5 / −0	+1.2 / +0.8	0.6 / 1.9	+0.8 / −0	+1.9 / +1.4	0.8 / 2.1	+0.8 / −0	+2.1 / +1.6	1.0 / 2.3	+0.8 / −0	+2.3 / +1.8	1.3 / 3.3	+1.2 / −0	+3.3 / +2.5
1.19–1.58	0.3 / 1.3	+0.6 / −0	+1.3 / +0.9	0.8 / 2.4	+1.0 / −0	+2.4 / +1.8	1.0 / 2.6	+1.0 / −0	+2.6 / +2.0	1.5 / 3.1	+1.0 / −0	+3.1 / +2.5	1.4 / 4.0	+1.6 / −0	+4.0 / +3.0

[a]ANSI B4.1-1967 (R1994).

11 Force and Shrink Fits[a]—American National Standard (continued)

Nominal Size Range, inches Over To	Class FN 1 Limits of Interference	Class FN 1 Standard Limits Hole H6	Class FN 1 Standard Limits Shaft	Class FN 2 Limits of Interference	Class FN 2 Standard Limits Hole H7	Class FN 2 Standard Limits Shaft s6	Class FN 3 Limits of Interference	Class FN 3 Standard Limits Hole H7	Class FN 3 Standard Limits Shaft t6	Class FN 4 Limits of Interference	Class FN 4 Standard Limits Hole H7	Class FN 4 Standard Limits Shaft u6	Class FN 5 Limits of Interference	Class FN 5 Standard Limits Hole H8	Class FN 5 Standard Limits Shaft x7
1.58–1.97	0.4 1.4	+0.6 −0	+1.4 −1.0	0.8 2.4	+1.0 −0	+2.4 +1.8	1.2 2.8	+1.0 −0	+2.8 +2.2	1.8 3.4	+1.0 −0	+3.4 +2.8	2.4 5.0	+1.6 −0	+5.0 +4.0
1.97–2.56	0.6 1.8	+0.7 −0	+1.8 +1.3	0.8 2.7	+1.2 −0	+2.7 +2.0	1.3 3.2	+1.2 −0	+3.2 +2.5	2.3 4.2	+1.2 −0	+4.2 +3.5	3.2 6.2	+1.8 −0	+6.2 +5.0
2.56–3.15	0.7 1.9	+0.7 −0	+1.9 +1.4	1.0 2.9	+1.2 −0	+2.9 +2.2	1.8 3.7	+1.2 −0	+3.7 +3.0	2.8 4.7	+1.2 −0	+4.7 +4.0	4.2 7.2	+1.8 −0	+7.2 +6.0
3.15–3.94	0.9 24	+0.9 −0	+2.4 +1.8	1.4 3.7	+1.4 −0	+3.7 +2.8	2.1 4.4	+1.4 −0	+4.4 +3.5	3.6 5.9	+1.4 −0	+5.9 +5.0	4.8 8.4	+2.2 −0	+8.4 +7.0
3.94–4.73	1.1 2.6	+0.9 −0	+2.6 +2.0	1.6 3.9	+1.4 −0	+3.9 +3.0	2.6 4.9	+1.4 −0	+4.9 +4.0	4.6 6.9	+1.4 −0	+6.9 +6.0	5.8 9.4	+2.2 −0	+9.4 +8.0
4.73–5.52	1.2 2.9	+1.0 −0	+2.9 +2.2	1.9 4.5	+1.6 −0	+4.5 +3.5	3.4 6.0	+1.6 −0	+6.0 +5.0	5.4 8.0	+1.6 −0	+8.0 +7.0	7.5 11.6	+2.5 −0	+11.6 +10.0
5.52–6.30	1.5 3.2	+1.0 −0	+3.2 +2.5	2.4 5.0	+1.6 −0	+5.0 +4.0	3.4 6.0	+1.6 −0	+6.0 +5.0	5.4 8.0	+1.6 −0	+8.0 +7.0	9.5 13.6	+2.5 −0	+13.6 +12.0
6.30–7.09	1.8 3.5	+1.0 −0	+3.5 +2.8	2.9 5.5	+1.6 −0	+5.5 +4.5	4.4 7.0	+1.6 −0	+7.0 +6.0	6.4 9.0	+1.6 −0	+9.0 +8.0	9.5 13.6	+2.5 −0	+13.6 +12.0
7.09–7.88	1.8 3.8	+1.2 −0	+3.8 +3.0	3.2 6.2	+1.8 −0	+6.2 +5.0	5.2 8.2	+1.8 −0	+8.2 +7.0	7.2 10.2	+1.8 −0	+10.2 +9.0	11.2 15.8	+2.8 −0	+15.8 +14.0
7.88–8.86	2.3 4.3	+1.2 −0	+4.3 +3.5	3.2 6.2	+1.8 −0	+6.2 +5.0	5.2 8.2	+1.8 −0	+8.2 +7.0	8.2 11.2	+1.8 −0	+11.2 +10.0	13.2 17.8	+2.8 −0	+17.8 +16.0
8.86–9.85	2.3 4.3	+1.2 −0	+4.3 +3.5	4.2 7.2	+1.8 −0	+7.2 +6.0	6.2 9.2	+1.8 −0	+9.2 +8.0	10.2 13.2	+1.8 −0	+13.2 +12.0	13.2 17.8	+2.8 −0	+17.8 +16.0
9.85–11.03	2.8 4.9	+1.2 −0	+4.9 +4.0	4.0 7.2	+2.0 −0	+7.2 +6.0	7.0 10.2	+2.0 −0	+10.2 +9.0	10.0 13.2	+2.0 −0	+13.2 +12.0	15.0 20.0	+3.0 −0	+20.0 +18.0
11.03–12.41	2.8 4.9	+1.2 −0	+4.9 +4.0	5.0 8.2	+2.0 −0	+8.2 +7.0	7.0 10.2	+2.0 −0	+10.2 +9.0	12.0 15.2	+2.0 −0	+15.2 +14.0	17.0 22.0	+3.0 −0	+22.0 +20.0
12.41–13.98	3.1 5.5	+1.4 −0	+5.5 +4.5	5.8 9.4	+2.2 −0	+9.4 +8.0	7.8 11.4	+2.2 −0	+11.4 +10.0	13.8 17.4	+2.2 −0	+17.4 +16.0	18.5 24.2	+3.5 −0	+24.2 +22.0

[a]From ANSI B4.1-1967 (R1994). For larger diameters, see the standard.

12 International Tolerance Grades[a]

Dimensions are in millimeters.

Basic Sizes		Tolerance Grades[b]																	
Over	Up to and Including	IT01	IT0	IT1	IT2	IT3	IT4	IT5	IT6	IT7	IT8	IT9	IT10	IT11	IT12	IT13	IT14	IT15	IT16
0	3	0.0003	0.0005	0.0008	0.0012	0.002	0.003	0.004	0.006	0.010	0.014	0.025	0.040	0.060	0.100	0.140	0.250	0.400	0.600
3	6	0.0004	0.0006	0.001	0.0015	0.0025	0.004	0.005	0.008	0.012	0.018	0.030	0.048	0.075	0.120	0.180	0.300	0.480	0.750
6	10	0.0004	0.0006	0.001	0.0015	0.0025	0.004	0.006	0.009	0.015	0.022	0.036	0.058	0.090	0.150	0.220	0.360	0.580	0.900
10	18	0.0005	0.0008	0.0012	0.002	0.003	0.005	0.008	0.011	0.018	0.027	0.043	0.070	0.110	0.180	0.270	0.430	0.700	1.100
18	30	0.0006	0.001	0.0015	0.0025	0.004	0.006	0.009	0.013	0.021	0.033	0.052	0.084	0.130	0.210	0.330	0.520	0.840	1.300
30	50	0.0006	0.001	0.0015	0.0025	0.004	0.007	0.011	0.016	0.025	0.039	0.062	0.100	0.160	0.250	0.390	0.620	1.000	1.600
50	80	0.0008	0.0012	0.002	0.003	0.005	0.008	0.013	0.019	0.030	0.046	0.074	0.120	0.190	0.300	0.460	0.740	1.200	1.900
80	120	0.001	0.0015	0.0025	0.004	0.006	0.010	0.015	0.022	0.035	0.054	0.087	0.140	0.220	0.350	0.540	0.870	1.400	2.200
120	180	0.0012	0.002	0.0035	0.005	0.008	0.012	0.018	0.025	0.040	0.063	0.100	0.160	0.250	0.400	0.630	1.000	1.600	2.500
180	250	0.002	0.003	0.0045	0.007	0.010	0.014	0.020	0.029	0.046	0.072	0.115	0.185	0.290	0.460	0.720	1.150	1.850	2.900
250	315	0.0025	0.004	0.006	0.008	0.012	0.016	0.023	0.032	0.052	0.081	0.130	0.210	0.320	0.520	0.810	1.300	2.100	3.200
315	400	0.003	0.005	0.007	0.009	0.013	0.018	0.025	0.036	0.057	0.089	0.140	0.230	0.360	0.570	0.890	1.400	2.300	3.600
400	500	0.004	0.006	0.008	0.010	0.015	0.020	0.027	0.040	0.063	0.097	0.155	0.250	0.400	0.630	0.970	1.550	2.500	4.000
500	630	0.0045	0.006	0.009	0.011	0.016	0.022	0.030	0.044	0.070	0.110	0.175	0.280	0.440	0.700	1.100	1.750	2.800	4.400
630	800	0.005	0.007	0.010	0.013	0.018	0.025	0.035	0.050	0.080	0.125	0.200	0.320	0.500	0.800	1.250	2.000	3.200	5.000
800	1000	0.0055	0.008	0.011	0.015	0.021	0.029	0.040	0.056	0.090	0.140	0.230	0.360	0.560	0.900	1.400	2.300	3.600	5.600
1000	1250	0.0065	0.009	0.013	0.018	0.024	0.034	0.046	0.066	0.105	0.165	0.260	0.420	0.660	1.050	1.650	2.600	4.200	6.600
1250	1600	0.008	0.011	0.015	0.021	0.029	0.040	0.054	0.078	0.125	0.195	0.310	0.500	0.780	1.250	1.950	3.100	5.000	7.800
1600	2000	0.009	0.013	0.018	0.025	0.035	0.048	0.065	0.092	0.150	0.230	0.370	0.600	0.920	1.500	2.300	3.700	6.000	9.200
2000	2500	0.011	0.015	0.022	0.030	0.041	0.057	0.077	0.110	0.175	0.280	0.440	0.700	1.100	1.750	2.800	4.400	7.000	11.000
2500	3150	0.013	0.018	0.026	0.036	0.050	0.069	0.093	0.135	0.210	0.330	0.540	0.860	1.350	2.100	3.300	5.400	8.600	13.500

[a]From ANSI B4.2-1978 (R1994).
[b]T Values for tolerance grades larger than IT16 can be calculated by using the formulas: IT17 = IT × 10, IT18 = IT13 × 10, etc.

Dimensions are in millimeters.

13 Preferred Metric Hole Basis Clearance Fits[a]—American National Standard

Basic Size		Loose Running			Free Running			Close Running			Sliding			Locational Clearance		
		Hole H11	Shaft c11	Fit	Hole H9	Shaft d9	Fit	Hole H8	Shaft f7	Fit	Hole H7	Shaft g6	Fit	Hole H7	Shaft h6	Fit
1	Max	1.060	0.940	0.180	1.025	0.980	0.070	1.014	0.994	0.030	1.010	0.998	0.018	1.010	1.000	0.016
	Min	1.060	0.880	0.060	1.000	0.955	0.020	1.000	0.984	0.006	1.000	0.992	0.002	1.000	0.994	0.000
1.2	Max	1.260	1.140	0.180	1.225	1.180	0.070	1.214	1.194	0.030	1.210	1.198	0.018	1.210	1.200	0.016
	Min	1.200	1.080	0.060	1.200	1.155	0.020	1.200	1.184	0.036	1.200	1.192	0.002	1.200	1.194	0.000
1.6	Max	1.660	1.540	0.180	1.625	1.580	0.070	1.614	1.594	0.030	1.610	1.598	0.018	1.610	1.600	0.016
	Min	1.600	1.480	0.060	1.600	1.555	0.020	1.600	1.584	0.006	1.600	1.592	0.002	1.600	1.594	0.000
2	Max	2.060	1.940	0.180	2.025	1.980	0.070	2.014	1.994	0.030	2.010	1.998	0.018	2.010	2.000	0.016
	Min	2.000	1.880	0.060	2.000	1.955	0.020	2.000	1.984	0.006	2.000	1.992	0.002	2.000	1.994	0.000
2.5	Max	2.560	2.440	0.180	2.525	2.480	0.070	2.514	2.494	0.030	2.510	2.498	0.018	2.510	2.500	0.016
	Min	2.500	2.380	0.060	2.500	2.455	0.020	2.500	2.484	0.006	2.500	2.492	0.002	2.500	2.494	0.000
3	Max	3.060	2.940	0.180	3.025	2.980	0.070	3.014	2.994	0.030	3.010	2.998	0.018	3.010	3.000	0.016
	Min	3.000	2.880	0.060	3.000	2.955	0.020	3.000	2.984	0.006	3.000	2.992	0.002	3.000	2.994	0.000
4	Max	4.075	3.930	0.220	4.030	3.970	0.090	4.018	3.990	0.040	4.012	3.996	0.024	4.012	4.000	0.020
	Min	4.000	3.855	0.070	4.000	3.940	0.030	4.000	3.978	0.010	4.000	3.988	0.004	4.000	3.992	0.000
5	Max	5.075	4.930	0.220	5.030	4.970	0.090	5.018	4.990	0.040	5.012	4.996	0.024	5.012	5.000	0.020
	Min	5.000	4.855	0.070	5.000	4.940	0.030	5.000	4.978	0.010	5.000	4.988	0.004	5.000	4.992	0.000
6	Max	6.075	5.930	0.220	6.030	5.970	0.090	6.018	5.990	0.040	6.012	5.996	0.024	6.012	6.000	0.020
	Min	6.000	5.855	0.070	6.000	5.940	0.030	6.000	5.978	0.010	6.000	5.988	0.004	6.000	5.992	0.000
8	Max	8.090	7.920	0.260	8.036	7.960	0.112	8.022	7.987	0.050	8.015	7.995	0.029	8.015	8.000	0.024
	Min	8.000	7.830	0.080	8.000	7.924	0.040	8.000	7.972	0.013	8.000	7.986	0.005	8.000	7.991	0.000
10	Max	10.090	9.920	0.260	10.036	9.960	0.112	10.022	9.987	0.050	10.015	9.995	0.029	10.015	10.000	0.024
	Min	10.000	9.830	0.080	10.000	9.924	0.040	10.000	9.972	0.013	10.000	9.986	0.005	10.000	9.991	0.000
12	Max	12.110	11.905	0.315	12.043	11.950	0.136	12.027	11.984	0.061	12.018	11.994	0.035	12.018	12.000	0.029
	Min	12.000	11.795	0.095	12.000	11.907	0.050	12.000	11.966	0.016	12.000	11.983	0.006	12.000	11.989	0.000
16	Max	16.110	15.905	0.315	16.043	15.950	0.136	16.027	15.984	0.061	16.018	15.994	0.035	16.018	16.000	0.029
	Min	16.000	15.795	0.095	16.000	15.907	0.050	16.000	15.966	0.016	16.000	15.983	0.006	16.000	15.989	0.000
20	Max	20.130	19.890	0.370	20.052	19.935	0.169	20.033	19.980	0.074	20.021	19.993	0.041	20.021	20.000	0.034
	Min	20.000	19.760	0.110	20.000	19.883	0.065	20.000	19.959	0.020	20.000	19.980	0.007	20.000	19.987	0.000
25	Max	25.130	24.890	0.370	25.052	24.935	0.169	25.033	24.980	0.074	25.021	24.993	0.041	25.021	25.000	0.034
	Min	25.000	24.760	0.110	25.000	24.883	0.065	25.000	24.959	0.020	25.000	24.980	0.007	25.000	24.987	0.000
30	Max	30.130	29.890	0.370	30.052	29.935	0.169	30.033	29.980	0.074	30.021	29.993	0.041	30.021	30.000	0.034
	Min	30.000	29.760	0.110	30.000	29.883	0.065	30.000	29.959	0.020	30.000	29.980	0.007	30.000	29.987	0.000

[a]From ANSI B4.2-1978 (R1994).

Dimensions are in millimeters.

13 Preferred Metric Hole Basis Clearance Fits[a]— American National Standard (continued)

Basic Size		Loose Running			Free Running			Close Running			Sliding			Locational Clearance		
		Hole H11	Shaft c11	Fit	Hole H9	Shaft d9	Fit	Hole H8	Shaft f7	Fit	Hole H7	Shaft g6	Fit	Hole H7	Shaft h6	Fit
40	Max	40.160	39.880	0.440	40.062	39.920	0.204	40.039	39.975	0.089	40.025	39.991	0.050	40.025	40.000	0.041
	Min	40.000	39.720	0.120	40.000	39.858	0.080	40.000	39.950	0.025	40.000	39.975	0.009	40.000	39.984	0.000
50	Max	50.160	49.870	0.450	50.062	49.920	0.204	50.039	49.975	0.089	50.025	49.991	0.050	50.025	50.000	0.041
	Min	50.000	49.710	0.130	50.000	49.858	0.080	50.000	49.950	0.025	50.000	49.975	0.009	50.000	49.984	0.000
60	Max	60.190	59.860	0.520	60.074	59.900	0.248	60.046	59.970	0.106	60.030	59.990	0.059	60.030	60.000	0.049
	Min	60.000	59.670	0.140	60.000	59.826	0.100	60.000	59.940	0.030	60.000	59.971	0.010	60.000	59.981	0.000
80	Max	80.190	79.900	0.530	80.074	79.900	0.248	80.046	79.970	0.106	80.030	79.990	0.059	80.030	80.000	0.049
	Min	80.000	79.660	0.150	80.000	79.826	0.100	80.000	79.940	0.030	80.000	79.971	0.010	80.000	79.981	0.000
100	Max	100.220	99.830	0.610	100.087	99.880	0.294	100.054	99.964	0.125	100.035	99.988	0.069	100.035	100.000	0.057
	Min	100.000	99.610	0.170	100.000	99.793	0.120	100.000	99.929	0.036	100.000	99.966	0.012	100.000	99.978	0.000
120	Max	120.220	119.820	0.620	120.087	119.880	0.294	120.054	119.964	0.125	120.035	119.988	0.069	120.035	120.000	0.057
	Min	120.000	119.600	0.180	120.000	119.793	0.120	120.000	119.929	0.036	120.000	119.966	0.012	120.000	119.978	0.000
160	Max	160.250	159.790	0.710	160.100	159.855	0.345	160.063	159.957	0.146	160.040	159.986	0.079	160.040	160.000	0.065
	Min	160.000	159.540	0.210	160.000	159.755	0.145	160.000	159.917	0.043	160.000	159.961	0.014	160.000	159.975	0.000
200	Max	200.290	199.760	0.820	200.115	199.830	0.400	200.072	199.950	0.168	200.046	199.985	0.090	200.046	200.000	0.075
	Min	200.000	199.470	0.240	200.000	199.715	0.170	200.000	199.904	0.050	200.000	199.956	0.015	200.000	199.971	0.000
250	Max	250.290	249.720	0.860	250.115	249.830	0.400	250.072	249.950	0.168	250.046	249.985	0.090	250.046	250.000	0.075
	Min	250.000	249.430	0.280	250.000	249.715	0.170	250.000	249.904	0.050	250.000	249.956	0.015	250.000	249.971	0.000
300	Max	300.320	299.670	0.970	300.130	299.810	0.450	300.081	299.944	0.189	300.052	299.983	0.101	300.052	300.000	0.084
	Min	300.000	299.350	0.330	300.000	299.680	0.190	300.000	299.892	0.056	300.000	299.951	0.017	300.000	299.968	0.000
400	Max	400.360	399.600	1.120	400.140	399.790	0.490	400.089	399.938	0.208	400.057	399.982	0.111	400.057	400.000	0.093
	Min	400.000	399.240	0.400	400.000	399.650	0.210	400.000	399.881	0.062	400.000	399.946	0.018	400.000	399.964	0.000
500	Max	500.400	499.520	1.280	500.155	499.770	0.540	500.097	499.932	0.228	500.063	499.980	0.123	500.063	500.000	0.103
	Min	500.000	499.120	0.480	500.000	499.615	0.230	500.000	499.869	0.068	500.000	499.940	0.020	500.000	499.960	0.000

[a]From ANSI B4.2-1978 (R1994).

14 Preferred Metric Hole Basis Transition and Interference Fits[a]— American National Standard

Dimensions are in millimeters.

Basic Size		Locational Transn.			Locational Transn.			Locational Interf.			Medium Drive			Force		
		Hole H7	Shaft k6	Fit	Hole H7	Shaft n6	Fit	Hole H7	Shaft p6	Fit	Hole H7	Shaft s6	Fit	Hole H7	Shaft u6	Fit
1	Max	1.010	1.006	0.010	1.010	1.010	0.006	1.010	1.012	0.004	1.010	1.020	−0.004	1.010	1.024	−0.008
	Min	1.000	1.000	−0.006	1.000	1.004	−0.010	1.000	1.006	−0.012	1.000	1.014	−0.020	1.000	1.018	−0.024
1.2	Max	1.210	1.206	0.010	1.210	1.210	0.006	1.210	1.212	0.004	1.210	1.220	−0.004	1.210	1.224	−0.008
	Min	1.200	1.200	−0.006	1.200	1.204	−0.010	1.200	1.206	−0.012	1.200	1.214	−0.020	1.200	1.218	−0.024
1.6	Max	1.610	1.606	0.010	1.610	1.610	0.006	1.610	1.612	0.004	1.610	1.620	−0.004	1.610	1.624	−0.008
	Min	1.600	1.600	−0.006	1.600	1.604	−0.010	1.600	1.606	−0.012	1.600	1.614	−0.020	1.600	1.618	−0.024
2	Max	2.010	2.006	0.010	2.010	2.010	0.006	2.010	2.012	0.004	2.010	2.020	−0.004	2.010	2.024	−0.008
	Min	2.000	2.000	−0.006	2.000	2.004	−0.010	2.000	2.006	−0.012	2.000	2.014	−0.020	2.000	2.018	−0.024
2.5	Max	2.510	2.506	0.010	2.510	2.510	0.006	2.510	2.512	0.004	2.510	2.520	−0.004	2.510	2.524	−0.008
	Min	2.500	2.500	−0.006	2.500	2.504	−0.010	2.500	2.506	−0.012	2.500	2.514	−0.020	2.500	2.518	−0.024
3	Max	3.010	3.006	0.010	3.010	3.010	0.006	3.010	3.012	0.004	3.010	3.020	−0.004	3.010	3.024	−0.008
	Min	3.000	3.000	−0.006	3.000	3.004	−0.010	3.000	3.006	−0.012	3.000	3.014	−0.020	3.000	3.018	−0.024
4	Max	4.012	4.009	0.011	4.012	4.016	0.004	4.012	4.020	0.000	4.012	4.027	−0.007	4.012	4.031	−0.011
	Min	4.000	4.001	−0.009	4.000	4.008	−0.016	4.000	4.012	−0.020	4.000	4.019	−0.027	4.000	4.023	−0.031
5	Max	5.012	5.009	0.011	5.012	5.016	0.004	5.012	5.020	0.000	5.012	5.027	−0.007	5.012	5.031	−0.011
	Min	5.000	5.001	−0.009	5.000	5.008	−0.016	5.000	5.012	−0.020	5.000	5.019	−0.027	5.000	5.023	−0.031
6	Max	6.012	6.009	0.011	6.012	6.016	0.004	6.012	6.020	0.000	6.012	6.027	−0.007	6.012	6.031	−0.011
	Min	6.000	6.001	−0.009	6.000	6.008	−0.016	6.000	6.012	−0.020	6.000	6.019	−0.027	6.000	6.023	−0.031
8	Max	8.015	8.010	0.014	8.015	8.019	0.005	8.015	8.024	0.000	8.015	8.032	−0.008	8.015	8.037	−0.013
	Min	8.000	8.001	−0.010	8.000	8.010	−0.019	8.000	8.015	−0.024	8.000	8.023	−0.032	8.000	8.028	−0.037
10	Max	10.015	10.010	0.014	10.015	10.019	0.005	10.015	10.024	0.000	10.015	10.032	−0.008	10.015	10.037	−0.013
	Min	10.000	10.001	−0.010	10.000	10.010	−0.019	10.000	10.015	−0.024	10.000	10.023	−0.032	10.000	10.028	−0.037
12	Max	12.018	12.012	0.017	12.018	12.023	0.006	12.018	12.029	0.000	12.018	12.039	−0.010	12.018	12.044	−0.015
	Min	12.000	12.001	−0.012	12.000	12.012	−0.023	12.000	12.018	−0.029	12.000	12.028	−0.039	12.000	12.033	−0.044
16	Max	16.018	16.012	0.017	16.018	16.023	0.006	16.018	16.029	0.000	16.018	16.039	−0.010	16.018	16.044	−0.015
	Min	16.000	16.001	−0.012	16.000	16.012	−0.023	16.000	16.018	−0.029	16.000	16.028	−0.039	16.000	16.033	−0.044
20	Max	20.081	20.015	0.019	20.021	20.028	0.006	20.021	20.035	−0.001	20.021	20.048	−0.014	20.021	20.054	−0.020
	Min	20.000	20.002	−0.015	20.000	20.015	−0.028	20.000	20.022	−0.035	20.000	20.035	−0.048	20.000	20.041	−0.054
25	Max	25.021	25.015	0.019	25.021	25.028	0.006	25.021	25.035	−0.001	25.021	25.048	−0.014	25.021	25.061	−0.027
	Min	25.000	25.002	−0.015	25.000	25.015	−0.028	25.000	25.022	−0.035	25.000	25.035	−0.048	25.000	25.048	−0.061
30	Max	30.021	30.015	0.019	30.021	30.028	0.006	30.021	30.035	−0.001	30.021	30.048	−0.014	30.021	30.061	−0.027
	Min	30.000	30.002	−0.015	30.000	30.015	−0.028	30.000	30.022	−0.035	30.000	30.035	−0.048	30.000	30.048	−0.061

[a]From ANSI B4.2-1978 (R1994).

14 Preferred Metric Hole Basis Transition and Interference Fits[a]— American National Standard (continued)

Dimensions are in millimeters.

Basic Size		Locational Transn.			Locational Transn.			Locational Interf.			Medium Drive			Force		
		Hole H7	Shaft k6	Fit	Hole H7	Shaft n6	Fit	Hole H7	Shaft p6	Fit	Hole H7	Shaft s6	Fit	Hole H7	Shaft u6	Fit
40	Max	40.025	40.018	0.023	40.025	40.033	0.08	40.025	40.042	−0.001	40.025	40.059	−0.018	40.025	40.076	−0.035
	Min	40.000	40.002	−0.018	40.000	40.017	−0.033	40.000	40.026	−0.042	40.000	40.043	−0.059	40.000	40.060	−0.076
50	Max	50.025	50.018	0.023	50.025	50.033	0.008	50.025	50.042	−0.001	50.025	50.059	−0.018	50.025	50.086	−0.045
	Min	50.000	50.002	−0.018	50.000	50.017	−0.033	50.000	50.026	−0.042	50.000	50.043	−0.059	50.000	50.070	−0.086
60	Max	60.030	60.021	0.028	60.030	60.039	0.010	60.030	60.051	−0.002	60.030	60.072	−0.023	60.030	60.106	−0.057
	Min	60.000	60.002	−0.021	60.000	60.020	−0.039	60.000	60.032	−0.051	60.000	60.053	−0.072	60.000	60.087	−0.106
80	Max	80.030	80.021	0.028	80.030	80.039	0.010	80.030	80.051	−0.002	80.030	80.078	−0.029	80.030	80.121	−0.072
	Min	80.000	80.002	−0.021	80.000	80.020	−0.039	80.000	80.032	−0.051	80.000	80.059	−0.078	80.000	80.102	−0.121
100	Max	100.035	100.025	0.032	100.035	100.045	0.012	100.035	100.059	−0.002	100.035	100.093	−0.036	100.035	100.146	−0.089
	Min	100.000	100.003	−0.025	100.000	100.023	−0.045	100.000	100.037	−0.059	100.000	100.071	−0.093	100.000	100.124	−0.146
120	Max	120.035	120.025	0.032	120.035	120.045	0.012	120.035	120.059	−0.002	120.035	120.101	−0.044	120.035	120.166	−0.109
	Min	120.000	120.003	−0.025	120.000	120.023	−0.045	120.000	120.037	−0.059	120.000	120.079	−0.101	120.000	120.144	−0.166
160	Max	160.040	160.028	0.037	160.040	160.052	0.013	160.040	160.068	−0.003	160.040	160.125	−0.060	160.040	160.215	−0.150
	Min	160.000	160.003	−0.028	160.000	160.027	−0.052	160.000	160.043	−0.068	160.000	160.100	−0.125	160.000	160.190	−0.215
200	Max	200.046	200.033	0.042	200.046	200.060	0.015	200.046	200.079	−0.004	200.046	200.151	−0.076	200.046	200.265	−0.190
	Min	200.000	200.004	−0.033	200.000	200.031	−0.060	200.000	200.050	−0.079	200.000	200.122	−0.151	200.000	200.236	−0.265
250	Max	250.046	250.033	0.042	250.046	250.060	0.015	250.046	250.079	−0.004	250.046	250.169	−0.094	250.046	250.313	−0.238
	Min	250.000	250.004	−0.033	250.000	250.031	−0.060	250.000	250.050	−0.079	250.000	250.140	−0.169	250.000	250.284	−0.313
300	Max	300.052	300.036	0.048	300.052	300.066	0.018	300.052	300.088	−0.004	300.052	300.202	−0.118	300.052	300.382	−0.298
	Min	300.000	300.004	−0.036	300.000	300.034	−0.066	300.000	300.056	−0.088	300.000	300.170	−0.202	300.000	300.350	−0.382
400	Max	400.057	400.040	0.053	400.057	400.073	0.020	400.057	400.098	−0.005	400.057	400.244	−0.151	400.057	400.471	−0.378
	Min	400.000	400.004	−0.040	400.000	400.037	−0.073	400.000	400.062	−0.098	400.000	400.208	−0.244	400.000	400.435	−0.471
500	Max	500.063	500.045	0.058	500.063	500.080	0.023	500.063	500.108	−0.005	500.063	500.292	−0.189	500.063	500.580	−0.477
	Min	500.000	500.005	−0.045	500.000	500.040	−0.080	500.000	500.068	−0.108	500.000	500.252	−0.292	500.000	500.540	−0.580

[a]From ANSI B4.2-1978 (R1994).

15 Preferred Metric Shaft Basis Clearance Fits[a]—American National Standard

Dimensions are in millimeters.

Basic Size		Loose Running			Free Running			Close Running			Sliding			Locational Clearance		
		Hole C11	Shaft h11	Fit	Hole D9	Shaft h9	Fit	Hole F8	Shaft h7	Fit	Hole G7	Shaft h6	Fit	Hole H7	Shaft h6	Fit
1	Max	1.120	1.000	0.180	1.045	1.000	0.070	1.020	1.000	0.030	1.012	1.000	0.018	1.010	1.000	0.016
	Min	1.060	0.940	0.060	1.020	0.975	0.020	1.006	0.990	0.006	1.002	0.994	0.002	1.000	0.994	0.000
1.2	Max	1.320	1.200	0.180	1.245	1.200	0.070	1.220	1.200	0.030	1.212	1.200	0.018	1.210	1.200	0.016
	Min	1.260	1.140	0.060	1.220	1.175	0.020	1.206	1.190	0.006	1.202	1.194	0.002	1.200	1.194	0.000
1.6	Max	1.720	1.600	0.180	1.645	1.600	0.070	1.620	1.600	0.030	1.612	1.600	0.018	1.610	1.600	0.016
	Min	1.660	1.540	0.060	1.620	1.575	0.020	1.606	1.590	0.006	1.602	1.594	0.002	1.600	1.594	0.000
2	Max	2.120	2.000	0.180	2.045	2.000	0.070	2.020	2.000	0.030	2.012	2.000	0.018	2.010	2.000	0.016
	Min	2.060	1.940	0.060	2.020	1.975	0.020	2.006	1.990	0.006	2.002	1.994	0.002	2.000	1.994	0.000
2.5	Max	2.620	2.500	0.180	2.545	2.500	0.070	2.520	2.500	0.030	2.512	2.500	0.018	2.510	2.500	0.016
	Min	2.560	2.440	0.060	2.520	2.475	0.020	2.506	2.490	0.006	2.502	2.494	0.002	2.500	2.494	0.000
3	Max	3.120	3.000	0.180	3.045	3.000	0.070	3.020	3.000	0.030	3.012	3.000	0.018	3.010	3.000	0.016
	Min	3.060	2.940	0.060	3.020	2.975	0.020	3.006	2.990	0.006	3.002	2.994	0.002	3.000	2.994	0.000
4	Max	4.145	4.000	0.220	4.060	4.000	0.090	4.028	4.000	0.040	4.016	4.000	0.024	4.012	4.000	0.020
	Min	4.070	3.925	0.070	4.030	3.970	0.030	4.010	3.988	0.010	4.004	3.992	0.004	4.000	3.992	0.000
5	Max	5.145	5.000	0.220	5.060	5.000	0.090	5.028	5.000	0.040	5.016	5.000	0.024	5.012	5.000	0.020
	Min	5.070	4.925	0.070	5.030	4.970	0.030	5.010	4.988	0.010	5.004	4.992	0.004	5.000	4.992	0.000
6	Max	6.145	6.000	0.220	6.060	6.000	0.090	6.028	6.000	0.040	6.016	6.000	0.024	6.012	6.000	0.020
	Min	6.070	5.925	0.070	6.030	5.970	0.030	6.010	5.988	0.010	6.004	5.992	0.004	6.000	5.992	0.000
8	Max	8.170	8.000	0.260	8.076	8.000	0.112	8.035	8.000	0.050	8.020	8.000	0.029	8.015	8.000	0.024
	Min	8.080	7.910	0.080	8.040	7.964	0.040	8.013	7.985	0.013	8.005	7.991	0.005	8.000	7.991	0.000
10	Max	10.170	10.000	0.260	10.076	10.000	0.112	10.035	10.000	0.050	10.020	10.000	0.029	10.015	10.000	0.024
	Min	10.080	9.910	0.080	10.040	9.964	0.040	10.013	9.985	0.013	10.005	9.991	0.005	10.000	9.991	0.000
12	Max	12.205	12.000	0.315	12.093	12.000	0.136	12.043	12.000	0.061	12.024	12.000	0.035	12.018	12.000	0.029
	Min	12.095	11.890	0.095	12.050	11.957	0.050	12.016	11.982	0.016	12.006	11.989	0.006	12.000	11.989	0.000
16	Max	16.205	16.000	0.315	16.093	16.000	0.136	16.043	16.000	0.061	16.024	16.000	0.035	16.018	16.000	0.029
	Min	16.095	15.890	0.095	16.050	15.957	0.050	16.016	15.982	0.016	16.006	15.989	0.006	16.000	15.989	0.000
20	Max	20.240	20.000	0.370	20.117	20.000	0.169	20.053	20.000	0.074	20.028	20.000	0.041	20.021	20.000	0.034
	Min	20.110	19.870	0.110	20.065	19.948	0.065	20.020	19.979	0.020	20.007	19.987	0.007	20.000	19.987	0.000
25	Max	25.240	25.000	0.370	25.117	25.000	0.169	25.053	25.000	0.074	25.028	25.000	0.041	25.021	25.000	0.034
	Min	25.110	24.870	0.110	25.065	24.948	0.065	25.020	24.979	0.020	25.007	24.987	0.007	25.000	24.987	0.000
30	Max	30.240	30.000	0.370	30.117	30.000	0.169	30.053	30.000	0.074	30.028	30.000	0.041	30.021	30.000	0.034
	Min	30.110	29.870	0.110	30.065	29.948	0.065	30.020	29.979	0.020	30.007	29.987	0.007	30.000	29.987	0.000

[a]From ANSI B4.2-1978 (R1994).

Dimensions are in millimeters.

15 Preferred Metric Shaft Basis Clearance Fits[a]—American National Standard (continued)

Basic Size		Loose Running			Free Running			Close Running			Sliding			Locational Clearance		
		Hole C11	Shaft h11	Fit	Hole D9	Shaft h9	Fit	Hole F8	Shaft h7	Fit	Hole G7	Shaft h6	Fit	Hole H7	Shaft h6	Fit
40	Max	40.280	40.000	0.440	40.142	40.000	0.204	40.064	40.000	0.089	40.034	40.000	0.050	40.025	40.000	0.041
	Min	40.120	39.840	0.120	40.080	39.938	0.080	40.025	39.975	0.025	40.009	39.984	0.009	40.000	39.984	0.000
50	Max	50.290	50.000	0.450	50.142	50.000	0.204	50.064	50.000	0.089	50.034	50.000	0.050	50.025	50.000	0.041
	Min	50.130	49.840	0.130	50.080	49.938	0.080	50.025	49.975	0.025	50.009	49.984	0.009	50.000	49.984	0.000
60	Max	60.330	60.000	0.520	60.174	60.000	0.248	60.076	60.000	0.106	60.040	60.000	0.059	60.030	60.000	0.049
	Min	60.140	59.810	0.140	60.100	59.926	0.100	60.030	59.970	0.030	60.010	59.981	0.010	60.000	59.981	0.000
80	Max	80.340	80.000	0.530	80.174	80.000	0.248	80.076	80.000	0.106	80.040	80.000	0.059	80.030	80.000	0.049
	Min	80.150	79.810	0.150	80.100	79.926	0.100	80.030	79.970	0.030	80.010	79.981	0.010	80.000	79.981	0.000
100	Max	100.390	100.000	0.610	100.207	100.000	0.294	100.090	100.000	0.125	100.047	100.000	0.069	100.035	100.000	0.057
	Min	100.170	99.780	0.170	100.120	99.913	0.120	100.036	99.965	0.036	100.012	99.978	0.012	100.000	99.978	0.000
120	Max	120.400	120.000	0.620	120.207	120.000	0.294	120.090	120.000	0.125	120.047	120.000	0.069	120.035	120.000	0.057
	Min	120.180	119.780	0.180	120.120	119.913	0.120	120.036	119.965	0.036	120.012	119.978	0.012	120.000	119.978	0.000
160	Max	160.460	160.000	0.710	160.245	160.000	0.345	160.106	160.000	0.146	160.054	160.000	0.079	160.040	160.000	0.065
	Min	160.210	159.750	0.210	160.145	159.900	0.145	160.043	159.960	0.043	160.014	159.975	0.014	160.000	159.975	0.000
200	Max	200.530	200.000	0.820	200.285	200.000	0.400	200.122	200.000	0.168	200.061	200.000	0.090	200.046	200.000	0.075
	Min	200.240	199.710	0.240	200.170	199.885	0.170	200.050	199.954	0.050	200.015	199.971	0.015	200.000	199.971	0.000
250	Max	250.570	250.000	0.860	250.285	250.000	0.400	250.122	250.000	0.168	250.061	250.000	0.090	250.046	250.000	0.075
	Min	250.280	249.710	0.280	250.170	249.885	0.170	250.050	249.954	0.050	250.015	249.971	0.015	250.000	249.971	0.000
300	Max	300.650	300.000	0.970	300.320	300.000	0.450	300.137	300.000	0.189	300.069	300.000	0.101	300.052	300.000	0.084
	Min	300.330	299.680	0.330	300.190	299.870	0.190	300.056	299.948	0.056	300.017	299.968	0.017	300.000	299.968	0.000
400	Max	400.760	400.000	1.120	400.350	400.000	0.490	400.151	400.000	0.208	400.075	400.000	0.111	400.057	400.000	0.093
	Min	400.400	399.640	0.400	400.210	399.860	0.210	400.062	399.943	0.062	400.018	399.964	0.018	400.000	399.964	0.000
500	Max	500.880	500.000	1.280	500.385	500.000	0.540	500.165	500.000	0.228	500.083	500.000	0.123	500.063	500.000	0.103
	Min	500.480	499.600	0.480	500.230	499.845	0.230	500.068	499.937	0.068	500.020	499.960	5.020	500.000	499.960	0.000

[a]From ANSI B4.2-1978 (R1994).

16 Preferred Metric Shaft Basis Transition and Interference Fits[a]— American National Standard

Dimensions are in millimeters.

Basic Size		Locational Transn. Hole K7	Shaft h6	Fit	Locational Transn. Hole N7	Shaft h6	Fit	Locational Interf. Hole P7	Shaft h6	Fit	Medium Drive Hole S7	Shaft h6	Fit	Force Hole U7	Shaft h6	Fit
1	Max	1.000	1.000	0.006	0.996	1.000	0.002	0.994	1.000	0.000	0.986	1.000	−0.008	0.982	1.000	−0.012
	Min	0.990	0.994	−0.010	0.986	0.994	−0.014	0.984	0.994	−0.016	0.976	0.994	−0.024	0.972	0.994	−0.028
1.2	Max	1.200	1.200	0.006	1.196	1.200	0.002	1.194	1.200	0.000	1.186	1.200	−0.008	1.182	1.200	−0.012
	Min	1.190	1.194	−0.010	1.186	1.194	−0.014	1.184	1.194	−0.016	1.176	1.194	−0.024	1.172	1.194	−0.028
1.6	Max	1.600	1.600	0.006	1.596	1.600	0.002	1.594	1.600	0.000	1.586	1.600	−0.008	1.582	1.600	−0.012
	Min	1.590	1.594	−0.010	1.586	1.594	−0.014	1.584	1.594	−0.016	1.576	1.594	−0.024	1.572	1.594	−0.028
2	Max	2.000	2.000	0.006	1.996	2.000	0.002	1.994	2.000	0.000	1.986	2.000	−0.008	1.982	2.000	−0.012
	Min	1.990	1.994	−0.010	1.986	1.994	−0.014	1.984	1.994	−0.016	1.976	1.994	−0.024	1.972	1.994	−0.028
2.5	Max	2.500	2.500	0.006	2.496	2.500	0.002	2.494	2.500	0.000	2.486	2.500	−0.008	2.482	2.500	−0.012
	Min	2.490	2.494	−0.010	2.486	2.494	−0.014	2.484	2.494	−0.016	2.476	2.494	−0.024	2.472	2.494	−0.028
3	Max	3.000	3.000	0.006	2.996	3.000	0.002	2.994	3.000	0.000	2.986	3.000	−0.008	2.982	3.000	−0.012
	Min	2.990	2.994	−0.010	2.986	2.994	−0.014	2.984	2.994	−0.016	2.976	2.994	−0.024	2.972	2.994	−0.028
4	Max	4.003	4.000	0.011	3.996	4.000	0.004	3.992	4.000	0.000	3.985	4.000	−0.007	3.981	4.000	−0.011
	Min	3.991	3.992	−0.009	3.984	3.992	−0.016	3.980	3.992	−0.020	3.973	3.992	−0.027	3.969	3.992	−0.031
5	Max	5.003	5.000	0.011	4.996	5.000	0.004	4.992	5.000	0.000	4.985	5.000	−0.007	4.981	5.000	−0.011
	Min	4.991	4.992	−0.009	4.984	4.992	−0.016	4.980	4.992	−0.020	4.973	4.992	−0.027	4.969	4.992	−0.031
6	Max	6.003	6.000	0.011	5.996	6.000	0.004	5.992	6.000	0.000	5.985	6.000	−0.007	5.981	6.000	−0.011
	Min	5.991	5.992	−0.009	5.984	5.992	−0.016	5.980	5.992	−0.020	5.973	5.992	−0.027	5.969	5.992	−0.031
8	Max	8.005	8.000	0.014	7.996	8.000	0.005	7.991	8.000	0.000	7.983	8.000	−0.008	7.978	8.000	−0.013
	Min	7.990	7.991	−0.010	7.981	7.991	−0.019	7.976	7.991	−0.024	7.968	7.991	−0.032	7.963	7.991	−0.037
10	Max	10.005	10.000	0.014	9.996	10.000	0.005	9.991	10.000	0.000	9.983	10.000	−0.008	9.978	10.000	−0.013
	Min	9.990	9.991	−0.010	9.981	9.991	−0.019	9.976	9.991	−0.024	9.968	9.991	−0.032	9.963	9.991	−0.037
12	Max	12.006	12.000	0.017	11.995	12.000	0.006	11.989	12.000	0.000	11.979	12.000	−0.010	11.974	12.000	−0.015
	Min	11.988	11.989	−0.012	11.977	11.989	−0.023	11.971	11.989	−0.029	11.961	11.989	−0.039	11.956	11.989	−0.044
16	Max	16.006	16.000	0.017	15.995	16.000	0.006	15.989	16.000	0.000	15.979	16.000	−0.010	15.974	16.000	−0.015
	Min	15.988	15.989	−0.012	15.977	15.989	−0.023	15.971	15.989	−0.029	15.961	15.989	−0.039	15.956	15.989	−0.044
20	Max	20.006	20.000	0.019	19.993	20.000	0.006	19.986	20.000	−0.001	19.973	20.000	−0.014	19.967	20.000	−0.020
	Min	19.985	19.987	−0.015	19.972	19.987	−0.028	19.965	19.987	−0.035	19.952	19.987	−0.048	19.946	19.987	−0.054
25	Max	25.006	25.000	0.019	24.993	25.000	0.006	24.986	25.000	−0.001	24.973	25.000	−0.014	24.960	25.000	−0.027
	Min	24.985	24.987	−0.015	24.972	24.987	−0.028	24.965	24.987	−0.035	24.952	24.987	−0.048	24.939	24.987	−0.061
30	Max	30.006	30.000	0.019	29.993	30.000	0.006	29.986	30.000	−0.001	29.973	30.000	−0.014	29.960	30.000	−0.027
	Min	29.985	29.987	−0.015	29.972	29.987	−0.028	29.965	29.987	−0.035	29.952	29.987	−0.048	29.939	29.987	−0.061

[a]From ANSI B4.2-1978 (R1994).

16 Preferred Metric Basis Transition and Interference Fits[a]— American National Standard (continued)

Dimensions are in millimeters.

Basic Size		Locational Transn.			Locational Transn.			Locational Interf.			Medium Drive			Force		
		Hole K7	Shaft h6	Fit	Hole N7	Shaft h6	Fit	Hole P7	Shaft h6	Fit	Hole S7	Shaft h6	Fit	Hole U7	Shaft h6	Fit
40	Max	40.007	40.000	0.023	39.992	40.000	0.008	39.983	40.000	-0.001	39.966	40.000	-0.018	39.949	40.000	-0.035
	Min	39.982	39.984	-0.018	39.967	39.984	-0.033	39.958	39.984	-0.042	39.941	39.984	-0.059	39.924	39.984	-0.076
50	Max	50.007	50.000	0.023	49.992	50.000	0.008	49.983	50.000	-0.001	49.966	50.000	-0.018	49.939	50.000	-0.045
	Min	49.982	49.984	-0.018	49.967	49.984	-0.033	49.958	49.984	-0.042	49.941	49.984	-0.059	49.914	49.984	-0.086
60	Max	60.009	60.000	0.028	59.991	60.000	0.010	59.979	60.000	-0.002	59.958	60.000	-0.023	59.924	60.000	-0.057
	Min	59.979	59.981	-0.021	59.961	59.981	-0.039	59.949	59.981	-0.051	59.928	59.981	-0.072	59.894	59.981	-0.106
80	Max	80.009	80.000	0.028	79.991	80.000	0.010	79.979	80.000	-0.002	79.952	80.000	-0.029	79.909	80.000	-0.072
	Min	79.979	79.981	-0.021	79.961	79.981	-0.039	79.949	79.981	-0.051	79.922	79.981	-0.078	79.879	79.981	-0.121
100	Max	100.010	100.000	0.032	99.990	100.000	0.012	99.976	100.000	-0.002	99.942	100.000	-0.036	99.889	100.000	-0.089
	Min	99.975	99.978	-0.025	99.955	99.978	-0.045	99.941	99.978	-0.059	99.907	99.978	-0.093	99.854	99.978	-0.146
120	Max	120.010	120.000	0.032	119.990	120.000	0.012	119.976	120.000	-0.002	119.934	120.000	-0.044	119.869	120.000	-0.109
	Min	119.975	119.978	-0.025	119.955	119.978	-0.045	119.941	119.978	-0.059	119.899	119.978	-0.101	119.834	119.978	-0.166
160	Max	160.012	160.000	0.037	159.988	160.000	0.013	159.972	160.000	-0.003	159.915	160.000	-0.060	159.825	160.000	-0.150
	Min	159.972	159.975	-0.028	159.948	159.975	-0.052	159.932	159.975	-0.068	159.875	159.975	-0.125	159.785	159.975	-0.215
200	Max	200.013	200.000	0.042	199.986	200.000	0.015	199.967	200.000	-0.004	199.895	200.000	-0.076	199.781	200.000	-0.190
	Min	199.967	199.971	-0.033	199.940	199.971	-0.060	199.921	199.971	-0.079	199.849	199.971	-0.151	199.735	199.971	-0.265
250	Max	250.013	250.000	0.042	249.986	250.000	0.015	249.967	250.000	-0.004	249.877	250.000	-0.094	249.733	250.000	-0.238
	Min	249.967	249.971	-0.033	249.940	249.971	-0.060	249.921	249.971	-0.079	249.831	249.971	-0.169	249.687	249.971	-0.313
300	Max	300.016	300.000	0.048	299.986	300.000	0.018	299.964	300.000	-0.004	299.850	300.000	-0.118	299.670	300.000	-0.298
	Min	299.964	299.968	-0.036	299.934	299.968	-0.066	299.912	299.968	-0.088	299.798	299.968	-0.202	299.618	299.968	-0.382
400	Max	400.017	400.000	0.053	399.984	400.000	0.020	399.959	400.000	-0.005	399.813	400.000	-0.151	399.586	400.000	-0.378
	Min	399.960	399.964	-0.040	399.927	399.964	-0.073	399.902	399.964	-0.098	399.756	399.964	-0.244	399.529	399.964	-0.471
500	Max	500.018	500.000	0.058	499.983	500.000	0.023	499.955	500.000	-0.005	499.771	500.000	-0.189	499.483	500.000	-0.477
	Min	499.955	499.960	-0.045	499.920	499.960	-0.080	499.892	499.960	-0.108	499.708	499.960	-0.292	499.420	499.960	-0.580

[a]From ANSI B4.2-1978 (R1994).

17 Screw Threads, American National, Unified, and Metric

American National Standard Unified and American National Screw Threads.[a]

Nominal Diameter	Coarse[b] NC UNC		Fine[b] NF UNF		Extra Fine[c] NEF UNEF		Nominal Diameter	Coarse[b] NC UNC		Fine[b] NF UNF		Extra Fine[c] NEF UNEF	
	Thds. per Inch	Tap Drill[d]	Thds. per Inch	Tap Drill[d]	Thds. per Inch	Tap Drill[d]		Thds. per Inch	Tap Drill[d]	Thds. per Inch	Tap Drill[d]	Thds. per Inch	Tap Drill[d]
0 (.060)			80	$\frac{3}{64}$			1	8	$\frac{7}{8}$	12	$\frac{59}{64}$	20	$\frac{61}{64}$
1 (.073)	64	No. 53	72	No. 53	...	...	$1\frac{1}{16}$	...	...	...	...	18	1
2 (.086)	56	No. 50	64	No. 50	...	...	$1\frac{1}{8}$	7	$\frac{63}{64}$	12	$1\frac{3}{64}$	18	$1\frac{5}{64}$
3 (.099)	48	No. 47	56	No. 45	...	...	$1\frac{3}{16}$	...	...	...	...	18	$1\frac{9}{64}$
4 (.112)	40	No. 43	48	No. 42	...	...	$1\frac{1}{4}$	7	$1\frac{7}{64}$	12	$1\frac{11}{64}$	18	$1\frac{3}{16}$
5 (.125)	40	No. 38	44	No. 37	...	...	$1\frac{5}{16}$	...	...	...	...	18	$1\frac{17}{64}$
6 (.138)	32	No. 36	40	No. 33	...	...	$1\frac{3}{8}$	6	$1\frac{7}{32}$	12	$1\frac{19}{64}$	18	$1\frac{5}{16}$
8 (.164)	32	No. 29	36	No. 29	...	...	$1\frac{7}{16}$	...	...	...	...	18	$1\frac{3}{8}$
10 (.190)	24	No. 25	32	No. 21	...	...	$1\frac{1}{2}$	6	$1\frac{11}{32}$	12	$1\frac{27}{64}$	18	$1\frac{7}{16}$
12 (.216)	24	No. 16	28	No. 14	32	No. 13	$1\frac{9}{16}$	...	...	...	...	18	$1\frac{1}{2}$
$\frac{1}{4}$	20	No. 7	28	No. 3	32	$\frac{7}{32}$	$1\frac{5}{8}$	...	...	...	...	18	$1\frac{9}{16}$
$\frac{5}{16}$	18	F	24	I	32	$\frac{9}{32}$	$1\frac{11}{16}$	...	...	...	...	18	$1\frac{5}{8}$
$\frac{3}{8}$	16	$\frac{5}{16}$	24	Q	32	$\frac{11}{32}$	$1\frac{3}{4}$	5	$1\frac{9}{16}$	...	...	...	...
$\frac{7}{16}$	14	U	20	$\frac{25}{64}$	28	$\frac{13}{32}$	2	$4\frac{1}{2}$	$1\frac{25}{32}$	...	...	...	...
$\frac{1}{2}$	13	$\frac{27}{64}$	20	$\frac{29}{64}$	28	$\frac{15}{32}$	$2\frac{1}{4}$	$4\frac{1}{2}$	$2\frac{1}{32}$	...	...	...	...
$\frac{9}{16}$	12	$\frac{31}{64}$	18	$\frac{33}{64}$	24	$\frac{33}{64}$	$2\frac{1}{2}$	4	$2\frac{1}{4}$	...	...	...	...
$\frac{5}{8}$	11	$\frac{17}{32}$	18	$\frac{37}{64}$	24	$\frac{37}{64}$	$2\frac{3}{4}$	4	$2\frac{1}{2}$	...	...	...	...
$\frac{11}{16}$	...	...	...	...	24	$\frac{41}{64}$	3	4	$2\frac{3}{4}$	...	...	...	...
$\frac{3}{4}$	10	$\frac{21}{32}$	16	$\frac{11}{16}$	20	$\frac{45}{64}$	$3\frac{1}{4}$	4	...	...	...	...	...
$\frac{13}{16}$	...	...	...	...	20	$\frac{49}{64}$	$3\frac{1}{2}$	4	...	...	...	...	...
$\frac{7}{8}$	9	$\frac{49}{64}$	14	$\frac{13}{16}$	20	$\frac{53}{64}$	$3\frac{3}{4}$	4	...	...	...	...	...
$\frac{15}{16}$	...	...	...	...	20	$\frac{57}{64}$	4	4	...	...	...	...	...

[a]ANSI/ASME B1.1-1989. For 8-, 12-, and 16-pitch thread series, see next page.
[b]Classes 1A, 2A, 3A, 1B, 2B, 3B, 2, and 3.
[c]Classes 2A, 2B, 2, and 3.
[d]For approximate 75% full depth of thread. For decimal sizes of numbered and lettered drills, see Appendix 18.

17 Screw Threads, American National, Unified, and Metric (continued)

American National Standard Unified and American National Screw Threads[a] (continued)

Nominal Diameter	8-Pitch[b] Series 8N and 8UN		12-Pitch[b] Series 12N and 12UN		16-Pitch[b] Series 16N and 16UN		Nominal Diameter	8-Pitch[b] Series 8N and 8UN		12-Pitch[b] Series 12N and 12UN		16-Pitch[c] Series 16N and 16UN	
	Thds. per Inch	Tap Drill[c]	Thds. per Inch	Tap Drill[c]	Thds. per Inch	Tap Drill[c]		Thds. per Inch	Tap Drill[c]	Thds. per Inch	Tap Drill[c]	Thds. per Inch[d]	Tap Drill[c]
$\frac{1}{2}$	...	...	12	$\frac{27}{64}$	...	...	$2\frac{1}{16}$	...	...	...	...	**16**	2
$\frac{9}{16}$	...	...	12[e]	$\frac{31}{64}$	...	...	$2\frac{1}{8}$	...	...	12	$2\frac{3}{64}$	16	$2\frac{1}{16}$
$\frac{5}{8}$	...	...	12	$\frac{35}{64}$	...	...	$2\frac{3}{16}$	...	...	...	...	**16**	$2\frac{1}{8}$
$\frac{11}{16}$	...	...	12	$\frac{39}{64}$	...	...	$2\frac{1}{4}$	8	$2\frac{1}{8}$	12	$2\frac{17}{64}$	16	$2\frac{3}{16}$
$\frac{3}{4}$	...	...	12	$\frac{43}{64}$	16[e]	$\frac{11}{16}$	$2\frac{5}{16}$	...	...	...	...	**16**	$2\frac{1}{4}$
$\frac{13}{16}$	...	...	12	$\frac{47}{64}$	16	$\frac{3}{4}$	$2\frac{3}{8}$	...	...	12	$2\frac{19}{64}$	16	$2\frac{5}{16}$
$\frac{7}{8}$	...	...	12	$\frac{51}{64}$	16	$\frac{13}{16}$	$2\frac{7}{16}$	...	...	...	...	**16**	$2\frac{3}{8}$
$\frac{5}{16}$	...	...	12	$\frac{55}{64}$	16	$\frac{7}{8}$	$2\frac{1}{2}$	8	$2\frac{3}{8}$	12	$2\frac{27}{64}$	16	$2\frac{7}{16}$
1	8[e]	$\frac{7}{8}$	12	$\frac{59}{64}$	16	$\frac{15}{16}$	$2\frac{5}{8}$	...	...	12	$2\frac{35}{64}$	16	$2\frac{9}{16}$
$1\frac{1}{16}$	...	...	12	$\frac{63}{64}$	16	1	$2\frac{3}{4}$	8	$2\frac{5}{8}$	12	$2\frac{43}{64}$	16	$2\frac{11}{16}$
$1\frac{1}{8}$	8	1	12[e]	$1\frac{3}{64}$	16	$1\frac{1}{16}$	$2\frac{7}{8}$	...	...	12	...	16	...
$1\frac{3}{16}$	...	...	12	$1\frac{7}{64}$	16	$1\frac{1}{8}$	3	8	$2\frac{7}{8}$	12	...	16	...
$1\frac{1}{4}$	8	$1\frac{1}{8}$	12	$1\frac{11}{64}$	16	$1\frac{3}{16}$	$3\frac{1}{8}$	...	...	12	...	16	...
$1\frac{5}{16}$	...	...	12	$1\frac{15}{64}$	16	$1\frac{1}{4}$	$3\frac{1}{4}$	8	...	12	...	16	...
$1\frac{3}{8}$	8	$1\frac{1}{4}$	12[e]	$1\frac{19}{64}$	16	$1\frac{5}{16}$	$3\frac{3}{8}$	...	...	12	...	16	...
$1\frac{7}{16}$	...	...	12	$1\frac{23}{64}$	16	$1\frac{3}{8}$	$3\frac{1}{2}$	8	...	12	...	16	...
$1\frac{1}{2}$	8	$1\frac{3}{8}$	12[e]	$1\frac{27}{64}$	16	$1\frac{7}{16}$	$3\frac{5}{8}$	...	...	12	...	16	...
$1\frac{9}{16}$	...	...	...	...	16	$1\frac{1}{2}$	$3\frac{3}{4}$	8	...	12	...	16	...
$1\frac{5}{8}$	8	$1\frac{1}{2}$	12	$1\frac{35}{64}$	16	$1\frac{9}{16}$	$3\frac{7}{8}$	...	...	12	...	16	...
$1\frac{11}{16}$	...	...	...	...	16	$1\frac{5}{8}$	4	8	...	12	...	16	...
$1\frac{3}{4}$	8	$1\frac{5}{8}$	12	$1\frac{43}{64}$	16[e]	$1\frac{11}{16}$	$4\frac{1}{4}$	8	...	12	...	16	...
$1\frac{13}{16}$	...	...	...	...	16	$1\frac{3}{4}$	$4\frac{1}{2}$	8	...	12	...	16	...
$1\frac{7}{8}$	8	$1\frac{3}{4}$	12	$1\frac{51}{64}$	16	$1\frac{13}{16}$	$4\frac{3}{4}$	8	...	12	...	16	...
$1\frac{15}{16}$	...	...	...	...	16	$1\frac{7}{8}$	5	8	...	12	...	16	...
2	8	$1\frac{7}{8}$	12	$1\frac{59}{64}$	16[e]	$1\frac{15}{16}$	$5\frac{1}{4}$	8	...	12	...	16	...

[a]ANSI/ASME B1.1-1989.
[b]Classes 2A, 3A, 2B, 3B, 2, and 3.
[c]For approximate 75% full depth of thread.
[d]Boldface type indicates Amrican National Threads only.
[e]This is a standard size of the Unified or American National threads of the coarse, fine, or extra fine series. See preceding page.

17 Screw Threads, American National, Unified, and Metric (continued)

Metric Screw Threads.[a]

Preferred sizes for commercial threads and fasteners are shown in **boldface** type.

Coarse (general purpose)		Fine	
Nominal Size & Thd Pitch	Tap Drill Diameter, mm	Nominal Size & Thd Pitch	Tap Drill Diameter, mm
M1.6 × 0.35	1.25	—	—
M1.8 × 0.35	1.45	—	—
M2 × 0.4	1.6	—	—
M2.2 × 0.45	1.75	—	—
M2.5 × 0.45	2.05	—	—
M3 × 0.5	2.5	—	—
M3.5 × 0.6	2.9	—	—
M4 × 0.7	3.3	—	—
M4.5 × 0.75	3.75	—	—
M5 × 0.8	4.2	—	—
M6 × 1	5.0	—	—
M7 × 1	6.0	—	—
M8 × 1.25	6.8	**M8 × 1**	7.0
M9 × 1.25	7.75	—	—
M10 × 1.5	8.5	**M10 × 1.25**	8.75
M11 × 1.5	9.50	—	—
M12 × 1.75	10.30	**M12 × 1.25**	10.5
M14 × 2	12.00	**M14 × 1.5**	12.5
M16 × 2	14.00	**M16 × 1.5**	14.5
M18 × 2.5	15.50	**M18 × 1.5**	16.5
M20 × 2.5	17.5	**M20 × 1.5**	18.5
M22 × 25[b]	19.5	**M22 × 1.5**	20.5
M24 × 3	21.0	**M24 × 2**	22.0
M27 × 3[b]	24.0	**M27 × 2**	25.0
M30 × 3.5	26.5	**M30 × 2**	28.0
M33 × 3.5	29.5	**M30 × 2**	31.0
M36 × 4	32.0	**M36 × 2**	33.0
M39 × 4	35.0	M39 × 2	36.0
M42 × 4.5	37.5	**M42 × 2**	39.0
M45 × 4.5	40.5	M45 × 1.5	42.0
M48 × 5	43.0	**M48 × 2**	45.0
M52 × 5	47.0	M52 × 2	49.0
M56 × 5.5	50.5	**M56 × 2**	52.0
M60 × 5.5	54.5	M60 × 1.5	56.0
M64 × 6	58.0	**M64 × 2**	60.0
M68 × 6	62.0	M68 × 2	64.0
M72 × 6	66.0	**M72 × 2**	68.0
M80 × 6	74.0	**M80 × 2**	76.0
M90 × 6	84.0	**M90 × 2**	86.0
M100 × 6	94.0	**M100 × 2**	96.0

[a]ANSI/ASME B1.13M-1995.
[b]Only for high strength structural steel fasteners.

18 Twist Drill Sizes—American National Standard and Metric

American National Standard Drill Sizes.[a] All dimensions are in inches. Drills designated in common fractions are available in diameters $\frac{1}{64}''$ to $1\frac{3}{4}''$ in $\frac{1}{64}''$ increments, $1\frac{3}{4}''$ to $2\frac{1}{4}''$ in $\frac{1}{32}''$ increments. $2\frac{1}{4}''$ to $3''$ in $\frac{1}{16}''$ increments and $3''$ to $3\frac{1}{2}''$ in $\frac{1}{8}''$ increments. Drills larger than $3\frac{1}{2}''$ are seldom used, and are regarded as special drills.

Size	Drill Diameter	Size	Drill Diameter	Size	Drill Diameter	Size	Drill Diameter	Size	Drill Diameter	Size	Drill Diameter
1	.2280	17	.1730	33	.1130	49	.0730	65	.0350	81	.0130
2	.2210	18	.1695	34	.1110	50	.0700	66	.0330	82	.0125
3	.2130	19	.1660	35	.1100	51	.0670	67	.0320	83	.0120
4	.2090	20	.1610	36	.1065	52	.0635	68	.0310	84	.0115
5	.2055	21	.1590	37	.1040	53	.0595	69	.0292	85	.0110
6	.2040	22	.1570	38	.1015	54	.0550	70	.0280	86	.0105
7	.2010	23	.1540	39	.0995	55	.0520	71	.0260	87	.0100
8	.1990	24	.1520	40	.0980	56	.0465	72	.0250	88	.0095
9	.1960	25	.1495	41	.0960	57	.0430	73	.0240	89	.0091
10	.1935	26	.1470	42	.0935	58	.0420	74	.0225	90	.0087
11	.1910	27	.1440	43	.0890	59	.0410	75	.0210	91	.0083
12	.1890	28	.1405	44	.0860	60	.0400	76	.0200	92	.0079
13	.1850	29	.1360	45	.0820	61	.0390	77	.0180	93	.0075
14	.1820	30	.1285	46	.0810	62	.0380	78	.0160	94	.0071
15	.1800	31	.1200	47	.0785	63	.0370	79	.0145	95	.0067
16	.1770	32	.1160	48	.0760	64	.0360	80	.0135	96	.0063
										97	.0059

Letter Sizes

A	.234	G	.261	L	.290	Q	.332	V	.377
B	.238	H	.266	M	.295	R	.339	W	.386
C	.242	I	.272	N	.302	S	.348	X	.397
D	.246	J	.277	O	.316	T	.358	Y	.404
E	.250	K	.281	P	.323	U	.368	Z	.413
F	.257								

[a]ANSI/ASME B94.11M-1993.

18 Twist Drill Sizes—American National Standard and Metric (continued)

Metric Drill Sizes. Decimal inch equivalents are for reference only.

Drill Diameter		Drill Diameter		Drill Diameter		Drill Diameter		Drill Diameter		Drill Diameter	
mm	in.	mm	in.	mm	in.	mm	in.	mm	in.	mm	in.
0.40	.0157	1.95	.0768	4.70	.1850	8.00	.3150	13.20	.5197	25.50	1.0039
0.42	.0165	2.00	.0787	4.80	.1890	8.10	.3189	13.50	.5315	26.00	1.0236
0.45	.0177	2.05	.0807	4.90	.1929	8.20	.3228	13.80	.5433	26.50	1.0433
0.48	.0189	2.10	.0827	5.00	.1969	8.30	.3268	14.00	.5512	27.00	1.0630
0.50	.0197	2.15	.0846	5.10	.2008	8.40	.3307	14.25	.5610	27.50	1.0827
0.55	.0217	2.20	.0866	5.20	.2047	8.50	.3346	14.50	.5709	28.00	1.1024
0.60	.0236	2.25	.0886	5.30	.2087	8.60	.3386	14.75	.5807	28.50	1.1220
0.65	.0256	2.30	.0906	5.40	.2126	8.70	.3425	15.00	.5906	29.00	1.1417
0.70	.0276	2.35	.0925	5.50	.2165	8.80	.3465	15.25	.6004	29.50	1.1614
0.75	.0295	2.40	.0945	5.60	.2205	8.90	.3504	15.50	.6102	30.00	1.1811
0.80	.0315	2.45	.0965	5.70	.2244	9.00	.3543	15.75	.6201	30.50	1.2008
0.85	.0335	2.50	.0984	5.80	.2283	9.10	.3583	16.00	.6299	31.00	1.2205
0.90	.0354	2.60	.1024	5.90	.2323	9.20	.3622	16.25	.6398	31.50	1.2402
0.95	.0374	2.70	.1063	6.00	.2362	9.30	.3661	16.50	.6496	32.00	1.2598
1.00	.0394	2.80	.1102	6.10	.2402	9.40	.3701	16.75	.6594	32.50	1.2795
1.05	.0413	2.90	.1142	6.20	.2441	9.50	.3740	17.00	.6693	33.00	1.2992
1.10	.0433	3.00	.1181	6.30	.2480	9.60	.3780	17.25	.6791	33.50	1.3189
1.15	.0453	3.10	.1220	6.40	.2520	9.70	.3819	17.50	.6890	34.00	1.3386
1.20	.0472	3.20	.1260	6.50	.2559	9.80	.3858	18.00	.7087	34.50	1.3583
1.25	.0492	3.30	.1299	6.60	.2598	9.90	.3898	18.50	.7283	35.00	1.3780
1.30	.0512	3.40	.1339	6.70	.2638	10.00	.3937	19.00	.7480	35.50	1.3976
1.35	.0531	3.50	.1378	6.80	.2677	10.20	.4016	19.50	.7677	36.00	1.4173
1.40	.0551	3.60	.1417	6.90	.2717	10.50	.4134	20.00	.7874	36.50	1.4370
1.45	.0571	3.70	.1457	7.00	.2756	10.80	.4252	20.50	.8071	37.00	1.4567
1.50	.0591	3.80	.1496	7.10	.2795	11.00	.4331	21.00	.8268	37.50	1.4764
1.55	.0610	3.90	.1535	7.20	.2835	11.20	.4409	21.50	.8465	38.00	1.4961
1.60	.0630	4.00	.1575	7.30	.2874	11.50	.4528	22.00	.8661	40.00	1.5748
1.65	.0650	4.10	.1614	7.40	.2913	11.80	.4646	22.50	.8858	42.00	1.6535
1.70	.0669	4.20	.1654	7.50	.2953	12.00	.4724	23.00	.9055	44.00	1.7323
1.75	.0689	4.30	.1693	7.60	.2992	12.20	.4803	23.50	.9252	46.00	1.8110
1.80	.0709	4.40	.1732	7.70	.3031	12.50	.4921	24.00	.9449	48.00	1.8898
1.85	.0728	4.50	.1772	7.80	.3071	12.50	.5039	24.50	.9646	50.00	1.9685
1.90	.0748	4.60	.1811	7.90	.3110	13.00	.5118	25.00	.9843		

19 Acme Threads, General Purpose[a]

Size	Threads per Inch	Size	Threads per Inch	Size	Threads per Inch	Size	Threads per Inch
$\frac{1}{4}$	16	$\frac{3}{4}$	6	$1\frac{1}{2}$	4	3	2
$\frac{5}{16}$	14	$\frac{7}{8}$	6	$1\frac{3}{4}$	4	$3\frac{1}{2}$	2
$\frac{3}{8}$	12	1	5	2	4	4	2
$\frac{7}{16}$	12	$1\frac{1}{8}$	5	$2\frac{1}{4}$	3	$4\frac{1}{2}$	2
$\frac{1}{2}$	10	$1\frac{1}{4}$	5	$2\frac{1}{2}$	3	5	2
$\frac{5}{8}$	8	$1\frac{3}{8}$	4	$2\frac{3}{4}$	3	. . .	. . .

[a]ANSI/ASME B1.5-1988 (R1994).

20 Bolts, Nuts, and Cap Screws—Square and Hexagon—American National Standard and Metric

American National Standard Square and Hexagon Bolts[a] and Nuts[b] and Hexagon Cap Screws.[c] **Boldface** type indicates product features unified dimensionally with British and Canadian standards. All dimensions are in inches.

Nominal Size D Body Diameter of Bolt	Regular Bolts					Heavy Bolts		
	Width Across Flats W		Height H			Width Across Flats W	Height H	
	Sq.	Hex.	Sq. (Unfin.)	Hex (Unfin.)	Hex Cap Scr.[c] (Fin.)		Hex. (Unfin.)	Hex Screw (Fin.)
$\frac{1}{4}$ 0.2500	$\frac{3}{8}$	$\frac{7}{16}$	$\frac{11}{64}$	$\frac{11}{64}$	$\frac{5}{32}$	...	...	...
$\frac{5}{16}$ 0.3125	$\frac{1}{2}$	$\frac{1}{2}$	$\frac{13}{64}$	$\frac{7}{32}$	$\frac{13}{64}$	...	...	...
$\frac{3}{8}$ 0.3750	$\frac{9}{16}$	$\frac{9}{16}$	$\frac{1}{4}$	$\frac{1}{4}$	$\frac{15}{64}$	...	...	...
$\frac{7}{16}$ 0.4375	$\frac{5}{8}$	$\frac{5}{8}$	$\frac{19}{64}$	$\frac{19}{64}$	$\frac{9}{32}$	...	...	...
$\frac{1}{2}$ 0.5000	$\frac{3}{4}$	$\frac{3}{4}$	$\frac{21}{64}$	$\frac{11}{32}$	$\frac{5}{16}$	$\frac{7}{8}$	$\frac{11}{32}$	$\frac{5}{16}$
$\frac{9}{16}$ 0.5625	...	$\frac{13}{16}$	...	...	$\frac{23}{64}$	...	...	...
$\frac{5}{8}$ 0.6250	$\frac{15}{16}$	$\frac{15}{16}$	$\frac{27}{64}$	$\frac{27}{64}$	$\frac{25}{64}$	$1\frac{1}{16}$	$\frac{27}{64}$	$\frac{25}{64}$
$\frac{3}{4}$ 0.7500	$1\frac{1}{8}$	$1\frac{1}{8}$	$\frac{1}{2}$	$\frac{1}{2}$	$\frac{15}{32}$	$1\frac{1}{4}$	$\frac{1}{2}$	$\frac{15}{32}$
$\frac{7}{8}$ 0.8750	$1\frac{5}{16}$	$1\frac{5}{16}$	$\frac{19}{32}$	$\frac{37}{64}$	$\frac{35}{64}$	$1\frac{7}{16}$	$\frac{37}{64}$	$\frac{35}{64}$
1 1.000	$1\frac{1}{2}$	$1\frac{1}{2}$	$\frac{21}{32}$	$\frac{43}{64}$	$\frac{39}{64}$	$1\frac{5}{8}$	$\frac{43}{64}$	$\frac{39}{64}$
$1\frac{1}{8}$ 1.1250	$1\frac{11}{16}$	$1\frac{11}{16}$	$\frac{3}{4}$	$\frac{3}{4}$	$\frac{11}{16}$	$1\frac{13}{16}$	$\frac{3}{4}$	$\frac{11}{16}$
$1\frac{1}{4}$ 1.2500	$1\frac{7}{8}$	$1\frac{7}{8}$	$\frac{27}{32}$	$\frac{27}{32}$	$\frac{25}{32}$	2	$\frac{27}{32}$	$\frac{25}{32}$
$1\frac{3}{8}$ 1.3750	$2\frac{1}{16}$	$2\frac{1}{16}$	$\frac{29}{32}$	$\frac{29}{32}$	$\frac{27}{32}$	$2\frac{3}{16}$	$\frac{29}{32}$	$\frac{27}{32}$
$1\frac{1}{2}$ 1.5000	$2\frac{1}{4}$	$2\frac{1}{4}$	1	1	$\frac{15}{16}$	$2\frac{3}{8}$	1	$\frac{15}{16}$
$1\frac{3}{4}$ 1.7500	...	$2\frac{5}{8}$	...	$1\frac{5}{32}$	$1\frac{3}{32}$	$2\frac{3}{4}$	$1\frac{5}{32}$	$1\frac{3}{32}$
2 2.0000	...	**3**	...	$1\frac{11}{32}$	$1\frac{7}{32}$	$3\frac{1}{8}$	$1\frac{11}{32}$	$1\frac{7}{32}$
$2\frac{1}{4}$ 2.2500	...	$3\frac{3}{8}$	...	$1\frac{1}{2}$	$1\frac{3}{8}$	$3\frac{1}{2}$	$1\frac{1}{2}$	$1\frac{3}{8}$
$2\frac{1}{2}$ 2.5000	...	$3\frac{3}{4}$	...	$1\frac{21}{32}$	$1\frac{17}{32}$	$3\frac{7}{8}$	$1\frac{21}{32}$	$1\frac{17}{32}$
$2\frac{3}{4}$ 2.7500	...	$4\frac{1}{8}$	...	$1\frac{13}{16}$	$1\frac{11}{16}$	$4\frac{1}{4}$	$1\frac{13}{16}$	$1\frac{11}{16}$
3 3.0000	...	$4\frac{1}{2}$	...	2	$1\frac{7}{8}$	$4\frac{5}{8}$	2	$1\frac{7}{8}$
$3\frac{1}{4}$ 3.2500	...	$4\frac{7}{8}$	...	$2\frac{3}{16}$	...	...	...	...
$3\frac{1}{2}$ 3.5000	...	$5\frac{1}{4}$	...	$2\frac{5}{16}$	...	...	...	...
$3\frac{3}{4}$ 3.7500	...	$5\frac{5}{8}$	...	$2\frac{1}{2}$	...	...	...	...
4 4.0000	...	6	...	$2\frac{11}{16}$	...	...	...	...

[a] ANSI B18.2.1-1981 (R1992).
[b] ANSI/ASME B18.2.2.-1987 (R1993).
[c] Hexagon cap screws and finished hexagon bolts are combined as a single product.

20 Bolts, Nuts, and Cap Screws—Square and Hexagon—American National Standard and Metric (continued)

American National Standard Square and Hexagon Bolts and Nuts and Hexagon Cap Screws (continued). See ANSI B18.2.2 for jam nuts, slotted nuts, thick nuts, thick slotted nuts, and castle nuts.

Nominal Size D Body Diameter of Bolt		Regular Bolts					Heavy Nuts			
		Width Across Flats W		Thickness T			Width Across Flats W	Thickness T		
		Sq.	Hex.	Sq. (Unfin.)	Hex. Flat (Unfin.)	Hex. (Fin.)		Sq. (Unfin.)	Hex. Flat (Unfin.)	Hex. (Fin.)
$\frac{1}{4}$	0.2500	$\frac{7}{16}$	$\frac{7}{16}$	$\frac{7}{32}$	$\frac{7}{32}$	$\frac{7}{32}$	$\frac{1}{2}$	$\frac{1}{4}$	$\frac{15}{64}$	$\frac{15}{64}$
$\frac{5}{16}$	0.3125	$\frac{9}{16}$	$\frac{1}{2}$	$\frac{17}{64}$	$\frac{17}{64}$	$\frac{17}{64}$	$\frac{9}{16}$	$\frac{5}{16}$	$\frac{19}{64}$	$\frac{19}{64}$
$\frac{3}{8}$	0.3750	$\frac{5}{8}$	$\frac{9}{16}$	$\frac{21}{64}$	$\cdots$	$\frac{21}{64}$	$\frac{11}{16}$	$\frac{3}{8}$	$\frac{23}{64}$	$\frac{23}{64}$
$\frac{7}{16}$	0.4375	$\frac{3}{4}$	$\frac{11}{16}$	$\frac{3}{8}$	$\frac{3}{8}$	$\frac{3}{8}$	$\frac{3}{4}$	$\frac{7}{16}$	$\frac{27}{64}$	$\frac{27}{64}$
$\frac{1}{2}$	0.5000	$\frac{13}{16}$	$\frac{3}{4}$	$\frac{7}{16}$	$\frac{7}{16}$	$\frac{7}{16}$	$\frac{7}{8}$a	$\frac{1}{2}$	$\frac{31}{64}$	$\frac{31}{64}$
$\frac{9}{16}$	0.5625	$\cdots$	$\frac{7}{8}$	$\cdots$	$\frac{31}{64}$	$\frac{31}{64}$	$\frac{15}{16}$	$\cdots$	$\frac{35}{64}$	$\frac{35}{64}$
$\frac{5}{8}$	0.6250	1	$\frac{15}{16}$	$\frac{35}{64}$	$\frac{35}{64}$	$\frac{35}{64}$	$1\frac{1}{16}$a	$\frac{5}{8}$	$\frac{39}{64}$	$\frac{39}{64}$
$\frac{3}{4}$	0.7500	$1\frac{1}{8}$	$1\frac{1}{8}$	$\frac{21}{32}$	$\frac{41}{64}$	$\frac{41}{64}$	$1\frac{1}{4}$a	$\frac{3}{4}$	$\frac{47}{64}$	$\frac{47}{64}$
$\frac{7}{8}$	0.8750	$1\frac{5}{16}$	$1\frac{5}{16}$	$\frac{49}{64}$	$\frac{3}{4}$	$\frac{3}{4}$	$1\frac{7}{16}$a	$\frac{7}{8}$	$\frac{55}{64}$	$\frac{55}{64}$
1	1.0000	$1\frac{1}{2}$	$1\frac{1}{2}$	$\frac{7}{8}$	$\frac{55}{64}$	$\frac{55}{64}$	$1\frac{5}{8}$a	1	$\frac{63}{64}$	$\frac{63}{64}$
$1\frac{1}{8}$	1.1250	$1\frac{11}{16}$	$1\frac{11}{16}$	1	1	$\frac{31}{32}$	$1\frac{13}{16}$a	$1\frac{1}{8}$	$1\frac{1}{8}$	$1\frac{7}{64}$
$1\frac{1}{4}$	1.2500	$1\frac{7}{8}$	$1\frac{7}{8}$	$1\frac{3}{32}$	$1\frac{3}{32}$	$1\frac{1}{16}$	2a	$1\frac{1}{4}$	$1\frac{1}{4}$	$1\frac{7}{32}$
$1\frac{3}{8}$	1.3750	$2\frac{1}{16}$	$2\frac{1}{16}$	$1\frac{13}{64}$	$1\frac{13}{64}$	$1\frac{11}{64}$	$2\frac{3}{16}$a	$1\frac{3}{8}$	$1\frac{3}{8}$	$1\frac{11}{32}$
$1\frac{1}{2}$	1.5000	$2\frac{1}{4}$	$2\frac{1}{4}$	$1\frac{5}{16}$	$1\frac{5}{16}$	$1\frac{9}{32}$	$2\frac{3}{8}$a	$1\frac{1}{2}$	$1\frac{1}{2}$	$1\frac{15}{32}$
$1\frac{5}{8}$	1.6250	$\cdots$	$\cdots$	$\cdots$	$\cdots$	$\cdots$	$2\frac{9}{16}$	$\cdots$	$\cdots$	$1\frac{19}{32}$
$1\frac{3}{4}$	1.7500	$\cdots$	$\cdots$	$\cdots$	$\cdots$	$\cdots$	$2\frac{3}{4}$	$\cdots$	$1\frac{3}{4}$	$1\frac{23}{32}$
$1\frac{7}{8}$	1.8750	$\cdots$	$\cdots$	$\cdots$	$\cdots$	$\cdots$	$2\frac{15}{16}$	$\cdots$	$\cdots$	$1\frac{27}{32}$
2	2.0000	$\cdots$	$\cdots$	$\cdots$	$\cdots$	$\cdots$	$3\frac{1}{8}$	$\cdots$	2	$1\frac{31}{32}$
$2\frac{1}{4}$	2.2500	$\cdots$	$\cdots$	$\cdots$	$\cdots$	$\cdots$	$3\frac{1}{2}$	$\cdots$	$2\frac{1}{4}$	$2\frac{13}{64}$
$2\frac{1}{2}$	2.5000	$\cdots$	$\cdots$	$\cdots$	$\cdots$	$\cdots$	$3\frac{7}{8}$	$\cdots$	$2\frac{1}{2}$	$2\frac{29}{64}$
$2\frac{3}{4}$	2.7500	$\cdots$	$\cdots$	$\cdots$	$\cdots$	$\cdots$	$4\frac{1}{4}$	$\cdots$	$2\frac{3}{4}$	$2\frac{45}{64}$
3	3.0000	$\cdots$	$\cdots$	$\cdots$	$\cdots$	$\cdots$	$4\frac{5}{8}$	$\cdots$	3	$2\frac{61}{64}$
$3\frac{1}{4}$	3.2500	$\cdots$	$\cdots$	$\cdots$	$\cdots$	$\cdots$	5	$\cdots$	$3\frac{1}{4}$	$3\frac{3}{16}$
$3\frac{1}{2}$	3.5000	$\cdots$	$\cdots$	$\cdots$	$\cdots$	$\cdots$	$5\frac{3}{8}$	$\cdots$	$3\frac{1}{2}$	$3\frac{7}{16}$
$3\frac{3}{4}$	3.7500	$\cdots$	$\cdots$	$\cdots$	$\cdots$	$\cdots$	$5\frac{3}{4}$	$\cdots$	$3\frac{3}{4}$	$3\frac{11}{16}$
4	4.0000	$\cdots$	$\cdots$	$\cdots$	$\cdots$	$\cdots$	$6\frac{1}{8}$	$\cdots$	4	$3\frac{15}{16}$

aProduct feature not unified for heavy square nut.

20 Bolts, Nuts, and Cap Screws—Square and Hexagon—
American National Standard and Metric (continued)

Metric hexagon bolts, hexagon cap screws, hexagon structural bolts, and hexagon nuts.

Nominal Size D, mm	Width Across Flats W (max)		Thickness T (max)			
Body Dia and Thd Pitch	Bolts,[a] Cap Screws,[b] and Nuts[c]	Heavy Hex & Hex Structural Bolts[a] & Nuts[c]	Bolts (Unfin.)	Cap Screw (Fin.)	Nut (Fin. or Unfin.)	
					Style 1	Style 2
M5 × 0.8	8.0		3.88	3.65	4.7	5.1
M6 × 1	10.0		4.38	4.47	5.2	5.7
M8 × 1.25	13.0		5.68	5.50	6.8	7.5
M10 × 1.5	16.0		6.85	6.63	8.4	9.3
M12 × 1.75	18.0	21.0	7.95	7.76	10.8	12.0
M14 × 2	21.0	24.0	9.25	9.09	12.8	14.1
M16 × 2	24.0	27.0	10.75	10.32	14.8	16.4
M20 × 2.5	30.0	34.0	13.40	12.88	18.0	20.3
M24 × 3	36.0	41.0	15.90	15.44	21.5	23.9
M30 × 3.5	46.0	50.0	19.75	19.48	25.6	28.6
M36 × 4	55.0	60.0	23.55	23.38	31.0	34.7
M42 × 4.5	65.0		27.05	26.97	. . .	. . .
M48 × 5	75.0		31.07	31.07	. . .	. . .
M56 × 5.5	85.0		36.20	36.20	. . .	. . .
M64 × 6	95.0		41.32	41.32	. . .	. . .
M72 × 6	105.0		46.45	46.45	. . .	. . .
M80 × 6	115.0		51.58	51.58	. . .	. . .
M90 × 6	130.0		57.74	57.74	. . .	. . .
M100 × 6	145.0		63.90	63.90	. . .	. . .
High Strength Structural Hexagon Bolts[a] (Fin.) and Hexagon Nuts[c]						
M16 × 2	27.0	. . .	10.75	. . .	. . .	17.1
M20 × 2.5	34.0	. . .	13.40	. . .	. . .	20.7
M22 × 2.5	36.0	. . .	14.9	. . .	. . .	23.6
M24 × 3	41.0	. . .	15.9	. . .	. . .	24.2
M27 × 3	46.0	. . .	17.9	. . .	. . .	27.6
M30 × 3.5	50.0	. . .	19.75	. . .	. . .	31.7
M36 × 4	60.0	. . .	23.55	. . .	. . .	36.6

[a]ANSI/ASME B18.2.3.5M-1979 (R1995), B18.2.3.6M-1979 (R1995), B18.2.3.7M-1979 (R1995).
[b]ANSI/ASME B18.2.3.1M-1979 (R1995).
[c]ANSI/ASME B18.2.4.1M-1979 (R1995), B18.2.4.2M-1979 (R1995).

21 Cap Screws, Slotted[a] and Socket Head[b]—American National Standard and Metric

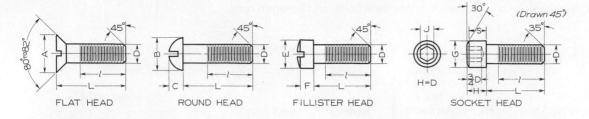

FLAT HEAD   ROUND HEAD   FILLISTER HEAD   SOCKET HEAD

Nominal Size D	Flat Head[a] A	Round Head[a] B	Round Head[a] C	Fillister Head[a] E	Fillister Head[a] F	Socket Head[b] G	Socket Head[b] J	Socket Head[b] S
0 (.060)	...	...	...	...	...	.096	.05	.054
1 (.073)	...	...	...	...	...	.118	$\frac{1}{16}$	.066
2 (.086)	...	...	...	...	...	.140	$\frac{5}{64}$	.077
3 (.099)	...	...	...	...	...	.161	$\frac{5}{64}$	.089
4 (.112)	...	...	...	...	...	.183	$\frac{3}{32}$	.101
5 (.125)	...	...	...	...	...	.205	$\frac{3}{32}$	.112
6 (.138)	...	...	...	...	...	.226	$\frac{7}{64}$	.124
8 (.164)	...	...	...	...	...	.270	$\frac{9}{64}$	.148
10 (.190)	...	...	...	...	...	.312	$\frac{5}{32}$	.171
$\frac{1}{4}$	.500	.437	.191	.375	.172	.375	$\frac{3}{16}$	.225
$\frac{5}{16}$	.625	.562	.245	.437	.203	.469	$\frac{1}{4}$	.281
$\frac{3}{8}$	.750	.675	.273	.562	.250	.562	$\frac{5}{16}$	.337
$\frac{7}{16}$	.812	.750	.328	.625	.297	.656	$\frac{3}{8}$	.394
$\frac{1}{2}$	.875	.812	.354	.750	.328	.750	$\frac{3}{8}$	.450
$\frac{9}{16}$	1.000	.937	.409	.812	.375	...	...	...
$\frac{5}{8}$	1.125	1.000	.437	.875	.422	.938	$\frac{1}{2}$	.562
$\frac{3}{4}$	1.375	1.250	.546	1.000	.500	1.125	$\frac{5}{8}$	.675
$\frac{7}{8}$	1.625	...	...	1.125	.594	1.312	$\frac{3}{4}$	.787
1	1.875	...	...	1.312	.656	1.500	$\frac{3}{4}$	.900
$1\frac{1}{8}$	2.062	...	...	...	...	1.688	$\frac{7}{8}$	1.012
$1\frac{1}{4}$	2.312	...	...	...	...	1.875	$\frac{7}{8}$	1.125
$1\frac{3}{8}$	2.562	...	...	...	...	2.062	1	1.237
$1\frac{1}{2}$	2.812	...	...	...	...	2.250	1	1.350

[a]ANSI/ASME B18.6.2-1995.
[b]ANSI/ASME B18.3-1986 (R1995). For hexagon-head screws, see Appendix 20.

21 Cap Screws, Slotted[a] and Socket Head[b]—American National Standard and Metric (continued)

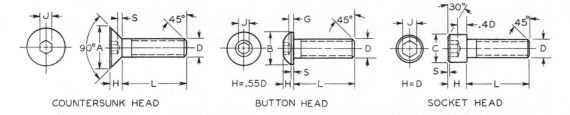

COUNTERSUNK HEAD   BUTTON HEAD   SOCKET HEAD

Metric Socket Head Cap Screws									
Nominal Size D	**Countersunk Head[a]**			**Button Head[a]**			**Socket Head[b]**		**Hex Socket Size**
	A (max)	**H**	**S**	**B**	**S**	**G**	**C**	**S**	**J**
M1.6 × 0.35	...	...	...	...	...	...	3.0	0.16	1.5
M2 × 0.4	...	...	...	...	...	...	3.8	0.2	1.5
M2.5 × 0.45	...	...	...	...	...	...	4.5	0.25	2.0
M3 × 0.5	6.72	1.86	0.25	5.70	0.38	0.2	5.5	0.3	2.5
M4 × 0.7	8.96	2.48	0.45	7.6	0.38	0.3	7.0	0.4	3.0
M5 × 0.8	11.2	3.1	0.66	9.5	0.5	0.38	8.5	0.5	4.0
M6 × 1	13.44	3.72	0.7	10.5	0.8	0.74	10.0	0.6	5.0
M8 × 1.25	17.92	4.96	1.16	14.0	0.8	1.05	13.0	0.8	6.0
M10 × 1.5	22.4	6.2	1.62	17.5	0.8	1.45	16.0	1.0	8.0
M12 × 1.75	26.88	7.44	1.8	21.0	0.8	1.63	18.0	1.2	10.0
M14 × 2	30.24	8.12	2.0	...	...	...	21.0	1.4	12.0
M16 × 2	33.6	8.8	2.2	28.0	1.5	2.25	24.0	1.6	14.0
M20 × 2.5	19.67	10.16	2.2	...	...	...	30.0	2.0	17.0
M24 × 3	...	...	...	...	...	...	36.0	2.4	19.0
M30 × 3.5	...	...	...	...	...	...	45.0	3.0	22.0
M36 × 4	...	...	...	...	...	...	54.0	3.6	27.0
M42 × 4.5	...	...	...	...	...	...	63.0	4.2	32.0
M48 × 5	...	...	...	...	...	...	72.0	4.8	36.0

[a]ANSI/ASME B18.3.4M-1986 (R1993).
[b]ANSI/ASME B18.3.1M-1986 (R1993).

22 Machine Screws—American National Standard and Metric

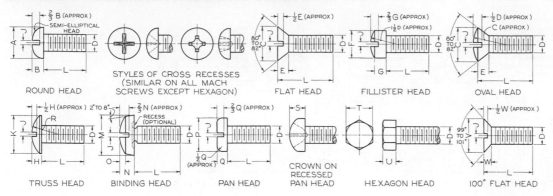

ROUND HEAD STYLES OF CROSS RECESSES (SIMILAR ON ALL MACH SCREWS EXCEPT HEXAGON) FLAT HEAD FILLISTER HEAD OVAL HEAD

TRUSS HEAD BINDING HEAD PAN HEAD CROWN ON RECESSED PAN HEAD HEXAGON HEAD 100° FLAT HEAD

American National Standard machine screws.

Length of Thread: On screws 2″ long and shorter, the threads extend to within two threads of the head and closer if practical; longer screws have minimum thread length of $1\frac{3}{4}$″.

Points: Machine screws are regularly made with plain sheared ends, not chamfered.

Threads: Either Coarse or Fine Thread Series, Class 2 fit.

Recessed Heads: Two styles of cross recesses are available on all screws except hexagon head.

Nominal Size	Max Diameter D	Round Head		Flat Heads & Oval Head		Fillister Head		Truss Head			Slot Width
		A	**B**	**C**	**E**	**F**	**G**	**K**	**H**	**R**	**J**
0	0.060	0.113	0.053	0.119	0.035	0.096	0.045	0.131	0.037	0.087	0.023
1	0.073	0.138	0.061	0.146	0.043	0.118	0.053	0.164	0.045	0.107	0.026
2	0.086	0.162	0.069	0.172	0.051	0.140	0.062	0.194	0.053	0.129	0.031
3	0.099	0.187	0.078	0.199	0.059	0.161	0.070	0.226	0.061	0.151	0.035
4	0.112	0.211	0.086	0.225	0.067	0.183	0.079	0.257	0.069	0.169	0.039
5	0.125	0.236	0.095	0.252	0.075	0.205	0.088	0.289	0.078	0.191	0.043
6	0.138	0.260	0.103	0.279	0.083	0.226	0.096	0.321	0.086	0.211	0.048
8	0.164	0.309	0.120	0.332	0.100	0.270	0.113	0.384	0.102	0.254	0.054
10	0.190	0.359	0.137	0.385	0.116	0.313	0.130	0.448	0.118	0.283	0.060
12	0.216	0.408	0.153	0.438	0.132	0.357	0.148	0.511	0.134	0.336	0.067
$\frac{1}{4}$	0.250	0.472	0.175	0.507	0.153	0.414	0.170	0.573	0.150	0.375	0.075
$\frac{5}{16}$	0.3125	0.590	0.216	0.635	0.191	0.518	0.211	0.698	0.183	0.457	0.084
$\frac{3}{8}$	0.375	0.708	0.256	0.762	0.230	0.622	0.253	0.823	0.215	0.538	0.094
$\frac{7}{16}$	0.4375	0.750	0.328	0.812	0.223	0.625	0.265	0.948	0.248	0.619	0.094
$\frac{1}{2}$	0.500	0.813	0.355	0.875	0.223	0.750	0.297	1.073	0.280	0.701	0.106
$\frac{9}{16}$	0.5625	0.938	0.410	1.000	0.260	0.812	0.336	1.198	0.312	0.783	0.118
$\frac{5}{8}$	0.625	1.000	0.438	1.125	0.298	0.875	0.375	1.323	0.345	0.863	0.133
$\frac{3}{4}$	0.750	1.250	0.547	1.375	0.372	1.000	0.441	1.573	0.410	1.024	0.149

Nominal Size	Max Diameter D	Binding Head			Pan Head			Hexagon Head		100° Flat Head		Slot Width
		M	**N**	**O**	**P**	**Q**	**S**	**T**	**U**	**V**	**W**	**J**
2	0.086	0.181	0.050	0.018	0.167	0.053	0.062	0.125	0.050	...	...	0.031
3	0.099	0.208	0.059	0.022	0.193	0.060	0.071	0.187	0.055	...	...	0.035
4	0.112	0.235	0.068	0.025	0.219	0.068	0.080	0.187	0.060	0.225	0.049	0.039
5	0.125	0.263	0.078	0.029	0.245	0.075	0.089	0.187	0.070	...	...	0.043
6	0.138	0.290	0.087	0.032	0.270	0.082	0.097	0.250	0.080	0.279	0.060	0.048
8	0.164	0.344	0.105	0.039	0.322	0.096	0.115	0.250	0.110	0.332	0.072	0.054
10	0.190	0.399	0.123	0.045	0.373	0.110	0.133	0.312	0.120	0.385	0.083	0.060
12	0.216	0.454	0.141	0.052	0.425	0.125	0.151	0.312	0.155	...	...	0.067
$\frac{1}{4}$	0.250	0.513	0.165	0.061	0.492	0.144	0.175	0.375	0.190	0.507	0.110	0.075
$\frac{5}{16}$	0.3125	0.641	0.209	0.077	0.615	0.178	0.218	0.500	0.230	0.635	0.138	0.084
$\frac{3}{8}$	0.375	0.769	0.253	0.094	0.740	0.212	0.261	0.562	0.295	0.762	0.165	0.094
$\frac{7}{16}$	.4375	...	...	...	.865	.247	.305	...	...	...	...	.094
$\frac{1}{2}$	.500	...	...	...	.987	.281	.348	...	...	...	...	.106
$\frac{9}{16}$	.5625	...	...	...	1.041	.315	.391	...	...	...	...	.118
$\frac{5}{8}$	.625	...	...	...	1.172	.350	.434	...	...	...	...	.133
$\frac{3}{4}$	.750	...	...	...	1.435	.419	.521	...	...	...	...	.149

22 Machine Screws—American National Standard and Metric (continued)

Metric machine screws.[a]

Length of Thread: On screws 36 mm long or shorter, the threads extend to within one thread of the head: on longer screws the thread extends to within two threads of the head.

Points: Machine screws are regularly made with sheared ends, not chamfered.

Threads: Coarse (general purpose) threads series are given.

Recessed Heads: Two styles of cross-recesses are available on all screws except hexagon head.

Nominal Size & Thd Pitch	Max. Dia. D mm	Flat Heads & Oval Head		Pan Heads			Hex Head		Slot Width
		C	E	P	Q	S	T	U	J
M2 × M	2.0	3.5	1.2	4.0	1.3	1.6	3.2	1.6	0.7
M2.5 × 0.45	2.5	4.4	1.5	5.0	1.5	2.1	4.0	2.1	0.8
M3 × 0.5	3.0	5.2	1.7	5.6	1.8	2.4	5.0	2.3	1.0
M3.5 × 0.6	3.5	6.9	2.3	7.0	2.1	2.6	5.5	2.6	1.2
M4 × 0.7	4.0	8.0	2.7	8.0	2.4	3.1	7.0	3.0	1.5
M5 × 0.8	5.0	8.9	2.7	9.5	3.0	3.7	8.0	3.8	1.5
M6 × 1	6.0	10.9	3.3	12.0	3.6	4.6	10.0	4.7	1.9
M8 × 1.25	8.0	15.14	4.6	16.0	4.8	6.0	13.0	6.0	2.3
M10 × 1.5	10.0	17.8	5.0	20.0	6.0	7.5	15.0	7.5	2.8
M12 × 1.75	12.0	…	…	…	…	…	18.0	9.0	…

Nominal Size	Metric Machine Screw Lengths—L[b]																				
	2.5	3	4	5	6	8	10	13	16	20	25	30	35	40	45	50	55	60	65	70	80	90
M2 × 0.4	PH	A	A	A	A	A	A	A	A	A											
M2.5 × 0.45		PH	A	A	A	A	A	A	A	A	A		Min. Thd Length—28 mm								
M3 × 0.5			PH	A	A	A	A	A	A	A	A	A									
M3.5 × 0.6				PH	A	A	A	A	A	A	A	A	A		Min. Thd Length—38 mm						
M4 × 0.7				PH	A	A	A	A	A	A	A	A	A	A							
M5 × 0.8					PH	A	A	A	A	A	A	A	A	A	A						
M6 × 1						A	A	A	A	A	A	A	A	A	A	A	A	A			
M8 × 1.25						A	A	A	A	A	A	A	A	A	A	A	A	A	A	A	A
M10 × 1.5							A	A	A	A	A	A	A	A	A	A	A	A	A	A	A
M12 × 1.75								A	A	A	A	A	A	A	A	A	A	A	A	A	A

[a]Metric Fasteners Standard. IFI-513(1982).

[b]PH = recommended lengths for only pan and hex head metric screws. A = recommended lengths for all metric screw head styles.

23 Keys—Square, Flat, Plain Taper,[a] and Gib Head

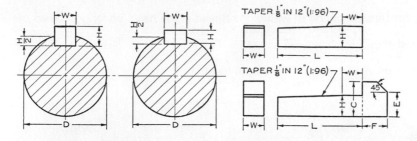

Shaft Diameters	Square Stock Key	Flat Stock Key	Gib Head Taper Stock Key					
			Square			Flat		
			Height	Length	Height to Chamfer	Height	Length	Height to Chamfer
D	W = H	W × H	C	F	E	C	F	E
$\frac{1}{2}$ to $\frac{9}{16}$	$\frac{1}{8}$	$\frac{1}{8} \times \frac{3}{32}$	$\frac{1}{4}$	$\frac{7}{32}$	$\frac{5}{32}$	$\frac{3}{16}$	$\frac{1}{8}$	$\frac{1}{8}$
$\frac{5}{8}$ to $\frac{7}{8}$	$\frac{3}{16}$	$\frac{3}{16} \times \frac{1}{8}$	$\frac{5}{16}$	$\frac{9}{32}$	$\frac{7}{32}$	$\frac{1}{4}$	$\frac{3}{16}$	$\frac{5}{32}$
$\frac{15}{16}$ to $1\frac{1}{4}$	$\frac{1}{4}$	$\frac{1}{4} \times \frac{3}{16}$	$\frac{7}{16}$	$\frac{11}{32}$	$\frac{11}{32}$	$\frac{5}{16}$	$\frac{1}{4}$	$\frac{3}{16}$
$1\frac{5}{16}$ to $1\frac{3}{8}$	$\frac{5}{16}$	$\frac{5}{16} \times \frac{1}{4}$	$\frac{9}{16}$	$\frac{13}{32}$	$\frac{13}{32}$	$\frac{3}{8}$	$\frac{5}{16}$	$\frac{1}{4}$
$1\frac{7}{16}$ to $1\frac{3}{4}$	$\frac{3}{8}$	$\frac{3}{8} \times \frac{1}{4}$	$\frac{11}{16}$	$\frac{15}{32}$	$\frac{15}{32}$	$\frac{7}{16}$	$\frac{3}{8}$	$\frac{5}{16}$
$1\frac{13}{16}$ to $2\frac{1}{4}$	$\frac{1}{2}$	$\frac{1}{2} \times \frac{3}{8}$	$\frac{7}{8}$	$\frac{19}{32}$	$\frac{5}{8}$	$\frac{5}{8}$	$\frac{1}{2}$	$\frac{7}{16}$
$2\frac{5}{16}$ to $2\frac{3}{4}$	$\frac{5}{8}$	$\frac{5}{8} \times \frac{7}{16}$	$1\frac{1}{16}$	$\frac{23}{32}$	$\frac{3}{4}$	$\frac{3}{4}$	$\frac{5}{8}$	$\frac{1}{2}$
$2\frac{7}{8}$ to $3\frac{1}{4}$	$\frac{3}{4}$	$\frac{3}{4} \times \frac{1}{2}$	$1\frac{1}{4}$	$\frac{7}{8}$	$\frac{7}{8}$	$\frac{7}{8}$	$\frac{3}{4}$	$\frac{5}{8}$
$3\frac{3}{8}$ to $3\frac{3}{4}$	$\frac{7}{8}$	$\frac{7}{8} \times \frac{5}{8}$	$1\frac{1}{2}$	1	1	$1\frac{1}{16}$	$\frac{7}{8}$	$\frac{3}{4}$
$3\frac{7}{8}$ to $4\frac{1}{2}$	1	$1 \times \frac{3}{4}$	$1\frac{3}{4}$	$1\frac{3}{16}$	$1\frac{3}{16}$	$1\frac{1}{4}$	1	$1\frac{13}{16}$
$4\frac{3}{4}$ to $5\frac{1}{2}$	$1\frac{1}{4}$	$1\frac{1}{4} \times \frac{7}{8}$	2	$1\frac{7}{16}$	$1\frac{7}{16}$	$1\frac{1}{2}$	$1\frac{1}{4}$	1
$5\frac{3}{4}$ to 6	$1\frac{1}{2}$	$1\frac{1}{2} \times 1$	$2\frac{1}{2}$	$1\frac{3}{4}$	$1\frac{3}{4}$	$1\frac{3}{4}$	$1\frac{1}{2}$	1

[a]Plain taper square and flat keys have the same dimensions as the plain parallel stock keys, with the addition of the taper on top. Gib head taper square and flat keys have the same dimensions as the plain taper keys, with the addition of the gib head. *Stock lengths for plain taper and gib head taper keys:* The minimum stock length equals 4W, and the maximum equals 16W. The increments of increase of length equal 2W.

24 Screw Threads,[a] Square and Acme

Size	Threads per Inch	Size	Threads per Inch	Size	Threads per Inch	Size	Threads per Inch
$\frac{3}{8}$	12	$\frac{7}{8}$	5	2	$2\frac{1}{2}$	$3\frac{1}{2}$	$1\frac{1}{3}$
$\frac{7}{16}$	10	1	5	$2\frac{1}{4}$	2	$3\frac{3}{4}$	$1\frac{1}{3}$
$\frac{1}{2}$	10	$1\frac{1}{8}$	4	$2\frac{1}{2}$	2	4	$1\frac{1}{3}$
$\frac{9}{16}$	8	$1\frac{1}{4}$	4	$2\frac{3}{4}$	2	$4\frac{1}{4}$	$1\frac{1}{3}$
$\frac{5}{8}$	8	$1\frac{1}{2}$	3	3	$1\frac{1}{2}$	$4\frac{1}{2}$	1
$\frac{3}{4}$	6	$1\frac{3}{4}$	$2\frac{1}{2}$	$3\frac{1}{4}$	$1\frac{1}{2}$	over $4\frac{1}{2}$	1

[a]See Appendix 19 for general purpose acme threads.

25 Woodruff Keys[a]—American National Standard

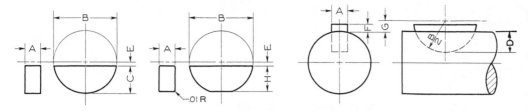

Key No.[b]	Nominal Sizes A × B	E	F	G	Maximum Sizes H	D	C	Key No.[b]	Nominal Sizes A × B	E	F	G	Maximum Sizes H	D	C
204	1/16 × 1/2	3/64	1/32	5/64	.194	.1718	.203	808	1/4 × 1	1/16	1/8	3/16	.428	.3130	.438
304	3/32 × 1/2	3/64	3/64	3/32	.194	.1561	.203	809	1/4 × 1 1/8	5/64	1/8	13/64	.475	.3590	.484
305	3/32 × 5/8	1/16	3/64	7/64	.240	.2031	.250	810	1/4 × 1 1/4	5/64	1/8	13/64	.537	.4220	.547
404	1/8 × 1/2	3/64	1/16	7/64	.194	.1405	.203	811	1/4 × 1 3/8	3/32	1/8	7/32	.584	.4690	.594
405	1/8 × 5/8	1/16	1/16	1/8	.240	.1875	.250	812	1/4 × 1 1/2	7/64	1/8	15/64	.631	.5160	.641
406	1/8 × 3/4	1/16	1/16	1/8	.303	.2505	.313	1008	5/16 × 1	1/16	5/32	7/32	.428	.2818	.438
505	5/32 × 5/8	1/16	5/64	9/64	.240	.1719	.250	1009	5/16 × 1 1/8	5/64	5/32	15/64	.475	.3278	.484
506	5/32 × 3/4	1/16	5/64	9/64	.303	.2349	.313	1010	5/16 × 1 1/4	5/64	5/32	15/64	.537	.3908	.547
507	5/32 × 7/8	1/16	5/64	9/64	.365	.2969	.375	1011	5/16 × 1 3/8	3/32	5/32	8/32	.584	.4378	.594
606	3/16 × 3/4	1/16	3/32	5/32	.303	.2193	.313	1012	5/16 × 1 1/2	7/64	5/32	17/64	.631	.4848	.641
607	3/16 × 7/8	1/16	3/32	5/32	.365	.2813	.375	1210	3/8 × 1 1/4	5/64	3/16	17/64	.537	.3595	.547
608	3/16 × 1	1/16	3/32	5/32	.428	.3443	.438	1211	3/8 × 1 3/8	3/32	3/16	9/32	.584	.4065	.594
609	3/16 × 1 1/8	5/64	3/32	11/64	.475	.3903	.484	1212	3/8 × 1 1/2	7/64	3/16	19/64	.631	.4535	.641
807	1/4 × 7/8	1/16	1/8	3/16	.365	.2500	.375	...	...	...	...	...	...	...	...

[a]ANSI B17.2-1967 (R1990).
[b]Key numbers indicate nominal key dimensions. The last two digits give the nominal diameter B in eighths of an inch, and the digits before the last two give the nominal width A in thirty seconds of an inch.

26 Woodruff Key Sizes for Different Shaft Diameters[a]

Shaft Diameter	5/16 to 3/8	7/16 to 1/2	9/16 to 3/4	13/16 to 15/16	1 to 1 3/16	1 1/4 to 1 7/16	1 1/2 to 1 3/4	1 13/16 to 2 1/8	2 3/16 to 2 1/2
Key Numbers	204	304 305	404 405 406	505 506 507	606 607 608 609	807 808 809	810 811 812	1011 1012	1211 1212

[a]Suggested sizes; not standard.

27 Pratt and Whitney Round-End Keys

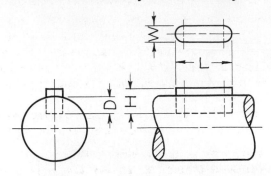

KEYS MADE WITH ROUND ENDS AND KEYWAYS CUT IN SPLINE MILLER

Maximum length of slot is 4″ + W. Note that key is sunk two-thirds into shaft in all cases.

Key No.	L^a	W or D	H	Key No.	L^a	W or D	H
1	$\frac{1}{2}$	$\frac{1}{16}$	$\frac{3}{32}$	22	$1\frac{3}{8}$	$\frac{1}{4}$	$\frac{3}{8}$
2	$\frac{1}{2}$	$\frac{3}{32}$	$\frac{9}{64}$	23	$1\frac{1}{38}$	$\frac{5}{16}$	$\frac{15}{32}$
3	$\frac{1}{2}$	$\frac{1}{8}$	$\frac{3}{16}$	F	$1\frac{3}{8}$	$\frac{3}{8}$	$\frac{9}{16}$
4	$\frac{5}{8}$	$\frac{3}{32}$	$\frac{9}{64}$	24	$1\frac{1}{2}$	$\frac{1}{4}$	$\frac{3}{8}$
5	$\frac{5}{8}$	$\frac{1}{8}$	$\frac{3}{16}$	25	$1\frac{1}{2}$	$\frac{5}{16}$	$\frac{15}{32}$
6	$\frac{5}{8}$	$\frac{5}{32}$	$\frac{15}{64}$	G	$1\frac{1}{2}$	$\frac{3}{8}$	$\frac{9}{16}$
7	$\frac{3}{4}$	$\frac{1}{8}$	$\frac{3}{16}$	51	$1\frac{3}{4}$	$\frac{1}{4}$	$\frac{3}{8}$
8	$\frac{3}{4}$	$\frac{5}{32}$	$\frac{15}{64}$	52	$1\frac{3}{4}$	$\frac{5}{16}$	$\frac{15}{32}$
9	$\frac{3}{4}$	$\frac{3}{16}$	$\frac{9}{32}$	53	$1\frac{3}{4}$	$\frac{3}{8}$	$\frac{9}{16}$
10	$\frac{7}{8}$	$\frac{5}{32}$	$\frac{15}{64}$	26	2	$\frac{3}{16}$	$\frac{9}{32}$
11	$\frac{7}{8}$	$\frac{3}{16}$	$\frac{9}{32}$	27	2	$\frac{1}{4}$	$\frac{3}{8}$
12	$\frac{7}{8}$	$\frac{7}{32}$	$\frac{21}{64}$	28	2	$\frac{5}{16}$	$\frac{15}{32}$
A	$\frac{7}{8}$	$\frac{1}{4}$	$\frac{3}{8}$	29	2	$\frac{3}{8}$	$\frac{9}{16}$
13	1	$\frac{3}{16}$	$\frac{9}{32}$	54	$2\frac{1}{4}$	$\frac{1}{4}$	$\frac{3}{8}$
14	1	$\frac{7}{32}$	$\frac{21}{64}$	55	$2\frac{1}{4}$	$\frac{5}{16}$	$\frac{15}{32}$
15	1	$\frac{1}{4}$	$\frac{3}{8}$	56	$2\frac{1}{4}$	$\frac{3}{8}$	$\frac{9}{16}$
B	1	$\frac{5}{16}$	$\frac{15}{32}$	57	$2\frac{1}{4}$	$\frac{7}{16}$	$\frac{21}{32}$
16	$1\frac{1}{8}$	$\frac{3}{16}$	$\frac{9}{32}$	58	$2\frac{1}{2}$	$\frac{5}{16}$	$\frac{15}{32}$
17	$1\frac{1}{8}$	$\frac{7}{32}$	$\frac{21}{64}$	59	$2\frac{1}{2}$	$\frac{3}{8}$	$\frac{9}{16}$
18	$1\frac{1}{8}$	$\frac{1}{4}$	$\frac{3}{8}$	60	$2\frac{1}{2}$	$\frac{7}{16}$	$\frac{21}{32}$
C	$1\frac{1}{8}$	$\frac{5}{16}$	$\frac{15}{32}$	61	$2\frac{1}{2}$	$\frac{1}{2}$	$\frac{3}{4}$
19	$1\frac{1}{4}$	$\frac{3}{16}$	$\frac{9}{32}$	30	3	$\frac{3}{8}$	$\frac{9}{16}$
20	$1\frac{1}{4}$	$\frac{7}{32}$	$\frac{21}{64}$	31	3	$\frac{7}{16}$	$\frac{21}{32}$
21	$1\frac{1}{4}$	$\frac{1}{4}$	$\frac{3}{8}$	32	3	$\frac{1}{2}$	$\frac{3}{4}$
D	$1\frac{1}{4}$	$\frac{5}{16}$	$\frac{15}{32}$	33	3	$\frac{9}{16}$	$\frac{27}{32}$
E	$1\frac{1}{4}$	$\frac{3}{8}$	$\frac{9}{16}$	34	3	$\frac{5}{8}$	$\frac{15}{16}$

^{a}The length L may vary from the table, but equals at least $2W$.

28 Washers,[a] Plain—American National Standard

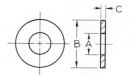

For parts lists, etc., give inside diameter, outside diameter, and the thickness; for example, .344 × .688 × .065 Type A Plain Washer. Preferred Sizes of Type A Plain Washers.[b]

Nominal Washer Size[c]			Inside Diameter A	Outside Diameter B	Nominal Thickness C
...	...		0.078	0.188	0.020
...	...		0.094	0.250	0.020
...	...		0.125	0.312	0.032
No. 6	0.138		0.156	0.375	0.049
No. 8	0.164		0.188	0.438	0.049
No. 10	0.190		0.219	0.500	0.049
$\frac{3}{16}$	0.188		0.250	0.562	0.049
No. 12	0.216		0.250	0.562	0.065
$\frac{1}{4}$	0.250	N	0.281	0.625	0.065
$\frac{1}{4}$	0.250	W	0.312	0.734	0.065
$\frac{5}{16}$	0.312	N	0.344	0.688	0.065
$\frac{5}{16}$	0.312	W	0.375	0.875	0.083
$\frac{3}{8}$	0.375	N	0.406	0.812	0.065
$\frac{3}{8}$	0.375	W	0.438	1.000	0.083
$\frac{7}{16}$	0.438	N	0.469	0.922	0.065
$\frac{7}{16}$	0.438	W	0.500	1.250	0.083
$\frac{1}{2}$	0.500	N	0.531	1.062	0.095
$\frac{1}{2}$	0.500	W	0.562	1.375	0.109
$\frac{9}{16}$	0.562	N	0.594	1.156	0.095
$\frac{9}{16}$	0.562	W	0.625	1.469	0.109
$\frac{5}{8}$	0.625	N	0.656	1.312	0.095
$\frac{5}{8}$	0.625	W	0.688	1.750	0.134
$\frac{3}{4}$	0.750	N	0.812	1.469	0.134
$\frac{3}{4}$	0.750	W	0.812	2.000	0.148
$\frac{7}{8}$	0.875	N	0.938	1.750	0.134
$\frac{7}{8}$	0.875	W	0.938	2.250	0.165
1	1.000	N	1.062	2.000	0.134
1	1.000	W	1.062	2.500	0.165
$1\frac{1}{8}$	1.125	N	1.250	2.250	0.134
$1\frac{1}{8}$	1.125	W	1.250	2.750	0.165
$1\frac{1}{4}$	1.250	N	1.375	2.500	0.165
$1\frac{1}{4}$	1.250	W	1.375	3.000	0.165
$1\frac{3}{8}$	1.375	N	1.500	2.750	0.165
$1\frac{3}{8}$	1.375	W	1.500	3.250	0.180
$1\frac{1}{2}$	1.500	N	1.625	3.000	0.165
$1\frac{1}{2}$	1.500	W	1.625	3.500	0.180
$1\frac{5}{8}$	1.625		1.750	3.750	0.180
$1\frac{3}{4}$	1.750		1.875	4.000	0.180
$1\frac{7}{8}$	1.875		2.000	4.250	0.180
2	2.000		2.125	4.500	0.180
$2\frac{1}{4}$	2.250		2.375	4.750	0.220
$2\frac{1}{2}$	2.500		2.625	5.000	0.238
$2\frac{3}{4}$	2.750		2.875	5.250	0.259
3	3.000		3.125	5.500	0.284

[a]From ANSI B18.22.1-1965 (R1981). For complete listings, see the standard.
[b]Preferred sizes are for the most part from series previously designated "Standard Plate" and "SAE." Where common sizes existed in the two series, the SAE size is designated "N" (narrow) and the Standard Plate "W" (wide).
[c]Nominal washer sizes are intended for use with comparable nominal screw or bolt sizes.

29 Washers,[a] Lock—American National Standard

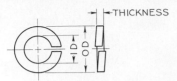

For parts lists, etc., give nominal size and series; for example, $\frac{1}{4}$ regular lock washer (preferred series).

Nominal Washer Size[b]		Inside Diameter, Min.	Regular		Extra Duty		Hi-Collar	
			Outside Diameter, Max.	Thickness, Min.	Outside Diameter, Max.	Thickness, Min.	Outside Diameter, Max.	Thickness, Min.
No. 2	0.086	0.088	0.172	0.020	0.208	0.027	. . .	. . .
No. 3	0.099	0.101	0.195	0.025	0.239	0.034	. . .	. . .
No. 4	0.112	0.115	0.209	0.025	0.253	0.034	0.173	0.022
No. 5	0.125	0.128	0.236	0.031	0.300	0.045	0.202	0.030
No. 6	0.138	0.141	0.250	0.031	0.314	0.045	0.216	0.030
No. 8	0.164	0.168	0.293	0.040	0.375	0.057	0.267	0.047
No. 10	0.190	0.194	0.334	0.047	0.434	0.068	0.294	0.047
No. 12	0.216	0.221	0.377	0.056	0.497	0.080	. . .	. . .
$\frac{1}{4}$	0.250	0.255	0.489	0.062	0.535	0.084	0.365	0.078
$\frac{5}{16}$	0.312	0.318	0.586	0.078	0.622	0.108	0.460	0.093
$\frac{3}{8}$	0.375	0.382	0.683	0.094	0.741	0.123	0.553	0.125
$\frac{7}{16}$	0.438	0.446	0.779	0.109	0.839	0.143	0.647	0.140
$\frac{1}{2}$	0.500	0.509	0.873	0.125	0.939	0.162	0.737	0.172
$\frac{9}{16}$	0.562	0.572	0.971	0.141	1.041	0.182	. . .	. . .
$\frac{5}{8}$	0.625	0.636	1.079	0.156	1.157	0.202	0.923	0.203
$\frac{11}{16}$	0.688	0.700	1.176	0.172	1.258	0.221	. . .	. . .
$\frac{3}{4}$	0.750	0.763	1.271	0.188	1.361	0.241	1.111	0.218
$\frac{13}{16}$	0.812	0.826	1.367	0.203	1.463	0.261	. . .	. . .
$\frac{7}{8}$	0.875	0.890	1.464	0.219	1.576	0.285	1.296	0.234
$\frac{15}{16}$	0.938	0.954	1.560	0.234	1.688	0.308	. . .	. . .
1	1.000	1.017	1.661	0.250	1.799	0.330	1.483	0.250
$1\frac{1}{16}$	1.062	1.080	1.756	0.266	1.910	0.352	. . .	. . .
$1\frac{1}{8}$	1.125	1.144	1.853	0.281	2.019	0.375	1.669	0.313
$1\frac{3}{16}$	1.188	1.208	1.950	0.297	2.124	0.396	. . .	. . .
$1\frac{1}{4}$	1.250	1.271	2.045	0.312	2.231	0.417	1.799	0.313
$1\frac{5}{16}$	1.312	1.334	2.141	0.328	2.335	0.438	. . .	. . .
$1\frac{3}{8}$	1.375	1.398	2.239	0.344	2.439	0.458	2.041	0.375
$1\frac{7}{16}$	1.438	1.462	2.334	0.359	2.540	0.478	. . .	. . .
$1\frac{1}{2}$	1.500	1.525	2.430	0.375	2.638	0.496	2.170	0.375

[a]From ANSI/ASME B18.21.1-1994. For complete listing, see the standard.
[b]Nominal washer sizes are intended for use with comparable nominal screw or bolt sizes.

30 Wire Gage Standards[a]

Dimensions of sizes in decimal parts of an inch.[b]

No. of Wire	American or Brown & Sharpe for Non-ferrous Metals	Birming-ham, or Stubs' Iron Wire[c]	American S. & W. Co.'s (Washburn & Moen) Std. Steel Wire	American S. & W. Co.'s Music Wire	Imperial Wire	Stubs' Steel Wire[c]	Steel Manu-facturers' Sheet Gage[b]	No. of Wire
7–0's	.651354	...	.4900	...	.500	...	...	7–0's
6–0's	.580049	...	.4615	.004	.464	...	...	6–0's
5–0's	.516549	.500	.4305	.005	.432	...	...	5–0's
4–0's	.460	.454	.3938	.006	.400	...	...	4–0's
000	.40964	.425	.3625	.007	.372	...	...	000
00	.3648	.380	.3310	.008	.348	...	...	00
0	.32486	.340	.3065	.009	.324	...	...	0
1	.2893	.300	.2830	.010	.300	.227	...	1
2	.25763	.284	.2625	.011	.276	.219	...	2
3	.22942	.259	.2437	.012	.252	.212	.2391	3
4	.20431	.238	.2253	.013	.232	.207	.2242	4
6	.16202	.203	.1920	.016	.192	.201	.1943	6
7	.14428	.180	.1770	.018	.176	.199	.1793	7
8	.12849	.165	.1620	.020	.160	.197	.1644	8
9	.11443	.148	.1483	.022	.144	.194	.1495	9
10	.10189	.134	.1350	.024	.128	.191	.1345	10
11	.090742	.120	.1205	.026	.116	.188	.1196	11
12	.080808	.109	.1055	.029	.104	.185	.1046	12
13	.071961	.095	.0915	.031	.092	.182	.0897	13
14	.064084	.083	.0800	.033	.080	.180	.0747	14
15	.057068	.072	.0720	.035	.072	.178	.0763	15
16	.05082	.065	.0625	.037	.064	.175	.0598	16
17	.045257	.058	.0540	.039	.056	.172	.0538	17
18	.040303	.049	.0475	.041	.048	.168	.0478	18
19	.03589	.042	.0410	.043	.040	.164	.0418	19
20	.031961	.035	.0348	.045	.036	.161	.0359	20
21	.028462	.032	.0317	.047	.032	.157	.0329	21
22	.025347	.028	.0286	.049	.028	.155	.0299	22
23	.022571	.025	.0258	.051	.024	.153	.0269	23
24	.0201	.022	.0230	.055	.022	.151	.0239	24
25	.0179	.020	.0204	.059	.020	.148	.0209	25
26	.01594	.018	.0181	.063	.018	.146	.0179	26
27	.014195	.016	.0173	.067	.0164	.143	.0164	27
28	.012641	.014	.0162	.071	.0149	.139	.0149	28
29	.011257	.013	.0150	.075	.0136	.134	.0135	29
30	.010025	.012	.0140	.080	.0124	.127	.0120	30
31	.008928	.010	.0132	.085	.0116	.120	.0105	31
32	.00795	.009	.0128	.090	.0108	.115	.0097	32
33	.00708	.008	.0118	.095	.0100	.112	.0090	33
34	.006304	.007	.0104	...	.0092	.110	.0082	34
35	.005614	.005	.0095	...	.0084	.108	.0075	35
36	.005	.004	.0090	...	.0076	.106	.0067	36
37	.004453	...	.0085	...	.0068	.103	.0064	37
38	.003965	...	.0080	...	.0060	.101	.0060	38
39	.003531	...	.0075	...	.0052	.099	...	39
40	.003144	...	.0070	...	.0048	.097	...	40

[a]Courtesy Brown & Sharpe Mfg. Co.
[b]Now used by steel manufacturers in place of old U.S. Standard Gage.
[c]The difference between the Stubs' Iron Wire Gage and the Stubs' Steel Wire Gage should be noted, the first being commonly known as the English Standard Wire, or Birmingham Gage, which designates the Stubs' soft wire sizes and the second being used in measuring drawn steel wire or drill rods of Stubs' make.

31 Taper Pins[a]—American National Standard

To find small diameter of pin, multiply the length of pin by .02083 and subtract the result from the larger diameter. All dimensions are given in inches. Standard reamers are available for pins given above the heavy line.

TAPER .25 PER FT

L (MAX)

Number	7/0	6/0	5/0	4/0	3/0	2/0	0	1	2	3	4	5	6	7	8
Size (Large End)	.0625	.0780	.0940	.1090	.1250	.1410	.1560	.1720	.1930	.2190	.2500	.2890	.3410	.4090	.4920
Shaft Diameter (Approx)[b]		$\frac{7}{32}$	$\frac{1}{4}$	$\frac{5}{16}$	$\frac{3}{8}$	$\frac{7}{16}$	$\frac{1}{2}$	$\frac{9}{16}$	$\frac{5}{8}$	$\frac{3}{4}$	$\frac{13}{16}$	$\frac{7}{8}$	1	$1\frac{1}{4}$	$1\frac{1}{2}$
Drill Size (Before Reamer)[b]	.0312	.0312	.0625	.0625	.0781	.0938	.0938	.1094	.1250	.1250	.1562	.1562	.2188	.2344	.3125
Length L															
.250	×	×	×	×	×										
.375	×	×	×	×	×	×									
.500	×	×	×	×	×	×	×								
.625	×	×	×	×	×	×	×	×							
.750	×	×	×	×	×	×	×	×	×						
.875	×	×	×	×	×	×	×	×	×						
1.000	×	×	×	×	×	×	×	×	×	×					
1.250		×	×	×	×	×	×	×	×	×					
1.500		×	×	×	×	×	×	×	×	×	×				
1.750				×	×	×	×	×	×	×	×	×			
2.000				×	×	×	×	×	×	×	×	×	×		
2.250						×	×	×	×	×	×	×	×		
2.500							×	×	×	×	×	×	×	×	×
2.750								×	×	×	×	×	×	×	×
3.000								×	×	×	×	×	×	×	×
3.250									×	×	×	×	×	×	×
3.500									×	×	×	×	×	×	×
3.750									×	×	×	×	×	×	×
4.000										×	×	×			×
4.250												×			×
4.500												×		×	×

[a] ANSI/ASME B18.8.2-1994. For Nos. 9 and 10, see the standard. Pins Nos. 11 (size .8600), 12 (size 1.032), 13 (size 1.241), and 14 (size 1.523) are special sizes; hence their lengths are special.

32 Cotter Pins[a]—American National Standard

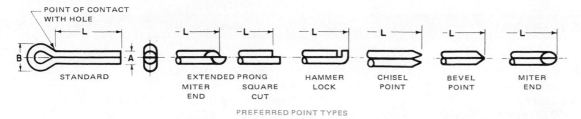

All dimensions are given in inches.

Nominal Size or Pin Diameter		Diameter A		Outside Eye Diameter B Min.	Extended Prong Length Min.	Hole Sizes Recommended
		Max.	Min.			
$\frac{1}{32}$	.031	.032	.028	.06	.01	.047
$\frac{3}{64}$	.047	.048	.044	.09	.02	.062
$\frac{1}{16}$	.062	.060	.056	.12	.03	.078
$\frac{5}{64}$	.078	.076	.072	.16	.04	.094
$\frac{3}{32}$	.094	.090	.086	.19	.04	.109
$\frac{7}{64}$	.109	.104	.100	.22	.05	.125
$\frac{1}{8}$	.125	.120	.116	.25	.06	.141
$\frac{9}{64}$	.141	.134	.130	.28	.06	.156
$\frac{5}{32}$	.156	.150	.146	.31	.07	.172
$\frac{3}{16}$	.188	.176	.172	.38	.09	.203
$\frac{7}{32}$	.219	.207	.202	.44	.10	.234
$\frac{1}{4}$	.250	.225	.220	.50	.11	.266
$\frac{5}{16}$	.312	.280	.275	.62	.14	.312
$\frac{3}{8}$	.375	.335	.329	.75	.16	.375
$\frac{7}{16}$	.438	.406	.400	.88	.20	.438
$\frac{1}{2}$	.500	.473	.467	1.00	.23	.500
$\frac{5}{8}$	.625	.598	.590	1.25	.30	.625
$\frac{3}{4}$	.750	.723	.715	1.50	.36	.750

[a]ANSI/ASME B18.8.1-1994.

33 Metric Equivalents

U.S. to Metric	Metric to U.S.
Length	
1 inch = 2.540 centimeters 1 foot = .305 meter 1 yard = .9l4 meter 1 mile = 1.609 kilometers	1 millimeter = .039 inch 1 centimeter = .394 inch 1 meter = 3.281 feet or 1.094 yards 1 kilometer = .621 mile
Area	
1 inch^2 = 6.451 centimeter^2 1 foot^2 = .093 meter^2 1 yard^2 = .836 meter^2 1 acre^2 = 4,046.873 meter^2	1 millimeter^2 = .00155 inch^2 1 centimeter^2 = .155 inch^2 1 meter^2 = 10.764 foot^2 or 1.196 yard^2 1 kilometer^2 = .386 mile^2 or 247.04 acre^2
Volume	
1 inch^3 = 16.387 centimeter^3 1 foot^3 = .028 meter^3 1 yard^3 = .764 meter^3 1 quart = 0.946 liter 1 gallon = .003785 meter^3	1 centimeter^3 = .061 inch^3 1 meter^3 = 35.314 foot^3 or 1.308 yard^3 1 liter = .2642 gallons 1 liter = 1.057 quarts 1 meter^3 = 264.02 gallons
Weight	
1 ounce = 28.349 grams 1 pound = .454 kilogram 1 ton = .907 metric ton	1 gram = .035 ounce 1 kilogram = 2.205 pounds 1 metric ton = 1.102 tons
Velocity	
1 foot/second = .305 meter/second 1 mile/hour = .447 meter/second	1 meter/second = 3.281 feet/second 1 kilometer/hour = .621 mile/second
Acceleration	
1 inch/second^2 = .0254 meter/second^2 1 foot/second^2 = .305 meter/second^2	1 meter/second^2 = 3.278 feet/second^2
Force	
N (newton) = basic unit of force, kg-m/s^2. A mass of one kilogram (1 kg) exerts a gravitational force of 9.8 N (theoretically 9.80665 N) at mean sea level.	

34 Welding Symbols and Processes—American Welding Society Standard[a]

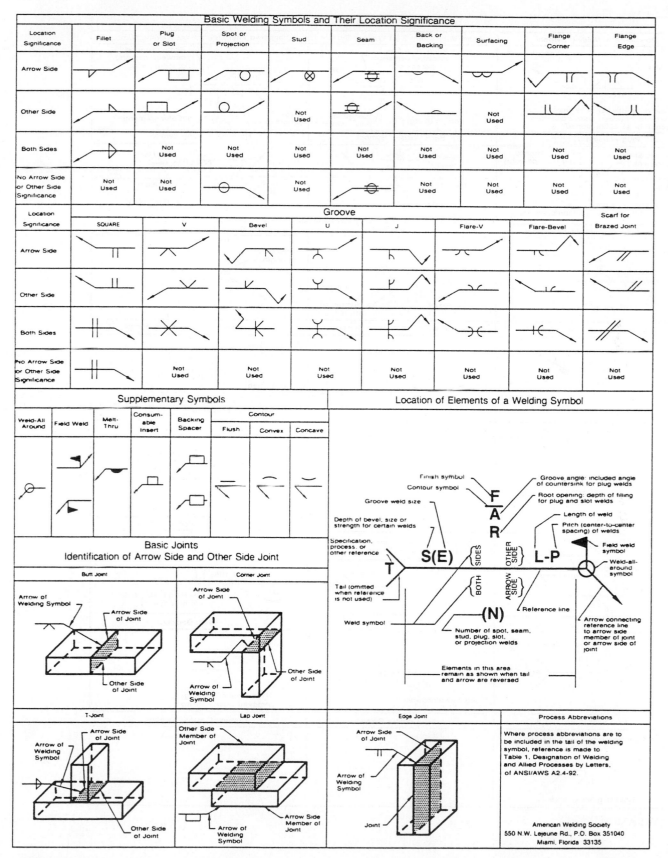

34 Welding Symbols and Processes—American Welding Society Standard[a] (continued)

Typical Welding Symbols

Double-Fillet Welding Symbol	Chain Intermittent Fillet Welding Symbol	Staggered Intermittent Fillet Welding Symbol

Double-Fillet Welding Symbol

Weld size — 1/4   6 — Length
1/16   4

Omission of length indicates that weld extends between abrupt changes in direction or as dimensioned

Chain Intermittent Fillet Welding Symbol

Pitch (distance between centers) of increments

5/16   2-5
7/16   2-6

Size (length of leg)   Length of increments

Staggered Intermittent Fillet Welding Symbol

Pitch (distance between centers) of increments

1/2   3-5
1/2   3-5

Size (length of leg)   Length of increments

Plug Welding Symbol	Back Welding Symbol	Backing Welding Symbol

Plug Welding Symbol

Included angle of countersink
Pitch (distance between centers) of welds
30°
Size (diameter of hole at root)   1   3/4   4
Depth of filling in inches (omission indicates filling is complete)

Back Welding Symbol

Back weld
— or —
2nd operation
1st operation

Backing Welding Symbol

Backing weld
— or —
1st operation
2nd operation

Spot Welding Symbol	Stud Welding Symbol	Seam Welding Symbol

Spot Welding Symbol

Size or strength — Number of welds — Pitch
RSW   025   (5)   4
Process

Stud Welding Symbol

1/2   6
(7)   Pitch
Size   Number of studs

Seam Welding Symbol

Size or strength
Increment length — Pitch
030   3-9   RSEW
Process

Square-Groove Welding Symbol	Single-V Groove Welding Symbol	Double-Bevel-Groove Welding Symbol

Square-Groove Welding Symbol

(3/16)   1/4
Weld size   Root opening

Single-V Groove Welding Symbol

Depth of bevel
1/2   (1/2)   1/8   Root opening
60°
Weld size   Groove angle

Double-Bevel-Groove Welding Symbol

Weld size
(1)
(1-1/4)
Weld size
Arrow points toward member to be prepared

Symbol with Backgouging	Flare-V-Groove Welding Symbol	Flare-Bevel-Groove Welding Symbol

Symbol with Backgouging

Depth of bevel
3/8   Back gouge

Flare-V-Groove Welding Symbol

(1/4)
Weld size

Flare-Bevel-Groove Welding Symbol

Weld size
(1/4)

Multiple Reference Lines	Complete Penetration	Edge Flange Welding Symbol

Multiple Reference Lines

1st operation on line nearest arrow
2nd operation
3rd operation

Complete Penetration

Indicates complete joint penetration regardless of type of weld or joint preparation
CJP

Edge Flange Welding Symbol

Radius
3/64   + 1/16
1/16
Weld size   Height above point of tangency

Flash or Upset Welding Symbol	Melt-Thru Symbol	Joint with Backing

Flash or Upset Welding Symbol

Process reference
FW

Melt-Thru Symbol

1/32
Root reinforcement

Joint with Backing

R
'R' indicates backing removed after welding

Joint with Spacer	Flush Contour Symbol	Convex Contour Symbol

Joint with Spacer

With modified groove weld symbol
Double bevel groove

Flush Contour Symbol

Convex Contour Symbol

G

[a]ANSI/AWS A3.0-94.

34 Welding Symbols and Processes—American Welding Society Standard[a] (continued)

MASTER CHART OF WELDING AND ALLIED PROCESSES

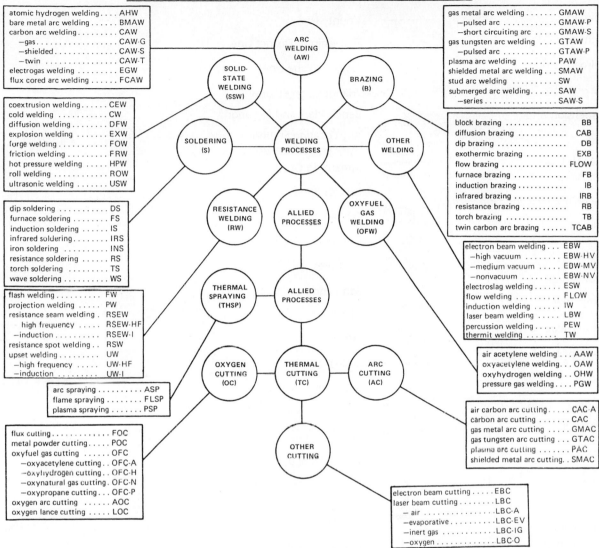

atomic hydrogen welding....	AHW
bare metal arc welding......	BMAW
carbon arc welding.........	CAW
—gas..................	CAW-G
—shielded.............	CAW-S
—twin.................	CAW-T
electrogas welding.........	EGW
flux cored arc welding......	FCAW

coextrusion welding......	CEW
cold welding..........	CW
diffusion welding........	DFW
explosion welding.......	EXW
forge welding..........	FOW
friction welding.........	FRW
hot pressure welding.....	HPW
roll welding...........	ROW
ultrasonic welding.......	USW

dip soldering..........	DS
furnace soldering........	FS
induction soldering......	IS
infrared soldering.......	IRS
iron soldering..........	INS
resistance soldering......	RS
torch soldering.........	TS
wave soldering..........	WS

flash welding.........	FW
projection welding.....	PW
resistance seam welding .	RSEW
high frequency.....	RSEW-HF
—induction..........	RSEW-I
resistance spot welding..	RSW
upset welding.........	UW
—high frequency.....	UW-HF
—induction..........	UW-I

arc spraying..........	ASP
flame spraying........	FLSP
plasma spraying.......	PSP

flux cutting............	FOC
metal powder cutting.....	POC
oxyfuel gas cutting......	OFC
—oxyacetylene cutting..	OFC-A
—oxyhydrogen cutting..	OFC-H
—oxynatural gas cutting.	OFC-N
—oxypropane cutting...	OFC-P
oxygen arc cutting......	AOC
oxygen lance cutting.....	LOC

gas metal arc welding.......	GMAW
—pulsed arc...........	GMAW-P
—short circuiting arc.....	GMAW-S
gas tungsten arc welding....	GTAW
—pulsed arc...........	GTAW-P
plasma arc welding........	PAW
shielded metal arc welding...	SMAW
stud arc welding..........	SW
submerged arc welding......	SAW
—series................	SAW-S

block brazing...............	BB
diffusion brazing............	CAB
dip brazing.................	DB
exothermic brazing..........	EXB
flow brazing................	FLOW
furnace brazing.............	FB
induction brazing............	IB
infrared brazing.............	IRB
resistance brazing...........	RB
torch brazing...............	TB
twin carbon arc brazing......	TCAB

electron beam welding...	EBW
—high vacuum........	EBW-HV
—medium vacuum......	EBW-MV
—nonvacuum..........	EBW-NV
electroslag welding......	ESW
flow welding..........	FLOW
induction welding......	IW
laser beam welding.....	LBW
percussion welding.....	PEW
thermit welding........	TW

air acetylene welding...	AAW
oxyacetylene welding...	OAW
oxyhydrogen welding..	OHW
pressure gas welding....	PGW

air carbon arc cutting.....	CAC-A
carbon arc cutting.......	CAC
gas metal arc cutting.....	GMAC
gas tungsten arc cutting...	GTAC
plasma arc cutting.......	PAC
shielded metal arc cutting..	SMAC

electron beam cutting.....	EBC
laser beam cutting........	LBC
— air.................	LBC-A
—evaporative..........	LBC-EV
—inert gas............	LBC-IG
—oxygen.............	LBC-O

[a] ANSI/AWS A3.0-94.

35 Topographic Symbols

Highway		National or State Line	
Railroad		County Line	
Highway Bridge		Township or District Line	
Railroad Bridge		City or Village Line	
Drawbridges		Triangulation Station	
Suspension Bridge		Bench Mark and Elevation	
Dam		Any Location Station (WITH EXPLANATORY NOTE)	
Telegraph or Telephone Line		Streams in General	
Power-Transmission Line		Lake or Pond	
Buildings in General		Falls and Rapids	
Capital		Contours	
County Seat		Hachures	
Other Towns		Sand and Sand Dunes	
Barbed Wire Fence		Marsh	
Smooth Wire Fence		Woodland of Any Kind	
Hedge		Orchard	
Oil or Gas Wells		Grassland in General	
Windmill		Cultivated Fields	
Tanks		Commercial or Municipal Field	
Canal or Ditch		Airplane Landing Field Marked or Emergency	
Canal Lock		Mooring Mast	
Canal Lock (POINT UPSTREAM)		Airway Light Beacon (ARROWS INDICATE COURSE LIGHTS)	
Aqueduct or Water Pipe		Auxiliary Airway Light Beacon, Flashing	

36 Piping Symbols—American National Standard

	FLANGED	SCREWED	BELL & SPIGOT	WELDED	SOLDERED
1. Joint					
2. Elbow—90°					
3. Elbow—45°					
4. Elbow—Turned Up					
5. Elbow—Turned Down					
6. Elbow—Long Radius					
7. Reducing Elbow					
8. Tee					
9. Tee—Outlet Up					
10. Tee—Outlet Down					
11. Side Outlet Tee—Outlet Up					
12. Cross					
13. Reducer—Concentric					
14. Reducer—Eccentric					
15. Lateral					
16. Gate Valve—Elev.					
17. Globe Valve—Elev.					
18. Check Valve					
19. Stop Cock					
20. Safety Valve					
21. Expansion Joint					
22. Union					
23. Sleeve					
24. Bushing					

[a]ANSI/ASME Y32.2.3-1949 (R1994).

37 Heating, Ventilating, and Ductwork Symbols[a]—American National Standard

———//———//———	High Pressure Steam
—·—·—·—·—·—·—	Medium Pressure Return
———FOF———	Fuel Oil Flow
———A———	Compressed Air
———RD———	Refrigerant Discharge
———RS———	Refrigerant Suction
———B———	Brine Supply

———·———·———	Soil, Waste or Leader (Above Grade)
———··———··———	Cold Water
———···———···———	Hot Water
———····———····———	Hot Water Return
—F———F—	Fire Line
—G———G—	Gas
———S———	Sprinklers—Main Supplies

Wall Radiator, Plan

Wall Radiator on Ceiling, Plan

Unit Heater (Propeller), Plan

Unit Heater (Centrifugal Fan), Plan

Thermostatic Trap

Thermostatic Float

Thermometer

Thermostat

Duct Plan (1st Figure, Width; 2nd Depth)   20X12

Inclined Drop in Respect to Air Flow   D

Supply Duct Section   S   12X20

Exhaust Duct Section   E   12X20

Recirculation Duct Section   R   12X20

Fresh Air Duct Section   F A   12X20

Supply Outlet

Exhaust Inlet

Volume Damper   Plan

Volume Damper   Elev.

Deflecting Damper

Turning Vanes

Automatic Dampers   M

Canvas Connections

Fan and Motor with Belt Guard

Intake Louvres and Screen

[a]ANSI/ASME Y32.2.3-1949 (R1994) and ANSI Y32.2.4-1949 (R1993).

38 American National Standard Graphical Symbols for Electronic Diagrams[a]

Common Schematic Symbols Used in Circuit Diagrams

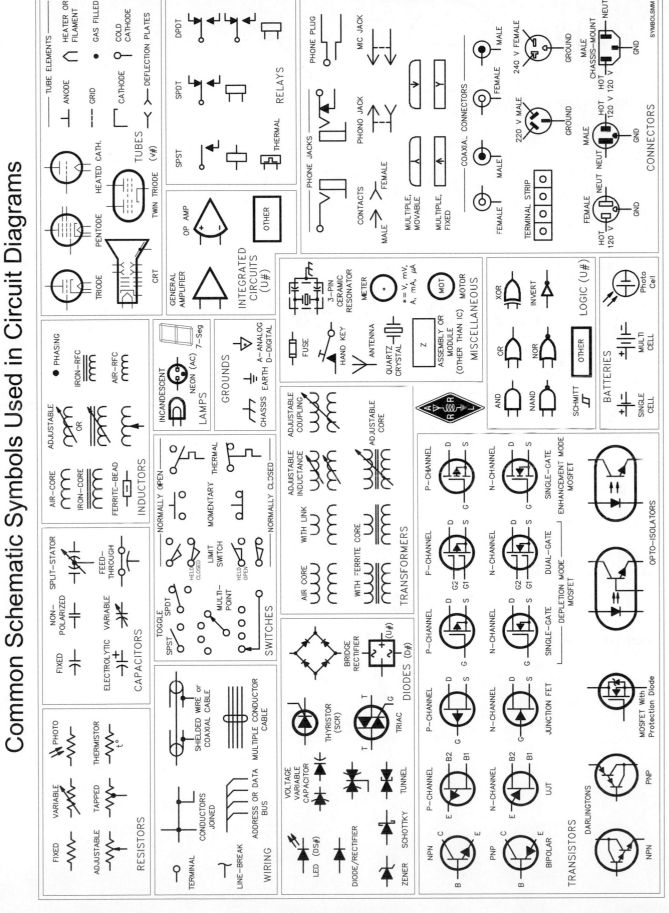

39 Form and Proportion of Geometric Tolerancing Symbols[a]

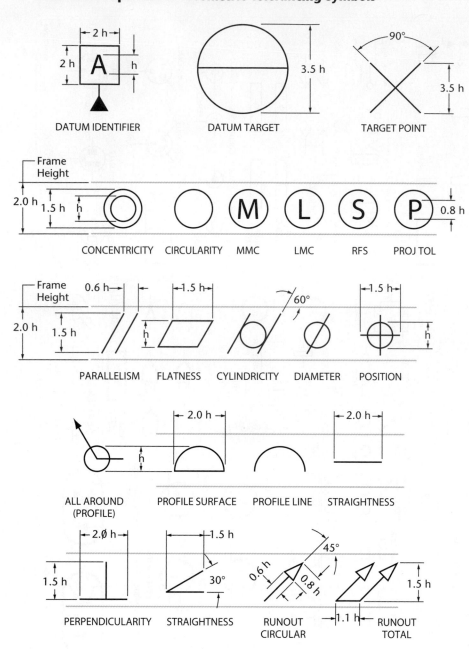

[a]ANSI/ASME Y14.5M-1994.

40 Wrought Steel Pipe[a] and Taper Pipe Threads[b]—American National Standard

All dimensions are in inches except those in last two columns.

Nominal Pipe Size	D Outside Diameter of Pipe	Threads per Inch	L₁ Normal Engagement by Hand Between External and Internal Threads	L₂ Length of Effective Thread	Sched. 10	Sched. 20[c]	Sched. 30[c]	Sched. 40[c]	Sched. 60[d]	Sched. 80[d]	Sched. 100	Sched. 120	Sched. 140	Sched. 160	Length of Pipe, Feet, per Square Foot External Surface[e]	Length of Standard Weight Pipe, Feet, Containing 1 cu. ft.[e]
⅛	.405	27	.1615	.2639	...	...	...	**.068**	...	**.095**	...	...	...	...	9.431	2,533.8
¼	.540	18	.2278	.4018	...	...	...	**.088**	...	**.119**	...	...	...	...	7.073	1,383.8
⅜	.675	18	.240	.4078	...	...	...	**.091**	...	**.126**	...	...	...	...	5.658	754.36
½	.840	14	.320	.5337	...	...	...	**.109**	...	**.147**	...	...	...	.188	4.547	473.91
¾	1.050	14	.339	.5457	...	...	...	**.113**	...	**.154**	...	...	...	.219	3.637	270.03
1	1.315	11.5	.400	.6828	...	...	...	**.133**	...	**.179**	...	...	...	.250	2.904	166.62
1¼	1.660	11.5	.420	.7068	...	...	...	**.140**	...	**.191**	...	...	...	.250	2.301	96.275
1½	1.900	11.5	.420	.7235	...	...	...	**.145**	...	**.200**	...	...	...	.281	2.010	70.733
2	2.375	11.5	.436	.7565	...	...	...	**.154**	...	**.218**	...	...	...	.344	1.608	42.913
2½	2.875	8	.682	1.1375	...	...	...	**.203**	...	**.276**	...	...	...	.375	1.328	30.077
3	3.500	8	.766	1.2000	...	...	...	**.216**	...	**.300**	...	...	...	.438	1.091	19.479
3½	4.000	8	.821	1.2500	...	...	...	**.226**	...	**.318**	...	...	...	...	.954	14.565
4	4.500	8	.844	1.3000	...	...	...	**.237**	...	**.337**	...	.438	...	.531	.848	11.312
5	5.563	8	.937	1.4063	...	...	...	**.258**	...	**.375**	...	.500	...	.625	.686	7.199
6	6.625	8	.958	1.5125	...	...	...	**.280**	...	**.432**	...	.562	...	.719	.576	4.984
8	8.625	8	1.063	1.7125	...	.250	.277	**.322**	.406	**.500**	.594	.719	.812	.906	.443	2.878
10	10.750	8	1.210	1.9250	...	.250	.307	**.365**	**.500**	.594	.719	.844	1.000	1.125	.355	1.826
12	12.750	8	1.360	2.1250	...	.250	.330	.406	**.562**	.688	.844	1.000	1.125	1.312	.299	1.273
14 OD	14.000	8	1.562	2.2500	.250	.312	**.375**	.438	.594	.750	.938	1.094	1.250	1.406	.273	1.065
16 OD	16.000	8	1.812	2.4500	.250	.312	**.375**	**.500**	.656	.844	1.031	1.219	1.438	1.594	.239	.815
18 OD	18.000	8	2.000	2.6500	.250	.312	.438	.562	.750	.938	1.156	1.375	1.562	1.781	.212	.644
20 OD	20.000	8	2.125	2.8500	.250	**.375**	.500	.594	.812	1.031	1.281	1.500	1.750	1.969	.191	.518
24 OD	24.000	8	2.375	3.2500	.250	**.375**	.562	.688	.969	1.219	1.531	1.812	2.062	2.344	.159	.358

(Middle columns grouped under heading **Nominal Wall Thickness**.)

[a] ANSI/ASME B36.10M-1995.
[b] ANSI/ASME B1.20.1-1983 (R1992).
[c] Boldface figures correspond to "standard" pipe.
[d] Boldface figures correspond to "extra strong" pipe.
[e] Calculated values for Schedule 40 pipe.

41 Cast Iron Pipe, Thicknesses and Weights—American National Standard

Size, Inches	Thickness, Inches	Outside Diameter, Inches	16 ft Laying Length Avg. per Foot[a] Weight (lb)	Per Length Based on	Size, Inches	Thickness, Inches	Outside Diameter, Inches	16 ft Laying Length Avg. per Foot[a] Weight (lb)	Per Length Based on
Class 50: 50 psi Pressure—115 ft Head					Class 200: 200 psi Pressure—462 ft Head				
3	.32	3.96	12.4	195	8	.41	9.05	37.0	590
4	.35	4.80	16.5	265	10	.44	11.10	49.1	785
6	.38	6.90	25.9	415	12	.48	13.20	63.7	1,020
8	.41	9.05	37.0	590	14	.55	15.30	84.4	1,350
10	.44	11.10	49.1	785	16	.58	17.40	101.6	1,625
12	.48	13.20	63.7	1,020	18	.63	19.50	123.7	1,980
14	.48	15.30	74.6	1,195	20	.67	21.60	145.9	2,335
16	.54	17.40	95.2	1,525	24	.79	25.80	205.6	3,290
18	.54	19.50	107.6	1,720	30	.92	32.00	297.8	4,765
20	.57	21.60	125.9	2,015	36	1.02	38.30	397.1	6,355
24	.63	25.80	166.0	2,655	42	1.13	44.50	512.3	8,195
30	.79	32.00	257.6	4,120	48	1.23	50.80	637.2	10,195
36	.87	38.30	340.9	5,455	Class 250: 250 psi Pressure—577 ft Head				
42	.97	44.50	442.0	7,070	3	.32	3.96	12.4	195
48	1.06	50.80	551.6	8,825	4	.35	4.80	16.5	265
Class 100: 100 psi Pressure—231 ft Head					6	.38	6.90	25.9	415
3	.32	3.96	12.4	195	8	.41	9.05	37.0	590
4	.35	4.80	16.5	265	10	.44	11.10	49.1	785
6	.38	6.90	25.9	415	12	.52	13.20	68.5	1,095
8	.41	9.05	37.0	590	14	.59	15.30	90.6	1,450
10	.44	11.10	49.1	785	16	.63	17.40	110.4	1,765
12	.48	13.20	63.7	1,020	18	.68	19.50	133.4	2,135
14	.51	15.30	78.8	1,260	20	.72	21.60	156.7	2,505
16	.54	17.40	95.2	1,525	24	.79	25.80	205.6	3,290
18	.58	19.50	114.8	1,835	30	.99	32.00	318.4	5,095
20	.62	21.60	135.9	2,175	36	1.10	38.30	425.5	6,810
24	.68	25.80	178.1	2,850	42	1.22	44.50	549.5	8,790
30	.79	32.00	257.6	4,120	48	1.33	50.80	684.5	10,950
36	.87	38.30	340.9	5,455	Class 300: 300 psi Pressure—693 ft Head				
42	.97	44.50	442.0	7,070	3	.32	3.96	12.4	195
48	1.06	50.80	551.6	8,825	4	.35	4.80	16.5	265
Class 150: 150 psi Pressure—346 ft Head					6	.38	6.90	25.9	415
3	.32	3.96	12.4	195	8	.41	9.05	37.0	590
4	.35	4.80	16.5	265	10	.48	11.10	53.1	850
6	.38	6.90	25.9	415	12	.52	13.20	68.5	1,095
8	.41	9.05	37.0	590	14	.59	15.30	90.6	1,450
10	.44	11.10	49.1	785	16	.68	17.40	118.2	1,890
12	.48	13.20	63.7	1,020	18	.73	19.50	142.3	2,275
14	.51	15.30	78.8	1,260	20	.78	21.60	168.5	2,695
16	.54	17.40	95.2	1,525	24	.85	25.80	219.8	3,515
18	.58	19.50	114.8	1,835	Class 350: 350 psi Pressure—808 ft Head				
20	.62	21.60	135.9	2,175	3	.32	3.96	12.4	195
24	.73	25.80	190.1	3,040	4	.35	4.80	16.5	265
30	.85	32.00	275.4	4,405	6	.38	6.90	25.9	415
36	.94	38.30	365.9	5,855	8	.41	9.05	37.0	590
42	1.05	44.50	475.3	7,605	10	.52	11.10	57.4	920
48	1.14	50.80	589.6	9,435	12	.56	13.20	73.8	1,180
Class 200: 200 psi Pressure—462 ft Head					14	.64	15.30	97.5	1,605
3	.32	3.96	12.4	195	16	.68	17.40	118.2	1,945
4	.35	4.80	16.5	265	18	.79	19.50	152.9	2,520
6	.38	6.90	25.9	415	20	.84	21.60	180.2	2,970
					24	.92	25.80	236.3	3,895

[a]Average weight per foot based on calculated weight of pipe before rounding.

42 Cast Iron Pipe Screwed Fittings,[a] 125 lb—American National Standard

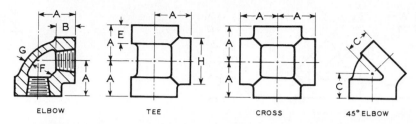

ELBOW   TEE   CROSS   45° ELBOW

Dimensions of 90° and 45° elbows, tees, and crosses (straight sizes). **All dimensions given in inches.** Fittings having right- and left-hand threads shall have four or more ribs or the letter "L" cast on the band at end with left-hand thread.

Nominal Pipe Size	Center to End, Elbows, Tees, and Crosses A	Center to End, 45° Elbows C	Length of Thread, Min. B	Width of Band, Min. E	Inside Diameter of Fitting F		Metal Thick- ness G	Diameter of Band, Min. H
					Max.	Min.		
$\frac{1}{4}$	.81	.73	.32	.38	.58	.54	.11	.93
$\frac{3}{8}$	.95	.80	.36	.44	.72	.67	.12	1.12
$\frac{1}{2}$	1.12	.88	.43	.50	.90	.84	.13	1.34
$\frac{3}{4}$	1.31	.98	.50	.56	1.11	1.05	.15	1.63
1	1.50	1.12	.58	.62	1.38	1.31	.17	1.95
$1\frac{1}{4}$	1.75	1.29	.67	.69	1.73	1.66	.18	2.39
$1\frac{1}{2}$	1.94	1.43	.70	.75	1.97	1.90	.20	2.68
2	2.25	1.68	.75	.84	2.44	2.37	.22	3.28
$2\frac{1}{2}$	2.70	1.95	.92	.94	2.97	2.87	.24	3.86
3	3.08	2.17	.98	1.00	3.60	3.50	.26	4.62
$3\frac{1}{2}$	3.42	2.39	1.03	1.06	4.10	4.00	.28	5.20
4	3.79	2.61	1.08	1.12	4.60	4.50	.31	5.79
5	4.50	3.05	1.18	1.18	5.66	5.56	.38	7.05
6	5.13	3.46	1.28	1.28	6.72	6.62	.43	8.28
8	6.56	4.28	1.47	1.47	8.72	8.62	.55	10.63
10	8.08[b]	5.16	1.68	1.68	10.85	10.75	.69	13.12
12	9.50[b]	5.97	1.88	1.88	12.85	12.75	.80	15.47

[a]From ANSI/ASME B16.4-1992.
[b]This applies to elbows and tees only.

43 Cast Iron Pipe Screwed Fittings,[a] 250 lb—American National Standard

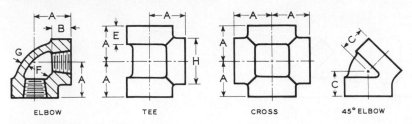

ELBOW   TEE   CROSS   45° ELBOW

Dimensions of 90° and 45° elbows, tees, and crosses (straight sizes). **All dimensions given in inches.** The 250-lb standard for screwed fittings covers only the straight sizes of 90° and 45° elbows, tees, and crosses.

Nominal Pipe Size	Center to End, Elbows, Tees, and Crosses A	Center to End, 45° Elbows C	Length of Thread, Min. B	Width of Band, Min. E	Inside Diameter of Fitting F		Metal Thickness G	Diameter of Band, Min. H
					Max.	Min.		
$\frac{1}{4}$	.94	.81	.43	.49	.58	.54	.18	1.17
$\frac{3}{8}$	1.06	.88	.47	.55	.72	.67	.18	1.36
$\frac{1}{2}$	1.25	1.00	.57	.60	.90	.84	.20	1.59
$\frac{3}{4}$	1.44	1.13	.64	.68	1.11	1.05	.23	1.88
1	1.63	1.31	.75	.76	1.38	1.31	.28	2.24
$1\frac{1}{4}$	1.94	1.50	.84	.88	1.73	1.66	.33	2.73
$1\frac{1}{2}$	2.13	1.69	.87	.97	1.97	1.90	.35	3.07
2	2.50	2.00	1.00	1.12	2.44	2.37	.39	3.74
$2\frac{1}{2}$	2.94	2.25	1.17	1.30	2.97	2.87	.43	4.60
3	3.38	2.50	1.23	1.40	3.60	3.50	.48	5.36
$3\frac{1}{2}$	3.75	2.63	1.28	1.49	4.10	4.00	.52	5.98
4	4.13	2.81	1.33	1.57	4.60	4.50	.56	6.61
5	4.88	3.19	1.43	1.74	5.66	5.56	.66	7.92
6	5.63	3.50	1.53	1.91	6.72	6.62	.74	9.24
8	7.00	4.31	1.72	2.24	8.72	8.62	.90	11.73
10	8.63	5.19	1.93	2.58	10.85	10.75	1.08	14.37
12	10.00	6.00	2.13	2.91	12.85	12.75	1.24	16.84

[a]From ANSI/ASME B16.4-1992.

44 Cast Iron Pipe Flanges and Fittings,[a] 125 lb—American National Standard

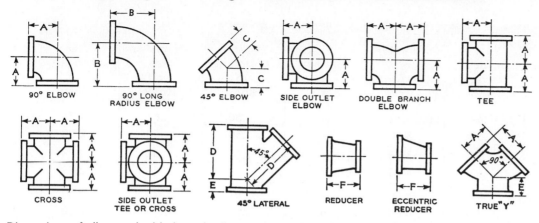

90° ELBOW   90° LONG RADIUS ELBOW   45° ELBOW   SIDE OUTLET ELBOW   DOUBLE BRANCH ELBOW   TEE

CROSS   SIDE OUTLET TEE OR CROSS   45° LATERAL   REDUCER   ECCENTRIC REDUCER   TRUE "Y"

Dimensions of elbows, double branch elbows, tees, crosses, laterals, true Y's (straight sizes), and reducers. **All dimensions in inches.**

Nominal Pipe Size	Inside Diameter of Fittings	Center to Face 90° Elbow, Tees, Crosses True "Y" and Double Branch Elbow A	Center to Face, 90° Long Radius Elbow B	Center to Face 45° Elbow C	Center to Face Lateral D	Short Center to Face True "Y" and Lateral E	Face to Face Reducer F	Diameter of Flange	Thickness of Flange, Min.	Wall Thickness
1	1.00	3.50	5.00	1.75	5.75	1.75	...	4.25	.44	.31
1¼	1.25	3.75	5.50	2.00	6.25	1.75	...	4.62	.50	.31
1½	1.50	4.00	6.00	2.25	7.00	2.00	...	5.00	.56	.31
2	2.00	4.50	6.50	2.50	8.00	2.50	5.0	6.00	.62	.31
2½	2.50	5.00	7.00	3.00	9.50	2.50	5.5	7.00	.69	.31
3	3.00	5.50	7.75	3.00	10.00	3.00	6.0	7.50	.75	.38
3½	3.50	6.00	8.50	3.50	11.50	3.00	6.5	8.50	.81	.44
4	4.00	6.50	9.00	4.00	12.00	3.00	7.0	9.00	.94	.50
5	5.00	7.50	10.25	4.50	13.50	3.50	8.0	10.00	.94	.50
6	6.00	8.00	11.50	5.00	14.50	3.50	9.0	11.00	1.00	.56
8	8.00	9.00	14.00	5.50	17.50	4.50	11.0	13.50	1.12	.62
10	10.00	11.00	16.50	6.50	20.50	5.00	12.0	16.00	1.19	.75
12	12.00	12.00	19.00	7.50	24.50	5.50	14.0	19.00	1.25	.81
14 OD	14.00	14.00	21.50	7.50	27.00	6.00	16.0	21.00	1.38	.88
16 OD	16.00	15.00	24.00	8.00	30.00	6.50	18.0	23.50	1.44	1.00
18 OD	18.00	16.50	26.50	8.50	32.00	7.00	19.0	25.00	1.56	1.06
20 OD	20.00	18.00	29.00	9.50	35.00	8.00	20.0	27.50	1.69	1.12
24 OD	24.00	22.00	34.00	11.00	40.50	9.00	24.0	32.00	1.88	1.25
30 OD	30.00	25.00	41.50	15.00	49.00	10.00	30.0	38.75	2.12	1.44
36 OD	36.00	28.00	49.00	18.00	...	...	36.0	46.00	2.38	1.62
42 OD	42.00	31.00	56.50	21.00	...	...	42.0	53.00	2.62	1.81
48 OD	48.00	34.00	64.00	24.00	...	...	48.0	59.50	2.75	2.00

[a]ANSI/ASME B16.1-1989.

45 Cast Iron Pipe Flanges, Drilling for Bolts and Their Lengths,[a] 125 lb—American National Standard

Nominal Pipe Size	Diameter of Flange	Thickness of Flange, Min.	Diameter of Bolt Circle	Number of Bolts	Diameter of Bolts	Diameter of Bolt Holes	Length of Bolts
1	4.25	.44	3.12	4	.50	.62	1.75
$1\frac{1}{4}$	4.62	.50	3.50	4	.50	.62	2.00
$1\frac{1}{2}$	5.00	.56	3.88	4	.50	.62	2.00
2	6.00	.62	4.75	4	.62	.75	2.25
$2\frac{1}{2}$	7.00	.69	5.50	4	.62	.75	2.50
3	7.50	.75	6.00	4	.62	.75	2.50
$3\frac{1}{2}$	8.50	.81	7.00	8	.62	.75	2.75
4	9.00	.94	7.50	8	.62	.75	3.00
5	10.00	.94	8.50	8	.75	.88	3.00
6	11.00	1.00	9.50	8	.75	.88	3.25
8	13.50	1.12	11.75	8	.75	.88	3.50
10	16.00	1.19	14.25	12	.88	1.00	3.75
12	19.00	1.25	17.00	12	.88	1.00	3.75
14 OD	21.00	1.38	18.75	12	1.00	1.12	4.25
16 OD	23.50	1.44	21.25	16	1.00	1.12	4.50
18 OD	25.00	1.56	22.75	16	1.12	1.25	4.75
20 OD	27.50	1.69	25.00	20	1.12	1.25	5.00
24 OD	32.00	1.88	29.50	20	1.25	1.38	5.50
30 OD	38.75	2.12	36.00	28	1.25	1.38	6.25
36 OD	46.00	2.38	42.75	32	1.50	1.62	7.00
42 OD	53.00	2.62	49.50	36	1.50	1.62	7.50
48 OD	59.50	2.75	56.00	44	1.50	1.62	7.75

[a]ANSI B16.1-1989.

46 Shaft Center Sizes

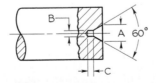

Shaft Diameter D	A	B	C	Shaft Diameter D	A	B	C
$\frac{3}{16}$ to $\frac{7}{32}$	$\frac{5}{64}$	$\frac{3}{64}$	$\frac{1}{16}$	$1\frac{1}{8}$ to $1\frac{15}{32}$	$\frac{5}{16}$	$\frac{5}{32}$	$\frac{5}{32}$
$\frac{1}{4}$ to $\frac{11}{32}$	$\frac{3}{32}$	$\frac{3}{64}$	$\frac{1}{16}$	$1\frac{1}{2}$ to $1\frac{31}{32}$	$\frac{3}{8}$	$\frac{3}{32}$	$\frac{5}{32}$
$\frac{3}{8}$ to $\frac{17}{32}$	$\frac{1}{8}$	$\frac{1}{16}$	$\frac{5}{64}$	2 to $2\frac{31}{32}$	$\frac{7}{16}$	$\frac{7}{32}$	$\frac{3}{16}$
$\frac{9}{16}$ to $\frac{25}{32}$	$\frac{3}{16}$	$\frac{5}{64}$	$\frac{3}{32}$	3 to $3\frac{31}{32}$	$\frac{1}{2}$	$\frac{7}{32}$	$\frac{7}{32}$
$\frac{13}{16}$ to $1\frac{3}{32}$	$\frac{1}{4}$	$\frac{3}{32}$	$\frac{3}{32}$	4 and over	$\frac{9}{16}$	$\frac{7}{32}$	$\frac{7}{32}$

47 Cast Iron Pipe Flanges and Fittings,[a] 250 lb—American National Standard

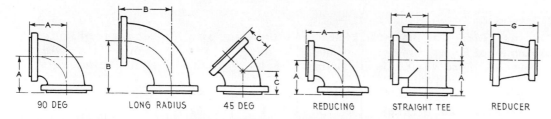

90 DEG   LONG RADIUS   45 DEG   REDUCING   STRAIGHT TEE   REDUCER

Dimensions of elbows, tees, and reducers. **All dimensions are given in inches.**

Nominal Pipe Size	Inside Diameter of Fitting, Min.	Wall Thickness of Body	Diameter of Flange	Thickness of Flange, Min.	Diameter of Raised Face	Center-to-Face Elbow and Tee A	Center-to-Face Long Radius Elbow B	Center-to-Face 45° Elbow C	Face-to-Face Reducer G
1	1.00	.44	4.88	.69	2.69	4.00	5.00	2.00	. . .
$1\frac{1}{4}$	1.25	.44	5.25	.75	3.06	4.25	5.50	2.50	. . .
$1\frac{1}{2}$	1.50	.44	6.12	.81	3.56	4.50	6.00	2.75	. . .
2	2.00	.44	6.50	.88	4.19	5.00	6.50	3.00	5.00
$2\frac{1}{2}$	2.50	.50	7.50	1.00	4.94	5.50	7.00	3.50	5.50
3	3.00	.56	8.25	1.12	5.69	6.00	7.75	3.50	6.00
$3\frac{1}{2}$	3.50	.56	9.00	1.19	6.31	6.50	8.50	4.00	6.50
4	4.00	.62	10.00	1.25	6.94	7.00	9.00	4.50	7.00
5	5.00	.69	11.00	1.38	8.31	8.00	10.25	5.00	8.00
6	6.00	.75	12.50	1.44	9.69	8.50	11.50	5.50	9.00
8	8.00	.81	15.00	1.62	11.94	10.00	14.00	6.00	11.00
10	10.00	.94	17.50	1.88	14.06	11.50	16.50	7.00	12.00
12	12.00	1.00	20.50	2.00	16.44	13.00	19.00	8.00	14.00
14 OD	13.25	1.12	23.00	2.12	18.94	15.00	21.50	8.50	16.00
16 OD	15.25	1.25	25.50	2.25	21.06	16.50	24.00	9.50	18.00
18 OD	17.00	1.38	28.00	2.38	23.31	18.00	26.50	10.00	19.00
20 OD	19.00	1.50	30.50	2.50	25.56	19.50	29.00	10.50	20.00
24 OD	23.00	1.62	36.00	2.75	30.31	22.50	34.00	12.00	24.00
30 OD	29.00	2.00	43.00	3.00	37.19	27.50	41.50	15.00	30.00

[a]ANSI B16.1-1989.

48 Cast Iron Pipe Flanges, Drilling for Bolts and Their Lengths,[a] 250 lb—American National Standard

Nominal Pipe Size	Diameter of Flange	Thickness of Flange, Min.	Diameter of Raised Face	Diameter of Bolt Circle	Diameter of Bolt Holes	Number of Bolts	Size of Bolts	Length of Bolts	Length of Bolt Studs with Two Nuts
1	4.88	.69	2.69	3.50	.75	4	.62	2.50	...
1¼	5.25	.75	3.06	3.88	.75	4	.62	2.50	...
1½	6.12	.81	3.56	4.50	.88	4	.75	2.75	...
2	6.50	.88	4.19	5.00	.75	8	.62	2.75	...
2½	7.50	1.00	4.94	5.88	.88	8	.75	3.25	...
3	8.25	1.12	6.69	6.62	.88	8	.75	3.50	...
3½	9.00	1.19	6.31	7.25	.88	8	.75	3.50	...
4	10.00	1.25	6.94	7.88	.88	8	.75	3.75	...
5	11.00	1.38	8.31	9.25	.88	8	.75	4.00	...
6	12.50	1.44	9.69	10.62	.88	12	.75	4.00	...
8	15.00	1.62	11.94	13.00	1.00	12	.88	4.50	...
10	17.50	1.88	14.06	15.25	1.12	16	1.00	5.25	...
12	20.50	2.00	16.44	17.75	1.25	16	1.12	5.50	...
14 OD	23.00	2.12	18.94	20.25	1.25	20	1.12	6.00	...
16 OD	25.50	2.25	21.06	22.50	1.38	20	1.25	6.25	...
18 OD	28.00	2.38	23.31	24.75	1.38	24	1.25	6.50	...
20 OD	30.50	2.50	25.56	27.00	1.38	24	1.25	6.75	...
24 OD	36.00	2.75	30.31	32.00	1.62	24	1.50	7.50	9.50
30 OD	43.00	3.00	37.19	39.25	2.00	28	1.75	8.50	10.50

[a]ANSI B16.1-1989.

INDEX